1 MONTH OF
FREE
READING

at

www.ForgottenBooks.com

By purchasing this book you are eligible for one month membership to ForgottenBooks.com, giving you unlimited access to our entire collection of over 1,000,000 titles via our web site and mobile apps.

To claim your free month visit:

www.forgottenbooks.com/free197859

ISBN 978-0-260-63353-8
PIBN 10197859

CRITICAL MANUSCRIPTS

TEENTH REPORT. APPENDIX, PART I.

THE

MANUSCRIPTS

OF HIS GRACE

THE DUKE OF PORTLAND,

PRESERVED AT

WELBECK ABBEY.

VOL. I.

Presented to both Houses of Parliament by Command of Her Majesty.

LONDON:

PRINTED FOR HER MAJESTY'S STATIONERY OFFICE,

BY EYRE AND SPOTTISWOODE,

PRINTERS TO THE QUEEN'S MOST EXCELLENT MAJESTY.

To be purchased, either directly or through any Bookseller, from

SPOTTISWOODE, East Harding Street, Fleet Street, E.C., and
32, Abingdon Street, Westminster, S.W.; or

MENZIES & Co., 12, Hanover Street, Edinburgh, and
88 and 90, West Nile Street, Glasgow; or

HODGES, FIGGIS, & Co., 104, Grafton Street, Dublin.

1891.

mentary :
utes—
iblic General, Session 1890. With Index, Tables, &c., &c. Roy. 8vo. **Cloth.**
                                                                          Price
cond Revised Edition. By authority. Vol. I. A.D. 1235–1713. 908 pp. **Vol.**
A.D. 1714–1800. 1,022 pp. Vol. III. A.D. 1801–1814. 966 pp. **Vol.**
A.D. 1814–1830. 1,122 pp. Roy. 8vo. Boards.   Price **7s. 6d.** e
vised Editions. Tables showing subsequent Repeals, effected by Acts of Sess
53 & 54 Vict. 1890. Roy. 8vo. 22 pp. Stitched.   **Price**
ronological Table and Index of. Eleventh Edition. To the end of the Se
52 & 53 Vict. (1889). Roy. 8vo. 1,690 pp. Cloth.   **Price**
atutory Rules and Orders other than those of a Local, Personal, or Temor,
Character issued in the year 1890. With a List of the more important t
Orders of a Local Character arranged in classes; and an Index. Ro
1,120 pp. Boards.   **Pri**
itutory Rules and Orders in force on 1st January 1891. Index to. **Imp.**
362 pp. Cloth.   **Price**
405.] MERCHANT SHIPPING (WATERTIGHT BULKHEADS). Report of Committee,
     Appendix (with Diagrams). 26 pp.   **Pric**
438.—I.] EDUCATION—ENGLAND AND WALES, 1890–91. Report; with Appe
     782 pp.   **Price 3**
444.—I.] EDUCATION—SCOTLAND. 492 pp.   **Pric**
450.] FISHERY BOARD—SCOTLAND. Ninth Report. 1890. Part I. 160 pp.
                                                                   Pric
450.—I.] FISHERY BOARD—SALMON FISHERIES. Part II. (with plate). 92 p
                                                                   Pri
450.—II.] FISHERY BOARD —SCIENTIFIC INVESTIGATIONS. Part III. (with pla
     432 pp.   **Price 4**
459.] RAILWAYS—SHARE CAPITAL, &c. General Report, 1890. 34 pp. **Price**
505.] SCIENCE AND ART DIRECTORY. Revised to June 1891. 288 pp. **Pric**
529] MINING ROYALTIES COMMISSION. Third Report, with **Evidence**
     Appendix. 246 pp.
533.] VETERINARY DEPARTMENT. Report. 1890. 267 pp.   **Price 1s**
537.] INLAND REVENUE. Thirty-fourth Report, 1890–91. 95 pp. **Pric**
, No. 268. RAILWAYS — RATES' AND CHARGES. Report of Committee,
     Evidence. Part I. 945 pp. Price **7s. 6d.** Part II. 8
     Price **7s. 2d**
ic Acts passed during the last Session are now published.
l and Private Acts passed during the last Session are in course of publication
KET RIGHTS AND TOLLS COMMISSION. Reports, Proceedings, Evidence, &c
14 Volumes, at various prices.   Cost of set, 2l. 1
s. Reports of Her Majesty's Inspecto   th Summaries c
tistic   Portion, under the provi   eg ulation Act,
w   Mines Regulati   s (Gunpowder)
                                                          cording to si

                                                  mber 1890.
                                                          P

HIRTEENTH REPORT, APPENDIX, PART I

THE

MANUSCRIPTS

OF HIS GRACE

THE DUKE OF PORTLAND,

PRESERVED AT

WELBECK ABBEY.

VOL. I.

LONDON:

PRINTED FOR HER MAJESTY'S STATIONERY OFFICE,
BY EYRE AND SPOTTISWOODE,
PRINTERS TO THE QUEEN'S MOST EXCELLENT MAJESTY.

And to be purchased, either directly or through any Bookseller, from
EYRE AND SPOTTISWOODE, EAST HARDING STREET, FLEET STREET, E.C., and
32, ABINGDON STREET, WESTMINSTER, S.W., or
JOHN MENZIES & Co, 12, HANOVER STREET, EDINBURGH, and
88 and 90, WEST NILE STREET, GLASGOW, or
HODGES, FIGGIS, & Co., 104, GRAFTON STREET, DUBLIN.

1891.

6474.] *Price 3s.*

INTRODUCTION

TO

VOLUME I.

OF THE

CALENDAR.

THE present volume contains a Calendar of one section of the large and valuable collection of manuscripts belonging to the Duke of Portland. It deals with twenty-two volumes of papers of the seventeenth century, which were found by Mr. Maxwell Lyte in a cupboard in the library at Welbeck Abbey, and were at once recognised by him to be the Collections of Dr. John Nalson and Dr. Philip Williams, from which he had seen extracts in Peck's *Desiderata Curiosa* and elsewhere. A twenty-third volume contains a list of the different papers in the others. While this Calendar has been in course of preparation, the original documents have been repaired and re-bound, but in the same order as before.

The Collection was formed by the Rev. John Nalson, LL.D., Rector of Doddington, and Canon of Ely. The chief source, both from internal evidence and his own statements,[1] appears to have been the papers in the office of the Clerk of the Parliament, from which he was apparently allowed to take almost anything he pleased, although in June 1684 the Clerk of the House wrote for a list of the books in his possession belonging to the office.[2] He also had access to the Paper Office,[3] though there he was apparently allowed only to take copies, and the Duke of Ormonde allowed him to see and copy the Ormonde papers, which now form the Carte Collection in the Bodleian. From these materials Dr. Nalson published two volumes, extending from 1639 to January 1641–2, the second appearing late in 1683, in the last words of which he expresses his

---

[1] *Collections*, ii., 790, 895.
[2] Tanner MSS., xxxii., 71.   [3] *Collections*, ii., 713.

U 61630.   Wt. 20512.   a 2

intention of continuing the publication, an intention frustrated by his death, at the age of 48, on March 24, 1685-6. He left no son, but his daughter Elizabeth married in 1690 the Rev. Philip Williams, also Rector of Doddington, and had by him a son, also named Philip, and some daughters. After Naison's death, his Collections appear to have been neglected, and a considerable part of them fell into the hands of Bishop Tanner, while he held a prebend at Ely between 1713 and 1724. Some notion of the number he obtained from the Collection may be obtained from the following fact. One volume, No. XI., consists of 356 transcripts by Nalson and Philip Williams, the elder. The originals of 164 of these are among the Tanner MSS., and doubtless came from Nalson's Collection; and in looking through the Tanner Catalogue one is continually struck by one part of a group of papers being there, while the other is here. For instance, four letters from Robert Wright were read together;[1] the first is in the Tanner MSS., vol. lx., fol. 337, the other three are here,[2] and no doubt the first also was once here. Again, Mrs. Gardiner, in the papers relating to Ogle's plot, published from the Tanner MSS., in the *Camden Miscellany*, vol. viii., mentions that the King's warrants to Devenish and Mosely are missing, both of which are here;[3] and these instances are only specimens.

It is even stated by Rawlinson, in the letter herein-after mentioned, that the whole Collection had been deposited in the Bodleian; but this seems to be an error caused by his mistaking the meaning of a letter of Bishop Tanner's brother to Archdeacon Knight. However, the documents left by Dr. Tanner came eventually into the possession of Nalson's grandson, Philip Williams, the younger, successively Fellow, Tutor, and President of St. John's, Cambridge, and Public Orator in the University. They were by him arranged and bound before 1730. Many of the documents were published between that date and 1735, by Peck, in the *Desiderata Curiosa*, and by Zachary Grey, in his *Examination of the Third Volume of Neal's History of the Puritans*, and in his *Examination of the Fourth Volume of the Same*, and they found the Collection in

---

[1] *Commons' Journals*, iv., 417.   [2] *Calendar*, pp. 323, 327, 335.
[3] *Calendar*, p. 166.

its present form, while on the other hand it contains one or two documents in Williams's handwriting. Dr. Williams married, and took the College living of Barrow, in Suffolk, in 1742, and died there in May 1749, leaving two daughters and one son, Philip, afterwards Fellow of New College, Oxford, Fellow of Winchester College, Rector of Compton, and Prebendary of Winchester. The Collections were offered through Thomas Carte to Richard Rawlinson,[1] but he apparently saw only the Index.

It is stated in Nichols's *Literary Anecdotes* [2] that the Collection came into the hands of the Rev. William Cole, of Ely (not his namesake, the antiquary), the son-in-law of Zachary Grey, and afterwards into those of his brother, Charles Nalson Cole, who died in 1804. The subsequent history of the volumes now at Welbeck is unknown, till they were discovered there by Mr. Maxwell Lyte in 1885.

There is a circumstance that throws some doubt on the above relation. After the death of Dr. Williams, of Barrow, his widow married the Rev. John Gordon, and had by him a son, the Rev. George Gordon, Dean of Lincoln from 1810 to his death in August 1845. From his library, four volumes, being XXIV. to XXVI. and XXVIII. of this Collection, were purchased in January 1846 by the British Museum. Hence, it is fairly arguable that the account in Nichols is incorrect, and that the Collection, or some part of it, continued in the possession of the Williams family. I have endeavoured, but without success, to ascertain whether Dean Gordon's library contained any other volumes of the Collection.

The first eight volumes consist of letters, except that occasionally some other document, such as a deposition, occurs as an enclosure.

Vol. I. contains 54 " Royal " Letters, *i.e.* from Charles I. and II., from the last both before and after his father's death, from the Elector Palatine, and his brothers Rupert and Maurice. Prefixed is the following note by Williams: "There are many " original letters and papers . . . which Bishop Tanner had " from this Collection of Dr. Nalson's, and which are now lodged " in the Bodleian at Oxon by his last will . . . as appears by

---

[1] Rawlinson to Owen, May 14, 1751, Rawlinson MSS , C. 989, fol. 109.
[2] ii., 549, and viii., 415.

" a letter of his brother and executor J. Tanner to Mr. Arch-
" deacon Knight, dated from Lowestoft, June 6, 1737." At the
end is a copy of the King's speech at the opening of the Long
Parliament.

Vol. II. contains 185 letters from the beginning of 1642, with
a few earlier ones, down to March 25th, 1643. At the end is a
copy of the printed letter, dated December 7th, 1681, of the
Earl of Anglesey to the Duke of Ormonde, in answer to his of
November 12th, concerning Lord Castlehaven's Memoirs.

Vol. III.contains 168 letters, to March 25th, 1645.

Vol. IV., 152 letters, to the end of October 1645.

Vol. V., 119 letters, to the end of March 1646.

Vol. VI., 80 letters, to the end of March 1648.

Vol. VII., 127 letters, to the end of March 1649.

Vol. VIII., 127 letters, to June 1660, and eleven others undated, but of earlier date. These I have succeeded in restoring
more or less exactly to their proper places in the Calendar.

Vol. IX. contains 301 documents, all but two or three relating
to the Uxbridge and Newport treaties. All, with one or two
exceptions, have already been printed, in *Lords' Journals*,
Rushworth, and elsewhere.

Vol. X. consists of 96 letters from Foreign Princes and States,
chiefly interesting for the autographs, which include one of
Louis XIV., several of Philip IV., of Christina of Sweden, of
Kings Christian and Frederic of Denmark, of the Prince de
Condé (including a holograph letter), and others.

Vol. XI. consists of transcripts of 356 letters, of which
the first 82 are by Philip Williams, the elder, and the rest by
Nalson. The originals of 164, as has been mentioned, are in the
Tanner Collection, and those of 119 are in this. The originals
of one or two of the remaining class must be in the Carte
MSS. The originals of the remainder I have been unable to
trace The last class, with six exceptions, two of which are copies
from Carte papers, occurs between No. 208 and No. 295, or
between April 1 and July 1, 1643, so I conjecture that by some
accident the bundle containing the originals for these months
was lost or destroyed. In the Appendix a Calendar is given of
those whose originals are neither in the Tanner nor in this
Collection. This volume also contains in the hand of the elder
Williams copies of 36 " Messages for Peace from the King,"

which are all printed in Rushworth or *Lords' Journals.* The transcripts by Williams were made in Nalson's lifetime, as appears by his notes upon them.

Vol. XII. contains 273 documents. Fourteen of these are Nalson's transcripts of other documents in the Collection, the rest are mostly letters ranging from 1641 to January 1660, many of them undated.

The next four volumes contain various documents, such as speeches, depositions, orders of one or both Houses, informations, accounts, &c., &c.

Vol. XIII. extends from December 1640 (with two earlier documents) to March 1643, and contains 210 documents.

Vol. XIV. extends to March 1646, and contains 234 documents.

Vol. XV. extends to March 1649, and contains 187 documents. About 20 at the end are undated, and range over the period from 1641 to 1649. Most of these also I have been able to date approximately.

Vol. XVI. contains 170 documents, going down to 1660.

Vols. XVII. and XVIII. contain documents relating to Foreign Affairs, the first 177, relating to France, Spain, and Portugal, the other 180, relating to Sweden, Denmark, the United Provinces, and other States.

Vols. XIX. and XX. consist respectively of 213 and 211 documents relating to Scotch affairs.

Vol. XXI. contains 137 documents relating to Ireland. This volume is in very bad condition, having at some time or other been exposed to wet, and consequently nearly all the documents in it have suffered, some being almost wholly illegible.

Vol. XXII. contains 167 documents, mostly petitions or the like. It also contains a large number of documents relating to the Assembly of Divines, including the original drafts of the *Directory* and of the *Larger* and *Shorter Catechisms,* being the identical papers presented to the House of Commons.

These twenty-two volumes, with the Index volume, constitute the whole of the Nalson Collection at Welbeck. The other eight were :—

Vol. XXIII., consisting of " Miscellaneous MSS. and Printed Proclamations 40–63, in very large folio," of which there were 107. Of these, Nos. 36 and 37 are printed in Peck, and

Commons' Journals, to which a reference is given on p. 407 of the Calendar. No. 62, " Proposals concerning the farming of the Post Office," is printed in Grey, iv., Appendix, No. 58, and Nos. 104 and 105 are copies of the Declarations of December 24, 1651, and January 31, 1651-2, calendared pp. 621, 626.

Vols. XXIV., XXV., and XXVI., being the original Journal of the Committee for Plundered Ministers, from January 1644-5 to January 1645-6; January 1645-6 to September 1646, and May to October 1647 respectively. Two other volumes of the Proceedings of this Committee are in the Public Record Office. See *Calendar of the Proceedings of the Committee for the Advance of Money, Preface,* vol. i., p. xvii.

Vol. XXVII., containing " Articles, Depositions, and Ejectments " against Malignant Ministers of the County of Lincoln from " July 29 to August 19, 1644."

Vols. XXVIII., XXIX., and XXX., containing the like for Cambridgeshire, Suffolk, and Essex, and the last also some particulars concerning the Reformation of the University of Cambridge.

Of these, XXIV., XXV., XXVI., and XXVIII., are in the British Museum, MSS. Additional, Nos. 15,669-72.

The numbers of the documents in each volume are taken from the Index, in which, however, there are omissions in nearly every volume; for instance, Wallis's five letters calendared at p. 683 are omitted. There are many mistakes too in the arrangement, and most of the volumes contain documents which either from date or subject should be placed elsewhere. Occasionally two copies of the same document occur in different volumes, sometimes with different titles. I take this opportunity of correcting a mistake noticed after the Calendar had gone to press. The document calendared at p. 35 as Additional Declaration against the King's going to Ireland, is a copy of that calendared last on p. 33, which is a draft in Pym's hand.

At the end of the Index volume are bound up extracts from the Earl of Manchester's Memoirs which Nalson states, in his printed work, that he procured through Lord Guildford. They are copied in the same hand as a large number of documents in the Collection, *e.g.* Lenthall's letters, the King to the Lord Mayor, " Advertisements what may content in London," Prince

Rupert's letter, the Earl of Northumberland's letter, Considerations, the Earl of Crawford's letter, Owen O'Neale's and Monck's letters, the Extracts from Dr. Stewart's letters, the Relation of the battle of Worcester, A. B.'s paper, and the address of J. S., pp. 28, 29, 218, 275, 302, 444, 493, 513, 534, &c., 616, 679, 697. I conjecture that the writer was a scribe employed by Nalson. The parts of the Memoirs not printed by Nalson, and not contained in a certain MSS. in the British Museum, are given at the end of the Appendix to this volume.

The interest of the following Calendar is much diminished by the circumstance that many of the most important documents have already been printed. For instance, of the eight original letters of Cromwell, those announcing the taking of Bristol,[1] Winchester,[2] and Pembroke,[3] the victory of Dunbar,[4] and the surrender of Edinburgh Castle,[5] and that about Colonel Lilburne,[6] have been printed ; while the other two,[7] concerning Major Gill and the commissions granted to Fleetwood and Whalley, are unimportant. The intercession of the Dutch Ambassadors for the King [8] has also been printed. Still, from the originals it has occasionally been possible to correct mistakes in the printed copies, and sometimes a change worth noting has been made from the first draft. For instance, in Cromwell's letter about Bristol, " who have *wrestled with* God for a blessing " is a correction for " *waited on* God," which the scribe originally wrote. Many of interest, however, remain, and the letters give a lively impression of the state of different parts of the country during the varying phases of the war. During the first years of the struggle, perhaps the most striking fact is the wretched condition of many of the Parliament's troops from want of pay and supplies, and their tendency to mutiny. It has sometimes been very difficult to ascertain whether a document has already appeared in print or not, and no doubt some have been over-looked. For instance, since the Calendar went to press, I have noticed that Sir John Meldrum's letter [9] is in the *King's Pamphlets*, E. 71, No. 22, and that abstracts of the letter of Sergeant-Major Rosse,[10] and of the examinations about the Earl of Antrim [11] are in the Appendix to the Fifth Report of

---

[1] p. 270.   [2] p. 282.   [3] p. 480.   [4] p. 534.   [5] p. 546.
[6] p. 560.   [7] pp. 535, 607.   [8] p. 509.   [9] p. 138.
[10] p. 113.   [11] pp. 120–123.

the Historical Manuscripts Commission. I shall now proceed to notice the most remarkable documents, taking first those that fall into groups, and then the miscellaneous ones in chronological order.

From December 1640 to the following summer are numerous papers that passed between the English and Scotch Commissioners, most of which have already been printed. One in June [1] refers to the alleged plots of Montrose and Traquair. The Royalist victories in the summer of 1643 obliged the Parliament to apply to Scotland for aid, and a copy of the address of the English Commissioners to the Convention of Estates will be found on p. 127. The Commissioners, in October,[2] describe their arrangements for garrisoning Berwick, and the state of affairs in Scotland. In January and February 1644 are notices of the entry into England of the Scotch army,[3] but before they were six months in England begins the series of complaints [4] that lasted for the next two years and a half. The Scotch complained with justice that they did not receive the pay and supplies that had been promised them. A specimen of their complaints will be found in Lord Leven's letter of July 8, 1645 [5]—" We are " called to march, march, that a plentiful country is before us, " where nothing will be wanting, but we find nothing by the " way but solitude—pleasant places indeed for grass and trees, " but no other refreshment." On the other hand the Scotch, deprived of their stipulated allowances, took the law into their own hands. All through the autumn and winter, and till midsummer 1646, occur numerous documents complaining of the oppressive assessments they levied, and the plunderings and other outrages they committed in Yorkshire and elsewhere.[6] On the other hand, the Parliament found it difficult to induce them to move or undertake any enterprise. In May and June 1645, the Scotch generals considered,[7] that before the siege of any town was undertaken it was necessary to dissipate the field forces of the enemy, and though at the end of July they began the siege of Hereford, they raised it after a month, on the King's approach, their army having been weakened by detaching the cavalry under Leslie in pursuit of the King, which cavalry on the news of Kilsyth had marched into Scotland. Full accounts

---

[1] p. 24.   [2] p. 136.   [3] pp. 167, 169.   [4] p. 181.   [5] p. 233.
[6] pp. 291–385 *passim*.   [7] pp. 224, 230.

of the progress and raising of the siege will be found on pp. 244, 248, 263, 271. Before the commencement of the siege, communications with the King had been entered into by some of the Scotch officers.[1] Meanwhile Montrose had been carrying all before him in Scotland, and raising the hopes of the sanguine Digby,[2] while the Committee of the Estates write on September 10 in despairing language,[3] they are " sensible of the many testimonies " of the brotherly affection received from the Parliament, but of " none more than this, that now they send up their prayers for par- " don and pity to us." Philiphaugh soon put an end to their fears, though for some time the English Royalists hoped that the defeat had been not decisive, and that Montrose would be in England at the head of an army before winter.[4] The strained relations between the army and the country where it was quartered culminated with the resolution of the Committee of the Northern Association of June 4, 1646,[5] that it be recommended to Sir Thomas Fairfax to go down into the northern parts with such forces as shall be thought fit for the preservation thereof. In the autumn of this year, and also in the spring of 1648, there are a good many papers, most of them already printed, concerning the negotiations between the Parliament and the Scotch. In January 1651, are two interesting letters from General Lambert from Edinburgh,[6] describing affairs in Scotland. In the following August are several documents about the Scotch invasion and the attempted rising in Lancashire under Lord Derby [7] (followed in October by the holograph petition of the latter four days before his execution [8]) and two characteristic replies to the summonses addressed to Dundee and St. Andrews by General Monck. Throughout the early part of 1652, numerous documents, mostly formal, concerning the intended union with England, occur, being the commissions to the deputies for the several counties and boroughs, and their assents to (and in a few instances their dissents from) the union, sometimes with statements of their desires.

With the outbreak of the Irish Rebellion in October 1641 begins a series of notices of Ireland. The earlier ones are mostly given

---

[1] p. 362. [2] p. 245. [3] p. 267. [4] pp. 281, 287.
[5] p. 368. [6] pp. 551, 552. [7] pp. 610–615. [8] p. 617.

in Nalson's printed work. The Mayor of Pembroke writes on February 17, 1641–2,[1] that hundreds of poor English had landed, and that he apprehends that the Rebels may attack the town. On the next page are letters from Chester showing the bad condition of the reinforcements for Ireland. On April 23,[2] the Lords Justices and Council write dissuading the King from coming, on account of the want of fit accommodation for him, and describing how wide-spread the Rebellion, and how weak the army was, and "the high and inexpressible extremities" the soldiers are reduced to for want of pay and supplies. A year later, comes a long account of the miserable condition of the Protestants and English there, who were "as it were breathing out their last breath."[3] Another letter, the following August, describing the arrest of Sir W. Parsons, Sir Adam Loftus, and others, tells the same tale—"All things here is very ill in the " highest degree, no expectation but ruin, and that all English and " Protestants will be quite rooted out of this Kingdom."[4] The conclusion of the Cessation brought no relief to the Protestants, who apprehended they were in more danger than at the beginning of the Rebellion.[5] The Scotch army in Ulster were, if possible, in worse plight, and three regiments had actually returned to Scotland in March 1644,[6] but the remainder were induced to stay at the earnest desire of the Scotch Privy Council. Their condition the next spring was even worse,[7] reduced, as they sometimes had been, to live on a pound of unground oats per man a day. The second Cessation concluded between Ormonde and the Irish through Digby's influence in 1646 brought no relief to the English Protestants,[8] and Lord Broghill about the same time urges the necessity of reinforcing the Parliament's forces in Munster with at least 5,000 foot and 1,500 horse, and of sending over money, victuals, and ammunition.[9]

To secure, if possible, the co-operation of the Confederate Catholic forces, Lord Clanrickard entered into an engagement on November 19th, 1646,[10] undertaking that all laws restraining the exercise of their religion should be revoked, that they should be left in *interim* possession of the churches and other ecclesiastical possessions they held, that a Catholic Lieutenant-General should

---

[1] p. 31.   [2] p. 36.   [3] p. 114.   [4] p. 125.   [5] p. 133.
[6] p. 172.   [7] p. 213.   [8] p. 388.   [9] p. 390.   [10] p. 396.

be appointed, and that a number of the Confederate Catholic army should be admitted into each of the garrisons held for the King. A month later, the Commissioners of the Parliament in a long report[1] describe the condition of Ireland, stating the portions held by the different parties, and the forces at the command of each, with suggestions for holding the places still in the Parliament's power, and for reducing the rest of the country. In March 1647, Mr. Baron reported to the Assembly at Kilkenny the result of his negotiations in France with Cardinal Mazarine and the Queen of England. This paper, which is a transcript by Nalson, probably from an original now in the Carte Collection, is unfortunately illegible in several places. The Queen, it appears, was at first inclined to comply with the requests of the Supreme Council, but was afterwards diverted by Protestant influence. On the departure of Lord Lisle, the Lord Lieutenant appointed by the Parliament, in April 1647, a dispute about the command of the army in Munster arose between Lord Inchiquin, and Colonel Sidney and Sir Hardress Waller, of which Inchiquin and Sir Adam Loftus and Sir John Temple give their versions.[2] In June, Sir Charles Coote and Lord Inchiquin give long accounts of raids into Connaught[3] and Waterford[4] respectively. The Parliamentary Commissioners in Dublin, in July, describe a high mutiny of part of their troops, in which some were killed and several hurt on both sides.[5] Part of the letter is printed in Haliday's *Scandinavian Kingdom of Dublin* (p. 165 note), from a copy in the Carte Collection.

Several letters in August, from Major-General Sterling, declare the intention of his army to stand for Presbyterial Government against the Independents in England.[6] Lord Inchiquin, in January 1648, describes the wretched condition of his army—" It will be difficult for me to resolve whether the " want of food or clothing be likely to prove most destructive to " us . . .our men die daily of their mere want."[7] This was followed by his declaring against the Parliament in April,[8] and the Scotch in June promised to support him,[9] and to conclude no peace without including him. In July, he invited Colonel Jones to join with him, who at first, with the privity of the Parliament,

---

[1] p. 399.   [2] pp. 418, 419.   [3] p. 422.   [4] p. 424.   [5] p. 429.
[6] pp. 433–435.   [7] p. 443.   [8] p. 449.   [9] p. 469.

negotiated with him in order to sound his designs and, if possible recall him to his obedience to the Parliament.[1] Jones, in August, describes his operations in Meath and his intention to fall into the enemy's quarters to destroy their corn as far as possible,[2] which up to October [3] he had not been able to do thoroughly. The only trace of Cromwell in Ireland are the Articles for the Surrender of Kilkenny [4] already printed, but there are letters to him in June 1650,[5] concerning Lord Broghill's operations in Kerry, who mentions that one of Lord Inchiquin's ships had been taken by some resolute troopers, who swam after her with their swords in their mouths and hands. A long Remonstrance by Lord Ormonde to the Popish Clergy at Jamestown in August charges them with being a main cause of the ruin of the nation, by not using their influence with the people to obey his orders, their disobedience arising indeed from the forgeries invented, the calumnies spread against the Government, and the incitements of the people to rebellion by very many of the clergy.[6] There are letters from the Roman Catholic Archbishop of Cashel and Lord Clanrickard in January and March [7] about Irish affairs, and the last mentions the arrival of the Abbot of St. Catherine,[8] the envoy of the Duke of Lorraine, whose mission and the Duke's expected aid are referred to in the letters of Colonel Plunket and Lord Taaffe.[9]

A year later, in January 1652, the Parliament still found it necessary to keep above 350 garrisons in Ireland, and their Commissioners [10] declare that about 100 more would be required, while in Ireland itself or under orders for it were above 30,000 men. The enemy on the other hand had nearly as many, and had great advantages from knowing the ways through the bogs, and having constant intelligence of the motions of the Parliament's forces, who seldom or never had intelligence of theirs from the natives, who were possessed with an opinion that the Parliament intended them no terms of mercy. They suggest that the fighting men be allowed to transport themselves to the service of any prince in amity with the Commonwealth, that something be held out to the peaceable inhabitants for the security of their lives and encouragement to follow husbandry,

---

[1] p. 485. [2] p. 493. [3] p. 499. [4] p. 522. [5] pp. 524, 525.
[6] p. 528. [7] p. 556. [8] p. 559. [9] pp. 563, 564. [10] p. 622.

that the Adventurers should at once begin to plant, and besides the well-known plan of the Pale behind the Barrow and Boyne, they propose another behind the Suir and More or Blackwater. They enclose a paper with a scheme of allotments to the Adventurers. In May, these particulars and others were again presented to the Council of State,[1] but the proposals for allotments and planting were disapproved of by the Adventurers for various reasons.[2] Meanwhile resistance was dying down, and the Irish forces were surrendering. Specimens of Articles will be found on pp. 645 and 648, and the Articles of Surrender in January 1653 of a fort on the remote Isle of Arran, one of the last that held out, on p. 668.

There is a copy of the Commission of the Earl of Essex[3] with the blanks in that printed in the *Desiderata Curiosa* filled up, and the Commission of Sir Thomas Fairfax,[4] being that delivered up by Rushworth when he resigned in June 1650. Of letters from the Earl of Essex there are none of any consequence, except that of June 28, 1643,[5] to Lenthall, desiring that the army may be paid and some one placed at the head of it in whom they may put confidence. Three from Sir William Waller, in November 1643,[6] describe his repulse from Basing House, and the mutinous spirit of his army, their utter want of necessaries (which is corroborated by a letter on the same page from Mr. Cawley) and a skirmish in Farnham Park.

There are several letters from the Commissioners with the Army. At the beginning of the campaign of 1644,[7] they describe a muster, noticing particularly the prevalence of disease among the horses. Just before the second battle of Newbury, they desire supplies for the army. After the taking of Bridgwater, they were much embarrassed " in labouring both to satisfy the " expectation of the soldier and continue the townsman [8] in his " propriety." Six weeks later, they send a narrative of the taking of Bristol,[9] where they find the disposal of the captured property still more troublesome, there being conflicting claims on it, and as to some on the part of the Admiralty and East India Company. They have also difficulty in providing the gratuity promised the army, in lieu of plunder, though " the general had

---

[1] p. 646.　　[2] p. 649.　　[3] p. 43.　　[4] p. 219.　　[5] Appendix, p. 715.
[6] pp. 154, 159, 163.　　[7] p. 177.　　[8] p. 236.　　[9] p. 268.

" neglected no expedient to sweeten the soldier with money,"
and for the supply of the garrison, and complain, that " for want
" of able ministers, *Directories* and orders for the use of the
" same, the people here sit in darkness, and the collegiate men
" still chant out the Common Prayer Book to the wonted
" height." [1]

A letter of Fairfax of July 6, 1645, is mostly about the
Clubmen.[2] Specimens of resolutions passed by those of Berkshire will be found on pp. 246, 247, and there are several
isolated notices of those in the West, and one each of those in
Wales [3] and Sussex.[4]

All through the Calendar from the summer of 1642 to the
spring of 1646, there are a great number of letters from Sir
William Brereton and others, describing the state of affairs, and
the operations in Cheshire and the adjacent counties. Of these
the most remarkable are those just before the outbreak of the
war,[5] showing how the rival parties endeavoured to raise forces ;
that of October 21, 1643,[6] describing the occupation of Wem,
the siege of Nantwich and their relief of it, the enemy's attack
on Wem and their relief of it, and their final defeat of the
Royalists at Lee-Bridge ; those of November 11 and 15,[7]
describing the forcing of the passage of the Dee, and the taking
of Wrexham and Hawarden Castle ; and others at the end of
that month,[8] describing how their hopes of taking Chester
had been disconcerted by the landing of forces from Ireland.
From the beginning of October 1645 onwards, till the following
February, are numerous accounts of the siege of Chester, including one of the rout of a relieving force at Denbigh,[9] and of
a sally of the besieged.[10] The last castle to surrender in North
Wales was Holt, which held out till January 1647.[11]

There are a good many papers about South Wales and the
neighbouring counties in 1645 and 1646. The first from
Captain Batten, in August, describes the defeat of the Royalists
in Pembrokeshire, and the taking of Haverford Castle by his
seamen,[12] and there is a whole series from General Laugharne
describing his operations.[13] Colonel Morgan announces the

---

[1] pp. 283, 308.   [2] p. 232.   [3] p. 270.   [4] p. 289.   [5] pp. 44, 46, 51.
[6] p. 141.   [7] pp. 151, 153.   [8] pp. 156–162.   [9] p. 301.
[10] p. 317.   [11] p. 406.   [12] p. 255.   [13] p. 286.

taking of Chepstow and Hereford,[1] in which subsequent documents show that he was assisted by the treachery of some of the officers of the garrison.[2] There are also several documents relating to the Royalist rising at Cardiff in February 1646, and its suppression.[3]

From Devonshire, at the end of 1642 and beginning of 1643,[4] are letters concerning the first invasion of that county by the Royalists, the forcing of a passage into Cornwall by the Parliamentarians and their subsequent repulse, the invasion of Devon by the Royalists and their repulse at Modbury, and several concerning the proposed treaty, with copies of the documents that passed between the Commissioners of Cornwall and Devon, and its final rupture. From time to time come letters from the besieged garrison of Plymouth, ending with the raising of the siege in January 1646.[5]

In 1642 and 1643, there are several letters from Hull, the earliest from the Committee there about the Magazine[6] and preparations for defence, and later on, from Sir John Hotham to the Parliament. Sir Christopher Wray and Captain Hotham, in November, describe their movements in North Yorkshire, and enclose intercepted letters from Sir M. Langdale and others[7] and Sir Hugh Cholmely, in January, narrates his skirmish with Colonel Slingsby at Gisbrough.[8] All through the winter and spring, there is a long series of curious letters from Captain Hotham to the Earl of Newcastle, beginning with one dated December 27.[9] Of several of these only transcripts exist, which will be found in the Appendix, where also is Mr. Stockdale's letter describing the defeat of the Fairfaxes at Aldwalton Moor. In September and October, are letters concerning the siege of Hull, and the raising of it.[10] The only trace of the campaign of Marston Moor is a letter of Prince Rupert to Goring from Liverpool, on his march northward.[11] In August 1645, are several letters describing the mutinous condition of the Yorkshire troops, and the writers' apprehensions of the consequences if the King should penetrate into the county.

---

[1] p. 328.   [2] pp. 395, 412.   [3] pp 348–352.   [4] pp. 77–111.
[5] pp. 330, 336.   [6] pp. 38, 41.   [7] p. 68.   [8] p. 90.
[9] p. 81.   [10] pp. 129, 138.   [11] p. 179.

There are a considerable number of documents relating to religious matters, most of which have already been printed. The first is a long series of Queries by some of the London Clergy, about the legality and meaning of the "*Et Cetera*" oath.[1] There are a great many papers presented to the House of Commons by the Assembly of Divines, including the original drafts of the *Directory*,[2] and of the Services for the Solemnization of Marriage, for the Burial of the Dead,[3] and the Visitation of the Sick,[4] which last is remarkable as showing the clauses struck out by the House of Commons, and also the drafts of the Directory for Admonition, Excommunication, and Absolution,[5] and of the Larger[6] and the Shorter Catechisms.[7] All through 1645 and 1646, papers occur concerning the controversies, which arose between the Assembly and the House about the power of Excommunication and about Church Government. Most of them have been printed, but occasionally the originals are of interest. For instance, it appears that in Questions concerning Church Government,[8] the Question "Whether any particular Church Government be *jure divino*, and what that Government is?" was an afterthought. By far the most remarkable is a Declaration of the House touching their proceedings in the matter of Church Government, which vindicates the right of the civil power to regulate, by appeal or otherwise, the power of Excommunication.[9] This was read a second time November 8, 1645, but laid aside in consequence of the opposition of the Presbyterians, and, as far as I know, it has not been printed or noticed by any historian. There is also a draft Declaration of Parliament, dated August 7, 1649,[10] which, as originally drawn, established a Presbyterian form of government, and public worship according to the *Directory*, but this clause was struck out. There are occasional notices of proceedings against Papists and Recusants, and also against the Clergy who were opposed to the Parliament. The King's party sometimes resorted to reprisals, for instance, the King's warrant to Goring in February 1645 [11] orders him to arrest Ministers who teach or countenance rebellion, who are not to be exchanged except for any of his Chaplains or other Orthodox Divines detained by the Rebels.

---

[1] p. 4.   [2] p. 194.   [3] p. 196.   [4] p. 197.   [5] p. 206.   [6] p. 439.
[7] p. 441.   [8] p. 357.   [9] pp. 296–300.   [10] p. 515.   [11] p. 212.

There are a very large number of examinations, depositions, informations, and the like throughout the Calendar. Of these the most remarkable are the examinations of Pollard, Ashburnham, Wilmot, and Goring, in June 1641, concerning the Army Plot,[1] the examinations of Michael Hudson and others in June 1646,[2] and the examinations of Thomas Coke in April 1651.[3] The second group relates to the King's journey to the Scots, the negotiations between him and them through the French Agent, the objects of Hudson's intended journey to France, &c. Peck printed in the *Desiderata Curiosa* as much of them as he or his copyist could read, observing " here follows a great deal more, but in so ill a hand I cannot read it." This description is quite correct, the papers being the statements of the witnesses taken down very hurriedly with numerous abbreviations, which for some words become a sort of shorthand. However, most of them have now been deciphered, though occasional words could not be made out at all, and others not with certainty. The third group reported on May 28, 1651, contains a full disclosure of the Royalist plots in England. The Council of State reports,[4] " Many have been apprehended, of " whom he hath informed, and many more yet to be apprehended. " His general scheme of the transactions of the King of Scots " hath much confirmed what we had before, and our intelligence " hath confirmed what he hath said to be truth. We also know " how to put together many things, which before were but " hinted and brokenly suggested." Many passages in the Nicholas Correspondence[5] show how the Royalists were thereby disconcerted, particularly p. 237, while Nicholas speaks of Coke's retaking as " as sad and fatal misfortune to the K. as hath " befallen him since his father's murder, and like to prove the " ruin of most of his Majesty's best affected subjects " Thomazon, the collector of what are now the *King's Pamphlets*, was one of those arrested in consequence, and the Duke of Richmond was examined before the Council on Coke's information[6]

Of miscellaneous letters and papers, the first that deserves notice is a copy of a letter in Spanish from the Earl of Strafford to some Spaniard of high rank, dated July 18, 1640, concerning

[1] pp. 15–25. [2] pp. 368–384. [3] pp. 576–603. [4] p. 604.
[5] *Camden Miscellany.* [6] p. 604. [7] p. 3.

the proposed loan of 400,000 crowns in exchange for Irish levies. From the endorsement, this letter apparently came into Pym's hands. A letter in French, of May 6–16, 1641, gives a foreigner's view of affairs just before Strafford's execution, and describes the marriage of the Princess Royal [1] The original of the well-known letter of R. E. to Mr. Anderton [2] is in the Collection.

The Hampshire Committee on August 12 describe the progress of the siege of Portsmouth,[3] and send news of its surrender on September 7,[4] while Captain Swanley [5] on August 28 narrates the securing of the Isle of Wight and the neighbouring castles for the Parliament. On the other hand the members for Oxford City early in September [6] describe the intended fortifications, the first occupation of the city by the Cavaliers, and what followed, and on November 21[7] is a detailed account of the seizure of Chichester for the King. Lord Edward Herbert, afterwards Earl of Glamorgan and Marquis of Worcester, on September 18 [8] desires to be excused coming to London, as he fears affronts of stopping and searching by the way, though his coming is " most " necessary for the accomplishing of that great and beneficial " waterwork in attaining the perfection whereof hath cost me " many thousands, not so much out of covetousness to gain unto " myself as to serve my country." Early in the following year, some one at Oxford [9] sends a sketch of affairs from a Cavalier's point of view to a friend at Cambridge, while " Philo-Brittanicus " (said to be Sir Thomas Peyton by Nalson, who had means of knowing, his wife being a Peyton) describes a slight put on the Lords by the Commons.[10] On March 2, 1643, the King writes a holograph letter to the Queen,[11] partly in cipher, which has been printed, but with mistakes now corrected in the Calendar. The cipher is the same as in the other letters between the King and Queen, printed in the *Appendices to the First and Sixth Reports of the Historical Manuscripts Commission*, pp. 4, 5, and p. 217. From this cipher I have been able to interpret a few words in the letter of January 25,[12] undeciphered in the printed copies. Another intercepted letter, from a Royalist agent at Rotterdam, in May [13] is chiefly concerned with the despatch of arms, &c. to

---

[1] p. 11.   [2] p. 29.   [3] p. 50.   [4] p. 61.   [5] p. 54.   [6] pp. 56, 59.
[7] p. 72.   [8] p. 62.   [9] p. 84.   [10] p. 94.   [11] p. 98.
[12] p. 93.   [13] p. 116.

England, and Strickland's proceedings in Holland. It is partly
in cipher, which I have deciphered, except some symbols for
proper names. Another long letter, partly in cipher, from a
Cavalier at Oxford, dated July 5,[1] to some one at the siege of
Exeter, is written in high spirits at the Royalist successes, and
shows that the current belief among the Royalists was that
Essex, Manchester, and others had offered to come over with
the whole army. The signature has unfortunately perished,
the paper being exceedingly worn and frail. At the end of
October and November, are several letters about the incursions of the Royalists into Bedfordshire and Northamptonshire,
and the occupation of Newport Pagnell,[2] and also three
from Sir John Byron to the Governor of Aylesbury,[3] making
proposals for its surrender to the King. A long intercepted
letter, partly in cipher, from Sir E. Nicholas to Lord Goring,
dated November 1,[4] relates to affairs in Holland, the arrangements for procuring arms and ammunition thence, and the
Queen's influence. It should have been noticed in the
Calendar that the draft Ordnance on p. 168 for the appointment of the first Committee of both Kingdoms was identical
with that appointing the second Committee, printed in
Gardiner's *Constitutional Documents*, p. 192.[5] In December
1644, Sir Anthony Ashley Cooper sends Essex an account of the
first relief of Taunton,[6] and expresses his astonishment at its
defence, the " works being for the most part but pales and
hedges and no line about the town." The paper of March 29,
1645,[7] headed " Advertisements of what may content in London,"
is curious as being apparently that to which the notes by Sir E.
Nicholas, printed in *State Papers, Domestic*, p. 373, were a reply.
On May 19, Digby and Prince Rupert order Goring to advance
to a junction with the King's army at Harborough.[8] " For God's
sake," says Digby, " use diligence and come as strong as you can.
In my conscience it will be the last blow in the whole business."
On June 15, the Prince of Wales writes to Goring about the
insolencies and injuries alleged against the officers and soldiers
who pretend to be under his command.[9] Digby, in his letters

---

[1] p. 123.   [2] pp. 139–148.   [3] pp. 139, 140, 144.   [4] p. 146.
[5] See *Great Civil War*, i., 404.   [6] p. 197.   [7] p. 218.
[8] p. 224.   [9] p. 227.

of July 4[1] and August 12,[2] to Goring, describes the King's plans
and prospects—in the second in his usual sanguine manner.
Unfortunately much of each letter is in a cipher, which I have
been unable to decipher. On July 6,[3] Fairfax writes to Lenthall
concerning the raising of the siege of Taunton and the enemy's
movements, and a month later Rushworth sends him an account
of the siege of Sherborne.[4] All through August, September, and
October, numerous letters from different parts of the country
occur, describing the rapid movements of the King and the
troops that pursued him down to his arrival at Newark in
October. A copy of a letter from Digby to Jermyn,[5] being one
of those taken at Sherburne, is the last from him before he
started on his expedition to Scotland, the final ruin of which
near the Solway is described in letters[6] from Sir John Browne
and General Vandruske. Two letters from Massie, of August 30
and September 12,[7] desire assistance on account of Goring's apprehended advance, and there are several from Culpeper to Goring
in September and October about affairs in Devon, and suggesting
that he should endeavour to break through with the horse to
Montrose or the King. These schemes were soon rendered
impracticable by the renewed advance of Fairfax, who took
Tiverton on October 19,[8] and on January 6[9] Culpeper writes a
long letter to Ashburnham apprehending that they will be
forced into Cornwall. The Royalist army had become thoroughly
disorganised, Culpeper observing that the horse would be very
good if they would fight more and plunder less. That the Parliament, however, were still by no means out of danger is shown
by the three remarkable letters of Robert Wright, their agent in
Paris, dated December 12 and 28, and January 9,[10] describing
the negotiations in Paris between the Royalists and the Scots
carried on by the Queen, and William Murray, and the plans for
sending a foreign army to the West under Goring and Sir William
Davenant. All these schemes failed, and the King was reduced to
fly to the Scots, at whose instance he ordered Lord Bellasis to
surrender Newark.[11] Through the summer notices occur of the

---

[1] p. 231.   [2] p. 245.   [3] p. 232.   [4] p. 242.   [5] p. 287.
[6] pp. 301, 302.   [7] pp. 262, 269.   [8] p. 292.   [9] p. 332.
[10] pp. 323, 327, 335.   [11] p. 358.

surrender of various places that still held out, and in September
Sir George Ayscue sends an account of the surrender of Scilly.[1]

In the summer and autumn of 1648, there are a great many
letters relating to the Royalist risings in different parts of the
country.[2] There are several about the rising under Langdale
from Lambert, the rising near Stamford, the insurrections in
Kent, and especially about the siege of Colchester, of which the
most remarkable is one to Lenthall,[3] unsigned, but probably from
a secretary of Fairfax, describing the beginning of the siege.
The rout of the Duke of Buckingham's party at St. Neots is
described in a despatch from Colonel Scrope.[4] There are also
several documents relating to the revolt of the fleet, including a
long narrative by Peter Pett [5] of what took place at Chatham.
The victorious army on November 16th presented their Remonstrance demanding justice against the King and others. The
original signed by Rushworth in the name of the army is in this
Collection.[6]

After 1648, down to the expulsion of the Parliament in April
1653, the character of the documents changes, there being fewer
relating to domestic matters, and many more concerning foreign
affairs. The earlier part of the Calendar indeed contains some
of the latter class, such as Strickland's letters narrating his proceedings in the United Provinces, the report of the skirmish in
May 1647 [7] between the English and Swedish fleets near the
Isle of Wight, because the latter would not strike their flag, and
the letter of the Queen of Sweden of April 18, 1646,[8] and the
papers presented to Parliament in May 1647,[9] concerning the
affairs of the Elector Palatine and the negotiations at Munster.
There is a very interesting series of letters from Blake and some
of his officers, relating to his operations against Prince Rupert's
fleet on the coasts of Portugal and Spain, the earliest being a
letter to the King of Portugal, March 10, 1650.[10] The most
important are two from Blake and Popham and from Blake
himself of August 15,[11] and October 14,[12] describing skirmishes
with Prince Rupert's ships, and the capture of the Brazil fleet,
and from Captain Saltonstall,[13] of November 22, describing the

---

[1] p. 392. [2] pp. 455-494. [3] p. 458. [4] p. 478.
[5] p. 459. [6] p. 504. [7] p. 437. [8] p. 356. [9] pp. 408-411.
[10] p. 519. [11] p. 531. [12] p. 536. [13] p. 543.

94 Brown	164 H. O.	219, 220, Will.
131 Duke	173 Hamilton	Murray.
132 Dutch	189 the King	226 Newcastle
138 (?)	192 K[enelm]	260 the Queen
140 Earl	D[igby]	269 Rebels
148 France	202 Mr.	300 Treat
159 General		324 York

b_3 is probably a mistake for $b_5 =$ "for." In another letter the symbol for "for" is given as 65, probably a misprint for b_5. d_5 and 138 occur without decipherment. The last probably means Essex.

The next two were undeciphered, but I succeeded in finding the key. The cipher of that on p. 116 is :—

15 a	29 (o)	and so on to 64 =
16 (b)	30 (p)	z. The letters in
17 (c)	31 (q)	brackets do not
18 d	32 r	occur in the letter
19 e	33 s	in question. Also
20 (f)	34 t	4 = by, 6 = with, 8
21 g	35 (u)	= to, 9 = of, kk =
22 (?)	36 (w)	letters. Besides
23 h	37 (x)	there are several
24 i	38 (y)	symbols denoting
25 (k)	39 (z)	words or proper
26 (l)	40 (nil)	names, which I
27 (m)	41 a	was unable to make
28 (n)	42 b	out.

The cipher of that on p. 123 is :—

1 m	15 e	32 y
3 m	16 f	35 w
4 l	17 e	37 t
7 i	18 f	39 u or v
8 k	19 d	41 s
9 i	20 c	43 r
10 g	22 c	48 p
11 h	24 a	50 o
12 g	25 a	51 n
13 h	26 b	52 o
14 e	30 x	

and 55 to 60 nils. Q and Z do not occur in the letter.

The symbols for words that occur in the Prince of Wales's letter on p. 446 are :—

79 although	110 have	151 self
82 against	111 hath	152 same
83 at	115 his	153 send
84 all	117 Instructions	154 service
85 and	118 in	155 to
86 any	119 it	156 the
89 command	122 King	157 this
90 commission	129 may	158 that
91 castle	130 Majesty	159 these
93 can	132 no	165 unto
94 could	133 not	166 when
95 Dover	137 of	169 with
97 do	138 or	170 which
98 done	140 our	176 will
100 Dominion	141 Parliament	177 would
103 fort	143 power	178 you
104 force	146 ready	179 your
105 for	149 Swan	180 yet
108 Governor	150 shall	

The key to the letter cipher is given in the Calendar.

Most of the references explain themselves. "Gilbert" is "*A Contemporary History of Ireland, entitled, An Aphorismical Discovery of Treasonable Faction,*" edited by Mr. J. T. Gilbert. "Grey iii." is "*An Examination of the Third Volume of Neal's History of the Puritans,*" by the Rev. Zachary Grey, and ' Grey iv." is *An Examination of the Fourth Volume of the Same.* When the King's Pamphlets in the British Museum are referred to the Press mark is given.

The second' volume of this Calendar, which will contain abstracts of many papers of the middle of the seventeenth century belonging to the Duke of Portland, but not forming part of the Nalson Collection, together with an index to both volumes, is in preparation.

It remains to express my acknowledgments to Mr. Heitland, Fellow of St. John's, Cambridge, for procuring for me from the

Rev. John E. B. Mayor, Fellow of the same College, information about Dr. Williams, to the Rev. E. Woode, Curate of Barrow, for a copy of Dr. Williams's epitaph there, and for an extract from the Register relating to his burial, to the Rev. R. Charles for a copy of Rawlinson's letter to Owen, now preserved in the Bodleian, and above all to Mr. W. A. Shaw, who first drew my attention to the four volumes in the British Museum.

F. H. BLACKBURNE DANIELL.

September 1891.

CALENDAR OF THE MANUSCRIPTS OF HIS GRACE THE DUKE OF PORTLAND.

Vol. I.

NALSON COLLECTION.

The names of all such persons as are certified to be in places of charge or trust in their several Counties, having wives, children, or servants that are RECUSANTS or NON-COMMUNICANTS, and therefore are vehemently suspected to be ill-affected in religion by reason of the acts of State.

1628, May 8.—William, Earl of Banbury, Lord Lieutenant of Oxfordshire.

Emanuel, Earl of Sunderland, Lord President of the Council of the North, and Lord Lieutenant of Yorkshire.

Viscount Savage, Justice of the Peace in Gloucestershire.

Viscount Newark, Commissioner of the Peace in Nottinghamshire.

Lord Weston, Chancellor of the Exchequer.

Sir William Wrey, D. L. for Cornwall.

Sir Thomas Lamplogh and Sir Edward Musgrave, Commissioners of the Peace for Cumberland.

Sir Henry Shirley, Commissioner of the Peace for Leicestershire.

Sir Charles Jones, George Melborne, and Edward Morgan, Commissioners of the Peace for Monmouthshire.

Sir William Yelverton, Commissioner of the Peace for Norfolk.

Sir Thomas Swinborne, Sheriff of Northumberland.

Sir John Clavering and Cuthbert Heron, Commissioners of the Peace for Northumberland.

Sir Richard Mulleneux and Sir Richard Haughton, Deputy Lieutenants for Lancashire.

John Brockholes, George Ireland, Sir Cuthbert Halsell, Richard Sherborne, and Edward Chiswell, Commissioners of the Peace for Lancashire.

Sir Thomas Riddell, Recorder of Newcastle-on-Tyne.

Arthur Brett, Serjeant-Major to a company billetted in Surrey.

Sir Henry Compton, K.B., D. L. for Sussex.

Sir John Shelly and Sir Garrett Kempe, Commissioners of Sewers for Sussex.

Sir Richard Titchborne, D. L. for Hampshire.

Thomas Otely, Commissioner of the Peace for Salop.

William Grosvenor, Coroner for Salop.

Richard Braithwayte, Justice of the Peace for Westmoreland.

Sir Marmaduke Wivell, Commissioner of Oyer and Terminer, and one of the Council of the North.

Sir Thomas Methame, D. L., and Colonel of Foot Bands in Yorkshire.

Jordayn Metham, Henry Holme, Michael Portington, George Cresswell, Thomas Danby, and Ralph Bingham, Commissioners of Sewers for Yorkshire.

Sir William Herbert, D. L., and Custos Rotulorum of Montgomeryshire.

Thomas Laier, Captain of Foot in Norfolk.

Sir John Conway, Commissioner of the Peace for Flintshire.

Robert Warren, Justice of the Peace, and Parson of Melford, in Suffolk, is justly suspected of Popery for the reasons given. [N. XIII., 1.]

Sir John Eliot.

[1628-9, January 28.]—Speech concerning religion. (This report differs in language, but is substantially the same as that printed in Forster, *Sir John Eliot*, ii. 412. An abridgement in Rushworth, i. 648.) [N. XIII., 46.]

John Williams, Bishop of Lincoln, to the King.

[1639(?).]—Petition. (Printed in *State Papers, Domestic*, p. 202.) *Copy.*

Observations of the Lord Keeper Coventry at the trial of the bishop in the Star Chamber.

1637, July 11.—With what limitations and how a man may meddle or tamper with such witnesses as he hath to deal with. (This is a report, slightly differing from that part of the one in Rushworth, ii. 1. 447, 448, from " for else if the witnesses be corrupted " to " perhaps he effects it not.") *On the same paper as the last.* [N. XXII., 159.]

The Duke of Lenox.

[1638, July 15.]—His [alleged] speech before his Majesty concerning war with Scotland. (There is an abstract of this speech in *State Papers, Domestic*, p. 564.) *Copy.* [N. XIX., 1.]

Doctor John Forbes of Corse, and others the Aberdeen Doctors.

[1638, July.]—" General demands concerning the late Covenant to be propounded to some Reverend Brethren, who were to recommend it to us and our people." (Manuscript copy of a pamphlet printed at Aberdeen by " Edward Raban, printer to his most excellent Majesty's famous University there." Apparently there is no copy of this pamphlet in the British Museum, though there are replies of the " Reverend Brethren " and rejoinders by the Doctors. There is an abstract in *State Papers, Domestic*, p. 270.) [N. XIX., 2.]

A List of the Scots pro et contra Regem.

[1638 or 1639.]—Showing 42 peers in the first class and 38 in the second. (Printed in Grey, iii. Appendix, Nos. 68, 69, pp. 110, 111.) [N. XIX., 4.]

" The Oath given to the Lords at York."

[1638-9, March.]—(Differing slightly from that printed in *State Papers, Domestic*, p. 637.) [N. XIX., 3.]

The Lords Leslie, Marr, Rothes, Montrose, Montgomery, Loudoun, and Forrester, to [the King of France].

[1639, May.]—Accrediting Mr. Colvile. (Printed in Nalson, i. 277.) *English Translation.* [N. XII., 271.]

SCOTLAND.

[1639, June 6.]—The humble Petition of his Majesty's Subjects. (Printed in Nalson, i. 232.) [N. XIX., 11.]

ARTICLES OF THE PEACE and SUBMISSION OF THE COMMISSIONERS.

[1639], June 17.—(Printed in Nalson, i. 239, 240, and Rushworth, ii. 2. 945, 946.) At the end is added "An assembly to be holden at Edinburgh the 6th of August next where his Majesty is to be present and that no consultations or meetings be made concerning it but such as be warranted by law. That whatsoever shall be agreed upon in the Assembly shall be ratified by Parliament. That a Parliament shall begin the 20th of August and an Act of pardon and oblivion to be made." *Copy.* [N. XIX., 12.]

Declaration of the PARLIAMENT OF IRELAND.

[1639-40, March 20.] — (Printed in Nalson, i. 283.) *Copy.* [N. XXI., 1.]

List of the Principal Acts passed by the PARLIAMENT OF SCOTLAND.

1640, June 11.—In the session that ended that day. 23 are enumerated. (See *Acts of the Parliament of Scotland*, v. 318.) Subjoined is " the substance of the petition after the Acts." (The whole document is identical with one calendared in *State Papers, Domestic*, p. 287, No. 73.) *Copy.* [N. XIX., 9.]

The EARL OF STRAFFORD to ———.

1640, July 18. London.—Your Excellency is not deceived in your confidence in my greatest diligence to form a league between the two Crowns which may be very firm and durable, not only for ourselves, while we live, but also for posterity, nor in believing, as far as regards my own inclinations, that I esteem in the highest degree the magnanimity and prudence of the Spanish nation, and desire its prosperity next to that of my own country. The King, my master, is no less satisfied with my zeal in his service, since I well know the strong inclination his Majesty discovers to me in private to form a firm friendship with that Crown, not only from his consideration of the advantage thereby to his subjects, but from his singular affection towards the person of his Catholic Majesty. To speak plainly to your Excellency, it appears to me that to effect everything we need nothing but mutual confidence ; this established by the diligence of the Ministers of the two kings, I do not see what can prevent these two monarchs who are so powerful, from being able to divide the world between them, without the one touching the interests of the other. Yet it is right to confess that this confidence has been for some years so weakened on this side, that words, without real and reciprocal acts moving *acquis passibus,* will not be sufficient to restore it. Let us apply ourselves then in every way to undertake this great work which is to turn out so happy and glorious for both kings and their peoples, and not allow the occasion to escape, which presents itself to us. We on our part will hasten the Irish levies desired by his Catholic Majesty, and that your Excellency—in case they cannot previously be drawn from Flanders, as is desired—may hasten the loan of 400,000 crowns, according to what has been proposed to the Ambassadors of his Catholic Majesty at this Court, and that this loan may be quickened (*se abrevie*) so much the more because unless it arrives here with all speed, it will lose entirely its grace and occasion, and also because these good offices being done to each other by the two kings, there will be more confidence, which will facilitate henceforward with equal suavity and efficacy those greater matters, of which your Excellency made mention in the postscript of your letter to Don Alonso de Cardenas. Your Excellency, in the same postscript, which Don Alonso showed me, is pleased to command me to serve his Catholic Majesty, particularly in the business of the levies, having accepted the employment, and I honour myself therein, assuring your Excellency that as far as the working at this shall concern me I will serve that Crown with all truth and promptitude as far as there shall be opportunity in both kingdoms, so as to confirm the confidence he has of my affections.

Finally having discovered to your Excellency my mind and inclination with all plainness and truth, you will be able thereby to know not only my anxieties that the treaty now proposed may repay the labour bestowed on it, but also the singular esteem I have for the person and natural gifts of your Excellency, and at the same time the real respect and veneration which I shall always pay to the correspondence and amity which he deigns to offer me with such generosity, so that I shall consider myself a most happy man, when your Excellency shall deign to command me in whatever my power suffices to serve him. God keep the most Excellent person of your Excellency many and happy years. In *Spanish*. *Copy*. *Endorsed* probably in Mr. Pym's hand " Spanish letter trans[cribed] (?) Sᵗ Th. Mallever (Mauleverer)." [N. XII., 1.]

Sundry of the Clergy of London Diocese and parts adjacent.

[1640, latter part of.]—Queries " touching the oath enjoined by the late Synod, Canon 6, wherein they unfeignedly desire satisfaction that so they may the more heartily and willingly take the said oath, when authority shall tender it unto them or by the Canon it is appointed.

1. Whether the Oath be legal so as to bind all the Clergy to it?" The ground thereof being that since 25 Hen. VIII. c. 19 the Convocation is bound from decreeing ought repugnant to the laws or customs of the realm, and we find not that the oath is warranted by the laws and we believe it to be contrary to the customs.

2. "What is meant by the doctrine and discipline or government of the Church of England?" The ground thereof being that we know not whether by doctrine the Synod mean the 39 Articles of 1562, or extend it to other doctrine, as his Majesty by his commission to the Convocation to make Canons seems to enlarge it, and if so, we cannot safely swear to it till it be declared, and then no further than it may be declared to be taken out of Scripture.

" Secondly we know not whether by discipline they mean only the Canons and Constitutions of the Church or other things besides. And if the Canons then what Canons, some of the ancient ones being grown out of use, and others altered, neither of which as we conceive ought to be, if the discipline be necessary to salvation. And the Canons being so many and at so many different times so far asunder made how can any man swear to that part unless it be . . . set forth what those be we swear unto, and if the discipline contain ought else, why is it not clearly expressed.

3. Whether it is meant that doctrine and discipline contain all things necessary to salvation *conjunctim* or *divisim*? If *conjunctim* we doubt of it, because we take all things necessary to salvation to be contained in the Articles of 1562 . . and not at all in the discipline as distinct from the doctrine" and admitting the discipline to be lawful we cannot concede it to be necessary to salvation, and he that swears it to be in both as we are required by the conjunction " and " and believes it to be in only one doth coast upon perjury. But if *divisim*, it must be understood of the doctrine only or discipline only or of both in different respects, in the last sense we think it needful that these respects be explained to take away ambiguity, but if it be meant of one only that ought to be expressed and the other cashiered as superfluous. And in any case to enjoin all to swear that the Discipline is necessary to salvation implies a condemnation of all Protestant Churches abroad as wanting what is necessary to salvation and the essential being of a true church. And it seems a large and wide step, since we have not heard of any such position in these terms so much as by bare assertion maintained, and the newness of the expression makes us afraid, especially considering the ancient Constitution under Archbishop Arundel against novel expressions about the faith.

4. " What is meant by the Clause 'nor will I ever give my consent to alter the Government of this Church by Archbishops, Bishops &c.' "

If this be sworn absolutely, so as no revocation or alteration herein that can be made by his Majesty in or out of Parliament at any time shall make us consent to such an alteration, we think it contrary to the oath of Allegiance and Supremacy, and a binding ourselves to resist authority, if any alteration be made on any occasion whatsoever. If it be intended only to bind us till such an alteration why is it so peremptorily expressed? Albeit the Casuists tell us that such an oath—even though unlimited—binds not if the Government be altered by authority, yet they dare not acquit him of rashness, who swears without such a limitation.

5. " Whether there be the same reason of not consenting to alteration of Government by Deans [and] Archdeacons as there is of not consent to alter that of Bishops " ? Because they were never esteemed as if they were of the same institution and foundation as Bishops, and therefore may more easily be changed, so that we see not cause to rivet them into an unalterable order by the sacred bond of an oath. The Canon of 1603 only requires acknowledgement that the Government is not repugnant to the word of God, which Canon is part of the Discipline established —as we conceive—and so the acknowledgement may suffice without an oath.

6. " What is meant by the ' &c.' " ? Because we never heard that an &c. was ever put into an oath either among Christians or Pagans, and believe it to be contrary to the perspicuity which ought to be in all oaths for either it implies some unnamed persons or things and then it is an ambiguous Clause, or else it signifies nothing at all, and then it is too vain and trivial for men to pawn their souls upon, and cannot be less than taking God's name in vain, which Clergymen of all others should most shun.

7. " What is meant by ' As it stands now so established, and as by right it ought so to stand ' " ? It is not clear whether the " now " be meant of any new establishment by the Synod, or the Establishment by Parliament in 1 and 8 Eliz.: " If the latter then it appears not what is that right by which it ought to stand, but only that which it hath by such establishment, viz. by the positive laws of the kingdom, which is a mere

tautology . . for who doubts but that which is established by the laws of the land ought to stand by the law of the land, and whether that will content the Reverend Bishops we much doubt, and if any other right be intended which we verily believe" then it ought to be expressed, especially in a point so much questioned and disputed of in the world and not positively decided in this Synod nor in any other in this Church of England.

8. "Whether our consent and suffrages are so involved in the new Canons and the Oath before mentioned that we cannot refuse" it? Because we conceive that the late Convocation ended with the Parlia-ment May 5th, And that by the Dissolution our votes and suffrages returned back to us again, especially considering that the first Commission granted to the Convocation on April 5th was of force only during the Parliament, and the Proctors had no new election by the rest of the Clergy, and no new writ enabling them to continue the Assembly, but only a new Commission to go on with the Canons not concluded before the Dissolution, and that this second Commission is dated May 12th, so that they were without a Commission to make one perfect Canon formerly begun by the space of a whole week after the dissolution.

"These queries we find cause to insist the more on, because of the last clause of the oath viz. That we must swear all this according to the plain and common sense and understanding of the same words and that heartily willingly and truly upon the faith of a Christian, which we cannot do till the former doubts be cleared, and the oath made so plain that we cannot mistake the meaning which is so ambiguous now, that we cannot understand" it "so as to adventure an oath upon it, in case it should appear to be lawful and meet—which we much doubt—to multiply oaths or decisions *de fide* beyond great and unavoidable necessity." [N. XXII., 1.]

The KING'S SPEECH at the opening of the Long Parliament.

1640, November 3.—(Printed in Nalson, i. 481; Rushworth, iii. 1. 12, with some differences, of which the most remarkable is that where the printed copies have "with this Protestation that if this accompt be not satisfactory as it ought to be" the MS. is "that if his account be not satisfactory, as wanting both time and conveniency to make it so full as it ought to be.") *Endorsed* "The King's speech . . . delivered to mee by Mr. Secretary Windebanke as a copie that the King himselfe avowes." [N. I., Unnumbered, at the end of the volume.]

The SPEAKER to all JUSTICES OF THE PEACE.

1640, December 7.—Directing them to prosecute Recusants, according to the order of that date. (See *Commons' Journals*, ii. 46.) *Draft.* [N. XIII., 2.]

The ENGLISH COMMISSIONERS to the SCOTCH COMMISSIONERS.

1640, December 9.—Reply to their fourth demand touching incend-iaries. (Printed from a copy in Lord Braye's papers in the *Tenth Report of the Historical MSS. Commission, Appendix, part* vi. 138.) *Copy.* [N. XIX., 13.]

The SCOTCH COMMISSIONERS to the ENGLISH COMMISSIONERS.

1640, December 14.—Delivering the grounds of their charges against the Archbishop of Canterbury and the Lord Lieutenant of Ireland (which charges are printed in Nalson, i. 681, 686), and desiring that they may be put to trial *per viam inquisitionis*. *Copy.* [N. XIX., 14.]

The Scotch Commissioners.

[1640, December 16.] — Paper containing their eight demands. (Printed in *Lords' Journals*, iv. 111.) *Copy.* [N. XX., 206.]

The Same.

Same date.—Charge against the Lord Lieutenant of Ireland. (Printed in Nalson, i. 686.) *Copy.* [N. XIII., 47.]

The Documents of the Scotch Commissioners.

[1640, December 18.]—(Printed in *Lords' Journals*, iv. 111, and Nalson, i. 689.) [N. XIX., 21.]

The Scotch Commissioners to the English Commissioners and their Reply.

1640, December 30.—Concerning the restoration of ships and goods. (Both printed in Rushworth, iii. 1. 366.) *Copies.* [N. XIX., 15, 17.]

The English Commissioners to the Scotch Commissioners.

1640, December 30.—Declaration in his Majesty's name. (Printed in Rushworth, iii. 1. 366.) *Copy.* [N. XIX., 16.]

The English Commissioners to the Scotch Commissioners.

1640[-1], January 7.—Concerning the restoration of about fourscore Scotch ships. (Printed in Rushworth, iii. 1. 366.) *Copy.* [N. XIX., 18.]

The Scotch Commissioners to the English Commissioners.

1640[-1], January 7.—" We would be no less willing to bear the losses, if we had ability, than we have been ready to undergo the hazard. But because the burden of the whole charges doth far exceed our strength, we have—as is more fully contained in our papers—represented our charges and losses, not intending to demand a total reparation, but of such a proportionable part, as that we may in some measure bear the remanent, which we conceive your lordships, having considered our reasons will judge to be a matter not of covetousness, but of the justice and kindness of the kingdom of England." [N. XIX., 19.]

The Same to the Same.

Same date.—Setting forth at great length their reasons for their demand. [N. XIX., 20.] *Annexed:*

    Schedule, the first part showing the public charges and burdens under which the whole country lies amounting to 514,128*l*. 9*s*. 0*d*., the second part divers other great burdens sustained by the Kingdom of Scotland amounting to 271,500*l*. represented to prove how much they are thereby disabled from bearing any great part of this burden which otherwise they would have willingly undergone.

(Printed in Grey, iii. Appendix, No. 70, p. 112. See Rushworth, iii. 1. 366.) *Copy.* [N. XIX., 10.]

The EARL OF BRISTOL.

[1640-1, January 12.]—Speech delivered at the Conference between the two Houses, concerning the treaty with the Scots. (See *Lords' Journals*, iv. 130.) [N. XIII., 5.]

The KING's SPEECH to both Houses at the Banqueting House.

1640[-1], January 23.—(A fuller report than that printed in Nalson, i. 735.) [N. XIII., 3.]

Information against Doctor CHAFFIN.

[1640-1, January 23.]—(Printed in Grey, iii. Appendix, No. 9, p. 13.) (See *Commons' Journals*, ii. 72.) [N. XIII., 4.]

ANONYOUS Speech.

[1640-1641.]—Beginning " Our Ancestors were accustomed to hear propositions from other nations of honour and greatness. We represent unto you a very distressed estate, sad things dishonourable to our Nation." . . . Ending " This is that I had in command to say unto you." Concerning the demands of the Scots. [N. XIII., 6.]

The SCOTCH COMMISSIONERS to the ENGLISH COMMISSIONERS.
The ENGLISH COMMISSIONERS to the SCOTCH COMMISSIONERS.
The SCOTCH COMMISSIONERS to the ENGLISH COMMISSIONERS.

1640[-1], January 26.—(All three papers are printed in *Lords' Journals*, iv. 145.) [N. XIX., 22, 23, 24.]

The SCOTCH COMMISSIONERS to the ENGLISH COMMISSIONERS.

1640[-1], February 5.—(Printed in *Lords' Journals*, iv. 153.) N. XIX., 26.]

The SCOTCH COMMISSIONERS to the ENGLISH COMMISSIONERS and their Reply.

1640[-1], February 8, [10]. — Concerning the seventh demand. (Both printed in *Lords' Journals*, iv. 159.) [N. XIX., 27, 25.]

The SCOTCH COMMISSIONERS to the ENGLISH COMMISSIONERS.

1640[-1], February 10.—Concerning the eighth demand. (Printed in *Lords' Journals*, iv. 159.) [N. XIX., 28.]

The SCOTCH COMMISSIONERS to the HOUSE OF COMMONS.

[1640-1, February 1-14.]—Reminding them that on the 16th instant 52,000*l.* is due to the Scots out of the Northern Counties and New-castle, and desiring to know when they may expect it. [N. XIX., 29.]

The HOUSE OF LORDS.

[1640-1, March 3.]—Paper concerning Berwick and Carlisle to be delivered at the Conference with the House of Commons. (Printed in *Lords' Journals*, iv. 175; *Commons' Journals*, ii. 98.) *Draft.* [N. XX., 205.]

INDEX of the REMANENT HEADS contained in the EIGHTH DEMAND.

1640[-1], March 9.—Concerning unity in Religion, the appointment of Scotchmen to places about the King and Royal family, the employment of none about the King and Prince who do not profess the Reformed Religion, the choosing of Counsel and Session in Scotland, naturalization and the mutual privileges of the subjects of both kingdoms, customs, freedom of trade, manufactures, coin, fishing, an Act of Oblivion, the ratification of the treaty by Act of Parliament, the prevention of any taking arms without the consent of the Parliament of his kingdom, the prevention of either of the two nations engaging in foreign war without the consent of both, their mutual assistance against foreign invasion, extradition, execution of decrees of the Courts of one kingdom in the other, the Borders and Middle Marches, and the trial by the Triennial Parliaments of both kingdoms of all wrong done by either nation to the other. (See *Lords' Journals*, iv. 216.) *Copy.* [N. XIX., 30.]

The SCOTCH COMMISSIONERS to the ENGLISH COMMISSIONERS.

1640[-1], March 10.—Desires concerning Unity of Religion. (Printed in *King's Pamphlets*, E., 157.) [N. XIX., 31.]

The ENGLISH COMMISSIONERS to the SCOTCH COMMISSIONERS and the SCOTCH COMMISSIONERS to the ENGLISH COMMISSIONERS.

1640[-1], March 15.—Answer to the paper of the 10th instant, and reply to that answer. (Both are abstracted from copies among Lord Braye's papers in the *Tenth Report of the Historical MSS. Commission, Appendix, part* vi., p. 139.) (See *Lords' Journals*, iv., 216.) *Copies.* [N. XIX., 32, 33.]

The SCOTCH COMMISSIONERS to the ENGLISH COMMISSIONERS.

1640[-1], March 16.—(Printed in *Lords' Journals*, iv. 187.) [N. XIX., 34.]

———— ROBERTS to CHARLES ALLEN.

[1641], March 26.—"Our Master's new work at Paris is in good forwardness in so much that he has divers times written to me to furnish him with 12 workmen such as you be, and to this purpose I have written to the place from whence you come, and if you please to be one of the number upon the intimation of your willingness I will not fail to put you upon the list. I am of opinion the June air of Paris will advantage your health." (See letter of the same dated May 7th.) [N. XII., 269.]

The SCOTCH COMMISSIONERS to the ENGLISH COMMISSIONERS.

1641, March 29.—Paper concerning Commerce and Trading.
(The last clause beginning "Forasmuch as the several jurisdictions" was with slight alterations incorporated in the Treaty, and is printed in Rushworth, iii. 1. 372.) *Copy.* [N. XIX., 35.]

The SCOTCH COMMISSIONERS to the ENGLISH COMMISSIONERS.

1641, April 1.—Concerning the reciprocal assistance by one nation to the other, in case of war, not to exceed 10,000 men with horse in the proportion from England of 100 horse to 1,000 foot, and from Scotland of 50 to 1,000. *Copy.* [N. XIX., 37.]

The Scotch Commissioners to the English Commissioners.

1641, April 1.—Paper "for conserving of Peace betwixt the two Kingdoms." (Incorporated for the most part with the treaty, being the part printed in Rushworth, iii. 1. 370, 371, 372, but with some additions and omissions.) (See *Lords' Journals*, iv. 216.) *Copy.* [N. XIX., 36.]

The King to the Lords Justices and Council of Ireland.

1641, April 3. Westminster.—Humble suit has made to us by the Parliament of Ireland that they may obtain the benefit of certain Graces promised by us in the 4th year of Our reign. For which purpose We require you to transmit bills for securing to our said subjects the following particulars.

First, that all kinds of corn may be freely exported, subject only to duty, from Ireland to our other dominions and to those of friendly powers, except in time of dearth.

Secondly, a bill for limiting the title of the Crown to sixty years, such as that passed in England in the 21st year of the reign of our father.

Thirdly, according to our princely promise in the 24th and 25th articles of the said Graces and in performance of the engagements of our father and Queen Elizabeth to secure the estates or reputed estates of the inhabitants as well of Connaught as of the County of Clare or Country of Thomond as of the Counties of Limerick and Tipperary and to free them and their said estates or reputed estates from all titles accrued to us or our predecessors and to forego our intended plantations therein notwithstanding any office then found . . we are graciously pleased that their estates be secured in Parliament and require you forthwith to transmit an Act for settling the said Province and Counties according to the tenor of the said 24th and 25th Articles.

Fourthly, that a bill be transmitted for the future prevention of Warrants of Assistance.

Fifthly, that a bill be transmitted for securing to our subjects the benefits of the 31st article and of all other parts of the said Instructions and Graces not herein expressed. *Copy.* [N. XIII., 8.]

The English Commissioners to the Scotch Commissioners.

1641, April 8.—Reply to the paper of April 1st "for the conserving of peace." (See *Lords' Journals*, iv. 216.) *Copy.* [N. XIX., 8.]

The Same to the Same.

Same date.—Reply to the paper of March 29th concerning commerce. *Copy.* [N. XIX., 39.]

The Judges.

1641, April 10.—Opinions. (Printed in *Lords' Journals*, iv. 212.) [N. XIII., 7.]

The University of Cambridge to the House of Commons.

1641, April 11.—(Printed in Rushworth, iii. i. 272.) *University Seal.* [N. II., 1.]

The Scotch Commissioners to the English Commissioners.

1641, April 12.—Pressing for payment of the arrears and Brotherly Assistance and desiring them to acquaint Parliament therewith. *Copy.* [N. XIX., 40.]

The ENGLISH COMMISSIONERS to the SCOTCH COMMISSIONERS.

1641, April 12.—"That his Majesty commandeth us to adhere to his former answer, and conceiveth it most just you should acquiesce therewith." (See *Lords' Journals*, iv. 216.) Two *copies*. [N. XIX., 41.]

CATALOGUE of the papers received at the report of the Conference.

[1641, April 15.]—Containing those mentioned in *Lords' Journals*, iv. 216. (See *Lords' Journals*, iv. 218.) [N. XX., 1.]

The SCOTCH COMMISSIONERS.

1641, April 28.—Paper. (Printed in *Lords' Journals*, iv. 231.) *Signed* "Adam Blair." [N. XIX., 44.]

The COMMITTEE AT NEWCASTLE to ———.

1641, April 30.—(Printed in *Lords' Journals*, iv. 243, and in Nalson, ii. 237.) *Extract.* [N. XIX., 43.]

Answer of the DEAN and PREBENDARIES OF DURHAM.

[1641, April, after the 8th.]—Stating why they cannot produce their book of Chapter Acts. (Printed in Peck, *Desiderata Curiosa*, ix. 4.) (See *Lords' Journals*, iv. 211.) [N. XV., 185.]

Examination of MARY BROWNE.

1641, May 6.—Stating that the Queen's plate at Somerset House was packed up the week before Easter, but that most of it had been unpacked to be used the previous Sunday at the Lady Mary's marriage, and was now at Whitehall. [N. XIII., 9.]

J. DU PERRON to the MARQUIS DE FONTENEY, Conseiller d'Etat et Maréchal des camps et armées de Sa Majesté. A Paris.

1641, May [6-]16. London.—"C'est pour vous asseurer que M. de Montereuil se tiendra extresmement honoré de vous suyvre en quelque condition qu'il vous plaise le mettre. Il est vray que l'employ qu'il à eu tant sous Monsieur de Bellieure que depuis son retour en qualité d'agent du Roy et mesme à Rome aupres du Cardinal Anthoine duquel il à esté domestique deux ou trois ans et duquel il à receu des marques d'agrement de ses services par un canonicat de l'eglise cathedrale de Toul qu'il lui à donné, luy eust fait desirer de vous cette grace si non d'estre le premier au moins d'estre en quelque sorte d'egalité avec l'autre. Toutefois il remit le tout à vostre volonté à laquelle il propose de se conformer entierement. Il est tres bien faict et de cors et d'esprit il scait les belles lettres et est d'une conversation egalement agreable divertissante et complaisante. J'espère, Monsieur, que vous en serez servy autant bien que vous le pouvez souhaiter, cependant je vous remercie tres humble de ce qu'il vous à pleu agreer la supplication que je vous avois faicte pour luy. Il est vray que la Chambre basse à signifie à la haute qu'elle trouvoit le viceroy d'Irlande criminel de Leze Majesté et desiroit que la justice en fust faite. Le Roy alla Samedy dernier au parlement pour dire que dans tout le proces la il ne trouvoit aucun chef qui le peust convaincre du trahison et partant qu'il ne pouvoit consentir à sa mort, qu'il n'empeschoit pas neanmoins qu'on ne l'eloynast de la cour et des affaires s'il se trouvoit chargé de quelque autre faute. Lundy dernier le peuple s'assembla à Westmonster au nombre de six ou sept mille hommes demandans que les Mylors leurs fissent justice du deputé. Cela continua encor le Mardy, et la chambre la leur ayant promise, ils se retirent. Le mesme Mardy, les deux chambres firent un serment ou protestation que tout le monde jura, excepté les Catholiques. Je vous en envoye la copie en Francois. On dit qu'il aproche fort du convenant d'Ecosse. Aujourdhuy se devoit donner le jugement du viceroy d'Irlande, mais je pense que cela est differé cependant sur un soubcon que le parlement à eu qu'on vouloit faire evader le dit viceroy de la Tour de Londre ou il est prisonnier, et qu'un nommé Sir Jean Suclin levoit des gens pour y faire entrée, et que le Roy faisoit aprocher son armée qui est à York. Le parlement à prié le Roy de commander que tous les officiers de la cour eussent à ne point sortir d'Angleterre et de la Cour sans permission particulier. Cela faict croire qui le parlement veut rechercher les autheurs de ce conseil, Mr Germain et Mr de Percy frerr de Madame de Carlille estans particulierement regardés en cela. Ils se sont retirez d'icy hier apres midi de resolution de passer la mer et eviter le malheur dont on les menacoit. Dimanche dernier se firent les noces de la Princesse Marie avec le jeune Prince d'Oranges, mais sans ceremonie ny danses ny autres rejouyssances. La Reyne Mere y assista et disna de mesme table, avec le Roy, la Reyne, les deux fils et deux filles de leurs Majestez et le Prince d'Orange. Elle ne se trouva pas au souper. On mist les jeune mariez à coucher ensemble une heure durant, mais de presence des Majestez des ambassadeurs et autres. Les ambassadeurs Hollandois furent traictez à part. Le Prince Palatin se trouva à la noce, mais non pas au disner ny souper. Mr Rosseti, agent du Pape s'en va d'icy car sa place (?) n'est plus tenable (?) pour luy ny pour les Catholiques. Je suis de grande peine de n'avoir aucune nouvelle de Mr de Chavigny touchant mon voyage, car les affaires [sont] si troublées icy et menacent de si grands malheurs si Dieu n'y mit le main, que nous ne sommes point * et moy principalement ; je vous supplie de luy en vouloir dire un mot. Je croy que vous aurez [reçu] les deux dernieres couvertures que je vous ay envoyées par M. du Prim (?)." *Seal.* [N. XVII., 2.]

——— ROBERTS to ———.

1641, May 7.—Commending the two bearers, Mr. Tirrell, "your countryman," and Mr. Allen, of whom he will write more particularly in his next week's letter. "They be hopeful every way and proper for the employment for which you desire them." *Addressed* "Pour mon maistre, Paris." (See the examinations of Charles Allaine and Clifton Thorold on May 31st.) [N. XII., 268.]

JOSEPH, C[lericus ?] C[armelitanus ?] to his much respected BARNABIE BURNE, Aleman, at Dublin.

1641, May 8.—"I have receaved yours of the last February of as little satisffaction as your formers. . . . You may saye" my necessities "are not soe great as to require such changement. I graunt that what I wrote to you in formal termes maye be such, but what you should suppose to be besydes and virtually included in them, which circumstances of tym etc. hindereth to laye down in writing, should induce you to graunt soe just a petition. You know full well that I am not haltered here, and perhaps better welcome than ever I may

———————————————————————————

* Blank. Paper torn.

expect to be thear. This being soe you might conclude that I have other motives to aske to goe hence then what you see by writing. I am certaine that if we weare boeth debating this matter before the great diffinitors that you would be convinced not to behave your selfe towards me according the prudent and charitable spirit of superiour maiors. Would you have me, if I have any of many motives for which change-ment is lawfull amongest us, or if I have many of them together, to sett them in writting to you, *temporibus et rebus sic stantibus ut sunt.* I am assured, that if I be as deare to you as the rest of your subjects that you cannot be but wholye persuaded in your selfe that it is not for lyghtnesse nor without good ground I doe soe insist, yea that I have as good raisons hereunto as any other these many years. That being, why should I be worse dealed with all then they? Am I onely a bastard amongest your children? You maye saye, I am necessarie heer, lett others stay as long as I and they will be more. You saye in yours to me you feare a ruine of our bodye; you may feare it well, when some are oppressed and wronged. I would I had another place to goe to then thither, I would never make this instance. I am not so burnyng to goe see friends or country, God be praised, and I pray His Divine Majestye that if I be not fitt for them parts that I never goe, but I am resolved absolutly not to stay heer, inasmuch as a raisonable will of a subject maye have place. If I could cast my eye on this hard deeling in my behalfe I would find in my hart to goe backe for ever to my province, but I have pitty on the weecknesse of this poor bodye, and see well that those that are not fitt heer maye doe some good thear and contrariewise. This much I thought meseife obliged to impart to you asking most humbly part in your holye prayers. I remaine yours br[other] Joseph C.C." [N. XII., 2.]

—— to PETER HAYWOOD.

[1641, May, before the 13th.]—Describing the arrest of a priest and his committal to Lancaster Gaol. (See *Commons' Journals,* ii. 145.) *Extract.* [N. XIII., 10.]

The SCOTCH COMMISSIONERS.

1641, May 26.—Paper representing the prejudice caused by so many cessations and so much delay, and especially that since the charge of their army exceeded the 25,000*l.* a month a great part of the 300,000*l.* of the Brotherly Assistance would be thereby exhausted, and therefore desiring that the business might taken so into consideration as to bring about a speedy and happy conclusion. *Copy.* [N. XIX., 45.]

The SCOTCH COMMISSIONERS.

1641, May 28.—The affection of Parliament in granting the Brotherly Assistance we can never forget; the difficulties to find money in a short time for both armies cannot be unknown to us, and we are so sensible of the diligence used that we are ready to accept most willingly what we conceive in any competency may serve for our present necessity and for the disbanding of our army, being no less confident of the payment of the residue in due time than if it were presently delivered; but when we look on the long time since our Commanders were first taken on, the great charges of the maintenance of the army, besides what is allowed for the relief of the Northern Counties, the hopes we have given of full pay before disbanding and the expectation of ship masters for rigging and their ships who are come from Scotland on our promise to receive money and in the meantime must cease from all trade, we are constrained to insist and still to desire that the Parliament may be pleased to extend themselves beyond the proportion of 80,000l., which cannot be sufficient for so many burdens. We therefore earnestly entreat that this may be considered and the trade of our merchants set up by the payment of so much money in Scotland or the Eastern Counties as may make up their stocks, which they have exhausted by advancing money within the kingdom and by furnishing commodities abroad, and that the security of the remanent be so agreed on as may move the better acceptance of the proportion to be presently delivered. *Copy.* [N. XIX., 46.]

Examination of CHARLES ALLAINE.

1641, May 31.—Stating that he had been five years abroad mostly at Cambrai and Douai, that he had been a twelvemonth in England, that when in Derbyshire he received this letter from Mr. Roberts, and that the word Master in it means either Cardinal Richelieu or the Bishop of Chalcedon, that he was told both by Mr. Thorold and Roberts that Mr. Thorold was to go with him to the Bishop of Chalcedon. [N. XIII., 11.]

Examination of CLIFTON THOROLD.

Same date.—Stating that he had served in Flanders, and was going to France to serve there, that he met Allen by chance, and does not know Roberts. [N. XIII., 12.]

The SCOTCH COMMISSIONERS.

[1641, June 2.]—As in our last paper we gave our reasons for considering that the 120,000l. of arrears, and the 80,000l. on account of the Brotherly Assistance would be insufficient for paying the debts of the counties and disbanding the army, so we have represented to the committee at Newcastle the great charge of the kingdom, the difficulty of finding such great sums and the diligence of the Parliament in providing them, endeavouring thereby to move them if possible to accept the Parliament's offer, from whom we shortly expect an answer that we hope may be satisfactory. And therefore we desire that in the mean time the treaty may proceed for answering our demands of the 1st April, and also that the Parliament would let us know the security and terms of payment of the remanent of the Brotherly Assistance, and what part thereof may be offered beyond seas and upon what conditions. *Copy.* [N. XIX., 47.]

The HOUSE OF COMMONS.

1641, June 3.—Votes concerning the Scotch treaty. *Draft* with amendments, with two copies of the last article. (Printed as amended in *Commons' Journals*, ii. 166.) [N. XIX., 48.]

SIR PAUL PYNDAR and others to the HOUSE OF COMMONS.

1641, June 4.—Petition stating according to a particular annexed their advances upon assignments of the customs and other duties and praying that the same might be made good to them. (See *Commons' Journals*, ii. 168.) [N. XXII., 67.]

SIR HENRY VANE.

1641, June 11.—Speech against episcopacy. (Printed in Nalson, ii. 276.) [N. XIII., 13.]

Examination of Captain POLLARD.

1641, June 14.--" (1.) That hee did not know of what Commissary Wilmott saide to him as hee went upp to the Committee Chamber.

(2.) Being examined if there were not discourses amongst them, that is Mr. Peircy, Mr. Wilmott, Ashburnham, Pollard and others, that they were disobliged from the parliament and not from the king, Hee answeared there was noe discourse att all concerning that pointe and that hee did not thinke himselfe disobliged from the parliament, nor heard them say soe much. Generall wordes there were but not the particular. *This there was: That the parliament had dealt severely with us, and that the Scotch had better pay then wee had.*

(3.) Being asked; whether they did not resolve uppon this, to make some expression of serveing the king in all things that were honorable for him, and themselves, and agreeable to the fundamentall lawes of the Realme, and that soe farr they would live and dye with him.

To this hee answeared; If Mr. Peircy were here *hee would not deny but that hee was the first proposer of it.* Hee *did propose it unto us and never left speaking to undertake it.* Hee *proposed it first out of some paper of his,* which I thought to bee rediculous more of folly then of daunger. *Hee spake of it here in the Hall.* Wee mett first in his chamber att Whitehall about the begining of Lent; I cannot say punctually to the tyme but as I guesse it was thereaboutes. *Mr. Peircy made the first proposicion* and desired us to come thither and sent his man unto mee. These proposicions were to mentaine the Bishopps, the King's Revenue, and keepe a foote the Irish Army till the Scottes were disbanded. Hee said it was good for the king and kingdome. Wee did dislike it, all of us. Mr. Wilmott, nor Mr. Ashburnham never approved of it, nor ever did anything from that tyme to this. Wee were diverse tymes with Mr. Peircy since that tyme, not about it, yet talked of it sometimes, but of noe reall designe. I will not tell a lye to save my life.

(4.) Being asked if this were not agreed amongst them hee answeared; Noe, I never agreed unto it; neither was there ever any agreement.

(5.) And being asked whether Mr. Peircy by theire consent was not to tell the king from them thus much, answeared: Noe, I never did consent nor anybody else to my knowledge.

(6.) And being asked: whether the matter was to bee soe ordered as that the king might apprehend this as a great service, hee answeared, Hee never heard him say soe much, nor gave him such direccions nor ever loved to heare more of it.

(7.) Being asked: whether they were not most confident to engage the whole Army thus farre but further they would not undertake because they would not infringe the lawe, and whether every one of them consented unto it; uppon which Mr. Peircy drew a noate in writeinge of the heads.

Hee answeared such discourses there might bee, but not any agreement, but the particular discourses hee doth not remember. That hee undertooke nothing att all, it was an impossibilitie.

(8.) Being asked whether Mr. Peircy haveing theire sence, drew not the heads up in a paper, hee answeared It was drawen before wee mett: true hee read a paper. I tould you the heads of them. There may bee more. but I remember not. It was about Episcopacie, the Irish Army, and I believe the king's Revenew. What was meant by the king's Revenew I understand not, unless how to improve it. I heard the paper read but I gave noe consent. I did dislike it att that tyme when it was read. I did not meane to intermedle att all with it. I did not wish him to informe the king of it. I doe not remember hee did say to us hee would informe the king.

(9.) Being asked: whether they did not by oathe promise one to another to bee constant and secrett, hee answeared

I did take the oathe att Mr. Peircyes chamber—the first tyme—before ever the proposicions were made. It was of secrecie onlie that wee should say nothing of what passed there att that tyme, and I confesse till of late I thought that oath did binde mce. Before such tymes as hee propounded any proposicion the inducementes were merely a secrecie.

Mr. Peircy, Mr. Wilmott, and Mr. Ashburnham, Mr. O'Neale, and my selfe did all of us take the oathe, and Sir Jo. Barkley. There was noe body else tooke it, but those six and noe more persons were then in the chamber. This oath was taken before the proposicion and Mr. Peircy can produce the oath, and you will finde it to bee an oath of secrecy only. Wee tooke it uppon the Bible as all other oathes are taken. Mr. Peircy did read the oath out of the paper. It was only an oath of secrecie—That wee should keep secrett the debate that then passed. The doore was locked, noe servantes were there. I know not well whether the doore was locked or noe. Hee had noe commaund to give the oath that wee knew of.

(10.) Being asked; what particulars were propounded to Mr. Peircy whereby hee might bee enabled to serve them, he answeared I know nothinge of it, nor any thing from any of these gentlemen.

(11.) Being asked whether in theire particular discourses they did not fall uppon a peticion to the king and parliament for monyes there being soe much delay, hee answeared there was a peticion which Mr. Peircy had prepaired, which hee did dislike and resolved of noe such thing. Never sawe it before nor since. One parte of the peticion was for pay of monyes directed to this house as I remember, or rather to the parliament in generall, pressing our wants. The manner of draweinge it wee did not like, nor of the way of it. It was to show noe discontent but a peticion for our pay. The peticion was brought with the proposicion att the same tyme or—as I remember.—a day or two after.

(12.) Being asked ; whether the preserveing of the Bishopps' function and theire votes in parliament and not disbanding the Irish Army, and the endevour to setle the king's Revenue to the proportion it was formerlie, was proposed, and that if the king required theire assistance as farre as they could they would contribute unto it, without breaking of the lawe of the kingdome, hee answeared ;

There was nothing agreed uppon. Such things were discoursed uppon, and diverse other discourses that I remember not, but noe agreement by any one of these gentlemen nor any thing intended. I thinke there were noe more proposicions in that paper. I wish they were all seene, the originall I meane. I thinke the oath was in the same paper where the proposicions were, or in severall papers.

(13.) Being asked whether they did acte and concurre in this as well as Mr. Peircy hee answeared, I know noe acting; there was such a thing proposed, but noe pursuance of it by us. I see these proposicions written in a paper, but see noe body write them ; wee mett a hundred tymes since that tyme but never mett about this but that night when Collonell Goringe was there wee were desired to bee there att that tyme, where Mr. Jermaine was alsoe.

(14.) Whether, this being all imparted to the king by Mr. Peircy from them, hee perceived the kinge had beene treated withall concerninge something of our Army but inclined to a way more high and sharpe not agreeing with our way, not haveinge limittes either of honour or law. Hee answeared, hee never heard of any of these proposicions.

(15.) This clause being read unto him : that Mr. Peircy saide the king would leave all other proposicions and take theires and that hee desired Col. Goring and Mr. Jermaine might bee admitted amongst them and that the king did presse it soe much as that att last it was consented unto, hee answeared they were to come to us that night to meete and speake of some business I knew not then of. Hee sent to mee to bee there to meete Mr. Goring and Mr. Jermaine. Hee tould mee wee should know to what end wee came there, when wee were there. *They spake to us there of a way of bringing of the Army. It was somewhat concerneing the Army about makeing a Generall of the Army. There was proposed—whether by Goring or noe I know not— to bring upp the Army hither, because if there should bee a disagreement between the king and the people that then the Army might bee here.* I meane suche people as should oppose the king in just thinges. I heard of noe proposicions of putting any condicion uppon the parliament. I doe not remember any particulars att all. Those three beades formerlie mentioned were not then propounded. Noe other things were then in proposicion. There were wilde extravagant discourses. But being askcd what hee meant by nameing a Generall hee answeared;

Some of us desired my Lord of Essex, some my Lord of Holland, others my Lord of Newcastle. I was one of those that *named my Lord of Essex.* · *Mr. Peircy named my Lord of Holland. Mr. Jermaine named my Lord of Newcastle.* Saith there was no proposicion of armeing the Frenche or papistes; nor of the clergie findeinge a thousand horse; nor of my Lord of Newcastle's meeting with a thousand horse , nor no proposicion was made how to mentaine the Army. *I never consented to the bringing of them upp nor ever disputed more of it.*

They were there an houre att a supper, but not a minuittes tyme was spent in disputing of this. There were waiters at the table, but wee did not speake of this before them. Both before and after supper wee discoursed. Wee were takeing of tobacco. It was in a great roome : some were att the window, some elsewhere. *Colonell Gouring had the oath given him on the table nere the fire. Mr. Jermaine was sworne att the same tyme when Goring was* sworne, but I cannot tell how long tyme it was betweene the first meetinge and the second, but not many dayes. There was an unwillingness of these two men's comeing in. Wee were *affraide to know theire proposicions,* and that was the truth of it. I did not care who knew oures. *I had heard theire proposicions were of ill nature. Mr. Peircy tould me of them ;* the particulars I doe not know. Wee disliked them because Sir John Suckling and they were in it. Wee heard they were ill proposicions and wee did not desire to medle with them. Wee did not very well like the men, for *Suckling,* Jermaine and Davenant were in it. I remember *noe more persones in it.* They were not made acquainted with oures. Wee did not debate our proposicions together. They did speake of theire proposicion.

I have named unto you what Mr. Peircy propounded. I tould you they talked about makeing a Generall of the Army. Wee tooke the oathe before hee made any proposicion unto us. I doe not know of any one of us that did signifie to Collonell Goringe that wee had taken the oath. I did see him take the oath ; the other gentlemen were in the roome ; how nere I doe not know. *Mr. Peircy did dislike* the *bringing upp of the Army.* Mr. Wilmott and Mr. *Ashburnham disliked it* because inconvenience *might happen to the king and subject by it. Wee did not agree* to bring upp the Armie by our owne pro-

posicion. Collonell Goring saide nothing to it. I never agreed to the proposicion to mentaine Bishopps etc., nor ever undertooke it. Mr. Jermaine and Mr. Goringe propound[ed] them ; Mr. Goring spoke about a Generall. I cannot remember what hee did propose. I doe not remember the particulars of the discourse. I doe not remember wee directed Mr. Peircie to propound any thing to Mr. Goringe.

(16.) This being reade unto him: viz. 'where I remember Col. Goringe made answer hee was soe engaged with Suckling that hee could doe nothing without him. But wee would not medle with him att all, but Col. Goring and Mr. Jermaine desired hee might bee brought in yet in the end, soe wee would not oppose Sucklynes imployment in the Army, they would passe it by. Then wee *tooke upp the way* proposed, the which tooke a great debate, and theires, *I will say,* differed from oures in violence and height.'

To this hee answered, There was debate in laying aside Suckling but I doe not remember of speaking of this to the king. Wee went away altogether ; one, one way and another, another way.

(17.) This being read unto him : viz. 'They left mee and Jermaine and to speake to the king and the king tould him those wayes were vain and foolish and would thinke of them noe more. Then Goring asked how the cheife commaundes would bee disposed of ' . . ." [N. XIII., 14.]

Examination of Commissary WILMOT.

[1641, June 14.]—"Being asked what hee said to Captain Pollarde, as hee went into the Committee Chamber, hee answeared that hee beleeveth it would much prejudice them to answeare suddenlie to such a business, but Mr. Pollard made noe answeare to mee againe. Being asked what discourse hee had with Mr. Peircy and the rest of being disobliged from the parliament, Hee answeared ; Mr. Peircie did putt many things into his head, that the parliament had disobliged us, and that it *concerned us in honour to regard the advantage of our Army,* declareing what I spoke in this House uppon occasion of an order made to lessen the sommes intended for the king's Army. But I doe *not remember any discourses of being disobliged from the parliament.* I should doe him and my selfe wrong if I should say any thing positivelie in this. I doe not remember it.

Being asked what agreement there was betweene him and Mr. Peircy etc., *concerning the undertakeinge of any particular proposicion as to mentaine the votes of Bishopps ; to keepe afoote the Irish Army ; and to keepe upp the king's Revenue,* To this hee answeared, Mr. Peircy did propound this to mee and to others before, any consent I must deny. The first tyme hee *spoke of this was in this House* tenn or twelve dayes after hee did speake to mee to come to his chamber. I cannot possiblie remember what hee said then. I beleeve many thinges of this nature you propound hee spoke then.

They *were propounded* in *Mr. Peircyes* chamber. I never mett them anywhere else. I beleeve there was some thinge written but whether this or somewhat else I cannot remember.

There were present there, Col. Ashburnham, Pollard, Barklett, O'Neale and *my self* and *I remember noe body else* but Mr. Peircy. *All that* wee spake of was concerninge the *Army.* They were *many tymes* spoken of butt *never resolved uppon.* An oath of secrecie was propounded but I did not conceive I might discover it, though now I thinke I may. *I confesse I did take* the oath and it was Mr. Peircie's jealousie to presse us to an oath because wee should not reveale it.

I tooke it in a solemne manner yet remember not I laid my hand uppon the Bible. It was an oath not to reveale what was there said, and that *noe oath under heaven* should absolve mee. It was in *our covenant* one with *another that nothing* should bee done by us to the prejudice *of the parliament* or *saveinge of Straforde.* There was *never any agreement* made amongst ourselves. I was never with them since. Wee were there debateinge these things. Some *liked it,* others disliked it. I heard Jermaine did *take the oath.* There were many things propounded there not justifiable for if they were *wee should have consented unto them.* I remember nothing but to *serve the king* and moderate *things of our owne,* which I hope will be justifiable.

I know not whose proposicions they were; either Peircy, Jermaine or Goringe, but who made them I know not I tooke notice of those *proposicions I* had a mynde to. I rememb[er] in generall wee never consented to any thing but what *was according to the fundamentall* lawes and of my duty to this House. *Mr. Peircy made* the *three proposicions.* I made none myselfe. I *never heard anything* of bringing upp *the Army* hither, nor of makeing *a Generall. My conceite* was if any partie in England should oppresse *the king* then wee *would serve the king in any just thing.* I never heard any *proposicions* of the French. I suppose it doth runne in another streame.

I never heard of the bringing the Prince to the Army till *within this fourteen* dayes or three weekes I meeting the Prince asked *him if* hee would goe to the Army who answeared with all his heart if his father would *give him leave.* I did it to see of what condition he was made. I remember my Lord *Newcastle* that night Mr. *Goring was there* was *named to bee* Generall by some of us, not by those among us but by *Goringe.* I propounded *Essex, and others, Holland,* and next day I *sent and acquainted Essex* with the *proposicion* for him *to bee Generall. I* heard nothing of Newcastle with *a thousand horse* nor of the clergie's thousand horse." [N. XIII., 15]

Examination of Colonel ASHBURNHAM.

[1641, June 14.]—" Being asked what discourse he had with the rest concerneing his being disobliged from the parliament and of engagement, etc.

Hee answeared; The occasion of such discourse—if there were any— was about the tyme when the Tenn thousand pound was kept backe from the king's Army. But *when Peircy spoke to any of us,* it was *in a slight manner, and hee did it without any acceptance of it. I never engaged my selfe to those particulars. Mr. Peircy had proposicions of his owne but I hope* my heareing of that discourse shall not make mee guiltie. Hee had severall proposicions. When I *was in his chamber :* hee sent for mee. I did not knowe what hee would have proposed. Hee laide as a ground : *If absolute disorders and confusion happened* there must bee some way or other. I tould him thus: Mr. *Peircy,* what would you have by this? I know not if you have anything to say to me. *If it bee dishonourable or dishonest* or stopping the free Justice by parliament or to doe service to the Earle of Straford, I will not medle in it.

Hee said to mee that hee conceived it was safest *for this kingdome the Irish* Army *were continued till the* Scoche Army *were disbanded.*

Hee spoke of the Kings Revenue, and saide those were just things; hee never spoke of any particular; nor was it inquired after, and except that in the paper I never heard of.

I was att Mr. Peircyes chamber when Mr. Jermaine and Collonell Goringe came there. That was the first tyme I ever spake with them together, before nor since.

There was some *extravagant discourses. I sate by the fire* and did not come into the discourse, but we had something of *wilde discourse.* But I remember they were of that *wildness* that they were *discented* from. I shall not att all connive att the business; much of wildness passed, for it was *excepted against* by Wilmott, *Pollard*, and myselfe. Wee never would nor ever came to condiscend unto it. *It did concerne discourses* about the Army. I would answeare with all my heart if I knew the particulars. I never heard that propounded of *bringing upp the Army* hither.

They spoke of the disposicion of the Army, and about commaunders. My Lord of Essex was spoken of, for the king and the countrie, and if my Lord of Northumberland did not goe, to perswade my Lord of Essex. I never hearde a worde *concerning the Frenche*, nor *of the horse* of the clergie. I can remember nothing of it *but a disposicion of the Army. If confusion did happen,* *the king to goe one way, and the people another way.* They saide if all sortes of law or (blank) stopped upp; that wee should breake in a confusion and the king one way and the *people another. I cannot say those were the words;* they were in generall. I never heard a worde of bringing the Prince to the Army. Mr. Peircy did endevour to perswade us if any thing might bee *undertaken by us to give* informacion *unto the king.* I never heard from the king. Hee did say hee would speake unto the king. I never saide anything that hee should propound our condicions. They spake of the peticion the Army should send. I never see any other writing but that of the proposicions." [N. XIII., 16.]

Examination of Colonel GORING.

[1641, June 16.]—" Sir John Suckling was the first that ever made such overtures unto mee. It was *att my lodgeing*, about three monethes since. I desire nothing else then to give a perfect relacion. *Suckling tould mee as I* remember *that there were purposes* of putting the Army *in a posture of serveing the king. That the Army should* marche towardes *London.* But I must aske your pardon if I doe not remember directlie the words or the place, but either there they were spoken or in some other place or in both places. Hee tould mee that my Lord Newcastle was to bee Generall and that I might be Lieut.-Generall if I would accept of it. I tould him I *would heare uppon what terme* it was and then I would give my resolucion. This was the discourse hee had with mee. Hee did *not discusse the particulars* unto mee then, nor att any other tyme, but heard of it afterwards in the consultacion. It was but the day before wee entered into the consultacion. It *was uppon a Sunday morning.* I said nothing, for I did conceive it had beene by publique authoritie, by the king's commaund ; though I never heard that my Lord Newcastle should bee Generall, or that I should bee leiuetenant-generall. I did not question but that it had beene by authoritie, and *goeing to* court, I found that there was noe such purpose for *either of* us. Being asked *if the Army* was to bee putt in a posture to *interpose in the proceedinges* in parliament, Hee answeared : *This was spoken* in generall termes by him. I hearkened to the proposicions of the misery of the souldiers, being the first stepp to this. And a

---

* This is crossed out in the original.

peticion to the parliament was to bee drawne for pay to the Army. I spoke something concerneing this to my Lord Dungarven within few dayes after or the very same day. That there were some officers of the Army that had *a greater zeale to the proceedinges* of this House then they did *thinke* of. I heard that there was an intencion some officers should meete about something concerning the Army. I came to Mr. Peircyes chamber with Mr. Jermaine, where they lett us know there was some thing *ought to bee* discussed of, and that it *was necessary* wee should take an oathe of secrecie before wee did it. Mr. Peircy tould us soe. This was in Mr. Peircies chamber. *Himselfe, Wilmott*, Pollard, Jermaine, Ashburnham, *Bartlett*, O'Neale and my selfe being present. Hee saide it was necessary to take an oathe and that theire consultacions were for the good of the Realme. Noe *proposicion offered* till the oath was taken. The oath was not *directlie* nor indirectlie ever to acknowledge any parte of *the consultacion*, nor ever to thinke our selves *disolved* from the oath by any other oath that should bee imposed uppon us hereafter. It was *tendered out* of a paper, and *Jermaine and I laid our* hands uppon the Booke when wee tooke the oath. The *rest said they had taken it before*. There was nothing said but that they might heare. They were about the table. I remember not theire particular posture. Those three proposicions were made unto us by Peircy.

I doe not remember any particular discourse of the Irish Army, nor any generall discourse att all of it. It may fall out that where seven or eight are together that some two of them may speake one to another and others not heare it. It was a generall proposicion of Mr. Peircies, read in a paper. I shall as nere as I can reporte the discourse but lett mee not bee tyed to words, least I prejudice others. I found when I was there, it was a very tickle and nice pointe to interpose in any the proceedings in parliament. Either I or Jermaine asked whether the Army was to marche towards London or noe, for I did not know it. They answeared *all that it was not theire intencion the Armies should* marche towards London *till the Declaration had beene* first *sent upp to the* parliament. I, thinking it to bee a nice pointe to interpose in the proceedings in parliament, I asked them what inconveniences would ensue of the Acte, and to informe my selfe and rebuke theire intencions, I propounded some difficulties in it to allay the business that was the sense *of our* discourse there, *Whether to marche towards London.* I asked what amunition they had: whether they were sure of the amunicion in the Tower, and how they intended to goe through with it if there should bee such disorders as might bee expected. *They answeared they had noe purpose to goe to London for the surprise of them att London would bee to conquerr the kingdome; which was said by Wilmott.* Ashburnham, and generally those that were there *wee found averse unto* it. All that I propounded there, it was not possible to effect it for I propounded impossibilities to diverte them from theire thoughts, to give over all other consultacions. Wee did not proceed to particulars.

There was another meetinge, and the matter *being impious on* the one side and foolish *in the other*, therefore my thoughts were to rej[e]ct it; and howsever I tooke my selfe out of it. I did declare my selfe att that very tyme I was there, both in speaking in contempt of the councell which I am confident will bee justified by them. This was att the first meetinge. I cannot distinguish betweene the one tyme and the other. I doe thinke the second meeting was the next night *after the first or next* night *after that*. And the reason why I propounded as I tould you was to diverte them from a thing *unjust, by propounding a thing* impossible, for that was my purpose from the begininge. For how could the Army that lodged in severall quarters in such a distance one from another, an Army unpaid and discontented. It was impossible to gather them soe suddainlie into a body to surprise them before they came upp I did speake as a souldier, not accordinge to the sence of my owne hearte, and particularly *Wilmott and Ashburnham* said *theire purpose was not to marche towards London*, for if *that were done* and that they *had the Tower in theire hands*, that were to *conquer the kingdome*, whereas theire *intent was to present theire greivances:* that if they had the Tower they would not make use of it, for the kingdome was conquered if they had noe ammunicion. This was the debate of the second meeting. My declaration was to have nothing to doe in the business. I tould them there was noe *intencion of* violence, and uppon this, we broke of that meetinge, being in the same roome and same company.

Beinge asked some further questions hee answeared There was discourse of marcheing towards London by himselfe and Mr. Jermaine, but whether his purpose was to informe himselfe I know not. They *saide before they gathered themselves together they would send upp the Declaracion.* Every *person that was there was absolutelie against the bring upp of the* Armies. I did not heare any body consent to any thing for there was nothing concluded. Suckling was not att all with us Hee only brought mee a generall nocion of the business.

Being asked upon the reading of Mr. Peircyes letter entered in a paper severall other questions distinctly, hee made this answeare : I desire I may bee excused to name such persons as I have confarred withall, being not safe for mee to speake it, but confident noe member of this house, nor of the lords' house spoke to mee in this business —except as aforesaid—.

I must rely uppon the testimony of some noble Lords and others, how I protested against all this in the birth of it : My Lord Newporte, my Lords Say, Mandevile, and Bedford. I tould it them altogether. The tyme was the next day after wee broke of from the last conference. I appeale likewise to my Lord Dungarven what I saide unto him. I doe not remember any consultacion att all of Portsmouth. Being asked further questions upon Mr. Peircies letter beinge read unto him, answeared,

I and Jermaine did make objeccions against theire designes, and whereas Mr. Peircy saith that I did solicite for the commaund of the Army by letters and sending downe persons none can produce that ever I sent or writt for any commaund : nay, I can make it appeare I did write to the contrary when they of the Army did make it a proposicion unto mee.

I did not know att all when Captaine Chudley went downe to the Army, nor doe not know what hee went downe withall for I was out of towne then, and a captaine brought a letter signed with severall officers of the Army to shewe theire willingness to accept of mee to bee theire leiuetenant-generall. I never see Chudleigh's face but that tyme. This letter came to mee att Portsmouth three weeks after Suckling told me of that.

Being asked if Jermaine propounded the bringeing upp of the Armie and what reasons hee offered for the same, answeared,

As I remember it *was Jermaine* that did propound it but I remember noe groundes nor reasons. *Hee seemed to resist* theire mocion, they propounded theire proposicions and wee came to heare what they said. There was a discourse of a Generall. Some named Essex ; some Holland. Jermaine and I propounded Newcastle. Jermaine and I

came together there. I mett with Jermaine in the Queene's drawing
chamber. I doe not remember any discourse betweene us from thence,
but to harken to theire proposicions. Hee spoke to mee the day
before, and then afterward said, It must not bee till next night, and
wished mee to meete him att the Queene's drawing chamber, and I mett
with him either after the first meetinge or second in the litle gallory in
the Q[ueen's] chamber. Mr. Jermaine tould mee The reasons you dislike
these proposicions is not but that you are as ready for any wilde mad
thing as any other, but you dislike the persons in it. Afterwardes hee
mett mee in St. James' Park, and tould mee there would bee noe more
meetinge.

Being asked concerninge the Tower and of theire comeing upp,
answeared,

That the whole kingdome would bee upp in armes against them,
and they would bee accounted as enemies and rebells. There was no
such thing voted of the Tower. They said they had amunicion. I
said if they seized uppon the Tower, it had beene to conquer the
kingdome. It was by the way of question, whether they had the
Tower in theire hands. I and Mr. Jermaine did aske them whether
they had the Tower in theire hands showing in *tyme of confusion* they
could doe nothing without it.

They said they would send a Declaration first, and would come up
if not satisfied."* (See *Commons' Journals*, ii. 177 ; and Rushworth,
iii. 1. 253, where there is another report, but differing considerably from
this.) [N. XIII., 17.] All these examinations are in Rushworth's
hand.

Mr. PURY's Speech.

1641, June 15.—Against Deans and Chapters. (Printed in Nalson,
ii. 289.) [N. XIII., 44.]

SIR JOHN WRAY's Speech.

[1641, June (?).] — Concerning Bishops. (Printed in *King's
Pamphlets*, E. 198, No. 8.) [N. XIII., 45.]

The COMMITTEE ON ARMY ACCOUNTS.

1641, June 17.—Report. (Printed in *Commons' Journals*, ii. 177 ;
and in Nalson, ii. 292.) [N. XIII., 18.]

Examination of NICHOLAS LOVE.

1641, June 25.—Deposing that " a little before Easter in Sir Richard
Harrison's house he heard Mr. Richard Nevile say much in commenda-
tion of the Earl of Strafford, and inveighed much against the citizens
of London, and said that they deserved to have the city burned about
their ears and . . that it were easy for six or seven of them to get into a
chamber and fire it. He said further that he would bring his troop
into Berkshire and plunder them if they would not pay. This he
conceives that Mr. Nevile spoke in a light way."

And

Examinations of SIR RICHARD HARRISON and FRANCES HARRISON his wife.

1641, June 25 and July 2.—The first deposing that " on Easter day
last he heard Mr. Richard Nevile say at " his " house that the Earl
of Strafford should not die, and that before that should come to pass

---

* The italics represent passages underlined by someone who has been perusing
the depositions. In several places a ☞ has been inserted by the same person.

we should see a strange thing happen which was that London should be set on fire or fired or words to that effect." The second deposing to the same effect. *All three Signed and attested by* the Earls of Bath, Warwick and Essex and by Lord Howard. [N. XIII., 19, 20, 21.]

The Scotch Commissioners.

1641, June 25.—The occasion of the narration made by the Scotch Commissioners proceeded from the letters and informations sent from the Committee of the Parliament of Scotland, showing that there have been wicked and false calumnies invented against the Parliament and Earl of Argyle, and some plots contrived by the Earls of Traquair and Montrose with the assistance of Lord Napier, Sir George Sterling of Keir, and Sir Archibald Stewart of Blackball to make a faction and division in that kingdom, and that there have several passages passed betwixt the Earls of Traquair and Montrose and instructions have been given by them to Colonel Walter Stewart to that effect, which were, that the Earl of Montrose desires the king to come down to Scotland to hold the Parliament in his own royal person, disband the armies and keep all offices and places in state undisposed of till then, to be conferred on the Earl of Montrose and his confederates as they should deserve, and further the instructions were that the Duke of Lennox was desired to combine with their faction and to be accessory to their plot. In the instructions are also some malignant expressions laying imputations against the Marquess of Hamilton, and showing that they have bad intentions and designs towards him. The names in these instructions are set down in a mystic way by letters of the Alphabet and the names of beasts, as the lion, elephant, dromedary &c.

The reason the Scotch Commissioners discovered these passages to the English was to move them to mediate with the king for removal of these incendiaries from the Court, nor do we find anything which proves that the king has been upon the knowledge of this plot, although Colonel Walter Stewart averred that the Earl of Traquair reported to him that he had imparted the Earl of Montrose's designs to the king and received his answer thereon, which appeared clearly to be a calumny forged by Stewart or by Traquair to him for the encouragement of those who were upon that plot. As for delivery of the papers and informations we conceive this to be unfit as they were for our own information and are not to be used or intermeddled with by the Parliament of England, but in so far as they were used for removing the incendiaries from his Majesty's presence and the Court, which his Majesty hath from his own royal justice granted. (See Rushworth, iii. 1. 290.) [N. XIX., 49.]

Memorial from the Elector Palatine for Sir Richard Cave of that which Mr. Speaker of the Honourable House of Commons is to present to that House.

[1641, July 5.]—"That his Majesty having been pleased to recommend the Queen his mother, himself, his whole family and their very being to their propitious and grave consideration, he esteemeth that his Majesty could not have put his business in any so good a way, as that he and his people should join for so good and just a work as the restitution of the Palatine House.

That he entreateth them to believe that as he hath hitherto deferred to press the consideration of his business by reason of the weighty affairs of this kingdom which have been and are still in agitation so he should have yet longer foreborne had not necesssity pressed him to this importunity.

That he thinketh himself infinitely beholding to their affection and generosity, that notwithstanding the foresaid important affairs of this state they have been pleased so cheerfully and suddenly—as indeed the present difficulty of his affairs require—to take his business into their serious and favourable deliberation.

That he beseecheth them to persevere in their good intentions towards the Queen his mother, himself and his family, so far as the convenience and present posture of the affairs of this state will permit, and beyond those limits his Highness will never press them, supposing and believing that the care of the religion abroad, the peace of afflicted Germany, their own goodness and honour will persuade them to as much as he can desire.

That therefore his Highness concludeth as the king, his uncle did yesterday—when he recommended his Manifest unto them—that by the effects hereof the world shall see how well his Majesty and his people are together, for the continuance whereof his Highness heartily prayeth, as the greatest blessing which can befall the king his gracious uncle and this kingdom." *Signed* "Charles." [N. I., 49.]

Thomas Nesbitt to ——.

1641, July 5.—Stating that when the Scots entered England Mr. Long said "You may now see the business of them that would not furnish the king with money, but if the king were of his mind he would let them pillage the City of London," and, that "the King would do well to join with his good subjects the Scots, and plunder England and make it his own by the sword." [N. XIII., 22.]

Examinations of Thomas Askham and Thomas Thorp.

1641, July 13.—(To the same effect as Thomas Nesbitt's letter.) [N. XIII., 23, 24.]

Deposition of Andrew Kynaston.

1641, July 19.—Concerning the proceedings at the May Quarter-Sessions at Welshpool against Popish Recusants, and the conduct of Mr. Blayney in holding that they might traverse the indictment by attorney without personally appearing and in otherwise endeavouring to protect them. [N. XIII., 25.]

The Scotch Commissioners.

1641, July 30.—Paper touching the disbanding of their army. (Printed in *Lords' Journals*, iv. 336.) *Copy.* [N. XIX., 52.]

Propositions of the Scotch Commissioners and Reply of the English Commissioners.

1641, August 4.—(Both printed in *Lords' Journals*, iv. 344, 345. *Copies.* [N. XIX., 53, 54.]

The Scotch Commissioners' Answer.

[1641, August 8.]—Concerning staying the King's Journey to Scotland. (Printed in *Lords' Journals*, iv. 352.) *Copy.* [N. XX., 210.]

Antony Haselwood to William Lenthall.

1641, August 30. Maidwell.—Acknowledging his letter with the ordinances of Parliament for conveying the poll money to York and stating how much had been collected. *Signed. Seal.* [N. II., 4.]

The EARL OF HOLLAND, Lord-General, to the LORD VISCOUNT
GRANDISON.

[1641, September 3.]—Instructions. 1. You are forthwith to repair
to Edinburgh and let his Majesty know that I have received by the
Lord Macklyn (Maitland) the desires of the Parliament of that kingdom
according to the instructions his Majesty was pleased to sign with them
for the disbanding of the English army and removing the garrisons of
Berwick and Carlisle.

2. You are to declare the present state of this army, whereof the
horse troops are totally disbanded, and orders given for the disbanding of four regiments of foot by the 11th instant, and four more—the
remainder—by the 18th, and that I have delivered to Lord Macklyn a
memorial thereof.

3. You are to represent to his Majesty that the 8th article of the late
treaty imports no more than that the garrisons of Berwick and Carlisle
on the disbanding of the Scotch army now in England and of all such
forces as are in Scotland be likewise presently removed so as there
ought to be a precedent act on the Scotch part before they can require
the performance of this article on the part of England. The same concerning the fortifications.

4. In conformity to his Majesty's pleasure I have written to the Parliament for money for the payment and discharge of the said garrisons
and for ships to remove the ordnance and munition there. I must
receive some positive answer and directions how to proceed before I can
appoint any certain day for that work, but I have begun by giving
orders to the Governors to prepare their accounts and all other
requisites for their retiring.

5. You are to represent that the general expectation of this whole
kingdom is, that for the better establishing of peace and the removal of
all jealousies his Majesty will be pleased to take order that the
army in Scotland according to the example of this may be forthwith
and totally disbanded, and the fortifications reduced to the condition
they were in before the late troubles. (See *Lords' Journals*, iv. 388.)
Two *copies*. [N. XIX., 7 ; XX., 60.]

Certificate by SIR THOMAS BENDYSHE, SIR RICHARD EVERARD,
and SIR ROBERT KEMPE.

[1641, September.]—Of the names and places of such persons as were
searched for arms powder and ammunition by them according to the
ordinance for the speedy disarming of Popish Recusants and other
dangerous persons.

And

Similar Certificate by SIR HARBOTTLE GRIMSTON.

1641, September 17.—(Both on the same piece of parchment.)
[N. XIII., 26.]

Proclamation of SIR PHELIM O'NEILL and alleged Commission
of the King.

1641, November 4. Newry.—(Printed in Rushworth, iii. 1. 400.)
Copy read in the House of Commons, March 15, 1652-3. (See *Commons' Journals*, vii. 267.) [N. XXI., 2.]

Declaration of both HOUSES OF THE PARLIAMENT OF ENGLAND.

1641, November 4 —(Printed in *Lords' Journals*, iv. 422.) Two
copies. [N. XXI., 3.]

ORDINANCE.

1641, November 6. — Empowering the Lord Lieutenant to give Commissions. (Printed in *Lords' Journals*, iv. 424.) *Copy.* [N. XXI., 4.]

THOMAS CROMPTON and EDWARD MAINWARING to the LORD HIGH TREASURER, the CHANCELLOR, and the CHANCELLOR OF THE EXCHEQUER.

1641, November 8. Madeley, Staffordshire. — Certifying that Sir John Offley had resided most of the last year at Madeley, where he had paid 20*l.* the sum assessed on him in respect of the last two subsidies. Subjoined is a copy of the receipt dated the previous 14th of July. *Signed.* [N. II., 6.]

List of the SERVANTS of the PRINCE OF WALES, the DUKE OF YORK, and the PRINCESS MARY.

1641, November 8 —[N. XII., 32.]

The HOUSE OF COMMONS to the COMMISSIONERS ATTENDING HIS MAJESTY IN SCOTLAND.

[1641, November 8.]—Heads of instructions. (This is a fragment of the end of those printed in Nalson, ii. 616, and *Lords' Journals*, iv., 430, beginning with " Ministers as shall be approved of " in clause 8 and agreeing with the printed copies to the end of the paragraph. The con-clusion is different, being as follows: " And without this—although we shall always be faithful to his person and to his Crown in discharging that service and obedience to which by the laws of God and of this kingdom we are obliged—yet we cannot without breach of duty and trust to the state and to those whom we represent undergo those voluntary aids and contributions and that literal and affectionate engagement of our lives and fortunes which the necessity of those affairs do require, and which we have formerly professed, and—this our humble petition being granted —shall be ready to make good: but if his Majesty shall not think fit to comply with our faithful and humble desires we do hereby declare ourselves to be fully discharged and acquitted of those engagements except only for such sums as we shall for the present necessity borrow, which we intend to make good howsoever.") *Draft.* [N. XX., 65.]

Members of the Sept of FARRALL to VISCOUNT DILLON OF COSTELO.

1641, November 10.—(Printed in Nalson, ii. 898.) A note shows that it was read in the House of Commons on December 8. (See *Commons' Journals*, ii. 335.) *Copy.* [N. XII., 3.]

The PARLIAMENT to the KING.

[1641, November 15.]—Petition with instructions to the Committee attending his Majesty. (The Petition is printed in *Lords' Journals*, iv. 438, the instructions Nos. 1 to 6 in the same, 430, 431 ; annexed are the Ordinance printed in the same, 432, 433, and the Order for providing ships printed in the same, 425.) *Copies.* [N. XIX., 5.]

SIR EDWARD DERING.

[1641, November 20.]—Speech concerning the Liturgy and a National Synod. (Printed in his *Speeches*, § 14, p. 96.) [N. XIII., 51.]

SIR PHELIM O'NEILL to SIR WILLIAM HAMILTON.

1641, November 23.—(Printed in Nalson, ii. 895.) *Seal.* [N. II., 2.]

THOMAS COWPER, Mayor, and others, to the HOUSE OF COMMONS.

1641, November 27. Chester.—Concerning the speech delivered in the Cathedral on the 1st by William Clarke, a minor Canon, against Papists and Puritans and exhorting the congregation to sign the Petition for the continuance of the Book of Common Prayer. *Signed.* [N. XIII., 29.]

Enclosed :
    i. Four Depositions dated November 5, by persons who heard the said speech. [N. XIII., 28.]
    ii. A copy thereof. [N. XIII., 30.]
    iii. The examination of the said William Clarke. [N. XIII., 31.]

The LORDS JUSTICES and COUNCIL OF IRELAND to WILLIAM LENTHALL.

Same date. Dublin Castle.—(Printed in Nalson, ii. 903.) *Signed.* [N. II., 3.]

Informations delivered by SIR JOHN STRANGEWAYS and Mr. KIRTON.

1641, November 30.—Concerning an alleged design upon the House. (Printed in Nalson, ii. 790.) (See *Commons' Journals*, ii. 327.) [N. XIII., 33, 34.]

WILLIAM LENTHALL to SIR EDWARD NICHOLAS.

1641, December 3.—Two letters, desiring to quit the Chair, or to be recommended to the House for some satisfaction. (Both printed in Nalson, ii. 713, 714.) *Copies.* [N. XII., 4.]

Deposition of CAPTAIN WINTOUR'S BOY.

1641, December 13. Stranraer (?).—Concerning the Irish rebellion and Sir Phelim O'Neill. (See *Commons' Journals*, ii. 366.) Much of it illegible. [N. XXI., 6.]

The papers brought from the HOUSE OF COMMONS at the Conference.

1641, December 13.—Against the toleration of the Romish religion and concerning the Rebellion in Ireland. (The heads and the conclusion of the last paper are printed in Nalson, ii. 737.) *Copies.* [N. XXI., 64.]

The humble Remonstrance and Petition of the LORDS AND COMMONS.

[1641, December 16.]—(Printed in *Lords' Journals*, iv. 477, Rushworth, iii. 1. 458, Nalson, ii. 751, and parts in Clarendon, iv. § 59.) [N. XIII., 205.]

JOHN SLEIGH, Mayor, to WILLIAM LENTHALL.

1641, December 27. Berwick.—Acknowledging his letter and thanking him on behalf of the town for the care shown them by the House. We signified to Sir Thomas Widdrington, one of our members, that there were divers Papists living here for some years, and others resorting hither, and a common rumour of more, and the town, being now unable to resist any strong violence, we desired some order either for the expulsion of those already here, or at least to restrain others from coming, whereunto we were the more occasioned concerning some fears which might ensue in those dangerous times, wherein we are left a naked and indefensible people without arms, for having petitioned his Majesty for some arms and powder when he was in Scotland, he did not grant them, holding it—as I understand—a breach of the treaties between the two kingdoms. Since then I and the others appointed by the ordinance of Parliament searched all the Papist houses here for arms and ammunition yet found none of great offence. Have not had time since receipt of your letter to execute the orders of the House, but will do so as speedily as I can, according to the commission sent. Further there are divers persons have lived here divers years, who have repaired to church themselves and their wives and divers of their children and servants recusants, whom with all Papists here I shall charge to be gone or else take the oaths of Supremacy and Allegiance as I am commanded. *Signed. Seal.* [N. II., 7.]

EDWARD SPENCER to SIR GILBERT GERRARD and SIR JOHN FRANKLYN.

1641, December. Buckston.—Enclosing the excuse of Sir John Offley of Isleworth for not paying the full amount of Poll money assessed on him with remarks thereon. *Signed. Seal.* [N. II., 5.]

COMPLAINT.

1641.—That the Bishop of Winchester had, as Lord Almoner, claimed the estate of one Chomlie, a mercer in Paternoster Row, who had hanged himself, and had forced the creditors to compound with him for 250*l.* [N. XIII., 48.]

VISCOUNT SAY AND SELE'S Speech.

[1641.]—About the Liturgy. (Printed in *King's Pamphlets*, E. 198, No. 117.) [N. XIII., 43.]

Articles of HIGH TREASON against LORD KIMBOLTON and the FIVE MEMBERS.

1641[-2], January 3.—(Printed in *Lords' Journals*, iv. 501, Nalson, ii. 811, Clarendon, iv. § 148.) *Copy.* [N. XIII., 50]

The KING to the LORD MAYOR OF LONDON.

1641[-2], January 3.—(Printed in Forster, *Arrest of the Five Members*, p. 157.) *Copy* from Secretary Nicholas' papers. [N. XII., 6.]

R. E. to Mr. ANDERTON.

[1641-2, January 4.]—(Printed in *Commons' Journals*, ii. 369, and Clarendon, iv. § 204 note.) *Seal.* [N. II., 12.]

The COMMITTEE OF THE HOUSE OF COMMONS SITTING AT GUILDHALL.

1641[-2], January 8.—Vote beginning " That the actions." (Printed in *Lords' Journals*, iv. 504; *Commons' Journals*, ii. 370.)

Same date. — Vote beginning " As the necessity of providing " ending " with *Posse Comitatus.*" (Printed in *Lords' Journals*, iv. 504.)

Same date.—Appointment by the same of certain of their members with power to consult with the Common Council for the safety of the king, kingdom, and Parliament and City of London and particularly for the present defence of the city.

And

Propositions from the CITY and Answers and Resolutions of the said COMMITTEE.

Same date.— Concerning the Militia of the City, their serving outside the limits of the City and the appointment of the officers of the same. (All these votes and propositions were read in the House, January 27, 1645[-6]. See *Commons' Journals*, iv. 419.) [N. XIII., 35.]

The KING to SIR JOHN BYRON, Lieutenant of the Tower.

[1641-2], the 17th year of our reign, January 10. Whitehall.—Warrant forbidding him to leave the Tower without the king's permission. (See *Lords' Journals*, iv. 508.) *Copy.* [N. XII., 37.]

The JUSTICES OF MONMOUTHSHIRE.

1641[-2], January 13.—Warrant to the Mayor of Monmouth and to the Chief Constables of four Hundreds for raising 20 men to secure the magazine at Monmouth and to those of three other Hundreds for raising 9 others to secure the powder at Caerlyon. *Copy.* [N. XIII., 36.]

The SCOTCH COMMISSIONERS.

164[1-]2, January 15. — Paper offering mediation. (Printed in Rushworth, iii. 1. 498, and in *Commons' Journals*, ii. 383.) *Signed* " Ja. Prymerose." [N. XIX., 64.]

The SCOTCH COMMISSIONERS.

164[1-]2, January [21-]31.—Paper requesting that the Irish treaty might be speedily concluded. (Printed in *Lords' Journals*, iv. 554.) *Signed* "James Prymerose." [N. XIX., 60.]

The HOUSE OF COMMONS to the KING.

[1641-2, January 25.]—Petition. (Printed in *Commons' Journals*, ii. 395.) *Draft.* [N. XVI., 167.]

DAVID EVANS, WALTER THOMAS, and RICHARD SEYS, to the HOUSE OF COMMONS.

1641[-2], January 25. Neath.—Stating that the Poll-money within the three hundreds of Swansey, Llangevalach and Neath being their division, had been duly assessed and collected, and paid over to Robert Button Esq. late High Sheriff of Glamorganshire. Subjoined is an account showing how much was paid by each parish, parcel and hamlet. *Signed. Seal.* [N. II., 8.]

The DUKE OF RICHMOND.

1641[-2], January 26.—Apology.

And

Same date.—Protest of certain peers against accepting it. (Both printed in *Lords' Journals*, iv. 543.) [N. XIII., 37, 38.]

The QUEEN to the PARLIAMENT.

[1641-2, January 27.]—Answer to their message. (Printed in *Lords' Journals*, iv. 546.) [N. XV., 184.]

The KING to WILLIAM LENTHALL.

[1641-2], the 17th year of our reign, January 28. Windsor.— Enclosing his answer to a Petition presented by Mr. Pierrepont and others. (See *Commons' Journals*, ii. 402.) *Sign Manual.* [N. I., 10.]

Information of GEORGE COLLINS.

1641[-2], January 30. Bristol.—That coming through Brittany last week he met soldiers in small·companies bound for Brest, as he was told, and that English merchants at Morlaix told him that 23 great ships were at Brest, bound to assist the Rebels in Ireland, and that others were coming there. [N. XIII., 39.]

The HOUSE OF COMMONS.

1641[-2], February 2.—Votes concerning Sir Edward Dering and his book. (Printed in *Commons' Journals*, ii. 411.) [N. XIII., 40.]

The KING'S Answer.

1641[-2], February 11.—Concerning the Lieutenant of the Tower. (Printed in *Commons' Journals*, ii. 426.) *Copy.* [N. XIII., 41.]

The KING'S Message.

[1641-2, February 16.]—Concerning Lord Digby's letter to the Queen. (Printed in *Lords' Journals*, iv. 592.) *Copy.* [N. XIII., 136.]

JOHN POYER, Mayor, to SIR HUGH OWEN.

1641[-2], February 17. Pembroke.—I have sent you here enclosed the examination of William Lurtine master and owner of a ship of Liverpool, which confirms the former report of aid to be sent the Rebels in Ireland by the French, the Lord prevent them. Since my last letter sent you the 18th of January last there have hundreds of poor English landed in Milford stript by the rebels, who do increase daily. If aid be sent to the Rebels it is very likely some of them may be driven or willingly will come into the river of Milford, where 500 or 1,000 armed men, as I conceive, may possess themselves of the whole country, and fortify Pembroke town with the Castle and other strong places in the said county which will not so lightly be regained. "I desire you to move the House, that order may be taken that the Trained Bands and all other persons fit to bear arms in the town and liberties of Pembroke may be put in a posture of defence in these dangerous times, and that course may be taken with all persons that are rated at arms, and for providing of powder lead and match in this town—for many are backward in the service—. I desire that it may be speedily looked into. For the Trained Bands of the town and county of Pembroke in general for want of exercise are not fit for sudden service, if they should be required. Their arms are much defective, for punishment is not laid on the offenders. I likewise certify your worship that I lately viewed the arms of the store of the whole county of Pembroke kept in the town of Haverford. I assure you that those arms on a sudden service will not arm 200 men—as I conceive—they are so defective. I have divers times desired the Deputy Lieutenants of the County to deliver me arms for 40 or 50 musketeers with powder match and lead out of the same store for the safeguard of the town of Pembroke, if occasion should be offered, but they have refused to deliver me any, notwithstanding this town hath paid for the providing of the said arms powder and lead, neither have they given any order or directions for watch to be kept in this town, either by night or day. We have not in this brave river of Milford one piece of ordinance mounted, the Trained Bands are not exercised, arms provided, or power granted for punishing of persons refractory in this service." I desire you to acquaint the House with these particulars. [N. II., 9.]

The KING's Answer to the Petition concerning Lord Kimbolton and the five members.

[1641-2, February 18 or 19.]—(Printed in *Lords' Journals*, iv. 600, and in Rushworth, iii. 1. 520, where it is called an answer to the Militia Ordinance.) *Subscribed* as the next. [N. XIII., 135.]

The KING's Answer to the Petition of Both Houses.

[1641-2, February 23.]—(Printed in *Lords' Journals*, iv. 612.) *Subscribed* "Copia Vera, Jo : Browne Cleric : Parlamentor." [N. XIII., 49.]

Articles of Impeachment against GEORGE LORD DIGBY.

1641[-2], February 25.—(Printed in *Commons' Journals*, ii. 455.) [N. XIII., 42.]

DUDLEY WYATT to "my very good Lord" (the EARL OF LEICESTER, Lord Lieutenant of Ireland).

1641[-2], March 5. Westchester.—"The four troops of horse are now all come hither, but neither the arms nor that little sum of money of which we have heard often is arrived, which breeds great distractions here, nor will that sum cure them when arrived. Captain Baker is very much behind. The four troops which are gone hence have left a great debt, the company of firelocks makes strange complaints and besides all this the mayor and county are so perverse that they will not trust the soldiers. Abroad the Justices of the Peace are willing to do what they can, but they wonder that no order or notice or direction was sent unto them, but the Mayor of Chester, though he knows the Captains are exceeding careful to pay, yet he commands the town to trust no soldier beyond one meal, so that it is impossible for the Captain to subsist without pay, having no credit. If money were here I conceive it would be exceeding well to pay here and send all the troops both of horse and dragooners to Liverpool, especially if your Excellency will be pleased to send a letter to the mayor there and gentlemen of the country about to give them notice of the coming of these troops and to desire them to further their quartering and dispose of them, as they shall find it most convenient either in Liverpool or the country. It is absolutely necessary they should embark in that place, the other country which lies near Chester water and Birbett Wharf being so eaten up that it is almost impossible for one hundred horse to subsist in all Worrall which is the country between those two rivers. This if your Excellency will be pleased to give order to Mr. Battier to do this post, it will render the quartering, providing for and embarking of these troops exceedingly expeditious and convenient." A complaint is likely to be presented at the instigation of one Bevon, a mere common barrettour, who has persuaded the country of Worrall, that they will not be paid at all for the last troops. I have been much troubled to procure quarter for these four troops and to settle the dragooners, which proceeded from want of notice to the gentlemen of the county and want of pay in due time. I hope that this will hereafter be seen to. I apologise for troubling your Excellency with such particulars. " There is nothing extraordinary from Ireland, only a report which comes from many, but I cannot fasten it on any that I will deliver it from as assured ; that the Rebels have summoned three score thousand out of every division of the kingdom a proportion to fall upon Dublin as a design which may compass the utmost of their ends. As I am now writing Mr. Parsons says that the money made over by Mr. Loftus in several parcels is not yet heard of here at all, neither doth he know how it can be got, which makes the disturbance the greater, because it was reported money was come down and none is issued to the soldier or country." [N. II., 10.] *Enclosed :*

Captain Thomas Sandford to Dudley Wyatt.

1641[-2], March 5. Chester.—On removing from country quarters, " I adventure to this town in expectation that a common respect might be shown my men, but since Tuesday last was sevennight myself and company has importuned for quarter from the magistrates here, yet nothing can prevail. Some of my soldiers for entreating billet were threatened, others sent to the gaol with much abuse and sufferance. Above 50 of my men do yet want quarters, and abundance are lodged among extreme poverty and infection of the Pox, and many are so cruel that they thrust my men out of doors to perish in the streets. Money is wanting, and none will credit or deliver a pint of beer or a penny loaf to a soldier without payment for the same. It lies much in your power to work a redress therein. I have engaged my reputation to the mayor no inhabitant shall suffer by my men, yet nothing will prevail but ready money, and that being want-ing my poor men want all things, and I fear in a short time, unless you please to assist me, myself shall by reason of this their want of accommodation want some part of my men. I make bold to send you this written entreaty, whilst myself in person do endeavour to suppress disorder amongst my distressed men and their cruel landlords." [N. II., 11.]

Roger Puttocke and others.

1641[-2], March 8.—Appointing Henry Jones D.D. in their names and the names of all others their distressed brethren the clergy of Ireland their Agent and Attorney to present to the House of Commons the remonstrance of their lamentable condition, and receive and return the bounty of their brethren in England. (See *Commons' Journals,* ii. 556.) *Signed* by seven persons, and their *Seals* affixed. [N. XIII., 52.]

The Parliament.

[1641-2, March 9.]—Additional reasons for his Majesty's return. (Printed in Rushworth, iii. 1. 531, and Clarendon iv. § 342.) [N. XV., 176.]

The HOUSE OF COMMONS to the KING.

[1641-2, March 16.]—Declaration concerning Passes into Ireland. (Printed in Rushworth, iii. 1. 514.) Two *copies.* [N. XII., 44, 45.]

And

The KING'S Answer thereto.

[1641-2, March 21.]—(Printed in *Commons' Journals,* ii. 494, and Rushworth, iii. 1. 515.) *Copy.* [N. XIII., 50.]

LORD ESMOND to the EARL OF LEICESTER.

[1641-2, March.]—(Read at the Committee March 23.) Concerning the requirements of the garrison of Duncannon Fort. (The order of the Committee at foot concerning their pay and payments for other purposes is printed in *Commons' Journals,* ii. 502.) [N. XXI., 121.]

The PARLIAMENT to the KING.

[1641-2, March 22.]—(Printed in *Lords' Journals,* iv. 661, and Clarendon, v. § 13.) *Copy.* [N. XII., 226.]

And

The KING'S Answer thereto.

[1642, March 26.]—(Printed in *Lords' Journals,* iv., 686, and Clarendon, v. § 20.) *Copy.* [N. XIII., 55.]

The SCOTCH COMMISSIONERS.

1642, April 6.—Paper concerning the Irish treaty. (Printed in *Lords' Journals,* v. 1.) *Original* and *copy* the first *signed* " Ja. Prymerose." [N. XIX., 62, 63.]

SIR THOMAS GOWER to WILLIAM LENTHALL.

1642, April 8. York.—(Sent with the petition for Yorkshire printed in *Lords' Journals,* iv. 711.) " The names " of the signers " are not sent up, as well because that presented to his Majesty had not any, as also that very many are yet signing, but already above twenty baronets and knights, fifty esquires and one hundred gentlemen have set their hands besides freeholders. . . We had stayed to send up the petition and hands together but that we hear there is already false copies and rumours of other petitions gone up." *Signed. Seal.* [N. II., 13.]

The SAME to FERDINANDO LORD FAIRFAX.

Same date and place.—Requesting him to present the petition. *Signed. Seal.* Addressed "to the Lord Fairfax his lodging, over against the Dog in the Palace Yard in Westminster." [N. II., 14.]

The HOUSE OF COMMONS.

[1642, April 8.]—Declaration for preserving a right understanding between the nations. (Agreed to by the Lords, and printed in *Lords' Journals,* iv. 707.) [N. XIX., 56.]

The KING to the PARLIAMENT.

1642, April 8.—Declaring his intention to go to Ireland. (Printed in Rushworth, iii. 1. 560, and Clarendon, v. § 58.) Two *copies.* [N. XV. 172; XXI., 63.]

TIMOTHY TOURNEUR to WILLIAM LENTHALL.

1642, April 9. Haverfordwest.—"At my coming to hold the Great Sessions of the County of Pembroke this last week there was shewed unto me the examination of Hugh Molloy a Franciscan friar or Romish priest taken before the Mayor of Pembroke and another Justice. And finding therein sufficient grounds to proceed against him for treason upon the law made against men of his quality did cause him to be indicted arraigned and tried and the jury having found him guilty I gave judgment on the verdict as in case of High Treason." I have directed the sheriff however to stay execution, as he was stayed amongst other Popish Irish by command of the House, till the return of the messenger to receive their further commands. "The story of this man's life and behaviour to bring him within the case of High Treason is amply set forth in his examination." I ask pardon if I have done wrong in not waiting for the direction of the House. (See *Commons' Journals,* ii. 506, 558.) *Signed. Seal.* [N. II., 15.]

The PARLIAMENT to the KING.

[1642, April 14.]—Petition against his going to Ireland. (Printed in *Commons' Journals,* ii. 527, and Clarendon, v. § 4.) *Draft* in Mr. Pym's hand with amendments. The clause declaring that if he went they would not hold themselves bound to submit to the commanders he should choose is an addition to the petition as originally drawn. [N. XII., 46.]

AR. SANDFORD to SIR RICHARD LEY and SIR JOHN CORBETT.

1642, April 14. Drayton-in-Hales.—Information against Mr. Peter Maxfield of Meare in Staffordshire concerning the publication of certain scandalous verses. (Printed in Grey, iii. Appendix, No. 15, p. 24.) *Signed. Seal.* [N. II., 16.] (The verses are N. XII., 12.)

The KING to LORD LITTLETON, Lord Keeper.

1642, April 14. York.—Enclosing a message concerning Hull and the banishment of the six priests. (See *Lords' Journals,* iv. 722.) *Copy. Enclosed :*

i. WARRANT.

For banishing the said priests. *Copy.* [N. XIII., 59.]

ii. The said MESSAGE.

(Printed in *Lords' Journals,* iv. 722.) *Copy.* [N. XIII., 61.]

Additional Declaration of the LORDS AND COMMONS.

[1642, April.]—Against the King's going to Ireland because—

1. His "absence will cause men to believe that it is out of design to discourage the Undertakers and hinder the other propositions for raising money for defence of Ireland.
2. It will very much hearten the rebels there and disaffected persons in this kingdom as being an evidence and effect of the jealousies and division betwixt your Majesty and the people.
3. It will much weaken and withdraw the affection of the subject from your Majesty without which a Prince is deprived of his chiefest strength and lustre and left naked to the greatest dangers and miseries . . .

4. It will invite and encourage the enemies of religion and the state in foreign parts to the attempting and acting of their evil designs and intentions towards us.

5. It causeth a great interruption of the proceedings of Parliament."
Copy. [N. XXI., 65.]

JOHN METTCALFE to Serjeant-Major GIFFORD.

1642, April 18.—"Little news here in these parts; his Majesty of Denmark hath his ships in a readiness, and it is reported intending for Hull, but he is not over hasty, since he hears of our navy being out at sea; besides we report you are very strong, and if he come he will be bidden welcome; he is about rising our tolls at Gluckstadt, as well as in the Sound, but of that I refer you to the passengers."

At foot, "This is an extract of a letter written from Hamburgh by Mr. John Mettcalfe to Serjeant-Major Gifford at Hull compared with the original by us.—Stamford, Edward Aycoghe, Christopher Wray, Samuel Owfield, Thomas Hatcher." (See *Commons' Journals*, ii. 560.) [N. II., not numbered, at the end of the volume.]

SIR JOHN CULPEPER, and ANTHONY HUNGERFORD to WILLIAM LENTHALL.

1642, April 19. York.—(The substance appears from *Commons' Journals*, ii. 537, where also the enclosed answer from the King is printed.) *Signed. Seal.* [N. II., 17.]

Petition of the Gentry and Commons of the County of YORK.

[1642, April 22.]—(Printed in Rushworth, iii. 1. 566.) *Copy.* On the back are notes, being suggestions for the Report herein-after mentioned. (See *Commons' Journals*, ii. 540.) [N. XXII., 142.]

REPORT thereupon.

[1642, April 25.]—*Draft* substantially agreeing with the Report as printed in *Lords' Journals*, v. 15. [N. XXII, 154.]

The LORDS JUSTICES and the COUNCIL OF IRELAND to SIR EDWARD NICHOLAS.

1642, April 23. Dublin Castle.—We have received the King's letters of the 13th inst., a copy of his message to the Parliament in England, and your letters of the 13th, by which we observe his Majesty's gracious resolution to adventure his person in this kingdom for suppressing the cruel rebellion. We have written to him, to express our thankfulness. For his information we now send you an account of the present state of affairs.

(1.) We gather by your letters that it is believed that on his Majesty's appearance in this kingdom, divers great men who have hitherto sat still, will declare themselves heartily for him against the rebels. We know no great men here but such as have already declared themselves either for the King or for the rebels. The former have few or no English left, and their Irish tenants being Papists are openly or under-hand joined with the rebels. Both sides have put forth their full strength.

(2.) The rebellion has now overspread all parts of the kingdom, notwithstanding all our endeavours, and those of all those great men who are not joined with the rebels. The rebels are generally masters of the field.

(3.) The whole strength of his Majesty's army in this kingdom is about 9,000 foot and 1,200 horse, and 300 dragoons, besides the small forces in Munster, Ulster, and Connaught. They are in want of wholesome food, clothes, shoes, and medicaments. We have not money to buy them here, or to provide skilful chirurgeons. Many die daily, and in truth the number of fighting men cannot be accounted above 6,000.

(4.) The forces are disposed into several apt garrisons, as at Dublin, Drogheda, Dundalk, Athy, Catherlagh, and Naas. They have no more strength than is necessary for guarding those places.

(5.) We cannot, without deserting those places, draw together into the field a body of more than 2,000 men, and those not fully armed.

(6.) To pay all in list here and in the other three provinces, and other charges incident to the war, we have received out of England since the 23rd of October—when this rebellion began—only 37,000l., which has not paid a sixth of the charges due in that time. The soldiers have been " disappointed and reduced to high and inexpressible extremities." Those in the remote parts have not had one penny since these troubles began, except 1,000l. sent to Knockfergus. They undergo many hazards against the enemy, and at home they endure the misery of nakedness, cold, hunger, and thirst. We cannot therefore deal with disorders among them which arise to the oppression of the good subjects of this town, who have besides been despoiled by the Rebels, as severely as we would.

(7.) If the 2,000 men were drawn into a body to march, our stores would not victual them for above a month. We are in want of horses and carriages, nor is there much victual in the country, and that not to be gained but by fighting for it.

(8.) There is no fit accommodation here for the entertainment of the King and his retinue, all places near this City and for many miles round having been wasted partly by the Rebels' forces and partly by the King's in vengeance for the inhabitants adhering to the Rebels. The provisions here are not fit for his Majesty's table. Provisions for horses, and firing are equally scarce.

(9.) We have no 'money to buy provisions from England, his Majesty's revenues being wholly taken away by this Rebellion. We send a relation of our late good success against the rebels. Of the 9,000 foot mentioned above, no more than 3,400 came from England, the rest having been raised here with much difficulty. *Copy.* [N. XII., 13.]

The King to Lord Littleton, Lord Keeper.

1642, April 24. Beverley.—Enclosing message. Two *copies* [N. XII., 14, 15.] *Enclosed:*

The said Message.

Concerning his being refused admittance into Hull. (Both printed in *Lords' Journals*, v. 16.) *Copy.* [N. XIII., 57.]

The Scotch Commissioners.

1642, April 25. Westminster. — Paper touching the payment of the Brotherly Assistance. (Printed in *Lords' Journals*, v. 42.) *Signed* " James Prymerose." [N. XIX., 42.]

The King to Lord Littleton, Lord Keeper.

1642, April 28. York.—Enclosing his message concerning Sir John Hotham and Hull. Original with *Sign Manual* and *Signet* and two copies. [N. I, 1.; XIII., 56.] *Enclosed:*

The said MESSAGE.

(Both printed in *Lords' Journals*, v. 31, and in Clarendon, v. § 93.)
Two *copies*. [N. XIII., 60, 62.]

The KING'S MESSAGE.

Same date and place.—Concerning the Militia. (Printed in *Lords' Journals*, v. 31, and in Clarendon, v. § 80.) Two *copies*. [N. XIII., 58; XV., 176a.]

The PARLIAMENT.

[1642, April 28.]—Declaration concerning Hull. (Printed in *Lords' Journals*, v. 26, and Clarendon, v. § 95.) *Draft*. [N. XIII., 133.]

ROBERT THORPE, of Hull.

1642, May 3.—Information that he heard on the Bourse at Hamburgh on April 19th that fourteen of the King of Denmark's ships were ready to go to Hull, and that he had raised 14,000 men. *Witnessed* by the Earl of Stamford, Sir Edward Ayscoghe, Sir Christopher Wray, Sir Samuel Owfield and Thomas Hatcher. [N. XIII., 64.]

The MARQUESS OF HERTFORD to [the EARL OF ESSEX].

1642, May 3. York.—(Printed in *Lords' Journals*, v. 49.) *Signed*. [N. II., 18.]

The PARLIAMENT to the KING.

1642, May 5.—Answer to his messages concerning Hull. (Printed in *Lords' Journals*, v. 46, and Clarendon, v. § 106.) *Copy*. [N. XIII., 63.]

EDWARD LAWRENCE, High Sheriff of Dorsetshire, to WILLIAM LENTHALL.

1642, May 8. Grange.—Stating that he had in obedience to the order of the House dated the 19th of April summoned all such members as he knew were in the County to give their attendance in Parliament. *Signed*. [N. II., 19.]

The COMMITTEE AT YORK to WILLIAM LENTHALL.

1642, May 10. York.—(Printed in *Lords' Journals*, v. 61.) *Seal*. [N. II., 20.]

SIR EDWARD AYSCOGHE, SIR CHRISTOPHER WRAY, SIR SAMUEL OWFIELD, and THOMAS HATCHER to WILLIAM LENTHALL.

1642, May 10. Kingston-upon-Hull.—On receipt of the order of both Houses yesterday we instantly hired two ships, and this day put on board half the cannon with a good quantity of powder match and bullet, and prepared a considerable number of muskets to be shipped tomorrow morning with the rest of the cannon. We hope within a few days to have dispatched the greatest part of that which is most needful, having two men of war, part of the Earl of Warwick's fleet, ready to waft them to London, which arrived here on Sunday last sent for that purpose. We have likewise given the Sheriff the opinion of the House concerning his warrants of restraint. "There is much expectation of a great meeting at York on Thursday next by all the Gentry and Freeholders of the County summoned thither by his Majesty's appointment and by a warrant of so unusual and high a strain that we have thought it good to send you herewith a copy." (See *Commons' Journals*, ii. 571.) *Signed.* *Seal.* [N. II., 21.]

THOMAS ELLIOT and Mr. WINDEBANK.

1642, May 12.—Words spoken against the Parliament. (Printed in *Lords' Journals*, v. 180.) *Copy.* [N. XIII., 65.]

ENDYMION PORTER to WILLIAM LENTHALL.

1642, May 13. York.—Excusing himself from attending the House in obedience to their order of April 18th, on the ground that the King refuses permission. *Seal.* [N. II., 22.]

Petition of many thousands of peaceably affected subjects of the County of YORK.

[1642, May 13.]—(Printed in Rushworth, iii. 1. 618.) *Copy.* [N. XXII., 141.]

A brief information of the present estate of our County of MONMOUTH which is, as we conceive, in greatest and most imminent danger next to Ireland as may appear by these particulars.

[1642, May 17.]—(Apparently of the same date and complaining of the same matters, as the petition presented at that date to the House of Commons, the purport of which appears from *Commons' Journals*, ii. 575. At the end is written, "Sent to Mr. Cromwell.") [N. XV., 175.]

The PARLIAMENT to the COMMITTEE AT YORK.

1642, May 17.—(Printed in *Lords' Journals*, v. 69.) *Draft.* [N. XII., 16.]

The PARLIAMENT.

[1642, May 18.]—Declaration thanking the Privy Council of Scotland for their Declaration of April 22nd. *Draft* with amendments. (Printed as amended in *Lords' Journals*, v. 74.) [N. XIX., 61.]

The PARLIAMENT.

1642, May 19.—Declaration. (Printed in *King's Pamphlets*, E. 148, No. 17, and Clarendon, v. § 157.) [N. XX., 52.]

Paper concerning DELINQUENTS.

1642, May 19.—(Printed in *Lords' Journals* v. 75.) [N. XIII., 66.]

The PARLIAMENT.

1642, May 28.—Order for the Quiet of the Northern Parts. (Printed in *Lords' Journals*, v. 90.) *Copy.* [N. XIII., 67.]

Informations of Captain WILLIAM WEBB, HENRY DARRELL, RICHARD FOSTER, and RICHARD WIDOSON.

1642, May 30, 31, June 2.—Concerning the allegation of the said Darrell and Foster that Mr. Pym had taken a bribe of 30*l*. (See *Commons' Journals*, ii. 661.) [N. XIII., 68, 69.]

LORD WILLOUGHBY OF PARHAM to the KING.

[1642, June 6.]—(Printed in *Lords' Journals*, v. 116, being a copy signed by himself and enclosed in his letter to the Speaker of the House of Lords.) [N. II., 185.]

THE PARLIAMENT to the KINGDOM OF SCOTLAND.

[1642, June 15.]—Declaration. (Printed in *Lords' Journals*, v. 136.) *Draft.* [N. XII., 17.]

THOMAS CHEDLE, High Sheriff of Carnarvonshire, to WILLIAM LENTHALL.

1642, June 15.—Certifying that John Griffith, Vice-Admiral of North Wales, is unable to obey the order of the House of the 2nd instance, requiring the attendance of all members, as he is confined to bed by illness. *Seal.* [N. II., 23.]

GRIFFITH WILLIAMS and others.

Same date.—Deposition to the same effect. [N. XIII., 181.]

LORD WILLOUGHBY to LORD WHARTON, Speaker of the House of Peers.

1642, June 19. Lincoln.—(Printed in *Lords' Journals*, v. 155.) [N. II., 24.]

LORD PAGET to ——.

[1642, June before the 20th.]—(Printed in *Commons' Journals*, v. 152.) [N. II., 150.]

SIR WILLIAM ARMYNE, SIR EDWARD AYSCOGHE, SIR ANTHONY IRBY, SIR JOHN WRAY, SIR CHRISTOPHER WRAY, and THOMAS HATCHER to JOHN PYM.

1642, June 22. Lincoln.—Referring to the case of William Clarke of Grantham and enclosing the informations taken. (See *Commons' Journals*, ii. 641.) *Signed. Seal.* Addressed to Mr. Pym at his lodgings in St. Margarett's Lane in Westminster. [N. II., 27.]

SIR JOHN WRAY and others to WILLIAM LENTHALL.

1642, June 24. Lincoln.—We are sending up Edward Farmery, in custody of William King, servant of the Sergeant at Arms, a disturber of the peace, and hinderer of our proceeding in the Militia. *Signed.* [N. II., 28.]

HENRY ROBINSON to WILLIAM LENTHALL.

1642, July 1. From outside the House of Commons.—Relating to Mr. Curteene's cargo of salt petre, of which he secured the refusal by paying 5*l.* He is now pressed to conclude and therefore desires an immediate answer, whether the House will take it or no. (See *Commons' Journals*, ii. 647.) *Signed. Seal.* [N. II., 29.]

JOHN PYM.

[1642, July 1.]—Draft in his handwriting of the Preamble he was directed by the House of Commons (*Commons' Journals*, ii. 647) to prepare to the intercepted letter of Henry Wilmott to James Crofts, to which it refers "Amongst other evidences of the disposition of those in credit about the king." *Annexed:*

HENRY WILMOTT to JAMES CROFTS.

1642, June 22.—(Printed in *Lords' Journals*, v. 169.) [N. II., 25, 26.] A fair copy of the Preamble is N. XII., 47.

The COMMITTEE AT HULL to SIR PHILIP STAPILTON.

[1642, July 3–12.]—"Since our last of the 3rd of June (July. See *Lords' Journals*, v. 182), the *Providence* hath landed six great pieces of battery, whereof three are demi-cannon of 24 pound bullet. You may see by the Declaration that a speedy course of violence is intended against us here. We have by our former advertised you how unable without present supply of more men we are to subsist. We have, as we conceive, certain intelligence that this ship hath within her 24 pieces of ordinance besides 14 of her own, which, if she cannot get of herself off the sands, then they will have the addition of those. We believe they have at this instant together 300 horse and about 2,000 foot. They have arms, powder and other ammunition, and so take up all men that come. We believe that they will instantly, if not opposed, be a considerable body, yet of such men as, if the Parliament take a quick course—but it must be without delay—as will not hazard much for them. We shall, God willing, do our best, but our outwork being not yet tenable 'tis not much we can do without we suddenly have moe men sent us by sallies to hinder their approaches. You have oft had it reiterated from hence the necessity of a good Committee here, you have appointed some, but we are no better. We are not at this instant four. We desire you will be pleased to send down Sir William Strickland, Sir Hugh Cholmeley, Sir Philip Stapilton, Sir Henry Cholmeley. They are gentlemen that in these times may do good with their credit in the country. If, while you sit voting, these others be doing, you will soon find but a bad issue. Horse speedily sent down, whereof great use. We shall earnestly intreat you will take to heart this, as sent from them, whose utmost endeavour if you will enable them, shall be to serve you. *Postscript.*—We have certain intelligence, they intend instantly, if they can, to make quick work with us here." *Signed* " John Hotham, John Hotham, Jo. Alured, Peregrine Pelham." [N. II., 43.]

The EARL OF EXETER to the SPEAKER OF THE HOUSE OF PEERS.

1642, July 4. Burleigh. — (Printed in *Lords' Journals*, v. 177.) *Signed. Seal.* [N. II., 30.]

The HOUSE OF COMMONS.

1642, July 4 —Order for seizing horses going to York. (Printed in *Commons' Journals*, ii. 649.) [N. XIII., 73.]

The Inhabitants of STANWELL to ——.

[1642, July 4.]—Accusing Dr. Reeves, their parson. (Printed in Grey, iii. Appendix, No. 8, p. 13.) (See *Commons' Journals*, ii. 652.) [N. XIII., 71.]

The HOUSE OF COMMONS.

1642, July 5.—Order against publishing the King's Proclamations. (Printed in *Lords' Journals*, v. 182; *Commons' Journals*, ii. 652.) [N. XIII., 70.]

The EARL OF WARWICK to the KING.

1642, July 5. Aboard the *James* in the Downs.—"I have received your Majesty's letter of my dismission to this service and with it an Ordinance of Parliament for my continuation in this employment. I beseech your Majesty to consider into what a great streight I am brought between these two commands as also of the weighty trust your Majesty's greatest council hath put me in for the defence of your Majesty and your kingdoms wherein I shall ever be ready to sacrifice life and all I have to serve your Majesty. Yet, Sir, I most humbly beg your pardon that I did not lay down my charge, your Majesty's command not coming by that way that it was imposed on me. And I hope your Majesty hath always been as well assured of my fidelity as of Sir John Pennington's or any other. And therefore I shall humbly beg of your Majesty I may not be divided between two commands, whereby your Majesty will lay the greatest of favours upon your servant, that night and day prays to God for your Majesty's long life and happiness." (*Copy.* See *Lords' Journals*, v. 216.) .*Signed.* [N. II., 31.]

SIR JOHN WOLSTENHOLME to WILLIAM LENTHALL.

1642, July 5. Buntingford.—Complaining that on his way northward he had been stayed by the search and stopping of his waggon for money, plate and ammunition, and asking that it may be released, (which was granted, see *Commons' Journals*, ii. 653). *Signed. Seal.* [N. II., 32.]

Treaty between the SCOTCH and ENGLISH COMMISSIONERS for the reducing of IRELAND.

[1642, July 6.]—(Printed in *King's Pamphlets*, E. 324.) [N. XIX., 50.]

LAWRENCE BALL, Mayor, and others, to ZOUCH TATE and RICHARD KNIGHTLEY, Members for the Borough.

1642, July 8. Northampton.--In obedience to an Order of both Houses I have stayed two war horses with great saddles, going towards Yorkshire, one belonging to Captain Neville, the other to Mr. Boyses. Consequently a messenger has been to attach me and bring me before the King. Therefore I desire the directions of the House. *Signed.* (See *Commons' Journals*, ii. 663, 664.) [N. II., 33.]

Colonel GEORGE GORING to SIR PHILIP STAPLETON.

1642, July 8. Portsmouth.—Concerning certain brass pieces he had desired to be sent thither. *Signed. Seal.* [N. II., 34.]

The KING.

1642, July 9. Beverley.—Warrant for the apprehension of Watson and Ames. (Printed in *Lords' Journals*, v. 216.) *Copy.* [N. XII., 19.]

EDWARD COLMAN and JOHN GRIGG.

1642, July 10.—Informations accusing Frederic Gibb, the parson of Hartest and Boxted in Suffolk of publishing the King's Declaration both in church and elsewhere, and inducing several of the neighbouring clergy to do the same. (See *Commons' Journals*, ii. 684.) [N. XIII., 72.]

The DECLARATION sent to the NORTH.

[1642, July 11.]—(Printed in *Lords' Journals*, v. 201. These are two drafts of it, the first differing considerably from the printed one, the second after receiving numerous alterations in Mr. Pym's hand, being that ultimately adopted.) [N. XIII., 138, 139.]

The EARL OF DERBY and other the Commissioners of Array in CHESHIRE to the CONSTABLES OF STOCKPORT.

1642, July 12.—Warrant ordering them to summon all that stand charged with arms and all the trained soldiers in the township to appear before the Commissioners at Macclesfield on the 26th and to attend themselves. A second copy is addressed to the Constables of Northbury. [N. XIII., 74.]

Lieutenant WATERS to Captain SLINGSBY.

1642, July 12.—Yesterday walking in Westminster I heard people talk of you, and say how much Parliament was incensed against you. I met Sir John Mennes who told me he was newly cleared by the Parliament, but that they were much incensed against you. You have gained a fair name and much applause from such as wish well to the King. I exhort you to adhere to the course you have taken. (See *Lords' Journals*, v. 216.) *Signed. Seal.* [N. II., 35.]

SIR EDWARD NICHOLAS to the EARL OF WARWICK.

1642, July 13. Newark.—" According to your Lordship's request I have presented your letter to his Majesty, who I perceive is nothing satisfied with what your Lordship hath written, and commanded me to signify to you that His Majesty conceived that nothing could have induced your Lordship to commit High Treason." . . . . (See *Lords' Journals*, v. 216.) *Signed.* [N. II., 36.]

SIR EDWARD HARINGTON and others to WILLIAM LENTHALL.

1642, July 14. Oakham.—We have received the instructions of the House concerning the Militia &c., and have taken measures for securing the magazine. The Commission of Array being directed to men of great power in the county and the innovating clergy being very forward to publish the books that come from his Majesty and not those from the Parliament we fear the business may receive great prejudice. *Signed. Seal.* [N. II., 37.]

The SCOTCH COMMISSIONERS.

1642, July 15.—Paper desiring payment of the 80,000*l.* (Printed in *Lords' Journals*, v. 214.) *Signed* " James Prymerose." [N. XIX., 51.]

The Commission of the EARL OF ESSEX as Captain General.

[1642, July 15.]—(Printed in Peck, *Desiderata Curiosa*, viii 2. The blanks there are filled up thus (i) according to their ordnance; (ii) displace or continue.) [N. XIII., 131.]

The EARL OF WARWICK to the SPEAKER OF THE HOUSE OF PEERS.

1642, July 17.—(Printed in *Lords' Journals*, v. 216.) *Signed.* [N. II., 38.]

The KING to the PARLIAMENT.

1642, July 19.—(Printed in *Lords' Journals*, v. 235, and Clarendon, v. § 393.) *Copy*. [N. XIII., 75.]

The PARLIAMENT to the NATIONAL ASSEMBLY OF SCOTLAND.

[1642, July 21.]—Declaration. (Printed in *Lords' Journals*, v. 229.) *Copy*. [N. XIII., 140.]

The PARLIAMENT to the HIGH SHERIFF and DEPUTY LIEUTENANTS OF HAMPSHIRE.

[1642, July 22.]—(Printed in *Commons' Journals*, ii. 686.) [N. XIII., 130.]

The EARL OF WARWICK to WILLIAM LENTHALL.

1642, July 22. From aboard his Majesty's ship the *James*.—"This day came down a small vessel, which had a young man in her, and upon search we found she had brass guns, which the young man coming on board showed me a copy of an order of the House of Commons for the transporting of them to Portsmouth to Colonel Goring, and because copies may be easily counterfeit as also they were shipped in so slight a vessel as 16 tons wherein were only two men and a boy for the guard of them, besides the young man that went with them, I have thought good to stay the Bark till I may know the pleasure of the House." *Signed. Two Seals.* [N. II., 40.]

Information of HENRY WALLIS and others.

1642, July 24.—Against Mr. Stamp, Vicar of Stepney, and others. (The purport sufficiently appears from *Commons' Journals*, ii. 690.) [N. XIII., 76.]

The KING to Colonel GEORGE GORING, Governor of Portsmouth.

1642, July 25. Leicester.—Ordering him to man and provision a pinnace lying at Portsmouth. *Sign Manual. Remains of Signet.* [N. I., 2.]

EDWARD SMITH and other inhabitants of EDLISBROUGH (AYLESBURY) in Buckinghamshire to the HOUSE OF COMMONS.

1642, July, before the 26th.—(The purport appears sufficiently from *Commons' Journals*, ii. 690.) [N. XIII., 78.]

The PARLIAMENT's Answer to the KING.

1642, July 26.—(Printed in *Commons' Journals*, ii. 693, and Clarendon, v. § 420.) *Draft*. [N. XIII., 128.]

SIR WILLIAM BRERETON to OLIVER CROMWELL.

1642, July 27.—"By my enclosure you can perceive with what violence and severity the Commissioners of Array proceed against those who oppose them in order to strike terror into the minds of those well affected to the peace and liberty of the kingdom. They have convented before them divers of our best ministers, as Mr. Ley, Mr. Holford, Mr. Clarke, Mr. Oseley. Some of whom have been summoned by such warrants—whereof a copy is inclosed—as it would seem they intend to enawe or expel our best ministers to the discovery whereof they are guided by their refusal to publish such books warrants and commands in their churches as they have sent into them. Indeed it is most apparent they intend so much to enawe the country as that none should dare oppose discover or speak against their courses, whereunto they are much encouraged by the expectations of the king's presence in those parts for whose entertainment great preparation is made, and he is expected within this three days. Though there are two messengers here there are no warrants save only for Earl Rivers and Sir Thomas Aston and Sir Edward Fitton who are under the protection of so strong a guard of horse that it is not to be expected the messengers should be able to seize them or to bring them up if they were apprehended. Some of the inferior delinquents might have been more easily apprehended. Should Parliament find out any course for the enlargement of this man Thomas Bennett, who is a very honest man, it would be of great advantage to the cause. I have already taken order for demanding the *Habeas Corpus*. I desire that some such provision be made for the security and protection of our good ministers, and that they be not exposed to so much violence and discouragement, for, as Mr. Ouseley himself informed me, Sir Thomas Aston came to his house with no less than twenty horse completely armed, and it was said there were near 40 more not far distant. But they shut the doors of the house upon him and kept him out so as the worthy minister was not then delivered into their hands, but still remains very courageous." *Seal.* [N. II., 41.] *Enclosed:*

    i. THOMAS BENNET to SIR WILLIAM BRERETON.

1642, July 21, Chester.—Am glad you are in the county that the trouble which is like to come on many in Worall by the Commissioners of Array may be made further known by the vigorous execution of your Commission. I, being one of the Constables of Williston and being troubled in my conscience whether to obey the warrant or no, was resolved not to go to the place. The other constable did also stay at home. One of the trained soldiers was examined on his oath what was the reason I was not there. He said he knew no reason, but thought the Constables might be excused, the trained soldiers being there. The other was called and examined and he said he heard the other soldier say that I said I cared not if the warrant which came from the Head Constable was burnt. He also complained that his armour was not scoured and for his pay though he had it with him. Therefore why I was dealt with and the other Constable spared was I was against the Commission of Array. Also I would acquaint your worship with the passage of the Under Sheriff. Myself, Thomas Hickcoocke, [and] John Bevan were all in a warrant, and I supposed a friend had sent a letter to Thomas Hickcoocke, did meet him at the two miles, at 7 o'clock, and if John Bevan had been at home we both had been together. When we came there the Under Sheriff with bilies (bailiffs) was there to take us. We paid for the change of ale, then we paid for sack at the Sun tavern in Chester. We paid for his dinner at his house in the city and his man's and the beer that was drunk, and I thought all day he had intended to have took bail for us both, but after dinner he called Thomas to him in the chamber and was content to bail him, but would commit me and now I am in the Castle, but I hope it is for no evil that I have done. I desire your advice for my carriage." [N. II., 39.]

ii. HUGH CALVELEY, High Sheriff of Cheshire, to the CONSTABLE
OF CHESTER CASTLE.

1642, July 25.—Warrant to take and keep in custody Thomas
Bennett for opposing the execution of the Commission of Array.
Copy. [N. XIII., 77.]

iii. LORD RIVERS, SIR THOMAS ASTON, and THOMAS SAVAGE, to
Mr. O[u]s[e]LEY, Minister at Weram.

[1642, end of July.]—Summoning him to appear on Monday next
[the 25th] at the Cock at Budworth before them on their passage towards Maxfield (Macclesfield) to give bail for his appearance after next assizes. *Signed.* [N. VIII., 136.] N. XII.,
18, is a copy thereof enclosed in Sir William Brereton's letter.

Informations of JOHN BALDING and BENJAMIN BAKER.

1642, July 29. Norwich.—Concerning a paper of scandalous verses,
against the Parliament, Lord Kimbolton, and Mr. Pym. [N. XIII.,
80.]

Confessions of the MAYORS OF HERTFORD, SALISBURY, and ST. ALBANS,
with the depositions of two persons concerning the Mayor of Salisbury.

1642, July 29.—(See *Commons' Journals*, ii. 696.) [N. XIII,
79.]

And

Interrogatories for the Examination of the said three MAYORS.

[1642, July.]—[N. XIII., 81.]

SIR WILLIAM BRERETON to WILLIAM LENTHALL.

1642, July 30.—"So soon as we were assisted by the addition of some
other Deputy Lieutenants to join in the other Hundreds we proceeded
to assemble the Hundred of Northwich upon Tuesday last at Northwich ; where there was a full appearance about three hundreth and
twenty musketeers and four score pikemen well armed and near six
hundreth other volunteers, who, though they brought not arms so complete yet I believe their hearts as well affected as the other to the safety
and peace of the King and Parliament. And though the number was
not so great as in the former Hundreds, which were much larger and
more populous than this, wherein divers of the Trained Bands and some
others charged with arms absented themselves by reason of their relation to the Commissioners of Array, yet the number of those that were
completely armed was double to those that are ordinarily charged with
arms, besides the other 600 volunteers ; so as you may be confirmed in
the assurance of the good affection of many in this country if they receive encouragement and protection, and many more I am confident
would discover themselves if they were not enawed by their remoteness
from your assistance and exposed to more than ordinary peril in regard
to the disaffected in Wales, Lancashire, Nottinghamshire, and some other
neighbouring counties. . . . *Postscript.*—There remains a considerable
sum in the hands of the Head Constables, Petty Constables, and Church
Wardens collected upon the Act of Contribution who demur to pay it
to the Sheriff, because they observe how he stands affected to the Parliament, and therefore desire your direction. By the enclosed letter
subscribed by Sir Thomas Aston you will discern their designs to
enawe or ensnare our best ministers, four or five of whom have been

already convented and given security to appear at the Assizes. Thomas Hiccocke and Thomas Bennett were apprehended last week by warrant from the High Sheriffe for opposing the authority of the Commissioners of Array. The one is bailed, the other remains in prison, a copy of whose commitment I have sent to Mr. Cromwell. There is violent pursuit against John Bevan and Robert Harvie and others who dare not return to their houses, by the terror of which examples many are much discouraged, and the other party much animated to advance both in numbers and courage." (Probably the original summons to Mr. Ouseley, of which a copy was enclosed in his letter to Oliver Cromwell, was enclosed with this.) *Seal. Endorsed* "Read Aug. 1, 1642." [N. II., 42.]

EDWARD LAWRENCE, High Sheriff of Dorset, to the MAYOR OF DORCHESTER.

1642, July 30. Grange.—Requiring him in His Majesty's name to forbear to muster or train the militia of the town, to cease to fortify the town, and to demolish the fortifications already erected, and enclosing two Proclamations to be published. *Seal. Endorsed* "The information against Mr. Lawrence . . read Aug. 2." (See *Commons' Journals*, ii. 701.) [N. II., 44.]

Doctor ARTHUR DUCKE to WILLIAM LENTHALL.

1642, August 1. Chiswick.—Certifying his reasons for not giving Mr. Tutty institution and induction to the vicarage of South Mimms. *Seal.* (See *Commons' Journals*, ii. 701.) [N. II., 46.]

NICHOLAS SIMPSON, Mayor, to SIR EDWARD HALES.

1642, August 2. Queenborough.—Describing how he arrested Captain Allen Lockhart, and how his companion escaped in a wherry. Subjoined is Captain Lockhart's examination. *Seal.* (See *Commons' Journals*, ii. 701.) [N. II., 47.]

HANBURY BLOUNT and ROBERT GRAY.

1642, August 1 and 2. Norwich.— Informations against Robert Riches for using scandalous words against the Parliament, Mr. Hollis, Mr. Pym, and the Earls of Warwick and Holland. (See *Commons' Journals*, ii. 769.) [N. XIII., 82, 83.]

Information of Captain JOHN BIRCH and others.

1642, August 3.—Against Mr. Robert Yeamans. [N. XIII., 84.]

The KING to Doctor GOFFE.

1642, August 3. York.—Warrant empowering him to collect and give receipts for money or plate given or tendered for the King's service. *Sign Manual.* [N. I., 3a.]

The COMMISSIONERS OF ARRAY FOR WORCESTERSHIRE to SERGEANT WILDE.

1642, August 5. Worcester.—Commanding him on the 12th to bring those horses, arms and array he stands charged with to the Pitchcroft, near Worcester. *Signed.* Tho. Coventrye, F. Lyttleton, John Packington, Will. Russell, Henry Herbert, Row. Berkeley, Sam. Sandys, Franc. Finche (?), John Washbourne, Hen. Townshend. *Seal.* (See *Commons' Journals*, ii. 729) [N. II., 48.]

Amendments to the SCOTCH TREATY.

1642, August 6.—"The words which his Majesty is pleased to add in the 3rd Article, viz., 'or Commissioners of the Admiralty for the time being,' and . . . in the 10th Article 'the two Houses of' in two several places, the Parliament do agree shall stand.

The Parliament holds it fit that the words 'and Parliament of England' in the 6th Article should stand.

And in the 12th Article the words 'and Parliament of England' and that the words 'his Majesty' put in by his Majesty do stand with these words 'and both Houses of Parliament,' and in the same Article the words 'his Majesty' put in by his Majesty do stand with these words added 'and them.'

Which said amendments and additions are agreed to by both Houses of Parliament." (See *Lords' Journals*, v. 268; *Commons' Journals*, ii. 707.) Two *Copies*. [N. XV., 178 ; XIX., 53, the first undated.]

The KING to Colonel GEORGE GORING, Governor of Portsmouth.

1642, August 7. York.—Enclosing copies of a letter to the Mayor and Corporation of Portsmouth, of part of a Proclamation then in the Press, and of a letter to the Lieutenant-Governor of the Isle of Wight, stating that his name is to be inserted of the Quorum in the Commission of Array for Sussex and Hampshire, and inquiring what money is required for his assistance. *Sign Manual. Remains of Signet.* [N. I., 3.]

The PARLIAMENT to HENRY HERBERT.

[1642, August 8.] — (Identical instructions with those printed in *Lords' Journals*, v. 285, except that in the last the Deputy Lieutenants are joined with Mr. Herbert.) *Draft.* [N. XIII., 137.]

The GRAND JURY and others of SHROPSHIRE.

1642, August 8.—Declaration of their confidence in the King and their readiness to serve him. [N. XIII., 83.]

ORDINANCE.

1642, August 8.—Appointing Sir Henry Vane Treasurer of the Navy. (Printed in *Lords' Journals*, v. 272.) [N. XIII., 86.]

Informations of GEORGE WATSON, THOMAS HALL, PETER MEADES, and JOHN HOLLIS, junior, all of KILLESBIE.

1642, August 9. Northampton.—Concerning murders and abuses committed by the King's Troopers. (Printed in *King's Pamphlets*, E. 110, No. 6.) [N. XIII., 88.]

The KING to the SPEAKER OF THE HOUSE OF PEERS.

1642, August 9. York.—(Printed in *Lords' Journals*, v. 284.) *Sign Manual. Remains of Signet.* [N. I., 4.]

The SAME to the SAME.

Same date and place.—(Printed in *Lords' Journals*, v. 284.) *Sign Manual. Signet.* [N. I., 5.]

Moses Reade, Mayor, to Samuel Vassall.

1642, August 9. Newport in the Isle of Wight.—Asking him to present to the House of Commons the enclosed which had been composed in great haste. *Seal. Enclosed:*

Moses Reade, William Stephens, Recorder, and ten others to the House of Commons.

Same date.—We forward a writing signed by divers of the knights and chief gentlemen of the Isle, referring the same to the judicious consideration of the House. We are utterly destitute of powder there being scarce any in the Island except in the Castles whence we are not confident to receive it in time of necessity. We therefore pray a speedy supply of some twenty or thirty barrels. (See *Commons' Journals*, ii. 716.) [N. II., 49, 50.]

Ordinance.

[1642, August 10.]—Directing Mr. Herbert to repair to Monmouthshire. (Printed in *Lords' Journals*, v. 280.) *Draft.* [N. XIII., 137.]

William Gray and Henry Fairchild and others.

1642, August 10, 14.—Informations against Edward Jeffery, Vicar of Southminster. (See *Commons' Journals*, ii. 728.) [N. XIII., 92, 90.]

Examination of Martin Harvey of Weston Favell.

1642, August 11.—Concerning his being in the Commission of Array, whether he had taken the Protestation, his horses, &c. [N. XIII., 89.]

Matthew Bie and others to Michael Oldsworth.

1642, August 11. Sarum.—Describing the late practice of Mr. William Wroughton, ensign in Portsmouth, and what ensued thereon. He came from Shafton to Sarum, where his guide reported of 30 men he had entertained at Shafton for service at Portsmouth, who were to lie at Downton that night. Mr. Wroughton was arrested at Sarum on information of the same and placed in the gaol. Alderman Johnson went to Downton to stay the soldiers, but found some, hearing about Mr. Wroughton, had returned home, and the rest encouraged by the evil counsel of Captain Abarrou of Charford had gone on for Portsmouth, of which we gave notice to the Committee near that place, and hear the said soldiers are taken in consequence. (See *Commons' Journals*, ii. 721.) *Signed.* [N. II., 51.]

The Company of Volunteers at Canterbury to the House of Commons.

[1642, August 12.]—Petition stating that about thirteen years by reason of a sudden alarm that the enemy were landed at Hearue the young men of the City—both English and Walloones—solicited the Earl of Montgomery, the Lord Lieutenant, to grant a Commission to Thomas Belke as captain of as many of them as should volunteer, which he did, and the said Thomas Belke has ever since—with the other officers—exercised the said company in the Military Yard of the said City—the charges of procuring the said yard with the walling and

levelling thereof and the building of the Armoury having been chiefly
borne by the officers and soldiers of the said Company,—and praying
that the petitioners may persist in their military discipline as formerly.
(See *Commons' Journals*, ii. 717.)   [N. XXII, 149.]

THOMAS LAWES, Mayor, to MICHAEL OLDSWORTH.

1642, August 12. Salisbury.—Informing him that a servant of
Mr. John Arundell had been stayed and searched, and forwarding some
letters and other articles found on him. [N. II., 52.]

The HAMPSHIRE COMMITTEE to [WILLIAM LENTHALL].

1642, August 12.   Southwicke —We have not received the
ammunition you wished us by your letters of the 9th and 11th to expect
at Sir William Lewis' house by a troop that was to march westward.
Sir William Waller with 43 horse and Captain Hurrey with his troop
came hither on Wednesday last, which we presume you think not any
strength to impeach the preparations at Portsmouth, wherein the ships
that are fallen thither are of great use, being ready to fasten on all
opportunities to express their forwardness and affections to the service
they are in.   On Tuesday night last, one Mr. Browne Bushell, being
Master of Captain Martin's ship, manned out a long boat.   And his
boldness was such in encouraging his men as that they took in the
Maria pinnis carrying six pieces of ordinance, and thereby hath
prevented those prejudices that the coast was liable unto by her rovings.
And she is now laid up near Faireham, where we have given order to
have her unrigged and to unlade her of her ordinance.   On Wednesday
morning last we took a course for the surprising of two barks laden
with about 80 quarters of wheat by Captain Badd, and one Riggs, and
other ill-affected persons for the supply of Portsmouth, whereof those
hands that were employed in the service shared some part ; and five
quarters were allowed to be distributed among the poor along the coasts,
the better to encourage discoveries, if the like preparation were again
attempted, and the part we appointed to be kept for the use of our men
here as occasion shall require.   And on that day also we seized on two
great horses of one Mr. Waigrave's, a known great Recusant, having
received information that he provided them for Portsmouth, and that
they also stopt one Mr. White a Dorsetshire papist with his servant and
one Mr. Knowles, another papist who were going thither.   We presume
you have heard from Salisbury how that they have there in custody one
Mr. Wroughton, who had—in those parts—levied thirty men for the
service of Portsmouth, whereof our watches have yesterday morning
met with fourteen, who are now in hold.   We on Wednesday sent a
summons to Colonel Goring a copy whereof and of his answer thereto
we have here inclosed, it being the opinion of the commanders here
that it is scarce proper to send to require him to deliver up the town,
till we have forces fit for the assault thereof should he refuse us, and
that he could not but hang that trumpeter that should come to require
his soldiers not to yield him any further obedience with those other
commands that you have directed for the mayor and townsmen, which
hath made us respite to proceed thereon.   Goring hath so great a
confidence of speedy supplies that he hath swept into Portsmouth all
the provisions of cattle that were in the island of Portsea, and plundered
the houses of the inhabitants there and hath already mounted his
ordinance to batter down Gosport, which his threats make them hourly
expect. his quarrel to them and to the islanders being his jealousy of their
disaffection to his commands.

Sir, thus we are enforced to trouble you with the sad relation of our condition here, which makes such a distraction in the county, as that we do not find any horse—more than our own private horses—coming on to our assistance, and the ill impressions instilled into the people by some ill affected of the gentry, such as Sir John Mills, Sir Richard Norton, Sir Richard Gifford with others, hath slackened those foot supplies, which we were in hope of, and those that come hither expect pay, which will speedily exhaust the 1,000*l.* you sent down, so that we must entreat you to hasten down a far greater sum, if you hold a resolution to provide for the safety of this place, we hearing that the Marquess of Hertford is marching hither with a great strength of horse and the Earl of Southampton daily expected with the like, which we hope will quicken your intentions so as that you speed us down the residue of Sir William Waller's regiment of horse and a regiment of foot under some experienced commanders which we hope will be seconded with such forces here as shall give you a good account of what shall be directed to them.

Sir, our earnestness upon the outcries of the poor people here and the dangerous consequence that delay may bring by our want of timely supplies upon this part of the kingdom hath enforced the coming up of this bearer being one of us your servants here—whose assistance we shall want—to importune your despatch of our desires hereby . . .

Postscript.—We have such need of Arms here that we desire to be supplied with 400 muskets, bandileers, rests, and swords out of your storehouse."

Signed " Will. Lewis, Tho. Jervoise, William Waller, John Fielden, John Lisle, Ro. Wallop." [N. II., 53.]

LAWRENCE BALL, Mayor, to RICHARD KNIGHTLEY.

1642, August 12. Northampton.—We stayed last night here Mr. Harvey, Mr. Havers, and Mr. Smith as spies and intelligencers of the Earl of Northampton and countenancers of the Commissions of Array. Their examinations and two informations are enclosed, and also a warrant for summoning the Commissioners of Array taken from Samuel Wightwick, servant to the High-Sheriff, now in custody. We desire you to acquaint Parliament herewith and send us directions. (See *Commons' Journals,* ii. 719.) *Seal.* [N. II., 54.]

SIR WILLIAM BRERETON to RALPH ASHTON.

1642, August 13.—" As the Mayor and citizens of Chester knew not how to prevent us but by raising a tumult so it was also in the County. for when we had summoned an appearance for Nantwich Hundred upon Friday last, the Commissioners of Array being conscious to themselves of their own weakness to make any opposition in that Hundred sent out warrants for all their forces in the whole county. And the Sheriff extended his authority for the raising of the *Posse Comitatus* to suppress the rebellious assembly—so he stiled that which was appointed by us—not containing themselves in this county but brought forces out of Wales, Shropshire, Staffordshire and other parts. All which we should not much have valued, if we had been furnished with one troop of horse, wherewithout we were not enabled to encounter them, yet if this meeting had not been unhappily disjourned and disappointed by some of the Deputy Lieutenants and some Gentlemen of that Hundred—to whom the managing of the business in that Hundred was referred—who had the warrants signed for the meeting in their hands twenty days since, some whereof were so apprehensive of the disadvantage and danger to encounter the Commissioners' power in the whole county with a part of this single Hundred—whereof the rest were by some of them disjourned—as that upon some motions arising first from one of the other party they did conclude before my coming to town that both parties should mutually withdraw and that there should be no training that day on either part. Which agreement was performed upon our part, and whereunto I would not have assented, but that we were prevented of a great part of our force that would have appeared before us. But there was no manner of performance upon their part, but they came in a triumphing insulting manner through the town of Nantwich after our departure and our forces dismissed." I ask, "that we may receive some manner of intimation from you what to expect, for if it be so that you cannot spare us any Horse, it may not then in discretion become us to implunge this country into too great an engagement, seeing we cannot but expect that great assistance will resort to them out of Staffordshire, Shropshire, Lancashire, and Wales, and therefore I beseech your advice how to proceed herein. For though I doubt not but that we may baffle them and beat them off the ground yet we cannot hope to make good the undertaking many days without assistance ; so great multitudes will resort unto them out of Staffordshire, Shropshire, Wales and Lancashire and other parts. And this is our greatest discouragement and disadvantage that we cannot relieve and protect those that obey us, for they are imprisoned and that in the County Gaol, which is very near and convenient to carry them unto. But if we apprehend any malignant spirits for opposing our authority or for any other crime, we can take no other course but send them up to the Parliament, whom we cannot expect to be brought thither, but that they will be rescued by the way. I desire therefore to offer to your consideration whether it be not very requisite that we should have power to commit to common gaols, or rather that there may be some short order made and printed directed to the Lieutenant and Deputy Lieutenants and Constables of the County Palatine of Chester and all other his Majesty's loving subjects, commanding that no obedience be given to the Commissioners of Array, and that no officer or other presume to apprehend or imprison any man by virtue of any warrant or command from them, but that every man according to the Protestation should assist to protect and defend them from their arrest, and to rescue them out of their hands, and that no gaoler should detain any of those that are committed for no other cause but for not appearing before, or not yielding obedience to the Commissioners of Array. The reason why I omit to name in the Order or Declaration the Sheriff, Justices of the Peace and Head Constables is because the most of them are Commissioners of Array, and the rest are such as are very forward to advance that illegal commission. The bearer hereof, Richard Wirrall, was a late Head Constable who refused to obey their commands, and executed our warrants, who hath therefore thus many weeks been pursued by them, so as yet he durst not return to his own house. Many others are in the same predicament and it seems they intend—as they threaten—to fill all the gaols and prisons . . .

Postscript.—If relief come not down from you into Warwickshire and other counties you cannot make account of any better, but that they will be lost, for the people begin to despair of the Parliament's assistance, because they see nor hear of no force coming down for their relief. Therefore they conclude the Parliament wants power to protect them. I sent into Herefordshire to be informed touching the raising of Horse there and received information to this purpose. I beseech you excuse me that I have no sooner returned the acknowledgement of your respect in your letter, and let this be communicated to Mr. Ashurst and Mr.

Alderman Pennington and entreat their assistance for procuring such an order or declaration . . to be printed and sent down." *Signed. Seal.* [N. II., 55.]

The INHABITANTS OF WOODCHURCH in Kent to the
HOUSE OF COMMONS.

[1642, August 13.]—Petition. Against Edward Boughen, their parson, and praying that Mr. Robert Everdine be appointed to preach in the afternoon. (See *Commons' Journals,* ii. 719.) *Signed.* [N. XXII., 147.]

Information of WILLIAM KING.

[1642, August 15-18.]—When sent with a warrant from the House of Commons to apprehend the Bishop of Worcester, he refused to go with me saying he had the King's protection and would not obey the Parliament. On Friday last being August 12th I was present when the Commissioners of Array met at Worcester and saw Lord Coventry and other Commissioners with a great number of men—of mean and base quality as they seemed to me—and having hedgebills, old calivers, shep pikes and clubs. It was commonly affirmed that they intended to surprise Serjeant Wylde and Mr. Salwey and carry them to York . . Mr. Doldswell, an attorney in the Common Pleas, sent six horses and was a busy man in that service. (See *Commons' Journals,* ii. 729.) [N. XIII., 98.]

Resolutions of the HIGH SHERIFF OF SHROPSHIRE and the rest of the Commissioners of Array.

1642, August 16. Much Wenlock.—That they will oppose any that oppose the Commission of Array to the utmost of their power—that if the Gentlemen of the County and of Shrewsbury that seemed at their last meeting too much to affect those ordinances of Parliament where the king does not consent will comply with them in their Declaration of the last Assizes they will join with them and protect them,—and they desire that those gentlemen will esteem of them as their friends and neighbours that desire peace. (See *Commons' Journals,* ii. 737.) [N. XIII., 85.]

The MAYOR and JUSTICES OF NORWICH to WILLIAM LENTHALL.

[1642, August 17–September 15.]—Enclosing informations taken before them against certain persons for very foul and scandalous words against the Parliament and against particular members of the two Houses. We took recognizances of John Baldwyn, William Symonds and Robert Riches—the other two delinquents had fled to Yarmouth—and desire to know the pleasure of the House. Some of the expressions deposed to are : "That the Earl of Holland was a knave, and that he hoped to see him as far as my Lord of Strafford—A health to our gracious king, and confusion bring to factious Pym—If the king should go to the Parliament they would take away his Prerogative, and commit him to prison, and take off his head." *Signed* "William Gostlin, Mayor—Ric. Harman—John Tolye—Christopher Baret." (See *Commons' Journals,* ii. 767.) [N. II., 45.]

The PARLIAMENT to the EARL OF BEDFORD and others.

[1642, August 17.]—Instructions. (Printed in *Lords' Journals,* v. 299.) *Draft.* [N. XIII., 133.]

Extract from the Register of the PRIVY COUNCIL OF SCOTLAND.

1642, August 18.—Concerning uniformity in Church Government. (Printed in *Lords' Journals*, v. 323.) *Signed* "Archibald Prymerose." [N. XIX., 57.]

Information of PHILIP COTTON and WILLIAM IRELAND.

1642, August 18.—Against Abel Winckefield. (See *Commons' Journals*, ii. 726.) Besides the words there mentioned, he is also accused of saying "That this was for the Earl of Essex, he might be killed or hanged, his father was beheaded, and none of them died in their beds." [N. XIII., 91.]

Information of THOMAS HAWES and others.

1642, August 22.—Against the Chief Constable of Greenwich. (See *Commons' Journals*, ii. 731.) [N. XIII., 96.]

The PARLIAMENT to the STATES-GENERAL OF THE UNITED PROVINCES.

1642, August 22.—Letter and declaration. (Printed in *Lords' Journals*, v. 316.) *Copy.* [N. XVIII., 53.]

ARTHUR BASSETT to SIR SAMUEL ROLLE and to all the officers and soldiers of the regiment lately under his command.

1642, August 22. Great Torrington.—Announcing that by warrant dated the 5th instant he has been appointed Colonel of the regiment, and ordering them to disarm and disband. (See *Commons' Journals*, ii. 744.) [N. II., 56.]

Presentment of the GRAND JURY assembled at YORK and the KING'S Answer thereto.

1642, August.—(Printed in Rushworth, iii. 1. 646.) *Copies.*

And

The Proceedings of the HOUSE OF COMMONS thereon.

1642, August 23.—(Printed in *Commons' Journals*, ii. 734.) [N. XIII., 97.]

Examination of ABRAHAM HAYNES and Informations of THOMAS PALMER, RICHARD GOODENOUGH and THOMAS GOARE against him.

1642, August 24. Sherston in Wiltshire.—The first giving an account of himself, the other three deposing to a conversation in which the said Haynes spoke against the Parliament and for the King. [N. XIII., 94.]

The EARL OF SUFFOLK to Mr. LUCAS.

1642, August 27. Audley End.—(The substance appears from *Commons' Journals*, ii. 741.) *Seal.* [N. II., 57.]

Captain RICHARD SWANLEY to the EARL OF NORTHUMBERLAND.

1642, August 28. From aboard his Majesty's ship the *Charles*.— "Since my last I have Captain Torney of Cowes Castle in safe custody, and have put therein a sufficient guard. After that I sent Captain Wheller unto Yarmouth to demand that Castle, but Captain

Barnabe Burley stood so much upon His Majesty's commission, that he would not obey an ordnance of Parliament without His Majesty's consent of which I had notice. Presently myself with Captain Jorden went up in the ship *Censer* and anchored before the said Castle where we went ashore, thinking to have had a fair parley with the said Burley, but being before the Castle we saw him on the wall like a mad man, having a barrel of powder at each corner of the Castle with a linstock in his hands, saying that before he would lose his honour he would die a thousand deaths; and we, seeing him in that rage at present, gave him time to recollect himself, which after some consideration he proffered to come to parley on condition we would promise he might return safe into the Castle again, which we granted, and after some parley we suffered him to go into the castle and there to continue, we putting a sufficient guard over him, there to remain till further order. After that I sent Captain Jorden to Hurst Castle, who so much prevailed with the soldiers—the Captain being absent—that they admitted a sufficient guard of our men to keep possession for the King and Parliament and peace of the kingdom. And as for Sandown Castle the Gunner with other soldiers came aboard to me, desiring an order from me and they will keep the Castle from their Captain or any other malignant spirit for the peace of the island, yet notwithstanding the Captain remains in the Castle, but hath not any command there. These forts being secured to the great rejoicing of the inhabitants of the island, yet in a bodily fear, by reason that Colonel Brett with other cavaliers held Casbrooke (Carisbrooke) Castle, whereupon we took into consideration how we should dispossess the new made Governor, and with an unanimous consent we landed 400 men from the ships, who went with a full resolution not to return, until they had made the Colonel conformable to the Ordnance of Parliament The first night we marched up to Newport from whence I presently sent Captain Jorden and Captain Martin with a letter to give him notice of our intention which was, that, if he would resign up the Castle for the King and Parliament, he with the rest of the Cavaliers should have free leave to depart, but he at that time stood upon unreasonable demands, as by the inclosed it doth appear. The next morning we drew up our forces upon the hill near unto the Castle joining with two Companies of the town of Newport which put them in great terror, yet nevertheless to prevent spilling of blood myself with Captain Jorden went near unto the Castle bidding him good morrow, and if he would send forth a man we would parley with him Presently there came forth to us Captain Worsley who we gave to understand our resolution if the Colonel would not yield on fair quarter, whereupon he desired me to go into the Castle to treat thereof and I should be assured of my safe return which the Colonel protested on the faith of a gentleman, on which terms I went to him and after much debate it was surrendered on the conditions specified in the inclosed, so that now the i[s]land is in peace, and the Colonel with other Cavaliers are gone to their own houses, and the Countess (of Portland) remaining there until further order from the Parliament. In the mean time I have left forty seamen with ten men of the town of Newport to guard as well her person as the Castle under the command of Browne Bushell, until it shall be otherwise ordered. As touching the condition of Portsmouth I cannot at present give any full relation thereof, by reason I am yet at Cowes, only that I caused two Demi-Cannons and two whole Culverin to be landed at Gosport to make a battery against the town, which as yet I hear is not finished. All these my actions are not expressed in my commission, therefore I shall entreat your Lordship that you will be pleased to procure me an Order from Parliament to authorise me for what I have done if the same shall be approved of." (See *Lords' Journals*, v. 332 ; *Commons' Journals*, ii. 745.) *Signed.* [N. II., 59.] *Enclosed :*

The said articles of Surrender of CARISBROOKE.

1642, August 24.—*Copy.* [N. XIII., 95.]

THOMAS BRISTOW and sixteen others to SIR JOHN WRAY and SIR EDWARD AYSCOGHE.

1642, August 30. Waynfleet.— Referring to the landing of ten gentlemen at Skegness, who were seized with their trunks (See *Commons' Journals*, ii. 747), stating that other ships have been descried on the coast, who threaten to land, and asking them to present their distress to Parliament that Commanders may be sent down. *Signed. Seal.* [N. II., 60.]

LORD LITTLETON, Lord Keeper, to THOMAS WILLIS, Clerk of the Crown in Chancery.

1642, August 30. Nottingham.—(Printed in *Lords' Journals*, v. 341.) [N. II., 58.]

The HOUSE OF COMMONS to MARTIN SANDFORD, High Sheriff of Somerset.

1642, August 30.—(The purport sufficiently appears from *Commons' Journals*, ii. 744.) *Draft.* [N. XII., 24.]

JOHN BANNASTER and JOHN DAY.

[1642, August 30.]—Information against Richard Pauling, Rector of Wallingford. (See *Commons' Journals*, ii. 743.) [N. XIII., 99.]

NOTES mostly in Shorthand.

1642, September 2.—Of the proceedings against Dodswell. (See *Commons' Journals*, ii. 749.) [N. XIII., 102.]

JOHN WHISTLER and JOHN SMITH, members for the City of Oxford, to WILLIAM LENTHALL.

1642, September 3. Abingdon. — "We wrote last Monday, but as the Carrier's waggon was that day stayed, his trunks broken open and carriages, perhaps our letters miscarried. We therefore thought it our duty to acquaint you with the present state of the City of Oxford. On Wednesday the 10th of August the Earl of Berkshire, the Lord Lovelace, Sir John Curzon, Sir Robert Dormer, Mr. Branthwaite and Mr. Hone had a private meeting at the Star with the doctors of the University, and by a message—as we conceive mistaken—in the afternoon the Mayor and his brethren were sent for. At which time the Earl told us that the business did concern the University and not at all the City, and shewed us his Majesty's letters directed to him and others for the securing of the University, which were in effect the same which the King had formerly sent to the Sheriff of the County and the Mayor of the City, but withal advised us that howsoever differences had been between the University and the City we should now be at unity and peace and to consult with them for the public safety of the place to prevent sudden incursions for that the times were like to be dangerous.

The Mayor thanked him for his advice. The Lord Lovelace wished the doctors to be presently sent for to consult about it. We told their Lordships the manner of doing of it was a thing of more difficulty than could be suddenly digested and desired time to advise thereon. Thereupon the Lords wished us to give the doctors a meeting concerning it. That night the Vice-Chancellor sent word that the Mayor and his brethren should on the morrow morning give a meeting and withal sent word that Sir Richard Cave and another expert soldier would come with them and advised that if we had any men experienced in fortifications or matters of war we should bring them with us. On the morrow we met accordingly; and Mr. Vice-Chancellor made a long speech advising us to join in defence of the place. Then Sir Richard Cave discoursed of making a breastwork which he called a line with redoubts and a foot pace, and Dr. Pinck, the Vice-Chancellor, and he had much discourse of the nature thereof. After half an hour spent in their discourse we asked them where that line should be made. They said on the North side of the town from the Charwell to the Thames, for that they would leave out no colleges. Then we asked them in what time that would be done. Sir Richard Cave said presently, for that everyone would work having his portion of ground allotted him. We told him we had not shovels for 40 persons. Then we asked what the charge of such a work would be. Sir Richard Cave said he knew not that, but asked the stranger that was brought, who desired time to consider of it. Then we asked them how many men would man this work. Sir Richard Cave said a 1,000. We told them. the work being a mile in length at the least, we conceived many 1,000 men would not do it and that we had not arms for above 100 men, and told them plainly we did not like the business, and thought it would draw enemies upon us, and make it the seat of a war, so nothing at that time was concluded, but that we would join with them for the keeping a diligent watch both by night and day. That night Mr. Whistler's windows were broken, and it was generally given out that he should be mischiefed for speaking against that fortification.

After this many days together the Scholars and privileged persons with such weapons as they had, trained up and down the streets, in Christ Church College quadrangle, and other College quadrangles, and kept no good rule either by night or day.

On Tuesday August 23rd, the Vice-Chancellor caused another meeting, and discoursed only of unity and peace between the two bodies, which we did very well approve of, but told him we must then be used as brethren, and called to their council, otherwise we would not maintain their resolutions, which they said was reason and promised so to do. We told them our Constables were threatened and beaten, and other citizens abused, and required justice from him, which he promised, but as yet hath not performed.

We told them we heard that they had sent for Chivalleers, to come into the city. The Vice-Chancellor and Dr. Fell both denied it and protested against it. Notwithstanding all those promises that afternoon and the morrow the University—without our privity or allowance—made a bulwark of timber against the East Bridge under Magdalen College tower, and a redoubt or trench a little beyond Wadham College with a pentice of boards to sit dry, in which a watch was diligently kept and managed by the Scholars until Sunday night last. In regard to these promises and protestations and of the great defeat at Coventry we rested secure conceiving that the University would not bring in and that his Majesty could not spare any forces to trouble us but on Sunday last about 12 of the clock in the night at this redoubt they let in a troop of horse and at Smithgate the entrance into Cat Street they came suddenly upon the Watch, which, albeit it were not very strong, it staid them for a good space, until some part of the City were armed, but having so great a number before them and the Vice-Chancellor and his company being ready behind them the Vice-Chancellor commanded the watch to let them in, and bid the Chivalleers ' Welcome, gentlemen,' and said they were their friends and he, with Dr. Baily and others, did conduct them to their inns, and caused the inns to open their gates and entertained them. How they have broken up houses and pillaged citizens and others we doubt not but you have sufficiently heard already.

There was a noble gentleman of the House of Commons upon Sunday last sent us a letter of intelligence truly suspecting that these troops were bound for Oxon, which letter being sent by one of New College was kept from us until Monday night, which if we had had might have prevented the disaster, for that the number were not—as we conceive—200 whereof not above 160 some soldiers and the rest grooms and guides, and the most of those ragged starved companions, having lost their arms in their flight from Brackley, and their horses tired and spent with hunger and travel. Their behaviour hath been so injurious that many that stood indifferent before or were seduced by the persuasion of some scholars do now detest them, in so much as some of them attempting to pull down the bridge going to Bottley called Bull-stake bridge, the citizens did arm themselves and drove them away, and had the Mayor then done his duty by all likelihood they might have driven them out of town.

Some part of the County of Oxford near adjoining and a great part of the County of Berks are very well resolved and willing to afford us their best assistance, and do now so guard the country that the Chivaleers dare not scout abroad, as usually they did at their first coming. Most of the sober and religious gospellers have left the University and most of the gravest citizens have done the like, this dissolute crew having threatened that as they had lost by Roundheads—for by that reproachful expression they call men that fear God—they would repair their losses upon them. The city of Oxon and country adjacent is in great distress and likely to become desolate, unless God's mercies, with the assistance of the Parliament, shall in due time prevent it. Both of us have of late been publicly scorned and derided and direfully menaced, and Mr. Smith hath received some blows for no other reason but because he is of the Parliament. We both of us by the advice of our friends both of the University and City have for the present left Oxon. Your own estate, Mr. Speaker, lying near is concerned, therefore we shall not doubt of your best affection advice and assistance, and you knowing the place can help without our dark and weak expressions." *Signed.* Addressed to the Speaker " at his house near Charing Crosse." [N. II., 61.]

Captains ANTHONY WILLOUGHBY and THOMAS ASHLEY to the LORDS JUSTICES and COUNCIL of IRELAND.

1642, September 3. His Majesty's fort near Galway.—Forasmuch as we perceive that grievous complaint is made against us by the County and Town of Galway to the Earl of Clanricarde and we are able and were willing to justify all our proceedings before the said Earl and the Lord President of Connaught and Lord Forbes, our accusers being brought face to face with us, which offer being made to the said Earl and to the Mayor of Galway was refused, and whereas the County promise to the said Earl protection to the English amongst them and reparation of the injuries done by them provided we give satisfaction for the injuries done by us we desire that clause be rightly and equitably interpreted, and that all those that complain will enter into Bond to answer to any complaint of us or any of the English against them, and we hereby bind ourselves to answer any complaint against us and being found guilty of having done contrary to our Commission and instructions to make reparation. *Signed.* [N. II., between Nos. 61 and 62, but not numbered, or noticed in the Index.]

Thomas Norwood and John Malmes to Francis, Lord Dunsmore.

1643, September 5. [Northampton Gaol.]—On the 27th of August last Sir John Byron's troop with two of his brother's troops marched from Leicester and marched all night and all the next day till 4 o'clock at night without any injury committed to any man by us till we came to Brackley and there we were to be quartered 4 hours, but before we could get meat for ourselves or our horses, being almost all tired out by that long march, there was of a sudden a sound To horse, and our enemies coming so fierce on us before we could get horse that after a little scrimmage being but 3 hurt of our side, [we] was forced by the command of our captains to fly every man for his safety, and the country had got such force and strength of a sudden that separated us into several parts that before 8 o'clock next morning there was 44 of us taken, our captains and officers being fled towards Oxford, and so taken prisoners, our horses swords money and all our arms and other materials taken from us and so brought prisoners pinioned as traitors to the state to this lamentable place of prison. The Committee of Northampton allow us 6d. a day, but the gaoler is so hard that he constrains us to pay 4d. a man every night for our bed, so that we are almost starved for want of maintenance. We entreat your Lordship to make this our petition known to the King, and to our Colonel Sir John Byron hoping that we shall have some relief or order taken for our liberty out of this woeful place of prison. *Seal.* [N. II., 70.] This petition was annexed to the following letter.

Thomas Norwood to Francis, Lord Dunsmore.

1642, September 5. The County Prison, Northampton.— Stating that he had been apprehended at Daventry the day Sir John Byron's troop came by, and asking as his tenant to assist him in recovering his liberty, and stating that the same day John Malme of Bilton had been imprisoned at the instance of Bartholomew Gutteridge for speaking some words in your Honour's behalf. [N. II., 62.]

John Whistler and John Smith to William Lenthall.

1642, September 5. Abingdon.—" On Saturday last this printed paper enclosed was with trumpets and other solemnity in divers parts of the City of Oxford publicly proclaimed and pasted up in several places of the city, we know not by what warrant or authority. But as yet do not hear of any considerable success that it hath had.

The University are making new lines and fortifications over against St. Giles' church, where the scholars do night and day gall their hands with mattocks and shovels, and for that use have taken from the Star the shovels and mattocks provided for the County Magazine.

On Friday last the University had a Convocation for the taxing of Colleges, Halls, and privileged persons for the maintenance of these new come soldiers.

On Saturday last they procured the Mayor of the City to call a Council where he first proposed that the town should join with the University in the charge of making these fortifications, which upon long debate the citizens denied. Then the Mayor proposed that the City should join with the University in a defensive war. Some citizens demanded who was the enemy and what Delinquents the city had that were in fear. But on long debate nothing was done.

Many motions have been made and earnestly pressed for training the citizens with the scholars which as yet hath not been agreed on. Yesterday there came in a load of arms unto the Cross Inn; some say from my Lord of Danby, some say from Sir William Walter, the truth whereof we yet know not. The scholars generally feed themselves with an expectation of Prince Rupert's coming to their aid with a great army. Our Mayor's weakness we can neither defend nor excuse, which is a great part of our present misery. One of our Bailiffs—the honester man—is much distempered. His distracted thoughts sent unto us we have enclosed out of which at your leisure you may perhaps pick something of the occasion." We conceive that we may do better service here than in the House. *Signed. Seal.* (See *Commons' Journals*, ii. 754.) [N. II., 63.]

Sir Gilbert Pykeringe, Sir Richard Samwell, John Crewe and Edward Harby to William Lenthall.

1642, September 6. Northampton.—We admonished Edward Lord Mountague and others to desist from executing the Commission of Array. As he persisted, as appears by the enclosed warrants, we apprehended him and sent him up to Parliament and also Sir William Boteler and Sir Anthony St. Leger. (See *Commons' Journals*, ii. 755, 760.) *Seal.* [N. II., 64.] *Enclosed:*

i. Lewis More.

1642, August 30. — Information stating that on the 20th instant Lord Cokayne had taken a recognisance from him and his son to bring in armour belonging to the town of Lowick, and that Lord Mountague had taken a recognisance from him and his son to produce another of his sons the next day to go to Nottingham to the King. [N. II., 65.]

ii. The Earl of Westmoreland, Edward Lord Mountague, and Sir Christopher Hatton to Sir Gilbert Pykeringe and his Colleagues.

1642, August 15. Kettering.—Denying that they had put the Commission into execution and saying that they had only caused the Sheriff to summon a meeting of the Commissioners and proposing that the Parliament's Committee should restore the arms they had taken to their owners, and that both they and themselves should desist from further proceedings. *Signed.* [N. II., 66.]

iii. Edward Lord Mountague, William Williams, and William Tresham to the Chief Constables of the Hundred of Navesford.

1642, August 16.—Warrant commanding them to issue warrants to the petty Constables to summon all Baronets, Knights, Justices of the Peace, Clergy, Freeholders and all other persons charged with arms or horses, or having any arms to appear before us at Oundle on Thursday next. *Signed.* [N. II., 67.]

iv. EDWARD LORD MOUNTAGUE, CHARLES COKAYNE, JOHN SYERS and RICHARD KINNESMAN to the HIGH CONSTABLES OF COLINGBURY HUNDRED.

1642, August 11.—Forbidding them to execute any warrants summoning the Train Bands, unless they came from the Earl of Northampton and his colleagues. *Signed.* [N. II., 68.]

v. The SAME to the HIGH CONSTABLES OF HIGHAM HUNDRED.

Same date.—(A duplicate of the last.) [N. II., 69.]

Examinations of MICHAEL PHILLIPS and SIR WILLIAM DENNY.

1642, September 6. Norwich.—Concerning a certain writing. (See *Commons' Journals,* ii. 789.) On the back of the first is a summary of both made apparently for the Committee for Informations. [N. XIII., 100.]

JOHN FIELDER, SIR WILLIAM LEWIS, and RICHARD NORTON to JOHN PYM.

1642, September 7. Stubbington —Our troops were so successful as to take Southsea Castle on Saturday night last without any loss of blood on either side. This became such a disadvantage to Portsmouth in seconding a battery we had at Gosport that our ordinance from both places played so on the town, as to occasion a mutiny there, and brought Col. Goring on Sunday to write to Sir William Waller for a parley, which began on Monday last and ended to-day in the Articles enclosed, for which we have great cause to praise God, considering the great terrors the design there menaced not only [to] these parts, but the rest of the kingdom. We think that of the forces sent to our assistance we shall need to keep no foot and only one troop of horse. We desire that the money ordered for this service be hastened down, that we may be able to pay the soldiers and prevent their committing any outrages, and also that the orders for removing the Countess of Portland and certain Delinquents from the Isle of Wight be hastened. *Signed. Seal.* Addressed to Mr. Pym "at his lodging at Mr. Manley's house in Westminster near the King's Fishyard." [N. II., 71.]

Doctor PINKE, Pro-Vice-Chancellor of the University of Oxford, to the EARL OF PEMBROKE AND MONTGOMERY.

1642, September 7.—

And

The EARL OF PEMBROKE AND MONTGOMERY to Doctor PINKE.

1642, September 12.—(Both printed in Rushworth, iii. 2. 11.) *Copies.* [N. XII., 25.]

JOHN DORNEY to WILLIAM LENTHALL.

1642, September 9. Gloucester.—The Ordinance for the Militia for this City and County was put in execution on Monday last, and the Gentry Citizens and Trained Bands cheerfully submitted thereunto with the increase of a band of Volunteers and a troop of horse, which are to be weekly exercised, but the adjacent counties are much disaffected. I therefore desire you to further the safe conveyance of those pieces of ordinance concerning which some four Deputy Lieutenants lately wrote, and, if the House thinks fit, the horse in the inclosed shall be paid.

Postscript.—Being in great want of horsemen's arms we have written to Mr. Holford of the City of London for 20 cases of Petronels, which we conceive can hardly be obtained without an order of the House, which we therefore solicit. *Seal.* [N. II., 72.]

The PARLIAMENT to VISCOUNT SAY AND SELE, OLIVER ST. JOHN, and others.

[1642, September 12.]—Instructions for settling and preserving the peace in the City, County and University of Oxford. (See *Commons' Journals*, ii. 763.) Two *Drafts* or *Copies*. [N. XIII., 129, and XV., 177.]

NOTES mostly in Shorthand.

1642, September 12.—Of that day's proceedings in the House of Commons. [N. XIII., 93.]

SIR EDWARD NICHOLAS to SIR WILLIAM BOSWELL.

1642, September 15. Derby.—Describing the king's march from Nottingham and an encounter between the forces of the Marquess of Hertford and the Earl of Bedford. (Printed in *King's Pamphlets*, E. 118, No. 26, where the date of the king's leaving Nottingham should be *Tuesday* not *Thursday*, and *Stowell* should be *Stawell*. [N. II., 73.]

SIR CHRISTOPHER WRAY to WILLIAM LENTHALL.

[1642], September 17. Bury.—Concerning Mr. Chaplaine and an Alderman of Bury then in custody, explaining their motives for opposing Lieut. Boulston's raising men (See *Commons' Journals*, ii. 774), and stating that the town had already subscribed over 1,000*l.* in plate and money. *Seal.* [N. II., 74.]

SIR EDWARD HALES, and nine others, to WILLIAM LENTHALL.

1642, September 17. Rochester.—We met here on the 15th, and have put the Militia in good forwardness by making and giving commissions and appointing days of muster. We have provided watches and wards and for the repairing of beacons, and sent out summonses concerning subscriptions. *Signed.* [N. II., 75.]

SIMON SNOW to WILLIAM LENTHALL.

1642, September 17. Exeter.—Excusing himself for disobeying an order to attend the House on Tuesday next, as next week he must be at the tin coinage, and at Michaelmas has to receive the Earl of Bedford's rents in Devon and Cornwall amounting to about 8,000*l.* [N. II., 76.]

EDWARD [LORD] HERBERT to WILLIAM LENTHALL.

1642, September 18. Ragland.—I desire to wait on the House of Commons, " my coming to London being also most necessary for the accomplishing of that great and beneficial waterwork in attaining the perfection whereof hath cost me many thousands, not so much out of covetousness thereby to gain unto myself as to serve my country . . ." I would not stay, but that I fear affronts of stopping searching and abuses by the way, and ask for an order of the House to protect me.

Postscript.—My coachman comes from Gloucester with a copy of an Order of Parliament. (See *Commons' Journals*, ii. 763, 766.) The information given of my horses hath been false, they are none other than coach geldings. *Signed. Seal.* [N. II., 77.]

Lieutenant ROANE to the EARL OF ESSEX.

1642, September 18.— Petition stating that for executing his Majesty's Commission he had been apprehended stript and left destitute by the magistrates of Walshall in Staffordshire and desiring some competent allowance for his relief. At foot is an order for his removal from Northampton Gaol to London there to remain in safe custody. *Signed,* " Essex." [N. XXII., 68.]

Examination of JOHN ROANE, Yeoman Pricker to the King.

1642, September 19. Northampton.—That he was employed by Lieutenant-Colonel D'Ewes in a regiment assigned by Lord Paget to Colonel Bolls with a commission under the King's own hand to raise volunteers, which he shewed to the Mayor of Walsall who refused to let him beat up his drum and apprehended him. [N. XIII., 101.]

THOMAS WHITE to his son FRANCIS WHITE, a prisoner in Ilchester Gaol.

1642, September 21. Limerick.—It is vain to expect that Mr. Mansell and his company being 13 in number will be exchanged for you, inasmuch as Sir Geoffrey Gallway took him and his company prisoners for committing robberies in the river of Limerick and betraying Edward Gould and his ship to Captain Cole, who by Mansell's persuasion brought them prisoners to Cork. I cannot prevail to get Mr. Mansell disguarded, till he or his friends procure that you and the rest of our friends there committed with their goods be sent to Cork. Am sorry your imprisonment and that of others in England is like to prove a dear purchase, for others here are like to pay dearly for you. (See *Commons' Journals,* ii. 714, and letters of the Earl of Cork and John Ashe, dated September 30 and December 30.) [N. II., 78.]

JOHN NANSON to SERJEANT WILDE and HUMPHREY SALWAY, Members for Worcestershire.

1642, September 26.—Excusing himself for having intermeddled in the Commission of Array. (See *Commons' Journals,* ii. 791.) [N. II., 79.]

JOHN WASTELL to SIR HENRY ANDERSON.

1642, September 30.—Sir John Savile of Lupsett is taken prisoner to Pountfract Castle which is replenished with soldiers. Two of his servants were slain before he was taken. Upon Tuesday last Sir Richard Hutton put 800 men into Knaresborough Castle, as my uncle Arthur Beckwith told me yesterday. He came that way on Wednesday from Leicestershire . . . *Seal.* [N. II., 80.]

The EARL OF CORK to LATIMER SAMPSON, of Freshford in Somerset.

1642, September 30. Youghal.—Concerning the means for procuring the release of Mr. Mounsell. Had sent an Irish footman to Limerick with Francis Whyte's letters, who is returned with the answers. Those from the merchants of Limerick show what high and insolent demands they made for exchange. I suggest therefore that the order should be procured from the Parliament to apprehend Thomas Power, Francis Rice, Oliver Bourke, Edmond Bourke, and Thomas Stritch, merchants of Limerick, and one Carney, merchant of Kilmallock, now skulking in or near London, and am confident Mr. Mounsell will thus get freed on better terms than had been proposed. I have a commander of theirs, Captain Prendergast, in prison, but they refused to exchange Mr. Mounsell for him. *Signed. Seal.* [N. II, 81.]

SIR EDWARD RODES and Captain JOHN HOTHAM to WILLIAM LENTHALL.

1642, October 1.—Enclosing a most disadvantageous agreement both to the service of the kingdom and the safety of the County, and asking for instructions for raising horse money and plate, for money to be sent down and for two regiments and four troops to march to us with all speed, we being now but betwixt 800 and 900 foot and one troop of the Hull forces at Selby, having left 300 foot and the other troop at Doncaster. (See *Commons' Journals*, ii. 792.) *Signed. Seal.* [N. II., 82.]

WILLIAM CONSTANTINE to WILLIAM LENTHALL.

1642, October 5. Wimborne.—" This country was in itself divided, for a main party of the chief gentry laboured with all their industry to bring war into their own houses and to supply the Marquess of Hertford with men, victuals, and ammunition. But God . . . frustrated their endeavours and we see their party vanished. Our forces had no sooner left pursuing the Marquess, but they were—with great prudence—lodged in such towns here as had shown themselves violently ill-affected, where at leisure they gleaned up such of the great Malignants as were left behind; some were seized by force, others yielded voluntarily and now we see here a unanimous consent and joy to be pliable to the Parliament . . . . The horse troops behave themselves with great moderation, but the foot are something violent upon the Papists, several of whose houses they have endeavoured to plunder, but the commanders use all diligence to prevent them as too uncivil and not agreeable to the sense of Parliament. This day they all march towards London." *Seal.* [N. II., 83.]

The MAYOR and JURATS OF DOVER to WILLIAM LENTHALL.

1642, October 5.—Forwarding the examination of Richard Pay. [N. II., 84.] *Enclosed:*
The said Examination.
Same date.—That Matthew Hamon, sawyer, said of the King, " He is as no King; if he were a King, he would not murder his subjects." *Copy.* [N. XIII., 41.]

The EARL OF ESSEX, the EARL OF PETERBOROUGH, OLIVER ST. JOHN, PHILIP [LORD] WHARTON, EDWARD [LORD] MANDEVILLE, THOMAS [LORD] GREY, NATHANIEL FIENNES, SIR PHILIP STAPILTON, LORD ROBERTES, SIR ARTHUR HESILFIGE, ARTHUR GOODWIN and FER[DINANDO] [LORD] HASTINGS to the COMMITTEE FOR PUBLIC SAFETY.

[1642, October 12 (?). Worcester.]—Concerning the raising of subscriptions, the sequestering of the Michaelmas rents of Bishops, Deans, and Chapters, and also those of notorious Delinquents, and the stopping of the King's revenue from rents, fines, &c. (See *Commons' Journals*, ii. 808.) *Signed. Seal.* [N. VIII., 133 *b.*]

The Earl of Warwick to William Lenthall.

1642, October 14. On board the *James* in the Downs.—Concerning the garrisons and pay of the Castles of Sandown, Deal and Walmer, whereof he had been appointed Captain General. *Signed. Seal.* [N. II., 85.]

Philip Francis, Mayor of Plymouth, and others to ——.

[1642, October 14 (?).]—Giving the names of those who refused lend plate or money for the service of the Commonwealth. (See *Commons' Journals*, ii. 811.) [N. XIII., 139 *b.*]

Robert Reynolds and Robert Godwin to William Lenthall.

1642, October 17. Bristol.—" The 2,000 men long since designed for Munster for the raising whereof 2,000*l.* hath been paid to the Lord of Kerry above five weeks since are in no readiness as yet, neither do we hear of my Lord here, but it is reported . . that he intends to stay till he hath a Commission from the King. The officers of Colonel Bamfield's regiment lie at Bath, visit this town, take their pay and do nothing for it. Captain Constable hath been here with his ships ten weeks at 400*l.* a month, there is 1,000*l.* charge upon the State for lying still in safe harbour. He and Mr. Dobbins have made a protestation before a notary by which it will appear where the fault lies . . . The wisdom of the House will find a way . . that the Commonwealth may not pay for ships when they do no service. Last night came Captain Bellfore to this town, his men unruly and his horses out of case, but he himself very well affected to the service of the Parliament.

We both hasted them and saw them out of town this morning to go towards the Lord General with all possible speed. We find both the Mayor and many others very well affected to the Parliament, if we may judge by verbal expressions, but no horse, plate or money subscribed. We assembled the Mayor and Aldermen to day and put them in mind of their duties to assist in the saving of the Commonwealth at this time. After they had heard us with a great deal of regard and attention, they desired time to consider their answer.

We mean to treat with them touching the payments of their customs which they do forbear to pay to the ill example of other towns." *Signed. Seal.* [N. II., 86.]

Sir Nevill Poole to William Lenthall.

1642, October 18. Okesey Park.—Requesting a protection for Lady Elizabeth Stawell. *Seal.* [N. II., 88.] *Enclosed:*

Lady Elizabeth Stawell to Sir Nevill Poole.

Same date.—Requesting him to make known to the Parliament that she has sustained a great loss at one of her houses in Somersetshire where a company of troopers under pretence of searching for arms, have rifled her goods to the value of 400*l.* and upwards, and she still fears that the like may be done at her other house —which also hath been lately disarmed by Mr. Pine and Captain Pym—the same troopers and others ill affected being still in these parts, and intreating him to procure her a protection. (See *Commons' Journals*, ii. 822.) [N. II., 87.]

The last clause in the EARL OF WARWICK'S Commission. •

[1642, October 22.]—(Printed in *Lords' Journals*, v. 417.) *Draft.* A paper follows containing apparently jottings of phrases in the said Commission. [N. XIII., 132.]

Captain HENRY BELL to [WILLIAM LENTHALL].

[1642, October 28.]—Desiring a warrant to search at Lambeth for Leathern Ordnance, and also to search Lord Herbert's house. (See *Commons' Journals*, ii. 827.) [N. II., 183.]

The DEPUTY LIEUTENANTS OF KENT to WILLIAM LENTHALL.

1642, October 28. Rochester.—Complaining that the business was wholly deserted by the major part and of the scorns and affronts put upon them that appear in the execution of the Militia and subscription. *Signed* by ten persons. *Seal.* (Part torn and lost.) [N. II., 89.]

SIR RICHARD ONSLOW and ROBERT PARKHURST to WILLIAM LENTHALL.

1642, October 29.—Concerning Henry Asquith who read the King's declaration at Horsely Down, and dissuaded people from enlisting. (See *Commons' Journals*, ii. 826, where the name is spelt "Aiscough.") *Seal.* [N. II., 90.]

SIR JOHN HOTHAM to WILLIAM LENTHALL.

[1642, end of October. Hull.]—I wrote to you it was best for your service to send for Mr. Pelham to the House which you accordingly did. Had he obeyed I should not have needed to have gone any further. . . . I had then heard of mutinous words he had given out against the Grey Coats—which were those southern forces you had sent down—as that the town must keep a guard against them. . . . The gentlemen that command them are men of sober condition and do their utmost to restrain their men from doing wrong. Some few faults were committed in the county, which as far as our power gives—not having martial law— we have endeavoured to remedy. Six I have delivered to be tried and suffer according to law. But for any hurt done in the town or towards the townsmen I believe in any garrison never was less cause of complaint. On the receipt of your order I sent it to him, and expected a long time obedience to it, and if he had not proceeded in a great measure to have disturbed the peace of the town, I had left him to himself to have made his own answer. But you will perceive by the testimony enclosed . . . to what height his anger had drawn him to accuse me in plain open English that I meant to plunder the town, with other words at his pleasure. . . . I hope you all believe that accusation deserves no answer. If I had such an intent surely I chose a most unfit time, having at the same time 600 of my foot forces at Cawood Castle, my son with his troop of horse, my major I had sent in one of the ships riding here to Scarborough with 120 men more to surprise a hoy from Holland with 2,000 arms—which were gone just half a day before we could get thither—and I had yielded to Sir John Gell of Derbyshire to lend him 120 more of my men to give a beginning to settle the Militia in Derbyshire, which county rightly settled—as they have assured me with those men they quickly can—gives great security to Yorkshire, Derbyshire being the best pass into Yorkshire should any forces be sent from the King's army, and at that time Mr. Aldred's troop was wholly in town you will think not much amicable to me. Explaining the case of Mrs. Watkinson whom he was accused of turn-

ing out of her house, and inclosing a note generally signed by the town
The cause of Mr. Pelham's anger was my refusal to admit into the town
his brother-in-law Mr. Toppin, who had been concerned in the plot for
betraying the North block-house and setting the town on fire   By the
advice of Sir Hugh Chomley and Mr. Wharton I sequestered Mr. Pelham
and sent him by one of the King's ships now riding here to you to be
proceeded with as you should think fit.   Whilst I sent my men abroad
I had need have all occasions nipt in the head that shall mutiny the
town against me at home.   *Postscript*.—" I shall only propose to you my
Lord of Essex now being at Worcester with his forces, if one of the Aldermen of Worcester had said to the townsmen, my Lord of Essex intends
to plunder you, 'tis fit we stand upon our guard, if he had presently
called a Martial Court and hanged that Alderman could you justly have
blamed him?   One word of mirth.   Upon Sunday night last, as the
neighbours of Sherborne tell our men, they drew certain forces out of
York to have set upon my son's men at Cawood.   When they came in
Sherborne, a village three miles from Cawood, they espied a wind-mill,
which they took for my son's colours marching to meet them, and
certain stooks of beans which they took for his men in order.   Whereupon they returned in more haste than they came.   I enclose information of the proceedings of my Lord of Newcastle and their associates,
that you may see the necessity there is of somewhat to be done.   We
have long heard of two regiments, Constable and Fairfax, to come to our
aid, but none yet appears.   If they had come in any time I am confident
your business had been done before this." (See *Commons' Journals*,
ii. 863.)   *Remains of Seal.*   [N. II., 153.]

DENNIS WISE, Mayor, and THOMAS PURY to WILLIAM LENTHALL.

1642, November 1.   Gloucester.—80 watermen and 70 firelocks
came hither on October 21st.   They complain greatly at not receiving
their advance money and pay.   We have lent them some money for their
present necessities but fear they will mutiny, unless some course be
speedily taken for their payment.   This morning two regiments from
Worcester are come to be billeted here, and last night we received
Captain Charles Price and six others sent here by the Earl of Stamford.
Many dangers are threatened us on the West part by the Welsh and
on the East by the Cavaliers.   *Signed.   Seal.*   [N. II., 91.]

JOHN PEERS to his fellow servant GEORGE BAYNES.

1642, November 2.   Westminster.—We came into Thames Mouth
Sunday after we set sail from Hull.   My master (Mr. Pelham) was
very well received in Parliament.   The Houses think Sir John
(Hotham) is mad.   They hear of all his carriages.   I think ere long
he will be sent for . . .   There is a great many soldiers in the City
and trenches made about it.   They took 2,900 muskets at Lambeth
House on Saturday last and abundance of arms and money from those
who they suppose to be naught. (See *Commons' Journals*, ii. 863)
[N. II., 91 *b*.]

The NORTHAMPTONSHIRE COMMITTEE to WILLIAM LENTHALL.

1642, November 4.   Northampton.—Sending up 13 prisoners.   (See
Commons' Journals, ii. 840.)   *Signed* Jo. Crewe, Gil. Pykeringe,
Richard Samwell, Ed. Harby.   *Seal.*   [N. II., 92.]

The PARLIAMENT OF ENGLAND to the Kingdom of SCOTLAND.

1642, November 7.—Declaration.   (Printed in *Lords' Journals*, v.
430.)   Two *copies*.   [N. XIX., 58, 59.]

The COMMISSIONER-GENERAL to the HIGH CONSTABLES of the
Hundreds in which the parishes therein named in Buckinghamshire are situated.

1642, November 9.—Ordering them to bring forthwith to Prince
Rupert's head quarters 4,000 twopenny loaves, 4,000 weight of cheese,
50 firkins of butter and 40 quarters of oats and 10 quarters of old
beans. *Copy.* [N. XIII., 103.]

The KING to the MAYOR OF EXETER.

[1642], The 18th year of our reign, November 9. Maidenhead —.
Warrant charging him in obedience to the Proclamation of the same
date to apprehend all persons raising levies there without the King's
consent. *Copy.* [N. XII., 78.]

ORDINANCE.

1642, November 9.—For punishing soldiers. (Printed in *Commons'*
Journals, ii. 841.) *Copy.* [N. XIII., 104.]

LORD WENMAN, WILLIAM PIERREPONT and SIR JOHN HIPPESLEY to WILLIAM LENTHALL.

1642, November 10. Uxbridge.—(Identical *mutatis mutandis* with
the letter of the same date, which is printed in *Lords' Journals*, v. 440,
to the Speaker of the House of Peers.) *Signed. Seal. Enclosed:*

The KING's Answer.

(Printed *ubi suprà*.) *Copy.* [N. IX., 2.]

SIR CHRISTOPHER WRAY, Captain JOHN HOTHAM and THOMAS HATCHER to [the COMMITTEE OF SAFETY OF THE KINGDOM].

1642, November 12. Northallerton.—"On Wednesday . . the
9th we with our three troops and three companies of foot marched from
Tadcaster . . to hinder the relief that York could expect, both of
men and victuals, because we were certainly informed that divers Yorkshire gentlemen were gone to my Lord Newcastle to solicit him to
march with what power he could raise to York, and after he had cleared
the country, as they made themselves believe he would do, then to march
into Lincolnshire, and so to the King. The desire of preventing this
growing danger, so many troops being certainly raised and under con-
vict Recusants, made us resolve to try if a sudden venture upon them
might either dissipate or dissolve this their so hopeful a project, and
therefore leaving all our foot at Topcliffe 18 miles from Darnton where
their horse lay, we with our three troops and 20 dragoons marched night
and day directly towards them and upon Friday morning by daylight
came to Darnton, where Captain Pudsey's troop was drawn up at this
end of the town with intention to relieve my Lord Dunbar from our
troops, but meeting us at the town's end and thinking we had been
Captain Sare, another of his fellows, he came up directly to us, until he
found his error by our shooting bullets, which made him run too fast
for an honourable retreat. We followed with what speed we could, but
they were a great deal better horsemen, yet we got 10 prisoners with
their horses and pistols, and but for a large furze bush that hid him had
got the Captain too. Four or five troops that lay thereabouts ran all
presently into Durham, thinking the plain country too hot for them,
upon which we marched to Yarm, there to meet the gentlemen of the

North Riding, in order to give them encouragement which, we hope, hath done a great deal of good in those parts, as they informed us, and that by the countenance of our forces they should be able to raise a considerable strength. From thence we came to Northallerton to countenance the well affected gentlemen of Richmondshire, and they tell us that our dispersing the Papists and being near to cherish the good and awe the bad will bring in all that side of the country, so that we intend to hover up and down in these parts a while, and if it be possible to hinder this pestilent growing mischief, which if it increase, then we shall join all our forces together, and I hope make them run with a rattle, for I believe we shall be able to draw together 4,000 horse and foot. We send you here enclosed some intercepted letters which lay open their intentions, and certainly it would benefit the public much, if you would please they might be printed. At our first coming to North-allerton we met with a Danish Ambassador, that landed at Newcastle some three days before, and was going to the King. We durst not venture to stay him, although we thought it was not fairly done of him to bring 6,000 arms for the King, and Colonel Cockran, the Scottishman, that had been soliciting there to bring over strangers, as appeared by his papers. The Colonel we have put in safe custody, and desire to know what we shall do with him. We are certainly informed that the highland men in Northumberland, that are tenants to my Lord Northumberland and my Lord Gray, begin to get together and refuse to obey any commands from my Lord Newcastle, and divers well affected gentlemen of that county join with them, to prevent which Sir William Widdrington is marched from Newcastle with some drakes to bring them to obedience, but we hope the strength of the country and their good cause will protect them. Some report these honest men have possessed themselves of Alnwick Castle and that my Lord of Newcastle is drawing some battering pieces thither." *Original* and *Copy*, the first *signed*. [N. II., 95.] *Enclosed:*

i. Sir Marmaduke Langdale to Sir William Savile.

1642, November 9. Newcastle.—"We find my Lord of Newcastle very unwilling to adventure his honour and reputation in York-shire, until he be very well provided of soldiers and officers, whereof he is not yet sufficiently . . . Of that force which is requisite for the work he intends he hath not as yet 3,000 horse and foot, few or no horses for carriage, yet he is getting horses and men every day, and this day hath positively set down to begin his march upon Tuesday next. He hopes to raise as many men in Yorkshire, as may increase his army to 10,000, with which he hath some thought of marching southwards, when he hath settled Yorkshire. He promises to guide us into Lincolnshire to requite the kind visit of our neighbours Sir Christopher Wray and Mr. Hatcher, by whose only means our miseries were brought to this height. My Lord expects commanders every day from Holland, but if they come not he will keep his word for Tuesday next to begin his march, which he had begun sooner, if the commanders had come. He hath plenty of arms and ammunition for more than he can tell what to do withal, insomuch as he must be forced to have a greater guard than he intended for the safety thereof, yet I know he will not spare you either arms or ammu-nition. Sir William Widdrington is raising men about Alnwick, where he finds much resistance by the Earl of Northumberland's and the Lord Gray's tenants. He took with him some horse and dragoons and this day two field pieces are gone to him. My

Lord of Newcastle took this day an opportunity to see his children at Bottell Castle. It may be it was to be further in the county and to be near the danger to prevent the rising of the county, which, as is reported, some of the Highlanders in Tynedale and Risdale (Redesdale) begin to get into small bodies and deny to be raised by any power from my Lord of Newcastle. There is some bodies raised in Scotland, but it is for France as is alleged, but certainly they are in these Northern counties much infected with the hot zeal of Puritanism, and many of them that were raised, upon second thoughts will not come to Newcastle. The like stories Sir Timothy Fetherston tells us out of Westmoreland and Cumberland, alleging that the King hath got the worse of the day and they will not go to be killed. The Parliament is far too nimble for the King in printing; the common people believe the first story which takes impression in their minds, and it cannot be beaten out. I believe my Lord of Newcastle hopes us to raise men in Yorkshire. I must confess it will' be an infinite vast charge and trouble to our county, yet seeing our estates must be wasted, I had rather it were wasted by them that will ruin our enemies than to feed our enemies with our estates and save their own. We talk here much of the Queen's coming over and there is almost every day some coming from her and some from the King to her, and she sends many arms, ammunition, and some money, but I fear her coming is uncertain. There was an ambassador from the King of Denmark come upon Monday last which brought much arms and ammunition and, as is thought, 25,000*l.* in money, but he will not confess with money. He is this day gone post towards the King. It is reported he hath brought propositions to the King and Parliament whereunto if the Parliament will not condescend he will send great forces in the spring to aid his Majesty, so we are like to feel the miserable effects of our own disagreement the next summer, which is like to make this kingdom the seat of war for all the nations of Christendom, that as we were in part the first beginners of the wars in Germany, so, I fear, they will all come to make an end of it in this kingdom. We in Yorkshire should have some happiness if we could make an end of the troubles and distractions of our county and so divert the war southward, that whatsoever foreign nations come they may be employed in the South where the wellspring of our miseries began, and where there is pillage enough to satisfy many armies." Two *copies.* [N. II., 93, 94.]

ii. Sir Edward Osborne, Sir Marmaduke Langdale, Francis Tyndall and Richard Aldburgh to the Earl of Cumberland.

Same date and place.—Concerning the Earl of Newcastle's intended march. When he is to enter the County some provision of bread and other necessaries must be made at the confines. We believe this may be safely done, his Lordship having ordered divers troops of his forthwith to quarter on the frontiers, which will sufficiently secure them. Because there will be many urgent occasions for money, which here we cannot get by any means, we entreat that 200*l.* at least be sent hither with all possible speed, without which we must be bold to tell your Lordship that the service will very much suffer and we so discouraged that we shall desire to quit this employment. To-day his Lordship commanded us to send the enclosed declaration to York with his desire to your Lordship that it may be printed with all speed and 500 books be presently sent him and as many more dispersed in Yorkshire as your Lordship shall think fit. We are further moved by his Lordship that all the saddlers in York may be presently and only employed in making saddles for troopers, as light and short as can be, for which his Lordship will give them ready money. *Copy.* (See *Commons' Journals*, ii. 853.) [N. II., 94.]

JOHN BARTHOLOMEW, Mayor, to WILLIAM LENTHALL.

1642, November 12. Chichester.—Enclosing a Proclamation and Petition. (See *Commons' Journals*, ii. 850.) *Signed. Seal.* [N. II., 96.]

Several PERSONS almost all marksmen.

1642, November 12.—Certificate that some of them had seen Sir John Digby at Stokedry daily since the 16th of August last. [N. XIII., 105.]

The PARLIAMENT.

1642, November 15.—Order appointing Commissaries for valuing horses. (Printed in *Commons' Journals*, ii. 7.) *Copy.* [N. XIII., 106.]

The PARLIAMENT.

Same date.—Order. The same as part of the last, viz., from " in all places within the City " to " not being delinquents." It is signed " Jo. Browne Cleric : Parliament : " but does not appear in the Journals. [N. XIII., 107.]

The PARLIAMENT.

1642, November 17.—Order for associating the Northern Counties (Printed in *Commons' Journals*, ii. 854.) *Draft or copy.* [N. XIII., 108.]

The DEPUTY LIEUTENANTS OF GLOUCESTERSHIRE to [WILLIAM LENTHALL].

1642, November 18. Cirencester.—Complaining that Sir Richard Ducie, Sir Henry Frederick Thynn, Sir Robert Points, Thomas Veale, and Humphrey Hooke by their disobeying their commands and warrants much hinder the execution of the ordinance touching the Militia. *Signed* Ro. Cooke, Na. Stephens, Edw. Stephens, John Georges, John Stephens. (See *Commons' Journals*, ii. 867.) [N. II., 97.]

DENNIS WISE, Mayor, and seven others to WILLIAM LENTHALL.

1642, November 21. Gloucester —We acknowledge your care in the dispatch of our messenger for providing ordinance and ammunition which arrived in good condition. We have the greater part of two regiments quartered here under Colonel Essex, and earnestly desire your assistance to furnish money for their pay. The receiver of money and plate has received plate to the value of about 15,000*l.* We therefore entreat that order may be taken for its speedy and safe conveyance to London. *Signed. Seal.* [N. II., 99.]

EDWARD HIGGONS, WILLIAM CAWLEY, and HENRY CHITTEY to WILLIAM LENTHALL.

[1642, November 21. Portsmouth.]—" On Tuesday last, being the 15th of this month we called all the inhabitants of the City of Chichester together there, to let them understand wherefore we had fortified the city, which was to defend ourselves from being plundered by the King's army, and to know if they would all join with us to secure one another from being destroyed by them. There was a general assent in it not one contradicting but with several vows and protestations resolved to live and die in it. Upon which agreement we went out of the Town Hall where the meeting was. When we came into the street we perceived some swords drawn at the Northgate of the city—where one of the guns we had from Portsmouth was placed—which swords were drawn against the gunner. We endeavoured to pacify the rage of the people, but we could not, but they then overthrew the gun off from his carriage and possessed themselves of him, and from thence they went to the other parts of the city where the other guns were placed and possessed themselves of them also. When this was done the chiefest gentlemen in and about the city gave countenance to those that did this. After this the same night came Sir John Morley, Mr. Robert Anderson, Mr. William Wray, and Mr. Francis Shallett to the Mayor and demanded of him that Sir John Morley and twenty other gentlemen of the town might watch that night. The Mayor was unwilling to consent unto it but they pretending it was for the settling of the town in quiet and to allay the fury of the common people, upon this it was agreed that there should watch twenty of the gentlemen and twenty of the citizens and that Sir John Morley should have the command of the gentlemen and Mr. Higgons of the citizens, and that the keys of the city should be delivered to the Mayor. But when it came to the setting of the watch, there were at the least 30 of the gentlemen and near 50 of the meaner sort of people gathered together, and Mr. Higgons demanding of Sir John Morley that there might be but 20 gentlemen watch and that the other should depart to their several houses Sir John answered that it was not safe for him to speak and wished him to be quiet and denied that any should be discharged. He then gained the city keys into his hands and would not deliver them, but said they should be kept for the King. Upon the first combustion in the town there was a messenger dispatched to the High Sheriff to acquaint him how the state of the city stood, and to desire him to come thither and he should have free entrance. Upon this the Sheriff made warrants to the several Trained Bands that they should appear within half a mile of the City and aid him to go into it the next morning at 9 o'clock, at which time the Sheriff accompanied with a hundred horse met the Trained Bands and so marched into the city, where when he came he commanded the Mayor to proclaim the proclamation of pardon to all the County except Herbert Morley Esq. and Henry Chittey Citizen. The Mayor refusing they forced him to go to the Cross, and then the Sheriff commanded the Proclamation to be proclaimed. After that was done he made search in divers well affected persons' houses for arms and all they found they seized and took away and put the Commission of Array in execution and displaced Captain Chittey and in his place put Sir John Morley. Then Nicholas Wolfe took the charge of Captain Oglander's band and so settled the Commission of Array. To countenance and attend the Sheriff in this action there was Sir William Forde, Sir William Morley, who hath sent the Sheriff four horses completely furnished for war, Sir John Morley, Sir Edward Bishopp,

Thomas Leedes, one of your House, who is made Captain of the horse for Arundel Rape — Sir Thomas Bowyer hath sent a horse—Robert Anderson a lawyer, Nicholas Wolfe a Justice of the Peace, Francis Shallett, William May, Thomas Gunter, who was a troop in Portsmouth with Colonel Goring, John Apsley, William Rishton, two of Mr. Robert Heath's sons, Francis Pury, George Gunter, Philip King the Bishop's brother, and John King the Bishop's son, and Edward Osborne with divers others. They have seized the magazine which was for the country as likewise ten barrels of powder we had from Portsmouth by order from the Parliament. Upon Wednesday we came to Portsmouth and addressed ourselves to the Governor and the Committee making them acquainted in what condition we were in and how the guns and powder which we had from the Governor were wrested from us. The Governor being very sensible of the affront to the Parliament and to himself and apprehending that if there were some expedition used in the business it would be very feasible to regain the guns and powder, so that it were done before the Sheriff could call in the country, and to that purpose he despatched Captain Swanley and Captain Winnford with seamen and landsmen upon the Thursday to effect that service but it pleased God so to turn the wind that they could not gain the harbour that night. The next day they gained the harbour, but before they could come near the place they intended to land the tide fell, so that they could get no further that night than an island called Thorney. When Captain Swanley found how contrary the wind had been to him he dispatched away his lieutenant with a trumpeter to demand the guns and powder of the Mayor or any others that had the charge of them at Chichester. When the Lieutenant came there demanding where the Mayor was it was answered he was not to be spoken with and they told him he must go to the Governor of the City, by which name the Sheriff was stiled. He delivered his message ; the answer was that he had a command from the king to detain the guns and powder to his use, and until he had a command from the king to deliver them he would keep them. With this answer the lieutenant returned to Captain Swanley, informing him likewise how the city was up in arms, and that he conceived there were eight hundred or a thousand soldiers in the city. Upon this Captain Swanley and Captain Winnford took into consideration whether it were fit for them being not above two hundred strong to venture upon the city or no. In the close they resolved the Governor of Portsmouth should be made acquainted with the proceedings, as likewise to inform him what they heard the strength of the city was, which was that they had near 100 horse and 1,000 foot. The Governor being informed of these passages and knowing of what consequence Portsmouth is to the kingdom and what a weakening it would be to the town if he should lose either landsmen or seamen therefore gave directions that the Captains and their men should return back to Portsmouth. The Sheriff, having intelligence that there was some forces coming against himself from Portsmouth, made his warrants to all the country near the city and commanded all men instantly to repair to Chichester upon pain of death or of being plundered, pretending Prince Robert was coming and that if he were not resisted they were all undone. Upon this trick he gained the country to come into the city, where when he had them he locked the gates and set a strong guard at them so that they could not retire to their own houses, but were forced to abide in the city. The countrymen express they have no hearts to the service, but they are kept in with hopes that there will forces come from the king and it is given out the city shall be made a garrison. We hear there are both foot and horse come from the king into the city, but we 'have no certain information of the truth thereof. Divers houses are threatened to be plundered within and without the city, the Sheriff, being abetted by the gentlemen before named, is extreme violent in the Commission of Array. They have taken and imprisoned some men, and have cast irons upon one and thrust him into the dungeon. They set two pistols to the Mayor's breast and offered him to take an oath, but what the contents of the oath is we know not." We desire you to acquaint the House of all that has befallen us, and that Parliament will take into consideration what this may grow to. *Postscript.*—Captain Chittey and Edward Higgons were forced to fly to Portsmouth without any money and the Sheriff will not suffer any goods to be brought out. They desire that for the present they may have some moneys out of the Contribution Money. (See *Commons' Journals*, ii. 860.) *Signed.* [N. II., 102.]

The KING to the SHERIFF OF OXFORDSHIRE.

1642, November 23. Reading.—Warrant to him to order the collectors in that County under the Act for raising 400,000*l.* to pay to himself all monies they had or should collect under the same Act and to keep them till further order. *Copy.* [N. XIII., 110.]

SIR JOHN HOTHAM to WILLIAM LENTHALL.

1642, November 25. Hull.—Concerning a great ship laden with ammunition driven by stress of weather on the coast of Lincolnshire and then into the Humber and detained by him till he receives orders from Parliament, and suggesting that as the magazine at Hull had at first but 300 barrels of powder, which was now much lessened, both by their own consumption, and by sending to their neighbours by order of Parliament—without which none had been sent except five barrels to Manchester when they were in that extremity with Lord Strange— they should agree with the merchant in London for 200 barrels of the powder to be left at Hull, and also whatever match there was on board, and wishing to know the price of the muskets on board. *Postscript.*— "If you do not take some speedy course to send down money to pay this garrison and that in a good measure, all your affairs in the North is like to break to pieces. 6,000*l.* for 3,000 will be gone before it can arrive there." *Seal.* [N. II., 100.]

The EARL OF MANCHESTER to Mr. ROUSE.

1642, November 27.—Supporting the petition of the bearer against Mr. Downhalle, the minister of St. Ives. (See *Commons' Journals*, ii. 864.) *Holograph.* [N. II., 98.]

The HOUSE OF COMMONS.

1649, November 28.—Order concerning Sheriffs nominated by the King. (Printed in *Commons' Journals*, ii. 867.) *Two Copies.* [N. XIII., 109, 111.]

EDMUND PRIDEAUX to JOHN BRISCOE, Postmaster of Barnet.

1642, November 29. London.—After referring to the order of the House of Lords of November 25 concerning the Post Office (*Lords' Journals*, v. 459)—"I have thought fit to vindicate and assume the liberty of carrying and recarrying letters by way of Post, and have undertaken the managing of the Inland Letter Office, for carrying the weekly letters in such course as hath been formerly used by the Post-masters, and if you think fit to join me you shall receive such salary as is now allowed you." (See *Lords' Journals*, v. 485.) *Seal.* [N. II., 101.]

John Browne to the House of Commons.

[1642, end of November?]—Suggesting a method for raising supplies and forces for prosecuting the war—In the first place that all counties, cities &c. should pay one shilling in the pound on their annual rents—some regard being had to counties that had been plundered—for maintaining the war and securing the counties from being plundered, by quarterly payments by the tenant, or by the owner if no tenant. Next that people may know their money goes for the public good, and will benefit the county where their estate lies all counties shall maintain a number of horse and foot proportionable to their contribution. Kent for instance should raise and maintain 1,000 foot besides officers and three troops of horse containing about 75 to a troop besides officers, such forces to be employed as follows ;—All the foot and two of the troops shall be joined with the other counties' forces to keep the body of an army on foot, and with the consent of the general when the army of the adverse party shall fall upon that county they may retire into the same to preserve it, they knowing the county best, as being chiefly raised out of it, and as for the third troop, they may be kept in the county for these and other several employ-ments—first to disarm all Malignants, for which purpose the Captain of the troop should have a Commission as Justice of the Peace, secondly to make sudden seizures on the estates of those who refuse to pay the contribution and to cut off plunderers and raiders from the adverse army, third the troop being well exercised, would be able to supply officers to all the light horse of the county, fourthly, the troop continually moving about the county would learn the ways and passages so well, that if an army were to come thither the meanest could serve as guide. The regiment and 3 troops will be paid out of the county contribution, which in Kent will amount to above 50,000*l.*, and I am sure that less than 40,000*l.* will pay all the said forces, and the residue will go towards the extraordinary expenses of the war. The value of the rents must be given on oath, and Commissioners appointed who will not for fear or favour undervalue estates. The tenant must be authorised to deduct the contribution from his rent, and tenants should be rated on the value of their stock, and also such as are maltsters, brewers, shopkeepers &c. and all these must have their estates valued, and pay five shillings *per annum* on every 100*l.* and whereas I have heard that this Honourable Assembly have made an order to sequester all the Bishops' Delinquents' and Papists' rents. if this be honestly be done, I am sure that out of them and the contribution money they will not only be able to maintain the war, but to discharge the sums for which the Public Faith is engaged. This business must put in execution betimes. (Perhaps the proposition referred to a Committee on December 1, 1642. See *Commons' Journals*, ii. 870.) [N. II., 184.]

Francis Wren, Richard Lilburne, Thomas Midford and others to the House of Commons.

[1642, November. Durham.]—Petition, stating that, whereas your Petitioners are informed that the Houses have lately associated the seven Northern Counties (See *Commons' Journals*, ii. 854), the enemy grows strong and draws nearer every day, and this County is in that desperate and exceeding danger that the well affected are forced to fly from their houses, there not being any of the country forces now on foot to protect them, nor any visible authority that will grant commissions, and praying that the Parliament's Ordinance might be immediately sent down, and power given to grant commissions, and that in the mean time they may have the protection of the House for raising what force they can, as their lives and liberties are in extreme danger by the Papists and Malignants now gathered together in Westmoreland, whom they daily expect will break in upon them. *Signed.* [N. XXII., 134.]

Many Citizens of LONDON to the HOUSE OF COMMONS.

[1642, December 1.] — Humble Remonstrance and Petition. (Printed in *King's Pamphlets*, E. 130, Nos. 7 and 26.) (See *Commons' Journals*, ii. 870.) [N. XXII., 146.]

WILLIAM TYLER and JOHN BRANDLINGE, Bailiffs, to WILLIAM LENTHALL.

1642, December 1. Ipswich.—Concerning Edward Dawtry, Scholar of King's College Cambridge, who is accused of having spoken very scandalous words against the Parliament, and whom they are sending up to the Parliament. *Seal.* [N. II., 103.] *Enclosed:*

    i. 1642, November 30.—The Informations of William Dyer, Matthias Bradford, and Ralph Hastone against the said Dawtrie. [N. II., 103.]

    ii. A copy of very scandalous verses (about 120) written upon torn papers found in his pocket. They begin :—

        " What always hear ? always be vext ?
        With the harsh railing of a five hours' text,

and end :—

        " May Lentulus and all that cursed crew
        Be broacht for blood by some such slaves they slew."
        [N. II., 103.]

PHILIP FRANCIS, Mayor, and JOHN WADDON to SIR JOHN YOUNG.

1642, December 2. Plymouth.—We have several charges against Mr. Trelawney. 1st that owing to his influence many refused to subscribe to the Parliament ; 2nd that the Proclamation for the Commission of Array being brought to this town he persuaded the Mayor to publish it—though all the rest dissented from him—pressed the custom of the town to publish such things the next market day after the receipt and said that were he Mayor he would do it ; 3rd he refused to lend any money to the Parliament ; 4th the most part of his favourites here are very averse to our proceedings, but we are very confident—were he here—they would publicly declare their concealed intentions. We are at present almost surrounded by the Cavaliers under the command of Sir Ralph Hopton, Ashburnham, Slanning, and others. Their rendez-vous is at Plympton three miles off, they came there last night, and Colonel Ruthen with some 300 horse dared them upon the sands to battle, but they durst not undertake it, so they retreated to the town, where we mean, God willing, to spend the last drop of our blood in this so just a quarrel. If Parliament think that Mr. Trelawney shall have liberty to come amongst us in these times of our distractions we shall submit ourselves to their judgements. We beseech them to send money and munitions for our speedy relief. *Signed. Seal.* [N. II., 105.]

Colonel ARTHUR GOODWIN to WILLIAM LENTHALL.

1642, December 3. Wycombe.—Concerning the stoppage of certain waggons containing clothes linen and plate of the Earl of Carnarvon and others " or rather, as the servants termed them, of my Lady, which was under the more prevalent title, because here the feminine gender is more worthy than the masculine, and indeed so I think for the most part." (See *Commons' Journals*, ii. 875.) The plate is here all sent you. "If you please to turn it into His Majesty's pictures and so return it to the soldiers here I think they will fight with more courage for His Majesty and Parliament." . . Great numbers come here from different counties to help us, the danger only is of their falling off again for want of money.

The want of some of the gentlemen of those counties, out of which the honest country fellows come, is a great discouragement. *Seal*. [N. II,. 106.]

SIMON KNOCKES and JAMES CONNOR to the HOUSE OF COMMONS.

1642, December 5. Dartmouth.—Concerning the voyage of the *Crescent* from Dublin and the refusal of the Master to obey the Captain's orders, for which see the latter's letter dated the 13th. *Sealed with Captain Plunkett's seal and in his hand, the writers being marksmen.* [N. II., 107.]

ALEXANDER STAPLEHILL, Mayor, and ROGER MATTHEW to WILLIAM LENTHALL.

1642, December 5. Dartmouth.—Sir Ralph Hopton with an army of 5,000 men is now drawing towards us, Plymouth being not feasible for his entry. A Commission of Array was sent forth by Sir Edmond Fortescue—titling himself High Sheriff of this County—to all the parishes hereabout to meet tomorrow at a place called Madbury, but 10 mile distant from us. What appearance he will find we know not, yet doubt too many, in regard almost all the gentry in these parts are for the Commission of Array, and begin to threaten the ruin of this poor town which if taken from us will be of that disadvantage to the Cause of Parliament both by land and sea as cannot be conceived, but by those who have duly considered, besides the ruin of our trade and ships which hath brought great benefit to the state, our hearty desires to the service. [We] by ourselves and friends sent above 1,700*l*. contribution. We have again and again solicited our Deputy Lieutenants to send us some speedy help of men and arms being of ourselves not able to arm above 300 men. . . . We beg that a speedy command come forth for our relief both by land and sea. . . Yesterday here arrived from Ireland Captain Plunkett in the [*Crescent*] whom we find very willing to assist us; we humbly beseech that a command may come for his better encouragement together with his company. (See *Commons' Journals*, ii. 884.) *Signed. Seal.* [N. II., 104.]

The PARLIAMENT.

1642, December 7. — Order clearing persons proclaimed traitors by the King. (Printed in *Lords' Journals*, v. 478) *Copy.* A note states that this order is to apply to Sir George Chudleigh, Sir John Northcote, Sir Samuel Rolle, and Sir Nicholas Martin. [N. XIII, 112.]

The HOUSE OF COMMONS to [FERDINANDO] LORD FAIRFAX.

1642, December 8.—Letter directing him to allow all letters from and to the Secretary of State or the Chancellor of Scotland or the

Council there to and from the King and also their letters to and from the Scotch Commissioners in London and also the merchants' packets from Edinburgh to London and back again to pass freely. (See *Commons' Journals*, ii. 902.) *Copy.* [N. XII., 32.]

SIR WILLIAM LEWIS, SIR THOMAS JERVOISE and others, to WILLIAM LENTHALL.

1642, December 11. Portsmouth.—Intreating the house to respite for the present the attendance of the members for Southampton, as they are of much use there. *Signed. Seal.* [N. II., 108.]

DENNIS WISE, Mayor, THOMAS PURY and others to VISCOUNT SAY AND SELE, Lord Lieutenant of Gloucestershire.

1642, December 12. Gloucester.—Certifying that according to his order they had delivered to Colonel Berrow towards the raising of his regiment in the Forest in plate subscribed the greater part of 1,100*l.* and also paid out of the subscription money to Captain Hill above 300*l.*, and for the maintenance of two regiments under Colonel Essex for divers weeks 400*l.* per week, and also spent about 1,000*l.* for fortifications and ammunition for the defence of this place, and desiring him to procure an ordinance for 500*l.* out of the subscription moneys of the City and County for completing the fortifications and other preparations for defence. (See *Commons' Journals*, ii. 895.) *Signed. Seal.* [N. II., 109.]

Captain THOMAS PLUNKETT to the HOUSE OF COMMONS.

1642, December 13. Dartmouth.—I was appointed Captain of the *Crescent* by the Lord Justices and the Committee at Dublin, of whom I had a commission, and withal a straight charge to go to the Bay of Wexford, and there to wait for 8 sail of the rebels' vessels which were to come out richly laden with butter, hides, tallow and wool, and when it would blow that we could not ride there, we were to cross the Channel to keep all aid and relief from them there or other such places as the rebels did inhabit. The next day, afore I left Dublin, the wind being north-west and the only wind to help out the rebels, I desired my officers that we might lay off some 7 leagues to the southward that we might perceive all the sail that came from Wexford, Tramore Bay and Dungarvan. The Master and Gunner told me plainly they would go home, and said that he had the charge of the frigate, and that the King had none left but the *Crescent* and the *Lidia*, and that he would go home to discharge himself, and said in the presence of good people that my commission is not worth a tobacco pipe. Being between Scilly and Landsend we met with an Irish bark came from Crookhaven, laden with 2,000 hides besides some 22 pieces of frieze cloth. I manned the said vessel with 6 men, desired them according [to] the terms of my commission to go for Dublin, to which the master would not condescend, so we were furst (? forced) into this faithful town, and so desires my [ship] to remain till further order from you. (See *Commons' Journals*, ii. 886.) *Seal.* [N. II., 110.]

SIR GEORGE GRESLEY, SIR JOHN GELL, THOMAS GELL and NATHANIEL HALLOWES to WILLIAM LENTHALL.

1642, December 13. Derby.—We have at the present about 700 men under Sir John Gell, but not all armed and not one week's pay aforehand. We have been lately pressed by my Lord Fairfax to send him some forces, and by the Northamptonshire men to do the same by them.

Also our neighbours in Nottinghamshire have desired help from us against the Malignants there. We were and are willing to help them all to our power and are confident we could have done it if Sir John Cooke, one of the knights of the Shire, would have been forward in it, but the truth is we have many Malignants in this County and men of great power with whom he is more conversant than with us, and we considering the present occasion thought it requisite to put in execution the Ordinance of Parliament for the Militia, that so we might have in readiness in our garrison at Derby as many men as we should part withal upon the forementioned occasions, for otherwise in the absence of our men the Malignants would seize Derby and so undo us and the whole country, and then become masters of this and two or three other neighbour counties, which yet by our small forces are kept safe from them. To this purpose we drew warrants—one of which is inclosed—set our hands to them and desired Sir John Cooke to join with us, but he absolutely refused, for what cause we know not but believe it is his dislike of the business, and that this is a means to displease the Commissioners of Array and some other Malignants with whom he is very familiar. Other instances of his lukewarmness are given, and the whole is submitted to the judgement of the House. (See *Commons' Journals*, ii. 892.) *Signed. Seal.* [N. II., 111.]

FRANCIS PIERREPONT to his brother WILLIAM PIERREPONT.

1642, December 13. Nottingham.—Requesting that the persons mentioned, who were arrested by Captain Charles White, one of the captains appointed by the Earl of Essex, may be allowed to give bail. (The names are given in *Commons' Journals*, ii. 914.) *Seal.* [N. II., 112.]

[Articles for the surrender of WINCHESTER CASTLE.]

[1642, December 13.]—That the whole force now in the Castle be forthwith brought forth into a field at the town's end near the Castle, and that they leave their horse and arms behind them in the Castle.

That no violence or incivility be offered to the Commanders and other Gentlemen and that they be preserved as far as in us lies from all plundering and rioting.

That we represent to the Lord General, the Earl of Essex, the reasons that the Lord Grandison and the rest allege why they should be returned again to the king's army, having given up themselves and the Castle on these conditions. *Signed* " Grandison, Richard Willis, Ralph Hebberne." *Copy.* [N. XX., 59.]

SIR EDWARD AYSCOGHE, THOMAS GRANTHAM and WILLIAM ELLIS to WILLIAM LENTHALL.

1642, December 17. Lincoln.—" We have put the Propositions in execution in this county in some places with very good success, but we find not all of the same opinion. We had an Order of both Houses of Parliament to send Sir Anthony Irby and his Dragooners into Yorkshire with all speed and to pay them out of the moneys raised upon the Propositions, and accordingly we sent out our warrants to the Treasurer, but find them crossed by commands from the Earl of Lincoln who hath an order from the Committee for the safety of the kingdom to receive all moneys as well raised upon the Propositions as the 40,000*l.*, so as by that order all the commands you gave us for the security of this county are made frustrate, which, if ever, require our speediest care and resolution for their preservation. My Lord of Newcastle is in his march towards us, and the Malignants in the Counties of Rutland, Leicester and Nottingham are raising both horse and foot, and ours in this county are very insolent, and have carried their horses out of this county to be employed against us, which doth much affright the people, and call on us to raise the forces of the county, but if we be disabled to receive any moneys the county of necessity must suffer, and be in extreme danger by those forces, therefore we earnestly desire to know your resolution herein. We extremely want officers, and therefore we have written to Captain Savile being in the county to stay here, promising him to acquaint you with the reason of his stay, assuring ourselves that in this extreme danger you will not only give him leave to stay with us, but send us more officers arms and ammunition, which you may send to Boston with safety." We earnestly desire you to send down with all speed Lord Willoughby our Lord Lieutenant and his regiment of horse, and that you would command Sir Christopher Wray and Captain Hatcher to come with their troops. It is much desired by us and by the county generally that Sir William Armyn should be sent down with all speed. His presence will do much service in those parts where he liveth and where of all parts it is most needful. (See *Commons' Journals*, ii. 894.) *Signed. Seal.* [N. II., 113.]

Captain John Hotham to the Earl of Newcastle.

1642, December 18. Cawood.—Stating there is a difference in his opinion between prisoners taken in their houses, and taken in arms, and offering to release as many prisoners as the Earl has released without an exchange. *Seal.* [N. II., 114.]

The Same to [the Same.]

1642, December 19. Cawood.—After acknowledging his letter with many compliments " I shall with confidence rely upon your word, and wait upon your Lordship in any place or in any fashion that you in your judgement shall think fit, as to the condition we now stand in, and not to bring suspicion upon it. I should humbly offer it thus, that if you please to appoint some gentlemen of quality to meet and treat for the prisoners, I shall use the matter so as I will be the man on our side and then either your Lordship may privately be there or appoint some other place, for I have some odd people to please here." [N. II., 116.]

Thomas Toll to William Lenthall.

1642, December 19. King's Lynn.—Advising of the despatch of four chests of plate the previous Friday to the Guildhall at London by way of Cambridge, three of them raised at Lynn of the value of 1,102l. 7s. 2d., the other out of the county, value 804l. 8s. 10d. It is 14 days since I was at Norwich ; there had then come in in money and plate :—

	£	s.	d.
In the City of Norwich	5,000	0	0
Out of the County in Plate	3,403	16	1
Mr. Howlet received at Lynn	804	8	10
Mr. John Corey had then received	3,212	6	9
At Yarmouth	2,000	0	0
In Lynn to this day	1,624	9	3
	16,045	0	11

I have stayed two horses of Sir John Burrell, a Lincolnshire knight, who, as I am informed, was very active in the Commission of Array there, and there are also at Lynn 35 good horses taken from Papists in the neighbourhood, about all which I desire instructions. *Seal.* [N. II., 115.]

ANTHONY NICOLL to the EARL OF LINCOLN.

1642, December 20.—(Written in pursuance of the order of the House of Commons in *Commons' Journals*, ii. 894, where the substance is given.) [N. II., 117.]

Order for Associating NORFOLK, SUFFOLK, ESSEX, CAMBRIDGESHIRE, HERTFORDSHIRE, and the City of NORWICH.

[1642, December 20.] — (Printed in *Lords' Journals*, v. 505, and elsewhere, with some variations. In the printed copies Lord Grey of Wark is designated as Major-General, but here Robert Earl of Warwick.) [N. XIV., 168.]

The KING to WILLIAM HOWARD of Tandridge.

1642, December 21. Oxford.—Warrant authorising him to receive contributions of money plate or other valuables from the well affected in the County of Surrey. (See *Commons' Journals*, ii. 949.) (Printed in Grey, iii. Appendix, No. 7, p. 12.) *Copy.* [N. XII., 33.]

The HOUSE OF COMMONS to [FERDINANDO] LORD FAIRFAX.

1642, December 23.—Thanking him for his services against the Earl of Newcastle, stating that 20,000*l.* had been appointed for the payment of his army, and approving of his billetting his soldiers on the country. (See *Commons' Journals*, ii. 917.) *Draft.* [N. XII., 34.]

Articles for Neutrality in CHESHIRE.

1642, December 23.—(Printed in Rushworth, iii. 2. 100, where Mr. Norton should be Mr. Morton, Dasbury, Daresbury, and Stopford, Stockford.) *Copy.* [N. XIII., 113.]

The EARL OF WARWICK to WILLIAM LENTHALL.

1642, December 24.—Desiring to know the pleasure of the House with regard to the seventeen prisoners brought from Portsmouth by the *Maidenhead*, with list (probably) enclosed. (See *Commons' Journals*, ii. 902.) *Signed. Seal.* [N. II., 118; XIII., 114.]

Pass to SIR WILLIAM SHEFFIELD.

1642, December 26.—To go to Rotterdam. [N. XIII., 115.]

Captain JOHN HOTHAM to [the EARL OF NEWCASTLE].

1642, December 27. Cawood.—"Your free and noble expressions of doing me so many great and real favours shall make me endeavour, either to requite them or be extremely thankful for them. The gentleman I wrote to is very sensible of those offices you were pleased to promise, and will not I hope be wanting in anything that befits an honest man or a good subject, but the business being of so high concernment as his good name and very being he desires to have some time to consider with himself before he can give a full and perfect answer, and it shall be with all the convenient speed that is possible. In the mean time he wished me to assure your Lordship, that whatsoever others may whisper to his Majesty, it shall be found that he hath none more real and firm unto his person and service than he and his family will be, and that he hopes that his Majesty conceives that what he hath done was only to discharge the public trust imposed upon him and not any disaffection to his service. He likewise returns your Lordship many thanks for your nobleness in not forgetting your old friend, as too many in these troublesome times take occasion to do. I hope a little delay can be no great prejudice to the business, but that you will be pleased not to think that there is anything intended to his Majesty and the Commonwealth by your Lordship's most humble servant." [N. II., 119.]

Sir Richard Saswell, John Crewe, and Edward Harby to Willia Lenthall.

1642, December 27. Northampton.—Mr. Francis Gray of Wellingborough was seized the last night being one that hath not contributed towards the defence of the kingdom and was supposed to nourish a faction against the Parliament, of which now there is good proof, for upon his apprehending the town rose in arms and killed two of our men. More forces being sent presently from Northampton to suppress those in arms Mr. Sawyer a Deputy Lieutenant and Captain for the town of Northampton that went with them was shot in the neck and fell from his horse, but we hear there is hope of his life. This so enraged the soldiers against Mr. Gray, who—as they conceive—was the occasion of this ill accident that befell their captain, that they generally declare they will pull down the house where he is and kill him. We therefore thought it fit—the tumult still continuing at Wellingborough—to remove him from thence and desire that he may be kept in safe custody. (See *Commons' Journals*, ii. 904.) *Signed. Seal.* [N. II., 120.]

Henry Nevill to the Inhabitants of Liddington, Stoke, and Bisbrooke.

1642, December 28. Holt.—"I being your neighbour, and hearing of the calamity that hath befallen Wellingborough, lately plundered by the soldiers of Northampton and took all they could carry away I could no less than give you notice of it, that you may provide to defend yourselves. Upon Tuesday last they did it, and have declared themselves that they are for these parts before they return." [N. II., 121.]

Francis Pierrepont to his brother Willia Pierrepont.

1642, December 28.—Interceding for the prisoners mentioned in his letter of the 13th. *Seal.* [N. II., 122.]

John Ashe to Willia Lenthall.

1642, December 30. Freshford.—I forward these letters from Ireland, from the Earl of Cork, one written by himself the other two from the rebels of Limerick (two of which are those of Thomas White and the Earl of Cork, dated September 21 and 30, *ante*, p. 63). The reason I send them is that about the end of June upon the petition of Mr. Latimer Sampson, Mr. Mounsell's brother-in-law, you ordered that two Irishmen taken on suspicion at Minehead, named White and Clansy should be kept in safe custody till the House ordered their enlargement, which was done to gain the release of the said Mr. Mounsell. This order Judge Foster when on circuit respected and told the gaoler to keep them in safe custody and advised them to labour with their friends at Limerick for the release of Mr. Mounsell, it appearing that one was a son and the other a kinsman to those that kept him in prison, and that they were here employed as factors and agents for those and others the principal rebels of Limerick. They thereupon wrote to their friends in Limerick by Thomas Moore, the bearer of this, Mr. Moun- sell's man, to obtain his release, but they also wrote to their friends in London, and obtained through them an order for their enlargement (See *Commons' Journals*, ii. 714), much beside mine and my friend's expectation. This Mr. Mounsell now in miserable captivity is my father's sister's son, and hath lost an estate in Ireland near the value of 10,000*l.*, out of which he was to pay his brothers' and sisters' portions, who are now all undone and live upon the charity of their friends. I request therefore that you will issue an order for the apprehending and imprisoning all those mentioned in Lord Cork's letter, and also the said White and Clansy in case they can be taken.

Postscript.—The bearer will present you with a certificate from the Commissary of Munster, showing that he hath delivered into the store house at Youghall 49 barrels of his master's beef at the price of 56*l.* 5*s.* 0*d.* which money he could not get in Ireland. I therefore request that he may receive the money from the officers appointed for the service in London. [N. II., 123.]

Colonel ARTHUR GOODWIN, HENRY BULSTRODE, SIR RICHARD INGOLDSBY, SIR WILLIAM ANDREWES, RICHARD SERJEANT, THOMAS TYRRILL, and SIR THOMAS SANDERS to WILLIAM LENTHALL.

1642[-3], January 2. Aylesbury.—Enclosing intercepted letters. (See *Commons' Journals*, ii. 915.) "The Collectors of the Subsidy in this county have received the like commands, which, as it is a violation of an Act made this very Parliament corroborated by Protestations since published in his Majesty's name so it is in a more particular measure prejudicial to many of this county who have advanced the money beforehand for the benefit of the kingdom, and are designed that money to reimburse themselves. Wherein we humbly beseech some course may be taken for the indemnity of ourselves, and of those of this county who have been assisting herein." *Signet. Seal.* [N. II., 125.] *Enclosed :*

i. The KING to the HIGH SHERIFF OF SUFFOLK.

1642, December 3. Oxford.—Warrant commanding him to take into custody from the collectors for that County such portion of the 400,000*l.* as was in their hands. *Sign Manual. Signet.* [N. I., 6.]

ii. The KING to JOHN, BISHOP OF PETERBOROUGH.

[1642], in the 18th year of our reign, December 28. Oxford.— Warrant desiring him to collect and remit immediately to Oxford his own Tenths, and the Tithes of his Diocese. *Sign Manual. Signet.* [N. II., 11.]

Captain JOHN HOTHAM to [the EARL OF NEWCASTLE].

1642[-3], January 2. Cawood.—"Since I could not be so happy as to attend you myself without a whole country's talking, a fitter mean could not have been found than by this noble gentleman whom you will find to deal really and plainly and not like a pedant, and, my Lord, it shall not need for to do otherwise, for with faith and honour to serve the King and the Commonwealth is all our ambition, and to leave that to posterity which our ancestors left us, an untainted name. We have Cæsars and Solomons as highly deceived as yours, although our Secretary Stockdale thinks he knows all as he directs all to our General. I shall not need to trouble your Lordship but leave all that to the bearer, only bewail the unhappiness of these distractions, that hinders from attending upon your Lordship your most faithful humble servant." *Seal.* [N. II., 126.]

BRIAN MIDDLETON to SIR WILLIAM SHEFFIELD.

[1642-3], January 3.—Acknowledging his note conveyed by Mr. Banks now a prisoner in Leeds. "There are not any rents received nor are you to expect any—as I fear—this long time. The payments towards His Majesty's army are great, York 12,000*l.* besides assessments very heavy to poor tenants. P. B . . . was redeemed from imprisonment by payment of 100*l.* besides plundered at T. by the other side. If God relieve not speedily, this country is wasted by plunderings, pillaging, robbing in the highways, and common charges, so as you are not to expect moneys from hence, till these storms be over." *Seal.* [N. II., 127.]

PETER SEALE, Mayor, and JOHN BENGER, Sheriff, of Southampton, to WILLIAM LENTHALL.

1642[-3], January 3. Southampton.—Enclosing several proclamations concerning which they ask directions. (See *Commons' Journals,* ii. 915.) *Signet. Seal.* [N. II., 128.]

Captain ANTHONY WILLOUGHBY to the PARLIAMENT.

1642[-3], January 5. His Majesty's fort near Galway.—Commending the bearer William Boughton, who had been there about six months, and had given directions for some outworks lately made about the fort. He will be able fully to inform you of the situation of this fort and what advantages may be taken against it, either by the town or other enemies. [N. II., 129.]

—— to HENRY MULLINER, Taylour, at his house over against Magdalene College, Cambridge.

1642[-3], January 7. York. [? Oxford.]—"Though it was our men's misfortune to be so treacherously used at Winchester, yet to give them their due, no men could show more gallantry then they did in that action, for when they saw the enemy draw up so strong, being all engaged Sir Richard Willis, Sir Jhon Smith—men of undaunted resolution—with 18 : more stood, whilst my Lord Grandison with the other forces made their retreat, and being thrice charged by entire troops still bravely repulsed the enemy and broke them in Winchester ; they spoiled the Church to the value of 7,000*l.* and which hath not been heard amongst heathen, they broke the leaden tombs wherein the bones of the Saxon Kings were kept for a great monument of Antiquity, and with these they broke and defaced all the glass windows.

At Chichester they used the same perfidious treachery they had formerly shown at Winchester, and notwithstanding Sir William Waller who commanded in chief their forces—consisting of 2,500 horse and foot—had subscribed these articles, that the gentlemen commanders should go out of the town on horse back with their swords, the common soldiers on foot, leaving their arms and colours behind them undefaced—for they had burnt them at Winchester—yet when he entered he observed none of these, but presently seized upon all the commanders as prisoners, and pillaged them of everything: the only thing the besieged wanted was powder, and the true affection of the Townsmen who basely forsook them : the chiefest loss was the persons of the Bishop and some of the chief gentlemen of the country, with my Lord Crawford's troop consisting of 40 : and no more, the choicest men of that Troop being here, either actually imployed, or expecting imployment in the army : all the soldiers there were not above 300 : too great a loss ; that same weeke some 1500 of them came into Banbury, we having 400 in the castle, but upon Prince Rupert's approach on Friday was seven night they left that place, stealing away in the night; yet we took one of their colours and 20 : prisoners.

On Saturday last there fell in some 2,000 of them—out of Ciscister (Cirencester)—into Sir John Byron's quarter at Burford whom he put to the flight with 14 men, killed 20 : not granting quarter to any. In this night service Sir John got a noble scar in the face. The same day the mint came hither with good store of money already coined, and plate, his Majesty hath given his foot a week's pay.

On the Wedensday following the Aldermen come hither with their nonsensical petition. His Majesty asked them how they could so confidently secure him, who could not secure themselves : wise Alderman Garret told the King that he had many times promised to secure their religion, laws and liberties. Sir, said he, could we be but secure and assured that your Majesty would do so, we should soon make an end of this business; at which all the court blurted right out, the Gracious King sweetly replying; I know not how to make you confide in me ; you shall do well to believe those that lie least. The King would not return his answer by them, but sent one Herne with it, who went in coach with them, they promising his Majesty that Herne should read it publickly at a Common Hall, because there hath been formerly such art used to smother his Majesty's other gracious answers. Having taken their leave of his Majesty as they came through the *court de guard* they offered the soldiers a piece. They answered bravely that his Majesty suffered them not to want money, yet if they had been as bare as the Parliament soldiers are, till they gave a better testimony of their affection to his Majesty they scorned to take any Roundhead's money in England. Which high piece of bravery pleased his Majesty so well, that he hath sent to inquire who it was that made the answer that so he may reward them. There is great hopes the prentices will give up to his Majesty these 4. grand incendiaries that he hath pitched upon. Either the last clause of denying his protection to the merchants will work, or inevitable prove the ruin of all trade. It is a high strain and of dangerous consequence, but no course must be left unattempted if this work not with the merchants nothing will. On Thursday there came a prentice to the King with a copy of their petition, and of their band of association ; now it begins to work like a Scottish prank. This day Hampden's lieutenant-colonel was taken by a party of my Lord Northampton's men who lie at Banbury. We hear that the man is a gallant old soldier and an honest man, and that he was not unwillingly taken, having given notice before that he intended to go that way to London. That which confirms me is that now he is a prisoner only in Sir Jacob Ashly his house, too honourable a lodging for any traitor.

The great newes are expected from Scotland, there was a general meeting of all the Estates there on Wednesday last, the result of which will let us know how they intend to behave themselves in this great business, whether the King's superlative goodness hath taught them a new lesson of obedience, or whether they intend to return to their old trade : one scurvy symptom of which is that it being put to vote at the council table, whether his Majesty's answer with the Parliament's incentive to rebellion by desiring their brotherly assistance should be printed together and read in all churches—being the only favour his Majesty desired—it was carried for the King but by one voice, so prevalent belike amongst them is the Parliament's golden rhetoric. But I hope though all the traitors there were devils—I am sure they are not far from it except they mend their manners—there will still be found in that kingdom so many loyal hearts as will make them eat their bread in order. In this vote Argyle and Chancellor Loudoun showed themselves plainly against the King; I could name a third as pernicious as either though he thinks he walks in the clouds. The Scots Commissioners are now here with his Majesty, one of them, my Lord Lothian is going in an embassy to France sent by the kingdom, and is here now expecting his Majesty's approbation. I think the King will not be very difficult in the suite, as glad to be rid of him.

I have not need to write London news, though our intelligence even of their actions is not inferior to yours. The rencontre betwixt my Lord Say and Northumberland, his resolute answer, and the other's pressing to have him called to the bar—which he could not effect— together with the vast sum of 600*l*.—3 : by Kimbolton, 2 : by Brooke, and one by old Say—subscribed by the Lords—for as for Rochester his 5,000*l*. is all one as if he had subscribed 50 : beeng able to pay neither—I know is as old with you as that my Lady Essex hath brought my Lord a young heir. When his Majesty read the first news of it, In troth, said his Majesty, I think he is no more the father of it than I am, and, Gentlemen here I clear myself of it before you all.

On Wednesday last as old Say went to the House the prentices came flocking about him for an accommodation ; Gentlemen, says he, this is not the way. God, my Lord, said they, this was the way, and this shall be the way.

Yesterday the Prince marched from hence with 5 regiments of horse, 2 of dragouners to Burford where he was to joine with the Marquess of Hertford his forces—consisting of 600 : horse, 250 : dragouners, and 1,500 : foot. The design is for Ciscister (Cirencester), with God's blessing. I question not the success, if the rogues run not before we come, they have in the towne 2,000 men and 3 piece of cannon. Do but think what a case I am in, my horse being lame.

I got Mr. Baly created doctor, but made him promise 5*l*. for books to our library.

Fail not to send every week, for now we shall have daily store of action. Oxford and Reading are so strongly fortified that we should not be afraid of Essex' whole army before either place. Yesternight a number of the chief gentlemen of Her[t]fordshire presented to his Majesty a brave petition for his Majesty's assistance and protection against all seditious schismatical rebels which the king accepted most graciously and hath returned a brave answer.

I hope the high sheriff brings both along with him, as he doth the London petition, and his Majesty's answer together with my Lord Digby his brave apology." [N. II., 132.]

SIR GILBERT GERRARD, Governor of Brill, to the HIGH CONSTABLES OF COTTESLOE HUNDRED.

1642[-3], January 7 and 8.--Warrants, the first requiring them to summon the Trained Bands and all able-bodied men to appear with such arms as they can provide at Brill on Wednesday next, the second requiring them to have 100 men there on Thursday next with spades and pickaxes, or to provide payment at 10*d.* a day for every man short. [N. XIII., 116.]

HUMPHREY DITTON, Mayor, to MICHAEL OLDSWORTH.

1642[-3], January 8, Salisbury.—Narrating the escape of Mr. Wroughton from the gaol by means of eight or nine soldiers part of a body that were passing through to Exeter to be under the command of Colonel Northcoat. *Seal.* [N. II., 130.]

Captain JOHN HOTHAM to [the EARL OF NEWCASTLE].

1642[-3], January 9. Cawood.—"You may if you please peruse this inclosed Copy, and by it perceive what is already done, an other to that purpose went from an other place. I hope no just nor honest man can dislike it for he that desires not a good peace deserves ill of this poor country that hath given him his subsistence. My Lord, there is no man that hath any reasonable share in the commonwealth can desire that either side should be absolute conquerers, for it will be then as it was betwixt Cæsar and Pompey whosoever had the better the Roman Liberty was sure to have the worse. I honour the king as much as any and love the Parliament, but do not desire to see either absolute conquerors, it is too great a temptation to courses of will and violence. My Lord, there is one thing more, which I fear much, that if the honorable endeavours of such powerful men as yourself do not take place for a happy peace the necessitous people of the whole kingdom will presently rise in mighty numbers and whosoever they pretend for at first, within a while they will set up for themselves, to the utter ruin of all the nobility and gentry of the kingdome. I speak not this merely at random, the west part of this county affords mighty numbers of them, which I am very confident you will see necessitied and urged to rise in far greater bodies than these. The armies that are already gathered here, necessity teaches to seek a subsistence, and if this unruly rout have once cast the rider, it will run like wildfire in the example through all the counties of England. I shall humbly desire your pardon for this great digression, and for my overweening to propose these things to a judgment so much greater than mine, but your Lordship's favours as they have obliged so they have imboldened Your most faithfull affectionate servant." [N. II., 131.]

SIR GILBERT PYKERINGE and SIR EDWARD HARTOPP to ——.

1642[-3], January 9.—When Lord Grey demanded of Mr. Nevil of Holt that all those in his house who had taken up arms should be delivered up, he proposed that his Lordship should permit the gentlemen to leave the house that the men who were there might fight it out, and also said that "he believed the force brought against him to be such that he was ill able to resist. Notwithstanding rather than yield to dishonourable propositions he would make his house his grave, and therein give an example to the rest of the gentlemen of that county to stand out in defence of their liberty." [N. XIII., 117.]

The House of Commons to Several Counties.

[1642-3, January 10.]—Ordering them to get in and send to London the arrears of the 400,000l. and the Poll-money. (See *Commons' Journals*, ii. 920.) *Draft*. [N. XII., 36.]

Colonel Arthur Goodwin, Sir Richard Ingoldsby, Thomas Tyrrill, and Richard Serjeant to Bulstrode Whitelocke and Richard Winwood.

1642[-3], January 11. Aylesbury.—Concerning the attempt by Prince Rupert on Cirencester, and the 100l. seized by them due from Mr. Henley to Mr. Coker, and enclosing two warrants of Sir Gilbert Garratt, Governor of Brill. (Printed in Grey, iii. 396.) *Signed. Seal.* [N. II., 133.]

Captain Richard Lee to William Lenthall.

1642[-3], January 11. Upnor Castle.—Enclosing by the Mayor's desire a Proclamation, and desiring the House's pleasure whether it should be proclaimed or not. [N. II., 134.]

The Parliament to the King.

1642[-3], January 12.—Petition against adjourning the Term to Oxford. (Printed in *Lords' Journals*, v. 548, and in Rushworth, iii. 2. 146) *Draft* and *copy.* [N. XII., 35, 39.]

Richard Beacon, Francis Goodere, William Ellis, and Doctor George Seaton.

1642[-3], January 12.—Examinations concerning the Hertfordshire Petition to the King. (See *Commons' Journals*, ii. 928.) [N. XIII., 119.]

Colonel William Strode to John Pym and William Strode.

1642[-3], January 13, 11 at night. Tavistock.—(To the same effect and in parts in the same words as the next letter). *Seal.* [N. II., 135.]

Francis Buller, Colonel William Strode, and John Pyne to the Earl of Stamford.

Same date and place.—"We have now opened our desired way —New Bridge—into Cornwall and have entered that country with our forces and persons this afternoon, a work of some difficulty by reason of the arch that was broken down, and the strong guards and works against us, which we obtained by passing a party of dragoons and horse by a ford and facing and playing upon them with our foot till they were both ready to fall on together which they did very bravely, killed two of them, forced Captain Hartgill into the river, where he was drowned, and took 41 prisoners, whereof Lieutenant Greenway was the principal man, besides 40 horses and 50 muskets at least. . . . . The bridge we have made good with some of our foot and returned to this place, whence to-morrow we intend to march on New Bridge into Cornwall to Cargreen with all our forces—except Major Worth's company which we leave to guard that bridge and this town—to join with Colonel Ruthen for Saltash or what else he shall appoint. We find our soldiers very stout and prompt to fight and had we your Lordship's presence we should think no work in Cornwall too hard for us to do. We had only

one man shot in the arm and hope [he] will soon be cured." *Signed.*
Seal. In the Margin ; " I am now, by God's assistance, on my march
and hope to be with the van of my army to-morrow night. In the
mean I shall not be wanting with my best industry to accomplish this
good work, and so I send you this letter to confirm my hopes.
Stanforde." [N. II., 136.]

SIR CHRISTOPHER YELVERTON, SIR GILBERT PYKERINGE, JOHN
CREWE and RICHARD KNIGHTLEY to WILLIAM LENTHALL.

1642[-3], January 14. Northampton.—"My Lord Spencer mustered
and trained to-day one-half of this county here. . . . The Trained
Bands made a full appearance and were very well armed." The
volunteers were of two sorts, some armed to the number of about 550,
others unarmed, who expressed great affection to the service. These
were not numbered, but were thought to be many more than the others.
We go to-morrow to Kettering and the next day to Oundle. *Signed.*
Seal. [N. II., 137.]

JOHN HOCKEWILL and others to WILLIAM LENTHALL.

1642[-3], January 14. Exeter.—Stating that their late disbursements on fortifications, ammunition and soldiers' pay had far exceeded
the 300*l.* allowed them, that they had raised and expended over 3,000*l.*
by way of rate, and that their charges still continue, and therefore
petitioning that the subscriptions of the inhabitants on the Propositions
be allotted for these services. (See *Commons' Journals,* ii. 931.) *Signed.*
Seal. [N. II., 138.]

Colonel ARTHUR GOODWIN, HENRY BULSTRODE and THOMAS TYRRILL
to the EARL OF ESSEX.

1642[-3], January 14. Aylesbury.—Explaining that Serjeant-Major
Browne had seized Sir William Drake's horses, not knowing that he had
a protection from the Speaker, and that they had been sent back.
(See *Commons' Journals,* ii. 920, 921.) *Signed. Seal.* [N. II., 139.]

Captain JOHN HOTHAM to [the EARL OF NEWCASTLE].

1642[-3], January 15. Cawood.—" I have not yet heard from
London since the letter went, but expect it every hour. I doubt not
but there may come very good fruits of it and the continued endeavours
of such men as desire peace with the King's honour and the public
security, and that I hope to see effected through all opposition. . .
You are now great in power with his Majesty, and your advice will
sway much, which if you please to make use of to him incline to peace
the whole kingdom would be obliged to you, and for the greatness of
the work it is the more honour if it be effected, and he that begins well
hath half done; nothing is so hard as it seems at first. The propositions
for peace go on fast, and I hope the jugglers will be deceived, although
I believe cunning enough on all sides. For my part, if I can serve the
King and the commonwealth, as a gentleman should do, and be esteemed
worthy your Lordship's friendship, it is all I expect, and I shall think it
honour enough. I hear of two converts in the Parliament, Hollis and
Pierrepont. Our general here thinks you raise men as the sand, and
the King of Denmark in a string. It was not like your business at
Sheriff Hutton should thrive better, being conducted by three such
cavaliers; you will find more such among my countrymen. Our
senators here think of saving themselves, as you may well see, we are

now so quiet. For the wishes of those gentlemen to me, I thank God, I never thought them valuable ; if I had, I could have had them cheap enough. . . . You are he, that I set my rest on as my noble friend, and you shall command me, for I know nothing will come from you but of honour, and you shall never find more truth and gratitude in any that you have obliged than in your most affectionate humble servant." [N. II., 140.]

SIR HUGH CHOLMELEY to WILLIAM LENTHALL.

1642[-3], January 16.   Gisbrough.—You have heard of my drawing some forces to Malton, and the defeat they gave the Earl of Newport's troops. "Upon information that Colonel Strickland and Colonel Slingsby were marched to Gisbrough, the principal town in Cleveland, with some troops of horse, and that they called together the Trained Bands of those parts and had summoned Whitby a sea town sixteen miles from that place to receive a garrison, Sir Matthew Boynton being come to me to Malton with two troops of dragooners, I joined to them one more of mine, one hundred and thirty foot and my own troop of horse, and—leaving a garrison in Malton—with these we marched unto Cleveland, and this day purposing to assault the enemy who laid in Gisbrough—as we are informed—with four hundred foot and a hundred horse, they were so confident of their strength as they advanced a mile out of the town to encounter us, and placed their musketiers under hedges in places of advantage. But after two hours' skirmish we beat them, first from the hedges and then out of the town of which we are now possessed. We have taken above one hundred and twenty prisoners, amongst which Colonel Slingsby and twelve Frenchmen that were troopers ;—and praised be God—we have not lost a man nor but two wounded with cuts in the head. I have this night information from Captain Bushell—who I left to command the garrison at Malton—that he hath intelligence the enemy with new forces from York intends suddenly to assault that place, so that I fear I shall be drawn from hence before this country be well settled or my men refreshed. I have now near eighty horse and a troop of dragoones one hundred and thirty foot with me newly raised here, besides the garrisons at Scarbrough and Malton. You will judge these forces must needs require an expense of money. I have drawn what I can from the country, and if supply come not speedily from you, all will dissolve instantly. I have received two hundred pounds of my brother's rents, which I desire may be speedily repaid. I hope my diligence and other carriage in these affairs will shew my former actions did never deserve those representations of them which were in print, nor any belief of them. But as nothing can divert me from serving the Parliament with all fidelity whiles I am in their employment yet I profess it grieves my heart to see how these calamities increase and how I am forced to draw my sword not onely against my countrymen but many near friends and allies some of which I know both to be well affected in religion and lovers of their liberties. And therefore I most humbly beseech the House that they will be pleased to lay hold of all occasions that may produce an accommodation between the King and Parliament, as that the circumstance of time may be considered when his Majesty began to withdraw himself at so great a distance from the Parliament and what person may be conceived to have the greatest power and interest to persuade him to condescend to such propositions as may conduce best to the quieting of these troubles, and if our religion be but firmly settled whether it be not better to let go some things that in right belong to

the subject then by insisting upon them have the king and so great a
party in the kingdom so unsatisfied as it must produce a civil war."
(See *Commons' Journals*, ii. 938.) [N. II., 141.]

SIR WILLIAM SPRING and others to WILLIAM LENTHALL.

1642 [-3], January 17. Bury St. Edmunds.—(The effect appears
from *Commons' Journals*, ii. 934). *Signed. Seal.* [N. II., 142.]

The KING to the MASTER and WARDENS OF THE COMPANY OF
WATERMEN.

1642[-3], January 18. Oxford.—Warrant ordering them to assemble
all the Members, Freemen, and Apprentices of the Company at their
Common Hall and to read to them the Petition lately received from the
City of London with the King's Answer, and his letter to the Sheriffs
and the Masters and Wardens of the several Companies. *Sign-Manual.
Signet.* [N. I., 7.] (N. I., 8, and 9, are warrants of the same date,
identical *mutatis mutandis* with this, addressed to the Master and
Wardens of the Barber-Surgeons' and Carpenters' Companies
respectively.)

SIR EDWARD HARINGTON, EVERS ARMINE, CHRISTOPHER BROWNE,
ROBERT HORSMAN, and JOHN OSBORNE to WILLIAM LENTHALL.

[1642-3, January, after 19th. Rutland.]—Enclosing two intercepted
letters to show why they had not as yet returned estreats upon the
payment of the great tax of 400,000*l.* fearing that it might be diverted
and misemployed, and desiring the directions of the House, as they
feared some of the collectors might be prevailed to part with their collected moneys upon the said letters. *Signed. Seal.* [N. VIII., 131.]
Probably *Enclosed :*

W. BODENHAM, Sheriff of Rutland, to —— SHIELDS.

1642[-3], January 19. Pyall.—Warrant ordering him by virtue of
the King's letter, whereof a copy is enclosed, to pay over to
himself all sums collected by him on account of the subsidy of
400,000*l.* or other sums lately raised in the County. *Signed.*
(The enclosed letter is in the same terms as that to the Sheriff
of Suffolk, enclosed in Colonel Goodwin's of the 2nd instant.)
[N. II., 143.]

SIR THOMAS WROTHE to JOHN PYM.

1642[-3], January 20. Plymouth.—"The Earl of Stamford hath
been all this week at Plymouth, in which time he hath been very active
and industrious in viewing the works and fortifications of this town,
giving and sending of orders and dispatches to his forces in several
parts of this county, Cornwall, and Somerset. He hath also passed the
river here to Salt Ash and Millbrooke, two towns which the enemy
hath lately been possessed of, and in which are now two garrisons of ours
placed. He hath been at the house of one Mr. Edgecombe, called
Mount Edgecombe . . who is a great Malignant and sides with the
Hoptonians. There are many marks of the battery of our ordnance
upon the said house as are also in the town of Salt Ash, but little hurt
is done to either . . . Mount Edgecombe is thought to be so considerable for fortification, and to annoy those that shall attempt this
town that there is a guard of musketeers protects it and some works
are intended speedily to be made there to make it more defensible. Near
unto this is a strong and impregnable island called St. Nicholas' island

committed to the trust and care of Colonel Carew, is well guarded both with musketeers and ordnance, and of this my Lord General did likewise take a view, and in all these places I attended on him. Concerning the strength of this town I must assure you that it is so fortified both by natural situation and industry and art of men, that it is not inferior in my opinion to any fort in this kingdom; and there is at this time great store of ships lying in the harbour. . . . . Happily I have given you some content in the preceding relation, but I must desire you to take it as a preparation . . to digest the sequel. . . . After the enemy had forsaken Saltash and Lanisdon, it was conceived they would draw towards Pendennis Castle for their refuge and safety. Whereupon our [forces] had order to bend and march that way, and accordingly were quartered at a town in Cornwall, between 8 and 10 miles from Saltash called Liskeard, the enemy being within 3 miles of the same. Yesterday in the morning, our forces . . . . marched towards the enemy, all the way being narrow and very dirty lanes, and, as it appears, had neither the help of guides nor scouts, so that on a sudden after their march of 3 miles they fell into an ambush of great disadvantage unto them, which the enemy had laid in a thick wood of a park of my Lord Mohun's joining to the way. As our forces marched beside a dangerous bog and a very high hill and the enemy in number treble beyond ours besides their ordnance, which we wanted, and I fear encouraged by some intelligence of the height of our strength; having all these advantages, the enemy charged furiously upon our forces, and they as magnanimously resaluted them, but in a short time the courage of our forces was abated, and surprised with such a panic fear that both our horse and foot were suddenly routed, and every man divided and dispersed, and ran and rode as fast as fear could carry them towards Saltash. The enemy pursued them eagerly, and in this chase got no small number of our arms, which the fugitives let fall in their flight, and the commanders as well as others tried the goodness of their horses in this chase. Four choice pieces of ordnance we have lost; what number of men is not yet certainly known, but I doubt not a few are taken prisoners; yet it is thought there are but three or four slain. Had our forces delayed this enterprise one day longer, four good pieces of ordnance, which came yesterday too late, with more soldiers had come up to them, and then I am confident that through God's assistance and good advice we had had a glorious victory on the Hoptonian rebels. But the late good success against these wicked ones made some chief commanders depend too much upon the arm of flesh, one cause of the miscarriage of this rash undertaking. Besides this attempt was not only without but against the order of my Lord General. Last of all, and not the least but the greatest of all, I doubt we have not been thankful enough for the late and former deliverances, and therefore God did in this action withdraw himself from our assistance. I doubt that one man of note is either slain or taken prisoner, for we yet miss him. His name is Sir Silston Calmady. . . . . *Postscript.*—Your son is now here very well, and so I hope is my brother . . . We are not so dejected, but we are preparing to pursue our enemies with as much courage and power, both by sea and land, as ever." [N. II., 144.]

JOHN WOGAN to RICHARD ALDWORTH, Mayor of Bristol.

1642[-3], January 20. Wiston.—The desperate condition of this county requires me to apply to you for its relief. "The Malignant parties . . are already come so near unto our doors, that they have already plundered the estate of Captain Gunter in the very heart of our county, and driven away all his cattle by night under the conduct of one Captain Henry Crowe of the county of Carmarthen, which injurious outrage we know that county would never have dared to attempt against us, but that it is put on by a stronger hand than its own. . . . We have certain intelligence that my Lord Herbert of Ragland with the Earl of Carbery are suddenly raising a force of 8,000 men to make a strong invasion upon us, under all which we are like to suffer. . . . I beseech you to be a means, both by yourself and by moving the chief commanders . . . in your noble city that present supplies may be sent us from your parts. If we had but 2,900 or 3,000 foot and draggoneers to what we have, we would not only drive them out of our country, but make them glad to sit down in their own. It is most requisite that 300 or 400 be instantly sent us, that we may make a defensive business of it till stronger supplies come. It is not our livelihood they aim at, so much as their surprise of our haven of Milford . . . . whereby a door may be opened to receive foreign forces to prejudice the troubled state more than themselves can." *Postscript.*— Desiring that a copy may be sent to the Parliament. [N. II₁, 145.]

HENRY BULSTRODE, THOMAS TYRRILL, and RICHARD GRENVILE to RICHARD WINWOOD and BULSTRODE WHITELOCKE.

1642 [-3], January 20. Aylesbury.—Concerning 100*l.* paid in by Sir Heneage Proby, and 1,000*l.* due from Sir Thomas Saunders. (Printed in Grey, iii. 379.) (See *Commons' Journals*, ii. 944.) [N. II., 146.]

KENELM SMYTH.

1642[-3], January 21. Northampton.—Information, describing the preparations for the defence of the house of Mr. Nevil of Holt, and of the adjoining church and steeple. [N. XIII., 118.]

The KING to the QUEEN.

[1642-3], January 23—February 2. Oxford.—Acknowledging her letters of December 29th and January 9th, and describing how he "was persecuted concerning places." A fragment in cipher is "con-
t h e Dutch treat(y)
cerning 45: 31: 7: 4: 132: 300: I will answer thee in thy own words. *Je le remetteray à vous respondre per bouche.*" (Printed in *King's Pamphlets*, E. 102. No. 6, p. 74.) *Copy.* [N. XII., 73.]

PETER SEALE, Mayor, and eight others to WILLIAM LENTHALL.

1642[-3], January 24. Southampton.—Desiring repayment of 2,000*l.* advanced by the town for paying the soldiers, (See *Commons' Journals*, ii. 945) and requesting that the members might be allowed to come down, as their presence would be useful in many ways. *Signed. Seal.* [N. II. 147.]

THOMAS HILMAN and 15 others to WILLIAM LENTHALL.

1642[-3], January 28. Coleraine.—Expressing their gratitude to the Parliament for bestowing on them 500*l.*'s worth of wheat and pease, whereof 400*l.*'s worth had already arrived, and for granting a collection for them in London and its suburbs, and also complaining of the conduct of Captain Thomas Church, sent by them with Captain Michael Beresford and Mr. Griffin Harverd to negotiate their affairs in England

who had traduced his two colleagues, and disclaiming his further intermeddling in their affairs. (See *Commons' Journals*, iii. 47.) *Original*
and Copy. [N. III., 113 ; II., 148.]

ALEXANDER BENCE, ROGER TWEEDY and PHINEAS PETT to the COMMISSIONERS OF THE NAVY.

1642[-3], January 31. Woolwich.—Desiring that 20 caulkers be
sent, stating the *Convertine* and *Bonadventure* were ready to take
in victuals, and concerning other naval matters. *Signed.* [N. II., 151.]

SIR GILBERT PYKERINGE, JOHN CREWE, EDWARD HARBY and EDWARD FARMER to WILLIAM LENTHALL.

1642[-3], January 31. Northampton.—Sending up Mr. Henry
Nevill and others named in *Commons' Journals*, ii. 953, the first of
whom had fortified his house against the Parliament, and the others
were there with him. *Signed. Seal.* [N. II., 152.]

SIR WILLIAM BRERETON to JOHN PYM.

1642[-3], February 4. Nantwich.—"Our enraged enemy lay in
wait and had prepared an ambuscade for our destruction, but the Lord
was pleased to watch over us, and to deliver 100 of them into our hands,
both men horses and many arms, amongst which there were three or
four captains and divers other considerable prisoners, who do much
increase the burden of our care how to dispose of them, seeing we have
no place of strength whereunto to retreat, nor where to dispose of them,
save only in the Nantwich, which we are about to fortify. We find
and hear every day of more and more of their slain and wounded men."
Complaining that two of his best horses with their saddles and pistols,
500 or 600 of his sheep at Chester and many horses had been
seized, his house at Chester plundered, and divers of his goods
conveyed away and feather beds sold for 20s. apiece. " There are four
independent troops here, Mr. Booth's, Mr. Mainwaring's, Mr. Duckinfield's, and Captain Edwardes'. I am in want of some 20 pair of pistols,
which if they were supplied I hope I should make my troop near 100.
I beseech that Sir John Corbett and Sir Thomas Midleton be sent
speedily into Shropshire and Derbyshire to raise some regiments there,
to hinder their forces from being employed against us here in this
county." *Seal.* [N. II., 154.]

The EARL OF STAMFORD and others to the COMMITTEE OF LORDS AND COMMONS FOR THE SAFETY OF THE KINGDOM.

1642[-3], February 6. Plymouth.—Commending the bearer, Mr.
Moses Goodyer, and referring them to him for information of the state
of the town and country. *Signed.* [N. II., 155.]

THEOPHILUS PHILO-BRITTANICUS to ——.

[1642-3, February 9.]—" Noble Sir, since your departure from hence
I wrote you a letter . . . if I had known of your bosom friend's
coming to you I should have sent and imparted that which now I
cannot, but since you have the conveniency and safety of Mr. Collard's
return hither pray let me receive a final determination and hang no
longer in suspense whether anything is to be done or no in that business
we spoke [of]. I want nothing but money to effect it, but in case

there be either a difficulty in the thing, or a dislike or distrust of me for the action pray let me know. And in case there be some reason which I am ignorant of to hinder what we spoke of, then Mr. Coll[ard] can tell you somewhat I wished him to write to you, which upon the receipt of money I shall bring along with me to you speedily. In a word 350*l.* will serve to effect that which will be an extra-ordinary benefit and advantage, if not a final happy conclusion to what we both desire, which money if you will give Mr. Collard order to furnish me with I'll give him that land and colliery which I spoke to you in security for the same, and speedily come to you well prepared where I shall take a full order for your satisfaction. However pray let me know your positive determination, and of what account and reckoning—if any at all—I am there, which how bad or small soever it be I would willingly repay by this or some other notable way wherein I might be instructed. Your candidness herein I shall take for an extraordinary evidence of your friendship. . . . . The news here is that the Commons yesterday carried up their votes to the Lords with reasons declaring their disassent from concurring with their Lordships in a Cessation of Arms and a Treaty. And that upon these reasons the Commons had voted the disbanding both armies presently, and till that were done no Treaty upon the Propositions; which, if his Majesty would assent unto, there should be a Treaty and Cessation of arms as towards a disbanding. One particular circumstance I will acquaint you with in the carriage of this business, which was remarkable. After the Lords had voted a Cessation of arms and a Treaty, the next morning they sent a message to the Commons for a conference to acquaint them with their votes. While the messengers tarried for their answer—which usually is very short, either they will, or they will send an answer by messengers of their own—it was so ordered that Colonel Mannuringe, Captain Hamy, Captain Titchburne, Captain Underwood, Captain Gore, and divers other citizens with Mr. Case and Mr. Woodcock and Burrough with other ministers came to the House of Commons, and desired to be heard, and so delivered some reasons they had, in the behalf of the City, against a Cessation of arms and a Treaty. Whereupon there was a present resolution to call them in, but a debate of almost an hour whether they should be called in before the conference with the Lords or no. After several votes the House was divided, and by ten voices carried to call them in first, and, so they had the preheminence of the Lords. When they were called in Colonel Mannuringe was their spokesman and tendered a paper containing the reasons, but they were commanded to withdraw, and after some debate the paper was received and they returned thanks. You may judge by this what likelihood there is [of] another end save by the sword. If . . I come to you I shall more enlarge than I dare write. We hear his Majesty had made Sir Ralph Hopton Baron of Glastonbury, but he enjoyed his honour a short space, for he and 600 men more of his are slain before Plymouth. I have him that I send to. you upon the exchange yet, and the rest you know of ready to do as I direct them." . . (See *Commons' Journals,* ii. 959.) [N. VIII., 140.] (Nalson suggests that the writer is Sir Thomas Peyton.)

[SIR WILLIAM BRERETON] to Captain FRANCIS ROWE.

1642[-3], February 10. Nantwich.—" We have near upon 5 troops of horse in this County, but because they are independent troops and not subject to command it was and is my desire that there may be a major sent down, an honest and conscionable man. We are much disadvantaged for want of such an officer, who is able to order a regiment of horse and if you please to send me a commission to command them

I shall be thereby enabled the better to serve you and shall expect no increase of pay. Shropshire forces lie now at Whitchurch and threaten much to infest us, so also do the Welshmen out of Flint and Denbigh-shire. If Sir John Corbett were sent into Shropshire and Sir Thomas Middleton into Denbighshire with commission either of them to raise a regiment I hope we should be less oppressed and able to do you better service, and I hope we may be able to give them some assistance. It is exceedingly desired by very many in both counties who so groan under the oppression there that they would be ready to join any who would assist to deliver them out of the hands of their taskmasters. Stafford-shire also wants some officer to Command in Chief. There are 2,000 yesterday up in arms there against Stafford as it is said, to whom I was able to afford no more than six or seven commanders, whereby I am much weakened for by reason of the thronging in of foreign forces out of Shropshire and Wales and Lancashire, the Earl of Derby being now at Chester and making his strongest design for Chester, and the Manchester forces not attempting anything to divert him, we must be constrained to raise another regiment, and therefore we could much desire some more Commanders, otherwise for want of more forces the country will be in danger to be overrun and our forces disabled. *Postscript.*—Captain Barkeley, who commands the king's pinnace called the *Swan*, is very officious to the Commissioners of Array, and hath promised them two pieces of ordnance to guard Chester. It is said the Commissioners have given him 500*l.* or 1,000*l.* If some speedy care be not taken to prevent him he may do very much mischief. Take care I pray that there may be a Major to order a regiment of horse with some officers of foot sent down, for we have a great need of them, a Lieutenant-Colonel and Serjeant-Major of foot and some Captains and some Lieutenants of foot, and I pray acquaint my Lord Brooke that if he do not come down speedily he loseth a brave opportunity and loseth the hearts of Stafford-shire, whom I have much ado to support. Am forced to send every day to them.—Some old soldiers for serjeants would do wondrous well. Now that we have gathered our forces together, we are at extreme want of money, and therefore desire that we may have the benefit of the like orders for raising money in our county as hath been already granted for Yorkshire Buckinghamshire Leicester and in particular for Somerset-shire dated January 27, 1642, giving power also to assess Malignants' estates in the said County, which if it be not granted we shall be speedily very much distressed. The names of Commissioners I have already given who are to appoint assessors, Sir George Booth, Sir William Brereton, George Booth, Henry Brooks, William Marbury, Henry Mainwaring, Robert Duckinfield, Henry Vernon, Thomas Stanley, John Crewe, John Bradshaw, Ralph Arderne, Edward Hyde, John Leigh, Thomas Croxton Esquires." (See *Commons' Journals*, ii. 966.) *Signature torn off.* [N. II., 94c, but not noticed in Index.]

The HORSE OF COMMONS to LORD INCHIQUIN and the COUNCIL OF WAR.

1642[-3], February 11. — Acknowledging their letters with the account of the moneys and necessaries furnished by them for the soldiers in Munster to the value of 4,060*l.* and stating that as soon as possible they would take a course for their satisfaction. *Draft.* [N. XII., 40.]

WILLIAM LENTHALL to LORD INCHIQUIN.

Same date.—Acknowledging his letters of the 12th and 19th of January, to which the House of Commons had directed him to return this answer. They have shipped such a supply of victual and ammunition as was propounded to them by Sir Hardress Waller and others, to be with you within your time limited, and have taken a course.—already in execution in London and the adjacent parts—for raising further moneys throughout the Kingdom to be employed solely for the relief of the armies in Ireland, of which the Munster forces are to be ample sharers, so that you shall never be put to treat with the Rebels for a cessation of arms, or to relinquish your interests in that Province. The House is informed that the remains of the foot formerly commanded by Lord Forboys [Forbes] are come to you, and may serve to recruit your regiment, and that he himself is arrived in England, and left his command, which will take away all further competition between you and him. The House will make it their care that you may receive such fruits of your fidelity industry and valour, as may be for your encouragement and advantage. A good while since they voted you to be Governor of Munster and Captain General of the forces there, and presented their vote to the Lords for their concurrence, which they intend to do again, and when it is granted, will take care, that with the burden of that government you be invested with the privileges and profits incident thereto. (See *Commons' Journals*, ii. 961.) *Draft.* [N. XII., 41.]

Captain RICHARD SWANLEY to WILLIAM LENTHALL.

1642[-3], February 14. From aboard his Majesty's Ship the *Charles* riding in Cowes Roads.—Having acknowledged the letter of the 11th (See *Commons' Journals,* ii. 962), "The Dutch Commanders and myself accorded, and delivered to me the English that were aboard their ships, which seeing they had complied with the power I had, I kept but 10 and sent back the rest, and recalled the warrants I had put forth." *Signed.* [N. II., 159.]

WILLIAM LENTHALL to the MAYOR OF PLYMOUTH.

1642[-3], February 16.—(Written in obedience to the order of that date stated in *Commons' Journals*, ii. 967, where the purport of the letter is given.) [N. II., 160.]

The EARL OF ESSEX to the EARL OF MANCHESTER, Speaker of the House of Peers.

1642[-3], February 20. — (Printed in *Lords' Journals,* v. 614.) [N. II., 161.]

SIR MICHAEL LIVESEY to WILLIAM LENTHALL.

[1642-3], Saturday [February 25]. Gravesend.—Describing how and why he had arrested Sir William Sheffield, who had at first represented that he was a member of the House and afterwards admitted that he was not, whom he is sending up in custody. (See *Commons' Journals,* ii. 979.) *Seal.* [N. II., 124.]

WILLIAM LENTHALL to the COMMISSIONERS FOR THE ACT OF 400,000*l.* in the County of Bedford.

[1642-3, February 26.]—(A circular letter addressed to the Commissioners of the different Counties, probably that referred to in *Commons' Journals,* ii. 980 under the above date, directing them to take steps for the speedy raising of the money levied under the ordinance lately passed for a new loan and contribution towards the Relief of the Kingdom of Ireland.) *Signed.* [N. II., 149.]

The PARLIAMENT.

[1642-3, February 28.]—Propositions for a Cessation. (Printed in *Lords' Journals*, v. 625.) *Copy.* [N. IX., 19.]

The PARLIAMENT to the KING.

1642[-3], March 1. (So dated but true date February 17.)—Petition that the Assizes be deferred. (Printed in *Lords' Journals*, v. 609.) *Draft.* [N. XII., 42.]

The KING to the QUEEN.

1642-3, March 2-12. Oxford.—(Partly quoted in Gardiner, *The Great Civil War*, i. 110, and printed *in extenso* by Mrs. Everett Green, *Letters of Henrietta Maria* p. 174, where Berwick and Chester are mistakes for Warwick and Sisseter, *i.e.* Cirencester. Subjoined are the parts in cipher deciphered.

```
            (I)    (am)
" now the King is  m    a    k    i    n    g         all    t    h    e
  h 3 :  189  : e 3 : 42 : 17 : 25 : 27 : 39 : 21 : 66 : a 1 : 45 : 31 : 7 : 4 :
            (I)
     h    a    s    t    e    he may  t    o        s    e    u    d    m    y
  32 : 18 : 47 : 46 : 9 : 3 : d 4 : g 4 : 46 : 35 : 67 : 48 : 7 : 40 : 5 : 43 : 74 :
     n    e    p    h    e    u    R    u    p    e    r    t         t    o
  3 : 41 : 7 : 33 : 62 : 8 : 63 : 68 : 50 : 64 : 34 : 9 : 51 : 45  : 69 : 46 : 37 :
          t    h    e         p    a    s    s    a    g    e
  cleere 45 : 31 : 7 : 1 : 33 : 18 : 49 : 47 : 19 : 21 : 10 : 70 :
  b    e    t    w    e    e    n    e         and    York
  13 : 7 : 45 : 58 : 8 : 9 : 41 : 10 : this  a 2 :  324 : in the meane tyme
  t    h    e    r    is    a         d    e    s    y    n    e
  46 : 31 : 7 : 50 : e 3 : 20 : 3 : 6 : 8 : 48 : 75 : 41 : 9 : 2 : upon
  W    a    r    w    i    k    e         c    a    s    t    e    l
  60 : 19 : 50 : 61 : 27 : 26 : 7 : 69 : 12 : 19 : 47 : 45 : 8 : 24 . . . .
                                                        (me)
  Will:Murray doth w   r    y    t    e    t    o     the King  t    o
      219  :  b 3 : 58 : 51 : 75 : 46 : 7 : 3 : 45 : 37 : 2 :  189  : 46 : 38 :
      make Hamilton duke                            but    I
  1 : g 1 :   173   : 131 : which I thinke fit to be done  a 5 : 4 : 30 : 3 :
  would    have  t    h    e    e    h    a    v    e    t    h    e
  n 5 : d 3 : 46 : 31 : 8 : 10 : 2 : 32 : 18 : 64 : 7 : 3 : 45 : 31 : 9 : 66 :
  t    h    a    n    k    s    of    it         doth*
  46 : 32 : 19 : 41 : 25 : 48 : k 1 : e 4 : 67 : 69 : b3 : I am now confident
      Hamilton
  that    173   : is now right for my service.") *Holograph.* [N. I., 12.]
  N. XII., 50 is a copy.
```

ENDYMION PORTER to [the EARL OF NEWCASTLE].

1642[-3], March 2. Oxford.—" I beseech your Lordship not to wonder at this tattered Mercury . . . for we have had such ill-luck in our cavaliers, as we thought this way the best to secure letters . . .

---

* *Sic* in original, but probably a mistake for b5 = for.

I am extreme glad that the Queen is safe arrived at York, and now I hope your Lordship will not suffer Tadcaster to be fortified nor the rebels to domineer as they have done . . . I have long wished to place my wife in the Queen's bedchamber, I beseech your Lordship to do in it as you shall think best and oblige me according your accus-tomed goodness. I have sent your Lordship the Queen's letter here inclosed and with it a copy of excellent verses." [N. II, 165.]

(These letters were intercepted at Coventry (See *Commons' Journals,* ii. 997); the Queen's is the preceding.)

Captain JOHN HOTHAM to the EARL OF NEWCASTLE.

1642[-3], March 2. Beverley.—"There shall nothing that may any-way accommodate the Queen, receive the least impediment from me. If you please that any may be sent to Hull, the cellars shall all be open to them, and for the way of conveying it, if I may know how you intend it I shall give it all the furtherance I can. For Sir William Fairfax, although there be some truth in wine, yet it is not all truth. There was something in your last letter that something troubled me, which was some doubt that promise would not be kept upon the cessation. If you mean it of me, then am I very unhappy to suffer so much in your opinion which I so much value, for I confess I value my word above all [be]sides. I am very sorry to hear that your Lordship hath any intention to make this poor country the seat of war. I am sure the clamours of all our friends and neighbours undone by it will make us ashamed to be seen with those that are the actors in it . . . These counsels may get your soldiers pillages, yourself neither friends nor strength. I know well the fountain of these violent counsels, and am sure all his friends that was led to it sunk under the burthen. For myself and friends nothing can be of that bad consequence to us, as the utter ruin of all our friends tenants and neighbours, we can then be no worse, we are fitted for desperation. This is all submitted to your deep judgement." *Seal.* [N. II., 163.]

THOMAS [LORD] GREY to WILLIAM LENTHALL.

1642[-3], March 2. Northampton.—Sent with Mr. Henry Noell, second son to Lord Camden, and Mr. Henry Skipwith. (See *Commons' Journals,* ii. 989.) "I drew some troops and dragoons into " Rutland "and came to Lord Camden's house, where I stayed. There was great store of arms and ammunition, but it was removed a little before my coming. His Lordship was also gone from thence and his eldest son was then in Newark, where he still remains. Afterwards I marched to Mr. Henry Noell's house in North Luffenham, where" he "and Mr. Henry Skipwith with about 200 men, 120 armed with guns and the rest with pikes and clubs stood upon their guard At my first coming thither I sent a trumpeter to Mr. Noell to demand his person arms and horses who returned me answer, that he would stand on his defence while he had breath. Before I used any violence I sent to him the second time that the shedding of blood might be prevented. He sent me answer again, he would die before he would yield, and thereupon we had a skirmish about an hour and Mr. Catesby Lieutenant to one of my captains was shot from the house and died thereof. The next day a common soldier was shot dead, and some others hurt, but afterwards. the house being shot through, they called for quarter and yielded. and then I entered the house and seized Mr. Noell and his arms and Mr. Skipwith . . . With much difficulty I preserved their lives. but the soldiers were so enraged I could not save their goods." (See

Lords' Journals, v. 641, and 5th *Report of the Historical MSS. Commission*, p. 76.) *Seal.* [N. II., 162.]

PRINCE RUPERT to the EARL OF NORTHAMPTON at Banbury.

1642[-3], March 2. Oxford.—

And

The SAME to the SAME.

1642[-3], March 3. 12 at night. Oxford.—Concerning the design on Warwick Castle. (Both printed in *King's Pamphlets*, E. 102, No. 6. p. 74.) [N. XII., 43.]

SIR GEORGE CHUDLEIGH and four others to the COMMITTEE OF LORDS AND COMMONS FOR THE SAFETY OF THE KINGDOM.

1642[-3], March 3. Plymouth.—"The great blessing of God upon our late endeavours, hath rendered the undisciplined forces of this county manageable to defend it against a small invasion. But consisting chiefly of Trained Bands altogether incapable to follow our victory into Cornwall for many unanswerable reasons, as the case stands yet, therefore we have thought fit to accept of our enemy's importunity for a treaty, hoping to increase our volunteers, and to get supplies for our trained soldiers, whose affections to their families and husbandry carry them from us daily in very great numbers with their arms." We ask for arms and power to use Martial Law. (See *Commons' Journals*, ii. 991.) *Signed. Seal.* [N. II., 164.]

The Commissioners of CORNWALL and DEVON.

1642[-3], March 4.—Protestation. Two *Copies.* [N. XIII., 121 and 141*a.*]

The Commissioners of CORNWALL to those of DEVON.

Same date.—Eleven Articles propounded. [N. XIII., 122.]

The Commissioners of DEVON to those of CORNWALL.

Same date.—Six propositions propounded. [N. XIII., 123.]

The SAME to the SAME.

1642[-3], March 7.—Answer to their articles. [N. XIII., 123.]

The Commissioners of CORNWALL to those of DEVON.

Same date.—Answer to their propositions. [N. XIII., 123.]

The Commissioners of DEVON to those of CORNWALL.

1642[-3], March 8.—Reply to the answer of Cornwall. [N. XIII., 123.]

The Commissioners of CORNWALL to those of DEVON.

Same date.—Reply to the answer of Devon. [N. XIII., 124.]

The Commissioners of CORNWALL and those of DEVON.

Same date.—New Proposition of Cornwall and Answer of Devon.

The Commissioners of CORNWALL to those of DEVON.

[1642-3, March.]—Propositions of peace offered. [N. XIII., 125.]

The SAME to the SAME.

[1642-3, March.]—Answer to their Answer. [N. XIII., 126.]
(All these are copies. The Protestation is printed in Clarendon, vi.
§ 254, and it and the first five papers are printed in *King's Pamphlets,*
E. 94, No. 21.)

ENGAGEMENT

[1642-3, March.]—To be taken by the Commander of the Parliamentary forces in Devon not to advance into Cornwall, Somerset or Dorset
during the proceedings on the intended treaty and for three days after
their termination. *Copy* of a *Draft.* [N. XIII., 126.]

GR. PARK, Mayor, to the COMMITTEE OF LORDS AND COMMONS FOR THE
SAFETY OF THE KINGDOM.

1642[-3], March 8. Exeter.—" On Monday last the first cessation
for seven days expired, and then another for 20 days more concluded on,
and solemnly ratified and confirmed on each side by the reception of the
Blessed Sacrament. All things proceeded very well . . . but unexpectedly this instant came to my hands a letter from Plymouth dated
there this morning, by which I am certainly informed that yesterday on
the meeting of the treaters . . . the Cornish made new propositions
on their part, which hinders the proceedings of the treaty. In brief it
is this ; that the cessation shall be a stand still, but no removal out of
either county, so that Somerset and Dorset in case of danger cannot be
assisted. The consideration of the disbanding of the most part of our
forces the day before caused the treaters of our side to harken unto
them, and yield further to the Cornish, that a pacification for the four
counties of Somerset, Dorset, Devon, and Cornwall be endeavoured, and
an association made not to invade each other, but mutually to defend
each other against all forces whatsoever. To this end letters are sent
both by the Cornish and our treaters into Somerset and Dorset, and the
meeting concerning this business appointed to be here in Exeter Tuesday
next " being the 14th instant. (See *Commons' Journals,* ii. 998.) [N. II.,
166.]

THOMAS GEWEN, CHARLES VAUGHAN, TRISTRAM ARSCOTT, and
THOMAS BOONE, to FRANCIS ROUS and EDMOND PRIDEAUX.

1642[-3], March 9. Exeter.— . . . " Our County was almost
lost till their—Sir Ralph Hopton and his complices—retreat from
Exeter. The . . . . Earl of Stamford being a stranger in these
parts was soon waited on by a considerable army of the trained and
others to the number of 13,000 or 14,000 ; so well charging and scattering the enemy at Modbury that our greatest and worthiest gentry there
acknowledged their valour and resolution such as they might hereafter
well trust as of men willing to fight and spirited to the work. Yet
when the enemy fled in a small number from thence and from about
Plymouth unto Tavistock in a very weak and undone condition, where
without effusion of more blood . . . . the work might have been
finished for these parts . . . . there fell in—God knows how—a
treaty of cessation first for six or seven days and then renewed for 20 or
21 more. All the most certain information we have is that the
Cavaliers in Cornwall do still fortify themselves and prepare for us,
expecting—as is reported—further accesses of strength from Wales or
elsewhere. . . . We hear confidently spoken that this cessation
was not approved by our said Lord General nor by the chiefest of our
Deputy Lieutenants, and we are sure that some of them consented net.

. . . . The general dislike that we find both in city and county of
this cessation assures us that there is a strong party that will readily
observe the orders of the Parliament to the uttermost of their lives and
fortunes." (See *Commons' Journals*, ii. 998.) *Signed. Seal.* [N. II.,
167.]

RICHARD SAUNDERS and others to JOHN PYM.

1642[-3], March 9. Exeter.—Acknowledging the care of Parliament for the city and in particular "that late timely provision for
disappointing the Assize . . . . which had it not been prevented
had occasioned great jealousies what the issue might have been of so
great a concourse of people diversely affected. Now so it is that there
being a cessation of arms agreed upon for 20 days more between
the Commissioners of Devon and Cornwall, and during the said time a
treaty, the same is appointed . . . . to be held here . . . .
where . . . . the Commissioners aforesaid with Sir Ralph Hopton
and divers other gentlemen of Somerset and Dorset-shire are appointed
to meet on Tuesday next about an Association, as we are informed, but
of what nature we know not. We therefore considering how much the
safety of this city may be herein concerned in regard of the considerable
number of Malignant inhabitants; with the unavoidable concourse of
many people diversely affected likely to be in this city at that time
—whatsoever provision by fore-agreement be made to the contrary notwithstanding—and the daring, violent, and desperate spirits of the
prisoners within us, wherewith two prisons are full—some being men of
very dangerous considerableness—" desire you to represent the sum of
this to the House that we may receive such order as they may
think fit. (See *Commons' Journals*, ii. 998.) *Signed. Seal.* [N. II.,
168.]

SIR JOHN HOTHAM to WILLIAM LENTHALL.

1642[-3], March 9. Hull.—Thanking the House for voting 6,000*l.*
for the garrison and observing that unless he has it quickly he is no
whit the better. "Tomorrow being Saturday I shall make some shift
to pay, then either I must billet upon the town or the soldier must not
eat. . . . . The Queen is at York. The enemy keeps still the
passes at Stamford Bridge and Malton to pass into this East Riding at
their pleasure. We have at Beverley about 900 horse and foot, much
too weak if the enemy fall on to make good that town. They have
plundered all where they come, but above all Sir William Strickland,
and two near kinsmen of his. Sir William hath lost above 4,000*l.* in
his goods and all his evidence seized upon." (See *Commons' Journals*,
ii. 1000.) *Seal.* [N. II., 169.]

SIR JOHN HOTHAM to WILLIAM LENTHALL.

1642[-3], March 11. Hull.—Enclosing a packet of intercepted letters
from the Low Countries to Mr. Jermyn, and again pressing for money
to pay his soldiers. "My credit you have broke by not paying those
small sums my necessity here forced me for your service to take up."
Seal. [N. II., 170.]

The HOUSE OF COMMONS to the MAYOR and DEPUTY LIEUTENANTS OF EXETER.

1642[-3], March 11.—Forbidding them to admit Sir Ralph Hopton
or any of his adherents into Exeter. (See *Commons' Journals*, ii. 999.)
Draft. [N. XII., 49.]

RICHARD ALDWORTH, Mayor, to WILLIAM LENTHALL.

1642[-3], March 13. Bristol.—Desiring payment of 568*l.* 11*s.* expended by him for billetting and transporting Lord Kerry's regiment and of 400*l.* for the relief of Duncannon Castle, and stating that owing to the large sums the City had expended on works and ammunition and the 3,000*l.* lent on the Public Faith they were unable to advance the 2,000*l.* now demanded by Sir William Waller and also to supply Colonel Fiennes' necessary occasions for their own defence. *Signed. Seal.* [N. II., 174.]

SIR GEORGE GRESLEY, THOMAS GELL and NATHANIEL HALLOWES to WILLIAM LENTHALL.

1642[-3], March 13. Derby.—(For the substance of most of this letter see *Commons' Journals,* iii. 5.) This business is "when our Colonel Sir John Gell upon the sad occasion of the unhappy death of that noble Lord Brooke was sent for post to Lichfield to settle those then almost distracted soldiers, where yet the necessity of that service continues him, and though by his being there those soldiers were continned together and that town and divers prisoners—some of great quality—taken, yet those men would hence take an occasion to thrust him and all his forces out of this county." *Signed.* [N. II., 171.]

EDMOND PRIDEAUX and ANTHONY NICOLL to WILLIAM LENTHALL.

1642[-3], March 15. Exeter.—We arrived on Monday night, and gave your commands to the Mayor not to admit any of the Cornish that were to treat or any other that had borne arms against the Parliament into the city. He willingly obeyed and the next morning some of them, who came to the gates, were denied admittance and sent away under a convoy to an inn in a neighbouring village. The letter from the Earl of Stamford with the enclosed papers will give you a clear account of their full proceedings, of the Articles whereon they treated and of their reasons for undertaking it, and will show the advantage they hope to gain by it. Of those expected from Somerset and Dorset only Sir Thomas Trenchard, Mr. Browne and Mr. Fitz-james came, the rest were dispersed by Sir William Waller's forces. From Somerset there was none appearance of any. We find some difficulties punctually at present to observe your instructions, and presume we may claim a little liberty for the time and manner of putting them in execution. (See *Commons' Journals,* iii. 8, 11.) *Signed. Seal.* [N. II., 171*b.* Omitted in Index.]

The EARL OF WARWICK to MILES CORBETT.

1642[-3], March 16. Chatham —Concerning a warrant for staying certain horses and money pretended to be the Duke of Vendosme's, but which came from Somerset House from the friars. (See *Commons' Journals,* iii. 4.) *Seal.* [N. II., 172.]

[SIR JOHN HOTHAM] to WILLIAM LENTHALL.

1642[-3], March 17. Hull.—I shall do my best for the relief of Mr. Bastwick and Captain Ludlow, and shall send today a trumpeter to offer any two officers we have in exchange for them. They have heretofore insisted on the release of Commissary Windam for them, which I cannot agree to, as he is such a man that they have few like him. I enclose extracts of "two letters written to two merchants in this town of good quality from Hamburgh. If there be any danger from the Dane it will be needful we should be well provided here. I have written divers times for some ordnance . . . but yet can get none. I wrote this the rather, because a member of your House told a a shipmaster of this town that if they had not ordnance it was the governor's fault, for it was denied to no town in England. I hope yourself and divers of the House will witness it was not my fault and indeed we stand in great need of them. I wrote concerning the billetting of the soldiers . . . we think if the soldier have no money to buy meat he must eat somewhere, and that this town that now enjoys so much safety and trade may very well not think much for the billetting of so few soldiers for some time, till the House shall find fit to satisfy for it. The poor town of Beverley upon a single motion from myself and my [son] yielded to billet almost as many of our forces there till we can repay them out of an assessment we have laid in the East Riding for the subsistence of the forces we have abroad. The other day, divers Papists, as I have heard, made suit to my Lord of Newcastle to be employed to pillage a little house and   of mine, which accordingly they did and took away all my breed of horses and   that I had there, but in their return Sir Hugh Cholmeley with his troop of horse and dragoons charged them very gallantly, broke their horse all to pieces, killed divers, took prisoners " divers officers " who are now coming by water from Scarborough to Hull as prisoners. What I have lost in this business I know not, but I shall do my best, that upon these Papists I light they shall neither carry it to heaven or hell." (Parts torn and lost.) (See *Commons' Journals*, iii. 10.) [N. II., 173.] Probably *Enclosed:*

—— to ——

1642[-3], February 21. Hamburgh.—" Great preparations are made by his Majesty of Denmark both by sea and land. By report 20 sail . . is or very speedily will be ready. For my part I know not the design . . . We have it here for certain reported that" he " took up at the last Steel Mart 150,000 dollars at interest." *Extract.* [N. XIII., 120.]

ARTICLES OF CESSATION.

[1642-3, March 17.]—(Printed in *Lords' Journals*, v. 653 and Rushworth, iii. 2. 174.) Two *copies.* [N. XIII., 203 and 208.]

The PARLIAMENT to the COMMITTEES APPOINTED TO TREAT WITH THE KING.

1642[-3], March 18.—Instructions. (Printed in Rushworth, iii. 2. 175.) [N. XV., 169.]

The EARL OF ESSEX to WILLIAM STRODE.

1642[-3], March 18. Windsor.—Supporting Sir Hugh Pollard's petition to be released on bail. (See *Commons' Journals*, iii. 9.) *Signed.* [N. II., 175.]

SIR EDWARD BOYS to the COMMITTEE OF LORDS AND COMMONS FOR THE SAFETY OF THE KINGDOM.

1642[-3], March 21. Dover Castle.—Sending up a Scotch gentleman and a Frenchman, desiring money to build the wall of the Castle which is lately fallen, and to pay his soldiers, and asking what he is to pay his minister. *Signed. Seal.* [N. II., 176.]

Captain JOHN HOTHAM to [the EARL OF NEWCASTLE].

1642[-3], March 22. Hull.--"I have sent this other letter to excuse me for not granting Sir Marmaduke Langdale a safe conduct, and to deal freely with your Lordship he shall never have one from me, nor do I care to treat with him, I know him too well. For a letter to the Queen, that I will certainly come in and at such a time, I cannot do it. This enclosed you may show her, if you please, or else burn, for your Lordship knows that I ever said unto you that I would do anything which might further his Majesty's service in the peace of the kingdom, and that if the Parliament did stand upon unreasonable terms with him, I would then declare myself against them and for him, but otherwise to leave my party that I had set up with, and no real cause given that an honest man may justify himself for so doing before God and the world I never would do it, although I endured all the extremities in the world, for I well know no man of honour or worth will ever think such a man worthy of friendship or trust. For the prejudice you undergo for not spoiling the East Riding truly you have put an obligation upon me by sparing it thus long, but rather than your Lordship shall suffer anything of prejudice either in your honour or affairs I shall not desire the thing any longer, but you may take what course you please and we shall do so for our defence. For Sir Hugh Cholmley and his manner of coming in every man must satisfy his own conscience and then all is well, all are not of one mind. . . . If it please God that we ever join and that I be thought worthy your friendship, it shall be seen you have got a friend that will not leave you for every wind or hope or fear. . . We shall now soon see whether the King will be refused just things, which if he be, I shall take no long time to resolve. If the Parliament offer all fairness and it be obstinately refused truly I will not forsake them, come the worst that can come, for this I conceive is just and honest and from that ground it is not fit for him that values his honour to secede. For my Lord Fairfax I do not think Nevill will speed, for he cannot offer him to be so well as he is, and sure fear will never do it. . . I know your worth so great that you will not value less for his plain dealing your most humble affectionate servant. *Postscript.*—For my Lord of Dunbar's son he is delivered as a prisoner to the Mayor's prison for entertaining a priest, and so I cannot yet release him." [N. II., 177.]

Captain JOHN HOTHAM to the EARL OF NEWCASTLE.

1642[-3], March 22. Hull.—"I shall desire you to excuse me that I cannot grant a safe conduct to Sir Marmaduke Langdale, for I am sure his last coming to Malton set people's tongues too much at liberty. Besides if he should be admitted hither all the country hereabouts, that thinks he hath been the cause of their suffering, would all say that their suspicions are now grown certainties, seeing Sir Marmaduke Langdale admitted but within the walls of Hull. . . . *Postscript.*— And for the business it will be better done without such a meeting." *Seal.* [N. II., 178.]

SIR WILLIAM WALLER to the EARL OF ESSEX.

1642[-3], March 23. Malmesbury.—Describing his capture of the town. (Printed in *King's Pamphlets*, E. 94. No. 12.) [N. II., 179.]

FRANCIS PIERREPONT and others to GILBERT HOLLINGTON.

1642[-3], March 24. Nottingham.—Asking liberty for Captain Harold Scrimpshire or his lieutenant to transport 160 muskets. (See *Commons' Journals*, iii. 22.) *Signed.* [N. II., 180.]

EDMOND PRIDEAUX and ANTHONY NICOLL to WILLIAM LENTHALL.

1642[-3], March 21. Plymouth.—We came here today from Exeter. "On Friday last those of Cornwall departed from the place of their meeting near Exeter, having agreed with the Commissioners of Devon for a further . . cessation for ten days, which was done, as they affirm by the advice of the general here and of others very well affected to the . . Parliament. We having nothing from you in command concerning that particular, and we having made known your pleasure touching the treaty they adjourned the further proceedings on it until Wednesday last, and the place of meeting to be near Plymouth, hoping before that time to have received your full directions . . but those not coming they repaired hither according to their agreement, where we hear not of any progress they have made in that treaty, neither can we believe it be like to take any good effect . . For what preparations are making in Cornwall we cannot give you any certain account, reports being very various and doubtful. But for our preparations in Devon we wrote you in our last that the Council of War had resolved to raise three regiments, which we can now assure you is in a good forwardness of doing." *Signed. Seal.* [N. II., 181.]

SIR EDWARD AYSCOGHE and THOMAS GRANTHAM to WILLIAM LENTHALL.

1642[-3], March 24. Lincoln.—Desiring the assistance of certain gentlemen. (See *Commons' Journals*, ii. 20.) Grantham was "lately taken by the enemy, in which we had placed 300 or 400 foot for the sole preservation of that part of the country from ruin and desolation. If this county be not thought so considerable as to send us down some assistance, who these three months and more have undergone the sole care, never having received from you the least aid either in moneys arms or ammunition, which hath been very chargeable unto us, we shall humbly make our request, that you will please to recall us to the service of the House, and not make your commands a punishment to us, who by God's mercy, have hitherto helped to preserve this country from evident ruin, and shall still continue our endeavours, if we may receive encouragement from you in this particular, as also in the speedy furnishing the 2,000*l.* so long ordered for us and Nottinghamshire to supply us with arms." *Signed.* [N. II., 182.]

The PARLIAMENT.

1642[-3], March 24.—Votes concerning the Cessation. (Printed in *Lords' Journals*, v. 668.) [N. XIII., 53.]

The PARLIAMENT to the KING.

1642[-3], March 24.—Consenting to treat, though a Cessation had not yet been agreed on. (Printed in *Lords' Journals*, v. 668.) [N. XXII., 69.]

The EARL of ESSEX to JOHN PLATT, Cornet in Captain Baynard's troop.

1642[-3], March 24.—Warrant to seize in Kent forty horses of Papists and Malignants for mounting his troop. *Signed.* [N. XIII., 127.]

The KING's answers and the COMMITTEE's replies.

[1643, March 26—April 15.]—Touching the Revenue, Magazines, Towns and Forts, Disbanding, Ships, and Oaths. (This paper is a summary in a tabular form of the papers printed in Rushworth, iii. 2. 195–259, some of which are also printed in *Lords' Journals*, v. 688, 689, 699–703, vi. 5–7.) [N. XIII., 204.]

WILLIAM PIERREPONT, SIR WILLIAM ARMYNE, and SIR JOHN HOLLAND to WILLIAM LENTHALL.

1643, March 26, one o'clock in the night. Oxford.—(A duplicate of the Earl of Northumberland's letter to the Speaker of the House of Peers, printed in *Lords' Journals*, v. 677, with this additional Postscript, " We moved his Majesty for a safe-conduct for the messengers named in your instructions. Mr. Secretary Nicholas gave us one for Mr. Michael Welden, which we have sent you here inclosed, and will get safe-conducts for the rest as soon as we can." The whole letter is printed in Grey, iii. 35, and iii. Appendix, No. 1, p. 1.) *Signed. Seal.* [N. III., 1.]

Captain ROBERT MOULTON to the COMMITTEE FOR THE NAVY.

1643, March 27. Portsmouth.—Concerning the condition of the ships there, the completion of whose fitting out is delayed from want of carriages which I desire may be speedily supplied. On the 24th I went to Southampton and gave the Mayor notice I came to press some men and required his assistance, but he refused, and told me we could not press any and farther that he had received proclamations from his Majesty to the contrary, which he showed me, four in number, dated the 6th, 6th, 7th and 8th of March. He said he would proclaim them, if the sheriffs came. In my opinion he is a dangerous man to govern that town. Arrivals of merchant ships from St. Lucar, and Majorca are mentioned. *Signed. Seal.* [N. III., 2.]

The PLOT for surrendering BRISTOL.

1643, March 27, April 10, 7, 24, 12, 21, March 10, April 27, May 3, April 28, 21, May 8, April 24, 27, May 27, April 28, May 3, 5. Bristol.—Examinations of Edward Hungerford, Jacob Brent, Thomas Stephens, Richard Luckett, Edmund Dakers, Francis Belcher, Tobias Goodyeare, John Pester (two copies), Nathaniel Streete, George Bowcher (four), John Bowcher, James Sterry, John Cary, William Pope, Captain Jeremy Buck, Moses Longman and Robert Hawkesworth, Griffen Batten, John Peverell, Edward Taylor, William Evans, Nathaniel Blanche, James Host, John Birkin, Thomas Browne, George Teague (three), Robert Yeamans (two copies), Thomas Hitchcock, Edward Hunt, William Reed, Edward Blinman, and William Haynes concerning the said Plot for surrendering the city to Prince Rupert. (The most important of these are printed in *King's Pamphlets*, E. 104, Number 4.) *Copies.* [N. XIII., 151 and 155–171 and 190]

PROCLAMATION.

[1642-3, March.]—" All inhabitants of the Bridge, the High Street, and Corn Street keep within your doors at peril of your lives. All other inhabitants of this City that stand for the King, the Protestant Religion and the liberties of this City let them forthwith appear at the High Cross with such arms as they have for the defence of their lives, their wives, and children, and follow their leaders for the same defence " *Copy* in the same hand as some of the above examinations. [N. XIII., 210.]

The Earl of Manchester, Speaker of the House of Peers, to the Earl of Northumberland.

1643, March 27.—(Printed in Rushworth, iii. 2. 181.)   *Copy.* [N. XII., 51.]

The Parliament.

[1643, March 27.]—Reasons concerning the Cessation. (Apparently a draft of the paper printed in *Lords' Journals*, v. 673, and Rushworth, iii. 2. 182, with some verbal differences   Also the last two clauses, and the end of the preceding one are omitted.) [N. XIII., 206.]

The Parliament to the Commissioners.

1643, March 27.—(Printed in Rushworth, iii. 2. 181, where it is misdated the 29th.) [N. XIII., 147.]

The King to the Mayor and Corporation of Weymouth.

1643, March 28. Oxford.—Requiring them to supply his forces and subjects in the Isle of Portland. (See *Commons' Journals*, iii. 37.) *Sign Manual.* [N. XIII., 153.]

The House of Commons.

1643, March 28.—Order for Sir William Brereton to satisfy his losses out of the estates of Sir Edward Fitton and Thomas Leigh. (See *Commons' Journals*, iii. 22.)   *Draft.* [N. XIII., 143.]

The Earl of Northumberland to the Speaker of the House of Peers.

1643, March 28. Oxford.—(Printed in *Lords' Journals*, v. 680.) *Signed.* [N. III., 3.]

William Pierrepont, Sir William Armyne, Sir John Holland and Bulstrode Whitelocke to William Lenthall.

1643, March 28. Oxford.—(A duplicate of the last.)   *Signed. Seals.* [N. III., 4.]

Papers relative to the King's Magazines.

1643, March 28 and 29.—(Bring those numbered, 3, 4, 5, and 6 in *Lords' Journals*, v. 688 and printed on the next page and in Rushworth, iii. 2. 198.)   *Copies.* [N. XIII., 145.]

Paper concerning the Cessation.

1643, March 29.—(Printed in Rushworth, iii. 2. 185.)   *Original* signed by the five Commissioners. [N. XIII., 146.]

William Pierrepont, Sir William Armyne, Sir John Holland and Bulstrode Whitelocke to William Lenthall.

1643, March 29. Oxford.—(A duplicate of the Earl of Northumberland's letter printed in *Lords' Journals*, v. 682, except that for " the King's proposition " it reads "the King's first proposition.")   *Signed. Seal.* [N. III., 5.]

Captain JOHN HOTHAM to [the EARL OF NEWCASTLE].

1643, March 30. Beverley.—I thank you for your two letters " in that you are pleased soe favourably to interprett the actions of your servant, and if your Lordship knew my reall intentions you would be farre from blaming me. I confesse I am very tender of my honor, for I know itt is like a woman's honesty, not to be repayred if once toucht, and to forsake my party when I can say nothing for itt but to please my ambition or lightnesse is to me a terrible thing. I know you would not desire to see itt in any man you esteemed worthy your friendship, although for the present itt may disadvantage your affayres. You have gotton by Sir Hugh Cholmley's turning when he could give noe reason for itt but an old castle, which will cost you more keeping then it is worth, his captaynes and soldiers are all here and have left him naked enough, wee say not sixty men. Wee made bold to stay two shipps of his at Hull, the one six pcice of ordinance, the other bringing him good store of provisions from the Parlement. Wee talke confidently of peace, and now 1 shall entreat your Lordship to laugh as hartely att our valient captaynes of the West that have quitt all their strong quarters without a shott as ever they did att others ; hie talking and strong drinking is not that that kills Sconderbag. I confesse when I heard itt first I did not much marvell att itt, as some did, well knowing that if itt had not beene for some they had never shott shott att Tadcaster when you came first, but I shamed them into itt, but noe man is valienter then he should be, nor noe woman honester, soe sayes the proverbe. For the businesse you writt of Portington, itt was thus. Sir William Savill and Lockby mett him and bad him tell Sir John that they were infinitely his friends and wished the peace of the kingdome. His answere was he was theirs,' and if he understood from them any propositions that were honest and honorable conducing to that end he should be glad to heare them and doe any office he could for the publicke good, this was all and indeed he did this to see what would come of it and soe lett you know as soone as itt was worth itt. I had sent you notice of this before but that I must send you a little more for I have had an instrument from Sir Marmaduke with long perswasions of his good will and what great things I should have. I gave him many thanks but told I was in such a condition as needed nothing, and soe there is an end I thinke. 1 could write some of our Southern newes, first peace, next Sir William Waller hath gott a greate victory, and my Lord Northampton slayne, and Colonell Hastings prisonnier att Stafford, but I am grown to believe nothing because I thinke our masters of both sides feed us with such meat as they thinke fittest for us." [N. III., 6.]

The HOUSE OF COMMONS to the EARL OF KINGSTON.

1643, March 31.—Asking for the loan of 2,000l. (See *Commons' Journals*, iii. 25.) *Draft* or *Copy*. [N. XII., 52.]

The EARL OF NORTHUMBERLAND to the EARL OF MANCHESTER,
Speaker of the House of Peers.

Same date.—(The beginning is printed in *Lords' Journals*, v. 687. It proceeds thus)—" Upon the Treaty upon the first Proposition. His Majesty with his Council have sat constantly, forenoon and afternoon, about the Cessation. We attended him until it was late this evening, but could not come to a full resolution in it within the time. Many difficulties did arise upon the third Article about removal of Quarters, which we did not conceive ourselves enabled to resolve, however we might believe the intention of the Houses to be. We hope this business will speedily come to a conclusion, and that your Lordship will receive it on Monday." *Copy.* [N. XII., 53.]

The House of Commons to the Earl of Essex.

Same date.—Concerning the Surrey Assessments. (The purport appears from *Commons' Journals,* iii. 25.) *Draft.* [N. XII., 54.]

Four Papers concerning the Change of Quarters.

1643, March 31.—(Printed in *Lords" Journals,* v. 691, 692.) *Originals,* the first and third signed " Falkland," the second and fourth by the Parliament's Commissioners. [N. XIII., 148 and 152.]

The Inhabitants of Stratford Bow to the House of Commons.

[1642-3, March.]—Petition praying for the removal of their curate Mr. James Coniers. *Signed.* [N. XXII., 151.] *Annexed:*

Articles exhibited against him.

Charging him with frequenting taverns, " quarelling fighting and such like uncivil carriage," with not reading the Protestation or other Ordinances or declarations of the Parliament, and with railing against the Parliament. [N. XXII., 110.]

The King's Message concerning the Cessation.

1643, April 4.—(Printed in Rushworth, iii. 2. 186.) (*Copy,* signed by John Browne.) [N. XIII., 154.]

Sir William Parsons and Sir John Borlase, Lords Justices, and the Privy Council to William Lenthall.

1643, April 5. Dublin Castle.—Concerning the petition of John Moody, owner, and John Webb, Master of the *Love's Increase* of Bristol on behalf of themselves and their crew 13 in number. The ship being partly laden was commanded to bring provisions for the relief of Duncannon Fort, and was afterwards ordered by Lord Esmond to the river of Rosse, to operate against the rebels and to attend the directions of the Marquess of Ormonde, in which service the ship with her cargo was lost. The petitioners then joined the army and in the battle assisted about the ordnance, in which John Moody was wounded. They therefore ask for relief and recompense. We find their allegation true, and therefore recommend them to the House. *Signed. Seal.* [N. III., 7.]

The King's Answer.

[1643, April 9. Oxford.]—Concerning the Cessation. (Printed in *Lords' Journals,* v. 711, and in Rushworth, iii. 2. 192.) *Sign Manual.* [N. XIII., 193.]

Richard Aldworth, Mayor, to William Lenthall.

[1643, April 9. Bristol.]—Desiring repayment of the moneys advanced to him (for an account of which see the ordinance for repayment in *Commons' Journals,* iii. 128) and enclosing a letter from Lord Inchiquin. (See *Commons' Journals,* iii. 38.) [N. VIII., 130.]

The LORDS to the COMMONS.

[1643, April 13 or 14].—"Message that the Lords conceive it necessary to send the reasons of the two Houses . . . why they cannot agree unto the Propositions offered in the King's message of the 12th April.

To express in the answer now to be made unto His Majesty that the endeavours of both Houses have been and ever shall be to put an end to these unhappy differences so as our religion, laws, and liberties may be secured.

That they would appoint the Committee formerly appointed to meet with the Committee of Lords this afternoon to consider the whole message, and to prepare such an answer as they think fit to offer unto the two Houses." (See *Commons' Journals*, iii. 44.) [N. XV., 12.]

Colonel HERBERT MORLEY to WILLIAM LENTHALL.

1643, April 24. Lewes.—"About 3 weeks since the Earl of Thanet passed the seas into France. The barque that carried him belongs to one Hayne of Brighthelmstone, which I have made stay of till I receive your pleasure, for I conceive it no small crime to transport those that have made war against the Parliament without your warrant. Friday last a party of my horse took one of my Lord Mountague's servants, that was ready to take barque for France. About him they found divers letters and scandalous pamphlets against the Parliament. I opened some of the letters, but finding the enclosed directed to himself and his lady, I send them to you sealed as I found them. . . ." (See *Commons' Journals*, iii. 67.) *Seal.* [N. III., 9.] *Enclosed:*

G. SWYNDINDRIS to VISCOUNT MOUNTAGUE at Rouen.

1643, April 12.— . . ."My Lord and Lady and theirs are well and the stirring man in these parts is—as it said—hemmed in a castle near Ross, not far from Monmouth, by His Majesty's forces. The Queen is thought will shortly be at Oxford. The City of London in much distraction amongst themselves, strong-holds most free, and no travel without much danger, and in a word if I should go from hence today, I know not where [to] go tomorrow. Mr. Stan: Br: is gone to Oxford, and, as 'tis reported, listed himself in Mr. Bennett's regiment." *Seal.* [N. III., 8.]

——————— to ———————

[1643, April 27.]—"The cessation and fruitless endeavours of treatie for peace with the treacherous Cornish being ended on Saturday last, some of the forces of Devon upon intelligence of advantage which celerity might obtaine, entred Cornwall the last Lord's day, sate downe before Lanceston about 9 in the morning, made and maintayned a brave assault upon the enemy till 10 at night, but the werke proving more difficult then was supposed, by reason of fresh supplies which came in to them, our men having much annoyed the enemy by the killing of Captaine Bassett and some others of quality and a considerable number of common souldiers, made so brave and honorable a retreat that they brought off all their men, ammunicion, and guns safe, lost but a few common souldiers and those in the assault only, made good the passe after them, so as the enemy durst not advance over the bridge till such tyme as our men had left their quarters at Lifton, and were for the better recruiting of their forces marched at Okehampton on Munday.

After which tyme—to witt—on Tuesday the enemy entered Devon and
came within three or four miles of Okehampton ; which being knowne
to our forces, they presently drew out their horse to face them, and
gave order that the foote should follow to charge the enemy. In the
close of that day our horse mett the enemy, gave them a brave charge
thorough and thorough, put their horse and foote into confusion, slewe
divers of them, tooke one captaine, three colours, three drumms, many
prisoners and sundry armes, but night and foule weather came on, they
were not able to pursue their charge, nor keepe the field, the enemy
being five or six thousand as is supposed, and our forces not two
thousand. Whereupon order was given that they should retreate backe
to Okehampton that night to refresh themselves, and on the morrow
with our artillery marched towards Exon with their prisoners, which
was done accordingly so that it is suspected the enemy will shortly
endeavour to invade our county to make his way toward Oxon. We
for the present are not of like strength with the enemy, yet your
neighbours and friends will not be wanting to rise all the strength
they can to assault the enemy and hinder his comming to you, but
least (lest) they should not be able to doe what they desire, doe
become sollicitours to you to take the present state of things into
serious consult of which this is a true relation, and to provide yourselves to assist us here or to make the best stopp you can to their insolent
attempts to invade your county, and we shall not be wanting to fall on
with you to the uttermost of our strengths.

(*In a different hand.*)—This was one of the first and best relacions
wee then had and this is the copy ; the letter sent into Somersett.
The relacion concerneinge Lanceston is very true." [N. XV., 183.]

The MAYOR and other Captains of the Seven Companies raised in LONDONDERRY to the HOUSE OF COMMONS.

[1643, April.] (See *Commons' Journals*, iii. 65.)—Petition stating
that the Lords Justices and Council had formerly appointed the said
Mayor and Sir John Vaughan Governors of the forces in the City and
County of Londonderry and that the last named had lately died, and
praying that the Mayor for the time being and Captain Henry
Vaughan, brother of the deceased, might be appointed Governors of the
said forces. [N. XXII., 150.]

The PARLIAMENT to the STATES-GENERAL.

1643, May 2.—(Printed in *Lords' Journals*, vi. 27.) *Draft.*
[N. XVIII., 60.]

WALTER STRICKLAND to [WILLIAM LENTHALL]

1643, May 4-14. The Hague.—After referring to his two former
letters for an account of the exceptions taken by the States-General to
the order of the House of April 7th complaining that two ships had
come out of Dunkirk under the Prince of Orange's license to serve
against the Parliament.—The result of much debate and discussion was
an order delivered to me last week the day after the post was gone, the
substance whereof is that they have resolved to write to the Parliament,
and because the information as far as concerns the Prince of Orange is
false and scandalous, they will receive no other information from me
without another order or till they hear from the Parliament. You will
please read the enclosed order (of April 7th) itself. What they say is
false and untrue. I know not what it can be except that Parliament

never received any such information, for nothing else is affirmed by the order nor by me in the remonstrance, but only that Parliament was so informed. The question therefore is not whether the thing be so or no, but whether Parliament was so informed or no, and it seems to me a good resolute as well as a harsh affirmation that it is untrue that Parliament was so informed, for it lies not within the cognizance of those that affirm it. This is the issue between the House and them, but my condition, though judged worthy to be suspended from the service I had the honour to do the Parliament, is yet better. The House commanded me to tell the States what they are informed, which I did as near as I could changing English into French. My fault would have been unpardonable, if I had not believed they were so informed, and obeyed them, nor was their information derived from me. "If I be wounded it is through the sides of the Parliament. . . . I am confident they will maintain my reputation, without which I am incapable of serving them. . . . I desire the House will so far do me right as to justify what I have done by their order, for whatever is said of the Prince of Orange is literally within the order, and nothing but that is here affirmed to be untrue. Then my reputation being made good I submit myself to the House whether they please to continue my service here or employ it upon some other"; and in the former case entreat them "to give me such a commission as may make me taken notice of as their servant. . . . I wish nothing but to be furnished with wings if they expect I should fly, but however must expect their justification in what I did by their order concerning the Prince. . . . The States of Holland much opposed the suspending me and have protested against the order that the States-General have made as to that fact. . . . Some write from London that the Dunkirk ships contracted with to serve the King are forbidden by Don Melos to serve against the Parliament, that they will keep the neutrality. This is written from a good hand as it was told me. The Admiral of Holland suffered a Newcastle ship laden with arms to come out, because he produced the Queen's warrant, as he himself confesseth and writes to know what he shall do in like case hereafter. I knew not what will be concluded hereupon. A man of war of the Hollanders took a Dunkirk, who had formerly taken an Englishman of Yarmouth, and brought him into Rotterdam. The Dunkirk shows a warrant from the Irish. The matter is not yet judged by the Admiralty, but I think notwithstanding his Irish Commission it will be adjudged a good prize. . . ." [N. III., 13.]

The EARL OF ESSEX to Colonel HENRY MARTEN and WILLIAM STRODE.

1643, May 5. Reading.—Concerning Patrick Stretley. (See *Commons' Journals*, iii. 73.) *Signed. Seal.* [N. III., 10.]

DECLARATION of the PARLIAMENT.

[1643, May 6.]—On the breaking off of the Negotiations with the King. (Printed in "*The Proceedings in the late Treaty of Peace*," pp. 77–103, in *King's Pamphlets*, E. 102, Number 6.) Apparently the copy used by the Printer. [N. XIII., 200.]

Sergeant-Major ROSSE to SIR HUGH CHOLMLEY.

1643, May 8. York.—"My Lord of Abuyn was gone from York before my here coming. Wherefore I will intreat your Honour to have such a care of the ammunition appertaining to my Lord of Abyn as your Honour shall have of my Lord of Antrim's ammunition, till such time as I either come myself or write to your Honour, for Mr. German (Jermyn) he desired me to write this line to your Honour, for I am commanded to go for Scotland." (See *Commons' Journals*, iii. 86.) [N. III., 11.]

Articles of Impeachment against ROBERT YEAMANS, WILLIAM YEAMANS, JOHN BOWCHER, JOHN THROOPE, THOMAS MILWARD, JOHN WALDEN, RICHARD POUNDE, WILLIAM GREENE, Doctor ROBERT MARKS, THOMAS COLE, and EDMUND DAKERS. Sentence on ROBERT YEAMANS, and Sentence on all the others except EDMUND DAKERS.

1643, May 8. Bristol.—(The sentence on Yeamans is printed in Rushworth, iii. 2. 154. That on the others was pronounced in their absence. Both are undated.) *Copies.* [N. XIII., 173, 174, 175.]

[SIR] F.[RANCIS] W.[ILLOUGHBY ?] to ROBERT REYNOLDS and ROBERT GOODWIN.

1643, May 10. Dublin.—These "are from one who desires to enforme you of the truth of busines here about Dublin, and though perhaps I shal not be beleived because you knowe not from whome it comes, yet be assured it is from one who desires and prayes for the peace of England and for the reducinge of this miserable kingdome of Ireland to the true religion, to obedience to His Majesty and his lawes, and to the late estate wherein it began to flourish and prosper . . . .

"Our estate here is now growen so extreamely miserable, that we are as it weare breathinge out our last breath, I mean the Protestants and His Majesty's best subjects. I doubt not but you have heard of the seige of Ballinekill in the Queen's Countie, which hath bine most valiauntly defended for above a month by Capt. Ridgway; we heare now it is taken by the rebells but are not very certaine of it. Here in Dublin we were above three weekes in getting some litle provisions to set forth a partie of fifteen hundred men to releive Ballinekil, and upon Friday last they were sent thetherward but with such discontent some of the officers beinge committed for refusinge to goe, before they went, and others with such murmeringes for want of provisions that if they come thether time enough which I feare they wil not, the successe is much to be feared, and if they shold miscarry there were an end of us here in al humane reason ; there were five hundred men sent after them on Sunday last since which time we have not heard from them. Our soldiers that remaine here in Dublin and nere unto it though they be not so many by farr as I thinke you make account of, yet very many of them are naked men both horse and foote ; our horse that are left beinge very weake and pore and few ; both horse and foote wantinge armes and have not many of them so much as a sword. The pouder in our stoare at Dublin—as I credibly heare—growes to so smale a quantitie that none can be spared to send any partie abroade any more unless the citie shold be left utterly destitute. The ship with pouder and match, which was so long agoe agreed for by the state here with four of our merchants after it had bine longe deteined about Caleis and after discharged and which we have longe loked for and hoped to have had here with us before this time, is not yet come though for theis fourteen dayes last past we have had a constant easterly wind and now it is reported that it is stayed in England by some directions from London : and victuales here are so scarce and our provisions in the stoare houses· so emptied and the soldiers so longe maintained by the citie of Dublin that now there is scarse anythinge left eyther for the soldier or other inhabitant in the citie. And some of the English protestants who dwelt here, by the sessinge of soldiers upon them are growen so miserably pore that they are enforced to leave the citie and betake themselves to country houses there to seke releife for to kepe them alive or to perish by the hands of the rebells. The ship wherein Dr. Jones came brought us victualls for the soldiers in and about Dublin only, but for eight dayes; al the out garrisons wantinge al manner of victualls as wel as we : so that it cannot be reasonably conceived that we can hold out longe but must starve and dye or run away or else be subject to the mercie of the rebells for our lives and goods and yeild to them upon what conditions they please. The best of theis choises in theis times is miserable but the necessities that lyes upon us wil despite of our harts enforce us to some one of theis, unles it can be thought that we can live without meate or fight without pouder and other amunition and armes.

The factions and divisions betwene and amongst the officers of our armye is such that it is plainely perceived that more regard and labour is had to put disgraces and affronts one upon another than to save this perishing kingdome ; and which amongst other wil be none of the least causes of our present distruction. I wold I cold write of the agreement at our counsel board, but I cannot heare of it nor doe I believe that the undermininge one of another which in former times have bine amongst many who have made a faire profession of unitie is clearly taken away from them. I wold it were. •

It is talked of here likewise that we are diserted by the Parliament, and that although the Londoners lent or gave a hundred and fortie thousand pounds for to be employed for the releife of Ireland yet none of it is converted that way ; and great jealousyes are here that your selves are not so zealous for that service as you protested here you wold be, and some think the cause to be the unkinde usage you received when you were here. And because we shold want nothinge to helpe forward our miseries ; the Wexford pirates and as they say some from Dunkirke with them doe dayly take our barkes cominge out of England which wold hove given us some litle helpe and sustenance of foode if they cold come safely to us which because they cannot doe many of them wil not stir from home.

When I had written thus farr, newes is certainely come of the takinge of Ballinekil : it was surrendered up on Friday last beinge the day our armye went out of Dublin ; and that there are seven hundred of the pore English come from thence and are within three or four miles of Dublin : Preston makinge it part of his agreement that they shold al come directly for Dublin, which no doubt he did that we might the soner eate up one another, for here are already so many pore English that of necessitie many must starve, the inhabitants here beinge growen so extreamely pore that the English protestants cannot releive them and we are sure and so finde it that the papists wil not. It is reported here that Preston is gone to beseige the fort of Marriburrow in the Queenes County, and no doubt wil sone take in al our garrison places nere Dublin in a short time if he be not prevented which how it may be I feare passes al our skills to tel you. Where the partie of our men is that went to releive Ballinakil we certainely heare not, but the most judicious men of ours here hold that they are not able nor is it safe for them to fight with Preston who is above treble the number—better armed and now grown into hart and courage. Preston hath amongst his other

great pceccs a demycanon against which none of our castles can hold out.

Thus I have truly related to you such thinges as have lately happened amongst us; and the miseryes with which we are so grievously oppressed, and the great and imiment daungers which we and this kingdome are in; what the daungers are which may happen to England if we here be utterly lost your selves knowe wel. I humbly beseach almightie God to send his peace and truth amongst you in England and that his Majestie and the parliament may before Ireland and the protestants in it be utterly lost resolve of some spedy supplies to be sent to it, which if they please to doe in time—and not let it alone as amongst other thinges we have done our sendinge to releive Ballinekil—before it be lost certainly. If Ireland be reduced to his Majestie's obedience it may pay al the costs that shal be bestowed upon it with treble interest.

Postscript.—The pore people of Ballinekil are come to this city as it is reported that Preston shold say that within a fortnight he wold send a strong armye into England " . . (See *Commons' Journals*, iii. 8) *Seal.* [N. III., 15.]

[The LORDS JUSTICES OF IRELAND] to the KING.

1643, May 11. Dublin Castle.—(Printed in Rushworth, iii. 2. 538, and Clarendon, vii, § 336.) *Copy.* [N. XII., 55.]

* SIR JOHN HOTHA꜔ and others to WILLIAM LENTHALL.

1643, May 12. Lincoln.—Concerning Serjeant-Major Purefoy, the Governor. (See *Commons' Journals,* iii. 86.) *Signed. Seal.* [N. III., 12.]

—— to ——.

[1643], May 13. Rotterdam.—" The first despatch I made to you was drowned with the ship and all the Company at Scarborough. Since then I have sent Archbut whose return and your answer thereto is very much expected, and all business for want thereof [is] under a great prejudice and therefore [I] pray the particular answer with full directions may be immediately sent.

R o t t e r d a m
57 : 54 : 59 : 34 : 45 : 57 : 44 : 41 : 52 : have well resolved but fall off for want of power to conclude according to the conditions propounded, grow shy, and think they are abused, therefore you are to hasten the sending such a warrant as may give credit to me to negotiate according to the way propounded and expected.

H a s d o n k
48 : 41 : 58 : 44 : 54 : 53 : 5[0] [w]ent away from a 101 :* the 24th April for 138 : since which time I have not heard of him.

H i s o t h e r a r m e s c o m e s
48 : 49 : 58 : 54 : 59 : 48 : 45 : 57 : 41 : 57 : 52 : 45 : 58 : 43 : 54 : 52 : 45 : 58:
with a r m e s
6 : 157 : 41 : 57 : 52 : 45 : 58 : which willibe at 101 : within 6 days and is

L e g e A r
already past all the hazards from 51 : 49 : 45 : 47 : 45 : and hope 41 : 57 :

---

* *Note.*—101 probably = Dunkirk.

c   h   b   u   t

43 : 48 : 42 : 60 : 59 : will come time enough to a 101 : for the same.

S   r   I   o   h n M   a   i   n   e   e   by   to

33 : 32 : 49 : 54 : 48 : 53 : 52 : 41 : 49 : 53 : 45 : 19 : was sent 4 : 123 : 8 : P : for

           c   a   r   b   y   n   e   s   h   u   n

65 : 77 : 72 : 74 : 43 : 41 : 57 : 42 : 63 : 53 : 19 : 58 : and two 48 : 60 : 53 :

d   r   e   d   f   o   u   r

44 : 52 : 45 : 44 : 167 : 79 : so much as amounts to 46 : 54 : 61 : 57 : 163 :

           b   i   l   s

82 : which was returned by 42 : 49 : 51 : 58 : hither and in four days

     to C   h   e   s   t   e   r   t   h   i   t   h   e   r

goes 8 : 43 : 48 : 45 : 58 : 59 : 19 : 57 : and 59 : 48 : 49 : 59 : 48 : 19 : 32 :

r   o   u   n d S   c   o   t   l   a   n   d

57 : 54 : 60 : 53 : 44 : 58 : 43 : 54 : 59 : 51 : 41 : 53 : 44 : and that appointed

by

4 : 123 : which came hither 7 days since by the coson (?) and *bon moeurs*

              letters   T   h   i   r   t

of 123 : who was sent with kk to 172 : and is gone. 59 : 48 : 49 : 57 : 59 :

y   f   r   i   g   g   o   t   s   r   e   a   d   y

63 : 46 : 57 : 24 : 47 : 21 : 54 : 59 : 58 : at 101 : are 57 : 45 : 41 : 18 : 63 : to

s   e   r   v   e   f   o   r   p   a   y   o   r   letters

58 : 19 : 57 : 60 : 19 : 1 : 65 : 46 : 54 : 57 : 55 : 15 : 63 : 54 : 57 : kk :

of m   a   r   t   p   a   y   i   n   g   a   s   t   h   e   i

9 : 52 : 15 : 57 : 59 : 55 : 15 : 63 : 49 : 53 : 47 : 15 : 33 : 59 : 23 : 19 : 24 :

r

57 : 65 : the first way security must be given which will be best and may be done if you will give power to 147 : to do as he shall think best but out of those things that may be best spared, but then there must be letters   r   u   b

kk to 71 : and to 105 : to do as shall be desired by 147 : for the 57 : 60 : 42 :

y   c   o   l : [lar]

63 : 43 : 54 : 51 : and such other things as may be useful, and giving him power to manage that business there may be good service ex-

                              l   i   s   t

pected for it is promised; 71 : will not R g + d 51 : 49 : 58 : 59 : for

               p   a   y

141 : without present 55 : 41 : 63 : which he cannot as yet have hence but expects it according to promise: and will do nothing of kindness to accommodate the present necessity. What you would have done here must be done by special warrants, otherwise it will be disputed Mr. Stric[k]land about 20 days hence gives in a memorial to the States-General, the sense whereof was that the Parliament had appointed him to complain of the Prince of Orange for giving a license to two frigates of Dunkirk, part of the 24 there hired for the King's service to pass by the Holland's fleet being loaded with ammunition for his Majesty and with this a comment of his own sense. The Prince complained to the States of the injury done him hereby, whereby Strickland was examined by what warrant he did this Upon which he produced an order of the House of Commons only,—and his credentials were from both Houses,—authorising Mr. Pym to give him instructions herein which order was not under Elsyng's own hand, so after 7 days debate with the States-General and by the particular provinces it was ordered by the States-General by the approbation of the particular provinces that Strickland's information was false and scandalous to the Prince, and that they expected reparation should be given the Prince from the Parliament, and that Strickland was not hereafter to propose anything by writing or otherwise until the States

did further or otherwise resolve therein, so he is ordered from all business whatsoever. There is some dispute how this order shall be sent to Parliament by letter or messenger, but both will be wa[i]ved to prevent the inconveniency they may thereby run into by any application to them, so that I believe the order and declaration shall be given to Strickland and no otherwise, and if any other way then 105 : will interpose to steer it so as the King thereby shall not be omitted, but be observed as he ought in their proceedings. 86 : for so much as concerned 84 : would not consent to but would have him continued. It is understood here that 84 : hath sent for 41 : 47 : 45 : 53 : 59 : 58 : to 43 : 54 : 52 : 19 : _{a g e n t s c o m e}
for every 55 : 57 : 54 : 60 : 49 : 53 : 43 : 19 : 147 : resolves to observe the order _{p r o v i n c e}
of 123 : in sending as he hath appointed. 157 : and the 112 : of 48 : 41 : 58 : 18 : _{H a s d :}
comes from 101 : together. My last letters were so full of all things necessary for the business to be done as I only here remember you rather than inform. The ship is going and am allowed no more time otherwise I should enlarge these to give you a more full account of all particulars here. Only this know that if I do not better serve you than these inform, it is not my fault, but that I am not qualified with such power as may make my actions more legible than good intentions can. I am by debt as well as affection, Sir, your most humble and most faithful servant.

Postscript.—My Lady Stanhup brought to bed of a son Saturday morning last. Gossips not spoken of it. 105 : begs your excuse for not writing, being surprised for time. Sir William Boswell upon the rumour that was made of the King's hiring ships at Dunkirk sent to Sir H. Devyc, the resident at Brussels, to have him inquire out the occasion of that report, whose answer is shewed to the States, which was, there was no such thing, nor any ground for that. It was an invention framed for the disservice of the king, like that of the Danish fleet. The Parliament hath bought in Flanders 20,000*l.* worth of arms."
[N. VIII., 139.]

The EARL OF FORTH to the COMMANDER IN CHIEF and COUNCIL OF WAR AT BRISTOL.

1643, May 16. Oxford.—Concerning Mr. Yeomans and others.

And

NATHANIEL FIENNES and others to the EARL OF FORTH.

1643, May 18. Bristol.—Reply.

And

The KING to the MAYOR and CORPORATION OF BRISTOL.

1643, May 29. Oxford.—On the same business. (All printed in Rushworth, iii. 2. 154.) *Copies.* [N. XII., 56, 57, 59.]

The Collectors of the Weekly Assessment in ESSEX.

1643, May 17. Chelmsford.—Return of the sums paid. [N. XIII., 176.]

The HOUSE OF COMMONS.

1643, May 19.—Order appointing a Committee concerning the Great Seal, &c. (Printed in *Commons' Journals*, iii. 92.) *Copy.* [N. XIII., 177.]

Lord Falkland to the Earl of Manchester, Speaker of the House of Peers.

1643, May 19.—(Printed in *Lords' Journals*, vi. 57.) *Holograph.* *Seal.* [N. III., 14.]

List of the Prisoners taken at Wakefield.

1643, May 20.—(Printed in Rushworth, iii. 2. 271.) *Copy.* [N. XIII., 179.]

The Scotch Commissioners to the Parliament
and
The Reply of the Parliament.

1643, May 20, 25.—(Printed in *Lords' Journals*, v. 59, 63.) *Copies.* [N. XIX., 65.]

Information of David Lawes, Mariner.

1643, May 22. King's Lynn.—That sailing from Scotland the captain of a man of war lying before Tynemouth told him that he had taken three or four Danish ships and sent them into Hull, and that he had been told by Danes taken out of the said ships that a hundred sail were fitting in Denmark to convey 10,000 or 12,000 men to England, and that the captain desired him to send notice thereof to the Parliament as soon as he reached Lynn. [N. XIII., 172.]

The Earl of Essex to William Lenthall.

1643, May 22. Reading.—Enclosing a copy of the desires of the Committee for the Associated Counties of Essex, Hertford, Norfolk, Suffolk and Cambridge, which they desire may be drawn into an ordinance for the more due payment of the forces sent thence to the army, and hoping their request will be taken into consideration. *Signed.* *Seal.* [N. III., 16.]

Ferdinando [Lord] Fairfax to William Lenthall.

1643, May 23. Leeds.—(Printed in Rushworth, iii. 2. 269. On p. 270 after "fortify the town" should be added "and pillage and utterly ruin all the religious people in those parts round about them," and after "Otley" "and there barbarously used some honest women of that town.") *Copy.* [N. XII., 58.]

Thomas Stockdale to ——.

1643, May 23.—Concerning the taking of Wakefield and the new Commissions under the Great Seal. (Printed in *King's Pamphlets*, E. 104, No. 13, p. 11.) [N. XIII., 180.]

Richard Powney to — Lovell at Reading.

1643, May 23.—Requesting him to acquaint the Commissioners appointed by the Lord General that he had heard that day that the Parliament had made an order against any further proceedings in any such Commission. [N. III., 25.]

Sir Richard Everarde and Thomas Hayward to William Lenthall.

1643, May 25. Chelmsford.—Certifying that they had called the Collectors for the weekly Assessment with the Committees of the

several divisions before them, and inclosing a particular of what is
paid in by every collector. "The greatest fault we find to be in the
Sub-Collectors, which the several Committees have promised carefully
to rectify." *Signed. Seal.* [N. III., 17.]

The HOUSE OF COMMONS.

1643, May 27.—Orders concerning the victory at Wakefield and
Lord Fairfax, General Goring, and Mr. Stockdale's letter. (Printed
or substance given in *Commons' Journals*, iii. 106, 7). On the back are
short notes in Mr. Pym's hand, apparently for a speech on the subject
of the victory. [N. XIII., 178.]

The COUNCIL OF WAR AT BRISTOL.

1643, May 28.—Warrant committing Prince Rupert's trumpeter, who
had come with a letter to stir up the citizens against the garrison. *Copy.*
[N. XIII., 175a.]

SIR GILBERT GERRARD, SIR HENRY VANE, OLIVER ST. JOHN, and JOHN PYM to WILLIAM LENTHALL.

[1643, June 4.]—Desiring that the House of Lords might be moved
to give leave for some of that Committee to speak with the Lords
Portland and Conway as they see occasion. *Signed. Seal.* [N. VIII.,
128.]

SIR RICHARD SKEFFINGTON and others to WILLIAM LENTHALL.

1643, June 24. Coventry.—"We have information that the Queen's
forces are advancing. On Thursday they surrounded Nottingham, as
was supposed with 3,000 horse and four or five regiments of foot. Some
2,000 foot were in the town, which we hear have done some execution
on the Queen's party. It is believed that she is advancing for Oxford."
(See *Commons' Journals*, iii. 146.) *Signed. Seal.* [N. III., 18].

ARCHIBALD PRIMEROSE to Mr. WELDEN.

1643, June 28. Edinburgh.—The Convention of Estates orders
true copies of the depositions of the Earl of Antrim, Shane Dick, and
James Stuart his servants, and of the letters written by the Earls of
Nithsdale and Aboyne to the said Earl, which were found on him when
he was apprehended, to be delivered to Mr. Welden that he may
acquaint the Hous[e]s of Parliament with them. *Signed. Enclosed:*

  i. Proceedings of a COUNCIL OF WAR under the Presidency of
    General-Major Monroe.

  1643, May 24. Carrickfergus.—Shane Dick, servant to the Earl of
    Antrim was accused of being accessory to taking the said Earl
    out of the Castle of Carrickfergus, called the Lord Chichester's
    house, where he was confined, being suspected of the rebellion in
    Ireland, and also, being found at Newcastle in Down in the
    said Earl's company, of traffiquing with the rebels, and putting
    himself in open rebellion with them, as evidenced by letters
    found on him and the Earl of Antrim at the time of their taking,
    and also of abusing the General in purchasing his pass under
    his hand and seal, under colour whereof he conveyed under
    silence of night by sea the said Earl away. Being desired
    according to his oath to disburden his conscience before death
    of anything he knew of the plot of the said Earl and his

confederates against the kingdom of Scotland or the Scotch army in Ireland, he confessed that he knew several letters passed concerning these matters betwixt the said Earl and the Earls Nithsdale, Montrose, Aboyne and others. He was not himself the carrier of the messages. He knew that there was a barque with ammunition and other furniture of war to be direct North to Lord Aboyne, and the Earl of Antrim's friends in the Highlands and Isles of Scotland, and another barque with the like was to be direct to Carlisle to the Earl of Nithsdale and his confederates, but that he knew not who they were. The Earl of Antrim told him that he and his confederates were resolved to do all the mischief they could by arms against the kingdom of Scotland, and to overthrow the Scotch army in Ireland as far as they might, and then to bring all the forces they could out of Ireland to assist the King and the Catholic army in England against the Parliament. He was then removed and being recalled was told that, in regard of his confession of the points he was accused upon, the Council with one voice had adjudged him worthy of death and to be hanged exemplarily to others.

ii. Examination of the EARL OF ANTRIM.

1643, June 12. Carrickfergus. — Asked what was the point to be prosecuted by him and his confederates in Scotland, he answers, they had resolved to levy forces for his Majesty's service in England, and condescends particularly upon the Earl of Montrose, the Earls of Airlie, Nithsdale, Aboyne and such others as would partake with them. The ammunition to be sent to Lord Aboyne was to be disposed of by him for the use of the regiment to be levied in the Highlands and Isles for the Earl of Antrim as for the forces by Lord Aboyne himself to be joined to the Newcastle army, as the rest of the foresaid forces were intended. The ammunition was first stopt at York and thereafter his Lordship upon his word got it sent to Scarborough where it was when his Lordship came for Ireland. At the earnest desires of Lord Aboyne he interceded with her Majesty for getting the ammunition stopt by her Majesty's forces sent away. He declares for clearing the postscript of Aboyne's letter of the 8th of May that the Earl of Montrose was not to join with them but in a legal way. Being asked who was the party who knew from whom he expected the wreitt he declares it was meaned by Lord Montrose who would not join in the raising of the said regiments. Cormock O'Seale, the Irishman, was the man passed betwixt his Lordship and Nithsdale. The rest who were for his Majesty's service were Lord Aboyne, Airlie, Nithsdale and such other friends as they could command. He declares that the deposition of Shane Dick, who was hanged, is false. Being asked if his warrant was immediately to Owen McKart and Sir Philomy (Phelim O'Neill) at Charlemont, or if they had a warrant to his knowledge for what they did or for joining with his Lordship he answers nothing to this interrogatory, but denies he knew of it. Being asked by whose warrant his brother was sent to Ireland to Owen McKart and Sir Philomy he acknowledges he had his directions from him, and declares the only warrant he gave him was to assure him with what surety his Lordship could come to Charlemont or any other part in Ireland, and gave him directions to stay there till his coming. He declares that he came into Ireland with Lord Newcastle's pass and private instructions for making of peace, having Lord Newcastle's promise if his Lordship could draw them to easy conditions my Lord Newcastle was to procure to him the King's warrant for proceeding therein. Being asked what end he had in offering 5,000*l*. sterling to the General-Major, he declares that offer was made conditionally if the General-Major would suffer him to return to England. There was no money in the barque. He knew no such man as Sergeant-Major Ross except he were in Lord Aboyne's company as one of his attendants, nor did he know of Colonel Blair.

iii. Further examination of the SAME.

Being asked what warrant Lord Newcastle could give him to levy forces in Scotland, having no power over the same, he answered that he had warrant to cause forces to be levied in any part of the King's dominions for his service, and that some of the English here would join their regiments to Lord Newcastle's army, which Lord Newcastle himself told him. Both the Englishes about Dublin and those here in Ulster had engaged themselves to Lord Newcastle to bring over regiments unto him.

iv. Examination of JAMES STUART, servitor to the Earl of Antrim.

1643, June 12. Carrickfergus.—Being interrogated upon oath to declare what he knew of the plot ingenuously under pain of torturing. He knew not what warrant the Earl of Antrim had, but he had the pass of the Earl of Newcastle and Lord Derby. He agrees with the other witnesses touching the ammunition to be sent to the North to Lord Aboyne, but knew not of that to be sent to Carlisle according to the other's deposition. The Scotch noblemen that the Earl of Antrim contrived with were the Earls of Montrose, Airlie, Nithsdale and Lord Aboyne. The Earl of Antrim's brother was sent by the Earl's direction, but he knows not what his commission was. The reason of their landing at Newry Castle was that they were informed at the Isle of Man their securest landing was there, it being in the hands of the Irish, and thence they expected a convoy to Charlemont. The Earl's brother had orders from him to deal with Coll Cittoch's sons to be of their party, but he was ignorant what speed he came. Alexander McDonell before his departure had shown him that he would use his endeavours to draw over Coll Cittoch's sons before the Earl's coming. As to men he expected to be his friends he knew of none but these the Commission was to be sent to, such as Aboyne, Sir Donald, Airlie and Nithsdale. The arms to be sent with the ammunition were five fielding pieces with 500 muskets with a quantity of ball, lead, and match. As to the officers sent North he knew of none, but that one Major Ross was there with Aboyne. The only servant that went betwixt Nithsdale and Antrim with the letters was one Cormock O'Sealle, an Irishman, who went with him from Carrickfergus at his escape. The man sent with the Irishman was one of the name of Maxweill whose name he knew not, a gross big man, not tall, redbearded, reddish haired, a little bald in the pate, aged betwixt 40 and 50. Asked what was meant by the hangings left at Carrickfergus he declared that

the Irishman told him at his return that the Earl of Nithsdale
being suspected for keeping correspondence with the Earl of
Antrim particularly by Sir Richard Graham was forced to allege
for an excuse that the barque was to be sent to Carrickfergus
for bringing away some hangings and stuff left there belonging
to my lady. Asked what was meant by the Lord of Montrose's
going back from that he promised at York he declared it was
openly reported in the town that he would fall back from them
and not stand to his promise. Concerning the stopping of the
ammunition to his judgement the reason was that the Parliament's ships laying before them it could not be brought away,
and that immediately Lord Aboyne and his followers went away
of the town, till they should resolve what way to get it away.
He knew nothing of the service undertaken by the Marquess of
Huntley, but that Lord Aboyne was the man talked of as ablest
for undertaking of the service. As to the parties who hoped
to be supplied by these arms he knew none other except Lord
Aboyne and Sir Donald, Nithsdale, and their confederates, and
the said Maxweill was the man to whom Aboyne's business was
committed, besides the letters with the said Irishman. Asked
what papers, commissions, moneys were in the barque that
brought them over or what was left there he knew of nothing
there of the like, and that nothing was left but his spurs and
the little money the Earl had upon him or his other man not
exceeding 30 pieces or thereby which Major Ballantyne got as
his share, and my Lord's barber and cook were to follow with
his clothes and sumptour and Ballantyne also got three little
cups and a salt cover. Asked if he knew by what warrant my
Lord had to tempt the General-Major with an offer of 5,000l.
sterling and of preferment under Newcastle's army he protested
that he knew nothing thereof neither was there any such sum
in the barque nor nothing else but the passengers. He knew
nothing of Major Ross or what he had undertaken, but he heard
he was to be sent away with the ammunition and arms. He
declared that he knew of no design for surprising the magazine
in Scotland or any principal persons in the government there.
Asked if he knew concerning any intelligence or correspondence
between the Marquess of Hamilton and the Duchess for interceding with the General for purchasing a warrant to take up
the rents due to Lord Antrim's brother for his proper use he
declared there was means used at Court by Master German
(Jermyn) and others to intercede with the Queen to speak the
Marquess of Hamilton for purchasing the like warrant from
the General. Lastly being threatened with the torture and
death except he should declare by whose warrant and direction
the Earl of Antrim and others undertook the employment he
declares that as the ammunition and arms was to be furnished
by the Queen's order and command so that he doubts not but
the Earl of Antrim's employment and others was directed by
her Majesty and others there, as was generally thought by all as
by him, and more he takes upon his conscience he knows not.
(All these are true copies, attested by Archibald Primerose.)
[N. XIX., 66.] Abstracts from duplicates sent to the House of
Lords are printed in the *Fifth Report of the Historical MSS
Commission, Appendix*, p. 94.

—— to ——

[1643], July 5. Oxford.—" My dearest dearest Jack, I have written
five times to thee since I received thy cipher which made S[ecretary]

Nicholas. Selwin's question from you amazes me, for by that I perceive you have received none of my letters. I gave you account of our
condition as we then stood. Now we are much hycr (higher) with this
great blow given in the North and Essex creeping—instead of coming to
Oxford—very weakly towards London yesterday, having had a good rap
on Sunday, coming to attempt the Prince's quarters at Buckingham.
We believe the Queen is this night at Ashby in Leicestershire, which is
no great distance from here. When she comes we intend to do great
matters on Essex. Then he should seek Cheapside for his sanctuary ;
but I say *piano, piano,* &c. In the mean time all our eyes and hopes
are placed on your Western affairs, which we conceive to stand in good
posture. We hourly look to hear of the render of Exeter to you and
then, after the joining of your forces, of Wawler's (*sic*) utter ruin and
consequently of all Roundheads. If God bless you with Exeter let me
intreat you to let the whole passage of the proceedings about that place
be sent me handsomely written at large with your names on all
occasions that command in chief, that I may have it printed, for though
I envy not the runnings over of any man's cup yet I cannot endure to
see my friend's cup denied a drop. Dear Rouge I have had something
to do in this particular, wherein I have not been a less friend to my
good friends with you than I hope they believe me. We are daily
frighted with what we hear concerning Poll[ard] and Portl[and], and
sometimes we are assured they will suffer the worst their friends can

[o]
N   e   w   p   r   t   c   o   m
fear. My Lord 51:15:35:48:43:37: is this day 20:50:3:and
                  l   o   r   d   e   s
hath brought with him an offer from the 4:50:43:19:15:41:55:
E   s   s   e   x   S   a   y   H   o   l   l   M   a   n
15:41:41:15:30:58:41:24:32:57:11:50:4:4: and 3:25:51:
c   h   e   s   w   h   o
20:11:15:41:tr Stapleton and others of turning that 35:11:50:
l   e   a   r   m   y   t   o   t   h   e
4:17:55:56:57:24:43:1:32:60:37:50:58:37:11:15:60:
k   i   n   g   e   s   s   e   r   v   i   s
8:7:51:12:17:41:57:41:15:43:39:7:41:59; a brave business
if it took and there is no doubt of it we lose not the matter by disputing
the manner. I shall be able within 4 or 5 days to give you a further
                              t   o   m   a   k   e
account for both sides are resolved 37:50:59:3:24:8:15:55:
   [o]   [it]   [n]
s   h   n   r   t   w   o   r   k   e   o   f   o   r
41:11:51:43:37:60:35:50:43:8:15:60,50:16:60:50:43:60:
o   n   n   o   t   t   h   a   t
52:51:55:60:Prince Rupert is 51:50:37:60:37:11:25:37:60:
g   a   l   l   a   n   t   m   a   n   w   e   t   o   o   k   e
10:24:4,4:25:51:37:3:24:51:60:35:15:58:37:50:52:8:17:
   h   i   m   f   o   r   P   e   r
57:13:9:1:56:16:50:43:60; you may judge it by 48:15:43:
c   y   s   h   i   s   c   h   e   e   f   f   a
22:32:41:60: being 11:9 41:60:20:11:17:14:18:60:16:24:
             .[n]
v   o   r   i   t   e   i   m   w   o   r   l   d
39:50:43:7:37:15:57:60:7:1:60: the 35:50:43:4:19:53.
       .   d   i   s   c   o   n   t   e   n
All our comrades here are highly 19:7:41:20:50:51:37:13:51:
t   b   e   t   t   e   r   t   h   e   a   r   e
38: God send you 26:15:37:37:15:43:37:11:15:24:43:15.
Wilmot and Percy were made Lords last week, but the latter for writing

the letter had the precedency with which I hear Mr. Wawler at London much comforts himself. Dear Jack farewell. Preserve me with my friends there, whom I love and honour, and shall, while I live and daily pray for their and your happy meeting with thy affectionate and faithful.

Postscript.—Sir Jacob is like now to peck over the perch again, so that it may be shortly I may be in employment. I long to hear what is become of my cousin James." [N. VIII., 143.]

Captain VALENTINE WALTON and JOHN GEORGES to SIR ROBERT HARLEY and other members.

1643, July 12. Oxford Castle.—Entreating on behalf of Mr. Alexander Gregory late Minister of Cirencester, who upon the taking of that town was spoiled of all his goods there, brought a prisoner hither, and since deprived of his rectory there, that, whereas the exchange arranged between Mr. Hartford, late minister of Banbury, and Doctor Turner, fellow of Merton College, had been frustrated by the death of the former, the Parliament would now exchange the latter for Mr. Gregory. (See *Commons' Journals*, v. 168) *Signed.* [N. III., 19.]

The PARLIAMENT to the ESTATES OF SCOTLAND.

[1643, July 18.]—Part of the Declaration of that date. (Printed in Rushworth, iii. 2. 467.) *Draft.* [N. XX., 64.]

ORDINANCE.

1643, July 19.—Appointing the Earl of Rutland and others as Committees to go to Scotland. (Printed in *Lords' Journals*, vi. 139.) Two *Copies.* [N. XIX., 67.] N. XIX., 101 is another *Copy* from a draft which contained the names of Lord Grey of Warke in addition to those of the Commissioners, and formed part of a larger whole, the end of a letter from the Earl of Loudoun dated March 6th 1644, preceding, and the beginning of a paper from Mr. Robert Meldrum following.

[JOHN RUSHWORTH?] to [SIR THOMAS BARRINGTON and the other Deputy Lieutenants of ESSEX].

[1643. July 25.]—Desiring them to send a regiment of foot and a troop of horse into Kent, to aid in suppressing the insurrection there. (See *Commons' Journals*, ii. 181.) *Draft.* [N. XII., 48.]

The COMMON HALL OF the City of LONDON.

[1643, August 2.]—Resolution. (The purport appears from *Commons' Journals*, iii. 193.) [N. XIII., 183.]

—— to ——

1643, August 2. [Dublin.]—One Brent, a most pernicious Papist, and, as they say, a lawyer, came over from England, and landed here the last of July, being sent to Lord Ormonde. On the next day, Sir William Parsons, Sir Adam Loftus, Sir John Temple, and Sir Robert Meredith, were committed to the Castle of Dublin. Report says that they do not know what their faults are. Their chiefest endeavours, they profess, have always been for the good of this Kingdom, the destruction of the Rebels and the King's honour, and they are not guilty of any other offences. Since their committal, the English are departing in great numbers, because the King has given too much countenance to natives of this most unfortunate Kingdom. The poorer sort of them fly for refuge into England, but they who have anything left go to the Low Countries, fearing to stay here since the committal of the above-named councillors. Within these few days, the Papists are growing very insolent, for the English Protestants are quite discouraged by the report of a cessation, assuring themselves that the rebels will be taken for the good subjects and the poor distressed Protestants for the rebels, for they daily see them accused of treason put at liberty and discharged out of the Castle, and men that showed themselves most real and hearty against the Rebels put in their room. The King's intention for the committal of these councillors was known at Kilkenny at least a fortnight before his letters came over, as appears by the examination which I send. It is credibly reported that the rebels seek earnestly the lives of these councillors. I am confident that they are innocent. The army, consisting of 4,500 foot and 500 horse has been lately abroad, but nothing has been done worth relating, only the rebels deserted an empty castle of Sir William Pooley. The Earl of Castlehaven, an Englishman and a rebel, has taken two strong castles near Catherlagh, which the English Protestants have kept ever since the rebellion, and a castle called Balli-lenan, in which were nearly a thousand English Protestants [is] strongly beseiged. Nevertheless the army returned yesterday to their several garrisons probably to remain in them all the summer. What will become of us English Protestants, I know not, for we are consuming away by little and little. Since the first bruit of this cessation we never prospered. Many Englishmen's houses have been burned this week within two miles of this city, and also part of the suburbs, but nothing has been done to prevent it or to defend these adjacent parts, which very much disheartens all the Protestants here who fear that they will be left as a prey to the rebels. "All things here is very ill in the highest degree, no expectation but ruin, and that all English and Protestants will be quite rooted out of this kingdom." (See *Commons' Journals*, iii. 213.) *Copy.* [N. XII., 63.]

[The FRENCH AGENT] to [the QUEEN OF FRANCE].

1643, August 3.—Informing her that the Houses of Parliament had at her request granted Sir Kenelm Digby liberty to go to France. *Draft.* In *French. Enclosed:*

> Undertaking of same date by Sir Kenelm Digby that he will not directly or indirectly negotiate, promote, consent unto, or concede any practise or design prejudicial to the honour or safety of the Parliament. (See *Lords' Journals*, vi. 153, 163, 206.) [N. III., 22.]

· SIR THOMAS PELHAM and others to WILLIAM LENTHALL.

1643, August 3. Lewes.—Today was brought before us "Mr. Thomas Cotton, a dangerous Papist. The inclosed warrant found in his man's saddle will clearly demonstrate his employment. By this and many other pregnant circumstances we are very sensible of our more than approaching danger, which to prevent we shall be willing to apply our utmost industry, but being conscious of our own inability to stand of ourselves we humbly address ourselves" to the House craving their advice and assistance, and that London and the adjacent counties may associate with us for our mutual defence. *Signed.* [N. III., 21.] *Enclosed:*

> SIR EDWARD FORD, High Sheriff of Sussex, to his kinsman THOMAS COTTON.
>
> 1643, July 19. Oxford.—Authorising him to persuade the well affected in Sussex and the parts adjacent to contribute horses,

arms, plate or money, for his Majesty's service and to receive and give acquittances for such contributions "that I may more clearly distinguish the well affected from cordial traitors and penurious neuters." *Signed.* [N. XII., 60.]

The GENERAL ASSEMBLY óf the Church of SCOTLAND.

1643, August 10.—Order empowering their Committee to meet and treat with the English Commissioners. *Signed* " Archibald Johnston." *Copy.* [N. XIII., 184.]

The ENGLISH COMMISSIONERS to the CONVENTION OF ESTATES.

1643, August 12.—We are commanded to remind our brethren of Scotland "that the Popish and Prelaticall faction which began with them about the yeares 1638 and 1639 and then intended to make way to the ruine of the Kingdome of England by theirs, Have not abated any part of their malice towards the Nation and Church of Scotland, nor are at all departed from their designe of corrupting and altering Religion through the whole Island, though they have inverted the manner of their proceedings conceiving now that they have an easier way to destroy them, if they may first prevaile over the Parlyament and King-dome of England. In which respect, it is the desire of both Houses that the two Nations may bee strictly united for their mutuall defence against the Papists and Prelaticall Faction, and their Adherents in both Kingdomes, And not to lay downe Armes till those their implacable enemies shalbee disarmed and subjected to the Authority and justice of Parlyament, in both Kingdomes respectively. And as an effectuall meanes hereunto, they desire their brethren of Scotland to raise a considerable force of horse and foote for their aid and assistance, to bee forthwith sent against the Papists and Prelaticall Faction, and Malignants now in Armes in the Kingdome of England.

And for the better incouragement of the Kingdome of Scotland to this necessary and soe much desyred union, Wee are by both Houses authorized to assure their brethren that if they shalbee annoyed or indangered by any Force or Army either from England or any other place, the Lords and Commons of England will assist them with pro-portionable strength of horse and foote to what their brethren shall now afford them, to bee sent into Scotland for the defence of that Kingdome. And they will maintaine a Guard of Shippes at their owne charges upon the Coast of Scotland for the securing of the Kingdome from the Invasion of the Irish Rebells, or other Enemies during such time as the Scottish Army shalbee imployed in the defence of the Kingdome of England. And to the end that nothing should bee wanting in the Kingdome and Parlyament of England to facillitate this worcke—wherein the true reformed Religion not onely in these two Kingdomes, but throughout all Europe, is so highly concerned,—Wee are further authorized to consider with their brethren the Estates and Kingdome of Scotland, of what other Articles or Propositions are fitte to bee added and concluded wherby this Assistance, and Union betwixt the two Nations may bee made more beneficiall and effectuall for the security of Religion and Liberty in both Kingdomes.

Seeing they have now so fully declared as by what they have done already so by what they are yet desirous to doe that the true state of this Cause and Quarrell is Religion, in the Reformation whereof they are and have bin soe forward and zealous as that there is not any thing expressed to them by their brethren of Scotland in their former or latter Declaracions which they have not seriously taken to heart, and earnestly endeavoured to effect—notwithstanding the subtill, malitious and industrious oppositions—that so the two Kingdomes might bee brought into a neare Conjunction, in one forme of Church Government, and Directory of Worshippe, one Catechisme, etc., and the foundation laid of the utter Extirpation of Popery and Prelacy out of both Kingdomes. The most ready and effectuall meanes whereunto, is now conceived to bee that both Nations shall enter into a strict union and League of mutuall defence, according to the desires of the two Houses. And to induce the perswasion of this—if there were cause—wee might observe that in the many Declaracions made by the Generall Assembly or States of Scotland to their brethren of England there have bin sundry Expressions manifesting the greate Necessity that both Kingdomes for the security of their Religion and Liberties, should joyne in this strict union against the Papists, Prelates, and their Adherents, As also in the Indeavours of a neare Conjunction betweene the Churches of both Nations, The apprehension and foresight of which hath caused the Popish and Prelaticall Faction in forraigne parts as well as in these his Majestie's Dominions strictly and powerfully to combine themselves to the hinderance of this so necessary worcke, and the universall suppression of the true Protestant Religion in Europe. A course not much different from that which they tooke in the yeare 1585, when the wisdome and zeale of this Nation to Countermine so wicked a Conspiracy, and from the due sense of the mutuall interest of these two kingdomes in religion and Liberty found a necessity of outring into a League of this Nature as well considering that thereby no lesse safety might bee expected to both Nations then danger by forbearing the same. And though no doubt but in so necessary and good a worcke many difficulties may arise to interrupt and retard the same, yet wee are as confident that the hearty and brotherly affection of this Nation to the Parlyament and Kingdome of England will easily breake through them and the rather because in the like cases of difficulty and danger not onely at the time of the League abovemencioned, but before and likewise since, when any opertunity hath offered it selfe, perticularly during the sitting of the present Parlyament, the Kingdome of England hath bin very ready and forward to lay to heart the dangers of the Kingdome of Scotland as their owne, and to decline no meanes in the reach of their power, for the redresse and prevention of the same." All which being taken into the serious consideration of the Lords and others of the Convention we hope many arguments will not be needed to persuade them to give their consent with all convenient speed to these desires of both Houses. *Copy.* [N. XIII., 185.]

The PARLIAMENT to the STATES-GENERAL.

1643, August 18.—Declaration in reply to the Exhibits of Sir William Boswell with the exhibits themselves. (Printed in *Lords' Journals,* vi. 186–190.) *Copies.* There are two copies of some of the exhibits. [N. XVIII., 54.]

SIR MILES HOBARTE and others to WILLIAM LENTHALL.

1643, September 4. Norwich.—Desiring that all moneys raised in this county may be employed for the present for the pay of the troops and other extraordinary expenses connected with the siege of Lynn and one good ship at least may be sent to lie at the mouth of Lynn Deeps to blockade the town. We have ventured to send round there the *Cygnet* frigate, but understand that she is inadequate for the purpose. *Signed.* (See *Commons' Journals*, iii. 232.) [N. III., 24.]

THOMAS RAIKES, Mayor, and others to WILLIAM LENTHALL.

1643, September 5. Hull.—"The Earl of Newcastle is before our town, and hath beleaguered it round about with at least 10,000 men, so that now we stand upon our defence. . The great impediment which is here at present is the lack of moneys for the payment of my Lord Fairfax's soldiers which causes them [to] murmur much, and we fear hath been the great cause that they have deserted Beverley and left it with six pieces of Ordnance and a great deal of ammunition to the mercy of the enemy who have plundered it in a most tyrannous way. . We beseech" you " to furnish us with such things as is needful. We stand need of two or three ships in Humber to keep the enemy from planting by the river side" . . and debarring us from the sea and so hindering us of all relief that could come to our aid. *Signed.* [N. III., 28.]

SIR WILLIAM ARMYNE, HENRY DARLEY and SIR HENRY VANE to WILLIAM LENTHALL.

1643, September 6. Edinburgh.—"We have received the good news of Berwick being declared for the King and Parliament, by the means of sending one of our number thither Mr. Henry Darley, who so represented affairs to the town that unanimously they consented to receive in our forces . . without any resistance, which was no sooner done but upon the notice thereof we presently made the Remonstrance herewith sent to the Committee of the Convention of Estates, and were for a while in greater difficulties after the town had received in our forces than before, until at last after a long and serious debate between the Committee of Scotland and ourselves we agreed upon a result to be presented unto you, which if the two Houses approve of, we hope will be a good expedient to settle that town in security, and to the advantage of the mutual interests of both kingdoms." We enclose particulars, "and can only say this much, that we who are upon the place, could not find any other means to secure that town, and reconcile the mistakes, which else we discerned were like to have happened by reason of the large treaty." (See *Commons' Journals*, iii. 244.) *Signed. Seal.* [N. III., 26.]

MILES TEMPLE to ———.

1643, September 7. Dover Castle.—Concerning his meeting at Rochester the previous day with a brother of Captain Dawkes of Dover, who said that he had newly come from the King's army, to talk with his brother about keeping Dover Castle for the King, and that his brother was mad if he did not do so. [N. XII., 64.]

GEORGE TROTTER to ———.

1643, September 7. [Dover Castle.] — Concerning Lieutenant Dawkes' alleged intentions of seizing the Castle, and asking that he might be turned forth with all possible speed, and for a supply of powder and match. (See *Commons' Journals*, iii. 234.) [N. III., 27.]

The HOUSE OF COMMONS.

[1643, September 7.]—Declaration concerning the suspension of the Fifth Article of the Covenant. (See *Commons' Journals*, iii. 231.) [N. XIII., 198.]

The Coaaittee at Derby to the Speaker.

[1643, September 10.]—(The purport of part concerning Mr. Allestree appears from *Commons' Journals*, iii. 281.) Your extra supply of powder and arms came so seasonably that it frightened the Queen's army from making any attempt on us. By reason of our ill quarter at the late general Rendezvous at Nottingham many of our soldiers run from us. Our horse are wearied out with continual convoying of Lancashire and Cheshire carriers. Nottingham horse are gone to the general Rendezvous about Boston, which gives the Newark forces a better opportunity to come into our county. We beseech you to be a means that either Lancashire and Cheshire give over entire trading, or else that they may receive a troop or two of horse to convoy their own. We also entreat for more powder and match; part of our last we sent into Cheshire, and part we spent in taking Sir Richard Fleetwood's house in Staffordshire. . It was only through want of it we missed taking Tutbury Castle with Hastings and all his chief commanders. *Copy.* [N. XII., 30.]

Philip Francis, Mayor, Sir Shilston Calmady, John Howes, Robert Savery, Thoaas Arundell, Francis Godolphin and Richard Erisey to Willaa Lenthall.

1643, September 14. Plymouth.—Yesterday there was discovered to us a plot for betraying the *Providence* by her Captain, William Brook. *Signed. Seal.* [N. III., 29.]

Sir David Watkins to Willaa Strode.

1643, September 15.—Complaining of the malignancy and negligence of the searchers at Gravesend, by whose remissness many ships have passed by there unsearched to the great prejudice of the Parliament and kingdom. *Signed.* [N. III., 30.]

Colonel Herbert Morley to William Lenthall.

1643, September 16. Farnham.—I was lately in Hampshire and was ordered here by the Committee for the safety of the kingdom to await their further orders, which have not come. "This day I received intelligence that the Earl of Crawford with his own, Col. Ford's, Col. Bennett's, the Sheriff of Wilts', Sir Ed. Deering's and Crispe's regiments are designed to take in Southampton and are expected this day to sit down before it. The garrison there is not above 300, the soldiers in arrears, the town abounding with Malignants. If immediate course be not taken to relieve it that town in probability will be lost. My force being but 400 is very unable to resist so great a strength now they are united, though if I had been let alone I might have given some obstruction to their joining together. If you can forthwith send 2,000 horse and dragoons to join with me, I believe we may give them some remove if not defeat. You may now see how necessary it was for the Associated Brigade to stay in these parts, without which, or some considerable force instead of it, the Southern Counties will be all lost, then London cannot but be in danger. This approaching cloud, I fear, may raise a storm in Sussex, which county is full of neuters and Malignants; and I have ever observed neuters to turn Malignants upon such occasions." *Seal.* [N. III., 31.]

DOCTOR JOHN KING to WILLIAM LENTHALL.

1643, September 19. Hertford.—The Committee of Parliament for this County, having received a warrant from his Excellency for the speedy raising of 100 horse for a troop of Arquebusiers have commanded me to ask the deferring the execution of this warrant for some time, inasmuch they are now raising 300 light horse to be under the Earl of Manchester's command, and the County has recruited Colonel Middleton's regiment twice, and other Companies under his Excellency, and has lately furnished Sir W. Waller with many horse, and the Earl of Denby's (Denbigh) officers swept away many men's horses when they went through the County, and the County hath furnished at least 1,000 or 1,200 horse for the most part at their own charge, and now they are speedily to raise 120 horse for Dragoons to be sent to the Earl of Manchester. *Seal.* [N. III., 32.]

SIR EDWARD MONINS, SIR MICHAEL LIVESEY and others to
WILLIAM LENTHALL.

1643, September 21. Sittingbourne.—Concerning the carriage of Sir Robert Honywood. (See *Commons' Journals,* iii. 257.) *Signed.* [N. III., 33.]

JOHN HOBARTE, SIR JOHN POTTS, SIR MILES HOBARTE, FRAMLINGHAM GAWDY, FRANCIS FERING, SAMUEL SMYTHE and THOMAS SOTHERTON to WILLIAM LENTHALL.

1643, September 21.— Reciting the great charges this county, (Norfolk), had undergone for the public defence in maintaining horse in the Lord General's army and two regiments of foot in Lincolnshire all the summer, besides forces necessarily kept at home for suppressing disturbances, and that now a new burden has been imposed by the late ordinance for 600 horses and for increasing the foot, and requesting with the approval of the Earl of Manchester that the county might have the benefit of the sequestrations therein. *Signed.* [N. III., 34.]

SIR THOMAS ALSTON, SIR JOHN BURGOYNE, THOMAS ROLT and
EDWARD OSBORNE to WILLIAM LENTHALL.

1643, September 26. Biggleswade.—Concerning the raising of 200 horse charged on Bedfordshire. The county complains that we have not charged the Train horse according to the letter of the Ordinance. We conceive that Parliament intended to have regard to their horses and arms found, and not to charge them as if they had found none. We submit the course we have taken to Parliament. (See *Commons' Journals,* iii. 260.) *Signed.* [N. III., 35.]

HARBOTTLE GRIMSTON to WILLIAM LENTHALL.

1643, September 26. Colchester.—Requesting that Mr. Henry Farre, Lieutenant-Colonel to the Earl of Warwick, who had been left out of the last ordinance by the printer's mistake, might be added to the Committee for the County of Essex. (See *Commons' Journals,* iii. 260.) *Seal.* [N. III., 36.]

Captain TRISTRAM STEVENS to Colonel WHITEHEAD and the COMMITTEE
AT PORTSMOUTH.

1643, September 27. From aboard his Majesty's ship the *Charles* afore Hurst Castle.—" We have only this day's victuals left, and when that is done, we are to seek for more, God knows where. I understand by our Purser's letter that no money can be got for our victualling. I would desire to know from you speedily what is intended to be done about us. If to supply us anew with victuals, then 'tis high time it were on board already; if not, then there must be special care taken for the speedy sending of a certain number of soldiers for the assisting of Colonel Button in keeping of the Castle. Never hath ship been sent to sea, as we have, nor used worse than we are, nor so ill accommodated with all sorts of provision, when 'tis sent us, for we have had stinking beef, and pork, and also stinking beer a great part of this voyage, and unless such a business had been purposely intended, a man would have scarce imagined that a ship should be so badly fitted with necessaries as we have been." A Frenchman, one Jerome from Newhaven, I am informed, has arrived at Weymouth with 100 barrels of powder and other arms and ammunition for their supply there. If you had sent a ship to Weymouth Roads. as I desired, he might have been intercepted. (See *Commons' Journals*, iii. 258.) [N. III., 37.]

SIR THOMAS STANLEY, COLONEL RALPH ASSHETON, and others to the HOUSE OF COMMONS.

1643, September 28. Manchester.—Christopher Malone of Drogheda being indebted to John Hartley of Manchester had consigned goods to Laurence Mercer of Liverpool to sell and pay Hartley out of the proceeds, but such proceeds had been detained by Mercer by order of Mr. John Walker, Mayor of Liverpool, on the ground that Malone being a rebel the goods were forfeited to the Crown and that the Corporation under their Charter was entitled to them, but in fact the goods had been shipped on October 25, 1641 and for three weeks afterwards Malone had behaved as a loyal subject during which time the sale had taken place, all which we certify at the instance of Hartley who has always been faithful to Parliament, and submit to your consideration. *Signed.* [N. III., 38.]

SIR EDWARD BOYS to WILLIAM LENTHALL.

1643, September 28. [Dover.]—Supporting the desire of the town of Dover to raise a third band of volunteers, with the mayor, Mr. Edward Prescott, as their captain, and requesting some money out the sums raised in the County for his soldiers' pay, who are two months in arrear, though he has borrowed 250*l.* [N. III., 39.]

The HOUSE OF COMMONS to the EARL OF WARWICK.

1643, September 28.—In reply to his letter of the 22nd declaring that they will take speedy order for payment of the mariners of the merchant men, provision having already been made for his Majesty's ships, and thanking him for his care wisdom and valour. *Draft* or *Copy.* [N. XII,. 65.]

The HOUSE OF COMMONS.

[1643, September 29.]—Votes concerning the proposed cessation in Ireland. (These are drafts differing considerably from the form finally adopted, which is printed in *Lords' Journals*, vi. 238.) [N. XIX., 29.]

The PARLIAⅯENT OF ENGLAND.

1643, September 30.—Declaration concerning the Cessation. (Printed in Rushworth, iii. 2. 555.) *Draft.* [N. XXI., 5.]

WILLIAⅯ VEALE to WILLIAⅯ HAWKINS, Agent to the Lord Lieutenant of Ireland.

1643, September 30. Dublin.—The Cessation here "is now concluded, to the great joy of the Roman Catholic subjects, as now they are called," of which the Articles are inclosed. "Since this was concluded and proclaimed some of these good subjects have hanged some and killed others of our men within four miles of this place yet no satisfaction or course taken with them. What a miserable condition we that must remain here are in any reasonable man may judge, being left, as I may say, both by our King and Parliament to the mercy of these merciless and bloody villains. That which they are to pay will not relieve our army a month, if they were to continue all with us, but 'tis reported here and 'tis very probable that 10,000 of our soldiers are to go over to you in England, and that my Lord Marquess of Ormond is to be General of them, my Lord Inchiquin Lieutenant-General, and Sir Thomas Luckes General of the horse that goes from hence, then the Irish to fall all of them upon the Scots in Ulster, so we in this place lie at their mercy whensoever they please, except God miraculously deliver us, for if they stay their hands from sending us provision, and ours being tied that we cannot fetch it in if we had strength as formerly we did, then we shall soon perish. Shipping that would come with provisions cannot, being blocked up, as we hear by some that lately came over, some by the King's ships and some by Chester water and Liverpool by the Parliament's. Winter draws on and never was less provision of coals here than now; 'tis likely many a house will be pulled down and burnt for want of firing. Most of us here do apprehend more danger now than at the beginning of the rebellion. Then here there was shipping to carry over those that would into England, but now here is not any or any like to be, the Parliament who we took to be our friends having now forsaken us, that will not command so much as one ship to lie upon this coast to relieve those that are in distress. The Lord unite the hearts of our King and his subjects together, that we may have some relief, and not these bloody rebels to triumph over us." [N. III., 40.]

Captain RICHARD LEE to JOHN PYM.

1643, October 1. Rochester.—Informing him of the apprehension of Mr. Walter Montague and desiring to know the pleasure of the Houses therein. (See *Commons' Journals*, iii. 261, 266; *Lords' Journals*, vi. 250.) *Seal.* [N. III., 41.]

Colonèl EDWARD MASSIE to the EARL OF ESSEX.

1643, October 5. Gloucester.—The bailiffs of your manors in Herefordshire have been unable to get any of your rents, as the enemy forbids it on pain of plundering, and this must continue till I have a force to enable me to countermand, the nearest of your tenants lying too remote and Gudderidg (Goderich) Castle including them. "We have not heard of the enemy's reflux—since your Excellency gave them their passports at Newbury of which they boast but little—until Monday last, there being marched into Tewkesbury 400 foot and

3 or 400 horse. Report is also that considerable numbers are marched into Sudeley and towards Evesholme, and their full resolutions are to lie at Stroud, Painswick, and Cheltenham, on the Forest side at Newnam Mitcheldcane and Newent, and nearer also, so that your Excellency well knoweth how impossible it will be for us to maintain this garrison without supply of strength, many of the townsmen here being weary of the service, and the country already dare not or will not look upon us, being also likely to lose our markets, since we are not able to defend them from the enemy's seizure. To remedy all which I am bold to make this address to your Excellency by whose favour in a speedy order and command our succour may be full and timely, which if delayed till these settle and fortify themselves in their winter quarters it will be a thing of much hazard and difficulty to relieve us,

Postscript. October 6.—I am truly advertised by my scouts that those foot which were at Tewkesbury being of the Welsh forces are all marched away yestr-evening upon an alarm my troop of horse gave them, that they cried out ' The enemy from Gloucester was coming with 4 pieces of ordnance and 2,000 foot and horse,' and so in much confusion and haste quitted the town, and swore—being of the Welsh forces—that the Lord Herbert should never make them slaves again, nor bring them out of their own country on any pretence whatsoever, so took their way over Upton-bridge, and no persuasion of Colonel Vavisor or other officer nor the force of their horse could constrain them to stay and fortify Tewkesbury, as this day they should have begun, and now not one left there. I know that the enemy will do what possibly they can to take Tewkesbury for their winter quarter, if our care prevent them not, for we expect others in the room of the Welsh, who, I persuade myself, will hardly ever be brought so far again upon any service whatever. We hear nothing of Sir William Waller but hope our supply is cared for. Sir John Winter's house in the Forest is fortified and a large number of soldiers allotted to garrison there. Sir Ralph Hopton is said to be at Berkeley Castle and hath brought with him 3 or 400 more to garrison there." *Seal.* [N. III., 42.]

Sir Thomas Middleton to Richard Moore.

1643, October 6. Wem.—Importuning his help in the House for supply of money men and horses. " It hath pleased God to bring us safely to Wem where we find the country so plundered and pillaged both of money and horse that there is no possibility of raising either here for our present supply, and those moneys I took up upon my credit are long since spent and which is worse I can be trusted for no more, because the moneys are not paid in to them according to the Order of the Committee, so that I am for present left in a poor condition, being seated in the mouth of the enemy, and wanting both money and men to defend ourselves. The enemy is very strong and daily expect more forces from His Majesty, and this night we are informed there is a supply come to them, and every hour we look to be set upon, our forces being but very few, and those auxiliaries we have from Cheshire ready upon all occasions for want of pay to leave us, so that unless God in mercy look upon us, and put it into your hearts to send us speedy supply we are like to be swallowed up by the enemy. I need not inform you of how great consequence to the public the reducing of these parts are. The great opposition [that] is made and the care [that] is had to keep us out of Wales, makes me believe there is some greater end in it on the adversaries' part than we for present can imagine. I should not doubt . . but by gaining 1,000 foot and 300 horse, which I believe my Lord General may for a time spare, to reduce these countries and to settle an oppressed people in peace, who for present dare not nor do not show themselves, though we are in the heart of the country, because the enemy is so strong and we so inconsiderable a number to deal with them." I desire you therefore to use your best endeavours in the House to manifest our condition and to find a way of speedily supplying both men and money, whether by Lord Denbigh's speedy march, or by the loan of some forces from my Lord General, or by landing of some Scots in Lancashire, I refer to the Houses to consider, only desiring expedition. "The country is engaged against us by oath, which they have been forced to take, and in particular Wales, and my own tenants forced to swear to oppose me. The enemy hath fortified my castle against me very strongly. My Lord Capel hath caused my woods to be cut down, my farms and outhouses to be pulled down and sells the wood thereof. I hope, if God prosper the Parliament, as I doubt not of, his Lordship may be thought of and some satisfaction may be made out of his estate." (See *Commons' Journals*, iii. 277.) *Seal.* [N. III., 43.]

HARBOTTLE GRIMSTON and others to WILLIAM LENTHALL.

1643, October 6. Chelmsford.—Interceding for Lieutenant-Colonel Farre, and justifying his having taken away Brasier's commission for seizing horses. *Signed.* [N. III., 44.]

ROBERT JORDAN to WILLIAM WELLBOR.

1643, October 7. Cambridge Castle.—"I have received a commission from our most pious Major, the Earl of Manchester, for the Castle, but I want above a 100 muskets, swords and bandoleers, besides pikes for to arm my company, which he commands me to make up between 2 and 300. Likewise we want 50 barrels of powder at the least, for all our store will not last above 3 hours' fight. Our ditch goes very slowly on, notwithstanding without it the Castle is of little value, but if it were done . . . impregnable. We . . are above 9 weeks behind in pay; these things considered our case is very desperate, unless God be pleased to move the Parliament to supply us with moneys and arms and munition, for Oxford forces come within 20 miles and plunder at their pleasure, and how soon they may come and surprise us God only knows, for I am persuaded they know as well as ourselves what a condition we are in, we having so many malignant scholars and others. I beseech you therefore to do what possible may be to procure" from the House some speedy and instant way for providing for the soldiers' arrears and their future pay, "otherwise we shall never keep soldiers together, for they drop away most miserably for mere want, and if the enemy should but make a breach in here—believe me as a soldier—all the Associated Counties would not only be endangered to be lost, but even London itself." [N. III., 45.]

THOMAS COLE, SIR JOHN READE, ROBERT CASTELL, THOMAS DUCKETT, DUDLEY POPE, MATTHEW LINSEY, and GEORGE GAWSETT to WILLIAM LENTHALL.

1643, October 10. Cambridge.—"First our very subsistence is questioned and therefore we humbly desire the resolution of the House whether the institution of several Committees in each county according to the late Ordinance for associating Lincolnshire with those counties do null and make void this general Committee of the Association, as is conceived and objected by some. Secondly for the power, which by the late Ordinance you have entrusted us withal, we find it too short to carry on such various and weighty business effectually ; as not enabling us to imprison or any ways to secure dangerous Malignants, refractory persons, and such as disobey and abuse not only our authority but yours, nor to punish mutinous soldiers, by whom we have found both ourselves and this place much endangered. Thirdly the Committee is in danger of dissolution through the non-appearance of Commissioners. Fourthly we are utterly destitute of money in the common treasury for the defraying of such charges as concern the Association in general, as the payment of the garrison in the Castle, the payment of Scouts, guards, carriages, and many other like occasions, besides above 300*l.* which is owing to the Treasurer, we having often written earnestly to the several counties to send in their proportions without effect in most of them. For our dangers we have just grounds to fear not only domestic insurrections by reason of the abundance of active Malignants, both in town, country, and colleges, but also the attempts of remoter enemies, concerning which we receive daily advertisement,"—which we leave to the bearer to relate, " humbly beseeching you to take into your consideration the consequence of this place, being the heart—as it were—of this Association, and which the enemy does most aim at, as we daily hear, and have reason to believe, for both town and castle being fortified to their hands, it would be a safe rendez-vous for them to retreat unto, and an inlet into all the other counties and be a means to stop the passages of provisions for London." (See *Commons' Journals,* iii. 274, 278.) *Signed. Seal.* [N. III., 46.]

The EARL OF DORSET to LORD EDWARD HOWARD.

1643, October 10. Oxford.—Expressing his gratitude for services done him. *Seal.* [N. III., 47.]

SIR WILLIAM ARMYNE, SIR HENRY VANE, and HENRY DARLEY to WILLIAM LENTHALL.

1643, October 11. Edinburgh.—" In our last we gave you accounte of our securing the towne of Berwick, which hath since appeared to us a happy prevention of the enemy, who at the same time and ever since hath had a designe upon it. Severall alarmes have bin given by the enemy along the Borders betwixt Owler and Berwicke, whereupon the Estates of Scotland published this inclosed Proclamation ; and it was thought fitte that three troopes of Scottish horse should be taken into the towne of Berwicke, for the further security of it from dangers both within and without, and two hundred Scottish foote, which hath bin an unavoydable charge to us, without the imminent danger of the towne, as our Billes of Exchange upon Sir Gilbert Gerraid can testify. But the enemies' strength being not so greate as at first was apprehended, and wee willing to take the first advantage of easing the charge, tooke order that the troopes of horse should bee withdrawne, and some companies of foote placed in their roome. Thus stands the present condition of the towne. What the resolutions of the Houses are concerning the further setling of it, wee very much desire to heare, as being of no small consequence.

By late letters from Major Generall Monro to the Committie of Estates wee perceive that the busines of the cessation is now con-eluded in Ireland, the coppies of which letters and cessation wee send you heere inclosed. This hath put the English and Scottish there to greate difficulties which cannot bee resolved and remedied without the speedy advice and assistance of the Houses of Parliament as in our answers to the Committie of Estates two severall times wee have bin necessitated to declare, and to feede them with good hopes and expectations in the meane season, untill wee receive the pleasure of the Houses concerning the same. Our last paper to this effect wee send .you the coppy of, wherein wee were put to very greate straightes what to expresse to them, that might keepe the army in Ireland from taking some desperate courses, and exposing that kingdome wholly to the will of the cruell and bloody rebells. All which wee earnestly recommend to you for some speedy resolution, fearing that extremities will now come upon that army and the other forces so fast, upon this cessation, that they will not rest contented much longer with words. What course wee shall then take to give them satisfaction unlesse wee speedily heare from you will bee very difficult, they having bin eighteene moneths without pay, and being ready to sterve for want of necessary subsistance. The Covenant as it is sent over with the alterations from the Parliament is very well approved of heere, and tomorrow the Commissioners of the Church meete to appoint daies for the taking of it by the whole kingdome. It is said heere that the House of Commons and Assembly of Divines have already taken it in a very solemne manner, which gives greate satisfaction, and is very seasonable in one respect; because there is newly arrived a French agent, whose businesse is—as it is commonly reported—to perswade this kingdome from ingaging in the cause of England, and to mediate the Earle of Antrim's release, but it is conceived heere hee is come too late, all things being in very good forwardnesse if the mony most necessary for the setting forth and maintaynance of the army weere arrived. The men are leavyed in severall sheyres but cannot bee brought into a body, for want of mony, which is requisite therfore to .bee hastened away, by reason of the winters comming on so fast. This day the Commissioners of the Church have mette, who have very readily and cheerfully approved of the Covenant with the alterations sent from England, and are extreamely well satisfyed to heare of the happy progresse it hath already had in England. They have appointed Friday next for the Committie of Estates and themselves to take it, and that in the same solemne manner as in England when also it is expected that wee should take it with them, from the example of the Scotch Commissioners with you who without direction from hence tooke the Covenant in England and therefore they conceive wee may do the same heere, to give satisfaction to this kingdome, not doubting but as they have approved this action in their Commissioners, so the Houses will do the same in us. Upon the next Lord's day, intimation of the Covenant is to bee given throughout all the churches and the same day seavenight it is to bee taken and sworne by all the kingdome. A relation of the king's greate victory at Newberry by his Majestie's expresse command to the Earle Lannericke is sent to this citty of Edenburgh, whilst our information to rectify the same is onely a few printed papers casually come to our hands. Wee have this day received a paper from the Committie of Estates, which wee herewith send, wherein is expressed how necessary it is that one of our number should speedily returne to acquaint the Houses by word of mouth of the true state of affaires in Ireland and heere, which in regard of Mr. Hatcher's speedy returne hither, wee do believe wee shalbee necessitated to consent unto." *Signed.* [N. III., 48.]

The EARL OF MANCHESTER to WILLIAM LENTHALL.

1643, October 12. Horncastle.—Entreating him to acquaint the House of Commons "that the Earl of Newcastle having assisted the Lincolnshire forces with 40 troops of horse, which body being joined with as many of their own country they marched towards the relief of Bullinbrook Castle which I had besieged, being a place which did much annoy those parts of Holland that lie near about Boston. After that I had drawn up the horse to the top of Bullinbrook Hill word was brought me that the enemy with about fourscore colours of horse was marching towards me, whereupon I advanced with the horse to meet him and caused the foot and artillery to march as fast after the horse as they could." (The rest of the letter is the same *verbatim* as that from the Earl printed in *Lords' Journals*, vi. 25) from "but came not so near" to "scattered about the country.") *Signed. Seal.* [N. III., 49.]

Sir JOHN MELDRUM to THOMAS (*sic*) LENTHALL, Speaker of the House of Commons.

1643, October 14. Hull.—"Sir, I shall not wearie you much with the relation of some happie successes God hath blessed us with all since my arrivall att Hull knowinge that many pennes will be sett a worke whereby neither the truth in the narration nor the favor and mercie of God cann bee revealed. Upon Munday beinge the ninth of this instant, the reginalists about breake of day did with a great deale of courage beinge commaunded by Denton, Stricland and one Little a countryman of myne who commanded in cheife fell upon one of our out workes called the raged jetty, a place of great importance for the safe ridinge of our shippinge before the towne. But by the resolution of two Inglish commaunders and a countryman of mine, cosen Germaine to Sir William Cunningham, and the courage of the gunners and souldiers, they were—upon veiwe of a hundreth musqueteres which followed me from the mount—beaten out of the worke dri[ven] to a most shamefull retreite leiveinge the bodies of theire commaunders dead upon the place, many of their souldiers killed and wounded. Where-upon, upon the eleventh of October, my Lord Generall bid call a counsell of warr, where it was resolved for us to issue forth, and to beate them forth of their next workes approachinge to ours. The order was to fall out in two distinct bodies of five hundred musqueteres apeiee commaunded—under my charge—by two collonells, Lambert and Raines-borough, who with major Forbesse and Major Wrenn caryed themselves very bravely, marching alongst the enimies lyne of approach, on every side, the enimy abandoning one worke after another, untill wee made ourselves masters of theire ordinance. But as the sunn—in her greatest brightnesse—is subject to eclipes, soe it fell out that the forwardnesse and violence of our souldiers, was abated by a hundred pikes of the enimy, who charginge the van of our foote, scattered and in disorder did drive us backward againe, regained there ordinance and enforced us all to a shamefull retreate, the commaunders and m[y]selfe not beinge able to stopp any one man—if t   had beene att the stake—. In this retreate [Rainesborough] is either taken prisoner or killed dead and fallen into some ditch, but cannot bee found, his man's dead body is found. Upon my Lord Generall's order to shutt the gates and the sense of their owne carriage a body of foote was againe drawne upp, which fallinge againe with as much

animositye and beate as formerly they had retyred did drive them
againe out of their workes, recovered all the ordinance lost and
gayned a halfe cannon and a demy culveringe of brass which wee
had not possessed in the first charge. Upon this change of the
scene of affaires the Lord Marquiss' Leifetenant-generall Kinge brought
downe the whole army from the head quarter, wherewith—the two last
peices turned upon the body of their army—they were all forced to a
wretched retreat, and to stand att a distance untill wee sleighted their
whole lyne of approach. Wee brought of nine peice of ordinance, one
demy cannon called one of the Queenes Boes, a demy culveringe of
brass, t[w]o sacers, and foure or five drakes safely within our quarters.
After they perceived that they h[ad] lost the two brass peeces—which
they did imagine wee we[re] not able to drawe of—there whole body
of foote with forty colours drawes themselves within pistoll shott to the
raged jetty—where theire great was—being resolved to fall upon it
that night, but by the order they perceived was taken to keepe
two hundreth musqueteres without the jetty which could not have
beene donn, if they had had ordinance and puttinge so many resolved
men within the jetty, they took themselves to their heeles about midnight and retired to their head quarter ; my Lord Newcastle and
Leifetenant-generall Kinge were beholders of the second part of this
act, and as is reported, Kinge is wounded in t[w]o severall places. Our
ordinance hath donn them a great deale of mischeife, and if wee had
had a fresh body of foote they had beene put to a great strayte. In
their retyringe ther other god stuck in the dirt untill all the country
people were called to drawe her of. Amongst the captaines—who
deserved all well—Micklewhaite, Persons, Bethel and Hardstaffe for
the horse [and] Captaine Clayton, the bearer hereof, haveinge a generall
love of all the souldiers, did very good service. Captaine Salmond,
Captaine Sibbald, and Captaine Crookes for the foote did carry themselves very valiantly. I had [a] blowe on the side by a slugg of cutted
yron shott from the [Queen]es pcice but thankes to God am not the
worse. I believe he[r] Majestie if she had knowne where the shott
should have   would have checked the gunner for
not charginge full   were in service in Yorkshire.
Wee hard the noise of the encounter in Lyncolnshire whereunto God
hath pleased to give a happy issue whereby you may persave that
God is upon the stage and that Dagon must downe. Since the begin-
ninge of my letter we understand that Colonell Rainsborough is safe."
Signed. Seal. [N. III., 50.]

Sir John Byron to Colonel Aldrich, Governor of Aylesbury.

1643, October 16. Oxford.—"I have adventured upon the former
acquaintance I had with you, to send this messenger to you, whom I
desire you will do no prejudice to, howsoever you entertain the motion
I shall make to you, which is only this ; that if you please to employ this
or any other trusty person to pass betwixt us I shall propound something
to you both for your honour and advantage, and that with all imaginable
secrecy which shall be punctually performed." (See *Lords' Journals,*
vi. 284.) [N. III., 51.]

Gabriel Barbor to the Honourable Sir John Lentall, Speaker
of the House of Commons (*sic*).

1643, October 17. Hertford.—"Upon notice received from certain
persons fled out of Bedford that Bedford is taken, as this our scout can
relate, and who can tell the pains of Sir John Norwich, who twice

sending out his warrants for horse and foot in Bedfordshire had not above 18 men come in, both out of town and country, wherein the honourable House may perceive how prepared they are to welcome the enemy, and the like we may fear in our country, for that some captains —as I am informed—do dispatch their soldiers to join with the volunteers of our new militia, and malignant gentlemen and others do all they can to hinder that business for the preparing a freer ingress for the enemy. I hope you will call in this our honest neighbour, who can more particularly relate, and I hope the House will be pleased speedily to promise some aid from his Excellency to Sir John Norwich, who disarmed and brought with him all the Malignants' arms, in and near Bedford. We doubt not you will command our Deputy Lieutenants to come down and give their assistance, lest the Malignants presently take the opportunity to draw the enemy into our county to receive their rents and sequestration business." [N. III., 52.]

John Sleigh, Mayor, to John Rushworth.

1643, October 19. Berwick.—Acknowledging his letter. "Thank God it was upon my resolution, though much against the mind of some of our Aldermen and others. I could certify you how much I have been opposed. . . The work is done, wherein I bless God I have been a main instrument. At that time and since I am grumbled at exceedingly by many of our neighbours, but weigh it not." Have against my will accepted the office of Mayor for the present year in order to prevent a Malignant being chosen. *Seal.* [N. III., 53.]

The Earl of Essex to William Lenthall.

1643, October 19.—Desiring that Mr. Henry Nott be appointed Guardian of the Fleet prison. (See *Commons' Journals.* iii. 283.) *Signed. Seal.* [N. III., 54.]

Sir William Brereton to [William Lenthall].

1643, October 21. Nantwich.—Desiring that the King's, Queen's, and Prince's revenues in Cheshire might be applied for the supply of the necessities of the soldiers there, and also that Mr. Henry Cockson might be appointed by the Committee for Sequestrations Solicitor for that County. (Printed in Grey, iii. 48.) [N. III., 55.]

Sir John Byron to Colonel Aldrich.

1643, October 21. Oxford.—"I have acquainted his Majesty with your letter, and only him, who is graciously pleased to give you assurance of his acceptance of your service by his own hand. His Majesty hath reason to be cautious in regard of the late failure at Poole upon a treaty of the same nature; and therefore what you propound in this business let it be done with that clearness and ingenuity, that it may not undergo any such suspicion. His Majesty would not have you go suddenly to attempt this business, as thereby to do any prejudice to it, but leaves both the time and manner of doing it to your own discretion, who being on the place can best judge of those circumstances. What you think fit to be done on this side, shall be punctually observed with all secrecy ; it rests only now that you declare yourself more particularly, and lay the design so that in human reason—leaving the success to God—it may not fail."

At foot in the King's hand :—" I approve of this letter. Charles R."
[N. III , 56.]

Sir William Brereton and Sir Thomas Middleton to William Lenthall.

1643, October 21.—"Wee with the forces could bee spared out of Cheshire having seised on Wem, a markett towne in Shropshire we endeavoured the entrenchment thereof as a comodyous and fitting place for our retyrement, if occacion should enforce us. The Lord Capell and counsell att Shrewsbury—sensible as it seemes of our intencions, and of the dangerous consequence would thereon happen, if they should permitte us quietlye to fortefye and entrench it—endeavored all they could to prevente and oppose us in it, and to that purpose havinge procured all the assistance that Lichfeild, Dudley, Worcester, Chester, Shropshire and Walles could make they drewe uppe into one bodye mette nere Ellesmire in Shropshire, had three cannons, two drakes, and one great morterpeece that carryed a thirty pound bullet, had one hundred and twenty odd waggons and carriages laden with bread, biskett, beare, and other provisions, and theire armye being formydable as consistinge of ncere five thousand, as the prisoners since taken by us doe relate, the enemye tooke the feild and encamped uppon yesterdaye sevenight all night in the feild ncere Culmeere aboute the middway betwixt Ellesmyre and Wem towards us; but [at] Lappington a place not so soone to bee forgotten by them, remarkable for their late crueltye in hurninge of the church, and of the currageous opposicion made there against them by a very small party of ours—as in our former lettres wee have signified about sixteen dayes past—the enemye altered his course—though that were the next fittest and rediest way for his advance to Wem—and marched backe and soe to a side slippe towne called Welsh Hampton intendinge to have marched thence the rediest way over a place called Blackhorse Ford towards us ; but a partye of our horse being sent forth, and facing him, hee made a stand in the open feilds there aboute Hampton, came not as we expected, stayed all that night ensueinge being Saturday in the open feilds againe and the small villages, and uppon the Sabbath day in steed of advanceinge towards us the enemye with all his said forces, luggage and carriages wheeled to the left hand into Maylor a parte of Flintshire, and directly over a place or great common called Fens heath hee marched into Whitchurch ; where the towne being malignant entertayned him for that night, rung bells for demonstracion of his welcome and added unto him a further supply of souldiers. . . . Notice thereof beinge given us in Wem wee advanced thence about twelve of the clocke in the night with our carriages and ordynance after him, sett our armye in battalia uppon Prees heath by breake of daye, and being in that posture within two myles of the enemye, wee lay there in expectacion till aboute noone, that the enemye would have waged battell with us. During which tyme wee oulie tooke two prisoners both Welsh, and of the enemyes scouts, by whom wee gott intelligence that the enemye understandinge of our beinge was that Monday morninge earlye advanced with his whole Armye and forces for the surprise of Namptwich in hope that all the garrison forces were out of towne with us, and that thereuppon they should fynd noe resistance. Whereuppon wee advanced speedelye after the enemye with the bodye of our whole armye, in hope eyther to gett betwixt him and the towne of Namptwich, or els to fall on him in the reare, but the enemye being not to bee overtaken, and the night approachinge, for avoydance of ambuscadoes and other danger that might occurre in the darke unto us, we diverted our ccurse, and marched on the right hand from a towne called Ashe in Shropshire unto Drayton, and thence agayne after a short repast advanced for Namptwich whither with all our forces wee came by breake of day uppon Tuesday morninge last for the townes relcife. But it soe hapned that the enemye having receaved unexpected entertaynement from the towne of Namptwich uppon his approach thither which was about eleven of the clocke in the aforenoone of the Munday; having receaved a great repulse, and losse of about forty of his men being taken prisoners —notwithstandinge hee had with his forces seised on Haghton Church and Dartford Hall both within halfe a myle of the towne and there had intended to raise his batterye—nevertheles what with the despaire hee hadd of attayninge the towne by reason of the courages of the defendants and of the intelligence hee received the approch of our armye from Drayton to its succour aboute twelve in the night the enemye rose with all his carriages and in haste backe unto Whitchurch, whither by breake of daye hee came with his armye; in his way having miserablye spoyled and plundered the cuntrye accordinge to his usuall course; whence agayne after a matter of three or four howres refreshment of himselfe and forces, hee advaunced straight for the towne of Wem; and aboute two of the clocke uppon Tuesday last sate down with his whole armye upon the east and north sides thereof—the other two sides of the towne beinge overdrowned by reason of our entrench-ments soe that hee could not come to the town on eyther of those partes for to assault it. — But such was our souldiers' wearines by reason of the foresaid long marches the two nights and day before that notwithstandinge our industrye and best endevours to have contynued in pursuite of the enemye and to have prevented the seige, yet by noe means could any perswacion at all avayle with them, untill they should have a day of refreshment which of necessitye wee were compelled to condescend unto. And thereupon wee advanced from Namptwich uppon the Wednesday morninge very earlye in pursuite of the enemye, and for the succour of Collonell Mytton, Mr. Mackworthe, Captayne Thomas Hunte and other of our friends in Wem; whoe though they had not within the towne above three hundred men to defend the towne and outworkes, yet soe valiantlye behaved themselves that they defended the walls of the towne—mauger the furious assalte of the enemyes—who likewise came on currageouslye, untill the enemye uppon the Wednesday having intelligence of our approch raised his seige, and hasted with all his carriages and ammunicion for Shrewsburye, whom after a fifteen myles march our forces eagerly and most currageouslye pursued as farre as Lee Bridge aboute four myles from Shrewsburye where there was great opposicion made by the enemye whilist theire carriages were in going into Shrewsburye. But aboute twelve of the clocke on Wednesday night after much and great fight, it pleased God to get the victory to our men, whoe having won the bridge pursued the enemye above a myle further, and in the pursuite tooke divers prisoners, and thereuppon by reason of the night, and the danger of the enemyes ambuscadoes which were that night very frequent with him, wee with our whole armye after a twenty myles march retreated into Wem; where wee found all our friends theire left in health, having had but three men slayn in the towne during the seige; whereof Majour Marrow was one. In the fight att the Bridge wee lost five men, and had aboute fifteen wounded. None of ours were taken prisoners, of the enemye many were slayne, whereof ten wee found together slayne att the end of the bridge. Wee tooke there and that night one Captain Chapman a man formerly exchainged, and many other officers and common souldiers. Wee tooke alsoe Collonell Scriven's Captain-Livetenant, prisoner. If the night had not hindred us wee had entred att leastwise into the subburbs of Shrewsburye before our returne; and putt a period to the trouble of that countye, in regard of the great discomfiture of the enemye and that hee fledd before us, many of his greatest comaunders being either slayne, or wounded, and the rest soe overwearyed with longe marches, nightlye watchinges and our pursuites that wee verely conceave they have now cause to forsweare theire raisinge any more in armes. Collonell William Wyn of Llanvar in Denbighshire, whoe was the pryme comander of the Welsh forces and had broughte downe out of Wales with him about seven hundred musketeers in his regyment, was slayne outright with a shott from the towne, Collonell Scriven was shott in the shoulder, and as wee heare it credibly reported is since dead, though not of that wound yet of another hee received att the Bridge. One Captayne Wyn was slayne, Collonell Wyllis hurte, one Captayne Davys mortallie wounded and taken, his livetenant taken one Captain Ellys sore hurt and wounded, and by report of the prisoners one Captayne Manley is alsoe wounded with many more, besides manye common souldiers and others were slayne in the seige from the towne, and lefte in the open feilds dead and unburyed whose naked bodyes wee sawe miserably torne with the shott and lyeing in the feilds neer the towne, which wee gave order to bee buryed. Wee heare likewise that Majour Broughton, Majour Trevour, Captayne Bread, and others of the enemys are alsoe sore wounded, and that the enemye att his retreat from Wem carryed alonge with him four cartloads of wounded officers. Thus you may evidently perceave how God hath helped us, and in what case wee now stand for the reducinge of the whole countye of Saloppe, which in itselfe is rotten, there having not bin soe much as one of them that have joyned or taken up armes with Collonell Mytton since his coming into the countye for its defence or preservacion, and likewise for the reducinge of all Northwales, from whence the maggazyne of all his Majestie's provisions of victualls and men doe proceed, and alsoe of Chester whoe by reason of the cessacion of armes in Ireland dalye expecte the rebells landing and arrivals. Wee want but only five hundred horse and five hundred foote to helpe us, and a matter of 3,000l. in mony. Therwith if you will please to move the House in to afford us, wee doubt not but by God's assistance wee should then bee of abilitye to reduce all these whole cuntryes speedelye. Wee have a designe in hand, wherein if it please God to blesse us with successe, it may prove very advantageous for the state, wee only now want monyes, and for further present supply for the prosecution of the enemye, and reducing of the whole countye of Salopp and the countyes adjacent. And without monyes there is noe good to bee expected of the souldiers." *Signed. Seal.* [N. III., 57.]

Sir David Watkins to John Rushworth,

1643, October 23.—" The Committee chosen in London for the affairs of Ireland are extremely discontented that they could not obtain the favour of the House to read their propositions annexed to their Petition, that all the House might have judged the candour of their actions, and extreme willingness to promote the affairs of Ireland in this sad and distracted time. I pray entreat Mr. Speaker to promise them to be read this morning, which will give great satisfaction to the Adventurers, and I am confident will greatly conduce to the safety of Ireland by opposing that horrid cessation." *Seal.* [N. III., 58.]

The Earl of Essex to William Lenthall.

1643, October 26. St. Albans. — Concerning his having released Sir Henry Barclay in exchange for Lieutenant-Colonel Hungerford. *Signed. Seal.* [N. III., 59.]

Sir John Byron to Colonel Aldrich.

1643, October 26.—"I have acquainted his Majesty with your last letter, who approves of your caution, and would not have you adventure anything but upon sure grounds. We are now marching towards Newport with a great part of our horse to secure the fortifying of that place, wherein we hear the enemy intends to give us some interruption. If you can now find a fit opportunity to execute our design I shall be quartered near Buckingham, where I have taken order your letter shall find me if you think fit to write, and shall be ready to come with such a proportion both of horse and foot as you shall prescribe, but—as I formerly wrote to you—you, who are upon the place are the best judge of the circumstances, both now and when this business is to be done, and therefore my request shall still be to you not to precipitate anything, but to lay the designs so that—with God's blessing—we may effect what we intend." [N. III., 60.]

The Earl of Essex to Sir Oliver Luke, Sir Gilbert Pickering, and others.

1643, October 29. St. Albans.—"Having sent out a considerable party of horse and foot from my army for the clearing of the counties of Bedford, Bucks, Northampton, and Hertford, from the ravage and spoil of the enemy, which hath occasioned the enemy to quit the towns of Newport and Bedford, and is in the field drawn out, by God's goodness my forces are in Newport. I thought good to acquaint you that I hold it fit that a garrison should be drawn into Newport to be raised and maintained by the aforesaid counties, therefore I desire you forthwith to send two committees such as are appointed by the Parliament in each of the aforesaid counties, giving them instructions in the behalf of that county from the which they are sent, to consult upon such ways and means as may speed the aforesaid service, and for the better expediting of it I desire that you would meet tomorrow in St. Albans, where my quarters are, that so they may have my directions in the settlement of that garrison." (See *Commons' Journals*, iii. 295.) *Signed.* [N. III., 61.]

Sir Samuel Luke to John Pym.

1643, October 29. St. Albans.—"By his Excellency's command I make bold to give you an account how graciously the Lord hath dealt with him in delivering up into his hands the town of Newport, which might have been defended by the forces which were in it against far greater forces than he had [sent again]st them, but though theirs was great bo[th hors]e and foot, and the King and Queen's guard interested there, yet their want of arms and ammunition was such that upon Thursday night last they forsook the town and drew themselves into a body between it and Stony Stratford in the fields, where they stood all that night and a great part of the next day, and are still hovering up and down thereabouts. His Excellency's desire is that some gentlemen of the Associated Counties may come down to him and some out of each of the Counties of Bedford, Buckingham, and Northampton, for the

Serjeant-Major-General by his Excellency's command is now finishing those works which were there begun, and before he leaves it will victual the town sufficiently, so that there will need a conference of the Associated Counties both for putting in a garrison and maintaining it afterwards." *Seal.* [N. III., 62.]

The EARL OF ESSEX to the SPEAKER OF THE HOUSE OF PEERS *pro tempore.*

1643, October 30. St. Albans.—"Although the foot have been weakened more for want of pay than they were at the battle of Newberry Wash, and the rest of the march, and the horse much wasted by continual fight and duty, yet it pleased God so much to advance the cause, as that although the enemy was possessed at Newport with greater force than we could spare to send thither against them—it being thought unfit by the Council of War to move with the whole army by reason of the deepness of the ways—yet such a panick fear possessed them, as that they quitted the place, we being upon our march, and your forces are possessed of it. But without a present considerable supply of money to pay the army, it will quickly be consumed, we being not able to recruit it, and it was well known to all that, though the army had but a little pay allowed them, and some clothes, how many of the old soldiers came in to us when we went for the relief of Gloucester. And, my Lord, soldiers that have done so good service will expect duly their pay if not reward.. In the second place I have to acquaint you how gallantly and faithfully Colonel Aldrich, Governor of Aylesbury, hath discharged his duty, having had such great temptations to have done the Parliament so great a disservice, which your Lordships will perceive by these enclosed. And if the Parliament please to take notice of it, it will be a great encouragement for others to do them service in letting that garrison be paid, it being a frontier and he rewarded or at least his arrears paid him. *Postscript.*—I thought not fit to publish the business concerning Aylesbury, till we were possessed of Newport." (See *Lords' Journals*, vi. 289.) *Signed. Seal.* [N. III., 63.]

WILLIAM GOLDINGHAM, RICHARD HARLAKENDEN, and others to WILLIAM LENTHALL.

1643, October 31. [Saffron] Walden.—Desiring the speedy passing of an Ordinance offered from them by Mr. Grimston for levying money in the county. *Signed.* [N. III., 64.]

JOHN LADE, Mayor, SIR JAMES OXINDEN, and others, to WILLIAM LENTHALL.

1643, October 31. Canterbury.—"What our Cathedrals have been, how prejudicial to the public weal, is a thing so well known, as that we shall need to say no more." We are constrained by the daily complaints of the scandalous and seditious preachments in the Cathedral to request that they also may be sequestered and some more religious and judicious preachers appointed. (See *Commons' Journals*, iii. 299.) *Signed. Seal.*

> Enclosed:—"Such and so scandalous, have the preachments of the Cathedral of Canterbury, especially of late, been, that one Dr. Jackson, Senior Prebend, was himself in person with Mr. Mayor of the said city, and wished the gates of the church might be shut up, that there might be no more such preaching. *Signed* 'John Lade, Mayor.'" [N. III., 65.]

Colonel RALPH ASSHETON and others to WILLIAM LENTHALL.

[1643, October. Manchester.]—" The appearance of our dangers by these and the like intelligence of the common enemy the Irish by sea or the Isle of Man together with the eminency of so potent a force upon our Borders from Yorkshire, and our county being so long in extent and so abundant in Papists and persons ill affected, who are no longer quiet than they are overpowered and upon the least commotion ready to bestir themselves to our general destruction at home enforces us, together with the sending up of these letters . . intercepted from Ireland to move the due consideration of our so general perils, which we humbly conceive cannot be more probably prevented them by the hastening of the Scottish forces in to our assistance and prevention of the total loss of the North parts, if it be much longer delayed." We also desire the benefit of our County Palatine Seal and that a Sheriff be appointed. *Postscript.*—For our better securities from dangers out of Yorkshire and facilitating any service we may be able to do our friends expelled thence in the recovery of their estates, we much desire the Lord Fairfax might be accommodated with a better strength of foot to discourage the greatest body of the enemy from falling on our borders." *Signed. Seal.* [N. VIII., 129.]

SIR EDWARD NICHOLAS to LORD GORING.

1643, November 1. Oxford.—" I have acquainted the king and queen with your Lordship's of the 29th of October st[ilo]n[ovo], who were both very glad to hear of your Lordship's safe arrival, as having often spoken solicitously concerning the danger of your passage. Their Majesties are extremely joyed at the good news you write of the Princess Royal's being so much grown, and of her Highness being so well pleased with the tender care of the Prince and Princess of Orange towards her. The French Ambassador—Mons. de Harcourt—hath been here at Oxford almost this fortnight, and we are here so entered into the Treaty, as that upon what the Ambassador delivered there to the king there have
b e n e p r o p o s i t i o n s
12:26:17:58:25:29:30:5:33:36:21:18:31:43:62:45:46:48:
d e l i v e r e d t o
39:26:16:18:4:26:30:58:13:7:51:5: him, whereof your Lordship
    c o p p y
shall by my next have a 10:36:29:33:22:47: Their Majesties would not have your Lordship to go from Holland, till you hear again from me, which shall be by the next. His Majesty very well approves of your prudent intimation given concerning his Majesty's
r e s e n t m e n t of the d i s
32:26:21:$_{58}$: 17:31:28:58:45:51:47 : 526 : 609 : 39:43:21:
h o n o r   h e a r
27:5:45:36:32:47: done him on that side by their 44:58:11:32:
i n g of S t r i c k l a n d
18:17:19:25:526:21:31:30:18:10:6:16:56:39:48: and I am
  the i r Ambassador s
confident 609:18:30:3: 365 :21:25: will find it if they
c o m e   i n
35:5:37:58:23: that their Majesties are very sensible of that 18:17:
d i g n i t y   T h i n
13:43:19:45:43:51:66:7: Your news of the Lady 51:44:18:45:
    the i r Majesty s
47: was news indeed to me, and it made 609:18:30: 500 :46: merry

By that gross lie you may judge of the rest of the intelligence you find there, but falsehoods have been the foundation of the present Rebellion and miseries here, and without the continuance thereof they cannot support
the i r Majesty s command
their wickedness. Both 609 : 18 : 30 : 500 : 21 : 7 : have 398 :
e d m e t o the i r p l e a
26 : 13 : 7 : 28 : 58 : 31 : 62 : signify 609 : 18 : 32 : 7 : 29 : 16 : 26 : 11 :
s u r e to i n
46 : 54 : 32 : 26 : 47 : 602 : your Lordship that you use all possible 18 : 17
d u s t r y b y the Prince of Orange
13 : 4 : 21 : 51 : 32 : 22 : 48 : 12 : 22 : 609 : 256 : 526 : 246 : and
u n d e r h a n d
otherwise handsomely 4 : 17 : 13 : 26 : 30 : 23 : 44 : 24 : 45 : 39 : to
h i n d e r the c o m i n g o v
27 : 18 : 45 : 13 : 26 : 32 : 47 : 609 : 10 : 5 : 28 : 18 : 45 : 19 : 7 : 5 : 54 :
e r of Ambassador s the s t a
26 : 32 : 48 : 526 : any 365 : 21 : 47 : from 609 : 21 : 31 : 56 :
t e s that they
51 : 26 : 46 : 48 : for it is here apprehended 604 : 7 : 607 : will do here
m o r e h u r t g o o d
37 : 36 : 30 : 26 : 7 : 44 : 54 : 30 : 51 : 47 : than 41 : 36 : 62 : 39 : 7 : 25 : As
b r i n g i n h[g]
concerning the proposition for 55 : 30 : 18 : 17 : 19 : 61 : 17 : 44 : 23 :
of c o a l e s t o Holland Newcastle The
526'. 35 : 5 : 57 : 16 : 26 : 46 : 7 : 51 : 62 : 197 : 48 : from 241 : 151 :
King Nicholas (me) command
approves of it so well as he hath given 240 : 7 : 398 : to
I s h a l l
send a warrant as 467 : 21 : 27 : 11 : 16 : 38 : 23 : do tomorrow to my
Lord of Newcastle
490 : 526 : 241 : to take order that it may be permitted to such
persons as your Lordship shall contract with, and his Majesty's
pleasure is that your Lordship proceed in that business with effect to
f u r n i s h e arm s and m u n i t i
9 : 4 : 30 : 17 : 18 : 21 : 27 : 26 : 25 : 369 : 46 : 361 : 28 : 4 : 17 : 18 : 31 : 43 :
o n England c o a l e s send
5 : 45 : 57 : into 48 : 149 : for 7 : 10 : 5 : 11 : 16 : 26 : 46 : 47 : What you 579 :
for the Irish sent to D a r t m o u t h
434 : 609 : 480 : must be 580 : 602 : 13 : 11 : 30 : 31 : 28 : 5 : 4 : 31 : 27 : 3 :
W e y m o u t h o r Dublin
14 : 26 : 22 : 37 : 36 : 54 : 51 : 44 : 7 : 5 : 30 : 23 : 91 : and for what is to
go the North
444 : into 609 : 47 : 519 : 48 : your Lordship is to receive directions from
Lord of Newcastle
490 : 526 : 241 : I humbly thank your Lordship for my son; I pray
he may be as capable to serve you as I am desirous to do it here. I
S r
have acquainted the King and Queen with the good service 21 : 30 : 23 :
C h a r l e s H a r b e r t
10 : 27 : 11 : 30 : 16 : 26 : 21 : 47 : 27 : 24 : 30 : 12 : 26 : 32 : 31 : 7 : hath
done in Holland, which their Majesties take very well, and would not
have him come over, till your Lordship go for France at soonest. Since
Digby · Secretary Nicholas i s i n
129 : hath been 7 : 585 : your 240 : 18 : 21 : not so much 18 : 17 :
[e]
e s t e e m t with the Queen
26 : 21 : 31 : 26 : 58 : 28 : 51 : 47 : 632 : 609 : 560 : as he was, but notwith-

I   a   m   the   the Queen
standing 467 : 11 : 28 : 7 : 609 : same man still. I assure you 609 : 549 : 7 :
p   o   w   e   r   a   s   e   u   e   r
hath as much 29 : 5 : 14 : 26 : 30 : 47 : 11 : 21 : 26 : 4 : 58 : 30 : The
French Ambassador   to   m   a   k   e   a   quarrel in
164   365 :   hopes 602 : 28 : 11 : 6 : 26 : 7 : 57 : 47 : 559 : 458 :
the army I   he   n   o   t   b   e   a   b   l   e
381 : 467 : doubt 455 : will 17 : 5 : 31 : 48 : 12 : 26 : 11 : 12 : 16 : 26 :
e   f   f   e   c   t   P   r   o   p   o   s   i   t   i
7 : to 26 : 9 : 40 : 58 : 10 : 31 : 7 : it. 29 : 30 : 5 : 33 : 36 : 21 : 18 : 31 : 43 :
o   n   s   to the French Ambassador t   o
62 : 17 : 21 : 48 : are by us delivered 602 : 609 : 164 : 365 : 48 : 31 : 5 :
f   u   r   n   i   s   h   e   Irish with money arms   a   n   d
9 : 4 : 30 : 17 : 18 : 21 : 27 : 26 : the 482 : 632 : 512 : 369 : 11 : 17 : 13 :
m   u   n   i   t   i   o   n   sent them   France
7 : 28 : 4 : 17 : 18 : 31 : 43 : 5 : 45 : and he hath 580 : 610 : 47 : into 163 : to
t[h]e   n   c   e   d   i   r   e   c   t   i   o   n   s
receive 31 : 26 : 17 : 10 : 58 : 7 : 13 : 18 : 30 : 26 : 10 : 51 : 43 : 5 : 17 : 21 :
a   o   n   s   w   e   a   r   s   to g   i   v   e
48 : what 11 : 5 : 17 : 21 : 14 : 26 : 11 : 30 : 59 : 47 : 602 : 19 : 18 : 5 : 26 : 48 :
to them
602 : 610 : My Lord Duke and his Duchess are firmly yours and will be
glad to receive your letters, when your Lordship hath leisure. You
may boldly affirm that all the forces that are arrived or sent for from
Ireland are only the English soldiers, Protestants who are not able to
live there for want of supplies, and that they were sent for as well to
preserve them from starving as' to make use of them here. If the
rebellious city of London had as much disposition to peace, as we that
are in Oxon, you would see a happy end of the present intestine troubles
here. I hear that your son the Colonel is sent back into the North to
be exchanged, but I have it not from so good a hand, as to give your
Lordship assurance of the truth of it." . . . [N. III., 66.]

Major-General PHILIP SKIPPON to the EARL OF ESSEX.

1643, November 2, one p.m. Newport.—"Our party of horse is
well returned . . . without loss of one man, as far as I yet hear.
The passage to the enemy's quarters at Alderton within two miles of
Towcester was so narrow that but one horse—as they say—could pass at
once, and the enemy was very vigilant, yet Col. Middleton—a very
worthy sober man—with only Col. Harvie's regiment—for Col. Turner's
he left to make good the passage behind him, and Col. Norris' regiment
being to watch this night went not—charged in with their guards, killed
—as they say—about 20 men have brought away as many prisoners with
a lieutenant of horse all which and some other prisoners taken at our
coming hither shall . . be sent to-morrow to St. Albans. All the
officers of both the regiments of horse that lay at Alderton viz. that
which was Carnarvon's now Nelvill's and Sands'— excepting his
lieutenant and lieutenant-colonel—were there, but kept close in the
houses so that it was not thought fit to stay so long—the enemy at
Towcester having taken the alarm—as to break into them. 'Tis
reported they intended to have visited some of our quarters, and now the
rather being provoked. I hope we shall be provided for them if they
come, and all shall be well by the help of our God, on which I wholly
rely. The Lieutenant that is prisoner says that as soon as they have
fortified Towcester all shall to their winter quarters except Sir Charles
Lucas with his brigade consisting of 2,500 horse, who is to go to

Huntingdon, and so into Suffolk, Norfolk &c. I have not yet heard what Northampton horse have done last night,—who were resolved to try on their side also—therefore I cannot yet inform your Excellency. . . 'Tis a thousand pities the enemy should nestle so near us. If I had a competent strength . . . I would have a bout with them, but as I am, and this place being yet so very open, it is not counselable, for the enemy hath 12 regiments of horse 3,000 foot at least, six pieces, one a demi-culverin, and many commanded foot out of Oxford being come unto them,—if our intelligence be true—.I beseech your Excellency cause four good scouts to stay here with me, for I have none but by chance, and be pleased to call upon the Committee of Hertfordshire, and let Sir Samuel Luke do the like to those of Bedfordshire that we may have money to pay our old soldiers on Saturday next, or we shall be but in an ill condition with them. Good my Lord think upon us and there shall be nothing wanting here by the help of God to hold all in good order. There is a rumour that there is money come to St. Albans for the army. If so, and we should want here, all our soldiers will leave us and go thither." . . . *Seal.* [N. III., 71.]

The Earl of Essex to William Lenthall.

1643, November 2. St. Albans.—Stating that the Committees of Northampton, Buckingham, Hertford and Bedford, had agreed to pay eight fourteenths of the cost of the garrison of Newport, and suggesting that Cambridge, Huntingdon and Essex ought to contribute proportionally. (See *Commons' Journals,* iii. 300.) *Signed. Seal.* [N. III., 67.]

Sir John Potts, Sir John Palgrave, Framlingham Gawdy and others to William Lenthall.

1643, November 6. [Norwich.]—Certifying on behalf of Sir William Doyly that he had appeared, and given reasons for not having returned sooner from Holland. *Signed. Seal.* [N. III., 68.]

Roberton Thoriton, Mayor, William Stewart, Sir Frederick Hamilton, Robert Stewart, Robert Sanderson, Thomas Staples, James Galbrithe, Thomas Dirdo, Sidney Cunningham, Archibald Colvill, Edward Hartwell, Robert Lawson, James Erskyn, Henry Vaughan, Simon Pask, Henry Finch, Henry Osborne, and John Kilner to the Lord Chancellor of Scotland and others.

1643, November 8. Londonderry.—"Amidst the many sad resolutions of our affairs, it is not the least addition to our sufferings that after our best endeavours employed against the bloody and barbarous rebels, as with happy success so with great expense, at last our sun should so far set in a cloud, as we should be misunderstood by your Lordship of most eminent place and quality in that kingdom, to whom next unto God and our king, and the Parliament and State of England it is our desire to approve ourselves. If we could dispense with the loss of our estates, yet the blood of our dearest friends and countrymen, so cruelly, treacherously and abundantly shed, cannot but still sound a loud alarm in our ears. And if that also could perhaps be passed by in silence, yet we hope the divine mercy will never suffer us to fall into such security, as to make light account of the great hazard which may ensue unto the true worship of God in this kingdom by the prevailing of that bloody and heretical party.

If your Lordship and the rest of that most honourable State may be pleased to afford a serious view of our present condition, and what the strength may be of our small and scattered forces consisting of men robbed of their estates at first, and since exhausted of their credit by two years' service without any considerable pay, your Lordships will find many inevitable necessities cast upon us for the intermission of action this short time past, amongst which your Lordships' resolution to withdraw the forces commanded by Monroe, joined with our own absolute want of ammunition, victuals and all other necessaries is not the least. Neither could it be expected from us that when General-Major Monroe thought fitter to retire with his forces into his quarters upon intimation of the cessation, we should still have kept the field especially in this season of the year, which of itself inforceth a cessation to men so meanly accommodated in all respects. Yet some of us being necessitated to go to Dublin gave order that our men should stay upon the fields to destroy or gain the rebels' corn. And if it shall please God to incline your Lordships and the State of Scotland to a brotherly and tender feeling of our condition, and to a just sense of the annoyances of our extirpation hence, and to be pleased to continue your army under Monro, and to take into your care our present wants of victuals ammunition &c., till we can be otherwise supplied and to be a means to hasten those supplies promised and provided for us by the Parliament in England—all which we most humbly desire—and also to recommend our wants and dangerous estate and condition to the King's Majesty and Parliament of England, your Lordships may rest assured we shall want neither affection nor zeal to the prosecution of these rebels, so long as there runneth a drop of warm blood in our veins, whereunto we are also warranted by his Majesty's favourable Commissions." *Copy.* [N. III., 69.]

Sir Michael Livesey and others to William Lenthall.

1643, November 9. Rochester.—Stating they had sent up some of Sir Edward Hales' servants in pursuance of the Order of the 3rd. (See *Commons' Journals*, iii. 301.) *Signed.* [N. III., 70.]

Colonel Wardlaw, Governor of Plymouth, to William Lenthall.

1643, November 11.—Describing the taking of Mount Stanford. (Printed in *King's Pamphlets*, E. 76. No. 11.) *Signed. Seal.* [N. III., 72.]

The Earl of Warwick to William Lenthall.

1643, November 11. Downs.—If the Houses " do not speedily send some more men to Plymouth, and a careful faithful commander to command the island there, and the House lay their commands on the Mayor and Committees to let the Governor command the Magazine, which now, as I hear, they keep from him, and that there be powder great shot of all sorts, and small shot sent with all speed, otherwise the town will be in danger to be lost." *Signed. Seal.* [N. III., 73.]

———— Cunyngham to the Earl of Warwick.

1643, November 11. Gravesend.—Desiring him to recommend Captain Hodges' business to the Houses, that the prize-money of the two Bristol vessels he has taken may expeditiously distributed. (See *Commons' Journals*, iii. 314.) *Seal.* [N. III., 74.]

Sir William Brereton to William Lenthall.

1643, November 11. Wrexham.—"Wee drewe out upon Tuesday last five Cheshire foote companies and three or foure troopes of horse and three or foure companies of countrey dragooners, which were all we could spare—consideringe them at Stafford and att Wem—wherewith theire joined five companies of Lancashire foote and one or two troopes of horse and one or two companies of dragooners under the comand of Colonell John Booth and Leutenant-Colonell Peter Egerton, and about twoe hundred foote and one troope of horse of Sir Thomas Myddelton's, with which wee advanced that night to Farne which is a little towne on Cheshire side—over against the Holt in Wales, wherein the enimy kept a garrison in the castle and had contracted all the strengthe and powre of Wales for our resistance for which purpose they runge their bells backeward and fired the becons throughout Wales to maintaine that passage against us beinge our onely way into Wales for which end they had alsoe made a towre and drawbridge and stronge gates upon the bridge soe as both they and wee conceived it verie difficulte if not altogether ympossible to make way for our passage over the bridge and therefore our designe was to face them upon the bridge and in the meane tyme to attempt by boates to lande over some of our foote; to prevent which our enimy was soe watchfull and circumspecte as that they placed theire ambuscadoes in the hedges and soe soone as our boates appeared on the water they gave fire and beate our men from their boates, soe as wee were in much danger to loose them, when there remayned unto us noe other way but to march downe the riverside with our foote towardes some cariages of ours—wherein wee had turnells which wee had purposely provided to amaze the enimy—as though we had intended to have forced our passage there alsoe. To interrupt and prevent which intended designe of ours they brought theire foote all alonge the riverside soe farre remote from the bridge as that they gave us the opportunitye to make a desperate assault upon the bridge by placeinge ladders to the toppe of the drawbridge and cuttinge the ropes. Which beinge done and the bridg falling downe wee had accesse to the gates and casting over some hand granadoes amongst the Welsh men —who there remayned—which strucke such a terror into them as that they all run away and could not be obtained to returne. Whereby wee had a verie faire opportunitie to force open the gates; which being done the enimy was without much difficultie beaten from theire double workes within the gates; whose runinge away did soe exceedingly amaze theire forces who were otherwise verie much encouraged by repulsinge our men and by theire hopes to gaine our boates att which tyme the most of our men were exceedingly discouraged, when it pleased God by this unexpected entrance to open a doore into Wales. Soe as the glorie thereof is wholly to be ascribed to God to whom alone the same is due, and who is able to make way for the advancement of his own worke through the greatest difficulties, yea such indeed as in humane apprehension seeme impossible: such was the entrance over the bridge which they judged an impregnable place. There was Colonell Ellis' regiment of foote, Major Trevor his regiment of horse and all the forces which could be raised in the adjoineing partes of Wales. Whom wee pursued, and routed both horse and foote, tooke about fouretie comon prisoners, one captaine, foure or five leyfetenauntes one cornet and some say one of them is a Leutenaunt-Colonell whom wee have not had tyme yet to examine. In this fight and pursuite wee lost few or none. And aboute six of the clocke upon Thursday eveninge wee entred Wrexham which is one of the chiefe townes in these partes of Wales and lyes within seven miles of Chester verie comodious to hinder all the passages to Chester. The enimy fly apace and begin to remove all their goodes out of these partes, but Holt Castle holds out, butt is beseidged. Wee have likewise obstructed the passages neere Chester on the other sides att Tarvin and Wirrall soe as I hope through Gods mercie wee may be able to give a good accoumpt thereof if care may be taken that the kinges forces may not fall downe upon us to oppresse and swallowe us up and that some from my Lord Generall's armye may waite upon and imploy them." *Signed. Seal* torn out. [N. III., 75.]

The MAYOR and JURATS OF SANDWICH to WILLIAM LENTHALL.

1643, November 14. Sandwich.—Stating that the ministers appointed by the House to the parishes of St. Clement and St. Peter there required the parents of any children to be baptized to give them satisfaction of the faith they hold themselves, that a seaman refused to give such satisfaction to the minister of St. Clement's, and had his child baptized by Mr. Alderson, that the minister then demanded that Mr. Alderson and the seaman should be punished, and desiring the direction of the House in the premises. *Seal.* [N. III., 77.]

WILLIAM GOULD to WILLIAM LENTHALL.

1643, November 15. Plymouth.—" Since my coming hither with Colonel Wardlaw . . and those few men we brought with us . . we have met with many difficulties, chiefly in the settling of the authority of the said Colonel to the command of the Militia here, which hath been mainly opposed by some of the town, who strive to uphold the Mayor in the managing of the military affairs, which he is not capable of, and the soldiery will not submit unto. This occasioned the loss of Mount Stanford . . . upon which loss, for the prevention of further mischief I was enforced to take the fort and island, the most considerable strengths in the West, out of the hands of the townsmen, who had long kept them without any care of providing them with sufficient garrisons, provisions and ammunition—wherewith I have now stored them—to the inevitable loss of both, if it had not been thus prevented, for the town cannot be safe without their safety, nor will be useful to the enemy though taken, these places being secured. What I have done herein I desire may be approved by the House, and do pray that further care may be had . . for the preservation of this town, now a long time closely besieged . . for we want men, money, ammunition, and arms, the 500 men brought down by me being near half killed, wounded and sick, and besides those left, few fighting men in the town." *Seal.* [N. III., 79.]

The EARL OF WARWICK to WILLIAM LENTHALL.

1643, November 15. Downs.—Complaining that the ship keepers at Chatham have been without victuals for the last ten days, concerning Captain Hodges and his prizes, and forwarding the complaints of merchants of Dover and elsewhere that all their foreign letters have been opened at Rochester, and through the carelessness of the clerks many letters and bills of exchange have been "imbezilled." (See *Commons' Journals*, iii. 314, where the date is misprinted 5th.) *Signed.* [N. III., 80.]

Sir William Brereton to William Lenthall.

1643, November 15. Hawarden Castle.—"Upon Saturday last Sir Thomas Middleton and myself, with some nine troops of horse and two small foot companies, marched from Wrexham towards Chester, leaving the city two miles on the right hand, and advanced to Hawarden Castle, which is a strong castle, and in very good repair, and is commodiously situated for blocking up Chester, which was so unprovided as that upon summons it was delivered up unto us, and the gentlemen and others thereabouts did submit themselves and are admitted into the Parliament's protection. Sir T. Middleton is returned to Wrexham to a general muster appointed upon Monday, myself remaining here in the Castle, which is unfurnished and wants a new Draw Bridge, which I desire to secure and victual with 'all possible speed. The whole county hereabouts tremble and dare not make any opposition and Colonel Davies and Colonel Mostyn are fled and their commanders dispersed, only we hear that the Bishop of York, and the Bishops of Chester, St. Asaph, and Bangor, and the Grandees of the country are at Conway, which they have 'exceedingly fortified, forming the body of an army and expecting the landing of the Irish army, under the command —as they report—of the Earl of Ormond, but I rather believe of Colonel Moncke or Colonel Gibson, whom they daily expect with 3,000 or 4,000 old soldiers, besides the Irish rebels; if the coming over of these could be prevented or they repulsed I doubt not, through God's assistance, to be able to give a good account of Chester, as also of all these parts of Wales. But I received certain intelligence from Dublin that 11 Bristol ships and 15 Wexford barques were on Tuesday November 7th come to the Bar of Dublin to transport 3,000 or 4,000 soldiers to the relief of these parts. I do therefore present this my humble request, that if these foreign forces throng in upon us, or if any part of his Majesty's army fall downwards into Staffordshire or Cheshire, that then some considerable part of my Lord General's army suitable thereunto may be designed to wait upon and attend their motions, whereby we shall not only be much enabled and encouraged to do the better service, but it may also contribute very much towards the settling and composing of all these parts of the Kingdom of England and Dominion of Wales. *Postscript.*—Since I concluded this letter I have received several advertisements of this Bristol fleet hovering upon the coasts of Ireland. Some report they have taken some of your ships bound for Liverpool laden with arms and ammunition, which though it be uncertain whether it be a true report, yet it is most certain that these will intercept and seize all those that come from London to Liverpool, and it is not to be expected that your small fleet at Liverpool should be able to afford them any protection or relief, besides the danger of conveying over the Irish army, which I make bold to present to your consideration, and do humbly beseech that it may be recommended to my Lord of Warwick to give some speedy order herein." *Signed. Seal.* [N. III., 81.]

[William Lenthall] to [Sir William Brereton].

[1643, November 16.]—By order of the House thanking him for his services, refusing his request about the King's, Queen's, and Prince's revenues in Cheshire, contained in his letter of October 21st, but promising an equal sum if proposed in a more convenient way, and enclosing an order concerning Eccleshall Castle. (See *Commons' Journals*, iii. 313.) *Draft.* [N. XII., 87.]

[Sir William Waller] to [William Lenthall].

1643, November 16. Farnham.—"When I came to the generall rendevous att Farnham, I tooke a view of the army, which consisted of 18 troopes of Horse, 7 companyes of Dragoones, three citty regiments, mine own—yet imperfect and not above three hundred strong—and four companyes of Colonell Jones his regiment. With these I marched to Alton with intention to have proceeded on to Winchester, where the body of the enemy then lay. But I there received information from good hands—some out of the citty, and some out of the country—that there were very considerable forces drawn out of [the] King's army to cutt off my retreat. Whereupon I [altere]d my resolution, and marched to Basing; up[on the gro]und, that if the intelligence were true [I should] either fight with them singly—before any [other par]ty should joyne with them—or if I found my [sel]f too weake, make a safe retreat to Farnham, but a few miles distant from thence. If it were false, I might either make an assay upon that house—which by all men was represented to me to be but a slight peece and if I could carry itt, itt would have been a great encouragement to the soldiour—or otherwise I might advance towards Winchester, which that way was but two dayes march and the most direct way from Alton thither was no less. Att my first coming to Basing I received an assurance that there was no danger could threaten me—for the present—from Oxford, whereupon I resolved to attempt that place. I was first guided to the north side of the house which was most commanded and fittest to batter but upon a triall I found that the enemy had fortified most strongly on that side, with diverse retrenchments one under the command of another. Wee tooke in some outhouses adjoyning to their workes, but the enemy fired them so that wee were faine to quitt them. Wee lost in that fight twelve or thirteen men, and as many more hurt. This and the coldness of the night with fowle weather was a great discouragement to the London regiments, who were not used to this hardness in so much as the officers came to me and made itt their request they might be drawn off, with an intimation that many of the souldiours were hirelings, and their mouye being spent, they began to thinke of their returne. The first remonstrance in this kinde was made by the field officers, the second by the captaines and inferiour officers. This was a great surprise to me, but the weakness of my condition without them, inforced me to yeeld upon condition they would give me in their desires under their hands which they did. Upon this, I drew the army into Basing Stoke to refresh itt for two or three dayes. In the meantime I seised upon the Vine—an house so called belonging to Mr. Sands—and putt some forces into itt, intending to fortify itt, and in regard of the neerne[ss to Basing] to make itt a bridle to that place, to cutt off their contributions, and   subsistence. The army beeing sufficiently refreshed, I resolved to [have ano]ther fling att Basing, upon an information I had received of a place that might give me some advantage. I intended to have fallen on before day, but the sluggishness of the soldiours was such that itt was afternoone a good while before I could come upp. The order was to give the ennemy allarums on all sides, and to fall on, on two sides, the one thorough the Parke, the other on the side towards Basing towne. Att this last place I sett upp my rest where Major Strahan,—a gallant brave gentleman as drawes a sword—fell on with his dragoones, seconded by mine own regiment, and the four companyes of Colonell Jones, and the petardier with them. This was performed with as much courage and resolution as could be don by men. The ennemy had quitted one of

their workes, our men gained the rampart, and the petardier applied
his petard, but unluckily mistooke the place; for whereas he should have
applied to a place in the ould wall which was but a brick and a half
thick, he sett it against a doore that was bricked upp and lined with
earth, so that itt tooke no effect. In the mean time that squadron of the
red regiment that should have fallen on upon the Parke side on a worke
that flanked us, and where there remained but six musketiers, the rest
beeing runn away, could not be drawn upp, only they fired out of
distance, and so fell off againe. This gave the ennemy new courage,
so that they fell againe into their workes and beat our men off. I lost
in this service, thirty men upon the place, and neere upon one hundred
hurte. That night fell out so fowle that I could not possibly keep my
men upon their gards, so that I was forced to draw into Basing. The
ne[xt morning] early my scowtes came in, and gave me advertisement
that Sir Ralph [Hopton with his] whole strength was upon his march
within six miles of me, and by a party [which I] had sent out towards
Reading, I was informed that Sir Jacob Ashly had drawne a considerable body of horse and foot out of Reading and the parts thereabouts, and was not farr from me. Whereupon I speedily drew the
army into the field, and sent out fresh partyes on all sides to discover
what way the ennemy held, for by some prisoners which my men fetch't
in I was informed that Sir Ralph struck out of the road towards me,
and marched Newbery way towards Kingscleare,—which was to joyne
with the Reading forces—. When the regiments were drawn out, as I
was riding about to give orders, I was saluted with a mutinous cry
among the citty regiments of 'Home, Home.' So that I was forced to
threaten to pistoll any of them that should use that base language, and
an ennemy in the field so neere. With this they were all very well
accquietted. I then sent for all the field officers, to take advice with
them concerning my proceeding. There were three propositions moved.
The first, to march upp to the ennemy, and fight with him; the second,
to march to Winchester, and seise upon that; the third to retire to
Farnham and to preserve the country from thence, untill further
supplyes came to strengthen us. The first was carried cleere, and the
officers dismissed to their severall charges. But they were no sooner
returned to their regiments, but the mutiny broke out againe, with a
protestation those of the citty would not march one foot further. Upon
this I was enforced to retire to Farnham where I now am. A great
part of those regiments are already gon to London, and the rest threaten
to follow immediately, so that I am in a deserted condition. What I
can do with my horse, and an handfull [of foot] I will, God willing,
perform with my uttermost endeavours. Itt [grieves m]y soule that
I can do no more. I have some requests to make which w[ith
reason]ableness, I shall tender to you. The first is that those regiments, which are levying for the West, may be immediately compleated,
and sent upp to me with all possible speed. 2^ly that wee may have
some monyes sent to releeve us, for wee are all in a most wretched
degree of want. 3. That command may be given that what forces may
be spared out of Kent, and the neighbour countyes may be dispatched
away to me indelaidly. I have written to them, but I suppose some
signification from the House would quicken them. 4. I desire that
what I have written concerning the London regiments may not be taken
in such a sence as might have a reflection of dishonour either upon the
citty unto which I owe all service and respect and particular obligations, or upon all the regiments, for there be many worthy gallant men
amongst them. But the truth is, amongst the hirelings which were
promiscuously taken upp, I have reason to suspect there [were]
Malignants, that putt themselves upon this service only to overthrow itt,

and they are the men that have blowne these coles. 5. [That there]
may be some exemplary punishment inflicted upon runnaways; And
lastly, that you will vouchsafe to pardon my many fa[ilings in this
ser]vice which are not only my fault but my punishment." *Partly
torn. Signature torn off.* [N. III., 82.]

Captain ANTHONY STAPLEY to WILLIAM LENTHALL.

1643, November 18. Chichester.—Acknowledging his letter of the
16th, directing that the rents and estate of Sir William Morley were
not to be taken. (See *Commons' Journals*, iii. 313.) " If you please to
discharge this estate or any other and not to provide otherwise to pay
these men under my command, you will, I hope, give me leave to
provide for myself and men as I can, and to quit the employment,
when I cannot longer serve you in it." *Seal.* [N. III., 83.]

SIR THOMAS STANLEY, Colonel RALPH ASSHETON, RICHARD HOLLAND, and ROBERT HYDE to WILLIAM LENTHALL.

1643, November 20. Manchester.—" We have now received certain
intelligence from Colonel Moore that 11 ships laden with Irish soldiers
are discovered near our coast, and already landed in Worrall.
Another letter from a friend concerning the same thing reports the
number of the ships to be 19 discovered by himself and by two captains
at sea, And that one who was in Dublin the last Thursday night gave
information that 10,000 are intended to be landed in these parts. We
have also received information from several Lands but especially from
the Committee at Derby of the Earl of Newcastle's advance with a
great force both horse and foot and many carriages into Derbyshire,
where they spoil and destroy all before them in their accustomed
manner, and at Derby they expect them daily. It is conceived that
Hastings is joined with them, and whether their intent be indeed for
Derby or to fall down into these parts is not yet discovered. Our
assistance and march towards them is earnestly desired by the Committee,
the rather, in regard Sir William Brereton and Sir Thomas Middleton
having their forces now in Wales, and intending to besiege Chester, if
not prevented by the landing of the Irish, cannot for the present help
them without prejudice to their present designs, and we for our parts
are as unable to answer their expectations as well in regard of the
arrival of the Irish as also because of a strong garrison—being 30
colours—now lying in Halifax by reason whereof we are forced to keep
a strong and constant guard upon all the east border of our county.
Besides we are vehemently threatened to be visited by a party raised in
Westmoreland being—as is reported—2,000 or 3,000 in a body. Being
thus environed all that can be expected from us at present is the
preservation of our own borders—if possible—wherein we shall employ
our utmost and leave the success to God . . . We earnestly desire
that some course . . . . may be thought of for the prevention of the
further landing of the Irish and suppression of those already landed,
and likewise that directions may be given to the Earl of Manchester's
forces to fall upon the enemy in Derbyshire or Yorkshire, and further
that upon the first opportunity " some ammunition may be sent us.
(See *Commons' Journals*, iii. 320.) *Signed.* [N. III., 84.)

SIR WILLIAM BRERETON and W. MANWARINGE to WILLIAM LENTHALL.

1643, November 21.—Since my last letter " there are two Bristol
and Barnstaple ships and four others which have hovered these three

or four days upon our coasts. If their men be not landed this day there are not many of them come on shore. It is reported by some that have been amongst them that there are three regiments under the command of Sir Michael Earneley, Sir Foulk Hunckes and Colonel Gibson, and that so soon as the ships are cleared of them, they are to return into Ireland to transport 8,000 or 10,000 more. If these had stayed but ten days longer, it is conceived the city of Chester could not have subsisted, whereas now we are constrained to draw our forces together and to unite them into stronger bodies to prevent their landing, which they seem not yet to attempt—whatsoever they intend— upon our Cheshire coasts, but on the Welsh shore about 16 or 20 miles below Chester. The Earl of Newcastle's forces press very hard upon the other side of our county which adjoins to Yorkshire. Derbyshire is much infested with them, and it is said that the Cavaliers are fortifying Chesterfield. It is also reported that the Earl of Newcastle's forces draw downwards towards Halifax, and that there are 30 foot companies thereabouts whereby the Lancashire forces are employed so as it should seem there is some correspondence and combination betwixt these and the Irish forces at one and the same time to attempt and distress these parts which were in a very fair way to have been settled and reduced entirely, if this shipping had not come out of Ireland. I shall presume therefore humbly to present this request that the Scots may be hastened and speeded before the countries be wasted and destroyed, and that some considerable number of shipping able to command and master the fleet, which now infesteth these coasts, may be speedily sent down, otherwise you may conclude these ships of yours which are six men of war which we have prepared will be in danger to be taken, Liverpool your only haven will be hazarded, and all these parts of the kingdom of England and Wales miserably distressed and ruined, if not subdued." *Signed. Seal.* [N. III., 85.]

Sir William Brereton to William Lenthall.

(A duplicate of the last, in Sir William's own hand throughout, except that the following postscript is added.

" I am informed that these ships have taken Lurtine's ship, wherein was the ammunition sent down, part for me and part for the Lancashire men. It is my humble suit that when you send a fleet to clear these coasts there may be sent down 100 pair of pistols, 300 muskets, and 200 or 300 firelocks. These are not to be procured upon any terms in this country wherein I could raise good store of men if I could arm them. We desire also some 30 or 40 barrels of powder, whereof we have great use, having been in continued action in Shropshire and Wales ever since Colonel Mitton came down, which was in the middle of September.") [N. III., 89.]

Torrell Jocelyn, Abraham Burrell and others to William Lenthall.

1643, November 21. Huntingdon.—Desiring that the county may be excused the two months' weekly assessment now demanded, on the ground that they had not previously heard of the ordnance imposing it, and the other heavy demands upon them. *Signed. Seal.* [N. III., 86.]

Sir William Spring, Sir John Rous, William Heveningham, Sir Roger North and others to William Lenthall.

1643, November 21. Bury St. Edmunds.—Recommending the bearer Edward Lelam as a fit person to be Clerk in Chancery. *Signed. Seal.* [N. III., 88.]

The Earl of Warwick to the Speaker of the House of Peers.

1643, November 22. Downs.—(Printed in *Lords' Journals*, vi. 313, with a few misprints, of which the chief are " Mariners *again* taste once," should be " Mariners *against you* taste once " and " Committee *for the* Safety," should be " Committee *of* Safety.") *Signed.* [N. III., 90.]

Colonel Thomas Mytton, Humphrey Mackworth and others to the Earl of Denbigh.

1643, November 22. Wem.—"We cannot believe after so many expressions of your care of this country that you will desert it. . . . We beseech you pardon our boldness if we now lay claim to that power the . . . Parliament upon our solicitation have invested you with in reference to our safeguard, for certainly we shall have little benefit by it, if speedily it be not put forth in these parts. The rebels are now landed in Flintshire about Mesten (Mostyn) to the number of 3,000, as is reported, and Lord Capell is preparing to receive some part of them into Shrewsbury, his confidence being more in them than the foot of this county. Our garrison serves but for a present resting place, but cannot resist a puissant enemy, yet such is the interest we have in the people's affections, and such is the general distaste . . . Shrewsbury and the generality of the inhabitants of this county have conceived against Lord Capell's forces, that did your Lordship with a body of horse appear you would soon be master of the field, and have a confluence to you of a sufficient number of foot, might they have arms . . . All our labours is lost, if many days be spent before you come, and we of necessity must either quit the country and expose our friends to ruin or perish ourselves with them." *Copy.* [N. XII., 62.]

Colonel Thomas Mytton, Humphrey Mackworth, and others, to Richard Moore.

1643, November 22. Wem.—"Our want of a Commander-in-chief arms and horse makes us now useless and our condition desperate. Had we conceived the Lord of Denbigh would have thus neglected us, we would not run ourselves into such a danger. God hath hitherto exceedingly preserved us, but we cannot expect safety longer, if we have no better means of subsistence. The rebels are now landed in Wales and are hastening into Shropshire where there is preparation of the Lord Capel to receive them. The care that every country hath of itself will leave us destitute of help, and deprive us we fear of that little aid that for the present is left us to keep us this garrison, for since this news the Cheshire commanders sent to withdraw the companies they lent us, and which are the only stay of our garrison. As you tender the safety of this county and the prevention of much mischief in the kingdom which must needs happen, if the rebels here receive not a stop, we beseech you hasten forces into these parts, with store of arms and ammunition. Foot enough may be raised here, but our arms are lost and lent to our auxiliary friends, and none left us to arm new forces. We desire therefore 1,000 muskets and snaphances may be sent us, and if the Lord of Denbigh come not the four case of drakes and all his arms and ammunition . . . *Postscript.*—We hear the Lord Byron with a great force is coming against us. If horse be intended for Herefordshire I pray you let it be hastened down." *Signed.* *Seal.* [N. III., 91.]

WILLIAM CAWLEY to WILLIAM LENTHALL.

1643, November 23. Farnham.—Acquainting the House " in what extreme sad condition I both hear and find Sir William Waller's army proceeding especially from want of pay, whereby they are altogether disabled for the present to do the Parliament that service, which if supplied with moneys may be expected from them. The soldiers, both horse and foot, want clothes, boots, shoes and almost all necessaries for their subsistence, yea their exigency is such and so great that when they are commanded upon any service—be the expedition ever so emergent—many of them cannot stir for want of money to shoe their horses . . . If speedy course be not taken to supply this so considerable an army with a round sum at least 10,000*l.*—for a small sum will rather discontent than satisfy—it's much feared by those who best know that a sudden ruin of this brigade will inevitably follow. I find Sir William Waller . . . very much troubled that he cannot punish the abounding vices and enormities of his soldiers for fear of mutinies and desertions to which for want of pay they are too apt, which not only produces a contempt of their officers, but great discontent also to the country, from whom they are sometimes necessitated to take that for their livelihood which the people can ill spare." *Seal.* [N. III., 92.]

SIR SAMUEL LUKE to the COMMITTEE AT COVENTRY.

1643, November 23.—Informing them by the Earl of Essex' command " That on Wednesday night last there lodged at Ainxton some 10 miles from Oxford not far from Chipping Norton some 2,000 or 3,000 of the King's forces, horse and foot, commanded by the Lord Dowens and Byron, who report themselves 5,000 and that they were to march into Shropshire, or else Sir William Brereton would gain the whole county. If you find they design for any other place, you will give notice thereof and strive to prevent them." *Copy.* [N. XII., 66.]

SIR WILLIAM WALLER to WILLIAM LENTHALL.

1643, November 23. Farnham.—Having acknowledged the readiness of the House to take care for the preservation of this poor Brigade and protested their faithfulness I " crave leave to offer to your consideration the necessitous condition under which we labour. Want of money and want of clothes have produced want of obedience and want of health, I had almost said want of heart in this army ; working like a malignant fever upon the spirits of our men, and dulling the edge of our swords, though I am confident the metal is unaltered. I cannot but take notice with humble thankfulness of 5,000*l.* voted for our supply, but I beseech you give me leave without offence to tell you it is impossible for this sum or less than double the proportion of this sum to stop the clamourous wants of our soldiers, for the last payment was so small that that it would not enable them to buy themselves so many necessaries as they wanted for this winter service and their hopes being fixed upon this supply, if this should fall short, it would instead of a satisfaction prove an irritation to them. God knows, I write this with a sad sense, but I have reason to doubt what command I shall be able to retain upon those,

whom I can neither reward nor punish. I humbly desire there may be
some present course taken to supply the army. I have presumed to send
some parties to Godalming and Midhurst to take up some coarse cloths,
linen, shoes, boots and stockings for the soldiers, and if there may be
any assurance given to pay for their commodities, I am confident it would
be best both for the soldiers and the country." (See *Commons'*
Journals, iii. 319.) *Seal*. [N. III., 93.]

The EARL OF WARWICK to WILLIAM LENTHALL.

1643, November 24. Downes.—Stating that he had ordered the
Ordnance in Upnor Castle to be brought to the Tower, as the Castle
might be easily taken, and these guns might then turned on Chatham
Dock, but that the gunners there refused to allow their removal alleging
they had some prisoners there "as though ordnance were fit weapons to
guard a few prisoners," and desiring the House to give order for their
immediate removal. (See *Commons' Journals*, iii. 248, 345.) *Signed*.
Seal. [N. III., 94.]

ARTHUR STAVELEY, THOMAS HESELRIGE and others to WILLIAM LENTHALL.

1643, November 24. Leicester.—"This garrison of Leicester lies
between Ashby and Belvoir, two strongholds of the enemy within this
County, besides Newark and Warton House, confining close upon us,
as also the road to Nottingham Derby and Manchester, so that the small
strength of horse that is left us is continually employed either in convoys
of ammunition and other commodities betwixt North and South or in
service against .the enemy, wherein—by the blessing of God—we have
been always successful. Nevertheless they being too strong in horse
for us take our friends, gather our rents, and hinder the collection of the
weekly taxes, by reason whereof our soldiers are in great want of pay, so
that the other day they refused service till we had taken up a great sum
of money to satisfy them for the present upon our own engagement.
Our humble suit . . is that all such money as we can raise in this
county may be disposed of for the maintenance of our forces." *Signed*.
Seal. [N. III., 95.]

Colonel THOMAS MYTTON, HUMPHREY MACKWORTH and others to the EARL OF DENBIGH.

1643, November 24.—Our remoteness and the environment of our
enemies prevents us from having answers to our letters, or knowing if
our messengers have come safe to you. If you think these countries
worth the gaining, you would with speed repair to us with your Body of
Horse, though you want foot. We dare assure you, your regiment may
be speedily completed here. We want only arms, which we hope you
will supply us with. Sir Thomas Middleton hath taken the Fort
Wrexham, Harding Castle and divers other places, all the Welsh are
fled and dispersed, not an enemy near him save the Castle of Holt, which
can have no relief. Chester is beleaguered round and can have no
assistance. 500 Horse will clear this county and bring the country to
subjection, which done, the towns will soon yield, but delays will prove
exceeding dangerous, and make an easy work difficult, the men flying to
strongholds and making every house a garrison. Sir William Brereton
and Sir Thomas Middleton are both so engaged in their own countries
that we cannot rely upon assistance from them. They have wholly left
us to ourselves, and to your protection to which they advise us to have
recourse.

Postscript.—We humbly desire you to send us all the arms that can be spared, we can raise 1,000 foot in one week had we but arms ; the country comes in exceedingly. Our Auxiliary friends have got a great part of our arms. *Copy.* [N. XII., 68.]

WILLIAM LENTHALL to SIR WILLIAM WALLER.

1643, November 25.—Acquainting him with the vote of the additional sum of 5,000*l.* (See *Commons' Journals,* iii. 319, 320.) *Draft.* [N. XII., 69.]

Colonel HENRY MILDMAY, SIR THOMAS HONYWOOD and others to WILLIAM LENTHALL.

1643, November 25. Chelmsford.—Stating that five of the Committee had audited Sir Thomas Barrington's accounts and found them correct, and desiring that he should receive some acknowledgment for his services, and asking that Colonel Long should be caused to give an account. *Signed.* [N. III., 96.]

Colonel THOMAS MYTTON, HUMPHREY MACKWORTH and others to the EARL OF ESSEX.

1643, November 26. Wem.—"The landing of 2,000 at least from Ireland, and the sending of the Lords Byron and Molyneux with a great force of horse and foot from the King to Shrewsbury, and none in the field to relieve us, hath exposed us to certain ruin, if your wisdom and timely care of these countries prevent not. This county of Salop hath a strong party for the Parliament in it, durst they show themselves, and many of the great ones we are assured would come in and submit, if a person of eminence were here to command in chief with some considerable force. We have yet encouraged our friends and feared the enemy with the hope of the Earl of Denbigh's coming. We and our friends and also the Cheshire and Staffordshire gentlemen do much desire him. And we are most humble suitors to your Excellency to betrust him with some strength of foot and horse for the preservation of this part of the kingdom, which, as it hath yielded great supplies to his Majesty, if once cleared would send more to your Excellency, we being able, before the Irish landed, in this county to have raised 2,000 horse and foot, had we had arms for them, and could soon have had the possession of Shrewsbury, many friends there having made a good way for our admittance." . . . We doubt our former letters have "miscarried and do now again renew our humble petition for your warrant for 200 case of pistols, 200 dragoons, and 600 muskets with 50 barrels of powder, by the help of which arms and the coming of the Earl of Denbigh with some considerable forces, we doubt not yet, but through God's blessing these parts will be preserved and the enemy scattered, we being resolved to improve all the interest we have in this county, and to adventure our own lives still as we have done for the Parliament's service." *Signed. Seal.* [N. III., 97.]

SIR HENRY MILDMAY to WILLIAM LENTHALL.

1643, November 27. Wanstead.—(The purport of the first part is given in *Commons' Journals,* iii. 321.) Desiring that the House may be reminded to provide for Dover Castle and the other castles on the coast of Kent, concerning which the Earl of Warwick had charged him to be solicitous with the House, "lest some of them be eaten out by the sea this winter, and the rest possessed by any enemy that will come and pay the soldiers" ; and stating that the County of Essex grumbles much that there should be so great a sum in arrears, "not less than 36 or 40,000*l.*, and the honest part still put to pay the new payments before the old are cleared, which will most light upon the Malignants and the neuters." [N. III., 98.]

The EARL OF MANCHESTER to the SPEAKER OF THE HOUSE OF PEERS.

1643, November 27. Cambridge.—(Printed in *Lords' Journals,* vi. 327.) *Signed. Seal.* [N. III., 99.]

Colonel JOHN BARKER and others to the EARL OF ESSEX.

1643, November 27. Coventry.—(Printed in *Lords' Journals,* vi. 321.) *Signed. Seal.* [N. III., 100.]

Colonel RALPH WELDON to WILLIAM LENTHALL.

[1643], November 27. Blackfriars.—Desiring that the House of Commons be informed of the sad condition of the garrison of Plymouth for want of pay, they being more than 22 weeks unpaid since January last. If not suddenly relieved the soldiers must leave the place or starve. Had already remonstrated this to the Committee of Safety. *Seal.* [N. III., 101.]

Major JOHN BRYDGES to Colonel PUREFOY.

1643, November 28.—Desiring him to inform the Earl of Denbigh and the Committee that the Worcestershire men have called in of the County, with which and those few forces they have, it is said, 600. They are set down before Coughton Court. You know how we are concerned to give them speedy relief; if that place is lost, all that part of the country is gone. Our men have little ammunition, therefore, I beseech you get orders that all the horse and foot that can possibly be spared be sent, and we will use all diligence to be ready to go with them. *Copy.* [N. XII., 67.]

SIR WILLIAM BRERETON to his brother, SIR RICHARD SKEFFINGTON, at Coventry.

1643, November 28.—"The condition of these parts are not so hopeful as of late when God was pleased to make way for us into Wales through great difficulties, and by our proceedings there to make way for the recovery of Chester and reducing . . all these parts . . . likewise the Lord Capell's army being almost routed, so as we had no opposition in Wales nor our proceedings against Chester till the Irish army landed . . . which consists of more than 2,500 foot, and these ships are returned by whom is speedily expected Colonel Berne, an Irish rebel, with 3,000 rebels. The Earl of Newcastle's army presses near upon us upon the other side of the county, so as we were recalled out of Wales to defend our own county, . . . and expect daily invasions on each side. Our condition may therefore be accounted very desperate . . . By the concurrence of these dangers unless some speedy aid be sent by sea to prevent the landing of any more forces out of Ireland the preservation of these parts . . . may be much endangered. More cannot be expected from us than is possible in our power, who have with a small strength and without any supplies or assistance of the main body or almost of any neighbouring counties made our part good and defeated many supplies from the King's army. But if still multitudes of fresh forces, not only domestic but foreign, increase upon us, we can do no more than we are able . . . Lancashire men, whom we had to our assistance when we were in Wales, deserted us in our greatest extremities, or otherwise we might . . . probably have prevented the landing of this enemy, whereas now he is as near and expected as much to make invasions out of Wales into this county as he was expected to land . . . We are gathering into a body speedily and resolved to go towards the enemy if they come not to us . . . If it come in your way procure relief to be sent to us. Hasten the Lord Denbigh, and assist us with all your means.

Postscript.—Mr. Mackworth will inform you at large if he reach Coventry, who is going to meet the Earl of Denbigh." *Copy.* [N. XII., 70.]

Dom Antonio de Sousa, Portuguese Ambassador, to William Lenthall.

1643, November 28.—Complaining that no answer had been sent to the memorial he had presented eight days ago concerning the Press and Type seized at Richard Herne's house. (See *Commons' Journals*, iii. 322.) *Seal.* [N. III., 102.]

Sir Thomas Barrington and others to John Lenthall, Speaker of the House of Commons. (*Sic.*)

1643, November 28. Chelmsford.—(The purport appears by the resolution in *Commons' Journals*, iii. 326.) *Signed. Seal.* [N. III., 103.]

[The Earl of Stamford] to Mr. Lisle.

1643, November 28. London. — Desiring that the Committee appointed to examine his charges against Mr. Nicoll would excuse his attendance that day "being somewhat indisposed by an extreme cold." (See *Commons' Journals*, iii. 327.) *Seal.* [N. III., 104.]

Sir John Sedley, Colonel Ralph Weldon, and others to William Lenthall.

1643, November 28. Westerham.—Declaring their apprehension of the unsupportable proportion which they hear is likely to be charged on their county for the maintaining of his Excellency's army, and desiring a respite till some members of the House then employed in the defence of that county which is even ready to be invaded, may be permitted to represent the condition thereof. *Signed.* [N. V., 44.]

Sir William Waller to William Lenthall.

1643, November 28. Farnham.—"Yesterday morning I had notice by my scouts that the enemy showed himself in a party of about 300 horse upon the heath a mile and a half from me. Whereupon I sent out a party to visit them who entertained them with a warm skirmish for near two hours. In this time we discovered their whole body advancing. Whereupon I drew out that small stock I had into the Park under the favour of the Castle. Besides foot I had not above ten troops with me, the rest being quartered in villages more remote, where they can find provisions, came not up to me till towards evening. The enemy drew up in a full body before us upon the heath, as near as we could judge about 5,000 horse and foot, and after a while advanced into the Park to us with their foot and some horse within musket shot, but we gave them such entertainment with our pieces that they thought it their best course to retire to the heath again, where they made a stand, but were quickly driven from thence in disorder by our culverins, whereupon they all retreated. I sent some parties of horse and dragoons

L 2

after them, who charged them in the rear and beat them off the down into the lane. We took some prisoners and killed some men and divers horses. If my horse had come up time enough I might have done good execution upon them. That night the enemy quitted Crundall and retired further off towards Hook. I have sent out parties after them to discover which way they move. The Kentish troops came last night hither from Guildford to quarter with me. There came with them likewise five companies of Sir Arthur Heselrig's regiment. But to allay this accession of strength I am now informed that the London Regiments resolve to be gone to-morrow or the next day at the furthest, but I hope they will not. I humbly desire there may be some course taken that they may stay, till some other strength come up to me, otherwise I am left at sixes and sevens, neither able to follow the enemy nor defend myself, and my old friend is so gallant an enemy, that he will quickly take his advantage [of] it to my destruction. I have received information that [his] Majesty is drawing this way. *Postscript.*—I am informed that Colonel Carr's soldiers, which were about 200, are turned out of their quarters and thereupon all disbanded and gone, to the great discontent of the officers who raised the men out of their means, and yet never received their full fortnight's pay. If they had received any help the Regiment might have been completed before this. I desire I may not be deprived of his service, for he is an honest man and a brave old soldier." *Seal.* [N. III., 105.]

The EARL OF ESSEX to WILLIAM LENTHALL.

1643, November 30. Essex House.—Urging the claims of Captain Charles Fleetwood to be appointed Receiver of the Court of Wards. *Signed.* [N. III., 106.]

SIR RICHARD HARDRES and others to WILLIAM LENTHALL.

1643, November 30. Rochester.—Concerning Mr. Robert Fowler's opposition to taking the Covenant. (See *Commons' Journals*, iii. 338.) *Signed. Seal.* [N. III., 107.]

The PARLIAMENT to the ESTATES OF UTRECHT, OVER-YSSEL, and HOLLAND.

1643, December 7.—(Printed in *Lords' Journals*, vi. 331, 332.) In *Latin. Copies.* [N. XVIII., 55, 56.]

The COMMITTEE AT GOLDSMITHS' HALL and the COMMITTEE OF IRISH ADVENTURERS.

1643, December 14. — Resolutions upon the propositions concerning the supply of the Scotch Army in Ireland. (Mostly printed in *Commons' Journals*, iii. 349, where line 4 should run " Committee at Goldsmiths' Hall, the Committee of Irish Adventurers are of opinion that for money, &c.") [N. XIII., 186.]

Colonel RICHARD NORTON to WILLIAM LENTHALL.

[1643, December 18 (?). Southampton.]—Enclosing a vow and protestation, put to the inhabitants, in which he has met with a better concurrence than he expected. . . " Some devilish spirits there are that have refused it, but I shall pare their nails." And asking the House to allow them the Customs of this place for a short time. (See *Commons' Journals*, iii. 347.) *Seal. Enclosed:*

The said Vow and PROTESTATION. (Both letter and vow are printed in Grey, iii., Appendix, No. 2, pages 2 and 4.) [N. VIII., 138.]

THOMAS [LORD] GREY to WILLIAM LENTHALL.

1643, December 25. Leicester.—" Upon Friday last it happened that Colonel Waite sent out 20 horse to scout out toward Belvoir, who having intelligence that two troops of the enemy's horse were quartered in a town called Waltham did ride up to the sentries and fired upon them, and fell into their quarters, where they took some prisoners and 11 horses. The governor of Belvoir and the rest of the commanders there . . . . next day drew out . . . . . eight score horse, and marched within a mile of Col. Waite, according to their accustomed manner plundering the country, and swearing that if he did not speedily quit Rutland, they would not leave a town unplundered. The Colonel immediately drew out three score horse, six of whom were musketeers horsed, and with extraordinary courage marched to the view of the enemy, and being resolved to win the horse or lose the saddle, sent a trumpeter to sound a challenge. The enemy refusing to answer, made a retreat, our body pursuing them, and on Sproxton Heath the enemy drew up into a body, which no sooner they had done, but our men were ready to charge them and did. The first charge we had something the better, the second charge we routed them wholly, and chased them to the very Castle walls. Herein Major Plucknet, a notorious plunderer, was slain, with divers others, but the number of them I do not as yet directly know. The governor of Belvoir run into the face and shrodly cutt; forty-six prisoners, who make themselves all common soldiers, but I hope that we shall find some officers amongst them. We took three score and odd horses, redeemed one hundred and forty head of cattle, and divers plundered horses. We lost not a man, only Col. Waite's Captain-Lieutenant was shot in the thigh, and three more wounded, but they are not mortal." *Seal.* [N. III., 108.]

The EARL OF FORTH to SIR WILLIAM BALFORE.

[1643, early in.]—I have showed his Majesty your list of Prisoners for exchange. He is not yet resolved what prisoners he will have exchanged, but when it is resolved I will send you a trumpet of my own. Lord Grandison has promised to send his own trumpet with his answer. At the ending hereof he sent his answer to me which you shall receive enclosed.

Postscript.—Thanking him for getting Lord Essex' pass for his wife, though it came too late. *Copy.* [N. XII., 200.]

SIR JOHN SACKVILLE'S Case.

[1643.]—Stating that he had been falsely accused by a defaulting tenant, who resisted eviction, of being a Malignant, that his farms at Wasperton near Warwick had been consequently sequestered, and desiring that the Speaker should be induced to write to the Committee at Coventry to "shew them how he hath been wronged and they misinformed by a lewd deboyshed fellow," and move them to unsequester the said farms. [N. XIII., 209.]

List of various ORDINANCES and ORDERS.

[1643.]—[N. XIII., 201.]

List of some Estates sequestered in ESSEX.

[1643.]—[N. XIII., 202.]

ORDER.

[1643.] — Directing the Committee for raising money for the assistance of our brethren of Scotland to pay to the Committee of both

Houses residing with them their expenses up to 100*l*. per week. [N. XIII. 144.]

The KING to the LORD MAYOR and CORPORATION OF LONDON.

1643[-4], January 2. Oxford.—(Printed in *Lords' Journals*, vi. 371.) *Copy.* [N. XII., 71.]

The ESTATES OF SCOTLAND.

164[3-]4, January 9.—Commission to the Earl of Loudoun and others. (Printed in *Lords' Journals*, vi. 411.) *Two copies.* [N. XIX., 82, 85.]

Captain JOHN HOTHAM to the HOUSE OF COMMONS.

1643[-4], January 11.—Petition praying either to be tried or released on bail, and desiring some relief of money. (See *Commons' Journals*, iii. 366.) *Signed.* [N. XXII., 144.]

The KING to THOMAS DEVENISH, Keeper of Winchester House.

1643[-4], January 12. Oxford.—Approving of his intention, of which he has heard from Thomas Ogle, of raising 200 men, under the command of his son Silas Devenish, to be sent to Windsor Castle, and promising to pay expenses. (See *Lords' Journals*, vi. 394.) *Counter-signed* "George Digbye." *Sign Manual. Impressed Seal affixed.* [N. I., 13.]

The KING to Lieutenant-Colonel MOSELY.

[1643-4], January 12. Oxford.—Having been informed that he desires to apply himself to his King's service and expiate former faults by some eminent testimony in the way of advancing the same, in case he gives testimony of his fidelity by surrendering the town of Aylesbury, not only a free pardon is promised him, but the command of his regiment and other marks of favour. (See *Lords' Journals*, vi. 394, and *Camden's Miscellany*, vol. viii.) In the hand of George Lord Digbye, and counter-signed by him. *Sign Manual. Impressed Seal affixed.* [N. I., 15.]

LORD ROBERTES to the EARL OF ESSEX.

1643[-4], January [before the 15th].—(The effect is given in *Lords' Journals*, vi. 350). *Seal.* [N. III., 109.]

Captain THOMAS SHILBURNE to the EARL OF ESSEX.

[1643-4], January 15. From my quarters at Adington.—"In behalf of the country, being so earnestly pressed by them I do humbly beseech . . that some forces may reside near this place, they fearing that if your Excellency should be pleased to command us away, they shall live under the same slavery and bondage as they did before we came, which was intolerable, but as soon as we came near them they ran away and would not abide to hear the sound of our muskets and drums, except we should have gone to Oxford or Banbury, so base and cowardly are they. I hope we have spoiled the two regiments which Colonel Dinton and Colonel Smith was to raise, the one of them having but three soldiers, as I am credablely informed, the other having officers enow for a regiment, but not above 30 soldiers, which are to hard for us at running away." [N. III., 110.]

[The House of Commons.

1643[-4], January 22.—Order disabling Sir John Fenwick from sitting. (See *Commons' Journals*, iii. 374.) [N. XIII., 137.]

WILLIAM, EARL OF LANERICK, to the HOUSE OF COMMONS.

[1643-4, January 23.]—Petition. (Identical, *mutatis mutandis*, with that to the Lords, which is printed in *Lords' Journals*, vi. 388. See *Commons' Journals*, iii. 373.) *Signed.* [N. XXII., 132.]

General GEORGE GORING to WILLIAM LENTHALL.

1643[-4], January 25. The Tower.—Desiring that so much of a letter from his father, which he hears is in the Clerk's hands, as concerns the payment of some money to himself, may be communicated to him. [N. III., 112.]

Examination of JOHN CHAMBERLAYNE, Mariner.

1643[-4], January 26. King's Lynn.—He was taken by a man of war and carried into Newcastle. Sir Thomas Glemham, the Governor, is now with his forces in Northumberland, and Sir John Morley, the Mayor, is Deputy Governor, and has in garrison only 500 men, all townsmen. The High Castle is fortified, but no other place within the town. The forces there have demolished a fort raised between the Uplight and the town, and there are but two other small works about the town called the Spanish work, and the Lower Light Fort. Tynemouth Castle is fortified, and has in garrison about 400 men. No arms or ammunition have been brought to Newcastle for the last ten weeks except 150 barrels of powder, and some small pieces brought about 8 days since from Amsterdam in a Danish ship and 500 muskets from Scarborough in two cobles. Browne Bushell is at Newcastle and has been there 6 or 7 weeks. A little before he took the *Ipswich Sarah* a prize, and she is now laden with coal for Holland to fetch arms thence. There are five men of war at Newcastle, and a ten gun ship lately run ashore on Coquet Island and was lost, but her guns were carried to Sir Thomas Glemham at Alnwick. They daily expect two ships from Holland with arms and ammunition. Till Tuesday last Sir Thomas Glemham was quartered at Alnwick, but then retreated six miles towards Newcastle, and the Scots marched in the same day. His forces are reputed 5,000 horse and foot, but half are unarmed. Many of the inhabitants of Newcastle are well affected to the Scots. There is much coal on all the stairs in great plenty. The examinant came yesterday from Newcastle. [N. XIII., 188.]

ORDINANCE.

1643[-4], January 30.—For fitting up Worcester House for the Scotch Commissioners. (Printed in *Lords' Journals*, vi. 404.) [N. XIX., 84.]

The HOUSE OF LORDS.

1643[-4], February 1.—Draft Ordinance appointing a Committee of the two Kingdoms. (This differs considerably from the form finally adopted. In particular after the names of the Commissioners it proceeds thus " or any three of them, whereof a member of each House to be present so that with the Committees and Commissioners " &c. as in the final form down to " concerning the same," and then proceeds:

" And do further give full power unto the members of both Houses above named, and to " the Earl of Loudoun, Lord Maitland, Sir Archibald Johnston, and Robert Barclay, " or any seven of them, whereof a member of each House to be present, as a Committee to order and direct whatsoever doth or may concern the managing of the war, keeping good intelligence between the forces of the three Kingdoms, and whatsoever may concern the peace of his Majesty's dominions and all other things in pursuance of the ends expressed in the said covenants and treaty and the Committee of both Houses are to observe such orders as they shall from time to time receive from both Houses." There is no limitation of time.) [N. XIX., 68.]

Information of MILES CAUSTON, Master of the *George*.

1643[-4], February 1.—Coming from the West Indies he was taken and carried into Dartmouth, and his ship and goods made prize of; they saying that all Londoners were rebels, and that it was their mercy they did not commit him longer to prison, because he resisted on their boarding him. In Dartmouth there are divers men-of-war ready for sea and others preparing, some of them intending, as he understood, to go for the Canary Islands and Madeira and the Azores to seize on any English ships there, and thence to the Isle of May and the Cape de Verde Islands, and so to seize all the English shipping there, and thence to the Barbados and the other Caribbee Islands to surprise all English ships found trading there, and to secure all those plantations to themselves against the King and Parliament, and so to pass northwards by Virginia, New England, and Newfoundland, there to take all fishermen that are for the Parliament, with which ships and men they intend to make a compiete fleet to set on against the Parliament, and to master the Narrow Seas, and for this purpose four are now setting forth, and the rest will do so as soon as they hear the Parliament ships are coming. Some Bristol men there told him there were also ships at Bristol about to sail for the same purpose. The Governor of Dartmouth had ordered a ship or two to relieve the Castle of Guernsey. Captain Smith and his Vice-Admiral have two Biscay shallops to row in and take such pillage as they can under the shore, and are likewise bound for the Trades, there to take all the Scotch and English that shall pass that way. [N. XIII., 191.]   Extracts from the above are N. XVI., 103.

ORDINANCE.

[1643-4, February 2.]—Enjoining the taking of the Solemn League and Covenant. (Printed in *Lords' Journals*, vi. 411.) This is a draft, amended in the form ultimately adopted. [N. XIII., 192.]

Mr. WHITTACRE's Report.

1643[-4], February 2.—Concerning the alleged affront to Sir Thomas Walsingham by Dillon, a servant of the Dutch Ambassador, and giving Dillon's version of the matter. "We desiring the Ambassadors' answer to the request of the House of Commons, which was that they would give way that he might be examined by a Committee . . . or by the House itself ; M. Bourrell answered he must avow the man to be his servant, and that he was now to attend him to Oxford, and that he much marvelled, if these things being done 3 or 4 days since it should not be complained of till now upon the very time of their providing to go to Court, and professing an unwillingness to have him further examined as was desired." (See *Commons' Journals*, iii. 384, 386.) [N. XVIII., 57.]

SIR WILLIAM ARMYNE, THOMAS HATCHER, ROBERT GOODWIN, ROBERT
FENWICK, HENRY DARLEY, and RICHARD BARWIS to WILLIAM
LENTHALL.

1643[-4], February 5. Morpeth.—"The Lord General advanced with
his army to Newcastle, where upon Saturday morning being the third
of February he shewed himself before the town, and the Committees of
both Kingdoms thought fit to send a letter to the Mayor Aldermen and
Common Council," whereof we enclose a copy and their answer. "The
Marquess of Newcastle, whom they call the King's General, came late
into the town the night before which was unknown to us, and upon the
approach of some of our soldiers to a work of theirs without the town,
—where some few were slain—they within set on fire and burnt down all
the streets and houses lying without the walls on the North side of the
town, by which and the other circumstances we gather that they are
resolved obstinately to hold it out to the last. All the county of
Northumberland on the north of Tyne is now in the power of the
Parliament, where if care were taken for the settling of a good ministry
you might hope for better fruits from thence, than you have hitherto
reaped.
Postscript.—We hear that General King and the Lord Witherington
are also in Newcastle." *Signed.* [N. III., 114.] *Enclosed* :

i. The MARQUESS OF ARGYLL and SIR WILLIAM ARMYNE to the
MAYOR and CORPORATION OF NEWCASTLE.

1643[-4], January [*sic* February] 3.—Summons.

And

ii. The MAYOR and CORPORATION to the MARQUESS OF ARGYLL.

1643[-4], February 3.—Reply. (Both printed in Rushworth, iii. 2.
613.) *Copies.* [N. XII., 72, 76.]

The SCOTCH COMMISSIONERS.

164[3-]4, February 5.—Paper. (Printed in *Lords' Journals*, vi.
410.) Two *copies.* [N. XII., 90 ; XIX., 99.]

The HOUSE OF COMMONS.

1643[-4], February 7.—Ordinance appointing a Committee of the
two Kingdoms. (Draft in the form finally adopted as printed in *Lords'
Journals*, vi. 430.) [N. XIX., 68.]

The SCOTCH COMMISSIONERS.

1643[-4], February 9.—Paper. (Printed in *Lords' Journals*, vi.
417.) *Signed* ".John Donn." [N. XIX., 69.]

SCHEDULE.

1643[-4], February 10.—Of the goods of such Delinquents as are
obstructed within the liberties of Westminster. [N. XIII., 195.]

Reasons presented at the Conference by the COMMONS and by the
LORDS.

1643[-4], February 13.—(Printed in *Lords' Journals*, vi. 424, 425,
423.) Two *Copies*, the first in shorthand. [N. XIII., 196.]

Account.

[1643-4], February 13.—Showing how the 12,000*l.* sent to St. Albans (See *Commons' Journals,* iii. 375) had been spent. A balance remained of 1,941*l.* 16*s.* 2*d.* [N. XIII., 189.]

Abstract of the CHARGE and PAYMENT of his EXCELLENCI'S ARMY for fourteen days.

1643[-4], February 14.—Amounting to 15,037*l.* 2*s.* 8*d.*, with a statement of the sums paid and remaining due. (See *Commons' Journals,* iii. 399.) [N. XIII., 194.]

The HOUSE OF LORDS.

1643[-4], February 15.—Draft Ordinance for appointing a Committee of the two Kingdoms, in the form ultimately adopted, except that the time is limited to six weeks instead of three months. (See *Lords' Journals,* vi. 427.) [N. XIX., 70.]

The HOUSE OF COMMONS.

1643[-4], February 16.—Order concerning Church Government. (Printed in *Commons' Journals,* iii. 401.) [N. XXII., 2.]

Paper of SCOTCH COMMISSIONERS and Reply of the PARLIAMENT thereto.

1643-4, February 17 and March 9.—About the Covenant, and supplies for their services. (Both printed in *Lords' Journals,* vi. 460, 461.) [N. XIX., 72, 71.]

Oath to be taken by the COMMITTEE OF BOTH KINGDOMS.

1643[-4], February 20.—(Printed in *Commons' Journals,* iii. 403.) [N. XIII., 197.]

The HERTFORDSHIRE COMMITTEE to the HOUSE OF COMMONS.

1643[-4], February 22. Petition.—(The purport appears from the order thereon, printed in *Commons' Journals,* iii. 405.) [N. XXII., 70.]

——— to ———

1643[-4], February 23. Shrewsbury.—"Prince Rupert on Friday morning sent out Major Legg with six troops of horse and 150 foot, who not only faced those at Wem at their own ports, but brought away between 20 and 30 loads of hay out of their quarters, they not so much as sending out a man to hinder him. On Saturday three musketeers of the late Irish defeated at Nantwich and gone into Wem, came hither with their arms. By these we know the state of the town, and that their first fear is lest the Prince should cut a great pond out of which they fill their ditches with water. To prevent which they summon in the country to cast up a tumultuary sconce for defence of it. The Prince's care is to draw together the dispersed forces, whilst his own regiment of foot marches to him from Bristol, whence they are set forward and convoy 200 barrels of powder, to employ which he hath put some ordnance and bullets to the casting. This afternoon 1,500 of those Irish which last landed in Wales are come into this town, so that we can already draw together 3,000 foot. Lord Byron is also this afternoon come hither whose army—as himself affirms—is in a very good condition in Cheshire, so that within this month we hope to be 7,000 or 8,000 men in field, besides which we hear that some Lancashire gentlemen have about 3,000 men ready for the Prince." *Extract.* [N. XII., 75.]

Sir Henry Anderson to John Rushworth.

[1643–4], March 4.—Entreating that copies of all orders relating to him be sent to him, and stating that he had no money or man to send about his business, having been now 18 weeks a prisoner. [N. III., 165.]

John Curtis to John Rushworth.

[1643–4], March 5. Bramford, near Ipswich.—Desiring him to use his influence in support of his application for the places of Collector of Excise and Receiver of the King's Rents for the whole or part of Suffolk. [N. III., 115.]

The Parliament to Walter Strickland.

1643[–4], March 6. Instructions. — (Printed in *Lords' Journals,* vi. 452.) *Copy.* [N. XVIII., 58, 59.]

Sir Henry Anderson to John Rushworth.

[1643–4], March . The Tower.—Entreating him to deliver the enclosed petition to the Speaker, stating his want of money and clothes, and that he had not received anything under the order for paying him 40s. a week (See *Commons' Journals,* iii. 339), and asking for the loan of 10l. to be sent by Jerome Couch, Captain Hotham's man. [N. III., 164.]

Sir Henry Anderson to John Rushworth.

[1643–4], March 9. The Tower.—Praying him to deliver the enclosed to the Lieutenant of the Tower, and to intreat Mr. Speaker to get his petition read and considered. [N. III., 166.]

The King to Richard Lowe, of Yateley.

1643[–4], March 17.—Privy Seal for borrowing 20l. (In the form of that printed in Rushworth, iii., 2. 580.) [N. I., 14.]

The Earl of Lindesay to Lord Maitland and the other Scotch Commissioners in London.

1644, April 6. Easington.—Have forwarded your letters of March 14th and 19th, with the enclosures, to Scotland, as the matters are so important that the answer should come from the Convention of Estates. The enclosed will inform you of the endeavours made for supplying the Scotch army still in Ireland, three regiments of horse being already landed in Scotland. 10,000l. in money has already been sent over, besides some clothes and ammunition. We again remind you of the great scarcity of money in the army. [N. III., 116.] *Enclosed:*

i. Viscount Montgomery, Arthur Chichester, Sir John Montgomery, Arthur Hill, Theophilus Jones, Arthur Gore, and
   Owen O'Connally to the Committee of the English Parliament with the Scotch Army.

1643[-4], February 21. Newtown [Ards].—By our last of
December 16th, we made known our good affections, and represented our great necessity and the danger of our regiments
disbanding for want of victuals, wherefore we entreated you to
mediate with the State of Scotland for so much meal as would
supply our six regiments for two months only, till the Parliament should provide better supplies. We received no answer
in writing to our modest request, but were told that you would
not mediate with Scotland, having no commission from the
Parliament to that effect, but that you would represent our
desires to the Parliament, and send our other letter to the Committee of Adventurers. We have with all patience waited for
their and your answers, but hungry bellies make pressing
tongues. We think it therefore fit to let you know our wants
have been so far from being any way yet supplied that the Scotch
army, being likewise reduced to want of victuals, has been laid
upon our poor exhausted quarters for their relief, whereby both
our forces and the country people will inevitably starve or
forsake the country, unless very speedily both the Scotch army
be supplied hereafter, and relief sent us, not only to repay the
country what has been taken from them for the support of the
Scotch army, but likewise so to maintain us that they may be
eased of the burden they have lain under. This we again
earnestly recommend to your care to do it either by mediation
with the State of Scotland or otherwise, and ask you to let
us know what answer you have had from the Parliament or
Committee of Adventurers to our last, for if their answer
with the supplies does not come very soon, and such as may
prove satisfactory to the country people, officers, and soldiers,
this country—now the best strength and stay of the Protestant
subjects of this kingdom—will be wholly lost to the Rebels.
Copy. [N. XII., 74.]

ii. Major-General Robert Monro to [the Committee of the
    Estates of Scotland].

164[3-]4, February 23. Carrickfergus.—"Lest your resolutions of
the army's stay or removal should not answer unto the present
exigency what may befall us of the army or what hereafter may
befall unto our country for want of timeous advertisement according to my bounden duty and the intelligence I have of the wicked
applotments of him most bound to guard us under God I have
thought fit in all haste to acquaint your Lordships that the
Marquess of Antrim now loadnit with titles of honour from his
Majesty in hope to do good service against us—Amongst others
his titles he is called Chief Justice and Commander of the Isles
of Scotland and General of the Catholic army of the Rebels
in Ireland, as I understand by several intelligences from our
noble friends from Dublin and elsewhere—That he is marching
with a strong army against us of Rebels, whereof he is the chief,
and is clad with commission to persecute the Scotch army, who
were sent to be under the Parliament's pay of England, and it

is thought they will spare none of the Scotch they can be masters
of. For my part I shall think myself happy in the rencounter
hoping my fortune may be to catch him the third time to vindicate
myself from the aspersion of the wicked, for which I will strive
to the utmost of my power with God's assistance to prove a loyal
servant to my country in despite of envy. What relief or supply
your Lordships are able to send unto us would come timely
being of great consequence for us and your own safeties, for if
the arme be disenablit, as God forbid, the body will be in danger.
Howsoever it is my earnest suit unto your Lordships that, since
the Rebels are provided of shipping for carrying their victuals
—without which it will be hard for them to victual an army
in the Province of Ulster—that your Lordships will consider
that after their victuals is disloadnit they may make use of their
shipping to intercept our victuals and our correspondence with
your Lordships. That your Lordships would be pleased timely
to direct forth some shipping from the West to prevent this
inconvenience, and with God's assistance we shall strive to
hinder their going to you and their supplies to their faction in
England. We have also defect of arms and ammunition, which
in all haste with other supplies would be securely convoyed unto
us .   .   .   .
Postscript.—For your Lordships' better information consider of
the enclosed, coming from one of our noble friends. The like I
received from Dublin also." *Copy.* [N. XII., 95.]

iii. Major-General ROBERT MONRO and the other Commanders to the
PRIVY COUNCIL and COMMITTEE OF THE ESTATES OF SCOTLAND.

164[3–]4, March 14. Carrickfergus.—" I having in conformity
to the Act of transportation resolved the removal of the army and
sent three regiments already to Scotland, we have the 11th of
this instant received a letter from Captain McGill, showing it
to be your earnest desire and pleasure that we should stay in this
land, where also your Lordships against the last of March
promised to assure us for our enablement in this service, and
notwithstanding all our bygone extremity to testify our great
respects to your Lordships and the good of our country we have
delayed our further removal till the first of April, and have sent
Major Borthwick . . to show our conditions and minds
anent the service . . . Therefore we expect your care towards
us and the service in despatching your answer against the said
day." *Copy.* [N. XII., 98.]

iv. The OFFICERS OF THE SCOTCH ARMY IN IRELAND to the
COMMITTEE OF THE ESTATES OF SCOTLAND.

164[3–]4, March 14. Carrickfergus.—" Their former sufferings
are the most assured testimony of their desire to do what in them
lies." Illegible in many parts. *Copy.* [N. XXI., 10.]

va. The COMMITTEE OF THE ESTATES OF SCOTLAND to ———.

164[3–]4, March 16.—The Committee " haveing taken the demands
of the Scotis armie in Ireland to their most serious consideration
doe returne this answer.

To the first concerneing the sixtie thousand pounds sterline with
ten thousand suites of cloaths and mantenance in tyme comeing, mentioned in their former instructions with Gedeon Murray

and now redemanded, the committie does acknowledge that the armie may verie justlie crave this soume as a part of their arreares due to them for their bypast service and promeist by the Englishe commissioners to have been payed before the first of Februar last by past. The not performance querof is a verie great dissappointment yitt are we confident that the officers of the armie are so judicious and reasonable in their desyres—which they have verie honestlie and kyndlie exprest in their late declaration—as they will not urge nor expect from this kingdome more then is possible for us to performe or that they thinke we are able instantlie without the assistance of the Parliament of England to delyver to them that sixtie thousand pounds sterline which not withstanding we acknowledge is far lesse then their deservings or our desyres. But as it is the verie carnest desyre of this kingdome that the armie may stay in Ireland for defence and preservation of the protestant religion and Brittishe plantation and for diverting of manie evills which will follow upon the relingquisheing of that kingdome to the rebells, so are we confident that in a verie short tyme suche supplies will be sent to the armie frome the houses of parliament in satisfaction of their former demands with what is and will be givin to them by this kingdome—who will leave nothing undone for their subsistance which is in their power—as may bothe enable and encourage them to stay and prosecute the warre in Ireland. And haveing out of the furst moneyis could be raised their sent to them ten thousand pounds sterline with so much cloath as could for the present be had readie heir, and als haveing sent victuall both by the north and west sea as some effectuall begining of the supplies promeist by us to thame our earnest desyre and order in behalfe of the estates of this kingdome to them is that they may be yitt content to stay in Ireland till the   daye of Apryle nixt, to the effect that the estates of this kingdome at their ensuing meetting which is to be upon the tent of Apryle nixt may resolve upon such present and solide course for entertanement and mantenance of that armie frome the Parliament of England and this kingdome as may enable them to the active prosecution of the warre in Ireland. And as we have writtin to our commissioners in England and the committie with our armie to be instant with the houses of parliament for that end, so is it our desyre that such persons may be sent frome that armie in Ireland as they shall think fittest to the convention of the estates against the tent of Apryle who may be witnesses to our actions and the realitie of our intentions in doeing everie thing which is in the reach of our power for the mantenance of that armie, for resolveing upon the best and most effectuall wayes for prosecuting the warre, for rectifieing anie former oversight or omission which hath been in the power or maner of commanding, and for everie other thing possible which may conduce to the subsistance and good of that armie. We sall be carefull to represent to the estates the prejudice the service susteans by the absence of the collonells or other officers of that armie and that there may be such a way takin as may serve for the encouragement and advancement of the officers who ar present as there service and valour does justlie deserve.

Wheareas it is desyred that these regiments of the armie in Ireland who ar come to Scotland may be continued and not removed till they be recalled to the armie, or the armie brought hither, it is our resolution that these regiments sall for cloathes and money be putt in equall footting with the other regiments that are in Ireland. And in the meane tyme quill they are heir we trust they will be content we mak the best use of their service for repressing the insolencies of malignants who are knowin enimies to religion and their countrie, and defending of this kingdome against forraine invasion. And incase we sall find a necessitie for the good of the caus querin both that armie and we are ingadged that their regiments be imployed ellis where it sall be in that way which we think will have approbatione of all who love religioun and the caus querin we are ingadged for yow may be confident that we will be no lesse carefull of the preservation and strenthing of that armie and there just interest then of our owne saiftie. And since we are both in on shipe and ingadged in one and the same caus we are persuaded yow will with the same sinceritie be willing to contribut your best furtherance in everie thing may tend to the advanceing of the caus and secureing and strenthneing of this kingdome.

That which is meaned by the keeping of a garrison in Carrick-fergus without the dominution of the armie is that if the armie be transported frome Ireland—as we hope in God it will not in haist—there may be als many of the Brittishe in Ireland brought over in place of the Scots that sall be left in the garrison as may compleit the armie to be ten thousand besydes these to be left in the garrison to be under the command of Generall-Major Monro or his deputs."

v*b.* [The COMMITTEE OF THE ESTATES] to [the OFFICERS OF THE SCOTCH ARMY IN IRELAND.]

Same date.—

" RIGHT HONORABLE,

We haveing receaved your letter frome Major Borthwicke and haveing considered your instructions to him and demands to us we cannot bot acknowledge what yow have done in sending over these three regiments is warranted by the act for trans-portation which the estates did meane of extreeme necessitie for preservation of the armie bot would have beene verie loath to remove the armie if there can be a competencie of meanes afforded for your subsistance there. We take your stay upon our letters sent by Captaine McGill as a verie reall testimonie and demonstration of your affection and obedience to the desyres of this kingdome which is also a verie powerfull motive to make us with the greater diligence and sheerefullnes to goe speedilie about the reall and effectuall performance of suche meanes as may enable and encourage yow to subsist and prosecute the warre in Ireland. And what we are not able to doe of our-selves we sall be earnest intercessors to procure the same frome the parliament of England and the estates of this kingdome, who are to meitt upon the tenth of Apryle nixt, and who as they have more power and auctoritie to injoyne and raise suche meanes as may serve for the supplies then we have, so we are most confident they will leave nothing undone which is in their power for your satisfaction and putting yow in suche a posture and condition as yow may activelie goe about the pro-secuting of the warres in Ireland against our common enemies. We have returned ansere to your instructions and demands sent by Major Borthwicke, and our earnest desire to yow is that yow would stay in Ireland till the 24th day of Apryle nixt, and that yow would send suche persons as yow thinke fittest from the armie to the convention of estates to be heir the tent of Apryle nixt who may be witnesses to the proceedings of the estates and of the realitie of their desyres to performe everie thing in their power for the subsistance and weelfaire of that armie and as may enable them most for the prosecuteing of that service that both yow may reach the just recompence of your service and both kingdomes the fruits of your labours which we are confident—frome the frequent experience we have found of your willingness to obey the desires of this kingdome—yow will not deny to doe. And then yow may certainelie expect frome both kingdomes that supplee which may enable yow to goe activelie about that service wheirin yow have both done and suffered so much or if that sould faill—as we hope it will not— have suche a honourable and warrantable call for your removall, as may serve most for your reputation and employment ellis where, so yow may be most usefull for the good of the caus querin both kingdomes are so deeplie ingadged, and shippes and barkes will be sent for your transportatioun, And yow may rest assured that in following the advice of the estates of this kingdome and there committies there will be afforded to yow a competence of mantenance for following the warres in Ireland or at least yow will be putt in the same condition with your native kingdome and our armeis heir and in England for as our caus is one and hes commoun freinds and enemieis, so we must resolve with Godis assistance to stand and fall together. And for our firmer union the commissioners of the generall assemblie and we have sent Mr. James Hamiltoun a faithfull minister in this kingdome and whois integritie is well knowin in Ireland with the covenant to be sworne be the officers and souldioures of our armie and all suche others of the Brittishe as sall be willing to enter into this covenant which is alreadie universallie receaved in this kingdome and by the houses of parliament and their armeis and is ordained to be takin by all sortis of persons in England. Concerneing the fittest tyme of sweareing this covenant we remitt it to your owne discretioun and the messinger sent with it but the soouner yow doe it we thinke it so muche the better which will confirme the confidence this kingdome hes in yow and will be a character to difference betueenc the well and disaffected. In the meane tyme we trust that yow and suche of the Brittishe forces as love the religioun and saiftie of thir kingdome will stand the best way yow may upon your guarde against the invasion of the rebells. The reason why we did not ansere the Generall-Major his desyre for exoneration of his bygane service and call heir is becaus of the desyre we have of his contning in that charge there. But if the armie be recalled he will find suche ane approbation of his by gane service and employment for the future as may witnes the gratitude of this kingdome and the constant resolution we have to continue." *Copies.* . [N. XIV., 45.]

---

* Note.--These are all in the same hand except the third, and are probably " the five papers concerning Irish Affairs " mentioned in *State Papers, Domestic*, p. 137, in connection with the letter of April 6th and ordered to be reported to the House of Commons by Sir H. Vane, the last two letters being copies on the same paper.

The Scotch Commissioners to Lord Wharton.

1644, April 8.—(Printed in *Lords' Journals*, vi. 506.) [N. XIV., 1.]

A true relation of the routing of the Earl of Carberie and his forces out of the County of Pembroke.

[1644, April 12.]—(Printed in *King's Pamphlets*, E. 42, Number 19.) [N. XIII., 199.]

Sir Henry Anderson to John Rushworth.

[1644], April 19. The Tower.—Asking what hinders his petition from being read and answered, and declaring that he is often without meat, having been now six months a prisoner. [N. III., 167.]

[The Parliament] to [the Earl of Essex].

[1644, May 20.]—(Printed in *Lords' Journals*, vi. 562.) *Draft* in Rushworth's hand. [N. XII., 182a.]

Harcourt Leighton and Thomas Herbert to Sir John Trevor.

1644, May 23. Reading.—"On Monday by 8 in the morning we got to Henley, where the foot drew out to muster—which I oversaw—and the horse near Marlow and Maidenhead thicket, which Mr. Leighton and Colonel Pinder viewed. Part of the horse muster was deferred till Wednesday, when we mustered near Harrison's barn at Reading. The train of artillery was mustered with the foot, the several particulars of which we have, as taken in the field, but know not whether 'tis expected that we should certify the Parliament or Committee concerning it, but by the way we may be bold to acquaint you that some regiments are very thin, and some troops few and ill-armed, and especially we thought good to complain of the recruit horse. Few of them but were diseased with farcy and glanders or such infectious diseases, and generally very poor and reasty. By reason of the suddenness of the muster 'twas very confused, and impossible to be well viewed by so few, the foot mustering at one time in so many places, and for the horse we think it would be very helpful to the truth of mustering and prevent borrowing one of another, if the several troops were marched with distinct characters upon the near side, and to bring all their arms to the muster to be viewed and certified. . . . *Postscript.*—We are marching forward. . . . By reason the army marched so suddenly after muster, and that the rolls could not be closed, there is only ¾ allowed the horse." *On the back.*—"The inconvenience both city and country and army may suffer by Greenland House is known to all. Saving my Lord General's consideration, we beseech that a guard may be set upon them by his Excellency, or that the city would please to send a regiment or two under command of Colonel Browne or some other. The place is excellently situate for battering in three places, and the pieces may be brought by barges very near the place—but let them be good ordnance as demi-cannon and culverin, and not small, such as be for campagnia—and especially employ seamen, who are best provided for such service, and with a gunner, and fit to scale or enter breaches." *Signed. Seal.* [N. III., 117.]

SIR WILLIAM CONSTABLE to WILLIAM LENTHALL.

1644, May 25. Hull.—"I have not hitherto taken the boldness to present you with a few lines from hence having nothing worthy of you, but this present which I now send you gives me a little more boldness being a proper service to the house to send you your members. (Mr. Bellassys and Sir J. Ramsden, see *Commons' Journals*, iii. 511.) I have only the sending of these, but shall be glad to bring you in more of the same quality." *Seal.* [N. III., 118.]

Colonel MARTIN PYNDAR, HARCOURT LEIGHTON, THOMAS HERBERT, and JOHN POTTER to WILLIAM LENTHALL.

1644, May 27. Abingdon.—Concerning the numbers and movements of the Earl of Essex' and Sir William Waller's armies, their want of arms and apparel, and some abuses committed by the soldiers, especially a plunder and murder near Wickham. (Printed in Grey, iii., Appendix, No. 38, p. 63.) [N. III., 119.]

Instructions concerning CONVOY.

1644, May 28.—Convoy to be afforded both to subjects and strangers, taking from the last acknowledgement according to the value of the goods and number of vessels, and from the first according to custom. (See *Commons' Journals*, iii. 509.) [N. XIV., 2.]

The EARL OF WARWICK to the SPEAKER OF THE HOUSE OF PEERS.

1644, May 30.—Concerning the relief of Lyme Regis. (Printed in Rushworth, iii. 2. 680.) *Copy.* [N. XII., 79.]

Colonel HERBERT MORLEY to WILLIAM LENTHALL.

1644, June 5. Arundel.—"Amongst the goods taken from the Dunkirk ships we have found certain pictures which contain most gross idolatry; upon one, the Trinity pictured in monstrous shapes like giants; upon another is painted the Virgin Mary as sitting in heaven with her babe in her arms, underneath is the Pope, on whose left hand stands our King perfectly limmed and completely armed, with his cavaliers attending him; on the Pope's right hand stands the Queen accompanied with her ladies, the King tenders his sceptre to the Queen, she accepts it not, but directs it to be delivered to the Pope. This picture was intended to be set up in the chief church of Seville in Spain, as appears by the direction on the outside of the box, in which it is inclosed. I look upon this picture as an hieroglyphic of the causes and intents of our present troubles, and the opinion of the neighbouring nations concerning them, and if the House please to command the picture to London and there permit it to the public view, I conceive 'twould very much convince the Malignants, and open the eyes of all that are not wilfully blind." *Seal.* [N. III., 120.]

EDWARD DUNCOMBE to WILLIAM LENTHALL.

1644, June 6. Croke Castle.—Complaining that the committee of his county disputed his right to fell timber on his lands at Croke, held under lease from the Bishop of Durham. *Seal.* [N. III., 121.]

CHARLES LODOVIC, ELECTOR PALATINE, to Mr. HARINGTON.

1644, June 13–23. The Hague.—M. de Servien, one of the French Plenipotentiaries at Münster, has requested me to procure a pass from the Parliament for half a dozen horses or geldings for his own use. Being desirous to gratify him I request you to use your best endeavours to procure the pass, and also immunity from paying Custom for the horses. *Signed* " Charles." *Seal.* [N. I., 48.]

PRINCE RUPERT to General GEORGE GORING.

1644, June 18. Liverpoole.—" I intend to be to-morrow at Ormis Kirke with all my forces, and if it please you to let the Earl of New-castle know that I am upon my march towards him and that no time shall be lost you will do me a favour. As soon as I shall have a copy of your cipher I will do it myself. *Postscript.*—I beseech you to hasten the Westmoreland and Cumberland forces and do not spoil our quarters." *Sign Manual.* *Seal.* [N. I., 40.]

SIR HENRY HOLCROFT and others to WILLIAM LENTHALL.

1644, June 24. Chelmsford.—Referring to the orders received from the Committee of both Kingdoms for raising their Trained Bands and other forces remaining in the country and requesting two things ; First that these additional charges might not thereafter be less considered, because they forbear to press them at present, and secondly, that they might forthwith receive the long desired ordinance. *Postscript.*—Suggesting that some gentlemen be sent for two or three days into the several counties of the Association, and hoping that Sir William Waller is following the King's forces " which we conceive, under God, the chief means of our preservation." *Signed.* *Seal.* [N. III., 122.]

WILLIAM LENTHALL to the [EARL OF ESSEX], LORD GENERAL.

1644, July 1.—I am commanded by the House of Commons to return your Lordship thanks for your respects to the Commissioners of both Houses attending your army. Notwithstanding, it appearing that they have received many discouragements and obstructions in performing their duties by several public and scandalous affronts from Dr. Dorislaus and Colonel Harvy, this House desires your Lordship that they may be sent up to this House to answer the informations made against them. (See *Commons' Journals*, iii. 543.) *Draft.* [N. XII., 80.]

The COMMITTEE AT NORTHAMPTON.

1644, July 3.—Warrant for raising horses for Sir William Waller's army. (See *Commons' Journals*, iii. 554.) [N. XIV., 3.]

The SCOTCH COMMISSIONERS.

1644, July 4.—Paper. "Whereas it pleased the . . Parliament by their votes of the 11th of April last . . to . . appoint that 30,000*l.* as the remainder of the 60,000*l.* formerly promised should be . . sent away by the last of June to the Scotch army in Ireland, upon which they might depend as a necessary supply after they had endured so much, and their subsistence hath been so heavy a charge to the Kingdom of Scotland these two years and above, and that the sequestration money should not be diverted to any other use upon any pretence whatsoever,

We entreat your Lordships and these noble gentlemen to represent to the Parliament that notwithstanding the constant endeavours of the Committee at Goldsmiths' Hall there are not any of these moneys as yet provided, neither out of the sequestrations nor in any other way, and to desire that some speedy and effectual course may be taken for providing and sending away the said 30,000*l.* and for the future maintenance of the armies in Ireland, conform to the votes above mentioned, which were long ago sent to the Kingdom of Scotland, and upon which those armies depend." (See *Commons' Journals,* iii. 555.) *Signed* " Jo Cheislie." [N. XIX., 73.]

The EARL OF LOUDOUN, the MARQUESS OF ARGYLL, the EARL OF LAUDERDALE, and ARCHIBALD JOHNSTON to SIR WILLIAM ARMYNE, and the other Commissioners at Sunderland.

1644, July 12. Edinburgh.—Desiring that satisfaction might be made to George Wesum, skipper, for five pieces of cloth taken from him at Sunderland that he had bought for his own and his companies use. *Signed.* [N. III., 123.]

The GRAND JURY to the JUSTICES OF STAFFORDSHIRE at Quarter Sessions.

1644, July 12.—Petition stating that they are over taxed beyond the rest of the Association, and complaining of free quarters, and that all their forces are drawn out of the county, whereby there will not be men to gather in the hay and harvest, and praying that some effectual means be used for the speedy calling home of their men, and that the members would present these their grievances to both Houses and to the Committee of both Kingdoms. (See *Commons' Journals,* iii. 565.) [N. XXII., 72.]

The PARLIAMENT to the COUNTIES OF THE EASTERN ASSOCIATION.

1644, July 12.—(Printed in *Lords' Journals,* vi. 636.) *Copy.* [N. XII., 81.]

The PARLIAMENT OF SCOTLAND to the PARLIAMENT OF ENGLAND.

1644, July 16. Edinburgh.—Receipt for 30,000*l.* paid on account of arrears due to the Scotch army in Ireland. *Signed* " Alexander Gibson." [N. XIV., 6.]

ORDINANCE.

1644, July 19.—For regulating the proceedings of the Committee of both Kingdoms. (Printed in *Lords' Journals,* vi. 641.) [N. XIX., 74.]

The SCOTCH COMMISSIONERS.

1644, July 22.—Paper on behalf of the Earl of Roxburgh stating that he had taken the Covenant within the prescribed time, and is very useful to the common cause, and therefore insisting that all his goods and those of his deceased lady, which had been seized by order of the Parliament, should be delivered to such persons as he shall appoint, who shall be no further troubled in the peaceable possession thereof. *Signed* " Jo. Cheislie." [N. XIX., 75.]

Sir Adam Hepburne and Thomas Hatcher to the Committee of both Kingdoms.

[1644, July 25.]—Representing the condition of the Scotch army in the North, and their wants and necessities due to payments not having been made according to the treaty, and desiring that the same be represented to the Parliament, that they may find out effectual means for raising considerable sums of money, whereby that army may be enabled to prosecute the service while the summer lasts, they at present having neither money, clothes, nor means to subsist. (See *Commons' Journals*, iii. 572.) *Copy.* [N. XIX., 76.]

The Scotch Commissioners.

1644, August 1.—Paper referring to the paper of July 25th, and, as the House of Commons has passed some votes for supplying the Scotch army with money and clothes, desiring that the House be put in mind of the growing extremities they are in, that some speedy and effectual course may be taken for providing what has been voted. *Signed* " Jo. Cheislie." [N. XIX., 77.]

Sir William Armyne, Richard Barwis, and Robert Fenwick to William Lenthall.

1644, August 1. Sunderland.—Some gentlemen of the Scotch Committee, Sir William Armyne, and Mr. Barwis, by Lord Calander's desire repaired to Leeds to General Lesley for the affairs of Northumberland, Durham, and Newcastle. On our return we heard that Hartlepool and the Castle of Stockton had surrendered to Lord Calander, and found Major Douglas, son of the sheriff of Tividall, appointed Governor of the former with six companies of foot, and that a Captain with six score men had been sent to Stockton. " Lord Calander himself with all his forces marched towards Newcastle, and with a strong party of commanded men possessed themselves of Gateshead, and have made some works to stop up the passage of the bridge, and my Lord himself lies with the rest of his men on the top of the hill, not far from them . . . If no forces from Prince Rupert, Goring, Montrose and his crew, who are endeavouring to raise men in Cumberland and Westmoreland do not interrupt us (*sic*), we are in good hopes to give a good account of the town of Newcastle. We have written formerly to know the pleasure of the House, how we shall demean ourselves to my Lord Calender and his army. We are daily called upon for many things, and hitherto we have endeavoured to accommodate him with all things in our power or what the country may afford for the use of his army, which we conceive will not be unacceptable service to you, and therefore till we know your further pleasure we shall continue." We enclose a letter from the President of the Parliament of Scotland, dated July 17th, and for the present are unable to satisfy the desires therein contained. We have also received a letter from some of the Scotch Lords concerning 5 pieces of cloth taken by the small catch, sent out of Sunderland by our direction, called the *Robert* of London. We desire that satisfaction may be given, and that they may be compelled to give us an exact account of all they have taken. *Signed. Seal.* [N. III., 124.]

M. de Sabran to the Speaker of the House of Peers.

1644, August 4–14.—(Printed in *Lords' Journals*, vi. 657.) *Signed.* N. XVII., 3.]

The SALE to WILLIAM LENTHALL.

Same date.—(Identical, *mutatis mutandis*, with the last.) [N. XVII., 4.]

GEORGE [LORD] DIGBYE to General GEORGE GORING.

[1644], August 5. Liskeard.—Am very glad to hear you came last night to Exeter. I enclose a warrant to the Commander at Oke-hampton to convoy you to Launceston, whence to us here there is no danger . . . "It is most necessary you should be with us to-morrow night, for we shall draw to-morrow out of this town toward the enemy and probably we may fight the next day." *Seal.* [N. III., 23.]

SIR WILLIAM ARMYNE, RICHARD BARWIS, and ROBERT FENWICK to WILLIAM LENTHALL.

1644, August 5. Duresme (Durham).—Had convened a meeting to-day at Durham of the well affected gentlemen of the Bishopric, at which were also present some colonels and other officers who received their commissions from Lord Fairfax. (The purport of most of what follows is given in *Commons' Journals*, iii. 593, and in addition the meeting desired that a High Sheriff and some Justices of the Peace should be appointed for the County Palatine). *Signed. Seal.* [N. III., 125.]

The EARL OF ESSEX to the SPEAKERS OF BOTH HOUSES.

1644, August 8. Listithiel.—(Printed in *Lords' Journals,* vi. 670.) *Signed. Seal.* [N. III., 126.]

The COMMITTEE [AT YORK] and the COMMISSIONERS OF BOTH HOUSES.

1644, August 8.—Order that all the lead found in the city at its surrender, which had been brought thither by the Earl of Newcastle, should be sold, compensation being afterwards made to such of the owners thereof as were well affected and proved their title within six months. [N. XIV., 5.]

Colonel FRANCIS THOMPSON to the HOUSE OF COMMONS.

[1644, before August 10th.]—Petition stating his services, his wounds received at Edgehill, and his disbursements for his regiment and praying for payment. (See *Lords' Journals,* vi. 666; *Commons' Journals,* iii. 587.) *Signed.* [N. XXII., 138.]

Colonel JOHN BINGHAM, Colonel JOHN FITZ-JAMES, Major WILLIAM SYDENHAM, and four others, to WILLIAM LENTHALL.

[1644, August 10. Dorchester.]— Praising the services of Sir Anthony Ashley Cooper and desiring that he may be added to their number. (See *Commons' Journals,* iii. 589.) *Signed. Seal.* [N. III., 127.]

[The EARL OF WARWICK] to the SPEAKER OF THE HOUSE
OF PEERS.

1644, August 10. Plymouth Sound.—(Printed in *Lords' Journals,*
vi. 671, where "Behere" is a misprint for "Behre.") [N. III., 129.]

The EARL OF ESSEX to the SPEAKER OF THE HOUSE OF PEERS.

1644, August 10. Listithiel.—*Signed.* [N. III., 128.] *Enclosed :*

i. PRINCE MAURICE and the EARL OF BRAINFORD to the EARL
OF ESSEX.

1644, August 9. Boconnock.—*Signed* "Maurice." "Brainford."
[N. I., 47.]

And

ii. The EARL OF ESSEX to PRINCE MAURICE.

1644, August 10.—*Copy.* [N. XII., 82.] (All three are printed
in *Lords' Journals,* vi. 671, where in the first "day" is omitted
after "every.")

CHARLES, Duke of Lorraine, to the HOUSE OF COMMONS.

1644, August 24.—Complaining of the treatment of his agent,
and desiring redress. (See *Lords' Journals,* vi. 699.) In *French.*
Signed. [N. X., 33.]

Articles against THOMAS MIDDLETON of Horsham, a member
of the House of Commons and one of the Committee for Sussex.

[1644, before August 26.]—Alleging that in the latter end of
December last when the King's forces lately invaded Sussex, and had
taken Arundel town and castle, pretending himself sick, he would not
in any ways show himself against the King's forces, but discouraged
the countrymen that took up arms for the Parliament when the King's
forces were within few miles of Horsham, and that he was in all
probability consenting to the bringing of some of the King's forces to
take Horsham. It is mentioned that on the 11th December some of the
King's forces were seen within four miles of Horsham riding towards
it in the night, and that there was a garrison of the cavaliers at Wiston,
and various statements are made to show Mr. Middleton's disaffection to
the Parliament. (23 articles in all.) (See *Commons' Journals,* iii. 609.)
[N. XVI., 36.]

GEORGE [LORD] DIGBYE to General GEORGE GORING.

1644, August 30. Boconnock.—"Till Sir Richard Cave's return I
shall have nothing to write unto you more than to give you thanks for
the excellent punctual accounts, which you give us here of your condition there, which pray continue. God send your dragooners every
day as good a breakfast as it seems they had yesterday morning."
Addressed "to his quarters at St. Austell." *Seal.* [N. III., 130.]

FRANCIS BACON, SIR THOMAS BARNARDISTON and others to
WILLIAM LENTHALL.

1644, September 4. Bury.—Desiring that the difference betwixt
two Clerks of the Peace for the County of Suffolk may be speedily
heard and ended. *Signed. Seal.* [N. III., 131.]

SIR SUILSTON CALMADY and others to WILLIAM LENTHALL.

1644, September 7. Plymouth.—Certifying to the valiant conduct of the Plymouth regiment " at the late disaster at Foy." *Signed.* [N. III., 132.]

The KING to PLYMOUTH.

[1644, September 10.]—Summons. (The substance in Rushworth, iii. 2. 712. *Copy.* [N. XII., 31.]

SIR EDWARD MONINS, HENRY OXINDEN and others to WILLIAM LENTHALL.

1644, September 13. Knoll.—Supporting the petition of Mr. Edward Hales, grandchild of Sir Edward Hales, for his release. *Signed. Seal.* [N. III., 133.]

Alderman JOHN TOWSE and the other Commissioners of Excise to SIR PHILIP STAPILTON and RICHARD KNIGHTLEY.

1644, September 13. Excise office.—Acknowledging their letter reminding them of the vote of the House, dated June 21, for the advance of 1,000*l.* to the English and Scotch Reformado Officers, and asking them not to expect that all payments and exigencies of that kind should centre in the Excise which is unable to bear them. *Signed. Stamp.* [N. III., 134.]

The EARL OF ESSEX to the COMMITTEE OF BOTH KINGDOMS.

1644, September 19. Portsmouth.—Having described the importance of the place, " I find the defect here to be great both by reason of the decay of the fortifications, the small number of men, and the want of a magazine of victuals to prevent the danger of a sudden siege. For the first the works are in very great decay and will cost a very considerable sum to repair which I hope your Lordships will be a means shall be provided so that the work may be put in a good forwardness, whilst my engineers are hereabouts, and brought to such a perfection before winter come too far on as may prevent the breaches from growing greater. How the men come to be so few this bearer must satisfy, but I find they are not above 400 men, where as indeed I conceive 1,000 are too few, and should be glad they were recruited to a considerable regiment of 1,000 men, whereof the one half may attend my army when the place is out of danger, and it is very necessary in my opinion that the town should be constantly furnished with 2,000 quarters of corn at least in store. Lastly I conceive that both for convoys and bringing in intelligence from abroad it were very fit there were a good troop of horse allowed to the garrison, which methinks might well be raised and paid by the county." (See *Commons' Journals,* iii. 638.) *Signed. Seal.* [N. III., 135.]

SIR JOHN MELDRUM to the COMMITTEE OF BOTH KINGDOMS.

1644, September 19. Montgomery Castle.—Commending the services done and the sufferings endured by Lord Herbert of Cherbury. (See *Commons' Journals,* iii. 636.) *Signed. Seal.* [N. III., 136.]

The PARLIAMENT to LORD INCHIQUIN and others.

[1644, September 20.]—(Printed in *Lords' Journals,* vi. 711.) *Draft* or *Copy.* [N. XII., 23.]

The Earl of Essex to William Lenthall.

1644, September 26. Portsmouth.—"Receiving now this fresh intelligence from Sir William Waller, and Quarter-Master-General Dalbier, I desire that those things which were promised this army both for horse and foot may be sent, any delay from taking the field being very prejudical at this present. In the mean time I have done what is in my power and that upon any summons from Sir William Waller I shall join my horse with his to make any impediment to the enemy if they march this way." (See *Commons' Journals*, iii. 642.) *Signed. Seal.* [N. III., 139.] *Enclosed:*

i. Sir William Waller to the Earl of Essex.

1644, September 24. Shaftesbury.—"His Majesty and his whole army quartered the last night at Chard, and I make no question but they will advance speedily. A gentleman that saw them drawn up speaks confidently they are not above 10,000 Horse and Foot, and 17 pieces." *Seal.* [N. III., 137.]

ii. Quarter-Master-General Dalbier to [the Earl of Essex].

[1644], September 24. Burgett.—"The trumpeter which I sent for Captain Grenville is returned . . He has left the enemy near Chard. Their head-quarters was on Monday night at Chard. They esteem themselves 10,000 men, horse and foot; they have 20 pieces of ordnance, but he says they have very few carriages or wagons. He could see not above twelve. He says that they give out to besiege Lyme, and yet they have sent 300 men to plunder Axminster, which makes me believe the contrary. The country people say 'they intend to march over Black Down, which is unlikely, unless they intend to pass at Minehead the sea and go to Wales. Sir William Waller has had a trumpet there too, who is marched through all their army . . . Your Excellency should make all the haste possible to get your foot armed that you may take a convenient post before the enemy be too near. The most part of our officers are absent, things will not be carried as it should. *Postscript.*—If they march over Black Down, it is their best way either to Taunton or Bridgwater. That they have so few carriages makes me consider that they are for no enterprise, rather for a great journey. I pray your Excellency will be pleased to let me know what is become of Prince Robert's forces, likewise where my Lord Manchester is. If the King takes the way of Bridgwater then he is for Bristol or for Oxford." [N. III., 138.]

List of Gunner's Stores delivered out of the *Leopard* for the use of the Army in Pembrokeshire.

[1644], October 6.—*Signed* "Richard Swanley." [N. XIV., 12.]

Sir William Armyne, Richard Barwis, and Robert Fenwick to William Lenthall.

1644, October 8. Penrith.—"We have endeavoured all we can for the present to settle all the people in Cumberland and Westmoreland in their obedience to the King and Parliament, and humbly offer to the consideration of the House the settling of the militia there, and the appointing of Sheriffs, . . and that Justices of the Peace may be appointed for both counties. Carlisle continues still obstinate, but they have been of late kept in that the country hath received little damage by them. Only the charge is very great to maintain such forces, as must of necessity be about Carlisle for the keeping them in on all sides. Sir Philip Musgrave, Sir Henry Fletcher, Sir William Dalston, Sir Thomas Dacres, Sir Timothy Fetherstonhaugh, and divers others remain still in Carlisle though they have been fairly invited forth by us. We have endeavoured by all the ways and means in our instructions and according to the Ordinances of Parliament to raise what money these parts will afford for the pay of the forces now there. Four regiments of horse are marching out of the country and two . . are left behind to join with the forces in the country to block up Carlisle, and preserve themselves from any ordinary party that might suddenly fall upon them. The Covenant is well embraced in these parts, and we hope shortly to give you a good account of it. The Mayor and Aldermen of Kendal have been twice with us, and seem very cordial for the Parliament and are raising some forces for their own " and the country's "defence. Sir Edward Musgrave,—who calls himself Sheriff of the County of Cumberland—keeps in Scaleby Castle, a house of his own not far from Carlisle, and will not come out. Sir Richard Graham, his father-in-law, is in Carlisle. The General-Major David Lesley hath taken Thirlwell Castle in the edge of Cumberland, but Naworth Castle and Millum Castle, both in the said County, hold out still against us. Sir John Lowther, Sir Patritius Curwen, Sir Richard Sanford, and Sir Thomas Sanford and divers others of the prime gentlemen of both Counties have taken the Covenant and submitted to the Ordinance of Parliament. We forbear to trouble with the relation of beating the enemy from Penrith, and chasing them to Carlisle, which was done at the first coming in of the Scottish forces. . . We find a great want of good ministers in these parts, as in the rest of the Northern parts, which, if not supplied, there is little hope of bringing the people out of that ignorance they have so long dwelt in. We send the names of several gentlemen . . that we thought fit to be Justices of the Peace . . and out of them High Sheriffs for each county may be appointed," namely :—

In Cumberland—

Sir Wilfrid Lawson, } of Iseild.
William Lawson, Esq. }
William Briscoe, counsellor at law, of Crofton.
Thomas Cholmely, of Little Salkeild.
Mr. Thomas Lamplugh, fit to be High Sheriff.
Mr. John Barwis.
Mr. William Orfuer.
Mr. John Skelton.

In Westmoreland—

Sir John Lowther, Bart.
Sir Richard Sandford, Knight.
Colonel Edward Brigges, Esq., fit to be High Sheriff.
Mr. Richard Branthwate, Esq.
Jervis Benson, Mayor of Kendal.
Gowen Brathwaite, Esq.
Colonel James Bellingham, son to Sir Henry Bellingham.
Mr. John Dalston.
Mr. Christopher Dudley.

(See *Commons' Journals*, iii. 678.) *Signed.* [N. III., 140.]

THO&AS TRAPHAM, Chirurgeon to Serjeant-Major-General Skippon,
to the HOUSE OF CO&&ONS.

[1644, October 10.]—Petition, stating that for his affection to the
cause he had lost his estate at Abingdon, and had served under the
Lord General, first in Colonel Hampden's regiment, and since it was
reduced he hath yielded his best services "to the said Major-General
and all the wounded soldiers in this last service in the West, and praying for payment of his arrears." (See *Commons' Journals*, iii. 658.)
[N. XXII., 135.]

SIR HENRY HOLCROFT, SIR WILLIA& MASHA&, and others to
WILLIA& LENTHALL.

1644, October 10. Chelmsford.—"It appears by the inclosed, that
by an order of the House some necessary works were raised by Sir
Harbottle Grimston's care for the defence of Harwich and six gunners
and twelve warders were appointed to attend the same by day and
night their pay amounting to 3*l*. 3*s*. per week. The town is very poor
and not able to bear the charges, and therefore they humbly desire
that Parliament will assign the Excise of their own town for defraying "
it, which request we support. *Signed*. [N. III., 141.] *Enclosed :*

> 1644, August 24. Harwich.—"The report of Sir Harbottle
> Grimston concerning the town of Harwich, how and by what
> order the works there were made, and the eighteen men there
> in garrison paid." This is signed by John Hunter the captain
> of the town. [N. III., 142.]

The Information of FREDERICK FABER and WILLIA& JONES, Commissioners for the Excise in Durham.

1644, October 11.—Stating that Major Rickarton had caused the
door to be broken open where was some tobacco they had seized, and
the same to be carried away in contempt of the ordinances of Parliament, and in defiance of the Commissioners, though they showed him
a copy of the Lord General's warrant, which he refused to obey.
(Printed in Grey, iii., Appendix, No. 18, p. 26.) [N. XIX., 78.]

The YORKSHIRE CO&&ITTEE appointed by the order of August 22nd.

1644, October 11.—Report that 7,000*l*. per month was as much as
could be raised for the land rate on the county and city of York, and
town of Kingston-upon-Hull, 1,000*l*. each upon Durham, Northumberland and the town of Newcastle, and Cumberland, 600*l*. on Westmoreland, and 1,753*l*. 6*s*. 8*d*. on the county and town of Nottingham, that
all the revenue from assessments, sequestrations, excise, King's and
Queen's revenues in these Northern Counties would be short by
25,000*l*. per month of the 31,000*l*. to be paid to the Scotch army and
25,000*l*. to the forces to be raised under Sir Thomas Fairfax and
suggesting that the compositions with Delinquents throughout England
be applied to make up the deficiency. (See *Commons' Journals*,
iii. 659.) [N. XIV., 7.]

PROPOSITIONS to the KING.

1644, October 14.—(Draft of those printed in *Commons' Journals*,
iii. 662.) [N. XIV., 8.]

ORDINANCE.

1644, October 14.—For raising money for arms for General Cromwell's Regiment. (Printed in *Lords' Journals*, vii. 24.) [N. XIV., 9.]

The EARL OF WARWICK to WILLIAM LENTHALL.

1644, October 14. Holborn.—Enclosing the subscription of divers commanders, officers, and persons at Duncannon in Ireland to the National Covenant, and also a letter from the Governor and a particular of their wants, and hoping the House will give them encouragement and supplies, " that the soldiers pretending to be provided for the service of the King of Spain, as by another of the enclosed appears, may be the better kept in and so more disabled from any prejudicial acting against the Parliament." *Signed.* [N. III., 143.]

The SIXTH QUALIFICATION of the FOURTEENTH PROPOSITION.

1644, October 14.—As altered. (Printed in *Lords' Journals*, vii. 56 as the fifth. The alterations consist in adding " Common or Civil" after " Law " throughout, inserting " Doctors, Advocates, and Proctors," and adding the paragraph about bishops and clergy.) [N. IX., 2a.]

PROPOSITIONS, ORDER OF REFERENCE to Mr. Reynolds and others, and ORDER OF REFERENCE concerning the Propositions desired by the City.

1644, October 15.—(Printed in *Commons' Journals*, iii. 668, 669.) [N. XIV., 42.]

Articles against SIR WILLIAM DARCY and his answer.

1644, October 16.—[N. XIV., 10.]

The COMMITTEE OF BOTH KINGDOMS.

1644, October 16. (Misdated July.)—Report desiring that the ordinance of June 15th may be continued, reporting papers from the Scotch Commissioners, and desiring that the Commissioners of Excise may hasten the payment of 500*l.* to the Wagon-Master-General. (See *Commons' Journals*, iii. 668, and *State Papers, Domestic*, p. 48.) [N. XIV., 4.]

The charge against SIR JOHN CONYERS and his answer.

1644, October 22.—[N. XIV., 11.]

Colonel MARTIN PYNDAR and THOMAS HERBERT to WILLIAM LENTHALL.

1644, October 24. Reading.—" Upon Thursday last my Lord Generall advanct to Southwick—Colonel Norton's house—wher drawing all his late divided regiments into one body, notwithstanding that the weather grew stormy and for three dayes and nights rayne fell incessantly, our foot marcht with extraordinary diligence and cheerfulnes—through deep wayes and entertaynd in late and penurious quarters—to the generall rendezvouz att Basingstoke, the joy to joyne with that gallant army counterpoising their wants and nothing more overcomming the difficultyes of the march than hopes to fight with their Cornish enemyes whose barbarisme will never be pardond till some proporcionable requitall. Next day the three armyes drew up and we are confident there never was in England a gallanter army either respecting the being well armd or courage of the men, who were overjoyed to hear the enemy was drawing towardes them. All next day wee spent in expectacion but the king wheeld about toward Newberry, so as we could not gett him ingaged. Howbeit our horse beat up their quarters and tooke above one hundred horse and foot prisners. Wee are now at Reading.

Touching the necessities of our owne army, give us leave to represent some thiugs to your consideracion. The army most parte of this march from Portsmouth has suffred in want of provision, partly through the indigency of the country through which wee past and partly through want of commissaries whose contynued absence is of extraordinary prejudice it being an imployment both of care and paynes; and tho a deputy may endeavor, yet wanting the reputacion the worke fayles much in the practize. Wherfore wee beseech you to take some course both to expedit the commissaries of provisions—both which are and have long been absent—to attend their charge, and if the house seam pleasd, to hasten some bisquitt and cheese hither, the passage being safe, the way not bad, and the souldyer therby would be exceedingly cheered. The commissaryes of the musters, both of horse and foote, are likewise at London. 'Tis fitt no money be issued out without muster. Wee are constrayned to complayne, for the servyce suffers much by their absence. The residence of an advocate would be advantageous to us here, for some exorbitances fall out now and then, which require a councell of warr, but by want of a judge advocate passe uninquird and unpunished. To supply the wants of our trayne and in order to the ordinance of parliament, the Isle of Wight voluntarily proffered fifty horse to my Lord Generall and accordingly this day he sent thither to quicken them, both to take an occasyon of retorning thanckes, and better providing for the teams who in these parts are so hardly to be gott, that of a dozen warrants for teems, not above one or two come in tho never so strictly commanded. The new trayne of artillery adds much to the contentacyon of our army. Wee are told ten or twelve more are designd which wee conceave may better be spared till Spring, the season affording little use, and the state if sent necessarily putt to excessive chardges.

Wee have no addicion, save that my Lord Generall has byn ill of late by an excessive flux and vomiting, but is better at this tyme." (See *Commons' Journals*, iii. 676.) *Signed. Seal.* [N. III., 144.]

The HOUSE OF COMMONS to the COMMITTEES of the Counties appointed to contribute to the maintenance of the garrison of Newport Pagnell.

1644, October 28.—Desiring them to send in their proportion of men and arrears of money. (See *Commons' Journals*, iii. 679.) *Draft.* [N. XII., 84.]

The SCOTCH COMMISSIONERS to the COMMITTEE OF BOTH KINGDOMS.

1644, October 28.—(The purport appears from *Commons' Journals*, iii. 681.) Signed "John Cheislie." *Original* and *Copy.* [N. XIV., 13.]

SIR JOHN HOTHAM to the HOUSE OF COMMONS.

[1644, October 28.]—Petition. After referring to his services, stating that " he received his commission from the House in these words annexed to the petition, and had from you no other law, direction, or rule to square his actions by but this particular commission. That he never received from this house or any other any signification or commands concerning Martial Law nor was it ever published in his garrison or the Association of Yorkshire, Durham &c., and that your petitioner finding some unruliness in his garrison did by a letter to you solicit you to send him some commands concerning Martial Law, but was by you denied it by an order in these words ' That such persons under Sir John Hotham as shall offend against any law shall be punished by law, but for such as offend against the safety of the town and peace of the Army as mutinies and such like them he shall commit to prison till upon information to this House further course may be taken.'

That the Ordinance of Martial Law whereby he received his summons and the instructions thereof are a law made 14 months after his pretended crime was committed, and therefore humbly conceives, it cannot be extended to the trial of it.

That he had his commission and instructions only from you, by you he was trusted and conceives himself bound solely to answer it to you, that he returned all his addresses to you, and was always your immediate agent, therefore craves leave not to submit, nor to be put upon any trial, but immediate by you, that to you and to your judgments he submits his estate life and honour, he confesses many errors, and lays himself down at the feet of your justice, and anything else that can be against him, he will willingly embrace a trial by any law extant or known to him, when they were committed, for where no law is, there is no transgression.

All this he humbly presents to your just thoughts, with a full and true relation of his whole government of Hull, which he craves it as a favour from you that you would grant, which he doubts not but you will grant him considering that he has laid now 15 months prisoner in silence and has not interrupted your business with the least word of petition for his private advantage." (See *Commons' Journals*, iii. 679.) *Holograph*. [N. XXII., 137.]

The EARL OF WARWICK to WILLIAM LENTHALL.

1644, October 29. Holborn.—After my several representations of the necessitous condition of the Navy during my absence at sea I hoped the House would have found time and means for the consideration and supply thereof. But on my return I found it in the same state, and therefore thought it my duty again to remind you of my representations in my letters of July 1st, and August 12th concerning the defective stores and materials. Without a speedy supply the Winter Guard cannot be completed nor a fleet set forth next summer. I have caused an estimate—not including the gunner's stores—of all the stores and materials necessary for setting forth the Winter Guard and the next summer fleet to be made, amounting to 15,078l. Great inconvenience arises from want of timely provision of money, which causes not only ships after coming in to lie at the State's charge in the river amounting lately to above 100l. a day, but also a long interval between the coming in of the summer fleet and the going out of the Winter Guard, and hence the guard of the sea is neglected, the enemy's ports opened, trade endangered, and the convoy of some of our own ships transferred to the Hollanders. Besides sellers are discouraged from giving provisions of proper quality by the non-performance of their contracts. The debts of the Navy, so far from being discharged, daily increase, and by the clamour attending them the officers of the Navy are disabled from doing their duty without distraction, which is the more considerable, because the Customs, whereby the expenses of the Navy are to be principally supported, have been anticipated, and hence great sums have to be borrowed, and a great charge for interest incurred. By not passing an Ordinance for the Commissioners of the Navy to act under me, they are discouraged from further acting and resolved to desist from the same as by the inclosed will appear, so that the business of the Navy will receive obstruction unless some sudden course be taken. I desire you to represent all this to the House. *Signed. Seal.* [N. III., 146.] *Enclosed:*

ROBERT TWEEDY and the other Commissioners of the Navy to the EARL OF WARWICK.

 i. 1644, October 24.—(The purport sufficiently appears from the previous letter.) *Signed. Seal.* [N. III., 145.]

And

 ii. The said Estimate. [N. XIV., 232.]

SIR THOMAS MYDDELTON to WILLIAM LENTHALL.

1644, October 30. Redd Castle.—"Having intelligence of the enemye's intention to raise newe forces in Wales, and of theire dailie pressings of men, and howe they intended to fortefie Ruthyn, and so make it a garrison towne—it beinge a place of great ymportance—I resolved to interrupt theire proceedinges the best I could and thereupponn drewe out a small partye both of horse and foote and marched to Ruthyn, it beinge three dayes march from Redd Castle, and extreame wette weather. Att three dayes ende wee came thither, and founde Collonell Trevor and Collonell Trafford with about four hundred horse and foote whoe withstoode our entrance into the towne but after some exchainge of shotte wee beate in uppon them, and beate them out of the towne. The enemyes foote ran into the castle, and theire horse towards Denbigh. Wee lost never a man att that tyme. Wee killed one of theirs, tooke a cornett, a doctour, and a quartermaster, with some twenty troops. I hope wee have scattered them, and distracted them soe that they will not easelye rayse men agayne. The enemye intends to raise great forces in these parts against the Prince's comynge which they expecte daylye, with ten thousand armes and five hundred barrells of powder. The cuntrye comes in reasonablye well in Mount-gomerieshire where I am, but wee wante armes exceedinglye and are like soe to doe, if our armes that wee provided and sent downe, both by sea and land shalbee taken from us, as they are, and wee lefte destitute and naked now in tyme of neede. Att my last cominge downe I sente by sea to bee landed att Liverpoole a parcell of armes —as by the particulars enclosed you may perceave—but are all taken from mee by one Captayne Tatum, without warrant as I conceave, and if our armes shalbee taken away att every man's pleasure that are to come to furnish these remote partes, it is but follye for any man to attempte the reducinge of them. I brought one thousand armes to Namptwich and att the last seige they were all taken awaye, and twenty-eight barrells of powder and I can neither gett my armes agayne, nor any satisfacion for them. I humbly desire that Captayn Tatum and Sir William Brereton and the Cheshire committee may bee ordered either to returne mee soe manye and soe good as they had of myne, or satisfacion for them, or that the honorable howse wilbee pleased to furnishe mee with fifteen hundred muskettes as many swords belts, snapsacks, and bandalyers, with fiftye barrells of powder, eight of shotte, and one hundred and fifty bundells of matche, all which they tooke away of myne, else I shall not bee able to proccede in the worke I have begunne, nor to doe yow any more service in these partes. For excepte wee maye have armes, wee can doe nothinge; and seinge I have entrenched uppon your patience thus farre give mee leave, I beseech yow, fullye to disgorge myselfe. I have offen pressed yow by my letters for releefe, both of men, armes, and moneys, but such hath byn my unhappines, that I have not receaved any satisfaction in any one of them. Nay, when motions have byn made for releefe, and the motion graunted yet it hath byn crossed, and stopped. I assure myselfe the wisdome of the howse had sufficiente grounde for what they did, but the commonwealth and myselfe suffer in the meane tyme. It is nowe six monethes sithence I came downe. I had 1,000*l.* of the howse att my cominge awaie, and sithence that tyme never a pennye. What I had before my cominge awaye was laid out att London, as will appeare by the accomptes when yow please to call for them. I have loste more then the one halfe of my men for wante of moneye though I have stretched my credditte to borrowe all the moneye I could gette to paie the souldiers. I am much troubled that yow have noe better thoughts of these partes. Sure I am that from these partes the kinge first raised his powerfull armye, and Prince Ruperte a second, and a third, and if care bee not spedelye taken to prevente, they will raise another armye as great as any of the former. I am disabled to prevente it, for I have neither men to spare, nor money to paye those that I have, nor armes to arme those that are willinge to come in unto mee." I request therefore leave to lay down my Commission and that some one else be appointed in my stead. *Enclosed* is a list of the armes and ammunition on board the *Marmaduke* and the *Cretian* and taken by Captain Tattam. *Postscript.—* Asking that 3,100*l.* a legacy of Lady Campden's for buying impropriations might be granted him as ready money to supply his occasions. *Signed.* [N. IV., 150.]

My Ladye Cambells 10,000: which nowe lyes dead.

General GEORGE GORING to Major-General PORTER.

[1644], October 31. Oxford.—Concerning his exchange with Major Carre who is too ill to journey to London. (See *Commons' Journals*, iii. 709, 711.) *Copy.* [N. XII., 83.]

SIR JOHN BOYS to SIR WILLIAM WALLER.

1644, November 2. Donnington Castle.—I have released Captain Masterton in accordance with your request, and desire Captain Bennett in exchange, or, if he be dead, Lieutenant Kylborne. [N. III., 147.]

PRINCE RUPERT to Major-General PORTER.

1644, November 4. Oxford.—Promising to exchange for him with Sir William Waller, Major Carr and Captain Maisterton. *Sign Manual.* [N. I., 41.]

The FIRST PROPOSITION and the FIFTH QUALIFICATION of the FIFTEENTH PROPOSITION.

1644, November 8.—(Identical with those printed in *Lords' Journals* of that date, vii. 54, 56, as the First Proposition and the fifth qualification of the Fourteenth Proposition.) *Copies.* [N. XXI., 128.]

The EARL OF MANCHESTER and others to the COMMITTEE OF ROTH KINGDOMS.

1644, November 11.—(Printed in *Lords' Journals*, vii. 62.) [N. III., 148.]

WILLIAM LENTHALL to SIR THOMAS FAIRFAX.

1644, November 12.—Thanking him in the name of the House for his services. (See *Commons' Journals*, iii. 691.) *Draft.* [N. XII., 85a.]

The PARLIAMENT to several COUNTIES.

1644, November [13.]—Circular to quicken the payment of arrears of assessment. (Printed in *Lords' Journals*, vii. 63.) *Draft.* On the same piece of paper is a copy of another letter to the same effect. [N. XII., 86.]

F. SEYMOUR, SIR E. FORTESCUE, and 42 others to——

1644, November 14. Exeter.—The sad condition of this County moves us of this County now assembled at our general meeting at Exeter to move you that the unhappy differences that are now and have been for too long a time between us may be happily composed. The reunion of you to us will so much advance your own and our peace that thereby exceeding great commerce and profit in these distracted times will redound unto us both. That and the sense of the miseries that befall you and us by this unnatural difference hath occasioned us thus to invite you to a treaty for peace, and that there may be some commissioners appointed of each side to endeavour a happy accommodation between us. (Probably referred in Lord Robertes' letter of the 16th.) *Signed.* [N. III., 149.]

The AMBASSADORS OF THE STATES-GENERAL to the SPEAKER OF THE HOUSE OF COMMONS and the same to the SPEAKER OF THE HOUSE OF LORDS.

1644, November 15.—Duplicates, asking exemption from Excise on Provisions; the first with the order of the House thereon. (The letter is printed in *Lords' Journals*, vii. 65, the order in *Commons' Journals*, iii. 723.) [N. XVIII., 98, 99.)

PRINCE RUPERT to [the EARL OF ESSEX].

1644, November [1] 6. Malingborough.—Sending two safe conducts from the King with a view to his receiving Propositions for Peace. *Copy. Enclosed* is a copy of the safe conduct. (Both printed in *Lords' Journals*, vii. 68.) [N. XII., 85.]

The EARL OF ESSEX to PRINCE RUPERT.

1644, November 16.—Concerning the exchange of Major-General Porter for Major Carre and Captain Maisterton. *Copy.* [N. XII., 88.]

LORD ROBERTES to WILLIAM LENTHALL.

1644, November 16. Plymouth.—Had long since represented what might be done here were a sufficient force sent to take the field. As they were otherwise employed, I conceived I might have been spared here, "had I not received some advertisements of the enemy's practice upon this place as much by fraud as force, against both which I was most willing to oppose my uttermost. Of the latter this day produced somewhat, which I herewith send whereby you see the enemy leaves nothing unattempted. Of the former I hope care will be taken to prosecute the victory . . else the splinters of a broken army may wound our sides." I desire the ammunition I asked for should be sent with all speed, and also that money be supplied for the garrison. " Had not a ship of fish and some lyncloth been taken, which for the instant necessity of this garrison we were forced to sell, I do not know how dangerous our condition had been. Here is now but one ship belonging to the state. I conceive that very good service might be done . . were there 6 or 8 small ships such as the *Providence* here, the enemy making use of this season for his supplies." *Signed. Seal.* [N. III., 150.]

The DIRECTORY FOR PUBLIC WORSHIP.

1644, November 21.—(This is the identical paper presented by Dr. Burges (See *Commons' Journals*, iii. 701) as " The humble Advice of the Assembly of Divines concerning a Directory for the Public Worship of God in the three Kingdoms." These words have been struck out and " A Directory for the Public Worship of God in the three Kingdoms" substituted. Against each clause is written R. for Resolved. It is signed by William Twisse, Prolocutor, Cornelius Burges and John White, Assessors, and Henry Robrough and Adoniram Byfield, Scribæ.

The only noteworthy changes made by the House of Commons are, in the direction for the Administration of Baptism the addition of the last line to the Exhortation to the Parent and the omission of the next clause which was as follows: "It is recommended to the Parent or Christian friend to make a profession of his Faith, by answering to these or the like questions, 'Dost thou believe in God, the Father, Son, and Holy Ghost ? Dost thou hold thyself bound to observe all that Christ hath commanded thee, and wilt thou endeavour so to do ? Dost thou desire to have this child baptized into the Faith and Profession of Jesus Christ ? ' " and in the direction for the celebration of the Communion or Sacrament of the Lord's Supper the omission of the following clause : " None are to be admitted thereunto but such as being baptised are found upon careful examination by the Minister, before the other Church Officers, to have a competent measure of knowledge and ability to examine themselves, and do profess their willingness to submit themselves to all the ordinances of Christ, and are of approved conversation according to the rules of Christ. The ignorant, the scandalous, the obstinate are not to be admitted ; nor those of another congregation, except they have sufficient testimony, or be very well known.") (See *Commons' Journals*, iii. 710.) The Preface is wrongly put with N. XXII., 5; N. XXII., 51 is another copy of the Preface. [N. XXII., 6.]

The EARL OF LAUDERDALE to the COMMITTEE OF BOTH KINGDOMS.

1644, November 22. Edinburgh.—Requesting that the plate and goods of the Earl of Roxburgh, seized at St. James', might be restored to him. (See *Commons' Journals*, iv. 1.) [N. III., 151.]

EDMOND JORDAN, Sheriff, and others, the Committee for Sequestrations for Surrey, to WILLIAM LENTHALL.

1644, November 23. Kingston.—Concerning Captain Withers and Mr. Andrewes' cause. The former had been given possession of the latter's estate to repay his losses from the King's forces, which he put at 2,000*l.*, whereas Mr. Andrews hath made it appear to us that his losses are not above a quarter of that sum, and that he has already been recouped out of the profits received by him. *Signed. Seal.* [N. III., 152.]

SIR JOHN WITTEWRONGE, SIR JOHN GARRARD, and others to WILLIAM LENTHALL.

1644, November 30. St. Albans.—The letter of the House dated October 28th represents there hath been a great negligence on our part for the supply of Newport Garrison. We are very sorry we should be so misunderstood in declaring the pressures of our County as that in desiring relief we should be rendered neglectful of our duty. Since receipt of your letter we have sent to Newport 500*l.*, which we borrowed, and appointed two of our Committee to go with it, and take an account out of the Treasurer's books there what we have paid and what other the Associated Counties have paid. We find we have paid for that garrison more than all the Association as appears by the inclosed account. Our humble suit to the House is that our County may be relieved of its insupportable burdens, which are as follows :— First, the County hath been set at above half in many ordinances with Essex when they ought not to have been above one third, and yet they have conformed in all obedience to pay their rates; Secondly, the great weekly disproportion of the ordinance for the Earl of Manchester for the maintaining of the associated forces, which amounteth in this County to 112*l.* 10*s.* weekly above their just proportion with Essex, which hath been continued now near 12 months, which in the whole year amounteth to 5,400*l.*; Thirdly, the great and insupportable burthen of the free quarter during his Excellency's army the last winter on them, amounting in only two Hundreds to 10,760*l.*—the other three not being yet cast up,—besides the great damage that befell them during that quarter; Fourthly, the heavy burthen to the County in the passing and repassing of the Parliament's forces for the most part on free quarter. Besides all this the County hath sent out upon the commands of the Committee of Both Kingdoms their own domesticall forces, which have cost them over 9,000*l.*, besides the great hindrance that hath accrued to them by the miss of their men. Many more are the pressures, which we forbear to mention. We therefore humbly pray that the County may be relieved in their former disproportions, and freed from that disproportion that is and hath continued on them in the Earl of Manchester's Ordinance, and specially that that great and grievous charge of the quartering of the army may be speedily repaid, and other the Associated Counties may be brought up to equalize them in Newport Garrison. The County is no way able to beare such charge as they now are under, it having cost them 3,800*l.* a month the last year, besides the free quarter, the excise, the fifth and twentieth part. *Postscript.*—We desire that the Committee or any two of them may be given power to make distress on all persons who disobey their warrants in paying the levies laid on them for the use of the armies as they pass

and repass, for the charge of our imprest soldiers, and for such like services, as are of necessity to be done upon any emergency. *Signed.*
Annexed is the following account :—

		li.	s.	d.
November 2do, 1643	Received out of Hertfordshire	200	00	00
20°	Received out of Hertfordshire	200	00	00
January 27°	Received out of Hertfordshire	300	00	00
March 26th, 1644	Received from Cambridge	300	00	00
August 2do	Received of Norfolk	250	00	00
	Received of Suffolk	250	00	00
	Essex	250	00	00
	Received of Huntingdon	090	00	00
	Received of Cambridge	112	00	00
November 8°	Received of Hertfordshire	500	00	00

This account we received from the Treasurer of Newport, written with his own hand. *Teste* William Love, William Dany.
So it appeareth Hertfordshire have paid more than either Essex, Norfolk, or Suffolk by 0950 00 00
Besides we paid Colonel Ayloffe out of the treasury at Hertford, while he lay at Newport with his forces to help keep that garrison :—

4 January 1643	0117 18 11
29 January	0145 14 10
22 February	0040 00 00
And more we sent to Cambridge to pay Colonel Ayloffe's forces while he lay at Newport of the money raised upon Newport Ordinance	0900 00 00

2153 13 9

So it appeareth that though any of those counties be valued at three times as much as Hertford in magnitude yet taxed but equal to us, they of that tax imposed are short of us. [N. III., 153.]

The Earl of Essex to William Lenthall.

1644, November 30.—Concerning the exchange of Major-General Porter and Major Carre. (See *Commons' Journals,* iii. 658, 709, 711.) *Signed.* [N. III., 154.]

M. de Sabran to William Lenthall.

1644, December 2.—(Identical, *mutatis mutandis,* with his letter to the Speaker of the House of Peers, which is printed in *Lords' Journals,* vii. 79.) [N. XVII., 5.]

The humble Advice of the Assembly of Divines.

1644, December 4.—Concerning the Solemnization of Marriage. (See *Commons' Journals,* iii. 715.) *Signed* as their paper of November 21st. [N. XXII., 7.] N. XXII., 49 is another copy, being the draft passed by the Assembly, showing the alterations they made.

The Committee of both Kingdoms in reply to the propositions of the Scotch Commissioners.

1644, December 7.—Touching the ascertaining of the payment of their armies and also concerning the pay and establishment of Lord Fairfax's army. (Some of these proposals were adopted by the House of Commons, and are printed in *Commons' Journals,* iii. 717, 723, iv. 10.) [N. XIX., 80.]

The A𝔫BASSADORS OF THE STATES-GENERAL to the PARLIA𝔫ENT.

1644, December 12.—(Printed in *Lords' Journals*, vii. 99.) In *French*. *Signed*. [N. XIII., 97.]

The humble advice of the ASSE𝔫BLY OF DIVINES.

1644, December 13.—Concerning the Burial of the Dead. *Signed* as their papers of November 21st and December 4th. [N. XXII., 9.]

[SIR ANTHONY ASHLEY COOPER] to the EARL OF ESSEX.

1644, December 15. Orchard.—" The last night we brought all our carriages safe to Taunton with our horse. We find the Castle in no great want of victual only of powder and salt. The town began to be in great distress, and it is almost a miracle to us that they should adventure to keep the town, their works being for the most part but pales and hedges and no line about the town. The enemy endeavoured twice to force it, but were repulsed, and since they have only kept them in by a quartering round about the town at a mile or two distance. Notwithstanding the townsmen made daily sallies and got in store of victuals without which it had been impossible for them to maintain such numbers of unnecessary people. The enemy on Friday last have quitted their garrisons in Wellington. Wycraft, and Cokum houses. The two last they have burnt, and, as I now hear, they have quitted Chideock house, whether it be out of fear or to make a body able to encounter with us we cannot yet understand, but Sir Lewis Dives coming up with his horse to the Bridgwater forces argues the latter. However, we are in a very good condition if they receive no assistance from the King's army, which we most fear, this county being of so great import to the enemy that it will be worth their engaging their whole army which may prove a successful design to them, if we have not a considerable strength ready on all motions of the enemy to advance to our assistance." (See *Commons' Journals*, iii. 734). *Signature torn off. Seal.* [N. III., 155.]

The humble Advice of the ASSE𝔫BLY OF DIVINES.

1644, December 16.—Concerning the Visitation of the Sick. This shows the Clauses omitted by the House of Commons for which was substituted the part in the printed copies from " And if the sick person shall declare any scruple " to " door of hope to every penitent believer." These omitted clauses are as follows :—" Exhorting him to declare what burden or trouble lyes upon his conscience, what sense he hath of his sinnes, what scruples, doubts, temptations are upon him ; and shall accordingly instruct and releive him. If the minister bee unacquainted with his conversation, he shall inquire of it, and what communion he hath held with God in his publique ordinances, how hee hath prized the Gospel and the meanes of grace, what care he hath had of private duties and of keeping a conscience void of offence towards God and man, and what evidences or hopes he hath gotten of the pardon of his sinnes, and his peace with God.

If he find that he hath not walked as becometh the Gospel, he shall endeavor to convince him of his sinnes, of the guilt and desert of them, the filth and pollution which the soule contracts by them, and of the curse of the Law, and wrath of God due to them, that hee may bee duely affected with and humbled for them, letting him know the danger of deferring repentance and of neglecting salvation at any time offered.

thereby awakening his conscience and rowsing him out of his stupid and secure condition to apprehend the justice and wrath of God, before which no man can stand but hee that being lost in himself, layeth hold upon Christ by faith.

If hee hath endeavored to walk in the wayes of holynes and to serve God in uprightnesse, although not without many failings and infirmities, or if his spirit bee broken with the sense of sin, or cast down through want of the sense of God's favour, the minister shal labour to rayse him up by setting before him the freenes and fullnes of God's grace, the sufficiency of righteousnes in Christ, the gratious offers in the Gospel that all who repent and beleive with all their heart in God's mercy through Christ, renouncing their own righteousnes, shall have life and salvation in Him.

Hee shall further endeavor to strengthen the sick person so qualified, against the feare of death, as haveing in it no spiritual evil to be feared by those that are in Christ, because sin, the sting of death, is taken away by Christ Who hath delivered all that are His from the bondage of the feare of death, triumphed over the grave, given us victory, is Himself entred into glory, to prepare a place for His people, so that neither life nor death shalbee able to separate them from God's love in Christ in whom such are sure, though now they must be laid in the dust, to obtayne a joyfull and glorious Resurrection to eternal life.

If weaknes disable the sick person from giveing cleare expressions of his repentance and obedience to the Gospel, the minister—with all prudence and discretion—shall advise him as to beware of an ill grounded perswasion on mercy, or on the goodnes of his condicion for heaven; so to disclayme all merit in himself, and to cast himself wholely upon God for mercy in the sole merits and mediation of Jesus Christ Who hath engaged Himself never to cast off them who in truth and syncerity come unto Him. The minister also is to take care that hee cast him not down into despaire by such a severe representation of the wrath of God due to him for his sinnes, as is not mollifyed by a seasonable propounding of Christ and His merits for a doore of hope to every penitent beleiver." [N. XXII., 8.]

The COMMITTEE AT GOLDSMITHS' HALL.

1644, December 23.—Report recommending that they should have the managing and regulating of the coal trade at Newcastle and of all the coals and coalpits belonging to Delinquents, and that they for the next four months should pay to the Scotch army in and about Newcastle 7,000*l.* a month out of the coals and collieries of Delinquents and the tax on coals. [N. XIV., 16.]

The EARL OF LOUDOUN to the RECORDER OF LONDON.

1644, December 24. Worcester House.—Desiring him to acquaint the Houses that Lord Warriston and Mr. Barclay begin their journey to Scotland to-morrow, and that it is our earnest request that they would return a speedy answer to our papers concerning the Scotch Armies in England and Ireland which have been so long laid aside and delayed to the hinderance of the public service. A note of those particulars is inclosed, and if there be any other thing concerning the Army or cause which the Houses shall think fit to represent to the Parliament of Scotland, it shall be either sent along with them or so as to overtake them. *Signed. Seal.* [N. III., 156.]

The Clauses substituted in the VISITATION OF THE SICK for those omitted by order of the House of Commons.

1644, December 28.—(See *Commons' Journals*, iv. 3.) *Draft* with a few alterations. At the end are some scraps of various orders in Parliament, including some extracts from the Ordinance calling the Assembly of Divines and the Ordinance of October 12th 1643, made for drawing up the Narrative of April 21, 1646 which is N. XXII., 45, and the order of September 13, 1644 concerning tender consciences, which is printed in *Commons' Journals*, iii. 627. [N. XXII., 50.]

ORDINANCE.

1644, December.—For the taking away of the *Book of Common Prayer* and for the establishing and putting in Execution of the *Directory*. (Printed in Rushworth, iii. 2. 839.) *Draft*. *Annexed* is the preface to the *Directory*. [N. XIV., 14.]

[The COMMITTEE FOR IRISH AFFAIRS] to [the PARLIAMENT].

[1644.]—Proposing to raise the Excise on Beer imposed by the Ordinance of September 11th, 1643, explained by that of October 17th, from 2s. a barrel to 3s., the additional revenue to be paid to them for the maintenance of the Parliament's forces in Ireland, because, " it is manifest from the date of the said Ordinance the retailers did advance one farthing upon the quart . . by colour of Excise, and so continued till farthings would not pass in payment. It is certain that two thirds of a farthing do implete the duty of 2s. . . and the other third part . . is exacted contrary to the Ordinance and produceth half as much in the gross sum as the rest. . . The Commons take this to heart that so much should be exacted from them and detained to the benefit of tapsters and retailers and not to be converted to the supply of the State's service, and so prevent such further impositions as might be raised on the subject for that purpose, and this doth often beget controversies. . . Since there is an equal number of statute quarts in a barrel with that of farthings in 3s. . ." if the duty be raised to 3s. a barrel " it would give abundant satisfaction to the subject, and the retailers be left without any just cause of complaint, whose insolency is grown so great that since farthings pass not in payment they now usually take 2d. for the quart of beer, which before was sold for six farthings, which raiseth the Excise to the Commons 6s. upon the barrel and 4s. to the retailers' benefit." [N. XXI., 13.]

BRIAN DAWSON, of York, to the HOUSE OF COMMONS.

[1644.]—Petition stating that of the lead brought to York by the Earl of Newcastle about 34 fother belonged to the petitioner, which was sold and the proceeds applied to the use of the Parliament's army, and praying that some money be immediately paid him and the rest allowed out of the Customs and Excise on such of his goods as be imported or exported into or out of Hull. [N. XXII., 139.]

THOMAS LAWE, Mayor, EDWARD BYLES, NORRIS CANE, JOHN HOBSON, JOHN BROWNE, SAMUEL CUST, and JOHN WHITINGE to WILLIAM LENTHALL.

[1645. Boston (?).]—We take the opportunity of Mr. Pelham's being here to represent the state of this place. From the beginning of these troubles we have been forward to advance the cause of the Parliament. 'I is very well known of what consequence this garrison is not only to this County but also to the whole Association. It hath notwithstanding been of late so much forgotten that the soldiers though not half so many as are necessary are many months in arrear, and therefore ready to mutiny. The want of pay for their quarters hath so impoverished the inhabitants that they are no longer able to bear it in respect of which and their late great losses of ships and goods as also that they have been put to great charges in making great and chargeable works, which they are unable to finish or hold without the assistance of the house. Wherefore we pray that a competent garrison may be established, and the arrears discharged, which are above 2,000l. *Signed. Seal. Endorsed* " from Lincolne."

> (This letter is probably from Boston, as a Thomas Lawe was Mayor there in 1652-3 and no such name occurs in the list of the Mayors of Lincoln. It was probably sent up with the letter from Lincoln of August 4, 1645, *post*, p. 237. (See *Commons' Journals*, iv. 263.) [N. V., 106.]

Breviate of the SCOTTISH PAPERS.

[1644, December.]—(See *Commons' Journals*, iii. 717, 723.) 1. That some solid way may be taken for securing the payment of the 31,000l. monthly.

2. That the assessment, sequestrations, excise, King's and Queen's revenues of the six Northern Counties, and whatever other means are or may be assigned for the payment of the Scotch army, be ascertained and secured against being otherwise applied.

3. That the deficiency of the 31,000l. be otherwise secured by Parliament.

4. That the Northern Counties where the Scotch armies are be not over-burdened with new levies and quartering of troops which consume the entertainment and accommodation of the Scotch army in those barren and wasted counties, and being under no command commit great disorders, and that such as are raised be removed to other places where they should be upon service.

5. That, in respect the 31,000l. for the monthly pay of the Earl of Leeven's army will not much exceed a fortnight's pay, it is desired that the Parliament, upon whose invitation the Earl of Calendar came into this kingdom, should resolve on some means of entertainment of those forces.

6. That victuals and provisions sent from London to the Scotch Army be sold at a reasonable price and be free from Excise. [N. XIX., 103.]

The COMMISSIONERS OF THE CHURCH OF SCOTLAND.

1644[-5], January 1.—Paper desiring an account of the Proceedings concerning the Church. (See *Commons' Journals*, iv. 7, 11.) *Signed* "John Donn." [N. XIX., 81.]

The COMMITTEE OF BOTH KINGDOMS.

1644[-5], January 3.—Proposed answer to the King's message of December 13th. (Printed in *Lords' Journals*, vii. 123.) [N. IX., 3.]

ORDINANCE.

1644[-5], January 4.—Appointing certain days for recreation. Namely the second Thursday in each month from ten in the morning till five in the evening. Any on that day found guilty " of the beastly sin of drunkenness or alehouse haunting " to be deprived of the benefit of the Ordinance for one whole year following in addition to the other penalties for drunkenness. *Draft*, read a first time on the above date. (See *Commons' Journals*, iv. 10.) [N. XIV., 17.]

HUGH MORRELL to GILES GREENE, Chairman of the Committee for the Navy and Customs.

1644[-5], January 6. London.—Desiring audience, having waited near eight months, in order to answer the pretended charge against him. [N. III., 157.]

The COMMITTEE OF BOTH KINGDOMS at Essex House.

1644[-5], January 8.—Reporting the orders made by them dated 1644, November 26, December 6, 20, and 23, concerning the keeping of the Line and the quarters of the forces. (See *Commons' Journals*, iv. 13.) [N. XIV., 15.]

The MINISTERS OF THE ASSEMBLY OF DIVINES to the HOUSE OF COMMONS.

1644[-5], January 8.—Petition for payment of their arrears and for provision for the future. *Signed* by 45 ministers. (See *Commons' Journals*, iv. 13.) [N. XXII., 10.]

The COMMITTEE OF BOTH KINGDOMS.

1644[-5], January 8.—Report by Mr. Solicitor-General. (For the first part see *Commons' Journals*, iv. 19 ; the second recommends that the counties therein named should provide 1,100 horses for dragoons for the Western expedition.) [N. XIV., 19.]

The COMMITTEE OF BOTH KINGDOMS.

1644[-5], January 9.—Report recommending arms to be sent to Sir John Price. (See *Commons' Journals*, iv. 19.) [N. XIV., 20]

The SCOTCH COMMISSIONERS.

1644[-5], January 9.—Paper. (Printed in *Commons' Journals*, iv. 19.) *Signed* " Jo. Cheislie." [N. XIX., 86.]

The NEW MODEL as reported from the COMMITTEE OF BOTH KINGDOMS.

1644[-5], January 9.—(See *Commons' Journals*, iv. 15, and Bushworth, iv. 1. 7.) [N. XIV., 21.]

The COMMITTEE OF BOTH KINGDOMS.

1644]-5], January 13.—Report concerning the Treaty. (Printed in *Commons' Journals*, iv. 18.) [N. IX., 12.]

List of ASSESSMENTS.

1644[-5], January 13.—To be levied *per mensem* for the maintenance of the Army. (The amounts appear by the resolutions printed in *Commons' Journals*, iv. 17, 18.) [N. XIV., 41.]

CO☐☐ISSION.

1644[-5], January 14.—Appointing Lord Inchiquin Lord President of Munster. (Printed in *Lords' Journals*, vii. 137.) *Copy*. [N. XXI., 9.]

The HOUSE OF CO☐☐ONS.

1644[-5], January 14, 15, 23.—Resolutions touching Church Government. (Printed in *Commons' Journals*, iv. 20, 21, 28.) [N. XIV., 18.]

The GRAND JURY OF NORTHU☐BERLAND to the ESTATES OF SCOTLAND.

1641[-5], January 15. Alnwick.—Remonstrance informing them "of the miserable poverty this county is brought unto by the continual thefts and robberies daily perpetrated by the inhabitants . . . . . of the dales and borders of both kingdoms, that . . . . Colonel Welden, the High Sheriff, with his regiment apprehended and committed to prison . . 200 of them, by reason whereof the county hath since enjoyed much quiet and security in their houses and goods, yet . . divers of the most notorious are fled into your borders and thereby do decline the course of justice, and that other evil disposed persons of your borders do likewise frequently infest our country by thefts and recepting such evil persons" and asking them to take order "for the apprehendings of such Englishmen as are mentioned in" the accompanying list "and such other Scotchmen of your Borders, who are in the like evil carriage and pertakes with them and alike noisome to you and us that both may receive condign punishment, without which course all we have or can do will nothing avail, and the Borders inevitably suffer ruin." *Copy*. [N. XIX., 83.]

The CO☐☐ITTEE OF BOTH KINGDO☐S.

1644[-5], January 15. — Report stating that the 1,100 dragoon horses formerly reported might be spared, and desiring that 50 barrels of powder with match and bullet proportionable be provided for the Pembrokeshire forces. (See *Commons' Journals*, iv. 22, 23.) [N. XIV., 23.]

The CO☐☐ITTEE OF BOTH KINGDO☐S.

1644[-5], January 16.—Report by Sir Philip Stapilton. (See *Commons' Journals*, iv. 23.) [N. XIV., 24.]

The PARLIA☐ENT and the SCOTCH CO☐☐ISSIONERS to the KING.

1644[-5], January 17.—Further answer to his message of December 13th (Printed in *Lords' Journals*, vii. 143.) *Copy*. [N. IX., 15.]

The PARLIA☐ENT.

[1644–5], January 17.—Letter to be written by the Lord General. (Printed in *Commons' Journals*, iv. 24.) [N. XII., 89.]

DOM ANTONIO DE SOUSA, Portuguese Ambassador, to WILLIA☐ LENTHALL.

164[4-]5,* January 20. London.—Desiring a pass for himself and attendants to Oxford or wherever his Majesty may be and back thence to London, as he has occasion to see him on his master's business. *Signed. Seal.* [N. XVII., 90.]

---

* It is uncertain whether he is using English or Portuguese style. In the former case it would be 1645[-6].

The Scotch Commissioners.

1644[-5], January 20.—Paper stating that they would represent to the Parliament of Scotland the desire of the Houses for the advancing of the Scotch army and their intention to raise 30,000*l.* for the purpose, and desiring to know what account they shall give to the Parliament of Scotland of the passing and execution of the ordinance for the 31,000*l.* monthly, and when they may expect the payment of the 30,000*l.* for the Earl of Leven's army and the 10,000*l.* for the Earl of Calendar's. (The purport of the rest appears by the orders thereon, printed in *Commons' Journals*, iv. 41.) *Original* and *copy*, the first *signed* " Jo. Cheislie."

The same.

Same date. Second paper.—Asking for arms and clothing for the Scotch army. (The purport appears by the orders thereon, printed in *Commons' Journals*, iv. 41.) *Signed* " Jo. Cheislie. [N. XIX., 87.]

List.

1644[-5], January 21.—Of the attendants on the King's Commissioners at Uxbridge. (Printed in *Lords' Journals*, vii. 151, and Thurloe, *State Papers*, i. 57.) Two *copies*. [N. IX., 1, 4]

List.

Same date.—Of the names of the King's Commissioners. (Printed in *Lords' Journals*, vii. 157.) *Copy.* [N. IX., 6.]

List.

Same date.—Of the attendants on the Parliament's Commissioners to Uxbridge as returned from Oxford. (See *Lords' Journals*, vii. 150) (Printed in Thurloe, *State Papers*, i. 58.) [N. IX., 10.] N. IX., 7, 8, 9 and 11 are lists of the names of attendants of individual Commissioners all included in the general list. Another copy, being that read and reported January 17 (see *Commons' Journals*, iv. 23) is N. IX., 14.

List.

Same date (?).—Of the attendants on the Scotch Commissioners to Uxbridge. [N. IX., 13.]

Thomas Webb to Sir Oliver Fleming.

[1644-5, January.]—Sending a list of the attendants of the Duke of Richmond and the Earl of Southampton, differing in some respects from that in Nos. 1 and 4. "These are all I can remember at present besides cooks, grooms and footmen, but you shall have a more exact note, though I cannot forget your Commissioners were not stinted to number nor restrained in Company at Oxford." [N. IX., 5.]

The King to the Parliament and the Scotch Commissioners.

1644[-5], January 21.—Propositions. (Printed in Rushworth, iii. 2. 858.) *Signed* " Edward Nicholas." *Sign Manual.* [N. I., 16.]

Prince Rupert to the Earl of Essex.

1644[-5], January 21. Oxford.—(Two letters, both printed in Rushworth, iii. 2. 857.) *Sign Manual.* [N. I., 42, 43.]

Lieutenant-Colonel LOFTUS.

1614[-5], January 21.—Proposition that he may be allowed to discover Papists' and Malignants' personal estates in London and Westminster to the amount of 5,000*l.* and apply the same, after rewarding the makers of the discoveries, for the relief of the fort of Duncannon. [N. XXI., 8.]

PRINCE RUPERT to the EARL OF ESSEX.

1614[-5], January 26. Oxford.—(Printed in Thurloe, *State Papers,* i. 59.) *Sign Manual.* N. I., 44.]

The COMMITTEE OF BOTH KINGDOMS.

1644[-5], January 27.—Reporting the order and instructions made by them on November 11th concerning the differences between Colonel Hutchenson, the Governor of Nottingham, and some of the Committee there, and the subsequent conduct of the parties concerned. [N. XIV., 25.]

ORDINANCE.

1644[-5], January 28.—Empowering the Commissioners to treat with those of the king. (Printed in *Lords' Journals,* vii. 159.) *Draft.* [N. XIV., 26.]

The SCOTCH COMMISSIONERS.

1644[-5], January 29. — Three papers concerning the treaty with the King. (The first is printed in *Lords' Journals,* vii. 161, the others in vii. 163.) *Originals* and *copies,* the first all *signed* " Jo. Cheislie." [N. XIX., 90, 88, 89.]

The PARLIAMENT to their COMMISSIONERS.

1644[-5], January 29.—Instructions. (Printed in *Lords' Journals,* vi. 163.) Two *copies.* [N. IX., 16.]

Powers of the COMMISSIONERS OF THE PARLIAMENT.

1644[-5], January 30.—(Printed in *Lords' Journals,* vii. 166.) [N. XIV., 22.]

LORD WENMAN, SIR HENRY VANE, DENZELL HOLLES, WILLIAM PIERREPONT, BULSTRODE WHITELOCKE, JOHN CREWE and EDMUND PRIDEAUX to WILLIAM LENTHALL.

1644[-5], January 30, 12 at night. Uxbridge.—(Identical, *mutatis mutandis,* with the letter to the Speaker of the House of Lords, which is printed in *Lords' Journals,* vii. 166.) *Signed.* [N. IX., 17.]

The SAME to the SAME.

1644[-5], January 31. Uxbridge.—(Identical, *mutatis mutandis,* with the letter to the Speaker of the House of Lords, which is printed in *Lords' Journals,* vii. 167.) *Signed. Enclosed :*
Copies of all the documents printed on the same and the next page. [N. IX., 18.]

The humble abvice of the ASSEMBLY OF DIVINES.

[1644-5, January.]—Concerning Church Government and the Officers and Assemblies of the Church, and a Directory for Admonition, Excommunication, and Absolution, and for Ordination of Ministers. (The part relating to Admonition, Excommunication, and Absolution is identical with that presented on February 4th.) *Signed* as the Directory, *ante*, p. 194.

Examinations of SAMUEL HUDDLESTON and HUGH JACKSON.

1644[-5], February 1 and 7.—Describing how Mr. Hudson of Maryn on the Hill, in Lincolnshire, had prevented their distraining upon a tenant of his for payment of the assessment.

And

Admission by Mr. HUDSON.

1644[-5], February 7.—That he had advised Lieutenant Wetherall, a Delinquent, how to take advantage of a clause in the Ordinance for Sequestrations. (See *Commons' Journals* iv. 60.) [N., XIV., 34, 35.]

ORDINANCE.

1644[-5], February 1.—For ten Commissioners to be a Quorum. (Printed in *Lords' Journals*, vii. 168.) [N. IX., 20.]

LORD WENMAN, WILLIAM PIERREPONT, DENZELL HOLLES, SIR HENRY VANE, BULSTRODE WHITELOCKE, EDMUND PRIDEAUX, and JOHN CREWE to WILLIAM LENTHALL.

1644[-5], February 2. Uxbridge.—(Identical, *mutatis mutandis*, with the letter of the same date to the Speaker of the House of Lords, which is printed in *Lords' Journals*, vii. 172.) *Signed. Seal.* [N. IX., 21.] *Enclosed:*

Copies of twenty-one papers which are printed in *Lords' Journals*, vii. 169-172. [N. IX., 31-39.]

The SAME (except Sir Henry Vane) to the SAME.

Same date, 12 at night.—(Identical, *mutatis mutandis*, with the letter of the same date to the Speaker of the House of Lords, which is printed in *Lords' Journals*, vii. 172.) *Signed. Seal.* [N. IX., 21a.]

The SAME to the SAME.

1644[-5], February 3. Uxbridge.—(Identical, *mutatis mutandis*, with the letter to the Speaker of the House of Lords which is printed in *Lords' Journals*, vii. 175.) *Signed.* [N. IX., 22.] *Enclosed:*
The five Papers, including the King's Commission, which are printed in *Lords' Journals*, vii. 175, 176. [N. IX., 40, 41.]

The SAME to the SAME.

Same date.—(Identical, *mutatis mutandis*, with the letter to the Speaker of the House of Lords, which is printed in *Lords' Journals*, vii. 176.) *Signed. Seal.* [N. IX., 22a.] *Enclosed:*
The Paper concerning Church Government printed in *Lords' Journals*, vii. 176. [N. XXII., 3.]

PRINCE RUPERT to the EARL OF ESSEX.

1614[-5], February 3. Oxford.—I am informed that Sir William Reddall, contrary to the articles of surrender of Tynemouth Castle, is carried up to London and imprisoned there. I enclose a copy of the articles, and request that your Lordship will cause Sir William Reddall to be allowed to return home or to join his Majesty as he pleases. A like request is made for the Mayor of York and some Aldermen and Ministers, who are also sent up and detained prisoners contrary to the articles of surrender. *Sign Manual.* [N. I., 45.]

The Humble Advice of the ASSEMBLY OF DIVINES.

1644[-5], February 4.—Concerning Excommunication. [N. XXII., 12.]

The Humble Advice of the ASSEMBLY OF DIVINES.

Same date.—Concerning a Directory for Admonition, Excommunication, and Absolution. (For both these see *Commons' Journals*, iv. 41.) Both *signed*. [N. XXII., 13.]

Examined Copies of SEVEN PAPERS that passed between SIR WILLIAM ARMYNE, Commissioner of the Parliament of England, and the ESTATES OF SCOTLAND, all at Edinburgh.

1. From SIR WILLIAM ARMYNE.

1644[-5], February 4.—Announcing his appointment to attend the Parliament of Scotland, and desiring that Commissioners from both nations be appointed to take the accounts between the inhabitants of England and the soldiers of the Scotch army since their entrance. [N. XIX., 94.]

2. From the SAME.

Same date.—Desiring that no protection be given by the Scotch army to any English subject against the orders of the Parliament, and in particular that the order of the House of Commons, dated November 19th concerning Delinquents in Newcastle, be put in execution. [N. XIX., 91.]

3. From the SAME.

1644[-5], February 7.—Whereas the Parliament of England have appointed the Excise and Sequestrations in the Northern parts for the maintenance and pay of the Scotch Army, desiring that orders may be given to the said army not to hinder, but on the contrary to assist, those appointed by Parliament for that service. [N. XIX., 96.]

4. From the ESTATES.

1644[-5], February 12.—It was agreed by the Committee of both kingdoms at Newcastle that such persons should be employed for working the coals there as were able to do so, for the maintenance of the army, some of whom are within the said order of November 19th, not from any intention to protect them, but from mere necessity for upholding the coal works, which necessity still continues, notwithstanding which the Estates agree that the said order be put in execution, except as regards persons included in the capitulation of Tynemouth Castle. [N. XIX., 92.]

5. From Sir William Armyne.

1644[-5], February 13.—Whereas the burthens of the kingdom of England are so great that they have not been able to pay the Scotch army the monthly sum of 31,000*l.*, desiring that the Estates would reduce their forces in England to such an establishment by lessening the number of regiments and officers that the money that is or can be provided may be disposed of to the best advantage, seeing it is one part of the treaty that the Kingdom of Scotland should manage their army in England as for themselves. [N. XIX., 95.]

6. From Sir William Armyne.

1644[-5], February 18.—Whereas the paper of the 4th instant consisted not only of a particular desire concerning the Delinquents of Newcastle—to which the answer of the 12th has given satisfaction—but also of a general desire, desiring that all Protections already given to Delinquents without the consent of the Commissioners of Parliament be limited to their just intention, which is conceived to be restraining the soldiers from all acts of violence, and not extended to the prejudice of any order or power of Parliament, and that no Protections be given or Capitulations made in future without the consent of the Committee with the Army, or in more difficult cases of Parliament itself, if possible. [N. XIX., 93.]

7. From the Estates.

[1644-5, February.] — In reply to the last paper all Protections complained of or to be complained of shall be revised by the Committee of both Kingdoms on the place, and on review of the list of Delinquents they shall take such course for removing them out of the Counties or securing them by imprisonment or caution for their good behaviour as they shall find most necessary, and for the future we agree with the said paper, but where the generals of our army think it necessary to delay the execution of any orders of Parliament or their committees, such necessity be represented to the Committee of both Kingdoms on the place, and to our Commissioners in London for preventing mistakes, without prejudice to keeping and falsifying (*sic*) the conditions in necessary Capitulations not being against the laws of the Nation or the National Covenant and whereunto the advice and consent of the Commissioners of the Parliament of England should be craved if possible.

In reply to the paper of the 4th we have ordered the Committee that goes with that Army to appoint some of their number or others to concur with the English Commissioners or with whom they shall appoint for the ends therein mentioned.

In reply to the paper of the 13th we have appointed the Committee of Estates to go really about the recruiting and reforming of the army, who we are confident will go heartily about it.

In reply to the remonstrance of Northumberland concerning the moss-troopers [*ante*, p. 202] we have given direction to the Colonels and Committee of War on the Scotch Borders to apprehend those mentioned in the list, and any others they can try to be partakers in those robberies, or their resetters, and to do justice to the satisfaction of the English Border Counties, with whom they are directed to concur, and the Committee of Estates have been appointed to write to the Lord General, that by the advice of Colonel Welden or any other instructed for Northumberland all possible concurrence may be done on our behalf for that effect.

In reply to the paper of the 7th we doubt not that the Lord General and the Committee with him will concur to further all ordinances of Parliament, especially those for the Excise and Sequestrations. [N. XIX., 97.]

PAPERS.

1644[-5], February 4–6.—Concerning the Militia. (Being the eighteen printed in *Lords' Journals*, vii. 181-184.) *Copies.* [N. IX., 42-50.]

The ESTATES OF HOLLAND AND WEST FRIEZELAND to the PARLIA-
MENT.

164[4-]5, February 7. The Hague.—(Printed in *Lords' Journals*, vii. 210.) In *Latin. Seal.* [N. X., 43.]

The PARLIAMENT OF ENGLAND to the PARLIAMENT OF SCOTLAND.

1644[-5], February 8.—Desiring that their army should advance southward. (Printed in *Lords' Journals*, vii. 185.) *Draft.* [N. XII., 91.]

LORD MAITLAND, ARCHIBALD JOHNSTON, and ROBERT BARCLAY,
to WILLIAM LENTHALL.

1644[-5], February 9. Worcester House.—Having been here ten days we must give an account of our diligence to the Committee of Estates, and therefore desire you to communicate the enclosed paper to the House of Commons. *Signed.* [N. III., 158.]

LORD WENMAN, WILLIAM PIERREPONT, DENZELL HOLLES, SIR
HENRY VANE, OLIVER ST. JOHN, BULSTRODE WHITELOCKE, and
JOHN CREWE to WILLIAM LENTHALL.

1644[-5], February 11. Uxbridge.—(Identical, *mutatis mutandis,* with the letter to the Speaker of the House of Lords which is printed in *Lords' Journals*, vii. 187.) *Signed. Seal.* [N. IX., 25.] *Enclosed :*

Copies of the ten papers which are printed in *Lords' Journals*, vii. 188, 189. [N. IX., 51-59.]

SIR WILLIAM WALLER to the COMMITTEE OF BOTH KINGDOMS.

[1644-5, February 11.]—" Upon an information that the enemy had three regiments of horse with some dragoons quartered att Andover, I gave order to a party of my Lord Generall's horse, and some regiments of mine owne to advance to Roply intendinge from thence to march with them, and to attempte the beatinge up of that quarter. But when I came thither I received advertizement that the enemy— by some intelligence from Old Alsford—had taken the allarme, and was retired to Newtontony neare Amesbury. The enemy from Salisbury have sent out there warrants for the bringinge in of cariages upon paine of death, which is a cleare implication that they intend to march, and I

guess itt wilbee westwarde, in regard I heare Majour-Generall Holburne hath ingaged Sir Lewis Dives' forces. It wilbee of very great
consequence to dispatch away forces to there present releife, with a
strength answerable to so great a worke. I am now labouringe to gett
the foote heere to march, but I know not how farr I shall prevaile
with them. I heare nothinge yet of Ailisbury regiment, neither is
Colonell Morleyes foote yet come to me. The comissioners cann give
you an accounte how farr 1 fall shorte of the number of my horse. If
all his Excellencyes foote might bee drawen out of Reddinge, and
a course taken to secure that place in there absence, I shall—by God's
assistance—bee inabled to bee master of the field, and goe thorough with
that worke in the west, which I looke upon as the greatest service in
the field that now lyes before you ; whereas if through the weakeness
of this partie, I should receive any blow, itt would bee very dangerous
to the East and West. I humbly desire that the particulers mentioned
in my former letters may be imediately dispatched unto me." (See
Commons' Journals, iv. 46.) *Signed. Seal.* [N. III., 159.]

The SCOTCH COMMISSIONERS.

1644[-5], February 12.—Paper asking for a supply of muskets and
ammunition. (See *Commons' Journals*, iv. 52.) In Sir John Cheislie's
hand. [N. XIX., 98.]

The KING to the HIGH SHERIFF of the County OF SOUTHAMPTON.

1644[-5], February 13.—Thanking him for his services in raising
soldiers and pioneers, and procuring bread and other necessaries for the
army under Lord Goring, and desiring that he would employ his best
diligence in raising the soldiers to be levied in that county against the
time appointed, and would take care that the contributions of that
county be assigned for the use of the garrisons only in that county and
not of any out of the county, which are to be paid according to the
establishment of the city of Bristol, and urging him to use all
diligence in collecting the arrears of the letter money and contribution,
and to continue the assistance formerly given to the army. *Copy.*
[N. XII., 92.]

'LORD WENMAN, WILLIAM PIERREPONT, DENZELL HOLLES, SIR HENRY VANE, BULSTRODE WHITELOCKE, and JOHN CREWE to WILLIAM LENTHALL.

1644[-5], February 14. Uxbridge.—(Identical, *mutatis mutandis*,
with the letter to the Speaker of the House of Lords which is printed
in *Lords' Journals*, vii. 195). *Signed. Seal.* [N. IX., 25.]
Enclosed :

> Copies of the twenty-six papers, including the King's Commission,
> which are printed in *Lords' Journals*, vii. 195-200. [N. IX.,
> 60-84.]
> N. IX., 24 is another copy of the twelfth of these papers.

WILLIAM PIERREPONT, DENZELL HOLLES, OLIVER ST. JOHN, BULSTRODE WHITELOCKE, and JOHN CREWE to WILLIAM LENTHALL.

1644[-5], February 15. Uxbridge.—(Identical, *mutatis mutandis*,
with the letter to the Speaker of the House of Lords, which is printed

in *Lords' Journals*, vii. 201.)   *Signed.   Seal.*   [N. IX., 26.]
Enclosed:

    Copies of the nineteen papers which are printed in *Lords' Journals*
vii. 201, 202, 203.   [N. IX., 85–102.]

JAMES HARRINGTON to the HOUSE OF COMMONS.

1644[-5], February 17.—Humble remonstrance concerning the
affairs of the Elector Palatine.   Stating the former orders of Parliament
and the Committee of the Revenue on the subject, the obstructions to
their execution, and the distressed condition of his Highness. (See
Commons' Journals, iv. 58.)   [N. XVIII., 176.]

LORD WENMAN, WILLIAM PIERREPONT, DENZELL HOLLES, SIR HENRY VANE, OLIVER ST. JOHN, BULSTRODE WHITELOCKE, EDMUND PRIDEAUX, and JOHN CREWE to WILLIAM LENTHALL.

1644[-5], February 18.   Uxbridge.—(Identical, *mutatis mutandis*,
with the letter to the Speaker of the House of Lords, which is printed
in *Lords' Journals*, vii. 211).   *Signed.   Seal.   Enclosed:*

    Copies of the twenty-one papers which are printed in *Lords'
Journals*, vii. 211–215.   [N. IX., 103–121.]

Report from the COMMITTEE OF BOTH KINGDOMS and Order thereon.

1644[-5], February 18.—Concerning Sir William Riddell and the
Lord Mayor and Aldermen of York.   (See *Commons' Journals*, iv. 52.)
[N. XIV., 43.]

List of PRISONERS taken at MOUNT STANFORD.

1644[-5], February 18.—(Printed in *Lords' Journals*, vii. 256.)
[N. XIV., 27.]

Account of the reception of SIR THOMAS FAIRFAX in the House of Commons.

1644[-5], February 19.—(Printed in *Commons' Journals*, iv. 54.)
[N. XIV., 28.]

LORD WENMAN, WILLIAM PIERREPONT, SIR HENRY VANE, OLIVER ST. JOHN, BULSTRODE WHITELOCKE, EDMUND PRIDEAUX, and JOHN CREWE to WILLIAM LENTHALL.

1644[-5], February 20.   Uxbridge.—(Identical, *mutatis mutandis*,
with the letter of the same date to the Speaker of the House of Lords,
which is printed in *Lords' Journals*, vii. 223.)   *Signed.   Seal.*
[N. IX., 28.]

LORD ROBERTES to the EARL OF ESSEX.

1644[-5], February 20.—Describing the action at Mount Stanford
in almost the same words as in his letter of the same date printed in
Lords' Journals, vii. 255.   *Signed.   Seal.*   [N. III., 160.]

PAPERS.

1644[-5], February 20-22.—(Being the nineteen printed in *Lords'
Journals*, vii. 244–354.)   *Copies.*   [N. IX., 150–168.]   Another copy
of part of number 15 is N. XXI., 127*a*.

LORD WENMAN, WILLIAM PIERREPONT, DENZELL HOLLES, SIR HENRY VANE, BULSTRODE WHITELOCKE, and EDMUND PRIDEAUX.

1644[-5], February 21. Uxbridge.—(Identical, *mutatis mutandis*, with the letter to the Speaker of the House of Lords, which is printed in *Lords' Journals*, vii. 230.) *Signed. Seal. Enclosed:*

Copies of the thirty-one papers printed in *Lords' Journals*, vii. 231–238. [N. IX., 121*b*–149.] A second copy of the last but one of these is N. XIV., 29.

The PARLIAMENT.

1644[-5], February 21.—Instructions to the Commissioners about the Militia. (Printed in *Lords' Journals*, vii. 219.) [N. XIX., 100]

LORD WENMAN, WILLIAM PIERREPONT, SIR HENRY VANE, OLIVER ST. JOHN, BULSTRODE WHITELOCKE, EDMUND PRIDEAUX, and JOHN CREWE to WILLIAM LENTHALL.

1644[-5], February 22. Uxbridge.—(Identical, *mutatis mutandis*, with the letter to the Speaker of the House of Lords, which is printed in *Lords' Journals*, vii. 239.) *Signed.* [N. IX., 30.] *Enclosed:*

Copies of the two papers printed in *Lords' Journals*, vii. 239, and Rushworth, iii. 2. 921, 922. [N. XII., 93, 94.]

CHRISTOPHER HUDSON to the HOUSE OF COMMONS.

[1644-5], February 22.—Petition stating though one of the Committee for Lincolnshire he had been committed to prison by his fellow Committeemen merely because he with others had signed a Petition to the House of Commons, and praying to be released and that a Committee of the House should inquire into the miscarriages of Lincolnshire. (See *Commons' Journals*, iv., 60.) [N. XXII., 71.]

The AMBASSADORS OF THE STATES-GENERAL to the HOUSE OF COMMONS.

1644[-5], February 24.—Concerning the Uxbridge negotiations. (Identical, *mutatis mutandis*, with their paper to the Lords, which is printed in *Lords' Journals*, vii. 240.) In *French* with *English* translation, the first *Signed.* [N. XVIII., 100, 101.]

Twenty REFORMADO OFFICERS to the COMMITTEE OF BOTH KINGDOMS.

1644[-5], February 24.—(Date of reading.) Petition, stating that they had done good service since the beginning of the war, that since last April when they were reduced they had received only the payments mentioned in the enclosed particulars, and that they had all served under the Earl of Essex in the war in Cornwall, and the second battle of Newbury, and praying that some speedy course may be taken for their relief. Enclosed are a few lines to some person not named, asking him to remind his Excellency of the petition as three of them are fallen sick and like to famish. Annexed is the particular referred to. [N. XXII., 74.]

Sir William Armyne to William Lenthall.

1644[-5], February 26. Newcastle.—Have 'delivered the letters committed to me and several other papers grounded on my instructions to the Parliament of Scotland, where I stayed near a month. I had stayed longer, but my health and my desire to return to my former charge in the affairs of the Northern Counties did not permit it. The multitude of business in which the Parliament was engaged hindered my receiving answers to some of the papers I presented, but Mr. Bowles shall shortly give you an account of it. I have sent the letter about the army marching southward to be presented by Lord Wariston. I desire a recompense be made to Mr. Bowles. *Signed. Seal.* [N. III., 161.]

Sir William Armyne to the Earl of Manchester and the Earl of Lauderdale.

1644[-5], February 27. Newcastle.—Had received your letter of the 19th instant and despatched it to Lord Wariston, whom I desired to present it to the Scotch Parliament in my absence. "For after my stay above a month in Scotland, and having performed what I was sent for thither, I returned back to Newcastle, on Saturday the 22nd . . being necessitated thereunto in regard of the 26 foot regiments that lie in the Bishopric of Durham, Newcastle, and Northumberland, that are in so great extremity, that if the Parliament take not a speedy course to supply them with some moneys, the countries will be spoiled and the army ruined. This I have often represented to the House in sundry of my former letters, and at this present there are gentlemen here of the country attending upon the Parliament and your Lordships for redress of their miseries, which if not suddenly helped will be past recovery." (See *Commons' Journals,* iv. 68.) [N. III., 162.]

Christina, Queen of Sweden, by the Regents of the Kingdom to the Parliament.

1644[-5], February 28.—Informing them that she had declared war on the King of Denmark on account of his illegally raising the Sound dues to an unprecedented amount, and declaring her intention to restore trade to its former liberty, and referring them to the bearer Hugo Moatt for further information. (See *Lords' Journals,* vii. 295.) In *Latin* with *English* translation subjoined. *Signed* by the Regents, Peter Brake, Count of Wissenborg, James de   , Marshal of the Kingdom, the Chancellor and Treasurer Oxenstierna, and Claudius Fleming, Vice-Admiral. [N. X., 7.]

The King to George Lord Goring.

1644[-5], February. Oxford.— Being informed there are yet within our quarters divers ministers, who either by their doctrine teach or by their behaviour countenance Rebellion, we command you to make strict enquiry for all such Clergymen within your quarters, and to apprehend them immediately, and send them to Oxford, if possible, or otherwise to keep them in custody till further orders, purposing that none of such persons be exchanged but for such of our Chaplains and other orthodox Divines, as for loyalty are detained by the Rebels at London and elsewhere. *Counter-signed* "George Digbye." *Sign Manual.* [N. I., 17.]

Colonel EDWARD KING to Mr. YARBOROUGH and others.

[1644–5, February.]—"God . . . since my coming to London hath unexpectedly driven on the cause. That which should have been my ruin will, I hope prove an advantage to the country . . . If now you will come and a considerable number with you and justify your Remonstrance and remove the clamours, shame will overtake our enemies."

And

Divers gentlemen, freeholders and other THE INHABITANTS OF the County of LINCOLN, to the HOUSE OF COMMONS.

[1644–5, February.]—Petition. Referring to their former petition for the restoration of Colonel King to his command, and to their petition and remonstrance expressing the grievances they suffered while they were deprived of his command, and praying for redress in the premises. (See *Commons' Journals,* iv. 60.) *Copies both on the same sheet.* [N. XXII., 148.]

The COMMITTEE OF BOTH KINGDOMS.

1644[–5], March 1.—Report concerning the Aldermen and Ministers of York. (See Report of February 18th.) [N. XIV., 30.]

Colonel GEORGE MONRO and Major WILLIAM BORTHWICK on behalf of the Scotch Army in Ireland to the COMMITTEE OF BOTH KINGDOMS.

[1644–5, March 3 (?).]—Setting forth the extreme necessities of the army, who had at times been reduced to live on a pound of unground oats per man per day, and desiring that if they are to be continued on that employment various necessaries—of which a list is subjoined—might be presently provided. (See *State Papers, Domestic,* pp. 333, 334.) [N. XXI., 125, 126.]

The COMMITTEE OF BOTH KINGDOMS.

[1644–5, March 3.]—Seven resolutions concerning the Scotch army in Ireland. (Printed in *State Papers, Domestic,* p. 333, and numbered 16 to 22.) *Signed* "Jo. Cheislie." (See *Lords' Journals,* vii. 282.) [N. XXI., 127.]

M. DE SABRAN to the HOUSE OF COMMONS.

1644[–5], March 4.—It appearing that the conference was broken off rather than finished, and more by the shortness of the time than by the design of the Deputies or the two parties, and since the King in addition to the offers he made during the last days has desired a prolongation, allow me, persevering in the duties imposed on me by the orders and affection of their Most Christian Majesties of watching incessantly over everything that can facilitate a peace, to represent that if the expiration of the time fixed for the conference, when the said offers from his Majesty and marks of his good intentions were received at Uxbridge and by the Parliament, has hindered your taking the resolution you might perhaps have taken, it is better worth trying by a new prolongation of the conference to shorten that of the war than by its termination to augment the mutual distrust of the two parties. And if

you judge me a fit person to be entrusted with your answers and intentions on that subject I will very willingly delay for four days my
departure to the King of Great Britain, which I had fixed for to-day, in
order to await your resolutions. (See *Commons' Journals*, iv. 68.)
In *French*. *Signed*. [N. XVII., 6.]

JECADIAH ABERCROMY to the EARL OF ESSEX.

1644[-5], March 5. Adington.—"The Sunday following I sent out a
small partie command[ed] by Hugh Campbell, my cornet, who met with
a partie of the enemie at Bister taking up contributione moncy, skirmished and took four of the enemie prisoners. The next Tuesday
being the 27 : of Feb : I went out and took good stor of provision goeing
to Bostoune guarded by some musquetiers who run into a wood so could
no be had. On Weddensday next at night the 28 : of Feb : I went to
Nook with my oune hors and dragounes, leaving my dragounes at Eislip
Bridge for our saver retreat. We entered the hous and took some
armes with other things necessarie for men and horses—belonging to
the enemie—out of the hous. We pursued the enemie through the hous
to the leads quher ther was a narrow trapp and a double door so we
could goe no further. I did not stay long, it being day before I came
to Nook, I retreated close by the King's troops, losing but two horses
which was nothing in respect of what we got. Sunday the second of
March, I borrowed from Sir Samuel Luk one hundred hors and that
same night marched towards Kidlingtone wher the King his troops
quartered. We made our passage over the river with faggotes at Eislip
Mill with the on half of the partie commanded by my self to get
betwixt them and Oxford, so that I was in the village befor they knew.
The rest of the partie I sent to Casworth Bridge—commanded by on of
Sir Samuell his captaines—to brak open a chain with a lock, and a turn-
pick with another verie strong lock which was the way of our retreat.
This troope consisting all of gentlemen wer quartered at Oxford. Som
of them gon that afternoon befor I cam thither, leaving ther servants
and horses at ther quarters. We took six or seven prisoners with on
of his Majestys commisaries betwixt thirtie and fourtie horses with
manie pistoles [and] carabines; we gave them a strong alarme at
Oxford, and all the countrie round wher the enemie ar quartered.
Cononell Palmer—on of the enemie—with his regiment made a show of
pursuing us, but at verie great distance. Ther is on of the enemie—a
sarjant—came to me out of Bletchington hous, another yesternight out
of the King's troope who affirmeth the enemie to be verie feared so
that they ar gon from Nook to Bletchingtone hous, sinc we bate ther
quarters up at Nook. Ther is eight scor of the enemie in Bletchingtone hous which if it wer under the comma[nd] of the parliament
—being thought a verie considerable place—who ever should be in it
wer able to doe good service commanding all for the most part betwixt
Oxford Wister and Banburrie." *Signed*. *Seal*. [N. III., 163.]

The Humble Desire of the ASSEMBLY OF DIVINES.

1644[-5], March 6 —Concerning the settling of a preaching ministry
and the keeping of scandalous persons from the Sacrament. (See
Commons' Journals, iv. 71.) [N. XXII., 14.]

The PRINCE OF WALES to GEORGE LORD GORING.

1644[-5], March 8. Bath.—Stating that he will be at Bristol on
Monday and desiring to receive there an account of his condition with

regard both to his own strength and to that of the enemy, and of his plans. *Counter-signed* " Richard Fanshawe." *Sign Manual.* [N. I., 23.]

The COMMITTEE AT GROCERS' HALL.

1644[-5], March 8.—Reports by Mr. Scawen. Being detailed estimates of a month's pay for the army, of the requisites for the train of Artillery, and of the arms &c. to be provided for the Magazine. (See *Commons' Journals*, iv., 73.) At the foot of one is written

" Earl of Essex' foot	3048
" Earl of Manchester's	3578
" Total	6628
" To recruit unto 14400	7774
" Sir William Waller	0600
	7174." [N. XIV., 38-40.]

The COMMITTEE AT GROCERS' HALL.

1644[-5], March 8.—Report by Mr. Scawen. (The purport sufficiently appears from the Orders made thereon, which are printed in *Commons' Journals*, iv. 73.) [N. XIV., 31.]

The COMMITTEE AT GROCERS' HALL.

1644[-5], March 8.—Report by Mr. Ellis. (Printed in *Commons'* *Journals*, iv. 74.) [N. XIV., 32.]

The EARL OF MANCHESTER to the EARL OF CLARE.

[1644-5], March 10. Cambridge.—"I have received your Lordship's letter, and have according to your Lordship's desire sent you a warrant for the receipt of your rents in Lincolnshire." *Seal.* [N. III., 168.]

TITLE of the DIRECTORY, and ORDINANCE for establishing it and taking away the *Book of Common Prayer.*

1644[-5], March 10.—(This is the copy sent up to the Lords and approved by them.) (See *Commons' Journals*, iv. 73.) [N. XXII, 4, 5.]

Colonel GEORGE MONRO and Major WILLIAM BORTHWICK to the COMMITTEE OF BOTH KINGDOMS.

[1644-5, March 11.]—Having already represented the condition of the Scotch Army and nothing having been done towards their supply, our time being nearly expired, we are obliged to represent in the name of that army that they must provide for their safety and preservation, and if they shall thereby be necessitated to desert that service, we hope that whatever may be the inconvenience or consequence thereof it may not be imputed to that army, and we again entreat that a satisfactory answer may be given to our just desires within the time limited for our stay here. (See *Lords' Journals*, vii. 282, and *State Papers, Domestic,* p. 341.) *Copy.* [N. XXI., 143.]

[WILLIAM LENTHALL] to Colonel PINDAR and other the
Commissioners with the Army.

[1644–5, March 13.]—Enclosing the votes of that date concerning the
army (see *Commons' Journals*, iv. 76) with the names of the four
captains of the Lord General's regiment selected as captains in the new
list. *Draft.* [N. XII., 97.]

Colonel SAMUEL JONES.

1644[–5], March 14.—Answer, desiring that his former answer be
delivered to the House, claiming that the Parliament should not dishonour him by putting him out without cause, and offering if the
gentlemen of the County that appear for him, be invested with power
equivalent to their opponents to perform the propositions they make.
(See *Commons' Journals*, iv. 91.) [N. XIV., 33.] Probably *Enclosed:*
The said propositions commending his services and desiring his
continuance as Governor of Farnham Castle. [N. XIV., 37.]

The HOUSE OF COMMONS.

1644[–5], March 15.—Resolution concerning the Aldermen of
York. (Printed in *Commons' Journals*, iv. 81.) [N. XIV., 44.]

The SCOTCH COMMISSIONERS.

1644[–5], March 17.— Paper concerning the Earl of Roxburgh's
plate, &c. (Printed in *Lords' Journals*, vii. 278.) *Signed* "Jo.
Cheislie." [N. XII., 100.]

The SCOTCH COMMISSIONERS.

1644[–5], March 19.—Paper concerning the wants of their army in
Ireland. (Printed in *Lords' Journals*, vii. 282). *Signed* " Jo. Cheislie."
[N. XII., 101.]

Account of what is paid by the Treasurers at GOLDSMITHS' HALL
towards what was promised the Scotch Army in Ireland.

1644[–5], March 19.—Amounting to 80,395*l.* 10*s.* 7*d.*, of which 800*l.*
was for the garrison at Berwick. [N. XIX., 102.]

[WILLIAM LENTHALL] to Major-General BROWNE at Abingdon.

[1644–5, March 20.]—(The purport appears from the votes printed
in *Commons' Journals*, iv. 85.) *Draft.* [N. XII., 96.]

The AMBASSADORS OF THE STATES-GENERAL to the KING.

1644–5, March 23. Oxford.—After expressing the gratification the
States-General will feel at the manner in which his Majesty has received
their propositions, and the interest they take in the maintenance of the
Protestant religion in England and of the laws of the kingdom regarding
the rights and prerogatives of the king and the liberties and privileges
of all his subjects, they proceed thus : But all human actions, even the
best and the most just are subject to men's judgment and to various and
sometimes sinister misconstructions. It is more than a year since we
have been in the kingdom, and since we addressed ourselves to the

Lords and Commons of the Parliament at London. After demanding for some months our admittance, which was at last granted, we declared the sincere intentions of our lords and masters in order to be able to offer our mediation for the settlement of the distractions of these kingdoms. We have been for five months soliciting an answer, and when we obtained it at last we found it couched in such general and obscure terms that we did not know what to make of it. We have by letter informed our said lords of everything, and they, having learnt by a second reply of the Parliament, that they did not as yet declare themselves plainly, have ordered us in that case to repair to your Majesty, charging us to declare that they find themselves greatly honoured and obliged by the confidence your Majesty has deigned to show in their devoted services and their duties, to be employed by us their Ambassadors for the good of your Majesty and all the subjects of his kingdoms. And, since it has not pleased the great God of peace to terminate the present distractions by some way of accommodation, committing themselves to divine Providence, they will not cease taking the best opportunities and suitable means, which may tend to a good termination of the present distractions, that they may see themselves overwhelmed with satisfaction at your Majesty, once more united with his people, enjoying perfect peace, the love of his subjects, and all the grandeur and happiness that the great friends and sincere allies of your Majesty and his Crowns could wish him. In *French. Copy.* [N. XVIII., 102.]

The PRINCE OF WALES to GEORGE LORD GORING.

1644[-5], March 23. Bristol.—Will send Lord Capel and Lord Culpepper to you the next day to Wells, to arrange for pursuing Waller and prosecuting the business of Taunton. You, however, are not to abandon anything which would be frustrated by this meeting. *Countersigned* "Richard Fanshawe." *Sign Manual.* [N. I., 24.]

The COMMITTEE FOR IRISH AFFAIRS to the PARLIAMENT.

1645, March 25. Grocers' Hall.—Proposing to raise 6,000*l.* for the Scotch army in Ireland upon the goods of the Duke of Buckingham at York House, and a like sum to be repaid to those who should advance the first sum, in repayment of former advances, any deficiency to be made up out of Delinquents' lands. (See *Commons' Journals,* iv. 94.) [N. XXI., 11.]

[The COMMITTEE FOR IRISH AFFAIRS] to [the HOUSE OF COMMONS].

[1645, March 25.]—Desiring that an ordinance presented on August 27, 1644, and now delivered to Colonel William Jephson for raising money for the service of Ireland might be considered. (See *Commons' Journals,* iv. 94.) (N. XXI., 12.]

The ASSEMBLY OF DIVINES to the HOUSE OF COMMONS.

[1645, March 25.]—Expressing the particulars of that Ignorance and Scandal, for which they conceive that persons ought to be suspended from the Communion. (See *Commons' Journals,* iv. 89.) [N. XXII., 15.]

Sir Nathaniel Bacon and others to William Lenthall.

1645, March 27. Bury St. Edmunds.—Commending the Petition of the inhabitants of Lowestoft (Laystoft). *Signed. Seal.* [N. IV., 1.]

ADVERTISEMENTS WHAT MAY CONTENT AT LONDON.

1645, March 29.—1. "That a constant moderator in the Church will be agreed to at London, and that business so quieted.

2. That for Ireland no more is required but that the Act already passed concerning that may remain in the Parliament's power, as it was past; and it will be declared that no extirpation is intended in Ireland.

3. That the Militia may be committed to an equal number of the King's and Parliament's nomination for a reasonable time to secure the fears of the kingdom.

4 And because the King and the Houses at London make difficulty who shall first offer, it is desired the Queen may make the proposition and it is assured it shall be agreed unto at London."* *Copy.* [N. XIV., 46.]

The Assembly of Divines to the House of Commons.

1645, March 29.—Further answer concerning what is the competent measure of understanding concerning God, without which none shall be admitted to the Sacrament of the Lord's Supper. (See *Commons' Journals*, v. 92.) (The answer agrees with the first resolution of April 1, in *Commons' Journals*, iv. 95.) [N. XXII., 16.]

Don Alonso de Cardenas to the Parliament.

[1645, March 31.]—Complaining of the depredations of Captains Jackson and Tayler in the West Indies. (Printed in *Lords' Journals*, vii. 301 in English.) In *Spanish* with *English* translation. [N. XVII., 32.]

The Earl of Essex to [the Committee for naming of the Officers that shall stand].

[1644-5, end of March or beginning of April.]—Had marked on the list received from them the names of those he knew to be fit. Those thought fit to be colonels will be best able to give an account of their captains. It will be a great encouragement not to remove without just proof those officers whose regiments continue. *Holograph.* [N. VIII., 133.]

Albert Joachimi, Ambassador of the States-General, to William Lenthall.

1645, April 1-11.—Asking the restitution of the ship *Northolland* of Hoorn, which was taken in December last by some of the Parliament ships at the mouth of Waterford Harbour. In *French. Signed.* [N. XVIII., 96.]

---

* NOTE.—This appears to be the paper to which the "Notes by Sir Edward Nicholas headed, the King's answer," printed in *State Papers, Domestic*, p. 373, is a reply.

ORDINANCE.

1645, April 1.—Appointing Sir Thomas Fairfax Commander-in-Chief. (Printed in *Lords' Journals*, vii. 298.) This is signed "H. Elsyng" and is endorsed "delivered to the House by Mr. Rushworth 26 June 1650." (See *Commons' Journals*, vi. 438.) [N. XX., 54.]

The GRAND COMMITTEE OF RELIGION.

1645, April 2, 10, 15.—Resolutions reported April 17th. (Printed in *Commons' Journals*, iv. 113, 114, down to "acquaint the Assembly of Divines with this last.") [N. XXII., 18.]

The COMMITTEE OF BOTH KINGDOMS.

1645, April 2.—Report concerning the money for Abingdon, the payment of the expenses of the Committees of the Eastern Association, the sending of the rest of the 40,000*l.* to the Scotch Army, and letters from Lancashire and Salop. (See *Commons' Journals*, iv. 99.) [N. XIV., 47.]

The PARLIAMENT to PRINCE RUPERT.

1645, April 3.—Concerning his executing a number of English prisoners equal to the number of Irish executed by the Parliament's orders. (Printed in *Lords' Journals*, vii. 306.) *Draft* as passed by the Commons. [N. XII., 102.]

The COMMITTEE OF BOTH KINGDOMS.

1645, April 4.—Report, being paragraphs 2, 3, and 9 of their proceedings, printed in *State Papers, Domestic*, p. 385. (See *Commons' Journals*, iv. 100, 101.) [N. XIV., 48.]

The COMMITTEE OF BOTH KINGDOMS.

1645, April 8.—Report. (Printed in *Lords' Journals*, vii. 347.) [N. XIV., 49.]

The ASSEMBLY OF DIVINES to the HOUSE OF COMMONS.

[1645, April 10.]—Further answer concerning the particulars mentioned in the order of April 1st. (Identical with the resolution, beginning "that they have not a competent measure of understanding" and ending "everlasting punishment" printed in *Commons' Journals* iv. 113, 114.) [N. XXII., 17.]

The COMMITTEE AT GROCERS' HALL to SIR HENRY VANE, the elder, and the rest of the Committee appointed to treat with them.

1645, April 10. Grocers' Hall.—Having protested their disinterestedness and willingness to contribute, and stated that no man can set up a trade without a stock or credit. "The committee to supply the army in Ireland heretofore are run in debt, which their creditors have long forborne with no little clamour to us, as if it concerned our private interest. . . . To redeem all, and to put us in esteem and capacity again to serve you and this business of Ireland . . . we humbly propose it as necessary . . . that either that ordinance may pass—whereof we have delivered a draught to Colonel Jephson—in such manner as shall be thought fit, or that some other like expedient may be found out to be a foundation of credit at all times to this Committee to answer your orders . . . for supply of moneys and provisions for the affair, which is the course hath been observed at Goldsmiths' Hall . . . and by which means they have done the state that faithful service there, which hath outgone all expectation, and we further crave humbly to represent our opinions in this particular that until some such course be taken that the subscriber may be satisfied and see a way laid before him to support that war, and that the Parliament is resolved to go on with it, the expense of their former disbursements for the service with so little fruit have put them out of all comfort that any good will be done by any such supplies which are only small—as we say—from hand to mouth and which dishearten the soldier also cheerfully to proceed, when he sees not how to be supplied again after the expense of that little which he thus receives. It must be also the assurance of these goods in York House propounded for to raise moneys and provisions to be put into the hands of the Committee by ordinance with power to dispose and sell, and likewise the remainder of the money to be collected upon the ordinance of 80,000*l*. after that 80,000*l*. satisfied, which will engage the Committee or whom they shall treat withal to lend money or make the provisions desired, which, if you shall be pleased to cause to be speedily done, so as they may sell them for the best advantage of the state and answer the values in what moneys they shall thus lend and provisions they shall thus make, and that these may be added to the other ordinance to make one work of all, for the better encouragement of any one concerned in this business." (See *Commons' Journals*, iv. 94.) *Signed. Seal.* [N. IV., 2.]

The NATIONAL CHURCH OF SCOTLAND.

1645, April 11.—Paper. (Printed in *Lords' Journals*, vii. 317.) *Signed* "John Donn." [N. XXII., 19.]

The GRAND COMMITTEE OF RELIGION.

1645, April 21, 22, May 1.—Resolutions reported May 3. (Printed in *Commons' Journals*, iv. 131.) [N. XXII., 20.]

CHRISTIAN IV., King of Denmark, to the PARLIAMENT.

1645, April 22. Copenhagen.—Letter of Credence. (See *Commons' Journals*, iv. 308.) In *Latin. Seal embossed. Signed* "Christianus R." [N. X., 18.]

The MARQUESS OF ORMONDE to ———

1645, April 22. Dublin.—Transmitting the heads of two bills to which he desires the Great Seal may be affixed, and that then they should be returned to be passed by the Parliament of Ireland. The bills are :—

i. An Act for the avoiding of all doubts concerning the validity of the late cessation and the indemnity of his Majesty's good subjects for having commerce and trade with the contrary party.

iĩ. An Act declaring his Majesty's Grace and Goodness to his subjects of this his kingdom of Ireland.

The first clause grants a remittal of rents, &c. as in the bill mentioned in Lord Digby's letter, printed in Carte, *Life of Ormond*, vol. iii. p. 362, No. 347; the second converts the tenure *in capite* to tenure in socage for the undertakers, servitors, and natives, in the five escheated counties of Armagh, Tyrone, Fermanagh, Donegal, and Cavan ; the third (which is in parts illegible) limits the benefit of the Act to such as have been obedient since October 23, 1641 to the authorities established by his Majesty in Ireland, and to such as shall be received into grace and favour ; the fourth empowers the Lord Lieutenant to receive into grace and favour such persons and towns corporate as shall be deemed fit objects of his Majesty's mercy, and enacts that thereupon they shall be adjudged to be in possession of all lands, &c. in such manner as they enjoyed them on the 20th of October 1641, and shall be restored to their bloods and be in the same condition as on that day. *Copy.* [N. XXI., 15.]

JOHN DAVIES.

1645, April 23.—Propositions for the supply of the Scotch Army in Ireland. (Printed in *Commons' Journals*, iv. 120. [N. XXI., 14.]

SIR SAMUEL LUKE to WILLIAM LENTHALL.

1645, April 28. Newport.—The time appointed by the Ordinance for calling up the members now expiring, before leaving the place I will acquaint you with its condition. I desire that "you will take some care for providing some money for fortifying, soldiers, and workmen, not knowing what effects necessity and change of a governor may work amongst them. You have here 1,100 foot and 250 horse belonging to the garrison, which if I am not deceived have been raised and paid with so little a charge that none of the counties will have cause to complain when their Committees have been here and taken their account. I confess the keeping in of my Lieutenant-Colonel, who is their countryman, will be a great means to keep them together, but without money they cannot long subsist." *Seal.* [N. IV., 3.]

ALBERT JOACHIMI, Ambassador of the States-General, to WILLIAM LENTHALL.

1645, May 1-11.—(Identical, *mutatis mutandis*, with the letter to the Speaker of the House of Lords which is printed in *Lords' Journals*, vii. 345.) In *French*. *Signed*. [N. XVIII., 104.]

The SAME to the PARLIAMENT.

1645, May 2-12.—In *French*, with *English* translation.—(The last printed in *Lords' Journals*, vii. 351.) [N. XVIII., 103.] A duplicate signed is N. XVIII., 105.

The PARLIAMENT to the EARL OF LEVEN.

1645, May 3.—Desiring him to advance southward. (Printed in *Lords' Journals*, vii. 350.) *Draft.* [N. XII., 103.]

CHARLES, Duke of Lorraine, to the HOUSE OF COMMONS.

1645, May 4. Brussels.—Promising that any future agent he may send will not be an Englishman, and asking that while his present resident Fortescue continues he may enjoy the privileges of his position. In *French*. *Signed*. [N. X., 34.]

The HOUSE OF COMMONS.

1645, May 7.—Order printed last in *Commons' Journals*, iv. 133. [N. XXII., 21.]

The COMMITTEE OF LORDS AND COMMONS FOR THE SAFETY OF THE ASSOCIATED WESTERN COUNTIES.

1645, May 8.—(Report, identical with the resolution passed thereon which is printed in *Commons' Journals*, iv. 136.) [N. XIV., 51.]

List of the OFFICERS and SOLDIERS exchanged from Bristol, and now in London.

1645, May 9.—[N. XIV., 50.]

The COMMITTEE OF LORDS AND COMMONS FOR THE KING'S CHILDREN.

1645, May 12.—Report advising that a list of the servants to be retained and of those to be discharged be presented to the House, stating that the expense, including 3,000*l*. to the Earl of Northumberland is estimated at 13,000*l*., and suggesting how it should be raised, and recommending that the Countess of Dorset's allowance should commence from last Michaelmas. [N. XIV., 52.]

The PRINCE OF WALES to the OFFICER IN COMMAND IN THE ABSENCE OF LORD HOPTON.

1645, May 12. Bristol.—Whereas upon the late inroad of the enemy into this county we appointed for the present all the marching forces to be under the command of Lord Goring and recalled Lord Hopton —being one of our Council—to attend us and his charge of Governor of this city, we order you to apply for orders to Lord Goring. *Counter-signed* "Richard Fanshawe." *Sign Manual*. [N. I., 25.]

The SCOTCH COMMISSIONERS.

1645, May 13.—Paper. (The purport appears from the reference in *Commons' Journals*, iv. 140.) *Signed* "Jo. Cheislie." [N. XIX., 104.]

Captain WILLIAM TYNTE to the COMMITTEE OF BOTH KINGDOMS.

1645, May 14.—Petition. Stating his services and losses in the war in Munster, and praying that he may receive the two months' pay as Captain ordered in October last.

And

Colonel WILLIAM HERBERT to the SAME.

Same date.—Petition praying that his Commission from the Earl of Essex to raise 1,500 men in South Wales may be renewed, offering that if he may have 1,000*l*. imprested to him with leave to beat his drums within the line of communication to raise 200 volunteers and equip and transport them to Pembroke, and offering that if the 1,000l. cannot be imprested to advance it on repayment at six months with interest being secured on the Excise.

And

The COMMITTEE OF BOTH KINGDOMS to the HOUSE OF COMMONS.

Same date.—Reporting the last two petitions which they recommend should be granted, except as regards part of the first, recommending that Sir John Henderson, who is in very great distress, should be allowed to send his servant to Holland for maintenance, and advising that the Committee for the Army should sit daily. [N. XXII., 75, 76, 77.]

The SCOTCH COMMISSIONERS.

1645, May 15.—Paper, desiring payment of the arrears of the Scotch reduced officers. (See *Commons' Journals*, iv. 145.) *Signed* "Jo. Cheislie." [N. XIX., 105.]

Colonel EDWARD MASSIE to WILLIAM LENTHALL.

[1645, before May 16.]—(See *Commons' Journals*, iv. 145.) I refer you to the bearer for the state of our business here, and the particulars of our late success in the Forest (of Dean). I understand there is a petition to be presented against me by the Committee of Gloucester. I desire the enlargement of Captain Browne. *Seal.* [N. V., 107.]

The PRINCE OF WALES to GEORGE LORD GORING.

1645, May 16.—Enclosing letter that he may furnish, if proper, such furtherance to the proposals therein as he can spare from the forces under his command. *Counter-signed* "Richard Fanshawe." *Sign Manual.* [N. I., 27.]

The COMMITTEE OF BOTH KINGDOMS.

1645, May 17.—Report on the question whether a seizure of goods entered for Spain, but shipped on a vessel cleared for Holland was lawful. [N. XIV., 54.]

The EARL OF CALANDER to the SCOTCH COMMISSIONERS in LONDON.

1645, May 18.—(The substance of the first part appears from the paragraph of the Scotch Paper printed in *Lords' Journals*, vii 391, second column, beginning, "This letter coming to the Earl of Leven." It continues thus) : " We should be forced to march upon his rear, and have little or no entertainment for our army, since all the provisions of the country would be eaten or destroyed by the enemy. If we should abandon Yorkshire and go into Lancashire this county would lay open to the enemy, and in all probability the City of York would be lost, besides many other inconveniences. If we stay here the King is left at liberty to go into Lancashire, where he may increase his army to a very great number by reason of the many disaffected persons in that county. We have offered to my Lord Fairfax to go into Lancashire, if his Lordship with his own forces, the assistance of the 2,500 horse and dragoons from the south, and the rest of the English forces from Derbyshire and those parts would undertake the defence of this county, or if his Lordship with those forces would secure Lancashire we offered to defend this county. But his Lordship declares he can do neither. It is altogether impossible for us to defend both being a line of above 80 miles, the ways and passages also between those counties being such as the forces in the one county cannot without great difficulty and marching a long way about give assistance to the other, and the King left at liberty to march into the one or the other, as he shall see his best advantage. The King's speedy march northward will, in all probability, hinder the coming up of many of those forces designed for our assistance, and for ought we can learn of Sir William Brereton's purpose we shall have little or no assistance from his forces. He conceives it will be necessary to put all his foot into their garrisons, otherwise" they "will be lost. And it seems he intends also to detain not only his own, but my Lord Fairfax's horse for the defence of the garrisons and counties where he is. Howsoever upon certain intelligence which way the enemy bends his course, we shall take the best ways and means in our power for opposing them. But we humbly conceive we needed not to have been put to so many difficulties and to bear so great a burthen of the war, when the Parliament have a strong army in the South, which might have followed the King on the rear, and we being before him by God's blessing might make an end of the war. And we also think, when a puissant enemy is ranging through the kingdom acquiring strength and subduing whole counties, that it is not reasonable to employ armies for the reducing of towns and licing down before strengths, but that it were much better for the security of the kingdoms and putting an end to our troubles to pursue the enemy in the field." (See *Lords' Journals*, vii. 386.) *Copy.* [N. XII., 104.]

[George Lord Digby] to [George Lord Goring.]

[1645], May 19. Newport. —" The bearer is despatched so suddenly and I have written . . . so largely to the Prince's Council and in private to Lord Culpeper . . . that I have only time to tell your Lordship that the orders which you will herewithal receive from Prince Rupert to march presently with all the strength you can make to Marred Harborugh (*sic* Market Harborough) in Leicestershire are dynt (*sic* ? sent) you by the unanimous advice of all here as a thing most absolutely necessary to our preservation, the Rebels setting up their whole rest upon encountering and distressing this army, where the King's person is, as will appear to you by their particular forces drawn this way whereof I have given an account in my letter to the Prince's Council. If their aims had been at the West all things had been laid aside to succour you and now *vice versa* you must do the like. For God's sake use diligence and come as strong as you can. In my conscience it will be the last blow in the business. Bring with you what powder and match you can possibly, and it is necessary that your design be kept very secret, and that it may be understood that it is for Surrey and Sussex."

And

[Prince Rupert] to [George Lord Goring.]

Same date and place. "I shall desire your Lordship to march immediately with all the horse and foot your Lordship can possibly can (*sic*) leaving a convenient and competent number within foy (*sic*) the garrisons the[re]. I shall expect by your Lordship at least 3,500 effectual horse, and all the foot as well Grenvil's as your own not staying for the new levies. I shall desire your Lordship to bring with you the lerche (*sic*) my train and all the powder and match you possibly can. It is conceived the best way to direct your course to Harborough in Leicestershire, and you will do the least hurt to our quarters about Oxford and near Northampton, but I refer the election to you."

Postscript.—" The reasons your Lordships will fully [understand] by the Lord Digby." *Copies.* (The originals probably wholly or partly in cipher, hence the mistakes.) [N. XII., 77.]

DOM ANTONIO DE SOUSA, Portuguese Ambassador, to the HOUSE OF COMMONS.

1645, May 21.—My master has received a letter in the name of the Parliament of England, but it having been delivered by a private person, he cannot be sure from whom it is, and cannot give a suitable answer. He therefore commands me to say that the person mentioned in the said letter, who had already left Portugal when the letter arrived, had gone there for objects different from those alleged in the said letter. He has also ordered me to request the two Houses, that, should anything else require to be represented for the good of the two Crowns, to avoid similar doubts which might cause delay, they would represent it through myself, assuring themselves that his Majesty will endeavour not only to preserve the good understanding between the two Crowns but also to give satisfaction to the Parliament, without prejudice nevertheless to his Britannic Majesty, with the affection which is natural between the two nations. For my part I shall certainly proceed with the sincerity I ought and the neutrality I profess. In *French. Signed.* [N. XVII., 89.]

The COMMITTEE FOR THE EASTERN ASSOCIATION.

1645, May 21.—Resolutions. (See *Commons' Journals*, iv. 149.) [N. XIV., 53.]

The SCOTCH COMMISSIONERS.

1645, May 23.—Paper stating that they had not had time to prepare an answer concerning the advance of the Scotch Army, but would do so to-morrow; and asking that the business might be deferred till then. (See *Commons' Journals*, iv. 153.) *Signed* " Jo. Cheislie." [N. XIX., 106.]

The SCOTCH COMMISSIONERS.

1645, May 24.—(Paper printed in *Lords' Journals*, vii. 390.) *Signed* " Jo. Cheislie." [N. XIX, 107.]

Colonel EDWARD MASSIE to WILLIAM LENTHALL.

[1645, May 27.] Eveshalme.—Evesham " we yesterday morning assaulted by storm and took in, when we took the Governor, Colonel Robert Legge, Colonel Foster, Lieutenant-Colonel Bellingam, Major Travillian, 13 captains, 16 lieutenants, with other officers and soldiers to the number of about 545. Of ours was only slain about 7 or 8 and of the enemy about 12. The assault was hot and the defence not to be disparaged." I desire that the Government of this place be settled by Parliament with all speed, to enable me to march to the West, where Parliament has commanded me, and also that there may be taken further settlement of Gloucester. *Seal.* [N. V., 109.]

The Prince of Wales to George Lord Goring.

1645, May 29. Bath.—Desiring him in exchange for 500 fixt muskets lately sent from Bristol to his army to return the like number of unfixt. *Counter-signed* "Richard Fanshawe." *Sign Manual.* [N. I., 26.]

Luke Nurse, Mayor, to the Lord Mayor, Aldermen, and Common Council of the City of London.

1645, May 29. Gloucester.—(The substance is in *Commons' Journals*, iv. 168.) [N. IV., 4.]

The Parliament to Several Counties.

1645, May 31.—Desiring them to make provision for the Scotch army on their march. (Printed in *Lords' Journals*, vii. 404.) *Draft.* [N. XII., 105.]

Sir Thomas Widdrington.

1645, June 3.—Report concerning the stay of the *Hopewell*. (See *Commons' Journals*, iv. 160.) [N. XIV., 55.]

The Parliament to the Committee of Essex.

1645, June 5.—About raising men for Sir Thomas Fairfax's army. (Printed in *Lords' Journals*, vii. 414.) *Draft.* [N. XII., 106.]

The House of Commons.

1645, June 6.—Order concerning Lord Inchiquin's letters. (Printed in *Commons' Journals*, iv. 160.) [N. XXI., 17.]

The Parliament to the Committee with the Scotch Army and to the Earl of Leven.

1645, June 7.—Desiring that the army might march Southward. (Printed in *Lords' Journals*, vii. 419.) *Draft.* [N. XII., 107.]

The Common Council of the City of London.

1645, June 7.—Order to their Committee to attend the House of Commons, and deliver and support the letter and information concerning Gloucester. (See *Commons' Journals*, iv. 168.) [N. IV., 5.]

The Scotch Commissioners.

1645, June 7.—Paper. In reply to the order of the House of Commons of the 6th we answer that besides writing with an express we have lately sent two of our number earnestly to desire the speedy advance of the army Southward, and leave to the wisdom of Parliament or their committee to consider what further invitation and encouragement they will be pleased from themselves to send to the army for the hastening of their march. *Copy.* [N. XIX., 109.]

The COMMITTEE OF BOTH KINGDOMS.

1645, June 10.—Report desiring that 1,000*l*. be appointed for the garrison of Northampton, that the public stores of arms and ammunition may be refilled in order that the Committee may be able to supply the demands of several places, and reporting the particulars concerning the garrison of Windsor resolved at the Committee on May 13, and the information given by Mr. Salway and Mr. Greensmith. [N. XIV., 56.]

Considerations concerning the Province of MUNSTER.

1645, June 10.—Stating the condition of the Province, and suggesting that the foot there be raised from 1,500 to 3,000 and the horse from 300 to 600 or 700. (Probably the report of the Committee of Adventures mentioned in the next.) [N. XXI., 16.]

VOTE.

1645, June 10.—Appointing a Select Committee of both Houses to consider propositions for the relief of Munster and the rest of Ireland and to report to each House. [N. XXI., 17.]

The COMMITTEE OF BOTH KINGDOMS.

1645, June 12.—Order reporting concerning the negotiations for delivering up the enemy's forts, &c. *Annexed:*

    i. Paper given in by LORD WARISTON with the LORD CHANCELLOR OF SCOTLAND's Declaration. (Printed in *Lords' Journals,* vii. 428, 429.)

    ii. Orders of the Committee, dated April 12th, May 6th and 7th, concerning the sub-committee appointed to carry on such negotiations. [N. XIX., 110, 111.]

Desires of the SCOTCH OFFICERS.

[1645, June 12 (?).]—(See *Lords' Journals,* vii. 430; *Commons' Journals,* iv. 174.)

That they may have immediately paid them for their present necessities and for their despatch to the Scotch army the fifth part of their arrears according to a late order of the House of Commons to that effect.

That they may have the public faith for the remainder.

That they may have a present and positive answer from this honourable Committee, an absolute denial being better than a delay. *Signed* by about 130, among whom General Middleton, Major-General Crauford, Colonel Wemyss, Generals Holburne and Von Drüschke are the most notable. [N. XIX., 6.]

The PRINCE OF WALES to GEORGE LORD GORING.

1645, June 15. Barnstaple.—During our late stay at Dunster Castle we received many great complaints from the inhabitants of those parts of the insolencies and injuries they undergo by officers and soldiers who pretend to be under your Lordship's command, the sum and grounds whereof we send you enclosed, and we earnestly recommend the redress thereof to your Lordship, presuming that your Lordship having informed us of your prohibiting the levying any money by your soldiers in that country—as indeed the condition thereof requires—will take such course that the poor people, who pay their contribution, assist that army with provision, and do all other duties very cheerfully, may not be discouraged by such usage. And we desire your Lordship to direct some examination to be taken what prisoners remain in the hands of any of your soldiers taken from their houses for no reason but to compel them to redeem themselves for money, all whom we doubt not but your Lordship will cause speedily to be set at liberty. *Counter-signed* "Richard Fanshawe." *Sign Manual.* [N. I., 28.]

PARTICULARS.

1645, June 16.—Of several sums of money paid by the contracted Farmers into the Exchequer, and upon assignments by tallies to several men. [N. XIV., 57.]

The SCOTCH COMMISSIONERS.

1645, June 17.—Paper. (Printed in *State Papers, Domestic,* p. 596, last entry.) *Annexed* are the Particulars therein referred to, namely :—

To call for Mr. Lisle's report.

To pass the Ordinance for raising a month's pay for the Scotch army.

The Houses declaring that the Ordinance for billeting the Scotch army extends to the forces left in garrisons and before Carlisle, as well as to the Army marching Southward. That the Scotch officers be speedily dispatched, and the reports from the Committee of both kingdoms concerning Lieutenant-General Middleton be called for, and a letter from the Commissioners to Mr. Tait.

That if the Houses think fit a letter be written to the Parliament of Scotland to be sent with the Lord Chancellor.

That the Houses will be pleased to appoint Commissioners to reside with the Scotch Army according to the Treaty. (See *Commons' Journals,* iv. 178.) In Sir John Cheislie's hand. *Endorsed* "for Mr. Wallop." [N. XIX., 112.]

The ASSEMBLY OF DIVINES to the HOUSE OF COMMONS.

1645, June 17.—Humble Petition and Request that, whereas there are many other scandalous sins besides the seven mentioned (see votes of April 17th) that do justly deserve abstention from the Sacrament, the Ordinance may be so drawn up that the Ministry and Elders may be sufficiently enabled to keep all such as are justly and notoriously scandalous from partaking. *Enclosed :*

A List of Instances of other Scandalous Sins. (See *Commons' Journals,* iv. 176.) [N. XXII., 22.]

The COMMITTEE OF CUMBERLAND.

[1645, June 20 (?).]—Paper bringing charges against certain of the Scotch army of outrage and extortion. (See *Commons' Journals,* iv. 180.) Part *illegible.* [N. XX., 209.]

The SCOTCH COMMISSIONERS.

1645, June 20.—Paper. (Printed in *Lords' Journals,* vii. 442.) *Signed* "Jo. Cheislie." [N. XIX., 113.]

Mr. Lisle's Report concerning the COAL TRADE.

1645, June 20.—(Printed in *Commons' Journals*, iv. 174.) [N. XIV., 58.]

The EARL OF LEVEN, the EARL OF CALANDER, and A. HAᴊILTON to the COᴊᴊITTEE OF BOTH KINGDOᴊS.

1645, June 21. Nottingham.—" The continuance of a firme union and good correspondence between the kingdomes, is so much in our thoughts and wishes, as that without it wee can expect no better then the weakning, yea undoeing of this Common Cause, and the strenthning of the common enemyes. And although there be neither few nor small occasions of discouragements from the misrepresentation of our actions, and misapprehension of our intentions, from the coolling if not changing of that affection formerly exprest, both towards ourselves and toward divers of our countreymen, who have deserved weell for their abilities and faithfulnes in the publique, and from the usage, and entertainment of this army which is neither according to that which other armyes in this kingdome do receave nor according to the treaty between the kingdomes, nor at all certain, such as can avoyde the hatred and discontent of the people whose affections and goodwill wee desire to carry along with us: Yet notwithstanding all these and the like discouragements, our actions have been, are, and shall be reall testimonies of our constant resolution to persue actively the ends exprest in the Covenant, and to adventure ourselves and whatsoever is dearest to us in this cause. And that as wee had great reason to march into Westmoreland in regard of the intelligence both then and since confirmed to us, so wee have been as ready and willing to come southward, as wee were desyred by the honourable houses of parliament and by your Lordships. And wee have marched with more speed, and lesse interruption then is usuall in such cases, yea our march had been more speedy, if wee had not been stayed in some places for want of draughts and provisions. And now wee are with the assistance of God Almighty, to undertake any action which may be fittest for the cause and safety of both kingdomes. But if—which God forbid—for want of the conjunction, and assistance promised, or for want of necessary provisions, the public worke be retarded or disappointed, wee shall be blameles. And therefore wee doe recommend to your Lordships' most serious deliberation that some more effectuall and speedy course be taken for necessary provisions to this army, that both officers and souldiers may have in an orderly and constant way not onely a part of their pay in victualls, but also money for their other necessary uses, and in case of our conjunction with any other forces of the kingdome, that then the provisions of this army be no worse then of those other forces. Which things, as they are just in themselves, so they are the rather decyred, that this army may not be burthensome, nor hatefull to the countyes where wee come, and that wee may not be redacted to the unhappy necessity of not punishing strictly wrongs and disorders, which as wee have not only forbidden by the strictest edicts but have exemplarly and severely punished, so shall wee ever be ready upon complaint, and proof of the same either to punish the same by death, or other condigne punishment according to the quality of the offence. Wee further entreat and expect, that this warr might be managed according to the treaty by the committee of both kingdomes upon the place, and for that end, that a Quorum of the commissioners from the honourable houses of parliament may be constantly with this army. And that your Lordships may entertain chari·

table thoughts of our proceedings, confident, that according to the knowledge which God hath geven us in the matters of our profession, wee shall improve all opportunityes to the best advantage. Wee shall not need to put your Lordships in remembrance how necessary it is that before the armyes of either or both kingdomes undertake beseiging of any toun, they first endeavour a totall dissipation of all the forces which the enemy hes in the feilds, and so much the rather because by the blessing of God that dissipation shall be more easy if the armyes of both kingdomes be continually aiding and assisting each one to other, and that each act their part and attend the enemys motions. What wee have written to your Lordships wee desire it may be made knowen to both houses of parliament and above all, that your Lordships would with all earnestness presse the expediting of the reformation of religion and uniformity in church government, together with the speedy prosecuting and ending of this warr, that wee may returne home with the comfort of religion and peace settled." *Signed.* [N. IV., 6.]

The COMMITTEE OF BOTH KINGDOMS to the PARLIAMENT.

1645, June 21.—Stating that the particulars being unknown to them they can deliver no opinion thereon. [N. XXI., 21.]

The EARL OF LEVEN to the SCOTCH COMMISSIONERS.

1645, June 22. Nottingham.—Desiring to be acquainted with the resolutions of the Parliament concerning his army's next undertakings, and that the 10,000*l.* for the army be sent down all at once and not divided, for the convoying whereof there shall be a way appointed before it can be at Northampton. *Copy.* [N. XII., 61.]

The SCOTCH COMMISSIONERS.

1645, June 22.—Paper. (Printed in *Lords' Journals,* vii. 450.) *Signed* " Jo. Cheislie." [N. XIX., 114.]

The PRINCE OF WALES to GEORGE LORD GORING.

1645, June 23. Barnstaple.—We send herewith Sir Richard Greenvile, that by his presence the soldiers under his command may be more easily gathered up and kept together. We have directed him to receive orders from you and if you think it convenient he should make some quarter in Dorsetshire, we presume you will assist him with such horse and foot as may be necessary. We are of opinion that if you assign him those foot that were brought by him to Taunton it will be your best means to draw together all those who have left their colours. We have likewise sent directions to the Committees of Cornwall and Devon to take speedy and effectual course whereby both those who have forsaken their colours and those who are to be levied according to the agreement be immediately sent you that that great work may be finished before the rebels can draw any forces for their relief. *Countersigned* " Richard Fanshawe." *Sign Manual. Seal.* [N. I., 29.]

The SCOTCH COMMISSIONERS.

1645, June 24.—Papers. (Printed in *Lords' Journals,* vii. 453.) *Signed* " Jo. Cheislie." [N. XIX., 115.]

The Scotch Commissioners.

1645, June 26.—Papers. (Printed in *Lords' Journals*, vii. 465.) *Signed* " Jo. Cheislie." [N. XIX., 116.]

The Members of both Houses who are members of the Committee of both Kingdoms.

. 1645, June 26.—Report concerning the Scotch putting a garrison in Carlisle, made in pursuance of the order of June 24. (See *Commons' Journals*, iv. 184). [N. XIV., 59.]

Impeachment of the Earl of Stamford, Henry Polton, and Matthew Patsall, their answers, and the Replication thereto of the House of Commons.

1645, June 28, July 21.—(Printed (except the Replication) in *Lords' Journals*, vii. 462, 502.) [N. XIV., 64, 63, 62, 61.]

Lord Savile to Mr. Gorden.

1645, July 2. The Tower.—Enclosing a paper accusing Mr. White-locke and Mr. Hollis. (See *Commons' Journals*, iv. 194, and Whitelocke, *Memorials*, p. 154.) [N. XIV., 65, 60.]

George [Lord] Digby to George Lord Goring.

1645, July 4. Ragland Castle.—"I have received your Lordship's letter by Stephens—which he says was delivered him on Tuesday—but being without a date we cannot so clearly understand where and when the enemy was in such and such places. As for your Lordship's resolutions his Majesty doth approve of them, so far as we at this distance can judge, but his Majesty doth not intend to interpose from hence any directions, but leaves it to you and to Prince Rupert, who we believe hath been with you ere this, to resolve and agree upon what you shall think best and accordingly to give directions unto 224 : 123 : 2 : 37 : 457 : u8 : 9 : and 3 : 7 : k8 : k10 : g2 : f6 : 239 : 312 : 502 : and 501 : His Highness will also have acquainted you with the resolutions taken at Barnstaple by the unanimous opinion of the Prince's Council there, in pursuance of which, that no time might be lost, orders were sent over to be instantly dispersed, in case the king approved of the resolution ; which his Majesty doing entirely the orders were issued, and 56 : 362 : 228 : are by this time drawing towards 490 : 188 : 457 : 9 : 73 : 11 : 22 : 60 : 31 : s : 61 : 186 : 362 : 185 : 478 : 362 : 287 : 18 : 96 : 236 : 67 : 17 : 95 : o3 : 33 : 87 : c6 : 23 : 69 : 340 : d10 : c9 : o : 69 : 83 : 11 : g2 : k4 : 79 : h6 : n10 : 93 : g7 : 14 : 15 : 11 : d10 : 8 : 31 : h9 : 4 : 36 : and k6 : h3 : 44 : c6 : 6 : 91 : o3 : Besides that c1 : k5 : 281 : o : 74 : 8 : q8 : especially 459 : 124 : 6 : 23 : 24 : y4 : m3 : 12 : 67 : d6 : c9 : d9 : 11 : 5 : 27 : k3 : e3 : 48 : f6 : 362 : 3 : 23 : c7 : 312 : so that of necessity the use which is to be made of 457 : 185 : e4 : 48 : 67 : 71 : u8 : 9 : and 3 : 8 : k8 : k10 : g2 : 361 : 439 : according as you shall direct. His Majesty is very well pleased to find himself so confirmed by the unanimous advice of Prince Rupert and the Prince of Wales' Council in that resolution which upon your advice he had before taken f6 : 75 : e2 : 9 : 14 : 361 : 11 : 511 : c1 : h1 : 8 : k5 : 9: which will be no longer deferred than till such time as he hear again from Prince Rupert.

In your preceding letter—which was the welcomest that ever I received from you—you insist upon a particular concerning Sir Richard Greneville's commission of Field Marshal, a thing which I never had any knowledge of till your letter. But since, having informed myself of my Lord Culpeper, I find that that commission of Sir Richard Grenville's concerns not my Lord Wentworth nor you at all, it being merely titular as to your Association and he is with you in the army quite in another capacity. It is true that when the command of the army under Prince Rupert and of the Association yet in my Lord Hopton shall be united in your person, as is intended, then possibly there may somewhat come in controversy how that commission of Sir Richard Greneville's shall stand in order to both your capacities. As for any difference in point of command between my Lord Wentworth and Sir Richard Greneville in your present army—if any difference there be—that will be wholly in Prince Rupert's judgment and power to determine, being improper for the King to interpose in . . *Signature torn off at end, but added to address. Seal.* [N. IV., 7.]

SIR THOMAS FAIRFAX to WILLIAM LENTHALL.

1645, July 6. Crookhorne (Crewkorne).—Concerning the Clubmen I enclose copies of their petitions, directions and letter delivered to me by Mr. Holles and others and my answer. "I believe I shall have occasion very suddenly to write more concerning this business, if such an appearance be made upon a warrant lately issued out as is expected. Our friends at Taunton—the Lord be praised—are now at liberty ; the enemy drew off upon the approach of the army, before we got to Beaminster, and is marched to Somerton, and part of their army towards Bath and Wells. They brake down the bridge, which hinders our falling on their rear. There is a strong party of horse and dragoons attends their motion." (See *Commons' Journals*, iv. 292.) *Signature torn off. Seal.* [N. IV., 8.] *Enclosed :*

    i. Petition to Sir Thomas Fairfax for passes for the delegates the Clubmen desired to send to the King and Parliament respectively. Subjoined are the delegates' names which are printed in Rushworth, iv. 1. 52. *Copy.* [N. IV., 9.]

    ii. Sir Thomas Fairfax's Answer dated July 4th at Dorchester. (Printed in Rushworth, iv. 1. 53.) *Copy,* but signed by Sir Thomas Fairfax. [N. IV., 10.]

ORDINANCE.

1645. July 11.—Giving instructions to their Commissioners to Scotland. *Draft* with alterations. (Printed in its ultimate form in *Lords' Journals*, vii. 514.) [N. XIX., 117.]

The PARLIAMENT to the COMMISSIONERS TO SCOTLAND:

1645, July 12.—Instructions. (*Draft* of part as sent from the Lords' that day, allowing that on the removal of the Scotch garrison from Carlisle and its replacement by an English one and the removals of the garrisons of Warkworth, Hartlepool, Stockton and Thirlwall Castles that a Scotch garrison should be continued in Newcastle for twelve months. This was not agreed to by the Commons. See *Lords' Journals*, vii. 515.) [N. XX., 63a.]

The PARLIAMENT OF ENGLAND to the PARLIAMENT OF SCOTLAND.

1645, July 12.—Letter of Credence for their Commissioners. (Printed in *Lords' Journals*, vii. 494.) *Draft.* [N. XII., 110.]

The SCOTCH COMMISSIONERS to the COMMITTEE OF BOTH KINGDOMS.

1645, July 12.—" We have very frequently represented . . to the . . Houses the hard condition of the Scotch army through want of necessary maintenance. Money is not given them whereby the country might be invited willingly to furnish them provisions and the endeavours of the Committees of the several Counties to bring them in without money . . . hath proved altogether ineffectual . . . and prejudices do inevitably follow, whereby the Army cannot encamp in the fields, but is forced to quarter at large in the villages, which subjects the Army to danger and the country people to those inconveniences from the soldier that otherwise might be avoided, and thereby makes the people everywhere look upon them not as Brethren to assist them, but enemies to take from them, while others pay for what they take. Two days of three are spent in procuring victuals for the Army whereas, being provided, they might proceed in a continued march; and when they shall come nearer the enemy will undoubtedly be reduced to greater extremities. The soldier is discontented, the country people disaffected, the public service disappointed, and the inconveniences every day so many, that the Army apprehends that either their condition is not rightly represented by us, or not believed by the Houses. We therefore earnestly desire that some effectual course may be taken for enabling them to perform the service that is expected from them, which in all probability must be in providing constantly money for the officers, and part money part provision for the common soldier. And that in the mean time power be granted for assessing the enemies' country, and places adjacent, till . . . a more regular and constant way of their maintenance be settled by the wisdom of the Parliament, without which we cannot see for the present how the war can be vigorously carried on in those parts, without being interrupted therein by daily wants before they be well begun. We desire also that the Houses . . . return an answer to the particulars presented the 4th . . . concerning that army and make known to them . . . their desires concerning their future undertakings, and that a Committee may be speedily sent to reside there, who at least may witness to the Parliament on the one hand the truth of this their hard condition from day to day notwithstanding the Treaty for their monthly maintenance, which is as obligatory and should be as effectual to them as any particular Ordinance is to any others, and on the other part the willingness and readiness of that army for the public service, if they were in any measure enabled and furnished with necessaries, while others are fully paid."

We enclose an extract of a letter received yesterday. (See *Commons' Journals*, iv. 205). *Signed* " Jo. Cheislie." [N. XII., 109.] *Enclosed :*

The EARL OF LEVEN and the COMMITTEE WITH THE ARMY to the SCOTCH COMMISSIONERS.

1645, July 8. Alcester.—We wrote to you from Birmingham the daily increasing hard condition of our Army. We desired from the Committee of Warwick and Coventry a constant way of entertainment, and in the mean time three days provision for marching and some money for officers under a Captain, but they have not done anything accordingly. We are now" here, "where we came yesternight a long march, and such we should make till we came where we might do service, but now we must stop here for want of provisions, for at the writing hereof the whole foot wants altogether officer and soldier alike, there being nothing to give the soldier and the officer having no money to buy anything. We think ourselves ill-used; we are called to march, march, that a plentiful country' is still before us, where nothing will be wanting to us, but we find nothing by the way but solitude—pleasant places indeed for grass and trees, but no other refreshment, the country people looking upon us as enemies to take from them without paying for it, as others do, and so eschewing to bring in any provision, all which have been endured hithertill with admirable patience by the poor soldier. We can hardly believe that you represent what we write, or that you are believed in what you represent. Certainly neither ye nor we will be long able to feed the pinching belly of this Army with words, and to starve them with fair promises. They desire that Articles might be kept unto them, and that they may not be destroyed for their desire to save others . . . . We are now in the Shire we were desired to march to within a little distance of Worcester . . . We shall be ashamed to be so nigh the enemy and do nothing worthy of the Army and yet we cannot contrary to the rules of reason and war, which require much order and great foresight, engage in any action from which we may be hindered or forced to leave from want of necessaries. We have so often given warning hereof that if it be not effectually and timeously remedied we cannot but apprehend —either in design or in consequence—the disableing and discrediting of this Army . . . Therefore represent fully and freely to the Houses of Parliament" [what is represented in the Commissioners' Paper above].

Postscript.—"Of the addition of forces promised . . we have not as yet seen any except two troops, as may appear by Sir John Gell's letter, and therefore desire you to use the greater diligence for procuring some part of our arrears to raise 1,000 horse to be constantly with us, seeing the enemies' strength is in horse. Necessity makes us so plain . . ."

Extract. [N. XII., 108.]

Informations and Examinations of LORD SAVILE and others, reported.

1645, July 17.—Concerning the charges made by him against Mr. Hollis and Mr. Whitelocke. (Apparently these are the notes taken down at the time, being hurriedly written with many abbreviations.) (See *Commons' Journals,* iv. 211, Whitelocke, *Memorials,* pp. 155, 161.) [N. XIV., 66, 67.]

The House of Commons.

1645, July 18.—Instructions to the Committee to reside with the Scotch Army.

They are to do their utmost towards the vigourous prosecution of the enemy and the preserving a good correspondency between the two kngdoms.

They are to acquaint the Scots " with the great straits we are in for want of money and that whatsoever failing of payments . . . have been from hence have not proceeded from any want of affection or intention to make good our engagements," and that a weekly assessment is now made for the maintenance of their army.

They are authorised to issue warrants for furnishing provisions to the counties where the army shall march, and to appoint sub-committees to assist them therein, account if possible to be taken of all such provisions that they may be charged on the pay of the Scotch army, and also to recruit horses for the army to replace those lost.

They are to take care that no protection be granted to any Delinquent, and the ordinances be put in execution against them.

They are to keep both Houses informed of their proceedings and observe any directions from both of them.

They are empowered, calling to their assistance the Committees of the Counties where such are appointed by the Parliament, to cause 200*l.* *per diem* in money and provisions to be furnished for the infantry of the army to be accounted as part of the 31,000*l.* per month.

The Lords' concurrence to be desired. (See *Lords' Journals,* vii. 500.) [N. XIX., 118.]

John Davies.

[1645, July 21.]—Offering on certain terms to send money and goods to the value of 10,000*l.* to Munster within six days. (See *Commons' Journals,* iv. 222.) *Signed.* [N. XXI., 19.]

Sir Thomas Fairfax to [Edmund Windham, Governor of Bridgewater.]

[1645], July 22.—Offering to allow the women and children in the town to leave it up to 4 o'clock in the afternoon. (See Rushworth, iv. 1. 58.) *Signed.* [N. III., 20.]

Eighth Article of the Ordinance.

1645, July 28.—(Printed in *Lords' Journals,* vii. 515.) [N. XIX., 108.]

Papers concerning Michael Crake.

1645, July 29. Read on that day.—(See *Commons' Journals,* iv. 224), being the order of September 14, 1642, (See *Commons' Journals,* ii. 766) and letters from the Commissioners of the Parliament with the Scotch army and the Earl of Leven, dated April 22nd and 25th 1645, to the Mayor and Corporation of Sunderland, and to George Lilburne respectively. [N. XIV., 68.]

The Humble Petition of the Assembly of Divines.

1645, August 1.—Again urging the exclusion of scandalous persons from the Sacrament. (See *Commons' Journals,* iv. 226.) [N. XXII., 23.]

John Lowry, Mayor and Member for Cambridge, to William Lenthall.

1645, August 1. Cambridge.—Giving an account of what had been done in compliance with the order of the House for the speedy sending in of the proportion of horse assigned upon the County of Cambridge to be employed at Grantham and likewise for our county's bringing in their recruits and old levies and also the moneys assessed upon our county for that worthy and successful commander Sir Thomas Fairfax. *Seal.* [N. IV., 11.]

ROBERT CHARLTON, HUMPHREY MACKWORTH, ROBERT CLIVE, and others, to WILLIAM LENTHALL.

1645, August 2. Shrewsbury.—"We long since having occasion to send forth a party towards Bridgenorth took prisoner one Sir Thomas Whitmore, who is able to afford a good ransom . . . We have by small means so far prospered that the county is settled in such a condition, especially on the Welsh side the river that no small force of the enemy can hurt us, the country now in those parts unanimously joining with us. There only remains some garrisons of the enemies, which we doubt not . . . but will in short time be reduced, but in regard this county hath lain long under the burthen of contribution on both sides and so much suffered by plundering and other hindrances it is so impoverished that we fail much of the weekly subsistence we expect for ourselves," besides our other great engagements and we therefore ask that Sir Thomas Whitmore's ransom may be granted us towards meeting them. *Signed. Seal.* [N. IV., 12.]

Colonel MARTIN PYNDAR, HARCOURT LEIGHTON, and THOMAS HERBERT, to WILLIAM LENTHALL.

1645, August 2. Bridgwater.—"We have been longe silent by reason of the multiplicity of business in these parts especially in this towne of Bridgwater where the nobleness of the Generall for the preservation of the place hath begott us much trouble—which wee forethinke not—in labouringe both to sattisfie the expectation of the soldyer and continue the townsman in his propriety. The rumor of riches here whorded up will fill your expectations with large returnes of our labours wherein wee have as the answere of a good conscience, soe the publique testimony of the country to certify you that in the first place the enemy himself seeinge to what he was reduced broke up all trunkes cabinetts and considerable places even in the time of parlie and tooke there all portable treasure which our poore honest soldyers let passe without riflinge, beinge accordinge to the Article; in the second place our owne soldyers notwithstandinge all the care wee could take beinge in number thousands to unity of us, over-maistered us, and soe made up theyr mouthes, who notwithstandinge will clamour for a share with the honestest of them that did nothinge; thirdly the numbers of persons upon oath attestinge both theyr propriety and necessity of securinge theyr goods in the place have wonne upon our judgments to deliver them such as are yet preserved from the fury of fire and warr upon easie and inconsiderable tearmes not worthy your trouble to take notice off. It remaines only that wee present you with what wee found valuable and could not for it find a markett considerable: which is plate and hanginges—wherof wee have sent you a schedule—which wee have herewith sent up, by the safest convoy wee could get; humbly desiringe they may be committed to the care of the treasurers to be turned into money and speedily returned to the army, to be joyned to other monies made of such goods as have proved lawfull prize and have been by us sould to that purpose, promised by the Generall, that every soldyer should have a share in it. The successes of your armies, with theyr deportment wee presume have been faithfully and lively presented by Mr. Aysh and Mr. Moore whose presence and paines in the army have been of singular use. Wee shall only adde that some omission ther is to the compleatinge of those reall intentions agreed upon by you and published by us and in the generall expected by the country, the paiment of all your forces equally, which notwithstanding, there are divers regiments out of the establishment who pretendinge want of pay doe both take free quarter and plunder horses most unreasonably, not only to the dishonour of the parliament, but alsoe to the evill example of all the rest of the army. A president wherof wee make bold to present you with, and cannot much except against where pay is not to be had, but wee find noe other soe carefull as this generall to give tiquetts. There are severall regiments of horse that pretend the like want, as Collonel Popham's, Collonel Fitz-James', Collonel Cooke's, and all Major-Generall Massie's forces, whose service wee cannot but recommend, and whose paiment wee earnestly solicett, that soe the reputation woune by your paiment of your army and the conquest wee have made over the Clubmen by paiment of our quarters may not be blasted by soe inconsiderable a party whome wee neither can pay or punish, deliveringe it as your knowne judgment that thousands have layed downe theyr armes merely upon the alteration of the soldyers' carriage, which worketh upon them more then lawes will. Yet wee humbly offer that it would much conduce to the perfectinge of the worke in hand, if wee might have your Declarations, Directory, the Cabinett of Letters, our instructions, and other thinges—fitt for the country to know—published in all places where wee march, the country hardly beleevinge you intend them either Liberty, Property or Religion, especially since you take away the *Common-prayer Booke;* which every soldyer doth practise to doe. Wee shall trouble you only with one thinge more : the hastning of your committees of sequestration and examination of the sufferances of the country : wee findinge the malignant rather to rule then to submitt even in this garrison. And because they enjoy liberty and property they thinke the bitternesse of death to be over and make use of theyr tongues, to the hearts' greife of the better part who have suffered by them." (See *Commons' Journals*, iv. 241.) *Signed*. [N. IV., 13.]

WILLIAM LENTHALL to the EARL OF LEVEN.

[1645, August 2.]—In the name of the House thanking him for his action with regard to Sir William Fleming's letter, and for recommending the Governor of Cannon Froome to the House, and stating that they were sending him a small remembrance in token of their love. (See *Commons' Journals*, iv. 229.) *Copy*. [N. XII., 182.]

The EARL OF CRAFORD AND LINDESAY to the ENGLISH COMMISSIONERS.

1645, August 4. Perth.—Desiring them to stay at Berwick for the present. (Printed in *Lords' Journals*, vii. 553.) Attested *Copy*. [N. XII., 111.]

List of the LEADERS OF THE CLUBMEN for Wilts, Dorset, and Somerset, taken at Shaftesbury.

1645, August 4.—(Printed in Grey, iii., Appendix, No. 36. p. 60.) (See *Commons' Journals*, iv. 234.) [N. XIV., 70.]

ROBERT MARSHALL, Mayor, THOMAS LISTER, Sheriff, and others to WILLIAM LENTHALL.

1645, August 4. Lincoln.—" We taking into our consideration the great and growing strength of the forces of Newark and also of the weakness of the forces in this county upon which they do and have lain these several years have thought good to intreat Mr. Henry Pelham . . to present unto the Honourable House how difficult a thing it will be to reduce Newark, unless it be speedily set on, before they shall have opportunity to get in their harvest, wherefore we beseech the Honourable House to take into their speedy consideration that the loss of this county is an inlet to all the Association, and consequently will be a ruin to those counties as also to Sir Thomas Fairfax's army, who are maintained from thence, to prevent which we humbly pray that some considerable forces may be speedily sent and commanded into these parts to join with our united forces for the blocking up and reducing of Newark." We also desire 60 barrels of powder, and want many other things which Mr. Pelham will represent to you. *Signed. Seal.* [N. IV., 14.]

EDWARD LEIGH, and others the Committee at Stafford, to WILLIAM LENTHALL.

1645, August 5.—The Governor of Dudly Castle has lately executed one and the Governor of Hartlebury Castle threatens to execute another of Colonel Fox's soldiers. We have therefore delivered to Colonel Fox two Irish soldiers, which upon this occasion we purposed to have put to death by the Ordinance of October 24th last, but, as they were not put to death upon their taking, but so long foreborne, we desire the pleasure of the Parliament. *Signed. Seal.* [N. IV., 15.]

THOMAS LEVET and others to WILLIAM LENTHALL.

1645, August 6. Burleigh.—"This last Tuesday being the 5th . . God was pleased to give our forces a great victory over a party of Newark forces commanded by Sir Robert Dallison, which came up into the country as far as Stamford . . . . to gather taxes, plunder the country and take prisoners. As soon as the alarm came to us Captain Allan . . drew out all our forces with much expedition which consisted but of fourscore horse and thirteen dragoons sent after and went to intercept the enemy in their retreat, which was accordingly done. At Carleby near Stamford Captain Allan fell upon them and there routed the enemy, who consisted of 200 horse, but they were reported 400. Notwithstanding our men was not daunted, and God crowned them with success, they took there in all 51 prisoners [names given], and fourscore horses and arms. Besides five slain upon the place divers which escaped were wounded, and crept into the woods, and all this was done without the loss of one man of ours. There was also rescued the Alderman of Stamford with 15 considerable countrymen whom the enemy had taken prisoners." . . (See *Commons' Journals*, iv. 236.) *Signed. Seal.* [N. IV., 16.]

The HOUSE OF COMMONS to the EARL OF LEVEN.

1645, August 6.—(The purport appears from the order directing it to be written, which is printed in *Commons' Journals*, iv. 231.) *Draft.* [N. XII., 116.]

The SCOTCH COMMISSIONERS.

1645, August 7.—Paper. "The pressing necessities of the Scotch army enforce us to represent . . to . . Parliament that notwithstanding the whole four months of the Ordinance be long since expired there is but a very small . . proportion of the money assessed . . as yet come into the Committee of Goldsmiths' Hall for repayment of the month's pay advanced by the City of London, and for satisfying the necessities of that army, which is reduced to that extremity in the present service wherein they are engaged that without the pease, apples, and wheat they gather from the ground they are not able to subsist. Some of the Counties, as Lincoln, Gloucester and Rutland desire to be excused and pretend their inability to afford any proportion of the money assessed upon them for that army, and little or none comes in from the rest of them.

It is above a twelvemonth since a month's pay was ordered by the House to be paid to the Scotch army out of the fines and compositions for Delinquents' estates immediately after the battle at Longmarston, a good proportion whereof is yet due, the payment of which is obstructed by several orders procured from the House for payments . . . for other uses out of those fines and compositions. Our earnest desire . . is that some speedy and effectual course be taken for bringing in of the moneys due . . for the four months past, that the ordinance may speedily be renewed, that the House will . . appoint the Committee of Goldsmiths' Hall, first to pay the remainder of that month's pay voted after the battle of Longmarston . . . notwithstanding any subsequent orders, and, that the Committee of Goldsmiths' Hall may be enabled for the speedy payment thereof and of the incident charges, that the House will call for their reports concerning those fines wherein they can proceed no further without the approbation of the House." *Signed* " Jo. Cheislie." [N. XIX., 121.]

The PARLIAMENT OF SCOTLAND.

1645, August 7. Perth.—Order adding to the former Commissioners for the treaty certain persons to treat with the English Commissioners. (Printed in *Lords' Journals,* vii. 689.) Two copies. [N. XII., 112; XIX., 119.]

HENRY BROOKE, GEORGE BOOTHE, and others, to WILLIAI LENTHALL.

1645, August 7. Nantwich.—Asking him to present to Parliament the Remonstrance of the County. (See *Commons' Journals,* iv. 254.) *Signed. Seal. Enclosed:*

" A Remonstrance of the Deputy Lieutenants and Gentlemen of the County Palatine of Chester of the condition of that county and of the great advantage the reducing of the City of Chester would bring to the State and their humble request thereupon," setting forth the services done and the charges borne by the County and praying That " it may please this honourable House —the wealth of the County being well nigh exhausted and not longer able to subsist—to afford such timely assistance of horse and foot as you in your wisdoms shall think fit for the reducing of Chester on which depends the well being of this County, Lancashire, Shropshire, North Wales and the North part of England and also of Ireland, and that these forces be not main. tained at the charge of the County. That shipping may be appointed for the guard of the Irish Seas to hinder the Irish from landing in England or Wales, who are daily expected, and Sir Marmaduke Langdale now sent into Wales with a power of horse to attend their landing. That our horse and dragoons be armed without which they cannot be serviceable and yet a charge to this County. That the Governor of Warrington may be commanded to relinquish the 29 towns lent him by this County for maintenance of that place, this County being now in distress, and that the money paid unto the said Governor since the serving of the order of this Honourable House for revoking of the said allotment be repaid. That some money may be afforded this County for payment of the horse and dragoons and procuring of ammunition which the County stands in great need of." [N. IV., 18.]

Lieutenant-Colonel RICHARD COKAYN to WILLIAM LENTHALL.

1645, August 7. Newport Pagnell.—(The substance in *Commons' Journals*, iv. 235.) *Seal.* [N. IV., 19.]

FRANCIS PIERREPONT and others to WILLIAM LENTHALL.

1645, August 8. York.—" In respect none of the Northern forces are yet come up and a great part of ours being engaged in the blocking up those castles which the enemy yet holds in our county and that work being brought to so good a perfection that we hope it will very shortly be finished we cannot for the present observe the commands of the House, unless we should either expose this county to the plunder of the enemies' garrisons or the remaining party, if we should advance them to Newark, to be beaten by the enemy there. The Committees have now reduced the greatest part of this army, but the want of money both for satisfying those many officers, who must of necessity be cast, and also those soldiers which stand, we fear will prove very prejudicial to the service. And this County by reason of its being so harrassed formerly by unpaid armies affords little money, and it being now the harvest time makes the husbandmen unwilling to part with any." After a reference to the mutiny of the horse at Skipton, " we fear the same from the rest, and have little or no money to satisfy either them or the foot, who though they have been much better paid than the horse yet cannot forget their old custom of mutinying. However we shall use our best endeavours to settle them, and then we shall advance the force we can towards the blocking up of Newark, and we doubt not but you will take order that considerable forces may be drawn out of the Southern Associations to join with them." We desire a power to choose general officers. *Signed. Seal.* [N. IV., 20.]

Colonel-General SEDNHAM POINTS to FERDINANDO LORD FAIRFAX.

1645, August 8. Skipton.—Concerning the taking of that town and the mutinous behaviour of the horse. (Printed in Grey, iii. Appendix, No. 42, p. 68.) [N. IV., 21.]

The SAME to WILLIAM LENTHALL.

Same date.—(The substance appears from the last and the letter of the same date to the Speaker of the House of Peers, which is printed in *Lords' Journals*, vii. 533.) [N. IV., 22.]

PHILIP FRANCIS to the COMMITTEE FOR PLYMOUTH, POOLE, AND LYME.

[1645, August 8.]—Petition. (The purport appears from *Commons' Journals*, iv. 269.) [N. XXII., 80.]

The COMMITTEE FOR PETITIONS and the COMMITTEE FOR PLYMOUTH, &c.

1645, August 8, 12, 13.—Three orders on the said Petition. (The last is printed in *Commons' Journals*, iv. 269.) [N. XXII., 81, is the originals of the first two; N. XIV., 73, is a copy of the last.]

The Humble Petition of the ASSEMBLY OF DIVINES.

1645, August 8.—Again urging the exclusion of scandalous persons, arguing among other things that that power cannot be called arbitrary which is not according to the will of man, but the will of Christ, or unlimited, which is circumscribed and regulated by the exactest law, the word of God, and that it is not in the least measure inconsistent with the liberties of the subject, it being exercised wholly and solely in that which is not part of Civil Liberty, the Sacrament, which certainly none can claim as he is a freeborn subject of any kingdom or state but as he is visibly a member of the Church. (See *Commons' Journals*, iv. 234.) [N. XXII., 24.]

The PROCONSULS and SENATORS OF HAMBURGH to both HOUSES OF PARLIAMENT.

1645, August 8.—Stating that the English Merchant Adventurers at Hamburgh had formed a league with those who are on the side of the Parliament, and that they had been warned by Mr. Avery, the King's resident, that the Adventurers were intending to hold a thanksgiving day for the late victory over the King's forces, which by the enclosed memorial he desired them not to allow, that hitherto the Adventurers had taken no part in the war, that whichever party they might join it might be dangerous for the town, that they had communicated with the Adventurers and obtained a delay to communicate with and learn the pleasure of the Parliament, and therefore desiring a speedy answer. In *Latin*. *Annexed:*

 The Memorial above referred to dated July 8. In *German*. [N. X., 73-74.]

RICHARD DARLEY and others to WILLIAM LENTHALL.

1645, August 8. York.—Are informed that the House has designed 5,000*l*. for this army here as also 5,000*l*. more towards the discharge of the arrears of the officers who are to be dismissed on reducing the army, who are in number above 480. The honour of the state, the necessities of those officers and the present miserable condition of this country press us to beseech you to present to the House, that if these moneys be not speedily sent away to be employed for the purposes intended, the discontentment of the discharged officers, as it hath already in part, will, as we easily foresee, suddenly produce sad effects in the country and kingdom, and the standing army, as it is now moulded, cannot possibly be kept together, if this be not done. *Signed*. [N. IV., 23.]

Captain TUTHILL to Captain STONE.

1645, August 8. Rushall.—"I have just now received intelligence from a man of quality. whose name I may not commit to paper, that the King is come to Bridgenorth this night, and hath with him 4,000 horse. His design is thought to be for the North. These are therefore, if you are doubtful of your strength at Tutbury, to intreat speedily to send them intelligence, that they may either be provided to fight or secure themselves . . . The next news is some forces for us have lately landed at Milford, routed Gerrard, taken four pieces and all carriages, the infantry routed, but the cavalry escaped." [N. IV., 24.]

Major-General EDWARD MASSIE to WILLIAM LENTHALL.

1645, August 9. Lyme.—Desiring that the gift of ironworks in the Forest of Deau to him should be made good, (See *Commons' Journals*, iv. 128.) and that he should himself be employed on active service. *Signed. Seal.* [N. IV., 25.]

WILLIAM LENTHALL to Lieutenant-Colonel COCKAYN.

1645, August 9. Westminster.—Continuing him in command at Newport till further order. (See his letter of the 7th.) *Seal.* [N. IV., 26.]

Colonel RICHARD NORTON to WILLIAM LENTHALL.

1645, August 9. Portsmouth.—Complaining of the want of stores there, out of which a whole cannon, a culverin, and other necessaries had been supplied to Sir Thomas Fairfax, and asking that his brother, now 12 months a prisoner, might be allowed to travel for a year or two into France or Holland. *Seal.* [N. IV., 27.]

[JOHN RUSHWORTH] to WILLIAM LENTHALL.

1645, August 9. Sherborne.—"I have litle newes to adde since my former, for the Clubbmen are quiett since their being well beat att Hambleton Hill. The armie still continues before Shereborne Castle: it proves a difficult peece of worke, wee are undermineinge as fast as may bee, and makeing gallories; by the time the amunicion come to us —which came yesterday by sea to Poole—wee shall bee in a good readiness to fitt the myne for springinge. Wee are very close under theire walls, and make good our ground, notwithstandinge theire many sallyes and throweinge of stoanes on our heads. The greatest hurte they doe us is by two keepers of parkes they have in the garrison, whoe in long fouling peeces, take aime throughe the loope holes in the wall,— for the most parte att commanders—. Captaine Horsey, a valiant honest gentleman was shott dead by one of them, likewise Captaine-Lieutenant Fleminge to Colonel Rainesboroughe whoe is alsoe dead, and both buryed with honour in Shereborne churche: Captaine Horsey, in the tombe there, where his ancestours were formerlie buried. Majour Doane, Captaine Crosse, and Captaine Creamer, all of them of that regiment likewise shott, but wee hope not mortall, most valiant men as any in the armie. Some of them were hurte in beatinge the enemie from a new batterie they were makeinge. Our peeces can doe noe good on the wall, it being twelve foote thicke, but when the great cannon comes, its conceived it will breake downe theire towers, and doe us great service. It is on the way from Poole. The mony is att Weymouth, and while the armee is mustered and paide—which will not bee till Wednesday att soonest, if wee had noe other worke to doe— wee must stay till that bee done and till our recruites of foote come upp, which wee heare are within two dayes marche, and then if wee cannot carry the castle wee must leave a partie to doe it and marche into Devonshire with the armie, for the sommer spends and wee have much worke to doe. But, when wee be come before Exeter, I wish the materialls, and such things soe long sent for to London in order to seidges (sieges) may bee more timouslie sent downe. The Lieutenant-General of the ordinance here saith hee can acquitt himselfe by letter after letter, for great gunne shott, granadoes, great morter peeces etc, but none is as yet come. This armie when wee come before a place, should not stay an houre for materialls. I desire you, Sir, to move —for the Generall above a moneth or five weeks since writt it—that great care bee taken to send downe things fittinge for seidges that being likelie to bee the business att the end of this summer. Goring lyes still and doth nothinge; within a few days I hope we shall rouse him.'

Postscript.—Since the writeinge hereof, newes is come our recruits are this night within seven miles and our gunns and shott nine miles of. I come now from the work. Wee are within tenn yardes and lesse of the castle wall. Our demy cannon are just now planted of a new battery, when the shott comes and the whole cannon, wee shall drive them to a narrow compasse. Wee have dismounted all theire old ordnance; beaten them from all the four towers. Theire grate play is throwinge downe of stoanes. I make noe doubt with God's blessinge, wee shall have them every man. Our newes now is that the king is comeinge to Bristoll, gatheringe all the strength hee can to joyne with Goringe with the Cornish to raise this seidge. I had rather thincke it will prove but a pretence to doe it. Yet the place as to his affaires, and supportinge of the three parties is more considerable then Bridgewater was to him other wayes." *Signature* torn off. *Seal.* [N. IV., 28.]

Francis Pierrepont and others to Willia\) Lenthall.

1645, August 11. York.—"We have seen a paper presented to both Houses . . . by the Commissioners of Scotland, occasioned by our letter to you concerning some informations we received from Cumberland, and although they charge us . . . with calumnies against them, and also put a very hard character and interpretation of our aims and intentions therein, yet by this enclosed, which we beseech you to acquaint the House with, we are cleared and hope to be vindicated in both." *Signed. Seal.* [N. IV., 29.] *Enclosed:*

Sir Wilfrid Lawson and others to the Co\)\ittee for the Northern Association at York.

1645, August 6. Wigton.—Concerning the exactions, demands and menacing language of the Scots. (Printed in Grey, iii. Appendix, No. 19, p. 27.) *Signed.* [N. IV., 17.]

Sir Willia\) Armyne, Thomas Hatcher, and Robert Goodwin, to Willia\) Lenthall.

1645, August 11. York.—"We have advised with the Committee of War at York, and with the Committees of the several Ridings in Yorkshire, and we perceive the number of horse you may expect from the Northern Association towards the blocking up of Newark will be 2,010 horse and 3,520 foot." (For the substance of the remainder, see *Commons' Journals,* iv. 241.) *Signed.* [N. IV., 30.] *Enclosed:*

i. List of Forces arising out of the several Counties of the Northern Association.

1645, August 11.—(See *Commons' Journals,* iv. 241.) [N. XIV., 71.]

ii. The Co\)\ittee of War at York.

[1645, August 11.] — Paper concerning sending forces for blocking up Newark, and suggesting that 1,000 horse be retained out of the forces formerly raised and maintained by the County beyond the number fixed by ordinance of Parliament, and be employed for that service. (See *Commons' Journals,* iv. 241.) [N. XIV., 72.]

Francis Bacon, Sir Thomas Barnardiston, and others, to
William Lenthall

1645, August 11. Bury St. Edmunds. — Stating that the garrison
at Lynn had no pay for a long time, and that their credit being now
exhausted a quarrel between them and the townsmen was to be expected
daily, and therefore desiring that pay might be speedily dispatched.
Signed. [N. IV., 31.]

Sir John Corbett, William Purefoy, Humphrey Salway, and
Edward Bainton to William Lenthall.

1645, August 11. From the Leaguer before Hereford.—" On Wednesday last was sevennight this army marched towards Hereford, and on
the next morneing the foote were drawne upp before the towne. The
Generall forthwith summoned it, and wee—by his advise--sent a letter
to the Maior and corporacion. The trumpeter which was sent could
not bee admitted into the towne but threw his message over the workes,
and wee have just cause to beleeve that our letter came not to the
maior's hands because wee have received noe answer thereunto. Since
wee came hither wee have found the countrey very backward in
assisting us. Though of what wee have assessed on the countrey for the
maintenance of the foote, the provision brought in hath been small,
wee cannot but say wee find a greate deale of chearefulnes and vigour
amongst the souldiers, and doubt not but—upon the first command—they
will bee ready to undertake any further enterprise against this place.
Divers of our men have been slaine in this seidge already, but none of
note save Lievetenant-Colonell Gordon of Colonell Stewart's regiment
who was killed with a greate shott, and is very much lamented in the
army, hee leaveing behind him the memory of a very gallant man. The
enimie hath yett made but one salley worth the takeing notice of, in
which they had two men slaine, and one taken prisoner, with noe losse
on our side. Much of the shott which they shoote are slugges out of
their muskettes, and crosse barr shott out of their ordnance. The
biggest gunn that wee can find to bee in the towne shootes a 12ʰ ball.
Att present the towne is streightly begirt on all sides in most places
within pistoll shott and wee doubt not but speedily to give you a good
accoumpt of Hereford, till which time—had wee not doubted what construction our silence might have mett withall the parliament haveing
comanded us to acquaint them from time to time with our proceedinges—
wee had a mind to have been silent. Wee are advertised that the king hath
been lately in Glamorganshire and other partes of Wales, but cannott
heare of any considerable force that hee is able to raise in those parts,
most of some considerable counties in Wales being of the same humor
with some of the western Clubmen, and now up for their owne defence.
His Excellency receiving certain intelligence of the King's being,
marched to Wolverhampton last night with about 6,000 horse and
dragoons, sent a party consisting of 8 regiments of horse, one of
dragoons and 500 commanded musquetteers on horseback under the
command of Lieutenant-General David Lesley and General-Major
Midleton to attend his motion." (See *Lords' Journals*, vii. 538.)
Signed. Seal. [N. IV., 32.]

The Committee of both Kingdoms residing with the Scotch Army
to the Earl of Leven.

1645, August 11. The Leaguer before Hereford.—Upon advertisement of the King and his forces being at Wolverhampton recommending
that a sufficient force of horse and dragoons be sent to attend their
motions. *Copy.* [N. XIV., 74.]

Sir John Broune to Lord Balierino.

1645, August 12. Rabbicol in Cumberland.—At my return from Newcastle to Cumberland, the Committee there did show me an express from the Committee at York, advising them not to assist the Scots with any entertainment, neither to contribute to any forces whatsoever except the Northern associated forces until such time as the Parliament had settled a garrison at Carlisle. . . . . . Be confident that I shall deport myself so that there shall be no just cause of complaint, although I well perceive and can evidence that the study of some here is to raise the country against me which hath been already attempted . . . Colonel Duglase hath also assured me that he will in no way trouble the country, until business be settled, seeing he can subsist a month. Within that time I hope your Lordship will think of the most convenient way for providing of that garrison, for the Parliament of Scotland doth think it incumbent to the committee with the army to take notice thereof but at this distance it cannot be expected that they will do anything therein. (See *Commons' Journals*, iv. 264.) *Seal.* [N. IV., 32*b*, not noticed in Index.]

George [Lord] Digbye to [George Lord Goring.]

1645, August 12. Lichfield.—"Not only your humble servant, but the King himself, is hugely revived by your cheerful letter of the 4th of August, and with the hopeful propositions made by you to the Prince of Wales' Council for the sudden raising and maintaining a gallant and a well disciplined army, of all which his Majesty extremely approves, as far as at this distance we here can judge of the constitution of those countries, but above all things that which joys us is to find you so resolved on your part to unite in the ways of the King's service heartily and friendly with the rest of his Ministers there, and may they be accursed, whoever they be, that shall not resolve to vie with you in compliance with one another. For what concerns our kind unkindnesses I shall say no more of them, for I am sure when we meet we shall both of us be forward to acknowledge our errors where really they have been. I send you here enclosed a copy of my letter to the Lord Culpeper, wherein you will find the state of the King's business in these parts and of his present resolutions." [N. IV., 33.] *Enclosed:*

[Lord Digbye] to [Lord Culpeper.]

Same date and place.—"Since you left us, we have . . . most luckily performed the second part of our wonderful retreat from Oxford the last year, the King's person with 3,000 horse and 300 musketeers having slipt by within four miles of the Scotch Quarters without ever awaking them so far as to be looked on by them in the rear, nor for ought we know did they so much as suspect the King's being gone till he was thus far. On Friday last, by which time we were at Bridgenorth, I am sure they knew not the king was removed out of Glamorganshire, which I do much attribute unto Sir William Fleming being near the Scotch army upon a secret negotiation with some of them daily pressing for an answer, which made them confident that the King had no intent of removing till he knew the effects of it. Whatever the cause was we are very luckily got thus far out of their reach free to pursue ,

362 : 338 : 95 : e7 : 79 : k4 : 14 : e7 : if they follow us not very quickly with their whole army—for we shall be strong enough by that time we are joined with Newark forces to beat their

horse and dragoons—and if they do we shall be able to lead them such a dance, as to make them lose all the summer in following us, and the King at last, and worst, be able to retreat and pass his winter where he please, besides the dishonour to them of quitting the siege of Hereford, having lost great store of men before it. If they do give us any competent leisure we have very good hopes given us 71 : 56 : 457 : 341 : 457 : 8 : e7 : o9 : 9 : 7 : d5 : 312 : e9 : 23 : 62 : 355 : f6 : 58 : 4 : e8 : 18 : 6 : 56 : k1 : 6 : c1 : 14 : f6 : 460 : 124 : 6 : 186 : m9 : 340 : 504 : 48 : and c1 : 14 : 457 : d6 : 6 : f6 : 405 : and 442 : and that we shall within very few days have up a considerable army of foot and possibly k5 : e1 : 75 : 9 : k4 : 79 : h6 : n10 : 374 : 6 : 79 : q7 : h7 : 186 : m9 : k6 : 31 : o : 79 : k9 : 6 : k8 : k10 : g2 : 231 : k3 : 6 : 1 : 48 : 458 : 56 : f6 : 462 : d4 : k9 : k3 : 8 : m1 : 12 : 79 : m5 : 79 : 8 : 457 : 409 : 6 : Over and above all this, our hopes from Scotland are such, as if all the rest should fail 476 : 457 : 267 : 6 : 209 : c1 : 14 : 504 : o : 208 : 69 : 83 : f6 : 228 : rr : e7 : h7 : 457 : 69 : 8 : 79 : 8 : 6 ꞌ We may reasonably promise ourselves 11 : 230 : 465 : 267 : 81 : e1 : k5 : 93 : 13 : h7 : 61 : to draw even this summer a powerful army thence, for I received but two days since two letters from the Marquess of Montrose, the one of the last of June wherein he tells me that he had reduced the rebels in that kingdom *ad Triarios,* and that if he beat them once more he should be in a condition 11 : 72 : 5 : *0 : 376 : and to send the King a better army thence than ever came against him, that however whether he had another blow at them or not he was now resolved 11 : 51 : 14 : 9 : 73 : 11 : 497 : 12 : 6 : 457 : k5 : 4 : 457 : 8 : e7 : 387 : 6 : f6 : 440 : Since this he writes me another of the 2nd of July relating his great victory that very day against Bayly wherein he killed 1,500 foot upon the place with the loss only of six on his side, whereof the Lord Gordon [was] one, that he was then in pursuit of their horse, which he had totally routed also, which was the reason that he could write no more at that time, but by this and the other letter laid together, I suppose we may imagine 240 : 95 : 1 : 469 : e7 : 87 : 181.

Thus, my Lord, you see what fair probabilities we have—as far as we seem to be chased from you—of looking back comfortably unto you ere this summer be over, if it please God that you in the West can but preserve yourselves from further mischiefs, of which we entertain here much more comfortable thoughts since I last heard from my Lord Goring, in a way of so much beartiness cheerfulness and résolution to draw with you kindly and industriously, whereunto his Majesty makes no question but you will give him all possible encouragement by all friendliness and compliance on your parts, without which good correspondence between you I am sure we must all be lost. God keep and prosper his Highness and bless and prosper your joint endeavours.'

Copy. [N. IV., 34.]

The peaceable MEETING ON COMPTON DOWN, near Ilsley, to the COMMITTEE FOR BERKSHIRE.

1645, August 12.—" Whereas we the knights, gentlemen, freeholders, and others the inhabitants of the County of Berks, who have been for a long time overpressed with the insupportable burdens and contrary commands of the many garrisons and several armies both of the King

---

* Throughout this letter and that of July 4th it is doubtful whether 0 or o is intended.

and of the Parliament . . . lately had a meeting to advise which way we might in the fairest way have but a livelihood and yield a competent proportion to the said garrisons until we might hear of a happy issue of our addresses both to the King and Parliament by our humble petitions now prepared and forthwith to be presented, to which purpose we then gave directions to the High Constables of several Hundreds . . . to give notice to the several inhabitants in the said Hundreds to give us a second meeting to the effect promised, and understanding that for the execution of this our request your Honours have—peradventure upon some misapprehensions—imprisoned John Hamilton of Tilehurst, the High Constable of the Hundred of Reading, we with one general consent earnestly desire that he may be speedily released." *Enclosed:*

DECLARATION.

" We, the miserable inhabitants of the County of Berks . . . foreseeing famine and utter desolation will inevitably fall upon us our wives and children, unless God of His infinite mercy shall . . be graciously pleased to put a period to those sad distractions are unanimously resolved to join in petitioning his Majesty and the two Houses of Parliament for a happy peace and accommodation of the present differences without further effusion of Christian blood. . . In the meantime we with one heart and mind declare that we really intend to the utmost hazard of our lives and fortunes :

1. To defend and maintain the true Reformed Protestant religion.
2. To join with and assist one another in the mutual defence of our laws liberties and properties against all plunderers and all other unlawful violence whatsoever.
3. We do hereby resolve and faithfully promise each to other that if any person or persons whatsoever, who shall concur with and assist us in those our resolutions happen to suffer in his person or estate in execution of the premises it shall be as the suffering of the generality and reparation shall be made to the party suffering according to his damage, and in case of loss of life provision shall be made for his wife and children and all this to be done at a conscionable rate and allowance to the uttermost ability of all the associates.
4. Lastly we do declare all such unworthy of our assistance as shall refuse to join with us in the prosecution of these our just intentions." [N. XXII., 79.]

The MEETING this present day at the bushes ON COMPTON DOWN to ——— ———.

1645, August 12.—" Whereas we are informed that the High Constable of Reading Hundred is lately imprisoned for sending forth tickets according to the general direction at the meeting on Ilsley Downs, when you were both present, it is earnestly desired by the like general consent that you would be pleased to repair together with Mr. Ilsley and Mr. Wilder to present the petition directed to the Honourable the Committees at Reading for his releasement. You are both earnestly desired to be at the next meeting which is appointed on Tuesday next, the 19th August instant." [N. XIV., 74a.]

SIR HENRY VANE, junior, SIR WILLIAM ARMYNE, THOMAS HATCHER, and ROBERT GOODWIN to WILLIAM LENTHALL.

1645, August 13. Newcastle.—" We have received this morning intelligence from the Committee of War at York, that the king is at

Lichfield with a considerable strength of horse, and as Sir John Gell gives notice, intends for Newark, and therefore we humbly offer it once again to the consideration of the House, whether it may not be thought requisite to keep on those horse we mentioned in our last letters of the 11th . . Besides we understand that there are very near 800 more that are scattered up and down in Yorkshire, and doubtless will draw to a head upon the first occasion, and no man knoweth for want of pay what party they may adhere unto." *Signed. Seal.* The letter bears several endorsements of the persons through whom it was transmitted. [N. IV., 35.]

SIR JOHN CORBETT, WILLIAM PUREFOY, EDWARD BAINTON, and HUMPHREY SALWAY to WILLIAM LENTHALL.

1645, August 13. From the Leaguer before Hereford.—Enclosing a paper delivered to them by the Committee of the Scotch Estates and their answer, and desiring that a copy of the treaty concerning the coming of the Scotch army, and of such orders as have been passed for their taking free quarter, and of the rules to be observed about the same, may be sent, and also enclosing a copy of the order by which Lieutenant-General David Leslie's party marched after the King. (See *Commons' Journals*, iv. 245.) *Signed. Seal.* [N. IV., 36.] Probably *Enclosed:*

i. The COMMITTEE OF THE ESTATES OF SCOTLAND and the LORD GENERAL to the COMMISSIONERS OF PARLIAMENT.

1645, August 5.—"Whereas the Scotch army at the earnest desires of both Houses, and on their manifold promises that provisions of all sorts should be in readiness for them have advanced southwards from Nottingham and now are engaged in a siege before Hereford, the Committee of Estates . . . . and the Lord General have thought it incumbent on them to acquaint the Commissioners . . . that during the whole time of their march they have been wrestling with extreme penury and want of victual for the soldiers. That they have had little or no assistance from the country of teams, which has been a great impediment to the march. That ever since the army's engagement before Hereford and the . . . Commissioners coming to reside with them, notwithstanding all the warrants issued for bringing in provisions the army's wants are a great deal more pressing than formerly, for in these eight days past there has not above one half day's provision been brought them, and the service they are now engaged in necessarily requires their constant attendance in Leaguer, so as they cannot go abroad to provide for themselves. And therefore . . . to desire that the said Commissioners . . . would condescend particularly what provisions of victual and ammunition the army may for this present service expect and depend upon, how much of the 200*l. per diem* promised . . . is in readiness and when to be received, what number of teams and what assistance from the country people for making of the works they will undertake to afford." *Signed* "John Prymerose."

ii. The ENGLISH COMMISSIONERS' Answer.

1645, August 8.—"Whatsoever failing of payments or provisions have beene to the Scottish army now in England have not proceeded from any want of affection or intention in the parliament to make good their engagements but from the greate straights they are in for want of money.

Att a consultation had with the Committee of Estates of Scotland and his Excellency at Micheldeane, 29th July last, the commissioners appointed by the Parliament of England to reside in the Scottish army agreed to lay seige to Hereford, being by them informed that by any intelligence they could gaine, the enemy had not a visible body to be pursued, but were devided into severall parties, which were adjudged inexpedient to be further followed with the whole army into soe mountainous a country, where a small part might miscarry and a greater could not with safety be spared from the army, nor have subsistence there.

If any wants of provision have happened to the army before the commissioners came to reside there, they can give noe accompt thereof, but are confident that those persons who were imployed by the Parliament for accommodating the army did theire utmost endeavours to effect the same and to advance the publicke service.

The army comming before Hereford last of July, the commissioners of Parliament caused their warrants uppon the place to be instantly issued forth, not onely to the high constables of all the Hundreds in the county of Hereford, but allso to the committees of the adjacent counties for the bringing in of 200*l. per diem* in money and provisions, much fruite whereof could not be expected in fower dayes' time, consideration being had of the malignancy of the country, and their distraction uppon the approach of this army, many high constables and petty constables absenting themselves and divers who appeared were fearefull and backward to execute the warrants which much retarded the service.

The horse allso taking free quarter in those parts, out of which the dayly provision was to be brought for the foote, not onely before the army sate downe at Hereford, but since, plundering of horses, taking away goodes and cattell of all kindes and some officers taking uppon them to send forth warrants for money and provisions of all sorts hath disabled many from providing and bringing in proportionable supplyes.

By all which the raising of provisions for the army is very much obstructed, and some provisions raised and uppon the way towardes the commissary have beene intercepted, and violently taken away by the souldiers.

And as for the proportions which are assessed upon Monmoth, Radnour and other counties, together with the remote parts of this county of Hereford, they cannot be had without a coercive power to obtaine them.

The commissioners are resolved to continue their best endeavours to cause 200*l. per diem* in moneys and provisions to be furnished for the infantery of the army, together with other necessaryes, and beleeve they shall effect the same, the obstructions above mentioned being removed.

And they concurre with the Committee of Estates of Scotland and his Excellency, the Lord Generall, that the true causes of the neglect of publique service—if any shall happen—may be knowne to the world for the exoneration of those who are engaged in it." *Signed* "John Cely." *Copy.* [N. XIX., 120.] A copy of the first is N. XIV., 69.

The House of Commons to the Earl of Leven.

[1645, August 13.]—Informing him of the King's advance to Lichfield, and desiring him to send a strong party of horse and dragoons to attend the enemy's motions. (See *Commons' Journals*, iv. 240.) *Draft.* [N. XII., 116a.]

The Prince of Wales to George Lord Goring.

1645, August 13. Padstow.—Desiring him to meet some of his Council and some persons of authority in those parts at Okehampton the following Monday in order to take measures for the recruiting of the army. *Counter-signed* " Richard Fanshawe." *Sign Manual. Seal.* [N. I., 30.]

Colonel Thomas Morgan to William Lenthall.

[1645, August 14 (?). Gloucester.]—It is well known to some members and also to a great part of this county what pains and travail I have taken since my coming here " in labouring to draw the distracted garrisons and discontented souldiers into any defensive posture, and indeede the onely means of our preservation hetherto . . hath beene in regaurd the enemy hath not had of late any breathing time to fall upon us before the last Lord's Day, at which time he having some inteligence of our weakness in horss, theire beeing only two or three broken troops in all the county, came out from Bristoll—Prince Ruport in parson—who joyning with the men of Bartcley maid up there number fourteen or fifteen hundreth horss and foote which violently and sudanly stormed a guard of ours two miles from Bartcley to keepe in that castle, put twenty of them to the sword in could blood, tooke the captain his ensigne with seven common souldiers prisonours, bourut the house and some other neare unto it, plundred and rainged up and dowen that part of the cuntrey, but upon Monday early I drew dowen all the foote I could, who joyning with the broken troopes faced and skirmished with them and tooke one lieutenant of horss to the Prince, slaying as maney of theirs, and withall sent speedy mesingers to Bath to intercept them —if possibley the could—in their retreate but they not staying longe nor adventureing to press further into the cuntrey in reguard I had stopped the narrow passages and lyned the hedges with musquetteers although they were farr stronger than wee espetially in horss yet they drew of for that time, but the like hazard we shall dayly be subject unto here-after to the greate dainger of the county, if wee have not a considerable body of horss to oppose against them. I have since my coming hither daily expected Collonel Cooke his coming with his regiment of horss, but I finde no certanty in it, moreover the burthen of the Scotch army quartering for a time in this county upon free billet hath much im-poverished a greate part of it, and our sending them three of our greatest peeces of ordnance, fifty barells of poudour, twenty whereof wee were enforced to fech from Malmesbury—it beeing for the publique good—with a proportionabl quantity of balle and match with teames and carriages for to tranceporte them to the leager neare Heriford, besides keepeing theire sicke men neare our garinson, hath not a litle charged and presed the county to crie out for suckour and support if they knew how to be remided and as though these prisniers were not suffitient to undowe and ruien a county wee are charged by the com-itioners residing about Heriford with 20*l. per diem* towards theire maintinance notwithstanding a great part of the county be under the power of the enemy. I dare not be too troublesome else I could say much to express the deplourable condition and bleedeing estate of this county. . . . *Postscript.*—Upon the closing of this letter I had news that the forces of Bath and those parts upon my advertisement fell upon the Prince in his retreat. What defeat they have given him I am not yet informed, but divers of them are come wounded to Bartcley and some my party met with and gave them Scotch quarter." (See *Commons' Journals,* iv. 248.) *Signed. Seal.* [N. IV., 48 should be 47.]

The Scotch Commissioners.

1645, August 14.—Paper. (Printed in *Lords' Journals,* vii. 539.) *Signed* " Jo. Cheislie." [N. XIX., 123.]

Sir John Gell to William Lenthall.

1645, August 15. Derby.—" I have given an accompte . . . of the Kinges motion from Bridgenorth unto Ashburne in our countye, and this last night his head quarter was at Chatsworth. I doe perceave that his intent is to goe into the remotest partes northward of this kingdome, by some letters that were found in some of the prysoners' pockettes that wee have taken. His strength is now most certeynly two thousand fightinge men, and of those, there is one hundred and twenty foot, two hundred dragoones. The rest, for the most parte, both ill armed and ill horsed. And truly, if upon my summons by request and upon my intelligence given unto Yorke, Collonell Rosciter, Nottingham, and Leicester with our owne have pleased to have joyned, I doubt not but to have rendred his Majestie unto his parliament. And yet if upon more serious thoughts, theise counties will followe, there is little doubt to bee made of takeinge his forces. Our horse, with parte of Stafford's are now joyned, and doe followe in the reare, but a forlorne of one hundred of ours were more valient then discreet, they charged five hundred of the enemies, tooke some sixteene prisoners, whereof Captain Blake, formerly a majour of foot, was one. Twentye more were slayne of the enemyes, wee had one slayne and ten more taken. Soe wee sent a trumpett for exchange which did take effect. The kinge was pleased to send for my trumpett, and did enquire what forces did follow him. The kinge did seeme to beleeve him and desired to knowe what they were, the trumpett answered a great strength of the Scottes horse. Now I have some hopes that Collonell Rosciter will joyne. . . *Postscript.*—Since I writt this letter I receaved intelligence from Lieuetenant-General Leasely whoe kept his Randevouz at Sturbridge in Staffordshire the 14th of this instant August and is marching as fast as hee can after the kinge." (See *Commons' Journals,* iv. 245.) *Signed. Seal.* [N. IV., 37.]

Colonel Henry Mildmay and others to William Lenthall.

1645, August 15. Trinity College, Cambridge.—Stating that 40 weeks' pay is due to the officers and soldiers, and the complaints made by the poorer inhabitants for money due to them for quarters. (Printed in Grey, iii. Appendix, No. 44, p. 70.) *Signed.* [N. IV., 38.]

William Lenthall to the Earl of Leven and the Committee of both Kingdoms residing with the Scotch Army.

[1645, August 15.]—(Printed in *State Papers, Domestic,* p. 67.) (See *Commons' Journals,* iv. 242.) *Draft.* [N. XII., 128.]

Several Yorkshire Gentlemen to [Ferdinando Lord Fairfax].

[1645, August 15th.]—*Colonel-General Poynts.*—The gentlemen, finding the election of officers was carried by partiality, crave you to move the House for an order empowering me to grant Commissions in future. *Mr. Pierrepont.*—Unless the Parliament by themselves or the Committee of both kingdoms appoint the officers to be continued in the New Model, and take some course for employing others as well deserving as any that may be retained we shall here run headlong to destruction. The most part of the horse we had drawn to Doncaster to oppose the enemy's coming into this county in a mutinous way left their guards there, and came towards York, giving out they would plunder the city and cut the throats of the Committee. *Mr. Chaloner.* —Here has been a week of much distraction, the officers not elected extremely discontented to be set by without pay, which was represented to us by some of them by way of remonstrance, which I suppose you have seen from Captain Harrison, who was a remonstrant himself. Colonel Overton likewise complained of an undue election by a combination of kindred—as he expressed it—in that Committee of the East Riding of their Foot Colonel. Yesterday morning came a letter from our Colonel-General of the mutinying of the whole army. They would be at no command of officers, they had set upon himself a guard of firelocks, nothing less than one month's pay would content them. *Mr. Farrer.*—Our army is in great distraction, and yesterday at Doncaster mutinied. The Dragoons began, and the Commander-in-Chief called for all the horse, intending to force them to obedience. But they joined the Dragoons and with a general consent took him into custody, and kept him in a chamber with many insolent speeches, that if he provide them not a month's pay by Saturday night they will all go to York, and plunder it, and all the Committees there, and to day sent some of the discreetest commanders to intimate so much to the Committees. It is generally suspected that some of our Commanders have occasioned this mutiny. *Mr. Stockdale.*—This unhappy distemper prevents us of the hope we had to be masters of these three Castles in a few days. The sieges are like to be deserted, and if the king's and the Newark forces come on they will be presently masters of the field in this county. *Mr. Thorp.*—Touching the election of officers and the reducement. *Colonel-General Poynts.*—On coming hither I tendered the horse 10s. a piece, which the Committee sent them, which they utterly rejected and fell into a general mutiny, horse, foot, and dragoons, swearing they would plunder York and hang up the Committee, and because I had promised them a month's pay set a guard on my quarters, requiring security for it of me, but with much ado I pacified them till I should intimate their desires to the Committee. Your Honour may imagine what encouragement I receive in this employment, and can expect no change till the Army is satisfied. *Mr. Hatter.*—Worse than this the foot, who have been constantly paid weekly, on the mutiny of the horse, are mostly run away, some whole companies marching none knows whither with their colours flying. The enemy cannot but know of it, and will certainly shortly take advantage of it, and then the North is in great danger to be lost. (See *Commons' Journals*, iv. 247.) *Extracts*, read by Lord Fairfax. [N. XII., 117.]

The English Commissioners to Scotland to the Earl of Lauderdale.

1645, August 16. Berwick.—(Printed in *Lords' Journals* vii. 566.) *Copy*. [N. XII., 113.]

WALTER STRICKLAND to WILLIAM LENTHALL.

1645, August 16-26. Leuerdin in Friesland.—Having communicated the Parliament's declaration to the assemblies of Guelderland, Holland, and Zealand and found that it much satisfied all who considered it, I went to Utrecht where the States were not assembled, and the Deputies who act when they are not assembled alleged they had no power to hear what my audience imported, but desired me to return where the States were sitting. I then came here where the States were not assembled, which usually happens only once a year in February, but the Deputies who act in their absence, gave me a fair and courteous audience and received the Declaration with thankfulness, as appears by the enclosed answer, not differing much from that of Guelderland. I was here eight days before the Deputies despatched me, all which time I spent in giving such impressions as the *Opening the King's Cabinet* furnished me with, which before my coming from the Hague I had got prepared for them in a language they understand. I am now going into Overyssel and then to Groningen. I express my gratitude to the Parliament for their great favours to me. *Seal.* [N. IV., 39.]

PETER TEMPLE, Sheriff, and others to WILLIAM LENTHALL.

1645. August 16. Leicester.—Sir Thomas Fairfax hath commanded a garrison of 1,000 foot and 500 horse to be maintained here. This town and county are altogether unable to pay such a force, nor are there horses left in this county nor money to provide them. Your order of 1,500*l.* to buy horse and arms out of Delinquents' estates comes too late for our present exceeding great wants. We earnestly entreat that some course may be taken for the payment of these out of the public, and also that 250 horse with saddles, bridles, and pistols be appointed for us, and also 100 carbines. This garrison securing all trade betwixt the North and South of England as some help towards the maintenance thereof we ask for an order to receive the King's and Queen's revenues, the excise money and the sequestrations, and all the uncollected moneys and arrears in this county belonging to the public, and also for an order to compound with those who appeared here in arms at the King's taking of the town, which caused great number of the common people to follow them, and had not Sir Thomas Fairfax put a sudden stop to those beginnings they had drawn the whole county from the Parliament. The garrison of Newark is so strong that we are not able to subsist by it without your help. We humbly entreat that whatever is thought fit may be done speedily, and lastly that a power be given us and the Governor to call a council and exercise Martial Law. (See *Commons' Journals*, iv. 257.) *Signed. Seal.* [N. IV., 40.]

The EARL OF LAUDERDALE to the COMMISSIONERS OF THE PARLIAMENT OF ENGLAND.

1645 (in one copy wrongly 1644), August 17.—Printed in *Lords' Journals*, vii. 553.) Two *copies.* [N. IV., 41 ; XII., 114.]

RICHARD HATTER to [FERDINANDO] LORD FAIRFAX.

1645, August 17. York.—"This morning Colonel Poynts wrote unto the Committee here . . that he had received intelligence that the King quartered on the 15th . . at Staley House belonging to Mr. Fretchvile, Governor of Welbeck, six miles from Sheffield, the number of his forces 3,000 besides the Newark 1,500 horse and 500 dragoons joined with him the 16th in the morning. It is supposed they intend for Halifax and so Northward. The chief commanders with him are Sir Thomas Glemham and Sir Marmaduke Langdale. Our forces are drawn from Sandall, Skipton, and Bolton. The horse quarters are along the South side of this river towards Turn Bridge and the foot at Brotherton and other towns on the North side. We are forced to decline an engagement of our forces, not daring to trust them alone at this time, in regard—besides they are fewer in number than the enemy— the great discontent they are in by the late reducement and for want of pay. . . . There is great necessity that the Parliament should take notice of the officers here, who are to be cashiered. If some order come not down for their encouragement there is very great fears that both officer and soldier will forsake the field, and that very shortly . . . Colonel Rossetter is in the Isle of Axholme coming towards us, but we are much troubled, for the enemy is interposed between Nottingham, Derby, and Stafford forces and us, whereby we cannot for the present join together, and we never had yet any assistance from the three North counties, and but a very few from Westmoreland and Lancashire. The cloud is very black; I pray God, if it be His will, it may blow over." *Seal.* [N. IV., 42.]

THOMAS CHALONER and others to WILLIAM LENTHALL.

1645, August 17. York.—"We have lately represented . . the dangerous constitution of this army as now it stands betwixt the condition of those reduced and the number elected to stand in this county, both parties being full of discontents for want of the arrears of pay, and for that cause they do join altogether in mutual mutinies against their commanders, whereof the enemies making advantage of the opportunity have drawn their forces to the borders of this country, and, as we understand, are quartered about the same parts where our forces lately quartered against Welbeck and Newark, and our men drawn off from thence and from all the sieges in this County are now retiring towards York, unless they find themselves able to make good some pass against the enemies' forces. But the discontents of our soldiers having been declared in so high a manner are such as we can have no assurance of their uniting and resolute opposition of the enemy, unless we were furnished with moneys to give them satisfaction according to their demands, and that being wanting we have no other way to prevent the universal ruin and loss of this country but by our humble address to the House to desire the speedy supply of those moneys formerly designed to us towards the satisfaction of the vast arrears of the commanders and soldiers." . . . . We further request that "two or three thousand horse and dragoons at least may be despatched from the Southern parts to follow the rear of the enemy's army to remorate their attempts in these parts, until the Parliament's forces can be drawn into a body and be able to give them a field. . . ." *Signed. Seal.* [N. IV., 43.]

SIR GEORGE GRESLEY and others to WILLIAM LENTHALL.

1645, August 18. Derby.—"How miserably this county hath been afflicted by the enemy is well known to all men, Newcastle's army, the Queen's, Prince Rupert's, Goring's and others having made prize of what they could get from our poor neighbours. The enemies have formerly had several garrisons in this county all kept by them for no other use but to oppress us. Though these be now recovered yet it was done by force, and not without great charge to the whole country. Ashby, Tutbury, Newark—and Welbeck of late—, all enemies' garrisons, have power and means still to compel contributions from us and ruin those that deny them. The army of our brethren of Scotland was for a time very chargeable to this county which since hath been a passage for other forces of our friends, who have all lived upon free quarter and supplied themselves with such horses as came in their way. The King's army is now amongst us; they have passed through and made spoil of a great part of this shire. Some of the Parliament party are already come to our help, and more we daily expect, all which will have free quarter at least, and for those few horses that are left their owners have little hope to keep them long." We ask the House to grant us the excise of this town and county for the present maintenance of our own soldiers.

Postscript.—"Just now our soldiers are in mutiny, and 200 of them gone away with their arms." *Signed. Seal.* [N. IV., 44.]

JOHN HOBARTE and TRISTRAM DYᴀOND to WILLIAᴅ LENTHALL.

1645, August 19. Wisbech.—We received an order of Parliament for raising within the county of Cambridge and Isle of Ely 32 Harque-bushiers to be employed about Grantham, and an ordinance of July 18th for   horses more within the said county and Isle. We sent out our warrants forthwith for levying the necessary money, but having only three days allowed us we advanced the money, amounting to 200*l.*, expecting to receive it again on our warrants. But the order not mentioning any distress to be taken the greater part of the inhabitants refuse to pay their proportions, wherefore, unless the House gives us power to distrain, it is more than probable we shall lose the greatest part of that money. There are two divisions in our Isle, North and South, and most of the Committee living in the South, the whole business and burden of the North lies upon us. We therefore desire the House to appoint some Committeemen for the Isle living in and about Wisbech. *Signed.* [N. IV., 45.]

Captain WILLIAᴅ BATTEN to [WILLIAᴅ LENTHALL].

1645, August 19. From aboard the *St. Andrew,* in Plymouth Sound. —Being sent by the Committee for the Admiralty and Cinque Ports to Milford Haven to displace Captain Swanley, and settle Captain Molton in his place, on account of some information given the Committee against him . . . he stands much on his justification, which being clear and the information found false, I am confident the House will vindicate him for the good service he has done. He was very obedient to the order, and during my stay there very forward in advancing the public good, and so had been, by report of the well affected, during his whole employment. " I arrived there the 29th July, which day the Maior-Generall had taken the feild, with about eight hundred foot and horse, for the pre-servacion of there corne, dayly threatned by the enemy to be fired, who lay neere Harfordwest and duble our number drew out to give them battle. The Mayior-generall hearing of my arrivall, sent unto me for my assistance wheruppon I sent upp the *Warwick* friggot with two hundred seamen to land within two myles of our army, the one halfe of them myne owne men. The enemy not knowing of the seamen's landing, drew out to give us battle, wherein it pleased our good God to give us the day by routing there whole army, takeing and killing neere as many of them as our army consisted of; fower gunns, fower barrells of powder, all there carriages and neere one thousand armes, with the losse of but one man on our parte—but many wounded—. This was performed in the compass of one hower, by two troops of horse, and one hundred foot which had the forlorne hope; our mavue body haveing not tyme to come upp. About one hundred and twenty of the enimies' forces fled into the Castle of Harford, which wee begirt three daies and a demy cannon sent upp from the *Lyon* for battery but did no execucion, the walls being so extreame thick ; which Captain Thomas perceaving tould the Mayior-Generall if he would give the seamen the plunder they would undertake to storme it—which was promised, but not performed— who presently made a great fire at the gate, scaled the walles in divers places, and so gott posesion of that towne and castle, and at my comeing away from thence, our forces were sate downe before Cary Castle, which was the 12th instant, and doubt not if the businis be well followed but you shall have a good accompt of all the small garrisons thereaboutes very shortly.

The prisoners being in number seven hundred were sent downe to me to secure them amongst the shipps, which I did accordingly, in which tyme I received letters from the Lord Inchequeene of the streightned condicion of Youhall—a coppie whereof goeth hereinclosed.—I have sent him four hundred and forty of the prisoners lately taken who have all taken the Covenant and expresse great forwardnes to serve against the Irish. I suppose they arrived the 13th instant. All the officers —two excepted—refused the Covenant, who are still in durance—so that I sent no officers with them.—I have sent him likewise out of myne owne shipp 8,000*li.* of bisket and ten barrells of powder, and out of the amunicion for Sir John Prise three hundred musketts onely, ten barrells of match, with bullett answerable and thirty barrells of powder out of the garrisons.

At my being at Milford, I received a letter from Sir Thomas Fairefax to let me know he had left six hundred souldiers about Bridg-water for Pembroakshire and desired shipping to be sent for them. Whereuppon I sent one shipp and three small barkques, but were not retourned at my comeing from thence.

The news at my comeing away was that the King was in Cardife the 8th of the moneth, who was demaunded by twenty thousand Club-men that are rissen, as they pretend to carry him to the parliament. There are many of good quallity amongst them, and well armed.

The king got away with a small party of horse to Ragland Castle. It is reported that the king endeavored to put the towne of Cardife into Papasts' hands to secure, which would not be indured, but on the contrary, the Welsh plundred them sufficiently. Those that escaped have sent there goods to Bristow.

The Clubmen likewise demaunded Gerrard and vow to cutt him in peeces for firing the corne and plundering the county of Penbrooke. That Sir Jacob Ashley is made Mayior-generall of South Walies in place of Gerrard, I saw in a letter under his owne hand.

That the seamen being forty in number prisoners at Cardife and Newport were released by the king without exchange, and some of them [were] at Milfourd Haven before my comeing from thence.

At my retourne from Milford I espied a saile to the seaboard of the Ilaud of Lundee. I sent Captain Thomas after her, who brought her in unto me, whom I found to be a Frenchman laden with salt, etc., and bound for Wexfourd. I shall take care to send her upp speedily." *Signed.* [N. IV., 46.]

WALTER POWELL, Vicar of Standish, to the HOUSE OF COMMONS.

[1645, August 20.]—Petition, stating that he had been plundered by the King's army of 400*l.* or 500*l.*, hath been used as a rebel for adhering to Parliament, hath waited almost twenty weeks to deliver a petition for the remedy of some grievances and for propositions for the raising of 1,000*l.* for the benefit of the State for the enlargement of his son-in-law Captain Bayly, now a prisoner in Hereford, and praying that the said grievauces and propositions might be referred to some Committee. [N. XXII., 82.]

Order of the HOUSE thereon.

1645, August 20. — (Printed in *Commons' Journals,* iv. 249.) [N. XXII., 83.]

Major-General MASSIE to the HOUSE.

(In support of the above petition.)   [N. XXII., 84.]

The COMMITTEE FOR PETITIONS.

1645, August 20.—Resolution on Sir Gregory Norton's petition. (Printed in *Commons' Journals,* iv. 269.)   [N. XIV., 75.]

The COMMITTEE FOR PETITIONS.

1645, August 20.—Resolution on the petition of the town and parish of Bradford.   (See *Commons' Journals,* iv. 269.)   [N. XIV., 76.]

The HOUSE OF COMMONS.

1645, August 20.—Order made on a letter from Colonel Morgan. (See *Commons' Journals,* iv. 248.)   [N. XIV., 77.]

The SCOTCH COMMISSIONERS.

1645, August 22.—Paper, recapitulating the charges and proceedings against Mr. Barwis, Mr. Lamplugh, Sir Wilfred Lawson, and others, and desiring that the informations of Mr. Osmotherly and Mr. Musgrave, the petition of Mr. Barwis, the letter from the Committee of York, our several answers and a letter from Sir John Broune herewith delivered, be referred to a committee on the place authorised by both kingdoms so far as may concern the Scotch army. (See *Commons' Journals,* iv. 264.)   *Signed* " Jo. Cheislie."   [N. XIX., 125.]

Lieutenant-General DAVID LESLIE to the COMMITTEE OF BOTH KINGDOMS.

1645, August 22.—(Printed in *Lords' Journals,* vii. 550.)   *Seal.* [N. IV., 48.]

THOMAS CHAMBERLIN, Mayor, and others to WILLIAM LENTHALL.

1645, August 22. Stafford.—Stating the inconvenience caused by the excessive number of officers which causes a want of pay, and that want discontent amongst them which hath au influence upon the soldiers and causeth daily irregularities. Six months ago. . . . we joined with the county in a petition to that Committee (of both kingdoms) that we might have power to reduce all our horse and foot—which at that time were about 700 and under six colonels—unto two regiments only one of horse another of foot.   This petition we hear hath been brought into the House, but . . . could not be taken into consideration unto this day, so that our forces remain all in many broken troops and companies to the discontent of the country and disadvantage of the public service. We therefore humbly desire power to reduce all our horse and foot into two regiments as aforesaid. *Signed.*   *Seal.* [N. IV., 49.]

Sir John Corbett and another to William Lenthall.

1645, August 22. From the camp before Hereford.—Acknowledging his letter with the expressions of the sense the House of Commons had of their despatching a party to attend upon the motions of the King's forces, and declaring that as on that occasion, so on every other they would do their best to make it evident that the common cause, according to the Covenant, was the chief desire of their hearts. *Signed.* [N. IV., 61.]

[William Lenthall] to Sir John Corbett and others, the Committee with the Scotch Army.

1645, August 23.—In reply to theirs of the 13th approving of their conduct and enclosing copies of the treaty and the letter to several counties desired therein. *Draft.* [N. XII., 120.]

The English Commissioners to Scotland to the Earl of Loudoun.

1645, August 24. Berwick.—Desiring him to effect that the Committee appointed by the Scotch Parliament might give them a speedy meeting. *Copy.* [N. XII., 121.]

The Ministers of London and Westminster and within the lines of communication to the Parliament.

1645, August 25.—Petition. (Printed in *Lords' Journals*, vii. 558.) On parchment. [N. XXII., 78.]

William Lenthall to the Earl of Leven and the Committee with the Scotch Army.

1645, August 25.—"Your horse and 3 or 4,000 of ours are in pursuit of the King. If they continue joined we doubt not but that, with God's assistance, they may within a few days give such an account of their design as may be much for the advantage of both kingdoms. If yours and ours should sever, the King who hath already taken Huntingdon may endanger the Association and be able quickly to go again Northward. The House of Commons thought it necessary to acquaint you herewith and leave it to your serious consideration." (See *Commons' Journals*, iv. 253.) *Draft.* [N. XII., 124.]

Colonel John Fiennes to the Committee of both Kingdoms.

1645, August 25.—"I endeavoured to keep my troops together being old soldiers and fittest for field service till the Committees of those counties where they quartered caused the country to rise upon them, and gave orders to the Governors of garrisons and captains of troops under their pay to fall upon them as enemies for no reason but because they took free quarter, a very harsh reward for soldiers that have done the State so good service as your Lordships know they have done. Though my officers did not at all fear what these men durst do against them, but could in despite of them and did keep their quarters till they received orders from me to remove, yet it was not fit for me to oblige them by orders . . . either to fight the Parliament's friends, or expose themselves to affronts and indignities not standing with the honour of soldiers to endure." I therefore resigned the command of the regiment and gave discharges to the officers of the several troops and now ask for a pass and discharge for myself. (See *Commons' Journals*, iv. 240.) [N. IV., 50.]

Lieutenant-General DAVID LESLIE to the COMMITTEE OF BOTH KINGDOMS.

1645, August 25. Stapleford.—Informing them of the King's movements and those of himself, Colonel-General Poynts and Colonel Rossiter. (Printed in Grey, iii. Appendix, No. 56, p. 90.) *Signature torn off. Seal.* [N. IV., 51.]

FRANCIS PIERREPONT and others to WILLIAM LENTHALL.

1645, August 26. York.—Concerning the mutinies in the army, and their difficulty in paying them. (Printed in Grey, iii. Appendix, No. 45, p. 71.) *Signed.* [N. IV., 52.]

Lieutenant-General DAVID LESLIE to the COMMITTEE OF BOTH KINGDOMS.

Same date.—Informing them of his intention to march to Scotland. (Printed in Grey, iii. Appendix, No. 57, p. 91.) *Seal.* [N. IV., 53.]

Lieutenant-General DAVID LESLIE to the SCOTCH COMMISSIONERS in London.

1645, August [26 misdated 22], Nottingham. (The first part is to the same effect as his letter of the same date to the Committee of both kingdoms. It proceeds thus:) " I had resolved to have taken but half my party and to have left Major-General Middleton with the rest to join with Colonel-General Poyntz to follow the King, but neither officer nor soldier was willing to stay, the soldiers professing openly they would all for their country, so considering their unwillingness to stay, and that the half of my party was not sufficient without a a conjunction of forces with me in Scotland to do the work without hazard, I resolved to go with all . . . I know some will censure me for this action, but, if they look on the business seriously I am confident it will be thought good service done to England, for if Montrose continue a while in Scotland without oppositions he would or long change the business in England, for though particular counties suffer for a time, if the public suffer not in general, that is not much. There be few horses left with our foot near Hereford. It were good for General Poinze and Colonel Rosseter with other county forces had order to attend the King's motions, and chiefly to interpose betwixt him and our army, yet I am confident the King cannot much trouble them. I entreat you to represent this to the Committee of both Kingdoms. . . ." *Copy.* [N. XII., 118.] *Enclosed :*

The EARL OF LOUDOUN to [Generals LESLIE and MIDDLETON].

1645, August 22. Berwick.—The Rebels " are now masters of the field running over and destroying the country, and will in all appearance prevail to do what they will, till God enable us to have an army in the field to oppose them, which if not speedily done—besides the ruin of this poor Kingdom—they will grow to such strength by Malignants, . . . and by pressing recruits in the country as may make a strong army, and invite the King to come . . hither, or they to march to him, and so increase the troubles and wars in both kingdoms. For preventing whereof and for preservation of Religion, liberties and this kingdom from destruction it is conceived there is no meane so

. . effectual, as the speedy return of our army from England, whom God has made so useful there, to march with all haste, for employing their whole strength and endeavours for opposing and suppressing these bloody Rebels, and recovery of their native kingdom. . . . For which end I or some other person of trust will be sent to you after our meeting tomorrow at Duns for advising what can be done in the meantime till the army comes. But till . . we have some body of an army on foot, to which the country's forces may resort, there will be no means of resistance made to the enemy. And therefore it is most earnestly desired that one or both of you may march hither with as great a strength of your cavalry as may be spared, securing the foot till the whole army come, with whom such forces shall be joined as can be raised in the country. The distress and danger of this kingdom, and the cause which we are sworn to maintain and your affection for both are so strong arguments for this public duty, as I trust will set you on present action to march hither." . . . *Copy.* [N. XII., 119.]

The EARL OF LOUDOUN and others to the ENGLISH COMMISSIONERS. 1645, August 26. Duns.—

The ENGLISH COMMISSIONERS to the EARL OF LOUDOUN and others.

Same date. —

Some of the SCOTCH COMMISSIONERS to the ENGLISH COMMISSIONERS.

[Same date.]—(All three printed in *Lords' Journals,* vii. 566.) *Copies.* [N. XII., 122, 123, 125.]

SIR RICHARD EVERARD, Sheriff, and others, to the COMMITTEE OF BOTH KINGDOMS.

1645, August 26. Chelmsford.—We send you our last from Colonel Mildmay at Cambridge. We desired your Lordships by our last to think upon some to order all our Associated forces which we are raising and repeat our desire that our Lord Lieutenant, the Earl of Warwick, be appointed to the command. *Signed.* [N. IV., 54.]

Colonel-General SEDNHAM POYNTS to the COMMITTEE OF BOTH KINGDOMS.

1645, August 27. Nottingham.—Informing them of Leslie's march to Scotland, and of his own intention to pursue the King's forces. (Printed in Grey, iii. Appendix, No. 58, p. 92.) *Seal.* [N. IV., 55.]

The SAME to the SAME.

[Same date and place.]—Stating that he had been hindered in his intended pursuit of the King by the mutiny of his whole army, who would not stir without pay. (Printed in Grey, iii. Appendix, No. 43, p. 69.) (See *Commons' Journals,* iv. 258.) *Seal.* [N. IV., 63.]

SIR HENRY VANE, SIR WILLIAM ARMYNE, THOMAS HATCHER, and ROBERT GOODWIN to [WILLIAM LENTHALL].

1645, August 27.—(Identical with that from Lord Wharton which is printed *mutatis mutandis* in *Lords' Journals,* vii. 566, except that five lines from the end " hear " is " see.") [N. IV., 56.]

JOHN LOWRY to WILLIAM LENTHALL.

1645, August 27. Cambridge.—"The king beat our forces at Huntingdon, and took Major Gibbs and some 60 prisoners being all common soldiers, which are sent to Cambridge in exchange of some of our prisoners, and not above 5 killed in the fight. We have had strong alarms within 4 miles of our town. We stood upon our guard and summoned all the counties to come in, which accordingly came in to our assistance—only Essex—not a man of which came in notwithstanding letters sent unto them divers times of our dangers. The last answer I had from them was that our town and castle was taken, and so thought not fit to come. I have been drawing all our forces these three nights into the fields, taking no posts, which I believe standing upon our guard both in town and field hath hindered the king of his design . . . For the present our fears are somewhat blown over. The king marched from Huntingdon yesterday unto St. Eoates (? St. Neots) and this morning we hear that he is at Bedford, and they are very much affrighted as appears by some prisoners we have taken. We hear that Colonel Rosseter with some Scots is come to Stilton, which is about 35 miles from us, and we have sent six troops of our horse in the pursuit of the king this morning . . . *Postscript.*—Since the sealing of my letter our six troops of horse are retreated where they were, ten miles from us, and they report that the enemy was there with a strong party. But how true I know not, which hath put us into new fears, yet however are resolved to stand to it for the safeguard of the town." (See *Commons' Journals*, iv. 257.) *Seal.* [N. IV., 57.]

PHILIP [LORD] WHARTON to the SPEAKER OF THE HOUSE OF PEERS.

1645, August 28.—(Printed in *Lords' Journals*, vii. 569.) [N. IV., 58.]

EDWARD NEWMAN, Sheriff, and others to JOHN CREWE.

1645, August 28, 4 past noon. Northampton.—We enclose a letter from the Governor of Leicester, which we thought good to speed, "because Colonel Thorney the last night coming by us told us the Yorkshire horse were gone back, but it appears by this they are marching forward. We shall not take upon us to advise, but we fear the Scotch horse being gone to Scotland the army before Hereford may be in want of them. The king marched yesterday from Woburn towards Oxford as is conceived. Our horse, Coventry and Newport being joined, pursued his force through Brickhill. We hear not from them since, only it is said they have taken many of his rear " . . . (See *Commons' Journals*, iv. 257.) *Signed.* [N. IV., 59.]

Instances of the Discipline of other Churches given by the ASSEMBLY OF DIVINES.

1645, August 28.—Wherein there is not a distinct and full enumeration of all the offences for which the Eldership may keep a person from that Sacrament. The instances are taken from the Bohemian Brethren, and the Church of Geneva, the French Church at Frankfort, the Dutch Churches in England, the Reformed Churches of Nassau, and the Church of Scotland. Citations are also given from Origen, Justin Martyr, Tertullian, and Chrysostom to prove that such was the practice of the early Church. Additional advice is given as to the method in which unworthy persons are to be excluded. [N. XXII., 25.]

WILLIAM LENTHALL to the COMMITTEE AT NANTWICH.

1645, August 28.—The House thought it not convenient for the present to make any resolve touching the assistance you desire for reducing Chester ; but have deferred it till September 8th, hoping our affairs before then may be in a more certain condition with relation to the forces now with the King, that give alarms to so many parts of this kingdom and by their speedy motions make all such undertakings hazardous. (See *Commons' Journals*, iv. 254.) *Draft.* [N. XII., 126.]

LORD BROGHILL, SIR JOHN CLOTWORTHY, and ten other Officers of the Army in Ireland to the COMMITTEE OF BOTH KINGDOMS.

[1645, before August 28th.]—(The effect appears from *Commons' Journals*, iv. 255.) *Signed.* [N. XXI., 20.]

LORD BALMERINO, ARCHIBALD JHONSTON, CHARLES ERSKINE, HEW KENNEDY, and ROBERT BARCLAY to WILLIAM LENTHALL.

1645, August 29. Derby House.—Enclosing a letter from the Scotch army, and stating that of the 200*l. per diem* assessed by the Commissioners of Parliament on the several counties for the maintenance of the infantry there is not one penny yet come in, and entreating earnestly that the month's pay voted to that necessitous army be speedily and effectually brought in, and that the ordinance upon the contract made with Mr. Davis may be speedily passed. *Signed. Seal.* [N. IV., 60.]

Major-General EDWARD MASSIE to WILLIAM LENTHALL.

1645, August 30. Bridgwater.—I wrote from Lyme on the 23rd, informing you of our present condition and the state of these parts, and desiring a supply and speedy assistance. I enclose a copy of General Goring's intercepted letter. "The Prince upon Thursday last, the 28th . . . came into Exeter, and the Cornish with him. Near Broad Clyst was that day a rendezvous held, where was 6 field pieces, 80 carriages and about 9,000 horse and foot, those come out of Cornwall not come up to him at that time. Their discourse tends to march eastward, supposing they shall have a good addition of strength out of Dorset and the east parts of Somerset amongst the Club[men]. I marvel not at it, and had much desired to have prevented it, yet however my counsels have been as much rejected in that as not desired in other things in these parts, which have concerned these parts, the kingdom and myself in the service intrusted, yet notwithstanding have I not failed in my duty towards the Parliament, nor will I by God's mercy ever do." *Postscript.*—Commending the case of Major Backhouse's widow. (See *Commons' Journals*, iv. 261.) *Signature torn off. Seal. Enclosed :*

GEORGE [LORD] GORING to SIR EDWARD NICHOLAS at Oxford.

1645, August 25. Exeter . . .—" This is only to let you know that the respite which the Rebels have given us hath advanced very much our recruits in these parts, for there is great hopes that we shall have a body of 10 or 1,200 men together within eight days. I believe you have more certain notice of the enemies' motions than we have. We conceive Fairfax is ready to engage before Bristol, and that we shall be able to make a very good attempt for the relieving of it within three weeks " . . . *Copy.* [N. IV., 62.]

[WILLIAM LENTHALL] to Colonel-General POINTS.

1645, August 30.—(The effect appears from *Commons' Journals*, iv. 258, 259. The place to which he was to march was originally Banbury.) *Draft.* [N. XII., 127.]

Colonel WILLIAM PUREFOY, HENRY HERBERT, and HUMPHREY SALWEY to WILLIAM LENTHALL.

1645, September 3. Maysmore, near Gloucester.—"In our last of 31 August we gave you an account of our doubtful condition concerning Hereford .... Yesterday morning the army rose from before Hereford and were upon their march to Fownehope four miles thence in the road towards Gloucester. That may seem strange to you as well as those parts of the kingdom. The grounds—as far as . . . we apprehend—were these. The Commissioners of Scotland have long pressed a necessity—to save their own kingdom—for this army's removal Northwards to whose importunities we agreed so far as to make preparation for a march, it being also . . recommended to the General in the meantime to use his best endeavour to reduce the town, whereto he engaged himself accordingly, and proposed in case it should be taken, we would provide how to keep it, that the Army might not be enforced to stay . . . Whereupon we . . . wrote letters to the adjacent garrisons for a supply of men, wherein we were confident of prevailing. But on Monday last his Excellency and the Commissioners of Scotland informed us of the King's coming to Worcester with 4,000 horse and dragoons .... They affirmed themselves ready and resolved for storm next day had not this intervened. What posture to be in to meet the King was proposed .... We urged whether an attempt by storm might not be made before the King could annoy them being then 20 long miles off. To which the General and commanders delivered their opinion that it was most dangerous and not to be attempted, because the batteries could not be finished before 2 o'clock by which time the King might be upon them. We then proposed whether the siege might not continue and yet draw out such a party of horse and foot as might encounter the King's forces, our information being that their horse were weary and not of that number as reported. To which the General and commanders declared it could not possibly be done, they had so few horse and the rather because—they said—that Major-General Middleton was gone with Lieutenant-General Leslie into Scotland with all their horse that followed the King. This being solely a military point we thought it not fit to contest with men of that experience in martial affairs, and lest by persisting for action here contrary to their judgments we should undergo the censure of what prejudice might befall this army we . . submitted to those votes . . . here enclosed . . . We cannot but inform you of the sad and most miserable condition of these parts . . . It much grieves us to see our friends . . . now ruined and all lost to the fury of a merciless enemy. If some speedy care be not taken for prevention, the King in all probability will again recruit himself hence to a great strength. What further is intended to be done by this army and which way they will march we shall with all speed acquaint you." (See *Commons' Journals*, iv. 266.) *Copy.* [N. XII., 131.] *Enclosed:*

The COMMITTEE OF BOTH KINGDOMS.

1645, September 1.—Vote. (Printed as part of the paper of September on or after 15th, and there marked C., *post*, p. 273.) *Copy.* [N. XII., 129.]

Sir William Armyne, Thomas Hatcher, and Robert Goodwin to William Lenthall.

1645, September 3.—(Identical *mutatis mutandis* with the letter of the same date from Lord Wharton to the Speaker of the House of Peers, which is printed in *Lords' Journals*, vii. 573.) *Signed. Seal.* [N. IV., 65 should be 64.] *Enclosed:*

The Same with Lord Wharton to the Committee of the Estates of Scotland.

1645, September 2. Berwick.—(Printed *ubi suprà*.) Certified *Copy.* [N. XII., 130.]

Humphrey Mackworth and others to William Lenthall.

1645, September 3. Salop.—"Since our late success before Lilshall and Dudley . . . it hath pleased God to give us a further evidence of his goodness by delivering into our hands 140 of the enemies' forces belonging unto Ludlow, who amongst others to the number of 300 were sent under the command of Colonel Davelier towards Bishop's Castle to plunder the country and to apprehend all such as stood affected to the Parliament. After some hurt done our forces consisting of 80 horse and 80 foot under the command of Major Fenwick, which quartered in Bishop's Castle for securing that town and parts adjacent, drew forth, and within a mile of that place with the assistance of some countrymen which were got into a body charged the enemy. Our forlorn retreated disorderly, but our horse did second them so gallantly that after a hot charge they wholly routed the enemy, took 120 horse, all their foot and arms, slew many, brought off all the prisoners to the number above specified, whereof almost 20 were Commission officers, and we are credibly informed that there came not above 40 back into Ludlow besides those which were brought wounded in carts." We desire that a sheriff be nominated for this county. *Signed. Seal.* [N. IV., 65.]

Lord Balmerino, Archibald Jhonston, and Charles Erskine to William Lenthall.

1645, September 3. Worcester House.— . . "Having certain information that the King's forces are marched towards Hereford, that Prince Maurice from Worcester and Sir Jacob Ashley from Wales are making all the preparation they can for their assistance whereby the Scottish army now in the absence of their horse—and those under command of Colonel-General Poyntz being few and at a great distance—may be brought into great distress, we do earnestly desire that you would be pleased to move the House to give order to Sir Thomas Fairfax for sending some forces for their relief and assistance." (See *Commons' Journals*, iv. 263.) *Signed. Seal.* [N. IV., 66.]

The Derbyshire Committee to the Committee of both Kingdoms.

1645, September 4.—(Printed from a copy among Lord Braye's papers, in the *Appendix (Part VI.) to the Tenth Report of the Historical MSS. Commission*, p. 159, where " Isbunds " should be " Mundy.") *Signed. Seal.* [N. IV., 67.]

The Elector Palatine to William Lenthall.

1645, September 5.—"How sensible I am of your busines and how loath to importune the House would sufficiently appeare, if the state of that which they have soe long agoe appointed for my supply were by those gentlemen unto whose care it was referred made knowne unto them. Wherefore I desire that you would put the House in mind to call for it, being myselfe unwilling to speake the language of those necessities which overburden your most affectionate friend." *Signed* "Charles." [N. I., 50.]

Court Martial upon Lieutenant Bridale *alias* Brydlf.

1645, September 5. Oxford.—Report, sentencing him to be shot for carrying himself tumultuously among the soldiers and disobedience to his superiors. (He was an officer in the Lord Keeper's regiment, and alleged he was to obey no orders but those that came through the Lord Keeper.) [N. XIV., 78.]

Colonel William Purefoy, Henry Herbert, and Humphrey Salwey to William Lenthall.

1645, September 5.—"In our last of the 3rd . . . we acquainted you with the rising of the Scots' army from before Hereford upon information of the King's approach to Worcester. . . . The General and whole army quartered last night at Highnam, and are now marching through Gloucester to Cheltenham 6 miles hence in the way to Warwick. We cannot certainly let you know what is intended, but we apprehend by former expressions of the General and Commissioners of Scotland a resolution to relieve their own distressed country and therefore believe them unwilling to engage their army in this kingdom, frequently urging an impossibility for them to recruit themselves, should they receive a loss. To whose importunities we so far consented as that necessaries should be provided for their march. But to the place where, the time when, or which way hath not yet been in proposition. We conceive it too high a point for us to decide and therefore most earnestly desire some speedy directions from the Parliament. . . . . . Should the army hold their march towards Scotland we shall humbly propose whether our employment be not at an end, not knowing wherein we may be further serviceable to you by our residing here. Solely to make provisions for the army we suppose you will not expect from us; the Committees in the several counties . . . . may be appointed for that purpose." *Signed. Seal.* [N. IV., 68.]

Colonel Charles D'Oilie and others to the Committee of both Kingdoms.

1645, September 5. Newport Pagnell.—Stating that the fifty prisoners lately taken with those they had before fill the prisons so full as to be dangerous to the garrison, and that, the allotted counties not paying their contributions, they have no money for their soldiers or for their prisoners' maintenance, and therefore desiring that the prisoners might be disposed of elsewhere and the counties made to pay. *Signed. Seal.* [N. IV., 68b; omitted in Index.]

The Earl of Warwick to William Lenthall.

1645, September 5. Lecze.—"Upon this alarm of the enemies coming to Huntingdon I drew up all the forces of Essex being 6,000 foot and 900 horse and 500 dragoons towards Cambridge as also 4,000 foot and 500 horse came out of Suffolk for the guard of Cambridge and the Isle of Ely. And upon the retreat of the enemy I dismissed them according to the order of the Committee of both Kingdoms, and sent 800 good horse of the Association and the 400 horse of Major Gibb's Regiment, as I was commanded by the House of Commons, to keep in the Newarkers from infesting the Association during the absence of Colonel Rossiter and his troops. I have caused the Counties to send a fortnight's pay with them, lest for want of pay they should take occasion to disband. The 400 under Major Gibb there is a course taken by ordinance to pay them, but for the 800 horse of the Association under Major Haynes they rely upon the promise of the House of Commons for their pay. I pray, Sir, move the House to take present order in it. 3,000*l.* per month will pay them." . . . (See *Commons' Journals*, iv. 265.) *Signed. Seal.* [N. IV., 69.]

LORD BALMERINO, ARCHIBALD JHONSTON, CHARLES ERSKINE, HEW KENNEDY, and ROBERT BARCLAY to WILLIAM LENTHALL.

1645, September 6. Worcester House.—Desiring that some portion of their arrears might be paid to divers officers of the Scotch nation who had been employed here in the service of the Parliament, and were now exceedingly desirous in the great distractions of their native country to repair thither. *Signed. Seal.* [N. IV., 70.]

The COMMITTEE FOR PETITIONS.

1645, September 6.—Resolutions on Bradshaw's Petition. (Printed in *Commons' Journals*, iv. 278.) [N. XIV., 79.]

The MEMBERS OF THE HOUSE OF COMMONS AT OXFORD.

1645, September 8.—Declaration that the Lord Dover's and the Lord Keeper's regiments were to do duty only in case of siege or other emergency, were not to be drawn out of Oxford except on sallies during the siege and were to be under officers of their own, by whom if necessary they were to be punished. That these regiments, consisting of scholars, gentlemen, and their servants conceive that, by a late sentence by a court martial on an officer of theirs, they may be thought subject to the same judgment, and the Commons being sensible of the great use of these regiments for the defence of the town conceive that this last judgment may have a very ill influence, and demand that their voluntary service, which they are forward to perform on extraordinary occasions, may not make them liable to be summoned by the military power, and that all other gentlemen and scholars with their servants may have it declared that they are not subject to a court martial, but for neglect of orderly duty to be punished by their own officers, and for anything that is capital by the civil power, and that the sentence on Lieutenant Brydall may be reviewed with some tenderness and execution stayed, they willingly affording him their favourable testimony, and conceiving themselves concerned in his sentence, because he is an officer in one of the regiments raised by their advice, and upon a dispute of jurisdiction undecided, and that for words spoken in that defence before his judges condemned as of mutiny. [N. XIV., 80.]

[WILLIAM LENTHALL] to [the EARL OF WARWICK].

1645, September 9.—In the name of the House thanking him for his recent services, and desiring him to convey their thanks to his countrymen. (See *Commons' Journals*, iv. 267.) *Draft.* [N. XII., 132.]

[WILLIAM LENTHALL] to [the Committees of several Counties in the EASTERN ASSOCIATION].

Same date.—Circulars in the name of the House forbidding them upon any occasion whatever to divert the monies collected for Sir Thomas Fairfax's army, but directing speedy payment thereof to be made according to the Ordinance. (See *Commons' Journals*, iv. 267.) *Draft.* [N. XII., 133.]

LORD BROGHILL to WILLIAM LENTHALL.

1645, September 9. Cork.—"The condition of this Province was desperate, before I arrived here with those supplies the Honourable Houses sent over by me, Youghal having been besieged three months, and notwithstanding all their miserable wants, constant and patient, the Lord President having done all that man could do for the preservation of so important a place for the Parliament, and God has so blest his endeavours that it is relieved with victuals and the enemy drawn off some five or six miles. The besieged made a fortnight ago a gallant sally, the rebels having possessed both points of the harbour and planted great guns on them, our soldiers made bold to kill betwixt 3 and 400 of them, seized upon their ordnance, spiked two brass demi-cannon, and flung them down a cliff into the sea, not being able to draw them off, took from them one brass saker and brought it with them, all this with the loss of two men. We do only expect Will. Jephson's arrival with the horse to give the rogues battle,—if they will stand us—. The season of the year is so far advanced there will be but little action. Next spring will, I trust in God, recover our losses of this summer . . . . I beseech your favour in any just desire that may be made to the House in the behalf of this Province, which, God willing, shall well merit the Parliament's care of them, being all resolved to sacrifice our lives and fortunes for their service." . . . *Seal.* [N. IV., 71.]

PHILIP [LORD] WHARTON to LORD GREY OF WARKE, Speaker of the House of Peers.

1645, September 10. Barwicke.—(Printed in *Lords' Journals*, vii. 581.) *Signed. Seal.* [N. IV., 72.]

The COMMITTEE OF THE ESTATES OF SCOTLAND to the SCOTCH COMMISSIONERS IN LONDON.

1645, September 10. Haddington.—"We have long tasted in these partis the bitter cup of Godes wrathe, whiche for our many provocaciones he hath in a large measour powred out among us and brought us verie lowe. The Lord in his mercie grant we may yet repent and turne from our evill wayes, and thane we hope he will repent him of the evill he intendit towardis us. We have reason to be exceiding sensibile of the many testimonies of the brotherlie affectioune we have receaved from the honourabill houses of the parliament of England, bot of none mair then that now in the day of our calamitie they send up their prayeers to God for pardoune and pitie to us. It is the greatest assistance can be given us, and we desyer you wald returne them heartie thankis for it from us. At the first meitting of the committee efter the Lordis hand was so heavie upon us at Kilsythe the Lord Chancellor was direckit bothe towardis our forces in England and the honorabill houses of Parliament there, fullie instructed with our conditioune and desyres frome bothe, whiche we ar confident ere this can come to your handes you will find from himselff, so that we have no wayes failled in our respectes to ather. Since his parting our faint hopes hes beine quicknod by the presence and assistance of Generall-Levtennant David Leslie and his forces, who after four hundrethe mylles marche in twantie ane dayes and aue dayes rest—whiche was indeid the Lordis day—in the Mers, hes advanceit with his forces towardis this place bothe for the saiftie and furder provyding the castell of Edinburghe and secureing our maga-zines of victuall in East Lowthiane.

The rebellis upoun Sunday last marched from Cranstonnriddell to-wardis Galowater from whence—as we ar this day informed—they caun towardis the Mers, and are now lying neir Stitchell within a myle or twa of the Castell of Home wherin we have put a garysoune, and find-ing great slownes and dissobedience to all publick orderes in the Mers and Teviottdaille it hes beine thought fitt for a tyme to secure the persones of the Earles of Home and Roxburghe." *Signed. Seal.* [N. IV., 73.]

Sir THOMAS HONYWOOD and others to WILLIAM LENTHALL.

1645, September 10. Chelmsford.—Thanking the House for the acknowledgment of their past services, and begging him to represent that in their confidence of having the arrears of the Association Assess-ments within their own county they had run themselves much in debt by these late alarms, and sending out their horse towards Newark, and asking therefore that the House should pass the ordinance prepared for that purpose. *Signed.* [N. IV., 74.]

HARCOURT LEIGHTON and THOMAS HERBERT to WILLIAM LENTHALL.

1645, September 10. Bristol.—"Four dayes being subtely spun out by Prince Rupert in treaty—either to compleat his workes, or from hopes of Goring's or the King's horse to raise our seige—this morning twixt 2 and 3 the whole army alarmd or stormd the lyne and forts every wher rownd the cittie. Collonel Welden's brigad fell on upon the south side towardes Ratcliff and for two full houres stood to it at lesse than pike's length of their lyne, neither fearing their nombers—though 1,500 were drawne thither—nor the difficulty of passing the trench and water which exceeded there, but with undaunted spiritts exposd themselves to the shott which abundantly was made at them. Albeit, by reason the ladders were not long enough—many that were longer being unhappily left behind at their quarter—they could not enter, both horse foot, and canon opposing them, notwithstanding they left behind them honorable signalles of fortitude, for L[ieutenant]-Collonel Durfee was slayne, Major Crumwell sore hurt in the groine, and about threescore private soldyers close under their workes who to gett up had scratcht the breast-work and exprest an extream desire to scale but could not. Collonel Mountague's brigad stormd the east part of the lyne and upon the very first attempt past over and most resolutely masterd Laffar (Lawford) gate and that part of the citty which joynes to the castle ; in which servyce—with the extraordinary assistance of the horse who on all sides kept pace with the musquetteers and seamd to emulate one another in courage and affection—Collonel Taylor, once a member of your house, was taken prisner and nigh two hundred other soldyers ; of which there are eight captains and leiftenants. Collonel Rayns-burrough's brigade alarumd the fort royall — wherein Leiftenant-Collonel Pride did bravely—and stormd Pryor's fort and after an houres fight with losse of three men conquerd it. Itt is under the royall fort upon the lyne and commands both the royall fort and castle. It was desperately defended by about seventy Irish, old soldyers, who all but twelve or fifteen were cutt in peeces by our men togeather with the Collonel or L[ieutenant]-Collonel—brother to Herbert Price some say—and in the fort we took four culverin and other armes. Hence the enemy are sufficiently gaid already, and truly this fort with four other wee took affoording nigh twenty peeces of cannon, a great comand to us and scanting the enemy, putts us in fayre hopes of overcoming the rest with lesse hazard and difficulty. In this storme wee have lost one hundred men and few lesse wounded. Major Bethell is one, a deserving gentleman and recoverable. Captain Lago with Major-Generall Skippon's men are sayd to enter the Prior Fort first and with him the rest of Collonel Mountagu and Collonel Hammon's. But to speak truth of all both officers and soldyers, I do not thinck a man gave back for fear or that ever any busines of this nature was managed with more heed or acted with more courage. What the enemy lost in the towne and forts as yet wee hear not but doubtless they had their payment. They are now burning that part of the citty which may give shelter or yeild approaches to us and their one thousand horse are circumscribed to the fort royall togeather with these lords: Rivers, Hawley, Barramore, Lumley, Crumwell, Newport, Cockayn, Grandison, Sturton, Capell, Bellassis, and others with abundance of gentry and ladyes, Prince Rupert's associates. The Generall has desyred Collonel Pindar to speed to Lyme, Taunton, and Bridgwater to furnish us here with what powder and other amunicion their magazines can spare for the dispatch of this busines. Pray hasten money to pay the army. They looke long after it; and, if ever any army, this deserves it. *Postscript.*—The rumor here is that the King is at Ragland, Goring in Devonshire recruiting. We heare now Prince Rupert will yeild up towne and forts upon other condicions, and departe tomorrow early." *Signed. Seal.* [N. IV., 75.]

REPORT.

[1645, September 11.]—Concerning the household of the Duke of Gloucester and the Princess Elizabeth. (See *Commons' Journals*, iv. 270.) [N. XIV., 230.]

ORDER appointing a Committee concerning the EARL OF STAI-FORD'S subsistence, and their REPORT.

1645, September 11 and October 13.—(The first is printed in *Commons' Journals*, iv. 271; the report proposes that 1,500*l.* per annum be allowed him out of the estates of Sir Thomas Jermyn and Thomas Jermyn.) [N. XIV., 90.]

WALTER STRICKLAND to WILLIAM LENTHALL.

1645, September 11-21. The Hague.—Praising Master Cooper, the late chaplain to the Queen of Bohemia, and commending him to the Parliament. *Seal.* [N. IV., 76.]

EDWARD FARMER, Sheriff, and others to SIR CHRISTOPHER YELVERTON.

1645, September 12. Northampton.—Concerning the composition of Mr. Edmond Sawyer for his Delinquency. (See *Commons' Journals*, iv. 281.) *Signed. Seal.* [N. IV., 77.]

Major-General EDWARD MASSIE to WILLIAM LENTHALL.

1645, September 12. Milverton.—"Since it hath pleased God to deliver Bristol into our hand . . . I humbly suppose that his Excellency will not longer repose himself there than necessity requireth,, but will pursue the service one way or other before the rain and cold make him unable either to keep the field or to march—winter drawing nigh—. And therefore where greatest advantage may be found that way I doubt not but the General will look. I am therefore both most humbly to mind—not counsel—the . . House . . of these Western parts, which require assistance; which had I had it or the country by any other hand sooner, doubtless the enemy had never recruited himself to so considerable an army as undeniable report doth render him. General Goring with a part of the army advanced yesternight as far eastward as Tiverton 3,000 strong, horse, dragoons, and foot and the body advancing up to them. My want of both dragoons and foot is that which rendereth me unserviceable or disabled to defend the country from ruin, or to stand or dispute it with the enemy, it being a country far more suitable for foot than horse to fight in, full of deep lanes and high hedges, &c. I therefore implore their speediest consideration that by a timely order to the General he may not be wholly engaged with the army in other parts, but may advance westward . . . at the only great service we may look after yet, before winter thrust the army into quarters. It is my faithfulness and zeal to the Parliament that bids me be importunate, for in the same I know no end or aim but my unfeigned desire to put an end to this bloody war, which I perceive can never be so long as we suffer a marching army to act its own desires without impeachment." *Seal.* [N. IV., 78.]

Colonel ROWLAND LAUGHARNE to WILLIAM LENTHALL.

1645, September 13. Haverfordwest.—" I have received 269 soldiers, most of them armed, from Sir Thomas Fairfaxe. Manie appeare to be this countreymen and desire to returne to their families. I praise God wee are in an indifferent state for foote, in horse vearie lowe. The other counties of South Wales of late entered a newe association and have raised a mightie multitude of Clubmen. I praie some of our next freinds maie be consigned to joine uppon our advaunce to Carmarthen- shire. I alreadie solicited,—but cannot prevaile—for a partie of the Mountgormrieshire horse. To engage this small remnant uppon soe vast disadvantages I dare not, and to rewarde, encourage or support them heere the countrey—soe wasted as it is—will not bee able without your favorable consideracion for addicionall supplies from the state in money and apparrell. The 3,000l. in money and provision alreadie sent, the comittee heere will rendor an accoumpt of, and I desire to pre- sent the acknowledgment of my thankfull obligacions. Mr. Arthur Owens by his constant integritie and resolucion for the publique merited our trust to agitate for us to the state. His addresses I desire may receive entertainment. Mr. Roger Lorte in our greatest exigencie deserted us, and in contempt of my comaunde for his staie, shipped himselfe for London, there—as I understand—makeinge Mr. Elliott of his faction, bestoweth himselfe in disgorgeinge private ranckor and malice against those whose merritt will endure the teste, and durst not appeare out of Pembrocke, when they both kissed the King's hand in Oxford. Since the takeinge of Haverfordwest, with the castell, wee have taken in Carewe, Manerbire, and Picton Castells, all the houlds the enemie had in this countie. The particuler accoumpt I refferr to the inclosed paper." *Signed. Seal.* [N. IV., 79.]

OLIVER CROMWELL to WILLIAM LENTHALL.

1645, September 14. Bristol.—(Printed down to "two hundred men" in *Lords' Journals,* vii. 584, and in full in Rushworth iv., 1. 85, and Carlyle, No. 31, where there are a few verbal errors not in the *Lords'*

Journals. Signed by Cromwell and here and there corrected by him, the most remarkable change being " who have *wrestled with* God for a blessing " instead of " *waited on* God." The passage from " Presbyterians, Independents," to the end is underlined, whether by Cromwell or not does not appear. In this passage the following mistakes occur in Rushworth and Carlyle:—" All *have* here " for all " *had* here "; " *have* no names of difference " for " *know* no names "; " *for* being united in forms," for " *as for* being "; " And *for* Brethren " for " and *from* brethren.") [N. IV., 80.]

SIR HENRY VANE, SIR WILLIAM ARMYNE, THOMAS HATCHER, and ROBERT GOODWIN to WILLIAM LENTHALL.

1645, September 15. Barwicke.—(The same *mutatis mutandis* as Lord Wharton's letter of the same date to the Speaker of the House of Peers, which is printed in *Lords' Journals*, vii. 592. *Enclosed* are certified copies of their letter to the Scotch Commissioners and the answer of the latter, and their letter to the Committee of Cumberland, all of which are printed in *Lords' Journals*, vii. 593.) *Signed. Seal.* [N. IV., 81, 82, 83; XII., 134.]

ALBERT JOACHIMI, Ambassador of the States-General, to the PARLIAMENT.

1645, September 15-25.—In *French.* (A translation is printed in *Lords' Journals*, vii. 580.) *Signed. Seal.* [N. XVIII., 105.]

[The COMMISSIONERS WITH THE SCOTCH ARMY] to ·———

[1645, September on or after 15.]—" Thursday, being the last of July the Scotts army satt downe before Hereford. The generall sent a summons for the surrender of the towne, which beinge refused, he layd close seidge to it, drew a line rounde within pistoll-shott of the wale, made all preparations of mines and batterys to take it by force, which was very hopefull; and spent most of our time. Munday the 25th of August, the Generall and Commissioners of Scotland enformed us that they had intelligence of a great defeate given by Montrose in Scotland, and that their country was wholly lost havinge noe visible means leaft to regayne it, but this army; the great raginge of the Plague ther addinge to their misery. Affayrs thus standinge, the Commissioners of Scotland desired our advice what to doe. Wee did—as wee had just cause—much condole their sadd condition, yet wee thought it fittest for them to propose the means of releife, they best knowinge their owne desirs and wants; for that time wee brooke off, not concludinge any thinge.

Tuesday, wee mett agayne, had the same debate, and weare much pressed for our advice which wee still avoyded, thinkinge some action heare first convenient, if not necessary. They at last—implicitly desiringe a removall of this army, but willinge, as wee conceave, to have us advise it—offered this proposition to be resolved, viz.:

A. The question is uppon the information received from Scotland, and uppon concideration of the posture of affayres in the north, what will be the most fittinge and conducible service for the good of both kingdomes at this time to be undertaken and performed by the Scottish army now before Hereford, the advice of the commissioners for the Parliament of England is hearin desired. That day ended in nothing but some seeminge discontent.

Wensday wee mett wheare wee alsoe had the same debate, and to the former proposition wee gave this answer, viz :

B. Wee shall be most ready as wee are bound by our league and covenant, to advise and act for the good of the kingdome of Scotland, as of our owne nation, whose welfares consist together, but before wee can give our advice to the question proposed, wee desire to bee satisfyed in these particulars followinge, as a foundation therof:

1° To knowe the condition and state of the army before Hereford, what probabillity ther is in takinge the same, and in what time, it beinge of concequence to this kingdome.

2° Wither it may consist with the safty of the kingdome of Scotland to stay some time to gayne Hereford, or wither the condition of that kingdome be such as doth require a present remove of this army.

Uppon this it was tould us that it seemed Hereford was of more concequence than the kingdome of Scotland, and they must thinke how to save themselves if they could have noe advice or assistance from us; of which wee thought our former answer a sufficient vindication, and we alsoe tould them till those particulars of ours weare answered, wee could not give any opinion. At last the Generall and Commissioners of Scotland enformed us that the towne of Hereford was very stronge, the moate deepe and the wals lined within, but our batteringe peeces weare smale, most of the mines fayled, and therefore 'twould be a worke of time, and that ther was a necessity for a speedy removall of this army to releive their owne country, havinge no other here. Wee pressed in what time the towne might probably be gayned. A weeke was agreed one as sufficient to perfect necessarys for a storme, uppon which this vote passed, viz.: August 27th.

The committee of both kingdomes uppon concideration of the present conjunction of affayrs, thinke it necessary that the Scotts' army before Hereford bee enabled for a march betwixt this and Wensday next, and doe recommend to the Lord Generall his Excellency to use his best endeavours for reducing of the citty in the meane time, who engaged himselfe accordingly.

All preparations weare made of mines and batterys and alsoe for their march, but the time when was never agreed to by us, the word enabled beinge of purpose inserted in the vote.

Thursday, accordinge to the Generall's desire, wee sent severall letters to the adjacent garrisons for men to keepe the towne beinge somthinge confident a storme would have taken it, and beinge willinge to correspond with our brethren of Scotland that they might not longer then necessary bee detayned heare, *wee had a promise of some men.*

Fryday, as an introduction to an attempt uppon the towne, the Generall sent a second summons for surrender to save effusion of blood, which receaved a slightinge answer, with denyall.

Saturday, the Generall enformed us that all the mines weare fayled, being drowned with water, and ther was but smale hopes, without longe time, of gayninge the towne. Wee then pressed an attempt by battery and storme without mines, to which the Generall answered all should be done that possibly could bee.

Munday, the first of September, the Generall and commissioners of Scotland enformed us of the King's approach to Worster with four thousand horse and dragones. They affirmed themselves ready next day to storme the towne, and had given orders accordingly, the ditch beinge miraculously—as they sayd—dryed upe, but this interveninge they thought new councells weare to be taken. The question was What posture to bee in to receave the King's forces if they came; in which debate wee urged wither an attempt by storme might not bee before the Kinge could come, beinge twenty myls off, to which the Generall and commanders delivered their opinions, it was most dangerous and not to be attempted, because the batterys could not be finished before 2 of the clocke, and should the Kinge—as he might—come uppon them as they weare storminge, 'twould ruine their army.

Wee then proposed wither they might not drawe off a party of horse and foote to secure them from the Kinge's forces, and yet leave the towne beseidged, and the ordinance one the batterys, *our information beinge, the enemy not to bee of that number as reported;* to which the Generall and commanders declared it could not possibly be done, they had soe fewe horse and the rather because they sayd Major-Generall Myddleton was gone with Lieutenant-Generall Leshley into Scotland, and ther weare not any that followed the King's motions. Ther came two letters alsoe of 27th and 29th from the committee of both kingdomes at London that the King's horse drew towards Bristoll as reported, which they thought fitt to lett us knowe, in case they should march towards the Scotts army, that wee might bee uppon our guard in a posture to receave them, but ther was not one worde of any that pursued the Kinge; and 'tis true wee knew nothinge of Poyntz' horse till wee came to Tewksberry. Sept^{ber} the 6th, and he was within five myls of us. The Generall alsoe affirmed the artillery and foote weare not to be separated, and that the canon could not be taken off the batterys with any safty, but in the night, these beinge soly military poynts. The Generall and commanders havinge first delivered their opinions, the five Commissioners of parliament agreed with these votes, viz.: 1° Septembris.

C. The committee of both kingdomes uppon advertisment of the king's forces beinge neare Worster yesternight, from which place they may bee att the leaguer to morrowe before the breaches can be made assaultable, thinkes fittinge and resolves that noe attempt shall be made against the towne of Hereforde for the present.

That the canon be drawne off the batterys this night.

Tuesday morninge, wee expected the army to bee in a posture fitt to receave the king's forces should they drawe towards them, beinge not without hopes of returninge to the towne agayne. But wee found the seidge wholy raysed and the army one their march to Founhope in the road to Glocester four myls. The words of the vote are that noe attempt be made against the towne for the present, which words weare inserted one debate and must have relation to their resolution of doinge it one Twesday, and drawinge of the canon that night because it could not be done in the day, if the king's forces should come; but for raysinge the seidge, marchinge away, or wither the army should goe or which way was never in debate, *much lesse consented to by us.*

Wee marched alonge with the army to Coventry, wheare some of the commissioners of Scotland tould us their intention was for Scotland and —supposinge wee would goe thence to London—they desired us to write letters to the severall committees, for their accommodations, which wee tooke into concideration, and findinge noe part of our instructions to march to Scotland, or to meddle with the affayrs of that kingdome, or whearin wee might bee further serviceable, wee tooke leave of the army one Fryday last, neare Bosworthfield in Leicestershyre, havinge writt letters to the severall committees as they desired, and are now repayred to London, leavinge all to the wisdome of the parliament." *Copy.* [N. XIV., 234.] N. XIX., 126, 122, are other copies of the Proposition and Answer in the above marked A. and B., and XII., 129, is a copy of the Votes marked C.

Sir Henry Vane, Sir William Armyne, Thomas Hatcher, and Robert Goodwin to Sir Thomas Widdrington.

1645, September 16. Barwicke.—Concerning Mr. Gilbert Swinhoe, who after his release on giving a bond did not appear when summoned, but "went into Scotland, and—as we are informed—endeavoured—with the Laird of Graden—to raise the Moss troopers or thieves of Tynedale and Redesdale to join with the Rebels of Scotland. He was surprised within a mile—as we hear—of Montrose's rendezvous within the borders of Scotland and being brought prisoner hither the Governor of Barwicke—in regard he is an Englishman—hath delivered him over unto us." (See *Commons' Journals*, iv. 291.) *Signed.* [N. IV., 86.]

Colonel RICHARD NORTON to the COMMITTEE OF BOTH KINGDOMS.

1645, September 16. Portsmouth.—Asking that money be provided for paying the garrison within a fortnight, as otherwise he must resign the command. (See *Commons' Journals*, iv. 280.) *Seal.* [N. IV., 87.]

JOHN [LORD] CULPEPER to GEORGE LORD GORING.

1645, September 17. 3 after dinner. Barnstaple.—"Just now I received from the Lord Digby this inclosed to your Lordship with one little one to the Council and a barren one to myself, wholly relating to a dispatch made by his Lordship to the Prince. Thereupon, finding as well by the complexion of my epistle as likewise by the discourse of the bearer many hints—but no particulars—of good news, I presumed to open the Prince's letter, a copy whereof—all but what is in cipher, whereof I have not the key—I herewith send your Lordship, hoping that this cordial may revive our drooping spirits, and much conduce to the work in hand. Neither in my opinion doth this success in Scotland and Wales make it more probable that Fairfax will advance to these Western parts, but rather that he should look towards the North. But your Lordship will be better able to form a judgment thereon . . . . *Postscript*—Cardiff is garrisoned for the King, and Wales is in much better temper since the raising the siege of Hereford, but I fear the loss of Bristol may relapse them. Your Lordship sees how much my Lord Montrose wants horse, and how much the enemy abounds in those cattle, and will—I presume—conclude with me that it is most necessary to preserve the body of horse with your Lordship If they were well joined with the King they might do great things, otherwise his Majesty's joining with the Lord Montrose will be very difficult. Second *Postscript.*—5 after dinner. Since the writing of this news, Mr. Hunsham of the Crown Office and Sir James Thynn are come hither, who report that the Clubmen were about Cardiff on Monday, and that the King is going from Wales, but whether to Oxford or Northwards they cannot tell. Prince Rupert marched to Oxford." [N. IV., 88.]

[WILLIAM LENTHALL] to the STANDING COMMITTEE of each County.

1645, September 17.—Circular directing them to consider how their county may be best divided into Classical Presbyteries, and what ministers and others are to be of each *classis*, and to divide their county accordingly. (See *Commons' Journals*, iv. 276.) *Draft.* [N. XII., 135.]

The ASSEMBLY OF DIVINES.

1645, September 18.—Paper reciting the Ordinance convening them and the Ordinances of October 12, 1643, and May 7, 1645, and stating that these Ordinances were never yet recalled. [N. XXII., 26.]

5

PRINCE RUPERT to the KING.

1645, September 18. Oxford.—(Printed in Warburton, *Memoirs of Prince Rupert,* iii. 186.) *Copy.* [N. XII., 136.]

WILLIAM LENTHALL to OLIVER CROMWELL.

1645, September 19.—Thanking him for his services in the name of the House, who "take it with much contentment to hear the unity mentioned in your letters, which they beseech God to continue. They are most joyed in your due and accustomed acknowledgments that all which is done was by the extraordinary Providence of Almighty God." *Draft.* [N. XII., 138.]

The SAME to SIR THOMAS FAIRFAX.

Same date.—In the name of the House thanking him and his army for their services. (See *Commons' Journals,* iv. 277, 279.) *Draft.* [N. XII., 139.]

The COMMITTEE FOR THE ADMIRALTY AND CINQUE PORTS.

1645, September 19.—Order concerning the *Becasse,* presenting a list of the Winterguard, and desiring that the Ordinance for Martial Law at sea be passed. (See *Commons' Journals,* iv. 280.) [N. XIV., 81.]

WILLIAM BROKETT to WILLIAM LENTHALL.

1645, September 20. From His Majesty's Fort of Castle Park.— " I received yours by direction from the . . . House of Commons with an inclosed from the Lord Digby, wherein under pretence of his Majesty's service poison lies sugared against my loyalty and conscience. When his Majesty's service is so Dagonized, who can but conceive the glory is departed from Israel, and who can but resolve to oppose such Philistines. My firmness in that resolution and my freeness from all intercourse with any who should tempt me to the contrary I could evince— my enemies being judges—by several demonstrations. But the insisting hereon unto you might seem to lessen the favour or distrust the confidence that Honourable House is pleased to make me an object of, both in clearing my innocence without dispute and intrusting me with the original of these letters. So ample testimony of their favour and confidence must further oblige me to the public service, if the bonds of conscience—which superlatively tie me to this duty—be capable of addition from other respects nor shall my continuance in that service be less than my zeal for it, for sooner shall the bonds of life than those of conscience be dissolved, or he prove either unfaithful to the cause of God, or undutiful to the commands of that honourable House, who is, your affectionate friend and humble servant." *Seal.* [N. IV., 89.]

SIR MATTHEW BOYNTON and others to WILLIAM LENTHALL.

1645, September 20. York.—"The forces of the Association are some of them coming in to our assistance, and others in a good way of preparation, so that we hope speedily to be in a condition not only to carry on the service in this county, but to be able and ready to . . . perform the orders we shall receive from the Parliament or the Committee of both Kingdoms for service in other parts. But by the speedy coming back of the Scotch army we are out of hopes of so sudden a conjunction as we expected, and if their abode be long in these

s 2

Northern parts, we shall not only be absolutely frustrate therein, but made utterly unable for the maintaining and continuance of our own forces, if any of the Scotch forces continue in Yorkshire. And in regard the time of the year for sieges is posting away, and the enemy's garrisons in this county are many and strong, it is of absolute necessity that we have considerable strength to join with us of the Association which by the late Ordinance are not to be burthensome to us." (See *Commons' Journals*, iv. 283.) *Signed. Seal.* [N. IV., 90.]

JOSEPH DALTON, Mayor, and others to WILLIAM LENTHALL.

1645, September 20. Hertford.— Representing that the extraordinary charges of the county were such, and that they, the committee for the county, besides their labours and charges have so far engaged themselves that they were unable by their own abilities or engagements to procure the money requisite for payment of the county's share of the 500 horse ordered to be raised by order of the 19th of May last, and therefore desiring to be excused. *Signed. Seal.* [N. IV., 91.]

Paper in form of a PETITION.

1645, September 20.—Reciting their perplexity and amazement that the great business of Church government should to this day remain unestablished, and praying that the Parliament would make all possible haste forthwith to establish by their civil sanction that government and discipline which Christ has left to his Church—a model whereof the reverend Assembly of Divines hath framed—and that when Church government shall be settled the Presbytery may have such power as may fully enable them to maintain all Christ's sacred Ordinances, especially the Holy Supper of the Lord in their highest splendour and purity. At foot. Resolved : " That this paper . . contains several matters scandalous to the proceedings of this House and untrue." *Signed* " H. Elsyng." (See *Commons' Journals*, iv. 280.) [N. XXII., 53.]

The HOUSE OF COMMONS.

1645, September 20.—Order appointing a Committee concerning a scandalous paper (the last). (Printed in *Commons' Journals*, iv. 280.) [N. XIV., 82.]

SIR HENRY VANE, SIR WILLIAM ARMYNE, THOMAS HATCHER, and ROBERT GOODWIN to WILLIAM LENTHALL.

1645, September 22. Berwick.—(Identical *mutatis mutandis* with the letter of the same date from Philip, Lord Wharton, to the Speaker of the House of Peers, which is printed in *Lords' Journals*, vii. 605.) [N. IV., 92.] *Enclosed:*

i. The ENGLISH COMMISSIONERS to the SCOTCH COMMISSIONERS.

1645, September 18.—(Printed *ubi suprà*.)

and

ii. The SCOTCH COMMISSIONERS to the ENGLISH COMMISSIONERS.

1645, September 20. Stirling Park.—We received your letter upon our march this day, and with great joy read the news of the surrender of Bristol. Some of us that waited on you at Berwick are now separated for a time for the better prosecuting of our late victory. We are to meet again on Friday next, God willing, at Perth, where there will be a full meeting of the Committee of Estates. Thence we will not fail to dispatch that elected number of Commissioners of Parliament which we appointed to treat with you. We must confess the reasons of this delay hitherto has been not less grievous to us than troublesome to you. Since they are in some part removed after this meeting we shall labour to give you all satisfaction. *Certified Copies.* [N. XII., 137.]

iii. The ENGLISH COMMISSIONERS to the SCOTCH COMMISSIONERS.

1645, September 22.—(Printed *ubi suprà*.) Certified *Copy.* [N. XII., 140.]

NICHOLAS LEEK, JOHN MUNDY, SIR SAMUEL SLEIGH, ROBERT WILLMOT, SIR EDWARD COKE, ROWLAND MOREWOOD, and FRANCIS MUNDY to WILLIAM LENTHALL.

1645, September 22. Derby.—Having referred to the letter of the House in reply to their's of the 4th instant reproving them for their neglect (See *Commons' Journals,* iv. 267) " for clearing of ourselves wherein we take the boldness to remonstrate unto you the whole particulars touching that affair. The first command by us therein seen was a letter directed to Sir John Gell and by him about the 4th of September shown to some of our Committee then sitting, who desired him to observe the same, notwithstanding that himself and some others . . . much urged that 100 horse might be by us stayed, unto which we no ways condescending we believe he gave—as was desired—present order for their march. It is true that by our letter of the 4th . . . we desired to represent the state of our county, but utterly refused to stay anything in obstruction of any command, only referring the after resolution of things to . . . that great Committee. Within two or three days after we received another from the Grand Committee mentioning the former command of sending, and that the horse were not then sent, and commanding again a sending of them. Whereunto we answered by one of the 8th. . . . —which we believe came not to their hands before the date of yours being the 10th—, wherein we humbly informed that those horse were before that time sent . . .
And . . . that you may be pleased to take notice what may be expected from us in disposal of military forces we . . . humbly inform that by the last ordinance . . . for our county all we have therein to do lies . . . in this clause, viz., that our forces shall not be drawn, kept, or continued, forth of our county without the consent of the Committee, 5 or more of them, particular directions of Parliament, Committee of both Kingdoms, or of Sir Thomas Fairfax. Wherein we humbly conceive as things with us now stand we have only a bare assenting power—in cases not excepted, as be the three last—to Sir John Gell, Commander in Chief's drawing out and no more. . . . " *Signed. Seal.* [N. IV., 93.]

The EARL OF WARWICK to WILLIAM LENTHALL.

1645, September 27. Westminster.—Excusing himself for having written to the Mayor of Sandwich touching the election of his son, Charles Riche. (See *Commons' Journals,* iv. 311.) *Signed. Seal.* [N. IV., 94.]

Colonel-General SEDNHAM POYNTS to WILLIAM LENTHALL.

1645, September 27. Chester Suburbs.—"In my last I promised a perfect list of our victory . . . which according to our common collection I have sent you inclosed. There are many considerable persons omitted being sent to Stafford and Shrewsbury, whereof I could receive no list. Sir Thomas Glemham proved to be Sir Henry Stradling, the late Governor of Carlisle. I hope you will pardon my mistake. The next morning after the fight I drew my forces out of the suburbs to Rowton Moor, where I remained till two of the clock in the afternoon, where I was counselled to quarter about Northwich, where I found a great inconveniency, so that I am moved this way, and do intend over the river into Wales, taking with me 1,000 foot to make good the Welsh side, and Colonel Jones on the other side, where I shall use my utmost endeavours in reducing this place, till I receive your orders to the contrary, and shall send about 1,000 or 1,500 horse to attend the King's motion with his ragged remnant. I desire there may be some further encouragement thought upon for the horse, for this hard march hath been very heavy duty to them." Seal. Enclosed is a list of the prisoners and slain, the former consisting of six knights and colonels, five colonels, the adjutant general, eight lieutenant-colonels, seven majors, eight gentlemen of quality reformadoes, twenty captains, sixteen lieutenants, seven cornets, four quartermasters, five trumpeters, seventeen of the King's Lifeguard, twenty gentlemen, 1,200 common soldiers, and 1,500 horse, and the latter of the Earl of Lichfield, and at least 300 commanders and soldiers besides. [N. IV., 95.]

JOHN [LORD] CULPEPPER to GEORGE LORD GORING.

[1645], September 27. Exeter.—Your desires in your letter to me shall be pursued by me before I go out of my chamber and I shall write very willingly, being much scandalized by Sir James Smyth's disobedience to your orders, and more at his disputing your power. I would willingly attend you to-night at Tiverton, but have despatches of great consequence on my hands, and expect the Prince's further commands to-night. But at 4 o'clock Sir John Berkley and myself will be at Thurverton in hopes of seeing you, which if your business prevents we shall attend you again tomorrow at any place you appoint. I take it for granted that my Lord Wentworth will come with you. [N. VIII, 137.]

The SCOTCH COMMISSIONERS to the ENGLISH COMMISSIONERS.

1645, September 27. Perth.—(Printed in Lords' Journals, vii 689.) Certified Copy. [N. XII., 141.]

Colonel-General SEDNHAM POINTS to the COMMITTEE FOR WAR AT YORK.

1645, September 29. Doddleston, near Chester.—"We hear the King has got a small body together, Prince Maurice and Sir Jacob Astley joining with him with all the forces . . . they could procure from Worcester, Hereford, and Wales. They are now about Denbigh and are moving this way with four fieldpieces intending to give us battle. I have written to London and to all our garrisons for assistance. One Nottingham regiment is returned and the rest with hard duty much discontented. We hear the Newarkers have orders to come this way. Therefore I earnestly desire you may give orders to the Yorkshire horse to attend their motion and to send your letters to Colonel

Rossiter and Colonel Thornhagh to the same purpose, for we hear the King hath vowed to raise this siege or lose England. He expects 5,000 Rebels to come over to him from Ireland." *Copy.* [N. XII., 143.]

SIR GEORGE BOOTHE and other the Deputy Lieutenants to
WILLIAM LENTHALL.

1645, September 29. From the Leaguer before Chester.—Since the House called up their members and committed the Militia to the Deputy Lieutenants,·though "we found the soldiers left in a mutinous condition for want of pay, and the country quite exhausted . . . yet it hath pleased God so to render our endeavours prosperous that the country and forces are now reduced to a cheerful and obedient condition ready and capable of any proportionable design that can be presented them for the service of the Parliament. . . Nevertheless we are informed there are some factious petitions presented to you, bearing the character of the whole county, but indeed being the act but of a few . . . intimating a necessity of Sir William Brereton's return and so insinuating an odium and scandal upon us and our actions to the disturbance of the present condition we are in and the hazard of the great attempts now in agitation . . . *Postscript.*—Major-General Pointz' horse with Colonel Jones' 500 horse are passed over the river and Colonel Booth and Colonel Duckenfield with such foot as we could spare to expect the King's attempt on the Welsh side." (See *Commons' Journals,* iv. 302.) *Signed. Seal.* [N. IV., 97.]

WILLIAM LENTHALL to Colonel-General POINTS

1645, September 30.—In the name of the House thanking him and his army for their services, and informing him that the House had voted 500*l.* as a free gift to him. *Draft.* [N. XII., 146.]

SIR MATTHEW BOYNTON and others to WILLIAM LENTHALL.

1645, October 1. York.—Sending Colonel Overton's letter and the articles of the rendition of Sandall Castle, stating that they were in very great want of ammunition to reduce the other castles in the county, and desiring that a good supply be speedily furnished. (See *Commons' Journals,* iv. 297.) *Signed. Seal.* [N. IV., 98.] *Enclosed:*

The said letter and articles. *Copies.* [N. XII., 144, 145.]

SIR ANTHONY ASHLEY COOPER and others to WILLIAM LENTHALL.

1645, October 1. Melcomb Regis.—Enclosing a communication "about the sad condition of Pool where the plague and famine busily contend for pre-eminence, and the distressed inhabitants impatient of either of their reigns threaten to break out to the inevitable danger of the loss of the garrison and ruin of the places adjacent," which we desire may be taken into present consideration on account both of the importance of the place and its affection to Parliament. We shall always be ready to contribute our best assistance, but "five of our great towns, Pool, Sherborne, Dorchester, Perret, and Week, being by the present contagion necessarily reduced to a just expectation of relief the county will not be able much longer to subsist under the intolerable burden of so many infected places and seven garrisons, especially when our weekly contributions shall be taken from us . . . ." *Signed.* [N. IV., 99.]

Sir William Armyne, Thomas Hatcher, and Robert Goodwin to William Lenthall.

1645, October 2. Newcastle.—"Our last letter to the Committee of Estates . . . of the 24th of September last hath prevailed so far as to produce a meeting on Monday next at Barwick . . . We shall not fail, God willing, to give them a meeting at the time and place appointed, and do therefore intend to begin our journey thitherwards tomorrow. We have not heard this week of any action between the forces of our brethren in Scotland and the Rebels. The Scotish army in England lieth in Cieveland, their head-quarters being at Stokesley. They have sent their train of artillery into this town, and the regiment of foot that convoyed it is quartered in the Bishopric. Some of their chief Commanders and officers are passed by this way into Scotland, and we hear that a great meeting is appointed this week at Jedburgh or Duns." *Signed. Seal.* [N. IV., 100.]

Colonel Thomas Morgan, John Fettiplace, and others to William Lenthall.

1645, October 3. Gloucester.—Recommending Lieutenant-Colonel Kyrle as Governor of Cannon Froom in place of Colonel Harley resigned. "After the departure of the Scots out of that country all things were left in such fear and confusion that had he not adventured far, and been very careful in the Governor's absence, the enemy had been now masters of that place." Also "he never had any command or requital answerable to that great service he did the State in gaining Monmouth to their obedience, which had it been as faithfully kept as he was active and zealous in reducing it the Parliament long since had been clearly masters of that part of the kingdom." *Signed. Seal.* [N.IV., 101.]

Sir Matthew Boynton and others to William Lenthall.

1645, October 3. York.—Complaining of the exactions of the Scotch army. (Printed in *Lords' Journals*, vii. 640, where in the second line of paragraph 2, "propositions" should be "provisions.") *Signed. Seal.* [N. IV., 102.]

Francis Pierrepont and others to William Lenthall.

1645, October 4. York.—(Printed in *Lords' Journals*, vii. 639.) *Signed. Seal.* [N. IV., 103.]

Sir John Gell to William Lenthall

1645, October 4. Derby.—"The king with some 2,000 in his army —whereof 1,500 fighting men—are this day passed our garrison about eight miles distant and so for Newark. The most now that is in his army are Irish. Those that have any religion in them at all run away, whereof we have two. There is now commanders with the King General Garrett (Gerard), Sir Marmaduke Langdale, Sir William Vaughan, and now the Lord of Loughborough. There is no other commander of note with the King, Prince Maurice being gone to Worcester, but left his Regiment with his Majesty." (See *Commons' Journals*, iv. 299.) *Signed. Seal.* [N. IV., 104.]

Sir John Gell to William Lenthall.

1645, October 4. Derby.—I sent to Colonel Rossiter to give him notice of the King's coming the Friday night before. I think it my duty to acquaint you with the enclosed, and what I did upon them, and to ask you to acquaint the House, the Committee of both Kingdoms, or whom else you please. "I was in a great strait what to do, all three of them being Committee men, and two of them soldiers, and the third —namely Mr. Clarke—only a Committee man, who likewise was well acquainted with all the former proceedings of Colonel Stockdale. At last" I resolved "to desire Mr. Clarke to go to the Earl of Leven and went to him to his lodgings to that purpose, but he seemed to be unwilling. Then I told him he needs must go and took him by the hand and wished him to go along with Colonel Stockdale. I was confident he being no soldier no harm would befall him, but that he would give satisfaction to General Leven in possessing of him of the truth of the proceedings in this business, and for the other two, being soldiers, I sent them not. He is since safe returned. If I had wholly refused, I know not what inconvenience might have happened, the whole Scots army at that time being at Nottingham and upon our county." If I have offended the House in this business, I am heartily sorry and beg pardon. (See *Commons' Journals*, iv. 303.) *Seal.* [N. IV., 106.] *Enclosed:*

The EARL OF LEVEN to SIR JOHN GELL.

i. 1645, September 15. Nottingham.—Concerning Colonel Stockdale. [N. IV., 84.]

The EARL OF LEVEN, the EARL OF CALANDER, and others to the GOVERNOR and COMMITTEE AT DERBY.

ii. 1645, September 15. Nottingham.—"We have been informed by Colonel Stockdale, whose regiment is a part of this army that whilst he was upon his march to us in June last some troops of your garrison fell upon him, pursued and robbed himself and his regiment. . . . As we are willing if any injury have been offered by him to give redress thereof to the full, so we desire and expect that restitution may be made of the goods and money, horses and arms taken from him, or otherwise that" those who commanded those troops be sent hither to their trial with the Colonel. (See *Commons' Journals*, iv. 303.) [N. IV., 85.]

The COMMITTEE AT YORK to the EARL OF LEVEN
and
The EARL OF LEVEN to the COMMITTEE AT YORK.

1645, October 4 and 6.—(Both printed in *Lords' Journals*, vii. 642, 643.) *Copies.* [N. XII., 147, 148.]

Information of GEORGE HIGGINS.

[1645], October 6. Nottingham.—(Printed in *Lords' Journals*, vii. 639.) [N. XIV., 36.]

JOHN [LORD] CULPEPER to [GEORGE LORD GORING].

[1645], October 6, at night. Launceston.—"My leter from the Lord Digby brought hither this morninge by Doctor Lloyd, Chaplaine to the Prince,—a copy whereof your Lordship will herewith receave—was written before his Lordship had heard of the London reports tochinge the Marquis Montrosse. But before he parted from the king—who was at Chirke Castle on Michaelmas day—, Mr. Spencer came from Oxford to his Majesty,—in his jorney over to Ireland—and towld the reports which came from London touchinge David Lesley and my Lord Montrosse much to the same effect as wee had them, which Mr. Lloyd sayeth was not beleived in the army, there haveinge been with the king an expresse from my Lord Montrosse with leters dated the 12th Septr. from Kelso, besides what my Lord Digby his leter mentiones from Kendalle. Doctor Lloyd sayeth that the expresse from Kelso affirmed that my Lord Montrosse did beate a considerable party of David Lesley his horse, and gave them the chace seventeen miles on English grownd. My Lord it is beyonde my power to reconcile all the particulars of this bussinesse. Uppon the whole I hope very well, yet ame not quite free of my former apprehensions. If your Lordship have any new intelligence which may cleare these mysteries yow will extreamely oblige me to convey them to me to Barnestable whither I ame goinge tomorrow, and where I shall continue untill Saterday morninge. I understand by another leter that his Majesty had a very good appareance of his horse at his private rendezvous at Chirk Castle 29th Septr., and that Prince Maurice came thither to the king with five hundred good horse—part of them came to him from Oxford and were of those that were at Bristoll and Berkely Castle—and—which your Lordship will not thinke fitt to impart to others—that the king intended to goe to Newarke by the way of Worcester. The government of Oxford is changed and Will. Llegg committed as you heard, but noe such thinge as any restrainte on p[rince] R[upert]. I perceave that it would be very acceptable to the king, if withoute hazard to these counties and with safety to the body of horse, they could be joyned with his Majesty. But this hath been sufficiently considered of, and cannot have a full resolution withoute further intelligence of Fairfax his motions." *Postscript.*—Desiring him to communicate this intelligence to Lord Capel at Exeter. *Signed.* [N. IV., 107.]

Oliver Cromwell to William Lenthall.

1645, October 6. Winchester.—Giving an account of his taking Winchester and enclosing the articles of Surrender. (Printed in Rushworth, iv. 1. 91, and Carlyle, No. 32, where "store of wheat and *beer*" should be "*beare*," *i.e.*, a sort of corn. There is also in the original a Postscript excusing himself for having given Mr. Chichley a pass to go to Cambridgeshire to see his sick wife, and stating that he had desired Mr. Peters to communicate some things about the army which may not be fit to commit to writing.) *Signed. Seal.* [N. IV., 108.]
Enclosed :

The Said Articles.

(Printed *ubi supra*, where in the 1st "function" and in the 5th "be in their own time" are misprints for "furniture" and "live at their own homes.") *Copy.* [N. XII., 155.]

Sir John Gell to William Lenthall.

1645, October 7. Derby.—"My men hath met with one Mr. Richard Johnson, Master of the Horse to the Lord Lichfield, who was prisoner at Nantwich, and had license to go to bury his Lord, and upon his parole for exchange, and so upon his journey from Newark did carry some letters, which I have sent to the Committee of both Kingdoms, with a Commission to my Lord Byron to be Governor of Conway and Field Marshal General of all North Wales with other expressions of great falsities. The King stayeth still at Newark, but intendeth the relief of Chester. The Lord of Linsey is also with the King.

Postscript.—This is part of my Lord Digby's letter to my Lord Byron :
According to what I wrote unto you at large from Chirk, his Majesty is advanced as far as Newark, and we hope it will have the wished effect.

68. his Majesty will 81. God send you may hold out till he come. If it should not be possible, for all that is possible I am sure you will do, you are then desired to apply yourself to 81 particularly to 68. I have received newly an express from Montrose who was betrayed and lost two or three hundred men at most, and since that he hath given D. Lesley a great blow. General Goring hath had a victory against Massey, and Fairfax is marched back into the West in great haste to encounter him. Newark, October 5." *Seal.* [N. IV., 109.] (The whole is printed in *State Papers, Domestic*, p. 174.)

Thomas Cole and others to William Lenthall.

1645, October 8. Bury St. Edmunds.—Reminding him that they had often informed the Parliament of the vast sums of money and number of horses raised in the county, and that they had engaged their credits for the service of the state whereby they had incurred a debt of 5,000*l.*, which by the last alarms is doubled, and desiring that they might have their arrears to pay their debts. *Signed.* [N. IV., 110.]

Colonel Martin Pyndar and Harcourt Leighton to William Lenthall.

1645, October 8. Bristol. — " The resolves of the General and Councell of Warr to fall on this citty hapned at a tyme when our treasure was at the lowest, yet not held a sufficient ground to divert such hopefull resolutions. The care for supply of the army in the meane tyme was committed to us amongst others, as Mr. Ash and Mr. Moore can sufficiently informe you, to which purpose wee issued out warrants to the countyes of Gloucester and Somerset to have provisions brought in, engaging ourselves the country should be satisfied for the same out of the pay of the army, and the successe was answerable to our desires and necessities ; but the irregularity of the soldyer hath prevented that just imposition on themselves, which by our instructions the honourable Houses of Parliament have ordered, and begott unto us much more trouble then is fitt to trouble you withall. Where wee can possibly reduce the charge by ticquett or oath to any regiment, troope, or company wee have upon moderate rates given debenters to the parishes for the same. Where wee cannot come to an exact rule, wee have left it to the committees of the countyes to allow out of contributions or asseasments upon the severall Hundreds, without which perticular persons will be utterly undon, because they cannot say who hurt them, not being able to say whither our army or the club armyes eate up theyr provisions which we find and saw to be devoured and destroied in an exterordinary measure, especially theyr h[ous]es which our foote soldyers were constreined to make use off in wett weather for hutts and in this also the club army had a proportionable share. What we now offer is the complaints brought in to us by the country who therefore apply themselves to us, because we have engaged ourselves for theyr satisfaction and say they are soe farre from receiving satisfaction for this dammadg', that the committees require greate contributions from them, and will not make any allowance thereout to the supply of the necessityes of these people, who in many places have had theyr cattle driven, ther houses fired, ther goods spoiled by the enemy, and that little remaynder eaten up by the great confluence of people comminge to the

leagure ; soe that without a present releife they will be in a perishing
condition. In perticular the committee for the citty of Gloucester
demaund to the very walls of this citty twenty-four mouthes contribution, and inforce it by driving the country, imprisoning the persons,
beating and wounding such as resist them in this violence, which they
complaining to us off, we were bould to adresse our letters to the committee, cloathed with the best arguments we could use from whome was
received such an answere soe seconded with the continuance of theyr
former outrages that wee cannot but present both our letter and theyr
answer to your honourable consideration humbly prayinge theyr may be
some speedy rule given us to remitt such contribution as the enemy hath
forced them to pay to this citty to repaire, such daumage as they have
suffered by our league before this citty, and that each garrison may be
bounded for contributions that one clash not against the other as now
they doe to which wee shall only adde that the visitation of this citty
increasing more and more wherby the soldyers are advisedly sent into
the same parts and parishes to quarter they may be dispensed withall
for a tyme that are thus burthened with quartering and interteining our
sick and wounded soldyers whom though wee equally doe undertake to
make satisfaction for, yet cannot be reimbursed by reason of that
extreame retarding of the supplyes appointed for the army, which
proveth of very dangerous consequence begetting daily mutinees, and
causing many honest and stout soldyers to dissert the service rather then
they will be a burthen to the country : which how farre it may exasperate the Clubmen and begett a new contest wee rather pray to prevent
then prophecy to ensue. The Generall hath neglected no expedient to
sweeten the soldyer with money and ere he marched hence did patch up
a weekes pay to the private foote for which wee your commissioners are
ingaged in this citty as also to make up the gratuity of Bridgwater
servyce all which must be paied ere we goe hence : where our imploi-
ment is to make up a second gratuity which the Generall was pleased to
engage himself to the soldyer, wherby to prevent that ruine which must
have fallen upon the citty by storming of it had not theyr apetitie been
cloyed by the expectation of this promise then which a more noble act
was not to be expected, nor more nobly entertayned both by officer and
soldyer, who obayed the Generall's commands therein to the full satisfaction of the citty. And the purchase of soe greate a benefitt to a
citty of such concernment wee presume to say was not deare at fourteen
dayes pay to the soldyer the collecting whereof hath byn committed to
our care supposing that the wealth of the enemy would have made good
the expected summe, which occasioneth us to present you also with an
account of our proceedinges herein. The citty wee finde to have byn a
den of theeves whither the enemy hath brought his plundred goods, and
where methodically they have placed the same to theyr owne advantage
becomming inhabitantes and housekeepers and well provided of hous-
howld-stuff, who being unrowsted (unroosted) by us have willingly left
theyr prey behind them save only such as was portable and by the
Articles permitted them to carry away soe that plate or mon[e]y we find
not in any proportion. The goods themselves soe farre as concernes
houshould affaires doe finde propriators for in abundance, whose affection
to your cause caused them to be plundred and faithfulness in your
servyce cause us to make restitution of what they can justly challenge
to be theyr owne. Much other goods wee find stored up and kept in
the citty, brought in while Collonel Fines was governour and doth belong
unto persons professing theyr integrity to the parliament though overpowred by the enemy whom we cannot esteeme as enemyes and therfore
cannot deny them theyr goods. Other goodes there are of that

nature that we may esteem prise because made soe by the enemy. Such is the corrall brought in by Mucknell and the Hanburgers' shipp with the goods there, both which are owned by instruments imploied to that purpose and are respitted by us untill theyr clayme by the allowance of the honorable house of parliament be made knowne to whome we have referred the state of theyr demaunds. Wee find also that Mr. Thomas Marsham of London hath brought in some quantity of goods which yet remayne unsould, but by a pretended property transferred to merchants in this citty for debt, which wce conceive to be purposely done to prevent that interest the army doth clayme in them, all which we humbly offer as arguments of necessity to annihilate the expectations of rich or vast prizes here to be had. Wee shall farther offer that wee have used all faire expedients to promote the gratuity which is of that necessary concernment that it is consistent with the being of the army and the preservation of any other citty or garrison we may storme hereafter, to the effecting whereof wee have layed open the honorable care our Generall tooke to preserve the citty from fire and plunder the one inducing him to give the Prince a passage which otherwise the wealth of the world could not have purchased from him, the other invitinge him to promise the soldyer that gratuity which would have cost the citty ten tymes as much had they byn theyr owne carvers. And to make theyr burth[en] lighter towards which we have offered unto them all prizall goods of what nature soever here found, provided they would only make good the promised gratuity which after many dayes deliberation produceth this effect only : that they denie to medle with any of the goodes in one kind or other, pretending theyr inability to lay downe money for the same, yet that it may appeare how ready they are to acknowledg the greate benefitt they are pertaker[s] of by that noble care of the Generall, they are willing to gratifie the army with the summe of 5,000*l.* towardes the fourteen dayes promised the soldyer, it being the uttmost of they[r] ability and more then they find any probable way to advance. Wherin we desire to subscribe unto them, our owne judgments evidencing unto us that whatever perticular persons aymed at in the countenancing of that party experience hath taught them that nothing but ruine hath accompanied them and dessolation would have byn the issue of such a government, it being manifest that the citty hath lost noe less of its wealth then of its reputation in the entertainment of such guests. What shall therefore want of the expected sum, which is computated by the Army to be near 12,000*l.* in all, and will not be advanced upon the Corall and other goods we pray may be added to the rest of your favours conferred on that army . . . and that it may be speeded unto them. *Postscript.*—[We suspect] Mr. Basset sometyme a member of the Howse of Commons and many persons of eminency both Lords and others to lurke in and have recourse unto this citty, which we conceive would soone be remedied were here a Standing Committee once settled." *Signed.* [N. IV., 111.]
Enclosed :

i. Colonel MARTIN PYNDAR and HARCOURT LEIGHTON to the GOVERNOR and COMMITTEE OF GLOUCESTER.

1645, September 27. Bristol.—Desiring that their ministers might forbear to molest the inhabitants of Henbury Hundred, till the ground of their demand be duly examined and cleared by order of Parliament, as from their sufferings during the late siege of Bristol they were wholly disabled from paying present contributions much less arrears. *Copy.* [N. XII., 142.]

ii. John Fettiplace, J. Bromwich, Willia Leigh, Willia
Shepheard, and Henry Jones to the Co issioners for
the Ar y in Bristol.

1645, September 29. [Gloucester.]—" We are as ready to believe
as let you know that we are sorrowful for those abuses which
have been committed in Henbury Hundred, and sensible of the
unruliness of the soldier as well as of the distresses of our poor
neighbours, but that you should free them from contribution
being behind almost two years and complain of us to the
Parliament for demanding it . . . is a precedent of such
dangerous consequence to the being of this garrison that we
- cannot admit it." Any injury to the poor people by any
minister of ours shall be censured and punished. *Signed.*
[N. IV., 96.]

Sir Henry Vane, Sir Willia Armyne, Tho as Hatcher, and Robert Goodwin to Willia Lenthall.

1645, October 8. Barwicke.—(Identical *mutatis mutandis* with the
letter of the same date from Philip Lord Wharton to the Speaker of the
House of Peers, which is printed in *Lords' Journals*, vii. 657.) *Signed.*
Seal. [N. IV., 112.]

Tho as Ga ble, Mayor, Francis Thornhagh, Sheriff, and others to Willia Lenthall.

1645, October 8. Nottingham.—Desiring that Colonel Ireton, Major
Lomax, and Alderman James, who had been by all former Ordinances
employed on the Committee for that county, but who had been left out
of the late Ordinance for the Northern Association, should be added to
the Committee. *Signed. Seal.* [N. IV., 113.]

The Marquess of Argyll, Philip [Lord] Wharton, and others to the Co ittee of both Kingdo s.

1645, October 9. Barwicke.—*Signed.* [N. IV., 114.] *Enclosed :*

i. George [Lord] Digbye to the Earls of Leven and
Kalender.

1645, October 4. Newark.—*Seal.* [N. IV., 105.]

ii. The Earl of Leven to the Chief Co ander of the Forces
now with his Majesty.

1646, October 9. Berwick.—(All are printed in *Lords' Journals*,
vii. 638.) *Copy.* [N. XII., 150.]

A Scout to Colonel Doyly.

1645, October 9.—(Printed in *Lords' Journals*, vii. 639.) *Copy,*
certified by Walter Frost. [N. XII., 149.]

Colonel Tho as Morgan to Willia Lenthall.

1645, October 10. Chepstow.—" Beeing informed uppon Satterday last
there was some riseing in the Counties of Glamorgan and Monmoth to
stand upon their owne gaurds under the command of Sir Trever
Williams and Collonell Mathews, with some shewes of beeing for the

parliament, I made use of that oppertunitie and drew out five hundred of my horss and four hundred foote from Gloucester towards Chepstow, with which I entred the toune and sommoned the Castle of Collonell Fitzmorris for the parliament's use, unto which he sent a very peremtorey answer saying he kept it for his master the king, but beeing very desirous to reduce that garrison unto dew obedience of parliament I still continewed in the toune with that partie, and sent to the governour of Bristoll for three hundred foote for my assistance in the bussenes, which he willingly did, who came up to me upon Thursday night. Then I raysed a battrey within halfe musquet shott of the Castle and planted two brass colvering and one of iron with which when I had made a resonable breach there came to my hand certaine intelligence of the enemys moveing from Worcester, Heriford, Lymster, Ragland, and Monmouth and intended to quarter two thousand horss and .foote this night at Aberganey, upon which I prepared with all possible speede to storme it, and for that purpose I drew out four hundred men and had sett them in a posture immediately to have faulne on, which the enemy discovered and bett a parley of which I admitted, and the then governour there send out a letter by his drumer desiring to treate, but because I would not admitt of aney delays, I appointed an officer to returne him this answer, viz., that I had not now time to send him an answer in wrighting, but if he would deliver up to me the Castle with all the armes, ordnance, amunicion, and other provitions therein, for the parliamentes use and render himself with all the officers and souldiers my prisoners hee and they should have faire quarter for theire lives, which he imbraced, and yealded himselfe and all with him my prisoners, and imediately marched out. The prisoners are Collonell Fitzmorris, Governour, Majour Bridgman Deputie Governour, Captain Hallome, Leiutenant Jones, Ensigne Dauson, and one hundred and six prisoners. I founde in the toune and castle, eighteen peeces of ordnance great and smale, fifteen barills of pouder, four hundred barills of butter, six hogsheads of bisquet with greate quantityes of other provitions. The countrey boeth here and in the Forest of Deane doe much rejoyce at our prosperous proceeding in the clearing this passage, by reson of the free traids they are now in hope to enjoye to London, Gloucester, Bristoll, and other parts of the kingdome, and I have appointed Collonell Heuges, Governour of the toune and castle of Chepstowe." *Signed. Seal.* [N. IV., 115.]

[GEORGE LORD DIGBY] to [LORD JERMYN].

1645, October 10. Newark.—" I hope mine from Bridgenorth is miscarried. It was more melancholy than upon second thoughts I would have written but . . . the loss of my Lord of Lichfield and the other gallant men and in the nick of that the Rebels' printed boasts of my Lord Montrose's total overthrow had put me into a fit of deeper melancholy and despair than I have ever before been subject unto. Since that I have received expresses from my Lord Montrose, wherein he relates the truth of his late misfortune . . . at Philiphaw . . . wherein he lost in all but 200 men, and bids us be assured that yet ere winter he will be in England with a gallant army. We since receive daily information from all parts in the North that he hath routed David Lisley, Colkito and his other forces being come up to him, for at Philiphaw he was only a small party invited to the Borders by Roxburgh and others who betrayed him. We shall no sooner receive an express of his good condition but we shall endeavour to get to him. In the meantime here we rest about Newark the unlikeliest place to be

besieged and the strongest if it be, and from whence the King may not
be hindered from marching away with his horse at any time, whither we
marched from Chirk without any interruption, Poyngs having it seems
been too much broken to follow us and opinatring since the siege of
Chester. If he give us leisure till we hear the certainty of Montrose he
will much oblige us. If not, I hope with that addition which we may
receive from this garrison, we may be able to fight with him for our
passage. We are in hourly expectation of an answer from the Scots
Army to those overtures made unto them whereof I advertised you
formerly, and we have cause to hope well of that negotiation. It were
impertinent to trouble you from hence with the westward news. . . .
If Goring hath given Massey such a defeat as is believed and that
Fairfax hath drawn back his army against him there will then be a fair
blow for the setting us as high again as ever. I hope that our mis-
fortunes will not make you faint there in soliciting all possible supplies
of money arms and ammunition, for whatsoever sudden damps may
seize us upon unexpected disasters, I hope upon recollection we shall
none of us doubt but God will in the end magnify his justice in the
prosperity of his Majesty's cause. Whatsoever happen let her Majesty
be assured that I in the discharge of my duty shall still make good the
confidence which she hath been pleased to have of me." *Endorsed :* "66
Digby to Germaine, but blotted out." (See *Commons' Journals,* iv.
324.) *Copy.* [N. XII., 151.]

Francis Pierrepont and others to William Lenthall.

1645, October 10. York. — Complaining that Colonel White at
London had protested the bills they had drawn on him for repayment of
600l. borrowed of the excise men at York when the soldiers were in
mutiny, because he had no funds, whereby their credit was injured, and
desiring that the House should allow them this money. *Signed. Seal.*
[N. IV., 117, should be 116.]

George Boothe and others to William Lenthall.

1645, October 10. From Chester Suburbs.—" Upon Monday last we
so straitly begirt the town on both sides the river, that none can get
forth or come in to them, of which Sir John Byron complained in two
letters, the one to his brother, the other to the Archbishop of York,
intercepted by us that day. Yesterday we again attempted the City by
storm. The most part of the day was spent in battery—after a parley
of 24 hours held with them—we fell to the storm a little before sunset,
which continued for the space of an hour and a half. The service was
very hot, in which attempt we spent very much ammunition, for which
the gentlemen of the County stand engaged. The service was performed
by the expense of some blood, yet no considerable man lost. Amongst
the wounded Lieutenant-Colonel Venables, a gallant man, received a
wound in the arm but not dangerous. The premises set out our necessity, and plead for a speedy supply of moneys, without which we cannot
continue in this posture. The help of the adjacent counties in provision
in a due way proportioned, will be necessary for our support otherwise
this overcharged county will be in danger to sink under the burden."
Postscript.—Praising Colonel Jones and Adjutant Louthiane and
desiring that some notice may be taken of them. (See *Commons'
Journals,* iv. 308.) *Signed. Seal.* [N. IV., 118, should be 117.]

Richard Darley and others to William Lenthall.

1645, October 10. York.—(Printed in *Lords' Journals,* vii. 642.)
Signed. Seal. [N. IV., 118.]

FRANCIS PIERREPONT and others to WILLIAM LENTHALL.

1645, October 11. York.—Stating on account of the report that the late reducement of the army is approved by the House and is to be presently executed, that as the late mutinies both of horse and foot were in some measure appeased by the late order for the continuance of the army in the same state for three months longer, so they cannot but fear that the present alteration of it may revive the distemper, representing the danger this may be in regard of the King's being at Newark, the forces of the other Associated Counties not joined with their own, and the last, both horse and foot, being too few for the present service, and therefore desiring that the House may take measures to allay or prevent the feared discontent. *Signed. Seal.* [N. IV., 119.]

WILLIAM CAWLEY to ROBERT SCAWEN.

1645, October 13. Chichester.—"By reason of the Clubmen's insurrection we can neither raise men or moneys for Sir Thomas Fairfax's army, or upon any other ordinance, they not suffering our officers to impress, or when impressed taking them away by violence, sending sometimes a Constable or Tithingman with the blood running about his ears so that of 67 to be impressed in this Rape, were brought in but 27, whom at a great charge we were forced to maintain for 14 days, and then sent them to Lieutenant-General Cromwell to Winchester, so that we want 40, which we shall endeavour to raise, if the House will authorise us to apprehend the principal fomentors, and so punish them that by their example others may be affrighted from attempting the like. And in no better case are we for moneys, it being one of their Articles to pay such taxes only as they please, the fruits whereof we are too sensible of, not an 100*l.*—though above 4,000*l.* due—being brought in since their first rising, no collector daring to distrain for fear of having his brains dashed out, 40 servants and women rising together armed with prongs and other weapons, so that of eight months' due upon Sir Thomas Fairfax's army not two months' yet brought in, all which may easily be remedied, if the Houses authorise the Committee to sequester their ringleaders, fine the rest, and disarm all, till which is done, in vain will it be for us to issue out our warrants, our persons being scorned and threatened, and your authority abused and derided." (See *Commons' Journals*, iv. 318.) *Seal.* [N. IV., 120.]

SIR JOHN GELL to WILLIAM LENTHALL.

1645, October 14. Derby.—"According to your command I gave order for my horse to march to Chester, and they went hence yesterday. I have only reserved three troops for defence of this county, in regard many of the King's horse quarter near our country. The King himself continues still about Newark, and makes a show of taking up his winter quarters there. He hath appointed the country people to come in to Newark this day to be healed of the King's evil, and either he will remove just against that time, as formerly he did, or else he will make a long stay in these parts. On Saturday last a party of the Yorkshire horse fell upon some of the King's in Warsopp, and took some prisoners and horse, but the certain number I yet know not. General Poynts continues still about Chester. . . The besiegers at Chester lately made an attempt against that city but lost about 18 men and had 80 wounded. At this instant I have intelligence that most of the King's horse are gone to Tuxford in the Clay. . . . *Postscript.*—

Is come to Welbeck (sic)." (See *Commons' Journals*, iv. 312.) *Seal.*
[N. IV., 121.]

SIR HENRY VANE and others to WILLIAM LENTHALL.

1645, October 14. St. Andrews.—(Identical *mutatis mutandis* with
the letter of the same date from Philip Lord Wharton to the Speaker
of the House of Peers, which is printed in *Lords' Journals*, vii. 649.)
Signed. Seal. [N. IV., 122.]

The HOUSE OF COMMONS.

1645. October 14.—Proceedings concerning trade with Denmark.
(Printed in *Commons' Journals*, iv. 308, from " The humble petition "
to " added to the same Committee.") [N. XVIII., 2.] *Annexed:*

Treaty between the Commissioners of the KING OF DENMARK and
Mr. Jenks and Mr. Skinner, COMMISSIONERS OF THE PARLIA-
MENT.

1645, April 26. Copenhagen.—Settling various matters connected
with trade, navigation, tolls, and customs. [N. XVIII., 1.]

The COMMITTEE OF BOTH KINGDOMS.

1645, October 14. — Order reporting certain letters and papers.
(Printed in *Lords' Journals*, vii. 638.) [N. XII., 181.]

WILLIAM LENTHALL to the EARL OF LEVEN.

1645, October 16.—Thanking him in the name of the House for his
conduct with regard to Lord Digby's letter. (See *Commons' Journals,*
iv. 309.) *Draft.* [N. XII., 152.]

Colonel EDWARD ROSSETER to WILLIAM LENTHALL.

1645, October 16. Grantham.—" Upon intelligence that Prince
Rupert with a party from Oxford was coming to Newark upon
Tuesday I drew to Melton with my own troops, and those under the
command of Major Baynes. About noon on Wednesday we lighted
upon Prince Rupert with his brother Maurice, the Lord Molineux, the
Lord Hawley, Sir William Vavasour with 300 in their party near
Waltham. Our forlorn hope skirmished with them, upon my advancing
to charge them they fairly faced about. We pursued them three miles
to the walls of Belvoir and killed many, took prisoners a major, three
captains and about three score gentle and others, six or seven score
horses. They had no colours, but we took the Prince's trumpet and
banner. The King amused us as if he had been for the North and
moved towards Welbeck to draw us over Trent. I hear he returned
to Newark on Tuesday with part of his force, but sent Sir Marmaduke
Langdale with a party Northwards. Colonel-General Poynts yesterday
came to Derby. The 1,000 horse and dragoons that came from London
to Leicester are marched to him." *Signed.* [N. IV., 123.]

Colonel-General SEDNHAM POYNTS to the COMMITTEE OF BOTH KINGDOMS.

1645, October 16. Ilkstone Moor.—(The purport sufficiently appears
from *Commons' Journals*, iv. 314.) [N. IV., 124.]

Sir John Gell to William Lenthall.

1645, October 16. Derby.—"This last night General Poynts quartered at Pisley in the midway betwixt Derby and Nottingham. Colonel Manwaringe quartered at Calveston within three miles of General Poynts, so that their forces are now united. Two days since the King's forces lay between Welbeck and Blyth, and had their rendezvous at Warsopp, from thence they marched towards Doncaster, and I am informed their intentions are to march Northwards. Upon this Colonel Copley retreated with his horse to Sherburne, where his foot lies, and he earnestly desires that the King may be pursued in the rear, in regard that his men have lately been in some discontent. Yesterday morning about 400 horse of the King's were at Harborough, their intentions was to go that night to Belvoir and so to the King. These came from about Banbury, and gave out that Prince Rupert and Prince Maurice were both with them, but that I conceive was but their report and little truth in it." [N. IV., 125.]

Francis Pierrepont and others to William Lenthall.

1645, October 17. York.—Enclosing a letter of the Commander-in-Chief of our horse and a list of the prisoners taken at Sherburne on the 15th. "Our foot was at first surprised, but this we are bold to say there wanted not our care and orders to prevent the same. . . . They were happily rescued by the horse, who, though their number was small and inferior to the enemy, yet their resolution and valour greater, and therefore merits all encouragement for so good service." We owe them a fortnight's pay by promise which we ask the House to supply speedily, and also to send some reward for their encouragement. By the enclosed from the Earl of Leven you may "perceive that the Scotch army are not in a present posture for their advance to Newark, though they have been several times earnestly solicited by us thereunto. We are the more earnest for money for our horse . . . in regard the former and present levies and billets by the Scots upon the North Riding have so exceedingly impoverished that large—and heretofore rich—part of this county that there cannot possibly be raised a competent subsistence for the horse and foot which necessarily are to be maintained in this county." (See *Commons' Journals*, vii. 316.) *Signed. Seal.* [N. IV., 126.]

The Committee for Sequestrations.

[1645], October 17.—Report concerning Mr. Cockshut, Exigenter of London, alleged to be a Delinquent, but of whose good affection towards Parliament they declared themselves satisfied. (See *Lords' Journals*, vii. 606.) *Part in duplicate.* [N. XIV., 185.]

Sir John Henderson to William Lenthall.

1645, October 18. London.—Desiring a safe conduct from the House to go to the King in order to deliver the King of Denmark's letter, and from thence to Scotland. *Seal.* [N. IV., 127.]

The Same to the Same.

Same date.—"I received yesterday morning an order from the Houses of Parliament commanding my sudden departure from this kingdom without any satisfactory answer to his Majesty of Denmark my master's desires, but that by their own Commissioners they would send their answer. In this I humbly acquiesce, entreating . . the House of Commons for a free pass to go to his Majesty of Great Britain for the delivery of his Majesty of Denmark's other letter " . . . and otherwise for permission to send one of my own servants or a trumpeter of theirs with the King of Denmark's letter and an open one of my own to the King. *Seal.* (See *Commons' Journals*, iv. 308, 328.) [N. IV., 128.]

Sir Thomas Jervoise and others to William Lenthall.

1645, October 18. Basingstoke.—Desiring that Captain Bettesworth, for whom they had written to the Committee of both Kingdoms for a commission to command their horse, and taken order for making him sheriff, should be appointed governor of Winchester Castle instead of Colonel Lower. (See *Commons' Journals*, iv. 314.) *Signed. Seal.* [N. IV., 129.]

Sir Thomas Jervoise and others to William Lenthall.

1645, October 20. Basingstoke.—Recommending Major Gifford, Major in Colonel Jephson's regiment of horse designed for Ireland, for his conduct at the storm of Basing House. *Signed. Seal.* [N. IV., 130.]

Sir John Bampfylde, Sir Samuel Rolle, Francis Buller, and Anthony Nicoll to William Lenthall.

1645, October 20. Tiverton.—" We came to the armie at Beaminster and from thence advanced with them to Chard the next day, where they remained some dayes in expectation of the recruites and mony for the armie and of monie for Majour-Generall Masseyes partie. Wee advanced thence to Hunningtou (Honiton) from whence before our advance the enemie retreated neere Exon till which time they plundered all the countrie of cattle. From Hunnington wee advanced to Collumton on Thurseday, on which day, Majour-Generall Masseye's partie came before Tiverton castle and summoned it, but received a refusall of obeying. Our noble Generall having notice of it, came on Friday with a parte of his armie hither, the residew hee sent to Bradnidge. Yesterday about two of the clocke after-noone, some batteries being made and all thinges being reddie for storming for which the souldiers with much cheerefullnesse prepared themselves, the Generall for the sparing of blood, with the advice of the councell of warre, resolved to sende them a second summons, which was written and signed and parties drawne out, who were reddie with theire scalinge ladders to storme, if a deniall were returned, but at that instant it pleased God so to derecte one shott that it cut the chaine of theire draw-bridge which instantly fell downe, and the souldiers spirrits were such, that they presently without ordre given, entred theire workes. The enemies heartes failed, and wee became suddenly masters of the church, and castle, and theire strong and reguler workes in which they confided. Wee tooke the governour, Sir Gilbert Tawbott, and two hundred and four officers and souldiers of which you have heere enclosed a list, four greate gunnes, thirty barrells of powder, with other armes which cannot bee particularized, they being dispersed. Wee loste not a man in the storming, nor put any to the sword. Wee saw so much resolucion in all the souldiers that wee cannot but make it our request that mony may bee speeded to them, without which, it is much doubted how they will bee supplied, the countrie where they advance not having in theire quarters wherewith to supply them. But if money bee wanting to pay in the market which is appointed to follow the armie with provisions from our reare, the market will faile. Majour-Generall Masseyes men have not mony to shoe theire horses. Goring is retreated to Chidleigh. What hee intends wee know not. Our industrious and vigilant Generall pittying the condicion of the contrie, who crie for his assistance and intending nothing more then the speeding of the worke, and the active Majour Massey resolve this day to advance in one body towerd Goring who is strong and wee can not devide the armie, unlesse Leiutenant-Generall Cromwell come up with his partie, with which its hoped they may devide and the more speedily finish the worke in the west, without which the whole armie must follow Goring or runne a great hazard, the Prince, Hopton, and Greenvill being entred Devon with four thousand foote and fifteen hundred horse as wee are informed." *Signed. Seal.* [N. IV., 131.]

Sir Henry Vane and others to William Lenthall.

1645, October 20. Anderweeke.—(Identical *mutatis mutandis* with the letter of the same date from Philip Lord Wharton to the Speaker of the House of Peers, which is printed in *Lords' Journals*, vii. 659.) *Signed.* [N. IV., 132.]

Thomas Salusbury and others to Gilbert Millington.

1645, October 22. Nottingham.—"There is now a very great force of horse in our county with General Poynts to straighten Newark, but the extreme poverty of our miserably harassed country, which hath so long been under the power of so potent enemies, and been forced so often to entertain numerous forces for and against the Parliament will not admit of delay to be supplied from adjacent counties or otherwise." We therefore desire the House to afford us speedy and seasonable assistance. *Signed. Seal.* [N. IV., 133.]

Charles White to Gilbert Millington.

1645, October 22. Southwell.—Asking him to solicit the Committee of both Kingdoms that if Newark shall be besieged this time, a standing Committee may be appointed out of all the adjacent counties to superintend and provide for the army, and that it may be maintained by the counties of Derby, York, Leicester, Rutland, and Lincoln, and that what foot shall be designed for this service may be speedily sent, otherwise the country shall be consumed before the work is begun, and stating the impoverished state of the county and army. "The King and the Princes are yet in Newark. General Poynts lieth at Southwell with our horse and foot and some other horse of Yorkshire, Gloucester, and the London Brigade. Welbeck is also straitened. Colonel Rosseter is now at Bingham. We cannot approach nearer Newark without foot." *Seal.* [N. IV., 134.]

Captain Robert Moulton to William Lenthall.

1645, October 22. King's Road, aboard the *Lion*.--Stating that when lately at Cardiff Sir John Strangewayes was brought into the town, who is now detained more or less at large there, and interceding for him, mentioning that there is at Cardiff one Culpepper, nephew to the pretended Lord Culpepper, against whom there is no proof, but it may be suspected that he may serve to convey intelligence, and enclosing a copy of two particulars he had written to the Committee of the Admiralty. • (See *Commons' Journals*, iv. 321.) This is written by a secretary and signed ; then follows in Moulton's own hand with a fresh beginning and end : "one thing or two I had almost omitted . . . Washington with about 1,500 horse and foot fell down into the skirts of Monmouthshire, but by the timely rising of the Glamorganshire Clubmen, and happy intervening of Gloucester forces were put back and pursued as far as Hereford. The Clubmen about 6,000 remain still in the field . . . In my apprehension the multitude of general persons in these counties, each commanding in chief and absolutely, as Gloucester, Monmouth, Brecknock, Glamorgan, Pembrokeshire may in time cause some confusion if not prevented . . . I shall humbly propound . . . whether one whole Commander-in-Chief, appointed by his Excellency over all these counties with . . 500 commanded men—strangers to the place—to whom the rest to be subordinate would not be more conducing to the public service." [N. IV., 135.]

Sir Matthew Boynton and others to Williaj Lenthall.

1645, October 23· York.—Concerning the mutinous spirit of the army, their want of pay, and the impoverishment of the county caused by the Scotch army quartering on it. (Printed in Grey, iii. Appendix, No. 47, p. 74.) (See *Commons' Journals*, iv. 329.) *Signed.* [N. IV., 136.]

The Earl of Warwick and others to the Coajittee of Lords and Coajons for the Eastern Association.

1645, October 23. Chelmsford.—Concerning the pay of the three regiments of horse sent to Newark in July, August, and September, which is due the end of the month or early the next month, desiring that the counties not of the Association who are charged with a portion of the pay and also those counties of the Association that are slow to pay should be quickened, and that arrangements should be made for the future pay of these regiments, and also that when the Parliament accepts a composition for a sequestration a portion of the composition should be paid to the county which had the benefit of the sequestration. (See *Commons' Journals*, iv. 327.) *Signed.* [N. IV., 138.]

Sir Matthew Boynton and others to Williaj Lenthall.

1645, October 24. York.—Since the battles at Roughton Heath and Sherburne there hath been brought in to this city near 500 prisoners, most of whom were formerly commanders in the King's army, who marched Northwards as common troopers. We enclose a list of the most considerable. In regard of the small number of soldiers here, and the general disaffection of the inhabitants, we consider it very dangerous to continue them here and therefore desire the pleasure of the House. We hear that the horse which escaped from Sherburne, being about 800, were stopped in their passage towards Scotland and are retreating again into this county, so that if the said prisoners remain here it may be of very dangerous consequence. *Enclosed* is a list of the prisoners. (See *Commons' Journals*, iv. 329.) *Signed.* [N. IV., 139.]

The Coajittee for Petitions.

1645, October 24.—Resolution on the petition of John Abbott. (See *Commons' Journals*, iv. 354.) [N. XIV., 83.]

Colonel THO MAS MORGAN and SIR TREVOR WILLIAMS to WILLIAM
LENTHALL.

1645, October 24. Monmouth.—Describing the taking of the place.
(Printed in *King's Pamphlets*, E. 266, No. 12, and in Phillips, *Civil War
in Wales*, ii. 279.) *In Morgan's hand and signed by Williams.*
Seal. [N. IV., 139, should be 140.]

SIR MATTHEW BOYNTON and others to WILLIAM LENTHALL.

1645, October 25. York.—Forwarding by Sir William Allanson
divers letters taken at Sherburne and again desiring to know the
pleasure of the House touching the prisoners. *Signed.* `Seal.*
[N. IV., 140, should be 141.]

JOHN [LORD] CULPEPER to GEORGE LORD GORING.

[1645], October 25. Launceston.—Stating that on the receipt of
all Goring's letters to him he had answered them immediately. *Seal.*
[N. IV., 137.]

Colonel JOHN HUTCHINSON, GEORGE HUTCHINSON, CHARLES WHITE,
and others to GILBERT MILLINGTON.

1645, October 26. Nottingham.—Enclosing a letter from General
Poyntz, showing their extreme want of match and powder, and asking
that some considerable quantity of this may be furnished, and also
competent sums to recruit the loss of horses and arms in this present
expedition, and also reminding him of their former desire that the
adjacent counties might be speedily made to contribute to the maintenance of the forces met together in that county. (See *Commons'
Journals*, iv. 329.) *Signed. Seal.* Addressed " at the sign of the Pear
in the little Centrey at Westminster." [N. IV., 142.]

The EARL OF LEVEN to the COMMITTEE OF WAR AT YORK.

1645, October 26, at 6 of the clock at night. Ripon.—" I have
received your letter of this day, wherein you show me that Colonel
Rossetter has altered his intention of marching this way to prevent the
conjuncture of Prince Rupert with the King's forces at Newark, whom
I cannot conceive to have any considerable body, the King having with
himself 3,000 horse, being so oft defeat in several places. As for
bringing of this army before Newark, I can determine nothing of that,
till I know the resolution of the Convention of Estates now in Scotland.
Withal clothes were very necessary for them against the winter, before
they should be put upon such designs in this season of the year. I have
received intelligence that the enemy are gone towards Skipton and . .
have sent a party thither, and whatever assurance they bring me I shall
communicate to you. . . I have made all the haste I could to draw
together 1,000 horse and 2,000 foot, which shall be in a readiness to
execute what is most conducing for the safety of this country." *Signed.*
[N. IV. 143.]

GEORGE HUTCHINSON and others to [GILBERT MILLINGTON].

1645, October 26. Nottingham.—" Though we forbear in our letter
. . to prescribe a proportion of match and powder to be sent to us

yet . . . less than 100 barrels of powder and match answerable will not be sufficient for the managing of designs in these parts. And if this supply be not hasted—as also additional supplies from adjacent counties for the maintenance of the forces here—the country will be utterly undone, before the main . . business can be enterprised." *Postscript.*—Suggesting that supplying the ammunition from Lynn, Boston, or Hull would be the most expeditious way. *Signed.* [N. IV., 144.]

The EARL OF LEVEN to the COMMITTEE OF WAR AT YORK.

1645, October 26. Allerton.—Enclosing a copy of Sir John Browne's letter of the 24th. *Copy.* [N. XII., 153.]

SIR ANTHONY WELDON and others to WILLIAM LENTHALL.

1645, October 27. Maidstone.—Stating that they had received the commands of the House to send the troop of horse sent under Major Webb to Basing on other service, and that they conceive that the ordinance for raising them only enjoins sending them to the rendezvous at Farnham with pay till they come there, after that to be wholly at the disposal and pay of the Hampshire Committee, representing that upwards of 9,700*l. per mensem* besides the Militia and other necessary charges is charged on the county, which not only disables them from undertaking new charges, but which they will not long be able to continue, and complaining that while these charges take away one-third of the revenue of the county, Sussex escapes with a 10th, 16th, or 20th part. *Signed. Seal.* [N. IV., 145.]

SIR WILLIAM VAVASOUR to WILLIAM LENTHALL.

1645, October 27. Northampton.—Complaining that notwithstanding he had Sir Thomas Fairfax's pass after the surrender of Bristol to go out of England, and Colonel Rosseter's to return to Bath or Bristol, he had been taken prisoner near Daventry by a party from that garrison, and asking permission to go according to his pass, or to wait on him. (See *Commons' Journals,* iv. 326.) [N. IV., 146.]

The EARL OF LOUDOUN, LORD BALMERINO, and HEW KENNEDY to WILLIAM LENTHALL.

1645, October 28. Worcester House.—(Identical with the letter of the same to the Speaker of the House of Peers, which is printed in *Lords' Journals,* vii. 668, where also is printed the declaration of the York Committee, a copy of which is here enclosed.) *Signed.* [N. IV., 147.]

SIR MATTHEW BOYNTON and others to WILLIAM LENTHALL.

[1645, October 28.] York.—Enclosing a copy of the last-mentioned declaration. (See *Commons' Journals,* iv. 329). *Signed. Seal.* [N. IV., 148.]

The HOUSE OF COMMONS.

1645, October 28 and November 8.—Declaration touching their proceedings in the matter of Church Government, in reply to the Paper in form of a Petition of September 20th. (*Ante* p. 276.) After recapitulating the proceedings of the Parliament and the Assembly of Divines down to the latter's petition of August the 8th, and the petition soon after of the Ministers of London and Westminster (namely, that of

August 25th), to show the delay had not been attributable to the Parliament, and pointing out that the Assembly had been summoned only to advise the Parliament on such points as they were asked to give their opinion on, it proceeds: " Whilst we were in pursuance of our intentions and had almost brought them to a happy conclusion, some unquiet spirits, perceiving that . . . we were not like to knit up the power granted to the presbyteries . . . with a slip knot as they desired, whereby they or any other subject to the common corruptions of the sons of Adam might have liberty to vent their own passions and private interests or at least errors . . . under the stamp of God's holy ordinance . . . plotted and projected that pretended petition, wherein they intended . . . to muster up as it were an army of importunate petitioners against us, the multitude of whose hands they thought haply might prevail more on our affections and apprehensions, than the Divines had been able to do upon our reasons and judgements. Let any man now trace from step to step, from month to month, from day to day our proceedings . . . and then let him say, if he can, whether any delay or negligence can be justly charged upon us . . unless that shall be esteemed a delay and fault that we do not exactly without any debate . . confirm whatever the Assembly shall propose to us, because haply they are pleased to give it the name of Divine right. . . ." The forwardness that we perceive already in the people to receive . . . from their ministers—as this pretended petition may testify—the impressions of Divine right in things of this nature is no great inducement to move us to put a boundless power into the hands of those that are so eager to claim it by such a right, as being once fixed in them also . . . the Parliament shall never be able to resume again . . no, not so much as to regulate it by appeals or otherwise. The same principles that settle it in Presbyteries by Divine right . . undermine the foundation of all appeals to the Parliament. We are not ignorant neither that in all ages those that have got that spiritual weapon into their hands have fought their own quarrels with it, and usually interested the honour and cause of God even in the least punctilios of their pretended jurisdiction and authority. And what troubles and mischiefs ensued thereupon, all stories, especially those of this kingdom, are full. Neither are we only . . . to look upon the ministers of the City of London —although neither there are they all of one kind—but throughout the whole kingdom also, nor are we in the making of laws to have respect only to the present times, but to those also that may succeed. We can in no wise admit that Christ hath invested the presbyteries with an arbitrary power to keep from the Communion . . . whomsoever they shall judge unworthy, and that the magistrate ought to confirm such a power to them by his civil authority. They say, it is no arbitrary power which is according to the will of Christ and hath the Scripture for its rule, but if it be left arbitrary to them to judge what is the will of Christ and what the rule of the Scriptures, the matter will not be much amended. They say Communion . . doth not belong to any man neither as a man nor as an Englishman, and that therefore by abstention from it, he cannot be prejudiced in any of his liberties or rights . . , but so long as England is Christian he that shall be rejected from Christian Communion will have little countenance in any civil conversation, and less capability of any employment or preferment either in Church or State. Besides we know . . . in the model of Church government, pretended to be according to the mind of Christ, that the civil magistrate is to second the censures of the Church with his civil coercive power, and not suffer them to be contemned. Will they then call the magistrate to strike and will they not allow him an eye to see, but only by the eyes of others, or will they raise up out of the dust again that exploded piece of Popery, that churchmen must declare persons heretics, and then by an implicit faith the magistrate must hang and burn them? that the ecclesiastical Consistories are to excommunicate them, and then without any further debate the magistrates must imprison them, fine them, banish them? Civil function . . . concerns only the civil magistrate, who is to give an account thereof to Him that intrusted him therewith, nor will He hold him excused, if He shall not find him use the like care and caution in the things that more immediately concern His glory and the Communion of Saints, which he doth in the things that concern the profit and politic society of men. . . It is a maxim amongst all wise law makers to leave as little arbitrary as may be, and to make the rule, as . . . determinate as is possible, and we know that even in cases of treason . . . our law, though it acknowledge that divers cases may arise, which men cannot foresee, yet doth it not leave any indefinite power in the Superior Courts, but reserveth such cases to be declared in Parliament. And why should not the like be done, in point of keeping men from the Lord's Table? The ministers fear to partake in other men's sins, that shall communicate unworthily, and have not the Parliament as much and better cause to apprehend that they shall be partakers in other men's sins in keeping persons unjustly from that Sacrament . . ? And who doth not know that if there should happen any such supposed case, which neither the wisdom of the Synod nor of the Parliament can foresee, that it is much better that some or few men should continue still in Communion till the case be determined than that the rule should be left so loose as haply might give occasion to the depriving of many worthy communicants . . . especially when as it is clear that neither minister nor any other is made guilty by communicating simply with an unworthy person . . . . , but in so much as they shall not do their duties in removal of them, wherein they cannot be said to fail, while they are diligently pursuing it in an orderly way? . . . . What can the magistrate demand more reasonable . . than only to see what it is he giveth his civil ratification to before he grant it?" There is less need to insist on this so much at this time, when Parliament is sitting and not likely to discontinue soon or suddenly, so that application may be had to them to supply anything proved by experience to be defective in the rule. If any one cannot satisfy himself while the matter is determining, he will be liable to the like scruples while the matter of fact is depending, and when the case shall be overruled on appeal contrary to his sense. "Therefore every man must be satisfied that he hath done or is doing his duty, otherwise he will certainly plunge himself into a bottomless pit of inexplicable or irremediless scruples. For the examples of other churches and countries it is more wisdom in us to take warning by the smart of others than by following their errors to cast ourselves upon the same rock that they did. . Reformation in most churches besides this . . began rather by the influence of the ministers or the people, than by that of the magistrate . . and therefore it is no great wonder if the magistrate lost some of his right, and the people much of their power. But the examples of Queen Elizabeth and King Edward the 6th, presented to us in the front of the pretended petition we shall willingly take for our patterns. And as we esteem it a great honour . . . that God hath held us worthy to endeavour to perfect what they so happily began, so shall we be careful to tread in the steps of our ancestors . . in causing the Reformation to move from the Parliament, and carrying it on in a Parliamentary way ; without prejudice to the freedom of the Parliament while it is in doing, and without impairing the just authority thereof when it is done, whereby to the magistrate will be preserved his right and to the people their power, whereunto we know no means so effectual as by leaving as little arbitrary as may be . . for if it should be left to the discretion of every presbytery to keep whom they thought unworthy from the Lord's Supper, how far corruption might stir up men's spirits to quarrel and spurn against them, who knoweth ? But when . . they are not censured but upon such causes as upon solemn debate in Parliament have been judged just . . all men . . . will be readier to submit themselves . . and therefore if the ministers and presbyteries well consider it they will give us thanks for binding them to a prescript rule . . that they carry before them the buckler of public authority . . . . . For the mischiefs . . . that are said to arise from the not settling of Church government we cannot deny but in matter of opinion and affection several differences . . have risen, which we should wish rather than expect should have been otherwise, since it hath been incident to all reformations . . . But we must not on the other side pass by the mercy of God to us that those evils have neither been so many or so great . . . as upon the motions and stirring of Reformation . . . have broken forth in Germany and other places, neither can we admit . . that by reason of the not settling of Church government every man may do what seems good in his own eyes to the disturbance of the City . . . the City and other courts of justice in it being enabled to maintain the peace thereof and to restrain the licentiousness of any in it, if not so well, yet in a good measure without the aid of ecclesiastical discipline, and it were a great . . dishonour to the Parliament and all inferior courts . . . if we should grant it to be true that for want of Church discipline abominable damnable and blasphemous opinions either have or may be broached or raised without control. That the hearts of any godly should faint through hope deferred, or that any should have cause to look upon Reformation as more difficult and improbable than ever, whereas it is confessed to be so near the birth we do not understand, but by what hath been declared we presume few are ignorant where or in whom the obstruction lieth, neither can we believe that any of our neighbours should be astonished at our delays, and least of all that our brethren of Scotland should have any cause so to be, since most other places had their *interims* and unsettled conditions in that respect much longer than we . . and our brethren of Scotland, as they have been better acquainted with our diligence in this work from time to time, so they know that their own book of policy was hammering and perfecting in several meetings and general assemblies for almost as many years as we have been months about ours . . . Though we should seem in the space necessary for our deliberations . . for the right settling of Church government to endure some inconveniences, yet better an inconvenience suffered for a while than a mischief settled for ever. Then might our enemies indeed scorn us as possessed with a spirit of giddiness if having so lately . . . taken all civil power from Ecclesiastical persons, and pulled down the High Commission we should presently set up a Higher Commission or a power more arbitrary in every presbytery. To shut the door against such as are grossly ignorant or notoriously scandalous is our duty and desire, but yet in such sort as we may not by that means give power to others to shut the door against pious and painful preachers or any others, because they do not agree with them to a hair, as we have had late and sad experience . . . We know how apt men are to make that blasphemy and heresy which is contrary to what they hold, and to esteem their actions heinous whose persons they hate. We see how ready men are in our days to brand one another with the names of incendiaries, covenant-breakers, children of Belial, and fighters against the kingdom of God, because they do not agree with them in every particular, or consent presently to what they desire in things which in their own nature are indifferent or at least very disputable. Needless separations we dislike, and therefore desire to take away all occasions of them by providing that the causes of excom-munication shall be so just that none being thrust from Communion at discretion . . . may be forced to seek Communion where they may, because they are not suffered to enjoy it where they should. To such as plead·for a toleration of all religious opinions we shall not give an ear, but cannot deny the modest request and reasonable relief of tender consciences, in whose behalf we shall stretch out the line of charity as far as the word of God and the peace of the kingdom will bear. . . . Who doth not see that by such comments as in that printed paper are made upon God's actions . . what a door is opened to every one to make the like according to their several fancies ? The assistance of men's persons in their several callings and of their prayers may further their own honest desires and our public endeavours, but such petitions as this will neither further their own desires nor others, and they will certainly hinder the work of God in our hands, which by His grace we shall hasten with all the diligence that may be, wherein when we shall have done our duties to the utmost, if all others shall not also be careful to do theirs . . with a spirit of love and meekness we shall have little hope of the expected and desired issue of or of the ceasing of those schisms and troubles under which we labour." (Prepared by the Committee appointed September 20th, read a first and second time October 28th and November 8th, and not further proceeded with. See *Commons' Journals*, iv. 280, 326, 336.) *Draft*, with a few amendments. [N. XXII., 35.]

PRINCE RUPERT to the PARLIAMENT.

1645, October 29. Wyverton.—(Printed in *Lords' Journals*, vii. 671.) *Sign Manual.* [N. I., 45a.]

Colonel GEORGE PAYNE and others to WILLIAM LENTHALL.

1645, October 30. Abingdon.—Setting forth the services of the garrison and the importance of the place, and stating they cannot keep it longer without a speedy supply of men and money, nine months' pay being due to most of the officers and soldiers. *Signed.* [N. IV., 149.]

SIR THOMAS MAULEVERER and others to WILLIAM LENTHALL.

1645, October 31. York.—Complaining that the sequestrators or agents employed by the Committees of the several Ridings, and in particular one James Field, a sequestrator, when coming ·to York by order of the said Committees, are arrested on process out of the Sheriff's Court there, and desiring that such persons might be privileged from arrest *eundo, morando, et redeundo.—Enclosed* is a draft order for Field's release. *Signed.* [N. IV., 151.]

Sir Henry Vane and others to William Lenthall.

1645, October 31. Bishop Auckland.—Desiring that a sheriff might be appointed for the county. *Signed. Seal.* [N. IV., 152.]

The Committee of Privileges.

1645, October 31—Report on the Reading election. (Printed in *Commons' Journals*, iv. 346.) [N. XIV., 85.]

René Augier to William Lenthall.

1645, October 31.—November 10. Paris.—"Sir Henry Compton . . . knowing I have the honour to be employed in this Court from both kingdoms" entreated me to write on his behalf asking that the pass for three months granted him on the 10th of September last to go to Spa might be extended for nine months as the benefit of the waters can be enjoyed only in summer. (See *Commons' Journals*, iv. 371.) *Signed. Seal.* [N. V., 16.]

The Earl of Loudoun, Lord Balmerino, and Hew Kennedy to William Lenthall.

1645, November 1. Worcester House.—Enclosing the Earl of Leven's letter concerning the defeat of Lord Digby and Sir Marmaduke Langdale. " We are further informed that the votes of both Houses concerning the Scotch army with the declaration of the Committee of York and others of the like nature are read in the churches and churchyards at public meetings, and free quarter is denied to the army, whereby many inconveniences are like to fall out. . . . Most of the soldiers of that army are naked, some wanting clothes, others walking without stockings or shoes and many of the officers are reduced to a very hard condition. We do therefore earnestly desire the Houses would be pleased to give order for some money to be provided for them with clothes shirts, stockings, and shoes, and to the counties to afford them free quarter in the mean time." *Signed. Seal.* [N. V., 1.] *Enclosed:*

i. The Earl of Leven to the Earl of Loudoun and others.
1645, October 28. Allerton.—*Signed. Seal.* [N. V., 2.]

ii. Sir John Browne to the Earl of Leven.
1645, October 24. Carlisle.—Two *copies.* [N. V., 3 ; XII., 154.] Both describing the defeat of the forces under Lord Digby and Sir Marmaduke Langdale. (Both are printed in *King's Pamphlets*, E. 308, No. 8.)

Sir William Brereton to William Lenthall.

1645, November 2, at 11 at night. The Suburbs of Chester.—" That party of horse and foot sent into Wales . . . have routed the enemy, taken 500 or 600 horse, and 300 or 400 prisoners, and slain a hundred in pursuit, which was most eagerly followed seven or eight miles by the Warwick and Derby Horse, who behaved themselves very gallantly. This victory was obtained near Denbigh, where our forlorn hope consisting of about 500 or 600 horse commanded by Captain Otter, a very brave and valiant man, was only engaged, the enemy having made choice of such a place of advantage that the body of our army could not come up to fight." *Signed. Seal.* [N. V., 4.]

The EARL OF LOUDOUN, LORD BALMERINO, and HEW KENNEDY to WILLIAM LENTHALL.

1645, November 3. Worcester House.—We intended to have sent the enclosed on Saturday, but forebore doing so as it contained little but the relation of a tedious journey. We now present it because "we understand some have spread insinuations to the prejudice of that party of Horse sent from the Scotch army to pursue the enemy, as if they had not all this time removed from their quarters, but the enclosed copy of a letter from General-Major Vandruske, Commander-in-Chief of that party, to the Earl of Leven, we trust shall vindicate them from so unjust an aspersion." *Signed. Seal.* [N. V., 5.] *Enclosed:*

[General-Major VANDRUSKE] to [the EARL OF LEVEN].

[1645, October 25.]—"I divided my party and kept your Excellency's Regiment with me and joining with Sir John Browne marched over the river into Scotland another way than the enemy did, with intention to come before them and beat them out of Scotland again and I took the English regiments that came with me and some other forces of horse and foot of Cumberland to guard the passage of the river, that they might not come back again without being interrupted. And so I marched towards Annan, but the enemy hearing of my approach towards him and of some of my Lord Backlaughe's (Buccleugh's) men retreated back again towards the passage of the river where he came over. I, thinking myself very happy to have once the occasion to have met with him, marched as fast as I could after him, hoping that the English according to their promise would have kept the pass. But they, as soon as I was marched towards Scotland left their posts, and went their ways, and so by that means the enemy got leave to pass over again. I marched after them as fast as I could, and came over the main water by night time, but within three miles of that there was another river, which I could not pass being then sea water, and so I was forced to stay and give the enemy leave to be a great way before me. They be gone towards Millain Castle and by reason that our horses are extreme weary with so tedious a march I have sent a party to follow them, for I am not able to follow with all, seeing that I have marched so long, and in so evil ways that I believe no horse before have marched it." *Copy.* [N. V., 6.]

The EARL OF NORTHUMBERLAND to ONE OF THE ENGLISH COMMISSIONERS TO SCOTLAND [? SIR HENRY VANE].

1645, November 4.—Referring to the return of the Commissioners, the negotiations with the Scotch about their keeping garrisons in England, and the refusal to engage and the oppressions of their armies, the laying down of their commissions by Prince Rupert and his friends, who desire a pass, Lord Digby's defeat, and the letters taken in his coach at Sherburne, and the Western army. "By the multiplied blessing which God hath bestowed upon us our affairs are in a prosperous condition at present, but I shall still think them subject to alterations, unless we fix upon some more solid and settled way than yet doth appear to me." *Copy.* [N. XII., 156.]

The Scotch Commissioners.

1645, November 6.—Paper. "Several votes of both Houses with declarations of private Committees being published in Yorkshire which very much reflect on the Scotch army and wherein all provisions and supply for their necessary subsistence is prohibited, on pretence that they are to depend upon the course settled for their pay by ordinance of Parliament, which affords them no entertainment, we have found it necessary before the Lord Chancellor's return to Scotland . . . again earnestly to desire a speedy answer to our former papers, that we may have an opportunity to vindicate the Scotch army from the calumnies . . . cast upon them, and give satisfaction concerning any prejudices taken against them, and be able to give some account to the ensuing Parliament of Scotland of our proceedings here." *Signed* "Jo. Cheislie." [N. XIX., 127.]

The Committee of the Navy.

1645, November 7.—Report concerning the Treaty with Denmark. (The purport appears from the votes thereon printed in *Commons' Journals*, iv. 339.) [N. XVIII., 3.]

Sir Thomas Mauleverer and others to William Lenthall.

1645, November 7. York.—Complaining of the extraordinary burthens and grievances the poor inhabitants groan under by many officers and soldiers of the Scotch army notwithstanding the care and readiness of the Earl of Leven upon complaints to redress the same. "By the continuance of that army in these parts the life-blood of the poor country-man's estate is now drawing out, the little remainder of the oil in the cruse, and of the meal in the barrel is now spending, and before that be quite spent—which will be in a short time—we cannot but acquaint you that with sad thoughts we do foresee some fatal inconvenience is like to fall out by the discontented country. By means of that army lying among us a third part of the subsistence of the soldiery of this country is wholly taken away, and the residue much lessened by the infection of many places, there being at least three score towns of the most wealthy part of the county for trading in the West Riding visited besides divers parts of the North and East." The supernumerary officers, whose three months are nearly expired, have also lain upon the country for the poor maintenance they have had, and have received no relief from the moneys designed by Parliament or otherwise. "By means of all which the country lies under inevitable ruin, and the soldiers are in continual mutinies and refuse to obey any orders. And as one instance that way . . . within these two days the officers and soldiers that were commanded on the design for the reducing of Skipton . . . did refuse to march till we were enforced to engage for their accommodation as for the rest of the army." . . We desire that it be represented to the House how necessary it is:

1. "That the Scotch army be speedily removed out of this county.
2. That the moneys ordered for the supernumerary officers and soldiers who are of this country be speedily sent down and that there be care taken for their maintenance for the time to come in regard they have deserved very well of the State.
3. That the excise of this county should be paid to the Treasurer of Yorkshire and disposed of towards the defraying of the public charge here." (See *Commons' Journals*, iv. 338.) *Signed. Seal.* [N. V., 8.]

M[ICHAEL] OLDISWORTH and others to WILLIAM LENTHALL.

1645, November 7. Cardiff.—" The gentlemen of this county, whom truly we may not name without the ascribing much to their good affections and endeavours in the way of the Parliament having thought fit to address their bearer Mr. Philip Jones unto you with such instructions as being effected we conceive . . . may conduce much to the public good and not a little to the welfare of this county we cannot be . . . silent of his pains and good endeavours here. . . . We are yet . . reasonable quiet in these parts, and shall assist to our utmost to preserve the country in such a condition. The gentlemen of best affection in Brecon, finding some untuneableness or not such reality as they had cause to expect in those parts have written to Major-General Laugharne to assist them with his forces, which he is with much forwardness drawing down accordingly and we doubt not but . . may prove a very good and effectual expedient for the reduction of those parts, for the which, as they have desired, this country doth cheerfully offer them their best assistance, and is in preparation to come in under the command of Colonel-General Russell, a gentleman of much worth and hearty affection to the cause." . . *Signed.* [N. V., 9.]

Colonel WILLIAM SYDENHAM to WILLIAM LENTHALL.

1645, November 8. Melc[ombe].—" Being chosen a burgess . . . for this place I apprehend it my duty to recommend the care of the Garrison " to Parliament. . . " Ability, faithfulness, and diligence will be requisite in a succeeding governor—especially till Portland be reduced which I have already blocked up."—I beseech the House that the many well affected persons, from whom in case of great extremity I have borrowed, and also the artificers and labourers also who are not in a condition to forbear payment may receive at least some competent satisfaction. *Seal.* [N. V., 10.]

FRANCIS PIERREPONT, SIR WILLIAM LISTER, and JOHN ALURED to WILLIAM LENTHALL.

1645, November 8. York.—" By our former letter we desired some present course might be taken for ordering so much moneys as would make up the month's pay to the troops promised them by Colonel-General Poynts, which we conceive will amount to 3,000*l.* or thereabouts. They now refuse duty for want thereof which doth exceedingly trouble us at this time especially in regard we are in so happy a way —if this obstacle were removed—to clear this country of the enemy." We again complain of the heavy burthens laid by the Scots on the country. We enclose Colonel Lascelles' letter and the articles for the surrender of Bolton Castle. *Signed. Seal.* [N. V., 11.] *Enclosed :*

The said LETTER.

1645, November 5.—Enclosing the articles, desiring to know their pleasure as to the Castle and the guns taken and resigning his command. (See *Commons' Journals,* iv. 338.) *Seal.* [N. V., 7a.]

SIR WILLIAM BRERETON and ROBERT DUKENFIELD to WILLIAM LENTHALL.

1685, November 8. From my quarters in the suburbs in Chester.— In my last I advertized you of that victory at Denbigh, November the

1st, " when the enemies' whole body was routed and dispersed and at least 600 horse taken and brought away, but not altogather soe many prisoners. But soe many thereof as was brought into the countie I have herein enclosed sent a lisst of theire names, the addicion of which number to those wee had before, doth much add to our trouble and charge, haveing not only soe many as all our prisons and garrisons are capable of but wee are forced to disperse them into severall townes and parishes in open quarters as Stockport, Gropnall, Middlewich, Northwich, and Congleton, where wee are constrained to command the countrey to guard and secure them.

Of which trouble and charge it is humbly desired this countrey may bee eased soe soone as conveniently may bee.

Wee are still endeavouring to draw a line from water to water on the Welsh side, wherein were it not that wee have received some interruption by a Royall Mount of the enimies lately made before wee tooke the suburbes, and also by the extreame fowle weather—which is soe violent that our men cannot endure out of doores—it might have beene in much more forwardnes then now it is.

Howsoever noe dilligence nor endeavour shall bee ommitted that may conduce to the advance of this service, touching which I know not what more to add. Since wee cast upp one mount at our bridg to secure it and another mount higher to confront theire Royall Mount, they can receive noe releife at all, beeing our men are quartered at Poulford, Bretton, Doddleston, Eccleston and Brewers Hall which doth soe blocke upp that side that noe releife at all is brought or attempted to bee brought into the citty, which on the Cheshire side is sufficiently begirte for wee keepe our guards close to theire walls, and have cast upp and made such defences and brest workes against theire gates and sally-ports as that there is noe great daunger of theire issueing out to annoy and offend us in our quarters, wherein provision of victualls begin to bee wanteing, this countrey beeing wholly exhausted and Lancashire and Darbyshire affordeing noe manner of assistance for provisions. And Wales which is most plentifull stored and lyes most convenient contributes very spareingly wherein the people remaine soe disaffected as that they rather preferr to bury and destroy or to carry away then that our men should partake thereof or our leaguer receive any benefitt thereby.

The only expedient that I can propose for the prevencion of what mischeife may ensue hereupon is : that either collonel Mitton may bee ordered to lye about Ruthin or Denbigh, who may send in provision of beeves, muttons, and corne, out of that plentifull countrey to our leaguer here at Chester : or that there may bee a considerable partie sent from hence that may have authority to quarter therebouts, and send in provision for the supply of our army here. . . . . *Postscript.*— I received this enclosed letter last night from Helbree, being a copy of Mr. Dalbee his letter, touching the taking of Captain Bartlett's ship, which as I am informed is a ship of strength, and carries 20 pieces of ordinance with a little pinnace besides." *Signed. Seal.* [N. V., 12.] *Enclosed :*

WILLIAM DALBIE to [SIR WILLIAM BRERETON (?)].

1645, November 7.—Captain Clarke, commander of the *Joslinc*, has just brought in here Captain Bartlett's ship, the *Swan*, and another, both stolen out of harbour. In Bartlett's vessel they have taken about 20 seamen, and 12 soldiers' firelocks set to keep her. [N. XII., 157.]

Colonel-General SEDNHAM POYNTS to WILLIAM LENTHALL.

1645, November 9. Bingham.—"Since the reducing of Shelford, it pleased God to assist us in the gaining of Wiverton House, the strength whereof moved me to give them fair quarter to march away with bag and baggage. . . The foot ordered to me for the siege of Newark are not as yet come from the Eastern garrisons which retards my going against it. The garrisons of Welbeck, Tickhill, and Bolsover are disgarrisoned by consent." I enclose Colonel Bethell's letter, who received many wounds at Rowton Moor, and the only man that stuck to me at my march out of Yorkshire to that service.

I make no question but the House will think on him and his deserts. For my own part I never received anything for intelligence, and am above 400l. out of purse. (See *Commons' Journals*, iv. 344.) *Signed. Seal.* [N. V., 13.] *Enclosed:*

Colonel HUGH BETHELL to General POYNTS.

1645, November 4. Nantwich.—Giving an account of his progress towards recovery. *Seal.* [N. V., 7.]

Edward LEIGH and others to WILLIAM LENTHALL.

1645, November 10. Stafford.—"Upon Thursday last we sent out Captain Stone's troope to Wrotesly House, a garrison which we have lately erected neare Dudly Castle. That night by theyr scouts they understood where Sir Thomas Aston quartered who was then upon his march towards Worcester, and on Friday morning Captain Stone's and Captain Backhouse's troopes from Wrotesly marched towards Sir Thomas Aston whom they overtooke betwixt Bridgnorth and Kidderminster and found him drawne up in a place of advantage with about an equali number of horse to them both, redy to fight with them. Our troopes made the first charge and were stoutly receyved, but at last they routed Sir Thomas Aston's party, and put them to flight in which Sir Thomas Aston often rallyed with such as he could procure to stand, and engaged for the safetie of his men untill our troopes slew above twentie of his men upon the place, whereof Captain Aston, sonne to Sir Arthur Aston, and Captain Moore were two, and tooke prisoner Sir Thomas Aston himselfe, his lieutenant, cornet, quartermaster and corporalls, one Captaine George of Worcester, and forty troopers and eighty horse which they brought to this garrison.

We have herewith sent such papers as were found upon Sir Thomas Aston and such as he much valued. He had likewise with him a commission to be major-generall of horse under Prince Rupert and a commission for a regiment in the west, and an other commission to place a garrison at Kinnsbery or Nuneaton in Warwicksheire, which we have sent to the committee for that county at Coventry.

There do yet remayne in this county three strong garrisons of the enemie; Lichfeild, Tutbury and Dudly Castles, which command a large contribucion weekely from a greate part thereof, and in the absence of the greatest part of our forces now at Chester leaguer where wee have according to command six hundred horse and foote, the enemie from these garrisons doe much oppresse the country neare them. The Brittish monie required of us is 30l. per weeke and at present we are charged with provision for the leaguer at Chester to the value of 160l. per weeke. Two Hundreds of this county—which is divided into five Hundreds—are so much under the power of the enemie that we can get little or none of these provisions from them nor any pay for our owne souldiers but by force. Aud one of the Hundreds which is most contributary to us was wholly plundred and spoyled of above 20,000*l.* worth of goods by the king's armie this last spring when he had quartered ten dayes within five miles of this garrison, and the other two Hundreds are much exhausted by the free quarter of all those forces as passe this way towards Chester or northwards." To add to our straits, divers Delinquents, whose estates have in great part supported our Militia, are now endeavouring to compound at Goldsmiths' Hall. We cannot continue the forces we had raysed without some supply of money. We therefore ask you to inhibit three persons named from compounding at Goldsmiths' Hall and to empower us to compound with them and certain lesser offenders so as to raise 3,000*l. Signed. Seal.* [N. V., 14.]

The COMMITTEE OF BOTH KINGDOMS.

1645, November 10.—Report concerning an amendment in the Pass for Prince Rupert and the rest. (See *Commons' Journals,* iv. 338.) [N. XIV., 86.]

JOHN ASHE to WILLIAM LENTHALL.

1645, November 10. Autree (Ottery).—" Touching elections as yet I have not proceeded far, only at Shafton and Weymouth, where for three vacant places there stood seven men, and so many speeches made against strangers and unknown persons that if three townsmen had stood they had carried it against all that interposed, for they rejected four able men and chose a poor simple townsman. He told them that by the Statute they ought to choose burgesses inhabitants, and I hear that they in Somerset are in like manner provided 3 or 4 for one place, wherefore I shall advise you to write your letters to Sir John Bampfeild, Sir Samuel Roll and Mr. Nicoll, for if you send them writs they have more places than men to supply them. . . . Sir Samuel Roll complains that the country is not able to undergo the quarter of the soldiers and he that was so eager to have the army come into Devon is now as willing to be discharged of them—at least of the charge and burden of them. As for the business itself we may hope that the enemy may be vanquished without blows. A few days will show us their resolutions, for they have been kindly saluted by us, and many things offered to their considerations. *Postscript.*— . . . I find the General exceeding healthy and cheerful, I believe much the better for the company of his good Lady." [N. V., 15.]

SIR GEORGE GRESLEY, Sheriff, SIR JOHN GELL, and others to WILLIAM LENTHALL.

1645, November 11. Derby.—Stating that many of their countrymen who had been in arms against the Parliament were now in Newark and other garrisons, and now desired to lay down their arms and live in their own country and desiring directions therein. *Signed.* [N. V., 17.]

SIR MATHEW BOYNTON, FRANCIS PIERREPONT, and others to WILLIAM LENTHALL.

[1645], November 12. York.—" Many of our officers that marched with Colonel-General Poynts into Cheshire . . are now returned into Yorkshire and desire their proportion of money granted by Parliament equal to the rest notwithstanding they received at Northampton 2,000*l.,*" affirming that Colonel-General Poynts declared it was a gratuity for their willingness to march. We desire to know the pleasure of the House herein. *Signed. Seal.* [N. V., 13.]

The EARL OF LOUDOUN and LORD BALMERINO to LORD GREY OF WARKE, Speaker of the House of Lords.

1645, November 12. Worcester House. — (Printed in *Lords' Journals*, vii. 697.) *Signed. Seal.* [N. V., 19.]

The EARL OF LOUDOUN. LORD BALMERINO, CHARLES ERSKINE, and HEW KENNEDY to WILLIAM LENTHALL.

1645, November 12. Worcester House.—(A duplicate of the last.) *Signed. Seal.* [N. V., 20.]

The PARLIAMENT to the MARQUESS OF BRANDENBURGH.

1645, November 12.—Stating the complaints of the English trading to his Highness' dominions in the Baltic especially as to the late enhancement of the customs at Pillau and Koningsberg contrary to the ancient pacts of Prussia and the ancient treaties between the Crown and his predecessors, and, as they have lately transacted like grievances with the King of Denmark and have obtained the reduction of the increased Customs in the Sound to their ancient limits, not doubting that his highness will be a conserver of the rights and liberty of trade. The rest is referred to the bearer Richard Jenks to whom they intreat his Highness to give full credit. (See *Commons' Journals*, iv. 339.) *Draft.* [N. XVIII., 166.]

The PARLIAMENT to the KING OF DENMARK.

1645, November 12.—Concerning the taking of English ships by pirates, freedom of trade, and tolls. (See *Commons' Journals*, iv. 339.) *Draft*, as passed by the Commons. [N. XII., 158.]

The humble advice of the ASSEMBLY OF DIVINES.

1645, November 12.—Touching some more particulars to be added to the Catalogue of scandalous offenders. (See *Commons' Journals*, iv. 339.) [N. XXII., 29.]

The PARLIAMENT OF ENGLAND to the PARLIAMENT OF SCOTLAND.

1645, November 13. — Demanding the removal of the Scotch garrisons. (Printed in *Lords' Journals*, vii. 703.) *Draft*, as passed by the Commons and fair *copy*. [N. XII., 159, 160.]

Colonel MARTIN PYNDAR and HARCOURT LEIGHTON to WILLIAM LENTHALL.

1645, November 13. Bristol.—In our last of the 8th of October we presented you with "the supply of the army from the country during the seige with our engagements for theyr paiment making up theyr accounts and giving debenters for the same, which money the country are in daily expectation to receive, and not without need, theyr pressures being encreased by the quartering of soldyers upon them ever since, and that upon free quarter which Collonel Birch doth require for the Kentish regiment who he sayth are wholly unprovided for otherwise. Some other new raised companyes follow the same example which giveth oportunity to Major-Generall Skippon's regiment and Collonel Fleetwood's troope of horse to expect the like, who wee dare and doe check in that perticuler, being within the ordinance of our instructions and acknowledge theyr care to observe our order therein, which those other will not looke upon, or be observant of. The like pressure the country complaines of by the committees of Gloucester and Somersett, who urge for contribution without any consideration of theyr present and by-past sufferings; which maketh us bould to presse upon the honorable Howse of Commones for some rule for the countrie's satisfaction, the rather because we see the treasure of the army cannot admitt of such large allowance for arrears as these adjacent parts have justly due unto them. And the garrison of this citty cannot subsist unless it be bounded with contribution from the Hundreds round about it: the welfare of which garrison is of noe small concernment and the reduceing of it to a cheerefull obedience must be a worke of greate judgment, the people in our appearance expressing strange discontents at the present; the qualifying whereof is one majore cause of our stay hoping to se Major-Generall Skippon soe settled that all things may be ordered to the rule of warr and it become to them a citty of peace. We shall now make bold to present yow with an accompt of the being and welbeing of such wounded men as were left here, after the taking of the citty and Barclay Castle, for whome according to the Generall's order, and our best judgment, we appointed an hospitall and placed therein soe many as the house could conteine, with nurses and chirurgiens fitting for them, and as our number increased we added house-roome and attendants to them: which though a house of great receipt yet not sufficient to hold all our foote soldyers, we caused the horse to be quartered in the country which hath byn one addition to theyr burthen, though not in giving free-quarter—which we have paied in money for the most part—yet in disquiet of theyr houses, distruction of theyr beddinge, linnen, and consumption of theyr fiering, which hath byn the more enforced, the generallity of theyr wounds being fractures of bones and dismemberinges by plugg-shott from the enemy, expressing height of malice, rather than martiall prowesse. Sir, we bless God the greater number are returned to the army, well recovered. Such as have dyed of theyr woundes, we have seen decently interred. amongst whom were two gentlemen of worth for theyr valour in health, and Christian conversation in sickness, Majour Bethell of horse, Majour Cromwell of foote, both which had such honorable buriall as the place and theyr rank did require; for whose attendance in theyr sickness and buriall as for all other charges about the care, attendance, and diett, of the rest that were wounded, we have taken speciall care, and all that have gone to the Army wee have supplied with monyes and other accommodations to carry them to theyr coulers. What we now humbly crave of the honorable Howse is that as your bounty extended itself to those that were wounded at Naseby and left at Northampton; soe you will please to reach forth your arme of comfort to these poore men whose pay will be farr short to defray theyr charge and expenses in this theyr extremitie, whom we affirme—as eye wittnesses—to have been noe lesse patient in theyr sufferings and constant in theyr resolutions, then they were couragious in theyr undertakings. Sir, we have kept constant musters of them, and did constantly visit them, though to the hazard of our lives, in this place and time of visitation, and can thereby the better judg of theyr wants and deserts, for whome we pray there may be some such course taken, as may encourage them and all others that willingly offer us theyr lives in your service, and we shall assure you to see all theyr scores cleared and every of them paied whatever you shall thus order to the uttmost penny. Hitherto we have issued monies to and for them out of the money collecting in this citty towards the gratuity promised by the Generall which we finde a worke of difficultie

to obtaine, and the more obstructed by a suddaine damp of money and in our judgmentts not unworthy your honorable consideration, which is the crying downe the ryalls of eight, which wee found plentifull and currant at 4s. 6d. a peece, when we first began this worke of collecting. But since the officers of the customo-house and excise refusing to take them at any rate, it not only daunteth the merchant who affirmes the passing of them to be much consistent with the being of trade, the meanes to bring money into the kingdome, which is now carried all into France, and will be more and more unless it be permitted to pass at 4s. 6d., but alsoe is a great prejudice to the publique and perticularly to our proceedings that whereas we did in eight dayes receive 300l. towards the gratuity, we have since spent twice soe much time and not received half soe much more and what we doe receive is in royalls of eight at 4s. 6d. which should   (line torn off)
                to which we shall humbly adde that a report from London concerning the alteration of the present government of this citty and the passing an ordinance to fine and sequester them hath put a period to our hopes of making any considerable progress in the collection ; some questioning our authority to collect, others threatening the present mayour, to bring him to a councell of warr for asseasing, and all neglecting the Generall's warrant for our proceedings herein. We have engaged ourselves to the citty, to give the parliament an account concerning the ryalls of eight and humbly crave it may admitt a debate and resolution, whether they shall pass currant at all and at what rates. For a result whereof, the citty much depend on us. How necessary it is that this gratuity be made good to the soldyer we refer to your wisdoms, and for effecting whereof we crave some aditionall assistance ; the goodes falling short of the Generall's expectation, even much of that which hath been apparent, and on which we did much depend being claimed by other powers, and intended to other purposes, such as the corrall, which the committee of the Admiralty ord[ered] us to secure for the East-India Companie's use. Soe are the ships, which we found here at the key when wee took the citty and accompted them ours. These are demanded by Captain Moulton and intended to be disposed by him for the use of the Admiralty which doth soe lessen our hopes to give any reasonable satisfaction to the army, that we cannot but present them to your honorable consideration. Many other hinderances there are to this worke which hapning [through] that libertie the officers take to themselves, who denying that assistance to us which your ordinance apoints doe dispose to theyr owne private use, whatever they lay hands on, which we are not able to prevent, being soe far distant from the Generall. Wee heartily wish to see Major-Generall Skippon setled here, of whom there is great need, both for our furtherance in this work, and reall preservation of the place which hitherto hath been—especially since Collonel Fleetwood went hence— much neglected. We shall only adde that for want of able ministers, *Directories* and orders for the use of the same, the people here sitt in darkness and the collegiate men still chaunt out the *Common-Prayer booke* to the wonted height and in private pariches they thinke of noe other discipline, here being hardly three sermons in the whole citty, on the Lords-day, and but one upon the last fast, the late holly-dayes being more solemnly observed then the Sabath." *Signed. Seal.* [N. V., 21.]

THOMAS DUCKETT, THOMAS PARKER, and others to WILLIAM LENTHALL.

1645, November 13. Cambridge.—" We have sent out our proportion of Horse and Dragoons for the straitening of Newark under the command of Major Gibbs, Major Haines, and Major Le Hunt," and borrowed great sums on the credit of the Ordinance of Excise to equip and pay them. The officers now require more pay, but we cannot raise more money out of our county without an ordinance. We "beseech you to consider the extraordinary charges this county has been put unto by alarms. It was agreed by the Committee of the whole Association at Bury that those frontiers to which alarms first come should make all possible defence . . without regard of proportions, and that the whole charge should afterwards be borne by the whole Association. Upon hope of having this Ordinance long since . . we got credit to borrow divers great sums " now long since due. "We had yesterday an alarm, and we wish the Houses would take notice how unable we are for want of moneys to make any considerable defence." *Signed. Seal.* [N. V., 22.]

[The EARL OF LOUDOUN and others] to WILLIAM LENTHALL.

1645, November 13. Worcester House.—The bearer Andrew Love and Donald Campbell about 18 months since delivered to the garrison of Londonderry 600 barrels of barley amounting to 600*l.* for satisfaction whereof these poor men have been petitioners to Parliament above a year. We therefore earnestly desire you to procure an order from the House referring these moneys to be paid by the Committee of Goldsmiths' Hall out of the fines of Delinquents' estates or otherwise. *Signature torn off. Seal.* [N. V., 23.]

The PARLIAMENT.

1645, November 14. — Order concerning differences of Church Government. (Printed in *Commons' Journals*, iv. 542.) [N. XXII., 28.]

The ASSEMBLY OF DIVINES to the HOUSE OF COMMONS.

1645, November 14.—Approving of Mr. Rous' Psalms. (See *Commons' Journals*, iv. 342.) [N. XXII., 30.]

The GRAND COMMITTEE FOR RELIGION.

1645, November 14, 21, 28, December 3, 5, 1645[-6], January 16, 17, 19. — Resolutions reported January 21. (Printed in *Commons' Journals*, iv. 412, 413.) [N. XXII., 32.]

Captain HENRY STONE and others to WILLIAM LENTHALL.

1645, November 14. Stafford.—Desiring that a new sheriff be appointed for the county in place of Colonel Rugley, who had been sheriff above a year and a half, and suggesting three persons as fitted for the office. *Signed. Seal.* [N. V., 24.]

The SCOTCH COMMISSIONERS.

1645, November 14.—Paper. (Printed in *Lords' Journals*, vii. 707.) Two copies both *signed* " Jo. Cheislie." The first misdated 1644. [N. XIX., 79, 129.]

Examination of ROBERT BOSTOCK, Stationer.

1645, November 15.—(The effect of the first part appears from *Commons' Journals*, iv. 348 ; but the rest is omitted, which is :—but for the second impression of the book it was given to him by Mr. Cheesley at

Worcester House, who sent for him to print the book again, and the words " now corrected and published with their knowledge and consent" were put in by Mr. Cheesley's direction, who wrote those words himself in that copy for the second impression, and the preface was not in the first impression nor licensed by Mr. Crauford.) [N. XIX., 130.]

Sir William Brereton to William Lenthall.

1645, November 16. Nantwich.—(Most of the letter, describing the taking of Beeston Castle, is identical with that to the Committee of Both Kingdoms, which is printed in *Lords' Journals*, vii. 719. It contains in addition the following. " The day before the Castle was yielded, great preparation was made and many carriages in readiness at Holt to relieve the same. It is humbly desired that the money and ammunition may be speeded down, and that there may be a supply of provisions more large and constant for the Liguer before Chester from the neighbouring counties and especially from Wales, whereby we shall be better enabled to carry on the work . . Shropshire and Staffordshire have sent in some provisions already.") *Signed. Seal.* [N. V., 25.]

Sir William Brereton to the Committee of Both Kingdoms.

1645, November 17. Nantwich.—(Printed in *Lords' Journals*, vii. 719, except the conclusion which is the same as the part printed of the last.) *Signed. Seal.* [N. V., 36.]

Sir Anthony Weldon and others to William Lenthall.

1645, November 17. Maidstone.—Desiring a continuance of their power of Martial Law which was then expiring. *Signed. Seal.* [N. V., 26.]

Prince Rupert to the Parliament.

1645, November 17. Enclosing his desires.—(Both printed in *Lords' Journals*, viii. 1.) *Copies.* [N. XII., 161.]

Nine reduced Dutch Officers to William Lenthall.

[1645, November 17.]—Petition praying for payment of their arrears. Stating among other things that "we like camelions were merely fed with wind," and "if there should be any that are a hinderance of our despatch, we humbly commend unto them the 4th of *Ecclesiasticus* from the beginning unto the 7th verse, and although it be in the *Apocrypha*, yet it is soundly seconded by the *Old* and *New Testament*." (See *Commons' Journals*, iv. 370.) *Signed.* [N. V., 27.]

Major-General Rowland Laugharne to William Lenthall.

1645, November 18. Carmarthen. — Desiring that the Earl of Carbery's delinquency might be remitted, in regard that on account of his great influence in those parts he had invited him to return with assurance of protection. (See *Commons' Journals*, iv. 444.) *Seal. Original* and *Copy.* [N. V., 28; N. XII., 162.]

Sir William Brereton to William Lenthall.

1645, November 18. Chester Suburbs.—Enclosing a copy of a summons sent in to the besieged, to which they promised to send an answer by a trumpeter of their own, but they had not yet done so. (The summons proposes the appointment of Commissioners on both sides to treat for surrender.) *Signed. Seal.* [N. V., 29.]

The House of Commons.

1645, November 18.—Orders concerning the answer to the Scotch papers. (Printed in *Commons' Journals*, iv. 347.) [N. XIX., 131.]

The Style, Audience, and Substance of the Oration of the Pope's Nuncio at Kilkenny.

1645, November 19. — "*Dominus Johannes Baptista Renuccini, Dominus Archiepiscopus et princeps Farmanus*, Apostolic Nuncio Extraordinary to the Confederate Catholics, had audience at the Castle of Kilkenny . . where he showed his credentials and declared the reasons of his coming, which was only to establish according to his power the Roman Catholic Religion, to preserve their liberties, and lastly to serve their Prince and Sovereign, which he did express with a great deal of sense and feeling in these words viz. '*Et serenissimo vestro Principi meipsum devoveo*' clapping his hand upon his breast, but yet that for their religion they should fight and maintain it against all the world. He said High Mass in the Church of Kilkenny upon St. Andrew's Day." [N. XV., 179.]

Bartholomew Nicoll, Mayor, and others to Lord Robertes.

1645, November 19. Plymouth.—"We did conceive great hopes of our relief ere this by the near approach of his Excellency's army, but it is now despaired of until the spring . . . . for that we hear they are drawn into their winter quarters, so that our straits are the greater, and our siege the closer by apprehension of the frustrated expectation of our enlargement." We are in great want of money, the pay of the garrison being at least 1,000l. a week, and having no means to make up the payment for this week. (See *Commons' Journals*, iv. 355.) *Signed.* [N. V., 30.]

Sir William Brereton to William Lenthall.

1645, November 20. Chester Suburbs at my quarters in the Mayor's house.—Enclosing another copy of his summons to the besieged and their reply. "You may thereby guess that they either expect relief or suspect our weakness—unless stupid ignorance or stubborn infidelity possess them—or else trust in the strength of the city . . . Our siege is close, our soldiers resolved, our want is provision—one of the sinews of war—yet not so great, but it will endure a seasonable supply. . . I humbly recommend that the counties formerly allotted to contribute for our relief of victual may again be put in mind of former orders . . . The Counties of Stafford and Salop have contributed; from Derby and Lancashire—as yet—nothing, and very little from North Wales, from which we might expect a large supply, maintaining no soldiers but what horse are quartered amongst them." *Signed. Seal.* *Enclosed:*

    i. A Copy of Sir William Brereton's Summons.

    ii. A copy of the reply thereto of Lord Byron and Charles . Walley, the Mayor, for himself and brethren.

    "When we call to mind those antient and honourable privileges and immunities granted heretofore to the citizens and freemen of Chester for their loyalty to the Crown we cannot but wonder at your impertinency in urging that as an argument to withdraw us from our allegiance whereby . . . we are most obliged unto

it, even iu point of gratitude as well as conscience. The care
you profess to preserve the City, and to avoid the effusion of
blood is so much contradicted by your acts that you must excuse
us, if we give credit rather to your deeds than words. As for
the fire and sword and famine you threaten us with upon refusal
of your unjust demands we must tell you that—blessed be God—
we have less cause to fear them now than when you first sat
down before this City and doubt not of the continuance of Divine
Protection in the defence of this just cause, wherein our liberty,
religion and allegiance to our Sovereign—whose service is
unseparable from that of the kingdom — are so deeply
engaged." . .

iii. Sir William Brereton's reply to the last.

"Your rebellion and obstinacy is not the way to preserve the
antient privileges granted unto that city. I know not what
action of ours contradict my willingness to save the effusion of
blood and preservation of that city. But it matters not what
those people—given over to destruction and make lies their
refuge—write or pretend. By the tender of honourable conditions
I have discharged my duty and conscience. Your blood be upon
your head and not on your servant Will: Brereton." [N. V., 31.]

The Ministers within the Province of London to the Parliament.

[1645, November 20.]—Petition. (Printed in *Lords' Journals*, vii.
717.) *Signed. Annexed:*
The desires of the ministers presented to the Common Council.
(Printed in *Lords' Journals*, vii. 715.) [N. XXII., 42.]

Walter Strickland to the Committee of Both Kingdoms.

1645, November 20-30. The Hagh.—(Printed in *Lords' Journals*,
viii. 15. The blank in line 2 from the top should be filled up thus:
" and men to go to," and the other blank thus: " the Parliament.")
Copy. [N. XII., 166.]

Colonel Anthony Stapley and others to William Lenthall.

1645, November 20. Lewes.—Asking that Mr. Stephen Humfry, a
member of their Committee and treasurer for the sequestered rents
within the Rape of Chichester, now imprisoned by the Sub-Committee
for that Rape, might be speedily examined and justice done upon him
if he deserved it, or otherwise be repaired, and commending Mr.
Humfry's services. *Signed.* [N. V., 32.]

Colonel John Barkstead, Governor of Reading, to William Ball.

1645, November 20. Reading.—" My scouts inform me that the
King hath designed a plundering voyage into Middlesex, that he will
march through Uxbridge, that he hath appointed a set number of horse
out of all his garrisons in these parts commanding them to send off the
best horse they have." *Postscript.*—Desiring his commission from the
Committee of both Kingdoms. (See *Commons' Journals*, iv. 350.)
[N. V., 33.]

Captain Robert Moulton to William Lenthall.

1645, November 20. Bristol.—I should not " now have been
molestious unto you, but that the exigencie of distressed bleeding

Ireland—to whose relief that great senate hath never been wanting—doth now again implore by me their chaːitable assistance and helping hands, and if it cannot be from the general stock, yet from particular contributions of that mother city which hath already done so much by some recommendation from your Honourable House." Am encouraged to do this "in regard that having but made a private motion to the same effect here in this city it hath taken so well that both magistrates and the private inhabitants have put to their helping hands for the relief of Youghal especially; and albeit the collection consisting from some in money, oibers in food or apparel . . . be not yet all come in, I have yet cause to hope . . . that it will not be altogether inconsiderable especially to such as who wanting all things a little of each will be some refreshment." Am not without hope of the like from the city and county of Gloucester and sundry of the shires in Wales. *Seal.* [N. V., 34.]

Sɪʀ Thoᴊas Jervoise and others to Wɪʟʟɪᴀᴊ Lenthall.

1645, November 21. Winchester.—Enclosing certain letters. (See *Commons' Journals*, iv. 352.) *Signed.* [N. V., 35.]

Colonel Chrɪsᴛopher Whichcoᴛe to Wɪʟʟɪᴀᴊ Lenthall.

1645, November 22. Windsor Castle.—Stating the steps he had taken to defend the Castle, and the miserable condition of his soldiers who were in arrears of pay above 80 weeks, and had only a month's pay these 16 weeks, and asking a supply for their wants. [N. V., 37.]

The Scoᴛch Coᴊᴊɪssioners.

1645, November 22.—Paper. (Printed in *Lords' Journals*, viii. 9.) *Signed* " Jo. Cheislie." [N. XIX., 132.]

Major-General Rowland Laugharne to [Wɪʟʟɪᴀᴊ Lenthall].

1645, November 24. Brecknock.—The gentlemen of Brecknock and Radnorshires make as full declaration for King and Parliament as the Counties of Carmarthen and Cardigan have. The enemy's horse are quartered about Pembridge in Herefordshire. I send a party this night to fall upon their quarters. I dare trust those two counties beyond Carmarthenshire, and they are exceedingly importunate I should remain a while among them, but my occasions require I first look upon Aberystwith and secure that country. Some hopes are given me that the Castle will be yielded if the Governor may have away his money. I have given passes to Gerard's sisters and Whitley's to depart the castle. I heard from Anglesey that Captain Clarke has taken a Fleming worth 3,000*l.* and Captain Barkley's ship with 18 guns, some brass culverins. (See Dalbie's letter, *ante*, p. 350.) The lady of Ruffarname was robbed of all her cattle lately by the Rebels. There is small hope of peace thence or that any Irish can come over. The Earl of Glamorgan is gone for Limerick to take shipping for France. *Postscript.*—I desire Captain Pen may be ordered to keep the guns in Milford till I send for them. The party I sent fell into Colonel Gradie's quarters about midnight and slew six or seven, took prisoners near 20 and odds of 50 horse with their saddles and bridles. (See *Commons'· Journals*, iv. 365.) [N. XII., 163.]

The Parlɪᴀᴊent of England to the Parlɪᴀᴊent of Scotland.

1645, November 24.—Demanding the surrender of Belfast. (Printed in *Lords' Journals*, viii. 14.) Two *drafts*, the first apparently the form ultimately adopted, the second that sent to the Lords. [N. XXI., 21, 22.]

Order of the HOUSE OF LORDS on Mr. WATERS' PETITION, Report of the COMMITTEE OF SEQUESTRATIONS thereon, and Order of the HOUSE OF COMMONS on that Report.

1645, November 25, November 27, December 9.—(The orders are printed in *Lords' Journals*, viii. 11, and *Commons' Journals*, iv. 370, and all are printed in Grey, iii., Appendix, Nos. 35 and 37, pages 61 and 62.) [N. XIV., 89, 87, 88.]

Colonel NICHOLAS DEVEREUX to WILLIAM LENTHALL.

[1645, November 25.]—"The County of Wilts being late freed of the enemies' garrisons, I conceived it most advantageous to the State's service to place such forces as I have under command in the securest holds next adjacent unto the enemy who are powerful at Farrington and Radcourt, to prevent their incursions on these parts of Wilts. On Thursday last I sent a party of foot to Lechlade, which is near both their garrisons, whereunto were near quartered some Gloucester horse by agreement between Colonel Morgan and myself. Yesterday morning there came out a party of 30 horse from Radcourt to Lechlade to prevent us from fortifying there. Captain William Moore, whom I sent thither to command that party and some horse of Gloucester received them, and in the dispute which was but short, only Captain Aytwood on the enemies' side was shot through the thigh, whereupon they retreated calling our party damned rogues, &c., promising also to return soon with a greater party. The same night at 7 of the clock Major Duett with 120 horse and 100 foot went thither from Farrington to surprise—if he could—our party of foot; but our sentries firing at them gave the alarm to our foot. Whereupon Captain Moore drew out to a wall 60 musqueteers, who flanked the enemy as they came into Lechlade and after an hour and a half's hot dispute betwixt them and the enemy, they repelled them out of the town killing on the place six of them. Within half an hour after the Gloucester horse taking the alarm came into Lechlade, whence both horse and foot pursued the enemy, and close under Radcourt wall they encountered each other, where our forces killed of the enemy Major Duett . . . and twenty more upon the place, took 30 prisoners, whereof five of the King's life guard, one cornet, 26 horse, and about 60 fire arms. In this accident we lost not one man, only two hurt, not mortally, I hope." Shall send up by Wednesday "a most malevolent man, one Lieutenant-Colonel Nott, who hath been as mischievous in his actions as Duett. . . . He, as I am persuaded, drew the King's forces into our quarters at Cricklade, where we lately lost 40 horse. . . We have concluded to place another garrison betwixt Farrington and Marlborough where most of the remainder of the horse and foot of Wilts shall quarter this winter to wait on the Farrington forces, as they come abroad." *Signed. Seal.* [N. V., 40, should be 38, and so entered in Index.]

SIR THOMAS JERVOISE and others to WILLIAM LENTHALL.

1645, November 26. Winchester.—Presenting "a true character of Sir Humphrey Bennett late pretended Sheriff of Hampshire, in which office he was both very active and very cruel, and also as he was a commander in the King's army even to the undoing of many a godly and honest man," submitting "whether so dangerous a person be fit to be suffered to go out of the kingdom, or to live at liberty in it," and desiring that " Nicholas Mason whom he now employs as his solicitor in London, an active and dangerous Malignant might be secured and examined." (See *Commons' Journals*, iv. 367.) *Signed.* [N. V., 39.]

Sir Thomas Jervoise and others to William Lenthall.

1645, November 27. Winchester.—*Enclosing :*

i. Pass dated November 12th from Sir Thomas Fairfax to Sir Humphrey Bennett. *Signed. Seal.*

ii. Pass of same date from the same to Nicholas Mason. *Copy.* [N. V., 40.]

Sir Thomas Jervoise and others to William Lenthall.

1645, November 27. Winchester.—Enclosing a report of two of the Committee sent to Dunnington showing how slowly the work goes on, and that Colonel Dalbier himself says that there is no possibility of reducing it this winter, and asking that, if Dalbier will not, some of the forces that took Winchester and Basing, which they hear are now advancing out of the West, may undertake it, and also desiring that the moiety of the Earl of Devonshire's composition, which had been bestowed on them, might be sent. *Signed.* [N. V., 41.]

Sir John Strangeways to William Lenthall.

1645, November 28.—Enclosing his petition to the House, declaring he had relinquished all employment or service for the king since the 18th of October 1644, and asking that on account of his age and infirmities he might be allowed to be at large on his parole or on security. (See *Commons' Journals*, iv. 357.) *Seal.* [N. V., 42.]

Sir William Brereton to William Lenthall.

1645, November 28.—The besieged in Chester "remain still very obstinate, and do not seem inclinable to embrace any overtures made for their own preservation. They have not made many sallies on Cheshire side the water. But the most adventurous and gallant attempt that they ever made was upon Tuesday last. . . We cannot imagine upon what confidence they are induced to persevere in this stubbornness, unless it be so that Sir Francis Gamull and Sir Richard Grosvenor . . do enslave and inaw them hereunto, for, if it be true which I have heard, Sir Francis hath wounded one or two with his own hands that were suspected to desire the delivering up of the city, out of which we have heard very little. . . They are very curious and scrupulous to admit our trumpets, or our drums into the city wherein it seems those that command do most cruelly tyrannize over the poor inhabitants, as they dare not attempt anything . . . They are the rather encouraged by the Commanding Castle and by the Royal Mount which they have lately made which commands much on the Welsh side, and is very strong and almost impregnable." (See *Commons' Journals*, iv. 364.) *Signed. Seal. Enclosed :*

——— to [Sir William Brereton].

[1645, November 26.]—"Yesternight the enemy had a design to have burnt our bridge over Dee, and at the same time to have fallen upon our guards both of horse and beyond the water, and we verily believe, when we had been in that distraction to have sallied out upon all our quarters . . . . . They about 12 of the clock in the night issued out on the other side with a strong party of horse and foot, forced in our sentinels to the higher Mount, and came and charged our men within less than carbine shot of the Mount, which our men maintained valiantly, and our horse guard kept their ground, our foot gave them good store of shot, and after some of the enemy were fallen and others shot, they caused [them] to retreat before their relief came up to them, beat them into their Mount. All this being in doing, at the same time two boats came up the river with the tide, filled with gorse, tallow, pitch, powder, and other combustible matter, and underneath them, and upon the sides of the boat in a frame of wood about twenty pieces of carbine barrels scarce full length and others pocket pistol length charged with powder and carbine bullets. The one of these came within six yards of the bridge and there fired, which gave a report like a peal of muskets, so that we upon the higher ground did verily believe they had been a company of musketeers. A soldier stept in, cast off the gorse and took the frame and brought [it] up with some six or seven of the pieces not discharged. The other boat gave fire over against my Lord's bowling alley, and fired all the gorse and boat itself. We have found one of their men slain within 40 yards of the Mount, and believe more are slain and wounded We have found four or five of their hand grenadoes . ." *Copy.* [N. V., 43.]

FRANCIS PIERREPONT and others to WILLIAM LENTHALL.

1645, November 28. York. — Recommending Lieutenant-Colonel Henry Currer as governor of Skipton Castle, which they hope will be shortly reduced. *Signed. Seal.* [N. V., 45.]

FRANCIS PIERREPONT and others to WILLIAM LENTHALL.

1645, December 2. York.—Stating that the Committee for War and the Committees for the several Ridings had been necessitated to engage themselves to the value of 4,000*l.* or more for clothing for the soldiers, and asking that some course might be taken for repaying them the same, stating that the revenues assigned for the forces allotted to that county were far too short to do the work, and were much weakened by compositions and many other defalcations by orders from the House, and that the necessity of keeping multitudes of supernumeraries, and the extreme pressures by the stay and frequent marches to and fro of the Scotch army have and will disable them to satisfy even those of the last model, and asking for further supplies, and that some special course be taken for the maintenance of the garrisons of Scarborough and Pontefract Castles, which are particularly appointed by the House and are above the number of those appointed by the Ordinance for the County. *Signed. Seal.* [N. V., 46.]

The KING to the MARQUESS OF ORMONDE.

1645, December 2. Oxford.—(Printed in Carte, *Life of Ormonde,* iii. 433.) *Copy.* [N. XII., 167.]

Colonel EDWARD POPHAM and others to WILLIAM LENTHALL.

1645, December 2. Ilchester.—The Gentlemen and Freeholders being summoned here on the 1st to elect Knights of the Shire on the morning of the appointed day the High Sheriff " came not, nor sent the writ, but his County Clerk, who declared that the High Sherive had commanded him to adjourn the County Court to ⸌a small village called Queen Camell four miles distant, because of the sickness at Ilchester. Against which the gentlemen and freeholders present did all unanimously —except one—protest, whereupon the County Clerk did forbear to adjourn until George Horner, Esq., eldest son to the Shreive who had declared himself to stand for to be one of the Knights, did after eleven of the Clock, come into the Court and required the County Clerk to adjourn the Court, who thereupon pronounced the adjournment without mention of any time or place whereunto it was adjourned, and the freeholders being to a very great number present in Court did generally protest against it and declared their resentment thereof, as a breach of the freedom of their election, and an occasion if not design to hinder their free choice of Colonel Stanley and Mr. Harrington, for whom the greater number by far did publicly profess themselves, and many of them did not stick to say that upon the same reason the Shreive might adjourn this day to another place he might the next day change that place, and so tire them out of their attendance, and therefore refused to wait further upon the service. Some of the gentlemen and freeholders present . . . . did despatch two several messengers to the Shreive to have altered his intention and to have drawn him to Ilchester, assuring him there was no danger . . . . But the Shreive's first answer was that he had freeholders enough at Queen Camell to proceed to an election, if those here did not attend, and towards the afternoon sent another message that he did give us notice that he had adjourned the County Court at Queen Camell until eight of the clock the next morning, but before this message came many of the freeholders were returned homeward, and those that remained refused then to attend. These carriages seem to us to have no legal warrant and to entrench upon the freedom of elections and the due execution of the writ is hereby frustrate, as we humbly conceive, besides the great scandal and discouragement given to the well-affected party." We therefore humbly pray that a new writ may be speedily sent down with directions for a lawful summons and fair election at a certain time and place, and not to be interrupted by any adjournment, and that all further proceedings upon the present writ be vacated. (See *Commons' Journals*, iv. 369, 565.) *Signed.* [N. V., 47.]

Sir William Brereton to William Lenthall.

· 1645, December 3. Chester Leaguer.—" The increase of the enemy's wants is the greatest ground of our hopes, they beginning now to be more pinched than formerly and therefore are less active. However they have not as yet admitted of any parley." . . . . *Signed. Seal.* [N. V., 48.]

The Committee for Petitions.

1645, December 3.—Resolution on Richard Netheway's petition. (See *Commons' Journals*, iv. 371.) [N. XIV., 91.]

The Committee of both Kingdoms.

1645, December 4.—Report concerning Sir Trevor Williams and Captain Morgan, with letter enclosed. (Printed in *Lords' Journals*, viii. 80.) [N. XIV., 92.]

Sir Thomas Jervoise and others to William Lenthall.

1645, December 5. Winchester.—Representing "the sad condition of our country, still groaning under the oppressions of those of our own forces designed for Ireland, whose outrages, pressures, and plunders are numberless, of which we might suspect the common soldier only culpable had we not read these informations here enclosed." (Printed in Grey, iii. Appendix No. 38, p. 64.) *Signed.* [N. V., 49.] *Enclosed:*

    i. Information by WILLIAM KING and his wife of Up Clatford.

    1645, December 2.—That some of Colonel Jephson's soldiers said first that if they could meet any of the Committee anywhere out of Winchester they would take from them their clothes, horses, and moneys and laid many vile curses upon them, secondly that the Parliament was at great charge to send them to Ireland, but they intended no such matter, for many of them that are there already are gone to the Irish, and if they should go some of them should do the like, thirdly they hoped the King's party would not be long absent from those parts and then they should have employment here, and that they robbed several persons coming from Collingborne fair. [N. XIV., 106.]

    ii. Deposition of JOHN MARKS, one of the Collectors of Sequestrations in Andover division.

    1645, December 5.—Stating that his servant Floyd having been taken prisoner by Major Gifford in Colonel Jephson's regiment, he went to ask his release, but was himself searched, his linen and money taken, and himself detained prisoner half an hour, that the Major said he was a rogue and so were all the Committee, and that the regiment so oppresses the county that the people think themselves in a far worse condition than in the time of the king's garrisons there. [N. XIV., 105.]

THOMAS CLARKE to Colonel TERRILL.

1645, December 6. Aylesbury.—Concerning a letter directed to Major Shilburne in Aylesbury found on the Bicester carrier and brought to Captain Phipps, who opened it, and found it desired " the Major to send the enclosed to Borstall, . . . which likewise . . . they read. The contents were to a gentlewoman in the said garrison, of the same name as the Major there is of and therefore supposed to be his wife to advise her . . . to come away from thence for that the town would shortly be besieged, and that if she did come he would serve her in what he might &c., which Captain Phipps and his officers reading and finding both the letters subscribed by Colonel Fleetwood yet because directed to his Major thought good to deliver to him . . . concealing from him that he knew anything of the contents." (See Commons' Journals, iv. 370.) *Seal.* [N. V., 50.]

Colonel THOMAS HERBERT to WILLIAM LENTHALL.

1645, December 6. Chepstow.—"I was desired by the General to assist Sir William Fenton—the Lord Inchiquin's agent into England—to procure money and provisions for the reliefe of Youghall . . . According to which order . . . from Lyme I despatched 45 tun of beef, bisquit, and cheese, and from Bristoll a like quantity with above 1,000*l.* in money which Colonel Pindar and Mr. Leighton upon the Gen[eral's] letter furnished. In pursuit wherof I rode into Monmothshire hoping to fynd the affections of that county forward in a work so charitable and necessitous, but am exceeding short of my hopes, for the Glocester party that came this last week to Monmoth and marcht hence to Abergavenny, to Usk, to Chepstow and so to Monmoth without stay anywher save to a fruitless summons of the wel-affected about Abergavenny—which has cost them deere synee by the enemyes falling into that towne from Ragland with four hundred horse and foot where they kild three and have carryed away divers well affected gentlemen and others—the design being to garrison a house three miles from Ragland, but not suting for that purpose, Collonel Morgan retorned with all his horse and foot to Glocester. Synce which tyme the enemy has raged more than ever, and so overpowre the country with their horse that they awe the whole shire and raise their contribucion at leasure, infinitely to the terrour of our freinds and the daily hazard of Monmoth and Chepstow—the two keys and most considerable garrisons of South Wales—which are likely to fall suddenly into the enemies' power if such a nomber of false hearted cavaliers be contynued there under the governors who are sensible I suppose of the danger but know not well how to remedy it of themselves without some advice from the governors of Bristoll and Gloucester; which my cosen Herbert the knight of the shire is sufficiently convinct of and will represent, I doubt not, and that in season. Being of the comittee for this county I was obligd to this march of thers and have upon all occasions communicated the distresse of Youghall to many of them here who have subscribed largely towards their releife for to have given three hogsheads of beefe, 120 bushells of wheat and forty cheeses, which they are thrashing and will with all possible speed send to Cardiff, whither I am gone to raise all there I can, and hope with much more, advantage, being that I may ride there safely and the gentlemen send in their provisions, which in Monmothshire could not be effected. . . .

Postscript.—Yesterday upon the enemies' beating up our quarters at Abergany and Rosse—wher we lost some horse---the rumor was all over this county that Monmoth was surprized by the Ragland foot. Upon which the Governor of Chepstow drew all his men --scarce 100—into the Castle leaving the towne desolate, so that had the enemy come they might have entred without resistance. You see therforo in what too poore condition that place is in and so full of Malignants that Ragland has intelligence thence daily. The Earle of Worcester has a new commission to be General for the King. Aberustwith Castle is taken we heare, and puld down." *Signed. Seal.* [N. V., 51.]

JOHN BLAKISTON, Mayor, to WILLIAM LENTHALL.

1645, December 10. Newcastle.—Enclosing a particular of the *Hopewell* and her goods, with the examinations of some of the crew. *Seal. Enclosed:*

    i. The particular referred to, which adds nothing to Richard Etheriu's deposition of the 18th, *post*, p. 329, except the names of some of the Scotchmen on board, viz. Bishop Sand-scarff's son, Captain Blackchall, Lord Maxwell's brother, one Henderson, Colonel Cockburne's servant, and Captain Meldron.

    ii. Depositions by three of the crew. That of NICHOLAS MURSETT, gunner, contains all the facts additional to those stated in Richard Etherin's deposition. He sailed in May year from London in the *Hopewell* of London, Captain William Ayre, Master, and Captain George Martin, owner, as a man-of-war for the Parliament, and went first to Falmouth, where the Captain took a Letter of Marque from the King in June. They cruised till Michaelmas, when they put into Luckestadt and took divers vessels, of which the particulars are given. The rest of the deposition is to the same effect as that of Richard Etherin. [N. V., 66.]

The Answer of the PARLIAMENT to the Scots' Papers.

[1645, December 10.]—(Printed in *Lords' Journals*, viii. 34.) *Draft*, with numerous amendments. [N. XIX., 128.]

The COMMITTEE OF BOTH KINGDOMS.

1645, December 10.—Report concerning Colonel Underwood's and Colonel Webb's soldiers. (The purport appears from the orders thereon, printed in *Commons' Journals*, iv. 379.) [N. XIV., 93.]

The HOUSE OF COMMONS.

1645, December 12.—Instructions for John Earl of Rutland and others, the Committee to the Scotch army. (Printed in *Commons' Journals*, iv. 374.) *Draft*, with amendments. [N. XIX., 134.]

The COMMITTEE OF BOTH KINGDOMS.

1645, December 12.—Order reporting the Earl of Leven's letter, and the papers of the Scotch Commissioners, and concerning the passes to the four Colonels, and concerning pay for the regiment of the Tower Hamlets returning from Abingdon. [N. XIX., 135.]

Captain ROBERT MOULTON to WILLIAM LENTHALL.

1645, December 12. King's Road, from aboard the *Lyon Regis*.— Being yesterday at Cardiff, the Governor gave me leave to take the copies of some intercepted letters, which are here enclosed. " There are many men which I pray heartily that they might be removed . . . There is Shreene Thomas and his father and parson Edwards at Swansea, and there is Major-General Stradling and the Bishop of Armagh at St. Dannett's (Donat's), a place of great consequence, a strong castle and comes to the waterside, and there is the Bishop Pearce seized on but set at liberty upon bail, and, if I be not mistaken, Bishop Manwaring. In the sirquit (circuit) they are all very violent, which doth discourage the well affected, and being all knit in sanguinity no course is taken with them. Colpeper, whom you were pleased to send for is now not to be found, it's said is gone for London." . . (See *Commons' Journals*, iv. 378.) *Signed.* [N. V., 52.] *Enclosed:*

   i. RALPH [LORD] HOPTON to SIR B. THROCKMORTON.

1645, November 27. Truro.—" His Highness and all your friends about him are well at their winter quarters at Truro. The enemy has pretended to make some quarters the East side of Exeter and now Fairfax and Cromwell are drawing back towards the East, their army being much wasted with the sickness. I long much to hear of the state of my friends in Wales. Lord Garrard, I hear, has left the King, and now if friends in those parts would address themselves in some considerable number to the Prince I am confident he would dispose his counsels by all possible means to assist them. Let me hear from you what may be probably expected from them."

ii. The SAME to HUMPHREY MATHEWS, his cousin.

Same date.—To the same effect. From General Garrard, as I conceive, rose the discontents of your country, and indeed it was his interest in that command that was the impediment between you and the Prince of Wales.

iii. and iv. The SAME to LEWIS GILBERT, and his aunt, Mrs. THOMAS.

Same date.—On private and family affairs.

v. ELIZABETH [LADY] HOPTON to Doctor MARTINE.

1645, November 17. Ex[eter].—Concerning the health of herself and her grandchild. *Copies.* [N. XII., 164, 165.]

Colonel JAMES KERR to the COMMITTEE OF PARLIAMENT FOR THE SAFETY OF PLYMOUTH, POOLE, AND LYME.

1645, December 12. Plymouth.—Enclosing a letter from Sir John Digbye to him, dated December 3, and his answer.

And

JUSTINIAN PEARD and others to the SAME COMMITTEE.

Same date.—*Signed.* (All these are printed in *King's Pamphlets,* E. 314, No. 10. See *Commons' Journals,* iv. 394.) [N. V., 53, 54.]

Major-General RICHARD BROWNE to WILLIAM LENTHALL.

1645, December 12. Abingdon.—Stating that the little money he had brought had all been paid away at his coming, and asking that the money assigned him might be quickened. *Signed. Seal.* [N. V., 55.]

ROBERT WRIGHT to OLIVER ST. JOHN.

1645, December 12-22. Paris.—"The Queene of England is with all dillegence prepairing for recrutes of 8,000 foote to be sent from hence in the spring as vollonteers under the command of the Marshall of Gramond—who was with her on Munday last—and to bee payed from hence 5,000 pistoles a moneth, 3,000 by the eccleastiques assembled and 2,000 by the queene of France and Cardinall underhand, and for their setting foreth 30,000 pistoles are ro be raysed upon the farmers of the gabels for salt. They are to be transported by shipps from Holland by favoure of the Prince of Oring who hath faithfully promised all other assistance. The Queene had assurance of all this given her four dayes since by the commander Soueray—one of the Cardinall's great confidents—being sent to her from him and the Queene of France. The Cardinall indeavours by all meanes to obleige the Queene of England. He is now ill at Rome, and not well assured in France where the distempers are likely to increase. Perhapes he intends England for his retreate. He is not to be trusted by you. The life of this busines consists—so they say here—in the speedy dyspatch, and that they may be earely sturring is laboured by all industrie. The King is resolved to give the Scots or Independents or boath their condicons, if by that meanes he can ingage them against the Presbeterians. The desires of the first are daily solicited at St. Germaines by Mr. William Murray of the King's bedchamber now their agent. It behoves to have a vigillent eye to them and to Holland from whence Doctor Goffe—now agent there deputed by the Lord Jermyn, extraordinario ambassadour as well for these countrys as France—gives great hopes of assistance. For renmedy of all and for youre owne security, you are to divulge your resolucions for the setting forcth of forty sale of men of warres, to cause all your colliers shipps to be dubled maned, halfe deckes to be fitted in them, that each ship may carry ten or twelve gunns, but above all to use all possible meanes to gaine the Prince of Wales unto you for which purpose 100 thousand pounds will be well imployed with condicons to the contint of Culpeper and those others that have power to serve you therein. Generall Goring may be wrought upon. Both he and his father are much unsatisfied with the Queene and she with them. The Lord Percy and Lord Willmot are practising against you. Call them home. The first indeavours to compound the governer of Garnecsy Castell, which you may prevent by geveing the governer his condicons. The peece is worth getting. Mrs. Nevile, the Queen's convert—to be published at her retourne—is now in London, where Mrs. Jermyn, the wife of Mr. Thomas Jermyn, will also sudenly bee. Sir William Davenant, the poet—now the great pirott—and he that was the agent in projecting and bring[ing] up the northerne army three yeares since, would be putt into the exceptions for life. No one man hath don you more hurt, and hath been a greater enemy to the parliament. Mr. Walter Steward gives weekly intelligence from London and 'tis very straing you prevent not this weekly intercourse of letters from the King to the Queene and from her to him by the way of London and under the covert of Sabran and the like." *Remains of Seal.* [N. V., 57, should be 56.]

Robert Fenwick and others to William Lenthall.

1645, December 13. Newcastle. — Concerning the settling of presbyterial government in the county of Northumberland, where in 60 large parishes they cannot raise above one *classis,* and desiring that Parliament may provide sufficient maintenance and send down able ministers. *Signed. Seal. Enclosed :*

> Advice presented to the Committee of Northumberland by the Rev. Thomas Wolfall and the Rev. Nathaniel Burnand concerning the scarcity of godly and able ministers, the need for speedily sending the *Directory* to the several ministers that so "the *Common Prayer Book* may be called in, seeing it is and hath been the nurse of an idle and non-preaching ministry, &c." [N. V., 57.]

Sir William Brereton to William Lenthall.

1645, December 13. Chester Suburbs.—" We have had several strong alarms of the enemy's great preparations for their relief, in the belief whereof we have been the more confirmed by letters intercepted, one whereof is under Sir W. Vaughan's own hand . . which was an answer of a letter sent to him from the Governor of Dudley Castle, desiring some assistance to take in Rotchlie (Rugeley) Garrison lately erected in Staffordshire. Their extremities in the City are very great and their expectations of relief are no less, whereby they are encouraged in their obstinancy. We have made use of some mortar pieces, which we lately borrowed from Shrewsbury whereby great execution is done, and on the 10th . . in the night fired in three several places in the city and killed and wounded divers in their beds, yet this nothing at all works upon them, but they seem still to remain as stubborn as formerly, so as we judge it more easy as yet to fire and destroy then to reduce and subdue this strong city. The enemy hath prepared another fire-boat to set on fire our bridge over the river, for prevention whereof we have chained over the river, and keep an extraordinary strong guard." *Signed. Seal. Enclosed:*

SIR WILLIAM VAUGHAN to the GOVERNOR OF DUDLEY CASTLE.

1645, December 8.—" Having received his Majesty's commands for to attempt the relief of Chester, desiring to know of you what horse and foot can be conveniently spared for this present expedition, I being here now waiting for further orders from his Majesty, being willing to do you any lawful favours but for the present cannot spare any." *Copy.* [N. V., 58.] . .

SIR HENRY VANE and others to WILLIAM LENTHALL.

1645, December 13. Durham.— Enclosing a schedule certifying the division of the county into six distinct classical presbyteries and the persons nominated for each, and further certifying that of the many other churches in the county divers are destitute of any ministers, while the ministers in others are some so weak, and others so scandalous or malignant or both that they cannot as yet recommend any more to be added to the several *classis. Signed. Seal.* [N. V., 59.]

SIR WILLIAM BRERETON and others to WILLIAM LENTHALL.

1645, December 15. Chester Suburbs.—" Though you may from other hands have received advertisement of the enemy's drawing together from Oxford and divers others of the King's garrisons, yet . . . . we have thought meet to send you the enclosed . . . true copies of letters received from Coventry and Evesham, and of an intercepted letter of Sir Wm. Vaughan's intended for the Governor of Dudley Castle. All these hint the enemy's intentions to attempt the relief of Chester for their better encouragement wherein they have—as we are informed—lately received letters from the Earl of Glamorgan assuring them that he hath 10,000 men ready to transport, and hath sent 200 barrels of powder. But we hear not as yet of the landing of the powder. Nothing seems to be more probable than that the enemy will engage deeply for the relief of this city, which hath held out so long and so resolutely . . —this being of greater concernment to them than all the rest of the holds they possess in these parts of the kingdom—. Whereof we doubt not but that you will be so sensible as that you will endeavour to expedite to us such timely and considerable assistance as our condition requires . . *Postscript.*—We have advised the Lord Leven and General Poynts thereof." *Signed. Seal. Enclosed:*

THOMAS ROUS and others to SIR WILLIAM BRERETON.

1645, December 12. Evesham.—" A body of horse and foot, they say themselves 2,000, but others which viewed them 1,000 or 1,500 came in yesterday at 11 o'clock to Stow-on-the-Wold. some ten miles from this garrison. There and thereabouts they quartered last night. They talk of marching for Worcester which is not improbable, and the rather because Sir William Vaughan and those horse which stay formerly about Worcester are not yet advanced. It may be they intend to join and so pass on towards the relief of Chester. We have sent to Colonel Morgan—with whom most of our horse are at present—to advertize him of this body . . . *Postscript.*—The Lord Northampton commands the party from Oxford." *Copy.* [N. V., 60.]

SIR WILLIAM BRERETON and others to WILLIAM LENTHALL.

Same date and place.—(To the same purport and mostly in the same words as the last.) *Signed. Seal. Enclosed:*

i. THOMAS ROUS and others to SIR WILLIAM BRERETON.
1645, December 12. Evesham.—

ii. SIR WILLIAM VAUGHAN to the GOVERNOR OF DUDLEY CASTLE.
1645, December 8.—(Both printed above.) *Copies.*

iii. CHRISTOPHER HALES and others to SIR WILLIAM BRERETON.
[1645], December 12. Coventry.—" We have even now received intelligence that the King's forces are upon their march towards Evesham, and thence as we are informed towards Chester. They are about 1,500, rather more. We have given notice hereof to Col. General Poynts to the end he may do what he can to interrupt his passage." *Copy.* [N. V., 61.]

The GOVERNOR and COMPANY OF MERCHANTS OF LONDON TRADING INTO FRANCE to the HOUSE OF COMMONS.

[1645, December 15.]—Petition. (The purport appears sufficiently from the order thereon, printed in *Commons' Journals,* iv. 376.) *Signed* by about forty persons. [N. XXII., 85.]

REASONS

In support of the said petition.—[N. XXII., 86.]

Resolutions of the GRAND COMMITTEE FOR THE AFFAIRS OF IRELAND.

1645, December 15.—That the Government of Ireland be committed to such person or persons as shall be agreed upon by both Houses.

That the ordinance of the 11th of April 1644 concerning the command of the British and Scottish forces in Ireland is to continue no longer than during the pleasure of both Houses.

That seventeen members therein named be a Sub-Committee to consider and state what power the Chief Governor or Governors of Ireland have as things now stand.

December 20.—That so much of the ordinances passed the 9th of March 1643 and 11th of April 1644 as concerns the Government of the British and Scottish forces in Ireland by Committees of both Kingdoms or otherwise be determined and repealed.

1645[-6], January 5.—The question being put whether the Government of Ireland shall be committed to more persons than one, it passed in the negative.

Sir John Evelyn, Sir William Strickland,	tellers for the Noes, they were 61.
Mr. Holles, Sir John Clotworthy,	tellers for the Yeas, were 50.

That the Government of the kingdom of Ireland shall be committed to one person. [N. XXI., 23.]

Colonel CHRISTOPHER WHICHCOTE to WILLIAꞋ LENTHALL.

1645, December 16. Windsor Castle.—Enclosing examinations concerning the insolency of the enemy from Wallingford plundering your friends and fetching them away prisoners within two miles or less of Windsor, which he is not only unable to prevent, but is almost incapable of subsistence himself. *Signed. Enclosed:*

> Deposition of ADREY LYDGALL, of Sippinham, in Burnham Hundred, in Buckinghamshire, two miles from Windsor.
>
> At about 7 p.m. on the 11th nine or ten soldiers from Wallingford came to her house and after remaining an hour seized her husband William Lȳdgall, and five horses and three more from John Foord a neighbour of hers with pistols swords and a fowling piece,—three of which horses and the pistols belonged to troopers of Colonel Martin's Regiment quartered in their houses— all which with two of the troopers they carried away to Wallingford, where her husband remains a prisoner till the arrears of all such taxes they pretend to be due from that parish be paid and 10*l.* more to the party that fetched him away. Mrs. Foord sent her servant to Burnham to acquaint Lieutenant Ryder quartered there with a party of horse that some Wallingford soldiers were at Sippinham, and had carried away divers horses, and though a cornet and other troopers of Colonel Martyn's gave him information of the enemy's being in those parts and offered to join him in pursuit he refused to go pretending that he had a charge of money to look after, and would keep the house where " he and divers others of his troopers were found typpling in a very deboyce manner." She desires that some way may be found by the Parliament for her husband's relief and liberty and for reparation for her horses and damages. *Copy.* Two other depositions follow deposing to various of the facts above stated. [At the end of N. V. Not numbered.]

SIR WILLIAꞋ BRERETON and others to WILLIAM LENTHALL.

1645, December 17. Chester Suburbs. — Acknowledging with thankfulness the care of the House in expediting the last 10,000*l.* assigned for the payment of such forces as should be necessarily employed in reducing Chester, and stating that though that sum when first granted seemed competent yet the great endeavours to raise the siege have occasioned such accession of forces and the continuance of it has been so much beyond expectation that without further supplies they were in no way able to carry out the work, and giving particulars of their expenses and of the exhausted condition of the county. *Enclosed* is a detailed account of how so much of the 10,000*l.* as came to the county was employed. (*See Commons' Journals*, iv. 384.) *Signed. Seal.* [N. V., 62.]

· ROBERT WRIGHT to OLIVER ST. JOHN.

1645, December 18-28. Paris.—" The accorde so much desired betwixt the King and Scots is with all dilligence persued by Mr. Wm. Murray and the Queene is very confident it will sucede. The party of Montrose in Scotland will not hinder it, for if he be not sucesfull and of better consideracon he may be offered uppe there to stringthen the party. The King is resoulved alsoe to give the Independentes their condicons alsoe, besides the Lord Goring is now at St. Germaines and gives good hopes of a sucesfull army out of the west in the spring which with the recrutes promised out of France may give you great diversions. He is now prepairing for his cure—which is no other then for the pox—and promises to be backe in the west within two monethes. The queene is much pleased at the answer the prince gave to the answer of his letter by Sir Thomas Ferfax inviting him to his army: 'Rogues: Rebelles; are not they content to be rebells themselves, but would have me in their number.' You see how he is instructed, and his conncell having voted that in case he should be prest to goe out of England, that he come not to France, but to Holland or rather to Denmarke, you must by all meanes keepe him in the kingdome, and if possible—by giveing any condicons to those about him—to gaine him unto you for nothing can give you more security then his person. The treaty for the generall truce at Mounster goes on and in the opinion of wise men may sucede for indoutedly the queene of France desires nothing more—what mine soever she makes—and that wilbe the master peece of the cardinall, wherein he laboures hartely, and if it should so fall out, you having the warre on foote, be confident to make England the seate of warr for all Christendome. You know how doutfull the chaneh of warr is, and the security of religion, lawes, liberties, your lives and those of your wives and childrens must be in a setlement which must be don either by acorde with the king—for suffer not the Scots to make their peace and then be the mediatours for you as they pretend to be—who if once gained may prove as much for you as now against you, or by gayning the prince, one of which must not be neclected. Yet for your more security, the armyes must be very early in the feild this spring, and the fleet likwise at sea for 'tis that only that can keepe the French in any reasonable nutrality. If the comisioners be come from the king, make use of them, for here is much industry to keepe the warre on foote, which is most desired by the French and Catholiques who will underhand speedily give supplies both of men and munies; and you know reveng is sweet, which is only laboured and desired by those at Saint Germain's, and there's *a starre* that hath to great influance upon the king." [N. V., 62, should be 63.]

Colonel Thomas Morgan to Thomas Pury.

1645, December 18, at 12 at night. Hereford.—Narrating "the tak'ng in of this garrison though with great difficulty in regard of the season of the year and the deepness of the snow which was above a foot thick. My forces consisted of 1,100 horse and foot, and Colonel Birche's forces of 900 foot, which being joined upon Monday we marched from Gloucester, and thought to have reached Hereford that night, but our foot soldiers were so much spent by the time we came within six miles of Hereford that they were able to march no further, so was constrained to draw back towards Gloucester that the enemy here should take the less notice of any design. Upon Wednesday night we marched toward it again, and drew up our forces within musket shot of the town under a hill about an hour before day, and before sun rising made our attempt, which God did effect for us with very small loss. Divers of the enemy was slain in the streets and the rest taken prisoners. We have already in custody 120 lords, knights and gentlemen officers in commission which are to be sent to Gloucester.

The most of them are Papists. For common prisoners I am not able as yet to give a true list, nor of the arms, only 11 piece of ordnance, and a reasonable quantity of all sorts of ammunition. By this the Pope's nest in Hereford is spoiled. . . . . *Postscript.*—Captain Temple had the honour to command the forlorn hope of horse and behaved himself very gallantly." [N. V., 64.]

Colonel THOMAS MORGAN to WILLIAM LENTHALL.

1645, December 18. Hereford.—A less full account than the last of the capture of Hereford. (Printed in Grey, iii. Appendix, No. 77, p. 131. See *Commons' Journals*, iv. 381.) [N. V., 65.]

JOHN BLAKISTON, Mayor, to WILLIAM LENTHALL.

1645, December 18. Newcastle.—Enclosing the examinations of six seamen taken in the ship *Hopewell* that was driven ashore at Cammes, near Blith, and stating that the Earl of Leven came thither on the 16th, and that it was likely he would stay there that winter. *Seal. Enclosed:*

> Five depositions by six seamen of the *Hopewell*. The fullest is that of Richard Etherin, to which the others add nothing. He, being shipwrecked on the coast of Jutland, begged his way to Luckstatt (? Gluckstadt) where he joined the *Hopewell*, Captain Ayre, Master, and shipped on board her September 30th, 1644. They stayed there till March 31st, when the ship went to Hamburgh, and stayed there till the end of May rigging and revictualling the ship, which then went to sea as a man of war with a commission from the King. They took two prizes, a Dover and a Sandwich man, and returned to Luckstatt the end of June, and stayed there till November 24th, when they set sail laden with 30 single and 15 double barrels of powder, two dry fats of pistols and belts, three baskets with rapiers and swords, and some carbines, and a great quantity of match. He conceives they were laden by the Lord Ethen and Sir John Cockram, and the Master told him they were to carry the said goods to Aberdeen in Scotland. There were eleven passengers in the ship, all Scotchmen, and including the Captain the crew were seventeen. Being caught in a storm, and the ship being very leaky. they were found to run ashore at Cammes in Northumberland, where the Governor of Tynemouth Castle seized on the ship and ammunition and nine pieces of ordnance, the armament of the ship, which was one of 80 or 100 tons burden, and sent the crew and passengers as prisoners to the Governor of Newcastle. [N. V., 66.]

The LORD LIEUTENANT and COUNCIL OF IRELAND.

1645, December 20. Dublin.—Order appointing the Earl of Roscommon, Lord Lambart, and Sir James Ward to examine the Earl of Glamorgan. *Copy.* [N. XXI., 24.]

The COMMITTEE OF BOTH KINGDOMS.

1645, December 20.—Report concerning Prince Rupert's letter and Windsor Castle. (See *Commons' Journals*, iv. 383.) [N. XIV., 94.]

CLEMENT FULTHORPE and others to WILLIAM LENTHALL.

1645, December 20. Bishop Auckland.—Desiring that the County Palatine might be abolished, and knights and burgesses allowed them, and they put in the same condition as other counties. *Signed. Seal.* [N. V., 67.]

The COMMITTEE OF PUBLIC ACCOUNTS to the COMMITTEE FOR PETITIONS.

1645, December 22.—(For the effect of this letter see *Commons' Journals*, iv. 389.) *Signed.* [N. V., 68.]

The LORD LIEUTENANT and COUNCIL OF IRELAND.

1645, December 26. Dublin.—Warrant for the commitment of the Earl of Glamorgan. (Printed in Grey, iii. 220, note.) *Copy.* [N. XII., 168.]

The COMMITTEE OF BOTH KINGDOMS.

1645, December 27.—Report concerning a provision of money and a greater fleet. (See *Commons' Journals*, iv. 338.) [N. XIV., 95.]

Colonel J. DALBIER to the COMMITTEE OF BOTH KINGDOMS.

1645, December 28. Newbury.—Cannot believe the enemy intend to fortify Compton House, as though it has a moat round it, it lies in a bottom, and so could not be held against ordnance. "I am left in so miserable a condition that I am able to do nothing. Had I had means I had put the enemy in this Castle to great shifts, but as I am I must let them do what they please." *Seal.* [N. V., 69.]

JOHN WADDON to WILLIAM LENTHALL.

1645, December 30. Plymouth.—"On Saturday last a party of 500 commanded musketeers and 120 horse—most of them of the old Train Band men of the country—fell on Kinterbury work, four miles from the town, which they as soon took as attempted, it being a very strong work, but neither armed nor manned, 17 being only in it, who had quarter given them. From thence they marched to St. Budox's Church, when the enemy being near 100 horse and foot fought valiantly and stoutly for an hour's space, in which encounter we lost worthy Major Haines—a great loss—, and four or five more, and 16 hurt or thereabouts, but in conclusion Lieutenant Vaghan, Captain-Lieutenant to Sir Edmund Powell, forced them horse and man into the church, and though shot through the thigh entered with them, to whom with much ado and great pains of the commanders the common soldier gave quarter for their lives, but plundered them to their shirts. Lieutenant-Colonel Crocker commanded the party." . . . Enclosed is a list of the prisoners, 105 in all, and 45 horses. [N. V., 70.]

Colonel THOMAS MORGAN to WILLIAM LENTHALL.

1645, December 30. Gloucester.—Enclosing a list of the prisoners taken at Hereford, and desiring how they should be disposed of. Have not received Sir John Strangewayes into my custody. Have settled the garrison at Hereford. *Signed. Seal.* [N. V., 71.]

The ASSEMBLY OF DIVINES to the HOUSE OF COMMONS.

[1645.]—The Proofs of several additional Votes concerning Church Government. [N. XXII., 31.]

List of goods delivered to the Garrisons of PEMBROKE and TENBY out of the *Tulip* of London.

1645.—[N. XIV., 104.]

JOHN BLAKISTON, Mayor, to WILLIAM LENTHALL.

1645[-6], January 1. Newcastle.—Submitting to the House the claim of Sir James Lumsden, that he as Mayor was to provide him necessaries for his house as Governor, and desiring that directions be sent by the House for the well managing of the collieries of notorious Delinquents, that directions be given to the Mayor and Corporation to compound with Delinquents who are ready to comply with the orders of Parliament, and that some proportions of Delinquents' estates be assigned to help to support such as have been utterly ruined by the malignity of the enemy. *Seal.* [N. V., 72.]

ABSTRACT.

1645[-6], January 3.—Of the sums paid or suffered through assessments, free-quarter, &c. imposed by the Scotch army by certain towns in Nottinghamshire since November 28, amounting to 10,100*l.* 19*s.* 5*d.* (Printed in Grey, iii. Appendix, No. 62, p. 97.) [N. XIV., 96.]

JO[HN] R[USHWORTH] to WILLIAM LENTHALL.

1645[-6], January 4. Tiverton.—"A party was sent from Chidley house to Southams, took four constables, with the Prince's proclamation, a copy whereof I send you enclosed. . . . Some that come from Plymouth side say the Plymouth men have taken a church and 150 men of the enemy in it. . . . The country rises but slowly for the enemy, and I believe will vanish as fast as they appear. The weather now breaks, so we shall have opportunity to do something upon them. The General hath written to the Committee of the army about recruits, &c. The sooner that is settled, the sooner shall we march east." . . . [N. V., 73.]

J[OHN] R[USHWORTH] to WILLIAM LENTHALL.

1645[-6], January 5. Tiverton.—Enclosing a letter from Plymouth. "We are preparing to meet the enemy and doubt not to prevent their design. The clothes are come to Weymouth. I hope they will come seasonably to comfort the poor foot in their march." *Enclosed:*

Colonel JAMES KERR and others to SIR THOMAS FAIRFAX.

[1645-6], January 1. Plymouth.—After describing the taking of Kentarbury work and St. Bodeaux church (see above). "We hear certainly the enemy is advanced with 4,000 horse and 1,500 foot to Ashburton and their design is within 6 days to beat off your forces on this side the river Ex, and the enemy is to sally out according to order with 2,000 horse and foot at the same time. The enemy hath provided 2,000 bushels of wheat and other provision to carry into Exeter." (See *Commons' Journals*, iv. 401.) *Copy.* [N. V., 74.]

GERVASE PIGOT and others to the Lords and others, COMMISSIONERS AT GRANTHAM.

1645[-6], January 5. Nottingham.—Enclosing the petition of the inhabitants of that part of the county of Nottingham lying on the north side of Trent, which is printed in *Lords' Journals*, viii. 97. *Signed.* [N. V., 75.]

The EARL OF RUTLAND and others to the COMMITTEE AT LEICESTER.

1645[-6], January 5, Nottingham.—Warrant ordering provisions for the Scotch army in the form of that printed in *Lords' Journals*, viii. 97. The value *per mensem* to be contributed by Leicestershire was 1,000*l.* [N. V., 76.]

GEORGE [LORD] DIGBYE to LORD CULPEPER.

1615[-6], January 5. Dublin.—Referring him to his letter to the Chancellor Sir Edward Hide for an account of his adventures and of the state of the kingdom. [N. V., 77.]

The SAME to LORD GORING.

Same date and place.—To the same purport. *Seal.* [N. V., 78.]

—— to ——.

1645[-6], January 5.—" For Mr. —— it's acknowledged he was an extreme man for the King's party. But now he confesseth himself thoroughly convinced and will regain all by-past errors to do the Parliament service. To this purpose he informeth, that the King's intentions and councils move him to subscribe to all the Parliament's desires to come up to the Parliament, to put all things seemingly into an orderly and peaceable way till an opportunity be offered by our divisions and discontents to overturn all, and that he will recompense that losing party, which now suffer by compounding with the Parliaments. I shall send him up to the Committee of both Kingdoms to reveal some secret plottings and contrivances in Kent, which ought to be privately handled. It were not amiss for the City to take notice what Kentish gentlemen resort there." *Extract.* [N. XII., 170.]

[LORD CULPEPER] to [JOHN ASHBURNHAM].

[1645-6], January 6, 6 at night [so at foot, at head January 12, probably the date it was intercepted or deciphered].--" By the Lords' (of the Council) to his Majesty you will see the condition of his affairs at the date thereof, and by the postscript what accidents have intervened. Pray take special care that due secrecy be observed in these particulars, which you will find ought not to be divulged. I fear we must now be compelled—though as unwillingly as ever we did anything—to retreat to the other side of the Tamar. If the enemy be full of gallantry and follow us into Cornwall we shall then have a hopeful day with him —better than we could have expected in Devon,—but if he will be wise and stay in Devon, neither Exeter nor Dartmouth will be long secure, the first being in danger of famine and the other of force, the works being very imperfect, and we shall be so burdensome upon the Cornish, and General Goring's horse so disorderly, that I fear Cornwall will quickly be weary of us. Therefore we will do all we possibly can to continue in Devon.

Touching the Prince's going out of England be confident we will make good our words as is at large expressed in the shorter letter, but his Majesty must presently send his commands in a letter to all the Lords of the Council, to lie by us, and to be produced when it shall be seasonable. In that letter his Majesty must likewise give them the like

Counsellors
authority as 313 to his Highness when he shall be beyond the seas
as they now have, with directions to the Prince to be advised by them
and only by them—to exclude Long, Berckly &c.—in all his affairs
as well household of importance as others. It is further desired that
his Majesty's commands to the Prince to go beyond the seas and to the
Council to be assisting therein may be privately sealed with the Great
Seal and remain with the greatest secrecy somewhere in very safe
custody. When you consider the vast importance of this business you
will conclude with all us four that such cautions are most necessary.
Let me speedily hear from you touching all these particulars, for it may
fall out that we shall be suddenly pressed to put his Majesty's commands into execution. Your Scotch Treaty joys my heart. D[uke]
Hamilton may—probably—be made useful in it. He has lately sent me
word by Doctor Freaper that he will do anything his Majesty will have
him to do. You shall hear more from me upon this subject very
speedily.

[What followeth was written in Culpeper's own hand and in cipher
too.]

January 8. Tavistock.—Your severe postscript cannot long stifle
the extremity of joy which your most kind letter gave me. Touching
that harsh Catechism I acknowledge it so surprised me, that it was some
time before I could believe it signified anything but some piece of
raillery. But when upon the third and fourth reading of what I found
open, the continuation of that unusual stile had sufficiently convinced
me that you were in sober earnest, I entered into the strictest examination of myself what I had done or said capable to render me thus
unhappy and I could not guess at the matter. Then I fell to work
with your cipher, which quickly unriddled the business, and I assure
you—whatever your relish was when you wrote it—I was a glad man
when I read it. My reply is only a request to you to afford me a new
hearing and again seriously and unconcernedly consider the words you
mention, and compare them with the scope and context of the whole
letters, and then to ask yourself whether that unhappy ' you ' ought
                    Ashburnham
to be applied to   573   or to his Majesty's Counsellors. If you then
find it doubtful I a thousand times ask your pardon for any ambiguity
in such a tender point. But if upon second thoughts you clearly
conclude that I could mean nothing but to express my apprehensions of
the like mischievous designs to overrule the King and his Counsellors
                                                    yea re
and so to hurry [him] hoodwinked to his ruin as were the last 90 re
contrived. 373 and 407 &c. and cherished by a faint hearted party
amongst us and are like now—more rankly—to spring out of the increase
     Lordship's   Culpeper
of his 220 ill fortune; you will then pronounce 576 no ill friend
though you find him no good penman. My categorical answer is
I no more intended or suspected you than myself. Nay, if I were your
enemy I must profess it to all the world that I have received more solid
confirmation of constancy in this good cause from your conversation
and practice than from any other man living, and I should as soon be
jealous of myself to become anything that I most abhor as that you
could warp or cool in that well grounded resolution. I certainly know
you can have no reserve not warranted by the strictest rules of duty
            honour
honesty and 251.

At the Rendezvous this afternoon, the Cornish were very cheerful and expressed much forwardness to fight. We have 1,000 horse full of the guard, very well armed and mounted, which I am confident will do well when they come to service. The Lord Wentworth—besides 300 horse now [at] Bovy Tracey and Colonel I'r a turn tail regiment now beaten up—hath with those before Plymouth now drawn off 2,500 horse, which I would call very good ones, if they would fight more and plunder less. The enemy's quick soldier-like motion has hindered us from joining with 1,500 good foot in Exeter and 1,000 as good now sent to Dartmouth. Yet we have in a body full 4,000 good men. 576 remembers his service to you with many kind expressions of friendship. Your brother is well in Exeter recovered of a late mischance, a fall, which put his arm out of joint. We hear hopefully of the treaty at London.

Postscript.—When I sent you the letter I had not heard one word of the treaty." *Copy.* [N. XII., 171.]

SIR ROBERT KING to WILLIAM PIERREPOINT.

1645[-6], January 6. Belfast.—(Printed in *King's Pamphlets*, E. 322, No. 32, and in Grey, iii., p. 219.) [N. V., 72.]

The SCOTCH COMMISSIONERS to the PARLIAMENT.

1645-6, January 6.—Paper about the maintenance of their forces before Newark. (Printed in *Lords' Journals*, viii. 89.) *Signed* "Jo. Cheislie." [N. XIX., 137.]

Colonel J. DALBIER to the COMMITTEE of the three Counties of BERKS, BUCKS, and OXON.

1645[-6], January 7. Newbury.—"I see that none of my letters can prevail, which makes me think you do not believe that I am in a most sad condition. Three Companies of Farnham went away last week with their arms as far as Basingstoke, where the officers overtook them and persuaded them to come back again, but I wish they had let them go for their return has proved prejudicial, because they refuse to do duty and to their example the rest that are unpaid do the like. The men that are well paid are not above 400. You may judge in what case I am, the enemy have very good intelligence of all, so that I must fear every day to be overfallen. I beseech you not to lose the poor town, which by our coming is already ruined, our men being indebted to them 1,200*l.* Perhaps you think it impossible for the enemy to have such a resolution, for I know their forces are described to you [as] inconsiderable. I answer there is 300 horse in Faringdon, 200 horse in Wallingford, 50 horse in Denington who all can appoint a rendezvous at any time without our knowledge, and if they take but 200 musketeers behind their horse they are able to master this place, having no men to defend it. I may preach my heart out to the soldiers of the danger they are and put us all in with their proceedings, they cry Money, money, money, that is all the answer I get." (See *Lords' Journals*, viii. 92.) *Copy.* [N. XII., 172.]

Major-General RICHARD BROWNE to WILLIAM LENTHALL.

1645[-6], January 7. Abingdon. — Desiring that some one be appointed Governor in his place, and setting forth the necessities of

the garrison and their want of pay. (See *Commons' Journals*, iv. 418.)
Seal. [N. V., 80.]

Captain JOHN POYER to WILLIAM LENTHALL.

1645[-6], January 8. Bailiff's House, Westminster.—Complaining
that though he had been sent up by Major-General Laugharne and the
Committee he had been arrested on his way to Westminster by Captain
Swanley in two actions, and beseeching that the House might order his
enlargement, and might send for Swanley to show cause that he had so
maliciously arrested him. *Seal.* [N. V., 81.]

ROBERT WRIGHT to [OLIVER ST. JOHN].

164[5-]6, January 9-19. Paris.—"The treaty betwixt the King
and Scots is with all industry prosecuted by Mr. William Murray
with the Queene. She to gaine time entertaynes it with great hopes of
a faire and desired conclusion and is resoulved, if other expectacions
faile, to gaine them there desires. The obstuckle at present is the
difficulty of reconciling the party of Montrose with that of Hamilton
and Arguile, yet in case the parliament should—upon the King's refusall
of the proposicons now desired—proceede to the deposing of him, the
Scots' comissioners in England doe assure that those two parties shall
reconsile and declare with one consent for the King, which is the only
thing by her desired for having alsoe assurance—in that case—of a
party now with the parliament, she is confident that that is the only
way to re-establish the King to her content. The French to entertayne
the warre—untell they have don their buisnes in Flaunders—gives leave
to rayse six thousand volentires two *mile* in Normandy, three *mile* in
Bretaigne and one *mile* in Poictou for the seting foreth of all which
Q[ueene] of France and Cardinall have this last weeke given thirty *mile*
pistoles. The clargie gives the lik sum and both asuerance of 5 *mile*
pistoles monethy. 600 of the former number and (? are) within sixteen
dayes to be shipt at Newhaven and conducted to Dar[t]mouth by Sir
William Davenant, the grose in March, all to be commanded by
Generall Goring, who having now past his cure will make his florish
for twenty or thirty dayes in Paris, and so retourne for the West. The
Pope hath very lately not withstanding the warres of Itelay faithfull[y]
promise[d] to assiste the Irish, that they shall submitt to the King's
condicions and furnish him with one thousand men, all defryed. The
jarr now betwixt him and the Frensh not not (*sic*) hinder so pious a
worke—these are his wordes—. The Prince of Oring gives assurance of
shipping and all other in his powre—and assuredly he is and shall bee
very cordialle and usefull to the king—. Docter Goff is now with him
for that purpose. That that keepes in this fire is the hopes of the
Prince of Walles being sudenly with him, which must by all meanes be
prevented and you cannot buy him and his party at to great a rate.
Yet must ye not proceed so farr as to depose the King but draw on the
warr with all industry—in case the accomodacion cannot now he hadde
it wil be the most assured way for saiefty—so to lessen his party, to
which purpose you must be very early in the feild this spring with
your armys, and likwise with your fleet at sea ; for 'tis that that gives
the reputacion abroad. The King was resolved to slig[h]t Hereford,
draw those forces to Woster and so to indeavour with his strength to
releife Chestor which is not only to be prevented but the taking thereof
by all possible meanes to bee prosequeted, as likewise that of Newarke
where the Scots will doe you no service so that ye may have two
armyes, the one to attende the west, which must be very considerable,

the other, Oxford. You may bravely (?) treat with the King or offer him his desire for coming to London, for 'tis conceaved by the Queene —and she hath assurance thereof—that he will not conclude anything tell he shall see the effectes of one bataille more this springe. Your assurance of religion, lawes, libertyes persons and those of your deere wives and childrens must be in accomodacion—for the chance of warr is doutfull, and ite you should loose one bataille, the people would all forsacke you being now most wery of the ware besides it would give the King that reputation as his allies abroad would serve him faithfully, and beleave it, the cardinall of France is not really yours—which must by all modest and gentle wayes be by you sought. If the present oportunity faile, the Kingdome of England wilbe the feild of blood and all nations will ponir their wurst of men into that now most miserable kingdome. The Queene of England comes on Munday next to Paris, there to solithit (solicit) in her person. Ye must not dout of what is now sent you for I have it from a friend that cannot erre and one that is a faithfull lover of his religion, contry, lawes and libertyes." (Part printed in Gardiner, *History of the Great Civil War*, ii. 432, note.) *Copy.* [N. VI., 25.]

The distressed INHABITANTS OF CLEVELAND to the QUARTER SESSIONS OF THE NORTH RIDING.

[1645-6, January 12.]—Petition, stating that part of the said Wapentake had for eight months paid the Scotch army 4,000l. *per mensem* and upwards, and now a month's pay was demanded in advance, which they were unable to pay. (Printed in Grey, iii., Appendix, No. 26, p. 43.) *Copy.* [N. XXII., 91.]

The PARLIAMENT to the KING.

1645[-6], January 13.—(Printed in *Lords' Journals*, viii. 99.) *Copy.* [N. XII., 169.]

J[OHN] R[USHWORTH] to WILLIAM LENTHALL.

1645[-6], January 13. Totness.—Enclosing a letter with the news of the raising of the siege of Plymouth. "A great part of the army is now before Dartmouth—hard duty this cold weather. This night some attempt will be made by storming it." *Seal.* [N. V., 82.] *Enclosed :*

Colonel JAMES KERR and others to [JOHN RUSHWORTH].

1645[-6], January 12. Plymouth.—"This day the enemy hath quitted all their strongholds before us, in much fear, but they were too strong in horse for us to deal with. The enemy left at Plimstock two great guns, at Newbridge two, at Fort Arundel 33 muskets and four barrels of powder, and we conceive if the enemy be pursued [they] will continue in their flying posture. They are gone as we believe towards Tavistock." *Copy.* [N. V., 83.]

SIR WILLIAM BRERETON o WILLIAM LENTHALL.

1645[-6], January 14. Chester Suburbs.—Enclosing a summons to the besieged and the correspondence that followed. "It seems many of the citizens remain still so enthralled and enawed as that they dare not oppose nor resist; many more so deeply engaged to hold out the city, as that they can expect no less than inevitable ruin, were there no more guilt and charge upon them, but to make reparation and satisfaction to those honest men, whose estates they have seized and possessed after they had turned them out of town. Hence . . all former fair tenders have been rejected, and such is the strength of the city, being a very compact piece, and the walls so high and strong, as that upon the Cheshire side our cannoniers could not find any convenient place to fix a battery to do execution either upon the walls or over the walls upon the houses in the city, though there hath been near forty barrels of powder spent in one day. And when a small breach hath been made and our men entered by storm, they have been beaten back with loss, whence the enemy also is encouraged to hold out. Nothing hath been so formidable to the enemy nor done so great execution as a mortar piece which we borrowed from Shrewsbury, for which if we had been furnished with shells, we should have been able to have given you a better account. . . *Postscript.*—We have sent a strong party consisting of three Cheshire foot companies under the command of Colonel Massie, and one of Colonel Mitton's under the command of Lieutenant-Colonel Twisleden, who have blocked up Hawarden, and secured those passages, and they are likewise seconded by the regiments of Cheshire and Derbyshire horse. We have sent another party this day to block up Holt by means whereof Chester will be deprived of all intelligence." *Signed. Seal. Enclosed* are several communications between Sir W. Brereton and the besieged which are printed in *King's Pamphlets,* E. 327, No. 30, p. 33. [N. V., 84.]

JOHN COSYN and others to WILLIAM LENTHALL.

1645[-6], Newcastle, January 15.—Have made but little progress in the commission directed to us to examine what money, billet, goods or other provision have been raised or taken by the Scotch army within this town and county. We desire to know whether the plunder taken in the storming of this town comes within the compasss of our commission as the Scots conceive it does not. *Signed. Seal.* [N. V., 85.]

The COMMITTEE OF BOTH KINGDOMS.

1645[-6], January 15.—Order reporting the letters of Mr. Annesley and Sir Robert King &c. to both Houses. (Printed in *Lords' Journals,* viii. 104.) [N. XXI., 25.]

The LORD MAYOR, ALDERMEN, and COMMONS OF the City of LONDON to the HOUSE OF COMMONS.

1645[-6], January 15.—Petition. (Identical with that to the House of Lords which is printed in *Lords' Journals,* viii. 105.) *Signed* "Michel." [N. XXII., 87.] *Enclosed:*

The Representation of the WARD OF FARRINGDON WITHOUT. (Printed *ubi suprà.*) [N. XXII., 88.]

Lieutenant-General DAVID LESLIE to the GOVERNOR OF PONTEFRACT.

1645[-6], January 15. Kelham —Demanding by what authority he had imprisoned some whom he had ordered to quarter there. (Printed in Grey, iii., Appendix, No. 31, p. 52.) *Copy.* [N. XIX., 136.]

The PARLIAMENT to [the DOGE and SENATORS OF GENOA.]

[1645-6, January 16.]—Concerning the arrest of the goods of the East India Company in their city by Sir Peter Ricaut, on account of a debt alleged to be due from the Company to him, the fact being that his interests in the Company had been sequestrated by the Parliament (see *Commons' Journals*, iii. 90), and desiring that the arrest should be taken off. (Printed in *Lords' Journals*, viii. 106.) In *Latin. Draft* or *Copy*. [N. XII., 198.]

Major-General ROWLAND LAUGHARNE to WILLIAM LENTHALL.

1645[-6], January 16. Haverfordwest. — " Aberystwith Castle opposeth as yet. My men by the vehemency of the weather and poverty of the place have very ill lying before it. The enemy, I suppose, are in no good condition within; their fuel is well nigh spent, and provision not very plentiful, and their water cut off. I have not yet drawn my guns before it, and the ground is not in this extreme weather pliable for raising of batteries. . . The supply in money and clothes the House ordered for my soldiers if received might much have furthered the service. . . . Mr. Lorte and Mr. Elliott the Committee's Agent are so wholly taken with prosecution of private malice they can spare no thoughts for the public good. I desire Mr. Arthur Owens . . . be entrusted with the dispose and conveyance of that and what other relief may be designed for us. I perceive Captain Poyer is molested by some gentlemen [who] in our distress were our greatest enemies and [whom] success only induced to profess our friendship." . . . . Having commended him highly "I humbly pray he may be remitted to his command of the Castle and Town of Pembroke " pledging myself to be responsible for his appearance. " I humbly pray the distressed condition of Pembrokeshire . . may be spared of the Excise ; no county in the kingdom, I am assured, is become such an object of pity;" and that if it be imposed on any other part of this Association, it may be assigned for the support of the public affairs here. *Signed. Seal.* [N. V., 86.]

The COMMITTEE AT YORK to the ENGLISH COMMISSIONERS WITH THE SCOTCH ARMY.

1645[-6], January 16.—Having formerly had no redress for our complaints of the great pressures on this county from the Scotch army, it has occasioned a much more exorbitant carriage not only in some of the Scotch, but—as under their command—even of our English with a mixture of Irish, and those all disaffected to the Parliament, to press upon the country with intolerable burdens and insolencies. Besides the two regiments of Horse lately come from Scotland about Thirsk and Northallerton, there is a regiment of 20 troops quartered about Rotherham and Tickhill, whose outrages and the grieved countrymen's occasions—in part to stay their violences—we desire you to take notice of by the enclosed Petition and Articles of charges, and by the enclosed copy of a letter. We request you to treat with the Scotch general that not only justice be done upon the offenders, but that their forces be removed out of this county. *Copy.* [N. XII., 173.]

J. HATFIELD to [JOHN] LAUGHTON.

1645[-6], January 17.—Giving an account of Captain Carse's journey with Richard Lane to the General of the Scotch army. He having read our petition and seen our grievances replied, " those your grievances have been insufferable and your petition is fair, but the action is such that I will revenge it upon your town, while I have a drop of warm blood in my body," and ordered Captain Carse to bring three regiments of Horse to quarter in our town, and they are expected every day. I therefore desire that a Petition be drawn to the Committees to acquaint them with our danger, that Colonel Bethell's men be directed to secure our persons and estates, or if not, some other of our Yorkshire horse, and that speedily, for danger is at the door. The General of the Scotch forces urged that we should have brought them to him which was impossible for us considering their army lay in the way. I have sent you Mr. Rolston's letter with an account of his and John Fleeman's journey to the Lords and Commons. Divers of the town will not come in to give evidence without warrants from the Committee or the Governor of Pontefract, so if you conceive them useful send warrants with speed. *Copy.* [N. XII., 174.]

The HOUSE OF COMMONS.

1645[-6], January 17. — Order concerning Sir John Fenwick. (Printed in *Commons' Journals*, iv. 409.) [N. XIV., 97.]

Muster of the SCOTCH ARMY.

1645[-6], January 17.—(Printed in *Lords' Journals*, viii. 186.) [N. XIX., 138.]

HENRY GOODING and others to WILLIAM LENTHALL.

1645[-6], January 17. Henley.—Complaining that Mr. Rodulph Warcoppe and his son, when summoned before them sitting as a Committee of Parliament to pay money due from them to their garrison, were arrested on a *Latitat* by the Under-Sheriff, and asking that the House should order that all persons may have liberty to come to them and return without arrest. *Signed.* [N. V., 87.]

SIR JOHN GELL to WILLIAM LENTHALL.

1645[-6], January 17. Derby.—"I ventured the other night with such forces as I have to fall upon Tutbury. We entered the town took seven score horses and eleven men ; the rest retreated to the Castle. We found but two dead men, the rest of the wounded were carried to the Castle. Since this Lieutenant Moore is come to me from the enemy with 22 men, he was the man that did us the most hurt when the King was last in our country. There is 20 more of the same troop gone to Sir William Brereton. Staffordshire forces made the like attempt against Tutbury lately, but was forced to retreat. Sir William Blackston is made Governor of Tutbury, the Lord Asteley is now there himself." . . *Postscript.*—Beseeching match and powder. *Seal.* [N. V., 88.]

Vice-Admiral WILLIAM BATTEN to WILLIAM LENTHALL.

1645[-6], January 17. On board the *Leopard* in Torbay.—"Having spent some time before Falmouth, and understanding that the Prince was gone Eastward for Dartmouth, which he endeavoured to do, but our forces lying in the way made him retreat for Cornwall again, where he now is, and for ought I hear hath no intention to go from thence, five sail I have left off Falmouth to attend his motion, and to secure our merchant ships out and home. On Tuesday last being in Plymouth Sound I received a letter from Sir Thomas Fairfax from Totnes, which signified his intent to fall on Dartmouth and desired my assistance. Whereupon I presently set sail, and came before Dartmouth the next day with eleven sail of ships and pinnaces, part whereof I left before the town, and went into Torbay with the rest, the siege from Plymouth being raised the day before came from thence.

On the 15th . . I sent away the *Providence* and *Robert* frigate to join with the *Expedition* and *Constant Warwick*, who were before Dartmouth, and the 16th in the morning the *Providence* brought me in a French vessel with these passengers and goods specified in the enclosed list, and the same day Sir Thomas Fairfax sent to me for some ammunition and 100 men, which I have accordingly sent him on shore." . . . . *Signed. Seal.* [N. V., 89.]

Colonel PURBECK TEMPLE, Governor, to WILLIAM LENTHALL.

1645[-6], January 18. Henley. — Complaining that the High Sheriff, being a member of the Committee, sits with them, and by his power as High Sheriff disenables them from discharging their duty. (See letter of the 17th from the same place.) *Signed* [N. V., 90.]

The KING to the MARQUESS OF ORMONDE.

1645[-6], January 19.—(Printed in Carte, *Life of Ormonde*, iii. 441.) *Copy.* [N. XII., 115.]

Major-General RICHARD BROWNE to the COMMITTEE OF BOTH KINGDOMS.

1645[-6], January 19. Abingdon.—"Colonel Rainsborough's regiment is come to us and consists of near 500 men. I have proposed conditions for Captain Williams with his brother and Mr. Jones the Minister, . . . which I believe will be accepted . . . This day I sent 40 horse under Captain Roe to alarm Wallingford, and so retreat The enemy pursued as far as Clifton, and—overpowering us with fresh and able horses—took 30 prisoners. But Major Blundell, whom I ordered with 100 men, to march over Chissleton Bridge, according as the design was contrived, surprised them in their return, relieved all our own, took 50 of the Wallingford horses, and near as many prisoners, of whom some escaped,—the night overtaking us—; 29 we have in custody, among whom one Lieutenant-Colonel, one Major, five Captains, lieutenants, cornets, ensigns, 14, most of them reformadoes. Lieutenant-Colonel Wilford that commanded their party is slain, with three more of their soldiers, but one of ours. The Lieutenant-Colonel of theirs who is taken is Sir William Lower, the Deputy Governor." (See *Commons' Journals*, iv. 416.) *Signed. Seal.* [N. V., 91.]

WILLIAM PIERREPONT, SIR WILLIAM ARMYNE, SIR EDWARD AYSCOGHE, and THOMAS HATCHER to WILLIAM LENTHALL.

1645[-6], January 20.—(Identical *mutatis mutandis*, with the letter from the Earl of Rutland to the Speaker of the House of Peers, which is printed in *Lords' Journals*, viii. 121.) *Enclosed* are the letter of General Leslie to the Commissioners and their reply, which are both printed as above. *Signed. Seal.* [N. V., 92.]

The JOINT COMMITTEES AT YORK to Lieutenant-General LESLIE.

1645[-6], January 20.—We wrote to you with the Articles enclosed about four days ago, when we first heard about the soldiers now in Pontefract for misdemeanours at Tickhill, and now acquaint you with the fears of the inhabitants there by menaces from some of your army, and the just ground of their danger by the intention of drawing some regiments of Scotch horse into that town, and desire you to order that charge and pressure to that particular place by any of your army be prevented, which will very much savour of revenge, the consequence whereof may extend to endanger the breach of that happy union of the two nations. *Copy.* [N. XII., 175.]

WILLIAM ASHBORNE to [LORD GREY OF WARKE.]

1645[-6], January 20. Chill[ingham].—Concerning the barbarous carriage of a regiment of Scotch horse under Colonel Frisell, and the storm, the like of which had not been known by any now living, (Printed in Grey, iii., Appendix, No. 22, p. 35.) [N. V., 93.]

The ENGLISH COMMISSIONERS WITH THE SCOTCH ARMY to Lieutenant-General LESLIE.

1645[-6], January 22. Grantham.—We have received very sad complaints of horse lately quartered at Stayncross and those parts in Yorkshire under Major Blair, how they took clothes and free quarter, and assessed great sums of money, take horses and when the owners redeem them for money take both horses and money, and that one of them committed a rape ; some said the Reformadoes of your army, committing many oppressions at Tickhill, were taken by the inhabitants to Pontefract Castle, of whom those of the Scotch nation the Committee have written to you shall be sent to receive justice at your hands, and the English Irish and French shall receive the punishment appointed by Parliament. This we perceive by the dates was before we were with you at the mustering of your army, of which you were pleased to say nothing to us. Tickhill and the Yorkshire Committees are informed that some regiments of your Horse are to come to Tickhill and that words were given out by some of ruin threatened to that town and to others for taking those soldiers. These things so much concern the public service against Newark and the good correspondency of both kingdoms, that we desire a speedy redress, and by this messenger to receive your answer, that we may send it into Yorkshire. *Copy.* [N. XII., 177.]

Lieutenant-General LESLIE to the ENGLISH COMMISSIONERS.

1645[-6], January 23. East Bridgeford.—In reply to the last. As for Major Blair's soldiers, the charges seem very strange to me, never having received any complaint of that regiment. I promise that if any such thing had come to my knowledge or shall be proved, I shall see them punished. As for the Reformadoes "I cannot but resent the affront done to me in taking of them, seeing they were under my command . . . and therefore I doubt not but that your Lordships will send them all to me to be punished if they be found guilty . . . according to the law of arms, and that you will punish those men of Tickhill for the wrong they have done to me. As to the information . . . of my purpose to quarter on that town and that out of revenge, the Lord knows I abhor revenge, and will your Lordships be pleased to quarter those regiments that are in Yorkshire in any other adjacent county, they shall go when you appoint them, so that if they lie any longer in that county it shall not be my fault but your Lordships.

I entreat your Lordships to give orders to the country people to bring their complaints first to me, when if they shall not be remedied, the fault to be imputed to me." *Copy.* [N. XII., 178.]

The ENGLISH COMMISSIONERS to Lieutenant-General LESLIE.

Same date. Grantham.—We have sent a copy of your letter to the Committee of Yorkshire and the Governor of Pontefract Castle that in all cases of complaint against any under your command our desires are and ever have been that the first address for remedy be made to yourself, and that such as were taken by the inhabitants of Tickhill and are of your army shall be transmitted for their trial to you, but for such as are not of your army we know it is your mind they should receive their punishment in such manner as by the Parliament is appointed, and we shall at every opportunity show how kindly we take your respect in leaving the business of the inhabitants of Tickhill to us. Our letter and instructions were far from imputing revenge to you, but that words of revenge have been uttered by some under you, which, as also the complaints made, will in due time be proved, or else let them suffer that have falsely accused. We have no authority to quarter your horse in other counties. *Copy.* [N. XII., 179.]

The MAYOR, ALDERMEN, and BURGESSES OF PORTSMOUTH to WILLIAM LENTHALL.

1645[-6], January 22. Portsmouth.—Desiring that a writ might be issued for the election of a member in the room of Colonel Goring. *Signed. Seal.* [N. V., 94.]

The COMMITTEE FOR ACCOMMODATION.

1645[-6], January 23 and February 2.—Votes printed in *Commons' Journals*, iv. 428. [N. XXII., 33.]

Colonel PURBECK TEMPLE to WILLIAM LENTHALL.

1645[-6], January 23.—Giving a fuller account of the arrest of Mr. Warcopp and his son. (See letter of the 17th from the same place.) *Signed.* [N. V., 96.]

SIR WILLIAM BRERETON to WILLIAM LENTHALL.

1645[-6], January 23. Chester Suburbs.—" The last night we took four of their spies, and by them and by letters intercepted from Sir Richard Lloyd to Watts the Governor of Chirk Castle we discover their designs and strong hopes of present relief, which, I believe did encourage them by Sir Edmond Varney and Major Thropp their Commissioners put out this day to make such high demands in their 36 propositions, whereof there cannot be six assented unto, and the rest some of them most high and unparalleled which were returned with as much scorn and disdain, as they were sent out with confidence. I tendered unto them my answer to Byron's letter, and such conditions enclosed as I thought fit to propose, neither whereof would they receive. Our bridge over Dee was— by breach of the weather—disordered and made unserviceable two days, after which time it was repaired. The enemy is possessed of strong hopes of relief by sea, and to that end have at Ruthland and Conway prepared several vessels laden with corn, bacon, and other provisions. For prevention whereof we have provided several small barques, which are manned with musketeers and furnished with ordnance, wherewith we doubt not—by God's blessing—to secure that passage, and to seize or repel those that come to their relief, whereof I have received strong assurance from Captain Rich. . . We are now again furnished with some grenadoes for our mortar piece . . . We are making a battery in the steeple of St. John's Church whence only—upon the Cheshire side—we can command and shoot into the city. But we are so unprovided of tackles and other necessaries for the firing and conveying up the great guns that we cannot yet perfect that work, which we hope a few days will finish. . . *Postscript.*—Whatsoever you have heard, I do assure you no relief—except a small proportion when our bridge was unservice-able—hath come into the city since I came down." *Signed.* *Seal.* [N. V., 97.] *Enclosed:*

i. Propositions sent out of Chester by Sir Edmund Verney and Serjeant-Major Thropp from LORD BYRON.

1645[-6], January 22.—(These, 36 in number, are the "very high conditions" mentioned by Rushworth, iv. 1. 137, and are much more favourable to the besieged, than those eventually agreed upon.) [N. XIV., 98.]

ii. [SIR WILLIAM BRERETON] to [LORD BYRON].

1645[-6], January 22.—" I should not have expected propositions of so high demands as those you have sent. . . . We know your wants are great, your hopes of relief desperate. . . . I will not trouble myself with answering the particulars of your unparalleled demands . . . yet to witness my desire for the preservation of the city I have . . . thought fit to tender these enclosed conditions for the performance whereof . . . commissioners may meet and treat. *Enclosed:*

The said CONDITIONS.

1 equals No. 13 of the articles printed in Rushworth iv. 1. 139, with the addition that the County Palatine Seal and Swords are to be delivered as well as the Records.
2, 3, and 4 equal Nos. 3, 5, and 15 of the said articles.
5. That such a sum as may be concluded upon by the Commissioners be raised and paid for satisfaction of the soldiery to prevent the plunder of the city.
6 equals No. 4 of the said articles from the beginning down to " violence of the soldiers."
7. That the Governor, noblemen, gentlemen, and soldiers, both English, Welsh, and Irish born of English parents, who did not take part with the rebels of Ireland, and such noblemen, gentlemen and citizens as are so minded and are now in the city—except those that have been members of this present Parliament and have deserted the same, and the Commissioners of Array for this county and city, and such as were of the Grand Jury and indicted many of the county for high treason against the King for their fidelity to the Kingdom—shall reserve free liberty to march away to the garrison of   in manner following. . . . The Governor with four horses and his arms and not above 50l. in money, any field officer two horses, captains of horse and foot and lieutenants of horse one horse apiece and none of them to exceed 5l. a piece in money, the lieutenants of foot, ensigns and other inferior officers with a sword only and no horse and 10s. in money, the common soldiers without arms and not above 5s. a piece in money.
8 and 9 relate to convoy and hostages. *Copies.* [N. XII., 176.]

OLIVER EJRY, Mayor, and others to WILLIAM LENTHALL.

1645[-6], January 23. Stafford.—" Yesterday Captayne Stone, our Governour, had intelligence that the force from Litchfield intended to come to Canock towne four myles distant from this garrison . . and that they would come stronge . . . Whereupon hee presently sent messengers to Rushall and Wrotesley two garysons in this countye to send what horse they could possibly spare to meete his owne troope at a place appointed, his troope coming to the place before them, and the enemye beeinge in Canock towne and havinge each discovered other, knowinge yf they stayed, the enemye havinge notice by their scoutes of theyr number would charge them, thought better to march to them, knowinge that the Lord doth not alwayes worke by probable, but often by small and unlikely meanes—as hee did in this—. The enemye had divided themselves into three bodyes, the one in the way our men were to march, and the other two on each side, every of the three bodyes beeing far biger than Captayne Stone's troope—that charged them—. They charged through the fyrst body, and then seeminge to fly before the enemye to recover some ground to set themselves in a fytt posture againe—which they did—faced about on those which pursued them, and charged them agayne, and routed them, and followed them soe close to their other two bodyes that they were all disperst. They pursued them some fyve miles At the charge and in the pursuite there were slayne tenne at least, there was taken two captaynes, two lyftenauntes, three coronetes, two trumpeters, twelve gentlemen reformadoes of the Lord Mulinax his troope, and about fyftye common troopers, one hundred horse, with the horse, cloake and hatt of Sir Thomas Tylsley and many armes, some souldyers bringing three horses and six swordes a peece. Sir Thomas himself who comaunded the party escaped—beinge unhorst as is conceyved—gott into some house and could not bee found. Wee lost not one man, onely six were wounded, but none mortally. There was betwixt two and three hundred of the enemye and not above eighty of oures. And as wee are informed by the prysoners, Sir Thomas havinge beene longe a prysoner in this garyson, and lately escaped, beeinge now by the Kinge made comaunder in cheif over the horse in this countye, knowinge the readynes of this troope to goe forth uppon any notice of the enemyes motion, made a pretence of fetching hay onely to drawe them forth to ensnare them. But the Lord was pleased to take them in their owne net, Sir Thomas himself narowly escapeinge."

We request that Captain Stone may have some competent satisfaction towards his charges in raising his troops. (See *Commons' Journals*, iv. 419.) *Signed. Seal.* [N. V., 95.]

ROBERT DODSWORTH to [LORD GREY OF WARKE.]

1645[-6], January 25. Chill[ingham] Castle.—I am much afraid you Lordship will find a good part of your Candlemas rents taken up. Colonel Welden's regiment has had 1,000*l.*, I am confident, out of your lends, himself and his men. I was sent to the General to get them put away, and he gave order accordingly, but Colonel Welden told him that he, being Sheriff, could not do any service without having two troops of horse to wait on him to curb the high lands men, so that as long as he continues Sheriff we cannot expect the charge to be lessened. Unless another be put in you nor any man need not expect any rents at all. It will be more by much than the land will bear. They have betwixt 700*l.* and 800*l.* per month out of this corner of the country, most whereof gees into their own purses. I have both spoken and wrote to him of several abuses, but nothing the better. Mr. Ashborne sent him your Lordship's letter. All that he had from him was that it needed no answer at all. The storm continues still so extreme that a great part of the sheep are likely to be lost ; they did already abundance of them. Corn gives small rates, rye 12s., heare 8s., oats 6s., and wheat 14s. They used to give double that rate not many years ago. We hear that in Scotland things are not likely to go well for reason of differences among the nobility. Montrose, it is said, draws to a great head again about the hills, in Murrowe Land. We are offered for Chivington 120l. per annum, little more than half the former rate, but the reason is that as yet men dare not venture upon stock, besides the easy rate of Delin quents' lands. [N. XII., 180.]

SIR WILLIAM BRERETON to WILLIAM LENTHALL.

1645[-6], January 26.—" The citizens discourse very familiarly and friendly, and say they will be no longer deluded. But their grandees, who have enriched themselves by those honest men's estates which they have seized and banished out of town, do know themselves in such a desperate condition that I cannot hope for the surrender of the town until they can hold out no longer, and the rather because they have an expectation of relief by Ashley and these forces that are preparing to join with him. To prevent the conjunction of the Welsh forces with them is that which is most necessary. To this end I have sent three regiments of horse, the Reformadoes, the Warwickshire, the Stafford-shire, and my dragoons, which party I believe will make near 900 or 1,000, whereof Colonel Mytton takes the charge and command, who marched yesterday towards Ruthin to find out the Lord St. Paul, who hath gathered about 700 or 800 horse and foot, many of them forced men, whom if we could disperse might much advantage us, and dis-appoint and discourage the enemy . . . *Postscript.*—Yesterday the Mayor . . sent out to desire my propositions might be sent unto the town, whereunto I replied, if the Lord Byron sent out a pass this day by noon for two gentlemen they should be sent in, for whom I have now received a pass to meet in the mid-way, but they will not admit them to come into town. The short note that I caused to be thrown over the walls expressing the conditions I offered . . . did produce very good effect." *Signed. Seal.* [N. V., 98.]

BUSSY MANSELL, EDWARD CARNE, and others to Major-General LAUGHARNE.

1645[-6], January 26. Cardiff.—" About the time of the receipt of yours of the 22nd of January . . we received intelligence of an increase of misery happened to " Monmouthshire by the sudden surprise of their forces by the enemy from Ragland at Carline (Caerleon) which without some speedy assistance hath laid that country open to the violence and rapine of that barbarous and bloody crew, now much animated by that advantage. The gentry of that county therefore and ourselves have instructed the gentlemen, hearers hereof, " to crave your best aid, and to let you know the condition of our both counties and the sad consequences of the pro-valency of the enemy, not only to insh as a torrent on that and the adjacent counties to their ruin, but likewise the danger of their moulding a new considerable power to the disturbance of the kingdom for the prevention whereof we desire as many forces as you can spare." *Signed. Seal.* [N. V., 99.]

Major-General ROWLAND LAUGHARNE to WILLIAM LENTHALL.

1645[-6], January 29. Carmarthen.—" Wind and weather proving unfavourable for conveyance of my guns much delayed my designs upon Aberys[t]with Castle, and the enemy's advantage of sending out some small boats in the long and dark nights from under the Castle prolonged their opposition . . . Ragland and Ludlow horse prove very active and much infest our friends within their reach. To guard Brecknockshire from the one I have settled my Lieutenant-Colonel with 300 foot and 100 horse to garrison the town of Brecknock, the other—I receive credible intelligence—purpose so sudden relief of Aberys[t]with, I march this day with all the horse I have unengaged to assist the siege and preserve my guns. The Governor of Hereford soliciteth me that some horse of mine may be in Radnorshire to prevent incursions upon the borders of that county and into Herefordshire. In all that I am able without hazard of loss at Aberys[t]with I promised, and resolve to answer his expectation. Glamorganshire forces,—though Captain Moulton hath so fully armed them partly out of my store by the spoil of the enemy at Colby Moor—will not be wrought upon [by any] extremity of mine or Brecknockshire gentry to stir a foot abroad or apprehend any sense of the danger of their neighbours, so that I am necessitated to have my hands more than full of action or expose some friends to the enemy's mercy. I have delivered propositions—and they are not disliked—to the gentry of Carmarthen and Cardiganshire for the speedy raising of 1,000 foot and horse with means to pay them to fit me for the field. I hope at two months' end to be in condition to receive and obey the commands of the House for more remote service." I ask for a renewal and enlargement of my powers and the hastening down of the money formerly ordered. *Signed. Seal.* [N. V., 110.]

The COMMITTEE AT GOLDSMITHS' HALL.

1645[-6], January 29.—Report concerning Lady Style and William Hill. (The purport appears from the order thereon, which is printed in *Commons' Journals*, iv. 573.) [N. XIV., 99.]

Colonel THOMAS MYTTON to WILLIAM LENTHALL.

1645[-6], January 29. Ruthin.—(Partly printed and misdated in *Mercurius Civicus*, 2042, *King's Pamphlets*, E. 322, Nos. 32 and 39, where "Fanrust" is a misprint for "Llanrwst." It concludes thus): —"This place is of extraordinary great consequence being one of the most fruitful places in all Wales, as also a place if obtained that no intelligence can come from Ireland toward the King, but it must come through the Parliament quarters, therefore to enable us to go on with this service . . it is humbly desired that the House will . . consider of the sad condition my forces are in, the leaguer before Chester having eaten up all the country from this place thither, insomuch that we cannot raise one penny towards the payment of my soldiers," who have received but 500l. from Sir William Brereton of all the money given by Parliament. My forces were the fifth part of those before Chester, and have received pay not according to the 20th part. (See *Commons' Journals*, iv. 429.) *Seal.* [N. V., 111.]

Colonel MARTIN PYNDAR to WILLIAM LENTHALL.

1645[-6], January 29. Bristol.—I am appointed by the General to present the House with his endeavours upon Lord Inchiquin's letter from Youghal to supply that place with such speedy relief of provisions and money as this city or our employment here could afford namely with such victuals as the Garrison could spare and with 1,000l. lent by us your Commissioners out of a gratuity given by the city to the army in lieu of plunder, which Lord Inchiquin promised to repay out of the first moneys collected by the Ordinances of Parliament for that part of

Ireland. I therefore beseech the House to order the Committee for Irish affairs speedily to return the said 1,000*l.* to the army, as the soldier bethinking the time misdoubts the purpose of the General, and also divers precious things such as the ships in the harbour belonging to strangers, and the things in the King's storehouse, especially the coral entered by the East India Company, are withheld from the soldier whereunto they plead right. The wounded men are miraculously recovered and returned to their colours, four only remaining out of near 400. The accounts of the free quarter during the siege have been taken which amounts to so great a sum that without your honourable encouragement of the poor country they will be undone and disabled to give assistance to this garrison or support themselves for whose satisfaction by the General's order we engaged ourselves. *Seal.* [N. V., 112.]

Colonel Anthony Stapley and others to William Lenthall.

1645[-6], January 29. Lewes.—Enclosing a petition from a considerable part of the county, asking repayment of part of the money lent by them towards the 200,000*l.* for the Scots' advance out of the sequestrations of the county, and for that purpose desiring that the garrison of Chichester, which is maintained out of the sequestrations may be dissolved as now useless, and supporting the request of the petition. *Signed.* [N. V., 113.]

Sir William Armyne and others to William Lenthall.

1645[-6], January 31. Grantham.—(The first part of the letter is identical with that from the Earl of Rutland to the Speaker of the House of Peers, which is printed in *Lords' Journals*, viii. 141. It continues thus) :—"We find so much difficulty in procuring the mortar piece from Reading, and—now the weather is broken—the ways so impassable that your service may suffer much before that come unto us. Wherefore we have sent for the casting two at Nottingham, and if you please to order the 350*l.* to us, and add somewhat more to it, we shall be able to pay for them and provide shells and other necessaries, and we hope to have no need of a Master of Fireworks to be sent, having with us one very expert, and others who have done very good service against Belvoir. We shall now apply our whole endeavours for the reducing of Newark." *Signed. Seal. Enclosed* are copies of the summons to the Governor of Belvoir and his reply, both printed in *Lords' Journals*, viii. 141. [N. V., 114.]

A Bill for Enacting the Propositions and turning them into an Act of Parliament.

1645[-6], January 31.—Read a first and second time on that date. (See *Commons' Journals*, iv. 424.) *Draft*, with alterations. Annexed are the Propositions themselves, with Mr. Whitelocke's addition to the preamble of the first in a different hand. (They substantially agree with those sent to the King at Newcastle, which are printed in Rushworth, iv. 1. 309, except that the order of some is different, the period that the Parliament is to have the command of the Militia is unlimited instead of 20 years ; some additional Acts, including one for abolishing the Court of Wards, and another for suppressing interludes and stage plays, are mentioned in proposition 12 ; there are some variations in the names of the persons in the first qualification, qualifications 9 and 10 are omitted, the parts of proposition 13 that relate to the Militia and Tower of London are omitted, and also proposition 14, concerning Grants under the Great Seal. On the other hand, there are some additional propositions concerning the Education and Marriage of the King's children, the uniting of the Protestant princes, and the restoration of the Elector Palatine, an Act of Oblivion, indemnity to Members of Parliament for losses sustained in adhering to the Parliament, and the disbanding of the Armies. [N. XIV., 100.]

The EARL OF CRAFURD AND LINDESAY, President of Parliament, to the LORDS and COMMONS IN THE PARLIAMENT OF ENGLAND.

164[5–]6, February 3. St. Andrews.—(Printed in *Lords' Journals*, viii. 178, being the first of the two letters there.) *Signed.* *Seal.* [N. V, 115.]

The PARLIAMENT OF SCOTLAND.

164[5–]6, February 3. St. Andrews.—Order appointing the Earl of Dunfermline and others as a Committee to attend the army in England. *Copy.* [N. XIX, 201.]

[Major-General ROWLAND LAUGHARNE] to [BUSSY MANSELL and others].

1645[–6], February 5. Aberystwith.—Since the receipt of yours of January 26th, I received information from the Brecon gentlemen of the enemy's late incursions into some part of your county, intimating their desire of my appearance amongst them. So far as it may suit with my other engagements I have promised the assistance of most of my horse to perfect that service. *Draft,* written within fold of Mansell's letter of January 26th, to which it is a reply. [N. V., 100.]

Colonel EDWARD PRITCHARD and others to Major-General LAUGHARNE.

1645[–6], February 6. Cardiff.—" This day the country here, being countenanced by many Malignants come unto them, being met at their rendezvous fell into mutinous expressions, and that party of them which were better affected being sent to quarters those under the command of Colonel Carne began to quarrel, and at length fell to declare for the king, and a troop of horse under the command of Captain Edward Gwin seised on the Colonel-General, your brother, Colonel Button   . .. . and many of the best affected gentlemen, and Colonel Herbert of Sir Thomas Fairfax's army, who was there by chance.   .   .   .   They do now besiege this town ; of them we have not the least fear nor consideration, but Ragland forces hearing of it may probably come down to them. Our desire is that you would dispose of your forces so as to hinder their joining." *Signed.* [N. V., 101.]

The Propositions and Demands of the County of GLAMORGAN to the GOVERNOR OF CARDIFF and his associates.

[1645-6, February 6.]—Contrary to our first agreement at our first rising for peace to keep both sides out of our country you have sent several messengers to bring a force into our country.

Contrary to our intents and wills the contribution of this country has been raised by Ordinance of Parliament from 67*l.* to 162*l.* per week, and some of quality have had their liberties restrained and their goods forcibly detained.

We require the town and castle of Cardiff with all the arms and ammunition therein to be suddenly and peaceably delivered to us, on which we shall to the utmost of our power, secure the governor in his estate and person, with his officers and soldiers, and keep the town free from plundering.

Men of mean quality and of little or no repute, fortune, worth or reputation, have been nominated and made Committees for this county, whereas baronets, knights, esquires, and gentry have been left out, and thereby slighted and vilified.

And

Colonel EDWARD PRITCHARD and others' reply to the last.

[1645-6, February 6.]—We never intended to desire any forces from abroad, but only to repel the attempts of the enemy at Raglan. If the county be grieved at the contribution we will join with them for redressing it. The Committee is appointed by Parliament, and why should they name those that never intended to act for them? if they premise now to do so, no doubt they will be added. For the rest the sum is that this county should be independent from all England, both King and Parliament, which if your army be such as you are able to do, send us word by what authority higher than that either King or Parliament by which you demand this town. Till then we will live and die in this town, and though you join Raglan forces with you we shall carry ourselves like soldiers and maintain it to the utmost. We wonder that Colonel Carne should revolt from that trust and those protestations to which he is as deeply engaged as any of us. As for detaining the gentry, send ours you shall have yours, or they may be exchanged at the bridge. . . . [N. V., 102.] N. XV., 170, is another copy.

The Declaration of the Gentlemen, Freeholders, and others, the inhabitants of the County of GLAMORGAN.

[1645-6, February 6.]—Whereas insupportable grievances and pressures by some officers and ministers were the cause wholly of our first rising in arms for our necessary preservation and defence, since the business hath been carried out by the practices and artifice of some few, who wrought their own ends under colour of public pretences, and instead of easing our sufferings have much increased them, as will clearly appear by these ensuing particulars :—

That the county's troop by strict summons attending upon the garrison at Cardiff were employed in no other service than seizing on divers of our persons, plundering our houses, and sundry other ways unnecessarily molesting us and our neighbouring counties.

That very mean men have been intruded into the Government of the county, passing by men of quality and worth.

That these men have put a character of malignancy and delinquency upon the better part of this county, nor could we conceive any of us secure, being equally obnoxious whilst they intend to the same power over us, as is evident they do, for, being pressed that they would declare not to look back, it was peremptorily denied.

That the weekly contribution of 67l. has been raised to 162l.

That the *Common Prayer-Book* hath been commonly traduced, and several Sundays omitted in Cardiff, which we apprehend as a forerunner of its final rejection, had some their desires, and were we not resolved by the help of God to continue it.

That divers of quality and known affections have without legal process or cause shown been restrained, most of whom we have been forced to enlarge by courses not sorting with our resolution.

That we are advertized of a resolution to bring an excise upon us, which we did ever most desire to avoid as the greatest pressure.

That their tyranny might not only extend to our bodies and goods, order was taken that our very souls should not be free, the Covenant already tendered in Carmarthenshire being to be shortly tendered unto us. the very taking whereof would render us guilty of perjury.

That schismatics of several kinds are of greatest trust with some in chiefest place of government in this county whereby our souls and lives, our liberties and estates must be at their desire.

Wherefore we appeal both to God and man, whether we have not just cause to take and persevere in these ways and courses, the laws at this time affording no redress, in regard whereof and of the premises we are confident no true lover of his God, his king and his country, but will cheerfully join with and assist us, and so persuaded are we of the justness of our proceedings as to desire all and singular parsons vicars and curates to read and publish this our declaration within their respective parishes and where need require to render the sense of it in Welsh and to pray that God would so bless us in our endeavours as they are intended for His glory, the King's honour, the peace and happiness of the kingdom and more particularly of this county.

And because some have a jealousy of receiving the King's forces in Monmouthshire to our assistance because they of the other side in Cardiff did and do still labour to bring in strange forces, we certify and declare that none are received or to be received but what mere necessity shall enforce us, and such as shall be necessary for reducing Cardiff, upon condition likewise that the said forces shall not offer to plunder or prejudice any man in the least degree, and likewise the said forces have bound themselves to depart, as soon as the reducing of the town and garrison of Cardiff shall be finished, and do promise to bring their own provision from Monmouthshire to avoid all trouble and charge to this land and also to receive orders from and be under the command of Colonel Carne. [N. V., 104.]

Amendments of the LORDS to the Propositions.

[1645-6, February 6.]—(See *Lords' Journals*, viii. 144.) (The effect of most of the amendments appears from the Report of the Conference printed in *Lords' Journals*, viii. 215.) [N. XV., 174.]

LORD CHARLES SOMERSET to the COMMANDER-IN-CHIEF and the rest of his Majesty's loyal subjects in GLAMORGANSHIRE.

1645[-6], February 13. Raglan Castle.—"Having received certain intelligence from Sir Charles Kemeys that your County of Glamorgan is unanimously by your means risen up in a body to the defence of his Majesty's rights and privileges against the insulting enemy . . . . I acknowledge with admiration those large testimories of your loyalty and encourage you . . to persevere therein. . . . I shall not be wanting upon any just occasion as well to engage my person as to venture my uttermost credit to serve you." As a proof of which "I have earnestly sollicited my Lord Ashley for his speedy assistance being now at Bromyard with a body of 3,000 men, conceiving it very probable that the enemy will be industrious to draw together all the force they can to come in our rear and thereby to hazard to distract, if not to destroy the forward way we are in, by God's assistance, to reduce all South Wales to their former obedience to his Majesty. I am confident that in a few days you will see the effects of these my labours to secure you, Lord Ashley being not only in honour but by a special command from his Majesty obliged to afford us assistance in this good occasion.

. . . Rather than you should want I have sent you a greater quantity " of ammunition " than I can well spare." [N. V., 103.]

Sir Thomas Fairfax to William Lenthall.

1645[-6], February 13. Crediton. — Recommending Sir Hugh Pollard to their favourable consideration both on account of the promise made by himself to him on the surrender of the Castle at Dartmouth, and also of the good report of his just moderate and fair carriage in his government both to the country in general and to the Parliament's friends thereabouts. (See *Commons' Journals*, iv. 495.) *Signed. Seal.* [N. V., 116.]

William Sprigge to Sir Henry Vane, junior.

1645[-6], February 16.—Recommending to him Mr. William Driden, who had been with him a year since touching the Island of Scilly. *Seal.* [N. V., 117.]

The Assembly of Divines to the House of Commons.

1645[-6], February 16.—Petition praying the House to take steps for setting up Classical Presbyteries so as to enable the many pious and learned persons willing to enter the ministry to be ordained. *Signed.* (See *Commons' Journals*, iv. 443.) [N. XXII., 34.]

The Elector Palatine to the Committee of both Kingdoms.

1645[-6], February 17. Whitehall.—" By this inclosed paper you will find my present condition to be such that I want means for my own subsistence and for the maintenance of my public Ministers in such negotiations as the urgent necessity of my affairs require. At this time it is the greater in respect that the Crowns of France, Sweden, and their confederates having seriously taken into their consideration the important interests I have in the present great affairs now in agitation at the general treaty of peace at Münster and Osnabrück, as also that no firm nor constant peace can be agreed upon—especially in the Empire—without the determining and settling of my affairs have earnestly and severally invited and desired me to send my public Ministers to the said places to manage my interests in all negotiations and stipulations which I cannot omit without a very great prejudice to the true Reformed Religion and cause in general as well as to my affairs and interests concerning my restitution in dignity and dominions, the advancement whereof since both kingdoms have ever embraced with so much affection, I doubt not but their sense will still be to provide for my present subsistence in a way most conducive thereunto in expectation of their more effectual advancement thereof. Therefore I thought fit to address my desires to be represented to the Parliament by you, who are best able to time the said business and to advance it by your serious recommendation." *Signed* "Charles Lodovic." *Seal.* [N. I., 51.]

Articles of Agreement between us and the Gentlemen and Officers in the town of Cardiff.

[1645-6, February 19.] — " The countrymen who march to their houses shall keep their own arms—we mean such only as they brought with them from their own houses—upon the engagement of all the gentlemen in the town of Cardiff that they shall not draw to any rendezvous without order or warrant from Colonel-General Bushy Mansell, and for all the Gentlemen and officers they shall march away with their horses swords pistols and cloakbags to any of the King's garrisons within 50 miles . . with such a convoy as shall guard them . . and such as shall stay at home shall have free protection from the violence of the soldier and, as far as it lies in us, for your persons and estates. We shall never urge any oath or covenant unto tender consciences.

We shall not only secure but honour and encourage the religious learned Clergy, they intermeddling only with the business of their function, and for the *Common Prayer-Book* we shall not, disturb any in the use of it.

The exchange of prisoners we wholly leave to Major-General Laugharne.

We . . yielding unto these particulars do require that the town of Cardiff with all the arms artillery and ammunition not before excepted be delivered into the Governor's hands for the use of King and Parliament by 10 of the clock tomorrow morning, being the 20th of February 1645.

We expect your answer within this hour or two at furthest and engage ourselves that Major-General Laugharne shall subscribe this before your surrender tomorrow morning and upon your return of a counterpart of this subscribed by all you gentlemen and officers we agree to a cessation of arms.

I subscribe to as much as concerns myself and my soldiers.

Rowland Laugharne."

[N. V., 105.]

Sir William Brereton and others to William Lenthall.

[1645-6, February. Chester.]—"The city itself is generally disaffected towards us, so that without a strong force we shall be unable to secure the city or ourselves, no less than 1,500 foot and 200 horse being sufficient for that work. It will also require a large sum of money to lay in a magazine of ammunition, to have a store well furnished with provisions and also to alter and strengthen the fortifications," which cannot be done without assistance from neighbouring parts, none, as we conceive, being more obliged hereunto than the nearer parts of North Wales which, " we must expect and shall desire to reduce by our own forces, Holt, Hawarden, and Flint being three castles that in a manner block up this city on the Welsh side for present, and the Parliament's forces in North Wales being so inconsiderable that of themselves they are not able to reduce these holds. Also these parts having constantly had their livelihood by their trade and commerce with this city will be most awed to the Parliament and secured in their estates by the forces maintained in this place." We therefore crave that we may have the command of at least twelve miles in North Wales to assist for the maintenance of this garrison. The poverty of this place is such on account of their want of trade and the exactions, and the county so exhausted by being for three years a seat of war, and finally by the burden of this long siege that they cannot without assistance bear the burden necessary to be imposed. *Signed. Seal.* [N. V., 109, should be 108.]

The Standing Committee of Northumberland.

1645[-6], March 2.—Testimonial. That to the best of their knowledge Sir John Fenwick had always adhered to the Parliament and not to the King. *Signed* by Robert Clavering, Sheriff, and by seven others. [N. XIV., 103.]

The Scotch Commissioners.'

1645–6, March 3.—Paper. (Printed in *Lords' Journals*, viii. 197.) *Copy.* [N. XIX., 139.]

Francesco Bernardi, Agent of the' Spanish Embassy, to the Parliament.

[1645–6, March 4.]—Concerning the seizure by Captain Plunket of ship called the *St. Nicholas* or *St. Peter.*

and

Michael Castel and others on behalf of the proprietors of the cargo of the said ship to the House of Peers.

[Same date.]—Petition praying for reparation. (Both printed in *Lords' Journals*, viii. 198.) [N. XVII., 33, 34.]

The Committee for the Admiralty and Cinque Ports.

1645[-6], March 5.—Report recommending a gratuity of 40*l.* to Robert Long, late master of the *Providence*, who had been dangerously wounded in taking one of the King's men-of-war. [N. XIV., 101.]

Sir Thomas Fairfax to William Lenthall.

1645[-6], March 6. Bodmin.—Recommending Mr. Glanvill to the favourable respect of the House. (See *Commons' Journals*, iv. 495.) *Signed. Seal.* [N. V., 118.]

The Committee of both Kingdoms.

1645[-6], March 9.—Report concerning Colonel Rainsborough, and the proposed surrender of a garrison of the King's. (See *Commons' Journals*, iv. 71.) [N. XIV., 102.]

William Pierrepont, Sir William Armyne, Sir Edward Ayscoghe, and Thomas Hatcher to Sir Anthony Irby and William Ellys.

1645[-6], March 12. Grantham.—Asking that no Colonel be appointed to the regiment lately under the command of Colonel Browne, it being unfitting for the county after the reducing of Newark to continue the pay of two regiments, and recommending that if the appointment is filled up, the present Lieutenant-Colonel should be promoted to it. (See *Commons' Journals*, iv. 475.) *Signed. Seal.* [N. VI., 31.]

Major-General Rowland Laugharne to William Lenthall.

1645[-6], March 17. Carmarthen.--Acknowledging the favour of the House in freeing at his suit the Earl of Carbery from all delinquency relative to his military employment or affairs, and desiring that, if this vote be not equivalent to a full and total remission of all crimes since the beginning of the war, such a remission might be granted on account of his Lordship's immutable compliance to the Parliament, and the influence this has been towards settling those parts, and because this course will induce many others to the Parliament's obedience. *Copy,* with footnote, signed "William Lenthall." "This letter remained with Mr. Speaker, and was never yet read in the House." [N. V., 119.]

The Assembly of Divines to the House of Commons.

[1645–6, March 23.]—Petition against the provision of Commissioners to judge of scandals. (Declared to be a breach of Privilege. The effect of the Petition appears from *Commons' Journals*, iv. 518.) (Printed in Grey, iii. Appendix, No. 54, p. 84.) *Original* and *Copy*. [N. XXII., 39, 36.]

The HOUSE OF COMMONS to the SCOTCH COMMISSIONERS.

1645[-6], March 23.—Answer concerning the unknown Knight and Robert Wright. (Printed in *Commons' Journals*, iv. 486.) [N. XXII., 37.]

The KING to the SPEAKER OF THE HOUSE OF PEERS *pro̍ tempore*.

1645[-6], March 23. Oxford.—(Printed in *Lords' Journals*, viii. 235.) *Copy* on back of last. [N. XXII., 38.]

HENRY HARPER to the HOUSE OF COMMONS.

[1645-6, March 23.]—Petition stating his good affection to the Parliament and his sufferings from the Cavaliers, and desiring to be relieved from his composition. (See *Commons' Journals*, iv. 486.) [N. XXII., 112.]

Lieutenant RAMSEY to Major-General VANDRUSK.

1646, March 26. Rednes.—" I am certainly informed that there are come to Couldsknoe the number of 200 foot, and doth threaten to put us forth of our quarters—which before they do some shall have bloody crowns—wherefore " I desire to know your will. *Endorsed:* " Read April 23 at Gainsborough." At foot : "19° April 1646. This letter was showed to Wm. Brooke at the time of his examination. William Brooke." [N. VI., 3.]

The COMMISSIONERS OF THE CHURCH OF SCOTLAND.

1646, March 26.—Paper. (Printed in *King's Pamphlets*, E. 333, No. 1, p. 16, being part of the volume ordered by the House of Commons to be burnt by the common hangman.) *Signed* "John Donn." [N. XIX., 140.]

The LORD LIEUTENANT of the one part and VISCOUNT MOUNTGARRET and the other COMMISSIONERS of the ROMAN CATHOLICS of the other part.

1646, March 28.—Defeazance of the articles of peace concluded that day. (The material part is printed in Carte, *Life of Ormonde*, i. 566.) *Copy*. [N. XXI., 46.]

The ENGLISH COMMISSIONERS to the SCOTCH COMMISSIONERS
and
The SCOTCH COMMISSIONERS to the ENGLISH COMMISSIONERS.

1646, March 28, 30.—(Both printed in *Lords' Journals*, viii. 344, 345.) *Copies*. [N. XIX., 141, 142.]

The PARLIAMENT to the PRINCE OF WALES
and
The PARLIAMENT to [SIR THOMAS FAIRFAX].

1646, March 30.—(Both printed in *Lords' Journals*, viii. 246, 247.) *Copies*, and *Draft* with amendments. [N. XII., 185, 186.]

SUMMARY.

[1645-6, March.]—Of letters from the Parliament of England to the Parliament of Scotland and to Colonel Home, and their replies concerning the giving up of Belfast by the Scotch, the last mentioned being Colonel Home's answer of February 17, 1645[-6], received about February 28th, concluding thus: "It is the desire and demand of the Parliament of England that the Commissioners of the kingdom of Scotland do immediately send order to Colonel Home or whoever else is the Commander of Belfast presently to deliver that town to such persons as the Parliament of England shall appoint." [N. XXI., 124.]

The PARLIAMENT to SIR THOMAS GLEMHAM.

1646, April 1.—(Printed in *Lords' Journals*, viii. 249.) *Draft.* [N. XII., 187.]

The GRAND COMMITTEE FOR RELIGION.

1646, April 1, 8.—Notes of their proceedings concerning the Breach of Privilege committed by the Petition of March 23rd. (Printed in Grey, iii., p. 142.) [N. XXII., 43.]

HENRY BROOKE, Sheriff, and others to WILLIAM LENTHALL.

1646, April 4. Chester.—Enclosing a petition and praying for a speedy remedy for the misery of the city and county. *Signed.* [N. VI., 1.]

The SCOTCH COMMISSIONERS to the ENGLISH COMMISSIONERS and their ANSWER.

1646, April 4. Lincoln.—(Both printed in *Lords' Journals*, viii. 345.) *Copies.* [N. XIX., 145, 144.]

The SCOTCH COMMISSIONERS.

1646, April 6.—Paper. (Printed in *Lords' Journals*, viii. 258.) *Signed* "Jo. Cheislie." [N. XIX., 143.]

The ENGLISH COMMISSIONERS to the SCOTCH COMMISSIONERS and their ANSWER.

1646, April 7 and 10. Collingham. — (Both printed in *Lords' Journals*, viii. 345, 346.) *Copies.* [N. XIX., 146, 148.]

Captain JOHN CROWTHER to [WILLIAM LENTHALL].

1646, April 9. Kingsroad.—Sending the news from Ireland. Captain Robert Moulton had taken and plundered Dingle de Couch, and Mount Rattie Castle, with Lord Turmount (Thomond). (Printed in *King's Pamphlets*, E. 333, No. 5, p. 7.) [N. VI., 2.]

Two papers of the ENGLISH COMMISSIONERS to the SCOTCH COMMISSIONERS and their two ANSWERS.

1646, April 10 and 17.—(All four printed in *Lords' Journals*, viii. 346, 347.) *Copies.* [N. XIX., 147, 149, 153, 154.]

The ENGLISH COMMISSIONERS to the SCOTCH COMMISSIONERS.

1646, April 15. Lincoln.—In reply to their first answer of the 10th. (Printed in *Lords' Journals*, viii. 347.) *Copy.* [N. XIX., 150.]

The PRINCE OF WALES to the PARLIAMENT.

1640, April 15. Scilly.—(Printed in *Lords' Journals*, viii. 295.) *Copy.* [N. XII., 188.]

The COMMITTEE FOR THE ADMIRALTY AND CINQUE PORTS.

1646, April 16.—Report recommending Joseph Bransby as captain of the *Hunter*. (See *Commons' Journals*, iv. 516.) [N. XIV., 109.]

The HOUSE OF COMMONS.

1646, April 16.—Resolutions appointing a committee concerning the Breach of Privilege. (Printed in *Commons' Journals*, iv. 511.) [N. XXII., 44.]

The LIEUTENANT-GOVERNOR OF ALDERNEY to the GOVERNOR OF GUERNSEY.

1646, April 16.—Two vessels of this island have lately come from Normandy, who report that there are certainly eleven ships English and Dunkirkers at Havre de Grace to transport soldiers into England for the King's service and that soldiers are approaching along the neighbouring coast of Normandy, who are also to embark. A person is also coming to Jersey on the King's behalf to take command of Castle Cornet, and he has orders to fire upon the town. In *French*. (See *Commons' Journals*, iv. 535.) [N. XVII., 9.]

The SCOTCH COMMISSIONERS to the ENGLISH COMMISSIONERS and their ANSWER.

1646, April 17. Collingham.—(Printed in *Lords' Journals*, viii. 347.) *Copies.* [N. XIX., 152, 151.]

CHRISTINA, Queen of Sweden, to CHARLES LOUIS, COUNT PALATINE, Arch-Steward and Elector of the Roman Empire.

1646, April 18. Stockholm.—We are gratified by the intelligence transmitted to us some months since by your Dilection through our Aulic Councillor, Paul Strasburg. We doubt not that your Dilection remembers our former answers concerning the weighty matter of the freedom of Germany and especially that of your Dilection and the whole Palatine House in reply to various letters of yours. When by God's blessing negotiations for peace commenced we straitly charged our plenipotentiaries to champion the cause of your Dilection, and to urge your restitution both to your provinces and dominions, and to your Electoral Dignity. The course of events shows that notwithstanding the greatest difficulties they have hitherto done their best to execute these commands. We are persuaded that from our example the Protestant Princes and States of the Empire will be more earnest for the restoration of the Electoral College, and the equality of the votes. We wish your Dilection to be assured that we feel deeply the afflicted condition of the Palatine House, so that we are resolved with God's help to promote your Dilection's honour and advantage both by arms and negotiations. For which purpose we shall again charge our plenipotentiaries to adhere firmly to our former commands, and to assist your envoys both those at Osnabrück and those at Münster on every occasion. And since it is known that the Duke of Bavaria uses his utmost endeavours with the Most Christian King, in order that by the opening of negotiations he may be relieved from the arms of the French and may with their assent transmit the Electoral dignity to his heirs and descendants, your Dilection being deprived of your ancestral rights and dignity, We therefore desire and endeavour to oppose in time, as far as we can, attempts of this nature as we have declared to the ambassador of the Most Christian King, M. de la Thuillerie, when he was here lately. But besides we think it advantageous as a friend to advise your Dilection that you should cause diligent application to be made to the Most Christian King for his co-operation in the general negotiations, that from his affection to the common cause he may by his plenipotentiaries at Münster so direct the proceedings that proper regard may be paid to your Dilection and the Palatine House and your Dilection's expectations and desires be satisfied in a fitting manner by the opposite party. We have impressed the same on our Ministers and Residents both in Germany and France. In *Latin. Copy.* [N. XVIII., 25.]

Proceedings of a Council of War of Colonel FRAZER's regiment.

1646, April 21. Laughton.—On several soldiers accused of rapes, robberies, and assaults. (It quite bears out the account of the proceedings in the letter of the English Commissioners of May 5th, printed in *Lords' Journals,* viii. 349, as to the evidence in many cases being the answers of the accused only. One who had formerly been sentenced to death for former misbehaviour was sentenced to be executed, another, Andrew Fraser, was acquitted on the charge of rape on the ground that the woman consented, being commanded by her father, who was threatened by the said Andrew, for which threatening the said Andrew is to hang by the hands two hours every day, and nothing of his body coming to the ground scarcely his toes in some convenient place, near the town of Tickhill, and this to continue during their abode there—except on the Sabbath day—upon which his ecclesiastical censure is to go on also.) (See *Commons' Journals,* iv. 558.) *Copy.* [N. XIX., 156.]

The HOUSE OF COMMONS.

1646, April 21.—Narrative of the matter of fact concerning the breach of the Privilege of Parliament. (Printed in *Commons' Journals,* iv. 518.) *Draft,* differing in some respects from the form finally adopted. [N. XXII., 45.]

The EARL OF CRAWFORD AND LINDESAY and others.

1646, April 22. Edinburgh.—Pass to Mr. George Haliburton. (See *Commons' Journals,* iv. 540.) *Copy.* [N. XIV., 113.]

The HOUSE OF COMMONS to the ASSEMBLY OF DIVINES.

1646, April 22.—Questions concerning Church Government. (Printed in *Commons' Journals,* iv. 519. This is the draft altered as ultimately adopted. The end of clause 1. "Whether any particular Church Government be *jure divino* and what that Government is" is an addition to the original draft.) [N. XXII., 40.] N. XXII., 52, is a *Draft,* the preamble and Clauses VI., VII. and VIII. differing in some respects from their final form.

THOMAS STEVENSON and others on behalf of themselves and other the inhabitants of ROCLIFF, SNAITHE, and other towns thereabouts to the COMMITTEE FOR THE WEST RIDING.

[1646, April 23.]—Petition. Stating that divers officers and soldiers formerly employed for the King are now among the petitioners, pretending that they are under the command of Major-General Vaudruske in the Scotch army, and commit great violences, and oppress all by grievous assessments, by reason whereof many leave their habitations, they being now in as great fear and as ill ease as when the enemy had the power of the country; among whom are Captain Lumsdale, late governor of Cawood Castle for the King, the two Poitingtons and others, who have been and still declare themselves disaffected to the Parliament, and praying that for redress the Committee would present these facts to the Lords and Commons, or the Committee of both Kingdoms. *Signed.* [N. XXII., 131.]

The ASSEMBLY OF DIVINES to the HOUSE OF LORDS.

[1646, April 25.]—Concerning Mr. Barton's version of the Psalms. (Printed in *Lords' Journals,* viii. 283.) *Signed.* [N. XXII., 46.]

List of such ENGLISHMEN as have served the enemy against the Parliament, and are either listed in or have sheltered themselves under the protection of the Scotch Army.

List of such in Major-General VANDRUSCHE'S Regiment as are found faulty by proof.

List of such in the SCOTCH ARMY as have committed divers misdemeanors and are complained of by the inhabitants of the Wapentake of OSGODCROSS.

1646, April 27.—(All printed in *Lords' Journals,* viii. 349, 350.) [N. XIX., 157, 158.]

A COMMITTEE OF THE HOUSE OF COMMONS.

1646, April 30.—Report suggesting what conditions should be offered to the garrisons that still hold out. (See *Commons' Journals,* iv. 537.) [N. XIV., 110.]

The COMMITTEE OF THE WESTERN ASSOCIATED COUNTIES.

1646, May 2.—Report. (The purport appears from the resolutions of the House thereon, which are printed in *Commons' Journals,* iv. 534.) [N. XIV., 111.]

The ENGLISH COMMISSIONERS to the SCOTCH COMMISSIONERS.

1646, May 5. Balderton.—(Printed in *Lords' Journals,* viii. 348.) *Certified Copy.* [N. XIX., 162.]

The KING to LORD BELLASIS.

[1646, May 6.] "8 of the clock.—Belasyse. Such is the condision of affaires att this present that I can give you no hope att all of releife, nor off better condisions than what I sent you last night, wherfore the best for my service will be that you conclude uppon them with all expedision the cheefe reason being that according to my dissigne I am necessitated to march with the Scoch army this day northwards, but cannot move till this agreement be consented to by you. I am hartily sorry that my business stands so as that I must impose such condisions uppon you. I am your most assured friend Charles R." *Copy.* On the outside is endorsed "His Majesty writt word to the Governor of Newark three weeks before the town was surrendered that upon assurances which he had received he intended presently to come to the Scots' army, and therefore he commanded him to keep the town till he came." (See *Commons' Journals,* iv. 580.) [N. XIX., 161.]

Articles for the surrender of NEWARK.

1646, May 6.—(Printed in Rushworth, iv. 1. 269.) [N. XIV., 112.]

DISCOVERY OF 4,000*l.*

[Before 1646, May 6.]—(See *Commons' Journals,* iv. 536.) Owing by Henry Poole to Sir Humphrey Tracy, both Delinquents, for the benefit of the city of Gloucester. [N. XIV., 84.]

The Examination of Major EDWARD SMITH.

1646, May 7.—Concerning the negotiations between the Scots and the King through Mr. Barry. (Printed in Grey, iii. Appendix, No. 59, p. 92, and in Webb, *Memorials of the Civil War in Herefordshire,* ii. 381.) (See *Commons' Journals,* iv. 569.) *Signed.* [N. XIX., 163.]

SIR THOMAS FAIRFAX to WILLIAM LENTHALL.

1646, May 7. Heddenton.—Enclosing and supporting the petition of Jane Atkinson, widow of Captain Henry Atkinson, who was killed when under his command at Wetherby. The petition is enclosed. (See *Commons' Journals,* iv. 550.) *Signed. Seal.* [N. VI., 4.]

The Account betwixt the COMMITTEE OF PARLIAMENT RESIDING AT SOUTHWELL and the SCOTS ARMY NOW BEFORE NEWARK from December 11th, 1645 to May 7th, 1646, being 21 weeks.

1646, May 7.—The total assigned to them amounts to 40,090*l.* 0*s.* 3*d.* [N. XIV., 114.]

The EARL OF LEVEN.

1646, May 8. Doncaster.—Proclamation against any who had served against the Parliament coming into the Scotch army. (Almost *verbatim* the same as that dated May 13th, which is printed in *Lords' Journals,* viii. 323.) *Copy.* [N. XIX., 164.]

The HOUSE OF COMMONS.

1646, May 8, 9, 13.—Votes about the Committee for the intercepted letters and concerning the examination of Mr. John Cheislie. (Printed in *Commons' Journals,* iv. 540, 541, 544.) [N. XIX., 165.]

The COMMITTEE OF THE ESTATES OF SCOTLAND.

1646, May 8. Edinburgh.—Proclamation against any leaving the kingdom till June 1st, without a pass. (Printed in *Lords' Journals,* viii. 323.) [N. XIX., 166.]

The EARL OF LEVEN.

1646, May 8. Great Markham.—Proclamation forbidding under pain of death any under his command to take away horses, cattle, or goods, or to compel service, or to do any wrong to the country people, or to exact moneys, or to have any dealing with those of the late garrison of Newark, or to engage any officers or soldiers that have been with the other party, and ordering them on notice of any such being in the army to signify the same to their superior officers that they may be removed. *Copy.* [N. XIX., 167.]

Colonel THOMAS MORGAN to WILLIAM SANDYS, Governor of Hartlebury Castle.

1646, May 9.—Summons to surrender Hartlebury Castle, much stronger garrisons, as Newark and Banbury, having surrendered.

And

WILLIAM SANDYS to Colonel THOMAS MORGAN.

Same date.—In reply admitting that if Newark be taken, he cannot probably expect relief, and desiring therefore so much time as may be sufficient to inform himself of the certainty thereof, and if he shall find it accordingly he will forthwith treat. *Copies.* [N. XII., 201.]

The ENGLISH COMMISSIONERS to the SCOTCH COMMISSIONERS.

1646, May 11. Lincoln.—(Printed in *Lords' Journals*, viii. 348.) *Copy.* [N. XIX., 168.]

The EARL OF LEVEN.

1646, May 13. Durham.—Proclamation. (Printed in *Lords' Journals*, viii. 323.) *Copy.* [N. XIX., 170.]

The COMMITTEE OF THE ESTATES OF SCOTLAND to the KING.

1646, May 13, 14, 15.— Four papers. (All printed in *Lords' Journals*, viii., 330.) *Copies.* [N. XIX., 171.]

Examination of Captain ADAM SHIPPERSON.

[1646, May 14.]—At Durham the day the Scotch army brought the king thither I met one David Bahannon, pretending to be Scout Master General to the Scots. I desired to know why they brought the king in such haste with their whole army northward. He replied that he could certify me in that particular as well as most men in their army could, and said that the Parliament had abused the king in denying him liberty to come safe to London and in voting him not fit to come to the Parliament, but to be sent to Warwick Castle to be kept in safe custody, and that he thought that rather than their army would suffer the king to take such dishonourable conditions of the Parliament as they had proposed, the Scotch army would protect the king against the Parliament and stand upon a defensive war against them.

And

Examination of Captain THOMAS LILBURNE and Lieutenant EDWARD SHIPPERSON.

1646, May 14.—Captain David Bahanon on the 12th instant said that the Parliament endeavoured to alter the form of government of this kingdom of England and to bring the kingdom under the government of petty kings and sought by all means to overthrow the power of King Charles, and that they endeavoured also to break the peace between the kingdoms of England and Scotland.

And

Examination of Cornet JOHN CARRUTH.

[1646, May.]—At Sherbourne I met with Sir Frederick Hambleton's son, a captain of horse in the Scotch army, and asked him why they marched so fast away with the king, and why they did not send him to the Parliament. He replied because the Parliament would send him prisoner to Warwick Castle, and before he should be a prisoner, and not placed in all his former power, throne, and dignities they would lose all their lives in establishing him therein. I replied they would have a shrewd party to fight against. He answered he knew that, for they had the Parliament of England to fight against.

And

Second Examination of the SAME.

1646, June 5.—At Monk Seton, in Northumberland, I met with a party coming from Scotland to recruit the garrison of Tynemouth Castle. I asked the officers what news in Scotland, who answered that in Scotland they were levying the 6th man. I replied, I hope we shall have peace, and then what will be done with those men ? They answered they were to be for his Majesty's service and at his command whenever he would command them. *Copies.* [N. XIX., 159.]

The House of Commons.

1646, May 15.—Order concerning the minute of the letter to the Prince. (Printed in *Commons' Journals,* iv. 546.) [N. XIV., 121.]

The Earl of Leven.

1646, May 15. Newcastle.—Proclamation in almost the same words as those of the 8th and 13th, with the addition that Major Trollop and the other officers named in the letter of the English Commissioners of the 11th are mentioned by name as persons to be removed from the army. *Copy.* [N. XIX., 172.]

The Examination of Michael Hudson.

1646, May 16. — (Printed in Peck, *Desiderata Curiosa,* ix. 9.) [N. XIV., 123.]

The Examinations of John Pearson and John Browne.

1646, May 18.—(Printed in Peck, *Desiderata Curiosa,* ix. 10.) [N. XIV., 115.]

The King to Sir Thomas Glemham, Governor of Oxford.

1646, May 18. Newcastle.—Authorising him to quit that city and to disband his forces upon honourable conditions. *Sign-Manual.* [N. I., 18.]

The King to the Committee of the Estates of Scotland.

1646, May 19. Newcastle.—" After so long and sad an interruption of the happy understanding betwixt us and our good subjects of our kingdome of Scotland—which hath exceedingly afflicted us—and least the sad effects thereof may have alienated the affections of many of that kingdome from us, and preferring nothing to the love of our subjects on which our safety and greatnes most depends, and without which wee propose not to ourselves any happines ; wee have thought fitt to labour to dispossesse them of all prejudices rather by shewing them our present resolutions, then remembring them of our former differences ; haveing come hither with a full and absolute intention to give all just satisfaction to the joynt desires of both kingdomes, and with no thought either to continue this unnaturall warre any longer, or to make a division betwixt the kingdomes, but to comply with our parliaments and those entrusted by them in everything for settling of truth and pease. Your commissioners have offred to us diverse papers in your name expressing your loyall intentions towards us, for which wee cannot but returne you harty thanks, and shall study to apply ourselves totally to the councels and advices of our parliaments. Wee have already sent a message to the two houses of our parliament of England, and your commissioners at London, which wee hope will give satisfaction. Wee have likewise written to all such within our kingdome of Scotland as have any commission from us to lay doune armes, disband their forces, and render their garrisons, and have written to our agents and ministers abroad for recalling all commissions issued forth by our authority to any at sea, against any of our subjects of either kingdomes ; and have sent letters to the governour of our city of Oxford to quitt that garrison upon honourable conditions, and disband our forces there, which being granted to him, wee have resolved presently to give the like order to all our other garrisons and forces within this kingdome. And that·the truth of these our royall intentions may be made knowne to all our good subjects in Scotland, wee desire a proclamation may be printed and published together with this letter at all convenient places, hoping none will beleeve but that this is our voluntary and cordiall resolution, and proceeds from no other ground than our deip sense of the bleeding condition of our kingdomes, and that our reall intentions are—with the blessing of God and his favourable assistance—to joyne with our par-liaments in seteleing religion here in purity—after the advice of the divines of both kingdomes assembled at Westminster—and our subjects of both kingdomes in freedome and safety. So expecting your councels and advices in everything wherein wee shalbe concerned, wee bid you hartily farewell." *Copy* in Sir John Chieslie's hand. [N. XIX., 173.]

HENRY HERBERT to ROBERT SCOWEN and THOMAS PURY.

1646, May 19. Bristol.—Enclosing the following examination. *Signed. Seal.* [N. VI., 5.] *Enclosed :*

The Examination of WILLIAM BARRY of Tregiett, in the parish of Lanrothell, in the County of Hereford.

1646, May 16. Chepstow.—" In the beginning of August 1645, when the Scots army laye at Mitcheldeane in Gloucestershire about 1,000 horse . . came on the Saturday before the siedge of Hereford to his house and carried him away prisoner . . . He . . was brought to Rosse to Liftenant-Generall Callender, and thence to Deane to Generall Leven where he was asked concerning the King's strength wherein hee gave them his best information. The Lord Leven then told him hee must go back with the Lord Callender to Rosse. That night hee was com-mitted, next day beeing Sunday, the Lord of Mountgomerie tould this examinant hee would gett him released and hee or the Lord Leveston gave him twenty shillings, and accordingly abowt six a clock that afternoone hee had his libertye, the Lord of Mountgomerie commanding him to come to his quarters which this examinant did. The Lord Mountgomerie then asked him whether hee would goe with a message to the King's Court to Sir William Flemin which—thong verie unwilling—hee under-tooke and carried a letter subscribed by the Lord Mountgomerie, the Lord Cinckclare, and the Lord Leveston to Sir William Elemin with direction in case hee were not at court to deliver the letter to the King's owne hande. This examinant, repairing on Munday to Rewperre in Glamorganshire, where the King then was, delivered the letter to Sir William Flemin who shewed the same to the King in the garden in the sight of this examinant. Upon reading whereof the King came to him and sayde, ' you are come owt of the Scott's armye. How strong are they?' This examinant replyed they were a greate armye, hee beelieved twenty thousand men, but thought they were his Majestie's faithfull subjects, some of them declaring themselves his Majestie's sworne servants. The King asked who were they; this examinant replyed that the Lord Levestone sayde hee had byn so this five yeeres. The King sayde it was true, so they parted. That night Sir William Elemin came along with him to Carlyeon, and next day beeing Tuesday to Monmoth and abowt fowre of the clock that daye neere this examinant's howse in a woode mett with the Lorde Mountgomerie, where after two howres' privat discoorse they parted. Then Sir William Flemin came with this examinant to his howse, and the Lord of Mountgomerie with the Lord Sinckclare and the Lord Leveston came thither in the night to Sir William Elemin, where after long discoorse, sitting up all night, at breake of day on Wednesday morning, that day they marched to Hereford to beesiedg it. The three foresaid lords repaired to theyr quarters and Sir William Flemin to the King. Abowt two dayes after, Sir William Elemin sent his man to this examinant to meete him at Monmoth, which hee did. Sir William Flemin then tould him hee must goe with a letter and deliver it to eyther of the three lords that mett at his howse. Hee accordingly went and delivered the letter to the Lord Mountgomerie at Dydley in Herefordshire, on Friday night as hee thinks, but the contents hee knowes not. The Lord Mountgomerie called for a mapp and after perusall towld this examinant hee wowld meete Sir William Flemin at Henllan, a place seaven miles from Hereforde. This examinant acquainted Sir William Elemin therewith, and brought him on Satyrday to the said place, where the Lord Mountgomerie was, and after an howre or two in discoorse parted, the Lord Mountgomerie commanding this examinant to bee at a place called New Inne next morning, heeing Sunday, that hee might consider of another meeting with Sir William Flemin. The Lord came not that daye, but Munday morning the Lord Mountgomerie sent his man Richard Storye to this examinant, who towld him hee had a message from his lord to Sir William Elemin, and desired him to go for him, which hee did upon the said Storye's horse, and Sir William Elemin beeing then at Gudderidg Castle, came along with this examinant neere New Inne, where Richard Story spoke with him, and after some discoorse, they parted, from which tyme this examinant never heard any more.

And this examinant farther saith that what hee did was only as hee thought for the goode of the Kingdome, the Lord Mountgomerie declaring that the busines they were now abowt with the King was to settle a happy peace." (See *Commons' Journals,* iv. 569.) *Signed.* [N. XIX., 187.]

The House of Commons.

1646, May 19.—Votes concerning the Scotch army. (Printed in *Commons' Journals,* iv. 551.) [N. XIX., 176.]

The Prince of Wales to the Receiver of the Duchy of Cornwall.

1646, May 20. Castle Elizabeth, Jersey. — (Printed in *Lords' Journals,* viii. 405.) *Sign-Manual. Seal.* [N. I., 31.]

Henry Ogle to Sir J[ohn] F[enwicke].

1646, May 20. . . .—" We have a regiment lately come in from Scotland, under the command of one Colonel Maull. . . They are very oppressing to our country, going up and down, burning towns, as the soldiers phrase it, receiving 3*l.*, 4*l.*, 5*l.*, and more according to the bigness and littleness of the towns, and where they quarter at night they demand, as I am told by a preacher their own countryman, who is sorrowful for their demeanour, for a captain 12*s.*, for a lieutenant 6*s.*, ensign 4*s.*, and for common soldiers 2*d.* a man, which they levy before their departure from their quarters. Their usual march is 5 or 6 miles a day, and not directly forwards neither. They have been some ten days in the country and are not above some 14 miles yet from the borders. The Committee is about to write to the General to certify him of their insufferable oppressing courses and hopes from him to get relief, else our country will be undone. There is not almost a week passes but forces are passing back and forth, so that our country is most pitifully harrowed. This hath been so often remonstrated and so little remedy that most despair, and so sit down in silence. . . . It would be beneficial to our poor country that a motion were made no more forces might come in amongst us, there being now a great levy of men which fears the country, these already come are so oppressing in their levies of moneys, much more if so many thousands follow as is here reported are coming amongst us. The letters and other carriages of our brethren, commissioners for that kingdom, gives all good satisfaction of their well intentions, but the oppressions and carriages of the common soldiers are very gross and oppresive, raising up the reproachful names of Roundheads, Parliament rogues, &c." [N. XIV., 116.]

Relation of ROBERT DODSWORTH, Steward to the Lord Grey.

[1646, May.]—Concerning Colonel Ma[u]ll's regiment, how they carried themselves after they came into England, describing how besides their quarters, they exacted contributions in money. [N. XX., 208.]

The MARQUESS OF ORMONDE to Major-General MONRO.

1646, May 21. Dublin Castle.—*Enclosed :*

The KING to the MARQUESS OF ORMONDE.

1646, April 3.—(Both printed in *Lords' Journals*, viii. 365, 366, and Rushworth, iv. 1. 272, 266, where it is misdated the 13th.) *Copies.* [N. XII., 189.]

The COMMITTEE FOR THE EASTERN ASSOCIATION.

1646, May 23.—Report. Recommending that the garrisons of Lynn, Cambridge, Bedford, Huntingdon, and the Isle of Ely be disbanded. and that the state of the garrison of Newport Pagnell be reported to the Committee of both Kingdoms. (See *Commons' Journals*, iv. 615.) [N. XIV., 122.]

The HOUSE OF LORDS.

[1646, May 25.]—Heads for a Conference. (The first paragraph of those printed in *Lords' Journals*, viii. 328.) [N. XIX., 175.]

The COMMITTEE OF THE ESTATES.

[1646, May 25.]—Papers concerning Mr. Ashburnham and Dr. Hudson. (Printed in Rushworth, iv. 1. 271.) *Copy.* [N. XIX., 169.]

The PARLIAMENT to the PRINCE OF WALES.

1646, May 25.—(The purport sufficiently appears from *Commons' Journals*, iv. 554.) *Draft* as passed by the Commons. [N. XII., 190.]

The COMMITTEE OF BOTH KINGDOMS.

1646, May 29.—Report desiring that arms and ammunition be sent to Guernsey. [N. XIV., 124.]

The COMMITTEE OF THE ESTATES.

1646, May 31. Newcastle. — Order disbanding General-Major Vandrusque's regiment. (Printed in *Lords' Journals*, viii. 366.) [N. XIX., 174.]

Information of JOHN GOODYEAR and GREGORY WILSON, Sequestrators for Langburgh Wapentake, presented to the Committee for the North Riding.

[1646, May.]—"That many officers and souldiers which were lately in the garrison of Newark and others the King's garrisons lately taken in are now mingled amongst the Scotts in their army and doe insinuate themselves into there companies and thereby draw the rudest sort of the Scottish army to comitt fearfull outrages in our countrey, which wee humbly certifie by credible informacion from our neighbors, wee not dareing to stay at home ourselves to stand to the mercy of those merciles men.

First it will bee proved that the sequestratours have bin sore threatned to bee bereavd of their lives and have had their goodes taken from them, and many of the inhabitantes have had their horses taken from them upon the highway and their purses and clothes, and some sore beaten and wounded.

That as wee are credibly informed they have taken divers horses belonging to Collonel James Mauleverer at Ingleby Arncliff, and allmost undone James Cliffton of Westlaythes by plundring, and on John Trewhit of Dounton, and as wee are informed fall cheifly upon them which are best affected.

That a poore woman of Dountou striveing to rescew some goodes of her owne was miserably murderd.

That one Thomas Spence of Gisborough, a man of good estate and credit, was lamentably murdered in his owne howse being run through with a rapier and, as if that had not bin enough, had allso his braines beaten out.

That the Scottish horse lay such excessive taxes on the countrey, that they are not able possibly to subsist, but are forced to suffer their goodes to bee taken—as it were legally—though noe such oppressive sesses bee imposed by the parliament comissioners or comittees for the county haveing legall power.

That the said sesses are generally layd on after the rate of about 90,000l. per month for Yorkshire, besides plundering, stealing horses, and free billitt.

By these courses our poore countrey will bee undone which formerly groand under the like—though not soe great tyranny—and for our parte it shall never greive us though wee bee allmost ruind in our estates, in regard wee are in so good hopes of a happy conclusion.

That none dare passe from towne to towne in regard soe many have had not only their money taken from them but allso their horses and clothes.

That an honest man of Egton striveing to rescew a horse which the souldiers would have taken from him had his hand stroken off." *Signed* [N. XIV., 229.]

The House of Commons.

1646, June 1.—Votes appointing Committees to consider of the raising of the 100,000*l.*, and to prepare an answer to the Scotch letter of May 20th. (Printed in *Commons' Journals*, iv. 560.) [N. XIX., 176.]

Deposition of Andrew Lumsdale, of Morpeth.

1646, June 1.—On May 24th " he saw a regiment of foot . . quartered in Morpeth, then newly brought into England from Scotland under command of Mr. Patrick Maule of the King's bedchamber." On the 21st he saw certain Scotch soldiers lately come over from Ireland . . quartered at Bowton in Northumberland, and on the same day " he was told " that a regiment of Scotch horse, who the night before had quartered at Kelso . . were come that day into Glendale, and that by common report in Northumberland he hath heard they are raising the fourth man to come into England." . .

And

Examination of John Dobson of Newcastle.

Same date.—(Part printed in Peck, *Desiderata Curiosa*, ix. 14. It continues thus) :—" Since the King came to Newcastle he heard that a ship laden with ammunition and arms was brought to Newcastle from beyond seas ; and he saw some round shot, part of that ship's lading, carried into one of the public magazines upon the Bridge at Newcastle."

And

Examination of —— Blackburne.

Same date.—(To the same effect as the last.) [N. XIV., 125.]

William Lenthall to Francis Crosse.

1646, June 3.—Pass. (Printed in Peck, *Desiderata Curiosa*, ix. 15.) The appearance of the original bears out the statement there as to the alterations in it. [N. XIV., 126.]

The Earl of Lincoln to the House of Lords.

[1646, June 3.]—Petition with certificate (on parchment) of the Committee for taking Accounts. (Both printed in *Lords' Journals*, viii. 353, 354.) [N. XXII., 152, 153.]

The Earl of Lauderdale, Archibald Jhonston, Hew Kennedy, and Robert Barclay to William Lenthall.

1646, June 3.—(Identical, *mutatis mutandis*, with the letter of the same date to the Earl of Manchester, which is printed in *Lords' Journals*, viii. 356.) *Signed. Seal.* [N. VI., end.]

Report of Mr. Stockdale's Committee.

1646, June 3, 4, 5.—Concerning-the misconduct of the Scots at Tickhill and elsewhere without their punishment, General Leslie's behaviour therein, the movements of the Scotch since the surrender of Newark, the number of English Papists and Delinquents in their army, their plundering and other misconduct, the numbers of the Scotch at the siege of Newark, their pay and what passed between them and the English Committee with their army, their taking free quarter and committing murders, rapes, and other outrages, their giving protection to those who formerly served in the King's forces, and particularly to

Mr. Ashburnham, their bringing new forces into England, and raising new levies in Scotland, their garrisons at Carlisle and elsewhere and the negotiations about them. (A brief abstract is printed in *Commons' Journals*, iv. 567.) [N. XIX., 178, 179, 181, 182.] N. XIX., 160 is rough notes for same. *Annexed* were (probably) the following :

i. Paper headed " TORTURES TICKHILL."

ii. The Inhabitants of ALFRETON against Quartermaster-General INNES' troop.

iii. Complaints of the grievances lately suffered from certain REFORMADOES pretending themselves to belong to the Scotch army.

[1645-6, January 12-15.] Tickhill.—

iv. The information of Captain THOMAS NICHOLSON and others. (All describing the acts of violence and exaction committed by Scotch officers and soldiers.) (All are printed in Grey, iii. Appendix, Nos. 28, 29, 27, 31, pp. 44–51.) [N. XIX., 177, 183, 184, 185, 186, the last two being slightly varying copies of No. 4.]

v. A true Account of the charge of the Town of WHITLEY.

1646, April 20.—" By being assigned as an assistant town to Captain Pott's troop in General-Major Vandruske's regiment since the 2nd of March last.

	£	s.	d.
Paid March 9th, for the first week's assessment in money	5	5	0
The soldiers that came to demand it spent the town	0	5	0
The Quartermaster forced the Constable to give him besides the Assessment	0	10	0
Paid the 18th for the second week in money	5	5	0
Before the payment of this week's assessment, Mr. Everingham was fetched prisoner to Hatfield because he refused to pay, and there detained till the money was paid, and further the Constable—Peter Marshall—who was ill beaten by the Quarter Master and prisoner likewise with him, was forced to pay the 4 men 10*d.* for fetching them.			
They spent the town 5*s.*, and their free billet when they came for the men	0	9	0
The Constable about this imprisonment was forced to spend at least	0	15	0
Two soldiers kept upon free quarter about a fortnight, and in ale for them 6*s.*	1	2	0
Paid the 28th in provision, hay, &c., to their quarters to the value of	5	5	0
Paid April 7th, for the 4th week's payment in provision 3*l.* 13*s.*, in money 32*s.*, and the Quarter Master for receiving it 6*s.*	5	11	0
More towards a fifth week's payment in provision, the 16th	2	0	0

All this paid by threats and compulsion.

£ *. d.

It cost the Constable about his attendance on them at several times and seeking after provision at least " - - - - 1 0 0

27 17 0

N. XIX., 155.]

The Committee for the Northern Association.

1646. June 4.—Order, reporting to the House of Commons: That the House be moved that all possible means be used for providing of the 100,000l. for the Scotch army, in order of their own vote; That it be recommended to Sir Thomas Fairfax to go down into the Northern parts with such forces as shall be thought fit for the preservation thereof. [N. XIX., 180.]

Colonel Robert Russell, Lieutenant-Governor of Guernsey, to the Earl of Warwick.

1646, June 4.—The morning of May 15th—it being a very great mist—four frigates from Jersey came near Castle Cornet with one pink and two boats, and by advantage of the dusk weather, put them into the Castle Cove, having in them provision and many Irish. The necessities of the soldiers in Sark are very urgent, and they much in arrear. Supply of powder, match, and demi-cannon and demi-culverin shot is desired with as little delay as possible. *Extract. Enclosed* are extracts from a letter from St. Malo with rumours about the intentions of the Prince. On the same paper are extracts from letters of Colonel Bethell and a merchant of St. Malo, on the same subject and about the state of the islands. [N. XII., 191.]

The Parliament.

1646, June 4, 17, and 9.—Resolutions concerning the Militia of London. (Printed in *Lords' Journals*, viii. 367, 372, and *Commons' Journals*, iv. 563, 579.) [N. XIV., 130.]

Captain Robert Moulton to William Lenthall.

1646, June 8.—Enclosing a paper sent by the Earl of Ormonde into Wales intercepted at Milford. *Seal.* [N. VI., 6.]

Examination of [James Thurbarne] Town Clerke of Sandwich.

1646, June 8.—" That Pitman came from Rochester with Hudson as he said to Sandwitch."

Examination of Doctor Francis Crosse.

Same date.—" That Hudson was with him and tolde him he coulde bringe the king to the parliament, and woulde undertake it upon his life. He desired to doe it privatly and have his intentions knowen to Mr. Pierpoynt and Mr. Hollis and to none of the Scotch commissioners. If they kuewe it, the king woulde be hurried away to Scotlande. He sayth he procured the passe for Hudson of the Speaker's Secretary. Hearing his good intentions he asked him to doe it without going into France, but he answered he woulde goe and have letters of credence from the Queene to the Scotch army. Then he conide better effe[c]te it. He said he woulde not stay above three dayes there."

Thursday or Wednesday last was the first time he sawe him and not this twelvemonth before. Then he sente for him to come to the Swan in Fish Streete to dine. Hudson had two men with him there. He kuewe not their names. He dined and supped with the said company at both diner and supper.

He knowes not of any company that he wente into or that came to him nor of any message or letter that he sente while he was in towne. He knowes not where he lay on Wednesday and Thursday nighte. He lay at his house one nighte.

Being pressed where he lay or whether at his house, he ansuered one nighte at his house, but after confessed two nights, the two firste nights that he sawe him after he came to towne. He sayth that the fiıst day he dined and supped with him at the Swane. The nexte day they dined and supped together at his house. His men satt with him at meals at the tavern. There was none other but his wife and a gentlewoman and Hudson and the man that was with him. The gentlewoman was Mrs. Mortimer. She lives in the Muse (Mews) is a widowe. He thinks Hudson sente for her, not he. After he wente from his house he wente to a cook's in Toolies Streete, and lay there, a poore house. Mr. Ed. Stevens and he wente to him thither. Hudson sente him for Stevens to come to him and there they spake of the busines of bringing the kinge to the parliament. He sayth his house is righte agaynste the Gate House. They were two or three honres drinking two pints of wine, and that was at the Blewe Anchor. He said Scotts were soe base and did soe abuse the English it was pitty but they shoulde suffer. They will suffer noe Englishman to come to him. He said he conceived the Scotts woulde undoc the King. He said Hudson said the Scotts woulde have thirty-six hundred thousande pounds for their danger by Montros and they have 10,000*l.* per month for customs, and the King as he thinks spends not above 100*l.* a month. He sayth he hath good ground from the King that he will goe alonge with him from the Scotch army. He said he wente to the Queene to make it her busines that the people mighte love him the more. He and Hudson both kuewe that the parliament had sente for him to the Scotts army. Hudson toulde him that the mayour had him in his custody and the Kinge sente for him and soe he escaped going upon his worde. He said he spake of these two members of the house, for he said they were rational men, and woulde carry it secretly that the design might not be loste. He did intend at his returne to comunicatt it to the King. He wente for the passe for himselfe the day after he was at the cook's and is dated the day he went for it, yet he had it not til the day after. He wente to him with his passe to the cooke's in St. Toolies, but from his house he wente with him to the White Lion in Tower Streete. Mr. Stevens wente with him when he carried tLe passe. He sayth at his coming away he desired the King not to ingage himself too far to the Scotts til he hearde further from him. Hudson, he thinks, was unsatisfied with the Scotts, for they woulde not let him stay with the King although they had promissed to the King he shoulde stay with the King. He sayth that the maiour of Newcastle and the Aldermen coulde not come to the Kinge, but making use of Hudson, they came to the King and kissed his hande.

He wente twice the first day for the passe and desired it for himself to traveil to improve himself for the languages. He said he tolde them he had taken the Covenent.

He had that letter from Hudson and knowes his hande.

The passe was in the deponent's name and he gave it to Hudson that soe he mighte passe freely.

He wente to Stevens his house to day and did whisper with his wife that he had a letter for Hudson and wished him to come to him.

A A

The serjant came to this deponent's house to search for Hudson but he was gone that morning thence.

He sayth that he hath spoken with none this day since he was taken but his keeper and sente for his wife whoo dined with him."

(The rest of the examination is printed in Peck, *Desiderata Curiosa,* ix. 16.)

And

Examination of JAMES THURBARNE, Town Clerk of Sandwich.

Same date.—"Laste nighte he was sente for by the Mayor and the jurats of Sandwich. When he came he saide he founde the mayour, Captain Peake and Mr. Foster, two jurats, and Lieutenant-Colonel Pitman and Mr. Hudson. When he came they were discoursing of Hudson's busines. He desired to heare agayne. They tolde this examinante that this man conveyed the King to the Scotch army, and fourteen days agoe he came from Newcastle to London, and Saturday nighte came to Sandwich with Lieutenant-Colonel Pitman, and Pitman lefte him that nighte and came to him one Sunday morning, and being ready one Sunday evening to take horse for Dover, Pitman sente for the maiour whoe came and apprehended him, asking him his design. He said he was going for France. Presently withal the inkeper where he lay brought in the passe here produced, founde in his servant's boots as the inkeper said. His name is Robert Barham. Upon further discourse he said his man was not in the passe for he was in the pay-sheets (?) and this man traveling by his owne name. Then I desired his design which he said was to goe to France to speake with the Queene, by whom he mighte be received to the Scotch army agayne, that he mighte gayne the King to come to the parliament. He said that his Majestie came from Oxford with Mr. Ashburnham and him. The King gave out that they were for London, and the lords knewe noe other. They came to Brainforde, ten miles from London. I asked if the King was not within the suburbs. He said that was a secret and desired to be excused. He saide he had the watch worde of N[ewcastle] from the captain of the guarde at Newcastle, and soe passed through the guarde very quietly and came to London yesterday was fourteen dayes. He said he came out of London as he beleives on Saturday and Colonel Pitman and he mette on this side Rochester, and came to Sandwich one Saturday. He said if the maiour and jurates woulde have a letter sente him he woulde sende it to two such gentlemen that shoulde carry the message to such parliament men that shoulde be satisfied. Being asked whoe they were, he said they were   men. Asked who they were, he said, Mr. Hollis, Mr. St. John, and Mr. Rouse." *Signed* " James Thurbarne."

And

Examination of EDWARD STEVENS of Westminster.

Same date.—" He hath knowen Michael Hudson nere twenty yeares. He sawe him in Auguste laste at the White Harte in St. Giles, where he lay above three quarters of a yeare. He wente in the habit of a scoller then   in grey suite with a blacke casocke. One Friday laste at nighte, by mere accidente he sawe him in Southwarke, and not before since Auguste. One Friday nighte aboute five a clocke, I was at a tavern under the Exchange in the Strande, and a brother-in-lawe of his came to me and asked me for Mr. Hudson. I asked him what he coulde doe with him if not arreste him. I protested I had not seene him. I desired him to see him. His brother and I wente downe. I wente into Southwarke and founde him and then he was going. We dranke a pinte of wine and then he wente away. I asked if he wente away with the King. He said I (aye). He said he was a prisoner at Newcastle and had got his liberty. He advised him to make his peace with the parliament, els he was undone. He assured me to come agayne within a fortnight. I wente to some friends to advise what to doe. This morning I acquaynted Mr. Rouse with it aboute 7 this morning and at 2 this afternone, and he said he was taken. I wente out today at six of the clocke and was never at home since. He sayth that after he hearde the King was gone he thoughte upon some speach betwixte Hudson and him heretofore aboute a yeare since, that the King was gone to Lynne. I tolde this to Mr. Rouse. He said that they had a design for Lynne and the Ile of Ely. Hudson had many suites. He was his solicitor for twenty. He said the Scotts woulde not suffer him to come to the King agayne; there was a fayr correspondency betwixte the English commitee and him as he said. They coulde not goe to the King, but he did often goe and they were loath he shoulde come away. Mr. Samuel Thornley, one of the committees at Westminster, was the man that he imployed to Mr. Rouse. He sayth in Auguste laste Hudson's judgment as he thinks was for the parliament. He had two livings but they were to be extended for debt and his rents given up, and was not sequestred though it be said he was sequestred. He is aboute forty yeares of age. I asked why he did not persuade the King to come hither as well as to the Scotts. He refused to ansuere. He said they lefte the King forty-eight honres til they wente to the Scotch army and returned. He did not tel where it was. They sente for a barber to trime them and he said they had almoste been discovered, for their hayre the barber said was cut with knives. He said they came within ten miles of London and dined there. He said the King was not in London. He wished me to be silent and said when he came backe he woulde say more to those he mighte truste. He was not disguised, but in a greene suite." *Signed* " Edw. Stevens."

And

Examination of Lieutenant-Colonel THOMAS PITMAN, an Officer for the King heretofore.

Same date.—" He was lately in Kente, his wife is there near to Sandwich. On Saturday laste, he wente to Sandwich from London. He knowes Mr. Hudson, but whether a parson (?) or noe he knowes not. He over-tooke one on Saturday laste on Rochester Bridge that called himself Dr. Crosse. He said he was for Flanders and I asked him if his name was not Hudson. He said noe, it was Dr. Crosse. I said I thought he was Hudson and he was with one. He said I (aye), then I was acquainted with him. I supped with him on Saturday nighte. He spake to me both Saturday and Sunday of many particulars of the King's intentions, which were, he intended to sende four propositions. 1. to yelde the Militia for   years to the parliament. 2. leave church govern-ment to the house. 3. he woulde stande for good tearmes for them that adhered to him. The fourth, I forgett : it was Irelande. His intention in going to France was for the good of the King and   . He came by London to acquaynte some parliament men with this as a message from the King. He shoulde have spoken with my Lorde Maiour, but coulde not, but sente a message to him in his time of being there. A friende of his got a passe in the name of Crosse, for him to passe as physician. His intention was for a letter from the Queene to give thankes to the Scotts for the receiving the King and desiring that he mighte be agayne readmitted. He said the deputy maiour broughte him out of the towne, and the captaine of the guarde gave him the worde before nighte. He tolde him that he had spoken with some parliament men for the King, and the man to whome he writte his letter can tell whoo they were. The firste time he sawe him was in Oxforde, and he undertooke then to goe to Warham and get it given up to the King. His way was he wente as a pursuivant (?) from the parliament to receive the King's rents, and at a weeke end he gott Warham. He let downe the bridge and this examinante then entered with his horse. He woulde ordinarily make the Speaker's passes and they wente   . I wente to church with him on Sunday, and dined with him, and we were at church twice in Sandwich. After afternone service he desired to be gone to Dover, for a packet boate was to put off that nighto. Aboute five at nighte his horses were ready, and his man Robert Baker, whoe was with him at Warham, and soe called himself there. Then, as he was going to horse, I desired him to drinke a pinte of wine and I sente John Witherborough D[eputy]-Constable (?) of the towne, to the maiour, to desire the maiour to come to me. He came and I layed my hande on his sworde and said he was a prisoner to the State and so was his man. I lefte the horses and armes with the maiour. He sayth he tolde him he lefte his horses there and his sworde and two peeces to come from his sister at whose house he lay and in whose house he was when he was searched for. His sister broughte him away to another place. He much desired to come to London." *Signed* " Tho. Pittman."

And

Examination of PHILADELPHIA CROSSE, wife of Doctor Crosse.

Same date.—" She sawe her husband this day at Spencer's (?) ; they dined together. She knowes Mr. Hudson. He was at her house and lay there two nights laste weeke and dined and supped there one day. It was Munday and Tuesday as she thinkes. Hudson's wife is her sister. He spake of bringing the king from the Scotts. Mrs. Mortimer dined with him when he was there. She sayth that he was not in her house that nighte. He said that he woulde acquaynte some members of the house with his purpos and he spake of Mr. Hollis and others whose names she forgetts." *Signed* " Philadelphia Crosse."

And

Examination of JANE STEVENS, wife of Edward Stevens.

Same date.—"She knowes Mr. Hudson, not Dr. Crosse. One Crosse was at her house today and said he woulde speake with her husbande and nothing els.

Ed. Stevens sayth that he spake not to him of any member of either house. Hudson said that the King would yelde the militia and Irelande, but the Bishops' lands the Bishops had soe satisfied his scruples he woulde not yelde, and Dr. Stewarde (?) had perswaded him to it. He said he desired the King not to ingage himself too far to the King (*sic* ? for Scotts).

Lieutenant-Colonel Pitman sayth that she wente away with him in a coach. He was seene by one and she put her hands before him that Dr. Dune mighte not see him. She sayth her husbande hired the coach that caryed him away.

Dr. [Crosse] sayth they wente in a coach to the White Lion in Tower Streete where they dined and supped.

Humphrey Crosse, father to the Dr., said nothing." [N. XIV., 127.]

Examinations of ROBERT BARHAM, ARTHUR CARINGTON, and HENRY RASTALL.

1646, June 9.—(Printed in Peck, *Desiderata Curiosa,* ix. 16.) [N. XIV., 120.]

Confession of MICHAEL HUDSON.

[1646, June 9.]—(Printed in Peck, *Desiderata Curiosa*, ix., 19.) [N. XIV., 118.] Another copy is N. XV., 180*a*, which is apparently that taken down from Hudson's mouth. In this the dates are given correctly, several of which are a day wrong in the other, where, for instance, Friday, April 2, should be April 3, and there are some verbal differences and also some additional matter, the whole of which is given in substance in the examinations of Hudson printed below. This last copy is headed, "Hudson's declaration under his hand, after that he was asked some general questions by the Kentish gentlemen that were members of the House of Commons."

The KING to the SPEAKER OF THE HOUSE OF PEERS.

1646, June 10. Newcastle.—(Printed in Rushworth iv., 1. 275, and in *Lords' Journals*, viii., 374.) *Sign-Manual*. [N. I., 19.]

The KING to the MARQUESS OF ORMONDE.

1646, June 11. Newcastle.— (Printed in Carte, *Life of Ormonde*, iii., 474.) *Copy* in Sir J. Cheislie's hand. [N. XII., 192.]

Examination of ANNE MORTIMER.

[1646], June 11.—" She sawe Mr. Hudson twice when he was laste in towne the laste weeke. Once at Mr. Crosse's, the other time at the Blewe Anchor, in St. Tulie's Street. He sente for her to Mr. Crosse's. He alsoe sente for her by a waterman to the Blewe Anchor. He sente for her thither to knowe where he mighte lay. There was none there but a lame man. He desired her to fetch a passe for him from Mr. Crosse's which she did accordingly. Noe body wente with the passe but herselfe. Mr. Crosse delivered the passe to her. She knowes not in whose name the passe was. When she was at Dr. Crosse's she dined with him, and there was then nobody there but the Dr. Crosse and his wife and another man that satt belowe Mr. Hudson ; whether he was Hudson's freinde or noe she certaynly knowes not. She thinkes it was not Hudson's freinde. She dined with him on Tuesday at Dr. Crosse's and on Thursday towards (?) the dining she caryed him the passe. He sente her with noe messages or letters, neither did he aske her.

1646, June 13.—She sayth she tolde me but one untruth laste time for she said Mr. Hudson wished that he coulde have spoken with my Lorde Maiour. She said she coulde not tell. He asked me if my Lorde Salton did not love the King. She said he was his cosen and had noe reason to the contrary. He said my Lorde Salton, it may be, can bringe you to the speach of my Lorde Maiour. Hudson desired to speake with him. I tolde my Lorde that a gentleman, a freinde of the King, did desire to speake with him. He said he woulde doe any service for any of the King's freinds. He desired that Mr. Hudson woulde appoynte a place of meeting. I said your Lordship may appoynte the place, and he appoynted the Hoope tavern on the bridge. My Lorde and he mette there and I was there. They were together not a quarter of an hower. My Lorde lyes at S   house in the Strande. My Lord Salton and Hudson mette at the tavern at eight at nighte. Then Hudson wente away. It was Friday nighte."

And

Further Examination of MICHAEL HUDSON.

1646, June 11.—The beginning is printed in Peck, *Desiderata Curiosa*, ix. 24. The words omitted at the end of clause 2 are " before he heard it from the King. She told me it one Saturday, and the Tuesday after the King told me of it." It proceeds thus :—" I came out upon his parol pretending to go to Gloster for an exchange. The 500 horse to meet at Harborough and the body of the Scots horse should meet the King between Newarke and Nottingham. This Nicholas tolde him and Ashburnham. He was ordered to goe to Southwell if the horse were not at Harborough.

The King acquaynted the lords at 10 at nighte of his purposes to leave Oxford and goe to London. Ashburnham and the King tolde Hudson that he tolde the lords that he woulde come to London. Otherwise if the Scots woulde not give him assurance he would goe to Paris.

He writte this after the members of the house of commons came to him.

While he was in London Mr. Stevens tolde him that he woulde acquaynte Mr. Rous, Mr. Densil Hollis and Mr. St. John, Mr. Whitlocke and Sir Gil. Gerarde with his purposes.

He was not with Mr. Stevens above an hower."

The Examination of Michael Hudson.

" After his letter writte to my Lorde Dunfermelin he was discharged within four dayes. On Wednesday, the 20th of May, he sente this letter by Mr. Archibald Hay to the King to be sente to my Lorde Dunfermling if the King thought fitt, he then being prisoner in the Maiour's house. He sayth the King himself reade it as Mr. Archibald Hay said. The King then delivered it to my Lorde Dunfermling.

Being asked whoe were ingaged in   he said it was one of the propositions of the Scots Commissioners to Mountrell at Southwell. Mountrell was for the King. One of the articles were that he and Ashburnham shoulde be secured. The Lords Commissioners at Southwell were the Lorde Dunfermling, Lorde Louthian and Sir Gilbert Carr as he believes. His Christian name he perfectly remembers not. These commissioners he knowes onely from Montrel, not of his owne knowledge. He sayth he came to Montrel on Wednesday, the first day— 29 April —. The Scots woulde not speake til servis were done. After servis, Montrel wente to them and he tolde him they said to him they could make noe conditions that woulde breake the covenent and treaty, but if the King pleased to come and trust them they woulde receive him in such an honourable manner as shoulde exceede the King's and Dunfermling's expectations. He said the General said he woulde creepe upon his knees if he would come to them. I tolde Munstrell if this was all, it was in vayne for me to stay longer. They must not expect the King to come to them ; he was resolved not to trust them except they woulde expresse the conditions and give it under their hande. I was pleased to take horse then. My Lord Dunfermling came to Munstrell. I sawe him come to the house but I spake not to him, neither did I heare him speake to Munstrell. Munstrell said my Lord Dumfermling desired that he woulde wait ane answere to the King till nexte day six at nighte for they woulde sende for some commissioners that were not then at Southwel and advise together at Southwell the nexte day, and sende the King a satisfactory answere. Munstell then sente for me and tolde me what Dunfermling had desired of him. I tolde him I coulde not stay soe long ; the King had commanded me to be with him the nexte day being Friday, at dinner, and he was 80 miles from the place, the King then being at Downham in Norfolke. Munstrel wente backe to them and tolde them they muste resolve sooner for he coulde not stay the messenger soe long, soe they appoynted one the nexte day and Munstell wente to them at one and at four brought me this answere, that the Scots would agree to perform the four propositions expressed by them in this matter and which were the same that the King and he had agreed at Oxforde. I tolde him these woulde not satisfie except they woulde give them under their hand for that was my instructions to see them under their hand. He wente backe to them, and they refused it. He said he desired the King to believe them, and I said he would not. Then he desired me to wrighte under my hande whatever I would want. He feared he said I would not make it fayrly for the Scots. When I was beginning to wrighte, he said I neede not, he woulde wrighte to the King himself and he gave me a litle note to this effect, open and written in English : ' the Scots have agreed to all the propositions agreed when I was with you in Oxforde. The particulars the bearer can more fully relate. I have great hopes, and were they any other people I coulde give you an assurance of what they promise. I desire your Majestie soe much to truste me as to beleive them.' Hudson, to avoide mistake, writte the propositions with his owne hande and sente it to the Scots by Munstrell and Montrel said they and he agreed and protested them. Montrel altered one of them with his hand by the Scots' directions as he said, which was for the King's freinds. The Scots woulde endeavour with the parliament that but four of them shoulde suffer and that shoulde be onely banishment. After he had mended that proposition he said that my Lorde Dunfermling tolde Muntrell as he tolde him that Dunfermling said that if the Scots did not fully performe these propositions according to their indenture, he woulde printe them and publish them to the world for their shame. Then I wente the King and was with the King at Mounforde in Norfolk on Friday nighte. I delivered to him Munstrell's note and tolde him the propositions and all the former passages, and he resolved then to goe to them. He parted with the King at Radaland (? Ridland) woods ende, and the King wente for Norfolke to Downham to the Swan. The King and Ashburnham had like to be discovered by a barber whoe said their hayres were cutt with a knife. He came backe to Downham and mette Skipwith upon the way whoe came from his Majesty and tolde him that if he had any friendes there they were gone to Montforde to the Cherry (?). The King sente me backe to Downham from Monforde to Mr. Skipwith for a coate and sworde, and I had it of him for him. I wente for the linnen but forgott it, and we sente backe for it by a trusty messenger.

When he came to Southwell he asked Montrell what was the reason of his confidence of the horse being at Harborough and they came not. He said he had his assurances from the Scotch commissioners at London. He asked Montrell—but I had noe instructions for it—what woulde become of Montros if a peace was concluded upon these propositions. He said the Scots had agreed that the King shoulde sende Montres into France by way of an ambassador for his   . When the king was at Newcastle, the king and they did much dispute about Montrosses disbanding. They then pressed that Montros shoulde submit to the justice of parliament in Scotlande, but the king woulde not yielde to it nor agree to his disbanding, til they agreed that he shoulde be sente away. Being asked why the king writte to Montros to disbande absolutely; and as to disbande upon conditions,* he saythe the reason was because the king and Scots had agreed that he and Ogleby and Craforde shoulde goe into France. This was tolde him by Cambel, when he himself was in prison and the king after tolde this examinante that Montros was to goe

---

* This is explained by the parallel passage in the Examination of June 9–10, N. XV., 180a, which reads " absolutely, and to his forces here to disbande upon honourable termes."

into France and to disbande, the king tolde him further what he had
sente to the houses and commanded him to tell it the Queene. Being
asked whether the king, secretary Nicholas, or Ashburnham did tell
him of an agreement betwixte the Scots and the king : the king, and
Nicholas and Ashburnham tolde him that the Scots and he were agreed.
The agreement was made at London by Montrel and the Scots commissioners, that the king shoulde goe to the Scotch army. All the agreement
with the Scots was made by Montrel that ever he hearde of.

Being asked why he wente not himself to the Scotch commissioners
he said his instructions were onely to goe to Montrel and to keepe myself' from being known to any. Never was he toulde by the king,
Ashburnham or Nicholas or any other that any did agitate any business
from the king either at London with the Scotch commissioners or any
in the Scotch army but onely Montrell. I never hearde from any that
any agitate[d] any business either here or at Southwell but onely
Mountrell.

Being asked how often he wente to the Scotch army he said the firste
time was, he wente to Harburgh on Wednesday 8th April, he went to
meete the party of horse which were to meete the king, finding them
not there upon the day, he wente to Southwell, and there I lay at an
inne and there Montrell was quartered in the Scotch General's lodgings
whether he wente to him imediately. Then he tolde him he coulde have
noe answere til Munday. I wente backe to Harborough and soe to
Woodstocke, intending to goe to Oxford, but finding noe convenient
passage I returned on Monday towards Southwell and came thither on
Wednesday 15 April.

Being asked why he wrights in his paper soe of the Scots he said it
was because of their fayling at Harborough which was the moste unworthy (?) thing that ever was done. If the king had been taken he
had been in a   . He thought the Scotts   were (?) very much.
26 April, Ashburnham came from Woodstocke where he was aboute
the treaty of surrender of Woodstocke. Ashburnham said he and the
two lords moved the parliament forces at Woodstocke to protect
the king in that army. They said they woulde not undertake it then.
Mr. Ashburnham said to me they muste goe my way for noe wayes
was safe. By way he meanes to goe disguised with a party of horse.
He, Mic[hael] (?), the king, Mr. Ashburnham were not in London
nor ever nearer than Harrowe on the Hill. He said the king gave a
warrant to Richmonde and Linsey to goe out of Oxford, and they
made use of that warrant, and wente to the Parliament's quarters and
tolde them of the king's going to the Scotch Army as we supposed.
This the king said when he sawe the bookes, whene we were
discovered. He had noe message from the king to any in this
towne, neither did he sende any to any but to Mr. Crosse, Mrs. Mortimer
and Mr. Stevens. He stayed in London from Munday til Friday nighte.
He came out of Newcastle the Sunday sennet (seven night) before.
He sayth the captayne of the guarde brought the king's groome, and a
smith and myselfe out of the guarde but the deputy maiour of Newcastle
kuewe nothing of his coming out.

Sir Henry Gibbs knewe of his coming out of Newcastle, soe he did
of Mr. Ashburnham's going away. Sir Henry Gibb woulde have had me
goe to Tinemouth, soe to Holland, and I desired to have the king's nagg
and I woulde goe to London. He sayth my Lorde Dumfrese and Lorde
Dunfermling knewe of his coming away, soe did the governour of Newcastle. Sir Henry Gibb and my Lorde Dumfres were against his coming
by lande for feare of being taken. My Lord Dumfres tolde me he was
with Ashburnham at Tinemouth Castle and stayed with him Munday

and Tuesday til nighte. Being asked how he kuewe that those two Scotch lords kuewe of his coming away, he said Dunfermling was with the king when he tooke leave, and he had of him 20*l.* in golde which my Lorde Dumfres delivered for silver. Dumfres said my Lorde Dunfermling said if I had neede I shoulde have 100*l.* in golde without silver.

My pretence cf coming away was that I mighte be free from a messenger of the parliament's. The deputy maiour let me goe to the king upon the king's desire, and there I stayed at the king's desire to the maiour.

The deputy maiour tooke me prisoner upon the bridge as I was going to Mr. Ashburnham to Sir Henry Gibb's howse by the king's commande to deliver a message to him, that the Scots would protect him noe longer; if he shoulde make all speede, he conide away. The messenger from the maiour came for me and I wente to him and while I was examined the king sente Mr. Savile (?) to desire that I shoulde not be committed prisoner nor sente away. Thereupon the maiour tooke me home to his house where I was prisoner a weeke before I wente to the king, but the king often sente to me. When I was prisoner the king sente to the Scotch commissioners to knowe whoe had moste interest with the maiour and he was tolde that Mr. Savile (?) had, soe he was sente to me. During the time of my imprisonment I was suffered to goe up and downe the towne with Mr. Dune, a maiour. I did wrighte to the king while I was prisoner. I did visit Mons^re Montrell dureing my imprisonment, Mr. Dune going with me, and I delivered a letter to him which I had writt to the king. This I writt by the consent of the maiour and aldermen. I in that letter sente to the king a counterfeit warrante which was broughte to me by a Scotchman for 40*l.* I writt a clause in my letter that I spake with some of the principal committee men in the towne that admired to heare of the vote which was said to be passed by the independents agaynst monarchy. They said it was not soe but it was a devise by some that had a design upon the king. The money that I had was money that we received of the maiour of Doncaster for rente due to the king.

He spake to the king that the maiour and aldermen of Newcastle mighte have accesse and they would convey a letter to the Prince from him if he pleased. This he did, hearing that Digby had been with him and was gone into France, fearing that he mighte come and gett the Prince thither which mighte prejudice (?) this kingdom both in victualles and armes." *Signed* " Mich : Hudson."

And

Examination of JOHN [LORD] BELLASSIS.

1646, June 11.—" He knew that the king intended to come to the Scotch army before he came thither. Being asked how long before he came thither did he knowe of it, he saythe he being beseged could not have often intelligences but aboute the 8th or 10th of April was the firste time that he hearde of it. The garison of Newarke kuewe it. My intelligence was from the king. He writte me worde that he thoughte he shoulde be with the Scotts and intended to goe to them. This letter was aboute the 8th or 10th of April. Being asked what directions he had from the king concerning the armies there he said the king lefte a latitude to him and seeing himself beseged and without hope of relefe he treated.

Hudson was sente to me from the king the nexte day after the king came hither. I hearde that the king was in the Scotch quarters. I received a letter in which were propositions worse then we had and a commande to deliver it upon these termes believing I conlde not have better. It was my difficulty that the king shoulde prescribe me con-

ditions before I knewe what I shoulde have. I answered to the king,
I wondered he shoulde prescribe me conditions which I coulde not
accepte of, that I desired him to leave me to the commissioners to
treate. The King sente to me to deliver the towne that nighte. I was
troubled at it, I believed I shoulde have better. The King sent Hudson
to me to hasten the treaty upon the former propositions that the King
sente to me. I sawe him not since in Newarke. He sawe him since at
his own howse in Lincolnshire at his owne howse. He came to me to
my owne howse. I then knewe not the parliament demanded him. He
came from the King to me and desired he mighte goe with me as one of
my servants. Being asked [he said] he did not acquaynte him with
any thing but that he was to goe into France.

He spake with Mr. Ashburnham in the Ilande the day that the King
marched away. He came thither and sente to desier to speake with
me. He tolde me that the King had endeavoured to have me waighte
on him, but coulde not prevayll. I never els spake with Mr. Ashburnham. He knewe not that the King woulde come, onely he writte he
intended it.

He knewe of the King's coming to Southwell within an hower after
he was there. A captayne came on his parol to me, and tolde it me and
wente backe to the King, and broughte me worde backe that he had
kissed his hande and he sente me worde that I shoulde heare of him
within three or four honres. I verily thinke the King was deceived
in his expectations in his going thither. A letter of the King's purpos to
goe thither came in a man's belly. He swallowed it in a billet and
voided it twice. I hearde out of the Scotch quarters signs of the King
being there.

He sayth that he knowes of noe gentleman of quality that wente
to the Scotch army from Newarke but some officers and souldiers of
fortune.

After he was beseged he often sente to Oxforde but not by the Scotts
nor through their quarters, but in the nighte and by olde women he
thinks sente before the line was finished.

He had advertisement from Oxforde by a ragged man whome he imployed as his agent, to be civil to the Scotch there, but at the firste I
sallyed equally to them and was as willing to beate the Scotch as the
English. I did not sally upon either after I was beseged because of the
plague among us. The English had better workes far then the Scotts.
The King's letter (?) to me in   was that the King intended
to goe to the Scotch army and he had assurance for his servants (?)."
Signed "J. Belasisse." [N. XIV., 127.]

Further Confession of MICHAEL HUDSON.

1646, June 12.—(Printed in Peck, *Desiderata Curiosa*, ix. 24.)
[N. XIV., 129.]

SIR JOHN BOURCHIER, Sheriff, and others to WILLIAM LENTHALL.

1646, June 12. York.—Complaining of the continual pressures of
the Scotch army in the North and part of the West Ridings, of which
they enclose particulars, and also a letter from the Scotch Lords at
Newcastle desiring to receive the accounts of their army and their
answer. (Printed in Grey, iii. Appendix, No. 23, p. 36.) [N. VI., 7.]

Further examination of MICHAEL HUDSON.

1646, June 12.—" He hath been knowen to the King, three-quarters
of a yeare and noe longer. I mette with one that tolde me that Sir
John Digby was to give up Newarke. He wente to the King then at

Newarke, and tolde him of it. Then as the King wente out of the towne, Sir John Digby committed me prisoner, where I was nine weekes, and I sente one to the King and he sente for my discharge. Then I wente to the King. I wente into Dorsetshire to Warham. One Colonel Philips spake of taking Warham. He and Dr. Ferrier (?) spake of me. Colonel Philips desired my acquaintance and he moved (?) me to goe into Dorsetshire and see if Warham was to be taken. I wente thither. He sente Pitman with me to Blaneforde (Blandford). I wente to Pitman where he had fifty men that would be the King's. I viewed Poole and tolde Secretary Nicholas that two hundred horse woulde take both Poole and Warham. The men that wente with me it. I lefte two within to let downe the bridge when I came. We wente ino and seised all. They thought them troope. He said at Warham he came to gather money for the parliament, in that county. An olde maiour came to examine me and I tolde him this. He writte a coppy of a warrant fiom Haberdashers Hall to gather the Duke of Richmond's rents. They were concealed rents.

The King imployed him about taking Ab[ingdon]. I tolde the King if the parliament had Ox[ford] and he (?) Ab[ingdon], it coulde stande ten dayes. A guide I intertained (?) came from Ab[ingdon] to me. My man tolde me most of them intended to come to the King. I directed their entry to the towne. My man was the chefe guide. My man's name was Charles. That was the time when they were beaten out. Thirty-one fierlocks entred; all the towne was in sleepe. That party sente backe his amunition. They entred, had noe powder. The King trusted him with the party. He sayth that he did procure the taking of Criclade. He was at Oxforde before, at Michaelmas twelvemonth, but not knowen to the King.

The firste nighte when they wente from Oxford and lay at Whithamstede the King helde out well. He was at noe gentleman's house but Mr. Cave's in Stamforde in all his journey. Mr. Cave knewe the King and Mr. Ashburnham. He hath been a prisoner most times (?). Furlong (?) was captain of the guarde that guarded the King, and he wente with Mr. Dune and the King , Cooke, and Duke his groome came to only (?) with him. Asking him what was his mayne worke into France over and above what he said yesterday, he said the King bid him tel the Queene that there was a greate party among Scots at Newcastle were more for him then the Caveliers were. He received good satisfaction from my Lorde of Lanericke of his charge for him in Scotlande, and that since my Lorde Calender came he received more respecte from the Scots then he did before. He sayth that Montrell tolde him at Southwell that the Scots woulde sende imediately into Scotlande for some of the lords to meete the King at Newcastle. I tolde them the King woulde not come. Therefore he sente a man with me to knowe the King's pleasure. The King sente noe answere, for our purpos was to alter our journey. We before proposed to goe by water but altered our minds for feare of being taken. But the Scotch lords were come out of Scotland to Newcastle the day before the King came thither.

The King tolde him that he sente his letter to the parliament by the advice or consent of the Scotch lords, wherin he had given them satisfaction, but not to the Ministers (?) for they woulde have him express to yelde to the Presbiterian government. Some Scots tolde me by discourse among (?) the Army (?) whome I knewe not, that if the King woulde yelde to a Presbiterian government all woulde be well, and if the parliament woulde not give the King satisfaction in other things tending to his honour, then the whole Kingdome of Scotland woulde rise with him as one man. He asked the King whether the Scots did observe the propositions agreed unto at Southwell. He said, noe, they were now upon other grounds. This question he asked the day before he came out of Newcastle. He sayth when the Scots and he came to Kelham the firste nighte, they tolde the King that they must observe their covenant. God must have the firste place, the King the nexte. This a tableman spake to the King. The King said he woulde observe his conscience. Lorde Lothian said, you will receive the humble desires of his people, I (aye), but doe nothing agaynst his conscience. The King at that time said he did not come upon these conditions to them or words to that effecte. I and Mr. Ashburnham were by and the Scotch commissioners and General were there. He sayth when he wente from Downham to the Scotch army, he wente to Montrell, being then at an inne in Southwell and he and I lay together. Being asked what discourse he had with Montrell, he being his bedfellowe, he said ; the Scots were loste, God had blinded their eyes to their destruction, in that they observed not the propositions that they made to the King from Harborough. He teling them that the King had greate hazards, they answered to him, that the English woulde have given the King and those with him, for Montrell at Newcastle told him that they kepte not terms with the King. Being asked what Montrell tolde him was the cause of his coming to Englande and whoe imployed him, he said the State of France, and it was to treate with the Scots for receiving the Kinge. He shewed me his commission from the King of France. It was not written with inke but with some water. He wetted it to reade. The effecte and substance of it was to treate with the Scots for their receiving the King.

Mr. Ashburnham tolde me that he tooke order with Skipwith to sende me to the King when I came, which he did accordingly, meeting me upon the h[igh] way and he lefte worde at the house.

I was prisoner at Rochester by warrant from the committee of Kent. I was alone and a lusty fellowe of Oxford followed me and came to me to Rochester and there were two scollers there in the house. They thought of rescueing me from the soldiers (?).

The King, Ashburnham and Nicholas tolde him that Montrel was here to treate with the Scots for him.

Pitman overtooke him on Rochester bridge. They ridd together to Citingbourne (Sittingbourne). He knewe me when he sawe me and asked me if that man before me was Mr. Robbin. I said noe, his name was Harry. He knewe me well, caryed me in all places to the King's freinds as he said, and where any were Roundheads he bad me take beede. He asked if I knewe not that he gave up Corffe Castle. I said noe. He said he woulde recompense the King if he coulde obtayne a pardon (?) from him for the King. And if the King woulde make him governour of Dover Castle he woulde get and keepe it for him. He said he woulde get the C   for the King. He woulde never fighte agaynst the King, but woulde have a commande in Irelande. Citingburne was Jennings', at Canterbury, Terry, and   General. At the King's coming to Southwell, Montrel came to meete us fifteen miles, but missed us. We came to Southwell to his chamber. The King lay downe to sleepe, and aboute two honres after Montrel came home, and then my Lorae Dunfermling came. Then came Sir Henry Gibb. We sente worde to Montrel the nighte before that we coulde come the nexte day. He sente worde to us that halfe a dosen of the Scotch commissioners woulde meete at the Trente side but they came not." *Signed* " Mich. Hudson."

And

FURTHER EXAMINATIONS.

1646, June 13.—" Pitman he lefte Hudson at 11 at nighte and wente home and came agayne. He confesseth he spake to him for a friend (?) that was to get what he coulde out of him.

Mr. Hudson sayth that these four propositions Mr. Stevens tolde him the parliament woulde sende to the King, denying anything that he saide of the King sending propositions. Hudson denyed all that Pitman said.

Hudson sayth that Pitman tolde him he was to have a regiment of foote and 100 (?) horse for Irelande and with them he woulde take Dover Castle.

Mr. Hudson sayth that nothing that he hath written or answered but he will speake it upon his oath. He may mistake a worde one the matter.

Hudson sayth that for propositions here at London the King lefte it to me to doe as I woulde. Asking him what propositions the King sente to the Queene, he was not to propounde anything to the Queene concerning her coming over or for his yelding. The King gave me a general power to doe as was beste for his advantage when you (he) was gone from London and at Grenwich I writt a litle note to the King that ' I had imployed an attorney to his city chapman and that I thoughte he woulde deale better with him then his chapman at Harborough. I was now going to my mistress to acquainte her what I had proposed and to prepare my way for my returne, and I intended to waighte on him within three weekes.' This letter he directed to Mr. Tod of Newcastle to deliver to Mr. Watson whoe was by agreement betwixte him and me to deliver it to the French agent to deliver to the King. The man he sente with it was Waterforde. He caryed it to the poste. By chapman he mente the parliament. The attorney he mente was Stevens. Chapman at Harborough were the Scots.

How can he tell the city chapman's minde. He said Stevens tolde him the four propositions agreed upon by the parliament were the Militia, Delinquents, Church, and Irelande. I desired that something mighte be proposed for the Queene and the mitigation of the proposition concerning Delinquents.

He hath not spoken to Crosse nor his wife, neither written or received any message from them or sent any to them. Being asked the grounde of his confidence for bringing the King, he said the King woulde truste himself with him, and he was not pleased with his being there. During his imprisonment he was twice with a keeper with Montrell and once came over to deliver a letter to him which the maiour sawe. The other was when he wente to the King. He sayth Mr. Durante the preacher there wente with him to the King and twice to Montrell and into the Ilande to a supper. To the Sheilds I wente with the maiour and aldermen to see Sir Henry Vayne's workes. We supped in the Ilelande upon the grasse ; they caryed colde meate with them."

And

Further examination of Doctor Francis Crosse.

Same date.—"The service he mente was to bringe the King from the Scots to the Parliament. By olde enemys he said not the now enemys but the ch   declare that they had been enemys. He sayth his brother Hudson tolde him that he made my Lorde Bellasis acquaynted with his intentions which were these that I declare here.

Upon his last examination, Hudson sayth that he hearde at Blanforde that Pitman was a carpenter. Pitman sayth that he did worke for his owne pleasure, but never wente abroade. He was never questioned for his life before any magistrate but a brother was, and he is deade but not hanged. He was killed at Bridgewater being on the King's side." [N. XIV., 128.]

Further examination of Edward Stevens.

1646, June 15.—"He hath neither scene nor hearde from Hudson since he came laste to towne, nor sente to him nor he to me, nor with Dr. Crosse, nor from him.

I asked him why he did not bringe the King to the parliament. Crosse said he may die that he adhered to it (?), yet I wished him to apply himself to the parliament in bringing him hither to discovering their counsels or perswading the King to yelde. He promised me to returne within a fortnighte then if I woulde persuade (?) him to goe to some parliament men that he mighte truste to communicate his mind to. I asked how he coulde doe any [of] this if he coulde not come to courte. He woulde satisfy their expectation. He said he had busnes into France and together with it he woulde procure a letter from the Queene to the Scots to suffer him to come agayne to the King, and withall he woulde come backe agayne from France to speake with these parliament men before he wente to the King, and he doubted not but he shoulde satisfy their desires. I did beleive what he said was true for he said he desired the King not to ingage too far to the Scots, for he said they woulde deceive him or els they woulde make him to yelde soe far that both he and this kingdom mighte be at their desires (?) or words to that effecte. *Signed* " Edw. Stevens."

Asking him his offer to the parliament, he sayth that to the utmoste of his power he hath served them. He said that aboute two yeares since he saved the Ile of Ely by intelligence that he had from him and he communicated it to Lieutenant-General Cromwell. *Signed* "Edw. Stevens."

Mr. Stevens sayth that he communicated all the news to him but Mr. Hudson lefte all to him to doe as he wil. He inclined to one noe more then other."

And Examination of Michael Hudson.

Same date.—" The King did not knowe that he intended to apply himself to any parliament men (?) neither did he directe him soe but the Kinge lefte him to use his discretion for his service. He still sayth that he tolde his designe to Mr. Belassis to bringe the King to the parliament from the Scots. He said nothing then but nexte morning asked me if he mighte speake it. He said he had one freinde that he mighte imparte it to if the motion was accepted he woulde come into France to him. He remembers not that he named any freinde by name.

He sayth that the King tolde his intention to the Duke and Prince Rupert on Saturday the day after that Montrell wente from Oxford. He hearde of it himself on Saturday at 2 by Mrs. Prior.

He wente from Kelham to Newarke by the leave of the General and the Scotch commissioners. I had my passe from Major-General Holberne. Our commissioners were not there. My pretence was to fetch the King's horse, but my errand was to speake to Bellasis about the rendering of the towne. My message was that he shoulde presently surrender the towne and get as good conditions as he coulde. I wente another time and the Majour-General gave way to it.

I passed with the King by a passe that I had from a captain whose name I knowe not. The passe was under the hands of Whaly and Norris." *Signed* "Mich. Hudson." [N. XIV., 128.]

Report concerning the Propositions touching the Militia.

1646, June 16.—(This agrees with the resolutions printed in *Commons' Journals*, iv. 578, 579, with some variations, of which the most

important are the omission of a clause restoring to the King after the expiration of 20 years the power over the Militia and of a clause making it high treason to levy forces without the authority of Parliament.)
[N. XIV., 131.]

Further examination of MICHAEL HUDSON.

[1646], June 17.—" Mr. Hudson for his voiage into France sayth that it was for his owne security and to acquaynte the Queen with what he had acquaynted us in his examination, concerning the King cominge to Newcastle and concerning the Scots and their usinge of him. When he came away the King intended to wrighte by the mariners of Jersey to the Prince that he shoulde not convey himself away out of Englande. He knowes the King intended it and I moved (?) it to him. The maiour and committee of Newcastle undertooke to sende this letter. I gott the King to sende for them and they kissed his hands.

When I came out of the Scotch army to goe to the King in Norfolke, at Stanforde he writte to Secretary Nicholas and sente it by a woman to Oxford—an olde woman. I gave her 50s. The letter was to Secretary Nicholas. ' Honest Ned, After my harty commendations rendered unto thee this is to let thee understande that I am in good health at the wrighting hereof and soe is my master Watson, and my brother Jack. This is to let thee understande that since we came to London—this I writt for the King tolde them he woulde goe to London—my master sente me to his ally at Harborough to knowe what he had done with his chapman aboute his lande there. His ally tells me that they have agreed upon the same conditions that my master and he had agreed upon at the last parting, but whether my master will accepte of these conditions or agree with his city chapman I can not as yet tell, but the chapman at Harborough promisses very fayre but, Ned, I neede not tell thee what a knave he is. I pray thee, Ned, doe not inclyne (?) yourself to any other master before, you heare agayne from me and I have sente thee the litel (?) six pence to drinke for a token.' This directed to my very loving frende Ed. Scrivenir. The woman was to deliver it to Secretary Nicholas with her owne hande. I sente by her a note to my brother Pollarde. I tolde him before I came out the meaning of these terms. We lay at Copingforde in Huntingdonshire one Sunday, 3 May. Wente not to church, but I reade prayers to the King and at six at nighte we wente to Stamforde.

(Marginal notes: The King. While he changed his habit they called him Master Watson (?). Ashburnham (?). Master, the King. — Alley, Muntrell; Chapman, the Scots; lande, the busnes conditions, the four propositions in my note. — Parliament. — He tolde the King of this letter when he came backe and the King approved it.*)*

I writte from Copingforde to Mr. Skipwith for a horse and he sente me one which was broughte to me at Stamforde. We wente out of Oxforde on Munday the 27 April, and came to the Scotch army, Tuesday morning the 5 of May. He did thinke the King woulde yelde the militia, but after we hearde that you had voted agaynst monarchy we thought this speich of propositions was but to fule the people, and that you never meante to sende any. He is considered he coulde have brought the King away. He was often private for an hower or two with the King and noebody was by. Secretary Nicholas woulde never heare of a treaty with the Scots till he hoarde of the vote agaynst monarchy. He never hearde the King or Nicholas or any other speake of any of either house or in the city that gave intelligence to Ox[ford].

At Doncaster the Scots broughte the printed order that it shoulde
be treason for any to conceale the King and shewed it to the King.

At Copingforde the King and we with my hoste and hostis and two
children were by the fire in the hall; there was noe other chimney in
the house. The King lay in a grande chamber, and Mr. Ashburnham
and I lay together at Whitbamstede.

He sayth Pitman was for the parliament at Bridgewator, and turned
to the King at Bristowe. He betrayed Corfe Castle to the parliament
and now proposed Dover Castle to doe the like for the King.

That what he tolde Mr. Bellasis and Dr. Crosse and Stevens was not
to save himselfe in case he shoulde be taken, but it was reall and that
he will sweare, and had not mine intentions been reall I coulde have
taken ship at Newcastle and not to have come thither. I made all the
haste I coulde, leaste you should fall fowle before I wente to the Queene.
Then I coulde doe noe good.

He offers to take his oath that all these answers are true, both these
and those before." *Signed* "Mich. Hudson." [N. XIV., 128.]

Sir Thomas Fairfax to William Lenthall.

1646, June 19.—Supporting the petition of Sir Francis Wortley.
Signed. Seal. Enclosed:

Sir Francis Wortley to the House of Commons.

Petition, setting forth his close imprisonment for two years in the
Tower, his sickness, his poverty, and his losses and his debts and
praying leave to go to Tunbridge for his health and to order
the Committees to pay his debts and allow him a livelihood out
of his own estate. [N. VI., 8.]

The Earl of Lauderdale, Archibald Johnston, Hew Kennedy, and Robert Barclay to William Lenthall.

1646, June 20.—Enclosing their answer to the paper of the House
concerning the accounts between the kingdoms. *Signed. Seal.*
[N. VI. end, unnumbered.]

The Committee for the Admiralty and Cinque Ports.

1646, June 23.—Report concerning the officers of the Vice-Admiralty
of Yorkshire. (Printed in *Lords' Journals,* viii. 398.) [N. XIV.,
132.]

The Scotch Commissioners.

1646, June 22.—Paper. (Printed in *Lords' Journals,* viii. 388.)
Signed "Jo. Cheislie." [N. XIX., 188.]

The Scotch Commissioners to the Parliament.

[1646, June 25.] — Concerning the Propositions. (The purport
sufficiently appears from *Commons' Journals,* iv. 589, second column.)
Signed "Jo. Cheislie." [N. XX., 4.]

The Scotch Commissioners to the Parliament.

1646, June 25.—(Printed in *Lords' Journals,* viii. 395, and Rushworth, iv. 1. 301.) *Signed* "Jo. Cheislie." [N. XIX., 189.]

The House of Lords to the Lord Mayor.

1646, June 25.—Order. (Printed in *Lords' Journals,* viii. 390.) [N. XIV., 135.]

And

The Lord Mayor.

1646, July 1.—Order made in pursuance thereof. (See *Commons' Journals,* iv. 597.) [N. XIV., 136.]

The King.

1646, June 27.—Answer to the Earl of Leven's petition. (Printed in Rushworth, iv. 1. 305.) A fragment, the first part missing. *Copy.* [N. XIV., 133.]

The House of Commons.

1646, June 30.—Instructions to the Judges. (Printed as amended in *Commons' Journals,* iv. 394. See also p. 393. The omitted clause about Church Government is "To let them know that their care of preventing an unlimited and arbitrary power to be exercised by the Church officers [of] the Church Government now in hand hath spent a great part of their time, the same having been a principal motive to them for the taking away of Episcopacy and the Bishops' Courts.") *Draft* with amendments. [N. XII., 184.]

The Committee for the Admiralty and Cinque Ports.

1646, June 30.—Order reporting the Prince's letter. [N. XIV., 134.]

The Committee for Ireland to the House of Commons.

1646, June 30.—Recommending that Colonel Jones' and Colonel Sydney's regiments be sent thither. (See *Commons' Journals,* iv. 600.) [N. XXI., 30.]

The Scotch Commissioners.

[1646, June.]—Paper concerning the accounts of their armies in England and Ireland. (See *Commons' Journals,* iv. 603.) *Signed* "Jo. Cheislie." [N. XIX., 190.]

A Particular of the County's sufferings by the Scottish Army.

[1646, June (?).]—Describing their outrages and exactions. (Printed in Grey, iii., Appendix, No. 21, p. 34.) *Copy.* [N. XII., 193.]

Notes of some things done by the Scotch Army and Officers.

[1646, June (?).]—Charging them with levying assessments, fortifying Tynemouth, interfering with the officers of the Customs and Excise, employing one Handcock, a Delinquent, and murdering three men, who resisted them or made complaint of their conduct. (Printed in Grey, iii., Appendix, No. 25, p. 40.) [N. XX., 2.]

The Parliament to the King.

[1646, July 6.]—Concerning the garrisons in Ireland. (Printed in *Lords' Journals,* viii. 417.) *Draft* with amendments. [N. XII., 197.]

Sir Wilfrid Lawson, John Barwis, Henry Tolson, and Thomas Curwen, to William Lenthall.

1646, July 7.—Enclosing a letter from the Lords and Committee of Scotland and their reply. " We cannot satisfy their expectations, we fear the country will be put to much damage by them, which indeed is already in great part made unuseful." (See *Commons' Journals,* iv. 623.) *Signed.* [N. VI., 9.] *Enclosed:*

The Earl of Leven and the Committee of the Estates to the Committee of Westmoreland.

1646, June 28. Newcastle.—Desiring them to send some of their number by the 9th of July in order to advise about the quartering and necessary maintenance of the Scotch Army. *Copy.* [N. XII., 194.]

The Committee for the Admiralty and Cinque Ports.

1646, July 9.—Report concerning the Earl of Bristol. (Printed in *Lords' Journals,* viii. 426.) [N. XIV., 137.]

The Marquess of Argyll, the Earl of Lauderdale, and others to the Speaker of the House of Peers *pro tempore.*

1646, July 11. Worcester House.—" The Lord Marquess of Argyll at his coming hither did represent to both Houses the extreme wants and necessities of the Scottish armies in England and Ireland. And being now to return with the Commissioners appointed by both Houses to present the propositions of peace to his Majesty it is our earnest desire that he may be enabled to give some assurance to those that sent him that the desires expressed in our paper of the 25th of June shall be granted; and that the Honourable Houses would be pleased to appoint Committees or take some other effectual way for expediting supplies to those armies, which is extremely expected from the affection wisdom and justice of the Honourable Houses. And sith it hath pleased God now after so many troubles and sad distractions to offer to these kingdoms such an opportunity of settling peace, we will not doubt but the Honourable Houses, as we have in two former papers earnestly desired, will in answer to his Majesty's letters give him such encouragement as may make him to grant the propositions and may further witness to all the world the reality of their desires for procuring a speedy and happy peace." (See *Lords' Journals,* viii. 433; *Commons' Journals,* iv. 616.) *Signed. Seal.* [N. VI., 10.]

John Ashe, M.P., to the House of Commons.

[1646, July 17.]—Petition. (The purport appears from the order thereon printed in *Commons' Journals,* iv. 619.) [N. XXII., 89.]

Colonel Thomas Morgan and others to William Lenthall.

1646, July 18. Gloucester.—Asking that the sequestrations of Lord Windsor and the Governor and Lieutenant-Governor of Hartlebury Castle might be taken off, in accordance with the articles of surrender of the same. *Signed.* [N. VI., 11.]

The Committee for Ireland to the House of Commons.

1646, July 18.—Recommending the payment of his arrears to Lord Blaney formerly Captain Edward Blaney. [N. XXI., 31.]

The SA**A**E to the SA**A**E.

Same date.—Recommending the payment of 300*l*. down and 200*l*.
per annum in future to Lady Blaney, whose husband had been killed at
Benburb. [N. XXI., 32.]

Account of Moneys paid by the TREASURERS AT GOLDSMITHS' HALL
for the Scots army in England from November 20, 1645 to May
7, 1646.

1646, July 20.—Amounting to 61,631*l*. 6*s*. 0*d*. [N. XIV., 138.]

The PARLIA**A**ENT to M. DE BELLIEVRE.

1646, July 22.—Pass and Letter. (Printed in *Commons' Journals*,
iv. 623.) *Drafts*. [N. XVII., 7.]

Report concerning JA**A**ES FENWICK, a Delinquent.

1646, July 24.—(See *Commons' Journals*, iv. 626.) [N. XIV.,
139.]

Report of proceedings at two COUNCILS OF WAR.

1646, July 23 and 30. Sherborne and Hinton St. George.—
Sentencing one trooper to be hanged for murder, another for not
endeavouring to prevent him to be cashiered, another to be burnt
through the tongue for cursing and swearing, and ordering other officers
and troopers to be tried at the Assizes for murder and highway robbery.
(See *Commons' Journals*, iv. 638.) [N. XIV., 140.]

The KING's Answer to the Propositions.

1646, August 1.—(Printed in *Lords' Journals*, viii. 460.) *Copy*.
[N. XIV., 41.]

SIR ROBERT HARLEY to the CO**A**MITTEE FOR IRISH AFFAIRS.

1646, August 1.—Stating in pursuance of the order of the previous
day (see *Commons' Journals*, iv. 632) that Colonel Birch's regiment in
Herefordshire might well be spared for the service of Ireland. *Original*
and *Copy*. [N. VI., 12 ; XXI., 33.]

The PRINCE OF WALES to the GOVERNOR and COUNCIL OF WAR of
PENDENNYS CASTLE.

[1646], August 6. St. Germains.—Acknowledging his despatches of
June 27 and July 7, and after referring to the miscarriage of the relief
at first intended hoping he has by that time received a considerable
supply which started thence a good while since. (Dated in the 22nd
year of the reign of our royal father.) *Sign Manual*. *Seal*. [N. I.,
31*a*.]

Reports concerning SIR CHARLES BOLLE, HENRY BARLOWE,
LAWRENCE BENTALL, JOHN NEALE, LADY ANNE FAR**A**ER, SIR
WILLIA**A** FAR**A**ER, and ADA**A** CLAYPOOLE, Delinquents.

1646, August 6.—(See *Commons' Journals*, iv. 636, 637.) [N.
XIV., 142-147.]

Order of the CO**A**MON COUNCIL.

1646, August 6.—Concerning the City Guards. (See *Commons'
Journals*, iv. 679.) [N. XIV., 148.]

Captain ROBERT CLARKE to WILLIAM LENTHALL.

1646, August 10. From aboard the *Swan Regis*, in Helbrea, near Chester river.—Enclosing copies of articles between the Earl of Ormonde and Macarth[y] the Irish general, and of a letter from a friend in Dublin. (See *Commons' Journals*, iv. 648.) *Seal.* *Enclosed:*

R. H. to Captain CLARKE.

1646, August 7. Dublin.—" I have not any newes to write unto you, only this, which greeveth the harts of all the poore distressed Protestants of this kingdome. The first day of this present August there was a generall peace proclamed betweene the Lord of Ormond in the behalfe of his Majestic and Denough MacCarthe, Lord of Musbry (Muskerry) and the Lord Mongarett and other commissioners of the Irish parte. The artickles I could not gett att any rate but I am suer you will have them within this sixe dayes att furthest. There is not anythinge that tends to any good of the English Prodestants but all to there utter ruen. There was a treatie between the Lord of Folleatt and the Lord of Ormond about the begininge of July last and it was thought that it would have produced to good effect had not the Lord Digbie come out of France. For as sone as Digbie came the Lord of Ormond doth nothinge without the aprobaton of Digbie. His Majestic sent a letter about that tyme stricktly commanding the Lord of Ormond to make noe peace with those unhuman rebells of Ireland, which he would have obayed had not the Lord Digbie perswaded him that his Majestie was prisoner and whatsoever he ritt now he was compeled to rite. Digbie cominge out of France brought with him 12,000 p. ½ pistolls which goeth in France for 10,000*l.*, and is reported that there followeth 150,000*l.* more in mony to mantaue the warr against the parliament and that 10,000 men is expected spedeley to be sent out of Ireland into Scotland and 10,000 men more out of France and 10,000 men more out of Denmarke; and that the Lord of Ormond shall sett from Dubline apone the 20th or 24th of this instant August towards the Lord of Insoquine (Inchiquin) and if he will not come in to his peace, I am afraid he will take such an army with him that without God's almightie providence he canot resist him, and Owin Roe O'Neall is to fall apone the Scottes whom he hath brought soe lowe alreadie that itt is to be feared he will overcome them without spetal and spedie ade from out of England." [N. VI., 13.]

The HOUSE OF LORDS.

1646, August 12.—Heads for a conference. (Printed in *Lords' Journals*, viii. 462.) [N. XIX., 191.]

Captain ROBERT CLARKE to WILLIAM LENTHALL.

1646, August 12. Helbrea, from aboard the *Swan Regis.*—Have heard from the Isle of Man that Lord Strange, the Earl of Derby's son, is gone over to Dublin, and that great store of English Papists do live in Douglas town who have license to go to mass there. [N. VI., 14.]

PETER DE BEAUVOIR and other inhabitants of GUERNSEY.

1646, August 15.—Testimonial in favour of Colonel Robert Russell, their Lieutenant-Governor. *Copy.* [N. XIV., 149.]

Captain RICHARD FORTESCUE to WILLIAM LENTHALL.

1646, August 16.—Enclosing the articles of the surrender of Pendennis Castle. [N. VI., 15.]

ORDINANCE.

1646, August 18.—To clear James Fawcett of his Delinquency. (Printed in *Lords' Journals*, ix. 46.) [N. XIX., 151.]

Statement of SIR JOHN TREVOR.

1646, August 18.—Complaining that he and his co-lessees had never received anything under their lease from the King of 12*d.* a chaldron payable to his Majesty for coals at Newcastle. [N. XIV., 150.]

The SCOTCH COMMISSIONERS.

1646, August 19.—Paper. "In answer to your paper of the 18th, . . . we desire to know if you have any power to agree with us upon a sum to be paid in present before the marching away of our forces, and for the future and at what times, in which case we are willing to concur. But if you have no power . . we cannot propose what is the least sum that can give satisfaction to be subjected to debate, yet are most willing and ready to confer with you in everything to give satisfaction to the desires of the . . House of Commons." (See *Commons' Journals*, iv. 649.) *Signed* "Jo. Cheislie." [N. XIX., 124.]

Articles for the surrender of FLINT CASTLE.

1646, August 20.—The castle to be surrendered on the 24th, the Governor officers and gentlemen to be allowed to go to their homes, and to have six months to make their peace with the Parliament, the common soldiers to march out with the honours of war and to go to their own homes without molestation, Colonel Mytton to use his best endeavours with the Parliament on behalf of Colonel Mostyn, the Governor, and Mr. John Mostyn. *Copy.* [N. XIV., 152.]

The NUNCIO and CONGREGATION OF THE CLERGY at Waterford to the SUPREME COUNCIL at Kilkenny.

1646, August 24.—Reiterating their objections to the peace and proposing propositions to be added thereto. (See Carte, *Life of Ormonde*, i. 579.) A *copy* from the original in the Carte papers. [N. XXI., 35.]

The State of the Accounts of the SCOTCH ARMY.

1646, August 27.—(Printed in *Commons' Journals*, iv. 654.) [N. XIX., 192.]

Articles between SIR THOMAS HOOPER and Captain FRANCIS LANGDON, Governor of Looe.

1646, August 28.—For the surrender of a shallop, called *The Castle of Pendennis.* [N. XIV., 153.]

The EARL OF WARWICK to WILLIAM LENTHALL.

1646, August 28.—Supporting the request of Colonel Robert Russell, his Lieutenant-Governor of Guernsey, for leave to come to England for three weeks on his private affairs. *Signed.* [N. VI., 16.]

Sir Thomas Fairfax to Major Rogers

1646, August 31.—Ordering him, in case Parliament order the great fort at Barnstaple to be slighted, to convey the arms and ammunition there to Bristol, unless Parliament should otherwise order, and then to rejoin his regiment with his men. *Copy.* [N. XIV., 172.]

Further Inducements to move a speedy answer to the [CHESHIRE] petition.

[1646, August.]—1. That the small County of Chester, since the beginning of the war, was necessitated to raise treble the number of forces it was able to pay or the neighbouring counties proportionately raised, whereby the County is in great arrears to the soldiers.

2. That the charge of the leaguer before Chester, being 19 weeks, was near 80,000*l.*, so that Sir William Brereton and the Deputy Lieutenants engaged themselves for great sums for provisions, which are yet unpaid.

3. That upon the reducing of Chester they were also forced to engage themselves in 18,000*l.* to satisfy the soldiers a month's pay, otherwise they would not have been restrained from plundering the City and County, of which there is near 80,000*l.* yet unpaid.

4. That then the reducing of the forces had been attempted but that many of the horse were ordered by the Committee of both Kingdoms into Wales and of the foot to the leaguer of Lichfield Close, whence they are all now returned and lie on free quarter expecting arrears and pay till they be reduced.

5. That some of the auxiliary forces yet unpaid of their month's pay promised at the reducing of Chester threaten to come and plunder the County for the same.

6. That the Excise is hitherto wholly obstructed and the people in a tumultuous manner have risen against the Commissioners and the soldiers express themselves against the Excise, so that there is little hope it can be set up till they are paid and reduced.

Subjoined are Extracts from several letters dated from July 23rd to August 1st showing the demands of the soldiers for their arrears, their mutinous behaviour and the miserable state of the county. [N. XII., 195.]

Lord Broghill to [the COMMITTEE FOR IRELAND] on behalf of the army in Munster.

[1646, August.]—The Lord President arrived about the 10th of July last with five thousand   hundred pounds part of the 6,000*l.* which by the order of this honourable Committee was to be disposed of to the officers and soldiers equally, but the said money will only be sufficient for about five weeks, 1,000*l.* having been spent on biscuit and salt to enable the army to march. Therefore the Committee will be pleased to ordain some constant supply of money and victual, a part to be sent without delay proportionable to the army you shall design for that service, otherwise that province is in great danger to be reduced to the power of the Rebels, since, First there is a peace concluded of late by the Earl of Ormonde, whereunto some of our party in that province and in other parts may adhere if some settled course be not taken for their livelihood, Secondly, the year being thus far spent, if supplies arrive not whilst the corn is in stack, which now begins to be reaped daily, the corn will not be gained from the Rebels without first gaining the Castles, under the shelter whereof they usually bring their corn, which will be hazardous tedious and chargeable, Thirdly, if there be not an army to keep the field and to leave the garrisons strongly defended the Rebels will deprive us of our markets and keep us within our towns, by which means they will be able to live on the corn within our quarters and to preserve their harvest, which otherwise we might destroy and thereby we shall be forced to expect every morsel of bread and other supplies out of England which otherwise we might in some reasonable proportion, if we had strength, gain from the Rebels, and if any accident happen by contrary winds or otherwise, whereby such supplies fail, the whole interest of the state there must fall into the hands of the Rebels unavoidably, Fourthly, The officers and soldiers there have endured such hardship and yet served valiantly and faithfully, expecting liberal supplies from hence, when this kingdom should be reduced, and now—they finding but little work remaining here to be done—it would be as well matter of great discouragement unto them as of joy to the Rebels, if we should not then find the fruit of such blessed effects here, and it is more than probable that the Rebels—who are exceeding heightened by their late successes—will apprehend their own danger, if they shall not suddenly bend all their power to destroy us before the forces and supplies which are designed shall arrive, and will propound to themselves the more strongly to set upon the work, which will be also the more facile, if forces speedily arrive not then, in respect that many of the Gentry and others who have during the Cessation stood at gaze, now the peace is there concluded will join with them heart and hand, whilst their armies are strong and ours weak, and if the footing we have there should be lost it would cost this kingdom more treasure and blood to regain the same than by the help of the footing we have already to subdue the Rebels; It is therefore humbly propounded that you will take into consideration the sad and dangerous condition of that part of the kingdom and hasten the supplies intended, which we humbly desire may be at least 5,000 foot and 1,500 horse for the present service, which is as little as may be for the preservation of the Parliament's interest there and preventing the annoyance which the Rebels might do to these kingdoms, considering the great numbers which the Rebels are able to bring into the field, they being at this time preparing an army of 20,000 for the subduing of the Parliament's forces in Munster—as appears by the depositions of divers who lately came out of Ireland—and considering also that many men are necessarily required to keep the towns and forts we hold,—and herein I desire that it may be understood that when the Parliament shall resolve of a thorough prosecution of that war there must of necessity be a far greater force of horse and foot and other warlike provisions transported there—and further that the Regiments already there may be speedily recruited, that there may an addition to the train of artillery and fitting carriages with ball, shells, and other necessaries, that a good proportion of powder be forthwith sent, the stores being already so exhausted by the field service and by the defence of Bunratty at the late siege—which was very strongly maintained—that very little remained in the Province at my coming away, that in respect of the great scarcity of iron there 20 tons may be presently sent thither, and that the former letters and propositions of Lord Inchiquin may be reviewed and such an answer given to what remains unanswered as to your Honours shall be thought fit. *Signed.* [N. XXI., 123.]

[The Scotch Commissioners] to [the House of Commons].

1646, September 1.—Paper. (This is made up of two parts, the first is answers to the four exceptions and the substance appears from the paper in Rushworth, iv. 1. 325, headed, "To these particulars the Scotch replied," where it is so put as to make it appear it was delivered before August 21st; the substance of the rest of the paper, with the exception herein-after mentioned, appears from the Scotch exceptions to the Parliament's estimate printed in Rushworth, iv. 1. 323, 324, 325.

The said exception is the following passage:—

"To the articles set doune in the debitor's side it is ansered that there is no such clause in the treaty as that the Scottish army should continne in England the numbers of 18,000 foote, 2,000 horse and 1,000 dragoones, but on the contrair the kingdome of England by the expresse words of the treaty is oblieged to pay towards their maintenance 30,000l. monethly, so long as it doth not amount to the full month's pay.

There is ommitted here about ten hundred thousand pounds which the committee residing with the Scottish army is able to make sufficiently appeare to be due by the kingdome of England.") In Sir John Cheislie's hand and signed by him. [N. XIV., 173.]

The Members of the HOUSE OF COMMONS who are members of the COMMITTEE OF BOTH KINGDOMS to the SCOTCH COMMISSIONERS.

1646, September 2.—Communicating in obedience to the vote of the House of Commons of that date the vote concerning the time and manner of payment of the 400,000l. (See *Commons' Journals*, iv. 660.) [N. XIX., 193.]

ORDINANCE.

1646, September 3.—Removing Dr. Baker from the vicarage of Southweald and appointing Nicholas Folkingham in his place. (See *Commons' Journals*, iv. 662.) [N. XIV., 174.]

The COMMITTEE FOR COMPOUNDING WITH DELINQUENTS.

1646, September 7. — Report concerning the composition of Mr. John Bellassis. (See *Commons' Journals*, iv. 687.) [N. XIV., 175.]

Paper of the SCOTCH COMMISSIONERS.

1646, September 10.—Stating that divers things having fallen into debate concerning the delivery of the garrisons and the marching of our forces out of the kingdom which were not foreseen when instructions were sent us, they were presently to send to the Committee of Estates for further instructions, and desiring that the sum to be presently advanced might be agreed on, and that the Houses would proceed to consider the rest of their paper of August 11th. *Signed* "Jo. Cheislie." [N. XIX., 194.]

The COMMITTEE OF BOTH KINGDOMS.

1646, September 11.—Report concerning Radnorshire forces. (Printed in *Commons' Journals*, iv. 686.) [N. XIV., 177.]

The COMMITTEE FOR THE ADMIRALTY AND CINQUE PORTS.

1646, September 17.—Order reporting to Parliament Sir George Ayscue's letter to them. *Enclosed:*

SIR GEORGE AYSCUE to the COMMITTEE.

1646, September 12. Aboard the *Expedition* in Carlisle Road.—
"In compliance to the Vice-Admiral's summons, the Governor of Sylly sent Commissioners to Falmouth to treat with such whom

he and Colonel Fortescue should appoint for the surrender of the place. Our first treaty proved not effectual in respect of the granting of their instructions, and therefore they desired to return to have them more enlarged. I consorted with the *Warwick*—who carried them to Sylly—and anchored in Crow Sound from the 30th of August till the Wednesday after, during which time I did employ my endeavours to ingratiate myself with the islanders which came aboard of me, by informing them of the Parliament's favourable intentions towards them who had been before deluded with reports that we intended to put [out] the old inhabitants, and to make a new plantation, but they were quickly undeceived and did afterwards believe so well of us that it proved much for our advantage. We are now agreed for the surrender of it, and this day the articles were signed by us. I have sent the *Constant Warwick* and the *Heart* to Sylly with one of their Commissioners to see the Governor sign. On Monday I intend to take Colonel Fortescue's soldiers aboard to transport them to Sylly and to take the surrender of it. I shall most humbly beseech your Honours to be mindful of the great advantage this place may be of, not only in securing merchant men but if you shall please to command serviceable frigates thither, there will not an Irishman be able to trade with France, besides the cleansing the Mouth of the Channel from the King's men of war, who, if they had well understood their advantage might have made that place a second Arger (Algiers), which the Lord Digby knew well, though too late " *Signed.* [N. XIV., 178.]

The COMMITTEE FOR THE ADMIRALTY AND CINQUE PORTS.

1646, September 24.—Report recommending that the *Kentish frigate* be restored to her former owner, Richard Shakerley. (See *Lords' Journals*, viii. 515.) [N. XIV., 180.]

The LORD LIEUTENANT and COUNCIL to the KING.

1646, September 26. Dublin Castle.—(Printed in *Lords' Journals*, viii. 528.) *Copy.* [N. XII., 215.]

The LORD LIEUTENANT and COUNCIL to SIR GERARD LOWTHER and others.

1646, September 26. Dublin. — Instructions. (Printed in *Lords' Journals*, viii. 523.) *Copy.* [N. XXI., 36.]

The LORD LIEUTENANT to the SAME.

1646, September 26 and 27.—Additional Instructions. (Printed in *Lords' Journals*, viii. 525.) *Copy.* [N. XXI., 37.]

The LORD LIEUTENANT and COUNCIL to the LORD MAYOR OF LONDON.

1646, September 26.—(Printed in *Lords' Journals*, viii. 527.) *Copy.* [N. XXI., 28.]

The EARL OF LOUDOUN and others to WILLIAM LENTHALL.

1646, September 28. Worcester House.—Supporting the enclosed petition of James Boswell, merchant, for repayment of the sums due to him for provisions sent to ireland amounting to 3,548*l.* The petition itself is enclosed. (See *Commons' Journals*, iv. 144.) *Signed.* |N. VI., 17.|

The Scotch Commissioners.

1646, September 29.—Paper desiring that 5,000*l.* which had been sent by the Treasurers at Goldsmiths' Hall to the Commissioners of both Houses then at Newcastle to be paid to the Scotch army, might be ordered to be delivered to the Treasurer of the Scotch Army, the Commissioners having left before the arrival of the 5,000*l.* *Signed* "Jo. Cheislie." [N. XIX., 195.]

The Same.

Same date.—Paper. (Printed in *Lords' Journals*, viii. 505.) *Copy.* [N. XIX., 196.]

Sir Robert King to the House of Commons.

[1646, October 1.]—Petition stating his services and losses and particularly the taking of his house at Boyle about August 1st 1646 by the Earl of St. Albans (Marquess of Clanrickard), and requesting that he might become tenant of the said Earl's estates at Summerhill and Barly in England at the rents mentioned in the Ordinance for the late Earl of Essex, and if these are otherwise disposed of that he may become tenant for 1,000*l. per annum* of Lord Capel's estate, and further showing that he became bound with Sir George Radcliffe in a bond for the penal sum of 1,600*l.* and desiring indemnity of Sir George Radcliffe's estate. *Signed.* [N. XXII., 145.]

The Commissioners from Ireland to the Governor and Deputy Lieutenants of Chester.

1646, October 3.—(Printed in *Lords' Journals*, viii. 526.) *Copy.* [N. XXI., 54.] A *copy* of the same with the note subjoined as printed above is N. XXI., 40.

The Committee for Ireland to the House of Commons.

1646, October 5 and 12.—Recommending that 21,000*l.* already taken out of the levy money for the pay of forces already in Ireland be supplied out of the receipts of Haberdashers' Hall and Goldsmiths' Hall. [N. XXI., 41.]

The Committee for Compounding with Delinquents.

[1646, October 8.]—Report concerning Lord Savile's composition. (See *Commons' Journals*, iv. 687.) *Enclosed:*

Order of December 30, 1645, concerning Mrs. Askwith. (Printed in *Lords' Journals*, viii. 75.) [N. XIV., 181.]

Order.

1646, October 12.—Appointing a Committee concerning the taking of the Covenant. (Printed in *Commons' Journals*, iv. 691.) [N. XIV., 182.]

Report.

1646, October 12.—Concerning Mr. Walter Kearle of Ross. (Printed in *Commons' Journals*, iv. 694.) [N. XIV., 183.]

The Assembly of Divines to the House of Commons.

[1646, October 13.]—Answer to the vote of October 9th. (Printed in Grey, iii. Appendix, No. 71, p. 120.) (See *Commons' Journals*, iv. 688, 692.) *Signed*. [N. XXII., 41.]

The Committee at Derby House to the House of Commons.

1646, October 14.—Report. (The effect appears from *Commons' Journals*, iv. 693.) [N. XXI., 39.]

The Committee for the Admiralty and Cinque Ports.

1646, October 15.—Report. (Printed in *Lords' Journals*, viii. 529.) [N. XIV., 184.]

Lieutenant John Freeman to the House of Commons.

[1646, October 15.]—Petition, stating that in February 1644, being in garrison at Burleigh, he had been sent with a party against some Cavaliers said to be at Okeham, and entering a suspected house had shot one John Halford, who was beginning to make resistance, of which wound he died, and that notwithstanding at the last Assizes he had been indicted for murder, and the grand jury had found a true bill against him for manslaughter, but the judge had admitted him to bail to appear at the next assizes, and praying the protection of the House

and

Order thereon.

(Printed in *Commons' Journals*, iv. 695.) [N. XXII., 95.]

John Osborne, Evers Armynne, and John Hatcher to Sir James Harrington.

[1646, October.]—Stating the facts of the charge against Lieutenant Freeman, and desiring him to move the House that the business might be referred to a Council of War. *Signed*. [N. XXII., 98.]

The Committee of both Kingdoms to the House of Commons.

1646, October 26.—Stating that Major Howorth and Captain Alderne, who were instrumental in surrendering Hereford, had been promised that two of the nearest allies of each of them should be freed from Delinquency and sequestration, and that they had accordingly named Roland Howorth, Charles Booth, Dr. Edward Alderne, and James Rodde. (See *Commons' Journals*, v. 113.) [N. XXII., 100.]

The Committee of both Kingdoms.

1646, October 26.—Report concerning Sir John Bridges, &c. (Printed in *Lords' Journals*, viii. 547.) [N. XIV., 186.]

Sir Thomas Fairfax to William Lenthall.

1646, October 26. The Devizes.—Concerning the disbanding of Major-General Massie's brigade, and recommending the officers and certain foreigners and reformadoes therein. (See *Commons' Journals*, iv. 728.) *Signed*. *Seal*. [N. VII., 113.]

Colonel Thomas Mytton to William Lenthall.

1646, October 28. Denbigh.—Sir William Middleton has been put into this castle as Governor according to your desire. *Signed*. [N. VI., 18.]

The LORDS to the COMMONS.

[1646, October (?).]—Message. They are of opinion upon the reading of the Lieutenant-Governor's letters to the Earl of Warwick, that since there is 400 men sent into Jersey it will be fit to send more force thither than the 1,200 men now desired for the reducement thereof, as also good store of powder match and bullet for the keeping of Guernsey and the recovery of Castle Cornett in that island, and that this may speedily be done, and that the House of Commons be desired to concur with the Lords for the speedy sending away Colonel Aldridge and the forces for the reducing of Jersey with him (See *Lords' Journals*, viii. 543.) [N. XV., 186.]

REPORT.

1646, November 2.—Showing what estates assigned for raising 6,000*l.* *per annum* for the Elector Palatine had since been otherwise disposed of. (Printed in Grey, iii. Appendix, No. 51, p. 78.) [N. XIV., 192.]

RESOLUTIONS.

1646, November 3.—Concerning persons within the Oxford Articles. (Printed in *Commons' Journals*, iv. 713.) *Appended :*

The COMMITTEE AT GOLDSMITHS' HALL to the COMMITTEE AT CHESTER.

1646, November 4.—Letter written on behalf of Orlando Bridgeman in pursuance of the second resolution. [N. XIV., 187.]

The COMMITTEE APPOINTED FOR RELIEF OF PERSONS MOLESTED for service done by the authority of Parliament.

1646, November 6.—Report advising that John Freeman be discharged from prosecutions at Common Law touching the death of John Halford. [N. XXII., 96.] *Enclosed :*

Depositions of ROBERT CANT, GEORGE REEVE, and JOHN CANT.

1646, August 6.—Describing the circumstances of the death of John Halford. *Copies.* [N. XXII., 97.]

ESTIMATE.

1646, November 17.—Of the charge for the Duke of York amounting to 7,580*l.* (See *Lords' Journals*, viii. 577 ; *Commons' Journals*, iv. 724.) [N. XIV., 188.]

The COMMITTEE CONCERNING THE SALE OF BISHOPS' LANDS.

1646, November 19.—Report. (Printed in *Commons' Journals*, iv. 725.) [N. XIV., 189.]

The Engagement of the MARQUESS OF CLANRICKARD.

1646, November 19.—"Upon the engagement and protestation of the General, nobility and officers of the Confederate Catholic forces hereunto annexed I . . bind and engage myself unto them by the reputation and hope of a peace and by the sacred protestation upon the faith of a Catholic in the presence of Almighty God that I will procure the ensuing undertakings to be made good unto them within such convenient time as securities of that nature which are to be fetched from beyond the seas can be well procured and at the furthest by the first of September next . . . or failing therein to unite myself to their party and never to sever from them and those therein interested till I have secured them unto you.

1. That there shall be a revocation by Act of Parliament of all the laws in force in this kingdom in as much as shall concern any penalty . . or restraint upon the Catholics for the free exercise of their religion.

2. That they shall not be disturbed in free enjoyment of their churches or any other ecclesiastical possessions which are in their hands at the publication of the late peace, until that matter . . . receive a settlement upon a declaration of his Majesty's gracious intentions in a free Parliament held in this kingdom, his Majesty being in a free condition himself.

3. I further engage myself never to consent to anything that may bring them in hazard of being dispossessed and never to sever from them till I free [? *sic*] them so secured therein either by concessions or by their trust and honour from his Majesty in the armies and garrisons of this kingdom, or to put them out of all danger of being dispossessed of them.

4. And further, that forthwith there shall be a Catholic Lieutenant-General of all the forces of the kingdom invested by his Majesty's authority, that the Generals or either of them signing to the said engagement shall be forthwith invested by his Majesty's authority with principal commands worthy of them in the standing armies of this kingdom and likewise in some important garrisons now under his Majesty's obedience, and that a considerable number of the Confederate Catholic army shall immediately be drawn into all the chief garrisons under his Majesty's obedience, and I further assure proportionable advantages to such of any other armies in this kingdom as shall in like manner submit unto the peace and his Majesty's authority.

5. That for the security of so many of these particulars as shall not be performed . . . by the Marquess of Ormonde . . I will procure them the King's hand, the Queen and Prince of Wales' engagement and an engagement of the Crown of France to see the same performed.

. . .

6. And further . . . that the Lord Lieutenant shall engage himself punctually to observe such free commands as he shall receive from his Majesty to the advantage of the Catholics of this kingdom, or during the King's want of freedom from the Queen and Prince of Wales or such as shall be signified unto him to the same effect to be the King's pleasure by the Lord Digby as principal Secretary of State, and further that while the King shall be in an unfreed condition he will not obey any orders that shall be procured from his Majesty by advantage of his . . want of freedom to the prejudice of what is undertaken.

7. . . . I shall never esteem myself discharged from this engagement by any power or authority whatsoever, provided that " it " be not understood . . to debar . . . his Majesty's Catholic subjects of this kingdom from the benefit of any other . . . favours his Majesty may be . . induced to concede to them upon the Queen's mediation . . or any other treaty abroad with his Holiness. And I further engage myself to employ my utmost endeavours . . to his Majesty to afford all the subjects of this kingdom that shall appear to have been injured in their estates redress in the next free Parliament.

8. I further undertake that all persons joining . . . in the present engagement shall be included in the Act of Oblivion promised in

. . the peace of every act done by them since the publication of the said peace unto the date of this engagement." *Copy.* [N. XXI., 42.]

The Committee appointed to confer with the Scotch Commissioners.

1646, November 26.—Report. (Printed in *Commons' Journals*, iv. 729.) [N. XIV., 190.]

Resolution.

1646, November 26.—Concerning the Earls of Northumberland and Pembroke. (Printed in *Lords' Journals*, viii. 578.) [N. XIV., 191.]

The Lords and Commons that are of the Committee of both Kingdoms to the Scotch Commissioners.

1646, December 1.—Two papers. (Both printed in *Lords' Journals*, viii. 592, and there described as "first paper" and paper explanatory of the first paper.) *Copies.* [N. XIX., 197.]

The Committee for Ireland to the House of Commons.

1646, December 2.—Report recommending that the officers therein named and all others belonging to the armies of Ulster, Munster, and Connaught then in England be dispatched away forthwith. [N. XXI., 43.]

The Scotch Commissioners to the Lords and Commons that are of the Committee of both Kingdoms.

[1646, December 3.]—(Printed in *Lords' Journals*, viii. 593, and there described as "Scots Second Paper.") [N. XIX., 38.]

The Committee for the Admiralty and Cinque Ports.

1646, December 3.—Two Reports (both printed in *Lords' Journals*, viii. 605), and account tendered by Mr. Johnson and Mr. Knight, which is referred to in the Second Report. [N. XIV., 193, 194, 196.]

The House of Commons.

1646, December 4.—Orders concerning obstructions to the Army Assessments and the Excise in Lincolnshire. (Printed in *Commons' Journals*, iv. 738.) [N. XIV., 197.]

The Committee of Complaints.

1646, Tuesday, December [8 or 15].—Resolution reporting to the House the enclosed petition and certificate. [N. XXII., 92.] *Enclosed :*

    i. Lord Abergavenny, Lord Stourton, Edmond Thorold, William Thorold, and John Paston on behalf of themselves and other Catholics residing in Oxford at its surrender to the Committee for Breach of Articles.

Petition, stating that they, conceiving themselves to be within the 11th Article, applied to the Commissioners at Goldsmiths' Hall for leave to compound, which they refused, because the House of Commons had given them no direction to compound with persons under the notion of Recusants, that they have since represented their condition to the House of Commons but as yet without success, and that taking notice of the late order to imprison persons that have been in any of the King's garrisons and have not prosecuted their Compositions with effect, and the late ordinance commanding all such persons to depart the Lines of Communication before the 18th of December they are likely to be imprisoned and suffer other inconveniences, and praying that some speedy course might be taken for admitting them to compound, and granting them protection in the mean time. *Signed.*

ii. HENRY IRETON, JOHN LAMBERT, THOMAS HARRISON and NATHANIEL RICH.

1646, November 30.—Certificate that they, being Commissioners on the part of Sir Thomas Fairfax in the treaty for the surrender of Oxford, declare that it was not intended that Papists or Popish Recusants then in Oxford should be excluded from the 11th or other articles of the said treaty. *Signed.* [N. XXII., 93, 94.]

Report of ARTHUR ANNESLEY, SIR ADAM LOFTUS, SIR WILLIAM PARSONS, SIR JOHN TEMPLE, and SIR HARDRESS WALLER.

1646, December 10.—" First as to the general, the Province of Leinster . . . is totally in the hands of the Irish and such as stand in opposition to the Parliament.

The Province of Connaught . . . is all in the power of the Irish except the town and fort of Sligo with 5 or 6 other Castles . . in the North. . . That county guarded with about 600 horse and 1,400 foot. . . .

For the Province of Munster the Parliament hath only therein the City of Cork and the towns of Kinsale Youghal and Bandon and a part of the County of Cork limited and in a manner guarded with these four strengths, the extent whereof is not above 30 miles in length and 20 . . in breadth, and much wasted and impoverished with the rebellion. All the rest of that large province . . . is all under the power of the Irish. . .

For the Province of Ulster the Parliament yet hath the command of all the maritime parts round about it, which is of great circuit. They have therein the City of Derry, the towns of Knockfergus, Belfast and Coleraine, the forts of Iniskillen and Culmore and several other small strengths on the seaside. This province consisteth of nine large counties in part of five whereof do inhabit such British as yet adhere to the Parliament. All the rest are utterly wasted, or in part, wherein viz. in part of Cavan and Monaghan many of the Irish do yet rest. The Irish have the Castles of Charlemount Dungannon and Montjoy, and those others now in opposition to the Parliament have the Newry and Greencastle, so as the most part of this Province may be said to be under the command of the Parliament, but of no benefit or advantage to them except the residence and some poor relief for their forces there, and the bare habitation of the few British above mentioned.

Touching the state of the Irish in general they have now under their power in a manner all the artillery of the kingdom except what is in Ulster and some in Munster. They have their men in a better order of war and better commanded by captains of experience and practice of war, than ever they were since the Conquest and these much emboldened by late successes, as well in the field as against fortresses. They are abundantly stored with arms and munition and have many good ports and harbours ready to import more and have all the horses in the kingdom both for service and carriage except what the Parliament have in Ulster, Connaught, and Munster.

Many of their bodies for service are well trained and manned and these well armed; the relations of the numbers of their armed men much vary, but the best estimate . . makes 20,000 foot and   horse, though certainly they have besides great numbers of horse and foot appointed to their ill ends. . .   The others now in opposition to the Parliament have about 2,000 foot and 500 horse.   The Parliament have yet in Ulster 17 regiments of foot containing about 8,000 men, whereof of the Scotch army intermixt with the inhabitants 3,500, and of the old British 5,000 or thereabouts, and 17 troops of horse about 50 in a troop, and in Munster about 4,000 and 300 marching horse.

. . .   For the preservation of such parties and places as are yet in the power of the Parliament . .   and to make further progress . . it is humbly offered as follows :—

First . . .   that the safety of their parties and places in Munster be first taken into care; and to that end that the Lord Lieutenant now residing here be with all convenient speed despatched thither . .   and carry with him the 3 regiments of horse and 4 regiments of foot already designed and may be made ready to be with him transported.

Secondly, whereas there is 30,000l. in pieces of eight at 5s. a piece in readiness to be sent with his Lordship, and some quantities of . . victuals arms and munition to be taken up upon the late ordinance of Excise ; . . .   that those provisions are so far short of what may be requisite to maintain the forces already there . .   and those now to be transported, as it is not be expected that they can subsist thereby but a very small time, specially the small territory about them being very much impoverished, and subject to daily inroads.

Thirdly . .   that the Parliament will . .   ordain a present monthly provision for support of those forces, and that some design-ment of money may be made for fortifying towns and places and for intelligence and extraordinaries.

And lastly . . .   that competent numbers of ships of force, whereof the most part to be of lesser burthens, may be designed to attend their ports there, as well for countenance and to beat off enemies' attempts as to be employed upon occasions and emergencies.

These things being thus provided . .   it is probably hoped that the parties and places in Munster yet under the command of the Parliament will be secured against the imminent danger which may happen through the discontent of our own soldiers and the now insolent forces of the Irish.

In the last place to provide for carrying on a war vigorously . . . against the bloody Rebels there and for regaining that whole kingdom into a just subjection to the Crown of England, in respect no part of Leinster at present stands for the Parliament, It is conceived . . . absolutely necessary to reflect also upon the present condition of . . . Ulster and Connaught and therein so to dispose (?) the said forces yet there as may preserve them from further distempers, and as far as may be . .   advance the service, which may be by furnishing some quantities of . . .   victual and a proportion of money to be sent to them in Ulster and Connaught . . .   and specially for Ulster, in regard the forces in Ulster seem now distracted under different com-mands, and so not so apt to be put into service nor to join to the requisite advantage thereof. . .   it will be fit a course be forthwith taken that they may be reduced into one command subject to the Lord Lieutenant ; and in order towards a full reducement it must further be

considered what additional forces are fit to be sent in due times into
the several Provinces of Munster Ulster and Connaught for enabling
the armies to march altogether at a due season, that so distracting and
disabling the Irish they may be distressed from several parts at one
time, in which . . principal care must be taken to impoverish and
destroy the several countries out of which they gather their subsistence,
and so frustrate them of maintaining considerable bodies to give
encounters." *Copy* by Nalson. *Torn and illegible in parts.*
[N. XXI., 44.]

ORDER.

1646, December 10.—Concerning Lord Grey of Warke. (Printed in
Lords' Journals, viii. 600.) [N. XIV., 198.]

ROBERT HUNT to the HOUSE OF COMMONS.

1646, December 11.—Petition. (The purport sufficiently appears
from the order thereon, printed in *Commons' Journals,* v. 10.) [N.
XXII., 90.]

The SCOTCH COMMISSIONERS.

[1646, December 12.]—Paper. We have considered the reasons for
the Houses adhering to their former vote touching the public faith to
be given for security of the last 200,000*l.* to be paid to the Kingdom
of Scotland, and must still insist that we may have the security agreed
upon by the treaty between the Kingdoms or some other particular
security. It is well known to the Houses how many and great the
troubles and sufferings of Scotland have been for these seven or eight
years past, and that within these two years by a cruel and barbarous
war divers counties have been wholly wasted and the rest of that
kingdom extremely exhausted and impoverished by the maintenance of
armies against the Irish Rebels and their Associates in Scotland. We
likewise desire the Houses to consider how great a proportion of the
Brotherly Assistance remains unpaid for those four or five years past
whereby the credit of some private persons of Scotland who were
assigned to that money, after long attendance here for satisfaction is
almost ruined and wholly extinguished.

There are other persons who out of their zeal for the cause adventured
their whole estates, and furnished arms ammunition and provisions
upon the coming of the Scotch Army into this Kingdom, and afterwards for six or seven months towards their entertainment, the country
being then in the enemies' power.

We have been often advertised from Scotland that the burdens of
those persons are still so great, as, if they be not supplied out of the
moneys due by this kingdom they will be suddenly ruined. And we
have received frequent directions to provide carefully for their relief
out of those moneys in such a certain way as they may depend upon
and may prevent their ruin. And seeing we know by experience both
in Scotland and here that none of their creditors will trust them upon
a general security,-unless they be ascertained in a particular way, we
most earnestly entreat that since we have made so good a progress in
other things, we may also berein receive such satisfaction, as we may
be enabled to give an account thereof to the Parliament of Scotland.

And whereas, whilst all garrisons here are reduced, and the forces of
the enemy subdued, Scotland is invaded and infested for their engagement with this kingdom by forces from Ireland, which with the
assistance of their Malignant associates in Scotland keep the hills,
possess garrisons, and abide in the fields expecting also further

assistance from Ireland, and seeing England is bound by the Large Treaty to prevent and by force to suppress all invasion of Scotland by the subjects of England or Ireland, it is earnestly desired and expected that the Houses will either according to the said Treaty pursue take and punish the offenders with all rigour, or give such a constant monthly supply and assistance for the forces that shall be continued on foot in Scotland upon return of our army, as may speedily reduce those rebels to obedience or drive them out of that kingdom without which it is to be feared they may grow to such a strength as to invade this kingdom. Wherein we are very confident England will out of their brotherly affection and sympathy of the troubles of their brethren of Scotland, and in order to the security and peace of this kingdom return so satisfactory an answer as may further witness their real intentions to preserve a happy union and firm correspondence betwixt the kingdoms.

Concerning your Lordships' desire that the Scotch army after receipt of their money may pay their quarters upon their removes and marches we have no power in that particular from the Army, and can say nothing therein, until they be acquainted. But as to your Lordships' desire touching the preservation and ease of the country in the passage of our army we are warranted to declare in the name of the general officers of the army that they shall have a very special care of the preservation of the country from any abuses or disorders of the soldiers in their passage and march out of the kingdom. (See *Commons' Journals*, v. 12, 18.) [N. XIX., 133.]

Sir Thomas Fairfax to William Lenthall.

1646, December 12.—Supporting the enclosed petition. *Signed. Seal. Enclosed:*

The said Petition of Twelve Gunners.

Asking to be appointed to the 12 vacant Feemen or Gunners' places in the Tower. [N. VI., 19.]

The Committee of the Army.

1646, December 14, and 23, 1646[-7], January 5.—Report concerning the charges against Colonel King, and his conduct. (See *Commons' Journals*, v. 46.) [N. XIV., 199.]

Report of Mr. Holles and Order thereon.

1646, December 16.—Concerning contractors. (Printed in *Commons' Journals*, v. 15.) [N. XIV., 200.]

The Scotch Commissioners.

[1646, December 17.]—Paper. Desiring alterations in the Articles of Agreement as printed in *Commons' Journals*, v. 13, namely, in the 1st Article to omit all after the words " by virtue of the said treaties," and in the 15th to substitute for " and that Berwick and Carlisle be slighted according to the large Treaty and not otherwise," " And that the works of Berwick and Carlisle be slighted, and the places dismantled, so as all monuments tokens and shows of hostility be taken away, according as is especially provided and agreed to between the two kingdoms by the articles of the large Treaty," and to add at the end " And likewise the Parliament of Scotland or any by them authorized are to appoint such persons, as they shall think fit to see this performed," and stating that they expected before this the answer of their paper delivered on

Saturday (*ante*, p. 401) and earnestly entreating that the Treaty may without further delay be brought to a speedy close. (See *Commons' Journals*, v. 18.) [N. XIX., 198.]

RESOLUTION.

1646, December 22.—Concerning the King's coming to Newmarket. (Printed in *Lords' Journals*, viii. 622, and Peck, *Desiderata Curiosa*, ix. 30.) [N. XIV., 201.]

Examinations of THOMAS DOUSE, Clerk to the Committee of Lincoln, and Colonel KING.

1646, December 23.—Concerning Colonel King. [N. XIV., 202, 210.]

SIR WILLIAM ARMYNE to WILLIAM LENTHALL.

1646, December 23.—Stating that the Earl of Leven had a quantity of arms at Newcastle, which he was willing to sell if the Parliament pleased to make use of them. *Seal.* [N. VI., 21.]

M. DU MOLIN to M. DE SABRAN.

1646, December 28. Dublin.—Recommending the bearer, Mr. Peter, uncle of Lord Peter, who is employing himself in some affairs important for the service of our Master. In *French*. *Signed*. [N. XVII., 8.]

NICHOLAS, BISHOP OF FERNS.

1646, December 31. The Friars' Monastery.—Order that the body of Francis Talbot, who died an obstinate heretic, be buried *in paenam hereseos et impenitentiæ nec non in terrorem aliquem* with only one candle at his grave at nine of the clock by night, without a bell in the church or street, without priest, cross, book, or prayer. Any person exceeding this manner of burial to incur Church censures. No wax taper or candle nor torch to be used. *Copy. Partly illegible.* [N. XXI., 45.]

The LORDS and COMMONS that are of the COMMITTEE OF BOTH KINGDOMS.

1646, December 31.—Order reporting the Articles of agreement and the Instructions for the Committee that are to go to the North. (See *Commons' Journals*, v. 36.) [N. XIX., 199.]

VOTE.

1646, December 31.—Concerning the King's coming to Holdenby. (Printed in *Lords' Journals*, viii. 628, and Peck, *Desiderata Curiosa*, ix. 30.) [N. XIV., 203.]

FRANCIS SYMPSON to WILLIAM LENTHALL.

1646, December 31.—Enclosing his petition to the House. *Signed Seal. Enclosed:*

The said petition, praying that in continuation of the force of the *Habeas Corpus* formerly granted he might be brought to the Bar, and receive his discharge. (See *Commons' Journals*, v. 5, 11.) [N. VI., 20.]

The Coᴍᴍɪᴛᴛᴇᴇ ꜰᴏʀ ᴛʜᴇ Aᴅᴍɪʀᴀʟᴛʏ ᴀɴᴅ Cɪɴǫᴜᴇ Pᴏʀᴛs.

1646, December 31.—Report. (Printed in *Lords' Journals*, viii. 672.) [N. XIV., 204.]

Colonel Thoᴍᴀs Oɢʟᴇ to [Sᴇʀᴊᴇᴀɴᴛ Wɪʟᴅᴇ ?].

[1646 end or beginning of 1647 (?).] (See *Lords' Journals*, viii. 571, ix. 111; *Commons' Journals*, v. 18.)—"My father[-in-law]'s importunity and my wife's sickness makes mė write . . . to you, before I can end the whole narration I intend. The sum is I had no plot, I know no plot, save that, because I was oppressed and hopeless of relief by the Parliament for my father[-in-law], [and] have spent so much in following the Parliament that we had neither meaus, meat, nor money left us, I petitioned to the King, and that it might take effect I mentioned that I would publish a declaration of the injustice [that] had been done me this Parliament by some men in action against the King, and come to Oxford to serve his Majesty with my life and estate bringing as many with me as I could, if his Majesty would do justice to us, and punish our oppressors and send me under his hand these . . . propositions following:

1. That he would maintain the Protestant religion, and never grant toleration of Popery, or dispense with the laws against Papists but by advice of Parliament.
2. That he would grant either an Act of Oblivion for what was past, or suffer the parties accused on both sides to be tried legally, as stood with privileges of Parliament.
3. That he would release all who have been oppressed, and particularly my father[-in-law] Smart, and punish our oppressors.
4. That he would never break the Acts of this Parliament, but govern by the laws, and not suffer the Queen to have any more priests or papists about her than the Articles of marriage allow.

This being given me for my satisfaction and relieved by his Majesty's justice, I hold myself and all others bound in conscience to serve him.

This is all the plot I know. For the money I was to have for my land, I would have paid my debts with [some], left some with my wife and children, and with the rest furnished myself and that company I could get to have gone with me to the King in as good equipage as I could . . . For any design upon the Parliament, City, or any particular member thereof, I protest I know of none.

So as, if it be treason to petition the King when the Parliament fails us, and to serve him upon his doing justice and to sell land to enable me the better to serve him I am a traitor. My former course of life, my service this Parliament may evidence sufficiently my love and constant zeal to religion and laws. This is all, and, when the larger is done, you shall have it. In the meantime, if that will procure me my liberty for the comfort of my father[-in-law] wife and children I have the less cause to complain; if not I am confident my usage will do my enemies more harm in the conclusion than me." *Signed. Endorsed:* "Delivered by Serjeant Wilde." [N. XII., 250*b*.]

The Coᴍᴍɪᴛᴛᴇᴇ ꜰᴏʀ Iʀᴇʟᴀɴᴅ to the Hᴏᴜsᴇ ᴏꜰ Coᴍᴍᴏɴs.

1646[-7], January 1.—Recommending certain persons as Privy Councillors. (The names are in *Commons' Journals*, v. 40.) [N. XXI., 47.]

The Earl of Lauderdale and others to the Speaker of the House of Peers *pro tempore.*

1646-7, January 2.—Enclosing a paper and letter from the Earl of Leven. (See *Lords' Journals,* viii. 641.) *Signed.* [N. VI., end.]

The Committee for the Northern Association.

1646[-7], January 2.—Report concerning Elizabeth Butler. (See *Commons' Journals,* v. 53.) [N. XIV., 205.]

Examination of Tobias Peaker.

1646[-7], January 7.—(Printed in *Lords' Journals,* viii. 665, and Peck, *Desiderata Curiosa,* ix. 31.) [N. XIV., 206.]

The Earl of Lauderdale and others to William Lenthall.

1646-7, January 9. Worcester House.—Asking that Lord Castle Stewart's petition might be considered to the end that some course might be taken to afford him the means of livelihood. *Signed. Seal.* [N. VI., 24.]

Hugh Morrell to William Lenthall.

1646[-7], January 11. Dover.—After a reference to a former letter concerning "a double malladie to this Commonweale, the one bv the unjust exportation of our woolls, and the other by a late most dangerous creeping-in corruption by forraine coyne"—"Who is ignorant of the greate decaies to our Marchants in their trading, of their many stopps—yeares together—through the false deceitpt of the manefactures in our king-dome. What is that Crowne Scale—though well intended—but became a meere approveinge of the shameles thefts of our nation. How comes it to passe that the Hollander and the French have soe exceedingly increased in their clothing of late yeares but through the deceitfullnes of ours—and partly through our exchange going so heigh : but of that more heereafter—, I doubt but this will bee confest to bee a desperate malladie and a cure for the same would bee very acceptable, which without presumtion I doubt not but to present unto your Honnours' hands though for doeing thereof I shalbee inforced to an unwillinge length.

Itt is now neere eight yeares past, that I presented an instrument to his Majestic under the Broad Seale of England in which much labour, care and paines was taken to settle a government in our manefactures. His highnes approved of the overtures I made then unto him concerninge the same, appointed a second commission of thirtie of the most expe-rienced marchants of London to consider thereof. They spent eighteene monthes in a weekely debate, consultacion and examinacion of many principall clotherers of the kingdome, and at length concluded on a report seigned under all our hands to bee presented unto this honnourable house of Commons, by the hands of Mr. Cradocke who was then chosen one of the burgesses for the cittie of London. Which instrument with the booke of our weekely transacctions and examinations will bee worthie of their vewe and much conduce to the publike good of the kingdome. Whether the hounourable house of Commons may not thinke good to reconfirme this commission of marchants or councell for trade to prepare matters of that nature fitt for them, thoire experience, knowledge and practice in most Christian kingdomes being capable for the same, to whome overtures will bee more freely presented—tendinge to the publike good—then they dare presume to doe to the parliament, and unto how many queries may bee proposed to consult on for the improveinge of commers, viz. :—

Queries—1. Why may not this kingdome beeing soe well situated, blest with soe many fitt and convenient harbours, bee made the magazine of Christendome, and how.

2. May not the establishing of a banke in the cittie of London—as is at Amsterdam—bee a good meanes to improve trade, and what course to effect the same.

3. What expedient may there bee found out for reduceinge marchants' course of exchange to a more equall ballance, because—as now—itt makes the French and Hollander undermine us in clothinge, and undersell us, which in tyme may bee the ruine of this kingdome.

4. May it not greatly quicken our exportacion and importacion to take of the greater part of the burdens on our manefactures, how may it bee done for the kingdome's most good and incouragement for trade.

5. Whether to take off customes from woulles imported from forraine kingdomes may not bee good for our kingdome, how farre it may and when not.

6. Whether the establishing of a marchants' courte, as in France, Spaine and Holland to deside matters and judge of accountts, bills of exchange, charterparties, contracts, bartars, buyings, selling betwixt them, or any matters of that nature amongst any other of the subjects of the kingdome, may not bee a greate improveinge of trade, preserve our marchants and others from ruine by longe law suites to inlarge ther opinions and reasons on this, in all particulers; as alsoe in case of appeale to any higher court, or on what penalltie or above what some it may bee fitt to appeale.

7. Whether if permission were given to marchants and others for transporting their billes of debt in buying other goods may not greatly improve trade throughout the kingdome, what order and for[m] may bee observed in this.

To the severall commissioners which are at Benboe's office concerninge the true makeinge of the manufac[tures] of our kingdome and trade bee considered by this committee of marchants or councell for trade and their report on a serious consultacion to bee reported to the parliament   The premises is most humbly submitted to your grave wisedomes." *Signed. Seal.* [N. VI., 22.]

The COMMITTEE FOR THE ADMIRALTY AND CINQUE PORTS.

1646[-7], January 12.—Paper concerning Sir George Asene. (Printed in *Lords' Journals*, viii. 672.) [N. XIX., 200.]

The COMMITTEE FOR IRELAND.

1646[-7], January 13.—Report. (See *Commons' Journals*, v. 150.) [N. XIV., 207.]

Colonel THOMAS MYTTON to WILLIAM LENTHALL.

1646[-7], January 13. Wrexham.—" After a twelvemonths' siege and a tedious treaty with the Governor of Holt Castle it is to be surrendered." My soldiers are much in arrear and out of employment and desire to be disposed of for the service of Ireland, or money be provided to disband. *Signed. Seal. Enclosed:*

A copy of the Articles of Surrender of the same date. [N. VI., 26.]

The EARL OF LEVEN.

1646[-7], January 18. Newcastle.—Order forbidding any cause of offence to be given to Major-General Skippon's party or convoy, but ordering his army to behave towards them as becometh brethren, and also strictly forbidding any to plunder or demand money. (This is the order referred to in his letter printed in *Lords' Journals,* viii. 702.) *Copy.* [N. XX. 5.]

Information of Captain JAMES WADSWORTH.

1646[-7], January 19.—Touching Popish reliques at Christchurch and Corpus Oxford, and elsewhere. (Printed in Peck, *Desiderata Curiosa,* ix. 33.) [N. XIV., 208.]

The STANDING COMMITTEE OF NORTHUMBERLAND.

1646[-7], January 20.—Certificate concerning the musters of their proportion of horse and foot at the dates and places specified. [N. XIV., 119.]

JOHN DRUMMOND to the TREASURERS OF THE MONEY TO ARISE FROM THE SALE OF BISHOPS' LANDS.

1646[-7], January 21 and February 3.—Two acquittances for 100,000*l.* each. (Printed in Peck, *Desiderata Curiosa,* ix. 36, 37, and in *Commons' Journals,* v. 87.) *Signed.* [N. XXIII., 36.]

Notes of the Proceedings against Colonel KING.

1646[-7], January 25.—[N. XIV., 211.]

The HOUSE OF COMMONS.

1646[-7], January 28.—Order concerning the pay of the Scotch army in Ireland. (Printed in *Commons' Journals,* v. 68.) [N. XXI., 48.]

Major-General PHILIP SKIPPON to WILLIAM LENTHALL.

1646[-7], January 31.—(Identical *mutatis mutandis* with the letter to the Speaker of the House of Peers, printed in *Lords' Journals,* viii. 700.) *Signed, Seal.* [N. VI., 27.]

SIR WILLIAM PARSONS and others.

1646[-7], February 2.—Certificates in favour of Sir Gerard Lowther and Sir Paul Davies. *Signed. Almost illegible.* [N. XXI., 51.]

SIR GERARD LOWTHER, SIR FRANCIS WILLOUGHBY, and SIR PAUL DAVIES.

[1646-7, February.]—Petition, apparently setting forth their services and their losses from the Rebels and desiring relief. *Mostly illegible. Signed.* [N. XXI., 47.]

The COMMITTEE FOR THE ADMIRALTY AND CINQUE PORTS.

1646[-7], February 2.—Report recommending Captain Crowther to command the *Bonadventure.* (Printed in *Lords' Journals,* viii. 705.) [N. XIV., 212.]

The COMMITTEE FOR THE ADMIRALTY AND CINQUE PORTS.

1646[-7], February 4.—Report of a letter from Captain Willoughby, enclosing an intercepted letter from Dublin to M. Le Tillier. (See *Commons' Journals,* v. 77.) [N. XIV., 213.]

The COMMITTEE OF THE REVENUE.

1647[-7], February 4.—Report concerning the establishment for the King at Holdenby. (Printed in Peck, *Desiderata Curiosa,* ix. 35.) [N. XIV., 216.]

The COMMITTEE OF THE REVENUE.

1646[-7], February 5.—Report concerning the Altar plate at White-hall, certain Bills of Exchange, and an estimate of the expenses of the King and his retinue. (Printed in Peck, *Desiderata Curiosa,* ix. 37. [N. XIV., 214.]

The SAME.

Same date.—Memoir concerning the Bills of Exchange returned from the Commissioners sent to the King. (See *Lords' Journals,* viii. 709.) [N. XIV., 215.]

WILLIAM LENTHALL to the COMMISSIONERS WITH THE KING.

[1646-7, February 6.]—(The purport sufficiently appears from the votes in *Commons' Journals,* v. 77.) *Draft* or *Copy.* [N. XII., 221.]

The COMMITTEE OF THE WESTERN ASSOCIATED COUNTIES.

1646[-7], February 11.—Report concerning Mr. William Boreman. (See *Commons' Journals,* v. 275.) [N. XIV., 217.]

Demands by the SWEDISH AMBASSADORS and those of the ELECTOR PALATINE.

[1646-7, February.]—(The substance appears by the next entry but one.) In *Latin.* [N. XVIII., 28.]

The Articles presented by the IMPERIAL to the SWEDISH PLENIPOTENTIARIES.

[1646-7, February.]—Though the Palatine question was excluded from the Edict of Amnesty and the treaty of Prague, yet since the peace of the Empire cannot be secure unless this controversy be settled without further dèlay, it is decided and agreed:

First, that the Electoral Dignity remain with the Duke of Bavaria and all the Guilhelmian line, as he has hitherto enjoyed it.

Second, that the whole of the Upper Palatinate remain and belong to the said Elector and all his descendants of the Guilhelmian line, in full discharge of the debt of 13 millions for which Upper Austria was pledged to the said Elector by the Emperor Ferdinand II. for which the said Elector shall execute a release.

Third, that on Charles Louis, the Count Palatine, rendering due obedience to the Emperor, he be equally admitted to the Electoral

Dignity but in the eighth and last place, but without any derogation from the rights of the Elector of Bavaria.

Fourth, that on his rendering due obedience as aforesaid, the Lower Palatinate be restored to him, without prejudice however to the feuds granted by the Emperor or the Elector of Bavaria, and on condition that the exercise of the Catholic religion established there be not interfered with and in particular that certain named monasteries should not be molested : and that the free nobles of the Empire in Franconia, Suabia, and the Rhine circle be left in their present state, and lastly that as the Bergstrasse was not formerly parcel of the Palatinate, but belonged to the Archbishop and Elector of Mainz, and was pawned in 1463 to the Palatines, subject to an express right of redemption, it, as it was restored by Ferdinand II. after the proscription of the Palatine Frederie to the Elector of Mainz, shall remain to his successors and the Archbishopric of Mainz, on condition of their repaying the sum for which it was pawned.

Fifth, that Charles Louis and his brothers for himself and his heirs whatsoever who shall succeed him in the Lower Palatinate shall renounce all claims to the Upper Palatinate while there continue legitimate heirs male of the Guilhelmian line. But if that line should fail, and there should be legitimate heirs male of the Palatine line surviving, the Electoral dignity held by the Duke of Bavaria shall revert to them, the eighth Electorate being abolished and the number of seven restored, and likewise the Upper Palatinate.

The Counter Proposals of THE SWEDISH PLENIPOTENTIARIES.

[1646-7, February.]—First, that there should be included in the Amnesty contained in this present treaty of peace the whole Palatine House, and all its adherents, who shall all be restored to the position they held before the outbreak of the Bohemian war. That the Palatine Electoral House, and the Elector Charles Louis and his brothers be restored as regards their former dignities, privileges, properties and rights, which belonged to the said House in 1618, and be in the same position and rights as the other Electors and Princes of the Empire both in sacred and profane matters, and enjoy the religious peace and whatsoever rights the other Evangelicals enjoy, Provided that the Electoral Dignity with all its rights shall continue to be held by Maximilian, Duke of Bavaria, for his life as he now holds it. Further as it has seemed good to his Imperial Majesty and the Diet of the Empire that an eighth Elector be added to the Electoral College, this Electorate shall be held by the Successors of Maximilian and his descendants of the Guilhelmian line, on whose extinction the eighth Electorate shall be suppressed, and the number of seven Electors, fixed by the Golden Bull, continue.

Secondly, the Elector Charles Louis, restored to his dignities and property, subject as is hereinbefore and hereinafter mentioned, shall bind himself to his Imperial Majesty by the same oath as the other Electors and Princes of the Empire, and on the death of Maximilian shall recover his former place of Electoral Dignity with all its rights and transmit it to his successors, yet so that during the life of Maximilian he shall equally enjoy the rights and prerogatives derived from the Electoral Dignity.

Third, that the whole of the Lower Palatinate be restored to the Elector Charles Louis and the Palatine House with all its appurtenances and the Bergstrasse, as well in Ecclesiastical as secular matters, all dispositions, grants of feuds &c. to the contrary notwithstanding. To this not only is the Emperor to pledge himself, both for himself and the King of Spain, but all others who claim any rights or interests are to declare their consent.

Fourth, that in like manner the Upper Palatinate be restored to the Palatine House except the Lordship of Cham up to the river Regen, which is to be left to the House of Bavaria on condition that it may be redeemed within an unlimited time for a fair sum. As to which the Palatines wish it to be understood, that though they might lawfully demand without exception whatever has been taken away from the Palatine House, and that though they consider that they are not concerned in or bound by the obligations between the Houses of Austria and Bavaria with regard to a certain sum of money yet to show their desire for peace and eagerness to defer to his Imperial Majesty, the Palatine House besides the concession already made about the dignity cedes to the House of Bavaria that district of Cham, and expects in return that his Imperial Majesty be released from his obligations, otherwise it insists on the restoration of the whole of the Upper Palatinate. In *Latin*. [N. XVIII., 32.]

PAPER.

164[6-]7, February 18-28. Osnabrück.—The Count of Avaux, the French Plenipotentiary, in answer to the question of the Swedish Plenipotentaries whether he approved of the articles proposed by the Emperor replied that " France greatly wished for peace, and inasmuch as the French had always recognised the Duke of Bavaria as Elector, and given him the Electoral title, and had disapproved of the Palatine's proceedings in Bohemia, and besides as the Duke of Bavaria was in high esteem everywhere, and had rendered good offices to the Crowns, they (the French) had declared both to the Imperialists and Bavarians that the Electoral Dignity ought to remain with the said Duke. As for the Upper Palatinate, as it had been bought for a large sum of money they could not take it from the said Duke; much less could they dispute against the Catholic religion in the Lower Palatinate."

To the deputies of His Serene Highness, the Elector Palatine, the said French Ambassador said " The French Ambassadors had sometimes spoken with those of the Emperor about the Palatine business, who were ready to agree to the French side under a certain condition which the French would not in any way assent to. They had declared their own intention to the Imperialists but had bound themselves to nothing. He promised to communicate further with the Swedes on the subject." When the Deputies of the Elector Palatine enlarged upon the unfairness of the articles, he replied in a chilling manner " He would use his good offices to obtain the Lower Palatinate. But as the Bergstrasse was ecclesiastical property, he could hardly speak for that, but left it to others to do this." As regarded religion he said " His King could not assist in the restitution if the Catholics were to be afterwards expelled (from the lands restored)." In *Latin*. [N. XVII., 10.]

The Reply of the IMPERIAL PLENIPOTENTIARIES to the SWEDISH proposals.

164[6-]7, [February 22-] March 4. Osnabrück. — To the first accepting as far as " Evangelicals enjoy," but substituting for " Evangelicals," " Protestants or adherents to the Confession of Augsburg ; " adding, Nevertheless on the restoration of the Palatinate the exercise of the Catholic religion shall be permitted to the vassals and subjects whether ecclesiastical or lay, nor shall they be compelled to adopt another religion under any pretext whatever; and insisting on their original proposal that the Electoral Dignity should remain with the Duke of Bavaria and all the Guilhelmian line for ever, and that the Count Palatine should be admitted to an eighth and last Electorate, and that on the extinction of either line the eighth Electorate be suppressed.

To the second, agreed to subject to the foregoing declaration.

To the third, agreed to, yet saving the rights of the Catholic religion, and the infeudations or grants made during the deprivation of the Palatines by the Emperor or the Duke of Bavaria, and likewise except-ing the Bergstrasse, viz. the Castle of Starckemburg with the townlets of Bentzheim and Heppenheim, and the Monastery of Lorsch with the villages and farms appertaining thereto, which belong to the Elector and Archbishopric of Mainz.

As to the fourth, since the Elector of Bavaria cannot be satisfied by the County of Cham for 13 millions spent on the war, and the Emperor is in no wise bound to make good that sum to the Elector in order to favour the Palatines by whose father he was forced into a defensive war, they adhere to their former proposal that Prince Charles Louis should either pay that debt in full or give up the whole of the Upper Palatinate. They accept that his Imperial Majesty be released from his obligation. The rest of this article must be limited in conformity to the foregoing declaration. In *Latin*. [N. XVIII., 32.] N. XVIII., 29, 30, 31 are separate copies of the 3 papers numbered XVIII., 32, which with the paper of February 18–28, are the papers numbered 1, 2, 3, 4, in the paper of the Elector Palatine presented to the Lords on May 4th and printed in *Lords' Journals*, ix. 174, 175.

The COMMITTEE FOR IRELAND to the HOUSE OF COMMONS.

1646[-7], February 20.—Concerning the payments to the Earl of Ormonde, and the forces to be sent over. (The purport appears from *Commons' Journals*, v. 94, 95.) [N. XXI., 55.]

The COMMITTEE FOR THE ADMIRALTY AND CINQUE PORTS.

1646[-7], February 23.—Two reports concerning Sir George Ayscue and the commanders for four ships. (Both printed in *Lords' Journals*, ix. 39.) Two copies of each. [N. XIV., 179, 202, 218, 219.]

The EARL OF CASSILIS to the SPEAKERS OF BOTH HOUSES.

164[6-]7, February 23. Edinburgh.—(The purport appears from *Commons' Journals*, v. 134.) *Signed. Seal.* [N. VI., 75.]

ROBERT GOODWIN and WILLIAM ASHURST to WILLIAM LENTHALL.

1646[-7], February 23. Edinburgh.—" We were forced to stay at Berwick with the hostages until . . . the 18th . . . . . before our messenger—by reason of the extremity of the weather and foulness and length of ways—could return to give us assurance of the marching away of the garrison from Carlisle, and all the Scotch forces out of that part of England . . . Upon Friday we went to Edin-burgh . . and came thither upon Saturday about two . . in the afternoon, the Parliament being then risen and adjourned unto this day." When they sat they sent a committee to acknowledge the respects of the Parliament of England and to bid us welcome in the name of the Parliament of Scotland. We delivered them our letters and desired a time and place to be appointed for us to represent what we had further in charge. *Signed. Seal.* [N. VI., 28.]

Captain W. Drumond to the Committee for Ireland.

[1616–7, February.]—Stating in the name of the Scotch Army in Ireland that he had been now eight months representing their pressing wants and humble desires but could get no answer, and that being now ordered to return he desired a present answer, otherwise he would be obliged to leave without any at all, " which how discontenting it will prove he leaveth to their serious consideration." *Signed.* [N. XXI., 57.]

The Committee for Ireland to the House of Commons.

1646[–7], February 25.—Reporting the above paper. (See *Commons' Journals,* v. 112.) [N. XXI., 56.]

The Committee for Foreign Plantations.

1646[–7], February 25, March 1.—Report concerning the Earl of Carlisle and the Caribbee Islands with their order reporting the same. (Printed in *Lords' Journals,* ix. 51, 53.) [N. XIV., 222, 221.]

Philip [Lord] Lisle, to William Lenthall.

1646[–7], February 26. Cork.—" [On Saturday eve]ning last I landed in Ireland.   came to this city, where in   I thought it necessary for the   of the moneys allotted for this [Army and the] preventing all abuse in the issuing thereof, to inform myself as exactly as I could what numbers of foot and horse were in the Parliament's pay in these parts, and have disposed of a thousand of them into outquarters until such time as the horse come over from Bristol, and the parts adjacent, who only stay for money to transport them hither." *In parts illegible. Signed.* [N. VI., 29.]

Major Epiphanius Howard and Captain Daniel Alderne to the House of Commons.

[1646–7, February 27.]—Petition desiring that they would concur with the Lords in agreeing to the report of the Committee of both Kingdoms dated October 26, 1646 (*ante*, p. 395). [N. XXII., 99.]

The English Commissioners to the Parliament of Scotland.

1646[–7], February 27.—Two papers. (Both printed in *Lords' Journals,* ix. 100, 101.) *Copies.* [N. XIX., 204, 203.]

Edward Leigh and others to the Chancellor of the Duchy of Lancaster.

1646[–7], February 28.—Recommending Mr. John Lightfoot for the vacant living of Fitanhill in Staffordshire. *Signed.* [N. VI., 30.]

The Committee Appointed March 16th, 1645–6.

[1646–7, February.]—(See *Commons' Journals,* v. 44, 61.) " An Alphabetical method of such offices Military or Civil or any other place, profit or advantage any members of the House of Commons or any in trust for them or any of them doe hold by any Authority from the Parliament according to such informations have been brought to this Committee appointed to take the same into consideration." [N. XIV., 107.] Of those informations this Collection contains the following :—

Sir Henry Cholmeley.

1646, March 30, April 29,—[N. XIV., 108, 117.]

SIR THOMAS JERVOISE, SIR PHILIP STAPILTON, JOHN HARRIS, SIR WILLIAM CONSTABLE, JAMES FIENNES, SIR EDWARD PARTHE-RICKE, SIR SAMUEL ROLLE, RICHARD WHITEHEAD.

1646, August 25, 27, 27, 27, 28, 28, 28, 29.—[N. XIV., 154, 155, 166, 167, 169, 170, 171, 157.]

BULSTRODE WHITELOCKE, JOHN WHADDON, JOHN ROLLE.

1646, September 2, 4, 8.—[N. XIV., 158, 160, 176.]

SIR WILLIAM STRICKLAND.

1646, September 10.—[N. XII., 199.]

SIR THOMAS PELHAM.

1646, December 30.—[N. XIV., 195.]

SIR WILLIAM LISTER.

1646[-7], January 6.—[N. VI., 23.]

THOMAS STOCKDALE.

1646[-7], January 23.—[N. XIV., 209.]

SIR THOMAS DACRES, SIR WILLIAM WALLER, SIR JOHN HIPPESLEY, FRANCIS DRAKE, JOHN LISLE, SIR EDWARD HUNGERFORD, WILLIAM WHITE and SIR THOMAS WALSINGHAM.

Undated.—Statements setting forth the places &c. enjoyed by them respectively. (Most of these particulars are given in the above "Alphabetical Method." Whitelocke's statement is printed in Peck, *Desiderata Curiosa*, ix. 29. In some cases the losses of the writer in consequence of his adherence to the Parliament are also stated, and Sir John Hippesley states the receipts and expenses of the Middle Park at Hampton Court and Marybone Park.) [N. XIV., 156, 159, 161, and 165; XIII., 182; XV., 166.]

The COMMITTEE FOR FOREIGN AFFAIRS to the PARLIAMENT.

1646[-7], March 2.—Order reporting proposed answer to the King of Denmark's offer of mediation. [N. XVIII., 4.]

The COMMITTEE FOR IRELAND to SIR GERARD LOWTHER and SIR PAUL DAVIES.

1646[-7], March 3.—In reply to their Petition expressing satisfaction at their conduct, and stating they will represent so much to the House. [N. XXI., 50.]

WILLIAM LENTHALL to [the COMMISSIONERS AT HOLDENBY].

1646[-7], March 3.—By order of the House enclosing votes and a transcript of a former letter. (See *Commons' Journals*, v. 104.) *Draft.* [N. XII., 202.]

The SAME to Major-General SKIPPON.

Same date.—Thanking him for his services. (See *Commons' Journals*, v. 104.) *Draft.* [N. XII., 203.]

The PARLIAMENT OF SCOTLAND to the ENGLISH COMMISSIONERS.

1646[-7], March 3.—(Printed in *Lords' Journals*, ix. 101.) [N. XIX., 205.]

The Scotch Commissioners.

1646-7, March 3.—Paper. (The effect appears from *Commons'
Journals*, v. 105.) *Signed* "Jo. Cheislie." [N. XIX., 206.]

The English Commissioners to the Parliament of Scotland.

1646[-7], March 8.—(Printed in *Lords' Journals*, ix. 101.) *Copy*.
[N. XIX., 207.]

The Committee for the Admiralty and Cinque Ports.

1646[-7], March 9.—Report recommending Commanders for the
summer fleet. (Printed in *Lords' Journals*, ix. 76.) [N. XIV., 226,
227.]

Information of Thomas Ringwood, a trooper, and Thomas Baker
of Halberton to the Standing Committee of Devon.

1646[-7], March 9.—That about 100 troopers and 100 horses pretending to be designed for Ireland, came the last Lord's Day and
quartered in that parish, and misused in manner specified certain
inhabitants therein named, that the said troopers when demanded for
their orders to quarter there drew out their swords and told the inhabitants that that was their order, and that there are two other troops
quartered in the country thereabouts, men very profane, full of cursing
and swearing. *Signed.* [N. XIV., 223.]

The Committee for Irish Affairs at Derby House.

1646[-7], March 12.—Reports reporting the propositions of Colonel
Robert Hammond, and desiring that Colonel Jones be furnished with
400 defensive arms. *Enclosed :*

The said Propositions.

They contain, besides stipulations for the pay and victualling of the
forces he is to bring over to Dublin, provisions that he is to be
Governor of Dublin and that the time of their employment there
should not exceed two or three months at furthest, and that
shipping be ready to transport them back 14 days before the
expiration of the term, and if relief come not " within 14 days
before the end of the said term then—whatsoever otherwise shall
happen—it shall be lawful for him and them to take shipping
seven days before the expiration of the said time and to return to
England." (See *Commons' Journals*, v. 112.) [N. XIV., 225,
224.]
And probably—

[Colonel Robert Hammond] to [the Committee for Irish
Affairs.]

[1646-7, March 12.]—" In case these propositions are accepted, he
desires to know and to be fully satisfied of the whole state of
that garrison and what provisions of war of all sorts are there
already, and what are intended thither for the defence thereof.
And he hopes that so he shall be able to satisfy your expectations
and the service of the kingdom, both in point of number of men
and defence of that garrison until the end of the said term or that
he be relieved." (See *Commons' Journals*, v. 112.) [N. XV.,
Unnumbered, between 178 and 179.]

The COMMITTEE FOR IRELAND to the HOUSE OF COMMONS.

1646[-7], March 13.—Report on the forces in and to be sent to Ireland. (The heads are given in *Commons' Journals*, v. 112, and the particulars of the forces to be sent in the same, p. 107. It states that there were in Ulster ten old regiments of foot and one old regiment and twelve troops of horse, in Connaught three old regiments of foot and four old troops of horse, in Munster eight old regiments of foot and three of horse. The total of the old forces, those newly sent, those ready to go and those designed amounted to 41 regiments and three companies of foot, thirteen regiments and eighteen troops of horse and two regiments of dragoons. The total annual charge including that of the artillery was estimated at 1,203,645*l*. 2*s*. 4*d*.) [N. XXI., 58, 59.]

The SAME to the SAME.

Same date.—Report concerning the discharge of the Scotch army in Ireland. (The same *mutatis mutandis* as the votes of the House on the 16th thereon.) [N. XIX., 208.]

WILLIAM LENTHALL to [the JUDGES].

[1646-7], March 13.—Enclosing an Order of the House. (See *Commons' Journals*, v. 109, 110.) *Draft* or *Copy*. [N. XII., 183.]

The PARLIAMENT OF SCOTLAND to the ENGLISH COMMISSIONERS.

1646[-7], March 15.—Two replies to their two papers of February 27th. (Both printed in *Lords' Journals*, ix. 101.) *Copies*. [N. XIX., 209, 210.]

The HOUSE OF COMMONS.

1646[-7], March 16.—Votes concerning the Scotch army in Ireland. (Printed in *Commons' Journals*, v. 113.) [N. XIX., 211.]

The LORD MAYOR and COMMON COUNCIL of the City OF LONDON to the HOUSE OF LORDS.

[1646-7, March 17].—Petition. [N. XXII., 101.] *Annexed:*

The humble PETITION of MANY THOUSANDS.
Copy. [N. XXII., 103.]

And

Votes of the HOUSE OF LORDS thereupon.
Draft. (All these are printed in *Lords' Journals*, ix. 82-85.) [N. XXII., 102.]

The ENGLISH COMMISSIONERS to the PARLIAMENT OF SCOTLAND.

1646[-7], March 17.—(Printed in *Lords' Journals*, ix. 102.) *Copy*. [N. XIX., 212.]

The SCOTCH COMMISSIONERS to [the HOUSE OF COMMONS].

1646[-7], March 18.—Paper. Stating that the Parliament of Scotland, as soon as they received the vote of the House of Commons of the 2nd instant, appointed instructions to be presently drawn, and Commissioners to be sent here to join in obtaining the King's assent to the Propositions, whereof we were advertised by letters of the 9th instant, and now hourly expect an express with further notice. (See *Commons' Journals*, v. 119.) *Signed* "Jo. Cheislie." [N. XIX., 213.]

The COMMITTEE OF THE REVENUE.

1646[-7], March 18.—Paper recommending Mr. John Nelthrop as Steward of the Manor of Barton. (Printed in *Lords' Journals*, ix. 103.) [N. XV., 48.]

Extracts from Mr. BARON's Report to the GENERAL ASSEMBLY at Kilkenny.

1646[-7], March 19.—" There was a letter from of January last signifying that late peace having both the Courts of France upon the public faith of the kingdom but that when informations were duly given and slight objections delivered by himself and Mr. Baron then the rejectment of that peace was endeavoured by the King and Queen of France and Cardinal Mazarine, yet when the [news] came to France of our forces returning from Dublin the good opinion was altered and an opinion of weakness and division took place, he desires that the said kingdom may join their forces again and set upon that place and make themselves masters of the kingdom and that thereby they will acquire and regain the goodwill of France and of Cardinal Mazarine; he signifies that the Prince and Queen of England are desirous to come unto Ireland. He desires their coming. We do not agree upon slighter terms than such as Mr. Baron will declare unto us, for he assures that when they come we will have our wills, and said that whosoever upon weak conditions will press an agreement before their coming, he will hinder the King's prospects and freedom.

A letter from the King of France of the 26th of September last imports the particular care he hath of what touched our interests, and that still he doth labour to contribute thereunto, to his uttermost endeavours, and by reason he is well informed of our inclinations and hath knowledge of the desire the kingdom hath in effect to show their affections to him he hath committed to the relation of Mr. Baron what he hath in charge to tell us in his name.

A letter from Cardinal Mazarine in September last signified the good intentions of his Majesty of France to give us assistance proportionable to his zeal to the Catholic Religion, had the state of affairs in France given way thereunto, and saith that it were an injury done to Mr. Baron to add anything to what he can lively represent unto us in the behalf of his Majesty.

By another letter from Cardinal Mazarine is signified that we can use no more effectual way to draw France to help us than to contribute our endeavours for the settlement of the affairs of his Majesty of England, and assures that what we do in this particular will work much with the King of France to advance what concerneth the good of our nation.

From Colonel FitzWilliams that the Scots had given up the King to the Parliament, that he is certainly informed, that as soon as the Scots quit England, the Presbyterians and Independents will fall into odds, which will prove advantageous unto us. By another letter from " him " is signified that he is informed that our propositions are at full and enjoins us in no way to descend from them, for he is sure we will have all; only he supplicates we may be pleased to leave one church open in Dublin for the King's religion, for he says the Parliament of England would be glad to get the like advantage to incense all those of England against the King, Queen, Prince and this kingdom for shutting up all our doors against them. He assures that the Pope directed 40,000 pistoles to be sent us from Rome and that Cardinal Mazarine promised himself shortly to send over unto us 6,000 pistoles.

This is the substance of the letters Mr. Baron brought with him. In the account of his negotiation, he saith that he presented the Supreme Council's letter to the Queen, and found her very willing to comply with his requests and accordingly promised him a great sum able to bring the service of Ireland to the wished period, and then parted with her well satisfied; but when he came again he found her as far from her former expressions as that she seemed to forget her answer to

being by Protestant
Council diverted   could prevail

with her, she being altogether about by that

one man whose name he craved the Queene's (?)
pardon.   There   found the

Queen full often willing in her expressions
was sorry he must say that he gained nothing
that the Cardinal had sent them 1,200 livres
which was all the supply he received since he went for France."
Torn and illegible in parts.   Copy by Nalson.   [N. XXI., 60.]

The Aᴍʙᴀssᴀᴅᴏʀ ᴏꜰ ᴛʜᴇ Sᴛᴀᴛᴇs-Gᴇɴᴇʀᴀʟ to the Pᴀʀʟɪᴀᴍᴇɴᴛ.

1646–7, March 22–April 1.—Announcing the death of the Prince of Orange. (Printed in *Lords' Journals*, ix. 98.) In *French*, with two copies of an *English* translation, the first *Signed*. [N. XVIII., 61.]

Cʜᴀʀʟᴇs Eʀsᴋɪɴᴇ, Hᴇᴡ Kᴇɴɴᴇᴅʏ and Rᴏʙᴇʀᴛ Bᴀʀᴄʟᴀʏ to the Sᴘᴇᴀᴋᴇʀ ᴏꜰ ᴛʜᴇ Hᴏᴜsᴇ ᴏꜰ Pᴇᴇʀs *pro tempore*.

164[6–]7, March 23.   Worcester House.—Desiring that satisfaction be made to Thomas Boyd, a Scotch merchant (whose petition they enclose), for wines taken by Captain Plunket in their transport from France to Carrickfergus. (See *Lords' Journals*, ix. 98; *Commons' Journals*, v. 122.) *Signed.   Seal.* [N. VI., 79.]   Probably *Enclosed*:

Tʜᴏᴍᴀs Bᴏʏᴅᴇ to the Hᴏᴜsᴇ ᴏꜰ Cᴏᴍᴍᴏɴs.

[1646–7, March.] — Petition, agreeing in substance and mostly verbally with that of the same petitioner printed in *Lords' Journals*, ix. 453, except that the fifth paragraph in the latter is omitted. [N. XXII., 73.] [N. XXII., 104.] is a second petition in identical terms addressed "to the Lords and Commons in Parliament."

The Eʟᴇᴄᴛᴏʀ Pᴀʟᴀᴛɪɴᴇ to Wɪʟʟɪᴀᴍ Lᴇɴᴛʜᴀʟʟ.

164[6–]7, March 24.   Whitehall. — (A duplicate of this letter, addressed to the Speaker of the House of Lords, is printed in *Lords' Journals*, ix. 105.) *Signed* "Charles Lodovic." *Seal.* [N. I., 52.]

The Cᴏᴍᴍɪᴛᴛᴇᴇ ꜰᴏʀ Cᴏᴍᴘᴏᴜɴᴅɪɴɢ ᴡɪᴛʜ DᴇʟɪɴQᴜᴇɴᴛs.

1646[–7], March 24.—Order staying proceedings on Lord Paulett's sequestration and directing the Lady Day rents to remain in his tenants' hands. Annexed is a statement showing the position of Lord Paulett and Sir John Paulett with regard to their compositions. [N. XIV., 228.]

Promise of the Lᴏʀᴅ Hᴇʀʙᴇʀᴛ ᴏꜰ Cʜᴇʀʙᴜʀʏ and Resolution thereupon.

1647, March 25.—(Printed in *Commons' Journals*, v. 125.) [N. XV., 1.]

The Committee of the Army.

1647, March 26.—Estimate of the moneys received and paid for Sir Thomas Fairfax's army. (Printed in Grey, iii., Appendix, No. 3, p. 5.) (See *Commons' Journals*, v. 126.) [N. XIV., 220.]

John Hobson, Sheriff, and others to William Pierrepont and four other Members.

1647, March 26. Lincoln.—Complaining of the conduct of Mr. King, who hindered the payment of the assessments by asserting that there were no ordinances which authorised them. *Signed. Seal.* [N. VI., 32.]

Colonel Richard Jones to William Lenthall.

1647, March 26. Laumihangell.—Vouching that the signers of the petition from Glamorganshire belong to "the godly party" and that the particulars therein are but part of their real grievances. [N. VI., 33.]

Charles Erskine, Hew Kennedy and Robert Barclay to William Lenthall.

1647, April 13. Worcester House.—Desiring that Scotch prisoners at Algiers might be included in the proposed agreement. (See *Commons' Journals*, v. 141.) *Signed. Seal.* [N. VI., 34.]

Statement by Captain Edward Wogan.

1647, April 13.—That Lieutenant-Colonel Pride had declared to him at an ordinary at Saffron Walden on March 25th last that those who would not sign the petition of indemnity should be blotted out of the rolls and excluded and counted as no members of the army. At foot John Farmer attests the truth of the above statement. [N. XV., 2.]

The Common Council of the City.

1647, April 17.—Answer to the Proposition of both Houses for borrowing 200,000*l*. (Printed in *Lords' Journals*, ix. 148.) [N. XV., 3.]

Lord Inchiquin to William Lenthall.

1647, April 17. Cork.—" The command of the army in this province being—in right of my commission . . from the Honourable Houses— returned into my hands at the Lord Lieutenant's departure out of this kingdom I esteem it my duty to give . . . some account of the condition wherein the province was left by his Lordship. . . . . I can only discover by a conjectural estimate from " the Treasurer's Deputy and from the Commissaries of the provisions and musters " that there was then remaining in the custody of the Treasurer's Deputy about 6,400*l*. in ryalls of eight at 5*s*. the piece, and provisions in the store of corn and victual to the value of 1,900*l*. or thereabouts,—part of which 6,400*l*. was raised upon the excise and customs—.All which —with what may be further raised upon the place—will not produce above five weeks' subsistence for the officers and soldiers already here, the constant charge whereof . . . viz. at three days' pay for the officers at 2*s*. 6*d*. the piece for the foot and 5*s*. for the horse being 2,200*l*. per week, besides the great addition of charge which must be expected . . upon the arrival of those horse and foot now lying at the waterside to be transported." I therefore make my humble suit that a reasonable supply of treasure be transmitted here, and having reason to apprehend that there may be endeavours to prejudice me in the good opinion of the Honourable Houses I have dispatched my secretary who, I doubt not, will be able to give satisfaction touching my proceedings. I also request that I may have the assistance of a Committee not only for the control of what may be raised or sent here, but for the satisfaction of the House in the conduct of their service. *Signed. Seal.* [N. VI., 35.]

Sir Adam Loftus and Sir John Temple to William Lenthall.

1647, April 23. Bristol.—Being safely landed, we inform you of Lord Lisle's arrival here. "About fourteen daies since, Colonell Sidney, the Lieutenant-Generall of the Horse, and Sir Hardress Waller, Serjeant-Major-Generall of the Armie, presented a peticion to the Conncell Board, wherein they declared their right to the comand of the armie in case of the absence of the Generall, and desired for the avoyding of future contestacons to the prejudice of the service, it might be soe setled before his Lordshipp's departure, and withall shewed to the Board at the same tyme a paper wherein it was testified that the Lord Inchiqune should tell Colonell Grey that in case the Lord Lieutenant left Colonell Sidney, the Lieutenant-Generall of the horse, behinde him that he had a freind who wold accuse him of treason, or declare him a traitour. This seemed a matter of soe high concernement as the Board thought fitt to take it presently into their consideracon, and findeing great divisions alreadie in the Armie about this particuler, much disaffeccion in the English officers and souldiers lately come over to the Lord Inchequine and the high contestacons which might happily ensue heereupon, after they had acquainted the Lord Inchequine heerewith, and received his Lordship's reasons for justificacon of his right to the command of the Armie, as President of Mounster, as also the reasons of the generall officers of the armie, and consulted with the colonells who were divided in opinion, they thought fitt for composeing of all differences for the present to settle the comand of the armie in four commissioners, vizt. the Lord Inchequine and the Lord Broghill, Generall of the horse of Mounster, being the two principall officers of the old armie, and the Lieutenant-Generall of the horse, and Serjeant-Major-Generall of the Armie of the whole kingdome, and these to continew only till the parliament should declare their pleasure therein. And this they were the rather induced unto because upon conference with Mr. Basil, the Attorney-Generall of the kingdome, they found it somewhat cleere that the extraordinarie power graunted unto the Lord President, whereby he claymed the right of a Commander in cheife was but dureing the pleasure of the parliament, which determined upon the passing of the Lord Lieutenantes commission, and could not be revived againe but by a new graunt from both howses. And yet soe desireous was the Board to give the Lord President all manner of satisfaccion as they offered his Lordshipp soe he would give his consent to this order, that any person whom he excepted against, should be left out of the comission ; which he seemed to take verie well, but made answer he could not give his consent without prejudicein[g] his owne right, but if the Board would make any such order, that it should be verie pleaseing and acceptable unto him, and that he wold willingly give obedience unto it. Hereupon, the Board after severall consultacons—leaving the civill power absolutely in the Lord President—made an order for setling the comand of the armie in the four commissioners afore-named till the pleasure of the parliament were further knowne, and delivered one part of it to the Lord President, and the other to the generall officers of the armie. But the

Lord President, the daie that the Lord Lieutenantes Commission determined, came and offered to his Lordshipp a Protestation against it, and the same evening would have returned to his Lordshipp the order which he refused to receive, telling him he was now a private person and could meddle no further with it, haveing as a publique minister done all that he thought could in that particuler tend to the settlement of quietness in the armie till the parliament was made acquainted therewith. And that he intended next daie to take shipping and so to returne into England : which accordingly he prepared himself to doe. And three of the commissioners haveing been with the Lord President next morneing and findeing that he absolutely refused to joyn with them, understandeing of the Lord Lieutenantes resolucion to leave Corke that morneing, they gave order to put his owne regiment only in armes to attend him out of the towne, which the Lord Inchequine interdicted and comanded by proclamacon by beate of drum, that they should laie downe their armes and repair to their quarters upon paine of death. But the officers of the regiment thought fitt to obey the comissioners and so stood in armes all that daie, whereby the Lord Lisle perceived that there would arise some trouble about this order, and therefore both he and the councell resolved to put off their goeing for that daie and to attend the composeing of the differences betwixt them, which they effected. Notwithstanding the Lord President—as wee heard—had the daie before sent for severall officers whom he confided in, to come to him from the out-quarters where they were laid with their companies to doe service upon the rebels, and had--as wee were further informed— gathered about him in his house neere two hundred officers—reformadoes that had been cavaliers—and soldiers, and comanded a troope of horse of his owne regiment to come into the towne; which the comissioners would not give entrance unto, but brought in some troopes of the Lord Broghil's regiment, and so had absolutely the comand of the towne, and full power in their bandes—as was confessed afterwardes by the Lord Inchequin's officers—to proceed to execute according to their comission : which, when wee of the councell sawe, and apprehending that matters might growe to some height betweene the Lord President and the three other comissioners who were resolved to stand upon their right according to the order of the Board, wee undertooke to mediate betwixt them, and at length so farr prevailed with the comissioners —by declareing our resolucion even to protest against them, in case they should use anie violence to maintaine their power—as they resolved —notwithstanding their right and power—to recede from their authoritie, and to suspend the execucion of their comission, and to come awaie into England to make knowne the Lord Inchequin's carriage herein to the parliament; and soe they causing all the horse and foot within the towne to laie downe their armes, wee have left all things in great quietnesse, and the full power in the Lord Inchequine, whom wee found so wedded to his own, as that no consideration of any hazard that might happen to the publique could draw him to any manner of accommodation." *Signed. Seal.* [N. VI., 37, should be 36.]

The Common Council of the City.

1647, April 27.—Order nominating 31 persons as a Committee for the Militia. (See *Commons' Journals*, v. 160.) [N. XV., 4.]

The Common Council of the City.

1647, May 3.—Opinion touching the advance of 200,000*l.* (Printed in *Commons' Journals*, v. 163.) [N. XV., 5.]

The charges against Colonel KENRICK.

1647, May 6.—Draft of the entry of them in the Journals. (Printed in *Commons' Journals,* v. 163.) [N. XV., 6.]

SIR THOMAS FAIRFAX to WILLIAM LENTHALL.

1647, May 12.—Recommending the petitioners, being the servants who attended the King in his household and were not engaged in hostility to the Parliament, to the House. *Signed. Enclosed:*

The said petition setting forth their distressed condition, and pray-ing that in pursuance of the 19th article of the surrender of ·Oxford, the Commissioners of the Revenue might be authorised to relieve them. [N. VI., 37.]

The COMMITTEE FOR THE ADMIRALTY AND CINQUE PORTS.

1647, May 13.—Report recommending that a letter of congratulation be sent to the Archduke Leopold, on his becoming Regent of Flanders. (Printed in *Commons' Journals,* v. 180.) [N. XV., 7.]

The EARL OF LAUDERDALE, CHARLES ERSKINE, HEW KENNEDY, and ROBERT BARCLAY to WILLIAM LENTHALL.

1647, May 17. Worcester House.—(Identical, *mutatis mutandis,* with the letter of the same date to the Speaker of the House of Peers, which is printed in *Lords' Journals,* ix. 199.) *Signed. Seal.* [N. VI., 38.]

The HOUSE OF LORDS.

[1647, May 20.]—Vote for removing the King from Holdenby to Oatlands. (See *Lords' Journals,* ix. 199.) [N. XIV., 233.]

Report of the Delinquency and Estate of FRANCIS NEWPORT.

1647, May 20.—(Printed in *Commons' Journals,* v. 179.) [N. XV., 8.]

Information of JOHN POWLE of West Wickham in Buckinghamshire, Hawker.

1647, May 22.—"That this day he was told" by Mr. Thomas Arnold "That there is a design of Independents to make head against the Parliament while the army is in discontent; That it hath been debated in their meetings and resolved upon and that it is now ripe; That some who within this fortnight were in their judgment against this way of proceeding are now for it; And that they have very strong argu-ments to back this way of theirs, that God hath put an opportunity into their hands, and that they will not let it slip; That it is so carried that it is impossible that any that is not of their way, should come to the knowledge of it . ." Affirmed before Sir John Gayer, Lord Mayor. (Printed in Grey, iii., Appendix No. 82, p. 138.) (See *Commons' Journals,* v. 196.) [N. XV., 9.]

SIR GILBERT GERRARD and others to WILLIAM LENTHALL.

1647, May 31. Chelmsford.—(Identical, *mutatis mutandis,* with the letter of the same date to the Speaker of the House of Peers, which is printed in *Lords' Journals,* ix. 228.) *Signed. Seal.* [N. VI., 39.]

The House of Commons.

1647, June 3.—Resolution re-appointing the Committee concerning members charged with receiving bribes. (Printed in *Commons' Journals*, v. 196.) [N. XV., 10.]

The Parliament to the Earl of Northumberland.

1647, June 4.—Desiring him to bring the King's children back to St. James'. (See *Commons' Jornals*, v. 198.) *Draft.* [N. XII., 204.]

Sir Charles Coote to the Committee for Irish affairs at Derby House.

1647, June 4. Londonderry.—"In obedience to your Lordships' severall directions to me since February last to divert as much as was possible for me the power of the rebels from Dubline or the garrisons under the command of my Lord of Ormond, I have indeavoured—though with much difficulty for want of things necessary—by severall incursions into the rebels' quarters to perform your Lordships' commands, whereof I have formerly given your Lordships an accompt in part, since which, haveing beene lately forth on an expedicion, I here inclosed humbly represent unto your Lordships a true relacion of what was done by your forces of Connaught and eleven hundred foote of the Lagan forces under the commaund of Colonell Mervine which joyned with us in that service, and as no man shall more readily obey your Lordships' commaunds in all things, so shall I most humbly beseeche your Lordships that the condicion of the forces in that Province may be taken into a tymely consideracion, for the extremityes we are reduced unto will not admit of delay. I have severall tymes, and by severall wayes represented unto your Lordships not onely by our agents but otherwise, the miserable condition both of officer and soldier there, who are not only naked for want of clothes, shooes, stockings and shirts, but dye for want of bread to susteyne nature, having not beene able for many monthes past to afford them but five and sixe pownds of oaten mealo a weeke, and if God had not miraculously blessed us this winter by getting beefe from the rebels with the litle salt which we had in the store, we had perished, and when the Lagan men came into Connaught to joyne with us in prosecution of the rebels I was able to afford the men but sixe pownds of oaten meale a man for twenty dayes which we kept the feilds in, and at this instant I have but fourteen dayes provission in the store after the same proporcion. The rebels know our wants as well as ourselves which will no doubt incourage them to fall on us, and then how unable we shalbe to defend ourselves so accomadated, your Lordships are well able to judge. To continue in the feild —our men being all naked and in want of all necessaryes—which is the only probable way for us to subsist by with so small a strength, the rebels haveing severall great armyes a-foote were rather desperation —whatever the successe might be—then justifiable before God or man. Which way to turne myself in so great exigencies, I professe I cannot tell, the Lord direct me, but to the uttermost of my power I shall not faile to indeavour the keeping the men together and preserving the parliament's interest there, humbly desyreing that some speedy course may be taken for our relief and howsoever it may please God to dispose of things my reall indeavours in your service may be accepted.

The sad condicion of the three newe companies of the Lord Folliot's regiment sent hither by the late commissioners being very deplorable, the meanes left them being quite spent, I was inforced to post hither to setle some course for their support for one monthe by layeing a taxe on the inhabitants of the citty and the lybertyes formerly overburthened by the tenn old companies of that regiment. Much adoe I had to effect it, and great clamour : the inhabitants conceaving it a very hard condicion that those sent hither for their comfort and preservacion should destroy them, which it will in one mouthe more undoubtedly, and inforce the inhabitants totaly to desert the place. I have severall tymes intimated this unto my Lord Folliot and our agents but have not receaved any answere thereunto. The soldiers are daily mutaning and running away and much adoe I have to keepe the towne from plundering and to keepe them and the townesmen from cutting one another's throats." If a speedy course be not taken to enable the men to prosecute the war I beg to be relieved of my command.

Postscript.—" I was lately abroad in Connaght with a reasonable party of horse and foote, my own, Mervine, and the Lagan forces joyning with us. We consisted of about 2,000 foot and some 400 and odd horse. We advanced as far as Ballenrobe in the county of Mayo, the rebels fiyeing before us into the mountaines of Owles and Erconaght with their catle, and haveing put our provisions into Balelaghan which was lately delivered unto us by Captaine Costolo, from Ballentobber-patrick we sent out a party of fifteen hundred men in two divisions comanded by [my] Majour and Colonell Mervine's who marched after the rebels and their Creaghts into the mountaines. My Majour with his party which consisted all of the Connaght men—onely some of Sir William Stuart's regiment with his sonne joyned with our brigade—had the good fortune to light on the most considerable prey for they brought with them two thousand cowes, killed severall straglers and marching back to our place of rendevous nere Castle Barre before they quitt the mountaines the rebels under the command of Sir Theobald Bourke, eldest sonne to the Lord of Mayo, and Lieutenant-Colonell O'Cahan, Lieutenant-Colonell to Rory McGuire, pursued my Majour with nine companies of the rebels part Ulster men and part Connaght, and about sixe of the clock after noone on the 12th of the last, they beganne to skirmidge with our party and without any long ado came gallantly up to push of pike and clubbing of the musquet which was a great providence of God, for our men's amunicion was by the extreamity of weather and illnesse of the wayes growne very wett. The number on both sides being equall, the fight for a pretty while was very doubtfull, sometymes inclyneing to the one side then to the other, the officers on both sides behaveing themselves very gallantly. In the end when Lieutenant-Colonell O'Cahan was killed, and Captaine and Captaine (*sic*) Edmond Bourke, sonne to the Lord of Mayo, Captaine McKenna and Captaine McMahonne taken prisoners which were the leading men—for Sir Theobald Bourke never came into the fight himself—the rebels betooke them to their heeles which stood them in good sted that day, yet it pleased God our men killed one hundred and eighty-seven of them in the place, besides such as dyed sence of their hurts which we understood to be many. And that which is most remarkable, of the rebels' officers being thirty-six from the best to the worst except Sir Theobald Bourke and one reformado sergeant there escaped not one but were killed in the place, but Captaine McMahonne, Captaine Costello, and Lieutenant Bourke who wee have still in our hands. We lost only Captaine Parker of my regiment, and one common soldier of Colonell Sanderson's. Severall of our officers and soldiers were hurt but I prayse God none dangerously. The next day after the fight my Majour came to our place of rendevouse with their prey the armes and plunder of the enemy. And the next day after,

Colonell Mervine's Majeur returned with his party with a good prey —but not so great as the other—haveing killed severall straglers but not encountred by any party of the rebels. Whilest they were abroad in the mountaines Colonell Mervine and I scoured the plaines with the horse and dragoones which we made of our bagage horses the foote officers' horses and the garrons we gott from the enemy, gott some catle and sheepe and killed severall rogues about their castles, and so haveing stayed as long as it was possible for us for want of bread for our officers and soldiers, the weather being extreame ill all the tyme of our being abroad, we returned safe home to Slygo, the Lord make us thankefull. This hath given the rogues a great cheque, for the Ulster men thought to carry all by falling in to the push of pike, but some such rancounters as they have now mett with may make them fall to some newe waye of fighteing." *Signed. Seal.* [N. VI., 40.]

The ARMY.

1647, June 4 and 5.—Representation of their dissatisfaction. (Printed in Rushworth, iv. 1. 505.) *Copy.* [N. XX., 53.]

The Scotch Commissioners to William Lenthall.

1647, June 5.—(Identical *mutatis mutandis* with their letter of the same date to the Speaker of the House of Peers, printed in *Lords' Journals*, ix. 240.) *Signed. Seal.* [N. XX., 3.]

The Earl of Dunfermline to William Lenthall.

1647, June 5.—(According to the resolution printed in *Commons' Journals*, v. 200.) *Seal. Enclosed:*

The Message from the King, which is printed in *Lords' Journals*, ix. 242. [N. VI., 41, 42.]

Lord Inchiquin to William Lenthall.

1647, June 6. Cappoquin.—"As soone as Dungarvan was taken I was forced to sitt still for a fortnight whilst bread was provided for us, during which tyme the army was payd in mony, Captain Swanly haveing then brought 5,000*l.* which was much about a fortnight's pay after that small proporcion that wee give pay, which is three dayes pay for a weeke to commission officers, 2*s.* 6*d.* to comon souldiers, and five shillings to troopers mounted, if unmounted but 2*s.* 6*d.* This course of paying the mony altogether I held most convenient; first, because the giveing out of provisions with it would have hindered the haveing any bread before hand without which wee could not march into the rebells' quarters; next, because I know that if I should issue monyes and provissions together, the officers and souldiers would bee discontented if they were not paid, as long as wee had mony, which would have bin a loss of that provisions that should have bin issued in respect of the present use of it. Againe by this meanes, the officers were the better able to take the feild, haveing had that tyme and some mony to provide for it; and lastly, because I saw that by keepeing the provisions to bee thus issued, I should not onely make the meanes that was in our hands last a forthnight longer, then otherwise it would, but also thereby enable the army for that forthnight to use what indeavours wee could to gaine further releife out of the rebells' quarters, for which purpose there was no place so convenient for us to lye at as this, because hither wee have our bread and pease—other provisions wee have none—brought by water, which wee have no carriages for, and heere is a convenient place for us, as well to make incursions dayly into the Irish quarters as to prevent their invadeing ours. As soone as the bread was delivered out, I sent away five hundred horse, under the comaund of Serjeant-Majour Banastree to prey the powren country, which was effected with good success and burned all the country, haveing gayned three thousand cowes, great and small, and four thousand sheepe, which would have bin a great releife to the army, had they not bin so imbezeild by the souldiers—some officers also being accessary—as they left us not above six hundred cowes and twelve hundred sheepe to bee converted to their publique use; wherein the state's service hath received soe great a prejudice as makes us earnest to find out those who are guilty, who being found, will receive condigne punishment. Wee understood from those that were uppon this party that they had not brought one of fifty that they saw, the cattle being sheltred by the woods and boggs, so as their horse could not come at them, which occasioned us to send out five hundred fresh horse with twenty-five hundred foote, under the comaund of Collonel Sterling, the Majour-Generall, hopeing with the helpe of those foote to have gayned much more cattle then wee had before. But the people had driven their cattle over the river Shure, soe as wee gott not above four hundred cowes and fifteen hundred sheep, the latter whereof were all devoured by the souldiers then abroad. Uppon this march there was no burning neither of houses or corne, the councell of warre haveing for divers reasons disadvised it.

Whilst these partyes were the last tenn dayes thus imployed, I lay heere to fall uppon the heeles of the rebells if they should draw out after our party from Clonmell and the parts adjacent where their Supreame Councell and a Nationall Synod now sitt, and all their army lye. And —that they might not stirr hence without my knowledge—I sent a hundred horse every day towards that towne to have intelligence. But yesterday those scouts that were out from these horse, being not so vigilent as they should have bin, the rebells were uppon them with four hundred horse and one thousand foote before they were aware so as they could not retreat before they were charged and routed being hotly pursued by the rebells till they came within two myles and a halfe of this towne. As soone as the newes came unto mee I went out with all the horse with mee, and though I made such hast to overtake them as tyred many horses in eight myles rydeing, yet I could not gett sight of them, but onely a few scouts within four myle of Clonmell and finding it to no purpose to goe further, I returned, causeing one to view the slayne which they find to bee thirty-four of our men, besides whom there were eleven priso[ners] taken; of theirs was onely one killed.

Wee find the divisions among the rebells disable them to fight with us, so as wee might probably carry any citty wee should attempt, if wee had provisions to subsist before it, but haveing onely so much bread as will enable the souldier with the helpe of some beefes reserved for them to spend twelve dayes in makeing incursions—to gaine what further helpe can bee had in the rebells' quarters towards our relcife,— I am inforced to imploy the army altogether for that end, and indeed I might not conveniently doe otherwise yett, though I had provisions, for I have not any men to spare from the feild. But if it shall please the state to send a competent nombor to garrison them, I doubt not wee shall gaine such townes before Michaelmus as will ease them of that charge they are now at, and cause great plenty of corne and all provisions in all our quarters." I therefore beg that Commissioners be sent with what relief is ready. *Signed*. [N. VI., 43.]

The Parliament to [the Commissioners at Holdenby].

[1647, June 8.]—Approving of their conduct on the 4th and stating that they had written to desire that the King be sent back to Holdenby.

And

The Same to Sir Thomas Fairfax.

Same date.—Expressing their satisfaction that the late act of the soldiers at Holdenby was done without his direction or encouragement, and desiring that the King should be returned to Holdenby and that the guards there should observe the orders of the Commissioners, and that he should investigate speedily the ground of that information con-cerning the surprise of the King, and who they are that those who gave in that paper enclosed in his letter undertake to make appear to be contrivers of such a design. (See *Commons' Journals*, v. 202.) *Drafts* as passed by the Commons and sent to the Lords. *Endorsed*, " Voted, not sent." [N. XII., 205.]

The House of Lords to the House of Commons.

Same date.—Message. (Printed in *Commons' Journals*, v. 203.) [N. XV., 11.]

Sir Thomas Fairfax to William Lenthall.

Same date. Cambridge.—(Printed in Rushworth, iv. 1. 550 with the following misprints, line 4, " with " for " which," last word of page, " them " for " the end " and " Childersey " for " Childerley.") *Signed*. *Seal*. [N. VI., 44.]

Sir Thomas Fairfax and the Officers of the Army to the Commissioners with the Army.

1647, June 10.—In Rushworth's hand.

And

The Commissioners to Sir Thomas Fairfax.

Same date.—(Both printed in *Lords' Journals*, ix. 253.) [N. XXII., 59; XV., 13.]

Pass for the Earl of Pembroke.

1647, June 11.—To embark two horses for France in exchange for one barb. (See *Lords' Journals*, ix. 303.) [N. XV., 14.]

Sir Charles Coote to the Committee for Irish affairs at Derby House.

1647, June 11. Londonderry.—I inclose a copy of my brother's letter out of Connaught, by which you may see the endeavours of your servants there " to prosecute the service and to gaine a poore subsistence from the enemy, which will not be possible for them to doe if not preserved by your Lordships' care in supplyeing of us with recruites both of men, horse and other necessaryes. . . . Within these four days here are severall long boats with four frigotes come to the mouth of this harbour to a place called Malin. They landed one day some three hundred men and killed some beasts they brought along with them in their boates, and having drest their meate ashore they returned to their boates and there lye still, and as I am this day assured, there are two frigotts and four long boates more come vnto them. We expect them to be highland men driven out of Scotland by the state's forces there, though we have no certainty thereof. Those that landed were excellently armed and had women and children with them. This begetts a great deale of feare in the poore inhabitants of these partes. What their designe may be we know not, but shall indeavour to prevent —by God's asistance—any prejudice. I am confident they will land at Broadhaven in Connoght, and so joyne with the rebels of that province. The rebels' friggots have taken above thirty small barques belonging to this kingdome and the kingdome of Scotland within this monthe which were fraighted with provisions and other commodities. The losse of these barques hath raised all things in these parts to excessive rates and ruined many families, and their not being any vessell of strength of the state's on these coasts will starve both inhabitants and soldiers and prevent any supplyes of comeing in safe unto us which shalbe sent if not speedily looked unto. There is one Mr. Thomas Costolo and Dudly Costolo—brothers—of an old English extraction, who have done divers considerable services to the Parliament in the province of Connaght since I had the honour to serve the Parliament there, by prosecuting the rebels vigorously, and in tyme of our greatest distresse continuing very faithfull unto us. They have surprised and taken severall holds of persons of great quallity which they still hold and preserve for the service of the state at their owne charge, and delivered Captaine Theobald Dillon, brother to the Lord of Costole, unto me whome they tooke prisoner, omitting nothing that lay in their powers which might advance the service, without any charge or burthen to this instant, but have suplyed our men in our tyme of extremity with mony, cowes, and baggage horses to the great furtherance of the service wherein they have meritted much. It is true they are Papists which is all can be said to their prejudice." I humbly ask they may receive some mark of favour. They only desire "to be receaved into the State's pay and to have the command of a troop of horse and a foot company which in effect they have already in the service and are well able at their own charge to raise and arm." . . . *Signed. Seal.* [N. VI., 45.]

THOMAS STAPLES and other officers of the British Army to [? the COMMITTEE FOR IRISH AFFAIRS at Derby House.]

[1647, June.]—Recommending Mr. Thomas Costolo and Mr. Dudly Costolo, who "though for the present Papists have proved very active and successful prosecutors of the rebels, and have lately taken three very strong holds, Castle Moore, Castle Manning, and Castle of Bally-laghan," and asking that they may have a company of foot and troop of horse confirmed to them. (See the last.) *Signed.* [N. VIII., 132.]

SIR THOMAS FAIRFAX and the ARMY under his Command

[1647, June 14.]—(Printed in Rushworth, iv. 1. 564.) *Signed by* Rushworth. [N. XXII., 62.]

The COMMON COUNCIL OF THE CITY.

1647, June 15. — Act. (The purport appears from *Commons' Journals*, v. 213.) *Copy.* [N. XV., 15.]

The Heads of a Charge delivered in the name of the ARMY

and

A paper delivered to the COMMISSIONERS OF PARLIAMENT from SIR THOMAS FAIRFAX and his ARMY.

1647, June 15.—Against the eleven members. (Both printed in Rushworth, iv. 1. 570, 572.) The second is signed by Rushworth. [N. XXII., 60, 61.]

The MARQUESS OF ORMONDE and the PARLIAMENT COMMISSIONERS.

1647, June 18.—Articles for the surrender of Dublin. (Printed in King's Pamphlets, E. 394, No. 14. See Carte, Life of Ormonde, i. 603–4.) Copy by Nalson. [N. XXI., 66.]

LIST.

1647, June 19.—Of the officers, who are in town and within the Lines of Communication who are not listed, and a Resolution thereon. (Printed in Commons' Journals, v. 217.) [N. XV., 16.]

[The COMMISSIONERS OF THE PARLIAMENT IN DUBLIN] to [the COMMITTEE FOR IRISH AFFAIRS].

1647, June 20, 21.—Recommending three persons as Physician, Surgeon-General, and Apothecary to the army (see Commons' Journals, v. 247), asking their influence in favour of the bearer, Mr. Hooke, for obtaining payment of about 1,000l. due to him for provisions supplied to the army in Leinster, in 1642, and desiring on behalf of Lord Ormonde that he might have an allowance for his expenses since the tenth of March last, the time of the last overtures for the delivery of the garrisons. Extract. [N. XII., 206.]

SIR THOMAS FAIRFAX and the ARMY under his Command.

1647, June 23.—Humble Remonstrance. (Printed in Rushworth, iv. 1. 385.) Signed by Rushworth. [N. XXII., 63.]

The PARLIAMENT to [the COMMISSIONERS WITH THE KING].

[1647, June.]—The two Houses, considering that the king was settled at Homeby by the consent of both kingdoms in order to the tendering to him there the propositions of peace by joint advice, and finding that, although the sudden removing of the king was without the knowledge of the Houses, yet many jealousies have risen thereupon tending to divide the two nations and to distract the people with fears of new commotions, to witness their great desire to keep a fairer correspondency with their brethren of Scotland, so that nothing might [prevent the conclusion] of a happy and speedy peace, have commanded us to send you this enclosed vote requiring you to see it put in speedy and effectual execution. Draft. (Probably earlier in date than the next.) [N. XII., 223.]

The PARLIAMENT to the COMMISSIONERS WITH THE KING.

[1647, June 29.]—(Printed in Lords' Journals, ix. 304.) Draft with amendments. [N. XII., 222.]

SIR JOHN COKE, JOHN CREWE, and RICHARD BROWN to
WILLIAM LENTHALL.

1647, June 30.—(Identical, *mutatis mutandis*, with the letter of the
same date from Lord Montague to the Speaker of the House of Peers,
which is printed in *Lords' Journals*, ix. 308.) *Copy.* [N. XII.,
207.]

ARTHUR ANNESLEY, ROBERT MEREDITH, SIR ROBERT KING, and
Colonel MICHAEL JONES, to [the COMMITTEE FOR IRISH AFFAIRS
at Derby House].

1647, July 6. Dublin.—" Wee have acquainted your Lordships with
the uncomfortablenesse of our imployment . . . in commanding men
guided neither by rules of reason or conscience, but hurried by their owne
lusts to what pleases their faneye, and gave unto your Lordships our apprehensions thereupon soe prophetically that it hath since accordingly
happened; for though to pravent as much as in us lay disorders daily
threatened by the insolent speeches of souldiers upon their guards, and
in their quarters wee—upon urgent supplication of the feild officers—
ordered a noble a peece to each comon souldier, towards the buying
them shooes, stockings and shirts, of which they were in great want, yet
on Friday last many of them fell into a high mutinie, and, casheiring
their officers, marched directly to Dammas (Dame's) Gate, adjoining to
the place where wee have our usuall meetings for dispatch of publique
affaires. Upon knowledg hereof, all dilligence was used by the
governour to crush an intemperance of soe dangerous example in the
first rise of it, and hee ordered out ymediatly a competent force of foot,
and severall troops of his owne regiment of horse, which wee must
againe lett your Lordships know is the greatest stay wee have to good
government in the army, and most cheerfully assisted to suppresse this
mutiny, and therefore wee cannot but continue with earnestnesse to
beseech your Lordships that present course may bee taken for satisfaction of the second payment due upon Colonell Jones his contract
which comes to 1,676*l.* 19*s.* 04*d.* least they being discouraged for want
of their due, should take in allsoe with the discontents of others to the
ruine of the whole. With the formencioned strength the governour
himselfe went against the mutineirs—the greatest part of them being of
Colonell Kinnaston's regiment accustomed to like practizes in North
Wales—and after some skirmishing—and comeing to push of pike—
wherein some of them were killed, severall hurt on both sides, the
governour endangered and Colonell Castle's horse shott under him, the
mutineirs betooke themselves to a place of advantage, a fortifyed hill,
neere the Collidg, and with them many of those called out to subdue
them, which occasioned the shutting the gates of the city, the stopping
others that were appointed to march, and calling in many of those that
were without, least the whole army—too inclinable to distemper—had
fallen into mutiny, which their language and carriage gave just grounds
to feare and to prevent the spreading of this contagion—if it should have
continued till morning—after they had defended the said hill till midnight, they were received to mercy upon their humble submission and
promise of amendment. By this great disorder which there have been
severall threatenings since of renewing, your Lordships will perceive
the necessity there is ot hastening a considerable summe of money hither
for contentment both of officers and souldiers—the numbers whereof the
inclosed lists will give you—who will not bee conteyned with that
allowance which we have hitherto made them, and gave your Lordships
notice of. If wee might bee bould to name a summe, wee could not
pitch upon lesse then 30,000*l.* which might in some proporcion answere

their expectations, and helpe to provide herring, beefe and other food for winter, and if your Lordships sent what money is intended for the Brittish in Ulster hither, wee suppose it might bee carefully and proffitably laid out for support of such of them as will move and joyne in the service here. Wee are not assured that the numbers of souldiers—of the old regiments which wee have reduced from eleven to seven—will hould, though upon the reducement wee had a generall muster of all your forces in one day, and tooke the strictest course possibly to prevent fraud, which if there bee any will bee discovered at their next muster which wee intend shortly, the generall transposcing of officers and confounding of companyes putting them out of the course of deceiveing us suddainly.

The horse are not yet reduced, but wee beleeve the twenty troops will be brought to ten or twelve, which wee shall endeavour to make the like numbers with the new troopes.

Wee humbly desire for the good of the service that all officers may bee comanded to their charges, for as wee allow noe pay to absentes so wee shall bee inforced to dispose of their comands whome wee have continued upon this new settlement unlesse they returne speedily.

Wee understand from Ulster that Sir William Stuart who commanded a regiment of foot, and a troop of horse in your service is lately deceased, and most of us knowing the great advantage would redound to the service by your Lordships giveing the Lord President of Connaght the power to dispose of the quarters hee held, and the rest in the Laggan, and to place a colonell and captaine in the severall charges void by his death, whome hee might bee sure would upon all occasions observe his commands in a cordiall conjunction with the Connaght forces for preservacion of the whole. And upon this occasion give us leave againe to interceed for speedy supplyes especially of money, both to his Lordship and the new forces at Derry, who cannot subsist by what is allready appointed for them, and have suffered as much, if not more, then any of your forces in this kingdome though hitherto most neglected, and especially wee cannot emitt to mention to your Lordships the Lord President's owne particular, whose condicion is soe sad that after the most exemplary devoating himselfe to your service in the midst of difficultyes not to bee parallelled, his life is become a burtheu to him. If 10,000l., a summe which hath been frequently afforded to other provinces, were but entrusted with his Lordship for the army there, wee are perswaded you would receive a better accompt of it then you have of many times soe much elsewhere.

Wee must againe in particular remember your Lordships of the great want here is of a traine of artillery, without which noe considerable service can bee done but to waste the enemye's corne, nor the rebells match't in the feild, though were wee provided thereof, wee should not doubt your army might bee masters in these parts, being able to draw out one thousand horse and three thousand foot leaveing the guarrisons indifferently manned. . . .

Postscript.—Since the writeing hereof we received a letter from the French Resident at Kilkenny, which wee send your Lordships here inclosed with our answere to it, and humbly desire to receive your resolution therein by the next, as also concerning the Lord of Ormonde's proposition for the 5,000 men." *Signed.* [N. VI., 46.]

WILLIAM LENTHALL to the COMMISSIONERS OF SCOTLAND.

" 1647, July 10 [should be 12].—Communicating Sir Thomas Fairfax's reply concerning their intercepted letters. (See *Commons' Journals,* v. 241.) *Draft.* [N. XII., 208.]

The Earl of Lauderdale, Hew Kennedy, and Robert Barclay, to
Willia☞ Lenthall.

1647, July 15. Worcester House —(Identical, *mutatis mutandis*,
with the letter from the same to the Speaker of the House of Peers,
which is printed in *Lords' Journals*, ix. 338.) *Signed. Seal.*
Enclosed:

Two papers both printed as above. [N. VI., 47.]

The Earl of Lauderdale, Charles Erskine, Hew Kennedy, and
Robert Barclay, to the Speaker of the House of Peers
pro tempore.

1647, July 22. Worcester House.—(Printed in *Lords' Journals*, ix.
350.) *Signed. Seal.* [N. VI., 48.]

The House of Co☞☞ons.

1647, July 30.—Order that the General should not advance his army
within 30 miles of London. (Printed in *Commons' Journals*, v. 259.)
[N. XV., 17.]

Ordinance.

1647, July 31.—For raising horses. (Printed in *Lords' Journals*, ix.
364.) [N. XV., 18.]

The Heads of the Proposals agreed upon by Sir Tho☞as Fairfax
and the Council of the Ar☞y.

1647, August 1.—(Printed in Rushworth, iv. 2. 731.) *Draft.* [N.
XV., 23.]

The Earl of Lauderdale, Charles Erskine, Hew Kennedy, and
Robert Barclay to the Speaker of the House of Peers *pro
tempore.*

1647, August 1. Worcester House.—(Printed in *Lords' Journals*,
ix. 367, and Rushworth, iv. 2, 738.) *Signed. Seal.* [N. VI., 49.]

The Asse☞bly of Divines to the Parlia☞ent.

1647, August 2.—Expressing their desire for peace. (Printed in
Lords' Journals, ix. 368.) *Signed.* [N. XXII., 47.]

The Lords to the Co☞☞ons.

1647, August 2.—Message. (Printed in *Commons' Journals*, v. 264.)
[N. XV., 19.]

The Parlia☞ent to the King.

[1647, August 2.]—Forwarding the Declaration, which is printed in
Lords' Journals, ix. 364. *Draft.* [N. XV., 20.]

The House of Co☞☞ons.

1647, August 2.—Resolution for appointing a Committee to communicate with the Common Council. (Printed in *Commons' Journals*, v.
264.) [N. XV., 21.]

THE PARLIAMENT to the COMMISSIONERS WITH THE KING
and
The SAME to SIR THOMAS FAIRFAX.

1647, August 2.—(Both printed in *Lords' Journals*, ix. 368.) *Drafts*. [N. XII., 210, 211.]

The PARLIAMENT to Major-General BROWN.

1647, August 3.—(Printed in *Lords' Journals*, ix. 373.) *Draft*. [N. XII., 212.]

The SAME to the COMMISSIONERS WITH THE KING.

Same date.—(Printed in *Lords' Journals*, ix. 373.) *Draft* with amendments as passed by the Commons. The form originally drawn up differs entirely from that ultimately adopted. [N. XII., 213.]

SIR THOMAS FAIRFAX to the EARL OF MANCHESTER and WILLIAM LENTHALL.

Same date. Colebrook.—(Printed in *Lords' Journals*, ix. 375.) *Signed. Enclosed:*

The Declaration of Sir Thomas Fairfax and the Council of War. (Printed *ubi suprà* and in Rushworth, iv. 2. 744.) [N. VI., 50, 51.]

The LORDS THAT WENT TO THE ARMY.

1647, August 4.—Engagement. (Printed in Rushworth, iv. 2. 754, and *Lords' Journals*, ix. 383.) *Signed* only by the Lords mentioned in Rushworth, but not by the Commons. [N. XV., 22.]

[The ARMY] to SEVERAL COUNTIES.

1647, July [? August] 12. Kingston-upon-Thames.—Circular intended to be sent. "Whereas the heavy burdens of tyranny and oppression . . . and the obstruction of free addresses to the Parliament for removal thereof occasioned you to desire this army to interpose between you and vassallage, and to endeavour the recovery and establishment of your native liberties. The consideration thereof hath begat in us a firm resolution freely to expose our lives and fortunes to the utmost hazard for the common interest of the free Commons of England. We therefore cannot but conceive a necessity of communion of Council in our preservation of these just and righteous ends. The grievances of every county are best apprehended . . . by themselves . . . and likewise various means of remedy for the same . . . being sometimes necessary for different counties . . . we conceive the most suitable means . . . may be with most facility apprehended by the counties themselves. We therefore desire that two or more . . . of every county that have called this Army by their late petitions to engage for their liberties—and are thereby equally engaged with us—might be chosen as Agitators in the behalf of the well affected in each respective county that they might constantly sit as gentlemen—during the time of the Treaty at least—at the Head Quarters to consider of all the infringements of their liberties and of expedients for relief and to propound them to the Council of War and Agitators for the Army, as also that both the Council of War and Agitators might communicate their propositions for the public good to them that from them all things might be communicated to the counties, that . . . the most exact scrutiny might be made to discover the foundations of our Oppressions Bondage and Misery to their everlasting overturning, and then a precious foundation for a glorious structure of true freedom righteousness and justice might be established immoveably." *Copy.* [N. XII., 209.]

Heads for a CONFERENCE.

1647, August 13.—About the Declaration from Sir Thomas Fairfax. (Printed in *Lords' Journals*, ix. 382.) [N. XV., 24, 25.]

The HOUSE OF COMMONS.

1647, August 14.—Order concerning the King's servants. (Printed in *Commons' Journals*, v. 274.) [N. XVI., 10.]

CHARLES ERSKINE, HEW KENNEDY, and ROBERT BARCLAY to the SPEAKER OF THE HOUSE OF PEERS *pro tempore.*

1647, August 17. Worcester House.—(Printed in *Lords' Journals*, ix. 387, where " by Sir Thomas Fairfaxe's soldiers " should be " by some of Sir.") *Signed. Seal.* [N. VI., 52.]

The COMMITTEE FOR THE REVENUE.

1647, August 19.—Report concerning the moneys for the King's Privy Purse mentioned in the annexed letter. [N. XV., 26.] *Annexed :*

EDWARD LORD MOUNTAGU and others to the said Committee.

1647, August 17. Oatlands.—" 100*l.* of the money last received was for the present delivered into the Privy Purse and his Majesty expects a further addition whereof we presume your Lordships will be sensible. The remainder of the money is already disbursed for the necessary charge of the household, which constrains us to send Mr. Cressett for a supply. We are also to desire that his Majesty's clothes and other accommodations mentioned in the paper we lately transmitted unto you, may be forthwith furnished according to the King's expectation, and his necessary use of them. Also that Table Linen may be provided both for the King and the Household, that which formerly you sent being worn out with the continual using of it." (See *Commons' Journals*, v. 284.) *Signed. Seal.* [N. XV., 27.]

[JOHN RUSHWORTH] to OLIVER CROMWELL.

1647, August 20. Kingston.—" The General commanded me to hasten this enclosed article, desiring you will be pleased to take a seasonable opportunity some time this day, if it be possible, to present this paper concerning the prisoners in the Tower, and to endeavour the obtaining as effectual an order for their relief" as the House will grant. *Signature torn off. Seal.* [N. VI., 53.]

Major-General ROBERT STERLING to his nephew, CORNELIUS CRAFORD.

1647, August 30. Cork.—" I know not what days may be here for us, since the Independents have got all in their hands in England, and we having declared all of us for the Presbyteral Government here to which purpose we have sent our declaration to London and the copy thereof to Leslie to let the State of Scotland know that we are against

Sir Thomas Fairfax his army and their government, and I am desired by this army to signify so much unto the General" . . *Seal.* [N. VI., 54.]

Major-General ROBERT STERLING to SIR PATRICK WEIMIS.

1647, August 30. Cork.—"I am presently tacking hors for the feild with our army towards the County of Tipperary wher we myud to atempt Clemell and Cashel, so far as God will inabill us. This last weik by past having certen intelligence from Ingland that Fairfax with his Independ army was possest of the Tower and Citty of London and moulding and modelling a new Parlament, giving them lawes and orders to what that army thought fitt, we heir the holl officers of this army upon long consideration and much debait all of us concludit to stand an with another according to the national Covenant in defenc of the king and former Parlament according as you may reid in this inclosit remonstrance, which is a trew coppy of that we have sent to the Parlament of Ingland. If the old Parlament ther, we sall have thanks, if a new on, they may judg of our intentions by our paiper, which is signat by all the officers both of hors and foot in behalf of themselves and soldiers. This much I am desirit to writ unto you, which if you think fitt and convenient to mak knowine unto Colonel Jones and the officers ther to know if theyre mynds, and lett me know by your letter, if that army did relish and lyke of the bussines, but if you fynd the army mor inclynabill to any new government I sall desyr you to destroy this letter and remonstrance and lett me receive your best advic herein that I may communicat it to our Lord President and other officers or so much as you sall think fitt. . . . . By the way I must assur you that our Lord President is a very honest and faithfull servant to King and Parlament . ." *Seal.* [N. VI., 55.]

Major-General ROBERT STERLING to his cousin, SIR JOHN CRAUFURD, of Kilburne.

1647, August 30. Cork.—(Most of it is to the same purport as the preceding) "all which I am desyrit by our Lord President, who is our generall and a faithfull servant to King and Parlament according to the Covenant and *no othirweyes* to let them know by my letter to the generall ther faithfullnesse to the Covenant, which remonstrance and letter to the generall I humbly desyr you present unto him and desyr his Excellenc to mak our faithfullness knowine to the stait of Scotland and to so many of the Parlament of Ingland as may bee for the present in Scotland, wher we heir ther is a grit many fled." . . I desire the bearer may be sent back with all speed with the best advice. We were all of one mind, but it was resolved that I only, as best known to Scotland and the general, should sign the letter which was written and read by them all. *Seal.* [N. VI., 56.]

Major-General ROBERT STERLING to Lieutenant-General MONTGOMERY at Ayr.

[1647, August 30. Cork.]—Concerning the resolution of himself and his army to stand for the Presbyterial government against Fairfax and his army. *Seal.* [N. VIII., 134.]

Lieutenant-Colonel MARSHALL to [SIR ADAM HEPBURN] LORD HUMBY.

1647, August 31. Cork.—Entreating his best assistance to "the real and faithful expressions of those who . . desire nothing more than the

King and kingdom's happiness and who will all . . .—except some few inconsiderable dissenting brethren—contribute their lives and all that is dear unto them to do you and that kingdom service in pursuance of the Covenant," and that he would be an instrument for the speedy dispatch by the bearer of the resolutions of our friends in that kingdom upon that which is imparted from this army to the Earl of Leven under the hand of Major-General Sterling. *Extract.* (This and the four Sterling letters were with several others, thirteen in all, intercepted by Colonel Michael Jones. See *Commons' Journals*, v. 307 ; *Lords' Journals*, ix. 445 (where two others and the Remonstrance are printed), 577.) [N. XII., 214.]

CHARLES ERSKINE, HEW KENNEDY, and ROBERT BARCLAY to WILLIAM LENTHALL.

1647, August . Worcester House.—Asking that the petition of Sir George Melvill, one of his Majesty's servants, who had been waiting for six months, might be taken into consideration. *Signed. Seal. Enclosed :*

The said Petition. [N. VI., 58.]

The MEMBERS OF BOTH HOUSES that are of the COMMITTEE OF BOTH KINGDOMS and the SCOTCH COMMISSIONERS.

1647, September 1 and 2.—Papers interchanged concerning the Propositions. (All printed in *Lords' Journals*, ix. 420.) The Scotch papers are the originals and there is also a copy of the first. [N. XX., 6, 7, 8, 9, 10, 11.] Other copies of Nos. 1, 2, 3, and 5 are N. XV., 28.

JAMES BRUCE to his uncle, THOMAS BRUCE, at Stirling.

1647, September 3. Cork.—Availing himself of Major-General Sterling's sending his servant to Scotland to write for news of his relations and friends. (Doubtless intercepted with Sterling's and Marshall's letters.) [N. VI., 58.]

CHARLES ERSKINE, HEW KENNEDY, and ROBERT BARCLAY to the SPEAKER OF THE HOUSE OF PEERS *pro tempore.*

1647, September 3. Worcester House.—(Printed in *Lords' Journals*, ix. 421.) *Signed. Seal.*
Enclosed : The paper signed John Donn, printed in *Lords' Journals*, ix. 422.
Annexed : The Resolution of the House thereon, printed in *Lords' Journals*, ix. 421. [N. VI., 59.]

The MEMBERS OF BOTH HOUSES that are of the COMMITTEE OF BOTH KINGDOMS and the SCOTCH COMMISSIONERS.

1647, September 4.—Papers concerning the Propositions. (All printed in *Lords' Journals*, ix. 424. The Scotch paper is the original.) [N. XX., 12, 13.]

Paper of the SCOTCH COMMISSIONERS.

1647, September 6.—(Printed in *Lords' Journals*, ix. 426.) *Signed :* "John Donn." [N. XX., 14.]

The PARLIAMENT to the LORD CHANCELLOR OF SCOTLAND.

[1647, September 6.]—Giving notice of their desire for the recall of the Scotch army in Ireland. (Printed in *Lords' Journals*, ix. 425.) *Draft*, with amendments. [N. XII., 196.]

The PARLIAMENT.

1647, September 7.—Vote approving of the papers of September 4th. (Printed in *Lords' Journals*, ix. 425.) [N. XX., 15.]

The EARL OF LAUDERDALE, CHARLES ERSKINE, HEW KENNEDY, and ROBERT BARCLAY to WILLIAM LENTHALL.

1647, September 8. Hampton Court.—(Identical, *mutatis mutandis*, with the letter from the same to the Speaker of the House of Peers *pro tempore*, which is printed in *Lords' Journals*, ix. 430.) *Signed. Seal.* [N. VI., 60.]

SIR JOHN HOLLAND, SIR JAMES HARINGTON, SIR JOHN COKE, and RICHARD BROWNE to WILLIAM LENTHALL.

1647, September 8. Hampton Court.—(Identical, *mutatis mutandis*, with the letter from the Earl of Pembroke and Montgomery to the Earl of Manchester, which is printed in *Lords' Journals*, ix. 428.) *Signed. Seal.* [N. VI., 61.]

ESTIMATE.

[1647, September 9.]—Of the arrears of the forces to go to Ireland. (See *Commons' Journals*, v. 298.) [N. XXI., 68.]

LORD INCHIQUIN to the EARL OF MANCHESTER.

1647, September 12. Cashel.—(Printed in *King's Pamphlets*, E. 409. An abstract in the *Appendix to the Sixth Report of the Historical MSS. Commission*, p. 198.) [N. VI., 62.]

The PARLIAMENT.

1647, September 16, 17, 18.—Resolutions concerning the army and garrisons in England and Ireland. (The first three are printed in *Commons' Journals*, v. 306, 307, 308, the last in *Lords' Journals*, ix. 448, the whole preceded by Mr. Scawen's report of the 9th (see *Commons' Journals*, v. 298), the purport of which appears from the Resolutions.) [N. XV., 29.]

SIR THOMAS FAIRFAX to the COMMISSIONERS OF PARLIAMENT.

1647, September 21.—(The heads are printed in Rushworth, iv. 2. 820.) [N. XXII., 64.]

The COMMITTEE FOR THE ADMIRALTY AND CINQUE PORTS.

1647, September 28.—Report concerning Captain Williams.

And

The HOUSE OF LORDS.

1647, October 6.—Order thereon. (Both printed in *Lords' Journals*, ix. 470, 468.) [N. XXI., 69, 71.]

The Committee of Foreign Affairs.

[1647, September 28.]—State of the matter of fact concerning the late difference between the English and Swedish ships, in obedience to the order of July 9th. (Printed in *Commons' Journals*, v. 239.) On Saturday, May 1st 1647, Captain Owen, Captain of the *Henrietta Maria* and Rear-Admiral of the fleet, having with him only the *Roebuck*, with 45 men, met near the Isle of Wight with a fleet of Swedes, Admiral, Vice-Admiral, and Rear-Admiral with three men-of-war more and nine to ten merchant ships, "who after several peeces of ordnance still refused to take in their flags, their topsailes being downe, whereupon Captain Owen sent his lieutenant aboard the Admirall to know his resolucion, who alleadged he had commission from the Queene of Sweden, comanding him not to stricke his flagg to the ships of any forreigne prince or state, except in his or their owne harbours, or roades, and declared himselfe resolved accordingly. Captain Owen, haveing received this answere, calls to his assistance two English merchant ships, then neare him, bound to the southward. But during the tyme of his consultacion with them, the Swedish Admirall boysed his topsaile, and was got soe farre on head of Captain Owen, that he had noe hopes to fetch him up before night, and therefore, being in duty and conscience bound not to deferre any opportunity of preserving the honour and just rights of this crowne in the soveraignity of those seas, beares to the Vice-Admirall and gives him a broadside within halfe pistoll shott. At the first answere from that ship, Captain Owen's tiller was shott asunder, which put him from his steerage, that he could not worke his ship, and thereupon was forced shortly after to stand off, till he had repaired his tiller, and soe then following them and perceiving to stand as for Diepe, he tackes in and stood for Portsmouth. The *Roebuck* alsoe, whose comander had told the Admirall that if he would not take in his flagg friendly, they should compell him or sinke by his side, did after his denying to doe it, make some shot at the Swedish ships, but night came on.

Captain Batten, Vice-Admirall and Comander-in-chiefe of the fleet, set forth by the Parliament, receiving advice hereof, on the second of May last, sailed out of the Downes with the *St. Andrew*, being the ship himselfe comanded, the *Guardland*, the *Convertine*, and the *Maryrose*, and on the third of May, in the morning, saw the Swedes lye at anchour in Bulloigne roads—haveing taken downe their colours before Captain Battin came in—, and by eight of the clock, came to anchour close by the Swedish Admirall. Whereupon, he sent unto them and they accordingly came on board, but declared that if their flags had beene up, they would not have taken them downe, by reason of the strictnes of their commission, given by the Queene of Sweden, which caused them to resist the Vice Admirall. Hereupon, Captain Batten brought onely the Vice-Admirall into the Downes, giving the rest liberty to repaire home, for that they wanted victualls, and had charge of a convoy. And after this, the other Swedish men of warre followed their Vice-Admirall into the Downes, declaring that they durst not goe home without her. Which matter, upon a report to both houses, was referred to the Committee of Lords and Commons for the Admiralty and Cinque ports, who on the 7th of May, gave Captain Batten order to release the ships, which being dispatched away unto him, the same night they were forthwith discharged." [N. XVIII., 26.]

The Parliament to the Queen of Sweden.

[1647, September 30.]—(Printed in *Lords' Journals*, ix. 455.) *Copy.* [N. XVIII., 27.]

The PARLIA) ENT.

1647, September 30.—Resolution about a further application to the king. (Printed in *Lords' Journals*, ix. 456.) [N. XV., 30.]

NICHOLAS, BISHOP OF FERNS, NICHOLAS PLUNKETT, and others,
to VISCOUNT TAAFFE.

1647, October 4. Kilkenny.—"The enclosed intelligence is certain confirmed by Colonel Warren, who upon parole came hither yesternight from Dublin. They are very strong in horse and foot by the joining of the Scots under Colonel Munro, now Commander-in-Chief of Ulster for the Parliament. It may be feared Inchiquin hath resolved a conjunction with them. You are therefore with your army to annear the borders of this province, as far as Cashel or Fethard, to hinder such conjunction. The enemy intends to put Ireland upon a day. You are to certify us by what day your army may be at Cashel, or Fethard, whereby to receive our further orders." *Signed.* [N. VI., 63.]

JEFFREY BARRON to [VISCOUNT TAAFFE].

1647, October 5. Kilkenny.—"It was an hour after nightfall when Major   and I alighted at the Council door last night and delivered your Lordship's and the Council of War's letter and being this morning called on presented the reasons of your resolutions with all the advantages I could, which were well received and admitted by the Council. They now only desire a party of 200 horse, which they think your army is able to spare, and which they believe would make the Catholic armies in Leinster matches for Jones, but on that I would not deliver any positive sense though I was often demanded. Some exception was taken at the stiffness of the phrase in the Council of War's letter, who did not seem to submit this their resolution unto the Council's determination. All other news are dead here. My other affairs are under debate at the Board. I put them here into great hopes of your success by the goodness of the party of horse and foot you now have, but most of all by your own good resolution. The miscarriages of the services of Cashel and the county of Cork are everywhere in the country much apprehended, but most of any at the Board, to which I think it would be very satisfactory to see your Lordship hath a just feeling." . . . *Torn and in part illegible.* [N. VI., 64.]

The Desires of the ARMY.

1647, October 15, 16. Putney.—1. That the Committee would move the House to determine under "what conduct the forces now appointed for Ireland upon the present establishment shall go, the uncertainty whereof is not a little discouragement to men from engaging in that service. And if the Parliament should think fit to leave the appointment thereof to the General we should then offer that all the forces to be continued under the present establishment both for England and Ireland shall be equally engaged without distinction to go for Ireland, when the Parliament shall require, and the Parliament only ordering what proportion of them they will at any time have sent the General to order what particular regiments shall go."

2 and 3. (The purport of these appears by the resolutions on them, which are printed in *Commons' Journals*, v. 341, top of left-hand column.)

4. Proposing that the 10*l.* *per diem* granted by order of the 4th instant be raised to 30*l.* [N. XXI., 70.]

Proposals reported by Mr. SCAWEN for the completing of the two bodies in England and Ireland, &c. from the Committee of the Army.

1647, October 15, 16. Putney.—(These proposals were turned into the resolutions printed in *Commons' Journals*, v. 340, 341.) [N. XV., 31, 32.]

JOHN RUSHWORTH to WILLIAM LENTHALL.

1647, October 20.—Enclosing a letter from the King to Sir Thomas Fairfax. (See *Commons' Journals*, v. 338.) *Seal.* [N. VI., 66.]

The humble Advice of the ASSEMBLY OF DIVINES concerning a LARGER CATECHISM.

1647, October 22.—(Printed in Grey, iii., Appendix, No. 12, p. 19.) (See *Commons' Journals*, v. 340.) Two copies both *Signed* "Charles Herle, Prolocutor, Cornelius Burges, Assessor, Henry Robrough and Adoniram Byfield, Scribæ." [N. XXII., 54, 55.]

ARTHUR ANNESLEY and SIR ROBERT KING.

1647, October 30.—Certificate stating that the Lord of Ormonde though entitled to have the bills of Exchange mentioned in the treaty accepted by sufficient merchants in France or Holland had at the persuasion of the Commissioners waived all farther security, relying on the honour of the Parliament. (See *Commons' Journals*, v. 350.) [N. XXI., 72.]

Propositions concerning DELINQUENTS.

1647, October 30.—Submitted to the House of Commons and disagreed to. (See *Lords' Journals*, ix. 506.) (The substance of them appears from *Lords' Journals*, ix. 476, except that Dr. Bramhall, Bishop of Derry, is added to the persons in the first exception, and except that nothing corresponding to paragraph 5 is in this paper, which on the other hand imposes on the King's menial servants a rate of composition proportionate to one-twentieth of their estates.) [N. XV., 33.]

Colonel JOHN BOYS to WILLIAM LENTHALL.

1647, November 2. Dover Castle.—Stating that Bennet, Lord Sherwood, an Irish Baron, and others had landed the day before at Dover, and that as they had no passes he had sent some along with them. *Seal.* [N. VI., 67.]

WILLIAM CLARKE, secretary signing by the appointment of the General Council of the Army, to WILLIAM LENTHALL.

1647, November 5. Putney.—"Whereas it is generally reported that the House was induced to make another address to the King by propositions, by reason it was represented to the House as the desire of the Army, from a tenderness to the freedom of Parliamentary actings this night the General Council of the Army declared that any such representation of their desires was altogether groundless, and that they earnestly desire no such consideration may be admitted in the House's resolutions in that particular." (See *Commons' Journals*, v. 352.) *Signed. Seal.* [N. VI., 68.]

[LORD INCHIQUIN] to WILLIAM LENTHALL.

1647, November 6. Cork.—I have secured Colonel Serle who is lately come into this Province, and who is by some suspected to have been interested in certain late actions not consonant to the pleasure of the Honourable Houses, and I desire their pleasure concerning him. *Signature torn off.* [N. VI., 69.]

SIR LUCIUS DILLON to VISCOUNT TAAFFE.

1647, November 6. Drumnishe.—"To inform your Lordship of the distracted condition of unfortunate Connaught would but take up too much room and add troubles to your thoughts, I will therefore defer the story thereof, and only let you know that all the friends you have in it are yet living and thats all. I have directed and recommended several captains with their companies to your Lordship. Which of them have appeared or how many I cannot say, but shall be glad to know and to have the favour of being advertised at full of the state of your army and affairs of that province with what else your Lordship pleases to impart unto me. The Commissary-General writes unto your Lordship. They are now in circuit in this Province, endeavouring to order the distractions thereof, but the confusion is so great, as if it come not from a high hand I expect to see no settlement this many a day to come ; though Mr. Darcye gives me better hopes, who is a convertent beyond belief, and promises to perform many good acts in this next assembly. I confess I am much taken with his professions, and shall be glad to know of your Lordship's resolve to be there. We are troubled with frequent marauds from the enemies of Sligo who, with the Lagan men, threaten destruction to us this winter, but they cannot hurt us more than the native robbers do. Lu[cius] went yesterday to the Boyle . . . he will do what he can to preserve the holds entrusted to his care." [N. VI., 70.]

Those whose names are subscribed on behalf of themselves, and all THE FREEBORN PEOPLE of ENGLAND to the SUPREME AUTHORITY of this Nation, the COMMONS in Parliament assembled.

[1647, November 9.]—Petition, showing " that the rights we claim in the Agreement, hereunto annexed, are our own both by birth and purchase.

That we see no other means—under Heaven—to preserve these rights unto ourselves and our dear fellow Commoners, than by so agreeing and declaring.

That this Agreement . . . shall be maintained with the same resolution of spirit and hazard of our lives wherewith our freedoms were —as we thought—recovered, rather than we will suffer ourselves by any force or fraud to be deprived of them, or any part of them.

That it is equally grievous to us whether we be enslaved by King or Lords, but to be in continual conferences and addresses offered up by those we trust into the hands of such as have manifested their tyrannical purposes towards us and towards you for our sakes, is a danger we can endure no longer.

That your extremely long forbearing to settle the people's peace and liberties upon your own authority—which indeed is theirs—without any just cause to hinder you,—your capital enemy being at your mercy and a considerable army at your commands—is matter of great jealousy, and hath necessitated us to betake ourselves to this extraordinary way of remedy. We do therefore most earnestly beseech you to join with your tried friends and natural countrymen in this agreement—any way tending to your weal and ours—and not with the King nor with any others by adventuring again the price of our blood upon the unsafe and groundless terms of accommodation with perfidious enemies." (See *Commons' Journals*, v. 354, and Rushworth, iv. 2. 867.) *Signed* by 21 officers. *Copy.* [N. XXII., 106.]

The KING to the PARLIAMENT
And
The SAME to Colonel WHALLEY
And
The SAME to LORD MONTAGUE.

1647, November 11. Hampton Court.—(All printed in *Lords' Journals*, ix. 519, 520.) *Copies.* [N. XII., 216, 217, 249.]

The PARLIAMENT to Colonel HAMMOND.

1647, November 16.—Instructions concerning the ·King's safety. (Printed in *Lords' Journals*, ix. 527, and Peck, *Desiderata Curiosa*, ix. 50.) [N. XV., 34.]

The Humble Advice of the ASSEMBLY OF DIVINES concerning a SHORTER CATECHISM.

1647, November 25.—(See *Commons' Journals*, v. 368.) [N. XXII., 56.]

Report by Mr. REYNOLDS.

1647, November 26.—(Printed in *Lords' Journals*, ix. 544; *Commons' Journals*, v. 370.) [N. XV., 35.]

The HOUSE OF LORDS to the HOUSE OF COMMONS.

1647, November 26.—The four Propositions concerning the Militia, for recalling the King's Oaths and Declarations, concerning Peers made since the Seal was taken away by Lord Keeper Littleton, and concerning the power of the Houses to adjourn. (See *Commons' Journals*, v. 370.) (These coincide with the Four Bills printed in Gardiner, *Constitutional Documents*, pp. 248–253, except that the last clause on p. 253 is omitted, and also the enacting parts.) [N. XV., 36.]

Information of WILLIAM HASLOPE.

1647, December 2.—Touching the meeting on November 13th at the Mouth at Aldersgate, giving the names of some of the persons there, there being about 150 altogether. One speaker is stated to have said "The same business we are upon is perfected in Naples, for if any person stand up for Monarchy there, he is immediately hanged at his door." (Printed in Grey, iii., Appendix, No. 76, p. 129.) [N. XV., 37.]

The humble Representation from SIR THOMAS FAIRFAX and the COUNCIL OF THE ARMY.

1647, December 5.—(Printed in *Lords' Journals*, ix. 556.) [N. XXII., 63.]

Divers of the PROTESTANT NOBILITY and GENTRY OF IRELAND to the HOUSE OF COMMONS.

[1647, December 11.]—Petition. (Identical *mutatis mutandis* with that presented to the House of Lords, which is printed in *Lords' Journals*,

ix. 568. See *Commons' Journals*, v. 380.) *Signed.* [N. XXII., 105.]

The COMMITTEE AT GOLDSMITHS' HALL.

1647, December 20.—Report in consequence of the General's letter, ordering that Sir John Poulett's fine be drawn up according to the Exeter Articles. [N. XV., 38.]

Major General ROWLAND LAUGHARNE to the HOUSE OF COMMONS.

[1647.]—Petition, stating his services and disbursements for the Parliament and praying that a debt of 5,000*l.* due to Thomas Marsham, a Delinquent, by the late Earl of Arundel might be paid by his executors to himself, and also that his accounts might be audited. *Signed.* [N. XXII., 123.]

The Affirmation of THOMAS GRIFFIN.

[1647 (?).]—(Printed in Peck, *Desiderata Curiosa,* ix. 38.) [N. XV., 187.]

WILLIAM LENTHALL to [Colonel RAINBOROUGH, Vice-Admiral].

1647[-8], January [1].—Enclosing the resolution of the House for his speedy repairing to the Isle of Wight. (See *Commons' Journals,* v. 413.) *Draft.* [N. XII., 220.]

The HOUSE OF COMMONS to the MAYOR and other well affected inhabitants OF NEWPORT.

1647[-8], January 1.—Thanking them for their conduct in suppressing the late mutiny and for the assistance they had given Colonel Hammond. (See *Commons' Journals,* ix. 414.) *Draft.* [N. XII., 218.]

VOTES.

1647[-8], January 1.—Concerning the safety and security of the king's person. (Printed in *Commons' Journals,* v. 414.) [N. XV., 39.]

VOTES.

1647[-8], January 3.—Concerning the Committee of both Kingdoms. (Printed in *Commons' Journals,* v. 416.) [N. XV., 40.]

The COMMITTEE FOR IRELAND.

1647[-8], January 4.—Reporting that they have no money available for the gratuities to Lord Inchiquin and others. [N. XXI., 73.]

SIR THOMAS FAIRFAX to WILLIAM LENTHALL.

1647[-8], January 6. Windsor.—Repeating his recommendation in favour of Major-General Laugharne. *Signed. Seal.* [N. VI., 71.]

The EARL OF LOUDOUN and others to WILLIAM LENTHALL.

1647-8, January 13. Worcester House.—Desiring that the gold, jewels, and plate of the Earl of Roxburgh, seized at St. James', that remain impignorated in the hands of Alderman Andrews be delivered back again, and satisfaction be given for such of them as had been disposed of. *Signed. Seal.* [N. VII., 119.]

List of ARREARS from MICHAEL HERRING, Treasurer at
Goldsmiths' Hall.

1647[-8], January 18.—(Printed in *Commons' Journals*, v. 436.)
[N. XV., 41.]

The HOUSE OF COMMONS to the COMMITTEE AT DERBY HOUSE.

1647[-8], January 24.—Order to suppress tumults and insurrections.
(Printed in *Commons' Journals*, v. 442.) [N. XV., 42.]

LORD INCHIQUIN to WILLIAM LENTHALL.

1647[-8], January 31. Cork.—Setting forth the distressed condition
of his army. "It will bee difficult for mee to resolve whether the want
of food or cloathing bee likely to prove most destructive unto us both
of them raigning most severely amongst us, so that our men dye
dayly of their meere want. . . . I must humbly offer to consideration that there is no visible humane meanes resting whereby"
the army "may bee expected to bee preserved from ruyue without
immeadiate supplies thence, save onely an intended expedition into
the county of Tipperary whether I resolve to draw the most considerable part of the army that can in any wise be able to march
and doe designe to place them in the townes of Fetherd and Cashell,
and to compell the country to affoard them free quarters, so long a
tyme as they are able which will not bee above a forthnight or three
weekes, the inhabitaunts being allready greatly wasted by our former
depredations and the Irish taxes heavily imposed on them . . . At
best wee cannot hope to find above 3 weekes or a monthes subsistannce
abroad haveing allready experienced that the like tyme exhausted and
destroyed all the provisions in the two countyes of Kerry and Lymerick,
so upon our comeing home, wee can expect no releife but what must
bee transmitted unto us thence, for our contribucions which formerly
were some stay unto us when lengthened out with supplyes thence, are
now for the most part anticipated and taken upp by the souldier comit-
ting disorderly wast and spoyle in his march or stragling from his
garrison which the officers cannot restrayne them from in theis necessitous
tymes with their utmost indeavours so as wee are forced according or
ingagement to allow most of our monyes arising that way to annsweare
and satisfy the prejudices done the country. And for the composi-
cions made with remoter parts, all wee can doe is to take hostages for
payment at such reasonable dayes as are allowed to rayse the monyes
in, without which they cannot bee levyed and so soone as wee march
out of the country compounded with where wee cannot stay and expect
they should levy the monyes, the Irish forces slipp in by partyes and
restrayne the country from makeing their payments by seizing the
monyes where they find any collected, imprisoning the collectors and
dealeing with those who contribute to us as with enemyes, so as all the
remedy wee have in this case is to hang upp the hostages which may
give some satisfacion to the eyes, but not to the stomackes of our
souldiers; whose necessityes have already growne to that height that
they frequently pilladge and plunder our houses and quarters and
rifle the people resorting to our marketts which deterrs them from supplying us that way so as on every hand wee are destitute of any
support to rest upon. And must therefore humbly beseech that
honnourable house so farre to compassionate our deepe distress, as
either to transmitt seasonable supplyes unto us, or to direct a competent proporcion of shipping to transport those soulders who desire to

returne to their native country, and to give admittaunce unto us to make the most moderate condicions wee can for the rest of the wretched English who cannot remove hence with their famiłyes but must submitt to a worse then Egiptian and Turkish servitude." *Signed. Seal.* [N. VI., 72.]

CONSIDERATIONS upon occasion of the Late Declaration of the Army to stand to the two Houses without and against the King.

1647[-8], February 1.—Though the King has granted such just laws as the parliament, when their debates were more sober and free, propounded, and which they held sufficient to redress the matters complained of, yet the same things are represented as reasons for the continuance of the persecution of the King. These matters complained of were scarcely sensible to the people compared with those, which the pretended reformers have laid upon them. These men persuade people that it is the public interest that the Kingdom be governed by military license and the King's just prerogatives are the swallowing up of all public interest in his sole power. The Parliament should have confined themselves to the power given them by the King's writ and the trust reposed by their Constituents. Had the King consented to the last address it would have been an absolute abdication, and he could not have discharged his conscience towards God, nor his care over his people. Nothing would have been left, but whether he should be called King or no. That they could not offer the King lower conditions without denying what God by the event of the war has borne such testimony to is a reason. beyond understanding. If success proves the justice of a cause, Turks and Pagans might use the same argument. The people were made believe they fought not against the King, and King and Parliament must lead an army against the King. It's the doctrine now that King-killing saints, not Kings, are the Lord's Anointed, and that David miscalled Saul when he so named him, and in sparing him denied that which God had borne testimony to. The people now feel the difference between the mild government of a King and the insolent tyranny of their fellows and inferiors. (Fourteen pages.) [N. XV., 43.]

The EARL OF ARDGLASS to "his kinsman," Lieutenant-General' OLIVER CROMWELL.

[1647-8, February 2.] Candlemas Day.—Desiring his favour in his poor business depending in the House, and stating that his estate had all been swept away by the rebels in the beginning of this war in Ireland and for these late years all his rents have been taken for the use of the Parliament forces, so that he has neither money nor credit, and his sureties are daily threatened with arrest for his second payment of 400*l.* "Let me not sink quite to the ground, if your power may hold up a falling house of the name, . . . Come to you I would, but I am told you would not be troubled where you are in Lincolnshire." *Postscript.*— "My Petition was once read in the House, and one made answer I was dead, but if you please to move me in it, I shall live again and prove successful." (See *Commons' Journals,* v. 437.) *Seal.* [N. VIII., 38.]

The PARLIAMENT to the STATES-GENERAL and to the ESTATES OF HOLLAND.

1647[-8], February 5.—Letters of Credence for Walter Strickland. (Both printed in *Lords' Journals,* x. 24.) *Drafts* with amendments. [N. XVIII., 62.]

The COMMITTEE FOR THE ADMIRALTY AND CINQUE PORTS.

1647[-8], February 17.—Report desiring that an ordinance for the settlement of the jurisdiction of the Court of Admiralty might be taken into consideration, as complaint is made by ambassadors that trade is much hindered by the want thereof, and also by commanders of ships that they cannot maintain discipline, and by owners that they cannot remove at common law a master who is part owner.

1647[-8], March 13.—Ordered that the above report be presented to the House of Commons. [N. XV., 44.]

SIR THOMAS FAIRFAX to WILLIAM LENTHALL.

1647[-8], February 17. Queen Street.—Desiring that the sequestrations of Colonel Sandys and Mr. Wightwick, the Governor and Lieutenant-Governor of Hartlebury Castle may be taken off according to the articles of surrender thereof. *Signed. Seal.* [N. VI., 73.]

SIR THOMAS FAIRFAX to WILLIAM LENTHALL.

1647[-8], February 22. Queen Street.—Enclosing the petition of divers officers and soldiers and desiring that the stating of their accounts might be expedited. *Signed. Seal. Enclosed :*

> The said petition, praying that their accounts might be referred to the Auditors to examine and audit, so that they might have the benefit of the Ordinance of the 1st of October last. [N. VI., 74.]

FRANCIS ALLEIN to WILLIAM LENTHALL.

1647[-8], February 24.—Enclosing a petition from Aldermen Averie and Packe and William Boothby, three of the Commissioners of Customs. *Signed. Enclosed :*

> The said petition, praying that in consequence of the absence of two other of the Commissioners their answer to certain accounts appointed for that day might be postponed to the Tuesday following. *Signed.* [N. VI., 76.]

Colonel MICHAEL JONES to WILLIAM LENTHALL.

1647[-8], February 26. Dublin.—" After one month's refreshing of these men since my coming out of the County of Wicklow and destroying the enemy's quarters in Westmeath, on the 3rd of this instant I marched into the County of Kildare with about 1,500 foot and 800 horse, where I have taken in 16 castles garrisoned by the rebels, whereby I have in a manner shut up the enemy's strongholds of Ballesonan and the island of Allan, and much more might have been done had not our naked men been so weatherbeaten through the unseasonableness of the time, whereby I was enforced back, having first placed 800 foot and two troops of horse in that county. I have not been wanting in improving my time and all advantages for gaining upon the enemy, wherein I have now more than I am able to make good, through the weakness of your army here, wanting men to hold what we have, much less to appear in the field with any competent number of strength, should occasion require, so as I am now almost at a stand, until I shall be thence supplied and enabled for further service, therefore make bold to desire your answer to my former letters, for without speedy supplies it is not possible for this army to subsist." I again represent the necessity of a Commander-in-Chief. *Signed. Seal.* [N. VI., 77.]

ROBERT GOODWIN, Colonel JOHN BIRCH and WILLIAM ASHHURST
to WILLIAM LENTHALL.

1647[-8], February 29. Edinburgh.—(Identical, *mutatis mutandis*,
with the letter of the same date from the Earl of Nottingham to the
Earl of Manchester, which is printed in *Lords' Journals*, x. 103.)
Signed. Seal. [N. VI., 78.]

The FRENCH AMBASSADOR to the PARLIAMENT.

[1647-8, February, end.]—Desiring a pass for some horses for the
use of the French King. (See *Commons' Journals*, v. 475.) [N.
XVII., 22.]

ORDERS.

1647[-8], March 1.—Concerning the Duke of York and the King's
other children. (Printed in *Commons' Journals*, v. 475, 6.) [N. XV.,
45.]

JOHN IRETON, executor of THOMAS SQUYER, to the HOUSE OF
COMMONS.

[1647-8, March 2.]—Petition, praying for the repayment of 3,236*l.*,
taken from his testator on pretence of authority from the Parliament.
(See *Commons' Journals*, v. 480, 485.) [N. XXII., 107.]

Instructions to the JUDGES.

1647[-8], March 3.—(Printed in *Lords' Journals*, x. 97.) *Draft*,
as passed by the Commons. [N. XXII., 108.]

The COMMITTEE FOR THE ADMIRALTY AND CINQUE PORTS.

1647[-8], March 7 and 13.—List of persons recommended to command certain vessels. (Corresponding with that printed in *Commons'
Journals*, v. 503.) [N. XV., 47.]

Seven or eight hundred OFFICERS and OFFICERS' WIDOWS to the
HOUSE OF COMMONS.

[1647-8, March 8.]—Petition, praying that the 9,100*l.* being the
balance of the said 10,000*l.* on Goldsmiths' Hall might be applied
towards the Petitioners' relief. (See *Commons' Journals*, v. 484.) [N.
XXII., 155.]

SIR THOMAS FAIRFAX to [the COMMITTEE AT DERBY HOUSE].

1647[-8], March 11. Queen Street.—Concerning the march of
Captain Wogan and his troop from Worcestershire to Scotland, he having
counterfeited an order to that effect from Sir Thomas Fairfax. (See
Commons' Journals, v. 408.) *Two copies.* [N. XII., 219.]

RICHARD LEE.

[1647-8, before March 15.]—Petition showing what was due to him
and asking for payment. (See *Commons' Journals*, v. 499.) [N.
XIV., 231.]

The PRINCE OF WALES to Captain WILLIAM SWAN, Governor of
Dover Castle.

164[7-]8, March [17-]27. St. Germain's.—Desiring him to forbear
declaring himself for him for the present, till he can become master of

the fort now commanded by Percival, and enclosing his Commission as Governor of Dover. *Sign-Manual. Seal. Enclosed:*

The said Commission. *Copy.*

(Both printed in *King's Pamphlets*, E. 435, No. 39.) (Most of the letter is in a cipher of which the following is the key. Single digits are unmeaning. 10 – 12 = y, 13 – 15 = x, 16 – 18 = w, and so on in groups of three to 76 – 78 = a. Then 102 words are represented by figures from 79 to 180 inclusive.) [N. I., 32, 33.]

The COMMITTEE FOR IRELAND and Major MATTHIAS WESTMORELAND.

1647[-8], March 17.—Articles of Agreement. (Printed with order thereon in *Commons' Journals*, v. 504.) [N. XXI., 74.]

The HOUSES OF PARLIAMENT to the ENGLISH COMMISSIONERS in Scotland.

[1647-8, March 17.]—Instructions concerning Captain Wogan's troop (being the second clause of the paper printed in *Lords' Journals*, x. 120, 225.)

And

The ENGLISH COMMISSIONERS to the PARLIAMENT OF SCOTLAND.

[1647-8, March 21.]—Paper in pursuance of their instructions. (Printed in *Lords' Journals*, x. 160, 225.) *Copies.* [N. XX., 43, the beginning of N. XX., 16 being the end of the paper, in fact 43 and 16 being parts of the same document, which sets out a number of communications on the subject.]

The HOUSE OF COMMONS.

1647[-8], March 19.—Order acquitting Lord Wharton from repayment of 2,000*l.* (Printed in *Commons' Journals*, v. 505.) [N. XV., 46.]

Information of Colonel THOMAS GALLOPPE taken before the Standing Committee of Somerset.

1647[-8], March 22.—That about Candlemas last year he met Colonel William Strode of Barington who said " ' Wee are now about to disband Sir Thomas Fairfax's armye' whereunto this Examinant said, ' What? will you disband such a gallant victorious armye without their pay?' The said Colonel Strode replied that the army should have noe pay for they had a president for that, there was none given in the Civill Warrs betweene Yorke and Lancaster, and said that those of them that would not soe disband, should either be sent into Ireland or hanged up here, and to effect this they had allreadye an armye in and about London of fortye thousand at command with which hee said ' Wee will destroy them all for Sir Thomas Fairfax wilbe deceived for parte of his armie will joyne with us, and besides the Scotts are very honest men and will come to assist us,' but he blamed the members of theire howse in not joyneinge with Mr. Hollis, Sir Phillip Stapleton, Sir William Lewes, Mr. Glinn, himselfe and others which if they had they would have effected this and much more. The said Colonel Strode farther said that the Independants should never bare office in Church or State —and rather then he would live amongst them he would goe into another countrye—for wee arc resolved not to leave one of the Independant paitie to live in this kingdome for they were all rogues and that he would never fight more, unlesse it were against this Independant armye. Whereupon one of the companye spake and said to his friends, 'I doubt this fellow is makeinge worke for the gallows,' and this examinant saith that not longe after this discourse, the said Colonel Strode was speakinge of Committees and in particular of Somersett committee and said of them that they were all rogues and said 'As for Pyne I make noe doubte but wee shall have him hanged and then what will become of the rest, the countrye will rise and knock them all in head, as soone as theire guard is gone, and that shalbe done very speedilye.'" *Signed.* [N. XV., 52.]

The PARLIAMENT.

1647[-8], March 22.—Orders concerning M. de Guyry. (Printed in *Commons' Journals*, v. 587; *Lords' Journals*, x. 125.) [N. XVII., 1.]

THOMAS [LORD] FAIRFAX to WILLIAM LENTHALL.

1647[-8], March 23. Queen Street.—Supporting the petition of Lieutenant Shreeve Parker, who had lost his limbs in the Parliament's service, for a pension. *Signed. Enclosed:*

The said petition. [N. VI., 80.]

SIR HENRY MILDMAY.

1648, March 25.—Report on the whole business between John Bland and Walter Fowke concerning the Receiver-Generalship of Yorkshire. (See *Commons' Journals*, v. 514.) *Annexed* are the order of the Committee of the Revenue dated October 5, 1647, referring the matter to Sir Henry Mildmay, and a paper with notes of cases on the subject. (All except the order of October 5, are printed in *Lords' Journals*, x. 170.) [N. XV., 50, 51, 49.]

The GRAND INQUEST at the Assizes held at Chard.

1648, March 27.—Presentment, declaring their resolution to adhere to the Parliament in prosecution of their late votes concerning the King, desiring that speedy course might be taken for settling the peace of the county and freeing it from the power of all Malignants, Neutrals and Apostates, "remonstrating" the great dearth of corn in the county and presenting "the excessive multitude of alehouses and maltsters . . . to be the great cause thereof, desiring your Lordships' (the Judges') orders to the Justices of the Peace . . . to suppress all unnecessary alehouses which are not within any market town and effectually to reduce the alehouses within the whole county unto a convenient number, to lessen the number of maltsters, and to put in execution the statutes against forestallers, regraters, and ingrossers and disorderly alehouses, licensed and not licensed" . . . complaining that not-withstanding divers ordinances to the contrary Delinquents and men of ill affection to the Parliament are chosen to and still retain offices of judicature and trust, and that they also practise as counsellors, attorneys and solicitors by whom frivolous and vexatious actions are brought and violently prosecuted against the well affected party. (See *Commons' Journals*, v. 534.) *Copy.* [N. XV., 53.]

The ENGLISH COMMISSIONERS to the PARLIAMENT OF SCOTLAND.

1648, March 27.—(Printed in *Lords' Journals*, x. 226, being the last clause of the paper printed in *Lords' Journals*, x. 172.) *Extract.* [N. XX., 16.]

The SAME to the SAME.

1648, March 31.—(Printed in *Lords' Journals*, x. 226.) *Copy.* [N. XX., 16.]

Captain JOHN CROWTHER to WILLIAM LENTHALL.

1648, April 5. Aboard the *Bonaventure* in Kinsayle Harbour.— (Identical with his letter of the same date to the Speaker of the House of Peers which is printed in *Lords' Journals*, x. 189, where also is printed from a copy the paper signed by Christopher Elsinge and others, of which the original is here enclosed.) *Signed. Seal.* There is also *enclosed :*

   i. Declaration by JOHN BENIWORTH, WILLIAM BATTELL, WILLIAM STOTESBURY, and JOHN GITTINGS dated April 7 to the effect that the several heads stated to have been propounded by Lord Inchiquin in his Presence Chamber on the 3rd instant were in the field on the same day propounded to them and the other officers of the army.

   ii. Declaration by THOMAS HEYFORD that Lord Inchiquin's declaration had been presented to him by Major John Crayford who used many arguments to induce him to comply with it. (All printed in *King's Pamphlets*, E. 435, No. 33.) (See *Commons' Journals*, v. 529.) [N. VII., 1.]

The EARL OF LOUDOUN to the ENGLISH COMMISSIONERS.

1648, April 8.—(Printed in *Lords' Journals*, x. 205.) *Copy.* [N. XX., 17.] *Annexed :*

Order of the PARLIAMENT OF SCOTLAND.

Same date. — (Printed in *Lords' Journals*, x. 205.) *Copy.* [N. XX., 18.]

The PARLIAMENT OF SCOTLAND to the ENGLISH COMMISSIONERS.

1648, April 12.—(Printed in *Lords' Journals*, x. 209, 226.) *Copy.* [N. XX., 21.]

The ENGLISH COMMISSIONERS to the PARLIAMENT OF SCOTLAND.

1648, April 14.—(Printed in *Lords' Journals*, x. 209, 226.) [N. XX., 20.] Part of another copy is part of N. XX., 19.

The HOUSE OF COMMONS.

1648, April 15.—Order referring Irish business to the Committee at Derby House. (Printed in *Commons' Journals*, v. 532.) (Written on back of vote of January 3, 1647-8.) [N. XV., 40.]

Informations of RICHARD PARNHAM, quartermaster, ROBERT BROWNE, cornet, and RICHARD TREWMAN, soldier, in Commissary-General Ireton's troop.

1648, April 15. Chichester.—Against John Coward, glover, that he said he was for God and King Charles, and that those who were not were rogues all. *Copies.* [N. XV., 54.]

BRIAN STAPYLTON and others to WILLIAM LENTHALL.

1648, April 18. Edinburgh.—(Identical *mutatis mutandis* with the letter of the same date from the Earl of Nottingham, which is printed in *Lords' Journals*, x. 223.) *Signed. Seal.* [N. VII., 2.]

SIR MARTIN LISTER to WILLIAM LENTHALL.

1648, April 19.—Desiring on account of his health to be excused from attending the call of the House on the following Monday. *Seal.* [N. VII., 3.]

The ENGLISH COMMISSIONERS to the PARLIAMENT OF SCOTLAND.

1648, April 18, 19.—(Printed in *Lords' Journals*, x. 223.) Two *Copies*, one of each date. [N. XX., 22, 23.]

Paper about SCOTCH transactions.

1648, April 19.—(Printed in *Commons' Journals*, v. 536, 7 beginning "a letter from the Commissioners" ending "tomorrow morning.") [N. XV., 55.]

MICHAEL JONES to WILLIAM LENTHALL.

1648, April 19. Dublin.—(Identical, *mutatis mutandis*, with the letter of the same to the Earl of Manchester, which is printed in *Lords' Journals*, x. 238.) *Signed. Seal.* [N. VII., 4.]

GEORGE BOOTHE to WILLIAM LENTHALL.

1648, April 20. Bradgate.—Desiring to be excused attending the call of the House on the following Monday. *Seal.* [N. VII., 5.]

The COMMITTEE AT DERBY HOUSE.

[1648, April 20 (?).]—Report. (Printed in *Lords' Journals*, x. 227.) [Separated, one part being the end of N. XX., 19, the rest N. XX., 48.]

The PARLIAMENT OF SCOTLAND to the PARLIAMENT OF ENGLAND.

1648, April 26.—Letter and Desires. (Both printed in *Lords' Journals*, x. 242.) Both *Signed* "Loudoun." [N. VII., 6; XX., 26.]

The ENGLISH COMMISSIONERS to the MAYOR OF CARLISLE.

1648, April 28. Edinburgh.—Giving him notice that the English Delinquents in Edinburgh were suddenly gone out and had some design on Carlisle, in order that he might use all means consistent with the Treaty between England and Scotland to prevent the same. The like sent to the Mayor of Berwick. *Copy.* [N. XII., 227.]

Papers concerning the DUKE OF YORK's servants and those of the DUKE OF GLOUCESTER, and the DUKE OF YORK's horses.

1648, April 29, May 1, and 2.—(All the information contained in them is summed up in that numbered 67, which is printed in full in *Lords' Journals*, x. 280, 281, except No. 64, an order of the Committee of the Revenue desiring to know the pleasure of the Houses concerning the Duke's horses, and No. 65 a list of the same.) [N. XV., 56-67.]

The ENGLISH COMMISSIONERS to the PARLIAMENT OF SCOTLAND

1648, April 29. Edinburgh. — Reiterating their demands for the surrender to them of Captain Wogan and his troop, Sir Philip Musgrave, Sir Thomas Glemham and Colonel George Wray contained in their letter of the 19th. (Printed in *King's Pamphlets*, E. 459, No. 21, p. 28.) *Copy.* [N. XX., 24.]

Ordinance concerning CHURCH GOVERNMENT.

1648, May 1.—Concerning the power of the *Classes*. Read a first time on that date. Nothing further apparently done regarding it. (See *Commons' Journals*, v. 548.) [N. XXII., 57.]

LUDOVIC EARL OF CRAFURD to DON ALONSO DE CARDENAS.

1648, May 1. Waterford.—Stating that he had raised troops according to the agreement between the King of Spain and himself, and had them ready for embarkation, but that in consequence of the ships of the Parliament on that coast it was impossible to sail, and requesting him to procure orders from the Parliament that their ships on the coast should not hinder the passage of the said troops and likewise a passport for himself. In *Spanish. Signed. Seal.* [N. XVII., 35.]

Captain ROBERT BATTEN, Governor of Holy Isle, to SIR ARTHUR HESILRIGE, Governor of Newcastle.

1648, May 2. Holy Isle.—Forwarding a copy of the letter received from Sir Marmaduke Langdale, describing the state of affairs in Berwick, and asking for repayment of money he had expended, and for coals and tools. [N. XII., 229.] *Enclosed:*

SIR MARMADUKE LANGDALE to Captain BATTEN.
1648, April 30. Berwick. — (Printed in Rushworth, iv. 2. 1106.) *Copy.* [N. XII., 228.]

The ENGLISH COMMISSIONERS to the PARLIAMENT OF SCOTLAND.

1648, May 2.—Concerning the seizure of Berwick. (Printed in *King's Pamphlets*, E. 459, No. 21, p. 29.) *Copy.* [N. XX., 25.]

The PARLIAMENT OF SCOTLAND to the ENGLISH COMMISSIONERS.

1648, May 2.—(Printed in *Lords' Journals*, x. 266.) *Copy.* [N. XX., 27.]

The COMMON COUNCIL OF THE CITY.

1648, May 2.—Answer on the order of the House for communicating the General's letter to them ; Thanking the House for doing so, and for their condescending to the humble petition of the City for the removal of the forces under his Excellency's command to a further distance therefrom and for confiding so far in the City and the places adjacent as to rest upon their guard and defence for the safety of themselves and the City and the other adjoining places, and declaring that the City will use their best endeavours for the guarding of the Parliament and for the defence of the same against any tumult or insurrection. (See *Commons' Journals*, v. 550. This differs considerably from the answer as given in Rushworth, **iv.** 2. 1101.) [N. XV., 68.]

The COMMITTEE AT DERBY HOUSE.

1648, May 5. — Report concerning the Lancashire forces. (See *Commons' Journals*, v. 552.) [N. XV., 69.]

The PARLIAMENT.

[1648, May 6.]—Vote for maintaining the Covenant and Treaties. (Printed in *Lords' Journals*, x. 247.) [N. XX., 31.]

The ENGLISH COMMISSIONERS to the PARLIAMENT OF SCOTLAND.

1648, May 9.—(Printed in *Lords' Journals*, x. 265.) *Copy*. [N. XX., 28.]

The HOUSES OF PARLIAMENT to the ENGLISH COMMISSIONERS.

Same date.—Instructions about the surprise of Berwick and Carlisle. (Printed in *Lords' Journals*, x. 250.) [N. XX., 44.]

Several thousands of REDUCED OFFICERS and SOLDIERS in and about London to the HOUSE OF COMMONS.

1648, May 10.—Petition praying that they may have the benefit of the former Ordinance for 3 months' pay, that such moneys as the House has already ordered may be paid them, and that they may have equivalent security with the Army for the remainder. (See *Commons' Journals*, v. 555.) [N. XXII., 114.]

The PARLIAMENT OF SCOTLAND to the ENGLISH COMMISSIONERS.

1648, May 10.—(Printed in *Lords' Journals*, x. 266.) *Copy*. [N. XX., 29.]

The HOUSE OF COMMONS to the ENGLISH COMMISSIONERS.

1648, May 11.—Instructions. (Printed in *Commons' Journals*, v. 556.) [N. XX., 46.]

The PARLIAMENT to the ENGLISH COMMISSIONERS.

1648, May 12.—Instructions. (Printed in *Lords' Journals*, x. 254.) *Copy*. [N. XX., 47.]

The ELECTOR PALATINE to WILLIAM LENTHALL

1648, May 12. Somerset house.—Soliciting the permission of the House to transport 1,000 of the prisoners taken in Wales for the service of the State of Venice under the command of his brother Prince Philip, the latter engaging that they shall not be employed to the prejudice of the Parliament. (Printed in Grey, iii. Appendix No. 49, p. 76.) (See *Lords' Journals*, x. 253.) *Signed* " Charles Lodovic." *Seal*. [N. I., 53.]

The COMMITTEE AT DERBY HOUSE.

1648, May 13.—Report desiring that more ships be sent to Berwick and that a store of arms and ammunition be laid at Newcastle, and that Commissions be given to such persons as have served the Parliament and are willing to serve again. [N. XV., 70.]

The COMMITTEE OF THE REVENUE.

1648, May 15.—Order appointing the High Sheriff of Yorkshire to act as Receiver. (See *Lords' Journals*, x. 258.) [N. XV., 71.]

The PARLIAMENT to the EARL OF LOUDOUN.

1648, May 15.—(Printed in *Lords' Journals*, x. 259.) *Copy.*
[N. XII., 230.]

The ENGLISH COMMISSIONERS to the COMMITTEE OF ESTATES.

1648, May 15, 18.—Two papers. (Both printed in *Lords' Journals*,
x. 284, 285.) *Copies.* [N. XX., 30, 32.]

The Knights, Gentlemen and Freeholders and inhabitants of SURREY
with the Citizens of SOUTHWARK to the PARLIAMENT.

[1648, May 16.]—Petition. (Printed in *Lords' Journals*, x. 260.)
At foot is added :—

The 8th of May 1648 it was resolved at Dorking on the meeting of
the Petitioners . .

1. That 500 copies of the Petition should be printed and sent to the
   gentlemen and the petitioners.
2. That on Tuesday the 16th the petitioners should meet on Putney
   Heath at 8 in the morning.
3. It is desired that those who shall subscribe the petition would
   show themselves in person in presenting it.
4. It is desired that all High Constables should in their several
   divisions make their returns of subscriptions of the said petition
   engrossed in parchment, one for the House of Lords and another
   for the House of Commons, and that they be delivered to Mr.
   John Evershed or such persons as he shall appoint, and that
   the original copies be left with the High Constables. [N.
   XXII., 113.]

The COMMITTEE AT DERBY HOUSE.

1648, May 18.—Report touching a plot. (Printed in *Lords'
Journals*, x. 262.) [N. XV., 72.]

Report of a Conference with the Lords touching the KING's
CHILDREN, and draft of Orders made thereon.

1648, May 20.—(Printed in *Commons' Journals*, v. 567.) [N. XV.,
56.]

The COMMITTEE OF THE MILITIA OF THE CITY.

1648, May 22.—Report. (Printed in *Commons' Journals*, v. 571.)
[N. XV., 73.]

Message from THE LORDS with paper presented by the EARL
OF THANET.

1648, May 24.—(Printed in *Commons' Journals*, v. 572.) [N..
XV., 74.]

The COMMITTEE AT DERBY HOUSE.

1648, May 24.—Report of the statements of the Earl of Thanet about
the condition of Kent, and his offer to go down. [N. XV., 75.]

BRIAN STAPYLTON and others to WILLIAM LENTHALL.

1648, May 24. Edinburgh.—Recommending to his favour Major
William Stewart and Colonel James Gray. *Signed. Seal* [N.
VII., 7.]

The ENGLISH COMMISSIONERS to the COMMITTEE OF ESTATES, and the PARLIAMENT OF SCOTLAND.

1648, May 25, June 1, 1, 6.—(Four papers all printed in *Lords' Journals*, x. 322, 323.) *Copies.* [N. XX., 33, 31, 35, 36.]

WILLIAM LENTHALL to [THOMAS LORD FAIRFAX].

1648, May 26.—Enclosing certain orders of the House, and desiring him if possible to come in person and forthwith to send some authorised person to consult with the Committee at Derby House. (See *Commons' Journals*, v. 574.) *Draft.* [N. XII., 231.]

The GENTLEMEN OF KENT to the COMMITTEE AT DERBY HOUSE.

[1648, May 27.]—In reply to their Instructions to the Earl of Thanet. (Printed in *Lords' Journals*, x. 290. The blank there should be filled up with the words, " nor suffers.") *Copy.* [N. XII., 232.]

The PROPOSITIONS to be sent to the KING.

1648, May 30.—(Printed in *Lords' Journals*, x. 308.) *Draft* with amendments as passed by the Commons. [N. XX., 49.] N. XX., 41 is another copy.

The LORDS to the COMMONS.

1648, May 30.—Message about the increase of the Committee at Derby House. (Printed in *Commons' Journals*, v. 578.) [N. XV., 76.]

Examination of JOSSELIN GATES, servant to Sir Anthony Aucher.

1648, May 30.—(See *Commons' Journals*, v. 579.) [N. XV., 77.]

PAPER.

[1648, May 20–31.]—After the letter of both Houses to the Chancellor of Scotland, concerning their desires of the 26th of April (see *Lords' Journals*, x. 259) was read by the Committee of Estates then sitting, the Lord Crawford and Lyndsay, Lord Treasurer, in their name wrote to the English Commissioners to this purpose, That the Committee of Estates desired to know whether the Parliament of England had sent unto them an answer of their desires of the 26th of April, whereunto the English Commissioners returned the ensueing answer. [N. XX., 207.]

SIR THOMAS MAULEVERER and others to WILLIAM LENTHALL.

1648, June 2. York.—(The purport sufficiently appears by the Order made upon it. See *Commons' Journals*, v. 584.) *Signed. Seal.* [N. VII., 9.]

THOMAS [LORD] FAIRFAX to WILLIAM LENTHALL.

1648, June 2. Maidstone.—(Identical, *mutatis mutandis*, with the letter of tne same to the Earl of Manchester, which is printed in *Lords' Journals*, x. 301.) *Signed.* [N. VII., 8.]

The COMMITTEE AT DERBY HOUSE.

1648, June 3.—Report. (Printed in *Lords' Journals*, x. 301.) [N. XV., 78.]

Colonel THOMAS STOCKDALE to FRANCIS THORP, M.P.

1648, June 3. Saturday morning, 9 o'clock.—"This morning early I understand Sir Marmaduke Langdale is coming down from Appleby and Kirby Stephen towards Barna[rd] castle and so to Yorkshire, and will fall upon our forces thereabout before our body get together, so Colonel Lambert is gone this morning to Otley to meet Colonel Harrison, whose regiment is still in Lancashire, and from thence marches towards the enemy who, it seems, prevents his design. This sudden accident may much alter and distract our resolutions yesterday, if the country be infested with the enemy. *Postscript.*—Sir M. L. brings 2,000 horse and 2,000 foot, if he be able." *Seal.* [N. VII., 21.]

THOMAS [LORD] FAIRFAX to WILLIAM LENTHALL.

1648, June 4. Rochester.—(Identical *mutatis mutandis* with the letter of the same date from the same to the Earl of Manchester, which is printed in *Lords' Journals*, x. 304, except that after "what they have undertaken" is added "and grant commissions to raise regiments, and the oath of secrecy which they took for the better management of their affairs" and that there is a Postscript recommending that some provision be made for the widow and children of Captain Price.) *Signed. Seal.* [N. VII., 11.]

The COMMITTEE AT DERBY HOUSE.

1648, June 5.—Report of the paper expressing the desire of the Lincolnshire gentlemen to raise a troop of horse. (See *Commons' Journals*, v. 384, 5.) [N. XV., 79.]

The COMMITTEE AT DERBY HOUSE.

1648, June 6.—Report with a list of the gentlemen that presented their service to the Parliament with Colonel Rosseter. (Printed in Grey, iii. Appendix No. 73, p. 125.) [N. XV., 80.]

The PARLIAMENT OF SCOTLAND to the ENGLISH COMMISSIONERS.

1648, June 7.—(Printed in *Lords' Journals*, x. 338.) *Copy.* [N. XX., 37.]

THOMAS [LORD] GREY to WILLIAM LENTHALL.

1648, June 7. Leicester.—(Printed in Peck, *Desiderata Curiosa*, ix. 45.) *Signed. Seal.* [N. VII., 12.]

WILLIAM BAINBRIDGE and others to WILLIAM LENTHALL.

1648, June 7. Leicester.—Representing to the House the good conduct of Lord Grey, in raising the well affected against the rising of Colonel Stiles. *Signed. Seal.* [N. VII., 13.]

THOMAS [LORD] GREY, WILLIAM BAINBRIDGE and others to WILLIAM LENTHALL.

1648, June 7. Leicester.—"We having notice of this rising about Stamford upon the last Sabbath day presently despatched Colonel Wayte with what horse were here, who marched presently to Burleigh and so to Stamford, where joining with other forces from Belvoir and Lincolnshire and Northamptonshire, he hath happily suppressed these rising spirits . . . After Colonel Wayte going from hence we presently ‹ent to some townsmen to invite the well affected to come in and join with us in defence of the country. And we found an extraordinary appearance here upon so short a summons, there being with us yesterday here above 300 horse and 200 foot who presently listed themselves for this service, and this town drew forth six foot companies. But the present work being done we dismissed them for the present, all but the horsemen, whom we this morning upon full information of the perfecting of the business dismissed with thanks for their goodwill to it." *Signed. Seal.* [N. VII., 14.]

BRIAN STAPYLTON, ROBERT GOODWIN, WILLIAM ASHHURST and Colonel JOHN BIRCH to WILLIAM LENTHALL.

1648, June 8. Edinburgh.—(Identical, *mutatis mutandis*, with the letter of the same date from the Earl of Nottingham to the Earl of Manchester, which is printed in *Lords' Journals*, x. 322.) *Signed. Seal.* [N. VII., 15.]

J[OHN] R[USHWORTH] to WILLIAM LENTHALL.

1648, June 8, 12 at night. Rochester. "In my last I acquainted you with the raising of the siege before Dover Castle by Colonel Rich and Colonel Hewson. That night being the 6th of June, the Mayor of Dover, in the name of himself and the jurates, officers, and inhabitants of Dover, sent a trumpeter to Colonel Rich for an act of indempnitie and other thinges least they should oppose him. Hee denied to grant them any because they refused itt when they might have had itt from the parliament, and soe march't into the towne expecting opposition, but the Mayor and three hundred more in armes, instead of resisting betooke themselves to the fort, which was summoned as soone as our guards were sett in the towne, and they imediately yeelded. Wheruppon hee sent a company of foote to possesse the fort, where hee found seaventy barrells of pouder, besides ordnance and armes. Hee sent another partie towards Sandwich which wee hope by this time is surrendred, and another partie to Deale and Sandon castles of which wee hope you will have a good account in the meanetime. Colonel Barkestead's regiment and the horse sent from the Generall under Commissary-General Ireton towards Canterbury as they march't this day neere Feversham mett with a letter from Sir Richard Hardresse —who lately besieged Dover Castle—,Sir Thomas Palmer, Sir William Man and divers other gentlemen of quallity, desiring a parley which by reason that the foote uppon this expedicion [is] designed into Essex, —where there is soe great neede—was condescended unto and the matter of the articles instantlie agreed to. But the messenger came away before they were putt into a forme and signed, one article was concluded, ' That at sixe of the clock tomorrow moīning wee were to enter the towne, and all the armes and amunicion are to bee brought into the cathedrall church.' You will receive a more exact account from his Excellency as soone as the articles are signed. I forgott to acquaint you that our partie march't with ladders instantlie to storme the place when the messenger mett them, and a partee of the enemies horse some four miles from the towne charged the van of our horse ; wee killed one and tooke twenty. I hope that Kent will bee totally reduced imediately which when the shippes doe know may bee a great inducement to them to returne to the obedience of the parliament. His Excellency hath sent unto them by such persons who may probably prevaile with them, assuring his indeavours for indempnity." [N. VII., 16.]

WILLIAM LENTHALL to [the COMMITTEE at LEICESTER]
And
The SAME to [THOMAS LORD GREY],
And
The SAME to Major BOTELEIR
And
The SAME to the GOVERNOR OF CROWLAND.

[1648, June 8.]—(The first, third and fourth are thanking them for their respective services against Hudson and Stiles' rising. The first two are printed in Peck, *Desiderata Curiosa*, ix., 46, 47. See *Commons' Journals*, v. 589.) *Drafts*. [N. XII., 225, 233.]

THOMAS ENGLISH, EDWARD CEELY, RICHARD TREVILLIAN and others to the SPEAKERS OF BOTH HOUSES.

1648, June 9. Ilminster.— Describing how "a Troop" who had slain a Malignant officer was condemned by a jury, "that we have cause to believe would have condemned all those that act for the Parliament," and hanged "to the great discouragement of those employed to do the Parliament service." (Printed in Grey, iii., Appendix No. 39, p. 65.) *Signed. Seal.* [N. VII., 19.]

The ENGLISH COMMISSIONERS to the PARLIAMENT OF SCOTLAND

1648, June 9. Edinburgh.—(Printed in *King's Pamphlets*, E. 459, No. 21, p. 49.) *Copy.* [N. XX., 38.]

BRIAN STAPYLTON, ROBERT GOODWIN, WILLIAM ASHURST, and Colonel JOHN BIRCH to WILLIAM LENTHALL.

1648, June 9. Edinburgh.— (Identical, *mutatis mutandis*, with the letter from the Earl of Nottingham to the Earl of Manchester, which is printed in *Lords' Journals*, x. 337.) *Signed. Seal.* [N. VII, 17.]

Captain JOHN COPPIN to WILLIAM LENTHALL.

1648, June 9, at 9 at night. From aboard the *Greyhound* frigate.— "I coming from the Norward as far as Yarmouth Roads, where we had intelligence of that unhappy revolt of that wicked perfidious crew, which I am confident are enemies both to God and man, and my company understanding this, the greatest part of them being Deal men, they carried me and my ship perforce into the Downs, so I perceiving this I complied with them, and coming aboard of she that wears the flag God directed me so that I seemed to join with them in their horrid design, till such times that it pleased God to work my deliverance out of their hands. So after much merriment at the Castle ashore I went aboard. So perceiving . . that most of my Deal men were ashore I consulted with my Master and the rest of my officers how we might get away from them, and Providence being our friend we resolved unanimously as one man with the hazard of our lives being some four or five and thirty in number and no more to venture to set sail and run away for Harwich. They no sooner perceiving that my ship was to sail being about 4 or 5 . . in the afternoon the 8th of this instant but presently two of their frigates cuts cable and made sail after me, which were the *Warwick* and the *Pelican*, and let fly at me several piece of ordnance, but the Lord was so pleased that we got away from them, and here I am arrived safe in Harwich, where I found three ships more for the Parliament, the *Providence*, the *Tiger*, and the *Adventure* frigates. I heard of from the late Boatswain, now Commander-in-Chief of she that wears the flag, that they will go and take colliers and sink them in the mouth of the river of Medway to prevent all those ships that are there from coming out." . . . (See *Commons' Journals*, v. 597.) *Seal.* [N. VII., 18.]

WILLIAM LENTHALL to SIR THOMAS BARNARDISTON.

1648, June 10.—By order of the House thanking him for his services, and especially in apprehending and sending up Sir Thomas Peyton and Mr. Swan. (See *Commons' Journals*, v. 592.) *Draft.* [N. XII., 234.]

ROBERT GOODWIN, WILLIAM ASHHURST, and Colonel JOHN BIRCH, to WILLIAM LENTHALL.

1648, June 13. Edinburgh.—The Parliament of Scotland adjourned on Saturday, leaving a Committee of Estates to whom they have given a very great power. Knowing that what you should resolve upon their answer of June 7th could not come before they were risen, we gave them the reply of which we enclose a copy. *Signed. Seal.* [N. VII., 20.]

—— to WILLIAM LENTHALL.

1648, June 14, 8 o'clock in the morning. From the Leaguer before Colchester.—"Yesterday the Generall marched from Coggeshall and about one of the clocke in the afternoone came before Colchester, whereupon the enemy drew out both horse and foot into the feild and lined the hedges thicke with muskettiers, and the Generall comaunded part of Colonell Barkestead's regiment and the draggoones to beat them from the hedges, which accordingly they did from feild to feild, and followed them close into the towne, doing execucion upon them and pursued them through the suburbs up to the verie gates.

The enemy perceiving the town would be lost if they should admitt our men to enter with their horse and foot that fled, shut the gates. Whereupon we tooke betweene two and three hundred prisoners, Sir William Layton and divers others of quallitie. The foot being thus farre engaged, it was conceived if they had two peece of cannon to breake open the gates wee might enter into the towne, the walls being too high to be stormed and besides a storme was not intended, soe accordingly two peeces of ordinance and more foote of Colonell Barkestead's and the Tower regiment was also sent. These were all the forces save some horse which made good the suburbs against all the forces of the enemy from three of the clocke in the afternoone till twelve at night.

A summons being sent in the afternoone to the Lord Goreing, he sleighted it, and the townesmen rise in armes in great numbers and joyned with Goreing, whereupon it was thought fitt to fire the gate in order to which to fire the houses next adjoyning, which being done proved to be our disadvantage by reason of the great light it gave the enemy to take aime at our men over the walls, in so much as about two of the clocke this morning it was thought fitt to drawe of from the suburbs and with the more difficulty and dainger wee brought off the cannons.

The army is now drawne upon the ground where wee first faced the enemy. All the bridges are pulled upp towards Suffolke, and the Suffolke forces are sent for to make good one part of the seige, Sir Thomas Honywocd and the other forces of this county another part, and this army to be devided into two parts more. If they have provisions in the towne—wee suppose they have not—it may make the busines take more time to reduce them this way, yet it is better then to cast away such gallant men against walls and bulwarks.

There is many of the enemy slaine and ours could not hold out that long service without losse. Colonell Woodham was shott in the legg, Captaine Laurence a captaine of horse shott in the body, Captaine Cocke shott and it is conceiv[ed] mortally wounded. Our souldiers are very hearty and would faine fall on againe.

Sir William Laiton told me when he was taken prisoner that in all the services he had beene in, he never see the like gallautrie by foot in the charge in the feild and into the towne. The enemy played with their great cannon all the day long from our first appearance before them but did veric little execucion. I never knew the Generall in so great dainger in these warres as in this charge. The enemy must betake themselves to sea for their is no escapeing and wee hear the country will come in verie freely to blocke them upp.

This is all the accompt I can give you at present being much wearied with the last night's continued service." *Unsigned. Seal broken.* [N. VII., 22.]

Report by Mr. KNIGHTLEY.

1648, June 14.—Concerning Banbury Castle. (See *Commons' Journals*, v. 598.) [N. XV., 82.]

SIR MICHAEL LIVESEY and others to WILLIAM LENTHALL.

1648, June 14. Canterbury.—"The bearer of these enclosed gave us great cause of suspicion, and upon search of his trunk we found the enclosed letters which in regard of the name of the person to whom they are directed we thought fit to transmit unto you, the bearer having a passport from the King of France." . . . . Until the Militia of the County may be reformed and recovered to a parliamentary interest we have improved the present opportunity, while any part of the army remains, to endeavour to raise some considerable strength to be engarrisoned in some few convenient places in case of the army's withdrawal. As this will probably be a work of charge we ask that whatever pecuniary punishment may be imposed on the Delinquents may, after making good the losses of the well affected, be employed for the use of the County. What moderation the House may use towards those who have been misled by others so as to difference them from the ringleaders we conceive will be a winning mercy upon ingenious spirits and an awful and exemplary justice upon such as are most unworthy of favour. (See *Commons' Journals*, v. 606.) *Signed. Seal.* [N. VII., 23.]

PETER PETT to [the COMMITTEE OF THE ADMIRALTY AND CINQUE PORTS ?].

1648, June 15. Chatham Dock.—"On Tuesday 23 May I came for Chatham and upon examination of divers of known integrity to the Parliament I perceived the designe of the Kentish petitioners to be so desperate that forthwith I sent an expresse to the Commissioners of the Navy, and desired them imediately to ympart it to your honours; which was the next morning presented to the Speaker of the House of Commons. The summe whereof was this, That if the Parliament did not presently either answere their desires, which I feared would proove unreasonable, or suppresse them by a power, the whole county would not only be up in armes forthwith but hazard Parliament and king-dome, for that the partie rissen was not only desperate in their resolucion but ymplacable in their malice, to which I received no answere at all. Wendsday the 21th, after I had sent downe the *Fellowshipp* at Gillingham for feare of their seizing of her, I mustered the ordinary men of the Navy and found as well divers officers of the shipps missing which were joyned in that horrid engagement to act as committee men with the pretended committee at Rochester as also many ordinary shipkeepers that had then taken up armes to se[r]ve the gentlemen of Kent and that committee. I caused them at present to be prick't out of victualls and wages but with this provisoe that if any of them would lay downe their armes, and come in to do their duty within two daies they should have their full allowance. But never an officer appeared nor above two ordinary men. This morning also the pretended Committee sent Mr. May, one of their committee men, with one Mr. Taylor with a threefold request to me. The first was to signe their petition, to which I answered that I would be so farr from signeing of it that I would not read it; the second was that I would give them leave to gett hands to it in the yard; to that I answered that it was a place of garrison, kept for the service of the Parliament and therefore I could not give way unto it without a manifest breach of trust; the third request was to borrow ordinance, to which I told them it was more I thought then a committee of Parliament would do without leave first had from the house. Therefore I durst not be so highly pre-sumptious to attempt any such thing, but advized them, if their affeccions were reall to the Parliament as they pretended, then not to dare to meddle with the Navy or anything thereunto belonging, for that I was confident the Parliament would take it as a large demon-stracion of mischeife intended either to themselves or kingdome. Their answere was that they knew the Committee would not staine their honours with such perfidiousnesse to the Parliament and that they would undertake that nothing should be meddled with. All which notwithstand[in]g, within two bowers after, they sent a party and tooke Upner Castle, carried away the captaine thereof to Rochester prisoner, and kept a guard of musketeirs and examined all vessells coming up or going downe.

Thursday, Fryday and Saturday being the 24th 25th and 26th of May, I expected orders either from your honours or the Commis-sioners of the Navy, for the transaction of the affaires thereof in reference to its safety in so dangerous a tyme, which failling of, the passages being stopt up, and for that the pretended committee sent a troop of horse to me to know whether I would lend them ordnance, to which I still gave my denyall, I thought it my duty in refference to my trust haveing no power to resist them, being forsaken almost by the whole Navy to write a letter to the pretended committee to this purpose, That they would be cautious in suffering any act to be donne by their instruments that might trench upon the honor of the Parliament and safety of the Navy which I was confident would not only be very acceptable to them and invite the honourable Houses the rather to a complyance with them in their just and reasonable desires, but also engage me. Their answere to which was that there was no intentions on their parts for an attempt prejudicous either to the honourable Parliament or Navy; that if there were any suspitions they did disavowe them and only protest their resolucion for the advancement of their just right of peticioning etc. Notwithstanding which, they sent a warrant that eivening to Captaine Jervas, comander of the *Fellowshipp*, for searching the ship, and the next day they sent another order to bring up the shipp to Upner Castle, and there they tooke out both pouder and victualls.

The 27th being Sundaye, they sent an order to gunner Pratt to fetch forty harrells of pouder out of the *Soveraigne* and *Prince* which they shewed me. I then told them the great danger of such an attempt as to themselves in obaying such an order, and the dishonour that would be putt upon the parliament in medling with pouder on bord those shipps stated as a guard to the Navy, besides the exposeing of the Navy to ruine and what a cleere contradiccion it was of their promises, at which tyme I staved them of. But the next day being Munday, because they intended to possesse themseves of all the Navy that they might make use both of shipps and stores, they sent a company of musketeers under the comaund of one Dirkin of Rochester, and ushered by some of the principall gunners of the Navy to the new dock. I caused the gates to be shutt, stood upon our guard, and parlied with them out of a window. I told them I was sorry to see them in that posture at this place and asked them by what order they came hither. They told me they had warrant from the committee, which when I had redd and blush't at the impudency of their committee and insolency of them to give and obey such an order for seizing of the yard and stores together with the *Soveraigne* and *Prince*, I askt them whether they thought that order would beare them out. and what was the reason their new masters were so perfidious as to promise me and declare to the world one thing one day, that they would not meeddle with the Navy, and the next to seize on all. They told mee they might as well breake their promise with mee as the parliament had done with them. I bid the wisest of them to tell me what the parliament had promised them since their rebellious riseing that they had not performed. They told mee that they had proclaymed them rebells and traytours, and they were resolved to defend themselves as long as they could; and when thev saw there was no coming into the yard they forthwith seized on the *Soveraigne* and *Prince*, left Dirkin to keepe the guard and sent up to their army some twenty-five harrells of pouder from thence ymmediately.

28th 29th and 30th, being Tuesday, Wendsday and Thursday, haveing as well posession of the shipps and ordnance as of the ponder, they carried away divers peeces of ordnance and were makeing of carriages for them, but through the infinite mercy of God in giveing successe to the Parliament's forces under the comaund of the Lord Generall at Maidstone on Thursday, they were so amazed as that on Fryday they began to shift for themselves, and the Lord Goreing together with divers of the pretended comittee gave warrant and order to one Captaine Bonner, Mr. Morland, and others to take possession of the *Fellowship* of which Captaine Gervas was comaunder, then rideing at Upner Castle, and comanded him to carry her away next morning, pilott and all things being ready, of which I hearcing on Fryday evening caused presently a court of guard to be kept at Chatham new dock with those few forces and men we had, and manned a beat of musketeeres, haveing consulted first with the carpenter and boatswain of the shipp, whom I found true to the Parliament, and seazed on the ship and captaine and brought him away, his brother and Morland, prisoners, and so saved the shipp, and the next day being Saturday, wee tooke possession of the *Soveraigne* and *Prince*. And then most of our Samaritan officers and comon men became Jewes, and would needs joyne with us; but because I found by experience their unparrallelled perfidiousnesse to the Parliament, divers of them haveing beene cheefe actors in this rebellion, and others by the way of signing the peticion, and takeing up of armes, engagement, I forthwith tooke a muster of all men both ordinary and extraordinary, belonging to the Navy and all which I found guilty I thought it my duty to give warrant to the Clerke of the Cheque to prick them out of victualls and wages till such tyme as they could cleere themselves, whose names I have drawne up in two listes ready to present to your honours." I offer it, whether it be not a thing very fit to purge the Navy of such ill members. [N. VII., 24.]

The Committee at Derby House.

1648, June 15.—Report concerning Upner Castle and Mr. Pett's letter. (See *Commons' Journals*, v. 605.) [N. XV., 81.]

Thomas [Lord] Fairfax to the Committee at Derby House.

1648, June 15. From the Leaguer before Colchester.—"The bearer hereof, Captain Harrison, cometh from the well affected of the Isle of Ely to acquaint your Lordships with the dangerous condition of themselves and that place especially the inner parts of it about Wisbech which are joined to Holland and Marshland and which is like to be the rendezvous and make the head for all the Malignant party of those parts if not prevented. The forces settled for the guarding of the island are all necessarily employed upon the frontiers of it and much too far for that service. . . . It is the desire of the well affected there—and I do earnestly wish that some order were given for it—that Colonel Hubbert of Well in that isle . . may have power to raise such forces for the guard of those parts as your Lordships shall think fit." (See *Lords' Journals*, x. 329, 330.) *Signed. Seal.* [N. VII., 25.]

Sir George Booth to William Lenthall.

1648, June 17. Dunham.—Enclosing a letter received the last post, the like of which in the name of four counties he had received the week before. *Signed Seal Enclosed:*

" Your loving friends of the City though nameless " to Sir George Booth.

1648, June 13. London.—"The prevailing party in the two Houses hath on Friday last voted the disarming of the kingdom, and intend to rule us by an arbitrary power and their army, if they can. The Kentish Trained Bands are dispersed by force and craft, but Sussex, Hampshire, and the adjacent counties are rising. We have a considerable army of resolved men now in Suffolk, and as it moves our disbanded soldiers and the Cavaliers gather to it. We doubt not but a little will lay Independent flat. Our City stands neuter. We desire you to interrupt publicly or privately, by force or otherwise, the proceedings of Duckenfield and his confederates that we may have a speedier end. You and Colonel Mainwaring may do much." *Seal.* (See *Commons' Journals*, v. 606.) [N. VII., 26.]

Declaration of Owen O'Neill and the Ulster Party.

1648, June 17. Athlone.—Against the Cessation. (Printed in Gilbert, i. 741.) *Copy.* [N. XXI., 76.]

The ENGLISH COMMISSIONERS to the COMMITTEE OF ESTATES.

1648, June 17 and 22.—(Both printed in *Lords' Journals*, x. 365, 366.) [N. XX., 39, 40.]

Order that the LORD HIGH ADMIRAL should write to the TRINITY HOUSE, Report of the COMMITTEE AT DERBY HOUSE, and of a SUB-COMMITTEE OF THE SAME AT SIR ABRAHAM WILLIAMS' HOUSE, and two letters signed ROBERT MOULTON and others and ELIAS JORDAN and others.

1648, June 17 and 21.—(All these are printed in *Lords' Journals*, x. 340, 343, 341, where the names of the subscribers to the last letter are omitted, and in the first line of it, "those" is a misprint for "us.") [N. XV., 83–85.]

The EARL OF WARWICK to the MASTER, WARDENS, and ASSISTANTS OF THE TRINITY HOUSE.

1648, June 19.—(Printed in *Lords' Journals*, x. 339.) *Copy.* [N. XII., 235.]

The PARLIAMENT to the STATES-GENERAL and to the ESTATES OF ZEALAND.

1648, June 20.—Concerning the revolted ships. (Both printed in *Lords' Journals*, x. 336, 337.) In *Latin.* Two *copies* of each. [N. XVIII., 64, 66.]

SIR ARTHUR LOFTUS to WILLAM LENTHALL.

1648, June 20. Westminster, in the Market Place.—Referring to his petition and stating he was then under arrest for debt. (See *Commons' Journals*, v. 609.) *Seal.* [N. VII., 27.]

Colonel WILLIAM DANIELL to WILLIAM LENTHALL.

1648, June 20. Chester Castle.—The governor being absent in taking steps for the payment of the assessments of some neighbouring counties allotted for the supply of this garrison was prevented from giving this first speedy relation. On Friday last, the 16th, "there was some discovery of a most deep and desperate plot to have betrayed this garrison . . into the hands of the Malignant party of the kingdom. This present Tuesday there hath been some further knowledge thereof, and yet are there so many examinations of engaged persons behind, that the bottom of the plot cannot for the present be presented to your Honour, only this much in general, that some of the greatest in this city and county that have served with and against the Parliament since the beginning of the late war are accused to be prime actors in the business, and that God Almighty hath frustrated their expectations and preserved this place in safety, and these parts of the kingdom from an open and desperate war, and the lives of many godly persons from the malice of unreasonable men." *Signed. Seal.* [N. VII., 28.]

The MASTER and WARDENS OF THE TRINITY HOUSE to the EARL OF WARWICK.

1648, June 21. Trinity House, Ratcliffe.—(Printed in *Lords' Journals*, x. 340.) *Signed.* [N. VII., 29.]

Colonel VALENTINE WAUTON (or WALTON) to the COMMITTEE AT DERBY HOUSE.

1648, June 21. Lynn.—I have had " severall advertisements of the designe of the enimie to surprise Lin and Crowland, in which they acted very farr. But there speciall eye is upon the Ile of Ely, a place of that concernment that if possest by an enimie where they might head a considerable armie with all provision for horse and man att there pleasure. According to the trust reposed in me [I] have settled Lin in a quiett posture for the present as to enemies within, and am repayring the woorkes which ware much decayed within the moate. Two forts more would be made upon the inward line to make that line regular that the new woorks which are large might be speedily slighted, for the small force I have are not sufficient for the towne. The out-works will require more men to man them then I have in the towne for that they lye open to invite an enymie, which may prove mischeavous. I have disburst mony for the repairing the inward woorkes which I am in hand with dayly, that some course may be taken for the reimbursing of that mony againe. I spent the last weeke in putting the Ile of Elye —the south part—into a posture of defence. I vewed all the passages into the Isle and caused breast woorkes to be made upon every pass, and all great boates upon the fresh rivers to be secured under our guards. I summoned in the auxcilliary forces who made a good appear-ance, about four hundred men, the captain and officers honest, ready upon all occasions to serve the publick but have spent upon theire owne estates all this warr. I conceive if some course were taken for their future incouragement to be paid the dayes they shall exercise their men on, and drawne forth to defend there frontiers, the charge is not considerable, they having noe feild officers. The auxcilliary souldiers are tracktable and willing to serve the commonwealth if they might receive there just pay due from those that find the armes who are much in arreere for former service. Soe that I was forcet for there present incouragement to send forth warrants for there speedy payment. For I find few that are there intrusted take care of the honor of the Parlia-ment, or their owne safety. Likewise the alarum tax which hath lyen two yeares in collectors' hands due to those souldiers I have caused to be broght in. I am setting forward to putt the north part of the lle into a postuie, those that may be trusted. But generally they are disaffected as Wisbich, March, and Whittlesey, whome I purpose to disarme, and to arme honest men if they may be found. Colonel Hubbert and Leiutenant-Colonel Dimond aie the only men for the Parliament, but over powred with Malignants. I cannot see how that part of the Ile can be secured without a troope of horse upon their frontieres. Colonel Hubbert would be the fittest to commaund them, who is a person of fidellitie and trust if itt be thought convenient. Crowland and Whittlesey workes are much decayed and part of Whittlesey fort not finisht, that if any enimie should rise within they cannot defend them selves against them, but for want of mony they are not made soe defensible as they might be. I had forty barrells of powder, match and bullett proportionable lately from the committe of the armie, which spends apace, being disperst to Ely, Whittlesey, Crowland and Boston, and for Lin guards, soe that if there should be any sudden occasion I know not from whence we could be timely supplyed. I have noe meanes to send out a scoute or for entilligence but all out of my owne purse, that any enimie may come under the woorkes before notice can be taken. I desire that ammunition may be with speede sent, and those other things taking into consideration, if thought necessary, the souldiers have great want of swords, not one hundred iu my regiment, alsoc drumes, about twelve wanting They have not bin recruted these three or four yeares. The committe of the armie allowed 13*l.* for fair coullers. There is yett wanting to compleat my regiment in Lin and the Isle of Ely, thre coullers." *Signed. Seal.* [N. VII., 30.]

WILLIAM FREEMAN, RICHARD YATES, and NICHOLAS SHEPPARD to the COMMITTEE AT DERBY HOUSE.

1648, June 22. Horsham. — We endeavoured to remove the magazine at Horsham to Arundel Castle on the 9th, but were resisted by the Bailiffs and Constable and disaffected party there, by whom the arms and magazine are still kept with a strong guard. They threaten to kill and plunder those who endeavour to remove them, using very high words against the Parliament. On Tuesday last a letter was delivered to the Bailiffs and Constables from Colonel Morley and Colonel Stapley requiring them to remove the magazine to Arundel Castle, but notwithstanding the said arms and magazine are still kept at Horsham with a strong guard, and the Bailiffs and Constables replied that they could not remove the same. "The Malignant party have given out speeches that they will arm themselves with the first arms and rise as one man against all such as have not joined with them in a petition called the Sussex Petition: they likewise refuse to pay taxes or to yield any obedience to the ordinances of Parliament. Till your lordships remove the obstructions we cannot safely meet for getting in taxes for the army or to doe the Parliament any further service. *Signed. Seal.* [N. VII., 31.]

Colonel RALPH ASSHETON to WILLIAM LENTHALL.

1648, June 23. Kendal.—The bearer Captain French is despatched by the officers and soldiers under my command to ask the House for an establishment of pay. "We have already reduced the enemies' garrisons of Dockerhall and Bertham and forced the retreat of the enemies' horse out of Westmorland, and in order to a further perfecting of the work are upon advance for conjunction with Major-General Lambert." [N. VII., 32.]

The PARLIAMENT to [Colonel MICHAEL JONES].

1648, June 23.—(Printed in *Lords' Journals*, x. 350.) *Draft* as sent from the Commons. [N. XII., 236.]

Colonel ROBERT HAMMOND to the COMMITTEE AT DERBY HOUSE.

1648, June 23. Carisbrook Castle.—(Printed in Peck, *Desiderata Curiosa*, ix. 47.) *Signed. Seal.* [N. VII., 33.]

ROBERT WRIGHT, Mayor, and others to WILLIAM LENTHALL.

1648, June 24. Chester.—The favour shown us by the House during the late plague here encourages us to address them. This city before its surprisal by the King's forces faithfully paid all assessments laid on it by Parliament being about one eleventh of what was imposed on the county, but since then about a fourth part is burnt, the rest almost wholly worn out by the king's forces in their time, and by the payment of great sums by the most able citizens to the use of the Parliament after its reduction, and also by the devastating plague, together with the want of trading all this while. And now in this most miserable condi. tion we are called on to pay assessments for the army and Ireland, winch we acknowledge are yet unpaid, not from disaffection but inability. We therefore ask that all arrears may be remitted, and that for the future the city may be charged at only a reasonable rate. *Signed. Seal.* [N. VII., 34.]

Sir Hardres Waller to William Lenthall.

1648, June 24. Exeter.—Have received no answer to my former inquiry how my prisoners were to be disposed of. In consequence of the soldiers not receiving their pay they are unable to pay for their quarters, which causes ill feeling between them and the country people. I therefore suggest as the best expedient that troops and companies should gather their moneys in the Hundreds where they quarter as assistants to the Constables, so that it being brought to the High Constable may be paid by him to the officer. Our next difficulty is the disposing of these forces in market towns and cities according to the ordinances of Parliament, which not being sufficient, an enlargement of quarters to the adjacent places became necessary, which however was much complained of, and further it is a generally received opinion that we are not suffered to march into Plymouth and by command expelled out of Exeter. I therefore desire a declaration or order of the House that all towns in these counties of Devon and Cornwall shall be free for their forces to march into upon all occasions. *Signed. Seal.* [N. VII., 35.]

Sir Hardres Waller to Sir John Temple.

1648, June 24. Exeter.—" Captain Richard Hart, who hath suffered much from the cruelty of Lord Inchiquin and his wicked party by being imprisoned and thrust out of his command and with much ado got from thence . . an honest, sober, faithful man, assured me that Lord Inchiquin and his forces are actually joined with the Irish, and that he hath sent a good party of his horse to join with Lord Taaffe and that Lord Taaffe had sent a great part of his foot to join with Lord Inchiquin's forces, and . . that their whole design of conjunction depends on coming for England, and that they resolve to land in Cornwall, that they knew long since that the ships would revolt, by means whereof they expect the Duke of York to come to them, or at least they assure themselves of those ships to come and bring them over, which design hath been to me so visible that I have given notice thereof some months since. They can well spare 2,000 horse and a large body of foot . . . Although it hath pleased God to enable me so to quell the enemies of the Parliament in these parts that they were never lower, yet they might be looked upon as merely under a force and that if any enemy of what quality or condition soever should land infinite numbers would presently resort to them, which my inconsiderable force cannot be imagined able to look upon. . . . *Postscript.*—Honest Sir William Fenton, gallant Lieutenant-Colonel Phane and some ten others are like to perish there as the Parliament's martyrs, if the House do not take some present course for their relief and release which in earnest I am so conscientiously sensible of that I cannot be silent in it, as I desire you and other real men may not be which are there upon the place from whence they may be relieved, as you will all answer it to God and the world." (See *Commons' Journals,* v. 620.) *Seal.* [N. VII., 36.]

Colonel Edward Rosseter to the Committee at Derby House.

1648, June 24. Lincoln.—" The late riseing of the disaffected party with Styles and Hudson neer Stamford was happily supprest before my comeing downe, yet was not this country therby freed from danger, the enimye much increasing at Pontefract, wherby their partie in these partes were incouraged to list men, and the better to carry on their designe, the most active of them had very frequent meetings in divers parts by which the peace of this county was much indangered. To prevent which I have with the assistance of the committee compleated a troope of horse ; save onely for armes, for supply whereof I humbly crave your Lordshipps' order, and by these I hope the country wilbe continued quiet within itselfe, though not protected from the growinge enimy, who is so increased at Pontefracte, as that he may without interrupcion march into any parte of this county. For the better security of these partes, I sent a party of horse into the Isle of Axholme with commission to an active gentleman to raise a company of foote for securinge those passes, the inlet into this county, but such was the aversnes of those partes as that they ernestly opposed their owne and the countrie's security, for which I feare they have by this tyme suffered, I haveing this night intelligence that a party of horse, foote and dragoones of about five hundred are ther entred, and I feare may settle in that place, to the great annoyance of this country, wee being no way able to make resistance, the inhabitantes being in no defensive posture, nor have they any provision of armes to protect themselves or offend their enemy, the magazeene of this county being removed to Hull whence without your Lordshipps' order wee can have no restitucion of any parte thereof. Provision is here made for securing of all places of strength in this county. The care of Belvoire Castle is committed to Captain Henry Markham, whoe is authorized to raise sixty foote for security of that place. Mr. Francis Fines is by the committee desired with fifty men to secure the Castle of Tattershall. Bullingbrooke is ordered to be demolished, and an ingineere appointed to effect the same the next weeke. Hougham House and Torksey are already slighted.

My Lords, perceiving that whilst wee endeavour severally to protect our divided counties, wee may successively meeto with our respective ruines, wee have agreed on Monday next to drawe to a randevouze in Newarke with the severall horse of this county, Nottingham, Derby, and Leicester, to prevent the enimies intended garrisoninge of that place if possibly wee can effect it, which indeed I much doubt, our conjoyned force being so much inferior to the enemy, and no way fitted for present service. So that without an addicion of some other force by your Lordshipps to be speedily ordered to our assistance, I cannot perceive how we should with this handfull of men be any waies serviceable to our country or the Kingdome." *Signed. Seal.* [N. VII., 37.]

Colonel ROBERT HAMMOND to the COMMITTEE AT DERBY HOUSE.

1648, June 25. Carisbrooke Castle.—(Printed in Peck, *Desiderata Curiosa,* ix. 48.) *Seal.* [N. VII., 38.]

Colonel JOHN SPARROWE to SIR HARBOTTLE GRIMSTON.

1648, June 26. From the Leaguer before Colchester. — "Our country now begins to be so exhausted of provisions that it may well be doubted 'that the poor will be compelled to rise for want of bread. And I cannot see any other remedy unless some pay may be advanced for the pay of the General's army, and . . then we should be supplied by way of markets here and other countries would readily send in for our money, whereas now all provisions are raised in our country.

both for the army and the Essex forces. The Suffolk forces are now come in and they are principally supplied from their own country for present, but now we have in a manner begirt the town of Colchester round, and then Tendering Hundred will be subject to supply them. I hope the enemy will soon be straitened and compelled one way or other to yield, though as yet they seem high and confident. I hear that Captain Lin and Captain Ayliffe, Sir Benjamin's son, have with a party, possessed themselves of your house at Bradfield and intend to garrison it, but I believe they will soon be compelled to leave it " . . [N. VII , 39.]

Colonel FRANCIS HACKER and others to WILLIAM LENTHALL.

1648, June 26. Leicester.—We have used the power given us by the Ordinance to raise forces in this County, in which we have had extraordinary assistance from Thomas Lord Grey and Peter Temple, Esq., who have personally gone through every Hundred. And the country thereupon coming in very freely had the choice of their officers and chose Lord Grey and Mr. Temple to be colonels in two Hundreds, and Colonel Beaumont, Colonel Hacker, and Colonel Heselrige for the other Hundreds. We are all much obliged to Lord Grey and Mr. Temple for their forwardness, and conceiving that their appearing in arms will be of considerable advantage, we recommend that, if the House please to give way they may accept of these places and commands accordingly, and act as occasion shall require. *Signed. Seal.* [N. VII., 40.]

The HOUSE OF LORDS.

1648, June 26.—Order referring to a Committee to consider of settling a Peace. (Printed in *Lords' Journals*, x. 347.) [N. XV., 86.]

The MAYOR, ALDERMEN, BURGESSES, and INHABITANTS OF KINGSTON UPON HULL, to THOMAS LORD FAIRFAX.

1648, June 26.—Praying that Colonel Overton may be removed from being Deputy-Governor, and either Colonel Mauleverer, the former governor, or Colonel Bethell be appointed in his place, as " we find him on every occasion so averse to anything we desire that unless we give up our reason as men and our religion as Christians we see no cause in the world why we should at all confide in him." *Copy.* [N. XII, 237.]

THOMAS PARKES and others to THOMAS LORD FAIRFAX at the Leaguer before Colchester.

[1648, June 27. Hull.]—Desiring that Colonel Overton may be continued as Deputy-Governor there. *Signed.* [N. VII., 41.]

RICHARD THORNTON and others to THOMAS LORD FAIRFAX.

1648, June 27. Hull.—Concerning the intrigues against Colonel Overton, which they allege to proceed from disaffected persons, and desiring that he should be continued as Deputy-Governor. *Signed. Seal.* [N. VII., 44.]

The ENGLISH COMMISSIONERS to M. DE MONTREUIL.

1648, June 27.—Pass. (Printed in *Lords' Journals*, x. 366.) *Copy* [N. XX., 50.]

Brian Stapylton, Robert Goodwin, William Ashhurst, and Colonel John Birch to William Lenthall.

1648, June 27. Edinburgh.—(Identical, *mutatis mutandis* with the letter of the same date from the Earl of Nottingham to the Earl of Manchester, which is printed in *Lords' Journals*, x. 365.) Signed. Seal. [N. VII., 42.]

P.   H.   to Joseph Mason at his father's house in Southampton.

[1648], June 27. [London.]—"The Saints are not well pleased to find every one desirous to send them to a place of bliss before they have a mind to go. At Colchester last week they lost many by the sword —some say 1,500 at one bout—more by deserting the colours. 'Tis thought 4,000 of the old army is all—if so many—left. On Thursday the General sent in propositions of peace, indemnity, deposition of arms, &c. The same were returned in offer to him again. Trinity House being consulted how to set out a fleet to reduce the revolted, made answer that the more were sent out the more would be lost, the defection being general. They desire a personal treaty to reduce all, which . . . I doubt they will not be induced unto, but by the sword, for I am confident the K. will not depose himself to get a treaty by first granting those bills, so often denied, and so much suffered for   By letters from Paris we understand of the Prince's journey to Callis, where the shipping attends him, and whither many from hence are gone. 'Tis thought he will hazard much, rather than Colchester suffer, which at present wants neither courage nor men and commands land and sea enough to support a relief. Pembroke also proves hard of digestion. The Saints there also multiply losses. . . The mutinous humours of the city continue of the old fashion to little effect—rail upon the Parliament and obey it, feast Cavaliers and suffer them to be imprisoned, long to see a personal treaty as some new strange thing." [N. VII., 43.]

The Committee of the Estates of Scotland to Lord Inchiquin.

1648, June 28. Edinburgh.—"We are very sensible of the great extremities the Lord Inchiquin hath been reduced to by the malice of the Independent party in England and it appears by the relation made unto us that his Lordship and the Protestant army in Munster have not been able still by force to oppose their common enemies, but have been necessitated to agree to a cessation with some of them, thereby to divide them among themselves to engage them in an active opposition one of another, and for the more vigorous pursuing of Owen Roe and that party that directly oppose the right of the Crown of England and laboureth a foreign interest whom he which might be trusted without a cessation with those who are guilty of the shedding of so much blood of the Protestants there, and to which it is protest his Lordship hath been necessitated by the withholding from him those assistances necessary for carrying on the war against them. The Kingdom of Scotland, though they cannot admit for their parts of any conjunction or association with the Roman Catholics there or any else under what pretences soever yet they will ever most cheerfully assist to their power the Lord Inchiquin and the Protestants with him, both against Owen Roe and all the party with him or who shall continue in their disobedience to the Crown of England, and likewise against the prevalent Independent party in England or Ireland and for that end we shall

henceforth include the said Lord Inchiquin, his army, and all such as
are or shall be joined within the solemn League and Covenant in all
treaties and agreements for peace which this nation shall make for [their
own] behalf, and we do expect his Lordship will make no agreement for himself and his party without including this kingdom and
including its interest. We leave to the Lord Inchiquin, concerning
his comportment to the Lord Clanrickard, the Lord Taaffe and the Irish
who are willing to submit to the King's authority, provided the terms of
that submission be not prejudicial to the Protestant Religion.

As for the Lord Marquess of Ormonde we look upon him as a person
so full of honour loyalty and good affection to religion as we conceive
the Lord Inchiquin and the Protestant army in Munster will do
themselves great right in acknowledging and submitting themselves to
the authority he hath from his Majesty. We shall employ some from
hence to reside there, and in the mean time shall desire the Lord
Inchiquin to continue a good correspondence with us" and the Scotch
army in Ulster. *Draft* or *Copy.* [N. XXI., 77.]

SIR THOMAS HONYWOOD and others to the COMMITTEE AT DERBY
HOUSE.

1648, June 29. Leaguer before Colchester.—"The rebels having
by the providence of God shut themselves into Colchester are now
by his Excellency's forces—with the weak assistance we have been
able to contribute—begirt on each side and near approached in sundry
places. Their obstinancy in the defence of that place sheweth plainly
that as they are the only visible force now in arms against the Parliament
in all the South parts of the kingdom, so they look upon themselves as
the last refuge of their party, and are resolved to venture to the utmost
for the upholding their dying rebellion. The bottom of their confidence
we conceive is from help of foreign assistance, which—as by themselves,
so also by the revolted ships and others—are daily threatened. The
concernment of the present affair . . is not unknown unto you. They
or we may justly expect certain ruin on the ground where we are. If
any help be afforded them it is like to be by the way expressed.
For the compassing of that the most opportune place is Harwich,
lying in the mouth of those parts, where the revolted Navy may
be easily fraught with disbanded soldiers." There are some ships
there of whose fidelity his Excellency is assured. Considering the importance of reducing the forces in these parts, we desire that your
Lordships should take order for the continuance and supply of these
ships there. We also desire that a considerable supply of money and
provisions be sent to the forces under his Excellency's command.
"The sad condition of our friends in durance presseth us to remind
your Lordships of a righteous resolution of sending to the head quarters
such a number of considerable Delinquents as may undergo the same
way of entertainment amongst us as our worthy friends do find among
the rebels, there being as yet but one come unto us. . . Our friends
are placed in such a house, as lies under the mouth of our chiefest
battery, so that we must either forsake our advantage, or at every shot
endanger the lives of those worthy persons." *Signed. Seal.* [N.
VII., 45.]

Votes concerning a TREATY WITH THE KING for Peace.

1648, June 30.—(Printed in *Lords' Journals,* x. 353.) [N. XV.,
88, 89.]

THOMAS [LORD] FAIRFAX to the COMMITTEE AT DERBY HOUSE.

1648, July 2. Leaguer before Colchester.—Concerning the differences at Hull between some of the townsmen and the Deputy-Governor, whom he praises, and the affronts offered to him by Mr. Boatman, the great incendiary in the town, concerning whom a paper is enclosed, and desiring that a good quantity of provisions for the Castle and Block-houses there might be speedily sent down. *Signed.* [N. VII., 46.] *Enclosed:*

A Breviate of certain articles against Mr. JOHN BOATMAN, minister to the Low Parish of Kingston-upon-Hull.

Charging him with speaking and praying against the Army, Lord Fairfax, and Colonel Overton. [N. XV., 167.]

[Major-General LAMBERT] to ———.

[1648], July 2. Brampton.—Since my last dated at Rickaby nothing considerable has happened. The country near Carlisle being altogether unable to furnish us longer with provisions it was thought fit to draw off at a little further distance yet so as to prevent provisions from going to the enemy. Accordingly on Friday last we drew off both horse and foot and marched to Brampton and Warwick Bridge and kept strong guards there and at other passes thereabout. Upon our drawing off the enemy with about fourscore horse troubled us in the rear and followed skirmishing about two or three miles. In this retreat Major Robinson, who brought up our rear and behaved himself very well received a shot in his face, though not dangerous, at a pass we went over, and the enemy following us to a second pass I appointed Major Haynes with a commanded party of Colonel Twisleton's regiment to draw up behind that pass upon the flanks of the pursuers where the ditch was so straight as a horse might leap it, and ordered him when they came up to career over and fall upon them, which he accordingly did, and the enemy immediately faced about with their whole party, and he had the pursuit of them almost as far as Stanwix. The enemy never stood but about twelve of them were taken prisoners, two slain, and divers dangerously wounded. After that we retreated very quietly. In this pursuit one Captain Sherburne, a Lancashire man and Papist, was taken, and the rest of them most gentlemen and reformado officers well mounted.

I received letters out of Northumberland from Sir Arthur Heselrige signifying that the enemy there increases much and summon in the country which come in freely, and thereupon sent Colonel Lilburne with three more troops of his regiment to join with the rest of ours there, and upon other letters I appointed Colonel Harrison with his own regiment and four of Lieutenant-General's troops should likewise go to their assistance, and accordingly he set forward yesterday afternoon. We this afternoon met with Colonel Ashton concerning the disposing of the remaining forces, which I conceive we shall draw up on the South of Carlisle. *Copy.* [N. XII., 250.]

Examination of ABRAHAM DOWCETT.

1648, July 3.—(Printed in *Lords' Journals*, x. 358, and in Peck, *Desiderata Curiosa*, ix. 49.) [N. XV., 90.]

The HOUSE OF COMMONS.

1648, July 4.—Vote concerning public debts and engagements. (Printed in *Commons' Journals*, v. 623.) [N. XV., 91.]

Colonel John Jones to William Lenthall.

1648, June [July] 4. Denbigh Castle.—"This last night this Castle of Denbigh should have been betrayed. The enemy that were to surprise it were in number about 80, of whom about 50 had entered the outer ward before the alarm was taken, having gained a corporal by promising him 100*l.*, and likewise two sentinels—who stood on that side where they were to enter—their confederates. The Captain of the Watch suspected treachery in the corporal by his neglecting to relieve his sentinels in due time, and therefore went himself the round and made the first discovery. The prisoners we took and the said soldiers which were in the design have upon their examination discovered the whole plot, as far as they knew being a limb of the general design of the kingdom. The chief contrivers yet discovered unto us are such as have perfected their compositions and were permitted to enjoy their estates as friends . . . . *Postcript.*—I was with the Governor in the Castle when the alarm was given and was an eye witness of the good posture and readiness of himself and soldiers although he had . . . . at that instant a greater number of prisoners in the Castle than soldiers." *Seal.* [N. VII., 10.]

Sir Anthony Weldon and others to William Lenthall.

1648, July 4. Rochester.— "We are in a daily expectation of new insurrections boldly threatened by the Malignants from several parts of the county whereunto they encourage themselves from the fresh remembrance of their own late formidable appearance, the only visible check thereof, the army, being now otherwise engaged, the nakedness of the well affected party by them disarmed, the delay of exemplary punishment upon themselves, their great hopes of succour by a foreign invasion, and the advantages thereto by the revolted ships and castles in the Downs together with the declared countenance of the Prince. All which mischiefs we are in this condition altogether unable to withstand by reason of the late plunderings and spoil of the Parliament's friends and of the county in general, the dissolution of the whole frame of the Militia, the imbezilling of the public magazines and moneys, besides the extraordinary and unproportionable burthen of taxes upon this county made use of by the Malignants to exasperate the people against the Parliament." We have therefore raised a regiment of horse and one of foot maintained upon free quarter in confidence the house will grant supplies for their maintenance which we suggest should be by applying the fines or sequestrations of the principal incendiaries in this insurrection. (Most of the rest of this letter sufficiently appears from the resolutions passed thereon. See *Commons' Journals,* v. 628. "The mitigation and exemption " there alluded to was proposed to be in favour of "such persons whose particular cases compared with their former actings for the Parliament may give just ground to believe that their compliance in this action was really forced.") *Signed. Seal.* [N. VII., 47.]

Sir Thomas Barnardiston and others to William Lenthall.

1648, July 4. From the Leaguer before Colchester.—"The forces of our county were so forward to serve you that four regiments of foot and seven troops of horse were advanced, besides those that kept the passes, and at our coming we found them in their approaches near unto the town, and they have since behaved themselves so gallantly, that after a hot dispute, where some of them lost their lives and many of them much blood, yet in the conclusion they beat the enemy out of their houses in the suburbs . . . so far as the East Bridge, which doth much straiten those within the town by hindering their sallies into Tendring Hundred. We are this day at their quarters with them, and are careful to send them in provision and to provide their pay. At their first rising there appeared in some of them a strange averseness to the service, but afterwards so unexpected a forwardness, and cheerfulness in all of them, that makes many wonder at it. and may make us all confident that God still appears for us. They labour under many difficulties, and the pay they have received we stand engaged for and doubt not of reimbursement at the public charge." . . . (See *Commons' Journals*, v. 624.) *Signed. Seal.* [N. VII., 48.]

SIR THOMAS HONYWOOD and others to WILLIAM LENTHALL.

1648, July 4. At the Leaguer before Colchester.—"The difficulties wherewith wee have wrestled in the late engagement, not onely continuing but alsoe growing upon us, dayly reports and informacions carving with them too much probability of further tumults intended, and forces to be levied for the reliefe of them besieged, giveing us just cause of feare that wee whoe were soe much overpowred by their first attempt shall no way be able in our present posture in the least measure to serve the Commonwealth or protect ourselves, wee are bold to give in our estate and desires to this honourable House, from which alone—under God—wee hope for assistance. The sad condicion wherein wee are will not give us leave to neglect or disbelieve the manifest intencions and knowne threates of our enemies, both in our owne county, the places adjacent and others remote, experience having convinced us that straitened power and small forces in such condicions as that whereunto wee are now reduced is the readiest and most expedious course for the ruine of the undertakers, wee are enforced to such a further engagement and advancement of the one and the other. Something wee heare is voted in order to the payment of the forces wee have already raised, which as wee receave with acknowledgment of your honourable care therein, soe it being onely for a month allready fully expired, wee cannot but informe your Honour that it will not reach to a supply of our necessities, without an addition at least of another month to be levied according to the continuance of our troubles, but indeed were that whole force of the old establishment, both traine and auxiliaries in the best posture they possibly can be settled in, it would be exceedingly short of what our present necessity calls for. Whilste our enemies were allwayes visible and at such a distance as wee might observe their motions towards us, the present power of the country especially considered as in association was not contemptible, but as to this tyme our feares ariseing for the future and our actuall troubles for the present from neighbours and formerly supposed friendes, many of the Trained Bands, both officers and soldiers, divers of the auxiliaries horse and foote, being seduced into the late rebellion, others refuseing or neglecting to come or send in to us, doth amount nere the one moity of the whole force, which the iminent danger of invasion from abroade for which our enemies are of late soe accomodated, nature itself continually prompting us to seeke the raising such a visible strength and the supporting of it by such a directing power, and meanes of supportance and maintainance as which with the blessing of God wee may oppose to the utmost endeavours. Our neighbour county of Kent, as wee humbly conceave, have given us as to the pointe of a boddy of horse and foote continually in pay and service, a desirable patterno. Lesse then what they have done, wee cannot apprehend wilbe u-full in any measure unto us." We therefore desire authority for levying such forces, and for enforcing an involuntary contribution from the estates of those who have contributed to laying the foundation of a second war. *Signed.* [N. VII., 49.]

[Major-General LAMBERT] to ————.

[1648], July 4. Wetherall, near Warwick Bridge.—I sent Colonel Lilburne with the remainder of his regiment to Northumberland with instructions to alarm and disturb the enemy in his levies, till I could settle affairs here so as to send a more considerable party. I also gave him instructions not to attempt anything upon the enemy, except God should put some clear opportunity into his hands by surprising, beating some quarters, or the like. According to his directions, bearing the enemy had summoned in the country near Cockett, in Northumberland, and had a great quantity of arms coming thither for the arming of such as should appear, he drew towards them in the night, intending thereby to give the country such an alarm that they should not appear the next day, but coming nearer and finding them in great security, and having either none or a very slight guard, he fell into their quarters. He took divers gentlemen of very good quality and account —according as the enclosed list will mention—, betwixt three and four hundred private soldiers and at least 600 horses, most of them very good. The enemy after this blow got together and made some parties in small bodies, and might probably have acted something upon him being diverted by his prisoners, and the soldiers upon their prey. Nevertheless they did not come on any farther.

I had upon further advice sent Colonel Harrison with his own regiment and four troops of Lieutenant-General Cromwell's for the relief of that county, most of which on that good success I hope to recall for defence of these parts from the enemy which I hope will be easy to be dealt withall, if they do not receive those supplies from Scotland, which they expect with very great confidence.

I understand from a very good hand, that partly by affections but chiefly by force they carry on the new levies in that kingdom, and have already drawn down to Dumfries, 25 miles from Carlisle, 3,000 horse and 6,000 foot, with arms, ammunition, victuals and other provisions of war, and this day Lord Calender and Major-General Middelton came thither, and gave out they intend for England this week. *Enclosed:*

> The said List of prisoners. (Agreeing generally with that printed in Rushworth, iv. 2. 1177. At the end " We lost not one man, nor killed any but three or four.") *Copy.* [N. XII., 250a.]

Major-General LAMBERT to his father-in-law SIR WILLIAM LISTER.

1648, July 4. Wetherall, near Warwick Bridge.—" The number of our forces are in all 23 troops of horse besides two in Northumberland and four in Yorkshire, but some very small, having divers commanded parties forth in other parts of the kingdom, many fallen sick, and abundance of horses sick and lame, and some run away upon the new raising of horse into Yorkshire and Lincolnshire, which amount unto about 2,300 horse and 1,200 foot besides Lancashire, which is about 1,000 foot and 300 horse. From Scotland we hear that the Malignants by force and power carry on their new levies very fast and have already in readiness 4,000 horse and 10,000 foot, which lie at Dumfries being of the new levies and 3,000 foot more which my information reports to be of the old army, which I understand not in regard I conceive all their foot was disbanded, and 3,000 more which they expect out of Ireland the 1st of July all which makes 16,000. Besides the horse aforementioned they have 2,000 horse of the old army and 1,000 more out of Ireland; great store of arms ammunition and oatmeal already brought to Dumfries. *Signed.* (*Seal,* a centaur with motto *Nosce Teipsum,* the same as that on the Margetts' letters in Lord Braye's collection. See *Sixth Appendix to the Tenth Report of the Historical MSS. Commission, p.* 169.) [N. VII., 50.]

The DUKE OF BUCKINGHAM, and the EARLS OF HOLLAND and PETERBOROUGH to WILLIAM LENTHALL.

1648, July 5 —(Identical, *mutatis mutandis,* with the letter from the same to the Earl of Manchester, which is printed in *Lords' Journals,* x. 367.) *Signed.* [N. VII., 51.]

The GRAND JURY OF the County of SOUTHAMPTON to LORD CHIEF BARON WILD.

1648, July 5.—Petition, complaining that notwithstanding the recent Act for easing the free quarter they still suffer heavily, as very many, pretending to be soldiers, under the proviso in the Act allowing free quarter for one night only, come successively one company after another. *Copy.* [N. XXII., 119.]

THOMAS [LORD] GREY to WILLIAM LENTHALL.

1648, July 5. Cotesbridge.—" Having intelligence from Colonel Rossiter that the cavaliers were at Lincoln I sent Colonel Hacker with about 200 horse being soldiers and countrymen who after following them three day[s] they took 100 or thereabouts passing over the Trent and I having intelligence that they were marching this way I sent in for the countrymen that were late listed and securing the passes last night drew them all to Cotesbridge to the number of 400 or thereabouts, and sending out parties from thence met with some of them, they being totally routed and running away in 30 and 20 in a company. I have sent parties every way to meet stragglers and am following that way the greatest part is said to be gone. The particulars you shall have more at large when the parties are all met and the officers drawn together. . . . *Postscript.*—The fight was at Widmorepoole in Nottinghamshire upon the confines of Leicestershire." *Signed. Seal.* [N. VII., 52.]

J[OHN] R[USHWORTH] to WILLIAM LENTHALL.

1648, July 5.—(Corresponding in substance and in many places *verbatim* with that printed in Rushworth, iv. 2. 1179. It adds that the sally was commanded by Sir George Lisle.) *Postscript.*—" Had we but old soldiers instead of these countrymen Colchester had not been out of your power at this hour, but you shall see God will give it us in good time " and recommending " honest Mr. Sleigh of Berwick." . . . " I have a list of 30 Coronels (Colonels), who are in Colchester, and have all formerly been coronels for the King, and now for the Covenant —as they say—in right of the King." Only the Postscript and address in Rushworth's hand. *Seal.* [N. VII., 53.]

Colonel THOMAS MYTTON to WILLIAM LENTHALL.

1648, July 5. Denbigh.—" Being here upon Monday night to meet Colonel Jones . . . . had it not been that God in his mercy prevented the enemies' design we had been all surprised, they having engaged a corporal, one Sutton, and two private soldiers, Williams and Ashmont, who stood sentinels that night to betray the Inner Castle unto them. The corporal was to have 100*l.*, the two private soldiers had no certain sum promised. We were all upon the pit's brink, they having effected their design so far as to be possessed of the outer works of the Inner Castle, and were got to a gate which cometh into the Inner ward which did not reach the ground by three-quarters of a yard, there being a piece of timber put under the gate to prevent any passage that way, which would have been quickly and without noise removed, the corporal having laid a wooden bar ready for them at the place to effect it, but it pleased God that, a sentinel having called divers times unto the corporal to relieve him and the corporal not answering, one Serjeant Owen being Captain of the watch that night . . . speedily went the round and coming near to the place where Williams stood, first heard a noise and then espied the enemy got into the tower where the sentinel stood, and gave the alarm. The Governor being not gone to bed, having parted with Colonel Jones and myself not half an hour before, got his men presently upon the works which when the enemy was aware of they made all possible haste to be gone, leaving many of their arms behind them in the Castle, and two of them fell under a drawbridge where they could not come out till they were apprehended as soon as it was day, who have confessed unto us much of the design and divers of the persons that were there that night . . . Williams fled away with them, the corporal and Ashmont we have taken, who have confessed how and by whom they were engaged. There is nobody that hath power to proceed against them by Martial Law, and this place hath more prisoners than soldiers in it, which I humbly desire may be taken speedily into consideration, it being of so considerable consequence that all the Parliament's interest in North Wales, excepting the county of Montgomery, will be lost next, if the enemy should possess himself thereof, Anglesey being in that posture it is yet in. The chief actors that we can discover as yet . . are Major Dollbin, Captain Dollbin, Captain Rutter, Captain Parry, Captain Hughes and Captain Charles Chambers, all of them commanders heretofore for the king, William Chambers and one Hughes both tradesmen in this town. . . ." *Signed. Seal.* [N. VII., 54.]

Sir Arthur Heselrig to William Lenthall.

1648, July 6 Newcastle.—" Upon the first notice of the prisoners that were taken I sent you upp a list as it then came to me and although they lost Sir Richard Tempest before the rest were brought to me, yet I find many gentlemen of qualitie and officers not mentioned in that list, in all full an hundred. Many of the officers and gentlemen are papists, and I am putt to very great charge and trouble in keepinge so many prisoners. It is not fitt to my understandinge that Collonel Grey and some of the most active and dangerous amongst them should be prisoners in their owne countie. I thinke Scarborough Castle or some other place might be more proper for them; and for those papists that have beene in armes I desire to know your pleasure whether yow will admitt of any exchange for them. Some of the private souldiers I have taken into service, others that were pressed men I have discharged, and there remaines about one hundred and fifty that I believe will never change their partie so long as they live. They are most of them troopers that have beene in the same service formerly with the gentlemen that are prisoners, and it is a very great charge to mainteyne them

and whensoever they are sett at libertie it will be an addielou of so
many stout desperate men to the enemies strength. I could heartily
wish that both they and such others as have formerly fought against
the parliament and have againe taken upp armes were sent to some
forraigne plantacions for they have noe estates and are sodainely
ready in every parte of the kingdome to rise upp in armes. This day
the Scottch forces that are raised bould their randezvous eight miles
from Carlile, and it comes to me from very good handes that they
intend to come into England on Satterday. I was tould by one this
day that came yesterday out of Scotland that the Scotts forces were
uppon their march towards their randezvouz, and that he was in their
quarters. And withall he told me that he heard divers ministers
preach both uppon the dayes appoynted for humiliation and other dayes
that the Curse of God would follow them. His wordes also were that
there was not an honest man in Scotland but was against their comeinge
into England. It would be of great advantage to this kingdome and to
your affaires if some forces of the army could speedilie come downe."
(The rest of the letter relates to Mr. Cole, a Delinquent.) *Signature
torn off. Seal.* [N. VII., 55.]

Colonel GEORGE TWISLETON and Colonel JOHN CARTER to
WILLIAM LENTHALL.

1648, July 6. Denbigh.—Suggesting in reply to the letter of June 8th,
which thanked them for their services against Sir John Owen, and asked
them to represent a way for remunerating the troops engaged in that
service, that pay should be granted them out of the sequestrations of the
estates of Sir John Owen's confederates, and asking for repayment of
about 3,000*l.* apiece due to themselves. *Signed. Seal.* [N. VII., 56.]

The COMMITTEE FOR LINCOLNSHIRE AND NOTTINGHAMSHIRE to
WILLIAM LENTHALL.

[1648, July 6. Nottingham.]—Desiring that some of the prisoners
taken in Colonel Rosseter's late victory be tried at the Assizes and the
rest sent over sea, and that the charge of keeping them and providing
for the wounded soldiers be provided out of their estates. (Printed in
Grey, iii. Appendix, No. 16, p. 24.) (See *Commons' Journals*, v. 629.)
Signed by William Drewry, Mayor, Gilbert Millington and others.
Seal. [N. VII., 57.]

Colonel EDWARD ROSSETER to WILLIAM LENTHALL.

1648, July 6. Nottingham.—"It hath pleased God to give us a
seasonable victory over the Pontefract forces, an increasing, active, and
resolved enemy. . . The timely advance of Sir Henry Cholmely
with those under his command—stopping their retreat by his lying on the
North side Trent—gave us this opportunity of fighting them. My present
indisposition occasioned by my wounds received in this sharp engagement will not give me leave to present you with an account thereof in
writing. I have therefore sent my Captain-Lieutenant to give you a
full narrative of the whole business." (Printed in Grey, iii. Appendix,
No. 17, p. 26.) *Signed. Seal.* [N. VII., 58.]

ORDINANCE.

1648, July 6.—Empowering the Committee of Huntingdonshire to
levy assessments for raising and maintaining a troop of horse. (*Endorsed:* "*Prima lecta* 6 Julii 1648, Laid by.") [N. XV., 92.]

Sir John Bourchier and others to William Lenthall.

1648, July 7. York.—Desiring that two of the collectors of the Revenue might be credited in their accounts with two sums of 59*l.* and 50*l.* respectively advanced by them for setting forth the Yorkshire forces sent against the enemy at Pontefract. *Signed. Seal.* [N. VII., 59.]

Thomas [Lord] Fairfax to the Committee at Derby House.

1648, July 8. From the Leaguer before Colchester.—Referring to his former letter concerning the differences between Colonel Overton and the townsmen of Hull, and stating he had since received by Alderman Ramsden and others another petition desiring his removal, but without mentioning any particular charge, nor had the gentlemen anything to say against him as a soldier. *Signed. Seal.* [N. VII., 60.]

The Committee of Estates to the English Commissioners.

1648, July 8.—In reply to their papers of the 17th and 22nd of June. (Printed in *King's Pamphlets*, E. 459, No. 21, p. 58.) *Signed* "Arch. Primerose." [N. XX., 42.]

Colonel Adrian Scrope to the Committee at Derby House.

1648, July 10. St. Neots.—" We after a very hard march came " here, " where we found the enemy, and early in the morning we fell into their quarters and had suitable success even according and beyond our expectation. The enemy when we entered the town were drawn up into three bodies, which my forlorn hope charged and routed before the rest of my horse entered, but when the rest came up the dispute was quickly at an end, for then they got out at all the passes and ran for it, but divers of them fell and some of the chief ones, and we have taken divers prisoners. . . . The Duke of Bucks escaped with about three score horse, who is gone—as I understand—towards Lincoln. I had marched all day Saturday and all night that my horse were unable to pursue further than Huntingdon, but I hope, if he goes that way, that he will be met with by Colonel Rosseter's forces. He is not at all considerable and unable to do anything." (See *Commons' Journals*, v. 633.) *Seal. Enclosed:*

" There were slain one Colonel and some other officers, which I cannot get knowledge of their names, with 40 soldiers or thereabouts. Prisoners taken,

The Earl of Holland,	Lieutenant-Colonel Goodwin,
Sir Gilbert Gerard,	Two Captains,
Colonel Skrimshere,	Lieutenant Wheeler,
Major Holland,	Quartermaster George Wheeler,
Mr. Stepkin,	Most of the Duke of Bucks' ser-

vants and the Earl of Holland's surgeon, Colonel Dolbere, who is mortally wounded, with about 100 private soldiers. There escaped away the Duke of Bucks, with Colonel Legge and threescore troopers. The Duke was the General. There were slain of my part two men only, my Captain-Lieutenant wounded and three more. Since the writing hereof was taken Colonel Legge and mortally wounded. I hear also that Sir Kenelm Digby's son is slain." [N. VII., 61.]

Colonel George Twisleton to William Lenthall.

1648, July 10. Denbigh.—On Monday night Major Dolbin and his party " came to that gate of the Castle where those centreys stood between 12 and 1 of the clock and by the help of two ladders were all received in by them . . and haveing the command of all the Outer Ward they came to the Inmost Gates. The Captaine of the Watch, Serjeant Owens, misseing the Corporall and suspecting something in that hee was absent and had not releeved those two centreys as hee had commanded immediatly went the round, and towards that tower where hee suspected danger. The centrey made him stand whilest he called the corporalls severall tymes before hee would answere and the centrey beeing one of them in the plott would not let him pass untill the corporall gave the word who heareing the captaine of the watch soe exceedingly storme, came as if hee had beene with reliefe to an other centrey, and hidd let him passe, but indeed as hee after himselfe confessed came from the gate where the enemy was, and hee was helpeing them to breake it open and that hee thought they had done enough to make all sure before the captayne could give the alarum, much more before the castle could take it. The captaine passeing presently looked over the wall, saw the enemy all within and at the gate called to this centry to fire. Hee did not, hee then called to armes. I bceing then up in my chamber with Collonell Jones came late that night beeing designed by the howse for some speciall service touching Anglesey, tooke the first call, and came directly to the gate where I knew the greatest danger lay. Against which a gun was placed where I fownd the enemy. God directed us to doe that and soe astonished the enemy that they were presently put to shift for themselves. The corporall should have let the enemy through the way wee sent out and releeved our centreys which was over a draw-bridge that I made of purpose very strong and secure. The captaine of the watch before by an imediate hand of providence leadeing him went a litle after the setting of these treacherous centreys, and findeing the draw - bridge unlockt, onely haspt on the inside, hee lockt a doore which secured the passage to the draw-bridge by which means the corporall could not come to it to let them in, which if hee had done as was plotted, wee had then beene all irrecoverably lost for they might have come all round the castle in private wayes and to the prisoners which were in number more then I had souldiers in the castle, whereof was Sir John Owen and others of great noate to the number of above one hundred, and let them out uppon us before wee cold have taken the alarum. Another speciall peece of providence was that neither the enemy nor the corporall should thinke of useing there great hammer with which one blow uppon the padlockes that lockt the bolts the corporall might have made way for them, and then they might all have rusht in a body. The enemy left behynd them near fifty armes, swords, bills, fowling peeces and suchlike weapons. Wee tooke a eleven (*sic*) prisoners first and last. The night was darke and rayny and my chardge within in respect of my prisoners was great, which was the cawse I would not sally untill I had secured all within. Then I did, but all the birds were flowen except two that wee tooke and by means of them gott a discovery of the persons that were both chiefe in and accessary to this plott. I have the corporall and one of the centreys in hold, and both of them did confesse all those particulars. I formerly mencioned they were to have an 100*l*. but had in hand litle, one 10*s*., the other 5*s*. I had informacion from Chester that the other centrey that came away with the enemy is apprehended there. They confesse noe more of my men in the plott, but I suspect many of the guard that was uppon the watch that night and have turned away some of them. Noe providence nor care can fence against treachery. I had ingadged all my souldiers seeing the desperatnes of the tymes in the inclosed ingadgement, had turned out and changed all—to the number of above threescore—that had beene cavaleers, and that had not morall principles of honesty at least to guide them. There was not the least discontent or shew of it in any, but duty readily and exactly performed according to as strict rules and orders as I could prescribe : yet these rogues were seduced who had served in these partes above four yeares, and never was of the enemyes party." *Signed.* [N. VII., 62.]

The Same to the Same.

Same date.—Enclosing the last, stating the weakness of the garrison, and asking for reinforcements, and for a sum of money out of the estates of these who attempted the surprise. *Signed. Seal. Enclosed* is a copy of the engagement taken by the garrison and alluded to in the previous letter. [N. VII., 63.]

Sir Michael Livesey to William Lenthall.

1648, July 10. Kingston.—"The inclosed coming to my hands I thought fit to send it to you, whereby you might perceive it is not a personal treaty will serve your enemies' turn ; but it is your lives and your estates they thirst after. . . . Those enemies are very high and in many places ready to rise. As yet they stop and imprison those that are your friends, some they have killed since the flight of the Lord Holland. If I should be commanded any further service here I will presently discover and secure them." [N. VII., 64.]

Oliver Cromwell to William Lenthall.

1648, July 11.—Announcing the surrender of Pembroke. (Printed in Carlyle, Letter 62.) *Signed. Seal.* [N. VII., 65.] Probably *Enclosed :*

The Articles of Surrender.

Same date.—(The substance in Rushworth, iv. 2. 1190, and in Phillips, *Civil War in Wales,* ii. 397.) *Copy.* [N. XV., 93.]

Sir Thomas Honywood and others to William Lenthall.

1648, July 11. At the Leaguer before Colchester.—Repeating their request that " amongst ourselves upon our own charge with the help of their estates who, we hope, have justly lost them by unjust labouring to possess other men's we may raise such a force," viz. a regiment of foot and another of horse and dragoons, " as whereby we may readily serve the Parliament in any such exigencies as they may be probably reduced unto and secure our own country fiom the like imbroilments, as that which it now wrestleth withall . . . . The sad condition of our worthy friends in Colchester . . . doth every day heighten our compassion, as indeed we were most unbowelled men, if we should not be afflicted in their suffering, besides such is the policy or rather cruelty of the enemy that they place them just under the mouth of our only advantageous battery. A bullet within these few hours notwithstanding all our care and declining our own advantage passed through the room where they are all in durance." (See *Commons' Journals,* v. 635.) *Signed.* [N. VII., 66.]

Sir Michael Livesey to [the Committee at Derby House].

1648. July 11. Kingston.—"I appointed two of my best troops to be at Deptford and Greenwich this morning by five . . . which

I am confident was done accordingly. As for the dragoons your Lordships write for, they are in Kent already. I am now marching up to the borders of Kent by the advice of the gentlemen of Surrey, leaving only two troops of horse behind me. Three carriages of ammunition I have left with the gentlemen of Surrey. . . . As for the countrymen's horses to be returned again I am confident there is not any one to be found in the whole brigade so taken save only the troop at Harborough, which had order to take such men's horses as were enemies to the State to supply the loss that troop had sustained in that service." . . *Signed.* [N. VII., 67.]

ROBERT SCAWEN, THOMAS HODGES, FRANCIS ALLEIN, and WILLIAM LEMAN to WILLIAM LENTHALL.

1648, July 11. Bury St. Edmunds.—" In observance of the order of both Houses (see *Commons' Journals*, v. 619) we came to the headquarters on Tuesday last, where we understood the great necessities the army in general was in for want of pay and for monies for the carrying on their works and other emergencies, as also the great burthen . . on the adjacent parts of Essex and Suffolk by furnishing provisions for the forces there, which by estimate amounts weekly to as much as would in money pay a month's pay to these forces." . . We have stopt all moneys in the Receivers' hands of the adjacent counties and converted it to the present occasion, but we find very little money in the Treasurers' or Collectors' hands. We have endeavoured therefore with the Commissioners of Essex at head quarters and with those of Suffolk at Ipswich and Bury for the speedy collecting and getting in of the arrears of the nine months' assessment and of three months' of the last six months', and are now going into Norfolk to do the like. *Signed. Seal.* [N. VII., 68.]

Colonel NATHANIEL RICH to WILLIAM LENTHALL.

1648, July 12. Walmer.—"After three weeks beleaguering of Walmer Castle and many fruitless attempts both by sea and land . . to disturb us here and relieve it, it hath pleased God to give it into our hands, and though we find in it such provision as might have enabled them within, being about 60 in number—enough to man sufficiently so compacted a place of strength—to withstand us three weeks longer, yet . . . I thought fit to hasten at present its regaining . . by giving the besieged the enclosed conditions, the sum of which is their protection from the soldiers' violence, not intending by any thing therein contained expressly or implicitly to anticipate your justice or favour. . . If I may presume . . to offer anything I think the Lord Admiral's presence in the Downs with some ships may be now as safe—riding under this Castle's protection—as advantageous to discountenance any foreign influence here and hasten the reducement of the other two, possessed for the most part by seamen, who I find rather capable of complying impressions from the successful appearance of your maritime affairs than of the land." (See *Commons' Journals*, v. 634.) *Seal.* *Enclosed :*

The Articles of Surrender. [N. VII., 69.]

The HOUSE OF COMMONS.

[1648, July 12.]—Answer to the London Petition. (Printed in *Commons' Journals*, v. 634.) *Draft.* [N. XXII., 109.]

The Earl of Warwick to Willia Lenthall.

1648, July 14. Chatham.—A messenger from the House came last night with a warrant to fetch up many of the officers that were in the late petition and insurrection of Kent. I had examined many of them and absolved some, the evidence against them failing, but if the House has anything against them more than the evidence brought before me they must submit to further examination. As some of them, whose names are in the margin, have been of great use to me in fitting out the ships, and as their going up will be a great hindrance I have ventured to keep them till I be got out. If you will have them before, I will send them though it will much hinder the service here. The rest come up with your messenger. *Signed. Seal.* [N. VII., 70.]

[Major-General Labert] to Willia Lenthall.

1648, July 14. Penrith.—"To-day I received a letter from Duke Hamilton desiring my pass for . . . Mr. George Halliburton . . . with letters to the " King and the Parliament from the Committee of the Estates of Scotland, which I accordingly gave, but perceiving he had other letters between private persons not within his instructions I ventured " in his sight to take a particular of the superscriptions of those letters which I have inclosed . . . and with it the letters themselves sealed up in one packet under his and my seal by this bearer, Lieu-tenant-Colonel Osborne. . . . . The letters, as I perceive by the superscriptions are many of them written in ciphers, and I believe may be of concernment. Here is also a cipher with the letters which the gentleman affirms was for his own use. . . . Since my last we have continued very still at our quarters at Penrith, little action being on either side, and the enemy beyond our expectation quiet, though doubtless their numbers be much more considerable than ours. They give out that they defer attempts upon us until they receive some forces —which they do expect—out of Ireland. I do also expect some addi-tional forces to mine here, which if they come to us, and we remain safe in the meantime, I hope we shall be in a condition to meet them in the field." (See *Commons' Journals,* v. 640, 643.) *Signature torn off.* [N. VII., 71.]

Colonel R[obert] Overton to Willia Lenthall.

1648, July 15. Hull.—" I have lately seized 388 case of snaphance pistols and 400 pair of holsters brought down from London to Hull in Roger Robinson's ship closely packed up in seven oil casks." From many circumstances it appears that the master and most of his men were privy to the plot. " They do not produce any bill of lading, only the master showed me the enclosed bill signed by William Boothe of Killingham in Lincolnshire, formerly in arms for the King, who con-fesseth that at the request of a friend he paid 5l. in hand and gave his note for 5l. more to be paid at Hull, but denies that he knew of these arms or what the freight was, but saith that he only disbursed " the money on behalf of his friend who cannot now be found or heard of. The witnesses to the bill are Mr. Readhead and Mr. Harbottle both formerly in arms against the Parliament. " Readhead, as the Master . . relates, should have come to receive these arms at Hull and thence conveyed them to Turnbrigge, where it was intended they should have been received by the enemy, and . . . there was in Lincolnshire 1,000 horse which would hereupon be immediately in armes for the King . . . I have fetched in Mr. Boothe, and shall secure his person until I receive further directions. . . . Readhead and Harbottle being more remote and having no horse under my command I could not conveniently pursue their quest." I ask an order of indemnity for the seizure, and that supplies of pay may be ordered for this garrison now 3,000*l*. in arrear of what is due upon several warrants charged upon the assessments of Lincolnshire and Yorkshire, as our soldiers are invited by the present levies from want of livelyhood to betake themselves to field employment. I also ask that what may appear to have been spent on repairs of this place may be paid out of the 500*l*. in the hands of the Committee of Sequestrations, and that speedy advance may be made of the 6,000*l*. ordered from the Excise. *Seal. Enclosed* are copies of the bill referred to, and of a declaration by Roger Robinson that it was signed by Mr. Boothe and witnessed by Mr. Readhead and Mr. Harbottle. [N. VII., 72.]

[JOHN RUSHWORTH] to WILLIAM LENTHALL.

1648, July 15, 12 at night. Leaguer before Colchester.—"In my last I intimated to you that wee hoped to gaine the Gatehouse, the workes about it, and churche, all which the enemy had fortified very stronglie. And it pleased God this afternoone about 5 of the clocke to deliver all these places into our hands. The manner was thus: wee discharged foure peece of cannon altogether which much amuzed the enemy in the works and then discharged foure more, and immediatlie our musquetiers fell on and stormed them (?) in the gatehouse with ladders, and threw in hand granadoes. The enemy opposed very stoutlie for a while, and threw downe severall of the ladders, but att last gave backe. Some held out theire handkercheefes, others fired very feircely, yet notwithstandinge our men gained the works and parte of the gatehouse, and throweing in a hand granadoe, where there was some of the enemy, stood to theire armes. It happened to lighte amongst their maggazine, consisting of about foure harrells of powder, and blew upp about forty of theire men. It pleased God that wee had but one man hurte with that blowe. All this eveninge our men have been diginge and pullinge out the dead bodyes of the enemy: findinge here and there a legg and an arme by itselfe. There were in the whole nomber as some of the prisoners whoe had quarter confesse, seaven score, and wee have but about sixty prisoners. Not any could escape—wee gettinge betweene them and home—soe the rest were putt to the sword, and distroyed as aforesaide. I send you he[rew]ith that you may see how they still persiste in theire venemous disposicion to shoote such things as may bee sure to ranker and poyson the flesh. The enemy was soe enraged att this losse—haveing totally by this meanes shutt themselves upp within the walles and not haveing any parte of the suburbs—that they sett the suburbs round the towne on fire and all this present there is the saddest spectacle to bee seene that hath fallen out in this age, there beeing now burneing in a grate plaine houses above a mile in length, and with that violence as it is a wonder to behold it. By this wee can conceive that they are desperately bent and will not only distroy the suburbs but even burne the towne alsoe. *Postscript.*—This day my Lord Generall had another pacquett boate, which came from Holland yesterday, and then the revolted shipps were there. Hee hath sent an expresse to Yarmouth to advise that towne to stand to their armes, one Johnson of Yarmouth, an Apostate, beeing newly come to the shipps, and whoe gives out hee hath made the towne sure for the King. If some members were sent doune thither it is very needful, and might bee of great use." (A short abstract of this letter is in Rushworth, iv. 2. 1191.) *Unsigned*, but in Rushworth's hand. *Seal torn off.* [N. VII., 73.]

The EARL OF WARWICK to [the COMMITTEE AT DENNY HOUSE].

1648, July 15. Chatham.— Concerning the landing of men from the revolted ships in the Downs, and the bad supply of his fleet. (Printed in Grey, iii. Appendix, No. 77, p. 131.) *Signed.* [N. VII., 74.]

SIR JOHN BAMPFYLD, SIR JOHN NORTHCOTE and others to WILLIAM LENTHALL.

1648, July 15. Exeter.—We have considered how our county may be put in a posture of defence, but find manifold defects, the chief being : 1. The ordnance is very defective; 2. The great want of arms both for horse and foot; 3. the distraction the county is in, occasioned by the diversity of rates unequally laid upon us beyond any other part of the kingdom, of which we give details. The remedies we conceive to be the speedy passing of the Grand Ordinance for the Militia, that 300 horse arms and 3,000 foot arms be speedily sent to us, that there may be but one rate for Ireland on foot at the same time, and that the Army rate being duly paid there may be some reasonable deduction for Free Quarter, and the deceitful way of Billet removed. *Signed. Seal.* [N. VII., 75.]

ROBERT CLIVE to WILLIAM LENTHALL.

1648, July 15. Stytch in Shropshire.—" I should spare to trouble you . . did I not apprehend the danger of losing this county to be far greater than others conceive it to be. There hath been special care taken to make all the houses which were thought to be tenable uncapable to harbour the disaffected party ; yet I much fear that if some speedy care be not taken for settlement of the Militia in this county, your friends will be enforced to seek for security in some place else. There have been orders granted long since by the Committee here for raising 1,200 foot, but I find they have been very little successful, and those who were the first that engaged for you altogether unwilling to appear ; this back-wardness of theirs arising not from any disaffection to you, but from discontent that those who have been least serviceable and that appeared but lately for you are most countenanced by those in authority here, and such who first engaged themselves for the Parliament and acted cordially to the last are very little regarded . . . There have been very lately with me many godly persons both clergy and others who acquainted me that within very few days many disaffected persons have left their habitations and great numbers are enlisted round about this part of the country for the King's service. Who the chief actors are I cannot yet learn, but I shall join my endeavours with theirs to find them out, if it be possible. There are many gentlemen of quality who have not prosecuted their compositions at Goldsmiths' Hall, and speak great words; if you would send a positive order for the speedy securing of them all it would much encourage your friends and may haply in a great measure prevent the enemies' design. There are 120 horse in pay which are lately raised, these . . have neither Captain . . nor any other officer. This is dissatisfactory to many of the soldiers themselves, and all the well affected that I have met with, who gave me assurance, that, if the Parliament would grant a commission to some faithful and active gentleman of this county to command the horse, in all cases of necessity they would not only engage themselves but all that had relation to them for the Parliament's service We shall the next week endeavour to put in execution the former orders of the Committee 'for raising foot, which, if not speedily done, I fear the enemy will take some encouragement to rise the sooner. Here are many that daily—to encourage the Malignants—raise false intelligence of the General's defeats in Essex, and the greatest successes of the enemy in all parts." ▪ . . *Seal.* [N. VII., 77.]

Sir Michael Livesey to William Lenthall.

1648, July 17.—Thanking the House for their order of the 12th instant. (See *Commons' Journals*, v. 633.) " I and my forces have had very hard marches and duties this fortnight, and are extreme weary, yet hope . . to advance up to Deal and Walmer Castles before the enemy lands, who lies ready to that purpose as you may perceive by this enclosed." *Signed. Seal.* [N. VII., 78.]

Thomas [Lord] Fairfax to William Lenthall.

1648, July 17. Leaguer before Colchester.—Suggesting on account ·of the late design on Denbigh Castle and the importance of the place the necessity of raising another company of foot of 80 men and also a troop of 60 horse to be under the Governor's command. *Signed. Seal.* [N. VII., 79.]

John Rushworth to Sir John Trevor.

1648, July 17.—Concerning the exchange of Mr. Ashburnham for Sir William Masham. (See *Commons' Journals,* v. 640.) *Seal.* [N. VII., 80.]

The Earl of Warwick to William Lenthall.

1648, July 18. Chatham.—Stating that in pursuance of the order of June 14th (see *Commons' Journals,* v. 599) he and the Commissioners of the Navy had investigated and determined the charges brought against several officers as actors and abettors in the late insurrection, that by a later order these officers and some others had been sent for by the House, and that though they had waited for some days they could not obtain a hearing, and desiring on account of their poverty that, if nothing fresh was proved against them, they might be remitted to himself, and he would render to every man according to his demerit. *Signed. Seal.* [N. VII., 81.]

Colonel Michael Jones to William Lenthall.

1648, July 19. Dublin.—"Haveing formerly received Inchiquine's declaration . . . with a letter to mee invitatory to the same course by him taken, of all which you have bin particularly informed, I did after on the 28th of June send to his Lordship that letter, the coppy whereof had bin first sent to you, beeing in returne to that of his accompanying his sayd declaracion. This I sent by Captaine John Parsons—a gentleman of approoved fidellity to the State, and some times of some intimacye with his Lordship—of whose soe sending, togeather with the private instruccions given him I have certifyed the honour[able] the co[mmi]tee of Lords and Commons at Derby House by my letter of the 28th of June last, the principall ends of all beeing, the assaying whether the Lord Inchiquine might bee drawen backe to his obedience to the parlyament, or dealt withall on condicions for resigneing to the parlyament the places by him held in that province or if that might not bee, to sound the depth of his Lordship's designes as much as could bee possible.

On the 18th present, Captaine Parsons returned with his Lordship's letter to mee—heere withall enclosed—wherein may appeare how farr hee is engaged in that his unhappy undertakeing destructive—as farr as in him may bee—to the interests of England heere, which I doubt not but the Lord will yet preserve to you, notwithstanding all combinacions whatsoever to the contrary.

Therein is withall found what expectacion there is of Ormond's nriveing heere and to what purposes, which is alsoe intimated in that declaracion lately published by Owen Roe and his partye, a coppye whereof is herewithall sent you.

By the sayd Captaine Parsons, I further find that Ormond and Inchiquine are confederate as with the Irish soe with the now ryseing party in Scotland, and with some Scotts in Ulster, and that there have letters lately arrived in Mounster sent from Scotland by an expresse, which have bin comunicated by Inchiquine to the Rebells' Councell at Kilkenny.

That upon Ormond's arivall, Inchiquine's cessacion is to end in a peace concluded with the Irish who are to yeild upp all to Ormond and hee to bee by them received on his former pretended commission as Lord Lieutenant. That it is resolved by the confederates in this cessacion and association to joyne against mee if not adhereing unto them after soe many invitations on all handes from them; which now —haveing gained that I intended by dallying with them hytherto—I am resolved to put them to; purposeing within a few dayes to appeare in the feild with what forces I can make thereby to destroy as much as I may possible, the rebells' corne now comeing on—this beeing theire future hope of subsistance—as I have in all this time by partyes of horse spoyled them of their cattell—more then four thousand cowes beeing within these two moneths taken from them—which was their present beeing. More then service of this kinde cannot bee heer expected, in the weake condicion I am, and yet is this of very great consequence duely considered. But I trust to bee by you in due time better enabled for further service to the more speedy ending of this warr.

To you is committed the management of this warr and God himselfe will therefore require at and by your hands the accompt of that innocent blood which hath bin heere inhumanely spilt and the cry of that destruction, burning, ravishing robbing and spoyleing the English heere is now shrill in God's care for vengeance against those cruell rebells. In the justice of which cause I have confidence even with this very inconsiderable party to appeare—if God will have it soe—against their whole powers.

This is the time for doeing the werke heere effectually, the divisions of the enemy every day more and more encreasing. . .

Postscript.—The necessity of the service and the preserving of your interests here hath—since the above was written—enforced me to the securing of those of Ormond's party here whom I conceived dangerous to us on his arriving, which is daily expected. Some of them I have now sent hence by Captain Pilgrim to be delivered at Chester, and to be disposed of as to you shall be thought fitting, the names and qualities of the prisoners are herewithall sent to you." *Signed. Seal.* [N. VII., 82.] *Enclosed:*

i. Lord Inchiquin to Colonel Michael Jones.

1648, July 15. Cork.—" I have received yours by Captain Parsons to whom I have communicated the grounds of our proceedings, wherewith I hope you will rest so well satisfied, as that you will with us contribute to establish his Majesty in his just rights, settle his authority over this kingdom, where probably we may suddenly restore the Protestant Religion to its former lustre and the laws to their force, and afford some assistance according to our oaths and professions towards the restoration of His Highness and the Parliament of England to their just rights, privileges and genuine freedom. My Lord of Ormonde is hourly expected here with great supplies of money arms and ammunition, and this army like to be paid constantly at a high rate, whereof I hope yours will make themselves capable to partake." *Signed.* [N. VII., 76.]

ii. List of persons secured as PRISONERS by Colonel JONES.

Sir John Gifford, Sir Maurice Eustace, Colonel Sir Francis Willoughby and six others to be sent to Chester, seven others to be prisoners in Dublin Castle, Lord Grandison, Sir Thomas Lucas, Sir Robert Byron and Major Billingsley to be secured. (See Carte, *Life of Ormonde,* ii. 36.) [N. XXI., 67.]

Captain ROBERT BATTEN to WILLIAM LENTHALL.

1648, July 19. Holy Island.—"I have been in a besieged condition near these six weeks. The enemy hath made a garrison of Haggerston House which is within two miles of this isle, which doth hinder all things from coming in for the relief of the poor inhabitants as well as the garrison, and they daily threaten to fall in and burn and plunder the town, so that we are forced thereby to extraordinary duty, and have not moneys nor provisions for the supply and encouragement of my soldiers, neither have I received any certain intelligence from the South this month, the Cavaliers being master of all the country hereabouts. This day the Scots came into Berwick with seven regiments of foot and some troops of horse. The English Cavaliers are marched forth. My drum being there saw Colonel Brandling deliver up his command unto the Scots' Governor. There is great need of a ship or two for my assistance. The guard of Berwick hath lien open these six weeks and many vessels have gone in thither, and at present there are three riding at anchor before that bar, but what they are I know not." . . . *Signed. Seal.* [N. VII., 83.]

PETER LOGAN, Mayor, and PETER MARFORD to ROBERT WALLOP.

1648, July 19. Winchester.—Concerning the probable danger to Southampton, if the revolted ships in the Downs carry out their plan of attacking the Isle of Wight and the places adjacent, especially since the declaration of the seamen at Portsmouth, and desiring that some speedy course be taken for the safety of the town. (See *Commons' Journals,* v. 647, 650.) *Signed.* [N. VII., 84.]

WILLIAM TATTNELL, ABRAHAM MELLO and JOHN DANIELL to Colonel WILLIAM WILLOUGHBY.

1648, July 20. Tilbury Fort. — Desiring a supply, as they had neither victuals or money and no fortifications. Though the guns are very good, there is but small store of ammunition and few men to man them, many being dismounted for want of carriages, and many other necessary things belonging to them being wanting. "We have 38 trusty and stout men, but the place is sickly and for want of fitting lodging some of them have gotten the ague already. . . Seeing no relief of victuals and money come unto them . . . they will be gone if a sudden order be not taken to supply them and accommodation be made for their lodging " . . . A postscript by Mello alone desires repayment of 4*l.* odd disbursed by him for necessaries for the soldiers. (See *Commons' Journals*, v. 649.) *Signed.* [N. VII., 85.]

Major-General LAMBERT to WILLIAM LENTHALL.

1648, July 20. Barnard Castle.—"On Friday night last presently after the sending away of Mr. Halliburton from Penrith the enemy with his whole body marched up to us, and pitched that night within a mile or two of Penrith, where we quartered; and taking into consideration our small numbers compared with theirs, the consequence to these parts and the whole kingdom, if we had been foiled by them, and not knowing the pleasure of the Parliament upon the coming of the Scotch army into this kingdom, we resolved to retreat towards Appleby and further as occasion should be. On Monday morning they followed with their whole body to Appleby . . and after some skirmish with them about maintaining of the pass against them there, which was gallantly performed by our foot, the loss of which dispute fell most on the enemies' part, of whom were slain about 40, divers wounded, some taken prisoners and 50 arms, our loss being Colonel Harrison wounded upon the first charge with our horse guard, Captain Cromwell's lieutenant slain, Lieutenant Sheeres taken prisoner and three or four foot soldiers wounded, we drew off the next morning and came to Kirby Stephen without any disturbance of the enemy and so we marched that night to Bowes, and from thence next day to Barnard Castle, our horse and men being very much tired and worn out with continual duty, hard marches, and bad weather, so that the soldiers are very much disinabled, and doubtless without some speedy addition of forces, supply of money, recruits of horse, arms and others necessaries . . . . the service of the Parliament is like to suffer very much by endangering the loss of all these Northern parts and permitting the enemy to recruit and grow greater every day, which with the small number of forces in these parts could not possibly be prevented." . . (See *Commons' Journals*, v. 646.) *Seal.* [N. VII. 86.]

Colonel THOMAS BETTESWORTH to the COMMITTEE AT DERBY HOUSE.

1648, July 21. Portsmouth. — Complaining that Mr. Cobb, the Receiver General of the County, does not pay the gunners and soldiers of the garrison, particulars of which will be given by the bearer Captain Joyce, and desiring that they will send their commands to the said Mr. Cobb and to Mr. Faulkenbridge of the Revenue office. (See *Commons' Journals*, v. 647.) *Seal.* [N. VII., 87.]

The COMMITTEE AT DERBY HOUSE.

1648, July 21.—Report. (The purport of part appears from the votes thereon printed in *Commons' Journals*, v. 646, the rest is that the Committee of Militia of Westminster have desired that the fair at St. James' be put off for this year, lest under colour thereof there be a meeting of many that may prove dangerous to the Parliament.) [N. XV., 94.]

SIR HENRY CHOLMELEY to WILLIAM LENTHALL.

1648, July 22.—. . . "Whilst I was attending the enemy towards Nottinghamshire they drew out 200 of their foot from Pomfract and

possessed themselves of Thornhill Hall, the late house of Sir William Saville, where they began to fortify, which being of itself defended with a moat was soon made strong enough to be maintained till cannon should be brought against it. Upon Sunday morning last my own regiment of horse and Colonel Fairfax's regiment of foot march[ed] up close to the house and presently possessed themselves of some out-houses which the enemy endeavoured to maintain. The dispute was hot for about an hour, and in that we had eight or ten men slain and twenty wounded, the enemy had their share of loss likewise. That night and the next day we endeavoured to draw away the water from the moat, and by Tuesday morning it was well nigh dried. I then sent a trumpet with some articles to them, but they refused them and desired a treaty, upon which it was at the last concluded that they should march away, leaving all their arms and ammunition bag and baggage behind them, only three horses and three swords being allowed to three of their officers. After the articles were signed the enemy by accident fired their powder, which killed five of their men, and blew up part of the house, which afterwards took fire, and burnt the house down to the ground. I marched the next day with the two regiments I had there to Wakefield, where they now lie to keep the enemy in on that side, and Sir Edward Rhoades' regiment of horse and 500 foot are at Ferribridge to attend the enemy's motion there. They are about 200 horse and above 1,000 foot in Pomfract and the Newhall. The regiments of foot commanded by Colonel Wasteil and Colonel Lassells are marched up towards Colonel Lambert, together with a troop of my regiment and another of Sir Edward Rhoades' regiment, and Colonel Bethell hath orders to march up with his regiment of horse likewise."
Seal. [N. VII., 88.]

The EARL OF WARWICK to the COMMITTEE OF LORDS AND COMMONS FOR THE NAVY AND CUSTOMS.

1648, July 22. Aboard the *St. George* in Sea Road.— "I have received notice of some distempers amongst the seamen at Portsmouth, particulerly of those in the *Guarland* and the *John.* Uppon the first intimation whereof—being on Tuesday last—I writt to the rere-admirall to discharge by ticketts such of the said two ships' companyes as were ill affected, and the rest—which seeme very fewe—to place aboard the other ships. Nowe I heare—that being offred—they are resolved not to stir out of their ships, till they receive their pay. I have therefore, uppon consultacion this day had with a councell of warr, resolved it to bee most convenient that they bee both paid off and dischaiged at Portsmouth, and that such of them as the captaines and officers shall approve of as well affected, bee invited to enter themselves aboard some of the other ships. I doe therefore recomend it to your Lordships, that a speedy provision of money may bee made for their pay accordingly, their continuing under an expectacion of it—considering their resolution not to oppose the revolted ships—tending meerly to contract further charge, though after the receiveing it, I feare there wilbee noe absolute security against their actings to the parlyamentes prejudice nor against the evill influences that their example may have uppon the other ships. I have signified to the Comissioners of the Navy my recomending of this to your Lordships, that they may attend and put in execucion what you shall thercuppon direct. Wee have alsoe this day resolved—as an expedient to the quicker manning of the fleete—to sayle with the *St. George* as high as Tilbury Hope, and to place the *Adven-ture* and *Nicodemus* neere my selfe, the *Unicorne* in the Medway betwixt the Hope and Gravesend, the *Fellowshipp* as high as Greenhithe, the *Hector* at Northflcete, and the *Greyhound* at Purfleete, for avoiding of some inconveniences which may otherwise present themselves ; the ships, one with another, being not halfe mannd, the *Adventure* and *Nicodemus* excepted." *Signed. Seal.* [N. VII., 89.]

JOHN COLLINGWOOD to Mr. SCOTT.

1648, July 24.—" This last week I heard of a petition . . set on foot by the reduced soldiery about London . . to the Houses of Parliament, wherein they set forth the cause of their first engagement, which was to reduce the enemies of the Commonwealth that the peace thereof might be settled ; the first being accomplished the second is still neglected, and they also left unsatisfied therein or in point of arrears, wherefore they have often petitioned, and in their attendance thereon many have perished for want; now their desires are that the Kingdom may be settled, and to that end that his Majesty may come with freedom and safety to London to treat according to the just desires of the City of London that so religion may be settled, the taxes taken off from the people, and general other desires looking that way, and then they will readily engage with the Houses again . . and so they go to desire to have their accounts audited and some present satisfaction . . of their arrears and security for the rest. They further say that their patience are tired, and therefore cannot defer longer the want of satisfaction herein, that is to say, to have the King settled in his just rights with religion and the liberties of the people, which if not accordingly done they shall be constrained to use all just means to accomplish." I replied that I misliked the petition as it mentioned anything besides arrears, had it been limited to them, I and divers others would have joined. " They made mention to me of something they intended to add, as the present engagement now began again, and something concerning the Scots, and this they told me, they were advised to do by some of their friends in the House, which if your members be of that mind I fear some desperate design.". . (See *Commons' Journals,* v. 646.) [N. VII., 90.]

Colonel R[OBERT] OVERTON to WILLIAM LENTHALL.

1648, July 27. Hull.—Informing the House of the revolt of Scarborough, of which he had sent notice to Lord Fairfax, the Army in the North, Newcastle, Nottingham, Lincoln, Boston, &c., and desiring that ships might be sent for the preservation of this town now in great distress for want of pay and endangered by the jealousies fomented by the agents of the disaffected party. *Seal. Enclosed:*

Captain ROBERT WITTIE to Colonel OVERTON.

1648, July 27. Beverley.—"This morning I came from Scarborough, where I find the affairs of that garrison very sad. Being brought before the Governor on Tuesday night at my first coming to town, he was pleased to utter many expressions of discontent against the Parliament and General in their more than ordinary slighting of him. He told me he had received the day before a letter from the Prince. What the purport thereof is doth too well appear by his declaring this day for the King, and his hanging out a red flag over the walls, which I am informed he had not usually done before. The Prince is expected daily to land in that harbour. Some officers there told me we should within a very few days hear of some men-of-war at Humber mouth . . . *Postscript.* — He hath expected Colonel Fairfax to come to him these two or three days, but he was not come this morning when I took horse." [N. VII., 91.]

SIR WILLIAM STRICKLAND to WILLIAM LENTHALL.

1648, July 28. Hull.—" I am right sorry nowe to accompany the rest of Job's messengers that bringe the newes of the trecherous and unworthy betraying of Scarborough Castle. I cannot acquaint you with many perticulers for my house being within twelve miles it was conceived in the countrie that their first action would be my surprisall, and therefore some well affected persons that gave me notice thereof yesterday late in the afternoone, perswaded me being sicke and haveing keept my chamber, imediately to remove and not to adventure the slowe pace of a coache with my wife and children, but in that weeke posture to come to Hull without any delaye, where I arrived att seaven att night. I heare the governour reported yesterday morning that he had received a letter from the Prince, then in Yarmoth roades. Generall rumours are this daye that the Prince is there, but that not certainely knowne. My designe is to adde to the sence of the House the dangerous couse-quence of this losse. The enimie had nue hold att sea untill nowe, this will give them all manner of accomodacion, and incorage their great partie here, to declare themselves and to leave you nothinge, and being owners of the North—as formerly—they will not dispaire of the South. If some present and vigorous course be used, your interest—by God's blessing—may yet bee regained. If you looke upon us and direct us there wilbe some life remaininge. Let me take the boldnesse to tell you that playing after games had lost you heretofore, if by miracles you had not bin preserved. We subsist by hopeing that Colchester is yours, which if soe, conceive it necessary to looke after Scarborough. Although with weak health, my poore desires and indeavours have not bin omitted in getting up your horse forces here, which are nowe in a convenient readinesse." *Signed. Seal.* [N. VII., 92.]

SIR ANTHONY WELDON and others to WILLIAM LENTHALL.

1648, July 28.—Acknowledging the votes of the 8th instant, and desiring power to be given to such persons as Parliament may appoint for fining or compounding with persons sequestered or sequestrable within those votes. (The orders made hereon are in *Commons' Journals,* v. 652.) *Signed.* [N. VII., 94.]

SIR JOHN BOURCHIER and others to WILLIAM LENTHALL.

1648, July 28. York.—" To all our former distractions we have this day the certain and sad report of the revolt of the Governor of Scar-borough declared in the face of the town by beat of drum. By this we expect no other than that the design of the enemy is ripe for the landing of the Prince's forces there or thereabouts, and the danger of the Parlia-ment's forces in the North by being between a body that may be landed there on the one side and the Scots on the other side, and so the hazard of these parts at least your wisdoms will easily apprehend. We are now necessitated to employ the forces this way that we intended for the North. And how to keep any of our force together for want of moneys we are utterly to seek. The care we perceive the Parliament hath taken that way lately we must humbly say we cannot see wee are like to receive any fruit of in any seasonable time. We humbly beg " for a speedy supply of horsemen and money, that Sir Henry Cholmeley's re.

quest for power of Martial Law may be granted, that ships may be sent down to secure the coast of Scarborough and Bridlington, and for 200 barrels of powder with match and bullet proportionable. *Signed. Seal.* [N. VII., 95.]

Colonel HENRY HERBERT to WILLIAM LENTHALL.

1648, July 28. Bergenenny.—"I was sent by the House into Wales where I have served them to my best ability in all faithfulness, having spent a great part of my time with Lieutenant-General Cromwell, and on Tuesday (25th) parted from him not far from Gloucester. I am now returned to Monmouthshire, where suddenly Colonel Horton and the gentry are to meet to put Wales into the best posture we can for the service of the Parliament, and truly I shall not want work, which I hope will excuse my attendance" at the call of the House for the 7th of next month. *Seal.* [N. VII., 96.]

SIR HENRY CHOLMLEY to WILLIAM LENTHALL.

[1648], July 28.—Describing his movements and the barbarous murder of two honest countrymen by two of his troopers, and desiring power of Martial Law. (Printed in Grey, iii. Appendix No. 48, p. 66.) *Seal.* [N. VII., 93.]

SIR THOMAS MYDDELTON to WILLIAM LENTHALL.

1648, July 28. Chirke Castle.—Desiring to be excused attending the call of the House for the 7th of August as "these parts being in some distempers and Anglesea having declared themselves against the Parliament" he has remained to defend his own house for fear of treachery, these parts being very Malignant and the people very apt to rise. *Seal.* [N. VII., 97.]

THOMAS TRENCHARD and others to WILLIAM LENTHALL.

1648, July 29. Dorchester.—Desiring to be excused attending the call of the House for the 7th of August being engaged in settling the Militia of the County pursuant to the Ordinance of Parliament. (See *Commons' Journals*, v. 656.) *Signed.* [N. VII., 98.]

WILLIAM DOBSON, Mayor, and others to WILLIAM LENTHALL.

1648, July 29. Hull.—Desiring "that a competent force of ships may lay before Scarborough and that two ships may be designed for Humber to keep the river open and to assist our ships as convoy." *Signed. Seal of the town.* [N. VII., 99.]

The PRINCE OF WALES to the MAYOR, ALDERMEN and COMMONS of the City OF LONDON.

[1648], July 29.—Enclosing his declaration. *Original* and *Copy*, the first with *Sign-manual* and *seal*. [N. I., 34; XII., 238.] *Enclosed:*

The said DECLARATION.

Same date.—*Original* and *copy*, the first with *sign-manual* and *seal*. [N. I., 35; XII., 239.] (Both are printed in *King's Pamphlets*, E. 457, No. 14.)

The Sale to the Company of Merchant Adventurers.

[1648], July 29.—(Printed in *Lords' Journals*, x. 417.) *Sign-manual.* [N. I., 36.]

The Lords to the Commons.

1648, July 30.—Message concerning the Committee appointed to treat with the King and order made thereon. (Printed in *Commons' Journals*, v. 651.) [N. XV., 95, 96.]

Lord Inchiquin to the Lord Mayor of London.

1648, August 1. Cork.—"If your Lordship shall please to interfere in soliciting those in power there, that an order may be conceived for the establishing of free trade and traffic betwixt that kingdom and this province with an assurance of safety and freedom to all such of the English nation, as shall have recourse unto us—not being men of war,—we shall then provide that none of that kingdom do suffer any prejudice by us or by our shipping or by any that correspond with us." *Signed.* [N. VII., 100.]

The Earl of Crawford and Lindsay to the Prince of Wales.

[1648, August 1 (?).]—Inviting him in the name of the Committee of Estates to come to Scotland. (Printed in Rushworth, iv. 2. 1230.) *Copy.* Endorsed "R[eceived], 21–31 Augusti 1648." [N. XII., 241.]

Several drafts of the Resolutions concerning the Treaty with the King.

1648, August 2, 3.—(Printed in *Commons' Journals*, v. 658.) [N. XV., 98.]

The Company of Merchant Adventurers to the House of Commons.

1648, August 3.—Petition. (Identical *mutatis mutandis* with that printed in *Lords' Journals*, x. 417.) *Copy.* Annexed is a *copy* of the Prince of Wales' letter printed *ubi suprà.* [N. XXII., 116, 117.]

[Colonel Humphrey Mackworth] to [William Pierrepont].

[1648, August 3.]—Enclosure describing the late attempted insurrection in Shropshire under Lord Byron. (Printed in *Lords' Journals*, x. 424.) [N. XII., 38.]

Colonel Michael Jones to William Lenthall.

1648, August 4. Dublin.—"By a party of 1,650 foot and 750 horse sent out the 28th past with Sir Henry Tichborne and commanded by Colonel Moncke, who was to meet them with 100 horse and 200 foot we have . . . possessed ourselves in the County of Meath of the Castle of Rafiin, the two strong forts of Nobber and Ardlonan—also Cruse's fort,—and of Lagan water Castle standing on a considerable pass. There is also taken the strong castle of Ballehoe, our men entering a breach made with above 40 great shot, and putting to the sword all therein found. Colonel Moncke is called off from us by some occasions requiring his presence at home, but our party is proceeding in the work for clearing that country of the enemies' garrisons and for thereby settling our quarters and enlarging them. The noise of Preston's advancing with 4,000 men—he being within 20 miles of our quarters—occasioned my not advancing with that party now abroad, that with the rest of the army I might attend the enemies' motions if breaking in upon us. The further purging also of the army from Malignants . . required necessarily my presence here for finishing that work. and for preventing any evil thereupon ensuing . . But all things settled I shall . . . with the whole army fall into the enemies' quarters and shall then perfect— what by a party only I am not but leading unto—the destroying the rebels' corn, as far as I may possibly do. Preston is with his army taking in those places Owen Roe held hereabouts, and is at present besieging the town of Athy, part of which he hath already taken, and is with four guns battering the principal hold in it. Clanrickard and Taaffe joined with some horse and foot of Inchiquin's have taken the Castle of Athlone by them besieged and held by Captain Gawley for Owen Roe, who for 500*l.* and the command of a troop of horse hath surrendered the place, it being delivered into the Lord Dillon of Costello's possession." I desire reinforcements, and that the money designed may be sent us with all convenient speed, there not being 100*l.* in the Treasury. *Signed. Seal.* [N. VII., 101.]

The COMMISSIONERS OF THE CUSTOMS to the COMMITTEE FOR THE NAVY AND CUSTOMS.

1648, August 7.—Declining the proposition made to them. (See *Commons' Journals*, v. 678, where "their moiety of their arrears" means "their moiety of the arrears owing by the East India Company for Customs.") *Signed.* [N. VII., 102.]

The COMMITTEE AT DERBY HOUSE.

1648, August 7.—Report recommending that Francis Bethan be appointed Provost-Marshall for apprehending such as are within 20 miles of London against the ordinances of Parliament. [N. XV., 99.]

Letter of Captain HAWKERIDGE and Examinations of HENRY CHALLONER and others.

1648, August 8 and 10.—(All printed in *Lords' Journals*, x. 432–434.) *Copies.* [N. XV., 100, 101.]

SIR MICHAEL LIVESEY to WILLIAM LENTHALL.

1648, August 10. Sandwich Down from my rendezvous.—"This morning Captain Batten came to the Prince with his ships; in them many land soldiers. They landed them this morning between Sandown Castle and my quarters at Sandwich where my outguard of horse and foot was in number 120, which beat them, took and killed 20 private soldiers and one quarter-master with the loss of one foot and one trooper of mine, who carried the cornet. I believe we shall be in action every day, by reason the ships are in such want of provisions. . . . . . Captain Greene, whom the Prince put so much trust and confidence in is a recusant, and hath been these five years a pirate at sea, and not any one hath done more mischief to your service than he hath." *Seal.* [N. VII., 103.]

WILLIAM RYLEY, Clerk of the Records, to the HOUSE OF COMMONS.

1648, August 11.—Petition. (Printed in Peck, *Desiderata Curiosa*, x. 50.) (See *Commons' Journals*, v. 555.) *Signed.* On parchment. N. XXII., 115.]

The House of Lords.

.1648, August 15, 16.—Resolutions concerning the treaty with the King. (Printed in *Lords' Journals*, x. 441, 442.) [N. XV., 102.]

Resolutions concerning the Treaty with the King.

1648, August 17, &c.—(Apparently this paper contains the resolutions as sent down by the House of Lords with the alterations then made by the House of Commons and finally altered to the form in which they passed both Houses. They are printed in *Commons' Journals*, v. 673, 674 and in *Lords' Journals*, x. 454. The same paper contains the Instructions to Colonel Hammond, printed in *Lords' Journals*, x. 454.) [N. XV., 104.]

The House of Lords to the Prince of Wales.

[1648, August 17.]—(Printed in *Lords' Journals*, x. 444.) *Draft* or *Copy*. [N. XII., 224.]

Colonel William Eyre and Captain John Waldron to Mr. Burr.

1648, August 18.—Declining to come to London alleging that from the confluence and increase of the Malignant party there they feared for their personal safety. (See *Commons' Journals*, v. 676.) *Signed*. [N. VII., 104.]

Information of Joseph Jackman of London.

1648, August 19.—Concerning an assault and robbery committed on him between Newbury and Kingsclere by troopers belonging to Colonel Ayres under the command of Colonel Marten. (Printed in Grey, iii., Appendix No. 41, p. 67.) (See *Commons' Journals*, v. 676.) *Copy*. [N. XV., 103.]

Informations of William Jones and Charles Garrard.

[1648, August.]—Concerning the seizure of their horses at Wellford and Lamborne by Colonel Martin's soldiers under the conduct of Colonel Ayres. [N. XV., 164, 165.]

Captain Robert Clarke to William Lyntoll, Speaker of the House of Commons.

[1648, August] 19. Chester Water.—Describing his capture of two.small barks betwixt Carrickfergus Bay and the coast of Scotland, in one of which were Sir David Cunningham and Captain John Steward, and 36 horses with riders for most of them, but arms for not a quarter of them, and stating that there is a most extreme want of money amongst Colonel Monck's men, so that they cannot go into the field, as I heard from Mr. Tobias Norris at Carlingford. Colonel Monck is at Leechnegurrie. We heard this morning by a Welsh barque that there is five sail of ships in Beaumaris. (See *Commons' Journals*, vi. 645, 676.) *Seal*. [N. III., 111.]

William Lenthall to the Committee of Kent.

1648, August 22.—By order of the House approving of their stay of Lord Andover, and ordering them not to suffer any person whatever to pass to the revolted ships without the order of the House. (See *Commons' Journals*, v. 676.) *Draft*. [N. XII., 240.]

REASONS to be offered to the Lords at the Conference.

[1648, August 23.]—(Printed with a few verbal alterations in *Lords' Journals*, x. 453 except the Instruction to Colonel Hammond, which is the conclusion of that printed on the next page. It is also printed in *Commons' Journals*, v. 681.) [N. XV., 97.]

[JOHN BROWNE and HENRY ELSYNG] to Colonel HAMMOND.

[1648, August 25.]—Enclosing his Instructions. (Printed in *Lords' Journals*, x. 455 and in Peck, *Desiderata Curiosa*, ix. 50.) *Draft.* [N. XV., 105.]

The PARLIAMENT to the KING.

1648, September 2.—(Printed in *Lords' Journals*, x. 486.) *Draft*, as passed by the Commons. [N. IX., 169.]

ORDINANCE.

1648, September 2.—Empowering the Committees to treat with the King. (See *Commons' Journals*, vi. 6.) [N. XV., 114.]

Title of the Instructions to the COMMITTEES APPOINTED TO TREAT WITH THE KING.

1648, September 2.—(Printed in *Lords' Journals*, x. 488; *Commons' Journals*, v. 697.) [N. XV., 110.]

The HOUSE OF COMMONS.

1648, September 2.—Votes concerning persons to be sent to the King. (Printed in *Lords' Journals*, x. 484.) [N. XV., 111.]

Instructions to the COMMITTEES APPOINTED TO TREAT WITH THE KING.

1648, September 2.—(Printed in *Lords' Journals*, x. 488; *Commons' Journals*, v. 697. This is the draft sent up to the Lords and returned with their alterations as ultimately adopted.) [N. XV., 112.]

The EARL OF WARWICK to all COURTS OF GUARD, POSTMASTERS, and others it may concern.

1648, September 5.—Warrant desiring them to permit certain French gentlemen of the Prince de Condé's army to travel from Dover to London and back, and to supply them with horses and guides. *Signed.* [N. VII., 106.]

The KING to the SPEAKER OF THE HOUSE OF PEERS.

1648, September 8. Newport.—The beginning is printed in *Lords' Journals*, x. 498. It continues thus " They not being persons under restraint in this Kingdom or in actual war against the Parliament by sea or land, or in such numbers as may draw any just cause of exception. In order to which we have dispatched the bearer, our trusty servant Richard Parsons, with letters unto the Committee of Parliament of that our kingdom of Scotland Authorising them to elect a convenient number of fit persons amongst them not exceeding the number of five and their servants speedily to attend us here. We do therefore pray you to give pass to the said Parsons freely to go thither and to return hither again, and likewise to send by him safe conducts with blanks for the persons and their servants who shall be chosen by the Committee in Scotland to attend us here.

For the particular names of the persons to be employed to us we could not insert them, being altogether ignorant of the state of that kingdom, and therefore we have referred it to the Committee there to choose whom they shall think fit." *Sign Manual at beginning and end.* [N. I., 20.]

Captain JOHN ARTHUR, Vice-Admiral of Dorset, to WILLIAM LENTHALL.

1648, September 9. Weymouth.—Enclosing an Examination and desiring that course might be taken for the preservation of the Isle of Scilly. *Signed. Seal. Enclosed :*

Examination of same date of WILLIAM COTTON of Weymouth, Mariner. Being Master of a bark of Weymouth, the *Magdalen,* about nine weeks since he was taken when bound from Portland to London by an Irish man of war, and carried to Barfleur, and turned ashore there. He then went to Shirbrook (? Cherbourg), and thence to Monville, where on September 1st a shallop arrived from Scilly with six men on board, one being Lieutenant to the Governor, who affirmed they were bound for the Downs with two letters, one for the Prince of Wales, and one for the Duke of York, the contents of which they affirmed were that in case the Prince should consent to the Articles therein the Governor of the Isle would deliver it up to him. *Copy.* [N. VII., 105.]

The PARLIAMENT.

1648, September 9.—Order, authorising Doctor Reeve and Doctor Ducke to go to the King. (See *Lords' Journals,* x. 494.) [N. XV., 115.]

SIR EDWARD WALKER to WILLIAM LENTHALL.

1648, September 12. Newport.—Desiring by the King's command passes for Doctor Harvey or Doctor Wetherborne, his physicians, and Humphrey Painter, his chirurgeon, to attend him there, and also for passes for three of his messengers, to be employed as messengers or doorkeepers. [N. IX., 170.]

The PARLIAMENT to the KING.

1648, September 13.—(Printed in *Lords' Journals,* x. 501.) *Draft,* as passed by the Commons. [N. IX., 171.]

The KING to the SPEAKER OF THE HOUSE OF PEERS.

1648, September 15. Newport.—(Printed in *Lords' Journals,* x. 501.) *Sign-Manual.* [N. I., 22.]

The Committee, Gentry, Ministry, and Inhabitants of the Town and County of LEICESTER to the HOUSE OF COMMONS.

1648, September 16.—Petition. (For the stating part see *Commons' Journals,* vi. 41), praying " that we may not be left in the dark concerning those suggestions and charges, which if true they may in the first place be made good . . . and proceedings accordingly, that we may not build our peace upon such . . foundations, but if otherwise, that his Majesty may be cleared so fully that we may neither fear your treating with him nor trusting him in the great and weighty affairs of these three kingdoms," and that since God " hath put the main principal enemies into your hands . . that impartial and personal justice may be speedily administered." *Copy.* The Speaker's answer (printed *ubi suprà*) is added at the end. [N. XXII., 118.]

The EARL OF WARWICK to the EARL OF MANCHESTER.

1648, September 17. From aboard the *St. George* in the Downs.—(Printed in *Lords' Journals*, x. 523.) *Signed. Seal.* [N. VII., 107.]

PAPERS.

1648, September 18, 19. Newport.—(Being the eight printed in *Lords' Journals*, x. 508, 509.) *Copies.* [N. IX., 172-179.]

PAPERS.

1648, September 19-25. Newport.—(Being the eight printed in *Lords' Journals*, x. 513, 514.) *Copies.* [N. IX., 180-184, 186, 187, 188.]

The COMMITTEE OF THE NAVY.

1648, September 20.—Report advising the release of the ship stayed at Dartmouth with 1,500 Barbary guns or birding pieces. (See *Commons' Journals*, vi. 27.) *Annexed:*

Order of the House referring the matter to the Committee. (See *Commons' Journals*, vi. 5.)

Order of the Committee referring to the Commissioners of Customs, with the report of the latter.

License from the Committee of Revenue, dated April 12, 1648, to export these guns. [N. XV., 116.]

Votes concerning passes to LORD CARNEGY and others.

1648, September 21.—(Printed in *Lords' Journals*, x. 505.) [N. XV., 117.]

The COMMISSIONERS AT NEWPORT to WILLIAM LENTHALL.

[1648, September 21.]—(Identical, *mutatis mutandis*, with that to the Speaker of the House of Lords, which is printed in *Lords' Journals*, x. 508.) *Copy.* [N. XX., 51b.]

The HOUSE OF COMMONS.

1648, September 23.—Order appointing a Committee concerning the Treaty with the King. (Printed in *Commons' Journals*, vi. 29.) [N. XX., 51a.]

The HOUSE OF COMMONS to the MEMBERS EMPLOYED ON THE TREATY.

1648, September 23.—Thanking them for their services, and informing them that the papers they had sent were under consideration, on which they would shortly receive their resolutions. (See *Commons' Journals*, vi. 30.) *Draft.* [N. IX., 185.]

The KING to the SPEAKER OF THE HOUSE OF PEERS.

1648, September 25.—(Printed in *Lords' Journals*, x. 514.) *Sign-Manual.* [N. I., 32.]

Examination of WILLIAM WARDEN, of Dover.

1648, September 25.—That morning a footman delivered him a letter from Captain Green enclosing one to the Prince, and desiring it to be sent to him to Helford Sluce, both which letters he left with the Mayor. [N. XV., 118.]

PAPERS.

1648, September 25, 28, 29. Newport.—(Being the three printed in *Lords' Journals*, x. 325, 326.) *Copies.* [N. IX., 189, 190, 191.]

ORDINANCE.

1648, September 28.—Attainting George Lord Goring (the Earl of Norwich). (See *Commons' Journals*, vi. 37.) [N. XV., 119.]

Colonel JAMES HEANE, Governor, to the COMMITTEE AT DERBY HOUSE.

1648, September 30. Weymouth.—Having at last got an addition of two companies I must disband them or see them perish for want of bread. "How impossible it is to keep these garrisons without them needs no demonstration. . . . The seas are pestered with Irish men of war . . . no less than 30 in a fleet, the Isle of Portland but this very week beset by some of them, and had I not had men ready there must needs have been taken. Had the enemy no possibility of proceeding a foot further, that Island is so convenient a receptacle for men of their profession that it will be a miracle if any ship pass safely either East or Westward." I therefore desire that these men be constantly paid, and 8 or 9 guns sent to Portland. (See *Commons' Journals*, vi. 45.) [N. VII., 108.]

PAPER.

[1648, September 30.]—Stating what is desired for the Garrison of Weymouth and Melcombe Regis and the Isle of Portland. (See the previous letter herein referred to.) [N. XV., 168.]

The PARLIAMENT to the COMMISSIONERS AT NEWPORT.

[1648, October 2.]—(Printed in *Lords' Journals*, x. 527.) *Draft.* [N. IX., 196.]

THOMAS [LORD] FAIRFAX to WILLIAM LENTHALL.

1648, October 2. St. Albans.—Asking that the sums already paid by Sir John Poulett and his father might free the former from any other fine. *Signed. Seal.* [N. VII., 109.]

THOMAS [LORD] FAIRFAX to Colonel ALEXANDER POPHAM.

1648, October 4. St. Albans.—"Sir Hardresse Waller having occasion in regard of the late revolt of the garrison at Scilly to draw away those foot of his regiment which have hitherto kept Bridgwater and Dunster, I desire you on sight hereof to give order for that company of foot commanded under you by Lieutenant-Colonel Raymond to march to Bridgwater, and there to continue to secure that town, and to send a party of foot with officers proportionable to Dunster Castle, for the securing thereof until further order." *Signed. Seal.* [N. XV., 122.]

Some of the Knights and Burgesses of SOMERSET.

[1648, October.]—Paper, desiring that the forces under Colonel Popham be disbanded as unnecessary. [N. XV., 123.]

And

Particulars presented to the COMMITTEE AT DERBY HOUSE.

[1648, October.]—Concerning the said forces and supernumeraries. (For these see *Commons' Journals*, vi. 59.) [N. XV., 121.]

Colonel MICHAEL JONES to WILLIAM LENTHALL.

1648, October 4. Dublin.—"I am lately returned from the enemies' quarters, where I have taken in their two main strengths in these parts, the strong fort of Ballysonan and the Island of Allan with some other considerable pieces, whereby our quarters are both enlarged and secured. My next work is to destroy all belonging to the enemy without us, which until now could not be done, neither is the time yet fully serving thereunto, most of their corn—by reason of the weather— not being yet made up, and not till then to be destroyed. In the spoil to be here necessarily made of corn will be taken from us all means of subsistence other than what must be thence or elsewhere acquired, which would be of timely consideration, that thereby no obstruction be to the service, and that the contracts to be made for us may be to the State's best advantage. As for money there hath not been so much as one penny in the Treasury for one whole month past." . . . The army is also short of men and horses. *Signed. Seal.* [N. VII., 110.]

The Committee at Derby House.

1648, October 9, 12, and 17.—Three reports concerning the dis-banding of forces in Somerset, Northampton, Kent, Herefordshire, Gloucestershire, Derbyshire, and Yorkshire, with papers expressing the desires of the gentlemen of the various counties thereon, for the general purport of which see the Resolutions of the House of Commons of October 23 in *Commons' Journals*, vi. 59. [N. XV., 124–130 and 132.]

Lord Wenman, William Pierrepont, Sir Harbottle Grimston, Sir Henry Vane, Sir John Potts, John Glyn, John Crewe, Samuel Browne, and John Bulkeley to William Lenthall.

1648, October 9. Newport.—(Identical, *mutatis mutandis*, with the letter to the Speaker of the House of Lords, which is printed in *Lords' Journals*, x. 536.) *Signed.* [N. IX., 203.] *Enclosed:*

Copies of the ten papers which are printed in *Lords' Journals*, x. 536–541. (The date of the paper concerning the Militia, printed on page 539, should be the 7th not the 9th.) [N. IX., 192–195, 197–202.]

The Same to William Lenthall.

1648, October 10. Newport.—Asking for the remainder of the 10,000*l.* (See *Commons' Journals*, vi. 51.) *Signed. Seal.* [N. VII., 111.]

The Merchant Adventurers to the Committee for the Navy.

[1648, October 10.]—Answer and petition stating that they find themselves in no capacity to undertake the loan of 20,000*l.*, and praying that "this ingenious discovery of their weakness and disability may be accepted to excuse them from this present service." (See *Commons' Journals*, vi. 50.) [N. XXII., 156.]

Lord Wenman, Denzell Holles, William Pierrepont, Sir Henry Vane, Sir John Potts, John Glynn, John Crewe, John Bulkeley, and Samuel Browne to William Lenthall.

1648, October 11. Newport.—(Identical, *mutatis mutandis*, with the letter to the Speaker of the House of Lords, which is printed in *Lords' Journals*, x. 544.) *Signed.* [N. IX., 205.] *Enclosed:*

Copies of the three papers which are printed in *Lords' Journals*, x. 544. [N. IX., 204, 206, 207.]

Lord Wenman, Denzell Holles, William Pierrepont, Sir Harbottle Grimston, Sir John Potts, Sir Henry Vane, John Glynn, John Crewe, Samuel Browne, and John Bulkeley to William Lenthall.

1648, October 14. Newport.—(Identical, *mutatis mutandis,* with the letter to the Speaker of the House of Lords, which is printed in *Lords' Journals,* x. 547.) *Signed.* [N. IX., 217.] *Enclosed:*

Copies of the nine papers which are printed in *Lords' Journals,* x. 547-550. [N. IX., 208-216.]

Sir Thomas Parker to William Lenthall.

1648, October 14.—Asking on account of illness to be excused attending the House next Tuesday. *Seal.* [N. VII., 112.]

Lord Wenman, Denzell Holles, William Pierrepont, Sir Henry Vane, Sir John Potts, John Glynn, John Crewe, John Bulkeley, and Samuel Browne to William Lenthall.

1648, October 17. Newport.—(Identical, *mutatis mutandis,* with the letter to the Speaker of the House of Lords, which is printed in *Lords' Journals,* x. 553.) *Signed.* [N. IX., 219.] *Enclosed:*

Copies of five of the six papers (omitting His Majesty's Propositions) which are printed in *Lords' Journals,* x. 553, 554. [N. IX., 218, 220-223.]

The House of Commons.

1648, October 17.—Order referring it to the Committee for Ireland to consider what more is to be offered to the King concerning Ireland. (Printed in *Commons' Journals,* vi. 54.) [N. XXI., 78.]

The Committee for Ireland.

1648, October 18.—Order, appointing a Sub·Committee to consider the reference and the Acts and Ordinances concerning Ireland, with powers to consult Irish gentlemen thereon. (N. XXI., 79.]

Papers.

1648, October 17-21.—(Being the fifteen printed in *Lords' Journals,* x. 560-563.) *Copies.* [N. IX., 219a, 224-237.]

The House of Commons.

1648, October 19.—Resolution concerning the computation of the 40 days appointed for the Treaty. (Printed in *Commons' Journals,* vi. 56.) [N. XV., 130.]

The House of Lords.

1648, October 21.—Votes for restoring the king to his dignity, &c. (Printed in *Lords' Journals,* x. 557.) [N. XV., 130.]

The House of Commons.

[1648, October 24.]—Resolutions and orders concerning the disband-ing of the Lancashire forces. (Printed in *Commons' Journals,* vi. 61.) *Annexed:*

Letter expressing the desire of the County for their disbandment. *Draft* or *Copy.* [N. XV., 120.]

LE PRINCE D'HARCOURT to the HOUSE OF COMMONS.

1648, October 27. Elbeuf (?).—Asking a passport for the bearer, his servant, to transport into France eight horses, which he has ordered him to buy. *Seals. Endorsed:* "Not opened till March 21, 1682-3." In *French.* [N. XVII., 12.]

The HOUSE OF COMMONS.

1648, October 27.—Votes upon the Treaty with the king. (Printed in *Commons' Journals,* vi. 62.) *Draft* of part, and *copy.* [N. IX., 238.]

The PARLIAMENT.

1648, October 28.—Orders, that the Commissioners present the *Shorter Catechism* to the King and for a prolongation of the Treaty. (Printed in *Lords' Journals,* x. 579.) [N. XV., 134.]

"The Names of the SEVEN PERSONS that are to remain in the First Exception in the Proposition concerning Delinquents."

[1648, October 28.]—Francis Lord Cottington, George Lord Digby, Sir Robert Heath, Kt., Sir Francis Doddington Kt., Sir George Radcliffe Kt., Sir Richard Greenvile, Sir Charles Dallison Kt. [N. XV., 135.]

The PARLIAMENT to the COMMISSIONERS WITH THE KING.

1648, October 28.—(Printed in *Lords' Journals,* x. 569.) *Draft.* [N. XII., 247.] *Enclosed:*

i. The MARQUESS OF ORMONDE to SIR RICHARD BLAKE.

1648, October 4. Cork.—

ii. ——— to Colonel MICHAEL JONES.

1648, October [? 10, date given as 20, but this must be wrong as it was enclosed in the next]. Maynooth.—

iii. Colonel MICHAEL JONES to WILLIAM LENTHALL.

1648, October 18. Dublin.—(All three printed in *Lords' Journals,* x. 568, 569.) *Copies.* [N. XII., 244, 245, 243.]

The COMMITTEE FOR IRELAND.

1648, November 2.—Order, reporting to the House the following paper in pursuance of the Order of October 17.

The PAPER referred to.

1. That an Act be passed for sale of the Rebels' possessions in the cities and towns of Dublin, Cork, Kinsale, Youghall and Drogheda according to the intent of the Ordinances of January 15th, 1647[-8] and June 5th, 1648.

2. That an Act be passed for the attainder and forfeiture of the Rebels, and also of all the hereditaments held by any of them by intrusion on any of his Majesty's possessions formerly reputed their inheritance.

3. That it be enacted that the loyal Protestant subjects shall hold and enjoy all the lands and hereditaments in Connaught, Clare, Limerick, and Tipperary, whereof they or those from whom they claim received the rents and profits before the Rebellion for their former estates therein.

4. That it be enacted that after disposition of the 2,500,000 acres intended for the Adventurers all the residue of the lands forfeited by

the Rebels or held by them by intrusion as aforesaid be disposed of for the further prosecution of the war there, for advancing the revenues of the Crown, &c.

5. That by Act of Parliament the same provisions be made against Jesuits, priests, friars, Papists and Popish Recusants in Ireland as are or shall be in England and all the laws made and to be made in England concerning such persons and their children be made of force in Ireland; And that all Papists and Popish Recusants be made incapable of being magistrates, officers or Commissioners in Ireland, and also of any practice in the Law, Common or Civil, either in public or private, or to sit as members in either House of Parliament in Ireland, or to have any military employment in that Kingdom.

6. That the Act intended for the due observation of the Lord's Day be made of force in Ireland.

7. That provision be made for the doing of such things during the intervals of Parliament as in the Act for the Adventurers are provided to be done by Parliament, and that the Commissioners of the Great Seal may do such things as in the said Act are to be done by the Lord Keeper or Lord Chancellor.

8. That there may be remitted to the loyal Protestant subjects of Ireland all rents &c. due to the Crown from Michaelmas 1641 till the Rebels be subdued and all subsidies due by virtue of any Act of Parliament in Ireland since the ninth year of his Majesty's reign except such as have actually been paid.

9. That the tenures and rents of all lands and hereditaments in the five escheated counties of Ulster be reduced to what they were in the beginning of the late Earl of Strafford's government, and yet then the remaining rents will be above double the rates intended by the Act for the Adventurers to be laid on lands in Ulster.

10. That the loyal Protestant subjects shall have and enjoy the lands and hereditaments held of them by the Rebels by lease, which leases will be now forfeited. [N. XXI., 80.]

The House of Lords.

1648, November 2.—Three Votes concerning the Treaty with the King. (Printed in *Lords' Journals*, x. 574.) *Copy.* [N. IX., 239.]

Lord Wenman, Denzell Holles, William Pierrepont, Sir Harbottle Grimston, Sir Henry Vane, Sir John Potts, John Glynn, John Crewe, Samuel Browne, and John Bulkeley to William Lenthall.

1648, November 2. Newport.—(Identical *mutatis mutandis*, with the letter to the Speaker of the House of Lords, which is printed in *Lords' Journals*, x. 575.) *Signed.* [N. IX., 249.] *Enclosed:*

Copies of the twelve papers which are printed in *Lords' Journals*, x. 575-578. [N. IX., 240-248; XII., 243a, 242, 246, the last three being those from Ireland.]

The Parliament to the Commissioners at Newport.

1648, November 3.—Concerning the prolongation of the Treaty for 14 days, and supplying them with money. (See *Commons' Journals*, vi. 68.) *Draft*, as passed by the Commons. [N. IX., 250.]

The Sa꜖e to the Sa꜖e.

Same date.—(Printed in *Lords' Journals*, x. 579.) *Draft.* [N. IX., 251.]

THO꜖AS [LORD] FAIRFAX to WILLIA꜖ LENTHALL.

1648, November 5. St. Albans.—Recommending to the House of Commons the exiles from Jersey. *Signed. Seal.* [N. VII., 114.]

LORD WEN꜖AN, DENZELL HOLLES, WILLIA꜖ PIERREPONT, SIR HENRY VANE, SIR JOHN POTTS, JOHN GLYNN, JOHN CREWE, and SA꜖UEL BROWNE, to WILLIA꜖ LENTHALL.

1648, November 6. Newport.—(Identical, *mutatis mutandis*, with the letter to the Speaker of the House of Lords, which is printed in *Lords' Journals*, x. 582.) *Signed.* [N. IX., 259.] *Enclosed:*

Copies of the seven papers, which are printed in *Lords' Journals*, x. 583, 584. [N. IX., 252-258.]

LORD WENMAN, DENZELL HOLLES, WILLIA꜖ PIERREPONT, and JOHN CREWE, to WILLIA꜖ LENTHALL.

1648, November 11. Newport.—(Identical, *mutatis mutandis*, with the letter to the Speaker of the House of Lords, which is printed in *Lords' Journals*, x. 589.) *Signed.* [N. IX., 263.] *Enclosed:*

Copies of the eleven papers, which are printed in *Lords' Journals*, x. 589, 590. [N. IX., 260, 261, 262, 264-271.]

MARGARET RANGSBOROUGH, widow, to the HOUSE OF CO꜖꜖ONS.

[1648, November 13, before.]—Petition, stating that her late husband had expended full 7,000*l.* in the service of the State, and desiring satisfaction out of the estates of Anthony Hamond and Captain Burgrane. (See *Commons' Journals*, vi. 100, 104, and Cary, *Memorials of the Civil War*, ii. 57.) [N. XXII., 111.]

The PARLIA꜖ENT to the CO꜖꜖ISSIONERS AT NEWPORT.

1648, November 15.—(Printed in *Lords' Journals*, x. 591.) *Draft.* [N. IX., 272.]

The PARLIAMENT to Colonel HA꜖꜖OND.

[1648], November 16.—Touching the King's Parole. (Printed in *Lords' Journals*, x. 593.) *Draft* as sent from the Commons. [N. XII., 248.]

LORD WEN꜖AN, DENZELL HOLLES, WILLIA꜖ PIERREPONT and JOHN CREWE to WILLIA꜖ LENTHALL.

1648, November 18. Newport.—(Identical, *mutatis mutandis*, with the letter to the Speaker of the House of Lords, which is printed in *Lords' Journals*, x. 597.) *Signed.* [N. IX., 277.] *Enclosed:*

Copies of the four papers printed in *Lords' Journals*, x. 597. [N. IX., 273-276.]

The humble Remonstrance of the Lord General FAIRFAX and his GENERAL COUNCIL OF OFFICERS.

1648, November 18.—(Printed in *King's Pamphlets*, E. 473. (70 pages small quarto.) A very short abstract in Rushworth, iv. 2. 1331.) [N. XXII., 66.]

Colonel MICHAEL JONES to WILLIAM LENTHALL.

1648, November 18. Dublin.—(Identical, *mutatis mutandis*, with the letter from the same to the Earl of Manchester, which is printed in *Lords' Journals*, x. 628. Enclosed is a copy of Major Harman's letter, also printed in *Lords' Journals*, x. 629.) *Signed. Seal.* [N. VII., 115.]

Examination of Doctor THOMAS GREY.

1648, November 21. Newcastle.—That about August 7th he met Colonel Carr about three miles from Holy Island, who told him he was going to meet Captain Batten on the sands to treat for delivering it up to the Earl of Lanerick, and that these had previously several messages between them for the purpose, and that after the meeting Colonel Carr was to ride post to Edinburgh to give Lord Lanerick an account of the business, and that the Colonel actually did so the next day.

And

Examination of Captain BATTEN.

Same date and place.—Stating that he had refused to give Colonel Carr a meeting on the sands and that he had written to Colonel Grey at Berwick only to ask for a pass to Holy Island for Mr. Clavering, who was skilful in setting bones. (See *Commons' Journals*, vi. 210.) [N. XV., 136.]

The PARLIAMENT to the COMMISSIONERS AT NEWPORT.

1648, November 21.—Enclosing their votes concerning Delinquents. (See *Commons' Journals*, vi. 82.) *Draft* as amended by the Commons. [N. IX., 280.]

The EARLS OF NORTHUMBERLAND and MIDDLESEX to the SPEAKER OF THE HOUSE OF LORDS.

1648, November 22. Newport.—(Printed in *Lords' Journals*, x. 603.) *Signed.*

And

LORD WENMAN, DENZELL HOLLES, WILLIAM PIERREPONT, and JOHN CREWE to [WILLIAM LENTHALL].

Same date.—(Identical, *mutatis mutandis* with the last.) *Signed.* [N. IX., 288.]

Enclosed in one or other of them :

Copies of the seven papers printed in *Lords' Journals*, x. 603–606. There are duplicates of all but the fifth and the last, being the enclosures in both letters. [N. IX., 278, 279, 281–287.]

LORD WENMAN, DENZELL HOLLES, WILLIAM PIERREPONT, and JOHN CREWE to WILLIAM LENTHALL.

1648, November 23. Cowes.—(Identical, *mutatis mutandis*, with the letter of the same date to the Speaker of the House of Lords, which is printed in *Lords' Journals*, x. 610.) *Signed.* [N. IX., 289.]

The PARLIAMENT to the COMMISSIONERS AT NEWPORT.

1648, November 24.—(Printed in *Lords' Journals*, x. 606.)   *Draft.* [N. IX., 301.]

PAPERS.

1648, November 25-27. Newport.—(Being the eleven printed in *Lords' Journals*, x. 621, 622, and numbered from 11 to 22 omitting No. 19, which is the same almost *verbatim* as the next.)   *Copies.* [N. IX., 290-300.]

Colonel ROBERT HAMMOND to SIR ROBERT DILLINGTON.

⟨ 1648, November 27. Carisbrook Castle. — Enclosing instructions. (Printed in Peck, *Desiderata Curiosa*, x. 28, and in *Lords' Journals*, x. 616.) [N. VII., 116.] *Enclosed:*

The said INSTRUCTIONS.

1648, November 27. — (Printed in *Lords' Journals*, x. 616.) *Annexed* is a copy of the instructions of August 24. [N. XV., 108, 109.]

Colonel HAMMOND to Captain BOWREMAN, and others.

1648, November 27.—Instructions. *Annexed:*

1648, August 24.—Instructions for Colonel ROBERT HAMMOND. *Copy.* (Both printed in *Lords' Journals*, x. 615, and in Peck, *Desiderata Curiosa*, x. 28, and ix. 51.) [N. XV., 106, 107.]

VOTES, RESOLUTIONS, and ORDERS of the HOUSE OF COMMONS touching the SECLUDED MEMBERS with their SOLEMN PROTESTATION and the DECLARATION of the House thereon.

1648, December 6, 7, 13, 14, December 18, 20; 1648[-9], January 4, 11, 29, February 1, 23 ; 1649, June 9, 6; 1648, December 11 and 15.—(All these are copies made to be read to the House on January 5, 1659-60. (See *Commons' Journals*, vii. 804.) The first four and that of June 6 are printed in *Commons' Journals*, vi. 93 and 94, 94, 96, 97, 225. The remainder were originally entered therein but were erased by the Orders of February 21 and 22, 1659-60. (See *Commons' Journals*, vii. 846, 848.) The declaration and protestation are printed in *Lords' Journals*, x. 631. The substance of the entries of December 18 and January 11 is in Rushworth, iv. 2. 1365 and 1366, 1390, that of the entries of January 29, February 1 and June 9 in Whitelocke, *Memorials*, p. 374. The substance of the remaining three is as follows : December 20.—*Resolved* that the former message to the General be renewed by the same Committee concerning the absent members. *Report* by Mr. Scot from the Committee to consider how the dissent of members to the vote of December 5th is to be entered. *Resolved:* That such as were present at the vote stand up and say that they dissent from it and that the clerk enter their names with their dissents, and that any members may have liberty to express their disapproval of the said vote. January 4.—*Report* by Mr. Serjeant Thorpe of the answer of the General Council of Officers concerning the late securing or secluding of certain members. February 23.—*Order* that no member . . . that hath not sitten in this House since the 31st of January last shall sit in any Committee till this House take further order.) [N. XV., 137-139.]

ORDINANCE.

1648, December 21.—For payment of 3,000*l.* to Lieutenant-Colonel Lilburne. (See *Commons' Journals*, vi. 102.) [N. XV., 140.]

THOMAS [LORD] FAIRFAX to WILLIAM LENTHALL.

1648, December 28. Queen Street.—Recommending the bearer; Mr.
John Morris, who had suffered much from the enemy during the siege
of Colchester, and desiring that some relief might be given him out of
Delinquents' estates in Essex. *Signed. Seal.* [N. VII., 117.]

Examination of GEORGE CLAVERING.

1648, December 29.—That in July last he delivered a letter from
Colonel Gray to Captain Batten, but knew not its contents and took no
message, and that on a Sunday, about August 10th, Colonel Carr sent him
to Captain Batten to desire him to meet him upon the sands on Monday
instead of Wednesday, the day Captain Batten had appointed, as the
examinant states, and that Captain Batten refused to change the day,
but whether they met or not, the examinant knows not. (See Examinations of November 21.) [N. XV., 141.]

ORDINANCE.

[1648.]—Concerning the appointment of the sub-collectors of the
20,000*l.* a month for Ireland to be raised by the Ordinance of the 16th
of February last. *Draft* or *Copy.* [N. XXII., 75.]

JOHN SICTOR, a Bohemian exile, to the HOUSE OF COMMONS.

[1648, end.]—Petition, stating that it was nearly two years since he had
presented to them 250 copies of his *Chronometræ* (a specimen of which
is probably among Lord Braye's papers, see *Sixth Appendix to the
Tenth Report of the Historical MSS. Commission*, p. 159), and other
poems on the events of the Civil War, and entreating a grant to enable
him to return to Prague, which had been—as was reported—occupied
by the Swedish army. In *Latin.* (The capture of Prague alluded to
was in October 1648.) [N. VII., 127.]

SIR WILLIAM FENTON and other officers from IRELAND to the HOUSE OF COMMONS.

[1648 or 1649.]—Petition. Having thanked the House for procuring their release by exchange they ask that some immediate relief
be afforded them out of the rents of Delinquents' Estates in Ireland, and
that their accounts may be audited, and one third of what is found due
to them be paid. (See *Commons' Journals*, vi. 254.) [N. XXI., 83.]
Probably *enclosed* in the next but one.

Lieutenant-Colonel PHANE BEECHER to the HOUSE OF COMMONS.

[1648 or 1649.]—Petition, stating his services and especially how he
had been twice sent over to Munster first to bring over Sterling and
Marshall, and secondly to exchange Lord Inchiquin's sons for the
gentlemen he had imprisoned for their fidelity to the Parliament, and
that his wife had been lately plundered by Lord Inchiquin's orders, and
praying that his arrears for his services in England may be paid and
secured and that he may be compensated for his charges and losses in
Ireland. *Signed.* [N. XXII., 136.] *Enclosed* in the next.

THOMAS [LORD] FAIRFAX to WILLIAM LENTHALL.

1648[-9], January 8. Queen Street.—Recommending the petitioners, who were long imprisoned by Lord Inchiquin, and also
Lieutenant-Colonel Beecher. *Signed. Seal. Enclosed* (not the
petitions referred to in the letter, which are the last two entries, but
apparently by mistake) :

Petition of SAMPSON SHEFFIELD.

Stating that he had been servant of the late King, who had put him out of his place because he would not adhere to him against the Parliament, for whom he had suffered much including a long imprisonment at Colchester, being one of the Committee for Essex, and praying that compensation be made him out of the late King's estate or otherwise. [N. VII., 118.]

The COMMITTEE OF THE REVENUE.

1648[-9], January 16.—Order that Lord Grey report to the House the statement of Baron Atkyns and Judge Godbold concerning the rights of the Lady Katherine Aubigny and others in a farm of the Aulnage granted to the late Duke of Lenox by James I. *Annexed :*
i. The said statement.
ii. Order of the House dated July 23, 1647, which is printed in *Lords' Journals,* ix. 351. [N. XV., 145-147.]

The COMMITTEE OF THE REVENUE.

1648[-9], January 16.—Order that Lord Grey of Groby report to the House the allowance of 7,450*l.* a year paid to the Earl of Northumberland for the maintenance of the Duke of Gloucester and the Princess Elizabeth, and also that of 3,000*l.* for himself. [N. XV., 143.]

Statement by Major JOHN MAYER.

1648[-9], January 28.—When he took Fenham House, which blocked up Holy Isle, he sent 22 prisoners to the Island to be secured by Captain Batten, nine of whom Captain Batten entertained as soldiers into the Castle. The Scots' army being then routed and Lieutenant-General Cromwell on his march northwards a little before Captain Batten sent his wife to Newcastle for relief, saying, if her husband had not a speedy supply he might be forced to deliver it up. Whereupon the Governor sent to Major Mayer to march into Northumberland with all possible speed, who accordingly marched to the Island, took and beat off the enemies' guards, and sent into the Island provision for the garrison for six months. When the Major came into the Island he found at least 200 sheep pasturing, a great warren full of rabbits and worth at least 100*l.*, and the cobles at sea bringing in great store of fish, besides that Major Sanderson not above two months before sent in provision for at least six months. [N. XV., 87.]

The STATES-GENERAL OF THE UNITED PROVINCES to WILLIAM LENTHALL.

164[8-]9, January [19-]29. The Hague.—Commending their ambassadors to his good offices. In *French.* [N. X., 47.]

The SAME to the HOUSE OF COMMONS.

Same date and place.—Letter of Credence for their ambassadors. In *French. Seal.* [N. X., 48.]

The SAME to THOMAS [LORD] FAIRFAX.

Same date and place.—Recommending to him their ambassadors who have been charged to see him and communicate to him the subject of their embassy. In *French. Seal. Endorsed* by Nalson " Not opened till March 21, 1682-3." [N. X., 45.]

The SAME to OLIVER CROMWELL.

Same date and place.—(A duplicate of that to Lord Fairfax.) In *French.* *Seal.* [N. X., 49.]

The AMBASSADORS OF THE STATES-GENERAL to WILLIAM LENTHALL.

1648–9, January 29 — February 8. — Enclosing their letters of Credence and desiring an immediate audience. (The translation is printed in Grey, iv. Appendix, Nos. 1, 2, pp. 2, 3.) (See *Commons' Journals*, vi. 124.) In *French.* *Signed.* *Seal.* [N. X., 44.] An *English* translation is N. XVIII., 107.

The AMBASSADORS OF THE STATES-GENERAL to the HOUSE OF COMMONS.

1648–9, January 30–February 9.—Interceding on behalf of the King. In *French* with *English* translation, the former subscribed "Spoken by the above Ambassadors in the House of Commons the above date." *Signed* "Adrien Pauw," "Alb. Joachimi." (Both are printed in Grey, iv. Appendix, Nos. 3, 4, pp. 4, 5.) (The above is the date of the delivery of the copy of the speech which was made the previous day, the 29th.) [N. X., 46; XVIII, 106.]

The HOUSE OF COMMONS.

1648[-9], January 30.—Order concerning the appointment to the Norfolk Shrievalty. (Printed in *Commons' Journals*, vi. 126.) [N. XV., 152.]

The Opinion of JOHN FRY touching the TRINITY.

1648[-9], February 3.—(Printed in Grey, iii. Appendix, No. 78, p. 133.) (See *Commons' Journals*, vi. 131.) [N. XV., 153.]

The COMMITTEE OF THE REVENUE.

1648[-9], February 3.—Order that Lord Grey report to the House the neglect of Mr. Middleton to pay the money due for his lands in Sussex. [N. XV., 144.]

The HOUSE OF COMMONS to the AMBASSADORS OF THE STATES-GENERAL.

[1648-9, February 5.]—Thanking the States-General for their good desires and assuring them that nothing had been done with regard to the late king but what was agreeable to justice and the fundamentals of this nation. (Printed in Grey, iv. Appendix, No. 5, p. 12.) (See *Commons' Journals*, vi. 132.) *Draft* with amendments. [N. XVIII., 67.]

WILLIAM CANN, Mayor, and RICHARD ALDWORTH to [WILLIAM LENTHALL].

1648[-9], February 5. Bristol.—Enclosing the informations of a Cornet and the master of a bark which arrived last night giving news from Ireland. *Signed.* [N. XXI., 81.] *Enclosed:*

The Information of JOHN PINE of Weymouth.

Same date.—On Saturday last he came out of Youghal, in company with the *Mary Constant.* It was reported that a peace was proclaimed in Waterford on the 27th of January between the English and Irish, the heads of whom are Ormonde and Inchiquin for the English and Antrim, Taaffe and Preston for the Irish. He hath heard that Inchiquin hath between 3,000 and 4,000 horse and foot. He knoweth that the Irish have forty frigates at least and two new ones are on the stocks at Wexford that are 100 foot by the keel almost. Prince Maurice was at Cork the last week, and Sir Pearce Smyth, the Governor of Youghal, told him that between Prince Rupert and Prince Maurice they had 28 sail of shipping. Captain Penn hath been in fight with the *Mary Antrim* and another frigate, and lost his mizenmast and boltsprit, but after made the *Mary Antrim* fly under Scilly, having killed eleven of her men. The cellars and storehouses at Waterford are full of Englishmen's goods, and the Irish there come and trade for them familiarly. The Irish forces at sea are most Dunkirkers, Fleming and English, and with them their frigates and men of war are most manned for commanders and seamen. They have at least 28 sail now at sea. A ship under the command of Captain Darsy is gone over into Holland to fetch the Prince over into Ireland.. Those Irish men of war lie constantly so in the throat of the Channel between Scilly and the Land's End that no ship can pass them in or out unless in the night or in a dusky dark time. A Wexford man of war lately took a ship of 500 tons of corn that was coming up to this port of Bristol. (See *Commons' Journals*, vi. 133.) *Signed* and *Attested*. [N. XXI., 82.]

The High Court of Justice.

1648[-9], February 7.—Order desiring papers &c. concerning the trial of the Earl of Cambridge and others. (Printed in Grey, iii. Appendix, No. 80, p. 136.) (See *Commons' Journals*, vi. 133.) [N. XV., 154.]

The Committee concerning the Funeral of the King.

1648[-9], February 8. Report.—(Printed in Peck, *Desiderata Curiosa*, x. 31.) *Draft*. [N. XV., 156.]

Forms of Oaths to be taken by the Commissioners of the Great Seal, the Chief Justice of the Upper Bench, the Sheriffs, and the Justices of the Peace.

1648[-9], February 8 and 15.—(Printed in *Commons' Journals*, vi. 135, 142, 143.) [N. XV., 157-160.]

Act.

1648[-9], February 9.—Forbidding the printing of the proceedings in the High Court of Justice for the trial of the Earl of Cambridge and others. (Printed in Grey, iii. Appendix, No. 81, p.137.) (See *Commons' Journals*, vi. 136.) [N. XV., 155.]

Ralph Jennison, Sheriff, to William Lenthall.

1648[-9], February 15. Newcastle.—Acknowledging his letter of January 30th enclosing an Act (namely that against the proclaiming of King Charles II.), and stating that he had caused it to be proclaimed at the accustomed places. *Seal*. [N. VII., 120.]

Proclamation of Charles the Second as King.

1648[-9], February 16. Carrick.—(Printed in Milton's Works, edited by Symmons, vol. ii., p. 354.) [N. XXI., 87.]

The COMMITTEE OF THE REVENUE.

1648[-9], February 16.—Order that Lord Grey report to the House the statement of Mr. Oliver St. John concerning the rights of the daughters of Sir Edmund Verney in 400*l.* a year payable out of the reserved rent of the Aulnage. *Annexed:*

    i. 1647, September 21.—Order referring the matter to Mr. St. John.

    ii. The Petition of Sir Edmund Verney's daughters.

    iii. Mr. St. John's Opinion of February 8, 1647[-8.] [N. XV., 148–151.]

REPORT.

1648[-9], February 19.—Of the arrears due to the Prince Elector, showing a total of 6,500*l.* being the 2,000*l.* voted in February 1644–5, and 4,500*l.* arrears on his pension of 8,000*l.* (Printed in Grey, iii. Appendix, No. 50, p. 77.) (See *Commons' Journals*, vi. 145.) [N. XV., 161.]

The COUNCIL OF STATE.

1648[-9], February 19.—Order for a report to the House concerning the members thereof that subscribed, and those who did not, with their reasons for refusing. (Printed in full in Peck, *Desiderata Curiosa*, x. 31, and in part in *Commons' Journals*, vi. 146.) [N. XV., 162.]

THOMAS [LORD] FAIRFAX to WILLIAM LENTHALL.

1648[-9], February 20. Queen Street.—Touching 500*l.* borrowed from the Sub-Commissioners of Excise. (The purport sufficiently appears by the Ordinance made thereon. See *Commons' Journals*, vi. 153.) *Signed. Seal.* [N. VII., 121.]

THOMAS [LORD] FAIRFAX to WILLIAM LENTHALL.

1648[-9], February 24. Queen Street.—Recommending the enclosed Petition to the consideration of the House. *Signed. Enclosed:*

> Petition of the DOMESTIC SERVANTS of the late King and his Children.

> Praying for payment of what shall appear to be due to them, and that provision be made for their future maintenance. (See *Commons' Journals*, vi. 170.) [N. XVI., 12, 11.]

A necessary Presentation of the present Evils and eminent Dangers to Religion, laws and liberties from the late and present practices of the Sectarian party in England by the PRESBYTERY OF BELFAST.

1648[-9], February 25.—(Printed in *King's Pamphlets*, E. 555; Milton's Works, edited by Symmons, vol. ii., p. 355, and elsewhere.) [N. XXI., 86.]

Mr. SAXBY's account touching the securing of the SCOTCH COMMISSIONERS.

[1648-9, February 28.]—On Monday [the 26th] about 3 o'clock the House gave Colonel Harrison the order, who desired Mr. Saxby to go with him. They went to their lodging and found they had gone two or three days ago to another house, and on inquiry there that they had gone to Gravesend on their way to Scotland. Mr. Saxby then went to Gravesend, and finding a Scotch vessel there ordered a Parliament frigate to attend her motion. Then he went in a boat and informed the master of the Scotch vessel that there was an order to stay some persons aboard his ship, but none should receive prejudice. He then took boat and in another boat sent the captain of the fort with eight musketeers with directions not to stir. Going on board he met Sir John Cheisly and inquired for Lord Lothian, to whom he showed the order, who having read it said he was his servant to wait upon him, but desired to stay aboard the ship that night. Mr. Saxby offered them to go anywhere on shore in respect of the coldness of the night or to the fort. Lord Lothian desired a copy of the order, and said they were public persons, and what was done to them was done to others, to which Mr. Saxby said he would not give an answer, and then they went on shore, and he waited on them to their lodging and there secured them. He came hither yesterday, but the House not sitting he resorted thither last night and stayed there till 11 o'clock. He moved them if they liked to take any house in the town it should be prepared for them, which they kindly accepted. (Then follows the Order for payment of Mr. Saxby's charges which is printed in *Commons' Journals*, vi. 152.) [N. XX., 45.]

Thomas [Lord] Fairfax to William Lenthall.

1648[-9], March 2. Queen Street.—Recommending the petition of the army. (See *Commons' Journals*, vi. 153.) *Signed. Seal.* [N. VII., 122.]

The High Court of Justice.

1648[-9], March 8 and 9.—Orders desiring that the House be moved to pay the balance of the expenses of the trials of the King and of the Earl of Cambridge and others and also recommending the Counsel and Clerks and Lieutenant-Colonel Beecher to the favour of Parliament. (Printed in Grey, iii. Appendix, No. 54, p. 140.) (See *Commons' Journals*, vi. 169.) [N. XV., 163.]

Thomas [Lord] Fairfax to William Lenthall.

1648[-9], March 8. Queen Street.—Interceding for the Earl of Holland and for Lord Capel. (See *Commons' Journals*, vi. 159.) In Rushworth's hand. *Signed. Seal.* [N. VII., 123.]

The Marquess of Ormonde to Colonel Michael Jones.

1648[-9], March 9. Carrick.—Inviting him to join him. *Signed.*

And

Colonel Michael Jones to the Marquess of Ormonde.

1648[-9], March 14. Dublin.—(Both printed in *King's Pamphlets*, E. 529, Number 28.) *Copy.* [N. VII., 124, 125.]

The Parliament.

1648[-9], March 21.—Order on the letter of Lord Fairfax of February 24th, and the Petition of the Domestic Servants of the late King and his children. (Printed in *Commons' Journals*, vi. 170.) [N. XVI., 13.]

Thomas [Lord] Fairfax to William Lenthall.

1648[-9], March 24. Queen Street.—Supporting the enclosed petition. *Signed. Seal. Enclosed:*

The Petition of Edward Hanchett late Usher of the Court of Wards and Liveries to the House of Commons.

Stating that he had purchased the office for 4,000*l.*, that the Committee of Examinations had awarded him 4,300*l.* on the abolition of the Court and that he was now utterly destitute and a debtor in the King's Bench and praying they should order the said 4,300*l.* to be paid him. [N. VII., 126.]

The EARL OF RUTLAND to the HOUSE OF COMMONS.

[1649, March 28.]—Petition. (The effect appears from *Commons' Journals*, vi. 175.) *Copy.* [N. XXII., 120.]

[WILLIAM LENTHALL] to [THOMAS LORD FAIRFAX].

1649, May 23.—Concerning Free quarter. (The purport sufficiently appears from *Commons' Journals*, vi. 214.) *Draft.* [N. XII., 252.]

General OWEN [ROE] O'NEALE to Colonel GEORGE MONCK.

1649, April 25.—Enclosing Propositions for peace.

And

[Colonel GEORGE MONCK] to [General OWEN ROE O'NEALE].

[1649, May.]—Replying to the last and enclosing counter-propositions and also proposals for a Cessation. (O'Neale's propositions and the proposals for a Cessation are printed in Gilbert, ii. 216, and all are printed in *King's Pamphlets*, E. 562, No. 1.) *Copies.* [N. XII., 251.]

An Estimate of the ANNUAL CHARGE issuing out of the PUBLIC REVENUE.

[1649, May 9.]—For pensions and fees for offices, amounting in all to 70,874*l.* (Printed in Grey, iv. Appendix, No. 60, p. 97.) (See *Commons' Journals*, vi. 205.) [N. XVI., 6.]

The PARLIAMENT.

1649, May 11.—Order declaring Thompson and others Rebels. (Printed in *Commons' Journals*, vi. 207.) [N. XVI., 1.]

The Information of WILLIAM ALSOP, THOMAS RUMBELOW and DANIEL MERCHANT.

1649, May 11.—Concerning the death of Dr. Dorislaus. (Printed in Peck, *Desiderata Curiosa*, xi. 9.) [N. XVIII., 69.]

Colonel HANS BEHR to WILLIAM LENTHALL.

1649, May 12. Hamburgh.—Congratulating the Parliament on their successes and requesting a special order for the payment of his arrears amounting to the small sum of 11 or 1,200*l.* In *French.* *Seal.* [N. X., 75.]

The COMMITTEE FOR THE REFORMATION OF THE UNIVERSITIES OF OXFORD AND CAMBRIDGE.

1649, May 21.—Order reporting resolutions. (The resolutions are printed in *Commons' Journals*, vi. 215.) [N. XVI., 2.]

The PARLIAMENT.

Same date.—Order to the Attorney-General. (Printed in *Commons' Journals*, vi. 113.) [N. XVI., 3.]

Captain WILLIAM BRAY to WILLIAM LENTHALL.

1649, May 22. Windsor Castle.—Requesting him to impart his third appeal to the House. (See *Commons' Journals*, vi. 168.) [N. VIII., 1.]

The House of Commons.

1649, May —.—Order to apprehend such persons engaged in the late rebellion as were at large. *Draft* (apparently not passed). [N. XXI., 89.]

Two Proclamations.

1649, May —.—The first ordering the apprehension of persons concerned in the late insurrection, the second declaring William Thompson a traitor. *Drafts.* [N. XVI., 4.]

Act.

1649, June 1.—Appointing a day of Thanksgiving. *Draft*, with numerous alterations. [N. XVI., 5.]

Account of the Estates of the several persons named in the Ordinance of June 5, 1648.

1649, June 2.—Showing that there was at the disposal of the trustees appointed thereby lands valued at 19,495*l. per annum* besides lands and tithes valued at 12,405*l. per annum*, and that they had since their appointment received 8,726*l.* [In fold of N. XXI., 90.]

The Council of State.

1649, June 5.—Order reporting their opinion concerning the solemnity tomorrow. (Printed in *State Papers, Domestic*, p. 174, paragraphs 20-23.) *Annexed* is the *Draft* of an Act empowering the Speaker to knight certain persons, of which there is an abstract in *State Papers, Domestic*, p. 175. [N. XVI., 7.]

The Committee for Ireland.

1649, June 13.—Report concerning Lord Lisle's accounts. (Printed in *Commons' Journals*, vi. 232.) [N. XVI., 8.]

Colonel Hans Behr to William Lenthall.

1649, June 13. Hamburgh.—Congratulating him on his recovery, and asking him to use his influence to procure payment of his arrears. In *French. Seal.* [N. X., 76.]

Cardinal Mazarin to William Lenthall.

1649, June 26. Amiens.—Stating that some troops levied in Ireland for the King of France had been taken on their passage and were still detained in England, and asking that they might be allowed to go to France, and stating that the Sieur de Gaumont who is charged with the affair will give more particular information, if it is desired. In *French. Signed.* [N. XVII., 11.]

The Committee of the Revenue.

1649, July 4.—Order reporting their opinion concerning the late King's servants. (The material parts are printed in *Commons' Journals*, vi. 264.) *Copia vera* by their Secretary. [N. XVI., 14.]

Recommendation.

1649, July 6.—To the House of Commons to pay certain sums to Sir William Parsons and others. (See *Commons' Journals*, vi. 254.) [N. XXI., 90.]

The Parliament.

1649, July 19.—Order concerning Sir Henry Mildmay. (Printed in *Commons' Journals*, vi. 264.) [N. XVI., 9.]

Declaration of the Parliament concerning the maintenance of Ministers and Church Government.

1649, August 6 and 7.—After a preamble stating that insinuations have been made that Parliament has laid aside all care for religion, they declare that it is their real intentions and shall be their constant endeavours to advance religion in its purity and to promote the sincere and powerful preaching and spreading of the "Ghospel" through the Commonwealth of England and Ireland and the dominions thereof, and they will give due encouragement and protection to all persons who shall conscientiously serve and worship God in the purity of his ordinances, and shall live peaceably and submissively under the present Government; That they will with all convenient speed make new laws, where need requires, and effectually provide for the due execution of the laws now in force for the suppression of popery, superstition, idolatry, prelacy, atheism and all manner of profaneness; That as they have reserved for sale—towards the augmentation of small livings and the advancement of the ministry and learning—all impropriations belonging to the late King, Queen, or Prince, to Bishops, Deans, and Chapters, which are of great yearly value, and many of those belonging to Delinquents, for which the Parliament have allowed out of the fines of such Delinquents who have compounded above 100,000*l.* and a further great sum out of the fines of others who have not yet compounded, and also have by Act lately settled 20,000*l. per annum* out of the public Revenue for these purposes, and they are resolved also to reserve for the same purposes such impropriations as belong to all Papists in arms and to those Delinquents whose estates are or shall be confiscated and such other impropriations as shall fall within their power to dispose : So they declare and promise that, when they shall change the present maintenance by tithes into some other way, yet they will first take care that no alteration shall be made therein until a certain and plentiful livelihood and maintenance—though perhaps to be more equally distributed—be visibly provided and firmly settled for maintaining such public ministry. (Then follow two clauses, the first concerning payment of tithes is printed in *Commons' Journals*, vi. 275, and with these preceding words " And therefore until the Parliament shall have liberty to take the same into consideration which within a short time they are resolved to do," was omitted by order on August 6th, the second, establishing a Presbyterian form of government and public worship according to the *Directory*, was omitted by order on August 7th) : Provided that all persons, who—upon conscientious grounds—cannot join in such public form of worship and Church government shall have freedom to worship and serve God in such other way as is warranted by the Scriptures, such persons walking holily, religiously and peaceably in their conversations ; Provided also that this privilege shall not extend to the toleration of the Popish religion, superstition, idolatry, prelacy, atheism, or the use of the late service book, commonly called the *Book of Common Prayer* in any place whatsoever within this Commonwealth. (See *Commons' Journals*, vi. 275.) *Draft* with numerous amendments. [N. XXII., 58.]

The Parliament.

[1649, August 16.]—Declaration touching the Thanksgiving for the victory in Ireland appointed for the 29th instant and narrative of the particulars touching the same. (Printed in *King's Pamphlets*, E. 1060, No. 55.) [N. XVI., 67, 68.]

The Proconsuls and Senate of Hamburgh to the Parliament.

1649, August 21.—Interceding on Colonel Behr's behalf. In *Latin*. *Seal embossed*. [N. X., 78.]

The Council of State.

[1649, August 23.]—Report of "the state of fact concerning free trade," &c. (Printed in *Commons' Journals*, vi. 284.) [N. XVII., 13.]

Colonel Hans Behr to William Lenthall.

1649, August 24. Hamburgh.—Again requesting payment of his arrears or at least a half or a third of them on account. In *French*. [N. X., 77.]

The Council of State to the Collectors of Prize Goods.

1649, September 15.—Ordering the discharge of the ship *Bommell*. (Following the terms of the order printed in *Commons' Journals*, vi. 295.) [N. XVI., 15.]

Thomas [Lord] Fairfax to William Lenthall.

1649, October 5. Kensington.—Recommending the enclosed petition of certain widows and others, who desire to be admitted to share in the benefit of the Act enabling officers to make discoveries to the public use and towards their satisfaction. (See *Commons' Journals*, vi. .303.) *Signed*. [N. VIII., 3.]

The Council of State.

1649, November 27.—Order to report concerning decayed ships. Printed in *Commons' Journals*, vi. 340.) [N. XVI., 19.]

The Committee for Sale of the late King's goods to the Council of State.

1649, November 28.—Reasons why we cannot conform to their order in delivering to the Earl of Pembroke the pictures alleged by him to be his. (Printed in Grey, iv. Appendix, No. 53, p. 89.) *Copy*. [N. XVI., 16.]

Declaration of the Marquess of Montrose.

1649, November.—(A somewhat fuller copy than that printed *State Papers Domestic*, pp. 415–417; *e.g.* in par. 1 the former reads " have harmlessly been involved and innocently inveigled, " the latter " have been innocently inveigled." In the last line but one " Crastinus' " should be " crastinus.") [N. XVI., 17.]

' Colonel ALEXANDER POPHAM and Colonel JOHN HUTCHINSON.

1649, December 3.—Two identical certificates to the effect that at the surrender of Newark the treaters for the Parliament had stated to those on the other side that the compositions for the estates of inheritance of all persons—not excepted by former Ordinances—then in the garrison should not exceed two years' revenue, and estates for lives or 21 years one year's value, and so proportionably. *Signed.* [N. XVI., 18.]

SIR JOHN HOLLAND, THOMAS SMITH and ROBERT THOMSON, Commissioners of the Navy, to the TRUSTEES FOR SALE OF THE LATE KING'S LANDS.

1649, December 21. Navy Office.—Specifying the number of trees and quantity of timber found fit for the use of the Navy, in the following parks and chases viz. Chestnut Park, Old Enfield Park, Enfield Chase, Nonsuch Great Park, Byfleet Park, Nonsuch Little Park, Bagshot Park, Richmond Park, and Oatlands Park. The trees mentioned are all oak, ash, elm or beech, except some pines in Chestnut Park, and some hornbeams in Enfield Chase. (See *Commons' Journals*, vi. 342.) [N. VIII., 4.]

List of OFFICERS serving with the Marquess of Ormonde.

[1649.]—The Earl of Roscommon, Lord Byron, Sir Edmund Verney, and others. [N. XXI., 84.]

The PARLIAMENT.

1649[-50], January 1.—Mr. Bond's report and the order thereon. (Printed in *Commons' Journals*, vi. 342.) [N. XVI., 20.]

[1649-50, January.]—The Confession of ABRAHAM GRANGER.

1649[-50], January 19.—The further voluntary Confession of the SAME.

[1649-50, January.]—The Confession of JOHN BOND, servant to Nicholas Greenway.

1649[-50], January 18.—The Examinations of JOHN STEPHENS and JOHN GRANGER.

1649[-50], January 18.—The Examination of NICHOLAS GREENWAY.

1649[-50], January 19.—The Second Examination of the SAME.

[1649-50, January.]—The Examination of JOHN STEPHENS.

1649[-50], January 21.—The Confession of JOHN COTTON. All concerning the frauds and forgeries committed by Granger, Greenway and others. (See *Commons' Journals*, vi. 390.) [N. XVI., 21, 22; XV., 142; XVI., 28, 29, 146, 24.]

' SIR CHARLES COOTE to WILLIAM LENTHALL.

1649[-50], January 24. Belfast.—" Since my last note by Colonel St. George I have been in the Laggan beyond Londonderry where I found my brother Colonel Richard Coote besieging of Castle Doe, the only seaport which was in the enemy's hands in this province of Ulster, which we had surrendered to us. My Lord Lieutenant having dispersed the forces of the enemy in the West a great part of them are falling down into this country to take up their winter quarters—if they may— which occasioned my return into these parts." The men under my command are destitute of clothes, shoes and stockings, and have no provisions except what they get by quartering on the inhabitants.' A great part of them are sick of the purple and other diseases, and some die every day. The Lord Lieutenant is so far from us, being in Munster, that we cannot expect any relief from him. I sent Colonel Venables to him about six weeks ago who took ship from Dublin but was driven back. If Parliament does not speedily supply us with necessaries the good success God has granted us will be lost. If money be sent us we can get provisions from other places with less charge and delay than if they were sent by long sea. *Signed. Seal.* [N. VIII., 2.]

The Council of State.

1649[-50], January 25 or 26.—Order to report concerning the *Santa Clara.* (Printed in *Commons' Journals*, vi. 359.) (Two copies, one bearing the first, the other the second date.) [N. XVI., 23, 25.]

The Council of State.

1649[-50], January 30.—Order to report concerning agents to Spain &c. (Printed in *Commons' Journals*, vi. 353.) [N. XVI., 26.]

The Committee for Advance of Money.

[1649-50, February 2.]—Report concerning the plot against Sir Jacob Garrett. (Printed in *Commons' Journals* vi., 354.) [N. XVI., 27.]

Examinations of Thomas Sherlock, John Flower, Mary Sandford and others.

1649[-50], February 7.—Concerning the plot against Sir Jacob Garrett. *Copies.* [N. XVI., 30.]

The Committee for Advance of Money.

1649[-50], February 7.—Order reporting concerning Mary Sandford, (Printed in *Commons' Journals*, vi. 454), and resolution that she be committed to Newgate to be kept in safe custody, till Parliament shall take further order. *Signed.* [N. XVI., 31.]

The Council of State.

1649[-50], February 8.—Order reporting concerning the reception of Ambassadors. (Printed in *Commons' Journals*, vi. 354.) [N. XVI., 32.]

The Council of State.

1649[-50], February 13.—Order reporting concerning daggers and pocket pistols. (Printed in *Commons' Journals*, vi. 366.) [N. XVI., 33.]

The COMMITTEE FOR RELIEF UPON ARTICLES.

1649[-50], February 27.—Report concerning Sir Gervase Scrope who prayed to have his composition reduced according to the Articles of Newark. [N. XVI., 34.]

The COMMITTEE FOR THE NAVY.

1649[-50], March 1.—List of merchant ships for the Summer Guard, (Printed in *Commons' Journals*, vi. 375), with details as to where some of them were, and also stating that the captains of some said that unless they might have the command of their own ships the owners would not lay out money on them. [N. XVI., 35.]

Articles for the surrender of BALLYSHANNON.

1649[-50], March 1.—Signed by Colonel John Hewson and Donnough Kelly. (See *Commons' Journals*, vi. 583.) *Original* and *Copy*, both nearly illegible. [N. XXI., 85, 91.]

The COMMITTEE FOR PROPAGATING THE GOSPEL IN IRELAND.

1649[-50], March 8.—Report. (The effect appears from the resolutions thereon, printed in *Commons' Journals*, vi. 379.) [N. XXI., 88.]

Admiral ROBERT BLAKE to the KING OF PORTUGAL.

1649[-50], March 10[-20]. From his Flagship.—As soon my fleet arrived in Cascaes Bay, hearing that Rupert and his fleet had not yet sailed I caused the letter from the Parliament to your Majesty to be immediately placed in your hands. Since your Majesty has been thereby acquainted with the object of this expedition and also apprised of their sincere friendship towards you I could not doubt that we shall find your Majesty favourably disposed to our undertaking, since there is nothing in our instructions and plans but what relates to the common advantage of nations, which is disregarded, unless pains are taken to exterminate pirates, that most nefarious tribe, the enemies of the world. Since the brothers Rupert and Maurice are an important part of them, who have now for several years been carrying on piracy with the ships of the English Commonwealth which were carried off by a treacherous revolt, and with some others they have captured, to the great damage of many, but to the greatest of our own countrymen, who cannot but deem it the work of some special Providence that they have been detained in your harbour till the arrival of our fleet? Your Majesty will, I hope, attribute it to our sense of duty and just feelings of revenge should any hostile attempt be made upon them while they are in harbour and it is impossible to make it otherwise: For that is certainly both allowed by the law of nations and requisite for our interests, and will be, as I hope, of no small advantage to your kingdom and people. I therefore trust that your Majesty will readily grant that we may freely use your port and will interpose no obstacle to so honourable an enterprise should an opportunity occur. I beg your Majesty to feel certain that we shall never do anything in the smallest degree inconsistent with the friendship between the two nations or which might give just ground of offence to your Majesty. I again earnestly entreat your Majesty to regard us in this light, and ask you to give a favourable hearing to the lieutenant of my flagship and to allow him soon to return to his duties. In *Latin. Copy.* [N. XVII., 91.]

WALTER STRICKLAND to the COUNCIL OF STATE.

1649-50, March 10--20. The Hague.—"The States of Holland took into consideration the things proposed by the Commissioner Shaep about his coming . . to reside at London to transact the affairs of Holland with the Commonwealth . . and being willing to give him some encouragement to counterbalance the apprehensions he might have from the great ones who might endeavour to take him off they have given him more than they formerly allowed him . ." with "leave once every year for some short time to come over to order his affairs here and to take order for sending over himself and his necessaries without any charge to him. This was done yesterday, so I believe he will shortly prepare for his journey and will bring such credentials as will be necessary in respect of acknowledging the Commonwealth. This seems to be no good augure to the Pretender's now coming hither, his best friends having omitted no endeavours to have carried it otherwise. I hope your Honours will allow him all the advantages of a public Minister . . ., and by giving him such audience and reception as may in some measure answer the like the States of Holland give me to the great regret of your enemies, I doubt not but such use may be made of this as may cut off the hopes of your greatest and most considerable enemies." (See *Commons' Journals*, vi. 384.) *Extract.* [N. XVIII., 141.]

Articles of agreement between JOHN MENDEZ DE VASCONCELLOS on the part of the KING OF PORTUGAL and CHARLES VANE on the part of Admiral BLAKE.

1650, March 28. New Style.—1. The said Admiral Blake shall not enter the port of Lisbon with his fleet nor pass the Castles of St. Julian and "*Capitis Sani*" without special permission in writing from his Majesty.

2. If forced by stress of weather, his Majesty allows the said fleet to enter and go up to the anchorage known as de Oeiras.

3. In the last case the said Admiral undertakes that he will neither commit nor allow any act of hostility either by sea or land against the English ships which are not on his side or their soldiers or sailors without his Majesty's permission in writing unless in self defence.

4. On the return of fair weather the said Admiral undertakes to return with his whole fleet outside the Castles of St. Julian and "*Capitis Sani*."

5. The said Admiral undertakes that while the fleet on account of stress of weather is at de Oeiras or nearer or further out to keep his men on board, forbidding them to land except a few to procure ueees-saries.

6. Other matters are reserved for further negotiation.

In *Latin*. *Copy* with several mistakes. [N. XVII., 93.]

A COUNCIL OF WAR.

1649[-50], March 23. On board the *George* in Weyres Bay.—Whereas the King of Portugal proposes that for a speedy accommodation between him and the Parliament's fleet in reference to Prince Rupert's fleet and for the removing of all jealousies some person of quality should be sent on shore to treat with such as he shall send, appointing Captain Robert Moulton, Vice-Admiral of England, for the purpose and empowering him to treat according to the following instructions:—

You are acquaint the King or his Ministers that this fleet was and is for the reducing or destroying of the revolted fleet now in this harbour, and there being no other way to attain that end but by the consent of his Majesty or by force you are insist on these particulars:—

1. You are to demand a restitution of all the ships now under Prince Rupert's command, and if that shall be denied;

2. You are to propose that liberty may be given unto the fleet here to seize on them by force of arms wheresoever we shall find them, and if that also be refused;

3. You are then to propose that his Majesty will within some short time give a positive command to both fleets to depart this harbour at one and the same time, and in case Prince Rupert and his fleet shall not conform themselves to the order at the time appointed then his Majesty will be pleased not to afford his fleet any longer protection, but to give this fleet liberty to seize on his ships by force of arms as opportunity shall be offered.

In case the King will not give his assent to any of the foresaid propositions which you are to insist upon with all instance and importunity as being just and reasonable;

4. You are to desire in the name of the Commonwealth—being in amity and league with this kingdom—the freedom and privilege of the harbour, and to ride where we shall find most safety for our ships and conveniency for obtaining the ends which we are employed about and whereof a most strict account will be required at our hands, we engaging ourselves upon the grant thereof not to do any act of hostility upon Rupert's fleet or any of them, while we are in this port, except they provoke us, or his Majesty shall give his assent.

5. You are to insist upon the aforesaid instructions to the best advantage of the Commonwealth the managing whereof we leave to your discretion in regard to some circumstances of time and place, provided that you recede not from their tenor and substance. You are also to give the best assurance to his Majesty that whatsoever scandalous reports are spread abroad concerning the design of this fleet there is no other intention of it but the reducing or destroying of the said revolted fleet and no evil purpose to his Majesty kingdom or people. *Copy*. [N. XVII., 92.]

ANTHONY ASCHAM to WILLIAM LENTHALL.

1650, April 3. New Style. Puerta Santa Maria.—" Nothing new having hapned since my landing, but my health and recoverie from a desperate feavour, I have the lesse worthy of your present advertisement. The $\frac{16}{26}$ of March, I landed in this place, as a necessary passage to San Lucar, where I intended my stand, till I should have answer from the King to your first letter, for my safe and honorable approach to him, if he please to admitt of it. But the Duke of Medina Celi governour both of San Lucar and of this towne, before I could cleare my things, sent his secretary and his coach to welcome me on shoare. I desired to kisse his handes in this my passage to San Lucar—where lodgeings were prepared for me—and to acknowledge his civilities to me in the first place which his secretary promised should be instantly done. But first he carryed me to a captaine's house in the towne where I by the Duke's order am lodged till he heare first from Court whether the King will admitt letters from the parliament or noc, etc. The Duke upon that ground desired to be excused from any visitt from me, till he knew what order the King would give about me, that he conceaved the King might be surprised at the newes of my arrivall, presuming he had received nothing from the parliament of their intents of addressing themselves to his Majesty in such a publique way. Otherwise his Majestie would have sent orders to the sea coastes about the reception and security of my person. Wherfore he absolutely declared that he could not yet permitt me to send any advise or letter of the parliament's, or any servant of mine to the Court, till his Majesty had first given answer to that expresse which he was imediatly dispatching to him, and to which he should have answer in eight dayes. Being under soe strict a hand, I could not send the gentleman of my owne which I intended ; but if by Monday—which is the eighth day—I have not my liberty, I hope to find some other sure hand for the dispatch and delivery of the letter which the Duke shall never know of till it be too late for him to hinder itt." *Signed. Seal.* [N. XVII., 36.]

Articles for the Surrender of KILKENNY.

1650, March 27.—(Printed in Gilbert, ii. 382.) *Copy.* [N. XXI., 93.]

Admiral ROBERT BLAKE to [CHARLES VANE].

1650, March 29. On board the *George*.—" I received yours . . last night. It is now evident enough that the King intends to do what he can in favour of Prince Rupert. And I take that message sent you as a preludium of some farther declaration against us when opportunity shall serve, for it being known to him that another fleet of English ships is prepared—as Rupert in his declaration saith—to join with this and there being no likelyhood at all in the world of any English men of war to come into this harbour to his assistance, but of the French daily expected and rumoured among them what other construction can be made of that message but that his purpose is to contribute what he can to the increase of Rupert's strength and to the lessening of ours ? And therefore my desire " and that of the Council of War is " that you would plainly speak to the King or to those which shall be sent from him, and to press them to give a clear and positive and universal answer to our propositions and to let them know that we should take it far better at his hand that he did openly declare for Prince Rupert against us than by such indirect policies to undermine us, and by uncertain and equivocal pretences of amity to entertain us and to lead us along by the nose any longer with an opinion of his neutrality, when as we may clearly perceive by that order given to his forts the contrary is intended." *Copy.* [N. XVII., 94.]

CHARLES VANE to [WILLIAM LENTHALL].

1650, April 3. Lisbon.—" Being sent by the Council of State to the King of Portugal with such instructions as they were pleased to charge me with I have held it my duty to give the Parliament an account of my safe arrival at Lisbon and my reception there by that King, who upon our advance with the fleet into the River of Lisbon was pleased to give order for my landing, and accordingly sent a Lieutenant-General with a coach with six horses to bring me to town where I have been these seven or eight days, and Friday last had my audience from the King, who, after general acknowledgements of the Parliament's kindness and expressions of his desire to maintain friendship with the state of England, for those other heads in my charge which I had represented unto him, he was pleased to refer me to his secretary to give them in writing. Their carriage hitherto is pretty fair, and they seem to grow weary of Prince Rupert's fleet. I have informed the Council of State of all particulars, and therefore shall trouble you no further, but to my power shall endeavour in these transactions to manifest my cordial affection to the Commonwealth of England and to yourself." (See *Commons' Journals*, vi. 396.) [N. XVII., 119.]

WILLIAM BASIL, Attorney-General of Ireland, to WILLIAM LENTHALL.

1650, April 4. Dublin.—(This letter is given in substance, and in parts *verbatim* in Whitelocke, *Memorials*, pp. 449, 450. The name of the officer killed at Kilkenny is Higbie not Higly, and the passage about the Earl of Castlehaven, which is shortened in Whitelocke, is as follows :—" the Earl of Castlehaven who about 12 days since came to Tecroghan, some say with seven score horse, and that Farralde is to join with him with his northern forces which have quartered the winter in the counties of Longford and Cavan; but hope the differences between them . . will hinder their conjunction, and in case they should join or that Farralde should move Southward—beside the party attending Castlehaven—Sir Charles Coote will be in his rear who already is or speedily will be in the field." It was the *Northern* Irish who had chosen the Earl of Antrim as their general. [N. VIII., 5.]

THOMAS PARKES and others to the COMMISSIONERS OF THE GREAT SEAL.

1650, April 6. Hull.—Enclosing the names of those who had subscribed the Engagement there, and also those of those who had refused. *Signed. Seal.* [N. VIII., 6.]

Captain OWEN COX to Colonel POPHAM, one of the Generals at Sea.

1650, April 7. From aboard the *Recovery*, now before Humber.—Concerning the capture of some of the fishermen by Montrose's soldiers in Orkney, and his forces and designs. (Printed in Grey, iv. Appendix, No. 13, p. 30.) [N. VIII., 7.]

THOMAS FELSTEAD and WILLIAM BARTON to Colonel BARKSTEAD.

1650, April 11. Yarmouth.—Concerning Montrose and the capture of the fishermen mentioned in the last, who were discharged by him. (Printed in Grey, iv. Appendix, No. 14. p. 32.) *Signed.* [N. VIII., 8.]

The ESTATES OF HOLLAND AND WEST FRIEZELAND to the PARLIAMENT.

1650, [April 25–]May 5. The Hague.—Letter of credence to their Commissioner Gerard Schaep. (See *Commons' Journals*, vi. 422.) In *Dutch* with *English* translation. *Seal embossed.* [N. X., 50.]

GEORGE BADON, Mayor, and others to WILLIAM LENTHALL.

1650, April 26. Bridgewater.—(The effect appears from *Commons' Journals*, vi. 407.) *Signed. Seal.* [N. VIII., 9.]

The Estates of Holland and West Friezeland to William Lenthall.

1650, May [13-]23. The Hague.—Recommending to him their Commissioner Gerard Schaep. In *Dutch. Seal embossed.* [N. X., 51.]

Richard Hutchinson and William Greenhill, treasurers for sick and maimed soldiers, to William Lenthall.

1650, May 13.—Beseeching that either money might be appointed to satisfy the post or that others be appointed in their stead. " Some threaten us that if they be hanged at our doors or shot to death, they will try whether we be pistol-proof or no." 10,000*l.* more will pay all that are listed. (See *Commons' Journals,* vi. 413.) *Signed. Seal.* [N. VIII., 10.]

William Atwood, treasurer of the Society of Merchant Adventurers of England at Hamburgh, to the Parliament.

1650, May 28.—Acknowledging their care for the welfare of the society by passing the ordinance confirming all their ancient charters and privileges, praising the services of the Resident, and beseeching them to admit the Society's petition which has been long before them for passing a bill formerly promised for the final confirmation of their ancient charters and privileges, especially since the Senate has hinted on complaint of breach of Privileges that the charters were granted by the late kings of England, implying thereby the necessity of having them confirmed by Act of Parliament. [N. XVIII., 148.]

William Lenthall to the Commissioners for Collecting 90,000*l.* *per mensem.*

1650, June 5 [4th according to the *Journals*].—(The purport sumciently appears from *Commons' Journals,* vi. 418.) *Draft.* [N. XII., 253.]

Colonel William Ryves to [Oliver Cromwell], Lord Lieutenant of Ireland.

1650, June 9. Cork.—Have sent to Nelson his commission as Lieutenant-Colonel of my regiment, who beyond my expectation gratefully accepts the same.

I desire your Excellency to hasten over Captain Nicholls with his company or else to send me conditions with commission for my Captain-Lieutenant John Payne to fetch me a new Company in his stead. " My Lord Deputy hearing an alarm of the enemy's being together in Connaught ready to advance hath sent for my Lord of Broghill to draw back out of Kerry, who . . was likely to finish his work there by this day. Ormonde and Inchiquin were on Thursday night last with about 4,000 men at Ennis . . . as intending to advance into Munster as is thought. By which appears their French voyage is not yet intended, unless Montrose's defeat hasten it. My Lord Deputy is about Catherlough, Duncannon, and Waterford with the army at present, from whence there is no news only that all is well . . and in a prosperous way. The Tory party in the West since the hanging of the titulary Bishop of Ross hath lost their courage and by the Lord of Broghill's march is dissolved." [N. VIII., 11.]

Lieutenant-Colonel John Nelsonn to [Oliver Cromwell] Lord Lieutenant of Ireland.

1650, June 9. Cork.—"My Lord of Bro[g]hill according to your Excellency's commands after the surrender of Kilmallock—which place my Lord Deputy committed to my care—advanced to Kilborlane Castle which I was before with 200 men and upon articles to surrender which was concluded upon his Lordship's appearing. The next day he advanced for Kerry and the Lord of Hosts hath been with him as your Excellency may perceive by the enclosed. My Lord Deputy being now before Carlow hath thought it conveighnient to recall my Lord of Bro[g]hill that there may be a conjunction of his party and the army, only leaving 6 companies of foot and a troop of horse with me in Kilmallock and 5 troops of horse and 3 of dragoons with Colonel Ingoldsby in the County of Limerick. The enemy are endeavouring to embody and Ormonde and Inchiquin were this week and [at] Limerick and very active endeavouring to garrison that place which as yet is not effected. The sickness which 30 men in a night died of before I came to Kilmallock the Lord hath so mercifully appeased for us that there hath not died 10 this 10 days, which manifesteth Him to be a wonderworking God in garrison and field. We may stand still and see everywhere the salvation of God. My Lord, it shall ever be my earnest desires at the throne of Grace that as you are honoured you may be humbled and every way fitted to be the Lord's instrument to the end for His own glory, that His love may be shed abroad in your heart making you all glorious within."

Enclosed:

Lord Broghill to Lieutenant-Colonel Nelsonn.

[1650], June 4. On our march to Castlemaine.—" We had by the blessing of the Lord brought our affairs in this county to very hopeful progress and had, I make no doubt, to a good issue, if you know what had not been sent to me. We have almost all the towns and castles in this County and every day a Barony comes in. We have taken two ships, one of my Lord Inchiquin's laden with iron which some resolute troopers swam after with their swords in their mouths and hands when she was under sail, and took her." *Seal.* [N. VIII., 12.]

The Council of State.

1650, June 10.—Order reporting to the Parliament concerning additional forces raised. (Abstracted in *State Papers, Domestic*, p. 197.) [N. XVI.. 40.]

The Council of State.

1650, June 12.—Order reporting to the Parliament concerning the Northern Expedition. (Printed in *Commons' Journals*, vi. 424.) [N. XVI., 41.]

Gerard Schaep, Commissioner of the Estates of Holland and West Friezeland, to the Parliament.

1650, June 14.—In *French* with *English* translation. (The last printed in Thurloe, *State Papers*, i. 133, where it is misdated January.) [N. XVIII., 108.]

The Council of State.

1650, June 17,—Order reporting the draft answer to Mynheer Schaep. (See *Commons' Journals,* vi. 424.) [N. XVIII., 70.]

William Lenthall to Gerard Schaep.

1650, June 18.—Reply in the name of the Parliament. (Printed in Thurloe, *State Papers,* i. 133, and in *Commons' Journals,* vi. 425.) [N. XVIII., 109.]

Robert Castell and others to William Lenthall.

1650, June 21. Cambridge.—Enclosing a return of the rents reserved and payable to the Colleges and other places exempted from the monthly assessment within that county according to the Speaker's letters of April 1, 1650. (See *Commons' Journals,* vi..390.) *Signed. Seal.* [N. VIII., 13.]

Lord Burghley, president of the Parliament of Scotland, to Thomas Lord Fairfax or other the Commander-in-Chief of the English forces.

1650, June 22. Edinburgh.—"The Estates of Parliament of this kingdom having intelligence of the marching of your forces towards their borders and being certainly informed that the English ships have searched diverse and seized upon some of the ships with the persons and goods therein belonging to this kingdom, and considering the large Treaty, which requireth a previous remonstrating of wrongs and seeking redress and giving of three months' warning before denouncing of war, which is also agreeable to the Law of God and practice of nations and conducible to prevent many dangerous consequences, they have written to Mr. William Lenthall Esq. Speaker of the House of Commons, and have thought fit to show unto your Lordship that they acknowledge on their parts their obligation and declare their resolution to observe that rule of remonstrating first the breaches of peace, of craving just reparation, of using all fair means and giving of preceding warning of three months' before any engagement of these kingdoms in war. And they desire to know whether your Lordship and those under your command do acknowledge yourselves obliged, or by your answer will oblige yourselves and declare your resolutions to observe the foresaid order upon your part to us, as also that your Lordship would plainly declare unto us, whether your marching be for defence or offence and whether with intention for keeping only within the borders of England or for coming within ours. Having thus cleared their intentions they desire to be cleared of yours by a speedy return to this letter with this express, being persuaded that God's justice will pursue whatsoever party of either nation that shall unjustly and unnecessarily invade the other kingdom." (See *Commons' Journals,* vi. 435.) *Copy.* (N. XII., 254.]

The Same to all Officers and Magistrates.

1650, June 22. Edinburgh.—Pass to Colonel James Grey. *Copy.*

And

G. Fenwicke to all Postmasters.

1650, June 24.—Warrant to supply Colonel Grey with two posthorses and a guide to Newcastle. *Copy.*

And
P. HOBSON to all POSTMASTERS.

1650, June 25.—Warrant to supply Colonel Grey as before to the Parliament of England. *Copy.* (See *Commons' Journals*, vi. 434.) [N. XVI., 42.]

THOMAS [LORD] FAIRFAX to WILLIAM LENTHALL.

1650, June 26.—Concerning the articles on the surrender of Pendennis Castle. *Seal. Enclosed:*

Report by HENRY WHALLEY and others.

1648[-9], March 16.—To the effect that on the confirmation of the articles the persons comprised in them were by virtue of article 10 to be freed from sequestration. *Signed.* [N. VIII., 45.]

Lieutenant-Colonel JOHN LILBURNE to the PARLIAMENT.

[1650, June 27.]—Petition stating that the security granted to him in March last had become totally invalid before half of the 3,000*l.* due to him was paid, the commissioners for compounding having by their order of May 28th granted the said lands to Lady Gibb for her jointure for her life, discharged from sequestration, and praying for payment of the said money. (See *Commons' Journals*, vi. 433, 441.) *Annexed* is a copy of the said order, and an account showing the amount claimed by Colonel Lilburne as still due. [N. XXII., 160.]

The COMMITTEE OF THE NAVY.

1650, July 5.—Resolutions concerning the Treasureship of the Navy. (Printed in *Commons' Journals*, vi. 440.) [N. XVI., 43.]

The COMMITTEE TO WHICH LIEUTENANT-COLONEL JOHN LILBURNE'S BUSINESS WAS REFERRED.

1650, July 6.—Resolutions. (Printed in *Commons' Journals*, vi. 441.) [N. XVI., 44.]

The COUNCIL OF STATE to Colonel EDWARD POPHAM and Colonel ROBERT BLAKE.

1650, July 13.—Instructions. After reciting at great length the events which had occurred at Lisbon and the negotiations with the King of Portugal they grant letters of reprisal against all the ships and goods belonging to the said King or his subjects and require the generals of the fleet in execution of the said letters of marque and reprisal to seize arrest surprise and take all such ships with the goods therein and to send the same into the custody of the collectors of prize goods that they may be valued judged and condemned in the Court of Admiralty for satisfying the loss and damages sustained by the Commonwealth in the premises in the said port and territories of the said King and of the charges incurred by the Commonwealth by reason of the neglect of justice of that King and the other defaults before mentioned, provided that any perishable goods or any ships ordnance or ammunition that may be necessary for the special service of the Commonwealth shall be inventoried and the former sold and the latter used for such service. And for that the Parliament were in probable expectation and would have been in a position to recover their said ships from Prince Rupert did not the said King still shelter him with the protection of his port, and for that the said King notwithstanding the often representations to him of the manifest iniquity and injustice on Rupert's part and the right and justice on the Parliament's part, " and notwithstanding the breaches of peace made by Rupert in the same port even to the infringement of the territory and dishonour of that King himself does yet persist to protect and defend Rupert in the same port and is the sole obstacle and impediment that the said ships are not again reseised and taken by the generals of the Parliament's fleet and doth it purposely to the end the General might not reseise them inasmuch as that King hath made it his desire to the general to remove afar off from the entrance of the port for that very end that Rupert might have hopes to get away, you shall therefore—the law of nations permitting it till that King remove the obstacle—continue to block up the said King's port and make stop of anything advantageous to him or tending to his commodity *retentionis causa* for caution only till he abstain from further protecting Rupert in that unjust detaining of those ships in his port and do *cavere per obsides* to hinder the Parliament no more in that their just design." (See *Commons' Journals*, vi. 525. *Copy*. [N. XVII., 95.]

Viscount Newburgh to [his mother-in-law].

1650, July 14.—Concerning the state of affairs in Scotland and the King's approaching coronation, and asking that robes may be sent him for it. (Printed in Grey, iv. Appendix, No. 41, p. 69.) (See *Commons' Journals*, vi. 448.) [N. VIII., 142.]

John Rushworth to William Lenthall.

1650, August 15 [*sic* probably July]. Newcastle.—Concerning the march of the army to Scotland, supplies, and their prospects in Scotland. They will either fight suddenly, or retire, "till their two generals, Captain Hunger and Captain Cold, do overcome us." (Printed in Grey, iv. Appendix, No. 15, p. 33.) *Signed. Seal.* [N. VIII., 15.]

The Committee for the Northern Association.

1650, July 25.—Report concerning Major George Gill and others. (Printed in *Commons' Journals*, vi. 450.) [N. XVI., 45.]

The Council of State.

1650, July 26.—Order reporting concerning Lord Newburg[h]. (Printed in *Commons' Journals*, vi. 448.) [N. XVI., 46.]

The Council of State.

1650, July 30.—Order concerning the garrisons of Newcastle, &c. (Printed in *Commons' Journals*, vi. 454.) [N. XVI., 47.]

The Marquess of Ormonde to the Popish Clergy at Jamestown.

1650, August 2. Roscommon.—"We received yours of the 24th of July on the 1st . . . and with much grief acknowledge that this nation is brought into a sad condition, and that by such means as when it shall be known abroad, and by story delivered to posterity will indeed be thought a fable ; for it will seem incredible, that any nation should so madly affect, and violently pursue the ways leading to their own destruction, as this people will appear to have done, and that, after the certain ruin they were running into was evidently and frequently discovered unto them, that in all times and upon all occasions have had power to persuade and compel them to whatever they thought fit. And it shall be less credible when it shall be declared . . . . . that the temporal spiritual and eternal safety even of those that had this power, and have been thus forewarned, did consist in making use of it to reclaim the people, and direct them into the ways of preservation . . . It cannot be denied but the disobedience we have met with, which at large we declared unto many of you, who with divers of the nobility and gentry were assembled at Loghreogh in April last, were the certain ready ways to the destruction of this nation, as by our letters of the first of May to that Assembly was made apparent.

Ancient and late experience hath made it evident, what power those of your function have had to draw the people of this nation to what they thought fit. Whether your Lordships have been convinced, that the obedience which we desired should be given to his Majesty's authority in us according to the Articles of Peace, was the way to preserve the nation we know not, or whether your Lordships have made use of all the means at other times and upon other occasions exercised by you to procure this necessary obedience we shall not now determine. Sure we are, that since the said Assembly not only Limerick hath persisted in the disobedience it was then in, and aggravated the same by several affronts since fixed upon the King's authority, but Galway hath been seduced into the like disobedience. For want of due compliance from these places, but principally from Limerick, it hath been impossible for us to raise or employ an army against the Rebels."

(The next clause is printed almost *verbatim* in Carte, *Life of Ormonde*, ii. 125, beginning " To attempt this," ending " have effected the work.")

" For want of such an army, which, with God's assistance might have been long since raised, if Limerick had obeyed our orders, the Rebels have without any considerable assistance from abroad taken Clonmel, Ticroghan, and Catherlagh, and reduced Waterford and Duncannon to great, and we fear, irrecoverable distress. The loss of these places and the want of any visible power to protect them, hath undoubtedly induced many to contribute their substance and personal assistance to the Rebels, from which whether they might have been withheld by your censures we know not, but have not heard of any such issued against them.

And lastly for want of such an army the Rebels have taken to themselves the contributions which might have considerably assisted to support an army and preserve this kingdom. If therefore the end of your consultation at Jamestoun be to acquit your conscience in the eyes of God, the amendment of all errors, and the recovery of this afflicted people, as by your Lordships giving us notice of your meeting is professed, we have endeavoured briefly to show, that the spring of our past losses and approaching ruin arises from disobedience, and it will not be hard to show, that the spring of the disobedience arises from the forgeries invented, the calumnies spread abroad against the Government, and the incitements of the people to rebellion by very many of the clergy. That these are errors frequently practised and fit for amendment is no more to be doubted, than without they be amended the affliction of the people will continue, and, is to be feared, end in their utter ruin and destruction, which if prevented by what your consultation will produce, the happy effect of your meeting will be acknowledged, without questioning the authority by which you meet." *Transcript* in Nalson's hand. [N. XII., 255.]

Captain ROBERT WYARD to the COUNCIL OF STATE.

1650, August 5. Yarmouth.—According to the command from the Rear-Admiral I lay at North Seas with the fishermen till the 23rd of July, and then went to the mouth of Humber to ballast and water. The merchants of Hull sent me letters that there were ready ten ships, six for London and four for Rotterdam. The London ships had stayed above ten or fourteen days for convoy. They prevailed with me to convoy them all into the Roads and to see the Rotterdam ships safe into harbour. I consented knowing the great necessity they had for a convoy, and that they had sent many letters to many of the ports on the North coast to be sent to the Rear-Admiral desiring one, which had not reached him, so they promising to acquaint your Honours I set sail out of Humber the 28th of July and gaining the Roads the 30th, where I left the London fleet to Captain Jones, "and my convoy setting sail upon the last of July with a bare wind contrary to my mind about 8 of the clock at night I came up with the headmost of them, whom I found to be very much in drink, and out of a bravado he fired three guns, the which I think it was the means to bring misery on us all, for before 10 of the clock there came up with us six great frigates. The Admiral had 26 guns, the Vice-Admiral 22, the Rear-Admiral 20, the rest 18 and 16. The least had too many guns for one poor ship to encounter with all at once and some of them, as I hear at Yarmouth by them that hath been taken by them very lately, that they have 250 men apiece. They coming up very fast with us, we immediately fitted our ship, little thinking they had been all frigates. I hailing the headmost, the which was the Admiral, he said he was of Amsterdam, and commanding him to come to leeward he would not, but said 'All friends,' so I fired at him. I had no sooner fired but he cried amain 'For King Charles the Second, you Roundheaded dogs.' I told him, our cause was good, I did scorn their words, for I had powder and shot enough for them. With that he fired a volley of small shot at me, I being upon the poop, and a whole broadside, and so did the other five frigates, they continuing so all night firing broadside for broadside that we were almost tired out. They came up with us so fast that our guns was so hot, I was afraid they would have split, we plied them so fast, but after they had tasted three or four broadsides apiece from us we bringing most of them by the lee in the night it was some ease to us for to refresh us. The fight began before ten in the night, the night being very light and the sea as smooth as the Thames all the time of the fight which continued till 12 o'clock at noon. I hoped to have had relief, knowing there was two ships in the Roads, but none came to our assistance. I spent 16 barrels of powder and 700 shot, beside musket shot, and barr shot in cases. I received 12 great shot in my mainmast, I have not one whole mast but my bowsprit, and I am sure in the hull, masts, sails, and rigging I have received about 500 great shot, so that 300*l.* will not make the ship good again besides powder and shot . . spent. The ship is so torn that, if it had not pleased God to send us fair weather, I had lost all my masts, for I had scarce two good shrouds on a side to hold them . . . Although the ship be mightily torn and battered I have received no hurt, but only two of my men. One is dead since we came to Yarmouth, but I hope the other will recover suddenly. I had eight men burnt with powder by a shot from the enemy. I hope in a short time they will be recovered . . . We were so torn in the fight that we had not one sail to help us but our foresail. All was shot down, yet it pleased God that I kept the ship all the time under command, and I kept my convoy 12 hours before I lost them, and they seeing me so torn, one of them struck, and the other being entered made no resistance, they having but 11 guns betwixt them, and after they were surprised the six frigates came up with me again thinking to have sunk me, the Admiral having 18 guns on the side next to us, they all gave us twelve broadsides before they left us, but we being ready to receive them we galled them so, that if any one ship had but come to have relieved us we had taken the best of them, for they were so torn that they lay three hours by the lee without any sail, four of the best of them. It will be the next spring[tide] before I can get my ship ready or shall have water out of the haven." (See *Commons' Journals*, vi. 454.) *Copy.* [N. XII., 256.]

Colonel ROBERT DUCKENFIELD to WILLIAM LENTHALL.

1650, August 11.—Desiring a reprieve for Major Cheadle condemned for the supposed murder of Colonel Buckley. (Printed in Grey, iii. Appendix, No. 12, p. 22.) (See *Commons' Journals*, vi. 455.) *Signed. Seal.* [N. VIII., 14.]

General DAVID LESLIE to OLIVER CROMWELL.

[1650, August —.] — Forwarding the Declaration of the General Assembly. *Enclosed :*

The said DECLARATION with Note by A. HENDERSON.

1650, August 13.— (Printed in *State Papers, Domestic*, p. 325.) *Copies.* [N. XII., 257.]

ROBERT BLAKE and EDWARD POPHAM, Generals at Sea, to [the COUNCIL OF STATE].

1650, August 15. From aboard the *Resolution*, riding off the Port of Lisbon.—" Wee suppose your Honours long ere this are acquainted by CaptaineBadiloe from Cadiz, howe in his way thither hee mett with some French men of warr and suncke one of them, the rest escaping out of their hands. Since that it hath pleased God in this place to exercise us with various and mixt providences, sustaining us with apparent evidences of his good will in our extreame straightes, and yet withoulding from us the fruit of the desire of our soules in our greatest hopes. The truth hereof, your Honours will perceive by the ensuing relation. The 26 of July betweene 9 and 10 in the morning, Prince Rupert after long preparation and much noise came forth of the Bay of Weyres with twenty-six ships, eighteen carvells, the wind at E.S.E., our fleet being then at anchor neere Cascais Roade. We forthwith weighed and stood of with them, they keeping the wind of us. Having gott a reasonable bearth from the shoare, wee haled our forsailes to the mast with our fleet which then consisted of ten saile beside the Brazeele ships, our Cales squadron being not returned, the *Hercules* and *Assurance* off at sea, the *Providence* at Virgo for water, and the *Constant Warwicke* on her way from England. The enemy still kept the wind, the French admirall with foure fireships being the headmost of their fleet, and a sterne of him about a mile, the *Reformation*. A little after, the wind coming to the South, wee filled our sailes, tackt and gott the wind which the enemy perceiving tackt likewise. Then wee bore away lardge uppon the Frenchman being betwixt us and the *Reformation,* and exchangd some shott with him, as alsoc did the *Phenix.* But as fast as wee bore uppon him hee bore away large in toward the harbour, and Rupert likewise—his mizen alway haled up—. Wee followed them till wee came into tenn fathome water neere the South Hetchoopes, and then it drawing toward night, having a lea shoare, and a leeward tide, and being in the indraught of the harbour, wee submitted to the present necessity, and stood off, the enemy coming to anchor betweene the two castles. That night was little wind and thicke. The next morning, the wind being easterly and but little, they gott under the forts of Cascais where the wind being as it was wee could not possibly fall on them, but kept faire in sight of them, that day being for the most part calme. In the evening wee gave order to the *Assurance* being then come to us to alarume them in the night thereby to keepe Prince Rupert in apprehension that hee might not steale away. The next morning being foggy and little wind wee espied the enemy under saile turning to and againe under the castles, and bore in soe neere that the castles shott at our frigot, being then alsoe calme. A little after, the wind at South, and very little, and the enemy seeming to make toward us, wee haled upp our sayles, till they had placed themselves in the wind of us thereby to drawe them to ingage. But they had noe minde to come to us, though wee lay many howres for them, nor could wee gett to them, they keeping the advantage of the shoare. At length about sixe in the evening wee discovered seven or eight saile in the offing, which the enemy likewise perceiving tackt and stood in. Wee not knowing whoe they were plyed toward them, and at breake a day they fell in among us, being our Cadiz squadron, which came very seasonably for us not having above fowre dayes drincke left in our fleet. After wee had releived our shipps with a little licour wee stood in toward them in Cascais Roade but could doe nothing, the wind being easterly; and at our approach, they running from us in toward the Barr, soe that wee lay short that night having resolved the next morning by breake of the day, if possible, to fall in among them. But when wee sought them they were all gone in to the great greife of our hearts, whoe longed for nothing more if it had stood with the will of God then to put an end to that great trouble and charge of the Comonwealth. This is a true and faithfull relation of what past in the whole bussiness. A fewe dayes after uppon the 4th instant, came to us the *Constant Warwicke* by which wee received your Honours' letters with further instructions for carrying on the service. In one of them wee find that your Honours have bin informed of the going in of a rich caracke from the East India after the seizure of the Brazeele ships and are pleased to note it as an omission of duty in us, whereat wee cannot but exceeding wonder seeing it was nine dayes before wee made a stop of the saide ships, and when shee past in wee knewe not whence shee was but conjectured her to bee a shipp come from Port a Port, neither had wee then any colour of authority to seize her,—having not received the King's finall answer—, nor if wee would, could wee possibly have done it, shee being to the windward, and keeping in close under the shoare, under comand of their forts. As to that which your Honours are pleased to intimate of sending some ships to lye off the Ilands for intercepting the Brazeele fleet, wee have debated it at a Councell of Warr and upon consideracion of many inconveniences which might arise from the seperacion of the fleet, the unfitnes of the Brazeele ships to stay out, which wee have therfore sent home, the unprovidednes of our owne, especially of drincke in supply wherof wee have mett with such hazardous difficulties, it was the resolution of the whole Councell that wee were in noe capacity for such a service. Touching the merchants mencioned in your Honours' letter, wee have in obedience to your comands used our utmost endevors to gett them of by sending a trumpett, and employing a captaine ashoare with proffers of exchange for them, and divers others in prison, but they utterly refused at first to exchange any merchants and wee have sithence prest it againe but have not yet received any concluding answere from them, though wee have wayted five dayes, neither doe wee thincke it safe in expectation thereof to delay the sending away these ships least wee bee brought into some distresse for want of drincke which is soe hard to bee gott, or by change of weather, which they are noe way fitted to endure in this place." *Signed.* [N. VIII., 17.]

RICHARD LITTLETON and EDWARD BULSTRODE.

1650, August 23. Bala.—Certifying concerning Major Cheadle. (Printed in Grey, iii. Appendix, No. 13, p. 18.) (See letter of August 11th and *Commons' Journals*, vi. 464.) *Signed. Seals.* [N. VIII., 18.]

The EARL OF NORTHAMPTON to the PARLIAMENT.

[1650, August 23.]—Petition praying that the composition formerly made may stand. (See *Commons' Journals*, vi. 458.) *Signed.* [N. XVI., 48.]

The COMMISSIONERS AT GOLDSMITHS' HALL.

[1650, August 23.]—Report on the Earl of Northampton's case. (Printed in *Commons' Journals*, vi. 458.) [N. XVI., 51.] *Annexed* are two copies of the former Report in the case, giving a lengthy narrative of all the proceedings therein. [N. XVI., 49, 52.]

JOHN RUSHWORTH to WILLIAM LENTHALL.

1650, August 27. Musselburgh. — Concerning supplies, and the Scotch army. (Printed in Grey, iv. Appendix, No. 16, p. 34.) (See *Commons' Journals*, vi. 461.) *Seal.* [N. VIII., 16.]

The PARLIAMENT.

1650, August 28.—Act and declaration concerning a Pamphlet printed at Edinburgh called "*a Declaration by the King's Majesty to his Subjects.*" (Printed in *King's Pamphlets*, Single Sheets, 669, f. 15, No. 52.) (See *Commons' Journals*, vi. 460.) *Draft.* [N. XVI., 161.]

The State of the TREASURY AT GOLDSMITHS' HALL.

1650, August 29.—(A more detailed account than that printed in *Commons' Journals*, vi. 461, giving the names of the particular persons entitled in the aggregate to 28,553*l.* 5*s.* 3*d.*) [N. XVI., 50.]

The PARLIAMENT.

1650, August 30.—Declaration of the reasons for appointing the 1st and 15th of September as Thanksgiving Days for the victories in Ireland.

(Printed in *King's Pamphlets*, Single Sheets, 660, f. 15, No. 53.) [N. XVI., 53.]

The Committee for Ways and Means.

[1650, September 3.]—Report. (Printed in *Commons' Journals*, vi. 461.) [N. XVI., 55.]

Oliver Cromwell to William Lenthall.

1650, September 4. Dunbar.—Announcing his victory. (Printed in Carlyle, No. 140. In some parts much faded and in others torn and illegible.) *Signed.* [N. VIII., 19.]

Richard Kift.

[1650], September 5.—Describing how he had intercepted a letter from Lord Willoughby from the Barbados to his wife. (The letter is probably the following.) [N. XIII., 27.]

[Lord Willoughby] to [Lady Willoughby].

[1650, ——. Barbados.]—A long letter mostly concerning his private and family affairs, and declaring his resolution to defend the island against the fleet of the Commonwealth. (Printed in Cary, *Memorials of the Civil War*, ii. 312.) *Torn and in parts illegible.* (Probably that referred to in the last.) [N. VIII., 141.]

The Council of State.

[1650, September 6.]—Report concerning the late King's children. (Printed in *Commons' Journals*, vi. 465.) [N. XVI., 56.]

Doctor Stewart, Dean of St. Paul's, to Sir Edward Nicholas.

1650, September 12-22. Louvre.—"From Jersey we are now come to Paris where we have been this fortnight. We are told the Duke shall [have] 600 pistoles from the State of France to carry him towards Holland. I believe that the Duke of York will make some stay at Bruxelles to advise with his father's honest councillors. Lord Hopton, Sir Edward Herbert, Mr. Windham, 'tis hoped, will be sent for, and no doubt Secretary Nicholas will be entreated to come thither; the journey is not great nor chargeable, and therefore I should entreat" him " not to fail, when he is sent for. The Duke . . . is very right set and you will see a change in his servants shortly. Queen of England will do little with him." *Extract.* [N. XII., 258, No. 1.]

William Basil to William Lenthall.

1650, September 13. Kilkenny.—"Within a few days after the surrender of Duncannon my Lord Deputy marched with his army into the county of Wicklow, where after part of our army had scoured the woods his Lordship divided his army, part whereof he sent back under the command of Sir Hardress Waller toward Limerick for the besieging thereof, and with the residue marched toward Tecrohan with intent there to victual, and so to march to Athlone, but our forces in the North having taken in Charlemont and advancing southward his Lordship sent an addition of forces toward Limerick and with the rest joined with the Northern forces and is marched to Athlone, whereof I doubt not but you will have—with God's blessing—a speedy and good account. The priests of Galway have lately interdicted Ormonde from meddling with any of the affairs of the Irish. Munster, Leinster, and Ulster are now wholly in our possession, only much infested with Tories, and I doubt not but we shall have speedy footing in Connaught." (See *Commons' Journals*, vi. 473.) *Seal.* [N. VIII., 20.]

HENRY HOPKINS, Warden of the Fleet Prison, to all MAYORS, &c. whom it may concern.

1650, September 14.—Warrant stating that whereas Richard Hairbread, a prisoner in the Fleet, had obtained liberty to go abroad on his urgent occasions till October 30th he, Henry Hopkins, had appointed three of his servants to attend him as his keepers and requiring all persons officers and lovers of justice to assist the said keepers in the execution of their duty. (See *Commons' Journals*, vi. 487.) [N. XVI., 54.)

The COUNCIL OF STATE.

1650, September 17.—Order reporting the letter to be sent to the King of France, and also desiring their approval of the list of the Winter Guard. (See *Commons' Journals*, vi. 469.) *Annexed:*

The said Letter.

After stating the care of the Commonwealth to preserve a right understanding between themselves and all other States and in particular with France, and their attention that due and speedy justice should be done between those of their nation and France, complaining that similar justice had not been done by France, as the debts contracted for their service by their Minister at Constantinople and due to English people had not been paid, and that English merchant ships and goods had been taken by the French in the Levant and adjudged prize and that they could get no redress, and declaring that they had therefore given letters of marque to persons interested in the said debts and losses, and had also given orders to all their commanders at sea to seize all French ships to be kept in deposit till the people of this nation receive justice from France ; but, before proceeding to adjudication they had thought it right to make one more demand for justice. [N. XVII., 15, 14.]

OLIVER CROMWELL to WILLIAM LENTHALL.

1650, October 2. Edinburgh.—" Colonel George Gill had a regiment under my command. I knew nor heard of anything but what was honest and Christian in the man, but if the Parliament was pleased to pass a sentence upon him and I commanded to discharge him from his regiment I did yield present obedience to your commands as became me ; since that time the man hath written unto me to desire I would mediate to some friends that he might have liberty to make his innocency to appear. I persuading myself that nothing would be more welcome to the Parliament than to hear and redress innocency which is so confidently stood upon by this man do in all humility desire he may be heard, and if it be found impudency in him he may have his punishment doubled. It is not my importunity in the person occasions this boldness, but because I durst not deny my [con]science. Craving pardon for this trouble I rest." *Signed. Seal. Enclosed:*

The Petition of the said GEORGE GILL.

Alleging that the 600*l.* which he was accused of having doubled (See Report from the Committee of the Northern Association in *Commons' Journals*, vi. 450.) were not arrears but money disbursed by him for the service of the Parliament which he was therefore entitled to double, but that he had in fact doubled only 400*l.* thereof and praying for a copy of the charges against him and a speedy examination of the matter. (See *Commons' Journals*, vi. 495.) *Signed.* [N. VIII., 21.]

ROBERT GUBBES, Mayor, to the COUNCIL OF STATE.

1650, October 11. Plymouth.—Enclosing the examination of Edward Witheridge late master of the *Defence* of London, who came into this harbour yesterday by contrary winds in a vessel of Lubeck from Lisbon. *Signed. Seal. Enclosed :*

The said Examination.

Same date.—Giving an account of Blake's victory over the Brazil fleet. (See *Commons' Journals*, vi. 483.) [N. XVII., 97.]

Doctor STEWART, Dean of St. Paul's, to SIR EDWARD NICHOLAS.

1650, October [12–]22.—(Printed in *State Papers, Domestic*, p. 384, and in Cary, *Memorials of the Civil War*, ii. 229.) *Extract.* [N. XII., 258, No. 2.]

THOMAS [LORD] GREY to the LORD PRESIDENT OF THE COUNCIL OF STATE.

1650, October 13. Grafton.—Concerning the musters, and the ministers' neglect of the last Thanksgiving Day. (Printed in Grey, iv. Appendix, No. 8, p. 17.) (See *Commons' Journals*, vi. 484.) *Signed. Seal.* [N. VIII., 22.]

Admiral ROBERT BLAKE to [the COUNCIL OF STATE].

1650, October 14. From aboard the *George* in the bay of Cadiz.— " From the last account which Colonel Popham and myselfe gave your Honours by the Brazeele ships sent for England till the seperation of our fleet, I suppose your Honours doe understand from him, what endeavours have bin used by us in your service, and with what successe. And that on the third of September wee were necessitated for want of liquor to part, the *Resolution, Andrewe, Happy Entrance* and five others to goe for Cadiz or Virgoe for a supply ; myselfe on the *George*, with the *Leopard, Bona Venture* and seaven others to keepe plying off the Rock. Powre dayes after our parting, being Saturday, about eleaven in the morning wee discovered a part of Rupert's and the Portugall fleet in a mist, and about fowre in the afternoone, wee found our selves—the mist clearing upp— very neare the whole fleet, consisting of of thirty-six sayle. I had onely with mee the *Phenix* and *Expedition*, having left the rest in the fogg. By God's good providence, the enemies' fleet was all to leiward of us, soe wee keeping the wind made toward them being resolved to encounter Prince Rupert, whoe was the headmost of the fleet. Coming within reach, wee gave him a broadside, soe did the two frigatts, which the Lord was pleased soe to direct, that his foretopmast was shott off by the capp. Wheruppon hee bore upp into the middest of the fleet and the thicke mist taking them againe out of our sight, wee stood off to secke the rest of our squadron, which wee mett with the next day. The Saturday following, early in the morning, wee discovered the Brazeele fleet bound for Lisbone, consisting of twenty-three sayle. I forthwith made towards the admirall, whoe being to nimble, I fell on the reredmirall, being a shipp of noe lesse force, and had above three howres dispute with him, it blowing very much wind, soe that wee could not use our loure tire. At length after losse of many of his men, hee yeilded, wee being soe neere that at going off, the head of our shipp receeved a cracke. Wee tooke in all seaven prizes having in them above four thousand chests of sugar, and neere four hundred prisoners. The vizeadmirall was burnt, being first boarded by the *Assurance*, whoo saved most of the remainder of his men. The wind being northerly and very neere spent, I bore upp for this pl[ace] whither by God's blessing we came all in safety. Wee were welcomed with much honour by the Admirall of Spayne whoo was at an anchor in the roade. After my coming, I sent away advice to Malaga to the fleet there to take the benefitt of a convoy, which many have followed. Three of the prizes being not fitt to goe to sea, I have unladen and removed their lading into other ships. The other fower I have sent home under comand of Captaine Bodiloe together with the *George, Assurance, Hercules* and the ship *Marchant*. The *Leopard* staies behind to repaire the masts which are very defective, but I hope in a fewe dayes shee wilbee made fitt to goe for England. I doe intend God willing in the *Bona Venture*, with the *Phenix, Elizabeth, Expedition, Constant Warwicke*, and the *John* to continue out yet a moneth or longer to doe the comon-wealth all the service I can hereabout, or elswhere as the providence of God shall direct mee." (See *Commons' Journals*, vi. 491.) *Signed.* [N. XVII., 96.]

RENÉ AUGIER.

1650, October 14–24.—Narrative and Certificate of the transactions with France. (Printed in *Commons' Journals*, vi. 494.)

And

The JUDGES OF THE ADMIRALTY COURT to the COUNCIL OF STATE.

1650, October 15.—Report thereon. We are of opinion that, as the fact is therein stated, the spoils therein mentioned of English ships and goods both at sea and in ports by French ships and the approbation thereof in the French Courts, as also the seizure of the persons goods and books of account of the English in their towns have been by the said Resident sufficiently represented to the proper French authorities as contrary to treaties and the free course of commerce, and that the said Resident having often demanded justice in vain represented to the proper authorities that unless within forty days reparation was fully made the Parliament would proceed to reprisals, but no reparation was made, that therefore justice has been sufficiently demanded, that no further demand is necessary, that the Parliament may justly proceed to reprisals and that it is necessary immediately to proceed to adjudication upon the ships and goods already seized. *Copies.* [N. XVII., 16.]

The CONSULS, PROCONSULS and SENATORS OF LUBECK to the PARLIAMENT.

1650, October 18.—Letter of Credence to John Grahe, sent to ask the release of the *Saint Matthias* and *Young Tobias* two Lübeck ships, which had been taken by English ships and carried into London, and also demanding the release of the said ships. In *Latin. Seal Embossed. Endorsed* "Not opened &c. till March 21 168⅔." [N. X., 94.]

The COMMISSIONERS OF YORKSHIRE to the COUNCIL OF STATE.

1650, October 18.—Concerning Mr. Richard Hairbread, a prisoner in the Fleet, who had received a pass from the Warden, and his keepers John Browne and Thomas Bridges (See *Commons' Journals*, vi. 487), requesting that three or four foot companies belonging to Colonel Alured's regiment now quartered at Pocklington be disposed of being ready and desirous to march, and stating that they had ordered Captain Hugh Savile to march with his troop, which would complete their forces to 1,000 Horse and Dragoons, besides officers. *Copy.* [N. XII., 259.]

[GEORGE DOWNING ?] to ———.

1650, October 18. Edinburgh.—Describing the march of the army to Glasgow and back, and the different factions into which the Kings' party was divided. (Printed in Grey, iv. Appendix, No. 19, p. 47.) [N. VIII., 23a.]

Doctor STEWART, Dean of St. Paul's, to SIR EDWARD NICHOLAS.

1650, October 19-29.—(Printed in *State Papers, Domestic*, p. 394, and in Cary, *Memorials of the Civil War*, ii. 230.) *Extract.* [N. XII., 258, No. 3.]

GEORGE DOWNING to WILLIAM ROWE.

1650, October 21. Edinburgh.—Objecting to the Duke of Gloucester being sent to Heidelberg, and giving an account of the siege of Edinburgh Castle and of the state of affairs in Scotland. (Printed in Grey, iv. Appendix, No. 20, p. 51.) *Seal.* [N. VIII., 23.]

ANTHONY MILDMAY to WILLIAM LENTHALL.

1650, October 28. Carisbrook Castle.—On behalf of the servants of the late Princess Elizabeth. (Printed in Peck, *Desiderata Curiosa*, xi. 10.) *Signed. Enclosed:*

The Petition of the said servants. [N. VIII., 24.]

The COUNCIL OF TRADE.

[1650, October 30.] — Propositions concerning the Levant trade annexed to their Report to the Council of State. (Printed in *Commons' Journals*, vi. 489.) [N. XVI., 57.]

[Admiral ROBERT BLAKE] to the COUNCIL OF STATE.

1650, October 30. From aboard the *Leopard* in the Road of Malaga. —" The day after I had despatched away Captain Badiloe with the *George* and other ships for England which was the 15th instant the *Hopewell* keteh came to me at Cadiz, by which I received your Honours' letters, and in order to the directions therein for improving all endeavours for advance of the public service, having got the four frigates cleaned and some victuals into them I went aboard the *Phenix*, and being at sea four or five days off the Straits' mouth met with a French man of war, who after some dispute yielded upon quarter. There was in her 36 brass guns and 180 men, the Captain, Chevalier de Lalande, commander of a squadron, (*Chef d'escadron*) brother to him that was sunk by the *Adventure* frigate. I intended to have taken the ship along with me to sea, but was necessitated to leave her at Cadiz upon intelligence given me that Prince Rupert was abroad, and had attempted to seize some of the merchant men here. I intend—God willing—to pursue him as far as Providence shall direct, and should have given . . a more full account of affairs had time permitted. Being under sail I crave your Honours' pardon " . . *Signature torn off.* [N. XVII., 43.]

WALTER MONTAGU to WILLIAM LENTHALL.

1650, November 1. Pontoise.—Asking that the Parliament should repeal his sentence of banishment (See *Commons' Journals,* vi. 289) or at least grant him a pass to come to England for a few months. *Seal.* [N. VIII., 25.]

WILLIAM BASIL to WILLIAM LENTHALL.

1650, November 4. Kilkenny.—Describing Colonel Axtell's victory at Meleek Island. (Printed in *King's Pamphlets,* E. 618, No. 3.) [N. VIII., 26.]

The COMMITTEE FOR REMOVING OBSTRUCTIONS.

1650, November 4.—Order reporting to the Parliament concerning Lilburne's claims. (Printed in *Commons' Journals,* vi. 549.) [N. XVI., 59.]

PRINCE RUPERT to "all or any of the CAPTAINS OF HIS MAJESTY'S FLEET."

1650, November 5-15. Formentera.—" Since you lost my company, I have taken one prize worth securing; and by reason her main-mast is shot away and other very great defects I am forced to go with her to the nearest place to this. You are appointed by your instructions to carry your prizes into the Isle of Sardina (?) (words erased and illegible). To that place you are to send all your prizes, and when you shall come near it yourself to send me word, that I may return you orders what to do. If the wind shall come Northward I intend to put into Calaris (Cagliari) Bay in the isle of Sardina, where you are to touch and see if I am not gone. You may take notice that I came to this place yesterday night, and if you shall not be all together when you find this paper, let it stand for the rest to see whither I am gone." *Sign-Manual.* [N. I., 46.]

Doctor STEWART, Dean of St. Paul's, to SIR EDWARD NICHOLAS.

1650, November 5-15.—(Printed in *State Papers, Domestic,* p. 414, and in Cary, *Memorials of the Civil War,* ii. 230.) *Extract.* [N. XII., 258, No. 4.]

Admiral ROBERT BLAKE to the GOVERNOR OF CARTAGENA.

1650, November [5-]15. From aboard the *Leopard* in the Road of Cartagena.—"The occasion of my coming hither is, I suppose, made known to you already. That is in pursuit of some of our enemies, part of that fleet which was so long protected against us in the port of Lisbon, but, I hope, will find no such entertainment here. The many and free expressions of goodwill towards this fleet, which I have received elsewhere by special command of his Catholic Majesty do assure me rather of the contrary, and common justice do require no less as against notorious pirates and destroyers of all trade. It is of very high consequence to the Parliament of England, and may be of no small concernment to his Majesty to give this business a speedy and present dispatch, that being master of those ships which are come into this harbour, I may be at liberty to pursue and by God's blessing seize upon the remainder of their strength before they join themselves unto the French, which is likely to be their last refuge. My desire therefore is that you would be pleased to send your answer forthwith by this bearer Captain Moulton." *Copy.* [N. XVII., 44.]

Admiral ROBERT BLAKE to the KING OF SPAIN.

1650, November [7-]17. Bay of Cartagena.—" There being at present for ought I knowe noe publicke Minister for the Parlyament of England residing in Madrid I have taken the bolducs by this imediate addresse to give your Majestie to understand : That on Sunday last, part of the fleet under my command did chace five sayle of Prince Rupert's into the Bay of Cartagena. One of them destroyd himselfe by fire without the harbor. The other foure went in where I supposed I should not have mett with any difficultie in seizing of them, being made confident before at Cadiz, that your Majestie had sent order to all your ports, not to admitt any of Prince Rupert's fleet. But I found it otherwise, being at my going in twice shott at by the Castle and after visited by the Alcalde, whoe required mee not to offer any force unto the said ships then lying under proteccion of the Castle. I did accordingly forbeare out of respect to your Majestie's authority, yet with much indignation against those wicked men for the great outrage and mischeife they had a fewe dayes before comitted against divers English marchants' shipps, and that within your Majestie's ports of Malaga, Veales, and Metrill, having taken two and burnt fowre. But what I was not then permitted to doe, Divine Providence did in a great measure accomplish shortly after, for the next day they were by a storme all driven ashoare, one of the men of warr beaten to peeces. The other as alsoe the two prizes are but in a little better condition. The ships might have beene most saved, had I been permitted to come nearer unto them, in time to use the meanes which was denyed me under pretence of expecting your Majestie's order. My desire therefore unto your Majestie according to the duty I owe to the parlyament of England, is that your Majestie wilbee pleased to send your comands, that the artillery, cables, anchors, and other furniture, and what remaineth of the two men of warr may bee delivered upp into my possession for the use of the parlyament of England, and that the goods which have been taken out of the two prizes to noe small value, and what remaineth of them may bee restored unto the right owners. Hereby your Majestie will acquire unto your selfe a name of justice and righteousnes in the world, and lay a very great obligacion uppon the parlyament and people of England to unite their affeccions and interests to your Majestie's which may bee of singuler importance unto both." Two *Copies.* [N. XVII., 42, 45.]

JOHN, King of Portugal, to the PARLIAMENT.

1650, November 9. Lisbon.—Letter of credence for Dom João de Guimãraes. *Signed* "El Rey." In *Portuguese. Seal Impressed.* [N. X., 4.] Copies in *Portuguese, Latin,* and *English* are N. XVII., 98.

The Powers conferred on the PORTUGUESE AMBASSADOR.

1650, November 9.—Giving power to capitulate with the Parliament and transact upon all doubts which have occurred between Portugal and England about the coming of the two princes Rupert and Maurice into this kingdom and also if necessary to confirm the peace covenant and commerce between the two nations in such manner and form and with such clauses and conditions as he shall think convenient. (See *Commons' Journals*, vi. 530.) *English* translation read in the Parliament, February 4th, 1650-1. [N. XVII., 102.]

Captain RICHARD BADILEY to the COUNCIL OF STATE.

1650, November 9. On board the *Happy Entrance* in the Downs. —"It pleased Colonall Blake . . . to send mee from Cadiz the 14th of October with order to ply my voyadge for England having asigned a squadron of shipps to accompany mee, vizt the *George*, the *Assurance* frigott belonging to the state of England, and the *Hercules* and *Merchant*, shipps imployed in the service, that soe I might bee the better inabled to take into my chardge and bee a safe convoy unto four prizes, ' to say, the *Peeter*, *Anthony*, *Lady Remidia*, and *Good Sheapeard*, that were lately taken from the Portugall in their homeward way from Brazeele laden with sugars and other commodityes. For an invoys whereof as alsoe what sugars is uppon the rest of our fleets, I humbly referr you to the inclosed packett from Colonall Blake. Ther came alsoe under this convey, twelve other mercharnt shipps, that laded at Leviorna (Leghorn) and Maligoe, and in their homeward way stopped at Cadiz for the aforesayd end. Now, therfore to advise your Honours that after many hazerds by stormy weather—which of late wee have often mett withall—through God's great mercy all the aforementioned shipps are safely arived in this rode, the *Anthony* prize excepted, which having broken some of her yards and splitt some of her sayles, in a storme neere Portland, she went away for a harbor in the night and that wee judge was Waymouth or the Ile of Whyt. The 28th of October, forty leages of the Land's End of England, I seased upon a Frenchman that came from St Cristopher's, laden with such goods as are specified in the inventory I send your Honours heerewith inclosed, but the shipp being soe leake, that the men I putt aboard her could hardly keepe her above water, two dayes since in a storme I bid them shift for themselfes and their lives, and soe venter for the shore although very thicke weather to find a harbor, and I doe not in the least doubt but shee is well arived either in the Ile of Whyt, or the adjacent places, and the next faire weather and oppertunitye of winds I sha[ll] indeavour with all the aborcsayd shipps to hasten into the river of Theames." (See *Commons' Journals*, vi. 491.) *Signed.* [N. XVII., 100.]

PHILIP IV., King of Spain, to Admiral ROBERT BLAKE.

1650, November [14-]24. Madrid.—(Translation printed in *State Papers, Domestic*, p. 429.) *Signed* "Yo el Rey." In *Spanish. Seal Embossed.* [N. X., 5.] Two *English* translations slightly varying are N. XVII., 46, 47, a third dated (probably by mistake) November 28 is N. XVII., 53.

The KING OF SPAIN to DON FRANCISCO FERNANDEZ DE MARMOLESO, Governor and Captain of War of the cities of Murcia, Lorca, and Cartagena.

1650, November [14-]24. Madrid.—After referring to Admiral Blake's letter of November [7-]17th, of which a copy is inclosed, it proceeds: "In the first place it hath seemed good to me that you give him to understand the satisfaction which I have of his good proceeding and to charge you . . that you take special care in well treating those ships which are there of the Parliament of England and the same of those besides which shall come as is meet to be done. And out of the desire that I have that with the Parliament and all that belong to them good and acceptable correspondence may be held in all my kingdoms, I have resolved, and it is my will, that the prizes which they shall have taken and in particular the vessels of Prince Rupert you cause to be returned entirely to those to whom they belong or to the Admiral in case that the owners be not there, that he may deliver them to them. Nevertheless this must be by public and judicial acts that the satisfaction which he hath received may appear. As to the point of losses and damages which the Admiral pretends to receive of the goods of those ships of Prince Rupert which I have commanded to embarr for the satisfaction of them to whom it belongs, as he mentions in his letter, you may declare . . . that my resolution is that satisfaction be made, and that to that purpose he have solicitors in Cartagena, that the matter may be tried before justice what they have lost by the invasion of Prince Rupert in Velez Malaga, telling him that I had before commanded to make that embarr to satisfy also for the offence which hath been received in my ports by the invasion of the Prince for having set upon a vessel defended by my artillery. You shall say with all sincerity to the Admiral . . that no order had been given that the ships of Prince Rupert should not be received into the ports in regard he had not as then given any offence, which they did in Velez in the invasion which they there made, and also that there was no agreement with the Parliament to forbear to receive them, so that it was the duty of my ministers to defend them under my artillery, as the Admiral saw was done in Malaga to those of the Parliament's party, and also that I have so much the more cause to thank the Admiral for the respect wherewith he proceeded for which I remain again obliged. This is all . . that I should say to you charging you again to treat and receive well those ships of the Parliament . . and to despatch courteously and friendly the Admiral in the manner aforesaid." At foot, "Received in Cartagena Monday [18–]28 November at 6 in the morning." A copy in Spanish and two copies of an English translation. [N. XVII., 99, 49, 50.]

The SAME to the SAME.

Same date.—" Besides that which the other despatches contain . . . it hath seemed good to me in this apart to tell you that I had resolved that those vessels which entered into the Port of Cartagena of those under Prince Rupert, that you should cause them to be disarmed, and that the men belonging to them which were come ashore should be shipped. And having afterwards understood the chance which those ships had to be lost that you cause the men of the said ships to be lodged in some place without the city of Cartagena, where they may be with safety, and may do no harm nor receive any, so ordering that they may have relief in their quarters. And for that which the ships of Prince Rupert did in Velez Malaga, and other ports . . . . I charge you that you send orders to the ports under your command that neither the ships of the prince nor his person be admitted therein for any pretence. As also I charge you that to those of the Parliament who shall enter therein all good reception be given, giving them to understand that it is my express will and command." A copy in Spanish and two copies of an English translation. [N. XVII., 106, 48, 51.]

The PROCONSULS and SENATE OF HAMBURGH to the PARLIAMENT.

1650, November 19.—Stating that they just heard of the Parliament's prohibition of trade with the Barbados, and adjacent islands, that several ships belonging to their citizens had been prepared and laden with goods suitable for that market and were on the point of sailing when the news arrived, and asking in general that their citizens might be allowed the freedom of trade to those places to which they had been accustomed and that in particular the ships already laden might be allowed to trade there, In *Latin*. *Seal*. [N. X., 79.]

The SA ɪ E to the SA ɪ E.

Same date.—(To the same purport and partly in the same words as the last.) [N. X., 81.]

CHARLES SALTONSTALL to ROBERT COYTMORE, Secretary to the Committee for the Admiralty.

1650, November 22. From aboard the State's ship the *John* in Carthagena Bay in the Straits.—" Since our sending home our left fleete from Cales with the shugar prizes in the company of Captain Boddiley our Reare Admirall, there now remaining of the Parliament's ships only seven saile vidt. : the *Leopard*, *Bonaventure*, *John*, *Expedicion*, *Elizabeth* frigott, *Phenix* frigott, and *Constant Warwick*, on the 20th November, (October) neere the Straight's mouth there was taken by the Parliament's ships one of the Kinge of France's men of warr with thirty-six brass gunes. Munday, the 28th October, wee had intelligence that Prince Rupert with his whole fleete being in all eight or nine saile was two daies since before Malligo. Our Gennerall therefor with the afforesaide seven ships imediately went into the Straights and the 30th October wee weare att Malligo and there heard that Prince Rupert was towards Alligant, and had burnt and sunke five or six ships att Veles Malligo Sipeone (? Estepona) and Muttrill. Wee staied nott two bowers but went after him. Satterday, 2 November, betwixt Cape Degatt and Cape de Paulo we tooke an other French with twenty gunes, and on the 3rd day November wee tooke the *Roe Buck* one of Prince Rupert's fleete neere Cape de Paulo, a ship of thirty-four gunes. On the 4 November the *Black Prince* of Rupert's fleete, the *John* being reddy to lay him abord, a ship of forty-two gunes, ran a shoare three leagues to the E. of Carthagene and there fired and blew up him selfe. The 5 of November, four more of Rupert's run ashoare in the Bay of Carthagen for feare of our forces and there are all cast away and bilged, having nott a mast standing. Satterday, 9th November, our Gennerall, Colonell Blake, sett saile to secke for the remainder of Rupert's flecte, being now only two ships, *vid.* the *Reformacion*, and *Swallow ;* and left mee here in the Bay of Carthagena with the *John* and two French prizes to bee Commander in Cheefe and to attend the King's answere conserning the gunes and amunition belonging to the ships putt ashoare. This day the Vice-roy of Murcia was abord the *John*, and signified I should have all things belong[ing]e to the ships, His Majestie's comands being come downe to Carthagene for that purpose, soe that I am now exceeding busie about looking after what may bee received and got together from these wracks for the State's use. Our Generall sett saile from hence twelve daies since intending to goe for the Islands of Mynyorcke, Mayyorcke, Fermitera and Iveney, where our (? their) instructions which wee tooke lead us unto that Rupert's rendevous weare att these places. I hope by this tyme hee may bee mett withall. Indeed the Lord hath proved us exceedingly since wee have had little of the arme of flesh amonghts us, I mean since our great and powerfull fleete of soe many ships weare reduced only to a little squadron of ten ships under the comand of Coll. Blake, for since then wee have taken the Brazcele fleete, and after that, our squadron being now butt three ships and four frigotts, wee have taken three French ships and distroyed and taken all Rupert's ships, seven in number, only two now remaining, and thus hath God owned us in the middest of our implakable cumies, soe that the terror of God is amonghts them, five chaseth a hundred and ten a thousand, which is marvilous in our eyes. The Spaniards are now exceeding kynd unto us and the Kynge of Spaine hath made large expressions to our Gennerall how acceptable our service hath beene unto him since our coming into the Straights, which I am to deliver unto him, so soone as hee shall arive heere att Carthagene. I expect him heere everie day." *Seal.* [N. VIII., 27.]

PHILIP IV., King of Spain, to the PARLIAMENT.

1650, [November 22]–December 2. Madrid.—Letters of Credence for his ambassador Don Alphonso (*sic*) de Cardenas, in which he expresses his regret at the murder of the Parliament's resident, Ascham, at Madrid, and his intention to take steps for the punishment of those concerned in it, and promising shelter to their Admiral and fleet in his havens. (See *Commons' Journals*, vi. 517.) *Signed* and *Countersigned* "Geronimo de la Torre." In *Latin.* [N. X., 2.] Another copy is N. XVII., 56, and an *English* translation is N. XVII., 54.

Extracts from two letters of Mr. FISHER.

1650, November 26. Madrid.—"Don Luis de Haro advised me of the utter ruin of Prince Rupert's fleet on the coast of Cartagena." And "Prince Rupert's ships being wrockt on the coast ought to be the King's, but he will grant them unto Colonel Blake for the respect he bears the Parliament and desire he hath of their amity." (See *State Papers, Domestic*, p. 479, No. 10.) [N. XVII., 52.]

—— to ——

[1650, November.]—After referring to Prince Rupert's attack on the Parliament ships at Velez Malaga it proceeds:—"His Majesty has received the resolution and advice of the Council of State, that to none of his ports within or without Spain should Prince Rupert or his ships be admitted for having violated with this hostility the security guaranteed in that port to those of the Parliament, and that to those of the Parliament all good reception be given with all care taking necessary precautions for their defence." [N. XVII., 111.]

Doctor STEWART, Dean of St. Paul's, to SIR EDWARD NICHOLAS.

1650, [November 28–]December 8.—Concerning the Duke of York's going to Popish services. (Printed in Cary, *Memorials of the Civil War*, ii. 230.) *Extract.* [N. XII., 258, No. 5.]

Colonel NATHANIEL RICH to WILLIAM LENTHALL.

1650, December 4. Norwich.—Concerning the insurrection in Norfolk to the same effect as the next. (Printed in Grey, iv. Appendix, No. 64, p. 105.) *Seal.* [N. VIII., 28.]

ROBERT JERMY and others to WILLIAM LENTHALL.

[1650, December 4.]—"In the first outbreaking of this insurrection the whole country seemed in a flame—and had been, had not the Lord even in the moment appointed for your and our sure overthrows showed he was God, Our God, who hath saved and would not now forsake us.— They had so many parties appointed and in so many places that we could apprehend no place safe, but our fears were soon past through the certain information they were all scattered and gone. They fled for fear of pursuers but none then pursued them but the terror of their own fault. We also transmitted some examinations which were the most material we had then taken, wherein there appeared somewhat of danger. We have since taken several other examinations, the principal . . . we humbly herewith present. The business seems so considerable to us upon the place that we take great care to search it to the bottom and make so clear a discovery that we may distinguish by this many secret enemies to the Peace of the Commonwealth, which no oath nor engagement would detect. There are many of power and eminency named as engagers with them but the ringleaders alone must manifest that. . . . But this is too plain that many yea we justly fear so many of the middle ranks of men are engaged in it, that it will be to no end to try them by jury, but either to make some exemplary by a martial trial, or by the High Court of Justice." . . . (See *Commons' Journals*, vi. 506.) *Signed. Seal.* [N. VIII., 29.]

Admiral ROBERT BLAKE to the KING OF SPAIN.

1650, December 5–15. Cartagena.—Thanking him for his answer, for his expressions of goodwill to the Parliament and fleet of England and "the real demonstration of the same by sending orders for the restitution of the two prizes in execution whereof much affection hath been used by your Corregidor in your kingdom of Murcia. . . . But as concerning the three other ships which your Majesty hath been pleased to embargo for the satisfaction of the parties interested I hope your Majesty will excuse me for taking the boldness to renew my former desire which was that the artillery cables anchors with other furniture and what remaineth of them may be delivered up for the use of the Parliament of England to whom I conceive they appertain. And that your Majesty will be pleased accordingly to send your order to your Corregidor here, whereby you will lay a more especial and direct obligation upon the Parliament and complete the work of justice so illustriously begun to our nation's abundant contentment and the perpetual honour of your Majesty. Two *copies* in *English*. [N. XVII., 55, 58.]

The COUNT OF EGMONT AND ZUTPHEN to WILLIAM LENTHALL.

1650, December 9. London.—Stating that he has charged M. de Circourt to present le sieur de Bertaire, his intendant, to him and the Parliament, and asking them to give him entire confidence on the subject with which he had charged him. In *French*. *Seal*. [N. XVII., 60.]

Colonel THOMAS BIRCH to Major-General HARRISON.

1650, December 10.—Requesting him to use his influence to prevent the sale of the lands of the Collegiate Church at Manchester. *Seal*. [N. VIII., 30.]

The LORD DEPUTY and Colonel LAWRENCE.

1650, December 12.—Propositions agreed to between them. (Printed in *Commons' Journals*, vi. 540.) *Signed*. [N. XXI., 94.]

The TRUSTEES FOR THE SALE OF FEE FARM RENTS to the COM-
MITTEE OF THE COUNCIL OF STATE FOR SCOTLAND AND IRELAND.

1650, December 14. Worcester House.—Certificate. (Printed in
Commons' Journals, vi. 520.) [N. XVI., 61.]

DOM JOÃO DE GUIMÃRAES to the PARLIAMENT.

1650, December [15]-25. [South] Hampton.—Announcing his arrival
at Southampton on a mission from the King of Portugal to the Parliament with full power to treat for the preservation and confirmation
of the ancient peace between England and Portugal, and to remove the
obstacles which by the defect of ministers rather than by the consent
of the King or of the Parliament have, he knows not by what fate,
lately happened, and desiring a licence to come to London. (See *Commons' Journals*, vi. 510.) In *Latin* with *English* translation. [N.
XVII., 107, 109.]

The SAME to the COUNCIL OF STATE.

Same date and place.—To the same purport as the last. (See
Commons' Journals, vi. 511.) In *Latin* with *English* translation.
[N. XVII., 108.]

The SAME to WALTER FROST addressed as "the Lord Secretary of
  the Parliament of the Commonwealth of England."

Same date and place.—To the same general purport as the last two.
(See *Commons' Journals*, vi. 511.) In *Latin*. *Seal impressed.* [N.
XVII., 110.]

The COUNCIL OF STATE to JOÃO DE GUIMÃRAES, public minister of PORTUGAL.

1650, December 16.—Acknowledging his letters from [South] Hampton
announcing his arrival, in which "you declare that you are sent from
the King of Portugal to the Parliament of the Commonwealth of England. But by neither of them do we understand with what title or
public qualification, whether as Ambassador or Agent, in which it is
our desire to be satisfied by a copy of your Credentials. And not
observing in the expression of your letters any intimation of power to
treat touching satisfaction for past injuries and damage done whereof
this Commonwealth hath just cause to complain we therefore desire to
know of you whether you have power in that behalf upon signification
whereof we shall proceed to give you further answer." *Copy*. [N.
XVII., 41.]

PEREGRINE PELHAM to BULSTRODE WHITELOCKE.

1650, December 23. Westminster.—Narrating his services in securing
Hull for the Parliament and otherwise, his losses, and necessities, and
desiring a present grant of money and in future what they shall think
fit out of Delinquents' estates. (See *Commons' Journals*, vi. 516.)
Signed. Seal. [N. VIII., 31.]

OLIVER CROMWELL to WILLIAM LENTHALL.

1650, December 24. Edinburgh. — Announcing the surrender of
Edinburgh Castle. (Printed in Carlyle, No. 161.) *Signed. Seal.*
  Enclosed are copies of Cromwell's letters to the Governor with the
replies of the latter and also the letter of Jaffray and Carstairs,

all of which are printed in Carlyle, Nos. 154–159, and supplementary matter thereto. [N. VIII., 32.] Other copies are N. XX., 55.

Also (probably) were enclosed a copy of a commission to Colonel Monk and Colonel White dated December 18th authorising them to treat with the Governor's Commissioners [N. XX., 56.] and a copy of the Articles of Surrender. [N. XX., 57.]

The Council of State.

1650, December 25.—Order reporting their opinion about the sale of Fee-Farm rents. (Printed in *Commons' Journals*, vi. 520.) [N. XVI., 62.]

Speech of Don Alonso de Cardenas to the Parliament.

1650-1, December 26 – January 5. — On presenting his letters of credence,—" His Catholic Majesty being the greatest and first king in Christendom, hath thought fit to oblige this Commonwealth by being also the first who should make this acknowledgment" solely on account of Spain's ancient goodwill towards England, and from his desire for friendship with this Commonwealth. I have special orders to declare his lively resentment at the unhappy accident of Anthony Ascham, the Resident, and also what he has done in prosecution of the cause against those who were guilty, wherein his Majesty and his ministers have not only done all that is permitted by the laws and customs of that kingdom, but have exceeded them by the particular diligence they have used, " as well with the ecclesiastical judge to make him declare that in point of appeal they are not to enjoy the benefit of the Church as with the secular, to the end that nothing of that may be omitted in execution of the chastisement, which the highest rights of justice permits, and he will not draw off his hand until he bring the business to an end, for which reason so much care is had" of the persons taken "that being as they are in a common gaol, he has therein for greater security put guards upon them." In all which I doubt not it will be shortly declared that the case could not be prest more if the dead person were a Prince, heir to the Crown of Spain. All which ought to assure the Parliament of the care to give them satisfaction on this point, as it is also desired may be given in everything else. Such has been the entertainment and shelter given in the Spanish havens to the ships of the Commonwealth which shall be continued. His Majesty has also ordered that neither Prince Rupert or his ships be admitted for they failed at Velez Malaga in the respect due to his standard, which on that fort and castle gave security to the English merchant ships, as the Parliament will more fully understand by the relation sent me, which I have thought fit to communicate. (See *Commons' Journals*, vi. 515, 517.) In *Spanish* with *English* translation, the first *signed*. [N. XVII., 57, 59.] *Annexed:*

A Relation of what hath passed in Velez Malaga and Cartagena between the ships of Prince Rupert and those of the Parliament of England.

[1650, December 26.]—" Foure English Marchant Ships being togeather in the haven of Velez Malaga, the captaines thereof warned Don Gaspar Ruys Alarcon, Lieutenant-Generall of that coast, that they mistrusted a fleete of eight ships, which was in sight, and that they had notice they were under the command of Prince Rupert, and that he would treate them ill because the said captaines and ships were of the Parliament's side. Don Gaspar

Ruys de Alarcon, having receaved this notice, sent Andrew Compero, treasurer of the souldiery belonging to that coast, as also an English interpreter, with a letter for the Prince to bid him wellcome, which when they had done, they delivered him the letter, and then the ordinary complements being past and having offered him what refreshment he should neede, they tould him that the Captaine Generall of that coast desired to know the reason of his comming thither because the captaines of the English ships were now in the haven and upon their guard, and had drawne to land, flying from him. To this he answeared, he came with order of the King of Great Britany, his cousin, to take all the ships he could meete with of English, his rebells, and that in conformity to this, he came to fetch away fowre ships which were in that roade. Wherupon, the said Compero entreating him he would not permitt any wrong to be done to those ships, being they were under the armes and protection of the King, his maister, and in his haven, the Prince gave answere, he could not comply with his order if he tooke not his advantage of the occasion he had lighted on, to find Captaine Morley, one of the foure and cheefest traytors, who had signed the sentence of death of the King of Great Britanie, his uncle ; that he had now bin three yeares in pursuite of him, and that the Captain Generall ought to deliver him, not to be guilty of the domages and inconveniences which might follow. To which Campero replyed, beseeching him in the name of the Captain Generall, not to attempt what he said, for in doing so he should be obliged to protect and defend the said ships which were in the haven. At length after many disputes, the Prince said that if those captaines did not give him occasion by shooting against him, he would also forbeare, seeing they were in his maister's haven, unto whom they should owe thanks that they perished not by his hand. Upon this Campero, having shewed the esteeme he made of this his answeare, said he accepted of the offer and that he would lett the captaines of the other ships know with what care and respect they were to comport themselves not to offer any act of hostility. And soe the said Campero, takeing his leave of the Prince, went aboard the other foure ships, and calling the captaines togeather, wished them to be carefull not to offend any ship of Prince Rupert's fleete, he having offered not to sett upon them, seeing they were in the King's haven. To which they answeared, they would proceed accordingly, but would be informed what they should doe if any fyre boates should draw nigh to scale or burne. To which he replyed, that were to breake the agreement, and in that case they might fight and defend themselves, and that the Captaine Generall would also endeavour to defend them if the Prince should offer to attacque them. This being past, in the darke of the night some of the Prince's fyre boates drew towards them, and burnt Captaine Morley's ship, and one other, the men that belonged to them having left them. The other two ships which defended themselves with healpe of those of the city, were saved.

On the [3rd-] 13th of November, betweene one and two of the clock in the morning, two English men-of-war of Prince Rupert's squadron, entered the haven of Cartagena, bringing with them two English prizes which they had taken ; and at breake of day, appeared at the mouth of the said haven another squadron of ten ships of war belonging to the Parliament, which came in chace of those others; and the same day. another man-of-war of Prince Rupert's fleete, called the *Black Prince* entered a crick called Perman, two leagues from the said city, who seeing themselves prest by those of the Parliament, forsooke the ship and sett it on fyre, and it was all burnt, except some litle wood which was saved. Fourty peeces of artillery were sunke; the mariners and others belonging to the ship fled into the said city. Next day, Robert Blake, Admirall of the Parliament fleete, put to shore a captain with a trumpet and letter to the city, to tell them that he came in pursuite of Prince Rupert's ships for to destroy them, because their only busines was to rove at sea, and make prizes of such ships as traded ; and therfore demanded, they would not protect them, but cast them out of their haven, or permitt him to enter and fetch them out; and that his Majestie would be well satisfied therwith. They of the city asked him whither he had any order from his Majestie to this effect, and he answering he had not, they replyed that the Prince his ships were come for shelter into that haven under the command of his Majestie his artillery, and that without his royal order they could alter nothing, entreating him that he would not trouble them; but if he wanted victualls or refreshments, they would afford them most willingly, and if he pleased to enter their haven with his ships as friends, they might doe it, observing the said order; but before he had received the answeare, he entered the haven, placing some of his ships very nigh to those of the Prince. Then the Licentiado Don Jacinto Barcarcell, high sheriff in that city, boarded the Admirall, and after that he had wellcomed him with all cheerfullnes, and offered him all good treaty, he intreated him not to trouble the Prince his ships, and if he had a minde to write to his Majestie, he would procure him a post. Then after some replyes he made insisting that he would permitt him to fetch out the ships, alleaging different pretexts, he satisfyed him in all, and finally brought him to that, that he would expect his Majestie his order before he would medle further, provided there should be no urgent cause obliging him thereunto, and that he would give an account unto the city of any accident that should happen. The same diligence was used with the captaines of the Prince his ships, who offered the same. Things being in this state, the Prince his ships perceaving their owne weakenes so far inferior to the strength of the Parliament, helping themselves with a south est wind which began to blow, they indeavoured to breake through, but were driven to land, and broken in peeces in the Baye of S. Lucy. The Admirall, Robert Blake, writt to his Majestie, giving him account of this successe, asking of him that he might have the artillery, decks, cables and other appertinences to the ships of war, and that the marchandise which was taken in the prizes; and other goods should be given to their true owners.

Upon this occasion, his Majestie gave order that an answeare should be sent to the letter, wherof here goes a copie, and commanded the Governor of Cartagena that he should lett the Admirall know how satisfied he was with his proceedings, and that he should affoord all good entertainment to him and his ships ; and that he should see entirely restored all the prizes which the Prince his ships had taken from particulars, unto whom they did belong, or unto the Admirall in case they were not there, to the end he might deliver them ; and that he should tell him that his Majestie was resolved satisfaction should be given to such as had suffered the losses and damages which the Admirall pretended to recover out of the wealth of Prince Rupert's ships ; and therefore proctors should be left to plead by justice for what was lost by Prince Rupert's invasion in Velez Malaga ; and that no order had bin given to hinder the receaving Prince Rupert's into his haven, because they had not offended before as they had now done in Velez ; and that it was never agreed with the Parliament, to forbeare the receaving of them, and therefore there was obligation in his Majestie's minister to protect them, when they came under his artillery, as it happened at Malaga with those of the Parliament side.

And after this, orders were sent to all the havens, forbidding them to admitt hereafter of any of the foresaid Prince his ships, by reason of the hostility offered by them in Velez Malaga, setting on the ships which were under the shelter of his Majestie's artillery." [N. XVI., 60.]

Henry Middleton to William Lenthall.

1650, December 26.—Concerning the Royalist plot in Norfolk, and the trials and executions of some of those concerned in it. (Printed in Grey, iv. Appendix, No. 65, p. 107.) *Seal.* [N. VIII., 33.]

Henry Ireton, Lord Deputy, to the Lord President of the Council of State.

1650, December 27. Waterford.—Concerning Ireland and the army there, and enclosing a paper of proposals for expelling the inhabitants from Waterford, Wexford, Kilkenny and other towns and planting them with English. (Printed in Grey, iv. Appendix, No. 47, p. 78.) (The paper enclosed is printed in *Commons' Journals,* vi. 546.) *Signature torn off.* [N. VIII., 34.]

Dom João de Guimaraes to William Lenthall.

165[0-]1, [December 27-] January 6. Forwarding to the Parliament a copy of his credentials. (See *Commons' Journals,* vi. 516.) [N. XVII., 101.]

Nevil Becke to William Lenthall.

[1650.]—Requesting assistance with thanks for his former benevolence. (See *Commons' Journals,* vi. 417, 454, 500.) *Seal.* [N. VIII., 135.]

The Committee for Answering the Spanish Ambassador's speech, &c.

1650-1, January 1.—Order to prepare a letter to the King of Spain, and draft letter to the same in *Latin.* (N. XVII., 63, is an *English* translation of the same. This letter was not adopted by Parliament. See *Commons' Journals,* vii. 520.) [N. XVII., 40.]

The Same to DON ALONZO DE CARDENAS.

[1650-1, January 1-6.]—*Draft.* (Also not adopted by Parliament.) [N. XVII., 61.]

DOM JOÃO DE GUIₐÃRAES to the PARLIAMENT.

165[0-]1, January [3-]13.—Objecting to the resolutions of the 1st instant (printed in *Commons' Journals*, vi. 518) concerning the manner in which audience was to be given him, mainly on the ground that they were of the nature. of an *ex post facto* law, being passed after his arrival in London and his application for an audience, beseeching them to provide for his admittance, desiring a speedy answer, and that they should appoint one or more commissioners, with whom he might discuss the question of an audience. (See *Commons' Journals*, vi. 519.) In *Latin* with *English* translation. [N. XVII., 112.]

Major-General LAₐBERT to ———

1650[-1], January 4. Edinburgh.—My last gave an account of the surrender of Edinburgh Castle. Nothing considerable has happened since but the Coronation of Charles the Second, which was performed with great joy and shooting of guns and bonfires on the 1st instant, and great preparations making towards the sudden raising of a great army which will consist wholly of malignant people. We hear their Parliament has passed an Act, assented to by their king, empowering him to call whom he thinks fit into their army and to hang and forfeit any who shall refuse or desert their colonels, and for this purpose their king is gone into the North, where he is to set up his standard. However this is most certain they have chosen all their new colonels being the most popular and beloved men, with whom we hear the people rise very willingly so that I think we may certainly conclude they will have numerous army before long. Massey has a commission and most English officers, and 'tis confidently reported they have encouragements and intend to send a party for England, which though we shall endeavour to prevent, yet it will be our duty not to be too secure at least in a preventing insurrections and risings in our own bowels, which I conceive is most to be feared. We have had great thoughts how to prevent these new levies, and if possible to have contrived a way for our getting over the water, but Providence denying that all this time makes me wait the Lord's leisure. . . Our great want besides the difficulty of passing over the river is want of victuals, our stores being wholly exhausted except a little cheese, and we in great straits what to do not hearing of the coming of any more. It will be of singular advantage to our affairs to have money and provisions sent us. *Copy.* [N. XII., 261, No. 1.]

DOM JOÃO DE GUIₐÃRAES to [WILLIAM LENTHALL].

165[0-]1, January [7-]17.—Acknowledging the receipt that afternoon of the resolution of the House affirming their former resolution concerning his audience, and expressing his willingness to comply, and therefore desiring a day and hour for the same might be appointed. (See *Commons' Journals*, vi. 520.) In *Latin*. [N. XVII., 113.]

The SAₐE to the SAₐE.

165[0-]1, January [8-]18.—Stating that he is informed that those who have the custody of the arrested goods of the Portugal merchants are resolved to make sale thereof to-morrow and desiring that the Parliament may by their injunction hinder the same lest it prove prejudicial to the peace on both sides desired. (See *Commons' Journals*, vi. 522.) In *Latin*, with *English* translation. *Impressed Seal.* [N. XVII., 114.]

Major-General LAMBERT to ———

1650[-1], January 8. Edinburgh.—Their young king is gone to Aberdeen, where, 'tis reported he sets up his standard. They will rise willingly, being very unanimous, yet the dumb man of Peebles makes signs that they will before long cut off the heads of some great ones. Truly I am confident they have filled the measure of their iniquities and the Lord will speedily judge them. Middleton is come in and 'tis thought will be received. Duke Hamilton is thought will be general; Massey has a regiment of horse. He must be they say for England and their army will be so numerous as they think to spare a considerable party with him. Straghan, we hear, is excommunicated and sundry others we believe will follow. We are labouring where we can to get a store of horsemeat to Leith. Something considerable I hope we may do, but not full to our purpose. *Extract.* [N. XII., 261, No. 2.]

Speech of João DE GUIMARAES at his audience by a Committee of Parliament.

[1650-1, January 10.]—Enlarging at great length on the ancient friendship between England and Portugal and the services rendered by the former to the latter especially against the Mahometans and against Philip II., and desiring that those imaginary clouds of discord should vanish as serving only to eclipse the clear light of their ancient amity which the importune sagacity of their common enemy would fain deprive them of and stating that he came with full powers from the King of Portugal to confer about the conservation of peace and removing all emergent obstacles to resolve and establish with the Parliament whatever shall be necessary for composing their present affairs. (See *Commons' Journals*, vi. 523, and Whitelocke, *Memorials*, p. 486.) In *Latin* with *English* translation. The first *signed*. [N. XVII., 103, 104.]

THOMAS BIRCH and others to WILLIAM LENTHALL.

1650[-1], January 10. Preston.— Asking him to represent to Parliament the ease of the widows and children of soldiers killed in the Parliament service by which their leases being for their life were determined, as many of the landlords, Delinquents who had compounded, refused to renew except on onerous terms. *Signed. Seal.* [N. VIII., 35.]

HUGH HORSOM, Mayor, and others to WILLIAM LENTHALL.

1650[-1], January 11. Barnstaple.—Praying that satisfaction and restitution be made to the town for the disbursements amounting to 16,000*l.* incurred by it for fortifications and soldiers for the service of the Parliament during the war. *Signed. Seal.* [N. VIII., 36.]

DOM JOÃO DE GUIMARAES to WILLIAM LENTHALL.

165[0-]1, January [13-]23.—Repeating his request that the sale of the arrested goods of the Portugal merchants be stopped or at least suspended. In *Latin*. [N. XVII., 115.]

The Committee for answering the Spanish Ambassador, &c.

[1650-1, January 15.]—Draft letter from the Parliament to the King of Spain. "By Don Alonso de Cardenas . . and by many other testimonies it seems clear how great an inclination your Majesty hath with kindness and civilities to oblige the Commonwealth of England. On our part that Royal affection which your Majesty expresseth towards us and our countrymen comes very acceptably to us . . and is to be cherished from henceforth with all due returns of neighbourhood and mutual friendship. Nevertheless we desire your Majesty and insist that public justice may now at length be satisfied in the case of Antony Ascham our Resident's wicked murder so much the rather, because after the authors of such a villainy have been duly punished we shall not doubt the sending an Ambassador from hence to your Royal Court, who may open such things as may be no less advantageous to your Majesty than to this Commonwealth. On the other side if we shall suffer that blood accompanied with so many weighty circumstances to pass unrevenged we know not how to deny to our just God nor to our native country a participation in the crime especially if we should venture another Englishman into a country where he may be assassinated and no man punished therefor." (See *Commons' Journals*, vi. 524.) [N. XVII., 37.] A *Latin* translation is annexed to the two copies of the King's letter which are N. XVII., 56 ; and N. XVII., 65, is a draft with alterations. The first part down to "this Commonwealth" closely agrees with the draft rejected on the 7th, the rest is an addition.

The Parliament to Don Alonzo de Cardenas.

[1650-1, January 15.]—"The Parliament . . have taken into their most serious consideration the letters and papers lately delivered unto them by your Excellency on the behalf of the King your Master, and have commanded us in their name to return this answer.

So soon as it pleased God . . . to restore this nation to the liberty and settlement now enjoyed in this present Government . . . it was their care and endeavour to maintain all good correspondence and amity with foreign Princes and States, the neighbours and former allies of this nation and particularly with the great and powerful King your Master for which purpose . . they dispatched their Resident unto the Court of Spain.

Upon the same grounds the Parliament doth well resent the respect now done them by the King . . . in qualifying your Excellency . . . as his Majesty's Ambassador here for acknowledging the authority and sovereignty of this Commonwealth to reside in this present Parliament.

The Parliament takes notice withal of the several favours and civilities extended to their Admirals and fleet upon the coasts of Spain by his Majesty and by his officers there in pursuance of his commands. Though the narrative delivered in by your Excellency be differing in matter of fact from what the Parliament hath received from Admiral Blake in his letters "—duplicates whereof are sent herewith—"and the desires of their Admiral thereupon made, the Parliament doth make them their own, recommending them to your Excellency for an effectual answer to be procured thereunto from the King. . . . And that all due encouragement and security may be given to the merchants of this nation in the managing of their trade and commerce.

They take notice further of a firm friendship and good correspondence which his Majesty is pleased to tender unto this Commonwealth, all which is entertained by the Parliament with very good acceptance and they are resolved not to be wanting on their part in expressing the same towards the King . . . with all due returns of amity and respect.

They also take notice how far proceedings have been had against the actors of that horrid murder upon their late Resident Mr. Ascham and do insist that justice be speedily and exemplarily done therein. For which purpose—among other things—the Parliament have thought fit to direct a letter expressly to his Majesty, which they desire your Excellency's care in causing it to be conveyed unto his Royal hands, and have commanded us to deliver you a duplicate thereof.

What your Excellency hath or shall have further to communicate the Parliament hath appointed the Council of State to receive the same and to return . . the resolution of the Parliament thereupon." *Draft* or *Copy*. (See *Commons' Journals*, vi. 524.) [N. XVII., 38.] The draft as submitted by the Committee and amended by the House is N. XVII., 62. N. XVII., 64, is another draft of the beginning of the letter.

DON ALONSO DE CARDENAS to SIR OLIVER FLEMING.

1650-1, January 20-30.—Stating that the state of his health prevents him from leaving the house and that he is therefore unable to comply with the order of the Parliament appointing Tuesday the 21st—31st, for his receiving their answer to the King of Spain's letter, and requesting him to inform the Parliament of the same. In *Spanish*. *Signed*. [N. XVII., 72.]

List under the hands of RICHARD SYKES and others.

1650[-1], January 20.—Showing the apportionment of 23,566*l*.1*s*.1½*d*. between the reduced officers late under the command of Ferdinando Lord Fairfax by virtue of an ordinance of October 10, 1648. (See *Commons' Journals*, vi. 47; vii. 174.) [N. XV., 113.]

Colonel OWEN ROE and others to the COMMITTEE FOR THE NAVY.

[1650-1, January 21.]—Proposing that the debts due to them from the State be allowed them out of the discoveries they shall make in manner therein stated. (See *Commons' Journals*, vi. 581.) [N. XVI. 78.]

The PARLIAMENT to the KING OF SPAIN.

[1650-1, January 22.]—" How much your Majesty hath been affected with the heinous murder of our Resident Anthony Ascham, and what hath hitherto been done toward the punishing of his murderers we have understood both by your letters and by Don Alonso de Cardenas. Nevertheless as often as we consider the foulness of that fact which takes away the very means of having or maintaining any commerce at all if the law of Embassy solemn with all nations shall without punishment so impiously be violated, we cannot but with all earnestness again request your Majesty that those parricides may with speed be brought to due punishment and that you would not suffer justice longer to be deferred by any delay or pretence whatever. And though we do very much value the friendship of so powerful a King, yet that the authors of so horrid a murder may not escape their condign punishment we ought to use our utmost endeavours. That courteous usage which by your Majesty's command our men have found in the ports of Spain since the injuries put upon us in the port of Lisbon as also your Majesty's good affection towards us which your Ambassador hath of late with much expression made known to us we acknowledge with all gratitude, neither shall it be unpleasing to us to render to your Majesty and the Spanish nation like friendly offices if occasion happen. But unless justice be satisfied without delay which we have now long sought we see not what ground of sincere or lasting friendship there can be, which notwithstanding to preserve and to further all free commerce no befitting means or opportunity shall be by us omitted." In *Latin* with *English* translation. *Draft* with Amendments. (See *Commons' Journals*, vi. 524, 526.) [N. XVII., 39.]

MILES CORBETT and other the Commissioners to Ireland to WILLIAM
LENTHALL.

1650[-1], January 25. Waterford.—Concerning the state of the army and the enemy and desiring that supplies might be hastened. (Printed in Grey, iv. Appendix, No. 49, p. 82.) (See *Commons' Journals*, vi. 530.) *Signed. Seal.* [N. VIII., 37.]

DOM JOÃO DE GUIMĀRAES to the PARLIAMENT.

165[0-]1, [January 27-] February 6.—Humbly demanding an answer with regard to his mission, since if he further delays to do so he will incur the suspicion of coming rather to attempt and commence than to complete the business, and that as a pledge of their good will they will stop or at least suspend the sale and condemnation of Portu-guese goods, concerning which he had applied to the Parliament by three letters to the Speaker, to which he had received no answer. (See *Commons' Journals*, vi. 529.) Duplicates in *Latin*. [N. XVII., 116, 118.]

The PARLIAMENT to DOM JOÃO DE GUIMĀRAES.

[1650-1, January 29.]—Reciting their grievances on account of the protection granted by the King of Portugal to the revolted ships and the steps they had taken to obtain redress by reprisals whereby a full reparation and satisfaction may be had both of the public and private losses, "which nevertheless they are not unwilling to receive by other ways agreeable to the honour and good of this Commonwealth . . when it shall appear to them how the same may be clearly and effectually concluded whereunto they are the more induced by these offers of friendship and amity by you made in the name of the King your Master to the Parliament . . who desire to be certified whether yourself are sufficiently authorised for this purpose. And that the powers given unto you on that behalf may be produced for the further satisfaction of the Parliament." (See *Commons' Journals*, vi. 529.) [N. XVII., 105.]

LORD MUSKERRY to [WILLIAM CANDLER], Governor of Macroom
Castle.

1650[-1], January 30.—"The Castle being in opposition to my party I thought fit according to my accustomed civilities to summon you to yield me the possession thereof by fair means and on honourable terms, which opportunity if you neglect I will endeavour to come otherwise by it, and acquit my own conscience of the inconveniences that may ensue . ."

and

WILLIAM CANDLER to LORD MUSKERRY.

1650[-1], January 31.—"You should do little to the reducing of the place if you did not attempt it with a piece of paper, in which I always expected more lines of terror than in those of your approaches, only I observe you resolve upon this refusal to recover this place otherwise than by fair and honourable terms. I believe I shall as easily acquit myself of the danger as you of the inconveniency. Pursue the ways of honour and safety to yourself, and you teach me my duty, which is to trust myself and this whole action to the mercy of Heaven and not yours." *Copies.* [N. XII., 263.]

THOMAS [WALSH, ARCHBISHOP OF] CASHEL, to Monsieur TIRELL, D.D., Superior of the Irish in the Abbey of Arras.

1650[-1], January 31. Limerick.—"Things fallen out most untowardly in this kingdom above ordinary expectation, through the faults of some which quitted " it " and others which remain in it, all the passages and tragedies whereof have been by your private and public letters often suggested to the Supreme Council before and in the time of your agency to the Court of France, and yet the current did go so strong for that faction, as th' other party could not prevail against it, nor your letters make any impression on them. All Ulster is lost, Leinster have not a foot but is for the Parliament, all Munster unto the City of Limerick and only the County of Clare is lost. Connaught is yet sacred and untouched by the enemy, and out of it we yet hope to recover Ireland by a general insurrection of all the Provinces, whose inhabitants are so graveled and yoked by the Parliament, as they are resolved rather to die honestly in the field than live basely at home. If the Cities of Limerick and Galway had submitted themselves unto those which desired the command of them, they had been lost as other cities and places are. Our new Deputy for Ormonde is my Lord Marquess of Clanrickard, of whom I may not yet complain, for he is not in government but since the 24th of December and there are hopes of his doing well. My Lord of Castlehaven is Lieutenant-General in Munster and in the field with a very considerable party of horse and foot. My Lord of Muskerry and Mr. David Roch, son and heir unto my Lord Roch, have a good party in the west of Ireland, Sir John Dungan, Captain Scurlock, Hugh mac Phelim and others [are] with a good party in Leinster. I hope this summer to be off or on, pray for us there hard." (See *Commons' Journals*, vi. 564.) *Copy.* [N. XII., 262.]

The PARLIAMENT.

1650[-1], February 4.—Order referring to the Council of State the letter of the Portuguese Minister. (Printed in *Commons' Journals*, vi. 530.) [N. XVII., 117.]

The COUNCIL OF STATE.

1650[-1], February 4.—Order reporting concerning the General's Life Guard. (Printed in *Commons' Journals*, vi. 530.) [N. XVI., 63.]

The ESTATES OF HOLLAND AND WEST FRIZELAND to the
PARLIAMENT.

165[0–]1, February [4–]14.—Asking for the restitution of the *St.
Matthias* and *Young Tobias* of Lübeck and their cargoes or for payment of the value of the same, they being the property of certain citizens
of Amsterdam. (See *Commons' Journals*, vi. 537.) [N. XVIII., 110.]

HENRY IRETON, Lord Deputy, to WILLIAM LENTHALL.

1650[–1], February 7. Waterford.—Explaining that he had not
written to him either for supplies or to narrate his proceedings as he
had done so to the Council of State and approving of the Parliament's
choice of Commissioners. (Printed in Grey, iv. Appendix, No. 48,
p. 80.) (See *Commons' Journals*, vi. 535.) *Seal.* [N. VIII., 39.]

HENRY IRETON, Lord Deputy, and the Commissioners of the
Parliament to WILLIAM LENTHALL.

1650[–1], February 10. Waterford.—In support of Lord Broghill's
petition that whereas an Act lately passed for settling on him and his
heirs an estate of 1,000*l. per annum* lately belonging to Lord Muskerry
is so drawn as to be altogether invalid the same may be amended.
Signed. Seal. [N. VIII., 40.]

The COMMITTEE FOR PLUNDERED MINISTERS.

1650[–1], February 13.—Exceptions against the Books entitled,
" *The Accuser Shamed*" and " *The Clergy in their Colours*" by Mr.
John Fry. (Printed in *Commons' Journals*, vi. 536.) [N. XVI., 64.]

The PARLIAMENT.

1650[–1], February 14.—Commission to Oliver St. John and Walter
Strickland as [Ambassadors Extraordinary to the States-General of
the United Provinces. In *Latin* and *English*. (See *Commons'
Journals*, vi. 535.) [N. XVIII., 71.]

The PARLIAMENT to the AMBASSADORS TO THE STATES-GENERAL.

Same date.—Heads of Instructions. 1. You are to repair forthwith
to the present Assembly of the States-General at the Hague and deliver
them your Credentials, and also to the States of the several Provinces,
if they shall be convened, and you find it be to the service of the
Commonwealth to do so.

2. You are to signify to the States-General that the Parliament have
thought fit to send you as Ambassadors Extraordinary to let them know
that though this Commonwealth have had but too much cause given them
to desist from their former endeavours to grow up into firm and near
union with that State yet to give a clear proof of the sincerity love and
goodwill which this Commonwealth bears to their neighbours of the
United Provinces and to show how acceptable the endeavours of the
States of Holland to hold a good correspondence with this State have
been to the Parliament, the Parliament have thought fit by you to tender
the friendship of this Commonwealth to the States-General and to let
them know that the Parliament is not only ready to renew and preserve
inviolably that amity and good correspondency that hath been anciently
between the English nation and the United Provinces, but are further
willing to enter into a more strict and intimate alliance and union with
them.

3. You shall represent to them how much the interests of England and the United Provinces are one, and how great an influence for good or evil the union or disunion between them must needs have upon the true Reformed Religion.

4. You are to make known to them that the Parliament is very highly sensible of the horrid murder committed upon Dr. Dorislaus, and if any of those murderers or accessories be known or found yet abiding within their jurisdiction, you are to press for justice against them and for all right to be done, and satisfaction given on that behalf to this Commonwealth.

5. If any person shall (in original draft "Whereas there is one Mr. Dowell a Scotchman that takes") take upon him the quality of Resident Ambassador or Agent there from the Scots' King usurping the name of the King of Great Britain, and endeavours to be received by the States-General in that quality, you are to declare how much the same is derogatory to the honour and rights of this Commonwealth, and therefore you are to do your utmost to hinder the same ; And if such person shall have audience in that quality before your arrival by the said States-General or any of the Provincial States you are to deliver your protest against the same, when you shall judge most convenient.

6. You are to perform all usual civilities to the public ministers of friendly or allied States there.

7. You shall apply yourselves to remove all misrepresentations of the Parliament and affairs of this Commonwealth, and shall from time to time by writing, printing, or otherwise declare the true state thereof, and endeavour to preserve a good understanding between the two States, and lay open the obstructions that have or may hinder the same, and make demands of just satisfaction for past grievances, according to the instructions you shall receive.

8. You shall have due regard to all such things, as may concern trade and commerce.

9. You are to pursue the present instructions and such as you shall receive, as necessity or advantage shall require, and shall frequently keep the Parliament or Council of State apprised of your proceedings. (See *Commons' Journals*, vi. 535.) *Draft* with amendments. [N. XVIII., 71.]

The PARLIAMENT to the STATES-GENERAL.

Same date.—Letters of Credence to Oliver St. John and Walter Strickland as Ambassadors Extraordinary. (See *Commons' Journals*, vi. 535.) *Draft* with amendment. [N. XVIII., 72.]

LORD WILLOUGHBY to LADY WILLOUGHBY.

1650[-1], February 15. Barbados.—Desiring her to come to him and concerning his private and family affairs. *Seal.* [N. VIII., 41.]

The SAME to EDWARD LINCOLN and another.

Same date.—Desiring them to send him the vessels and goods described. *Seal.* [N. VIII., 49.]

The Examination of WILLIAM MOWBRAY before the Commissioners for Compositions.

1650[-1], February 20.—He being at Breda about April and May 1650, saw the Earl of Oxford many times, viz., twenty and more with the King of Scots, and several times waiting at the said King's table, and also saw him go after the King into the withdrawing rooms, and at the same time he also saw Lord Craven with the said King several times and many times waiting at his table upon him. *Copia Vera.* [N. XVI., 65.]

Captain WILLIAM HARDING to Captain GEORGE BISHOP.

1650[-1], February 28. Weymouth.—" I am informed by a gentleman . . out of France that there are great preparations upon the King's interest to land soldiers in the West of Cornwall, and that there are 28 sail of ships with 4,000 soldiers near ready . . who are to come along with Sir [Richard] Greenfield, who is appointed their general, and there is one Harris or Harrison of the West of Devonshire or Cornwall, formerly in the Parliament's service, their correspondent, that is to give them inlet, and hath made a party in those parts to join with them." *Seal.* [N. VIII., 42.]

The MARQUESS OF CLANRICKARD to the EARL OF CASTLEHAVEN.

1650[-1], March 2. Portumna.—" Being upon my way yesterday morning to Athlone as far as the new fort, and having given order for the securing of that passage, . . . I received a despatch from Father George Dillon newly landed at Galway and with him one Monsieur St. Catherine, whom he calleth ambassador from the Duke of Lorraine. They have brought good supplies of money and overtures of large assistance, if we can agree, and a strong fleet at sea, and his letters and others from the Commissioners importuning my speedy repair to Tyrrelawe, I have turned faces about and will go from hence to-morrow to Tyrrelawe, though this weather doth somewhat pinch my teased constitution. This treaty being likely to be of matters of great difficulty and high concernment, it is necessary I should have the assistance of the ablest judgments and rightest affections. If your Lordship have a few days to spare and make a start to Galway it will be much of satisfaction to me, and perhaps your Lordship may thereby purchase a child's portion to carry back with you.

I have appointed a rendezvous of all my Connaught horse at Clonfert the 22nd of this month, only three troops sent to Sligo to make some diversions that way, and I am confident they will be about 500 effective horse. What posture they will be in then in Leinster to join upon any design, or whether your Lordship will be in a condition to stir about that time I speedily expect to know. The enemy is drawing strongly together about Killbeggan, but I cannot imagine what design they can have with their labour and spoil of horse, the Shannon, I presume, [being] very sure against any attempt they can make, and so having much of trouble and business on me I must hastily conclude.

Postscript.—I have heard nothing yet of your Limerick ambassadors. I hope they have taken better resolutions." (See *Commons' Journals*, vi. 564.) *Copy.* [N. XII., 264.]

The COUNCIL OF STATE.

1650-1, March 3.—Order reporting various matters to the Parliament. (Most of it is printed in *Commons' Journals*, vi. 544, and all in *State Papers, Domestic*, p. 68, paragraphs 4, 9, 10, 11.) *Seal.* [N. XVI., 66.]

Colonel SOLOMON RICHARDS to HENRY IRETON, Lord Deputy.

1650[-1], March 4.   Crock an Pill ; near Bristol.—Have shipped 80 men commanded by Major Poole.   Though I have received of the State 185*l.* to conduct my company to shipping I could give no account of it.   I durst not come near my men till my peace was procured and they on board.   I cannot stir hence till money comes, I am like to be divided amongst brewers, bakers and cheesemongers yet I hope to be at Milford ten days before any party of men can reach it.   (See *Commons' Journals*, vi. 564.)   [N. VIII., 43.]

OLIVER CROMWELL to WILLIAM LENTHALL.

1650[-1], March 8.   Edinburgh.—On behalf of Colonel Robert Lilburne.   (Printed in Carlyle, No. 168.)   *Signed.   Seal.*   [N. VIII., 44.]

OLIVER CROMWELL to WILLIAM LENTHALL.

1650[-1], March 11.   Edinburgh. — Concerning the proposed erection of a College at Durham.   (Printed in Carlyle, No. 169.)   *Copy.* [N. XII., 264*a.*]

Colonel JOHN HEWSON to ——.

1650[-1], March 14.   Finnagh.—Concerning the taking of that place and his other proceedings.   *Enclosed :*
        A list of Officers taken prisoners.
        The Articles of Surrender.
(The list and articles are printed in Gilbert, iii. 383, and also a letter of the same date from him to William Lenthall to the same effect but fuller than this.)   *Copies.*   [N. XII., 265, 266.]

Resolution of the STATES-GENERAL on the proposal of the Deputies of the Province of Holland.

165[0-]1, March [14, 15-]24, 25. — Concerning the precedency between the Commissioners of the States-General and the Lords Ambassadors of France, the former to take precedence in the house of the latter, but the latter to take precedence at conferences in the withdrawing room of the States-General.   [N. XVIII., 111.]

The STATES-GENERAL.

165[0-]1, March [15-]25.—Resolution upon the answer in writing of the Ambassador of Portugal, that all further conference be broken off with him and that he be no more acknowledged as an ambassador, but as a private person, and the States of Holland and West Friezeland are to declare to him that his freedom from Excise which he had enjoyed by virtue of the aforesaid quality be taken from him.   " The deputies of the province of Friezeland said they were not authorised to concur with the resolution and therefore could not agree to it."   [N. XVIII., 112.]

THOMAS MARGETTS to OLIVER CROMWELL.

1650[-1], March 17.   Whitehall.—By desire of the Council of War at Whitehall informing him that Colonel Nicholas Borlace, though within the articles of Truro, had had goods and cattle above the value of 500*l.* taken by the Sequestrators' agent, that notwithstanding several letters from the late Lord General Fairfax and from Cromwell himself he could get no relief, that the power of the Commissioners for relief upon Articles is determined and the faith of the army in the breach of the Articles is violated, and that the Council therefore desire that he would give him relief either by asking the Parliament to discharge his sequestrations and fine amounting to 320*l.* or otherwise. (See letter of October 10th following.) *Seal.* [N. VIII., 46.]

JOHN JAMES and others to WILLIAM LENTHALL.

1650[-1], March 17. Hereford.—Desiring that the persons therein named be added to their Committee. *Signed.* [N. VIII., 47.]

OLIVER ST. JOHN and WALTER STRICKLAND to the COUNCIL OF STATE.

1650-1, March 20–30.—Describing their voyage and reception in the Netherlands, and various matters there. (Printed in Grey, iv. Appendix, No. 50, p. 83.) (See *Commons' Journals,* vi. 554.) *Signed.* [N. XVIII., 76.] *Annexed:*

The ENGLISH AMBASSADORS to the STATES-GENERAL at their Audience.

1650[-1], March [20–30.]—"The Parliament . . . well knowing by the antient and successive treatyes and leagues of amitye betweene England and the Netherlands, as well before their restitution to their libertyes as since, and by the many and notable assistances given unto them, and sometymes received from them against the enemyes of each other that there hath alwayes bin a firme union and constant entercourse of freindshipp and reall affections betweene England and this state.

And withall, considering that the defence and ayde against forreigne enemyes, and the free entercourse of trade and traffick,—the common interests of states—, that first combined them in this happy league, doe still continue with the accession sythence of the profession of the true reformed religion and of the just libertyes and freedome of the people of equall concernment unto both, more then formerly.

And that God, who at first appointed unto all people the bounds of their severall habitations, by situation, likenes of manners and dispositions, commodityes ariseing by sea and land, shippinge and otherwise, hath not only inabled them to bee more usefull unto each for the mayntenance of the common interests then to others, but seemes likewise in those regards to putt a necessity uppon both to desire and effect the good of both.

And finding by long experience that breaches sometymes occasioned through misunderstanding have alwayes produced damage unto both, and likewise regrett and impatience till reconciliation, as if made for meet helps they could not bee well alone.

And further, observing that the signall blessing of Almighty God hath ever accompanied the actions of each, undertaken for their welfare wherby great additions of happines have bin derived unto both, for which they are bound ever to give thankes to God, and were noe doubt taken into the consideration of the high and potent lords of Holland, in their late good and acceptable endeavors for the continewance of a freindly correspondency betweene the two states.

As therfore they have cause from hence, soe the Parliament accordingly doe desire that this pious and strickt confederacy and league of amityc, derived from their ancestors unto them, may from themselves bee transmitted unto posterity, if God soe please. And such is the sincere love and good will, which the Commonwealth of England beareth unto their neighbours of the United Provinces, begotten and conserved uppon the grounds before expressed, that they are willing to enter into a more intimate alliance, and neerer union with them then formerly hath bin ; wherby a more reall and intrinsecall interest of each in other, may bee contracted for their mutuall good.

This, the Parliament of the Commonwealth of England, doth by us, their ambassadors extraordinary, declare and make tender of to you the high and mighty lords, the States Generall of the United Provinces of the Netherlands, and hath given us full power and authority on their part to bring to effect. And they have chosen this as the most seasonable tyme to acquaint your Lordshipps herewithall, when you are mett in this great and extraordinary Assembly to consult, as they suppose, matters of highest importance to your state, and which hath bin occasioned by remarkable acts of Divine Providence, and likewise when the Commonwealth of England, through the infinite goodnes of God, is in soe peacable and settled a condition under the present goverment, and freed in soe great a measure as now it is from enemyes abroad.

And although great alterations of goverment, how good and just soever, have alwayes bin accompanied with various and sinister constructions, tending to the disadvantage of the state concerned, wherof wee know the Netherlands have had experience as well as others, nor can it bee otherwise expected, because those without are not soe fully acquainted with the grounds and causes therof, and by reason of the severall interests, relations and dependencyes involved therin ; yet considering the place and persons where and to whom wee now speake, and the declarations of this state made at Utreckt, the 23rd of January, in the yeare 1579, and in this place, the 26th of July in yeare 1581, they thought it not needfull to bee particular upon this subject.

My Lords, in the severall and successive mutations of the affaires and conditions of the Netherlands, the treatyes and alliances betweene England and them, have alwayes bin continewed, and with the greatest expression of affection from England when this state hath stood in most need. And upon the present alteration in England, soe happily by the blessing of God ordered for the common good, your Lordshipps may see cause to continew and improve them to the neerest conjunction, a foundation being therby layd of makeing them more durable and advantagious then formerly, when they depended upon the uncertayntyes of the life, alliances, change of affections and private interest of one person.

My Lords, yow see the Commonwealth of England—notwithstanding the many discouragements they have found, and just cause given them of laying aside the thoughts of any further motion in this kind—have begun to you and in matters of highest concernment to both, led therunto—such is the mercy of God—not out of necessity but choyce. This, their good will, deserves all acceptacion on your part, with whom it now rests, and will, they doubt not, produce resolutions answerable and tymely, and whatsoever issue it shall please God in his wisdome to give, they shall alwayes have the satisfaction of haveing done what befitted them, and what the wellfare of the true reformed religion, and the other great and common interests of both states obliged them to doe." Concerning ourselves we would have you rest assured of our sincere affections to the welfare of this state. We desire that you would with all convenient speed appoint Commissioners to treat with us. Read in Parliament July 2nd, being No. 1. (See *Commons' Journals*, vi. 595.) [N. XVIII., 75.] Another copy read April 1st is N. XVIII., 79.

The SAME to WILLIAM LENTHALL.

Same date.—Also describing their voyage and reception and enclosing an order made by the States of Holland on account of the malicious language and insolent carriage of the old Malignants towards themselves. (Printed in Grey, iv. Appendix, No. 51, p. 86.) (See *Commons' Journals*, vi. 554.) *Signed.* [N. XVIII., 78.] *Enclosed:*

The ESTATES OF HOLLAND AND WEST FRIEZELAND.

1650[-1], March [19-]29.—Proclamation forbidding affronts or injuries to the Ambassadors or public ministers of Kings, Princes, or Republics under pain of corporal punishment but ordering on the contrary that all inhabitants give all honour respect and assistance to them. *Copy.* [N. XVIII., 113.]

The ENGLISH AMBASSADORS to the STATES-GENERAL.

1650[-1], March 20[-30].—Demanding satisfaction for the murder of Dorislaus. (Printed in Thurloe, *State Papers*, i. 174, and in Peck, *Desiderata Curiosa*, xi. 17.) Read in Parliament July 2nd being No. 2. (See *Commons' Journals*, vi. 595.) [N. XVIII., 73.] Another copy read April 1st is N. XVIII., 77.

Extract from the Register of the Resolutions of the STATES-GENERAL.

165[0-]1, March [21-]31.—Appointing Commissioners to treat with the English Ambassadors. (Printed in Thurloe, *State Papers*, i. 174.) Read in Parliament July 2nd being No. 3. (See *Commons' Journals*, vi. 595.) [N. XVIII., 74.]

WILLIAM KING to HENRY IRETON, Lord Deputy.

1650[-1], March 24. Loghguire.—Concerning the terms agreed on between Clanrickard and the Duke of Lorraine's agent, and Castlehaven's proceedings, and enclosing the abstracts of some letters that came to his hands about two days ago. (Printed in Grey, iv. Appendix, No. 7, p. 15.) (See *Commons' Journals*, vi 561.) [N. VIII., 48] *Enclosed:*

i. Colonel PLUNKET to the [Roman Catholic] ARCHBISHOP OF DUBLIN.

1650[-1], January 3. Brussels.—Lord Taaffe sends to you the Abbot of St. Catherine from the Duke of Lorraine, with a considerable sum of money, and promises of future supplies of more and of ammunition, arms, men and officers. None is more willing or better able to defend you than this Duke, who, in the presence of Father Dillon and me, assured Lord Taaffe that he would venture his treasure, his life and his estate, in regaining that part of the kingdom which is possessed by the enemy, if you call upon him unanimously to your assistance he protests that he will settle religion in that kingdom in as ample a manner as it is exercised at Rome. The Abbot of St. Catherine is one of the best gentlemen of Lorraine, and one of the Duke's Privy Council whom he esteems very much. If he return with satisfaction the Duke will effect that before the end of next summer your enemies will be dispossessed of their several holds in that kingdom. The Duke will be able to do it, for he is a wise prince and very rich. He wants neither good counsel nor commanders. He has a good army and the best horsemen in the world. He ordered Lord Taaffe to prepare a good magazine for the muskets, cannon, ammunition, etc. which he intends to send to be in readiness against the Abbot's return. He is also preparing ships for war to be sent with the first mission. If you encourage him, you will have 50 sails before the end of March. *Abstract.* [N. XII., 260.]

ii. Lord Taaffe to [the Irish Roman Catholic Archbishops].

Same date.—All I advise your Graces is not let slip his offered protection, for no other Prince in Christendom is either willing or able to assist you. You will therefore do well to direct the persons committed to your charge not to neglect so unexpected a blessing, whereby they may secure their religion loyalty and fortunes from their present dangers. I have procured such assistance from his Highness which I send by my uncle George. *Abstract.* [N. XII., 260 end.]

The English Ambassadors to the Commissioners appointed by the States-General.

1651, [March 25-]April 4.—"We propound that it be declared and agreed that in the ensuing treaty no article that shall be agreed and concluded upon by both sides shall be obligatory unto either unless the treaty be completed and brought to effect." Read in Parliament July 2nd being No. 4. (See *Commons' Journals*, vi. 595.) [N. XVIII., 80.]

The Same to the Same.

Same date.—"We do tender the friendship of the Commonwealth unto the . . . States-General . . . and do propound that the amity and good correspondency which hath anciently been between the English nation and the United Provinces be not only renewed and preserved inviolably, but that a more strict and intimate alliance and union be entered into by them, whereby there may be a more intrinsical and mutual interest of each in other than hath hitherto been for the good of both." Read in Parliament July 2nd being No. 5. [N. XVIII., 81.]

The Committee for the Sale of Delinquents' Estates.

[1651, March 25.] — Order reporting the case of Mr. Carew Rawleigh. (Printed in *Commons' Journals*, vi. 552.) [N. XVI., 69.]

The Committee for the Northern Association.

1651, March 26. — Resolution naming the persons to receive the 3,000*l.* (Printed in *Commons' Journals*, vi. 537.) [N. XVI., 70.]

The STATES-GENERAL to the ENGLISH AMBASSADORS.

1651, [March 28-]April 7.—Reply to No. 5. (Printed in *French* in Thurloe, *State Papers*, i. 176.) Read July 2nd being No. 6. [N. XVIII., 82.]

The COUNCIL OF STATE.

1651, April 1. (*Sic*, but not completely drawn up till the 3rd, as it refers to a paper dated April 3–13.)—Order reporting that in pursuance of the Order of February 4th the Council prepared a paper of demands in six Articles containing what they conceived to be requisite to be agreed unto on the part of the Portuguese previous to any further treaty of peace which paper (No. 1) was delivered to the Minister on February the 12th and at the same time a paper (No. 2) was delivered of the charge the Commonwealth had been at (214,640*l*.) in reference to their demands in general made in the fourth Article, as the same was certified from the Commissioners of the Navy.

That at the same time they received from the said Minister a paper (No. 3) containing three preliminary demands. Upon the receipt whereof they signified to him that the Council expected an answer to their six demands before they returned any to the paper received from him.

That the said Minister on February the 13th returned a paper (No. 4) replying to the six demands together with a paper (No. 5) of redemands of the charge of the Portugals (amounting to 900,000*l*.) which his answer to the fourth Article refers to.

That the Council finding therein nothing of satisfaction to their said six demands they sent him a second paper (No. 6) on February the 15th, in which they declared they were not satisfied. And they appointed the same Committee to meet with the said Minister and in conference to give reasons (No. 7) why the said papers were unsatisfactory. And also ordered that the State of fact of all the transactions at Portugal should be drawn up by Dr. Walker upon conference with Mr. Vane and with the Generals of the fleet there, which was accordingly done, and the said State of fact (No. 8) delivered to the said Minister and also the said reasons.

That at the same time the said Minister, after many verbal discourses delivered a paper (No. 9) to the said Committee, which was reported to the Council. And thereupon a third paper (No. 10) was sent to him on February the 25th declaring that the Council was not satisfied with his answer in that paper, and insisted upon their former demands.

That the said Minister on March the 3rd returned to the Council a paper (No. 11) as an answer to their third paper, upon consideration whereof the said Council, not finding satisfaction to their demands to the end no occasion or colour might be taken by him either to make ambiguous or insignificant answers or to draw the business into length upon pretence of difficulties that were not, on March the 6th sent him a paper (No. 12), explaining what might seem dubious to him in the first paper of demands and also showing wherein what he had yet offered was not satisfactory.

That on March the 10th the Council received from the Minister two papers (Nos. 13, 14) for answer to their last, in which there was an agreement in effect to the first, third and sixth Articles of their first paper but conditionated that the whole were agreed within fifteen days. But as to the second, fourth, and fifth—which were of greatest consequence—that to the second was not fully satisfactory, and those to the fourth and fifth to as little purpose as the former.

That therefore on March the 12th the Council sent him a fifth paper (No. 15) showing more at large why his answer to the second fourth and fifth demands remained still unsatisfactory, and gave him also such an answer to his three preliminaries as they conceived them capable of, having hitherto given no answer at all to them.

That on March the 18th the Council received from the Minister a paper (No. 16) in answer, containing at last an answer to the second Article of their first paper as explained in the fourth paper, but still under condition that the whole was agreed unto within 15 days, but as to the fourth and fifth offering nothing that was yet satisfactory.

The Council thereupon on March the 22nd sent him a sixth paper (No. 17) and received one (No. 18) on the 25th containing expostulation and not satisfaction.

They have therefore thought fit to report the whole to the Parliament, and to offer in one paper (No. 19), the first, second, third, and sixth demands with his answers that seem to have given satisfaction unto them, and in another paper apart the fourth (No. 20) and fifth (No. 21) demands with all his answers to them which considered in particular or in any result to be drawn from them all do not offer to the Council the satisfaction which they have thought fit to insist upon. All which they submit to the consideration and judgment of Parliament.

The report being prepared April the 1st the Council thought fit to signify their intentions herein to the said Minister (No. 22), that if he had any further matter to offer before the Report it might with the former be offered to the consideration of Parliament. As answer to which the Council received to day a paper (No. 23) dated April 3–13, the copy whereof is also herewith presented, with the Council's opinion that he hath not yet satisfied the fourth and fifth demands, and that as to the fifth demand to which nothing is said of further satisfaction in this paper there are many cases of great losses of many persons of the best affections to the Commonwealth which fall within that Article, which deserve very much commiseration, and which the Council is of opinion ought to be satisfied by the King of Portugal, to which he hath yet offered nothing satisfactory. (See *Commons' Journals*, vi. 556, 558.) (All these papers except No. 8 are in this volume numbered thus 1 = 130, 2 = 127, 3 = 131, 4 = 132, 5 = 128, 6 = 133, 7 = 146, 9 to 18 = 134 to 143 respectively, 19, 20 and 21 = 129, 22 = 144, 23 = 145. The articles (No. 1), the explanations (No. 12), and the conclusion of No. 15 are printed in full in *Commons' Journals*, vi. 558, 559, from the last of which the three demands of the Portuguese Minister appear.) [N. XVII., 120.]

The COUNCIL OF STATE.

1651, April 3.—Order reporting the treaty with the Portuguese Minister. [N. XVII., 121.]

The STATES-GENERAL to the PARLIAMENT.

1651, April 4. The Hague.—Stating that two Dutch captains had taken off the coast of Portugal a Portuguese ship laden with 600 chests of sugar, and that in the English Channel the prize being separated by a storm from her captors was taken by an English ship and carried into Plymouth, on the ground that there was no copy on board of the commissions of the two Dutch captains, and demanding the restitution of ship and cargo. In *French*. [N. X., 52.]

GEORGE CHAPPELL, Commander of the *Peter and Jane* of London, to the COUNCIL OF STATE.

[1651, April 5.]—Petition stating that arriving with the said ship at Lisbon at the time of the general sequestration there he was imprisoned above five months and the ship and cargo sequestered, that he procured liberty from the King to come to England with the said ship to bring home 68 English mariners, prisoners there, upon caution given by himself and five others for the immediate return of the said ship, and praying that either he may be permitted to return with his said ship, or that some other way may be thought of for the disobliging of his said friends. (See *State Papers, Domestic*, pp. 131, 225.) [N. XXII., 140.]

Extract from the Resolutions of the ESTATES OF HOLLAND AND WEST FRIEZELAND.

1651, April [9--]19.—The report of the insolencies and actual violence daily offered about the lodging of the English Ambassadors and also to their attendant gentlemen and servants being heard in the Assembly, it is resolved that the Lords of the Provincial Court shall be and are most seriously desired to cause proceedings without delay for the apprehension of such persons as are at present known to have acted such violence or insolencies, and for such as are not yet known to cause information to be made against them ; and likewise to cause proceedings against the person of Apsley, who is reported to absent himself, for the greater terrifying of others, who shall go about to undertake such enormities, and the said Lords shall not for any reasons neglect what is aforesaid and what else may further the security of the said Ambassadors but shall give account hereof to their Great Mightinesses.

The Magistrates of the Hague shall be and are likewise expressly charged to cause proceedings to be made by their officers against all such malevolent persons.

The Captain of the Guard of their High Mightinesses—besides the charge formerly given him—shall keep before his door a continued armed watch, always to have a careful eye to the lodging of the said Ambassadors, and he is to erect and keep a tent court of guard about the verge of the said lodging where it shall be judged best, and to put therein such a number of soldiers as he shall judge best : and he is charged to keep such order about the said lodging that no insolency or concourse of people happen there, but to cause them to depart ; and if they will not obey the said captain or others there commanding are expressly authorised, after warning, to fire upon them with bullets, which may likewise be done to any who may attempt a rescue of such as are apprehended.

And the several officers both of the said Court and the Hague are expressly charged to apprehend all such as shall go about to offer any outrage or insolency upon the lodgings of the said Ambassadors, their persons or servants, and the said captain of the Guard and his officers and soldiers are charged to assist them.

This resolution is to be communicated to the Ambassadors with request whether they require anything further for their security. (See *Commons' Journals*, vi. 561.) [N. XVIII., 114.]

The KING to every COLONEL OF HORSE in the Army.

1651, April 9. Stirling.—Warrant, ordering him to send out of each troop in his regiment one horse and man, the best armed and appointed in it, to make a troop for the Duke of Buckingham. *Copy.* [N. XII., 72.]

The COMMITTEE FOR THE ARMY.

1651, April 9.—Order reporting concerning the Army in Scotland. (Printed in *Commons' Journals*, vi. 562.) [N. XVI., 71.]

RICHARD SHUTTLEWORTH and others to WILLIAM LENTHALL.

1651, April 9. Preston.—Enclosing the following petition, which they support. *Signed. Seal. Enclosed:*

The most humble Petition of many hundreds of maimed SOLDIERS, WIDOWS and FATHERLESS CHILDREN in the COUNTY OF LAN-CASTER.

Showing that the weekly pensions formerly received by them out of the Sequestrations of the County had been discontinued since the 24th of June last, the Commissioners being required to pay the same into Goldsmiths' Hall, and praying that they might receive them as formerly. *Signed* by four marksmen and markswomen in the name of themselves and about 1,000 more. [N. XXII., 129.]

The PARLIAMENT.

1651, April 10.—Proceedings with regard to the negotiations with the Portuguese Minister. (Printed in *Commons' Journals*, vi. 558, 559, 560, beginning "The Parliament this day resumed the debate," ending "within six days after they are delivered to him.) [N. XVII., 122.]

The STATES-GENERAL to the ENGLISH AMBASSADORS.

1651, April [11-]21.—In reply to their letter of the previous day (printed in Thurloe, *State Papers*, i. 177) they declare that they have no other intention than to cultivate and entertain a sincere and perfect friendship and correspondence with the said Commonwealth, and to take away from the Parliament every ground of jealousy or umbrage about the expedition of Lieutenant Admiral Tromp towards the Scilly Islands or Sorlings, they further declare that they have given no orders or instructions to the said Lieutenant Admiral to conquer and make himself master of those isles, or to do anything to the prejudice of the said Commonwealth, but only to oblige the Governor and those of the islands to restore the ships and goods taken from their subjects and in case of refusal or delay to attack and take their ships and goods wherever he can. In *French. Original* and *Copy.* The first with *Seal.* [N. X., 53 ; XVII., 115.]

The ENGLISH AMBASSADORS to the STATES-GENERAL.

1651, April 15-25.—(Printed in Thurloe, *State Papers*, i. 179.) Read July 2nd, being No. 7. [N. XVIII., 83.]

The STATES-GENERAL to the ENGLISH AMBASSADORS.

1651, April [16-]26.—"The States-General . . . upon the report which hath been made unto them by their Deputies who have been the second time in conference with the Ambassadors . . . have declared as they do declare by these presents, That they will not only renew and observe inviolably the good amity and correspondence which of yore hath been between the English nation and the United Provinces, but also to enter into a more strait and intimate alliance and union by the means whereof they may reciprocally better find their interests for the good of both states than heretofore hath been done." Read July 2nd, being No. 8. [N. XVIII., 84.]

The ENGLISH AMBASSADORS to the STATES-GENERAL.

1651, April 17[-27].—" We propound that the two Commonwealths may be confederated friends joined and allied together for the defence and preservation of the liberties and freedom of the people of each against all whomsoever that shall attempt the disturbance of either state by sea or land, or be declared enemies to the freedom and liberties of the people living under either of the said Governments." (The rest is printed in Thurloe, *State Papers*, i. 179.) Read July 2nd, being No. 9. [N. XVIII., 83.]

The COUNCIL OF STATE to DOM JOÃO DE GUIMÃRAES.

1651, April 17.—Two papers embodying the final demands of the Parliament in accordance with the votes of the 10th and 11th for which see *Commons' Journals*, vi. 560. [N. XVII., 146, 147.]

The DOGE and GOVERNORS OF the Republic of GENOA to WILLIAM LENTHALL.

1651, April 18. Genoa.—Complaining of the seizure by the English fleet of a ship and cargo belonging to their citizens and demanding their restitution. (See *Commons' Journals*, vi. 612.) In *Latin* with *English* translation. *Seal embossed.* [N. X., 39.]

DOM JOÃO DE GUIMÃRAES to the COUNCIL OF STATE.

1651, [April 21-]May 1.—Enclosing his answers to the last demands and votes of the Parliament and hoping that they and the Parliament will approve thereof. In *Latin* with *English* translation. [N. XVII., 126a, 123.] *Enclosed:*

The said Answers.

Conceding all the demands in the six articles and concluding thus : " For as much as concerns the Truce of six months for finishing the treaty of this peace now that I have given full satisfaction to all the demands of the Parliament, and in regard a few days may suffice to end this treaty, I here present myself ready to put an entire period thereunto, and there shall be nothing wanting on my part to the present finishing thereof. Wherefore I beseech the Parliament that they will vouchsafe to dispatch this business which is of huge concernment thereby to prevent maturely any new troubles that may arise, whereof there shall be no occasion given by the King my master." (See *Commons' Journals*, vi. 565.) [N. XVII., 149.]

The SAME to the PARLIAMENT.

Same date.—Stating that he had forwarded his answer by the Council of State as he was ordered. In *Latin* with *English* translation. [N. XVII., 125, 124.]

The STATES-GENERAL to the ENGLISH AMBASSADORS.

1652, [April 22-]May 2.—(The purport appears from the English Ambassadors' paper of May 17-27, printed in Thurloe, *State Papers*, i. 183.) Read July 2nd, being No. 10. [N. XVIII., 86.]

An Estimate of the monthly charges of the forces in MUNSTER and LEINSTER and also of the monthly charges of the forces in ULSTER.

[1651, April 22.]—Amounting in all to 58,002*l.* The former forces then consisted of 17 foot regiments of 1,000 privates each, nine of horse of 500 each, two of dragoons of 1,800 each besides officers, three odd troops of horse, the life guard of 70 gentlemen, the train, and the general officers, the latter of three regiments and two troops of horse, and of seven regiments and two companies of foot, besides the officers of garrisons and the train. (See *Commons' Journals,* vi. 564.) [N. XVI., 75.]

THOMAS LEVESON to the PARLIAMENT.

[1651, April 23.]—Petition, stating that in 1645 he was appointed Governor of Dudley Castle for the king, and though the Castle was provisioned for three years he before any siege to avoid bloodshed offered to surrender it to Sir William Brereton, he with six other gentlemen having their estates quit of any sequestration, which the said Sir William Brereton refused concerning the said gentlemen but promised that he would endeavour that the petitioner might stand quitted or very well dealt with by the Parliament for his estate and thereupon the petitioner surrendered the Castle accordingly, yet he hears that he is exempted from making his composition and his lands are to be disposed of, and praying that his fine might be remitted or that he may at least be admitted to a favourable composition. (See *Commons' Journals,* vi. 566.) *Annexed :*

i. Certificate of Sir William Brereton.
ii. Affidavit of Edmond Ashenhurst, formerly a prisoner in Dudley Castle, and negotiator between Colonel Leveson and Sir William Brereton, both echoing the petition. [N. XXII., 161.]

The COUNCIL OF STATE to DOM JOÃO DE GUIMARAES.

1651, April 23.—Demanding a positive answer in accordance with the votes of the previous day. [N. XVII., 150.]

DOM JOÃO DE GUIMARAES to the COUNCIL OF STATE.

1651, [April 24-] May 4.—In answer to the paper of the Council of State brought to me on May 3rd, new style, I declare that the state of the treaty is now such as allows at present neither of the name nor nature of a Truce for as much as Truce or temporary Cessation of Arms is only agitated in the commencement of treaties, at the end of which we have arrived, as far as relates to disputed points therein, since I have finally satisfied all the demands and conditions of the Parliament by my consent to and approval of all and singular the six articles. It remains therefore that the treaty thus concluded be completely finished, and be confirmed and subscribed by both parties, which I am ready to do, and this done, I undertake, in the name of my King that on the day when it shall be made known at Lisbon by the Parliament's care and diligence—if they so please—the first and second of the said articles shall begin to be put in execution, and shall be completely carried out in a few days, from which day in like manner shall begin the complete cessation of arms which by this peace shall be illimited and perpetual. The remaining four articles shall be put in execution within such necessary and reasonable space of time as may be agreed upon between the Parliament or Council and myself by an amicable agreement to be inserted in the treaty. (See *Commons' Journals,* vi. 568.) In *Latin,* with *English* translation. [N. XVII., 126c, 151.]

The COUNCIL OF STATE to DOM JOÃO DE GUIMĀRAES.

1651, April 26.—In pursuance of the Resolution of the Parliament (printed in *Commons' Journals,* vi. 568), which it recites, demanding an answer in accordance therewith. *Copy.* [N. XVII., 152.]

The STATES-GENERAL to the PARLIAMENT.

1651, April 26. The Hague.—Complaining that nine of their vessels bound for Portugal had been taken in the Downs and carried to London, as having on board contraband of war, and demanding restitution. In *French.* [N. X., 54.]

Lord Commissioner RICHARD KEBLE to WILLIAM LENTHALL.

1651, April 29. Painted Chamber.—Enclosing the certificate of the High Court of Justice in Sir John Stawell's case. (See *Commons' Journals,* vi. 569.) *Signed. Seal.* [N. VIII., 50.] *Enclosed:*

The said Certificate.

(Printed in *Commons' Journals,* vi. 585.) [N. XVI., 76.]

DOM JOÃO DE GUIMĀRAES to the COUNCIL OF STATE.

[1651, April 30–May 10.]—The Council of State having given me to understand that the Parliament expects from me a more clear and positive answer, I answer that having understood that the Parliament was pleased to vote all my answers to the six Articles were satisfactory, and that there only remained to declare in what time and manner those promises should be fulfilled which I had made to the Parliament I now further say, that if it shall please the Parliament by our mutually signing these six Articles to conclude a peace by adding thereunto the Articles of Commerce I shall by all means endeavour to give the Parliament content in these particulars of the time and manner wherein full performance is to be made, and shall in the interim pawn my head and person for his Majesty's putting in execution all and every of the six Articles, as I have already promised and do now again promise, which I trust may be a sufficient encouragement to send away to Portugal some prudent person with the news of a peace signed by the Parliament and myself, the conclusion whereof may fill all the Englishmen there and all the Portuguese with a huge joy. As for the other Articles of Commerce or Trade—which *mutatis mutandis* may be the same or the like as those agreed upon in 1642, whereunto it seems to me the Parliament hath said they will add some few more—in regard these are not properly Articles of Peace but only of Commerce I am now prepared to confer about them with the Parliament or Council of State, and shall not easily dissent from their opinions knowing the propension of the King and myself to favour the English merchants therein, and I am not ignorant that his Majesty is desirous with affection and industry to promote their trade by all honest and possible means. Now as I have heard that some are of opinion that these Articles of Trade do appertain to those of Peace also, I therefore easily assent that we proceed to treat upon them, being ready to sign as we shall agree, before any ship go hence with the tidings of peace to Portugal, that the absolute and perfect certainty of peace may at once and altogether not by intervals of time arrive there, since it was for a peace I was sent hither expressly. For should any messenger arrive in Portugal with tidings of a cessation of arms for six months only, leaving his Majesty in suspense, although neither he nor myself can have any doubt of the sincerity of the Parliament, yet if I should stand blamed for having proceeded in that manner how I should clear myself I know not. And whereas it may be pretended by some that trade would flow in the interim of a six months' cessation as a pledge of peace between us, those six months would rather serve the merchants to draw away all the goods they have from Portugal, than encourage them to send any more thither, which would do more hurt than good unto the trade that would follow the peace. This I remit to the prudence of the Parliament and Council, and therefore beseech the Parliament to depute some chosen members to treat with me upon this particular of Articles of Commerce, which may be done in few days and signed by both parties together with the six Articles of peace already agreed upon. (See *Commons' Journals*, vi. 570.) In *Latin* with *English* translation. [N. XVII., 126b, 153.]

The COUNCIL OF STATE.

1651, May 7.—Order reporting concerning the Lincolnshire Militia. (Printed in *Commons' Journals*, vi. 593.) *Seals.* [N. XVI., 77.]

The COUNCIL OF STATE to DOM JOÃO DE GUIMÃRAES.

1651, May 7.—Communicating the votes of that date (printed in *Commons' Journals*, vi. 570), and demanding a clear and positive answer within three days. [N. XVII., 154.]

The DOGE and GOVERNORS OF the Republic of GENOA to the PARLIAMENT.

1651, May [9–]19. Genoa.—Complaining that a ship *Alexander the Great* chartered by their merchants at Lisbon and laden with their goods was, on the voyage to Genoa, taken by some English ships off the Island of Iviça and demanding the restitution of the cargo. (See *Commons' Journals*, vii. 5.) In *Latin* with two *English* translations. Trace of *embossed Seal.* [N. X., 40.]

The ENGLISH AMBASSADORS to the STATES-GENERAL.

1651, May 9[–19].—(Printed in Thurloe, *State Papers*, i. 181.) Read July 2nd, being No. 11. [N. XVIII., 87.]

The ENGLISH AMBASSADORS to the STATES-GENERAL.

1651, May 10[–20].—(Printed in Thurloe, *State Papers*, i. 182.) Read July 2nd, being No. 12. [N. XVIII., 88.]

DOM JOÃO DE GUIMÃRAES to the COUNCIL OF STATE.

1651, May [11–]21.—" I confess ingenuously that I had a great desire to be able also to assent to all those things which are contained in the last paper of the Parliament . . . as I have amply and without exception consented to the six articles. . . . But since in earnest I dare not do this, though I am most willing, it is not without sense of grief that I forbear to do it, and that I am compelled in this case which hath happened beyond my expectation to recur unto the pleasure of the king my master, assuring myself his Majesty is so propense to peace and to the Parliament that he will very speedily send me his last commands to satisfy those last desires of the Parliament, whereunto as I dare not fully assent so neither do I dissent. And for this purpose I earnestly beg time to certify the king . . . in what state the present treaty stands and to receive his Majesty's answer." . . . In *Latin*, with *English* translation. [N. XVII., 159a, 155.]

The Same to the Same.

Same date.—" In regard I cannot be certain whether I shall obtain the leave I ask of the Parliament to recur unto the pleasure of the king, . . . I thought it best to send in this my second paper, that thereby it may clearly appear unto the Parliament I have done as much as in me lies.

For love of Peace and of the Parliament . . . I answer clearly and expressly to the point above this second way. That I do give my consent to all the Particulars that are contained in the last papers of the Parliament and Council of State, for as much as concerns the execution of those things which are comprehended in the first and second Articles, and the six months' Truce; provided that the persons who shall be set at liberty or to whom shall be made restitution . . . shall give a convenient caution to the king my master of surrendering their persons and all their goods restored in the same state they were in before such restitution in case peace be not concluded within the time prefixed. And that this condition . . may yet be more subjected to the judgment of the Parliament I leave it to their arbitrament whether they will by any private writing—if they so please—secure me this shall be done or whether it shall be inserted into the treaty of the Six Articles. I ask moreover, that from the day these Six Articles shall be subscribed trade may flow freely on both sides, and the truce of six months begin from that very day wherein we shall begin to make restitution according as is agreed in the two first Articles." (See *Commons' Journals*, vi. 573.) In *Latin* with *English* translation. [N. XVII., 159c, 156.] (This and the previous paper are both dated May 21, *vet. styl.*, but this must be a mistake for *new style*, as the translations are endorsed as read on May 13th.)

The Council of State to Dom João de Guimãraes.

1651, May 13.—Communicating the votes of that date, which are printed in *Commons' Journals*, vi. 573. [N. XVII., 157.]

Dom João de Guimãraes to the Council of State.

1651, May [15-]25.—Understanding that the Parliament was not satisfied with my two last papers, because there is nothing more desired by me than that I may make an end of this difficult affair, "I have resolved to go in person to the king, my master, that I may give him an exact account of all that hath been done hitherto in this affair, and that I may personally allege unto his Majesty the weight and moment of those reasons whereby his Majesty may be moved to finish this peace and to assent unto the Parliament's desires," . . . as "it may be necessary that his Majesty's counsellors hear from me by word of mouth what I can be able justly to oppose and reply if they shall allege any reasons to the contrary. . . For this purpose I thought it necessary to make my mind known unto the Parliament and Council, and at once to desire their safe conduct for my going into Portugal and for my return, which I hope will be speedy." . . (See *Commons' Journals*, vi. 575.) In *Latin* with *English* translation. [N. XVII., 159b, 158.]

The ENGLISH AMBASSADORS to the STATES-GENERAL.

1651, May 17–27. — (Printed in Thurloe, *State Papers*, i. 183.) Read July 2nd, being No. 13. [N. XVIII., 89.]

DOM JOÃO DE GUIMÃRAES to the PARLIAMENT.

[1651, May 20–30.]—Desiring that if the Parliament cannot grant his requests, they would at least allow him a longer time for preparing for the journey and voyage. In *Latin*. *Seal embossed*. *Endorsed* "Opened May 28, 1683, *per me* Jo. Nalson." [N. X., 6a.]

Extract from the Register of the Resolutions of the STATES-GENERAL.

1651, May [21–]31.—Concerning the Queen of Bohemia's letter. (Printed in Thurloe, *State Papers*, i. 185.) Read in Parliament July 2nd, being No. 19. (See *Commons' Journals*, vi. 595.) [N. XVIII., 63.]

MARY [LADY] AYSCUE to WILLIAM LENTHALL.

[1651, May 22.]—Enclosing petition. *Seal*. *Enclosed:*

The said petition.

Stating that her husband Sir George Ayscue had petitioned against the Bill for making the river Wey navigable from Guildford to the Thames, that the matter had been referred to a Committee, to which Sir George was summoned, but public business had him prevented from attending and he had now sailed in command of the fleet to Barbados, and praying that consideration of the matter be deferred till his return or else a committee be appointed to hear evidence on his behalf. (See *Commons' Journals*, vi. 577.) There is also a proviso written on parchment apparently to be added to the bill for compensating Sir George for any damage to his wharf at Chertsey. [N. VIII., 52.]

DOM JOÃO DE GUIMÃRAES to the PARLIAMENT.

1651, [May 23–]June 2.—" When I asked a safe conduct to go for Portugal and to return . . I thought I had done the Parliament a service, but receiving my Passport for going only, without leave to return . . I am afraid that I have either expressed myself ill, or that I do not well understand the Parliament, and for this reason I beg leave not to make any use at all of the said passport, but rather to continue and to conclude the treaty of peace, for which purpose it seems to me precisely necessary that I have an authenticated copy of such votes as the Parliament hath passed concerning peace . . . and to the end I may consent to what the Parliament demands my best ground must be a certainty of a future peace, which happily may be found in the votes aforesaid. If so, the Parliament shall not doubt of having what they ask about the execution of the two first Articles and security for the exact performance of all the other four. Wherefore I beseech the Parliament also to vouchsafe me a copy of their other intended Articles of Peace, for if they be only such as were formerly about Commerce—*mutatis mutandis*—I hope we may immediately conclude a peace, or that I shall accept of cessation offered for six months, being then assured there can nothing hinder a happy peace to follow." (See *Commons' Journals*, vi. 578, 579.) In *Latin* with *English* translation. [N. XVII., 160.]

The Examination of JAMES, DUKE OF RICHMOND AND LENOX.

1651, May 24. Whitehall.—"Being demaunded whether the Letters now produced unto him of these severall dates viz. 16 June 1646, 5 July 1646, 4 August 1646, 1º October 1646, 8 October 1646, 15 October 1646, 2 November 1646, all of them dated at Newcastle, the first word in every of them beinge Richmond, and each of them signed Charles R. were sent to him the Examinant by the late Kinge, for answere sayth that hee doth thinke they were the letters of the late Kinge to him this Examinant, and doth thinke that they were sent to him, aud that they were found in a box belonginge to him this Examinant. Upon the letter dated 4 August 1646, being demaunded whoe that trusty bearer was and what were his instructions spoken of in that letter sayth that hee nether remembers the bearer nor his business. Upon the letter dated 1º October 1646, wherein are these words : ' I am very well pleased with any new friendshipps which you have, or can make, for it may make mee have a better opinion of them but not worse of you, as hopeinge that you might convert them in case they were not right and knowinge that you cannot bee deboished by them,' the Examinant being demaunded what those new friendshipps and whoe those persons were ther intended, sayth hee conceives it to bee intended of some civilities the Kinge might bee informed that this Examinant might have receaved from the Scottish Commissioners here.

The Examinant beinge demaunded to decipher the cipher in that letter sayth that he cannot readily doe it, and beinge demaunded whether ther were a cypher betwixt the late Kinge and him or noe, sayth that he remembers not, and beleives that there was none. Upon the letter dated the 8 October 1646, beinge demaunded whether he had not sent the late Kinge a letter, and what that letter did concerne, sayth, that hee beleives by the remembrances in that letter that hee the Examinant might send a letter, but cannot certainly say hee did. Upon the letter dated 15 October 1646, beinge demaunded whether William Murry was with him, the Examinant, and the substance of his despatch to him sayth that hee doth not remember that Mr. Murry was with him, and beinge asked whether William Murry did not bringe him that letter sayth that hee doth not remember whoe brought it, and sayth farther that he doth not remember or beleive that anythinge was imparted to him by or from Mr. Murry. Upon the letter dated 2 November 1646, beinge demaunded what that freedome was for which the Kinge ther thankes him, sayth, that hee cannot say positively what the Kinge might meane by it, and being asked whether hee did impart any advise or opynion to the sayd Kinge, which might occasion that expression of thankinge this Examinant for his freedome to him in the letter beleives he might speake his sence to the Scottish Commissioners in generall concerninge either what was then in agitation or like to bee, to this purpose wishinge that the Kinge would enlarge himself as much as might bee to give satisfaction to what might bee desired in very greate condiscentions.

Being shew'd the letter dated at the Hague 9–19 September directed thus, For my deare Cosen, the Dutchess of Richmond, and signed Elizabeth hee beleiveth it to bee the letter of the Queen of Bohemia, but sayth hee saw it not till yesterday that the same was shewed him before the Councell, saveinge that hee thinks hee might have a sight of it by the officer whoe came to search his house att Christmas last.

IInvinge heard the examination of Mr. Cooke read to him and beinge demaunded whether Mr. Cooke was with him aboute the latter end of July last or any time the last summer at his house called Cobham, sayth, that hee remembers not of Mr. Cooke's being ther then or at any other time, and being demaunded positively to make answere whether Mr. Cooke was with him or noe, sayth that he was not with him, nor did impart to the Examinant any such thinge as is mentioned in his information. Beinge demaunded whether hee was acquainted with the intention of the riseinge in Kent 1648, and moved to bee a generall for the Kinge ther before the same riseinge sayth, that he was not knoweinge of the same riseinge before the same was, nor was moved to bee generall for the Kinge in those parts.

This Examinant beleiveth the letter dated 9 June 1646, and sign'd John Ashburnham now show'd unto him and directed to him was a letter directed to him by Mr. Ashburnham and found amongst his this Examinant's papers.

Beinge demaunded whether he hath a pardon under the Greate Seale of England, sayth that hee doth not knowe, and being demaunded whether hee hath taken the Engagement appointed to be taken by Authority of Parliament desires to bee excused at the present from giveinge answere to it." *Signed* "J. Richmond & Lenox." [N. XVI., 73.]

The following papers contain the several examinations and confessions of THOMAS COKE of Drayton in Shropshire made on March 31st and in April and May 1651, the whole of which were reported together from the Council of State on May 28th. (See *Commons' Journals*, vi. 579.)

They are here entered under that date and numbered according to the numbers in the *Journals* and are given the titles under which they appear there. All those mentioned in the *Journals* are here except No. 7, the Duke of Buckingham's letter, and No. 9, the King's Instructions. The letter with a decipherment is in the Tanner MSS. vol. lv., Nos. 88, 89; and is printed in Cary, *Memorials of the Civil War*, ii. 418.

No. 1.

The several examinations and confessions of THOMAS COKE Esquire, taken in the month of April 1651, containing 18 leaves and one page.

THOMAS COKE to the COUNCIL OF STATE.

1651, March 31.—Petition. Showing "that your petitioner having not long since voluntarily and foolishly made an escape out of a messenger's custody, and not rendered himself according to the time prefixed stands now by Act of Parliament attainted of treason, and ought thereby to suffer and forfeit as in case of treason. Neither hath he anything legally to plead for himself why execution should not be laid upon him according to the said Act. He doth humbly cast himself and all relations that can belong to a person of his quality at the feet of the Parliament, humbly begging that by the intercession and mediation of this honourable Board . . . . the Parliament, who are masters of their own acts, may be induced to suspend the execution thereof, until . . . . this Board shall be fully informed of your petitioner's state and condition. He confesseth he hath formerly adhered to an interest in opposition to this Commonwealth, not out of any malignity but according to the principles which he had received, for which he perfected a composition, and since it hath pleased God to cast upon him some fortune by the death of his elder brother he hath desired to spend his days in quietness and submission to the Government under which God hath put him, and to that purpose he hath prosecuted another composition with effect for his delinquency according to such rules as are prescribed by parliament. And if this honourable Board shall think him a fit subject for mercy and pity he doth not only promise all future fidelity and submission to the present government, but will give all obligations that are possible for the true performance thereof. And as an earnest of his service he offereth herewithal an ingenuous discovery of his own condition, and of his whole knowledge at present of public affairs, desiring that his clearness therein may make some sort of expiation for his past crimes, and may be accepted as some testimony of his future intentions . . .

He doth therefore humbly implore your mediation for a reprieve of that sentence passed upon him by the Act." *Copy.* [N. XVI., 72, No. 1.]

Second Paper.

1651, April 1.—Concerning the Westerne Counties. "About a twelve-moneth or more agoe there was a meeting at Salisbury by two gentlemen of each of the sixe counties, concerning an association in the King's businesse. I thinke Sir Humphrey Bennet was there and Sir —— Courtney for Hantshire. Colonel Strangways one for Dorsettshire, Sir John Arundell for Cornwall, Sir Henry Carey and Sir Edward Seymor I think for Devon. The names for other places I cannot tell. There they agreed upon an association, and wordes or some other signes of sending from one to another are agreed upon. The Lord Beauchamp was designed for some commaund, and one Jonathan Trelawny, a Cornishman, to bee major generall. Other officers he cannot name. Cornwall then offered to furnish three thousand foote, if the other five counties would provide fifteen hundred horse. That body to meete at a rendevouz in Devon and so to march. But they all desired to have some forein force landed if possible for encouragement, and to that purpose, sent Mr. John Seymour to the King; who was sent by the King out of Scotland to the westerne partes againe before Christmas last. This deponent knowes all this not of his owne knowledge, but by relation from the said Mr. Seimour only, who further told this deponent upon his returne to London, that if the King should fortune to give any discountenance to the present army and they should heare from him, they would speedily bee in armes in the west, but without perticuler orders from the King they would not stirre. This gentleman lay in Middle Row in Holborne when I was in towne last terme, but acquainted me with his discourse att my chamber. The Scotch commissioners at Breda desired the Lord Roberts might be lieutenant generall of these westerne counties. They surmised some hopes of Plimouth by that meanes. The sayd Mr. Seymour told this deponent likewise, that the sheriffe of Barkes,—as I remember, his name was Boys,—and the sheriffe of Wilts would endeavour their interests as sheriffs to rayse the *Posse Comitatus* if there were occasion for that purpose.

One Captaine Canes, a Dorsetshireman told this deponent in Michelmas Terme last, there was some designe upon the garrison of Poole. The Duke of Bucks sent word out of Scotland in wryting, and by word of mouth. Doud—who brought it—told this examinant that one Captaine Stanley had beene there with him about some designe upon Langbor (Landguard) Fort in Essex, and was come into

England againe. But this deponent knoweth him not. Hee wrote·
further that they were all united in Scotland, and the army would
consist of twenty-five thousand men well officerd, that they would take·
each souldier foity dayes' provision, and make ther way into England
or else fight the English army. If they had any succes they expected
some part of England should rise and appeare speedily, especially about
London or the southerne partes for a diversion of the parliament's army.
This was the effect of the paper with that formerly related, which paper
Doud brought out of Scotland, about February last. This deponent
knowes no more of the businesse wherein the Lord Chandos was
mentioned then what was written last night. He beleeves Sir Henry
Linghen hath some interest therein because the Lord Chandos when he
was with him asked this deponent whether he knew such a man.
There is one Colonell Worden in towne expecting to engage with the
first opportunity in the King's service. He did ly neere the Palsgrave's
Head in the Strond, and with him Colonell Vernon and Colonell Crumwell upon the same score. They lodged sometimes in Milford Lane at
one Mr. Ainsworth's house, and allso where this deponent was taken as
he hath hearde.

The same day the rising was in Norfolke, one Curtis, Colonell
Blake's man, came to this deponent's chamber, and told him of that
rising. He, being angry at him, desired him to goe downe againe to
appease it if he could. Which I thinke he did for I never saw him
since. This deponent knew not any person engaged in that commotion.
He heard from that Curtis that Sir Henry Felton and Sir Raph
Skipwith were forward men in the King's service there, but he knowes
neyther of them. There is one Mr. Cob in Yarmouth, a great confident
of Colonell Blake's for delivery of that towne. In Cambridgeshire Mr.
Ayliffe, Mr.   * and Mr. Chicheley looked upon as persons that
prepare and will engage in the King's service upon occasion. The
later is only knowne to this deponent. In Staffordshire, Egerton,
Worsley, Bagot, and Bowyer. One of them—hee thinkes Bagot—hath
some designe upon Stafford and upon Coventry, in both places upon
the affections of some persons within the townes. Hee had intimation
hereof from Colonell Worden not long since. In Derbyshire, Mr.
Shalcrosse will bee the forwardest man to appeare if there bee occasion,
Mr. Fitzherbert, Sir Wolston Dixie, Mr. Eyre and perhaps Mr. Gell
with the high sheriffe. These two last counties should have assisted
Lancashire and Cheshire upon any rising when the King or any army
should appeare. Mr. Shalcrosse hath good interest in the miners
where he lives, and would speedily get men together, lives in the
borders of Cheshire.

Mr. Henry Howard, the Earle of Arundell's sonne, Mr. John Russell,
and Sir William Compton he beleeveth are engaged in the Lord Gerard's
designe for Kent, Surrey, and Sussex.

In Sussex, Mr. Middleton looked upon as a person that will engage,
as allso Mr. Leuknor, Sir Edward Ford and Mr. Gunter.

In Berkshire, Mr. William Hinton hath mannagement of affaires.

The westerne men expect the parliament should withdraw their forces,
or a great part of them, northward.

They waite for that advantage to get into a body.

Lord Belassis was designed generall of the horse for the northerne
counties, and lookt upon as a gentleman very able and forward to
serve.

* Blank in MS.

The wiser and lesse rigid part of the Scots at Breda did privately agree to receave in all interests as well papists as others and to that purpose this deponent beleeveth have emissaries in England, but he knoweth them not.

Sir Abraham Shipman came as this deponent beleeves from Scotland to the Lord Beauchamp. I met him since he came to towne at the Swan on Fish Streete, and he told me he was to goe into the west and was returned before his taking.

When Doud went into Scotland, being in Michaelmas Terme last, I gave him seventeene pounds and ten shillings, as I remember to buy him a horse and to beare his charges to the water's side at one Mr. Pennington's house in Lancashire. But Mr. Booth was the man that was to see him conducted in those partes, to whom I directed a letter to that purpose by the name of Francis Blith, and Doud at his returne told the examinant, he had bene with Colonel Booth and had his helpe in the busines.

My Lord Chandos desired to know where he might send to mee. I desired him to leave letters for mee at one Stanton's house, a barber in Ivy Lane, by the name of Thomas Dutton and I would send thither for them. He sent a note to mee by that name to come to his lodging to speake with him, but I never met him since, for I came not to towne in a fortnight after he sent the letter."

Endorsed " Mr. Cooke's second paper delivered in from the Tower by the Lieutenant to me 1º Apr. 1651 in a letter and paper sealed up." Marginal summary of each clause in same hand. [N. XVI., 72, No. 2.]

Third Paper.

1651, April 2.—" The letters showed to mee on Sunday night [March 30] att the Committee of Examinations, directed out of Holland to Mr. Glew or such name to Doude's House were I beleeve sent from my Lord Byron to Colonell Worden or some other of his correspondents here. You may by this discover it. They are written in a water which appeares not till it bee held to the fire neere warme coles, and then may plainly bee read. What is written in inke signifyeth little or nothing. I know intelligence is weekely conveyed in that manner from thence and betwixt those persons. If the letters bee still there it may speedily be tryed. I once receaved such a letter so written from the Lord Byron to have procured some money from hence for the Duke of Yorke's subsistence at the Hagh, but I returned no answeare nor ever had a penny of money upon any publicke account, nor endeavoured the procuring any. There was a little glasse full of the same water in my studdy att Gray's Inn upon a shelfe.

One Doctor Lucy, a divine living in Hantshire, was in towne here last terme, solliciting for money for the Duke of Yorke and did the like in the countrey, I beleeve, but what he got I cannott tell.

The paper written in cypher and shewed to mee the same night as from the Duke of Bucks, if the same were intended for mee and Captaine Bishop may bee sent with it to shew mee, I shall tell him and direct him how it may bee opened and discovered, and allso where he may have some other cyphers and papers if he thinko them materiall, which have layne hid a long time, yet perhaps may bee usefull.

The presbyterians had not long since a designe upon Hull to bee effected by the meanes of Mr. Stiles who was minister there and kept much correspondence with the ministers of London. Hee, upon Sunday in the afternoone, should have drawne all or most of the soldiers to church over the water,—he being a person much followed in the towne and preaching at that church on purpose in the afternoone—. During the sermon time with connivence and assistance of some in the towne the gates should be surprised and opened for a party ready without to bee let in. This I receaved from Alderman Bunce.

Upon discourse with Tomlinson, I found he had a great opinion of this Stiles and of the affection of many people in Hull, though wee had no talke of the particulers. But perhaps it may bee a discovery worth the prevention if it bee not allready prevented. It was intimated to me from Bunce, as if the Lord Fairfax should have some hand in disposing the men without.

There is one Mr. Weston, a papist, which I did not remember yesterday, engaged in the surprise of Langhor Fort with Captaine Stanley as the Duke wrote mee word. Hee lives in Surrey. And there are some soldiers now in the fort in pay by them against the time of surprise to bee then upon centery, but how many I cannott tell.

Curtis, Colonell Blague's man, told mee upon the last rising in Norfolke there would fifteen hundred foote and fifteen hundred horse appeare, which were in readinesse, and that they had one hundred barrells of powder, and much money att commaund, and that he receaved this information from Captaine Kitchinman, who was an actor therein. I never heard of one hundred men that appeared there yet. What the remainder signifyed, Captaine Kitchinman best knowes, for I know nothing thereof. The mention of so large a number betrayed mee into this miserable snare by sending toward Scotland to give the advertisement. Whether the remainder bee in any condition now to rise is wholly unknowne to mee, being totally a stranger to all persons there, and to all affaires others then what I have expressed. When Blague came over with mee, he brought blanke commissions under the King's great seale for sheriffs of those two counties of Suffolke and Norfolke, but how hee disposed them I cannott tell. He spake of Sir Henry Felton for Suffolke and one Mr. Paston for Norfolke, if he could get them to accept the same. But whether they did or no I cannott tell. The busines of those countries was wholly referred to him.

For reiteration of the busines concerning the Lord Chandos, hee sent a man, a countrey fellow living neere Stanes, into Scotland which Doud met there. That man acquaincted the King from the Lord Chandos that there [were] four thousand men in readinesse in some partes westward,—it was guessed about Gloucestershire—for his service. The Duke of Buckingham wrote to mee to acquaint my selfe with the particulers from the Lord Chandos. Whereupon I went to his Lordship and acquainted him with what I had receaved. Hee seemed very shy, not acknowledging nor altogether denying any such thing, I being a stranger to him, neyther did I presse him hard upon it. Hee desired only to know how and by what name he might send to mee. I gave him Thomas Dutton, to bee left at the barber's in Ivy Lane, whether he sent a note for mee to come to him shortly after. But I, being then out of towne, receaved not the note untill a good while after. Was since at his lodging in Covent Garden, but could not meete with him." *Signed.* *Endorsed* " Narrative of Mr. Tho. Cooke sent to me by the Lieutenant of the Tower 2º Apr. 1651 at night." Annotated like the last. [N. XVI., 72, No. 3.]

Fourth Paper.

1651, April 3.—" In one Mr. Hardie's chamber in Coney Court in Gray's Inn . . if a loose boord bee taken up under the window, there will bee found the instructions that I receaved from the King att Breda, wherein how the designe was then layd will appeare. And I shall give an account of what hath beene done by mee in every particuler or by my knowledge.

There bee allso some cyphers, one with the King himselfe, another with Duke Hamilton, and with Dr. Frazer in Holland. Another with the Duke of Bucks. By these cyphers you might know weekely, if I were in a possibility to bee thought to act any thing, the secret intelligence of all designes whatsoever, for I know they would all write mee word.

I employed one Major Hall att Royston to sollicite the people in those partes to joyne with the King, if there were occasion. He hath layne there and sometimes in towne here ever since I came over, and assured mee hee could have one thousand men in those partes att three dayes warning. They only want armes and ammunition, whereof they have little, especially of the latter. The designe is to seize upon the publique magazines on occasion att Hartford and Cambridge; but the countrey people have very many armes in their houses. Hee was to bee made lieutenant-colonell to Mr. Ayliffe, I mentioned yesterday. There is one Squire Cæsar, Mr. Gulston, Mr. Randall, and others I cannott now call to mind, will bee ready to assist in those partes. One Charles Baxton, an inkeeper in Royston that is active in stirring up the people to that purpose and one Thomas Turner, living likewise in that towne, goe up and downe the countrey to that end.

In Northamptonshire I employed one Mr. Kinsman, formerly an auditor of the exchequer, to give intelligence of those partes. Hee lives neere the Lord Mountague and hath assured mee of his great fidelity to the King, and that hee will stirre when there is occasion, but is very cautious. There are armes still left and ammunition in the countreymen's houses there. Hee hath employed one Col. Griffin, formerly a colonell in the King's army, to sollicite and prepare the people in the countrey and rayse them in those partes upon occasion. Hee did lately reside att Sir Edward Griffin's house att Dingley. Sir John Norwich will appeare.

The sayd Mr. Kinsman hath likewise by my direction employed one Major Knightley in Huntingdonshire to negotiate affaires there, who is there now, as this deponent beleeveth, but hath receaved no account, only in generall Mr. Kinsman told him as he came up last to towne that the people were forward enough to rise there upon occasion.

The towne of Northampton will bee very forward to declare for the presbyterian interest, if the Scots get any advantage. Sir William Harmer and Sir Charles Compton have good interest among such as have affection to the King in the towne. Captaine Barnard and his brother inclinable that way. Sir William Fleetwood lately come to live in that towne likewise. Alderman Gifford, good interest among the people. I know all the exchanges in Christendome are layd by Alderman Bunce for returne of moneys for the service of the designe now in hand in Scotland, and by correspondence he drawes from all other martes to Roterdam and Amsterdam."

(Then follow particulars about Foreign Affairs to the same effect as in No. 5.)

"I employed one Mr. Rogers in Surrey to try the affections of the people there. He gave me an account of Sir Francis Stidolph, Mr. Hiliard, Mr. Evelyn, [and] others I cannot at present call to mind, that would appeare upon occasion, and that the countrey people are very heartie for the King, but being so neere London could not appeare in a body unlesse they had some garrison. They spoke of Windsor Castle or else somebody to repaire to in Kent or thereabouts. I spake with yong Mr. Bish att my first coming over about the other end of the countrey where his father lives. He told me his father and he could have a 1,000 men in readinesse there upon the least opportunity, and that the people were mad to bee in armes, if there were but the least tumult to give them occasion. There is one Mr. Price of Esher in that countie, a man of good interest among the people that there was hopes of engaging but not actually done. Sir Richard Onslow would appeare fierce upon the Presbyterian score and also upon the King's, but he was thought to be so totally guided by the Presbyterian Ministers that the Cavaliers were not willing to trust him. I went last year into Sussex to Sir Edward Ford to enquire after the said Mr. Ford. I mentioned concerning the Lord Fairfax's business. He told me of the persons I mentioned in my former paper that would engage in that end of the countie, as also my Lord Lumley to my best remembrance, and Colonel Norton formerly Governor of Portsmouth for the other end of the countie. He thought his cosen Ashburnham was able to give the best account with whom I never spake. Before the Lord Gerard had the command for Kent and these counties, I had a perfect list of the modell of an armie in Kent for all officers and members which I received from Colonel Thornhill from Roterdam, but since he had the command, it is lost and gone. Perhaps upon recollection I may remember many other names. There were set downe the names of all that would assist in person reputation and purse. Duke of Richmond was desired to bee Generall but refused, thereupon Gerard nominated. Lieutenant-General, Lord Hopton or Lord Ashley; Major-General, Colonel Hamond (?); General of Ordinance, Sir William Compton; Colonels, Thornhill, Culpeper, Hardes, Boys, Sir Ambrose Monyngs, Sir Anthony Auger, Crispe in the Isle of Thanet, Sir George Stroud, Sir Henry Penton" &c. *Signed.* *Endorsed* "Fourth paper of Mr. Cooke 3 Ap. written in Whitehall." Annotated as before. [N. XVI., 72., No. 4.]

Fifth Paper.

[1651, April.]—"I was . . about February last att the Palsgrave's Head, where I met with Colonell Worden, Colonell Vernon, yonger son of Edward Vernon of Sudbury, Colonell Crumwell, Captaine Fitzherbert and Mr. Doud. Mr. Shalcrosse should have beene there, as Vernon said, who said Shalcrosse would engage. There it was agreed that Worden should goe into Cheshire, Vernon and Fitzherbert into Derbyshire and allso Shalcrosse, Crumwell into Staffordshire, and should stirre up the gentlemen mentioned in my former paper, the King's friends in those parts, to get what armes they could privately and to bee in a readinesse to joyne with Lancashire upon opportunity. Every of the counties was to meete at a rendevouz the night appointed with such horse as they could make, and to surprize the Cheshire countie troope if they could, and the next night to meete all att a rendevouz upon an heath neere Warrington, there to joyne with the Lancashire forces. ' Sacrifice' was agreed to bee the word to passe from one to another in the meane time, and likewise till they met at that place.

Severall pistolls and powder in barrells have beene sent downe by carriers in boxes and barrells, under the name of sope and other goodes, and are still, as this deponent beleeveth.

There is one Smith, a servant to Mr. Withering's at the posthouse in Bishopsgate Street, who hath often taken out letters directed to Doud and other persons, and not brought them to the Councell of State, though the whole letters were seized if the maile were but once opened. Mistress Doud knowes this very well. There came severall letters to mee the last yeare by the name of George Edwardes and other names. There lay a warrant at the posthouse a long time to apprehend such person as came for those letters. Notwithstanding this, Smith severall times sent those letters to mee by Doud. I perused them and sent them backe againe to the same place. I have been told Allibond would doe the like or some courtesies of the like nature at the other office, but I know not of my own knowledge.

The Lord Culpeper came from Russia to the Hagh where he now is, and brought eyther in money or credit a great summe with him for the King's service. The King hath ordered him to issue 1,000*l.* to such purposes as I shall appoint for his service here in England, and sent mee word that hee had so done. But I never yet made use of one penny thereof.

I met once not long since in Covent Garden, at Sir Joseph Seimour his chamber, the Lord Beauchamp, Sir John Arundell, Colonel Richard Arundell, and Sir Joseph Seimour. Att another time with all the last mentioned persons, the Lord Arundell of Warder, and one Mr. Pile, that lives in Hantshire, a chirurgeon, who lookes after some busines of that nature. I told the Lord Beauchamp that the King expected that if he had any succes against the parliament's army, that England should then appeare in some partes for his restitution, and particulerly the westerne counties—wherein he hath commaund from the King to bee generall of the horse—. Hee expressed all readinesse, as the rest did, to serve the King, and all resolved to send downe what armes they could privately. and to bee ready when there was occasion and as they had orders from the King. My Lord Beauchamp sent since to speake with mee but I met him not, hee staying in towne but two dayes. Sir Joseph Seimour went about three weekes since downe to my Lord from this towne with an account that I showd him out of Scotland of the affaires there, and Sir Joseph is since gone downe into Devonshire and those other westerne counties from my Lord Beauchamp, upon that occasion to prepare those counties to a rising. I drew a commission at Jersey for the Lord Beauchamp to bee generall of the horse for those westerne counties, but whether it were sealed or delivered to him or noe, I cannot tell. I beleeve he acts now by vertue of it.

Cornwall, the most considerable countie in the kingdome to begin a commotion in respect of Sylly behind, and three partes of the county surrounded by sea. The people generally disaffected and full of armes, and some of the smaller portes will assuredly upon the first rising revolt. What men they can procure at Sylley may bee landed any night from thence. The landing place intended for them is the towne of Pensants neere the Mount. There will meeto them att the time appointed foote enough with armes to make a body, the avenues of the towne being easily made defensible against any partie of horse untill the countrey comes in. There is little store of horse in the countrey; their strength consistes all in foote. Another party att the same time will rise about Saltash Trematon and Foye, to get to the borders of Devon, there to make good the passes untill horse can come to them out of other countreys. The first fort aymed to bee gotten there is Hellford. The gentlemen that will engage are Sir Charles Trevanion, a man of great power among the people, Mr. Arundell of Trerice, and his sonne, Colonel Richard Arundell, Sir John Arundell of Lanherne, though a papist yet much beloved, John Arundell of Seyny, Blacke William Godolphin, Mr. Noy, Sir Chichester Wray, Mr. Pendarvas who lives neere Pendennis Castle, and hath an eye upon that place. He [is] now with Sir Richard Greenvill at St. Malo. Sir Richard Greenvill is much desired there by the countrey.

The people lesse active, but which will immediately repaire to a body are Mr. Edgcumb, Mr. Covinton, Mr. Scowen, Mr. Rashley, Mr. Richard Prideaux, Mr. Tremaine, Mr. Polewheele, Mr. Bassett and many others. The sollicitors upon this designe are principally one Captaine Spry, and Mr. Piper. Mr. Gewen is a man much looked upon there by the presbyterians.

When the King of Scotts was at Breda last before his journey for Scotland, money being the principall want, the designe was to sell the Islands of Sylley to the Hollanders and to deliver them possession. The bayt was faire for the Hollanders as the most commodious place for trade in this part of the world. The ends of sale were first for money, secondly, to keepe the Hollanders out of the English portes, having that place of their owne to goe to, thirdly, to set enmity betwixt the Hollanders by that meanes and this commonwealth. Sir John Berkeley and myselfe attended the Prince of Orange severall times about it, who endeavoured to promote the bargaine on the King's behalfe, and told us that he thought it would bee effected, the Amsterdammers being very desirous of the accomodation of the place. The occasion of my comming for England when the King went for Scotland left the negotiation with Berkeley. What issue it had, I cannot tell.

When I came over into England, I brought with mee severall letters to bee directed to severall persons for lending money. Sir Richard Page had one to deliver to my Lord Coventry, but he refused to receave it. Captaine Mewes had another to the Bishop of Rochester who lent him thereupon fiftie pounds as hee told mee. The account hee gave mee of the money was that hee had disbursed it in armes and ammunition, which he had lodged in and at a village neere Oxford, against a time for the surprisall of that place.

In Devonshire, the townesmen of Exeter are looked upon as generally well affected to the King, and waite an opportunity to take an advantage of the garrison. Potter, Walker, Colston and Shapcote are leading men amongst them, all for the royall interest.

In the countie, Sir Hugh Pollard, Sir Edward Seimour and all the Seimours, Sir Ameas Ameredith, Sir — Fortescue, Sir Henry Carey, Sir Francis Fulford, Sir — Courtney, Sir James Smith, Sir Thomas Heale. Earle of Bath is endeavoured to bee engaged, and Sir John Christopher neere Barnstaple, etc.

In London, the designe is eyther upon a suddaine tumult or rising to repaire to Whitehall and destroy the Councell of State or parliament, or else if any body appeare neere to repaire in numbers speedily to that. Every house hath armes, and the apprentices and servants are apt enough upon the least commotion to doe any mischeife. The Cavaliers, officers and others, will bee apt to incite them and assist them in the execution of such a designe upon the Councell. It was in designe the last yeare to my knowledge. Sir Richard Page when he was here was looking after some soldiers for that purpose. Captaine Garraway offered to assist. A designe much pressed at the King's court, if ever any rising bee in England, to repaire immediately to Westminster to destroy the fountaine. I have often heard it, and my Lord of Holland blamed extremely for not doeing it when he rose about London in the yeare 1648.

The presbyterian designe is most carried on in London by some of the nobility and principally by the ministers, Calamy, Vines, Jenkins, Crauford, Love, Cawton, Gouge, Case, Fuller.

These correspond with all other in England, as with Dr. Burges att Wells. Ball at Northampton, Angell and White at Leycester, Swetnam at Derby, Cooke late of Ashby, Stiles at Hull, Clegate at Bury, Fowler in Gloucestershire are diverse others. I cannot now remember in all partes. They preach to their congregations according to their intelligence. They are very close in their transactions. They have an intelligencer att Yorke, one Swinburne—I thinke his name is—that maintaines from thence correspondence with Scotland. Titus and Banfeild were lately sent out of Scotland to come for London. They came into France to my knowledge, but whether they bee yet arrived or noe, I cannot tell." *Signed. Endorsed* "Fifth paper of Mr. Cooke." Annotated as before. [N. XVI., 72, No. 5.]

Sixth Paper.

[1651, April.]—"In London the designe was layd in generall as was mentioned in the last paper, eyther to surprise the Parliament and Council by a suddaine tumult, or else to repaire to such body as should first appeare neero at hand. The persons imprisoned in Windsor lookt upon, as cheifo heads for countenance. The ministers mentioned in the last paper with some others to stirre up the people for them by preaching, praying and intelligence. The citizens to furnish money and assist, that I can call to mind, were Langham, Whitmore, Adams, Pride, Ashwell, Viner, Cropley, Richard Eliab Harvey, or his brother. Sir David Watkins lookt upon as a presbyterian, but not confided in. These and many other names I received from Alderman Bunce who told me that some of these had furnished money, his brother Langham as I remember for one. But Mr. Hougarden, who was sent over on purpose to sollicite the citizens for money, was intrusted for that point. What monies hath beene raysed or returned I cannot tell. He told me he had private tokens from Bunce to goe to many citizens for money, and particulerly that he went to Whitmore, but what money was gotten I cannot say.

When Titus came over to Jersey, have brought (*sic*) a catalogue of many citizens that authorized his negotiations thither, and shewed them the King. I was told there were neere eighty of them, but never saw the list. He then offered the King from them that if he would agree with the Scots he should want neyther men nor money. The intent of his journey being to persuade the King from the presbyterians in and about London to that agreement.

Denzell Holles wrote a long letter of advice to the King at that time, to agree with the Scotts as the only meanes to restore him to his crowne of England, sent it by his cosen Gervas Hollis.

After the agreement, the King wrote to him to invite and require his attendance into Scotland, offered him any place of advantage, particulerly the Secretarie's, but he refused to goe.

The ladies lookt upon as active in the presbyterian designe are the Lady Carlisle, the Lady Peterburgh, the former, though in prison, yet kept weekely correspondence by cyphers till the King went into Scotland, with her brother, the Lord Percy, who allwayes acquainted the King therewith, and sometimes mee with his intelligence. His secretary—Mason—hath beene often in England upon that occasion. Hee is now comming out of Scotland as I beleevo. Hee was designed a good while since.

When Doud came last out of Scotland, he brought a letter from the King of Scotts in his owne hand to the Lady Peterburgh. Hee shewed mee the paper sealed, but whether it was delivered or noe, I never since asked Doud; but I veryly beleeve it was.

When I came into England I desired letters from the King to the Lord Manchester and Lord Roberts. The secretary told mee the King had written to them allready by other handes.

There was one Major Wood, as officer under Massey, that was an emissary into England and out againe for that partie. Where he is now I cannott tell."

(Then follows a passage about Mr. Pryn and his brother-in-law Clarke to the same effect as that in No. 4 below.)

" Tomlinson had beene at Frankfort Mart in Germany, for bookes as he sayd, comming backe through Roterdam, stayed with Alderman Bunce, who sent by him into England some letters from the King to the ministers of London. Bunce afterwards recommended mee to him by this token: that those letters were crossed at the bottome. He acknowledged the markes, and thereupon entertained discourse with mee most upon the subject of the Lord Fairefax, who was a little before displaced and Rushworth who was then gone downe with the army, and upon some division which might probably happen in the army, upon that occasion. Rushworth, by that discourse, appeared to bee a great confident of his, but the particulers, being now nine moneths since, I cannot certainly depose. Since that time wee were both shy one of another."

(Then follow statements about Mr. Potter, Sir Richard Page, and Mr. Povey more fully given in No. 10 below.)

" This examinant since met the sayd Mr. Povey at the Countesse of Devonshire's house in Bishopsgate Streete att dinner, not long before Christmas last, amongst much other company. Where after dinner, the said Mr. Povey discoursing with this examinant, hee tooke notice to him of a letter formerly brought by Sir Richard Page from the King of Scotland to the ministers of London, alledging as this examinant remembers that these ministers were not to bee blamed that they gave him no better satisfaction in that businesse, and that it was not want of affection in them, or to that purpose." *Signed. Endorsed* " Sixth paper of Mr. Cooke." Annotated as before. [N. XVI., 72, No. 6.]

Seventh Paper.

[1651, April.]—(The substance fully given in Nos. 3 and 4.) *Endorsed* " Seventh Paper of Mr. Cooke." Annotated as before. [N. XVI., 72, No. 7.]

Eighth Paper.

1651, April 8.—(The substance of the commencement is fully given in Nos. A, B, and C. It continues) :—" Before I came into England I had a designe in writing delivered to mee for the surprise of the garrison of Boston in Lincolnshire. As I remember the forces were to bee brought up in long botes by water in the night, and to bee landed in the middle of the towne, and so to have surprised the maine guard. One Mr. Booth living neere Grimsby was lookt upon as a person to have acted in it. But the Command of that countie being then otherwise designed for the Lord Willoughby the paper was taken from mee againe. The Earl of Lincoln and Rossiter were then lookt upon as persons that would freely engage upon the Presbyterian score." *Endorsed* " 8° Apr. 1651. Eighth paper of Mr. Cooke." [N. XVI., 72, No. 8.]

Ninth Paper.

1651, April 11.—" The discourse mentioned . . in the examination of George Thomazon now prisoner . . betwixt him . . and this examinant and the manner of their acquaintance—so much of the same examinacion being now read unto him, this examinant—is in substance and to the best of this examinant's remembrance true. And this examinant saith he comming forth of Holland and arriving at London upon the Munday before the end of Trinity Terme last, went within a weeke or thereabouts to the shop of the said Thomazon and asked for a booke called Tholosanus *De Republica* of about 12*s*. pryce, but quicklie after made himself knowne to the said Thomazon by the token mencioned in the said Thomazon's examinacion, who readilie acknowledged it, and they spent in discourse about an hower in which the examinant made knowne to the said Thomazon the substance of the King of Scots' agreement with the commissioners at Breda, and their promise of assistance for the restitucion of him to his rights here, and that they expected that their brethren of England should joine with them upon that interest, and told him that himself was imployed into England, and entrusted both by the King and commissioners and particularlie by Alderman Bunce to negotiate their affaires here and to setle a correspondence betwixt England and Scotland. And did intimate to the said Thomazon that the King did looke upon the ministers of London as persons that might doe him a great deale of service upon that interest, and did expect that they should stirre up their several congregacions to joine with him. And thereupon the examinant desired the said Thomazon to acquaint the ministers with the effect thereof. To which the said Thomazon then replyed in effect that he thought the King needed not to doubt of the ministers' good affections, giving this examinant good incouragement that way, speaking likewise of the fasts which the ministers had for the good success of that busines, and spoke particulerli[e] of Mr. Jenkins, the minister, how gallantlie he had behaved himself before a com[mittee] verie latelie and was hum'd up and that himself was behind Mr. Jenkins' backe al[l] the tyme and that he was banished twenty miles out of towne, and to the examinant's best remembrance, Thomazon said Mr. Jenkins intended for Scotland and spoke also of Mr. Cala[my] and other ministers in and about London, their good affection to the said cause, and did acknowledge that he had delivered the King's letters to some of the said ministers, and spake of Mr. Vines his good affections. And the examinant further saith that Alderman Bunce did shew to this examinant at Roterdam the copies of the King's letters to the ministers, which in substance as he remembreth were an invitacion of assistance and his desire of compliance with them. And this examinant saith he doth not perfectlie remember whether he had discourse with the said Thomazon more then once, but saith it was in the inner roome of the said Thomazon's shop, and in some of those discourses spake concerning the Lord Fairfax, John Rushworth and the armie to the effect by him this examinant sett downe in his former papers sent in to this committee. And further saith that the said Thomazon blamed the Lord Fairfax for laying downe his commission at that tyme. And the examinant conceived by that discourse which he had with him, the said Thomazon, and others, that that partie was not pleased with the said Lord Fairfax laying dewne his commission, as conceiving if he had continued generall they might have made some advantage, thereby to have wrought a division in the armie and to have drawne some of them over to the King, and that in case a division had bene the same might have occasioned a rising in the citie and theise parts. And the said Thomazon, speaking of the King's partie, said John Rushworth had done them verie manie civilities and had bene often in that verie roome—where the examinant and the said Thomazon were conversing—upon severall meetings where they had discoursed verie freelie about businesses, and said Mr. Calamy had great power and influence on the Lord Fairfax, as also the Lady Fairfax. And this examinant did acquaint the said Thomazon with his intention of setling correspondences and that himself was to goe down shortlie for Lancashire to setle that correspondence, and that he did expect to heare there forth of Scotland and if he did this examinant would acquain[t] the said Thomazon with it. . . . At the time of these discourses his brother Sir John Cooke was living, but dyed shortlie after." Taken down or copied in the same hand as the endorsements and annotations on the other papers. [N. XVI., 72, No. 9.]

Tenth Paper.

1651, April 11. Whitehall.—

" Cornwall :

Colonel Buller in the yeare 1650 in February being then exchang'd publiquely said that hee would never serve the Parliament againe, and did offer to serve the King. Sir George Carteret informed this Examinant.

Major Hammond Arundell of Cornwall, a man that will bee very active upon occasion.

Sir Peter Courtney, Lieutenant-Colonel to Sir Bevill Greenfild, one that is ready to serve upon any insurrection.

Charles Roscarrock, Lieutenant-Colonel, one ready for new action, and one that was formerly in the old service all alonge.

Devon :

Parson Mervin of Okehampton, parson heretofore, a very active man, and now engaged, being mostly a solliciter in the King's designes.

Sir John Acland, a very active man, forward for any engagement, observed by the Kinge to bee his greate friend, and was soe recommended lately to the Kinge by some of the Agents.

Roger Mallock of Exeter, very active and lookt upon as a friend to these designes.

Captain Pinchback was at Jersey with the King of Scotts and Mr. Windham.

Sir Francis Fulford, or his sonn were look'd upon as freinds.

Dorset :

Mr. John Tregunnell, junior, and Mr. Thomas Tregonwell were recommended to the King at Breda as friends, whom he might make use of and who would appeare upon occasion, and since in England. Mr. Nappier, one of Dorset, told this Examinant that they were very good friends for the King's designes.

Sir John Lawrence, the same that is sayd of Tregunnell, a man of much violence formerly.

Sir John Wilde is lookt upon as a friend to the designes of the Kinge. He turned from a Protestant to a Papist. Dorsetshire generally lookt upon a country well affected to the Kinge.

Sommersett :

The Marquess of Hartford and his sonne are lookt upon as persons of greatest interest for the Kinge in the County of Sommersett ; and left to their care, and those whom they should imploy as their agents by reason of which hee hath little lookt into that business.

Sir Charles Berkly of Bruton ⎱ persons affected and as he con-
Sir Edward Rodney ⎰ ceives imployed by the Marquess.

Captain Rodney, Sir Edward's brother, came to the Kinge whilst at Breda, and tendered to the Kinge service together with some recommendations of the King's friends in that county, and brought an account of the affections of the county to the King.

He conceives that there is a designe on Dunstarr Castle, because he hath heard Mr. Windham formerly Governor of Bridgewater speake of some hopes of men in that part of the country and hath agents thereabouts. He hath heard somethinge of the Holmes Islands in the river neere Bristoll to serve some designe in those parts, but remembers not anythinge more concerning it att present. For Bristoll, being masters of the field they thought that place would not stand out.

Sir Edward Berkly looked upon as hearty for the Kinge.

Colonel John Tynt was at Jersey with the Kinge of Scotts.

Wilts:

Mr. George Hide was at Bredagh, when the treaty was there, and constantly with the Kinge.

Colonel James Longe, nephew to Secretary Longe; a very active man formerly and depended upon to engage these designes. Secretary Longe told this Examinant oftentimes . . that the said James would engage upon occasion.

The Seymores generally sway in those parts, especially the Lord Seymore and the Marquess of Hertford.

Sir John Oglander of the Isle of Wight and his sonn John were lookt upon as great friends to the Kinge at the treaty.

Younge Worsely Esq. was in a designe for the escape of the late Kinge out of the Isle of Wight, when he was prisoner in Carisbrooke Castle, and prepared horses to receive him, as soone as he should come over the werkes. Captain Titus layd [horses] on this side of the water by Tichfield for his conveiance. Mr. Dillington told this Examinant that younge Oglander, Sir John's sonn and most of the gentlemen in the Isle of Wight were engaged in the then designe of the surprize of Carisbrooke Castle, and the late King's escape and blamed very much the revolted shipps for not appearinge before the island to give them an opportunity to rise for that purpose.

The Lord Commissioner Lisle's brother was sent from the island to the revolted shipps to come before the island and to land some men in order to the riseinge and escape aforesayde; as he remembers the said Mr. Lisle or Mr. Dillington did acquaint this Examinant with this particular.

Sir John Mewes was alsoe in the same designe, and is now looked upon as a friend for the King's service." *Endorsed* "11 Apr. 1651. At Whitehall. Mr. Tho. Cooke's further information touching several persons." [N. XVI., 72, No. 10.]

Eleventh Paper.

1651, April 24.—" This Examinant was directed by the Lord Byron and Duke Hamilton att Breda to goe to . . . Mr. John Booth as to a person that had power and interest in the partes where he lived, and as to one they thought had good affections to serve his Majesty, and should be useful for settling a correspondency with Scotland. This Examinant . . . . after his coming into England about August last went downe into Lancashire to meete with a person who should have come to him out of Scotland, thinking he should there have met also the sayd Colonel Booth. But this Examinant did not see tho said Colonel Booth during his stay in Latcashire he being not then in the country—as this Examinant was informed—. Colonell Worden—as he told this Examinant—afterwards meeting Mr. Booth . . by accident told him that this Examinant had been in the country to look for him. And thereupon Mr. Booth coming afterwards to London about Michaelmas last one Thomas Doud brought this examinant to the sayd Colonel Booth att the Holy Lambe taverne neere Clement's Inn, where they had some discourse ; the particulers this examinant doth not now remember, but there was mention of a passage to bee had for some person to bee sent into Scotland through Lancashire. And, as this examinant remembers, hee did, in the presence of Mr. Booth, aske Doud whether hee would undertake a journey into Scotland, if there were occasion, the sayd Doud consenting thereunto, the sayd Mr. Booth did, to this examinant's remembrance, expresse his willingnesse to doe the King service, and after desired that if this examinant had any businesse or newes to impart to him, that hee would direct his letter to him into the countrey, whither he was then going, by the name of Francis Blith. And when Doud was after sent towards Scotland, this examinant did send a letter by him to the said Mr. Booth, directed by the same name, desiring him in generall,—to this examinant's best remembrance—, to give Doud such assistance in anything as hee could with conveniency, and what moneys hee should furnish him withall, this examinant promised to repay. Doud, after his returne from Scotland, told this examinant that hee had beene at Sir George Booth's house to looke the sayd Colonell, but hee being not there, his sister, Mistress Elizabeth Booth,—to whom, it seemes, Doud had directions from the Colonell to repaire in his absence—, told him that hee was at Warrington, where Doud told this examinant ·that hee the next day did meete the said Colonell ; who did eyther direct or guide him to one Mr. Bradshawe's house about ten miles beyond Warrington. From whence the sayd Doud went, as he told this examinant, to one Mr. Pennington's house by the water side, with whom one Mr. Shakerley dwelt, that had formerly served the late King in these warres. And that from thence hee went to Workington in Westmorland, and there tooke shipping for the west of Scotland. But whether he had any directions or helpe from Mr. Booth in any of those passages, the said Doud did not relate to this examinant, neyther doth he know anything thereof.

And as concerning the design now said to be discovered in Lancashire and these parts this deponent acknowledgeth that he heard since Christmas last out of Scotland that the Earl of Derby was designed to come into those parts with some forces out of the Island of Man, that Sir Philip Musgrave was sent out of Scotland into Cumberland and Westmoreland to stir up those counties, and that Massey should come in with 2,000 horse out of Scotland to joyne with them and with such other forces as should have been raysed in Lancashire and the partes adjacent, and the design was by that meanes to have compleated a perfect body of an armie, and to have given opportunity to all those adjacent partes of England to have resorted to them. Preparations were designed likewise out of Derbyshire and Staffordshire to have come into their assistance. And this Examinant further sayth that the said designe was layd in generall upon the agreement between the King and the Scotch Commissioners at Breda, and hopes and encouragements were then and there given as well by the Presbyterians as the King's partie that some forces might be raysed in those counties, and a messenger was despatcht away from thence to the Earl of Derby in order to preparations for that purpose.

Having been permitted to read the Examination of George Thomazon of Aprill 23º I well remember that Alderman Bunce told mee att

Rotterdam that he had sent over into England the substance of the Treatie agreed upon att Breda with the Ministers' letters as is mentioned in that Examination." *Signed. Endorsed* "24 Ap. 1651. Mr. Cook's 11th Examination at Whitehall. Speaks of Col. Jo. Booth and of the Lancashire designes &c." Annotated as before. [N. XVI., 72, No. 11.]

No. 2.

Concerning Colonel John Booth.

(The same in substance and almost in words as the first part of the last paper.) *Signed.* [N. XVI., 72, No. 12.]

No. 3.

Concerning the Levellers—Dorislaus' Death—Colonel Layton—the Lord Finch.

" During the time of his attendance att Court and especially since John Lilburne was acquitted upon his tryall, there came severall overtures from the people that goe under the notion of Levellers, to the King of Scotland, both in France, Jersey and att Breda. The same were transmitted usually in letters from Sir Sackvile Crow to the Earle of Cleveland, by him to bee communicated to the King. It was the examinant's fortune sometimes to see some of the letters. But the particulers hee cannott now call to mind, it being so long since, but to his best remembrance, they did containe a demaund from the King of some assurance for a full and generall libertie, or to that purpose, and an offer upon those termes to give him assistance for the suppression of the present power. There was the number of two thousand men mentioned in one letter, as this examinant remembers. It was conceaved that John Lilburne had a hand in the letters, and that the intelligence came from him to Sir Sackvile Crow. Mr. Martin and one Wildmore,—as the examinant remembers his name—, were lookt upon as persons that together with John Lilburne had influence upon the spiritts of those men. This examinant further sayth that about the conclusion of the treatie betweene the King and the Scotch commissioners at Breda, there came thither one Marston, sayd to bee a leveller, who had escaped out of England after the slaughter of two or three men. Hee was carried to the said King by Secretary Nicholas or the Earl of Cleveland. The King conferred with him privately neere halfe an houre or thereabouts, to what purpose this examinant cannott tell, but the King tooke him along with him afterwardes into Scotland. And this examinant before his departure met the sayd Marston at the Hagh, where, upon discourse, hee sayd that the King had now the hearts of those which hee called the free people of England ; that they would fight for him—against the people that reigned here—upon a cleere score, without talking of rigid termes or propositions, or to that effect. But hee did not then appeare to the sayd examinant to bee a person of any great judgment or consideration. And since this examinant's comming into England, hee hath heard nothing more then common report of any persons that drive on that designe.

Concerning the death of Dorislaus, the examinant sayth his name was Whi[t]ford that committed the fact, and that he was told by one Robinson, an English preist, who was then confessor to the Portugall embassadour att the Hagh, that the sayd Whitford, being a papist—as the examinant conceaves,—came to him to bee resolved in point of conscience beforehand, whether he might lawfully committ the fact or noe.

What resolution he gave him, the examinant cannott tell. But the fact ensued. The said Robinson told this examinant moreover that the Portugall embassadour shewed his affection much to the King in that case, for that he was privy to the fact, and caused his doores to bee set open on purpose that hee might repaire thither for sanctuary after the deed done ; whither the said Whitford did repaire, and had shelter untill his passage was prepared into another province. From thence hee got to Bruxells, and where hee hath beene since the sayd examinant cannott tell.

Concerning Colonel Layton, this examinant sayth that hee came from Bruxells to Jersey, pretending some businesse from the Duke of Loraine, but what the particulers were the examinant cannott tell. The said Colonell, during his stay there, did make applications to all men of businesse concerning the affaires of England, and seemed very busie and active in discourses and arguments upon all occasions. Some suspected him because he had beene an enemye, others treated him with more confidence. He went from thence to Breda where he was very sollicitous to promote an agreement with the Scotts upon any termes. And this examinant did not observe any person to expresse so much joy and content att the accord as hee did. Very few were satisfyed what religion he was of, or rather, whether he professed any att all. He went along with the King into Scotland, and is there now, a very great confident of the Earle of Argyle. Hee keepes the King's signet and is in nature of a secretary to him for dispatch of affaires relating to England, and is the only man that transmitts businesses betweene the King of Scotland and the Earle of Argyle upon all occasions, as Thomas Doud informed this examinant when he came last out of Scotland.

Concerning the Lord Finche's applications in any kind, this examinant never observed that hee did intermeddle in any publicke busines eyther for conncell or action. The reason was conceaved because hee was not admitted to the King's privy councell after the death of his father, which the Lord Finch expected. But Sir Edward Hyde, who had then great influence uppon the yong King, thought his spirit incompatible with their way of councells, and upon that score it was thought the said Lord Finch was rejected. After that time he came seldome to court, unlesse it were for ceremonie, or formall service." *Signed.* [N. XVI., 72, No. 13.]

No. 4.

Concerning the Treaty with the late King at the Isle of Wight, and Sir John Gell, Mr. Pryn.

" The sayd examinant being required to set downe his knowledge concerning any passages att the treatie . . att the Isle of Wight saith .

The propositions and answeares together with all publicke transactions are upon record.

For any private driftes or aymes. In generall, as hee remembers, the presbyterians, upon the opening of the treatie, pressed the King without dispute to give in two or three dayes an implicite consent to every proposition, and thereupon they pretended presently to have him up to London, to the parlement before the armie could come southward, which was then eyther in Scotland or upon the borders. And, upon his presence att London and his passage thither, they would have made him beleeve that the citty of London would rayse an armie under the commaund of Major Generall Browne, and that other partes of the kingdome would rise for their assistance under the name and authority of the two houses of parlement, which had given life and power to that treatie. And by this meanes they contrived to have setled their owne power, and to have given what law they had pleased to the armie still in the north. The King had as little affection to the presbytery or to the yoke of those propositions as he had to the armie. Some things hee alledged hee could not doe in his conscience, and therefore would not encline to that councell, but drew up concessions of his owne, as large as hee then thought fitt to condescend unto, and sent them up to the two houses by Captaine Titus and upon those concessions offered to come to London. But neyther the commissioners for want of power, nor the two houses would receave these propositions, and thereupon that contrivance fayled and came to nothing.

After the armie was drawne neerer London to St. Albons, the presbyters still deluded themselves with a beleife that the name parlement bore such a sway in the kingdome, and the two houses such authority, that together with the countenance of their owne partie in the citty, they should yet bee able to give the law. Neyther would they beleeve the contrary, though the armie had then published a very high remonstrance.

The King foresaw the contrary, knew the spirrits of the cittizens, and that a rude giddy multitude could not subsist against a formed armie, apprehended equall danger to himselfe in their handes, as where hee then was. Thereupon some about him advised him to attempt an escape. Others of highest ranke, and those which were most neere him dissuaded it alltogether. So that in diversity of opinions, the councell was quickly discovered and made impossible, and the King having no other twig left to hold by but the credit and name of the two houses of parlement, was glad to lay hold on that reed which deceaved him in the end."

(Then follows a paragraph concerning the design of the Presbyterians to the same effect as No. 6 below.)

" For particuler persons and passages att that treatie which occurre at present, the examinant sayth :

That the Lord Say was of all the parlement commissioners the most inward man with the King, and undertooke most on his behalfe with his interest in the houses. The Duke of Richmond and hee were very intimate, and by him the Lord Say conveyed his intelligence still to the King. Hee was so confident of the successe of the treatie that hee had bespoke himselfe to bee Lord Treasurer, and places likewise for his sonnes and many of his kinred. One Mr. Thomas Temple, his kinsman, had there upon his instance a promise to bee made groome of the bedchamber to the King.

Mr. Hollis was intimate with the Earle of Lyndsey, and by him conveyed all his opinions and projects to the King. The office of Secretary of State was designed for him ; another great office for Mr. Pierrepoint. The King was often in conference how he should dispose the offices to please them all.

Mr. Browne had gained himselfe into a very good opinion there with the late King, and was designed for his sollicitor in the first place or to such other place of advantage towards the law as should fall. Sir Harbottle Grimstone was lookt upon as one heartily affected to the King, but expected not any preferment that the examinant heard of. Mr. Vines was lookt upon by the King as a person won to his interest.

Sir John Gell sent thither to tender his service and to desire a pardon from the late King for his former actions. The King gave him something to that purpose under his hand and signett. One Bowring, a servant to the Lord Commissioner Lisle, came downe to sollicite the businesse. What money was given for it, he best knowes.

There was one Clerke, brother-in-law to Mr. Prin, who came thither allso to offer his brother's service to the King, if it might bee accepted, which was done accordingly, as the said examinant was told by Sir Edward Walker, to whom hee applyed and who carried him to the King. The same man came afterwardes to the King of Scotland upon the same errand to Breda, and had a letter from the said King to Mr. Prin to invite him into Scotland, as the said examinant was told by Secretary Long. The examinant confesseth hee saw the sayd Clerke at the Isle of Wight and allso at Breda, and that hee heard him speaking at Breda what service his brother Prin was both able and willing to doe the King if hee might bee employed, or to that purpose.

When the parlement commissioners departed all from the Isle of Wight to London, the Governour Hammond undertooke to preserve the King's person there against all opposers, but only such as should come with a particuler order from the houses of parlement. Accordingly, when the governour was sent for to the armie, hee left orders and directions in writing to that purpose with the captaines of the trained bands, and with the captaines of all the fortes and other the officers in the Island. The day before the King was taken away, the examinant went to the captaines of the regiments of the trained bands, viz. Sir John Lee and Mr. Dillington, to know whether they and their regiments should defend the King's person in that place in case of opposition. They shewed the examinant the governour's orders to that purpose, and sayd they would, and did allso undertake for their regiments, that the greatest part of them should dy in his Majestie's defence. They had appointed a rendevous to that purpose the next day. But in the morning, the King was surprized and carried away to Hurst Castle." *Signed.* [N. XVI., 72, No. 14.]

No. 5.

Concerning Foreign Affairs.

" There is one Generall Carpe—so called—who was with the King of Scotland at Breda, and is now att Bruxells, who did offer,—and he beleeves doth still—, to furnish four thousand men to land in any part of England, if money and shipping might bee provided for their transportation. Money hath beene much pressed from the Duke of Lorraine for that purpose, but he refuseth upon that account, and prosecutes the interest of the papists in Ireland. My Lord Taffe and Mr. Brent are still with him, solliciting for men and money for their assistance. The said Duke did offer to advance 20,000*l.* for that service, and the examinant beleeves hee hath done it. Hee was a principall person that pressed the King to confirme the toleration of religion and the other large priviledges and demaunds which were granted to the papists in Ireland. And when the Scotch commissioners afterwards at Breda pressed the sayd King to declare that toleration and treatie with the Irish voyd, the said Duke wrote a long letter of advice to the King with many arguments to agree and condescend to the Scotts upon any termes and to sticke att nothing. Hee did likewise formerly att his owne cost and charge rayse many men with a designe to have compassed the redemption of the late King's person from the Isle of Wight, whilest hee was. in Carisbrooke Castle, and one Monsieur Romecour, an officer and commaunder in his armie, partly for his forward diligence in that designe and partly to engage his fidelity to advance the King's service with the Duke of Loraine for the future upon all occasions, was gratifyed with the patent and title of an English baronett att Breda. Whilest the Duke of Yorke was lately at Bruxells, the sayd Duke of Loraine was dayly with him, solliciting him to goe into the kingdome of Ireland into the hands of the papists there. But his brother sent him a positive commaund out of Scotland to the contrary, and that hee should discharge Sir George Ratcliffe, Sir Edward Herbert, and Secretary Nicholas, who promoted that designe, from further attendance on him, and that hee should repaire to Paris and abide there with his mother. He pretends that he cannot remoove now out of the Low Countreys for want of moneys, his principall subsistence being the profitts which come by the tenths and fifteenes of such prizes as are taken at sea by such persons as have commissions from his brother and himselfe as Lord Admirall under his brother, and who harbour att Sylly, Jersey and Dunkirke where the French King hath given leave to set up an Admiralty Court for adjudication of such prizes and tryall of maritime causes arising thereupon, by English judges and officers to bee named by the said King and Duke of Yorke in such manner as was formerly practiced in the Admiralty of England.

The sayd examinant further sayth that there came to Breda one Duke Wolmar,—as hee remembers his name—, base brother to the King of Denmarke, and delivered to the King of Scotland a proposition in writing which the examinant saw, wherein he proposed to furnish the sayd King with an armie of eight thousand men, horse and foote, out of the upper partes of Germany or thereabouts, all armed, with a traine of artillery and ammunition fitting, to bee brought readie to the water side and to land them in any part of the King's dominions where hee pleased to appoint and afterwardes they should shift for themselves, if threescore or but fiftie thousand pounds might bee advanced, and shipping provided for their transportation. The Lord Hopton, the Lord Gerard, Secretary Nicholas, and generally all those that were enemies to the Scotch interest, were very eager in the prosecution of that designe, but the money and shipping were not then to bee had, and principally the Scotch commissioners opposed the bringing in of such a great forein force, which then retarded the designe. But the Lord Hopton is now att Colen very earnest upon the same designe and courtes all persons he can in those partes to engage. And Secretary Nicholas is as earnest at the Hagh.

One Mr. Armourer, a querry to the King, was sent not long since out of Holland into Denmarke to sollicite supplyes for the King of Scotland. Three hundred Danes were sent by the King of Denmarke into Scotland with a recommendation to bee of the lifeguard of the King, but the Scotts would neyther entertaine them nor permit them to abide there, whereupon they were sent to the Island of Jersey where they now are.

The Queene of Sweden did mediate very hard and interpose very earnestly betweene the King and the Scotts for an agreement by letters which the sayd examinant saw. Shee sent likewise one Sir William Balladine, a Scotchman, to the King for that purpose. One Captaine Mead was afterwardes sent to Sweden to acquaint the Queene with the progresse of affaires and to sollicite supplies. But the sayd Sir William Balladine resides there, and is very active upon the Scotch interest. He is a servant to the Queene, of her privy chamber. The Scotts are very confident of supplies from that kingdome when they desire it and have lately renewed their ancient league with them." *Signed.* [N. XVI., 72, No. 15.]

No. 6.

The Design of the Presbyterians, &c.

" The designe of the Presbyterians is if ever they get power into their handes to set on foote the concessions made by the late King at the Isle of Wight which were afterwards voted in both houses to bee a ground and foundation for a peace, and to restore the parliament to the same condition and members as it had the day of their seclusion, viz. 4th December, 1648. The examinant doth beleeve the same to bee true, for that the Scotch commissioners at the treatie at Breda did on behalfe of the English, there presse a consent from the King to confirme all ordinances of both houses of parlement, consented unto by his father, which did include these concessions, and upon debate of that proposition did expresse themselves at large, that though neyther they nor the English presbyterians did owne or esteeme the present assembly at Westminster to bee a lawfull parlement, yet neverthelesse that the former parlement was still in being, not dissolved by the late King's death by virtue of the Act which did prohibit the dissolution of the same without consent of both houses. And though the members, the 4th of December, 1648, were by force remooved and secluded from meeting and acting att Westminster according to their duty, yet, that force being taken away, they might lawfully come together againe to their places and proceed upon the former session. That the body remained undissolved though the members were scattered. The examinant had many debates with the Lord Libberton and other Scotch upon this point, and did urge the same stiffly as the sense of the presbyterians in England. But because it was not a thing proper for commissioners from Scotland to take upon them to determine the lawes or parliamentary constitutions of this kingdome, thereupon they were contented that all matters relating to England should bee referred to a free parliament to bee called by the King's writt, when the condition of the kingdome would permit. The examinant sayth that he hath understood the returne of the secluded members to the parliament to bee the drift and opinion of most of the presbyterians in England as a thing avowed by them, from diverse persons whose names he cannot now call to mind. And that since the late King's death he had once a debate with Mr. Waller of Gray's Inn, a secluded member, who did upon the like grounds and arguments maintaine the same opinion."

Endorsed in the same hand. [N. XVI., 72, No. 16.]

No. 8.

Information against the Duke of Richmond.

" About the latter end of July last he arrived from Holland att Gravesend on Saturday night . . . —being brought over on a Holland man of warre, commanded by Captain De Liuda—. That on Sunday following in the afternoone he went from Gravesend to Cobham to . . speake with the Duke of Richmond, where meeting at the doore with a gentleman, whom he supposed to bee an attendant upon the said Duke demaunded to speake with his Lordship. The sayd gentleman was of a middle stature, a blacke complexion, with a locke on one side, as the Examinant remembers, and he thinkes he heard him called Washington, who taking notice as if he knew the Examinant, and had formerly seene him in the Isle of Wight, did thereupon carry him into a lower parlour of the sayd house, where after some stay the said Duke came to this Examinant. And after salutations, and some discourse of civility the Examinant to his best remembrance did acquaint him that he was lately come out of Holland where the Scotts and King were agreed upon a treatie at Breda. That the King was gone into Scotland, and that the Scots had given him some assurance that they would assist him in the recovery of his rights in his other kingdomss. That the Examinant was sent into England, to negotiate the raysing of forces to joyne with the Scots to that purpose, and that he did repaire to his Lordship by direction from the sayd King and his Lordship's brother the Duke of Buckingham, to know whether he would undertake the command of such forces as should be raysed for that end in the counties of Kent, Surrey and Sussex, to which command the King had designed his Lordship as Generall, if he would accept thereof, and that he, the Examinant desired to know his answer, to the end that the King might bee acquainted therewith. His Lordship to the Examinant's best remembrance seemed strange that the King should have any such opinion of him or should have him in his thoughts for any such employment, who was no soldier nor ever meddled in busines of that nature. That though he had receaved much kindnesse from the late King, yet that he never had anything to doe with his son or to that purpose, and did desire to bee excused from medling therein. The Examinant further sayd, to his best remembrance, the gentlemen of Kent, which were beyond the seas, as Col. Thornhill and Mr. Heath, did likewise propound his Lordship to the King as the fittest person and whom they thought the countrey people did well affect. His Lordship sayd he meddled not in any countrey affaires and did desire but to live quietly amongst them or to that purpose. And that Col. Thornhill had come to him upon the last rising in Kent upon the same errand, and that he then likewise refused to entermeddle therein. When the Examinant did presse his Lordship for his particular answer that the King might be acquainted with it, he did positively refuse the same, and did seeme to deehne all discourse to that purpose. Admonished the Examinant the danger himselfe would bee in, if he should negotiate or act anything of that nature against the present governement, and what a severe eye there was upon all endeavours of that nature.

The rest of the discourse was concerning newes, the acquaintance that this Examinant's brother and his Lordship had at Cambridge in the University and the Examinant's and his being together att the treatie in the Isle of Wight, and other matters not material to busines. This is substance of all, as neere as the Examinant can possibly call to mind, that passed betwixt them. After halfe an houre's discourse or more the Examinant departed, and never saw or heard ever from the said Duke since, neyther doth he know or hath heard of any correspondencies that hee hath kept up with the King or his brother the Duke of Bucks, or any other since the late King's death, neyther doth the Examinant beleave he ever had any." *Signed. Endorsed* in the same hand as the Annotations " 8 Information against the Duke of Richmoud." [N. XVI., 72, No. 17.]

No. 10.

Mr. Thomas Coke's further Information touching several Persons.

"About two dayes after that this Examinant had beene with Mr. Thomazon . . he repaired to the house of one Mr. Potter an Apothecarie in Blackfryers, to whom Mr. Alderman Bunce at Rotterdam had commended this examinant, as to a very active man in the cittie of London upon the Presbyterian interest, and one that had much acquaintance and correspondencie with the cheife ministers in London, and would transmit all affaires to them as there was occasion. The sayd Alderman further told this examinant that hee need not looke after any other persons in the citty of London, for the mannagement of affaires there, more then the sayd Thomazon and the sayd Potter for that they knew the affections of most of the citizens and allso of the ministers, and which of both would bee most forward to engage upon the Scotch interest. His further expression was—they were both very right men—. The sayd Alderman further gave this examinant a token, whereby he should repair from him to the sayd Mr. Potter, and he doubted not but the sayd Mr. Potter would thereupon communicate freely with him and give credit to him, this examinant. The token was, as this examinant remembers,—that Mr. Ratcliffe's or Alexander's letters were come safe to his bandes—, or to that effect. . By which Ratcliffe or Alexander was understood betwixt them,—as the sayd Alderman told this examinant—, one Mr. Drake who had formerly receaved subscriptions from severall persons in London, for sending of money to the King. And this examinant sayth that he did about the time abovesayd repaire to the sayd Potter from Alderman Bunce by the sayd token, to his house in Black-fryers, where the sayd Potter did acknowledge the token mentioned to him by this examinant ; and thereupon tooke him into an inward roome within his shop and entertained discourse with him necre halfe an houre, to his remembrance, the substance whereof was, to this examinant's best remembrance, that he acquainted him, the sayd Potter, with the agree-ment betwixt the King and the Scotch commissioners at Breda. How that the Scotts did intend to assist the King in the recovery of his other crownes, and how that this examinant was sent over by the King to negotiate some assistance to bee given here in England, and particulerly in London, to the Scotts in their intended designe for the King's restitution ; as allso for settling a correspondence betweene London and Edenburgh by private stages, for conveying of intelligence betweene Scotland and London ; and that this examinant was to goe speedily into the countrey for that purpose, or to this effect. The sayd Potter expressed some backwardnesse in opening himselfe upon the first sign to this examinant, as being a stranger to him. But, to this examinant's best remembrance, did expresse the affections both of the citizens in generall and of the ministers to the King upon the interest hee was now upon. And that the ministers did fast and pray for him in private meetings and for the succes of the businesse, though they durst not in there pulpitts. He did allso, to this examinant's best remembrance, expresse his owne discontent and the regret of very many of the citty att the present governement, and seemed desirous to have a way of correspondence setled, whereby they might both heare and send from Scotland ; and that this examinant would let him knowe when the same was setled, that letters might bee sent and receaved. And this examinant promised so to doe, and to come againe to him within a short time to acquaint him with such newes as hee should heare out cf Scotland, from whence this examinant then expected to have met a messinger. And this examinant went shortly after downe into Lancashire, but never spake with the sayd Mr. Potter since. But this examinant further sayth that before he went out of this towne he acquainted one Sir Richard Page, —who came over with this examinant out of Holland upon the same businesse—, with what had passed betwixt him, the sayd examinant, and. the sayd Mr. Potter, and desired the sayd Sir Richard Page to speake further with him in this examinant's absence, if he could with con-veniencie, and get further information concerning both ministers and citizens in particular. And after his returne to London againe, the sayd Sir Richard Page told this examinant, to his best remembrance, that he had at large spoken with the said Mr. Potter, and that one

Mr. Hougarden, a Dutch merchant who came likewise over with this examinant out of Holland, had brought the said Potter to the sayd Sir Richard's lodgings at the signe of the Death's Head in the Old Baylie, —where the said Sir Richard then lodged by the name of Mr. Smith—, and that the sayd Potter had given him great assurance of the affections both of the cittizens and ministers of London to the King and to the Scotch designe now on foote, and had likewise spoken very confidently and largely that hee did beleeve there was not one citizen of fiftie in London, that was pleased with the present governement, but that they wished the King here againe in their hearts, and the King should find that to bee true if ever there were occasion. But the said Sir Richard did not acquaint this examinant, to his remembrance, with any further particulers of the discourse that passed betwixt them. Only that the sayd Mr. Potter desired the sayd Sir Richard to conferre with one Mr. Povey of Gray's Inn about the said businesses, whom the sayd Potter offered to bring unto the said Sir Richard's lodging, alledging that hee would bee able to give full satisfaction in matters of that nature. But whether Sir Richard did ever discourse with the sayd Mr. Povey thi[s] examinant cannott say, for that the sayd Sir Richard went shortly aft[er] out of the kingdome. And this examinant further sayth that when hee and the sayd Sir Richard came into England, the King sent a letter by them to the ministers of London, directed to Mr. Calamy, Mr. Crauford and Mr. Love and to Mr. Jenkins, as this examinant remembers, to bee by them communicated to the rest of the ministers in or about the citty of London. The substance of which letter was, to this examinant's best remembrance, to acquaint the sayd ministers with his Majestie's agreement with the Scotts, and with what hee would doe for satisfaction in settlement of religion and presbyterian governement here in England; that confidence of their assistance was one motive that induced the agreement; that they would now joyne with him and with the Scots in the endeavour of his restitution; and that they, haveing influence not only upon their parishes but other parts of the kingdo[me], would stirre up their severall congregations, and other places where they had inte[rest] to joyne likewise with his Majestie to that purpose; and that they wou[ld] privately pray for him and his good successe, or to that effect. And this examinant further sayth that the said Sir Richard did after his arrivall here endeavour,—as he told this examinant—, to deliver th[e] said letter according to the direction, and to that purpose sent to one Mr. Cawton, a presbyterian minister who was formerly in prison with him, the said Sir Richard, in the Gatehouse, and desired him to acquai[nt] the said ministers that the King had sent such a letter to them and that it would shortly bee brought to some of their bandes. And the sayd Sir Richard further told this examinant that the sayd Cawton had acquainted the said ministers therewith, and that he had receaved some generall assurance of their affections thereupon, but they conceaved the sayd letter was nothing but a complement, and could containe nothing but wh[at] they had formerly understood. But whether the sayd letter was afterwardes delivered to any [of] them or noe, this examinant cannot tell, for that he went presently downe into Lancashire, and upon his returne heard of his brother's death and thereupon desisted any further prosecution of that businesse, and the sayd Sir Richard departed out of the kingdome without leaving any account to this examinant thereof.

This examinant further sayth that at such time as he was at Mr. Thomazon, his shop in Paul's Churchyard, he met there with one Mr. Edward Bish, who was formerly knowne to him, this examinant, and after he had discoursed with Mr. Thomazon, hee entertained some discourse with the said Mr. Bish and did likewise acquaint him in generall

that this examinant was lately come into England to negotiate some
assistance to bee given to the Scotts, and to the King in order to his
restitution, or to that effect, but did not acquaint him with any more
particulers, as farre as this examinant now remembreth. He told this
examinant the great hazard and danger of acting anything here of that
nature, and how severe an eye there was over all endeavours to that
purpose, or to that effect. This examinant replyed, to his best remembrance, that hee was neverthelesse come hither for that purpose, and in
the discourse desired to know of the sayd Mr. Bish what his opinion was
of the affections of the people in generall to the present govcrnement,
and particulerly in the countie of Surrey, where hee had an interest.
Hee replyed, to this examinant's best remembrance, that he thought the
people about London were generally disaffected to the present governement, and would embrace any occasion of rising for the change of it,
and particulerly that in the part of the countie of Surrey where he lived
the people were so distasted and forward to rise, that upon any tumult
or insurrection hee and his father could undertake to bring together a
thousand men in a very short warning. . . . He hath since several
times seen the sayd Mr. Bish but never spoke to him about any publicke
businesse."
Signed. Endorsed " Tenth Paper of Mr. Cooke from the Tower."
Annotated in the same hand. [N. XVI., 74, No. 1.]

A. B. C.

(Three papers concerning correspondence and intelligences marked iu
pencil A., B., and C. Of these B. is the latest in date, but C. is the
fullest and is therefore given below with supplementary matter in
brackets from A. and B. Of these A. is the " paper given in to the
Council this 28th day of May 1651," B. and C. are the " two papers
concerning Correspondencies and Intelligences.")
" Being required to set downe what correspondence he hath knowne
to bee held betwixt any persons professing to bee of the Parliament's
party and those on the other side, or what intelligences or applications
have beene made or given to the King of Scotland or any of his party
during these late troubles &c. saith:
It is not to bee thought that since the change of Government here,
any members should imediately send eyther intelligence or supplies to
the sayd King, but if any such thing hath beene the same was done
cautiously by third Handes which must bee driven out by relations and
circumstances.
The Lord Herbert, now Earl of Pembroke, was since his father's
death recommended to the sayd King by Dr. Morley for a person both
of affection and will to serve him [A. B. as the examinant was told at
Breda by Sir Richard Page the last year]. The recommendation of the
sayd Doctor came not without the sayd Lord's privity—as the Examinant beleeveth—. He was thereupon designed to bee Generall of South
Wales [A. and of such forces as should be raised there] in this present
Scotch Enterprize. But whether he have any such command or authority
at present the Examinant cannot tell. Upon discourse at Breda none
was thought so fitt. And thereupon the Examinant was directed when
he came into England to make an addresse to that purpose, but never
could have opportunity. His late forward appearance in the Parliament's service, — as the Examinant hath heard — may perhaps to
judicious persons not at all diminish the suspition.
Sir William Russell of Worcestershire and Sir Gilbert Talbot did use—
as the Examinant hath heard—to transmit intelligence to the Court under
other names. They are both very great with the Lord Powis, who is inward with the sayd Lord Herbert, perhaps he might tell what he knew,

and some of their intelligence might come that way. [B. Sir William Russell was wont to write to the Lord Jermyn, Sir Edward Walker and Endymion Porter, when hee was abroad.]" He "was formerly likewise a great freind of the Chief Baron of the Exchequer. Though they have lately very much differed seemingly, yet it hath beene thought some intelligence might come that way.

Sir Sackville Crow did use to transmit intelligence [to the Lord Cleveland] from the Levellers, as was mentioned in the former paper.

Mr. John Hall, now living at Richmond, formerly a servant to Mr. Secretary Long, and, as the Examinant thinks, to Mr. Cornelius Holland also was not permitted to attend in his place of Clerk Comptroller of the King of Scotts' house upon suspition of giving intelligence hither. [A. B. Hee was put away when the King went to Jersey.] How justly the Examinant cannot say. But he prosecuted Secretary Long's Composition here at Goldsmiths' Hall, where it was finished about a year since by the assistance of Mr. Holland and other freinds, whilst Mr. John Ash sat in the chair, though Long at the same time and also before and since acted as Secretary to the King beyond the seas. [A. B. Mr. William Loving, who is now Register of the Admiralty Court att Dunkirke for adjudication of English prizes taken by such as have Commissions from the King of Scotts', told this Examinant that he sent some of the money towards the payment of the said Composition.] Perhaps persons that would further his Composition here would probably send him intelligence beyond the seas. Truth may sometimes be discovered out of discourses and conjectures of this nature.

Mrs. Wheeler likewise, laundresse to the late King, was wont to bring letters to him to the Isle of Wight, but from whom the Examinant cannot tell.

There is one Mr. Ogle, a kinsman to Dr. Smart, who was very zealous for the Parliament at the beginning of those times came after to Oxford, where everyone supposed him an enemy, only the Lord Digby, then Secretary of State, tooke him into his particular care. He stayd not long at Oxford, but came back to London, from whence he hath been thought to give intelligence ever since. Hee came privately to Breda, stayd there not above a day or two, was carryed to the King, and returned again speedily for England. He was supposed an intelligencer, and is now in England. It may bee easily discovered to which of the Parliament or Councell hee makes applications.

There is one Colonel Hauley, formerly of the King's partie, who hath some neere relation to Mr. Chaloner, a member of the Parliament or Councell. Hee lives much about Whitehall. The Examinant hath heard, as if some intelligence should sometimes come out that way." [A. B. While "the Examinant was in Jersey there came thither about Christmas last was a twelvemoneth one Carter and with him a Chirurgeon living in London, whose name the Examinant cannot remember, who were it seemes employed from hence upon some designe concerning the islands of Sylley. So soone as they landed at Jersey they were imediately apprehended and imprisoned, the King having formerly receaved intelligence both of their names, their qualities and their employments. The intelligence came—as the Examinant there heard—imediately to the sayd King himselfe from some person with whom he kept correspondence by cypher, but who the same is the Examinant cannot tell. In the like manner when one Mosse was employed from hence into France the last yeare, and from thence backe into Scotland, the sayd King had intelligence both of his negotiation and intentions before he arrived in Scotland and of all circumstances necessary, as one Thomas Dond informed this Examinant who came out of Scotland in February last. But from whom or in what manner the said intelligence

came, or any other certainty concerning cyther of the same this Examinant doth averre that he cannot further expresse it. He hath heard
Secretary Nicholas boast of the good intelligence he had from Derby
House, when the Committee sate there, but from whom he never heard
him speake, nor knoweth anything particularly therein.]

He heard the Lord Lautherdale say in Holland that he or Duke
Hamilton had correspondence with Mr. Henry Darley, a member of the
House.

The Earl of Denbigh and the Lord Howard were lookt upon att Court
as freinds to the King's interest, and averse to the present way of
Settlement, but doth not know of any particular correspondencies kept
by either of them with any at Court. Hath only heard that the Earl of
Denbigh should keepe correspondence with his mother at the Queene's
Court. And hath heard private intimations at the King's Court as if
the Lord Howard should have done very good service but knows nothing
in particular.

He hath heard much talke likewise of summes of money that should
bee sent by the Speaker to Oxford, but knowes nothing of his owne
knowledge, and Mr. William Leg, to whom the late King disposed the
profitts of the Speaker's lands at Burford, was supposed to trade with
the Speaker for that purpose. He hath heard also Mr. Love esteemed
as a person much discontented with the present Government and a
wellwisher to the King's restitution, but knowes nothing of him particularly.

[B. Touching the Earl of Northumberland hee heard it credibly
reported at Oxford that he had an intention to have came thither soone
after . . the Earles of Holland and Clare came thither, if they had
liked their entertainment. As he remembers he had the same from
Blague, the governor of Wallingford, who went with a partie of horse to
Lord Paget's house, to fetch the sayd lords to Oxford. At Breda likewise the last yeare, when the Earl of Newcastle was designed for the
command of the Northerne Counties, he heard the Lord Percy murmure
as if his brother or himselfe had more command and interest in
Northumberland and those partes then the Lord Newcastle, and yet
were passed by which he seemed to take ill. The Examinant remembers
nothing else concerning the sayd Earle.

Sir John Hippesley was a man never in any ill esteeme at Court.
He was at Yorke and Nottingham at the beginning of the warre. But
the Examinant knowes nothing else of him particularly.

Sir John Danvers he hath heard spoken of as a person weary of the
present times, and much come off from the Parliament wayes, and as if
some intelligence should come that way sometimes, but cannot instance
anything in particular. He heard Sir Richard Page speak as if one
Wakeman, who hath relation to Sir John Danvers, were one of his
acquaintance, whom he put some confidence in, but knowes nothing
more in particular of him.]

The Lord Commissioner Whitelocke, when he came down to Oxford
with propositions from the Parliament was lookt upon as a freind, and
so treated by those that were neere the King. Sir Edward Hyde and
others visited him and conferred with him under that notion. And to
this day he is esteemed at the King's Court as a person that complyes
for his owne interest, and as one that is apt to shew civilities and
curtesies to the King's partie upon all occasions. There was a great
contest in the Parliament about two yeares since betweene him and Mr.
Martin, about the gardianship of the sonne and beire of Sir Charles
Blount in Berks, supposed to be a recusant, who had been Scout-
master-Generall to the King and was slayne by Langston (?) at Oxford.
The same was then voted to Mr. Martin, who sent the said Mr. Blount

over into Normandie att the same time as this Examinant went last into France, where he is bred up in the Popish religion, as the Examinant was there credibly informed.

Colonel Purefoy hath annuity or rentcharge of 200*l.*—as the Examinant thinks—*per annum* out of the Earle of Devon's estate granted about two yeares since, upon pretence of arreares due to him to bee satisfyed out of omissions or undervalues in the said Earle's composition. But there is a tacite condition therein to doe him all freindly favours and curtesies that shall ly in his power, eyther in Parliament or Councell upon all occasions. All this out of Mr. Hanson's mouth.

There was one Mrs. Whorwood, the wife of Mr. Broome Whorwood in Oxfordshire, that was wont to bring intelligence to the late King as well to Oxford as to the Isle of Wight. She was sent severall times of messages, and came in the last Scotch designe, wherein Duke Hamilton miscarried, from Scotland to Carisbrooke Castle privately to the late King &c.

[A. The Lord Cottington had a grant from the King of Lord Say's estate in Oxfordshire, which he protected from all damage and spoyle, so long as the King had any strength in those parts. The Examinant hath often heard at Oxford that his woods were not suffered to bee felled nor his grounds to pay contribution, but the same was still countermaunded by warrants from the late King upon Cottington's procurement. The Lord Say had likewise the Lord Cottington's house and estate at Hanworth from the Parliament, which was generally conceaved to bee protected by him upon the same termes by a mutuall consent.]" All *signed.* A. is *endorsed* " Mr. Cooke's paper given in to the Councell this 28th of May 1651," and C. is annotated in the same hand as the former papers. B. was drawn up after C. [N. XVI., 74, Nos. 2, 3, 4.]

Thomas Coke to Sir Henry Mildmay.

1651, May 28. The Tower.—" I was induced to the setting downe of the particular names and matters contained in this paper by expresse order from the Committee . . . and to give satisfaction of my cleere and ingenuous discovery of whatever came within the compasse of my knowledge or understanding I chose rather to set downe hearsayes and conjectures of mine owne without distinction of persons then to omit the expression of any thing that had relation to publicke businesse, the judgment being left entire to the Councell to take or reject as they saw cause. But when I was commanded by the Committee to make a review of those informations in respect of the generality and uncertainty of the same I thought fitt to omit very many of the particulars as conjectural only, and so uselesse, and not fit to bee published. Neverthelesse according to the command of the Councell of State this morning, I have here enclosed sent the same papers to you, submitting both myselfe and them together with all other concernements whatsoever to the favour and mercy of the Parliament." *Holograph. Seal.* [N. XVI., 74, No. 5.]

[The Council of State ?] to [the Parliament ?].

1651, May 28 read.—Mr. Thomas Cooke's information hath been made use of

Against the	Lord Beauchamp	Now Prysoners in the Tower of whom he hath given a large and particular Account.
	Lord Chandois	
	John Bellassis, Esq.	
	Sir Abraham Shipman	

Against { Captain Potter
{ Mr. Thomasin
{ Solely discovered and apprehended upon his information, which occasioned the first proceeds against the Treasons of some of those of the Presbiterian Judgment.

The Duke of Richmond inform'd against by him and confronted before the Councell.

Many in the several counties have been apprehended of whom he hath informed, and many more yet to bee apprehended, which the narrative will particularly manifest.

The King's Instructions to him, discovered by him where it was buried underground, doe singularly testify the generall agencies of designes, particularly the tradeings of the Ministers and the Presbiterian party with the King.

His general scheam of the transactions of the King of Scotts' designes hath much confirm'd what wee had before, and our intelligence hath confirm'd in those particulars what hee hath sayd to bee trueth. We alsoe know how to put togather many things, which before were but hinted and brokenly suggested, which may prove of good advantage.

The narrative itselfe will demonstrate what farther use is to be made of his discoveries and how farr hee may be serviceable in things which tyme hath not admitted to aske, or opportunity suggested, is left to your discretion to judge." This is in the same hand as the Duke of Richmond's examination and the paper numbered 10 of April 11th, with corrections in the same hand as the annotations in other papers. [N. XVI., 74, No. 6.]

[THOMAS COKE] to [SIR HENRY MILDMAY?].

[1651, May.]—Stating that " I do desire to unbowel my soul in everything I can discover " that " God . . . by this close imprisonment begins to open my eyes to see the error and vanity of my ways, and how that I have a long time danced in the net of destruction, wherein . . . I shall miserably perish, unless I be by the favour of your Lordship and the Honourable Council of State pluckt out thereof" and that " I cannot call to mind at present more than what I have set down in the enclosed papers. I hope there is enough to give your Lordship and the Council satisfaction that I do not prevaricate . . . It was a sin at the first to deny some things I knew." Rough *draft* in Coke's handwriting of a letter, instead of which he probably adopted that of May 28th. [N. XII., 250c.]

The GRAND-DUKE OF TUSCANY to the PARLIAMENT.

1651, May 27.—Concerning the ship *Alexander the Great,* which had been partly freighted by merchants of Florence, and demanding restitution of what belonged to them. (See letter of May 9-19.) In *Italian. Signed. Seal embossed. Endorsed* " Opened May 1, 1683, *per me* Jo. Nalson." [N. X., 23.]

The COMMISSIONERS FOR COMPOUNDING to the PARLIAMENT.

1651, June 12.—Certificate concerning the arrest of Sir Benjamin Rudyard when returning from attending before them. (See *Commons' Journals,* vi. 587.) *Signed.* [N. XVI., 79.]

Draft of a Treaty between the United Provinces and England proposed by the Commissioners of the States-General.

1651, June [14–]24.—1. There shall be a firm and inviolable and perpetual friendship between the two powers and their subjects, and a more intimate alliance than formerly.

2. They shall remain confederates for mutual defence, as hereinafter declared.

3. There shall be always sincere amity between the two powers and their subjects so that they shall be bound to behave peaceably and friendly towards each other, and may come freely by sea or land into the dominions of each other, and stay there as long as they please and buy and sell any victuals or other necessaries, and may return with their property and transact their business as they may do in their own countries and as the inhabitants of the country may do without any passport or permission.

4. They shall not do or attempt anything against each other by sea or land or succour any other to do or attempt anything to the prejudice of either but rather hinder the same.

5. They shall not aid the declared enemies of each other, but shall *bona fide* assist each other if required by arms, at the charges of the party requiring the same as shall be mutually agreed *pro re nata*.

6. They shall not aid the rebels of each other within or without their countries with counsel soldiers arms money ships ammunition or any other merchandize of contraband, as shall be hereafter more fully declared, nor shall suffer them to be assisted by their subjects or inhabitants respectively.

7. In case either make any treaty of friendship, alliance, or confederacy with any other state they shall comprehend the other therein on request.

8. The friends, allies, and confederates of either shall be included in the present treaty if named before the ratification if they desire it.

9. If during this alliance anything shall be attempted or done against this treaty by any one of those confederates or their subjects respectively or by the allies comprehended herein or their subjects, the said alliance shall not be broken, but shall remain in full force, and the persons only that have done or attempted as aforesaid and no others shall be punished.

10. The subjects and inhabitants of either may for trading travel within either country reciprocally with or without their goods, armed or unarmed, provided that there be not above 40 in company armed.

11. The subjects and inhabitants of either may sail and trade within the Caribee Islands and other places of Virginia, as they have formerly done, without distinction whether these islands were formerly or shall be hereafter possessed by the subjects of either notwithstanding any prohibition to the contrary.

12. Provides for settling as soon as possible, the boundaries of the possessions of either in North America.

13. Grants freedom of trade to the subjects of either between the usual and accustomed places.

14. The merchants, officers, and seamen and their ships and merchandises shall not be seized or arrested by any general or special warrant, or for any cause whatever of war, or otherwise, except in some unavoidable necessity and that for reasonable hire, and also saving arrests in the ordinary course of justice.

15. The subjects and inhabitants of either shall not be bound to pay any higher customs or impositions in either country than the subjects of that country.

16. The merchants and their servants, the masters and mariners on board their ships and going ashore shall be allowed to wear and use for the defence of themselves and their goods all sorts of weapons both offensive and defensive, but being come to their lodgings they shall leave them there, till they be ready to embark again.

17. The subjects and inhabitants of either shall be permitted to settle in either country, and to have their own houses and warehouses there, and to trade in all security enjoying the same privileges and immunities as the inhabitants of that country, it being understood that the seamen of both shall navigate and help freely one another on the ships of each other without any injury or hindrance.

18. The subjects of either shall everywhere without any license or pass go by sea and fish both herrings and all other kinds of fish, and the said fishermen being forced by storm, pirates, enemies or otherwise to come to land shall be courteously received in the ports of either, and be permitted to depart with their ships and cargoes, and if they have not broken their loads without any toll or imposition.

19. To make the navigation everywhere more secure neither shall suffer any pirates or searovers to be admitted maintained or lodged by their subjects, but shall pursue and punish as well the concealers as the pirates, and the ships retaken and the merchandises yet in being, without limitation of time, though already sold, shall be restored without any charges to the true owners, their assignees, or attorneys.

20. The private captains and owners of either shall, before going to sea, give sufficient security that reparation may be made in case they exceed their commissions and orders.

21. To repurge the sea of pirates and searovers, and to maintain the liberty of commerce, navigation, and free fishing of both, both powers shall every year provide a powerful fleet fully equipped, each under his own Admiral and flag to secure the said seas, being bound to board and take all pirates they meet, and restore the ships to the true owners, and in case of necessity to assist each other, each keeping his own booty and prizes.

22. The said fleets and also the other vessels of war and privateers of either shall act not only against the pirates, but also against every one that shall molest, hinder or exact of the one or the other, or against the Law of Nations annoy the said liberty of commerce navigation and fishing, provided nevertheless that the party damnified shall complain to the undamnified, procuring together by an amicable intercession that reparation be made by the causer of the trouble, which not being done the ships and goods of that state shall be attacked not only by the said fleets, but with all the forces they shall be able to bring to sea, continning till the party damnified has received full satisfaction.

23. The ships of war of either shall protect the merchant ships of the reciprocal subjects or of the allies comprised in this treaty, as long as both are sailing the same way.

24. If any ships belonging to any of the subjects of either or to any neuter be taken in any of ports of either by a third party, not a subject of either, then the owner of such port shall be bound to procure with the other party that such ship be pursued, retaken and restored to the owners, at however their own charges.

25. If any merchant ship belonging to the subjects of either by tempest, pirates or other necessity come to the harbour of either, they shall depart freely, without being compelled to go ashore, to unload, to sell their merchandises, or pay any imposition or custom, but it shall be enough in such cases to show their passes without further search.

26. The ships of war and soldiers shall not come to the ports of either in any number that may cause suspicion without permission from

the' owner of the port, unless compelled by storm or to avoid greater dangers at sea.

27. The ports and rivers of both shall always be open to the ships of war reciprocally, provided they shall not be in such number as to cause suspicion, submitting nevertheless to the laws and uses of the said places.

28. Exempting all men of war, and privateers from any search, except only to show their commissions when coming into the ports of each other.

29. Granting the same liberty to all private persons that sail with commissions from either, in respect both of their own ships and their prizes, to bring such prizes to the places where they are bound to bring them by their commissions, nor shall they be bound to give any notice of the said prizes to the officers of those places, or to pay any duty to them or others, but they shall only be bound to show their commissions.

30. The goods of the subjects of either found in enemys' ships shall be good prize.

31. The contractors shall not carry or allow to be carried from their countries to their enemies or rebels reciprocally any contraband articles (which are then enumerated) with this express clause that under the name of contraband be not comprehended wheat or other corn and grain peases beans salt wine oil nor generally all that belong to the food and maintaining of life, but they shall be reputed free, as also all other sorts of merchandises not forementioned; and the contraband articles specified found in the ships of either shall be confiscated by competent judges, leaving all the other merchandises and the ships themselves unquestioned and untroubled.

32. The subjects and inhabitants of either shall not transport in their vessels the goods of the Portugals from America, Asia, or Africa, into Europe, or from any of those parts into another, nor also *vice versa* from Europe to any of them, upon penalty of losing their vessels.

33. If any war or merchant ships be cast away on the coast of either, these ships or their wreck and the contents may be reclaimed within a year and a day by the true owners or their attorneys without any formalities, paying only the expenses of the recovery, disputes to be summarily settled by the officers of the places.

34. The Commissioners for search from either part shall regulate themselves according to the laws and ordinances as issued in the hand of either.

35. No letters of marque or reprisals shall be granted for any damage or wrong that either of the subjects shall have committed against this treaty, and all those already granted for any cause shall be void, but the whole shall be amicably agreed, if possible or settled *ordinaria via juris.*

36. All other treaties and alliances made by either party with other states shall remain in full vigour without derogating from them by the present treaty. *Copy*: Read July 2nd, being No. 14. [N. XVIII., 90.]

The ENGLISH AMBASSADORS to the STATES-GENERAL.

1651, June 16[-26].—(Printed in Thurloe, *State Papers*, i. 188.) Read July 2nd, being No. 15. [N. XVIII., 91.]

OLIVER CROMWELL to the LORD PRESIDENT OF THE COUNCIL OF STATE.

1651, June 17. Edinburgh.—"At my march into Scotland being destitute of general officers of Horse, I commissioned Colonel Fleetwood to be Lieutenant-General of the Horse and Colonel Whalley to be Commissary-General, and now understanding that the Treasurers make some stop of their pay by reason they are not within the establishment I thought fit humbly to recommend their case unto your Lordship desiring they may be put into the establishment. I crave pardon for this trouble and rest." (See *Commons' Journals*, vi. 592.) *Signed. Seal.* [N. VIII., 53.]

The STATES-GENERAL to the ENGLISH AMBASSADORS.

1651, June 19-29.—(Printed in Thurloe, *State Papers*, i. 189, where "21st" should be "24th.") Read July 2nd, being No. 16. [N. XVIII., 92.]

The ENGLISH AMBASSADORS to the STATES-GENERAL.

1651, June 20-30.—(Printed in Thurloe, *State Papers*, i. 190.) Read July 2nd, being No. 17. [N. XVIII., 94.]

The SAME to the SAME.

Same date.—(Printed in Thurloe, *State Papers*, i. 191.) Read July 2nd, being No. 18. [N. XVIII., 95.]

The ENGLISH AMBASSADORS to the STATES-GENERAL.

1651, June 20-30.—Concerning the Queen of Bohemia's claim. (Printed in Thurloe, *State Papers*, i. 189.) *Draft.* Read in Parliament, July 2nd, being No. 20. (See *Commons' Journals*, vi. 595.) [N. XVIII., 65.]

The STATES-GENERAL to the ENGLISH AMBASSADORS.

1651, June [20-]30.—Declaration. (Printed in Thurloe, *State Papers*, i. 191.) Read in Parliament, July 2nd, being No. 21. (See *Commons' Journals*, vi. 595.) [N. XVIII., 68.]

The STATES-GENERAL to the PARLIAMENT.

1651, June [20-]30. The Hague.—Letters Re-credential to the English Ambassadors on their return. In *French*. (See *Commons' Journals*, vi. 595.) [N. X., 55.]

The COMMISSIONERS FOR COMPOUNDING to the PARLIAMENT.

1651, June 24.—Certificate concerning George Ball and others. (Printed in *Commons' Journals*, vii. 61.) *Signed.* [N. XVI., 80.]

The STATES-GENERAL to the PARLIAMENT.

1651, [June 24]-July 4. The Hague. — Complaining that when two captains of Harlingen in Friezeland had exported corn to Whitby the money received for it had been unjustly seized, and demanding its restitution. In *French*. [N. X , 56.]

The ENGLISH AMBASSADORS TO THE STATES-GENERAL to the PARLIAMENT.

1651, July 1.—Recapitulation of their proceedings. (Printed in Thurloe, i. 193.) Read July 2nd, being No. 22. [N. XVIII., 93.]

The COUNCIL OF STATE.

1651, July 7.—Order that " Mr. Gurdon put this Parliament in mind of the letters now lying before them sent from the Lord Willoughby to his wife and trustees (being those of February 15th) and acquaint them with the Declaration now read . . being translated forth of the Dutch Copy and sent from the Barbados. And that the Parliament will be pleased to take the said Lord's condition as to the Act for sale of Delinquents' lands in reference to his former and later treasons into their consideration." [N. XVI., 81.] Probably *Annexed* hereto was:

The said Declaration of LORD WILLOUGHBY, Lieutenant-General and Governor of the Barbados and other Caribie Islands.

1650-1, February 18.—Serving in Answer to an Act of the 3rd of October 1650. (A version of this was printed in English also at the Hague, and is among the *King's Pamphlets*, E. 644, No. 4, and it is also printed in Grey, iv. Appendix, No. 12, p. 27.) [N. XVI., 58.]

The DOGE and GOVERNORS OF the Republic of GENOA to the PARLIAMENT.

1651, July 7. — Letter of Credence to their agent Francesco Bernardi, appointed with special reference to the restoration of the detained ships and cargoes. In *Latin*, with *English* translation. [N. X., 41.]

The STATES-GENERAL to the PARLIAMENT.

1651, July [8-]18. The Hague.—Complaining that a ship belonging to an Échevin of the town of Middelburg on her return from the Virgin Islands with a cargo of tobacco had been taken and carried into Yarmouth on the ground that by the resolution of the Parliament in last November the Virgin Islands were at war with the Parliament, although the said ship had sailed from Europe six months before the passing of the resolution, and desiring restitution of ship and cargo. In *French*, with *English* translation. [N. X., 57.]

The PARLIAMENT to the KING OF SPAIN.

1651, July 14.—Setting forth the complaints of the English merchants, who trade to the Spanish dominions, of the injuries done them by the governors and other officials of the ports to which they trade (of whom Don Pedro Carillo de Guzman is mentioned by name) particularly in the Canaries, contrary to the treaty of commerce, and asking that orders may be given to prevent the same in future, and for reparation. *Draft* or *copy*. [N. XVII., 66.]

EDMOND PRIDEAUX, Attorney-General, to the CLERK OF PARLIAMENT.

[1651, July 15.]—Receipt for papers given him by order of that date, being the Instructions from the King of Scots to Mr. Coke, and the paper containing his several examinations. (See *Commons' Journals*, vi. 604.) *Signed*. [N. XVI., 82.]

The STATES-GENERAL to the PARLIAMENT.

1651, July [18-]28. The Hague.—Complaining that a ship containing five bales of thread consigned by a citizen of Harlem to Leghorn had been taken by the English fleet in the Mediterranean and sent to London on some pretexts which in any case do not affect the goods in question, and demanding their restitution. In *French*. [N. X., 59.]

The COMMITTEE TO WHOM THE LIST OF THE LATE KING'S SERVANTS AND CREDITORS WAS REFERRED.

1651, July 22.—List of Abatements, Omissions, and Respites. (Printed in *Commons' Journals*, vi. 606.) [N. XVI., 83.]

DON ALONSO DE CARDENAS to the PARLIAMENT.

1651, July 25–August 4.—Asking on behalf of Colonel William Cobb, on account of his services to the King of Spain in Flanders, that his sequestration might be taken off. (See *Commons' Journals*, vi. 612.) In *Spanish*. *Seal*. [N. XVII., 67.]

The COMMISSIONERS FOR COMPOUNDING to the PARLIAMENT.

1651, July 29.—Certificate concerning Gamul's School. (Printed in *Commons' Journals*, vii. 61.) [N. XVI., 84.]

Certificate of the Estate of WILLIAM COBB, Esq., of Sandringham.

[1651, July 29.]—(See *Commons' Journals*, vi. 612.) [N. XVI., 85.]

The STATES-GENERAL to the PARLIAMENT.

1651, [July 25–]August 4. The Hague.—Asking the Parliament, inasmuch as Lord Craven, Colonel of a regiment in their service, has been cited to appear in London on September 3rd under penalty of confiscation of all his property and as, in consequence of the armies of the Elector of Brandenburg and the Duke of Neuburg being upon their frontiers, they have been obliged to issue an order that all the officers in their service should rejoin their regiments by a certain day in obedience to which order the said Lord Craven has come from Germany, and inasmuch as they cannot allow him as the senior Colonel of his nation to leave, to allow Lord Craven to appear by his attorney in the usual manner. (See *Commons' Journals*, vii. 5.) In *French*. [N. X., 59.]

The STATES-GENERAL to the PARLIAMENT.

1651, August [1–]11. The Hague.—Complaining that the ship *Amsterdam*, the property of merchants of Amsterdam, when bound from Bayonne to Sallee had been taken off Sallee by the English fleet, and sent to London, and on the voyage thither had been lost with her cargo worth more than 15,000 *francs* in consequence of too few men being put on board as a prize crew, and demanding restitution of the value of the ship and cargo. In *French*, with *English* translation. [N. X., 60.]

The KING to the EARLS OF CRAFURD, MARESCHALL, and GLENCARNE, and LORD BALCARRES, appointed by us and our Committee of Estates to remain at this time in Scotland for our service.

1651, August 1. Cumbernald.—Private Instructions :—
1. To keep frequent Committees of Estates for regulating and ordering public affairs in the kingdom.
2. To endeavour to raise as great forces both of horse and foot as possible for the good of religion and our service for driving any remainder of the enemy out of Scotland, for seconding us in this our design, and for preventing insurrections within the kingdom, such forces to be under such inferior officers as you are confident of both for their affection to religion and their loyalty to us.

3. Also to endeavour the speedy raising of the new levy already imposed.

4. To endeavour the continuing a good correspondence betwixt the Committee of Estates and the Commission of the Kirk, and that the civil authority concur for getting ready obedience to the ecclesiastical orders.

5. To be careful the act of the Committee at Stirling anent runaways be put in execution, they to be carefully brought together and so ordered as by advice of the Committee of Estates and those entrusted by us with the command of the forces shall be thought expedient.

6. To endeavour the careful bringing up all deficients in former levies and particularly those imposed upon the shire of Argyll.

7. To secure the persons of any who obstruct or oppose the public resolutions.

8. To be careful that the public dues imposed on the kingdom be effectually brought in, especially the voluntary contribution.

9. To recruit with all diligence Lord Balcarres' regiment and that of Sir John Browne out of the shires of Angus, Fife and Perth, and to arm them out of the readiest of those arms lately come from Sweden.

10. General Power to do everything you think fit for the good of religion, our service and the kingdom.

11. To give us frequent advertisement of your proceedings.

12. Further to be careful that none of those who have now laid down their charges or deserted our service be admitted to any place of power or trust. *Sign-Manual. Seal.* (See *Commons' Journals,* vii. 14.) [N. I., 37.]

The KING to JOHN, EARL OF CRAFURD AND LINDESAY.

1651, August 2. Cumbernald.—Commission appointing him Commander-in-Chief under the Earl of Leven of all forces raised or to be raised within the Kingdom of Scotland, such commission to continue as long as we and our army are out of Scotland or during pleasure. *Sign-Manual. Seal.* (See *Commons' Journals,* vii. 14.) [N. I., 38.]

The ESTATES OF HOLLAND AND WEST FRIEZELAND to the PARLIAMENT.

1651, August [2–]12. The Hague.—Asking them to dispense with the personal appearance of Lord Craven and to allow him to appear by his attorney. (See letter of July 25–August 4.) In *Dutch,* with *English* translation. [N. X., 61.]

The COUNCIL OF STATE.

1651, August 2.—Estimate of the charge of the forces in England, Scotland, and Ireland from March 24th last to the 20th of October next. (Printed in *Commons' Journals,* vi. 617.) [N. XVI., 86.]

The COUNCIL OF STATE.

1651, August 4.—Order reporting concerning the 4,000 foot to take the field, with an estimate of their pay. (Printed in *Commons' Journals,* vi. 616.) [N. XVI., 87.]

The STATES-GENERAL to the PARLIAMENT.

1651, August [6–]16. The Hague.—Stating that a ship called *Le Vieux Chariot* belonging to some of their subjects had been taken by a ship of the King of Scotland, and carried to Peterhead where she was again taken by two Parliament ships and carried to Leith, and demanding the return of the ship or at least her value, if she had been sold. In *French.* *Seal.* [N. X., 62.]

A)ERIGO SALVETTI, Resident of the Grand-Duke of Tuscany, to
WILLIA) LENTHALL.

1651, August 5. Great St. Bartholomew.--Having received letters from his Master and instructions to present them and make some additional representations he desires a time and persons to be appointed by Parliament for his reception. *Seal.* [N. XVIII., 143.]

The STATES-GENERAL to the PARLIA)ENT.

1651. August [8-]18. The Hague.—Complaining that a ship called *The Isle of Wiringue* belonging to some of their subjects had been taken on a voyage from France to the Netherlands by a Parliament ship and demanding restitution. In *French.* *Seal.* [N. X., 63.]

Major-General HARRISON to WILLIA) LENTHALL.

1651, August 11. About noon.—"This morning I had an express from Major-General Lambert dated the 9th about 12 at noon within ten miles of Pe[n]reth, and enclosed several letters, which he had taken, and therewith six of the enemy conveying them, whereof two were lairds. He desired my despatch of the letters to my Lord General, which accordingly I have done, but considering they came from Duke Hamilton, Lord Lauderdale and Lord Wentworth, and that the esteem they have of the Presbyterian party—whom Hamilton calls rogues, and Lauderdale thinks they are well rid of—and the pleasure they take in their present pure Cavalierish composition, may help to satisfy those displeased friends, I thought it my duty to transmit you copies of them, till his Excellency can send the originals, I being so much nearer than he is. I am confident the Duke speaks their very heart, not knowing the danger of the conveyance as the other did, who writ accordingly; and we expect day by day the Lord will more open their eyes to see the strait whereunto Himself in judgement hath led them, so as the terror of the Lord will prove a sorer enemy to them than we. Major-General [Lambert] will be this night I hope in their rear and close. I am hastening to get the van, and if possible to recover the middle parts of Lancashire before them, for which purpose I shall . . be this night at Skipton and so toward Preston or Manchester, as Providence shall direct. If the enemy keep constant motion he might be near Preston this night, lying at Kendal on Saturday, which is but about 35 miles distant, and so may a little put us to it to reach him, but I hope the Major-General and I know he will not let their rear go off quietly, whereby he may reasonably and easily clog their march. My Lord Howard's son commanded a troop at Carlisle, whom ere this I had avoided, but that he was his son. He took off with him but twelve of his troop, as the Major-General and Governor of Carlisle inform me, which would have been cashiered, had we had opportunity, and they stayed. The riddance of such are no loss to us, nor their accession strength to them." *Copy* in Dr. Williams' hand. [N. XII., 267.]

The COUNCIL OF STATE.

1651, August 11.—Order reporting concerning the precautions to be taken on account of the Scotch invasion. (Printed in *Commons' Journals,* vi. 620.) [N. XVI., 88.]

Anton Günther, Count in Oldenburgh, to the Parliament.

1651, August 15.—Letter of Credence to his Agent Hermann Mylius. (See *Commons' Journals*, vii. 44.) In *Latin. Signed. Seal. Original* and *Copy.* [N. X., 38 ; XVIII., 167.]

The King to the Earl of Derby, Captain-General of the County Palatine of Lancaster, &c.

1651, August 16. Our Royal Camp at Higher Whitny in Cheshire. —" We by reason of our quick march having not until now had time sufficient to send a particular summons to our subjects of that county, by which we might have expected to receive any satisfactory account, and being now resolved to pursue the enemy, whom—by God's help—we have forced from Warrington, and made him fly before us in a scattering and disorderly manner, together with such other advantages as may offer themselves, and having sent forth a general summons and invitation to all our subjects to join with us in this our present expedition and having in all places where we passed through that county been received with so great joy and acclamations of our people that we cannot doubt of their readiness to assist and join with us at this time--they having so good an opportunity for it— . . . require you to give notice to all inhabitants thereof from sixteen to sixty to appear at such times and places as you shall direct" with their horses arms and ammunition for the defence of the country, the reducement of the few refractory parts thereof and the recruiting of our marching army. We further command you to make no distinction of persons with reference to former differences, but in imitation of us according to their future carriage. For as we do most heartily forgive and forget and also interpret well the supposed disobligation passed to the Crown in such as shall now by their action make good their former professions, so we shall retain no good memory of those—though appearing at that time well deservers—who shall upon such an occasion as this—having means and opportunity for it—be wanting to us and their country so highly injured, and so miserably oppressed and enslaved in their liberties, their properties, and their consciences. We send our Declaration, our general summons to the kingdom and the brief state of our affairs before, at the time, and since we left Scotland, all which—together with this—are to be dispersed and published in all churches, chapels and markets within that county, particularly the towns of Manchester, Preston and Wigan. And as in our County Palatine of Lancaster, so in the rest of the counties comprehended in your commission you are to pursue the same course hereby prescribed to you. *Sign-Manual. Endorsed* " Papers Reported from the Council of State, 1 Sept. 1651." (See *Commons' Journals*, vii. 9.) [N. I., 39.]

The Earl of Derby.

[1651, August 16 (?).]—Articles to be observed by his officers and soldiers.

1. That none upon pain of death shall make any quarter for himself without an order from the Quarter-Master-General.

2. That none being quartered shall demand from his landlord any money &c. upon pain of death.

3. That none on a march shall leave the ranks to enter any house or to take anything thereout upon pain of death.

4. That none shall absent himself from his command or post upon pain of death.

5. That every soldier or officer on sound of trumpet or beat of drum shall immediately repair to the colours, upon pain of death.

6. That whatsoever officer doth cavil at the command of his superior be disgracefully cashiered, and any soldier mutinying or disobeying his officer shall die.

7. That whosoever doth not forthwith list himself under some commander shall not enjoy the benefit of any quarter, but be expulsed the army as useless and obnoxious to the same.

Lastly, that whosoever doth contrive or complot anything to the prejudice of the person or government of the Lord General shall die without mercy. (Two *copies* with slight differences.) [N. XVI., 117.]

DRAFT COMMISSIONS.

[1651, August 16 (?).]—For a lieutenant-general for Lancashire, Cheshire, Shropshire and the six counties of North Wales under the Earl of Derby, for a Major-General, a Colonel, a Captain, and for the surprise of a town. *Endorsed* " Patterns for Commissions found among the Earl of Derby's papers." [N. XVI., 118.]

A COUNCIL OF WAR.

1651, August 19. Warrington.—It is resolved that the forces to be raised throughout the whole County of Lancaster shall consist of 1,300 borse and 6,000 foot, viz., out of Leyland and Derby Hundreds 500 horse and 2,000 foot, and out of Amounderness and Lonsdale Hundreds, the same, the proportions to be raised out of the other two Hundreds to be considered of when his Lordship advances nearer unto them; the raising of the horse to be proportioned thus, entire horse, man and furniture to be rated at 12*l.*, the horse at 8*l.*, the man at 30*s.*, the saddle and furniture at 20*s.*, the sword and pistol at 30*s.*, every musketeer to be rated at 3*l.*, and every pikeman at 2*l.* 10*s.*, the man to be rated at 30*s.*, the firearms at 30*s.* more, the pike and sword at 20*s.*, two parts muskets and a third pikes. Where either man horse or arms are wanting these sums must be raised respectively from such persons by whom they ought to be brought in, and employed to the same purpose. A day of Rendezvous to be appointed for every company, and in case any man do not send in his numbers those which are drawn together are to be quartered upon such till they do bring them in, and when such companies are raised they are to repair immediately to the main body, or where else they shall have orders. During their march these companies are to have free quarter, and when they join the army to have provisions from the providers. An assessment either of provisions or money for the subsistence of our present force. In our march the horse and foot to be quartered as near together in barns or empty houses as may be, and provisions to be sent in from their quarters. All in their several allotments to search for arms and ammunition for furnishing their companies. Bryan Burton empowered to search for arms and ammunition in this town and a guard appointed to assist him . . An Account to be given every evening to my Lord of the officers' design of their several levies, and how they proceed in them. (The Council consisted of my Lord [of Derby], Lord Widrington, Sir Thomas Tillisley, Sir William Throgmorton, Sir Francis Gamull, Sir Theophilus Gilby, Sir Edward Savage, Colonel Vere, Colonel Standish, Lieutenant-Colonel James Anderson, Lieutenant-Colonel Hugh Anderson, Colonel Robinson, Colonel Legge. There is a second copy, slightly differing, of part of the proceedings.) [N. XVI., 89.]

Extract of the Commissions granted [by the EARL OF DERBY] IN LANCASHIRE.

1651, August 14-22.—To one Colonel, one Major, seven Captains and two Lieutenants including one to William Christian as Lieutenant of the foot Company of the Guard. [N. XVI., 90.]

ALEXANDER BARLOW, RICHARD HAWORTH, JOHN HARTLEY and JOHN GILLJAN to the CONSTABLES OF PENDLETON.

1651, August 21. Heaton Norris.—Warrant ordering them to summon all men between the ages of 18 and 50 in their township to appear armed on the 22nd before the Commissioners of Militia at Manchester to oppose the Earl of Derby and other enemies of the Commonwealth, and to furnish a list of all such men, and of all horses in their township. *Signed.* [N. XVI., 91.]

Names of certain gentlemen of LANCASHIRE.

[1651, August.]—Found among the Earl of Derby's papers. [N. XVI., 116.]

Ro. LUMSDAINE, Governor of Dundee, to General MONK.

1651, August 26.—" We ressavit yours, for answer quhairunto we doe by these acquent you, that we ar commanded be the Kingis Majestic to desyre you and all officeris and souldieris and schipis for the present in armes and oppositioun to the Kingis auctoritie to lay doun their armes to cum in and joyne with his Majesties forces in this kingdome, and receave protectioun from thame conforme to the Kingis Majesties declaratioun sent you heirewith whiche ift you will obey we sall continoue your faithful freindis and servauntis in the old manner." Added in Monk's hand, "This answeare I receaved from the Governor of Dundee in answeare to the summons I sent him." (See *Commons' Journals*, vii. 14.) [N. XX., 58.]

The PROVOST and BAILIES OF ST. ANDREWS to General MONK.

1651, August 27.—" We have hard of your generous behavior in your former services, and observing your courteous wretting at this tyme, holding foorth to us how unwilling you are to doe anything tending to the breache of Colonell Overtoun his proclamatione the dait whereof is not yet expyred, we intreat your Honour to consider the summons sent to us boeth now and formerlie . . . and our answer to the same. Truelle . . unlesse we would renounce the dictates of our consciences and the tye of the oath of God upon us we cannot acknowledge and come under the obedience of ane foirane power contrarie to our aledgiance and covenant. So . . againe we intreat your favour that no demands be laid upon us but what consistis with honestie and conscience." *Signed.* Added in Monk's hand, "This is the ausweare of the Provist and Baylies of St. Andrews in answeare to the summons I sent them." (See *Commons' Journals*, vii. 14.) [N. XX., 61.]*

The GRAND-DUKE OF TUSCANY to the PARLIAJENT.

[1651, August 29.]—Asking for the restitution of the goods of Captain Cardi, his subject, which had been on board a French ship taken by the English Admiral Hall, within the last few weeks, to Tommaso Bianchi, Cardi's agent. (See *Commons' Journals*, vii. 28.) In *Italian. Signed. Seal embossed.* [N. X., 28.]

The COJJITTEE FOR REMOVING OBSTRUCTIONS.

1651, September 4.—Order reporting concerning Sir John Stowell's case. (Printed in *Commons' Journals*, vii. 21.) *Copy.* [N. XVI., 92.]

---

* This and the preceding eight documents all have endorsements in the same hand as those on the examinations of Thomas Coke, as have also the King's instructions and Commission of August 1 and 2.

The STATES-GENERAL to the PARLIAMENT.

1651, September [8–]18. The Hague.—Complaining that the *Saint John*, belonging to merchants of Rotterdam, had been taken on her voyage from Brazil by Parliament ships and carried into Portsmouth, and demanding restitution of ship and cargo. In *French*. *Seal*. [N. X., 64.]

The COUNCIL OF STATE.

1651, September 9.—Order reporting concerning the apprehending of Charles Stuart. (Printed in *Commons' Journals*,vii. 14.) [N. XVI., 93.]

BULSTRODE WHITELOCKE, JOHN LISLE, OLIVER ST. JOHN and SIR GILBERT PYKERINGE to WILLIAM LENTHALL.

1651, September 10. Ailesbury.—"In pursuance of your commands we came the last night to Ailesbury where we found my Lord General, Lieutenant-General Fleetwood, Major-General Deane, and many other officers and gentlemen attending his Lordship. We thought fit that night to acquaint them with your pleasure wherein they seemed to receive great contentment. And my Lord General returned his humble thanks for the favour. His Lordship intends tomorrow to go from hence to Uxbridge and from thence on Friday by Acton and Kensington to London." (See *Commons' Journals*, vii. 15.) *Signed. Seal.* [N. VIII., 54.]

A CAVALIER PRISONER to ―――.

1651, September 17. Chester.—Relation of the battle of Worcester. (Printed in *State Papers, Domestic*, p. 436.) *Copy*. [N. XVI., 94.]

The ESTATES OF HOLLAND AND WEST FRIEZELAND to the PARLIAMENT.

1651, September [18–]28. The Hague.—To the same purport as the letter of September 8th–18th. In *Dutch. Seal Embossed. Endorsed* "Opened May 26, 1683 *per me* Jo. Nálson." [N. X., 65.]

CHRISTINA, Queen of Sweden, to the PARLIAMENT.

1651, September 26. Stockholm.—Letter of Credence to Peter Spiring Silverchrona. (See *Commons' Journals*, vii. 77.) In *Latin. Seal Embossed. Signed* "Christina." *Countersigned* "Andr. Gyldenklau." [N. X., 8.]

RICHARD CARTER and two others of the Committee of Cornwall and two of the Commissioners of Sequestrations to WILLIAM LENTHALL.

1651, October 10. Bodmin.—Desiring that the false allegations of Mr. Nicolas Burlace, an officer in the late King's army, and the answer thereto of Mr. John Jago and the great oppressions of the said Mr. Burlace be taken into full and clear examination. (See letter of March 17th.) *Signed. Seal.* [N. VIII., 55.]

The BURGOMASTERS and SCHEPPENS OF AMSTERDAM to the PARLIAMENT.

1651, October [11–]21.—Stating that one of their citizens had freighted a ship at San Lucar, which was taken by the Parliament ships and asking for the restitution of the cargo. In *French. Endorsed* "Opened May 26, 1683, *per me* Jo. Nalson." [N. X., 66.]

JAES, EARL OF DERBY, to the PARLIAENT.

[1651, October 11.]—Petition shewing that " Your Petitioner a sen-tenet prisoner in Chester has addrest several petitions to this supreme power, humbly begging your mercy upon the rendition of the Isle of Man ; but because he never heard anything of your pleasure concerning him he humbly begs again,—being now, without your mercy, within few hours of his death,—that the island may be accepted for his life ; which he shall ever owne to your mercy.

That he pleads nothing in excuse of his offences, but humbly casts himself at the feet of the Parliament, desiring pardon.

That if this may not stand with your justice and wisdom, you will in mercy and compassion to his soul allow him some further time to prepare himself to meet his God ; insomuch as to this very hour Col. Duckenfield has given him constant hopes his life would be granted upon submission of the island.

Your Petitioner most humly (*sic*) beseeches this Honourable House to hear his dying petition ; either that he may live by your mercy, or by your mercy may have a little time allotted him wherein he may be fitted for death." *Holograph.* (See *Commons' Journals,* vii. 27.) [N. XXII., 128.]

JAES EARL OF DERBY.

1651, October 15.—Speech on the Scaffold, &c. (All printed in Peck, *Desiderata Curiosa,* xi. 46.) [N. XVI., 95.]

The STATES-GENERAL to the PARLIAENT.

· 1651, October [16-]26. The Hague.—Repeating the demand made by the letter of July 8th-18th. In *French. Seal. Endorsed* "Opened May 26, 1683, *per me* Jo. Nalson." [N. X., 67.] An English translation is N. XVIII., 116. Probably *Enclosed:*

> DIRCK JANSON, on behalf of the LORD JOHAN BASSELIER of Middelburgh, to the PARLIAENT.
>
> Petition, praying for the restoration of the *Fortune of Middel-burgh* and her cargo, which had been seized for violating the Act prohibiting trade with Virginia, she having sailed from Europe before the Act was passed, and having again sailed from Virginia before news of the prohibition arrived. [N. XXII., 157.]

The STATES-GENERAL to the PARLIAENT.

Same date. The Hague.—Complaining that the *Moses* belonging to merchants of Amsterdam had been taken by a Parliament ship on her voyage home from Stettin and carried into Berwick and demanding restitution of ship and cargo. In *French. Seal. Endorsed,* " Opened May 26, 1683, *per me* Jo. Nalson." [N. X., 68.] An English trans-lation is N. XVIII., 117. Probably *Enclosed:*

> Deposition of MICHAEL GROENENBURGH, Master of the *Moses,* before the Burgomaster and Magistrates of Amsterdam.
>
> 1651, October [9-]19.—Stating that the said ship was owned partly at Stettin but chiefly at Amsterdam and when on a voyage from Stettin to Amsterdam, was taken by a certain sea rover who put the deponent and his crew into two fishing boats, and carried off the said ship and goods to Berwick, as the deponent is informed. *Copy.* [N. XVIII., 118.]

Don Alonzo de Cardenas to Willia) Lenthall.

1651, October 30.—Asking him to move the Parliament for an
answer to his letter of July 25–August 4. In *Spanish*, with *English*
translation. *Seal.* [N. XVII., 68, 69.]

Articles for the surrender of Castle Rushin and Peele Castle in
the Isle of Man.

1651, October 31.—(See *Commons' Journals,* vii. 35.) *Copy.* [N.
XVI., 96.]

Articles for the surrender of Clare Castle.

1651, November 4.—(Printed in Gilbert, iii. 261.) *Copy.* A footnote in a different hand states, "Carick Colla, another strong castle of
Sir Daniel O'Brien, the furthest point west in Thomond about the
mouth of the Shannon, was surrendered to the Lieutenant-General upon
the like conditions." [N. XXI., 95.]

The States-General to the Lord Mayor of London.

1651, November [5–]15. The Hague.—Recommending their ambassadors to his good offices. (See *Commons' Journals,* vii. 64.) In
French. Seal. [N. X., 69.]

The Same to Walter Strickland.

Same date and place.—Recommending their ambassadors to his good
offices. In *French. Seal.* [N. X., 70.]

The Same to the Parliament.

Same date and place.—Letter of Credence to their Ambassadors.
(See *Commons' Journals,* vii. 54.) In *French,* with *English* translation. *Seal.* [N. X., 71.] Copies of both attested by the Secretary
to the Embassy are N. XVIII., 123.

——— to ———

1651, November 6. Perth.—"We who are here convened by command
of our respective shires have found it most necessary to . . . invite
all shires and boroughs to ane joint correspondence for attending the
downcoming of the English Commissioners . . . For this end we
have drawn this draft of ane Commission . . . to be subscribed by
the shire to such Commissioners as shall be chosen by you . . . to
meet at Edinburgh the 21st of this instant, and therefore we . . .
intreat you . . . to send this letter with the . . . Commission
to the shires and boroughs next yours and desire them to choose Commissioners . . ." *Enclosed :*

The said Co))ission.

Empowering the persons chosen in conjunction with the other
Scotch Commissioners to meet the English Commissioners, and
treat with them with full powers for the settlement of these
nations. *Copies.* [N. XX., 62.]

John Billingsley on behalf of Thomas Billingsley.

1651, November 10.—

And

Thomas Withering, an infant, by Sir David Watkins,
his guardian.

1651, November 12.—Claims by each to be entitled to the office of
Postmaster for foreign parts. (See *Commons' Journals,* vii. 192.)
[N. XVI., 97, 98.]

WILLIAM JERVIS to the PARLIAMENT.

[1651, November 14.]—Petition, praying that his sequestration may be taken off, and himself rewarded for his services. (See *Commons' Journals*, vii. 110.) [N. XXII., 121.]

The form of OATH to be administered to every member of the COUNCIL OF STATE.

1651, November 28.—(Printed in *Commons' Journals*, vii. 46.) [N. XVI., 102.]

The COMMISSIONERS OF THE PARLIAMENT IN IRELAND.

1651, December 2. Dublin.—Order appointing in consequence of the Lord Deputy's death, Lieutenant-General Ludlow as Commander-in-Chief, till the pleasure of Parliament be known, or orders received from the Lord Lieutenant. (See *Commons' Journals*, vii. 49.) *Signed* "Miles Corbett, John Jones, John Weaver." [N. XXI., 96.]

The SAME.

Same date.—Order that Commissions granted by the late Lord Deputy should continue in force notwithstanding his death. [N. XXI., 98.]

DON ALONSO DE CARDENAS to WILLIAM LENTHALL.

1651, December 3–13.—To the same effect as that of October 30th. In *Spanish*, with *English* translation. *Embossed Seal.* [N. XVII., 70, 71.]

The COUNCIL OF STATE.

1651, December 4.—Order reporting with amendments the tenth and eleventh Instructions to the Commissioners to Scotland. [N. XX., 68.]

The COUNCIL OF STATE.

1651, December 8.—Order reporting the Articles of November 4th and other papers to the House. [N. XXI., 97.]

The PROCONSULS and SENATORS OF HAMBURGH to the PARLIAMENT.

1651, December 9.—Complaining that the *St. Paul*, belonging to their citizens, had on a voyage to Oporto been taken off the Isle of Wight and carried into Weymouth, where she was still detained, and asking for her restitution and compensation for the things taken out of her. In *Latin. Seal embossed. Endorsed* "Not opened till March 21 1682-3." [N. X., 80.]

The PARLIAMENT to OLIVER ST. JOHN and others, Commissioners to go into Scotland.

1651, December 11.—Instructions. (*Draft* with amendments, partly in shorthand, some signed by Whitelocke. See *Commons' Journals*, vii. 47, 49.) [N. XX., 63, 66.]

J. VAN VLIETS and JOHN OSTE, Secretaries to the Ambassadors, to WILLIAM LENTHALL.

1651, December [18-]28.—Enclosing the Letter of Credence from the States-General to their Ambassadors, and desiring an audience for them. [N. XVIII., 121.]

JAﻟES CATS' Speech to the Parliament at the audience of himself and his colleagues GERARD SCHAEP and PAULUS VANDEPERRE, Ambassadors from the States-General.

1651, December [19-]29.—In *Latin* with *English* translation. (The Latin with a Dutch translation was printed in Holland and is in the British Museum. The pressmark of the volume of pamphlets containing it is 8122 e e 4. A florid speech with numerous Latin quotations. The most remarkable part is where he touches on the similarity of Dutch and English, showing the relationship of the two nations, in proof of which he mentions many common words that are nearly the same in both, as bread, butter, cheese, wine, &c., and also the names of different parts of the body.) The Latin *signed* by the three Ambassadors. [N. XVIII., 119, 120.]

DON ALONZO DE CARDENAS to the COUNCIL OF STATE.

[1651, December 19.]—In *Spanish,* with *English* translation. (The last is printed in Peck, *Desiderata Curiosa,* xii. 1.) The original *signed.* [N. XVII., 73.]

The SAME to the SAME.

Same date.—In the late King's time letters of marque under certain conditions, one of which was that the prizes should be brought to England and appraised at their true value in the Court of Admiralty, were granted to certain of his subjects upon pretence of injuries done to them at sea by those of the King of Spain, but these conditions not being observed he revoked and annulled all letters of marque already granted, issuing a declaration in 1644 of which a copy is inclosed. And the King being dead and this Commonwealth established, the said Ambassador conceives it just that no use be made of the said letters without a new grant from the Commonwealth, but they, notwithstanding it was never granted by this Parliament, have been continued with great disorder in taking Spanish ships without bringing them into England, the goods being taken into France, Ireland, and Holland and sold there, being a notorious breach of the articles of peace. And though both the grant and recalling were derived from the said King they used the former not taking notice of the latter. The Ambassador therefore desires the Council to revoke all letters granted by the late King against any Spanish subjects, and not to grant new ones without notice to himself or other the Spanish Resident *pro tempore ;* and that the Judges of the Admiralty may be ordered not receive any informations or to examine any witnesses upon any injuries pretended to be done by Spanish to English subjects without acquainting such Ambassador or Resident, whereby a combined remedy may be applied against the great disorders and abuses that may happen hereafter in such cases. In *Spanish,* with *English* translation. The original *signed.* [N. XVII., 74.]

The SAME to the SAME

Same date.—Again demanding satisfaction in the matter of the *Santa Clara.* In *Spanish,* with *English* translation. (The last is printed in Thurloe, *State Papers,* i. 130, where it is wrongly dated 1649.) The original *signed.* [N. XVII., 75.]

The SAME to the SAME.

Same date.—The King his Master intending not only to maintain a good correspondence and amity with the Parliament but also to make it more strict upon all convenient occasions hath commanded him to endeavour the begetting of it by all possible and convenient means, and being conceived that the conjunction with one accord in some operation of mutual convenience to both nations in Spain, France, Portugal, or Flanders is a point towards the said strict amity the Ambassador desires that some few persons of the Council may be authorised to receive his addresses, which must be frequent and of different subjects and therefore unfitting the whole Council therewith to be troubled, who after debate on the propositions may conveniently report thereon to the whole Council. And though in all State matters the members of the Council observe secrecy yet in particular he desires that such secrecy may be kept in these points as the importance of the business deserves. In *Spanish*, with *English* translation. The original *signed*. (For all these four papers, see *Commons' Journals*, vii. 64.) [N. XVII., 76.]

The PARLIAMENT.

[1651, December 24.]—Declaration concerning the Settlement of Scotland. (Printed in *King's Pamphlets*, E. 659, No. 19.) (See *Commons' Journals*, vii. 56.) [N. XX., 204.]

The COMMITTEE FOR REMOVING OBSTRUCTIONS.

[1651, December 25.]—Report concerning the claims of the Earl of Salisbury. (Printed in *Commons' Journals*, vii. 56.) [N. XVI., 100.]

The COMMITTEE FOR REMOVING OBSTRUCTIONS

1651, December 25.—Report concerning the case of Alexander Ratcliffe. (The question was whether the tenant in tail being sequestrated for Delinquency and dying without issue the next in remainder should enjoy the land according to the entail.) [N. XVI., 101.]

PETER SPIRING SILVERCHRONA, the Swedish Minister, to WILLIAM LENTHALL.

1651, December 29.—Enclosing his Letter of Credence. *Signed.* (See *Commons' Journals*, vii. 77.) [N. XVIII., 33.]

JAMES CATS' Speech on behalf of himself and his colleagues to the COUNCIL OF STATE.

165[1-]2, January 1-11.—Whereas on December 29th we delivered to the Parliament the sum of the matters with which we are charged by the States-General we thought it needless to repeat the same. But as our Powers are demanded, we now present them, both the original and the copies. And in virtue thereof we earnestly desire that Commissioners be appointed to whom we may fully deliver all our charge, that so not only the ancient truces may be renewed, but also a closer bond strengthened. That so laudable a work may have a happy end we require of you according to the special commandment of the States-General that all intercourses between the two nations shall remain in the same state as they were left by the Ambassadors of the Commonwealth at their parting from the Low Countries, and that thereupon the Statute of this Commonwealth which was to be brought in practice on December 1st be abolished, or at least suspended, till an order shall be settled for the ensuing treaties between us, that such an excellent business should not be wronged with an ill prejudice in the beginning, but the sooner and happily be brought to a desired end. In the meantime we cannot pass over in silence so many complaints of our merchants and sailors from day to day delivered to the States-General and also to us here, because some of yours assault and rob their ships, taking away their merchandize, and bringing their ships into your havens under pretence of some letters of marque decreed against ours and the French, which the States-General no further with a good mind can behold, unless they would also suffer the undoing and perishing of all intercourses. We therefore require a speedy remedy, and the restoration of all the ships so taken with reparation to the sufferers for their damages and losses. (See *Commons' Journals*, vii. 64.) In *Latin*, with *English* translation, the first *signed* by the three Ambassadors. [N. XVIII., 122.]

FRANCESCO BERNARDI, the Genoese Minister, to WILLIAM LENTHALL.

1651[-2], January 2.—Asking him to present the enclosed Remonstrance to Parliament. *Signed. Seal.* [N. XVIII., 179.] *Enclosed:*
  i. The said Remonstrance.
    1651, December 31.—Complaining of the long delay in granting him an audience and demanding that a day be appointed for the same. *Signed.* [N. XVIII., 178.]
  ii. Copies of the orders of September 16th and 30th concerning him which are printed in *Commons' Journals*, vii. 19, 22. [N. XVIII., 177.]

The PARLIAMENT to the GRAND-DUKE OF TUSCANY.

[1651-2, January 2.]—The Parliament desiring to satisfy the Grand-Duke concerning the matters specified in the document delivered by his Resident Amerigo Salvetti on July 3rd, 1651, namely relating to Edward Hall the Admiral of the Mediterranean fleet, because after the said Admiral's return an investigation of his conduct in the port of Leghorn was instituted in the Court of Admiralty both as regarded himself and several others who were examined on oath, and their answers in so many important respects disagree with the allegations in the said document, that the Parliament can as yet arrive at no certain answer to return to the Grand-Duke and considers that the further discussion of the matter does not conduce to the friendship they are desirous of maintaining with the Grand-Duke—they therefore have decided that it is improper to examine into the matter more accurately at present, but rather to take care that all causes of offence for the future be provided against. The Parliament therefore returns this answer : that, as they ask and expect of the Grand-Duke that their ships which shall touch at his ports shall be saluted by his ports and castles in as ample and honorable manner as the ships of any Republic or Prince are, so they will give orders to the commanders of their ships whenever they touch at the Grand-Duke's ports not to do or attempt anything there that may hinder trade, but to behave there in so peaceful a manner, rendering due honours, as to give no just cause for offence or a rupture of the friendship between the Parliament and his Highness. (See *State Papers, Domestic,* p. 89.) In *Latin. Draft.* [N. XVIII., 146.]

EDMUND LUDLOW, JOHN JONES, MILES CORBETT, and JOHN WEAVER to [the COUNCIL OF STATE].

1651[-2], January 8. Kilkenny.—"The Parliament have in Ireland above 350 guarrisons which at present must bee continued being placed in port towns, walled citties and towns and in castles upon passes and in the other places of advantage for the keeping of this country in subjection, annoying the enemy and preventing—as much as may be—their conjunction there. Although the Parliament have now in pay in Ireland and in view as ordered already to come over upwards of 30,000 foot, yet in respect of the numerousness of the guarrisons now maintained and of the number of about 100 guarrisons more that must bee placed in the counties of Wicklow, Longford, King's and Queen's Counties in Leinster, Kerry in Munster, Galway, Roscommon, Mayo, Sleigo and Leitrim in Connaught, Tyrone, Cavan, Fermanagh, Monaghan and Armagh in Ulster, as these places shalbe reduced, the said number of forces must for some time be held up and the charge continued. The enemy now in armes are conceived to be noe lesse in number then thirty thousand men, all which—except those in the guarrisons of Galway, Sleigo, Roscomon, James Towne, and some other few small guarrisons—live in woods, boggs, and other fastnesses, yeilding them many advantages in order to their security and livelyhood, wherof they cannot easily be deprived, viz. :—

1. First, The countrey being allmost every where in the counties above mencioned interlaced with vaste great boggs in the middest of which there are firme woody grounds like islandes, into which they have passes or casewayes through the boggs where noe more then one horse can goe a breast, which passes they can easily mainteine, or suddainely break up soe as noe horse can approach them, and being inured to live in cabbins and to wade through those boggs they can fetch prey from any part of the countrey to releive themselves and prosecute their designes which are to robb and burne those places that yeild our forces subsistance.

2. Secondly, Those fastnesses being unpassable for horse, and into which foote cannot goe without some experience and hardship to wade in water and tread the bogg; such of our forces as attempt to goe are subject by cold to get the countrey disease which wastes and destroyes many of them and being gott into those places their unacquaintedness with the passes through the woods etc., renders them incapeable to pursue and subject to surprises.

3.   to   t of strength then because
they ca   [bes]eiged in them   Because they
their strength   to act their designes without hazarding the losse of the place.

4. Fowerthly, They have exact and constant intelligence from the natives of the mocions of any of our forces, and of opportunities to act their designes upon us. But our forces have seldome or never any intelligence of their mocions from the natives, who are possessed with an opinion that the Parliament intend them noe tearmes of mercy, and therfore endeavour to preserve them as those that stand betwene them and danger.

For the speedier breaking of their strength it is humbly proposed :—

1. First, That such of the contrymen now in proteccion as shall goe out into armes against the Parliament be declared to be excepted from pardon for life or estate.

2. Secondly, That such persons of the enemie's party as are now in armes—except preistes, Jesuites, and other persons excepted from pardon by any rules or qualificacions held forth by the Parliament—and shall, by a set day, lay downe armes, disband their men, and deliver up their armes in soone of our guarrisons, and ingage themselves to live peaceably and submitt to the authority of the Parliament, shall have liberty to

make sale of their horses, and to live under the proteccion of the Parliament, and shall have the benefit of such termes as the Parliament shall hold forth to persons in their condicion. And if the Parliament shall hold forth any termes to their prejudice, which they shall not be willing to submitt unto, or if they desire to serve any forreigne prince or state, they shall have   moneths time for to transport themselves into any of the partes beyond the seas, and shall have liberty in the meane time to transport—and to that end to treate with the agentes of any forraigne prince or state in amity with the Parliament and Commonwealth of England for the transporting of—such regimentes and companies as they can raise to carry over with them for the service of such prince or state and for their continuance in the command of them, being transported.

It is conceived that such termes as these would move most of their leading men to lay downe armes and carry away most of their fighting men which would add much to the security and peace of the inhabitantes here.

3. Thirdly, That guarr[isons]   [m]ay be to their fastnesses to disturbe   take away their preyes, and that the said fastnesses and [the parts n]ext adjacent to them be layd waste and none to inha[bit them] upon paine of death, to the end that releef and intelligence may be taken from them.

4. Fowerthly, That some thing may be held forth to such of the inhabitantes—as desire to live peaceably and are not guilty of blond and murther—in order to the security of their lifes and encouragement to follow husbandry if it be thought fitt.

For the more speedy lessening of the charge in maynteining the present forces.

1. First, That the Adventurers upon lands in Ireland doe cast lotts where their lands shalbe assigned them according to the proposalles in the annexed paper, to the end they may presently beginne to plant notwithstanding the warr is not ended, and may plant together, and thereby be strengthened which the Act doth not provide for them, and to the end the Parliament may more freely dispose of the rest of their land to publique advantage.

2. Secondly, That a Pale be made by secureing all the passes upon the Boyne and the Barrow, and the space of ground betweene them making those two rivers one intire line for the better securing the inhabitantes to plant and follow husbandry within the said line—the same being once cleered of the enemy—which wilbe effected by planting a strong guarrison in the fastnes of Wicklowe, and the like for the county of Waterford lying betweene the Sewer which falles to Waterford, and the More which goes to Youghall and many other places—which may be done without much charge and kept without increasing the number of the forces, inland guarrisons being lesse usefull when these lines are made—. Such lines being made, the countrey within them will in a short time be inhabited, and yeild more security to the people then now they have within a mile of the best guarrison wee possesse, and probably more profit to the Commonwealth then all the landes in Ireland now doth; whereas now while the countrey is open, the enemy have libertie upon the approach of our forces to fly out of one fastnes into another, and soe avoid engaging, and weare out our men and destroy those places that yeild our forces subsistance.

Thirdly, that all the forces may be fixed to their respective guarrisons and quarters, and may have landes assigned them as well for their arreares [as part] of their present pay to the end they may be [en-

couraged to follow hu]sbandry and to maintcinc their owne inteurest
as [well as that of] the Commonwealth. Provided that such of them
as marry with Irish [women] shall loose th[eir] commands and forfeit
their arreares and be made incapable to inhabit landes in Ireland." (*Torn
and partly illegible.*) *Signed. Enclosed:*

> The following paper signed and dated as above. The first lines are
> illegible but apparently propose that the allotments to the
> Adventurers be as follows:—
>
> 1. "The first allotment to consist of the Counties of Limerick
>   and Kerry in Munster and the Counties of Clare and Galloway
>   in Connaught.
> 2. The second allotment to consist of the Counties of Kilkenny,
>   Wexford, Wicklow, and Catherlogh (Carlow) in Leinster.
> 3. The third allotment to consist of the Counties of Westmeath
>   and Longford in the province of Leinster, and the Counties of
>   Cavan and Monaghan in the province of Ulster.
> 4. The fourth allotment to consist of the Counties of Fermanagh
>   and Donegal in the province of Ulster and the Counties of
>   Leitrim and Sligo in Connaught.
>
> And although it be conceived that there is in any one of these allot-
> ments more forfeited lands than will upon admeasurement satisfy
> the Adventurers according to the Act, yet that it may appear that
> not only full satisfaction is intended them but also an advantage
> of strength and security in having their several proportions
> assigned unto them together, which the Act did not provide for;
> It is further proposed that, if the first allotment chance to fall
> short upon admeasurement of giving the satisfaction intended,
> that then in such case the one moiety of such defect be supplied
> out of the forfeited lands in the County of Mayo, next adjacent
> to the Counties of Clare and Galway.
> 2. That the second allotment proving defective be supplied out
>   of the forfeited lands in the Queen's County and King's County
>   in Leinster next adjacent to the said second allotment.
> 3. That the defect of the third allotment be supplied out of the
>   forfeited lands in the County of Fermanagh in Ulster next
>   adjacent to the said third allotment.
> 4. That the defect of the fourth allotment be supplied out of the
>   forfeited lands in the County of Mayo in Connaught and of
>   Cavan in Ulster next adjacent to the said fourth allotment."
> *Signed.* [N. XXI., 130.]

DOROTHY, COUNTESS OF LEICESTER, to the PARLIAMENT.

[1651-2, January 8.]—Petition, showing that "the Lady Elizabeth
and the Duke of Gloucester . . . having—by order of Parliament
in June 1649—been committed unto the charge of the Petitioner, and after
by order removed to the Isle of Wight the Lady Elizabeth—before she
went from your Petitioner's house—deposited in the hands of your
Petitioner's husband . . . a jewel of diamonds declaring her will
how the same should be disposed in case she should die, which at her
death she confirmed giving the said jewel to your Petitioner, which
although thus disposed of by the said Lady and having never belonged
unto either King, Queen, Prince, or Crown, but was given unto her by
the late Prince of Orange at the time of his marriage with her
sister.
Yet your Petitioner's husband . . . as well as herself taking
notice of the late additional Act . . for sale of the goods belonging

to the late King, Queen, and Prince, and being both of them very scrupulous and fearful of any failing on their parts, the said Earl did —within the time limited by the said Act—make discovery thereof unto the trustees appointed by the said Act desiring your Petitioner might retain the same according to the gift and will, of which the Probate under seal was produced unto them : Notwithstanding which the said trustees upon the 23rd of December last . . . have valued the same at 2,000*l.* being at least twice the value thereof, and ordered . . your Petitioner's husband to pay the same within 7 days " . . And praying that " her just interest and right in the said jewel may be considered by yourselves and allowed, or that she may be admitted to make further proof thereof before such persons as you shall be pleased to appoint." *Signed.* [N. XXII., 126.]

The PARLIAMENT.

1651[-2], January 8.—Order thereon. (Printed in *Commons' Journals,* vii. 65.) [N. XXII., 125.]

Estimate of FEEFARM RENTS sold and to be sold.

[Same date.]—Amounting to 559,100*l.* 15*s.* 0*d.* (See *Commons' Journals,* vii. 65.) [N. XVI., 105.]

List of Persons suggested for REGULATING THE LAW.

[1651-2, January 9.]—(Printed in *Commons' Journals,* vii. 67.) On the back is a fragment of some accounts apparently relating to the Navy. [N. XVI., 104.]

DON ALONSO DE CARDENAS to the COUNCIL OF STATE.

1651-2, January 13–23.—In reply to the order of January 8th (see *Commons' Journals,* vii. 64), stating that all his authority and ,powers appear clearly in his Letters Credential presented to Parliament. In *Spanish,* with *English* translation. The original *signed.* [N. XVII., 77.]

The PROCONSULS and SENATORS OF HAMBURGH to the PARLIAMENT.

165[1-]2, January 15.—Letter of Credence to Leon de Aissema, whom they had charged with some matters concerning Hamburgh alone. In *Latin.* *Seal embossed.* [N. X., 84.]

The CONSULS and SENATORS OF LÜBECK, BREMEN, and HAMBURGH in their own name and that of the remaining Hanse Towns, to the PARLIAMENT.

165[1-]2, January 16. — Letter of Credence to their Resident Leon de Aissema. (See *Commons' Journals,* vii. 96.) In *Latin. Seals embossed* of the three cities. [N. X., 82.]

Mr. KILVAT, Mr. LOVELL, THOMAS BECHAM, and Mr. MILDMAY.

1651[-2], January 28.—Examinations before the Committee of Obstructions touching the alleged gift by the Lady Elizabeth to the Countess of Leicester. [N. XXII., 127.]

The COMMISSIONERS TO SCOTLAND.

1651[-2], January 31. Dalkeith.—Declaration annulling authority in Scotland not derived from the Parliament. (Printed in *King's Pamphlets,* E. 659, No. 19.) *Copy.* [N. XX., 67.]

The Co**ǝ****mmissioners** **to** **Scotland** to the **Deputies** of each Shire
and Borough.

[1651-2. February, beginning of.]—Summons demanding a full and
clear answer before March 18th. First as to whether they accept the
Parliament's tender of incorporation with England. Secondly as to
whether they will in the mean time live peaceably and obey the Parliament. Thirdly that they offer what they conceive requisite for effecting
the said Union. *Copy.* [N. XX., 69.]

List

[1651-2, February.]—Of the Shires and Burghs summoned with the
days for their Deputies' appearance. *Copy.* [N. XX., 70.]

The Co**ǝ****missioners** **to** **Scotland.**

[1651-2, February.]—Form of Order to such shires who having not
attended within the time limited yet apply for new summons. *Copy.*
[N. XX., 71.]

The Burgesses, Inhabitants, and Neighbours of Forres.

165[1-]2, February 3.—Commission to Thomas Warrand[er] as their
Deputy to the English Commissioners. Attested *Copy.* [N. XX.,
203.]

Assent of the **Kincardineshire** Deputies and also those of the
other Shires and Boroughs specified in *Commons' Journals*, vii.
105.

[1651-2. February 12–March 3.]—*Copies* attested by the Secretary
to the Commissioners to Scotland. [N. XX., 72–91.]

The **Deputies of the Boroughs** specified in *Commons' Journals*,
vii. 106, from **Edinburgh** to **Culross** inclusive.

165[1-]2, February 12–March 3.—Assents to the Union. (Brough
after North Berwick is not a separate place but goes with the preceding
words " North Berwick Burgh," " Elgmburgh " should be " Elgin
Burgh " and "Kylenym," " Kilrynnie." The first ten boroughs all sign
the same paper.) Attested *Copies.* [N. XX., 117–136.]

The Heretors, Rentallors, and Inhabitants of Orkney and Zetland.

165[1-]2, February 16. Kirkwall.—Commissions to George Ruthe-
vene and John Craigie as Commissioners to the English Commissioners.
Attested *Copy.* [N. XX., 198.]

Safe Guard to the Count of Oldenburgh.

1651[-2], February 17.—(In the same general form as that to the
Duke of Sleswick, which is printed in Thurloe, *State Papers*, i. 385.)
(See *Commons' Journals*, vii. 88.) *Drafts* in *Latin* and *English.*
[N. XVIII., 168, 169.]

Don Alonso de Cardenas to the Council of State.

[1651-2, February 17.]—After quoting part of the last paper
delivered by him on December 19–29 (*ante*, p. 620) it proceeds thus:
" Being desirous to manage that strictness by such means as I esteem
most convenient for both nations, before I descend to particulars it
seemeth just and reasonable that first . . . your Honours will be

pleased to declare likewise to me, whether the will and intention of the Parliament be in this point conform and corresponding to that of the King, my Master, for the knowledge thereof is necessary for me that with the greater confidence I may proceed in proffering to your Honours what I do conceive most conducing to that end.

Secondly I desire " you " to let me know, in case the intention of the Parliament be conform to that of the King, my Master, in this particular whether they intend likewise to come to a treaty and a con. elusion of some ajustation of union and interest for the common utility and convenience as well of his Majesty as this Commonwealth because upon the assenting to those two points as preliminary I may proceed to declare what I have to offer further." (See *Commons' Journals*, vii. 100.) In *Spanish*, with *English* translation. The original *signed*. [N. XVII., 78.]

Reasons for the Dissent of the DEPUTIES OF GLASGOW.

1651[-2], February 24.—1. "We who have had all divine and human rights to properties and to a self disposing power of our own government, and also have had the government of our Church settled. . . Let it be considered if we can actively consent to such a tender by which all these . . may be destroyed, and so make ourselves guilty of all the blood and treasure has been spent . . if . . we return by our own consent to put it without government, Covenant or what has followed upon them.

2. Because our acceptance of the Incorporation . . involves us . . in the approbation of the Parliament of England's disposing of all that's near or dear to us and of the grounds upon which they go in relation thereto.

3. Because it doth . . establish in the Church vast and bound- less toleration of all sorts of error and heresies without any effectual remedy for suppressing the same notwithstanding that there be moral and perpetual obligation upon us to suppress and extirpate heresy no less than profaneness. Like as these Declarations do allow diverse wayes of worshipping God under the name of Gospel ways.

4. Our consent is sought to an incorporation, and yet no time or way propont, when such a thing may be made effectual, nor any plot or draught of it holden forth, but we engaged to approve we know not what as also to give obedience to the Commonwealth of England . . . whereby we have no access to desire either the privileges which may be supponet to come by this tender, or to have any hand in framing the mould thereof if it should come, but bind up ourselves from having any government at all but what shall be derived to us." (See *Commons' Journals*, vii. 106.) Attested *Copy*. [N. XX., 102.]

SIR JOHN WAUCHOPE, Deputy for Edinburghshire, to the COMMISSIONERS.

1651-2, February 27.—Desiring that another deputy might be chosen, instead of his colleague who is sick. (See *Commons' Journals*, vii. 106.) *Signed*. [N. XX., 100.]

The desires of the DEPUTIES FOR EDINBURGH. PEARTH, DUNDEE, ABERDEEN, ST. ANDROIS, BANFF, MONROSS, JEDBURGH, BRECHIN, FORFAR, ABERBROTHOCK and WIGTOUNE.

1651[-2], February 25.—1. That the Protestant religion be established in uniformity throughout the whole island.

2. That not only forfeitures and confiscations be taken off, but an Act of Oblivion passed and all prisoners released.

3. That all merchants and traders may enjoy full liberties by sea and land, the same as those in England.

4. That the Boroughs may enjoy their ancient liberty of convening yearly by their Commissioners.

5. That such public judicatories as may be erected and their judges may be made and chosen by the Commissioners with the advice and consent of the Deputies of the shires and burghs.

6. That to relieve the country as many of the forces be removed as may consist with public safety.

7. That Manufactories of all sorts may be erected in the several shires of such commodities as each shire best produces. And to that effect that well qualified workmen may be induced to come from England and join with those of this nation in these undertakings, and that all encouragements privileges and helps may be tendered to such as shall undergo the same. And that an absolute restraint may be made of transporting wool, skins, hides, yarn or any of the like commodities till it be put to the best perfection in workmanship within this island.

8. That some effectual course may be taken for the advancement of the fishing.

9. That the Mint may be with all conveniency reestablished.

10. That the Boroughs may be exempted from payment of Cess.

11. That new elections be made throughout the boroughs of Magistrates Council and other officers.

12. That some certain time be fixed for perfecting the Union.

(See *Commons' Journals*, vii. 106.) *Signed.* [N. XX., 103.] N. XX., 140 is a copy presented on the part of St. Androis only.

The desires of the DEPUTIES OF the shire of ROXBURGH and burgh of JEDBURGH, DUMFRIES-SHIRE, and the shire and borough of SELKIRK.

1651[-2], February 28, 25, March 9.—(See *Commons' Journals*, vii. 106.) The first *signed*, the rest *copies*. [N. XX., 104, 105, 106.]

The desires of the DEPUTIES OF the shire and burgh of BUTE and the burghs of STIRLING and QUEENSFERRY.

1651[-2], February 28–March 2.—[N. XX., 93-95.]

The ENGLISH COMMISSIONERS to HENRY WHALLEY, RICHARD SALTONSTALL, and SAMUEL DESBROUGH.

1651[-2], March 1 and 3. Dalkeith.—Warrant establishing a Court of Admiralty for Scotland and appointing them judges thereof, and form of oath to be taken by them. (See *Commons' Journals*, vii. 106.) *Copies.* [N. XX., 115, 196.]

The ENGLISH COMMISSIONERS.

[1651-2, March.]—Form of the Commissions for Sheriffs, and of the oath to be taken by them. (See *Commons' Journals*, vii. 106.) *Copies.* [N. XX., 116, 197.]

The ENGLISH COMMISSIONERS.

1651[-2], March 1.—Order sending up Sir Henry Vane and Colonel Fenwick, two of their number, to the Parliament. (See *Commons' Journals*, vii. 105.) [N. XVI., 113.]

Speech of LEON DE AISSEMA, public Minister of the HANSE TOWNS, to the COMMITTEE APPOINTED TO RECEIVE HIM.

[1651-2, March 2.]—The Hanse Towns were persuaded to send an ablegation by the example of other nations, although such as follow a monarchical form of government, and in their heart hate all poliarchies and republics, but were dissuaded for want of an occasion, it being unnecessary to acknowledge the Republic like a thing newly acquired as it never was lost, it being clear the people were before the Prince. I shall therefore only touch two points. First as to trade. The ancient commerce between England and the Hanse Towns is to see by the houses constructed to lodge the Hanse merchandises so in London as elsewhere by name of the Steelyard in lieu of which places at Hamburgh and elsewhere the flourishing companies of this nation enjoy such rights and privileges that we also hope the restitution of the old rights and privileges in times past granted to the Steelyard House, being by those deprived of them who formerly directed all to the arbitrary power, an enemy to those that embraced a poliarchicy manner of government. The second is the same love of liberty with unity of inclination which is the strongest tie to friendship. Who knows not the wars which the Hanse Towns have had with their neighbour kings and princes for their liberty and the liberty of trade? Lübeck only once durst and could defend their liberty as well as that of Gustavus, a little afterward King of Swedland. I add to this the liberty in religion abhorring all monarchical Hierarchy, which with this nation we have so common, as can be said, that here it took its beginning from Saxony. These things being so well known it would be superfluous to make congratulation at least in the same manner as others. (See *Commons' Journals*, vii. 100.) In *Latin*, with *English* translation, the first *signed*. [N. XVIII., 158, 152.]

The doubts and scruples of the BURGESSES and NEIGHBOURS OF the burgh of LANARK.

1651-2, March 2.—While professing themselves willing for a Union they desire to be satisfied in these particulars:—"First we conceive ourselves bound by the law of God and the oath of Covenant . . . to endeavour the preservation of the liberties of this nation and just fundamental laws thereof, which we judge to be altogether infringed by the form of the now demanded incorporation which, though carrying along with it a change of the whole fundamental form of government . . . is not presented to the full and free deliberation of the people in their collected body, but first concluded without their advice and knowledge and now offered in a divided way without a previous condescension in what might preserve from the dangerous consequences that may follow so great a change if not carefully guarded against. But secondly, though we could be much denied to cut and carve in what concerns our own interest yet we dare not add to or diminish from the matters of Jesus Christ dearer to us than anything earthly, which is so far from being secured by anything offered for that effect that it is in diverse ways prejudiced and a foundation laid down in general and doubtsom terms of a vast toleration. We are far from the approving the persecuting of any of the truly godly, but how should we be exonered in the day of our wakening to give our full and sure consent to anything which opens a door to many gross errors contrary to sound doctrine" . . . *Signed*. [N. XX., 92.]

The ENGLISH COMMISSIONERS.

1651-2, March 2. Dalkeith.—Declaration to all assenting shires and boroughs that they are taken into the protection of Parliament, and form of Charter to assenting boroughs. (See *Commons' Journals*, vii. 106.) *Copy* and *draft*. [N. XX., 107, 108.]

The desires of the DEPUTIES OF the shires of LANARK and DUMBARTON.

1651[-2], March 2.—(See *Commons' Journals*, vii. 106.) [N. XX., 96.]

The desires of the DEPUTIES OF NAIRNESHIRE.

1651[-2], March 2.—*Signed*. [N. XX., 97.]

The desires of the DEPUTIES OF FIFESHIRE and STIRLINGSHIRE.

1651[-2], March 2, 3.—(See *Commons' Journals*, vii. 106.) *Signed*. [N. XX., 99, 98.]

OLIVER ST. JOHN, SIR HENRY VANE, ROBERT TICHBORNE, RICHARD DEANE, RICHARD SALWAY, and G. FENWICK, being the Commissioners for Scotland to the PARLIAMENT.

1651-2, March 3. Dalkeith.—" The Commissioners . . . having according to the Instructions to them given from the Parliament by conferences with the Deputies of the respective sheires and burroughs of Scotland that have beene choasen, and attended according to the summons on that behalfe, as also with divers other persons of the Scots' nation as by sundry other waies and meanes informed themselves, to the best of their power, of the state of things here, to the end that they might ripen their results thereupon for the consideracion of the Parliament, doe accordingly humbly offer, as followeth :

1. The major part of sheires and burroughes in Scotland, having by their deputies accepted the Parliament's tender of being one Common-wealth with England : It is offered to the Parliament to take into consideracion the passing of such Act or Acts, whereby the aforesaid incorporacion may be speedily made. That kingly power in Scotland and all lawes and oaths relating thereunto be taken away and abolished. And for the punishment of such as shall endeavor the restitucion of kingly power in Scotland, or that shall oppose or endeavor to subvert the government established upon the said Union, or the authority exercised in Scotland, in order thereunto, or in pursuance thereof.

2. That in the said Act, the Parliament would be pleased for the present to declare their minds as to England and Scotland's being represented in one Parliament : as to the particulers for the effecting thereof, and setling of the lawes and government in Scotland, and other things necessary for compleating the said Union. That the Parliament would likewise declare—if they thinke fitt—that the respective sheires and burroughes who accept the tender of Union, be authorized to elect the same number of persons as upon summons from the said commissioners they have lately done, with power to the said deputies—each of them having first expressed their consent to the tender of Union in such manner as the Parliament shall thinke fitt—to meete, and out of themselves to elect fourteene persons to represent all the said sheires and seaven persons to represent all the said burroughes : which one and twentie persons or anie seaven

or more of them are to repaire to the Parliament of England by the   day of   with full power on the behalfe of Scotland to effect the premisses. And it is humbly offered that the charges of the said persons in comming upp to London, and attending that busines may be defrayed by order of the Parliament of England out of the revenue of Scotland, or otherwise.

3. It is humbly propounded that the Parliament would more particulerly ascertain the persons whose estates shall incurr the penalty of forfeiture and confiscacion: and that by an Act of Grace all others which accept the tender of the Parliament for the said Union, and expresse the same by the   day of   in such manner as the Parliament shall thinke fitt, be secured in their persons and estates; so as the same extend not to hold upp bondage services, which shall hereafter be found needfull to be taken away. As also that it be declared by the Parliament that all confiscated lands in Scotland shall be lyable to the payment of debts, in such manner as other lands are by the lawes of Scotland.

That persons formerly desired for administracion of justice in Scotland be with all possible speed sent downe.

That twelve or more ministers be speedily sent down to reside in the severall guarisons and other convenient places in Scotland." *Signed.* [N. XVI., 112.]

The ENGLISH COMMISSIONERS to HENRY WHALLEY, Judge Advocate.

1651[-2], March 3. Dalkeith.—Commission to administer the oath to Magistrates of Edinburgh. (See *Commons' Journals*, vii. 106.) Attested *Copy*. [N. XX., 114.]

The CITY OF EDINBURGH.

165[1-]2, March 5.—Assent to the Union. (See *Commons' Journals*, vii. 106.) *Copy*. [N. XX., 109.]

SIR JAMES STEWART and others.

165[1-]2, March 5.—Protest that before the electing of the Council or Magistrates of Edinburgh the minds of the English Commissioners be known whether the last Council be the Electors or the meeting of neighbours that gave Commission to the last Council. (See *Commons' Journals*, vi. 106.) *Copy*. [N. XX., 110.] N. XX., 112 Entitled " Desires of certain persons in Edinburgh " is almost *verbatim* the same.

The Answer and Overtures of the DEPUTIES OF PEEBLES-SHIRE.

Same date.—*Copy*. [N. XX., 100.]

Several NEIGHBOURS OF EDINBURGH to the COMMISSIONERS.

165[1-]2, March 5.—Petition desiring them to choose the Magistrates themselves, and protesting against the validity of any election. (See *Commons' Journals*, vii. 106.) *Copy*. [N. XX., 111.]

Certain NEIGHBOURS OF EDINBURGH to the COMMISSIONERS.

[Same date (?).]—Praying that they would employ their power for God's honour and the advantage of his people by setting over them such governors as may be found men fearing God and loving righteousness. (See *Commons' Journals*, vii. 106.) *Copy*. [N. XX., 113.]

The State of the Receipt of DELINQUENTS' LANDS.

1651[-2], March 6.—Showing a receipt of 55,116*l*. 15*s*. 0*d*. and a balance of 10,116*l*. 15*s*. 0*d*. [N. XVI., 106.]

The State of the Treasury at GOLDSMITHS' HALL.

1651[-2], March 6.—Showing charges upon it amounting to 449,200*l*. 17*s*. 5*d*., and also an estimate of what may be expected to be received into it. [N. XVI., 107.]

Estimate of the charge of the FORCES IN ENGLAND, IRELAND, AND SCOTLAND.

1651[-2], March 8.—From December 25, 1651, to June 24, 1652, amounting to 689,959*l*. 17*s*. 6*d*. [N. XVI., 108.]

Account showing the receipts and payments of the TREASURER OF THE NAVY.

1651[-2], March 8.—From January 1, 1650[-1], to date, amounting on each side to 529,320*l*. 14*s*. 3½*d*., and 529,120*l*. 12*s*. 8½*d*. [N. XVI., 109.]

Certificate of the RECEIVER-GENERAL OF THE REVENUE.

1651[-2], March 8.—Showing payments already due 45,552*l*. and estimate of payments for the ensuing year charged thereon 30,430*l*. together 75,982*l*. towards which the estimated receipts for the year would be only 25,755*l*. 0*s*. 0*d*. A second account gives the yearly payments and estimated receipts in detail. [N. XVI., 110, 111.]

The Borough of ST. ANDREWS.

1651-2, March 8, 10.—Confirmation of their former commission to their deputy, Assent by him to the Union, their Petition and their Propositions anent the third article of the tender of Union. (See *Commons' Journals*, vii. 107.) Attested *Copies*. [N. XX., 137–139.]

The BURGESSES and NEIGHBOURS OF DUMFERMLIN.

165[1-]2, March 9.—Commission appointing James Reide as their deputy to the English Commissioners. (See *Commons' Journals*, vii. 113.) Attested *Copy*. [N. XX., 155.]

The GENTLEMEN and HERITORS OF the Shire of MURRAY.

1651-2, March 10. Elgin.—Setting forth their objections to the tender of Union, being among others that a wide door will be opened to toleration, that Church Government by subordination is by the declaration wholly cast loose, and the forfeiting and sequestration. (See *Commons' Journals*, vii. 113.) Attested *Copy*. [N. XX., 157.]

The PARLIAMENT to the QUEEN OF SWEDEN.

1651[-2], March 11.—Acknowledging her letter delivered by her public minister, desiring that the ancient friendship and commerce between England and Sweden might continue, and not doubting that the said minister's instructions were for the honour, and advantage of both nations, but as he had died before he had received an audience they had not been able to learn her Majesty's intentions, and stating they had therefore thought it best by this letter sent by Daniel Lisle Esquire to signify to her Majesty how acceptable her letter and minister were to the Parliament, and how eagerly they expect her friendship. (See *Commons' Journals*, vii. 103.) In *Latin*. [N. XVIII., 34.]

The HERITORS and RENTALLORS OF the Shire of MURRAY.

1651-2, March 12. Elgin.—Commission to Sir Robert Innes and Robert Dunbar to repair to the English Commissioners with their answer. (See *Commons' Journals*, vii. 113.) Attested *Copy*. [N. XX., 156.]

The PUBLIC MINISTER OF THE KING OF DENMARK's speech at his audience.

1651[-2], March 12.—Stating that " After four months' travel and a very difficult winter journey at last I arrived in England," and announcing his master's desire to see England flourishing and their ancient leagues with Denmark restored, he himself being sent to prepare for a more solemn Embassy. (See *Commons' Journals*, vii. 105.) In *Latin*, with *English* translation. [N. XVIII., 8, 5.]

Louis de Bourbon, PRINCE DE CONDÉ, to the PARLIAMENT.

165[1-]2, March 12. Agen.—Letter of Credence to the Sieur de Barriere who will explain " the justice of my cause and my designs, which are followed and approved of by all the *gens de bien* in this kingdom." (See *Commons' Journals*, vii. 112.) In *French*. *Signed*. *Seals*. [N. X., 33 should be 32.]

The HERITORS and RENTALLORS OF the Stewartry of KIRKCUDBRIGHT.

165[1-]2, March 13. Carlingwark.—Commission to William Gordon to repair to the English Commissioners to declare their dissent from the tender of Union because :

1. " The government of that nation by King and House of Lords was conceived by the Kingdom of England in 1643 to be the ancient government of that land . . which that whole nation together with this did solemnly engage to maintain. . . .

2. That we cannot without manifest perjury willingly accept that tender . . . may be sufficiently demonstrate from the third Article of the League and Covenant where we are tied to defend the person of the King in the defence of the liberties of the Kingdom. . .

3. Because the government we are required to accept . . . leaveth a latitude for superstition heresy and profaneness together with whatsoever may be contrary to sound doctrine, the extirpation of which we are bound to endeavour by the second Article of the League and Covenant.

4. Because by the second Article of the League and Covenant we are bound to preserve the Reformed Religion in the Church of Scotland in doctrine, worship, discipline, and government, all which shall be destroyed by this liberty which is granted to such as shall serve God in other Gospel ways, which we humbly conceive as a way which the Scriptures of God never knew of.

5. We are bound by the sixth Article of our League and Covenant never to suffer ourselves . . . to be divided from the Union then made."

(See *Commons' Journals*, vii. 111.) Attested *Copy*. [N. XX., 145.]

The Deputies of Glasgow.

Same date.—Assent to the Union with the desires of the borough. (See *Commons' Journals*, vii. 111.) Attested *Copies*. [N. XX , 146, 147.]

The Deputy of Kirkcaldy.

Same date.—Assent to the Union. (See *Commons' Journals*, vii. 111.) Attested *Copy*. [N. XX., 148.]

The Deputies of the Shire of Orkney and Zetland.

165[1–]2, March 15.—Assent to the Union and desires of the Shire. (See *Commons' Journals*, vii. 108.) *Copies*. [N. XX., 143, 144.]

The Deputy of the Borough of Dysart.

165[1–]2, March 16.—Assent to the Union and desires of the Burgh. (See *Commons' Journals*, vii. 107.) *Copies*. [N. XX., 141, 142.]

Edward Winslow and others to Colonel John Downes.

1651[-2], March 16. Haberdashers' Hall.—Enclosing the case of Sir Henry Frederick Thynne. (See *Commons' Journals*, vii. 109.) *Signed. Seal*. [N. VIII., 51.]

The Burgesses and Neighbours of Tayne.

165[1–]2, March 17. Tayne.—Commission appointing David Ross as their deputy to the English Commissioners. Attested *Copy*. [N. XX., 159.]

The Heritors and Rentallors of Ross-shire.

Same date and place.—Commission appointing Robert Monro as their Commissioner to the English Commissioners. Attested *Copy*. [N. XX., 160.]

The Deputies of Perthshire.

165[1–]2, March 17. Dalkeith.—Assent to the Union with the desires of the County. (See *Commons' Journals*, vii. 111.) Attested *Copy*. [N. XX., 150.]

The effect of the Conference between the English Commissioners and the Earl of Argyll.

1651[-2], March 18. Dumbarton.—" The first thing his Lordship desired was, that, if we had anything of prejudice against him to object he might know the particulars, and thereby have opportunity to give satisfaction therein. It was answered; We were sent to receive such desires as his Lordship had to make. He replied; that he was prevented in what he [had] to desire, in order to the settlement of [the] nation, and the good of the whole island, by the positive resolutions of the Parliament, expressed in their declaration, which he had no knowledge of, when he first desired [an] opportunity to communicate his mind, nevertheless, though he believed the Commissioners might not go contrary to what the Parliament had expressed, yet he thought it might be worthy consideration in order to the very ends propounded by Parliament that a number of select persons, who had in Scotland constantly with England opposed the common enemy might be permitted to convene and meet together for receiving and giving mutual satisfaction.

It was answered ; That the Parliament . . had declared their intentions concerning the settlement of Scotland by the union proposed, and that their Commissioners by their authority had given the people of Scotland opportunity to express their acceptance of the tender . . . declaring withal, if they accepted of that union, that then they would be ready to receive such overtures from them as might make the said union effectual and with best satisfaction to the people of Scotland. Ile desired to know what was expected from him, and how he might demean himself touching the premises, and what was intended concerning him. It was answered ; That we were present to receive his desires and not to tender propositions to him, the Commissioners . . not having thought meet to do anything of that nature to any individual persons in Scotland, and therefore must refer him therein to the Parliament's declaration ; yet since [he] insisted so much upon these particulars that if [he] pleased in writing to express them to the Commissioners we doubted not but they would be taken [into] consideration by them. That as he desired to be at some certainty concerning the premises so he had not resolved [to] demean himself otherways than peaceably towards [the] authority of the Parliament . . exercised in Scotland. And that if it should be found convenient for the settlement of Scotland that any places should be fortified in the Highlands, where he had interest, that upon notice given him—which he desired— he should be so far from opposing the same that he should be ready to give his advice and assistance therein. He farther declared that the shire of Argyle would with all possible speed send Commissioners to Dalkeith with full power and authority according to the Commissioners' summons . . and that although that shire was very unable to pay any cess by reason of the great devastations made by Montrose for their affection to the Parliament of England, as he alleged, and that the authority of Scotland found cause not to lay any burthen upon the said country ; yet to show how willing they were according to their ability to do anything that might express them with other shires to be under the protection of the Parliament . . they should be ready beyond their ability to pay towards the said Assessment." (See *Commons' Journals*, vii. 111.) [N. XX., 151.]

Other GENTLEMEN OF the Stewartry of KIRKCUDBRIGHT.

165[1–]2, March 18. Kirkegunzeu.—Declaration that they had not assented to the dissent from the tender of Union (*ante*, p. 634), and commission to George Maxwell and Andrew Lindsay to assent thereto. (See *Commons' Journals*, vii. 113.) Attested *Copy*. [N. XX., 158.]

The AMBASSADORS OF THE STATES-GENERAL to the PARLIAMENT.

1651-2, March 19-29.—Declaring that the States-General had, for guarding the sea and preserving the shipping and trade of the United Provinces, determined to fit out with all speed a fleet of 150 ships, besides those they had already ready, at the same time declaring that they did so with no intention of injuring with the said fleet any allied or friendly powers to the United Provinces. much less the inhabitants or subjects of this Commonwealth, but that on the contrary they were most anxious to maintain that friendship with all such inhabitants and subjects, as was fitting between neighbouring states, and that they equipped the said fleet with no other intention than to guard and defend their own subjects and their shipping and commerce. (See *Commons' Journals*, vii. 103.) In *Latin*. *Signed* by all three ambassadors. [N. XVIII., 124.)

. CHRISTINA, Queen of Sweden, to the PARLIAMENT.

165[1-]2, March 20. Stockholm.—Letter of Credence to Harold Applebohm, her minister. (See *Commons' Journals*, vii. 130.) In *Latin. Seal embossed. Signed* " Christina." *Countersigned* "A. Gylden'\lou." [N. X., 14.]

The DEPUTIES OF INVERNESS.

1651[-2], March 20.—Assent to the Union. (See *Commons' Journals*, vii. 111.) *Copy.* [N. XX., 149.]

The BURGESSES and NEIGHBOURS OF PEEBLES.

165[1-]2, March 22.—Commission appointing Peter Thomson as their deputy to the English Commissioners. Attested *Copy.* [N. XX., 163.]

The HERITORS and RENTALLORS OF INVERNESS-SHIRE.

165[1-]2, March 23.—Commission appointing Kenneth McKenzie and Alexander McIntosh as their deputies to the English Commissioners. Attested *Copy.* [N. XX., 166.]

The GENTLEMEN OF CAITHNESS-SHIRE.

165[1-]2, March 24.—Commission appointing John Sinclaire and George Monro as their deputies to the English Commissioners. Attested *Copy.* [N. XX., 172.]

The COMMISSIONERS OF THE NAVY.

1651[-2], March 24.—Estimate of the charge of the Fleets and Convoys at sea for the year beginning the 24th of December last, amounting to 717,714*l.* 13*s.* 4*d. Signed.* [N. XVI., 114.]

Several ELDERS and BRETHREN to the COMMITTEE FOR THE
PROPAGATION OF THE GOSPEL.

1651[-2], March 24.—Proposals closely resembling and for the most part agreeing *verbatim* ,with, those next following. *Signed* " Hanserd Knollys, John Simpson, Henry Jessey, William Consett, and Edward Harrison " for themselves and divers others. *Noted* " Received March 24, 1651." [N. XVI., 115.]

Several ELDERS and BRETHREN to the COMMITTEE FOR THE
PROPAGATION OF THE GOSPEL.

[Between 1651-2, February 10 and 1652-3, February 11.]—Offering proposals for the removal of the hindrances to the Gospel and for establishing what may promote the same. (Printed in Grey, iv., Appendix, No. 81, p. 144.) (See *Commons' Journals*, vii. 86, 258.) *Signed* " Richard Woollason, Hanserd Knollys for ourselves and others." [N. XVI., 37.]

Captain EDMUND CHILLENDEN, JEREMIAH JUES, and T. LODINGTON
to the SAME COMMITTEE.

[Between the same dates as the last.]—Offering other proposals for the same purpose. (Printed in Grey, iv., Appendix, No. 82, p. 149.) *Signed.* [N. XVI., 38.]

The DEPUTIES OF DUNFERMLIN, TAYNE, and ROSS-SHIRE.

165[1-]2, March 24 ; 1652, March 26.—Assents respectively to the Union. (See *Commons' Journals*, vii. 113.) Attested *Copies*. [N. XX., 154, 152, 153.]

Several GENTLEMEN OF the Stewartry of KIRKCUDBRIGHT.

1651-2, March 24.—Declaring their assent to the Union. (See *Commons' Journals*, vii. 113.) Attested *Copy*. [N. XX., 199.]

The DEPUTY OF the Burgh of PEEBLES.

1652, March 25.—Assent to the Union with the desires of the Burgh. Attested *Copies*. [N. XX., 162, 161.]

The PARLIAMENT.

1652, March 25.—Declaration in order to the Uniting of Scotland into one Commonwealth with England. (Printed in *King's Pamphlets*, E. 659, No. 19.) (See *Commons' Journals*, vii. 110.) *Draft* with amendments. [N. XX., 195.]

The GENTLEMEN OF ARGYLESHIRE.

1652, March 27.—Commission appointing James Campbell of Ardkinglase and Dowgal Campbell their commissioners to the English Commissioners. (See *Commons' Journals*, vii. 132.) Two *Copies*, one attested. [N. XX., 165, 185.]

WILLIAM LENTHALL to the COMMISSIONERS OF THE PARLIAMENT IN SCOTLAND.

[1652, March 30.]—(The purport sufficiently appears from *Commons' Journals*, vii. 111, 112.) *Draft*. [N. XII., 273.]

The FREEHOLDERS and RENTALLORS OF the Sheriffdom of ELGIN AND FORRES.

1652, March 30. Elgin.—Commission appointing Sir Robert Innes and Robert Dunbar their Commissioners to the English Commissioners. Attested *Copy*. [N. XX., 168.]

WILLIAM MAXWELL of Kirkhouse, and PATRICK MURDOCKE of Dumfries.

1652, March 30, [and (?) same date].—Declarations of their personal assents to the Union. Attested *Copies*. [N. XX., 173, 174.]

GEORGE MAXWELL and ANDREW LINDSAY, Commissioners from the Heritors of the Stewartry of KIRKCUDBRIGHT.

1652, March 30.—Assent to the Union. (Printed in Grey, iv., Appendix, No. 45, p. 77.) *Signed*. [N. XVI., 120.]

ANTON GÜNTHER, Count in Oldenburgh, to the PARLIAMENT.

[1652, March.]—Acknowledging their letter and Safe-guard brought back by his agent Hermann Mylius and thanking them for their profession of regard. (See *Commons' Journals*, vii. 88.) In *Latin*. *Seal*. [N. X., 95.]

The humble Petition of the Committee of ADVENTURERS for Lands in IRELAND.

1652, April 5.—Setting forth the sums advanced by them, and the extent of lands due to them in return namely 281,812*l*. on the First Propositions and 12,283*l*. on the Ordinance of July 14th, 1643, and 1,038,234 acres, with the proportions thereof to be allotted in each Province, and praying that the annexed proposals be taken into consideration, and if thought to conduce to the public good, be granted. (See *Commons' Journals*, vii. 115.) *Signed. Annexed:*

The said PROPOSALS and REASONS.

(The substance of these is printed in Prendergast, *Cromwellian Settlement*, pp. 19, 20.) *Signed.* [N. XXI., 131.]

Captain JAMES THOMSON, Governor of Dumbarton Castle, to Major-General DEANE.

1652, April 6.—Concerning the refusal of the magistrates at Dumbarton to take the oath when he tendered it to them. The Lord of Mackfarlinge is willing to become obedient to the Parliament, if his burden may but equal with that of his neighbours, whose oppression, he saith, has been the cause of his standing out. *Enclosed:*

The PROVOST and BAILIFFS OF DUNBRITANE to Captain THOMSON.

Same date.—Promising to obey the Parliament " as far as God's word is the rule to lead us therein " and to exercise justice faithfully, and entreating that more particular acceptance of the oath may be continued till they have greater freedom and light in conscience for performing the same. Attested *Copies*. [N. XX., 178, 177.]

The Undersigned DEPUTIES OF SHIRES to the ENGLISH COMMISSIONERS.

1652, April 6.—Desiring 1, that the inferior judicatures may be authorised to sit, 2, that for repressing the many robberies and murders on the Borders persons should be empowered to apprehend and imprison such as are guilty till criminal judges be appointed, 3, that for securing the shires that border on the Highlands from invasions of Highlanders the laws of this nation be with speed put in execution against all disturbers of the peace there and that the said shires be empowered to appoint armed guards or watches of their own inhabitants. Two attested *Copies*. [N. XX., 164, 175.]

M. DE BARRIERE, Agent of the Prince de Condé, to the COUNCIL OF STATE.

[1652, April 6.]—" Yeasterday I did make some propositions which were not within my wrighting, and because words may bee aisely forgotten this made me beeleeve that yours honnours should not taked it ill that I should give you in wrighting. I do beeseeche your Lordships to give mee a speedy ansswere concerning my wrightings and allsoe upon the demand which I have made to grant to his Highnesse, the Prince of Condé, to transport in this Commun Wealth some wines because the summer drawes necare and the heath is able to spoyle thos Burdeaux wines which should bee transported.

The Earle of Warsowye having commission from . . the Prince of Condé to rise 6,000 strangers soldgers, butt because the contrarye winds and bad weather hath beene forced to come into the harbour of Plimouth and to pass throng Ingland, at his arrivall in London hath bene many Inglish officers to see him and offred him to rise men, provided that the parliament will give them leave—bee publickly or secrettly—and if the parliament does grant this demand that hee may rise the soldgers without droume beating and thos soldgers may be freely transported in such shipps as he shall appoint which shipps and soldgers shall noe bee troubled by the parliament shipps or privat men of warre belonging to this Commun Wealth.

Allsoe your Honnois be pleased that the French shipps belonging to the City of Burdeaux, that they may come into this Commun Wealth freely without any molestation, because yours shipps does goe freely to traid at Burdeaux and does cary their guns before the said city, which hath not bene granted two hundreth yeares agoe and Burdeaux shipps having leave to come and goe hether ore in any plasse of this Commun Wealth that shall bee the cause that his Highnesse shall bee able to maintaine his soldgers because hee hath not other subsistence onely by the waye of the traid of the said citty." *Signed*. [N. XVII., 26.]

The SAME to the SAME.

(This is the French original of which the last is a translation with some unimportant omissions.) [N. XVII., 27.]

M. DU BARRIERE to SIR OLIVER FLEMING.

[1652, April 6.] Tuesday. London.—Requesting him to present the last two papers to the Council of State. In *French*. [N. XVII., 31.]

M. DE BARRIERE to the PARLIAMENT.

[1652, April 6 (?).]—" The Prince hath sent me to the Parliament . . to give them all assurances of his earnest desire to establish a good and sincere correspondence with them . . . his hopes being also to find " in them "a disposition to the same. His Highness gave me order to representate to them the true condition wherein he is and the reasons which made him to take up arms, which are so just that he is confident they shall be approved of by them, and that the justice of his cause shall procure him the help and assistance . . he demands . . and the rather because his Highness is persuaded it is not contrary to the interest of this estate to assist him against those who ever opposed this Commonwealth and are still of the same mind when they shall be in paoure to do it. Therefore I do hope that I shall with no great difficulty obtain what in that name we have already both by word of mouth and in writing demanded and do now demand again That the Parliament will be pleased to afford unto His Highness such succour of men and money which may enable him to oppose himself unto the attempts of his enemies to which he can very hardly resist if he be not speedily assisted specially in Guienne where he or in his absence the Prince of Conti his brother is brought to a very great strait. And we hope that the Parliament shall not willingly see the poor people of that Province utterly desolated, since the greatest trust of all that country next unto God is in some help from hence and that there is no doubt if the Princes should be totally oppressed that the miserable people shall be reduced under the greatest and hardest tyranny that can be imagined for the Cardinal shall never forgive, and in all human reason their preservation doth only depend of that of the Princes, by whose ruin not Guienne alone but all the rest of France shall be brought to the most hard bondage and slavery that ever was. What a great honour will it be besides for the Commonwealth of England after it hath so happily and so gloriously established the precious liberty at home to send their helping hands unto their craving neighbours for the same, whose obligation for that shall be eternal and the acknowledgment of it real and perfect.

And I do here offer and answer for the Prince that whatsoever shall be in his human paoure to do, and that this Parliament shall desire of him he shall do it in acknowledgment of their assistance. I do also demand in the same name that the Parliament may be pleased to establish the free commerce betwixt the city of Bourdeaux and all Guienne and the Commonwealth of England, as it was heretofore, that Province having never done anything that can move the English to that rupture for they had no part in the piracy . . which the Cardinal Mazarin brought in, they refused to admit those declarations which forbidded the receiving the cloth and all other manufactures of England, but contrary to that they have always received and used the English merchants and do still as their best friends, and are yet ready to receive all sorts of merchandises, which from England or other foreign parts shall be brought in the English ships, of which the City of Bourdeaux offers and is willing to make such public declaration as may be desired.

And by reason that the time of transporting their wine ·passes away, I had requested the Parliament to suffer that, whilst they shall be about the settling of the free commerce, the Prince may transport 5 or 6,000 tons, by which means his Highness shall receive some small benefit and money, of which above all things he stands in need at this present, having left his brother in that country in great wants, which makes me renew my earnest request to the Parliament for the grant of that speedily." . . . (See *Commons' Journals*, vii. 117.) *Signed.* [N. XVII., 23.]

The DEPUTIES OF SHIRES, who signed the paper of April 6th, to the ENGLISH COMMISSIONERS.

1652, April 8.—As they understand that judges are about to be appointed to the several shires desiring that all persons who have had conferred on them any jurisdiction or office whether heritable or *ad vitam* should enjoy and exercise their offices as formerly. Attested *Copy.* [N. XX., 176.]

The DEPUTIES OF INVERNESS-SHIRE.

1652, April 8.—Assent to the Union. Attested *Copy.* [N. XX., 167.]

The DEPUTIES OF the Shire of MURRAY.

1652, April 8.—Assent to the Union and certain overtures anent the same. Attested *Copies.* [N. XX., 169, 170.]

The DEPUTIES OF CAITHNESS-SHIRE.

Same date.—Assent to the Union and certain overtures anent the same. Attested *Copies.* [N. XX., 171.]

The ENGLISH COMMISSIONERS to the EARL OF ARGYLL.

1652, April 9. Dalkeith.—In reply to his letter of March 23rd desiring to know what is required of him referring him to the published declaration of the Parliament. (See *Commons' Journals*, vii. 132.) Attested *Copy.* [N. XX., 179.]

U 61630.

The DEPUTIES OF ARGYLESHIRE to the ENGLISH COMMISSIONERS.

1652, April 9.—Desiring that time should be granted to acquaint the shire with the particulars contained in the tender of Union. Attested *Copy.* [N. XX., 180.]

The COMMISSIONERS FOR IRELAND.

1652, April 11.—Exceptions to the Articles for the Surrender of Galway. [N. XXI., 101.]

REPLIES to these EXCEPTIONS.

1652, April.—Two copies, coinciding except as regards the reply to the second exception, the first by the Commissioners appointed by the Lord President of Connaught to treat, the second (apparently) by some of the inhabitants of Galway. (See *Commons' Journals,* vii. 133.) [N. XXI., 102.]

The PARLIAMENT to the KING OF DENMARK.

1652, April 13.—Acknowledging his letter of December last, and informing him that they are animated by the same spirit and desire of perpetuating the ancient ties of friendship and commerce between England and Denmark as he is, being aware that notwithstanding the change of government the same motives and advantages which was the cause of the former treaties continue. *Draft* as reported from the Council of State. (See *Commons' Journals,* vii. 119.) [N. XVIII., 6.]

The Answer of the COUNCIL OF STATE to the papers exhibited by the RESIDENT OF THE HANSE TOWNS.

1652, April 13.—The Parliament for the encouragement of the navigation and increase of the shipping of this nation having passed the Act in the Resident's papers mentioned, and the grounds thereof appearing clearly just and no injury to any their good friends or allies, we see no reason yet given for their relaxation thereof. As to the further desires in their papers of having the Hanse Towns included in any treaties between this Commonwealth and others for the better freedom and advancement of trade, and they may not be postponed to any others they may be well assured that the Parliament will do therein what is just and reasonable, and may testify the value and esteem they have of the friendship of such Protestant allies. And we declare ourselves ready to treat with the Resident concerning what may tend to these ends or conduce to more strict correspondence between this nation and these their ancient allies. Touching the abuses of the English cloths complained of by the Senate of Hamburgh, the Parliament have such grievances under their serious consideration, and will remedy them as their other weighty affairs may permit. Concerning taxes and assessments relating to the Merchants of the Steelyard the same is under consideration and care will be taken that right be done therein. Touching the cases of the two ships belonging to the Hanse Towns and another to Stettin now depending in the Court of Admiralty, to which a recommendation is desired for speedy justice to be therein done, the Council of State, taking notice that these businesses are in a way of a legal determination doubts not that right will done without delay. (See *Commons' Journals,* vii. 119.) In *Latin,* with *English* translation. [N. XVIII., 159.]

The Parliament to the Hanse Towns.

1652, April 13.—Acknowledging their letters of January 16th and reciprocating their friendly sentiments, and stating that for this particular business the Resident had been referred to the Council of State, and such answers and dispatches have there been given to his propositions as have been found just and reasonable. (See *Commons' Journals*, vii. 119.) In *Latin*, with *English* translation. *Drafts.* [N. XVIII., 160, 161.]

The Parliament to the Proconsuls and Senators of Hamburgh.

1652, April 13.—Acknowledging the receipt of their letters of January 15th by their Resident Leon de Aissema to whom they had given audience and whom they had referred to the Council of State, and desiring that in return the Senate will pay equal attention to what may be represented to them by the Resident of the Parliament. *Drafts* in *Latin* and *English*. (See *Commons' Journals*, vii. 119.) [N. X., 85; XVIII., 149.]

[William Clarke?] to William Lenthall.

1652, April 13. Leith.—Announcing the surrender of the Castle of Bradock in the Island of Arran in Scotland with a particular of the arms and ammunition found there. (See *Commons' Journals*, vii. 123.) *Seal.* The said particular is enclosed. Then follow the articles of the surrender of Fort Arkin in the Island of Arran in Ireland dated January 15, 1652-3. [N. VIII., 56.]

The Consuls, Scultets, Landamanns and Senators of the Evangelical Cantons of Switzerland, namely Zurich, Bern, Glarus, Basel, Schaffhausen, and Appenzell, and of the Confederates of the same religion in Rhœtia, Geneva, Saint Gall, Mulhausen, and Bienne, to the Parliament.

1652, April 14.—Expressing their regret at the differences that had arisen between them and the United Provinces, pointing out how important to the true religion it was that peace should be preserved between them, and offering their good offices. In *Latin*. *Seal* of Zurich *embossed*. *Endorsed* "Never opened till May 28, 1683, *per me* Jo. Nalson." [N. X., 90.]

Louis de Bourbon, Prince de Condé, to the Parliament.

1652, April 14. Paris.—Desiring them to place absolute confidence in the Sieur de Barriere, and promising to carry out whatever he and they may agree on. (See *Commons' Journals*, vii. 129.) In *French*. *Signed*. *Seals*. [N. X., 31.] An English translation is N. XVII., 30.

Thomas Warrander, Deputy of Forres.

1652, April 14.—Assent to the Union. *Copy*. [N. XX., 200.]

The Deputies of the Boroughs of Fife to the English Commissioners.

Same date.—Desiring that no oath be required of the Magistrates to be elected, "being conscious to ourselves of the breach of former oaths." Attested *Copy*. [N. XX., 201.]

The Burgesses of Dornoch and the Heritors and Rentallors of Sutherlandshire.

1652, April 15 and 20.--Commissions to Robert Gordon as their Commissioner respectively to the English Commissioners. *Copy.* [N. XX., 182, 184.]

Count Le Daugnion to the Parliament.

1652, April 21. Brouage.—Asking their protection against Cardinal Mazarin and desiring them to place entire confidence in the bearer. (See *Commons' Journals*, vii. 133.) In *French*. [N. X., 35.]

The Gentlemen of Argyleshire.

1652, April 22.—Commission empowering James Campbell of Arkinglas to act as sole Commissioner in case his colleague be unable to travel to Dalkeith. (See *Commons' Journals*, vii. 132.) *Copy.* [N. XX., 186.]

James Campbell, Deputy of Argyleshire.

[1652, April 26.]—Assent to the Union, with the desires of the shire anent the third proposition and the supplication of the same. (See *Commons' Journals*, vii. 132.) *Copies.* [N. XX., 187, 188, 189.]

The English Commissioners to James Campbell.

1652, April 27.—In reply to his supplication stating that the inhabitants of Argyleshire are now taken into the protection of the Parliament, and the desires with reference to the Marquess of Argyll shall be represented to Parliament. *Copy.* [N. XX., 194.]

The English Commissioners to Scotland.

1652, April 27, 28, 28.—Orders fixing the salaries of the Commissioners for the Administration of Justice, four to receive 600*l.* and three 300*l. per annum*, and for regulating and fixing the fees of the Court of Justice and for the payment of their salaries not to exceed 2,200*l.* *Copies.* [N. XX., 193, 192; XVI., 121.]

Considerations to be offered to the Parliament by Mr. Weaver, wherein their resolutions are humbly desired.

[1652, April 30.]—" To give an accompt unto the Parliament, in what manner and by whose hands their Revenue of Sequestrations, Customs. Tithes &c. are managed.

To hasten the Parliament's Resolutions concerning the Quallifications.

To hasten the Parliament's Conclusions with the Adventurers upon Irish Lands and to insist upon their enjoying by Lott one of the four parts of Lands proportioned, And that they bee engaged to plant such Proportions with English within   yeares and not to be freed from Contribution unlesse they will Secure the Countries.

To obtaine the Parliament's resolutions concerning Ormond's Articles on which will depend the forfeiture or not forfeiture of many Considerable Estates in Ireland.

To make knowne the Articles and Agreement with Colonell Fitz Patricke and his Partie and the grounds and successe thereof and Desire their Approbation.

That Instructions may be considered of for Stateing Souldiers' Accompts and Ascertaining payement thereof by Irish Lands and upon what tearmes.

To Acquainte the Parliament with the Declaration for putting out of Protection severall Counties and places in Ireland, And of their Declaring such of the Enemies' party who come into the Parliament's Quarters under the number of twelve to be Spies And of their Declaring such of the Enemy who after submitting to protection doe returno into Rebellion to be put to Death, And of their Orders for all Smiths, Sadlers, Cutlers, etc., to come into Some Guarrison of the Parliament's or within Musquett Shott Distance, by which Severall Declarations divers of the Irish are dayly knockt o' the head and put to Death.

To give an Accompt how Justice is Administred at present and to desire the Parliament Sending over more Judges.

To desire the Parliament's Consideration of what Debtes contracted by Delinquents before the Warre shalbe allowed out of their Lands or other Estates and what Joyntures or Dowers to be allowed.

To move that Captain Rich with his Friggott of forty Tunnes, nine Gunns, and twenty-five men now ymployed in this Coast may be paid by the Comittee of the Navy.

That Estates Taile may be made lyable to payement of Debts.

To knowe the Parliament's pleasure in giveing leave to Irish Comaunders to transpourt Irish Souldiers to Princes in Amitie with them and to allow of what hath been done therein already upon Capitulacion." (See *Commons' Journals*, vii. 127.) *Signed.* Two *copies.* [N. XV., 173, and XXI., 99.]

The Commissioners of Public Accounts.

[1652, April.]—Representation desiring to know whether in consequence of the Act of Oblivion Collectors, Receivers and Treasurers of money plate &c. on the Propositions and also the Collectors &c. of the several loans and contributions continue accountable or no.

And
The Same to ——.

Desiring him in addition to the representation to move that the Accounts of Sequestrations be determined by the Committee of Public Accounts as formerly instead of by the Commissioners for Compounding, that their former power concerning Discoveries be renewed, and that an allowance at the rate of 300*l.* a year be made to every member of the Committee from October 11th 1649 for two years and a half to the 11th of April last and that the same allowance be made in future. Annexed are several draft resolutions for carrying the above into effect. (Nothing appears to have been done by Parliament in consequence.) N. XVI., 39.]

The Deputies of the Burgh of Dornoch and the shire of Sutherland.

[1652, end of April or beginning of May.]—Assent to the Union. (See *Commons' Journals*, vii. 132.) *Copies.* [N. XX., 181, 183.]

Articles between Colonel Venables and others and Colonel Thorlagh O'Neill and others.

1652 May 1. Dundalk.—1. All non-commissioned officers and soldiers . . shall deliver up to the said Col. Venables or whom he shall appoint on the 3rd instant all their horses and arms without any spoil or embezzlement.

2. The said colonels officers and soldiers that shall deliver up their arms as aforesaid—except what is hereafter excepted—shall have protection for their lives liberties and personal estates, to live in such places as shall be thought fit by the said Col. Venables or the Commissioners of the Revenue, they acting nothing during that time to the prejudice of the Parliament of England.

3. As to their real estates—subject as is hereafter excepted—they shall have equal benefit with others under the like qualification in any offers that shall be hereafter held out from the Parliament.

4. Provides for paying them the value of their horses.

5. Empowers such as wish to serve any foreign state in amity with England to treat with its agents for such purpose and also to transport themselves thither.

6. Excepts from the benefits of the Articles any that have been guilty of murdering or massacring any of the English or any adhering to them since the 23rd of October 1641 and all priests and others of the Romish Clergy and any officer or soldier that hath taken away the lives of any of our party after quarter given or any of that party that hath formerly served the Parliament and deserted their colours since August 20, 1649 and any that sat in the first General Assembly or first Supreme Council, and provides that all persons included in these Articles that commanded in the first year of the Rebellion shall be liable to a trial at law for anything done by them since October 23, 1641.

7. Allows six weeks to all who come in upon these Conditions to apply to the Commissioners of Parliament for Ireland to procure what further favour they may grant.

8. Provides that true lists of the men and horses in each regiment be delivered.

9 and 10. Provides for hostages to be given to Col. Venables ; and for their restoration if the Commissioners of Parliament do not confirm these Articles.

11. If any one included in the Articles violates the same, he only shall suffer. (See *Commons' Journals*, vii. 133.) *Copia vera Concordans cum originali.* [N. XXI., 104.]

FREDERIC III., King of Denmark, to the PARLIAMENT.

1652, May 1. Copenhagen.—Letter of Credence to his Ambassadors Extraordinary Erie Rosencrantz and Peter Reetz. (See *Commons' Journals*, vii. 136.) *In Latin. Seal embossed. Signed.* [N. X., 20.] N. XVIII., 7 is a *copy* with an English translation.

HAROLD APPELBOOM, Public Minister of the Queen of Sweden, to WILLIAM LENTHALL.

1652, May 3.—Announcing his arrival, desiring an audience, and enclosing a copy and translation of his Letter of Credence (*ante*, p. 637). (See *Commons' Journals*, vii. 129.) *Signed. Seal.* [N. XVIII., 35, 36.]

Considerations to be offered by Mr. WEAVER to the COUNCIL OF STATE.

1652, May 4.—Concerning a supply of clothes &c. to the soldiers and the payment thereof.

"To consider with the Spanish Agent of a course to be taken for conveying the Irish for his master's service and to take care that such Irish as are raised may continue under their respective commanders sent with them.

Touching a Great Seal and others less for Administration of Justice.

To resolve of a convenient number of able physicians to be sent over to be placed in such garrisons and other places, wherein they may be most serviceable to the soldiery and the English.

To desire the Council to consider of encouragements to be held out to planters.

To endeavour the settlement of a constant monthly pay of 20,000*l.* &c. to be sent over to Ireland—without defalcation of any part for clothes or other provisions—for that notwithstanding the greatest part of the enemies' forces may submit yet there will be a necessity for some time to continue between 3 or 400 garrisons in Ireland for better securing the country and beating the enemy out of woods and mountains.

To endeavour the Parliament's assent—by the Council—to the particulars mentioned in our letter from Kilkenny of January the 7th 1651[-2] viz.:

For planting garrisons near the woods and fastnesses of the enemy.

That the Adventurers cast lots where their lands shall be assigned them.

That a Pale be made by securing the rivers of Boyne and Barrow and other places.

That all the forces may be fixed to their respective garrisons and may have lands assigned them, as well for their arrears as part of their present pay to the end they may be encouraged to follow husbandry, Provided that such of them who marry Irish women have no benefit &c." [N. XXI., 100.]

M. DE BARRIERE to the COUNCIL OF STATE.

[1652, May 4.]— . . Will not reiterate the propositions several times already made. I now only beseech you "to consider that the time doth extremely press and that the season doth come on, especially for the transporting of the wines of Bordeaux, for now we enter into the hot weather, which is a great deal sooner there than in this country, and which may hinder the transporting of the said wines. And as it is a thing which is profitable and necessary to all the world I hope the Parliament will grant this proposition . . . And as it was objected that the wines of Bordeaux could not be had without ready money I answer . . that those of Bordeaux are ready to receive all kinds of merchandises whatsoever, so that it is not to be feared that any money should go out of the kingdom. Further the said city . . . and the rest of the provinces of Gascoigne which are under the . . authority of . . the Prince of Condé do concur with his said highness, and earnestly desire to have a good and true correspondence with the Parliament . . . which the said city conjointly with his highness will perform and maintain against all declarations that may be made to the contrary by the King of France. I . . humbly beseech that if the Parliament will not establish this commerce suddenly to . . permit that in the meantime a certain quantity of wines may be transported." Duplicate in *French* and *English. Signed.* [N. XVII., 24, 25.]

The COUNCIL OF STATE.

1652, May 4.—Order referring to the Committee for Foreign Affairs the Order of Parliament of that date made on the Prince de Condé's letter (see *Commons' Journals*, vii. 129), and the letter itself. [N. XVII., 29.]

The COUNCIL OF STATE.

1652, May 5.—Order reporting M. de Barriere's paper. (Probably that of the 4th.) [N. XVII., 28.]

HAROLD APPELBOOM'S speech at his audience.

1652, May 6.—On hearing of the death of my predecessor, my mistress despatched me hither to express her resolution of perpetually preserving and enlarging the ancient friendships between the two countries, " which inclination in what occasions Her Majesty especially hopes to find on the Parliament side and again on her part is ready to show I shall more at large declare before Commissioners, which to that end I desire may be given me." (See *Commons' Journals*, vii. 130.) In *Latin*, with *English* translation, the first *signed*. [N. XVIII., 37, 38.]

The PARLIAMENT.

1652, May 11.—Resolution reviving the Committee for proposals from the Adventurers. (Printed in *Commons' Journals*, vii. 131.) [N. XXI., 132.]

The COMMITTEE FOR PROPOSALS FROM THE ADVENTURERS.

1652, May 11.—Resolutions. (These are nearly the same as parts of the Resolutions passed the next day, except one, that the lands to be assigned be all together, and that the Adventurers are given the choice only of Limerick, Kerry, and Cork, or Waterford, Wexford, Wicklow and Kilkenny, the third alternative Limerick, Kerry, and Tipperary being omitted.) *Copy.* [N. XXI., 133.]

The SALE.

1652, May 12.—Resolutions. (Printed in Gilbert, iii. 318.) [N. XXI., 134.]

Articles for the surrender of the LEINSTER forces.

1652, May 12. Kilkenny.—(These with several explanations and the places for disbanding the different regiments are printed in Gilbert, iii., pp. 94–99. The places for disbanding here differ from those printed by adding Birr, and some of the regiments are according to this paper to disband at different places from those at which they are to disband according to the printed paper.) *Copies.* [N. XXI., 105, 106, 107, 108.]

HAROLD APPELBOOM to the COUNCIL OF STATE.

[1652, May 12-22.]—As Her Majesty's "subjects have as well through the Northern as Western sea in several places hitherto been accustomed freely to have their commerce and navigation" she "undoubtedly hopeth that they shall henceforward likewise be free from being any way disturbed or infested by the subjects of the Parliament, and especially that the Parliament will permit them securely and without molestation to continue their aforesaid commerce in England and in the countries and lands thereunto belonging with their wonted free use of coming in and going out of their harbours." And she is confident that they will every way be courteously entertained there and that it shall be free for them to refresh and provide themselves of victuals and other necessaries for navigation, not only when they are directly bound for any of the ports of this Commonwealth, but also when, being bound for some other place they shall by tempest or otherwise be forced to run into the same. She declares that she on her part will ever in her dominions and harbours be ready to permit as much to the subjects of the Parliament. In *Latin*, with *English* translation. *Signed.* [N. XVIII., 40, 41.]

The Form of the Oath for the OFFICERS OF THE SCOTCH NATION

and

Their DECLARATION OF ASSENT.

[1652, before May the 14th.]—(See *Commons' Journals*, vii. 132.) *Copies.* [N. XX., 190, 191.]

The COMMITTEE OF THE ADVENTURERS to the COMMITTEE FOR PROPOSALS.

1652, May 14.—They dare not accept the proposals because " 1. That albeit they resolve to use all expedition they safely may to plant, yet considering the various dispensations of Divine Providence to root up and to pull down and the great disappointment which God hath already given to their hopes for a more speedy reducing of Ireland to peace that it might become a quiet habitation, they hold it presumptuous and a tempting of God to undertake to plant fully such a quantity of land absolutely within 3 years or within any certain time.

2. That, although they shall gladly attempt to their utmost endeavour to come up to the pleasure of the Parliament publicly declared, yet they cannot admit of such a tie upon them to plant all in such a manner as shall be directed by the Parliament for that there is no such direction given to them whereupon they may consider whether they be able to do it or not and for that they humbly conceive that the land—when set out —being their own by a dear purchase they may plant and build for their own convenience at their own discretion, and that it is their liberty and birthright so to do.

3. That albeit they neither do nor can plead for the Irish, yet for that the Parliament hath not declared their pleasure touching the natives, whether Protestants or others, the Adventurers can say nothing to the exempting or admitting of the Irish until the Parliament hath disposed of them.

4. The Counties propounded and sorted as they are for the Adventurers to make their election are so situated by reason of hogs woods and mountains so intervening that the Adventurers cannot plant together in a body to assist and guard one another in case of assault or danger, as was propounded . . and will therefore prove very prejudicial to the managing of. the work and safety of the workmen, nor are the Adventurers satisfied . . whether there be forfeited lands sufficient to satisfy the Adventurers in those counties, nor when or how they shall be cleared of the multitude of Tories that yet swarm in them, nor what protection the planters shall have during the worke or upon what terms.

5. The first proposition also mentioning an allowance of so much land only as their present Adventures amount unto, it is not clear to them whether it be meant only of what is due in Munster and Leinster alone, or of what is due to them in all the four provinces ; and whether that

which is due by Ordinances, as well as by Acts, seeing in the close of your Propositions mention is made of Acts only . . .

6. Although the addition of 500,000 acres be a large favour and is so acknowledged, yet to be tied to such building and planting and in such manner as the Parliament shall appoint . . . and not to have the same addition in the same provinces and yet to plant it also within 3 years from September next or to forfeit it all then not so planted and inhabited and all the said lands to be still subject to the several and respective rents reserved in the Acts of Parliament notwithstanding that this is upon a new contract. These are such conditions that the Adventurers dare not embrace were the addition much larger than it is. And as to that of the reserved rent they cannot yield unto it upon a new Contract for the reasons laid down to back their 5th proposal formerly tendered to be presented to Parliament."

7. (Of this clause only a few words are legible, the paper being here much torn and the ink in many places totally gone. It is apparently in answer to the 3rd Proposal concerning the demise of houses to the Adventurers.)

8. "The liberty of exporting commodities there, doth not thereby take in agents (?) without which they can neither plant or live in Ireland, nor doth it discharge Excise or other imposts as the Act of Parliament doth now grant the like immunity from Custom and imposts for goods being native commodities of the country from Ireland to England and the want whereof will make bad markets render their commodities cheap and the Adventurers poor, while in foreign plantations the Planters, who pay nothing to the State for the land, have greater liberties and privileges than was propounded by the Adventurers in their former proposals.

9. Although the proportion of land limited in the first proposition might be borne if all other things were granted which the Adventurers propounded, this safe there shall be so only a necessity to continue them ; yet seeing there is an intimation that a greater proportion may be required after ten years, and that this will not be granted for ten years but on accepting all the other propositions, and that all must be planted conveniently, inhabited, and husbanded, as the Parliament shall appoint within three years or forfeited, and the old rents also continued, they dare not undertake to pay so great a proportion.

10. Lastly observing that the three years allotted for the planting and full finishing and inhabiting of the same, as the Parliament shall direct, or to forfeit all which by that time shall not be so inhabited, planted and husbanded, and that the exemption from Customs for seven years are all to commence from the 29th of September next, and no assurance given or propounded that all or any of the Counties named in your Propositions shall be before that time cleared of Tories or of other Irish, which by the Propositions may not be admitted to be in the Plantation, although Protestants, and that there is no hint of any course to be taken for declaring and surveying the forfeited lands where they lie and of what quantity and quality they are, or for clearing up their estates who have not forfeited their lands, or how so many persons and families shall be provided for of any tolerable habitations while they are at work upon the plantation—which cannot be performed within three years by 40,000 men, who must also have their families with them—without all which no plantation can now be carried on ; The Adventurers humbly crave leave to say that it lies in their apprehensions as a thing no way feasible or possible to effect what this Honourable Committee propounds unto them, although not only all these Propositions, but all the Adventurers' own proposals and much more should be granted freely to them, and

they are of opinion that, if they should attempt the work on such terms, they must inevitably ruin themselves and destroy the plantation as to any considerable fruit which it might otherwise yield to the Commonwealth and render all that part of Ireland very mean poor and contemptible, and so they should, instead of promoting, extremely hinder the public interest strength and honour of the Commonwealth.

Wherefore if the Parliament shall think fit to grant their proposals formerly presented, the Adventurers shall readily enter upon the Plantation, so soon as the country shall be so far cleared of Tories and Rebels that the planters may sit down to the work in safety, and so soon as by Acts of Parliament it shall be declared what lands are forfeited and where they lie, and the same set out unto them, and that all men's estates not forfeited may be cleared and known, and that after all this done the season of the year shall be proper to begin the work which being begun they resolve with God's assistance to proceed in it with effect and with all possible speed and expedition." [N. XXI., 135.]

HAROLD APPELBOOM to the COUNCIL OF STATE.

1652, May 18–28.—Desiring favourable and speedy answers to her Majesty's letter and to his two propositions. In *Latin*, with *English* translation, the first *signed*. (See *Commons' Journals*, vii. 133.) [N. XVIII., 42, 43.]

The Fifth Clause in the QUALIFICATIONS.

1652, May 18.—(Printed in *Commons' Journals*, vii. 133.) [N. XXI., 103.]

CHRISTINA, Queen of Sweden, to the PARLIAMENT.

1652, May 22. Stockholm.—Commending to them Regiment's Quartermaster Bernard Killey, to whom she had given leave of absence to go to Ireland to recover his brother's lands, and desiring their good offices on his behalf. (See *Commons' Journals*, vii. 159.) In *Latin*. *Seal embossed. Signed* " Christina." *Countersigned.* [N. X., 10.]

Extract out of the Register of the Resolutions of the STATES-GENERAL.

1652, May 23.—Resolved in reply to the letter of the Evangelical Cantons of Switzerland dated April 14th to thank them for their affection towards this State, and their care for the conservation of the Reformed Religion and also for the continuation of peace between this State and the Commonwealth of England with a declaration that their Lordships will not fail to contribute all things necessary to promote the one and the other, and specially, a good correspondence with the said Commonwealth, hoping the same from them ; " that it is true that some extraordinary preparation of ships of war was made, but to no other intention as to the safety of the sea, and security of the navigation and trade of these countries." (See *Commons' Journals*, vii. 139.) [N. XVIII., 126.]

ROBERT MOULTON, junior, and four other CAPTAINS.

1652, May 24.—Certifying " the state of the business betwixt us and the Dutch fleet. Upon the 19th . . . we had intelligence that they were off the South Foreland consisting in the whole of about 42 sail. We paid up with our ships as fast as possible, and being off Foulston (Folkestone) espied the Dutch fleet to ride at anchor near Dover. As soon as the tide presented we plied towards them, whereupon they weighed and stood to the Southward three leagues to the windward of our ships We, thereby imagining they had not any intent to engage with us, laid our ships about, and within half an hour Vantrumph with ail his fleet bore up upon us, and being near, our general gave orders to fire at the Dutch flag to strike, which they refusing, we shot again. They still refused to strike, but shot a piece at our flag, and shot it through, we then being within musquet shot one of the other. Then . . . . the third time we fired a gun at his flag, which was no sooner done, but he fired his whole broadside at us, and so we engaged and went on fighting from " half past four in the afternoon till nine, " and then we anchored to fit our ships in a posture for the next morning, the Dutch fleet being to the Southward of us three leagues next morning directed their course for France, whereupon, seeing them do so, we plied up to the Downs." *Copy.* [N. XVI., 122.]

The DUTCH AMBASSADORS to the COUNCIL OF STATE.

1652, [May 24-] June 3.—(An English translation is printed in *King's Pamphlets*, E. 668, No. 1, p. 26.) In *Latin. Signed* " J. Cats, G. Schaep, P. Vandeperre." [N. XVIII., 128, No. 1.]

ERIC ROSENCRANTZ and PETER REETZ the Danish Ambassadors' Speech at their Audience.

1652, May 26.—Stating that their master after his father's decease bent his mind on nothing more than how in the great inconstancy and restlessness of this last age he might enter into and uphold a most strait League of amity with all his neighbours, and perceiving how great profit from the commerce between his kingdoms and England as also from the religious and near. union of friendship between them accrued to both nations, as soon as his own kingdoms were freed from those various difficulties whereunto new empires are obnoxious, endeavoured that the ancient amity between them might not be annihilated, but be kept inviolate, for which purpose he has sent them with full powers, and declaring their readiness to declare all that concerns that business to commissioners assigned them by Parliament. (See *Commons' Journals*, vii. 136.) In *Latin*, with *English* translation, the first *signed*. [N. XVIII., 9.]

The DUTCH AMBASSADORS to the COUNCIL OF STATE.

1652, [May 27-] June 6.—(An English translation is printed in *King's Pamphlets*, E. 668, No. 1, p. 35.) In *Latin. Signed* as their last paper. [N. XVIII., 128, No. 2.]

The PARLIAMENT to HAROLD APPELBOOM.

1652, May 28.—Declaring their anxiety to preserve and strengthen the ancient friendship between England and Sweden, promising that her Majesty's subjects are and shall be treated as friends in the ports and coasts under the jurisdiction of the Commonwealth, and expressing their readiness to treat about the manner in which the navigation and trade of both nations may be promoted and the mutual confidence of both parties increased so as to confirm the former treaties. (See *Commons' Journals*, vii. 137.) In *Latin. Copy.* [N. XVIII., 44.]

FRANCESCO MOLIN, Doge of Venice, to the PARLIAMENT.

1652, June 1.—Letter of Credence to Lorenzo Pauluzzi, secretary to their Ambassador to France, whom he is sending to London to procure the preparing of some ships and levying of some soldiery against the Turks, "who with a mighty arm do not cease obstinately to practise their perfidious hatred against the Christendom." (See *Commons' Journals*, vii. 142.) In *Italian*. Written on Parchment. [N. X., 96.] A copy with *English* translation is N. XVIII., 154, 155.

The PARLIAMENT to the QUEEN OF SWEDEN.

1652, June 2.—In *Latin*, with *English* translation. (The first is printed in Thurloe, *State Papers*, i. 206.) (See *Commons' Journals*, vii. 137.) *Copies*. [N. XVIII., 45.]

CHRISTINA, Queen of Sweden, to the PARLIAMENT.

1652, June 2. Stockholm.—Acknowledging their letter of the 11th of March last, and expressing her continued friendship towards England. (See *Commons' Journals*, vii. 159) In *Latin*. *Seal embossed*. *Signed* "Christina." *Countersigned* "A. Gyldenclou." [N. X., 9.]

The DUTCH AMBASSADORS to the COUNCIL OF STATE.

1652, June [3-]13.—(An English translation is printed in *King's Pamphlets*, E. 668, No. 1, p. 38.) In *Latin*. *Signed* as their last paper. [N. XVIII., 128, No. 3.]

The STATES-GENERAL to the PARLIAMENT.

1652, June [4-]14.—Letter of Credence to their Ambassador Extraordinary Adrian Pauw. *Copies*. In *French* and *English*. [N. XVIII., 129, 130.]

Narrative of the LATE ENGAGEMENT between the ENGLISH and DUTCH FLEETS.

[1652, June 5.]—

And

Information of Captain WILLIAM BRANDLEY and Examinations of BASTEAN TUNEMANT and several other Dutch officers dated May 22nd and VAN TROMP'S Instructions dated May [15-]25th.

(All these are printed in *King's Pamphlets*, E. 688, No. 1. The narrative is also one of the documents in the Appendix to the Declaration of July 7th.) [N. XVIII., 137, 125, 136.]

ADRIAN PAUW to the COUNCIL OF STATE.

1652, June [7-]17. Gravesend.—Announcing his arrival as Ambassador Extraordinary, that arrangements may be made for his reception. In *Latin*. *Signed*. [N. XVIII., 131.]

The SAME to ———

Same date.—Accompanying the last and to the same effect, and referring him to the bearer, the secretary of the Embassy, for further information. In *French*. *Signed*. [N. XVIII., 132.]

DON ALONSO DE CARDENAS to the PARLIAMENT.

1652, June 10-20.—Pressing for a favourable answer to his former application on behalf of Colonel William Cobb of Sandringham. (See *Commons' Journals*, vii. 141.) In *Spanish*, with *English* translation. The original *signed*. [N. XVII., 79.]

Speech of ADRIAN PAUW to the PARLIAMENT.

1652, June 11-21.—-(An English translation is printed in the Appendix to the Declaration of Parliament of July 7th which is in *King's Pamphlets*, E. 669, No. 19.) In *Latin. Signed.* [N. XVIII., 127.]

Colonel ROBERT VENABLES to Doctor HENRY JONES, Scout-Master General.

1652, June 17. Belturbet.—Describing a defeat of the enemy by Sir Theophilus Jones. (Printed in *King's Pamphlets*, E. 669, No. 8.) *Seal.* [N. VIII., 57.]

Articles between Lieutenant-General LUDLOW and LORD MUSKERRY.

1652, June 23.—For the surrender of the Island of Ross, and the forces under Lord Muskerry's command and explanations thereof. (Printed in Gilbert, iii. 324 from the part signed by Ludlow and the Parliament Commissioners. This is a copy of the part signed by Lord Muskerry and his Commissioners.) Much torn and injured. [N. XXI., 109, 110.] A list of the officers and soldiers included therein is N. XXI., 122.

Propositions of the COUNCIL OF STATE to the PARLIAMENT.

1652, June 24.—1. That the . . States-General . . pay and satisfy to the Commonwealth the charges and damages this State hath sustained and been put unto by the preparations and attempts this summer, the particulars whereof shall be in due time produced.

2. That upon payment of the sum to be agreed upon as aforesaid for charges and damages, or securing the same to the satisfaction of the Parliament, there shall follow thereupon a cessation of all acts of hostility and the ships and goods taken since the late differences shall be released.

3. The two former propositions being assented to and put in execution, the security which the Parliament does expect is by both states contracting a firm alliance and consistency of interests for the good of both, which the Parliament . . is willing on their part by [all] just ways and means to endeavour. (Passed with amendments. See *Commons' Journals*, vii. 145.) [N. XVIII., 138.]

ADRIAN PAUW to the PARLIAMENT.

1652, June 28–July 8.—Stating that he had received an express order to return that he might give a report of his negotiation, and therefore entreating them to give such an order for his audience that he might take leave tomorrow. (See *Commons' Journals*, vii. 145.) In *French*, with *English* translation, the first *signed.* [N. XVIII., 132, 140.]

JAMES CATS, GERARD SCHAEP, and PAULUS VANDEPERRE, to the PARLIAMENT.

1652, [June 29-] July 9.—Stating that they had received orders to return, that they might give an account of their negotiation, and asking an audience as soon as possible to take leave, and for a safe conduct. (See *Commons' Journals*, vii. 145.) In *Latin. Signed.* [N. XVIII., 134.]

The Danish Ambassadors to William Lenthall.

1652, June 29.—Desiring an audience. In *French. Signed.* [N. XVIII., 10.]

Adrian Pauw's Speech in his own and his Colleagues' names to the Parliament.

1652, [June 30-] July 10.—(An English translation is printed in the Appendix to the Declaration of Parliament of July 7th, which is in *King's Pamphlets*, E. 669, No. 19.) In *Latin. Signed* by all four ambassadors. [N. XIX., 133.]

The Roman Catholics to the Parliament.

[1652, June 30.]—Petition. (Printed in Peck, *Desiderata Curiosa*, xi. 10.) (See *Commons' Journals*, vii. 147.) *Signed. Endorsed* "Read and upon the question rejected." [N. XXII., 130.]

The Commissioners for Compounding to the Parliament.

1652, July 1.—Certain queries. (Printed in *Commons' Journals*, vii. 158.) [N. XXI., 123.]

The Danish Ambassadors' Speech to the Parliament.

1652, July 2.—Exhorting and entreating them in their Master's name not to suffer the difference betwixt them and the States-General of the United Provinces to break out into open war, but rather to give place unto amicable composition and pacification, with several arguments in support thereof. (See *Commons' Journals*, vii. 149.) In *Latin*, with *English* translation, the first *signed.* [N. XVIII., 11, 12.]

Declaration of the Parliament.

1652, July 7.—Relating to the affairs and proceedings between this Commonwealth and the States-General of the United Provinces. (Printed in *King's Pamphlets*, E. 669, No. 19, where are also printed N. XVIII., 137, 127, 130, 140, 134, 133.) [N. XVIII., 139.]

John, King of Portugal, to the Parliament.

1552, July 7· Lisbon.—Letter of Credence for his Ambassador extraordinary Dom João Roiz de Saa e Meneses, Count of Penaguião, his Lord Chamberlain. (See *Commons' Journals*, vii. 188.) *Signed* "El Rey." In *Portuguese. Seal embossed.* [N. X., 5b.] A *Latin* translation is N. XVII., 163.

The Case of Lord Brudenell.

[1652, July before the 13th.]—Stating the proceedings on the reference ordered on the 8th of July 1651 (see *Commons' Journals*, vi. 599), and praying that he may not for his conscience and religion be ranked amongst the highest offenders. (See *Commons' Journals*, vii. 153.) [N. XXII., 133.]

M. Gentillot to William Lenthall.

1652, July 18-28. Calais.—Stating the circumstances under which he had come to England, and how he had been ordered to leave by the Council of State. (See *State Papers, Domestic*, pp. 319, 324, 326.) In *French.* [N. XVII., 17.]

The Council of State to the Grand-Duke of Tuscany.

1652, July 29.—(The purport appears from the instructions for preparing it, printed in *State Papers, Domestic*, p. 316, No. 4.) *Enclosed* was a copy of the Parliament's Declaration. In *Latin. Draft.* [N. XVIII., 144.]

The Council of State.

1652, July 30.—Report concerning Colonel Hewson, and Adjutant-General Allen's proposal. [N. XXI., 114.] *Annexed:*

The said Proposal.

(Printed in *Commons' Journals*, vii. 162.) [N. XXI., 113.]

The Council of State.

1652, August 3.—Report. The first part is concerning the qualifications and suggests various amendments, of which the most important are the omission of the 2nd qualification, the substitution of a new one for the 7th (now 8th), and the addition of a proviso. All those amendments were incorporated in the Act passed on August 12th.

The second tenders a Draft Commission and Instructions for Irish affairs, and advises the repeal of the former Act and Instructions.

The third, relating to various Irish affairs, is printed in *Commons' Journals*, vii. 162. [N. XXI., 111.]

The Council of State.

1652, August 4.—Report concerning Major Adams. (Printed in *Commons' Journals*, vii. 163, and *State Papers, Domestic*, p. 355.) [N. XXI., 112.]

Christina, Queen of Sweden, to the Parliament.

1652, August 7. Stockholm.—Stating that the Swedish Muscovy Company had before the outbreak of the war between England and the United Provinces, chartered six Dutch ships to convey corn brought by them in the previous winter from Archangel to Batavia, and asking that orders should be given to the Admiral and captains not to molest the said ships, or that at least that her subjects as the owners of the cargoes should be indemnified. (See *Commons' Journals*, vii. 177.) In *Latin. Seal embossed. Signed* "Christina." *Countersigned* " Peter Lulig Coijett." [N. X., 11.]

The Count of Peniguião, Portuguese Ambassador Extraordinary, to the Parliament.

1652, August [11]–21. Plymouth.—Announcing his appointment as Ambassador Extraordinary. (See *Commons' Journals*, vii. 165.) In *Portuguese,* with *English* translation, the first *signed.* [N. XVII., 161.]

The Council of State.

1652, August 12.—Reporting the names of those recommended as Commissioners for Ireland. (Printed in *Commons' Journals*, vii. 164.) [N. XXI., 115.]

The Council of State.

[1652, August before the 18th.]—Report concerning the Ormonde Articles. (Printed in *Commons' Journals*, vii. 165.) [N. XXI., 116.]

The Grand-Duke of Tuscany to the Parliament.

1652, August 17.—Concerning Captain Cardi's ship and rice. (See *Commons' Journals*, vii. 192.) In *Italian*. *Signed*. *Seal embossed* [N. X., 24.]

The names of the Gentlemen who are nominated Commissioners for England for Boroughs and Counties.
[1652, August 20.]—[N. XX., 211.]

Frederic III., King of Denmark, to the Parliament.

1652, August 21. Copenhagen.—Letter of Credence to his Resident, Henry Williamsen Rosemving. (See *Commons' Journals*, vii. 178.) In *Latin*. *Seal embossed*. *Signed*. [N. X., 21.] N. XVIII., 13 is an *English* translation.

Constance Stringer, Widow of George Stringer, to the Parliament.

[1652, August 27.]—Petition. After stating to the effect of the report and orders printed in *Commons' Journals*, vi. 421, stating that in pursuance of the said orders she had made discoveries to the value of 511*l*. 0*s*. 8*d*., the net value of which, however, was only about 350*l*. that there still is due to her 1,092*l*. 17*s*. 4*d*., besides interest, and that, since by reason of the late Act of general pardon discoveries are taken away, the said orders are now fruitless to her, and praying that satisfaction may be made to her for the remainder of the principal with interest. (See *Commons' Journals*, vii. 171.) *Annexed* :
  i. The Orders of June 7th, 1650. (Printed in *Commons' Journals*, vi. 421.)
  ii. Certificate from the Treasurers at Goldsmiths' Hall, that she had received 511*l*. 0*s*. 8*d*., leaving the above balance still due. [N. XXII., 165, 166.]

Above 1,500 Distressed Protestants of Ireland to the Parliament.

[1652, August 27.]—Petition, stating that many of your Petitioners lost great estates in Ireland by the rebellion there ; that by the Act of Contribution passed in the 17th year of the late king near 50,000*l*. was collected for their relief, but not full 15,000*l*. has been distributed among them, but the rest has been employed about the affairs of the Commonwealth, as by the accounts of Sir George Whitmore and others may appear ; and, forasmuch as the Petitioners are able to procure not only a good sum of money, but also certain lands heretofore given to charitable uses to be discovered, which have sundry years been detained and not employed according to the intention of the donors, and also are able to discover several debts and sums of money due to divers of the bloody rebels in Ireland by persons dwelling in England, by whose means the Petitioners have been totally destroyed and ruined, praying them to grant to the discoverers of the premises the fifth part of such discoveries, as well out of such moneys as shall be raised out of the disposal of the said lands as out of the arrears of rent and sums of money given as aforesaid, and the remainder thereof to your Petitioners, and that such sums be paid to the Treasurers to be appointed and be issued by them to the Petitioners, as the Committee for Contributions for the distressed Protestants of Ireland may think most meet. And that what your Petitioners may discover as due to the said Rebels as aforesaid they may have the particular benefit thereof. (See *Commons' Journals*, vii. 172.) *Signed* by Eliza Leigh, Sara Mordant, Elizabeth Chichester, Susanna Stockdale, Anne Bastard, Dorothie Bolt, and Clairie Morton. *Annexed* is an unsigned letter, apparently to the Speaker, in support of the Petition. [N. XXII., 112.]

SAMUEL DISBROWE and RICHARD SALTONSTALL to WILLIAM LENTHALL.

1652, September 1. Leith.--Stating that according to the orders of the Commissioners of Parliament they had surveyed the Manor House and lands of Liddington amounting to 500*l. per annum* and set out the same to Commissary General Whaley, and also had surveyed the Manor House and lands of Kineale amounting to the same value, and had set out the same to Lieutenant-General Monk. *Signed. Seal.* [N. VIII., 58.]

The COMMITTEE FOR THE ARMY and COMMITTEE OF OBSTRUCTIONS.

[1652, September 7.]—Order reporting concerning the Northern reduced officers. (Printed in *Commons' Journals*, vii. 174.) *Copy.* [N. XVI., 124.]

The COUNCIL OF STATE to the GRAND-DUKE OF TUSCANY.

1652, September 16.—Hoping he had received their letter of July 29th, and again thanking him for the protection afforded at Leghorn to the English ships against the Dutch. In *Latin. Draft.* [N. XVIII., 145.]

The COUNT OF PENIGUIÃO to WILLIAM LENTHALL.

1652, September 28.—Forwarding a copy of his credentials, and desiring to know on what day the Parliament will give him audience. (See *Commons' Journals*, vii. 185.) In *Portuguese*, with *English* translation, the first *signed.* [N. XVII., 162.]

The COUNT OF PENIGUIÃO's Speech to the PARLIAMENT.

1652, September 30.—After enlarging on the ancient friendship between England and Portugal, and the present state of Europe it continues : Between these two nations only can peace be firm, being grounded both on past successes and present interests. As to the complaints and offences which have happened I would rather pass them by than repeat them, but since this course might imply a consciousness of error, while a plain narrative of the facts will disclose the cause of the injury, I will not hesitate to say that such events and accidents happened as to free us from the least blame as far as our intentions were concerned. The errors of commanders on both sides hindered the demonstrations. The dispute originally related to the Princes, and then it took the turn of satisfaction being demanded from us for the ships that were detained, thus making us parties to the issue where we had been judges thereof. Then followed the attack upon and the plundering of our fleet, which so enraged the people that they could not have been restrained by either reason or force without the compensation that was demanded. Hence what appeared a wrong was really a remedy.

The imprisonments [of the merchants] and sequestrations of their goods prevented the murder of the one and the robbing of the other. As soon as time permitted satisfaction was made them for their losses and injuries. João de Guimãraes was sent to England to settle the remaining disputes, and though received less cordially than we expected, as soon as the King saw any hopes of peace he immediately confirmed the Articles which regarded its commencement. The English in Portugal enjoy their liberty, their freedom from taxes, their privileges, and their property, and have been restored their ships and goods. I have been now sent as Ambassador to propose in the King's name what may be required to effect a peace, and considering your wisdom doubt not that you will approve the justice of my cause, which I trust will be recommended by the fact that I have always been a friend to your nation. (See *Commons' Journals*, vii. 188.) In *Portuguese*, with *Latin* and *English* versions, neither an exact translation and the last occasionally unmeaning. The above represents the general effect of the speech. [N. XVII., 165.]

The DANISH AMBASSADORS to WILLIAM LENTHALL.

1652, October 11.—"Perceiving by the success of their negotiation that they are not able to make any further progress in it," they find themselves obliged by their master's express command to return in order to report to him, and therefore ask an audience of Parliament to take leave. (See *Commons' Journals*, vii. 190.) In *French*, with *English* translation, the first *signed*. [N. XVIII., 14, 15.]

AMERIGO SALVETTI to the COUNCIL OF STATE.

1652, October 14.—Brief memorial asking the restitution of the goods of Tuscan subjects taken by the English on board French or Dutch ships, and in particular of the rice taken from Captain Cardi at Leghorn by Admiral Hall. (See *Commons' Journals*, vii. 192.) [N. XVIII., 146*b*.]

The DANISH AMBASSADORS to WILLIAM LENTHALL.

1652, October 16.—Pressing their request for an audience. (See *Commons' Journals*, vii. 192.) In *French*, with *English* translation, the first *signed* and *sealed*. [N. XVIII., 15, 18.]

The COUNCIL OF STATE.

1652, October 18.—Order reporting concerning Danish affairs. (See *Commons' Journals*, vii. 192.) [N. XVIII., 16.] *Annexed:*

i. The COUNCIL OF STATE to the DANISH AMBASSADORS.

1652, October 15.—Desiring an answer concerning the stay by the King of Denmark of English Merchants' ships at Elsinore and Copenhagen. *Copy.* [N. XVIII., 17.]

ii. The COUNCIL OF STATE.

1652, October 18.—Order that the Commissioners appointed to meet the Danish Ambassadors concerning their paper demanding the release of the Danish ships in the Thames stayed by order of the Parliament shall declare that the cause of such stay is the detention of the said English ships at Copenhagen, and demand what securities will be given for the safe return home of such ships. *Copy.* [N. XVIII., 19.]

iii. The Information of WILLIAM CRIPPS.

1652, October 15. Kingston-upon-Hull.—That he had been a sailor on board the *James* which with several other English ships has been for ten weeks at Copenhagen waiting for convoy ; that about five weeks since Captain Ball with 17 ships came to Lapland End as a convoy, and sent notice of their arrival to the ships at Copenhagen, which then prepared to sail but were stayed by the Danish Admiral for what cause he knows not ; that the masters then gave leave to their men to depart and make their passage to England as best they could ; that the informant got on board the *Antelope* one of the convoy ships, which was wrecked on the coast of Jutland, only the men being saved. *Copy.* [N. XVIII., 20.]

The DANISH AMBASSADORS to the PARLIAMENT.

1652, October 20.—After they at the Conference yesterday had declared in reply to the Commissioners' questions about the stay of the English ships that they were ignorant of the fact and circumstances but were convinced that when the cause of the said stay is known it will be found to give no ground for a breach of the amicable relations between England and Denmark, the Commissioners in the name of the Parliament demanded what security would be given for the safe return of the ships. To which the ambassadors reply it is not in their power to settle the question, and that they do not perceive their persons could be bound to give security. They promise however what lies in their power namely to use every effort that nothing be omitted that might conduce to the preservation of the friendship between their King and the Parliament. They therefore earnestly ask the Council that there may be no further delay in granting the permission to depart they have already requested. In *Latin. Signed.* (See *Commons' Journals,* vii. 192.) [N. XVIII., 21.]

The COMMITTEE FOR MARKETS.

1652, October 21.—Order reporting concerning a market at Smythick in Cornwall. (Printed in *Commons' Journals,* vii. 248.) *Signed.* [N. XVI., 125.]

CHRISTINA, Queen of Sweden, to the PARLIAMENT.

1652, October 23. Stockholm.—Letter of Credence to Benjamin Bonell, her minister. (See *Commons' Journals,* vii. 262.) In *Latin. Seal embossed. Signature* torn off. [N. X., 13.] N. XVIII., 39 is a copy.

The DANISH AMBASSADORS to WILLIAM LENTHALL.

1652, October 25.—Again pressing for an audience to take their leave. (See *Commons' Journals,* vii. 195.) In *French,* with *English* translation, the first *signed* and *sealed.* [N. XVIII., 22]

Captain RALPH GRUNDY to the PARLIAMENT.

[1652.]—Answer to the Petition and reasons of the Earl of Carbery. *Signed. Annexed :*
Copy of the Report and Order of October 17, 1649, concerning Captain Grundy, which is printed in *Commons' Journals,* vi. 309. [N. XXII., 163, 164.]

Captain RALPH GRUNDY to the COMMITTEE FOR PETITIONS.

[1652, October 28.]—Petition, stating that at the beginning of the Parliament he was the only person in Carmarthenshire that acted for them, published their declarations and remonstrances, and opposed the raising of arms against them, for which he was plundered, his brother murdered, and himself condemned to death as a traitor, but escaping to Pembrokeshire he there served the Parliament in arms, while the enemy enjoyed his estate, and also stating the steps he took after the county was reduced to obtain reparation, and that he had been engaged for the last six years therein, and praying that the Committee would take his deplorable case into consideration, which being formerly examined may be reported accordingly, and your Petitioner relieved. *Signed.* [N. XXII., 167.]

The DANISH AMBASSADORS' Speech to the PARLIAMENT on their taking leave.

1652, October 29.—Expressing the desire of their master to have that Ancient Amity betwixt Denmark and England established by treaty to the full as testified by his sending this embassy and by the declarations they had already made; regretting that his desire to go through with the treaty of confederacy has been impeded by difficulties unluckily fallen out ; stating that he had therefore determined to recall them, with a constant resolution however on the first opportunity which the inclination of the Parliament and future times shall offer to re-establish and fasten the said ancient amity with a closer knot of confederacy; and expressing their thanks to the Parliament and Council for their civilities with all good wishes for the prosperity of England. In *Latin*, with *English* translation, the first *signed.* [N. XVIII., 23, 24.]

The COMMITTEE APPOINTED TO CONFER WITH THE DEPUTIES FROM SCOTLAND.

1652, October 29.—Report. (Printed in *Commons' Journals*, vii. 202.) [N. XX., 202.]

JAMES, Duke of Courland, to the PARLIAMENT.

1652, October 31. Mittan.—Apparently Letter of Credence to his Commissioners, Philip Fisher and Thomas Corbett. (See *Commons' Journals*, vii. 243.) In *German. Seal embossed. Signed.* [N. X., 30.]

CHRISTINA, Queen of Sweden, to the PARLIAMENT.

1652, November 13. Stockholm —In *Latin*. (An *English* translation is printed in Thurloe, *State Papers*, i. 219.) *Seal embossed. Signed* "Christina." *Countersigned* "Peter Lulig Coijett." [N. X., 12.]

DON ALONZO DE CARDENAS to the PARLIAMENT.

1652, November 16-26.—Thanking them in his Master's name for removing at his request the sequestration of Colonel William Cobb. (See *Commons' Journals*, vii. 215.) In *Spanish. Signed.* [N. XVIII., 80.]

PHILIP IV., King of Spain, to the PARLIAMENT.

1652, November 27. Madrid.—Thanking them for their fleet having attacked that of the French, when the last was endeavouring to relieve Dunkirk, and hoping that there may be frequently occasions on which his and their united arms against the French might be successful. (See *Commons' Journals*, vii. 233.) *Signed. Countersigned* " Geronimo de la Torre." In *Latin. Impressed Seal.* [N. X., 3.]

The GRAND-DUKE OF TUSCANY to the PARLIAMENT.

1652 [November 27-] December 7. Pisa.—From my care that the English vessels should not be molested by the Dutch vessels, which are at present stronger and more numerous I received them within the mole of Leghorn taking a reciprocal engagement from both parties that neither would make any attempt on the other when within cannon-shot of the fortress, and after they had been discovered from the lighthouse, yet while this act of my goodwill has been accepted by Parliament with discreet courtesy, on the other hand a bad return was made for it by Captain Appleton, by whose command the frigate taken by the Dutch in the fight off Monte Christo has been surprised by night and carried off from them by an armed force, while they were in possession of it in good faith under my word, and in addition the said Appleton has used violence to the sentry posted at the end of the mole, with other accessory circumstances, which will be better represented to Parliament by my Resident. I have therefore been obliged to call on him to give account of his actions and to imprison him in this fortress, of which I immediately apprised General Bodoel (Badiley). I doubt not but the Parliament will approve of my resolution. I shall always continue to pay due regard to the Parliament, and will serve them on every occasion and will treat all English vessels courteously. It remains that Parliament who can easily imagine the arguments and clamour of the Dutch should give me the means of freeing myself from these troubles and giving them satisfaction, which I would much rather receive from the Parliament than by other methods. (See *Commons' Journals*, vii. 244.) In *Italian. Signed. Seal embossed.* [N. X., 26.]

JAMES, Duke of Courland, to the PARLIAMENT.

1652, November 28. Mittau.—Concerning his Commissioners Philip Fisher and Thomas Corbett, and complaining that notwithstanding his neutrality two ships, the *Pietas* and *Innocentia*, belonging to his subjects, with cargoes of wine, salt, elephants' teeth and other things had on their return voyage from France been taken and carried into Plymouth. (See *Commons' Journals*, vii. 243.) In *German. Seal embossed. Signed.* [N. X., 37.]

The GRAND-DUKE OF TUSCANY to the PARLIAMENT.

1652, [November 29-] December 9. Pisa.—At the request of Signor Bodoel (Badiley) I have placed Captain Appleton in his hands, wishing to show my respect to the Parliament, and hoping that my indulgence towards him, as far as concerns the offence to myself, should deserve that the Parliament should have regard to my engagement with the Dutch, not considered as such, but as persons who under my word have been defrauded. (See *Commons' Journals*, vii. 244.) In *Italian. Signed. Seal embossed.* [N. X., 25.]

The PARLIAMENT.

1652, November 30.—Proceedings on the negotiations with Portugal: (Printed in *Commons' Journals*, vii. 223, beginning " Sir Henry Vane " ending " that concern the Merchants.") [N. XVII., 166.] *Annexed:*

A report from the COUNCIL OF STATE of the negotiations from November 2nd to 22nd consisting of four columns, the first containing the six articles formerly propounded to Dom João d$_e$

Guimãraes, the second the replies of the Portuguese Ambassador to each, the third the observations of the Council thereon and their objections, and the fourth the Ambassador's replies to the last column. At the end is the reply of the Council to the last expressing their dissatisfaction and demanding that he should agree to the six articles as fully and clearly as Dom João de Guimãraes had formerly done, and demanding immediate payment in ready money of 65,753*l.* 8*s.* 6*d.* the balance of the 180,000*l.* after allowing for the reprisals, with a copy of Dom João's paper of 1651, April 17-27, and the Ambassador's reply obliging himself to perform all that shall be shown to appertain to the articles to which the said Dom João bound himself expressly, and thereto requiring the deliverance of his original writing, while as to the account of the sum which clearly appears to belong to the Parliament, if it cannot forthwith be tendered, he will declare the consignment thereof according to the will of the Council.' [N. XVII., 167.]

Louis XIV. to the Parliament.

1652, December 2. Paris.—Letter of Credence to his Ambassador, who is to declare his goodwill to them and to complain that some of their ships had taken French ships, and also of their issuing letters of marque to some merchant men. (See *Commons' Journals,* vii. 228.) *Signed* " Louis," and *Countersigned* " de Lomenie." In *French. Seal impressed.* [N. X., 1.] A copy is N. XVII., 18, and N. XVII., 19 is another copy beginning " Parliament de la Republique d'Angleterre" and addressed " au Parlement, &c." instead of the address to which the Parliament objected.

The Senate and Council of the free Imperial City of Köln to the Parliament.

1652, December 4.—Asking for the restoration of eight tons of Spanish wine the property of their Fellow Senator John Cnisten, which had been shipt at Malaga for Hamburgh on board the *St. George,* which had been arrested by the fleet of the Commonweath. (See *Commons' Journals,* vii. 252.) *English* translation. [N. XVIII., 165.]

The Six Preliminary Articles delivered to the Count of Peniguião.

[1652, December 7.]—(These are the articles drawn up in obedience to the vote of November 30th, which is printed in *Commons' Journals,* vii. 223, embodying the substance of the former proceedings with some alterations.) [N. XVII., 177.]

Don Alonso de Cardenas to the Parliament.

1652, December 8-18.—Asking for an immediate audience. (See *Commons' Journals,* vii. 227.) In *Spanish,* with *English* translation. The original *signed* and *sealed.* [N. XVII., 81.]

The Count of Peniguião to the Parliament.

1652, December 13.—The preliminary articles have now been satisfied by me. And as the final decision on the fourth is referred to Parliament, for this and other reasons I think it necessary to address them in person, and therefore ask them to fix a day and hour for an audience. In *Latin. Signed. Seal.* [N. XVII.,168.]

The COUNCIL OF STATE.

1652, December 13.—Order reporting to the Parliament their nego-tiations with the Portuguese Ambassador and stating that he had on that day sent to the Council the six Articles signed by himself with some alterations and additions, of which the only material one was adding to the fourth, " Concerning this Article I refer the determination of the same unto the determination of the Parliament, and have promised to stand to their judgment therein. But as to the time of payment I refer myself to that which I have writ in my paper." (See *Commons' Journals,* vii. 229.) [N. XVII., 170.] *Annexed:*

i. The AMBASSADOR to the COUNCIL.

1652, December 8.—Approving of the six Articles except the fourth concerning which he offers to the Council the annexed paper. [N. XVII., 169.]

ii. The LAST-MENTIONED PAPER.

Since the Commissioners have delivered a single paper containing a mixed sum amounting both from the ships seized and those taken, I do not think it the mind of the Council that I should altogether consent to what is contained therein, but only that I should certainly know of the goods which were confiscate.—(Argu-ments then follow to show that the true values of the Brazil and Per-nambuco ships and cargoes were much greater than as shown in the paper, the cargoes having considerably depreciated during their detention.)—I therefore propose that the Commonwealth and the King should each appoint a person to inquire into the condition of the ships and wares, whose arbitration shall be final. And lest it should be believed that I would burden the Commonwealth for those losses, in the name of the King I desist from that which —the Commonwealth being satisfied—by virtue of judgment given may be owing, and I will pay whatsoever shall be certainly found owing thereof, and in obedience to the Commonwealth I offer 25,000*l.* though nothing be owing, which the peace being made shall presently be restored. [N. XVII., 169.]

iii. The AMBASSADOR to the COUNCIL.

1652, December 13.—As to the sum demanded in the Fourth Article, I refer the decision thereof to the arbitration of the Council, and if they cannot change the resolution of Parliament I remit it to their judgment desiring that by them regard will be had to equity and justice. As to the manner of payment, I pro-pound three ways (which are then specified). [N. XVII., 170.]

iv. The SAME to the SAME.

Same date.—" I have satisfied the preliminary Articles in general, which were offered me by the Lords Commissioners. But having received from them that the Council wishes peace might be speedily confirmed, and that being signified in the last papers delivered to me, that answer being given to the papers the treaty shall begin, there remains nothing but that the day and hour be appointed me for the performance thereof." [N. XVII., 170.]

The Consuls, Proconsuls, and Burgomasters of Lübeck
to the Parliament.

1652, December 14.—Asking for the restitution of six tuns of
Spanish wine the property of their citizen John Lembke, shipt by his
kinsman at St. Lucar for delivery at Hamburgh on board the *St. Michael*,
which was intercepted by the English fleet and brought into London.
(See *Commons' Journals*, vii. 252.) *English* translation. [N. XVIII.,
153.]

Don Alonso de Cardenas to the Parliament.

1652, December 14-24.—Demanding the release of the *St. Salvador*
and *St. George* of Hamburgh and the *Sampson* of Lübeck with their
cargoes. (See *Commons' Journals*, vii. 229.) In *Spanish. Signed.*
[N. XVII., 82.]

The Count of Peniguião to the Parliament.

1652, December 16. Speech.—Peace being so preeminent an advantage, and the mutual alliance of our nations so much to the interests of
all Europe, I considered it more important than all considerations which
might have made me doubtful about the preliminary Articles or caused
me to delay giving my decision on them. I have therefore given satisfaction to the Articles propounded to me.

I have however hesitated at the fourth; because in the account
received from the Council no mention is made of the Customs' duties
paid in this port on the goods; 2. No allowance is made for the ships,
though it be not less just to restore the ships than the goods which
were in them; 3. No inquiry is made into what was unjustly seized.
Though these points are so clear and so important, rather than delay
the peace I preferred to leave them to the judgment of so prudent a
senate, and the generosity of such a magnanimous Commonwealth.

As to the time of payment may I hope that the Commonwealth will
be contented with my proposals.

With regard to the complaints of certain of his Majesty's subjects I
negotiated with the Council that their goods should be released, who
replied that orders had been given to the Admiralty to look into the
matter and stop the sale, but I found that that Court could not obey on
account of an old order of Parliament made before the restitution in
Portugal of all goods of the English to their lawful owners. I am
therefore obliged to apply to Parliament, being ready to prove, according
to the laws as administered in that Court that the goods demanded
belong to the King, my Master's, subjects, that they may be restored to
them. (See *Commons' Journals*, vii. 230.) In *Portuguese* and *Latin*,
the first *signed*. [N. XVII., 171.]

The Archduke Leopold William to the Parliament.

1652, [December 18-]December 28. Brussels.—Asking that the
three ships, the *St. Salvador*, the *St. George*, and the *Samson* might
be restored without litigation, especially as in consequence of their
detention the bills of exchange drawn by Spanish on Belgian merchants
were not paid, which caused inconveniences to the King's army. (See
Commons' Journals, vii. 243.) In *Latin. Signed.* [N. XVIII., 173.]

The Proconsuls and Senate of Hamburgh to the
Parliament.

1652, December 20.—Letter of Credence to their Resident Joachim
Petersen. (See *Commons' Journals*, vii. 252.) In *Latin*, with an
English translation. *Seal embossed.* [N. X., 83.; XVIII., 150.]

M. DE BORDEAUX, French Ambassador.

[1652, December 21.]—Speech at his audience.—The King has sent me to salute the Parliament on his part and to assure them of his friendship, being confident that he will find here a mutual correspondence to his good intentions. The union which ought to exist between neighbouring states does not depend on the form of their government. This kingdom can from a monarchy become a republic, but the geographical situation is not changed; the nations always remain neighbours and always interested in each other; commerce and the treaties between them bind peoples more than princes, having for their chief object their common advantage. Wherefore it appears that those at the head of two such powerful states ought to use the greatest care to obviate the inconveniences which might alter in any way the ancient alliances.

This consideration, which concerns your honour, your advantage and your repose as well as ours, has obliged the King to acquaint you by my mouth of the means of preserving so necessary a union by conveying to you his just complaints of the capture of his vessels, which he was sending to the assistance of Dunkirk, on the pretext of reprisals.

His Majesty has so scrupulously observed the treaties made by his predecessors with this Crown, and has forbidden his subjects under penalty of such rigorous punishments to carry on depredations on those of this state and his Council have done justice so uprightly to those who have demanded it, that he does not believe he can have given cause to grant with reason letters of reprisals against France. If some merchants, in consequence of decisions which were not in accordance with their desires, have sought and obtained from this Parliament permission to use them, this gives them no lawful title to capture and keep the vessels of the King of France. This right has been introduced and reserved by the treaties of peace in order to redress the loss of those to whom justice has been denied, by permitting them to revenge themselves on the property of private persons, but hitherto it is a thing unheard of, that any nation has extended it to the property of an allied Prince, or employed the forces of the state to put it in execution—otherwise there would be no difference between a declaration of war, and Letters of Marque.

This maxim being generally received, and neither the King of France nor his subjects having undertaken anything against what belongs to this Commonwealth, and further the principal result of the loss of his vessels being turned to the advantage of Spain, his Majesty is willing to attribute the cause only to the secret influences of that common enemy. You ought to regard him as a common enemy, since, considering the interests of the Parliament, he divides you from your ancient allies and tries to engage you in war with all your neighbours, in order not only during that war to repair his affairs, but also to reduce you to the necessity of depending on his assistance. The designs which at various times that nation has engaged in against England, their political maxims and counsels of conscience so contrary to your welfare and religion, ought to make you suspect the great zeal with which they have affected to seek your alliance.

If the King of France now demands redress of the wrong that has been done him by other means than those that have been employed by those in his position, it is not from fear of increasing the number of his enemies, but solely from the desire of preserving those whom he has believed to be his friends. It requires only to look at the history of past centuries to be convinced that France has nothing to fear except her own strength. Your divisions, in which she has not intervened, though she was in a position to foment them, and many reasons impelled her to do so, have made you acquainted with the frankness and sincerity with which his Majesty has been accustomed to treat his allies.

He has already given you marks of his entire acquiescence in the change which it has pleased God to introduce in those kingdoms, when in the most flourishing condition of his affairs after that famous battle of Rethel, he sent you proofs of his friendship. I can confirm to you these same sentiments now, when he has extinguished the fire which threatened his kingdom with complete ruin, when he has driven into the territories of his enemies those who kindled it, and when the only city which supported it by its revolt, breathes nothing but his mercy.

His Majesty does not doubt that the Parliament will not be able to reflect on the power of the King of France, on the manner in which he behaves towards the Commonwealth, on the treaties between the two nations, and the advantage of maintaining them, finally on their own interest, without repairing—by restoring the vessels in the same condition in which they were taken—the just grounds for complaint which he has against such a proceeding. This is what I am come to demand of the Parliament on the part of the King, my master, and to assure them that his Majesty who regards justice as the principal support of his sceptre, and the solid foundation of lawful empires, will not fail to do right to those of this state who have just claims against his subjects, and will embrace every means of maintaining a perfect correspondence between the two states. (See *Commons' Journals*, vii. 233.) In *French*. *Original* and *Copy* the first *signed*. [N. XVII., 20.]

The BURGOMASTERS and COUNCIL OF the City of ZURICH to SIR OLIVER FLEMING.

1652, December 24.—The Evangelical Cantons and their allies, having with much grief understood the great dissension between the Parliament and the States-General, whereby not only the said states are like to grow entangled in the great hazards and mischiefs of war, but the whole Evangelical cause abroad must incur the greatest danger it ever sustained since the Reformation, unanimously held themselves engaged by the common bond of religion and the affection they bear to both the said states to communicate to them their sad apprehensions in this regard. That this our joint address may be presented to the Parliament with all due observance, with the outward circumstances whereof we cannot be so well acquainted at so great a distance, we entreat you to deliver the letter enclosed in the best manner requisite, and most befitting so great a state. (See *Commons' Journals*, vii. 252.) *English* translation. [N. XVIII., 163.]

The CONSULS, SCULTETS, LANDAMANNS, and SENATORS OF THE EVANGELICAL CANTONS OF SWITZERLAND, &c., as in heading to their letter of April 14th, to the PARLIAMENT.

1652, December 24.—We hope our letter written early in spring (that of April 14th, unopened till 1683) was taken in good part. While we were still hoping that peace would be preserved, we received the sad news of a seafight between the fleets of the two Republics, and that war had begun. Without expressing any opinion on the merits we, with all the reformed churches, exhort you to put an end to this fratricidal war, so prejudicial to religion. (See *Commons' Journals*, vii. 252). In *Latin*. *Seal* of Zurich *embossed*. [N. X., 91.]

Louis de Bourbon, PRINCE DE CONDÉ, to the PARLIAMENT.

1652, December 26.—Further Letter of Credence to the Sieur de Barriere. (See *Commons' Journals*, vii. 251.) In *French. Holograph. Seals.* [N. X., 30.]

The COMMITTEE ON THE ACT FOR PLANTING IRELAND.

1652, December 28.—Report. (Printed in *Commons' Journals*, vii. 242.) [N. XXI., 117.]

The COUNCIL OF STATE.

1652, December 30.—Report recommending Viscount Lisle as Ambassador to Sweden. (Printed in *Commons' Journals*, vii. 240.) [N. XXI., 118.]

The PARLIAMENT to the DOGE OF VENICE.

1652, December 31.—Acknowledging the receipt of his letter of June 1st through Pauluzzi, and reciprocating its friendly sentiments. (See *Commons' Journals*, vii. 243.) *Draft.* [N. XVIII., 156.]

DON ALONZO DE CARDENAS to the PARLIAMENT.

1652-3, December 31—January 10.—Enclosing a letter from the Archduke Leopold William, Governor of Flanders (that of the 18–28th), which his bad health prevents him from delivering in person. (See *Commons' Journals*, vii. 243.) In *Spanish*, with *English* translation. The first *signed* and *sealed.* [N. XVII., 83.]

M. DE BORDEAUX to the PARLIAMENT.

[1652-3, January 4.]— " I see by your answer to the letter of the King, my master, that, persuaded of the advantage there is in maintaining a perfect correspondence and friendship between France and England, you are ready to employ the power which God has been pleased to place in your hands for the preservation of an ancient alliance. That disposition which his Majesty has always expected from your wise conduct and zeal for the welfare of your state obliges him to complain to you and to demand justice in order that, obtaining the satisfaction which cannot be denied him, he may also employ all his authority for the execution of designs so useful to two nations. The evident justice of his demand ought not to meet with any long delay, and to remit it to a long discussion would be in some manner to cause prejudice to the sincerity of your good intentions. Nevertheless, assuring myself that the reasons . . . of his Majesty will make the more impression on your minds the more they are deliberately considered, and that nothing will be capable of hindering the restitution of his vessels, I will willingly meet in a more particular conference those whom the Parliament shall find good, in order to make manifest his just pretentions. . ." (See *Commons' Journals*, vii. 243.) *Signed. Seals.* In *French.* [N. XVII., 21.]

Articles of Surrender of the FORT OF ARKIN, in the Island of ARRAN, in Ireland.

1652[-3], January 15.—(Printed in Gilbert, iii. 363.) (See *Commons' Journals*, vii. 253.) (Annexed by mistake to the letter of April 15th 1652, announcing the surrender of the Castle of Bradock in the Island of Arran in *Scotland*.) [N. VIII., 56.]

The COMMONWEALTH OF GENOA to the PARLIAMENT.

165[2-]3, January 16.—"The Mediterranean being in a manner quite blockt up by the frequent incursions and insufferable pillaging of pirates and . . their strength daily increasing to the obstruction of almost all commerce and correspondence . . . for the preventing of which damages and the securing of our trade we have some time since ordered certain ships to be prepared. . . . And in regard . . two ships which we ordered to be built at Amsterdam will be ready to set sail this next spring," we entreat you to give free passage to them with their goods arms and crews that are to bring them hither, we being to man them with our own men after their arrival here. (See *Commons' Journals*, vii. 261.) [N. XVIII., 180.]

The Information of SOLOMON HOUGHAM and TIMOTHY GOFFE.

1652-3, January 18. Copenhagen.—(Printed in Peck, *Desiderata Curiosa*, xiii. 1.) *Copy.* [N. XVI., 131.]

SAMUEL DISBROWE, RICHARD SALTONSTALL, and others, to
WILLIAM LENTHALL.

1652-3, January 18. Leith.—Stating that according to an order of Parliament they had surveyed and set out to Lieutennant-Colonel Cobbett, the Manor house and lands of Monquhanie late part of the inheritance of Major-General Lumsden. *Signed.* [N. VIII., 59.]

CHRISTINA, Queen of Sweden, to the PARLIAMENT.

165[2-]3, January 20. Stockholm.—In *Latin*, with *English* translation. (Printed in Thurloe, *State Papers*, i. 216.) *Seal embossed. Signed* "Christina." *Countersigned* "A. Gyldenclau." [N. X., 17.]

RICHARD HIGGINS to HENRY SCOBELL.

[1652-3], January 21. Plymouth.—Upon my new arrival from the Barbadoes. Describing the calling in of all the Books of Common Prayer there, the refusal of Mr. Charles Robson, formerly a Prebend in Salisbury, to obey, and the disturbance that followed. (Printed in Grey, iv. Appendix, No. 11, p. 24.) *Seal.* [N. VIII., 61.]

Speech of JOACHIM PETERSEN, Public Minister of Hamburgh, to
the COMMITTEE APPOINTED TO RECEIVE HIM.

1652[-3], January 28. — After congratulations and compliments expressing the desire of Hamburgh for the restoration of peace that "the fruit and freedom of commerce, so sadly shaken now by these storms to the imminent utter ruin of their people, may be revived yet . . to its ancient flourishing conditions," and desiring that time and place be appointed for him to propound the business with which he is charged. (See *Commons' Journals*, vii. 252.) In *Latin*, with *English* translation, the first *signed.* [N. XVIII., 151.]

' The COUNT OF PENAGIUÃO to the PARLIAMENT.

165[2-]3, January 31.—Concerning the goods of Portuguese subjects in the Court of Admiralty mentioned in his speech of December 16th previous. In *Portuguese. Signed.* [N. XVII., 172.]

The PARLIAMENT to the ARCHDUKE LEOPOLD WILLIAM.

1652[-3], February 2.—Stating that the three ships, the *St. Salvador*, the *St. George* and the *Samson*, had been taken as prizes and were now under adjudication in the Court of Admiralty to which the question rightly belonged and with which they should not interfere. (See *Commons' Journals*, vii. 251.) *Draft.* In *Latin.* [N. XVIII., 174.]

Information of ANONYMOUS.

1652-3, February 6. Copenhagen. — Concerning a plot to kill Bradshaw, the Parliament's Resident. *Copy.* (Printed in Peck, *Desiderata Curiosa*, xiii. 2.) [N. XVI., 130.]

Further information of ANONYMOUS.

1652-3, February 9. Copenhagen.—Concerning Christopher Nelson. (Printed in Peck, *Desiderata Curiosa*, xiii. 4.) *Copy.* [N. XVI., 129.]

Information of a SERVANT of the Same.

Same date and place.—(Printed in Peck, *Desiderata Curiosa*, xiii. 5.) *Copy.* [N. XVI., 130.]

INFORMATION.

Same date and place.—That George Wayte said when the Scotch King marched into Scotland he wrote thanking him for his many faithful services, and that he would have joined him in commission with Sir John Cockram into Poland, had not he begged his excuse considering it would be destructive to his trade, and that further the King had given him a large pass to all foreign Princes in testimony of his faithfull services. That he said that he had lately received letters from Major-General Massey from Holland, stating that he had received a new commission from the King, and that he was now busy in transacting his affairs.

That a Mr. Spark had sent him from Hamburgh Massey's letters, and he himself had corresponded both formerly and lately with Massey, and also for the King's affairs with Lord Hopton and Sir Edward Nicholas. He said he must now go and write letters to France, England and Holland, and spoke as if they were intended to the said King and his interest. He further said—seeing a letter of Sir John Henderson's that had some views in it to the advantage of Charles Steward—that it was not good to communicate it to any of the English skippers for they would inform the said Resident of it, and understanding that one Prince had notice of it, he sent charging him not to communicate it to the Resident. He further said that the King of Denmark's non-admittance of the English Resident to his presence was, because the King was a passionate man, who in his fury had killed one man. And this said Resident Bradshaw being of the same name with that Bradshaw that judged the King of England his kinsman, it was feared that the King in his rage should fall foul upon the said Resident and do the like to him as he had done to the man he had killed. He being moved to intercept the said Resident's letters, said it was not worth the while, for the said Resident had nothing in his packet but what he himself had in his, and that the Commonwealth had sent him to undertake a business which nobody else would, his hands being so tied, that they might as well have sent a herald. The said George being told that there was a piece shot at me through a window in my lodgings as I sat at supper and my landlord and landlady said it was English and Dutch, he replied that it would be none but the Resident's servants, and if the Resident were good at that we should be good enough for him. Subscribed by both parties in the presence of Samuel Misselden and Anthony Compton. *Copy.* [N. XVI., 128.]

SAMUEL MISSELDEN.

[1652-3, February.] — Substance of the message delivered in the name of the Resident to the Rixhoffmeister. (Printed in Peck, *Desiderata Curiosa*, xiii. 6.) [N. XVI., 132.]

DON ALONSO DE CARDENAS to the PARLIAMENT.

1652-3, February 9-19.—Enclosing the letter of November 27th from the King of Spain, which his ill-health prevents him from delivering in person and assuring them of his Majesty's great desire to show by real effects of gratitude his acknowledgement of the benefit which flowed from that action, both to his said Majesty, and to his dominions in Flanders. (See *Commons' Journals*, vii. 257.) In *Spanish*, with *English* translation. The original *signed*. [N. XVII., 84.]

Paper of CERTAIN MINISTERS.

[1652-3, February.]—" By the 13th Article we intend that no persons be suffered to preach or print anything in opposition to those principles of Christian Religion which the Scripture plainly and clearly affirms that without the belief of them salvation is not to be obtained, in the further explication of which proposal we humbly offer these following principles . . which we conceive to be generally received and therefore have not brought all the Scriptures—or any of them—singly to prove the truth of the principles themselves ; but to show that without the belief of them salvation is not be obtained." (Then follow 16 " principles " with several texts cited under each. At the end of the 11th are the signatures of John Goodwin, Philip Nye, John Owen, Sidrach Simpson, John Davies, William Greenehill, William Bridge, William Carter, George Griffiths, William Strong and John Stone. At the end of all Nye and Simpson sign for themselves and others.) (See *Commons' Journals*, vii. 258.) [N. XXII., 48.]

The CONSULS, SCULTETS, LANDAMANNS and SENATORS OF THE EVANGELICAL CANTONS OF SWITZERLAND, &C. as in heading to their letter of April 14, 1652, to the PARLIAMENT.

165[2-]3, February 16.—We have commissioned the bearer Stockar to ascertain how the offer of our mediation will be accepted by you and the United Provinces, and we again urge you with a view to the interests of the Reformed Churches to make peace with them if possible. (See *Commons' Journals*, vii. 279.) In *Latin*. Seal of Zurich *embossed*. [N. X.. 92.]

The Representation of the OFFICERS OF THE ARMY IN IRELAND against Mr. WEAVER.

1652[-3], February 18.—That even before the Lord Deputy Ireton's death, he had in a letter manifested a great dissatisfaction at a censure given concerning the dealing of an officer with a party of rebels by a council of officers, which letter being intercepted by the Irish in Scilly, where that officer was then a prisoner, was made use of to countenance their intentions to take away his life.

That after the Lord Deputy's death he had laboured to persuade the other Commissioners to keep the command of the Army to themselves, and not to intrust any single person therewith.

The dangerous use he made of an information—we fear set on foot by himself—that there was an Anabaptisticall Plot in the Army to bring in an Anabaptist General, whereon he advised the other Commissioners that the persons said to be in the said plot, who were the greatest part of the eminent godly persons in the Army, might be speedily sent for to prevent that design as he pretended, which, if agreed to, would have broken your Army in pieces, and he and his instruments so spread these aspersions that England and Ireland was filled with them.

His strange and unchristian carriage, at the Commissioners next coming to Kilkenny, to many honest men, refusing to pay them their salaries or to own them in their employment, besides his turbulent carriage to officers at the same time taking upon him to judge military actions and question a council of war for discharging their duty, and when Lieutenant-General Ludlow resolved to grant a Commission for Martial Law to the Deputy-Governor of Waterford, he told him that if he intended it from any power he had received from the Commissioners he must declare against it.

We therefore request first that Mr. Weaver be required to fix on particular persons and make good the charge he hath indefinitely laid upon the officers of the army.

Second, that he may not be continued as a Commissioner for Ireland.

Thirdly, that some eminent person be appointed in his stead. (See *Commons' Journals*, vii. 260, 261.) *Signed* " Hardres Waller," and by about thirty other officers sent over as a deputation. [N. XXI., 119.]

List of OFFICERS sent over as above with their INSTRUCTIONS. [1652-3, February.]—*Copy.* [N. XXI., 120.]

BENJAMIN BONNELL, Public Minister of the Queen of Sweden, to the COMMITTEE APPOINTED TO HEAR HIM.

[1652-3, February 24.]—After assurances of the friendly feelings of his Mistress and congratulations on the peace of the Commonwealth, desiring that Commissioners be appointed to confer with him concerning the business on which he is sent. (See *Commons' Journals*, vii. 262.) In *French* with *English* translation. [N. XVIII., 46.]

INFORMATION

1652-3, February 27. [Hamburgh].—Against Mr. Thomas Bellingham and Mr. Thomas Lee. That the former had said that when a Roundhead had refused to drink the King's—to wit Charles Steward's—health in his presence he himself had pulled down the State of England's arms which were in the same room, and again drank the King's health. Mr. Thomas Lee said that Resident Bradshaw understood that I was a Cavalier, and therefore sent to me to come and speak with him and the said Bellingham which I did. Then they told me that the Resident was so base a fellow that if I had not a great care of myself he would put me in chains and send me to England, to prevent which he hired a soldier for 15 stivers to go with me out of the town, that I might be out of his jurisdiction. He wished me to remember him to Charles Gerrard, sometime Lord Brandon, and believing that I was one of Charles Steward's agents, to assist me in my travels he offered me 20 dollars and what else I wanted, and at the same time he drank the King's health. Before this he said he wrote to Mr. George Waite at Copenhagen, signifying that the Dutch fleet was 90 sail, and the English but 60, and that he had received a letter from Mr. Spark to say that Major-General Massey was very busy in transacting Charles Steward's affairs.

February 28.—I have just this instant received from Lee and Bellingham 20 rix dollars to bear my charges to the King as they call him, which money they have mutually charged me not to let a man living know of besides Charles Steward, and further my right hand must not tell my left hand of it, because—as they say—they shall be accused of maintaining Malignants in their agencies. Lee further said that they had certain ships belonging to their company now in the service of the Commonwealth, and that when they were in fight with Sir George Ayscue their Masters saved themselves and received not a shot, but the rest of Sir George's fleet was much torn, and after that fight the said Masters sent their Merchants word in Hamburgh that they walked up and down with their broadswords about their necks and drank sack, but yet they would keep their ships safe. *Vera Copia.* R[ichard] B[radshaw]. [N. XVI., 127.]

The FRENCH AMBASSADOR.

[1652-3, March 1.]—Desiring license to transport 30 horses. (Printed in *Commons' Journals*, vii. 263.) [N. XVII., 22.]

The ESTATES OF HOLLAND AND WEST FRIESLAND to the PARLIAMENT.

165[2-]3, March [8-] 18.—Whereas the two nations, instead of thanking God for the benefits they enjoy, have given matter to the enemies of God and themselves to rejoice, and to hope that they will finally effect for them what they never could have done for themselves, and—what increases the evil—by the changes and daily varying successes of arms he who has the upperhand, considering the matter as a true Christian ought to hold his victory as mournful an event, as the other who seems to suffer the defeat, the said Estates prompted by pious zeal and the grace of God, and in no wise constrained by any other consideration have not scrupled to represent the above to the Parliament in order that, if they take the same view, what ought to be done for maintaining the honour and glory of God and for the welfare of both States may be taken into consideration, or if the Parliament be otherwise minded the said Estates having discharged their duty can with much more peaceful consciences await the issue. (See *Commons' Journals*, vii. 270.) In *Dutch* and *French*. [N. XVIII., 135.]

The COUNCIL OF STATE.

1652[-3], March 10.—Order reporting concerning horses impressed in Northamptonshire. (Printed in *Commons' Journals*, vii. 275.) [N. XVI., 126.]

The PARLIAMENT.

1652[-3], March 22.—Instructions to Philip, Viscount Lisle, Ambassador Extraordinary to Sweden. (This is the draft, submitted to Parliament as printed in Thurloe, *State Papers*, i. 227, and amended as appears by *Commons' Journals*, vii. 269.) [N. XVIII. 47.]

The PARLIAMENT to the QUEEN OF SWEDEN.

1653, March 30.—Letter of Credence for Philip, Viscount Lisle, as Ambassador Extraordinary. (See *Commons' Journals*, vii. 273.) In *Latin*, with *English* translation. *Copy.* [N. XVIII., 48.]

DON ALONSO DE CARDENAS to the COUNCIL OF STATE.

1653, March 30–April 9.—Requesting on behalf of the King of Spain leave to transport forty English horses into Flanders. In *Spanish*, with *English* translation. The original *signed*.

And

Order of the COUNCIL thereon.

Same date.—[N. XVIII., 85, 86.]

ISRAEL LAGERFELDT, Public Minister of the Queen of Sweden, to the COMMITTEE appointed to hear him.

1653, April 8.—Expressing the desire of his Mistress for peace between England and the United Provinces, and declaring her willingness to offer her mediation between them. (See *Commons' Journals*, vii. 277.) In *Latin*, with *English* translation, the first *signed*. [N. XVIII., 49.]

The COMMISSIONERS FOR THE NAVY.

1653, April 14.—Order reporting concerning widows and children of officers. (Printed in *Commons', Journals*, vii, 279.) [N. XVII., 133.]

JOHN JAMES STOCKAR, formerly Bailiff of Locarno, to [the PARLIAMENT].

[1653, April 15.]—After stating the cogent reasons in favour of peace, offering the mediation of the Swiss Republic, should it be of any service towards a pacification. (See *Commons' Journals*, vii. 279.) [In *Latin*. [N. X., 93.]

PAPER

1653, May 7. London.—Describing how a gentleman last Tuesday fixed up the Lord General Cromwell's picture with certain verses beneath to one of the pillars of the Exchange. (Printed in Grey iv., Appendix No. 51, p. 98.) [N. XVI., 134.]

CHRISTINA, Queen of Sweden, to the PARLIAMENT.

1653, May 18. Stockholm.—Commending the Lord Hieronimus in Radzieicwice Radzieiowsky, Senator and Vice-Chancellor of the Kingdom of Poland, who intends to visit England. (See *Commons' Journals*, vii. 299.) In *Latin*. *Seal embossed*. *Signed* "Christina." *Countersigned* "Cant Sersten." [N. X., 15.]

The CONSULS and SENATORS OF BREMEN to the PARLIAMENT.

1653, June 30.—Letter of Credence to Henry Oldenburg. (See *Commons' Journals*, vii. 292.) In *Latin*. *Copy*. [N. X., 88.]

FREDERIC, Heir of Norway, Duke of Sleswick, Holstein, Stormar, and Ditmarsh, Count in Oldenburgh and Delmenhorst, to the PARLIAMENT.

1653, July 14. Gottorp.—Letter of Credence to Colonel Paul Wirtz. (See *Commons' Journals*, vii. 305.) In *Latin*. *Seal embossed*. *Signed*. [N. X., 19.] A copy is N. XVIII., 171.

The Same to the Same.

1653, July 14. Gottorp.—Desiring that strict orders may be given to the English Admirals to observe the neutrality of his dominions, and declaring his friendly sentiments towards England. (See *Commons' Journals*, vii. 305.) In *Latin. Seal embossed. Signed.* [N. X., 22.] A copy is N. XVIII., 170.

The Grand-Duke of Tuscany to the Parliament.

1653, August 2. Florence.—Availing himself of the change of government in England to reassure them of his friendly sentiments towards that nation. (See *Commons' Journals*, vii. 315.) In *Italian. Signed. Seal embossed.* [N. X., 27.]

Instructions to Mr. Richard Lawrence, Agent at Constantinople.

1653, August 16.—(Abstract printed in *State Papers, Domestic*, p. 123.) (See *Commons' Journals*, vii. 301.) [N. XVIII., 142.]

Christina, Queen of Sweden, to the Parliament.

1653, September 11. Stockholm.—Interceding on behalf of the Earl of Leven now a prisoner, whose estates she hears are forfeited, on account of his good services to her father and grandfather from 1605 to 1638 in their Muscovite, Livonian, Prussian, and German wars. (See *Commons' Journals*, vii. 340.) In *Latin. Seal embossed. Signed* "Christina." *Countersigned* " A. Gÿldenclau." [N. X., 16.]

The Parliament to the Consuls, &c. of the Evangelical Cantons, &c. (as in the heading to the letter of April 14, 1652).

1653, October 10.—Having acknowledged and thanked them for their letter of December 24th last and complimented them on the early acquisition of their freedom and their excellent government:—whereas with religious affection you exhort us to peace that exhortation ought to us to be of very great moment both on account of the desirability of peace in itself and the authority of yourselves, who in the midst of the greatest wars have both yourselves maintained so long peace both at home and abroad and have been to all others both exhorters to peace and the best examples. Lastly in that you urge that which we ourselves not so much for our own interests as for the general good of the Protestant Religion have by our ambassadors and other public ministers industriously sought, namely amity and straitest league with the United Provinces, but they —especially the Orange faction, adverse to us, always devoted to the royal party, and itself also affecting tyranny at home—how they used our Ambassadors coming to them not about peace but about friendship and strictest union, what causes of war they afterwards gave, how in the midst of a treaty for such a near alliance they assaulted us with a prepared navy at our own doors, when we little expected such salutations from them you will fully understand by our public declaration herewith transmitted. As for us, our serious endeavour is neither to attribute anything to our own strength but all to God alone, nor to be lifted up with any successes, but to retain minds ready to embrace all good opportunities of making a just and honourable peace. You in the meanwhile, whose zeal it is to reconcile brethren at variance, are among men worthy of praise, and shall doubtless receive a blessing from God as peacemakers. (See *Commons' Journals*, vii. 329.) *Drafts in Latin and English.* [N. XVIII., 162, 164.]

The PARLIAMENT to the QUEEN OF SWEDEN.

1653, October 21.—Letter of Credence for Bulstrode Whitelocke, as Ambassador Extraordinary. (See *Commons' Journals*, vii. 336.) In *Latin. Copy.* [N. XVIII., 50.]

The PROCONSULS and SENATORS OF LÜBECK to the PARLIAMENT.

1653, October 24.—Complaining that five of their ships have been taken by two English men of war in the Narrow Seas and carried into London and Dover, and, though they do not doubt that the Parliament with its usual love of justice and equity will release them of its own accord, asking on account of the approach of winter and the fact that a delay of a day or hour may oblige them to winter abroad being detained by the freezing of the ports, inasmuch as the only ground for their detention is that two Dutch men of war were in their company who probably joined them without their consent, that they may be released and that strict orders may be given to the English captains not to interfere with them on their voyage home, and not to molest any other Lübeck ships. (See *Commons' Journals*, vii. 350.) In *Latin. Seal embossed.* [N. X., 87.]

The PROCONSULS and SENATORS OF HAMBURGH to the PARLIAMENT.

1653, October 25.—Complaining that their ships on their voyages to and from neutral ports were frequently seized by English ships, and sometimes the men on board tortured to obtain a false confession that they were bound for a belligerent port in order to give an excuse for making prize thereof, and further that goods belonging to their citizens were frequently unloaded, and detained to wait the result of an action in the Admiralty Court, by the great delays in which their citizens were much damnified, and desiring redress. (See *Commons' Journals*, vii. 350.) In *Latin. Seal embossed.* [N. X., 86.]

ISRAEL LAGERFELDT to the COMMITTEE appointed to hear him on his taking leave.

1653, October 26.—It is now the eighth month since in conference with the Commissioners of the Parliament, I in the name of my mistress urged a peace between England and the United Provinces and offered the good offices of her Majesty as a mediatrix. Since then the war has become yet more violent and sanguinary. It is a grievous matter that there should be so cruel and dangerous a war between two neighbouring nations both of the same religion, and to terminate it is the interest of not only the contending parties but all who profess the orthodox faith. My most gracious Queen pitying so much bloodshed, and influenced by the friendship which has existed between both nations from time immemorial, again and again urges a reconciliation, and offers whatever she can contribute to an object so necessary to Christendom, lest the war should spread and not only inflict greater losses on the belligerents, but also other States should be drawn into it. And since her Majesty has ordered me to return immediately I am bound to acquaint the Parliament therewith, that I may start as soon as possible with such an answer as her Majesty expects from the Parliament, and the ties of their mutual friendship require. (See *Commons' Journals*, vii. 340.) In *Latin. Signed.* [N. XVIII., 51.]

The PARLIAMENT to the QUEEN OF SWEDEN.

1653, October 29.—The Parliament has received your letter of January 20th, through your public minister Lord Lagerfeldt, and also a paper from him on April 8th, both showing how your Majesty has been affected by the differences between us and the United Provinces, and your desire for a reconciliation. This we recognise proceeds from your Majesty's desire for peace and the welfare of the Reformed Churches, who will give an opening to the machinations of their enemies, if they break out into slaughtering one another. The consideration of this and of other evils of war has influenced this Commonwealth to use its utmost endeavours both to avert them, and to terminate them on fair terms. The feeling of the Parliament remains the same, and they hope that God in his own time will in like manner influence the heart of the States-General, so that such a peace as shall be for the public benefit be established for the future. Meanwhile let your Majesty be convinced that this war shall on our side be carried on with all due care for preserving trade, especially that between this Commonwealth and your dominions, according to our directions both written and verbal to the said Lord Lagerfeldt, who we doubt not will on his return declare to your Majesty the evident proofs of the desire of the Commonwealth for preserving and increasing their friendship and good understanding with your Majesty, for the mutual benefit of both States. (See *Commons' Journals*, vii. 342.) In *Latin*. *Draft*. [N. XVIII., 52.]

The COUNCIL OF STATE.

1653, November 8.—Order concerning Lord Lagerfeldt's re-credentials. (Abstract in *State Papers, Domestic*, p. 236, number 8). [N. XVI., 135.]

The PROCONSULS and CONSULS OF DANTZIC to the PARLIAMENT.

1653, November 10.—Complaining of the capture of the *Hope*, belonging to some of their citizens, while sailing in ballast from Holland to France, and asking for her release. (See *Commons' Journals*, viii. 361.) In *Latin*. *Seal embossed*. [N. X., 59.]

JOHN THURLOE to HENRY SCOBELL.

1653, November 10.—Concerning the accidental omission of certain words in the letter to the Queen of Sweden. [N. VIII., 60.]

Safeguard to FREDERICK, Heir of Norway, Duke of Sleswick, &c.

[1653, December 1.]—(Printed in Thurloe, *State Papers*, i. 385.) (See *Commons' Journals*, vii. 361.) In *Latin*. *Draft*. [N., XVIII., 172.]

JOHN CAMPBELL to the PARLIAMENT.

[1649-1653.]—Petition, stating that 12 years since he lost his sight in Antrim, where he was born, whereby he was reduced to much extremity, so that he was forced to come over to England "to seek some means of livelihood for himself in craving the charity of well disposed people, but contrary to his expectation, he hath been often troubled here with dreams and fearful visions in his sleep, and hath been twice bewitched, insomuch as he can find no quietness or rest here," and praying therefore for a pass to return to Ireland. [N. XXII., 122.]

The JUDGES' Opinion.

[1653-4, January 16.]—On the demand of the Portuguese Ambassador that his brother, who was committed for murder, should be surrendered to him. (Printed in *State Papers, Domestic*, p. 360, with several variations or mistakes, of which the following corrections seem worth making . . p. 361, line 24, "the *modus* is" for "the murder"; line 33, "He may be tried, observing the rules of the law" for "by the law"; line 34, "*Jus*" for "*Comes*"; line 36, "privileges as to his person" for "privileges to"; line 39, "*subjiciatur*" for "*subjicitur*"; line 41, "it" for "I"; line 43, "is so triable" for "is triable"; line 48, "constable and marshall" for "constable marshall"; last line, "him" for "them"; p. 362, line 4, "local" for "legal.") [N. XVII., 173.]

The LORD PROTECTOR and the PARLIAMENT.

1654, September 19.—Declaration for a day of fasting and humiliation. (Printed in *King's Pamphlets*, E. 1064, No. 64. Abstract in *State Papers, Domestic*, p. 368.) [N. XVI., 136.]

An ELOGY written on the late unhappy accident which befell the LORD PROTECTOR.

[1654, October.]—
> "Foreign ill-tutored jades, had you but known
> Whom you rebelled against, whom you have thrown,
> You would have pined to nothing, loathed the day,
> And left the crows a memorable prey.
> O Life of three great realms; whose brains did hatch
> Successful plots, which no past age could match,
> Whose army braves the land, whose fleets the main,
> And only beasts did think unfit to reign,
> How near to fatal was your error, when
> You thought outlandish horses English men.
> Had the mild Britons dreamed your Highness meant,
> To pass through all degrees of Government,
> The all subscribing Parliament that sate,
> Would have prevented this sad turn of State;
> They would themselves have drawn the coach and borne
> The awful lash, which those proud beasts did scorn.
> 'Twould doubtless be to men free from affright,
> A most magnificent and moving sight
> To see the brother both of Spain and France
> Sit in the Coachbox and the members prance,
> To see Northumberland and Kent contest
> Which of their Representatives drew best.
> Make the slaves pay and bleed, let th'asses beare;
> The measure of the power is their base fear."

[N. XVI., 170.]

OLIVER CROMWELL to WILLIAM LENTHALL.

1654[-5], January 22.—Message that he desires to speak with the Parliament in the Painted Chamber. [N. VIII., 62.]

The LORD PROTECTOR and COUNCIL.

[1655, September 21.] — Orders for securing the peace of the Commonwealth, with Instructions to the Commissioners. (Abstract given in *State Papers, Domestic*, p. 346, where in clause 1, 16 December is printed for 16 November.) *Copy.* [N. XVI., 99.]

A. B. to the KING OF SPAIN.

[1655-6, Jannary.]—Seeing that Cromwell hath violated the peace and good correspondence betwixt Spain and England by sending his fleets both to the Indies and the coasts of Spain to intercept the galleons bringing home of the plate, A. B. has thought it his duty to represent to your Majesty how much it may import your service to declare in favour of the King of England, and endeavour to restore him to his Crown as the most efficacious means to diminish the power of Cromwell and increase your Majesty's for the following reasons.

1. Since Cromwell is resolved to make war against your Majesty, he will not fail to do you all the mischief he can, though you should not declare in favour of the said king, the King's loyal subjects both in England and abroad, and likewise many soldiers in Cromwell's own armies, now enforced by invincible necessity to serve under him, seeing your Majesty's declaration, would come over to you daily with a considerable strength, ships of merchandise, and men of war.

2. The greatest and best part of the soldiery embarked for the Indies formerly served the king and is still rightly affected to him, and they were sent out of England, because Cromwell could not confide in them, and should they have mastered any place in the Indies, on finding that your Majesty favoured their king they would easily have been persuaded to have taken arms under your Majesty against the rest who were not rightly affected, and also the rest of the English in the Barbadoes, Bermudas, and St. Christopher's which have stood right for their king, and maintained those islands for him, as long as he had a foot of land left in his three kingdoms. And if necessary your Majesty may capitulate as much with the king before you engage in his quarrel, and he must acknowledge himself infinitely obliged to your Majesty, in tendering such a motion to him.

3. Cromwell is so perfectly abominated in all the three kingdoms, and there is so great division in all his armies, that should they see their king assisted by your Majesty they would universally turn their arms against Cromwell, lest establishing him faster in that Government they should contribute to their own eternal slavery and be deprived of all commerce with Spain.

4. If your Majesty shall give permission to the loyal English to bring their fortunes into your service and dominions, and to live and traffic securely there, provided they bring passports from their king, undoubtedly many rich merchants would come over, with ships of merchandise and war, to avoid the danger they are daily subject to under that usurping government, which has no way but that of force to maintain his armies by sea and land, and all this at the expense of the rich and powerful merchants, which on the interruption of trade with Spain must impoverish the customs, the greatest part of his constant revenues, and they will fail him, and then h3 must grate upon the subject which must enforce them to revolt.

5. It is the best way to call away all the English, Scotch, and Irish, who at this day in great numbers serve the Crown of France against your Majesty.

6. The King of Denmark and the Hollanders on your Majesty's example would undoubtedly do the like, being both dissatisfied with the peace they lately contracted, and they say that if Cromwell be successful against your Majesty in the Indies, not only they, but all Europe would be ruined in their trade, and therefore in good policy all Christain Princes ought to join against Cromwell's designs.

7. It is well known that in Cromwell's armies and fleets there are very many that have their hearts right for the king, and if they knew whither safely to repair they would bring over a considerable part of the fleet to his Majesty's service, which they would do if your Majesty should only publish by declaration that all ships of war carrying the King of England's colours should freely be admitted and protected in all parts of your dominions with their prizes.

8. Your Majesty might very much advantage the Catholic faith in the three kingdoms interceding with the king that in case God should be pleased to restore him to his Crown he should give liberty of conscience to his Catholic subjects or at least that he should not execute the penal laws against them.

9. The sooner your Majesty declares yourself the better it will be, for Cromwell's ill intention was confirmed sufficiently by the retreat of his fleet from Cape St. Vincent and had he intended friendly he would have expected your Majesty's fleet, which went out of Cadiz, and that he designs taking San Domingo or Cuba, or both, is apparent enough, because he sent back the ships into England, which lately came out of England, to be sheathed, and it will be hard to unnest him, for his purpose is to transplant the English from Barbadoes, Bermudas, St. Christopher's, Virginia, and New England to San Domingo and Cuba, and by the shipping he will continually maintain there he will destroy the commerce betwixt Spain and the Indies, and so he doubts not but to oblige the inhabitants to traffic with him.

I conclude by saying again, that your Majesty can receive no prejudice imaginable by declaring for the king, for Cromwell will endeavour as much to endamage your monarchy, as if you had declared, and your Majesty shall do him more hurt by the very name of the king, than by the expense of millions of ducats, in regard of the great affection his subjects have generally towards him, who expect nothing but such an occasion to declare for his Majesty. (Compare the letter from Nicholas to Jane, dated February 1-11, 1655-6 in *State Papers, Domestic,* p. 159.) *Copy.* [N. XVII., 88.]

The COUNCIL AT WHITEHALL to the CLERK OF THE COMMONWEALTH.

1656, September 13.—Ordering him to deliver tickets only to such persons as being returned to Parliament were approved by the Council. (See *Commons' Journals,* vii. 425.) [N. XVI., 137.]

The LORD PROTECTOR and the PARLIAMENT.

1656, September 23.—Declaration for a day of fasting and humiliation. (Printed in *King's Pamphlets,* E. 1065, No. 10. Abstract in *State Papers, Domestic,* p. 115.) *Draft* with amendments. [N. XVI., 138.]

The LORD PROTECTOR and the PARLIAMENT.

[1656, October 4.]—Narrative of the late success against the Spanish West India fleet, and declaration for a day of thanksgiving for the same. (Printed in *King's Pamphlets,* E. 1065, No. 11.) (See *Commons' Journals,* vii. 440.) Two *Drafts.* The second draft contains the following passages which were finally omitted : " Besides the aforesaid narrative the ensuing relation was received from the said Marquess of Badex his eldest son, after he was taken prisoner. The Spaniards having exercised monstrous cruelties upon the natives of Peru—which the said Marquess for 14 years governed . . having his residence at

Lima, the chief city of that kingdom—by oppressing them in their consciences, persons, and estates—even those that are accounted freemen and profess the Romish religion—which made them to groan under their burdens, the cry thereof came at last to the ears of the Lord, for about five months since, presently after the Marquess his departing from Peru, there happened the fearfullest earthquakes and raining of fire from heaven in Peru that have been heard of in the world, insomuch that the whole city of Lima is swallowed up—as is also the island of Callao—in which there perished about 11,000 Spaniards and not above 100 Indians with them, the king of Spain having also lost by the earthquakes a 100 millions of plate in bars of silver ready wrought up. The famous mines and mountains of Potosi are also destroyed, so that there are no more hills to be seen there nor any further possibility of any gold or silver in Peru. This relation, though very wonderful, is affirmed to be true by the aforesaid relator." And after the words "the fierceness of thine anger:—" "And no less observable are the terrible things which God hath done in Peru—the place where the king of Spain had exercised so much cruelty and from whence he had so great a part of his riches—concerning which it may now be said as it was of Babylon 'The glory of his kingdom and the beauty of his excellency is as when God overthrew Sodom and Gomorrah.'" [N. XVI., 139; XVII., 87.]

JAMES NAYLOR, a prisoner in Bridewell, to the PARLIAMENT.

[1657.]—"That which I have suffered in this nation I complain not of. But that which is set before me to testify to you, who are now in authority, is this. That concerning my faith in Jesus Christ and His sufferings, it is no other than what the saints have witnessed in Scriptures who do confess Him in them, every one in their measure as they have received Him. How is it in my heart to take to myself any of His glory, but what He by His Holy Spirit shall put upon me, which is His free gift and not my desert, and without which I have no good thing in me? And therefore the glory of all I am or have I ascribe unto the eternal Spirit—and not to the perishing nature—of which all the children of light, who are born of the Spirit, are heirs with me, each one in our growth. And to set myself above the least of them I condemn as pride, owning Him alone to be Head over all, Who is in all, God blessed for ever.

And this in few words is the substance of my faith in Christ Jesus without hiding or dissembling, declared to you that none of you may be led by misinformation in this thing. So to the righteous principle of God, who is in you all, I commit you, that therein ye may receive power to answer His will in all things, without Whom you can do nothing, that He will accept you in, that before Him you may quit yourselves of your engagements, as to Him Who is the searcher of all hearts, and looks for truth in the inward parts, for there is great wrath felt against the nation, if God turn it not away for His mercy's sake." (See Neale, *History of the Puritans*, iv. 139-143.) [N. XXII., 158.]

The LORD PROTECTOR and the PARLIAMENT.

[1656-7, February 2.]—Narrative of the late attempt upon his life and declaration for a day of thanksgiving for his escape. (Printed in *King's Pamphlets*, E. 1065, No. 13, and in Grey iv., Appendix No. 63, p. 101.) (See *Commons' Journals*, vii. 484.) Two copies, the first the draft as amended, the second the fair copy presented to the Protector. [N. XVI., 140.]

The LORD PROTECTOR.

1657, April 21.—Paper delivered to the Committee containing observations upon the Humble Petition and Advice. (See *Commons' Journals*, vii. 523, Whitelocke, *Memorials*, p. 656.) (The substance of these appears from his speech in Carlyle, No. 13, with Carlyle's remarks thereon.) [N. XVI., 141.]

The LORD PROTECTOR.

Same date.—A second paper delivered to the Committee containing observations on the clause concerning the revenue. (This agrees almost *verbatim* with the report in Carlyle of the same speech from " The present charge of the Forces " to "for carrying on the same and for what time.") [N. XVI., 142.]

The LORD PROTECTOR.

1657, May 25. The Painted Chamber.—Speech on consenting to the Humble Petition and Advice as reported by the Speaker the following day. (Printed in *Commons' Journals*, vii. 539, and in Carlyle, *Appendix*, No. 30.) [N. XVI., 142b.]

The LORD PROTECTOR.

1657[-8], January 25. The Banquetting House, Whitehall. — Speech to the two Houses. (Printed in Carlyle, No. 17, with some variations. The most remarkable are p. 105:—Read " satisfaction enough to yourselves of that as a necessary thing" for "enough to yourselves as this;" p. 107, " what is there in all that part ? What is there in the other part of Europe " for " all the parts of Europe," and " interest of Europe " for " interests of England " ; p. 109, " If these things saved " for " And these things stated," and " I have told you. If you will judge it no danger, if you shall think " for " I have told you; you will judge, &c " ; p. 113, omit " that we are got again to peace," and read " let the pretences be what they will, the will " for " what they may " ; p. 116, add after " a peaceable people " " an honest people " ; p. 117, read " Liberty of the people " for " of the subject " ; p. 118, " If these things be not considered—I cannot doubt, but they will be considered—I say, I judge what the state of Ireland is. Should free quarter come, &c." for " If these things be considered, &c.," and " a popish and Spanish " for " the Spanish " ; p. 119, " if we have to look " for " while we, &c.," and " How should that man " for " how can any man " ; p. 120, " hold to nothing, like nothing, neither &c." for " hold to nothing neither " ; p. 121, line 4, after " peace " add " We have had four score years peace," and read " pretend what you will, if we run " for " pretend what we will, if you run "; p. 124, between " Government " and " that every " insert " That thereby liberty of conscience may be secured for honest people that they may serve God without fear." . As this is the form in which it was reported by the Speaker (see *Commons' Journals*, vii. 589), its authority is superior to that of the reports accessible to Carlyle.) [N. XVI., 143.]

[The LORD PROTECTOR] to the SPEAKER.

[1657-8, January 25.]—" I should have imparted a paper unto you, which indeed I have forgot. I have it not here. It is concerning the state of your moneys. You had lately an account of the public moneys, and we have been as good husbands thereof as we could. We have not increased the debt. But some supplies designed by you for public service, that of the buildings, hath not come in as was expected. The Paper shall be ready for you. You shall have it, when once you desire it. I desire you to acquaint the House with it." (See *Commons' Journals*, vii. 589.) [N. XVI., 144.]

The [so-called] LORDS to the COMMONS.

[1657-8, February 3.]—Message. (Printed in *Commons' Journals*, vii. 591.) [N. XVI., 145.]

JOHN WALLIS, Savilian Professor of Geometry, to the Reverend MATTHEW HALE, Minister of Michael's Quern, London.

1658, October 2, November 11, December 25, 1658-9, January 20, March 10. Oxford.—All except the last are concerning the results of examinations. The last also refers to a translation of the Bible into Lithuanian by "a Polonian," at Oxford. (All printed in Grey, iv., Appendix, Nos. 83-87, pp. 153-158.) [N. VIII., 62 *b, c, d, e, f.* Omitted in Index.]

A. DALE, Deputy-Sheriff of Lincolnshire, to WILLIAM LENTHALL.

1659, May 14. Lincoln.—Stating that he had caused his letter to be delivered to Mr. John Weaver. [N. VIII., 63.]

JOHN STRODE, Sheriff of Dorset, to WILLIAM LENTHALL.

1659, May 14.—Stating that Mr. John Browne, for whom he had received a letter enclosed in one to himself, had died in the preceding March. *Signed. Seal.* [N. VIII., 64.]

The PARLIAMENT.

1659, June 18.—Order to the trustees for sale of the lands of the late king, &c. (Printed in *Commons' Journals*, vii. 689.) [N. XVI., 147.]

The GRAND-DUKE OF TUSCANY to the PARLIAMENT.

1659, June 21. Florence.—Congratulating them on the restoration of their authority, and assuring them of his friendly feelings. (See *Commons' Journals*, vii. 729.) In *Italian. Signed. Seal embossed.* [N. X., 29.]

The COUNCIL OF STATE.

1659, July 1.—Instructions for the Commissioners for the governing of the affairs of Ireland. (See *Commons' Journals*, vii. 700.) [N. XXI., 137.]

FRANCISCO DE MELLO, Portuguese Ambassador Extraordinary, to WILLIAM LENTHALL.

1659, July 9. Wild Street.—Announcing the arrival of his credentials and asking for an audience. *Signed. Seal.* [N. XVII., 174.]

The DOGE OF VENICE to the PARLIAMENT.

[1659, July.]—Letter of Credence to his Resident, Francesco Giauavina, congratulating the Parliament on their restoration. (See *Commons' Journals*, vii. 769.) In *Italian,* with *English* translation. *Copies.* [N. XVIII., 157.]

The STATES-GENERAL to the PARLIAMENT.

165:), August 4. The Hague.—Praying them to expedite a hearing of a case the *Saint Mary*, in the Admiralty Court, in which some of their subjects are concerned. In *Latin*. [N. X., 72.]

LANCELOT LEE and others to WILLIAM LENTHALL.

[1659, August 6. Shrewsbury.]—Stating that in obedience to the Act of Parliament for settling the Militia they had met the previous day at Shrewsbury and had agreed that one foot regiment of 600 men and a troop of horse and one of dragoons of 600 men each besides commissioned officers be raised, and submitting the names of several persons as officers. *Signed. Seal.* [N. VIII., 124.]

GEORGE BLAKISTON and others to the PARLIAMENT.

Same date. Newcastle-on-Tyne.—Submitting a list of names for commissions. (Printed in *Commons' Journals*, vii. 756.) [N. XVI., 158.]

ROGER WHITLEY to MUTTON DAVIES.

1659, August 9.—By virtue of his Commission from the King as Colonel of a regiment of horse appointing him Captain therein. [N. XVI., 159.]

The DOGE and GOVERNORS OF GENOA to " The MOST SERENE PRINCE " [? LENTHALL].

1659, August 11. Genoa.—Congratulating the Parliament on their restoration. In *Latin*, with *English* translation. [N. X., 42.]

Articles of Agreement between Col. JEROME SANKEY, Col. DANIEL AXTELL, Major RICHARD CREED, and Capt. JOHN HATFIELD, Commissioners appointed by LORD LAMBERT, Commander-in-Chief of the Parliament forces in these parts, and Col. ROBERT BROUGHTON, Col. RICHARD LLOYD, ROGER GROSVENOR, Esquire, and Capt. RICHARD DUTTON, appointed by THOMAS MIDDLETON, Esquire, Governor of Chirk Castle.

1659, August 24.—Imprimis that Thomas Middleton Esquire shall on the 24th inst. at 10 a.m. deliver up the Castle of Chirk, and all arms, ammunition, horses, stores, etc. without embezzlement to Lord Lambert or his deputies. Item, that the said Governor and his Commissioners shall deliver themselves prisoners, and upon good security to be approved by Lord Lambert, shall have liberty for two months in which to make application to the Parliament for mercy, and that such of them as shall not obtain the Parliament's favour to continue within their territories shall have liberty to go beyond seas. Provided nevertheless that Lieut. Col. Edward Broughton shall not have the liberty upon security granted to the other officers until Lord Lambert's pleasure be further known. Signed and sealed by Col. Robert Broughton, and the other three Commissioners for the Governor. (See *Commons' Journals*, vii. 769.) [N. XVI., 160.]

ALFONSO, King of Portugal, to the PARLIAMENT.

1659, August 26. Lisbon.—Stating that he had been informed by his Ambassador Francisco de Mello of the deliverance to him of Antonio Vas a Portuguese, who had been sent with Dom Fernando Telles the Ambassador to the United Provinces, and had been implicated in the treasonable proceedings of the latter, and therefore thanking the Parliament for their conduct in the matter, and as the seas were covered with pirates, enemies to that crown, asking them to provide some convoy or security that so the said Antonio Vas might be conducted safely to Portugal. Written in the King's name, but *signed* "La Raynhu." *Seal embossed.* In *Portuguese.* [N. X., 6.] An *English* translation is XVII., 176.

Sir John Fenwicke, Sheriff of Northumberland, to William Lenthall.

1659, August 31. Stanton.—Acknowledging a letter to the Justices of the County touching the number of alehouses, inns, and taverns. *Seal.* [N. VIII., 65.]

General George Monck to William Lenthall.

1659, September 2. Dalkeith.—Concerning the officers of his own regiment, Major Hubblethorne of Colonel Talbot's regiment, and the state of the country, and professing his fidelity to the Parliament. (Printed in Grey, iv., Appendix No. 88, p. 160.) (See *Commons' Journals*, vii., 789.) *Signed.* [N. VIII., 69.]

Elizabeth [Lady] Booth to Sir Arthur Haslerig, President of the Council.

1659, September 2. Dunham.—"I hope this Gentleman, your messenger, will give you an account that he hath had free liberty to execute the order committed to his trust, and hath seized upon several papers, and amongst others I delivered to him one paper sealed up, and endorsed on the back with figures, which was given to me at London in the drawing room belonging to our lodging by Mrs. Mordant, wife to Mr. John Mordant, who afterwards presently left me upon the coming in of some other company without saying anything to me of it, which paper as it is now delivered to the bearer I received, and never showed the same to my husband or acquainted him with it." *Signed.* *Seal.* [N. VIII., 68.]

The Earl of Clare to Henry Martyn.

1659, September 2.—Thanking him for his services that day week (apparently in opposing the Bill promoted by the City for establishing a new market in Clement's Inn Fields). (See *Commons' Journals*, vii. 773.) [N. VIII., 66.]

Major Edmund Waring, Governor of Shrewsbury, to William Lenthall.

1659, September 3. Shrewsbury.—Stating that he had ordered the Clerk of the Peace to signify the instructions to the Bailiffs of the liberties, and that only three Justices of the Peace in the whole county had as yet taken the engagement.

Postscript.—" I am as yet daily employed in securing persons that have been in the late rebellion, that are of this county, and are now lurking in holes." *Seal.* [N. VIII., 78.]

Colonel Jerome Sankey to the Lord President of the Council of State.

1659, September 6. Chester.—Stating the loss of a ship on the passage from Ireland with Majors Bolton and Rawlings on board and other officers and men, the hardships and dangers suffered by the other troops in their passage from a storm, and their activity in the Parliament's service, and asking that the widows and children of those who were lost should be provided for, and six weeks' pay given to the troops. (See *Commons' Journals*, vii., 776.) *Postscript.*—" The landing of your forces in Wales prevented a general rising, which was intended to be the 18th of last month, which the Committee for Sequestrations have knowledge of." *Signed.* [N. VIII., 67.]

THOMAS HOWELL to WILLIAM LENTHALL.

1659, September 9. Plymouth.—Commending Samuel Northcote, the Mayor of Plymouth, and excusing his conduct in not publishing the proclamation proclaiming Sir George Booth and others traitors, his reason for not having done so being that the proclamation had been sent by the Constable of the adjoining Hundred to the petty Constables of Plymouth, and not by the High Sheriff to the Mayor himself according to the usual custom. [N. VIII., 70.]

WILLIAM LENTHALL to Colonel SANKEY.

1659, September 10.—By order of the Parliament thanking the officers and soldiers from Ireland for their services. (See *Commons' Journals*, vii. 776.) *Signed.* [N. VIII., 71.]

FRANCISCO DE MELLO to [WILLIAM LENTHALL].

1659, September 13-23. Wild Street.—About ten weeks ago the Council of State remitted to me Antonio Vas, a Portuguese prisoner who was guilty of High Treason against the King. I acquainted his Majesty therewith and yesterday received a letter from him (that of August 26th) for the Parliament thanking them for that favour, which I send that it may be delivered to the Parliament, and steps taken for the safe conduct of this man to Portugal according to the request therein. (See *Commons' Journals*, vii. 793.) In *Portuguese*, with *English* translation. [N. XVII., 175.]

Colonel THOMAS CROMPTON to [the COUNCIL OF STATE].

1659, September 14. Stoneby Lodge.—The previous day on receipt of a letter from the Council of State, the Commissioners for the Militia had written to the Council for instructions how they should raise money for paying off the soldiers. This morning I heard that the Commissioners had, the previous night, drawn up an order to disband my regiment and Captain Backhouse's horse from further service. When the soldiers understood it, it caused a high mutiny. The Judge of Assize, Lord Chief Baron Wild, who was ready to take horse, sent for the Commissioners and told them they could not dismiss the men before they had paid them off, and with much pains convinced them of their error. It was concluded that the order should be recalled, and that they should come again on Tuesday and expect an answer from the Council, and that the soldiers should continue to stand to their arms. I, and Captain Backhouse's troop accompanied his Lordship two miles, and returning half a mile from Stafford, saw my regiment drawn up, and the officer told me that the soldiers left in the town had seized on the Commissioners, and would do so to me if I went into the town. But after I told them the conclusion my Lord had had with the Commissioners they promised my protection and the Commissioners' release, and so at the head of them I marched into the town when I understood the trembling condition the Commissioners were in. I suddenly sent an officer to them, and conducted them out of the town very peaceably. I desire that some course may be taken that the soldier may have his pay and be dismissed till further order. (See *Commons' Journals*, vii. 788.) [N. VIII., 77.]

Lieutenant-General EDMUND LUDLOWE to WILLIAM LENTHALL.

1659, September 14. Dublin.—Concerning Majors Bolton and Rawlings and the others lost in the *Sea Flower* of Liverpool, and asking that provision be made for their wives and children, and the arrears of the army there. (Printed in Grey, iv., Appendix No. 62, p. 99.) *Signed.* [N. VIII., 72.]

CHRISTOPHER MARTYN and others to the COUNCIL OF STATE.

1659, September 16. Plymouth.—Stating that no money having been raised in pursuance of the Act for settling the Militia in either Devon or Cornwall, the Commissioners are unable to muster and pay off the Militia as directed by his letter of the 7th instant. *Signed. Seal.* [N. VIII., 73.]

THOMAS CROXTON and others to WILLIAM LENTHALL.

1659, September 21. Chester.—Asking that notwithstanding the nulling of the Ancient Charter of the city, such privileges as are grounded on equity and reason, and are consistent with the laws of the Commonwealth may be restored. (Printed in Grey, iv., Appendix, No. 69, p. 127.) *Signed. Seal.* [N. VIII., 74.]

WILLIAM ILLY and others, Commissioners for the Militia, to JOHN BRADSHAW.

1659, September 22. Stafford.—Describing how they had been seized the previous day by the common soldiers wanting pay and taken to the Shire Hall under guard, and kept there four or five hours, requesting him to procure an order of the House or Council of State for levying the necessary money with all speed, hoping that Parliament will see that they have reparation for the great wrong, disgrace, and danger put upon them, and stating that they had that day borrowed money to pay a great part of the foot soldiers, and engaged themselves to pay the rest in a few days. (See *Commons' Journals*, vii. 788.) *Signed. Seal.* [N. VIII., 76.]

EDWARD OXBOROUGH to BRAMPTON GURDON.

1659, September 23. Bury St. Edmunds.—Concerning his seizure and detention by some of the soldiers in Major Sparrowe's troop who declared they would not hold themselves dismissed, but would remain in town till they had their pay, and would be paid to the day that they should receive their pay. (See *Commons' Journals*, vii. 789.) [N. VIII., 75.]

WILLIAM STEELE, MILES CORBETT, and MATTHEW TOMLINSON, Commissioners for managing the Government of Ireland, to the COUNCIL OF STATE.

1659, October 5.—Concerning the continuing of terms and causes, and regulating the fees of judges and officers in Ireland. (See *Commons' Journals*, vii. 794.) *Signed. Seal.* [N. VIII., 79.]

Speech of GIOVANNI SALVETTI ANTELLIMNELLI, Resident of the Grand-Duke of Tuscany, to the Commissioners appointed to receive him.

[1659, October 11.]—Assuring them of the affection borne by his Master to the English Nation, and stating that to continue and confirm the same, he has been accredited to the Parliament, whom on their recontinuation and re-establishment after such an intermission of time he congratulates, felicitating the people of England on the return of their so long discontinued and much desired liberty, and assuring the Parliament of the Grand-Duke's readiness on all occasions to serve them and to oblige such of their subjects as shall come into his dominions, adding personally that "though I reside here as a public Minister from a " foreign prince; I owe my birth and education to this country to whom " I would prove too ungrateful, if I did not employ all my spirits and " faculties in her service." (See *Commons' Journals*, vii. 793.) [N. XVIII., 147.]

The COMMITTEE OF SAFETY to Major EDWARD WARING.

1659, December 14. Whitehall.—Enclosing a warrant for 120*l.* on the farmers of the excise for Herefordshire, Worcestershire and Shropshire for pay of the garrison of Shrewsbury. *Signed* " A. Jhouston (of Warriston) President." *Embossed seal affixed.* *Enclosed* is the said warrant of the same date. [N. VIII., 80, 81.]

Colonel SIR THEOPHILUS JONES and others to [the COMMISSIONERS OF THE ARMY at Portsmouth].

1659, December 15. Dublin.—Describing their seizing Dublin Castle and declaring for the Parliament. (Printed in *King's Pamphlets*, E. 1013, No. 8.) *Signed.* [N. VIII., 82.]

WILLIAM HARTWELL, Mayor, and others to SIR HENRY INGOLDSBY.

1659, December 20. Limerick.—" Major Wilson hath secured Limerick for the Parliament, and is at present chosen Governor. Lieutenant-Colonel Nelson frighted thence by the violence of the soldiers. Anabaptist officers decoyed and exploded. The city concurs with the garrison. *Postscript.*—We did the work on Thursday Dec. 15, 10 at night." *Signed.* *Seal.* [N. VIII., 84.]

Colonel JOHN WARREN, Colonel SIR THEOPHILUS JONES, and others to [the COMMISSIONERS OF THE ARMY at Portsmouth].

1659, December 24. Dublin.—Since our former letter all considerable places in this nation have owned this undertaking for the Parliament, and this, besides the active endeavours of your friends, must be ascribed in a great measure to the common soldiers and inferior officers in the several regiments and garrisons, by whom such of their superior officers as have been disaffected to you, have been for the most part deserted, where such did not at least seemingly comply, finding their being laid aside would otherwise have necessarily followed . . . We have judged it necessary to proceed forthwith to a new modelling of this army, so far only as to remove such as may be dangerous, and put others in their places of whose fidelity to the Parliament we are abundantly satisfied, until the Parliament's pleasure shall be therein declared, or that we shall have your Honours' orders. We ask for a right construction of our acts if we are obliged to lay aside some lately by the

Parliament's Commission or power placed in command here, the Parliament being at a distance having been guided by the misrepresentations of those who now act, declare, or practise against them, who laboured to strengthen their party by placing their own partisans at the head of regiments and in places of trust as sheriffs, justices of the peace, &c., and insinuating with Lieutenant-General Ludlow, they had by his means got into their power all the chief cities and places of strength particularly the Castle of Dublin. As for Lieutenant-General Ludlow we cannot but own the Parliament's power vested in him as our Commander-in-Chief, and as being one of your number for ordering the armies of this Commonwealth, yet our jealousies of him grow daily on your behalf, and as to a prosperous government of your affairs here. (The rest of the letter consists of ten heads of charges against Ludlow.) (See *Commons' Journals*, vii. 803.) *Signed.* [N. VIII., 83.]

Sir Arthur Hesilrige and Colonels Valentine Walton and Herbert Morley to Willia) Lenthall.

1659, December 25. Portsmouth.—" We are glad to hear Colonel Okey, Colonel Alured, and Colonel Markham are commissionated by you and head seventeen troops of horse. We shall with all speed possible march to London to wait upon you, and in order to that we are disposing of some of your forces to come with us for your better security. We entreat " to hear " what your thoughts are concerning the time of the House sitting, humbly conceiving it necessary that letters should be immediately sent to summon the several members." *Signed. Seal.* [N. VIII., 85.]

Richard Hicks, Mayor, and others to Willia) Lenthall.

1659, December 26. Coventry.—Stating that they have that day proclaimed the Parliament to be the supreme authority of this nation, and requiring the peaceable subjection of all persons thereunto. They have also sent to Colonel Hawkesworth at Warwick to do the same, who answered he would secure the garrison within a few hours. *Signed. Seal.* [N. VIII., 86.]

Thoas Basnet and others, Commissioners of the Militia, to Willia) Lenthall.

1659, December 26. Coventry. — Declaring that they retain an unimpaired affection and goodwill to the Parliament, and that this city had declared themselves for the Parliament. (Printed in Grey, iv. Appendix, No. 72, p. 136.) *Signed.* [N. VIII., 87.]

Sir John Norwich, Colonel Francis Hacker, and others to Wlia) Lenthall.

1659, December 28. Coventry.—Stating their arrival there with a party of horse, the feeling of the adjacent counties in favour of the Parliament, and the securing of Warwick and Belvoir, and desiring directions about raising forces in the counties of Northampton, Warwick, Leicester, Rutland, Lincoln, Stafford and Derby. (Printed in Grey, iv., Appendix, No. 73, p. 137.) (See *Commons' Journals*, vii. 801.) *Signed. Seal.* [N. VIII., 58.]

Robert Jermy to Willia) Lenthall.

Same date. Norwich.—Declaring that during the late interruption he had been up only to preserve the peace of the county, and declaring his readiness to obey the commands of the Parliament. (Printed in Grey, iv., Appendix, No. 76, p. 139.) *Seal.* [N. VIII., 89.]

WILLIA⁊ CHARLTON and others to WILLIA⁊ LENTHALL.

Same date. Bristol.—Stating that three companies of Sir Brice Cockrain's regiment there, and also the Mayor, Aldermen and Sheriffs had declared for the Parliament. (Printed in Grey, iv., Appendix, No. 74, p. 138.) *Signed. Seal.* [N. VIII. 90.]

Colonel EDWARD SAL⁊ON to WILLIA⁊ CURRER, Mercer in Lombard Street.

1659, December 28. Newcastle.— " The officers here seem to be unanimous, and very courageous. . . . Yesterday they met at a general council to seek the Lord for direction, and this day they met again, and have resolved to march southwards, and if the Lord do but show them their way, I do verily believe they will venture their all in doing that that may tend to his glory and his people's good." (See *Commons' Journals,* vii. 802.) *Seal.* [N. VIII., 91.]

JA⁊[ES] STE[PHENS] to WILLIA⁊ LENTHALL.

1659, December 28. Bath.—"We were so overjoyed with the Parliament's restoration and sitting, it makes us like men that dream. . . The town of Taunton and this city of Bath make very large expressions of their joy, and great content, as well by ringing their bells, and bonfires as in all other outward demonstrations." *Seal.* [N. VIII., 92.]

JOHN EBBESDON, Mayor, and others, to WILLIA⁊ LENTHALL.

1659, December 30. Lyme Regis.—(The substance appears from *Commons' Journals,* vii. 801.) *Signed.* [N. VIII., 93.]

Colonel THO⁊AS CRO⁊PTON to WILLIA⁊ LENTHALL.

1659, December 31. Stafford.—Excusing himself from attending the House being in a course of physic, and stating that since November 3rd he had been there with his regiment of foot, and troop of horse, having been commanded thither, as he confesses, by the late powers for the safety of the country against the common enemy, and that as soon as his troops " understood that the Parliament was sitting they all unanimously made great acclamations of joy, and said they would live and die under your command." (Printed in Grey, iv. Appendix, No. 77, p. 140.) (See *Commons' Journals,* vii. 801.) *Seal.* [N. VIII., 94.]

ROBERT WOOD to WILLIA⁊ LENTHALL.

1659, December 31. Stone.—Am sent from the officers in Ireland with letters to the Commissioners for the Army, and the City of London. Could they have understood the Parliament's sitting again they would, I am sure, have directed their first joyful addresses to yourself. I left Ireland (December 25) in so good condition at the Parliament's service that the officers commanded me to tell the Commissioners for the Army that they could, if need be, send over 3,000 or 4,000 men for the service of the Parliament. *Seal.* [N. VIII., 95.]

Colonel BLACK⁊ORE to WILLIA⁊ LENTHALL.

1659, December 31. Exeter.—"As soon as I understood there was a likelihood of the restoring civil authority into the Parliament's hands

I visited the foot officers of the three companies of Sir Brice Cockrain's regiment that quarter here. . . and we agreed to draw the foot and horse together. . . and at the head of them, in the presence of 1,000 citizens, I declared our owning, and being for the Parliament's Government, and that we were unanimously resolved to obey all orders. . . from them, rejoicing that the Lord had once more placed amongst us the face and majesty of civil authority in them. Unto all which the soldiers gave most cheerful concurrence by their loud acclamations and reiterated hollowes, which being also attended with some small gratuity from the officers they were dismissed and all things in this place are in much quietness, and the bad blood which was growing between the citizens and soldiers much allayed." *Signed. Seal.* [N. VIII., 96.]

EDMUND HOYLE and others of the foot regiment lately come from Ireland to WILLIAM LENTHALL.

1659, December 31. Beadle in Yorkshire.—" This day the regiment of foot that came lately out of Ireland unanimously declared. . . . for the restoring of the Parliament of England lately interrupted. And we are now upon our march both day and night until we are clear of the quarters of the rest of the forces. The Irish Horse and we have quartered at a distance of late by which means we have had no conferences with them, but we daily expect to hear of their declaring the same also. . . *Postscript.*—We direct our present march towards Tadcaster, and thereabouts do intend to remain until we receive your orders. This day about thirty of the Life Guards came in to us having likewise declared for Parliament." (See *Commons' Journals,* vii. 803.] *Signed. Seal.* [N. VIII., 106.]

Colonel GEORGE PLEY to WILLIAM LENTHALL.

1659, December 31. Portland Castle.—As I had no order of Parliament for raising the company which in Sir George Booth's insurrection I had commission to raise for the security of Weymouth, and finding the town peaceably inclined I kept myself to my charge here. The town of Weymouth lying on a headland, and very open to any foreign enemy and these parts being much infested by Ostenders, and other enemies of the Commonwealth, I think it my duty to state the necessity, if Parliament think fit, that one foot company be continued there. ' Yesterday the Ostenders put on shore between Portland and Weymouth . . where they were out of the command of my ordnance. And though I did what possible to keep them off with small shot, yet by the help of their great guns which they continually fired on us, they got away a ship from the shore, for their shot lighting on a beach of small pebbles, and having no shelter for my men we could not stand to do that execution upon them, as otherwise I might. I am at present in want of powder." *Seal.* [N. VIII., 99.]

ROBERT WASHINGTON to Captain JOHN PICKERING.

1659, December 31. Leeds.—" Divers known Cavaliers did yesterday buy furniture of war for man and horse at Cutlery and saddlery shops, and the Cutler. . told me that one of them said they hoped to be 1,000 horse ere Monday night. Some of them as young Hodshan had persons at his house last night, strangers, which were supposed to be come out of the Country to rise with those here, and by the preparations which [some] of these made of boots, spurs, breast bands for their horses,

X X 2

swo[rd-]belts, holsters all against the evening it was very supposed they intended to go out this night about midnight to the place of rendezvous. One of Mr. Tod's people came to give me warning to secure my money and arms and said it was certain they would rise this night, and that Lord Fairfax is to head them and seemed sorry that he was to have so many Cavaliers in his party. Whether he head them or Buckingham you will hear shortly. One went in the night to York with my letter to Colonel Lilburne or the governor present. We fear their design is upon York."

I write this before day. *Seal.* [N. VIII., 97.]

Captain JOHN PICKERING to WILLIAM LENTHALL.

1659, December 31. 10 A.M. Hague Hall near Wakefield.—Concerning the seizure of muskets and ammunition from the Skipton carriers, and sundry rumours of an intended rising under Lord Fairfax and the Duke of Buckingham, and enclosing the last. (Printed in Grey, iv., Appendix, No. 76, p. 139.) *Seal.* [N. VIII., 98.]

Captain DANIELL NICOLL, and others the officers of two Companies in Colonel John Briscoe's regiment to WILLIAM LENTHALL.

1659[-60], January 2. Chester.—We, who after the defeat of the enemy at Northwich and the reducing of Chirke Castle were ordered to lie at Chester, declare that we shall yield all due obedience to the Parliament as the supreme authority of this Commonwealth. *Signed. Seal.* [N. VIII., 101.]

Colonel THOMAS WAITE to WILLIAM LENTHALL.

1659[-60], January 2.—Expressing his joy at the restoration of the Parliament. *Seal.* [N. VIII., 102.]

Captain SAMUEL WISE and other the officers of his company in Colonel John Briscoe's regiment to WILLIAM LENTHALL.

1659[-60], January 3. Ripon.—We, who marched from Yarmouth to the encounter at Northwich and from thence were commanded to the North, declare our affections and promise our obedience to the Parliament. *Signed. Seal.* [N. VIII., 103.]

DANIELL JACKSON, Chaplain to Colonel Roger Sawry's regiment, to WILLIAM LENTHALL.

1659[-60], January 3. Ayr.—Desiring of the Lord to pardon him for having through ignorance and rashness given concurrence to those who had been lately against the Parliament. (Printed in Grey, iv., Appendix, No. 71, p. 135.) *Seal.* [N. VIII., 104.]

The COMMISSIONERS OF THE MILITIA FOR THE COUNTY AND CITY OF WORCESTER to WILLIAM LENTHALL.

1659[-60], January 3. Worcester College.—Expressing their joy at the restoration of the Parliament, and promising obedience to the same. *Signed. Seal.* [N. VIII., 105.]

JOHN TOPPING and others to WILLIAM LENTHALL.

1659[-60], January 5. Tynemouth Castle.—Stating that the officers of the garrison had on the 2nd and the privates and noncommissioned officers on the 3rd unanimously declared for the Parliament. *Signed. Seal.* [N. VIII., 107.]

SIR HARDRES WALLER to "his kinsman" [WILLIAƆ LENTHALL].

1659[-60], January 6. Dublin.—" When you were all lost as to the eyes of men there came a Spirit upon the people even as that in the wheel, which turned about universally the whole people here save a very few, as if there had been an enchantment in the word Parliament as those that once cried out ' Great is Diana of the Ephesians,' which went throughout the land, so that in a few days the Army, ministry, churches and the whole country save a very few owned the undertaking of a few poor little ones so that I may say a nation was born in a day, and the strong fort of Enniskillen sent me a surrender this night, and we have now no visible opposition, but at Duncannon fort, which is in an obscure nook that can defend nothing but itself, and is easily hindred from doing that. And nothing now hinders the completing of this work but the late arrival of Lieutenant-General Ludlow in this harbour of Dublin, to whom we applied ourselves earnestly that he would not land until . . the Parliament . . should make their pleasure known, that they were satisfied with his actings in England because of his late continuance and acting with that army which we looked upon as the Parliament's enemies . . . seeing clearly that his landing must unavoidably put all into blood, there being so general a protestation of the military and civil interest of the nation against his proceedings, which will further appear in a charge preparing both against himself and the Commissioners of Parliament, which is sent over to be tendered to the view of the House, and therefore I hope his prudence and conscience will direct his return for England, at least until . . . the pleasure of the Parliament be known, though we apprehend he may be gone towards Munster, expecting there a party to join with him. . . . The army have with great willingness and freedom owned me and to be under my conduct and command for the Parliament's service wherein this hath been and I hope shall be ever my end and aim to have them served by such officers who shall never dare to pull out a Parliament or pull in a single person" . . I recommend to you the bearers of this. *Signed.* [N. VIII., 108.]

W. BOTTERELL and others to WILLIAƆ LENTHALL.

1659[-60], January 6. Ludlow Castle.—I received in July last a commission by order of Parliament from the Council of State to raise 100 soldiers and take possession of Ludlow Castle which I did. We rejoice at your restoration. We request that provision be made for our considerable arrears. *Signed. Seal.* [N. VIII., 109a.]

The NON-COƆƆISSIONED OFFICERS and PRIVATES of the Garrison of CARLISLE to General MONCK.

1659[-60], January 9.—Declaring their resolution to stand by the Parliament, stating that they had secured their officers the previous night, and asking him to send them officers. *Signed. Seal.* [N. VIII., 109b.]

ISAAC TULLIE, Mayor, and others to General MONCK.

1659[-60], January 9. Carlisle.—Concerning the declaration of the garrison there for the Parliament, and asking that well affected persons might be appointed officers there. (Printed in Grey, iv. Appendix, No. 78, p. 141.) *Signed. Seal.* [N. VIII., 110.]

The COMMITTEE FOR THE NOMINATION OF JUDGES.

1659[-60], January 10, 14.—Order reporting the names of persons nominated. · (Printed in *Commons' Journals*, vii. 814.) [N. XVI., 162.]

The PARLIAMENT.

1659[-60], January 11.—Order concerning the report about nominating judges. (Printed in *Commons' Journals*, vii. 807.) [N. XVI., 163.]

Colonel GEORGE PLEY to WILLIAM LENTHALL.

1659[-60], January 11. Portland Castle. — Complaining that Mr. Hurst had been appointed Governor in his place, and justifying his conduct in the late troubles. *Seal.* [N. VIII., 111.]

General GEORGE MONCK to WILLIAM LENTHALL.

1659[-60], January 12. York.—Concerning the modelling of various regiments, specially of those lately under Colonel Lambert's command. (Printed in Grey, iv., Appendix, No. 69, p. 111.) [N. VIII., 112.]

ELIAS PALMER and others the Officers of the Ordnance to Major RICHARD LEWIN.

1659[-60], January 13.—Desiring him to return the arms formerly delivered to him for his Company in Colonel Thompson's regiment. (See *Commons' Journals*, vii. 813.) [N. VIII., 113.]

The COMMISSIONERS FOR THE ARMY.

1659[-60], January 14.—Order reporting concerning certain appointments. (Printed in *Commons' Journals*, vii. 814.) *Signed* "Arthur Hesilrige, Valentine Walton, Herbert Morley." [N. XVI., 164.]

[WILLIAM LENTHALL] to [General GEORGE MONCK].

1659[-60], January 16.—(The purport appears from *Commons' Journals*, vii. 813.) *Draft.* [N. XII., 270.]

General GEORGE MONCK to WILLIAM LENTHALL.

1659[-60], January 16. York.—Having thanked the Parliament for their favour expressed in his letter of the 7th, " In obedience to the Parliament's commands I am advancing towards London, and for the securing of Scotland I have sent thither a regiment of horse, and another of foot, which is all I can do at present. I had sent Colonel Clarke, but that I had no money to spare them; if they were furnished they might march presently for Scotland. I have appointed Major-General Morgan to stay here for the present till things are better settled, and if you please to supply us with monies, and send orders to him about it he will give Colonel Clarke orders for the march of his regiment thither. There is 1,800*l.* lies in the hands of Mr. John Ince, Deputy to the Treasurers at War, they are indebted for their quarters and I think as much more, so it would serve their turn to enable them to march and pay their quarters, till they have a further supply ; but if you cannot do any more, I desire that 1,800*l.* may be ordered to be paid out by Major-General Morgan's warrant to the forces here for taking them off from free quarter. I have ordered Colonel Fairfax's regiment to lie at York and put one of the companies of that regiment into Clifford's Tower. I am marching myself with four regiments of horse and three of foot towards you with what expedition I may. I have put the command of the Lord Lambert's late regiment of horse into Colonel Bethel's hands. He is an honest and faithful man, and was faithful and active for your interest in appearing for you with the Lord Fairfax. I have put out all the disaffected officers from the head of their troops and dismissed them, and I shall humbly desire that Commissions may be speedily granted for that regiment according to the list sent to your Commissioners for the government of the army, and that they may be sent to Major-General Morgan, and then, I think, all these parts will be well fixed for your service so far as I have gone yet. I could heartily wish the Militia of these parts were settled. I return you thanks for your being mindful of Colonel Saunders, Colonel Lytcott and Major Barton." *Seal.* [N. VIII., 114.]

[Colonel WILLIAM LOCKHART] to WILLIAM LENTHALL.

1659[-60], January 17. Dunkirk.—Recommending for promotion Captains Devereux and Ely. *Signature torn off.* [N. VIII., 115.]

ROBERT THOMSON and FRANCIS WILLOUGHBY to the COUNCIL OF STATE.

1659[-60], January 23. Navy Office.—"The Petty Warrant victuallers have, as they inform us, run out so much money that they are unable to proceed any further without a supply, so that we expect their total declining the service every day. We have been necessitated to send some provisions out of the sea stores to the Petty Warrant victuallers lest the seamen, for want of victuals, might have been put upon extravagancies. It is the same case in relation to the whole action of victualling for that the respective persons concerned herein do daily importune for supplies of money . . . Such is the condition of all your stores in reference to timber, plank, cordage, &c. in [the respective yards, that in case of any sudden emergency for speeding away the fleet, we fear it could not possibly be accomplished." (See *Commons' Journals*, vii. 830.) *Signed.* [N. VIII., 119.]

The PARLIAMENT.

1659-60, January 23.—Declaration. (Printed in *King's Pamphlets*, E. 1013, No. 24.) *Draft* with Amendments. (See *Commons' Journals*, vii. 819.) [N. XVI., 165.]

ROBERT THOMSON and FRANCIS WILLOUGHBY to the COUNCIL OF STATE.

1659[-60], January 25. Navy Office.—Referring to their former report of the 23rd concerning the victualling of the Navy, stating that they since heard from Plymouth that the contractors for victualling there had refused to furnish more provisions because the bills of exchange formerly drawn by them on the Navy Office were unpaid, and desiring that the customs and excise and the remains of the last assessment undisposed of in the Western parts be appropriated to the service of the Navy. (See *Commons' Journals*, vii. 830.) *Signed.* [N. VIII., 116.]

Robert Thomson and Francis Willoughby to the Council of
State.

1659[-60], January 27. Victualling Office.—Enclosing a letter
from Dennis Ganden with whom they had made a contract in September
last for victualling 4,000 men at the outports named for six months and
to deliver all the butter and cheese the State should require in London,
Portsmouth and Plymouth for this present year, by which the Council
will perceive that for want of money according to contract he is wholly·
disenabled to proceed any further therein and in no capacity to deliver
any more provisions to the fleet. *Signed.* *Enclosed :*

i. A copy of Mr. Gauden's letter.

ii. Order of the Council of State that the three letters of January
23rd, 25th, and 27th be reported to the House. (See *Commons'*
Journals, vii. 830.) [N. VIII., 120.]

Thomas Hill and others to William Lenthall.

1659[-60], January 30. Shrewsbury Castle.—Upon the 27th this
Castle was to be betrayed by a contracted party of Cavaliers within this
town as also of several persons out of the country. I had notice of the
business about 12 o'clock on Friday last in part, and making some preparation in the Castle for resistance, a soldier of our Company divulged
the business to a serjeant, which I then employed in strengthening the
lines with materials fit for their reception. I then privately strengthened
the garrison with our men that were without, and with a commanded
party marched out that night and apprehended some of those concerned
in the plot, whom I have sent to our Governor from whom you will
receive them. I desire the sense of the House as to the disposal of the
persons now in custody. *Signed. Seal.* [N. VIII., 117.]

The Officers and Soldiers of the five companies of Colonel Richard
Mosse's regiment now in the North to [the Parliament].

[1659–60, January.]—Stating that on the interruption of the 13th
of October last they had marched to Westminster by order from Sir
Arthur Hazelrigg, Colonel Morley, and Colonel Walton, and then remained
till dismissed by the Council of State, and trusting that Parliament would
judge them according to the integrity of their hearts, they promising
all faithful obedience for the future. *Signed.* [N. VIII., 100.]

Sir Henry Ingoldsby to William Lenthall.

1659[-60], February 1. Dublin.—Concerning the state of the army
there, and the appointment to commands of obedient and faithful
servants to the Parliament. (Printed in Grey, iv., Appendix, No. 79,
p. 142.) *Seal.* [N. VIII., 118.]

List of Commissioners and Judges for Scotland appointed by General
Monck.

1659[-60], February 6.—(See *Commons' Journals*, vii. 835.) *Signed*
" George Monck." [N. XXI., 136.]

George Moody, Alderman, to William Lenthall.

1659[-60], February 8. Bury St. Edmunds.—Enclosing a declaration found posted that morning, being market day, on the market cross.
[N. VIII., 121.]

Cornelius Holland to William Lenthall.

1659[-60], February 20. Creslowe.—Desiring to be excused attending the House on that day as ordered, on account of his infirmities. *Signed. Seal.* [N. VIII., 122.]

John Legh, Sheriff, to William Lenthall.

1659[-60], February 25. Boothes in Cheshire. — Certifying in obedience to his letter of the 21st (See *Commons' Journals*, vii. 841) that in the year 1648, the two knights for the shire were Sir William Brereton and Sir George Booth, and the members for the city William Edwards and John Ratcliff; that William Edwards was in Ireland, and that he had given notice to John Ratcliff to attend. *Seal.* [N. VIII., 123.]

The Council of State.

1659[-60], March 5.—Proceedings in the case of Colonel John Lambert. (Printed in *Commons' Journals*, vii. 864.) [N. XVI., 166.]

John Maudit to "Right Honourable Patriots and Christian Brethren" [the Parliament].

1659[-60], March 12. Penshurst in Kent. — Arguing, with many quotations from Scripture, against a sudden dissolution. (Printed in Grey, iv. Appendix, No. 70, p. 128.) [N. VIII., 125.]

John Owen, Stationer, to the Parliament.

[1659-60, March 15.] — Petition praying for payment for the stationery supplied by him since the previous May. (See *Commons' Journals*, vii. 878.) *Signed.* [N. XXII., 124.]

J. S., a relative of General Monck, to the King.

[1660, May 3.]—Address of congratulation. (*Copy.* Original is in the State Papers. See *State Papers, Domestic*, p. 5. Also printed in Grey, iv., Appendix, No. 44, p. 74.) [N. XVI., 119.]

The Committee of Discoveries

1660, May 19.—Report. (Printed in *Commons' Journals*, viii. 37.) [N. XVI., 168.]

William Lenthall to Sir Harbottle Grimston, Speaker.

[1660, June.]—Desiring him to offer to the House statements showing that his gains when Speaker were much less than was supposed. (Printed in Grey, iv., Appendix, No. 68, p. 125.) (See *Commons' Journals*, viii. 61.) *Seal.* [N. VIII., 127.]

Sir William Walter to Sir Thomas Chamberlaine, at Wickham.

1660[-1], January 2. Sarsdon.—Stating that lately in London the Lord Lieutenant of the County had blamed him for the state of the Militia, that he had sent out warrants to summon all the enrolled of Chadling Hundred to meet at Chipping Norton on Friday the 4th, and desiring Sir Thomas to attend as the nearest Deputy Lieutenant. [N. VIII., 126.]

Account.

[In or after 1660.]—Showing what part of the Adventurers' money raised for Ireland was used against the King, and what was employed in Ireland. "So that there was sent into Ireland . . . which the

rebels at Westminster seemed so much concerned for, but 154,003*l*.0*s*.9*d*."
In parts illegible. [N. XXI., 7.]

Presentment of the GRAND JURY OF THE COUNTY OF NORTHAMPTON.

[1683.]—Alluding to the late plot against the King and his brother (the Rye House plot), and to the seditious address presented by the disaffected of the County at the last election, which desired a change in the succession to the Crown, and suggesting that all ill affected persons to Government may give security for the peace, and particularly Ralph Mountague, Esq. *Copy.* [N. XV., 180.]

FRAGMENT IN DUTCH.

N. D.—(Consists only of 12 lines. The names of the Prince of Wales and General Cromwell occur in it.) [N. XVI., 169.]

PAPER.

N. D.—Stating in detail the authority of the governor of a garrison. In all military affairs he has the sole control independently of the Committee. If he be not thought competent complaint should be made to the General. [N. XXI., 129.]

Titles of Four ACTS OF PARLIAMENT.

N. D.—The first is for the speedy and effectual reducing of the rebels in Ireland, the others are amending Acts. [N. XXI., 18.]

ORDINANCE.

N. D.—Confirming orders made by the House of Commons or by Committees of Parliament concerning Papists' and Delinquents' Estates without the concurrence of the House of Lords, but declaring that such concurrence should be necessary in future. [N. XV., 171.]

A List of GENTLEMEN OF CUMBERLAND.

N. D.—[N. XV., unnumbered, preceding 183.]

——— to ———.

N. D.—" I have delivered the hopes you have given me of the speedy raising of a fortnight's pay to those troops so confidently that from this time I shall begin to punish all the disorders and violences committed by them as if they had shirts or boots. I conjure you therefore humbly to move the House on my behalf to hasten the letters after me, or I shall lose my reputation with the army and they will keep theirs with the country. I desire also very earnestly that the Gentlemen of the Counties through which I march may have order to meet me upon my march to assist me in gathering provisions of all kinds necessary to the troops, and to advise with me of securing the country from the Rebels' forces, and easing it from our own as much as may consist with the preservation of those forces committed to my charge, and I shall endeavour to give" a becoming "account to the House of my zeal to the King's service and respect to their orders." *Copy.* [N. XII., 99.]

FRAGMENT.

N. D.—Entitled " This concerns the present Government in England, who should have long since lifted up their heads according to the word of God, *Luc.* 21, and in their consciences considered the day of the Lord. 1 *Thess.* 5; *Apocal.* 3, 16, 17, 18, 22; *Dan.* 7, 12." [N. XVI., unnumbered between 165 and 166.]

Supplement.

Captain JOHN HOTHAM to the EARL OF NEWCASTLE.

1642[-3], February 11. Cawood.—" I am very sorry that you should have the least occasion to thinke that I am not mindfull of that freindship which I shall ever soe valew. I make noe question, but you will still honor me with your good opinion, untill you finde I doe some act unworthy of itt, which I know you never shall. I should thinke it happines enough to me and my posterity that any act of mine might prove an advantage to his Majestie and a settlement to this distracted kingdome, and whatsoever ill hap I have had to be scandald with his Majestic I hope to make itt appeare that his honor and safety are as deare and pretious to me, as to those that have made far greater braggs. For Sir Ralph Hopton's miracles or Sir Hugh Cholmley's defeat, they are noe motives to me. I should as soone doe what I thinke is fitt for an honest man to doe after my Lord of Essex had gott a victory as before. I confesse I pin my faith upon noe man's sleeve, nor will I follow any man's courses, if I be not satisfied that they sute with honor and justice. I hope to see the endevors of honest men prevayle soe far, now that the propositions are gone to the King, that wee shall once agayne see truth and peace in our dayes, and I wish with all my hart that which side soever will not condiscend to wave trifles for the settlement of Church and State that his owne side may leave him. For my owne part rather then be a slave to etheir I would live of bread and water in another kingdome. I am of your opinion if we agree not wee shall trouble one another to little purpose. But that I was turnd the wandering Jew you had heard before this from " me. *Seal.* [N. II., 156.]

The SAME to the SAME.

1642[-3], February 12. Cawood.—" I am glad for the prisonniers' sake that the time is soe neere. I make noe question but every man will contribute his endevors to a worke of soe great charity. All things promised shall be really performed by " me. *Seal.* [N. II., 157.]

The SAME to the SAME.

Same date and place.—" You are pleased still to increase the obligation of him that was before as much a servant to your person and worth as ever any freind you had in the world, and truly itt is a great comfort to me in the middest of these mighty disturbances, which every private and the publicke groanes under, that I have soe noble a freind to rely on in these great exigencies of the Commonwealth. I know your Lordship's quality estate and good affection in the country where you have lived may make you more happy than anything att Court can, although I well know your Lordship's great interest there. The cause is playne why those Cesars would fall into the East Riding more then into the West, because they thinke there will be fewer blowes then in the West, for there you shall constantly have their advice to fall on. I know them of old, your Lordship's respects to me is noe lesse for that, but I would I could meet with a knot of them single to make sport. You may remember Leeds and the Commaunder in Chief." [N. II., 158.]

The LORDS JUSTICES and COUNCIL OF IRELAND to the EARL OF ORMONDE,

1641, November 2.—(The substance is in Carte, *Life of Ormonde*, i. 193. The original is probably in the Carte papers.) [N. XI., 60.]

[Wᴵᴸᴸᴵᴬᴺ Lᴇɴᴛʜᴀʟʟ.] to [Sɪʀ Tʜᴏᴍᴀs Gᴏᴡᴇʀ.]

[1641–2, March 16.]—(Printed in *King's Pamphlets*, E. 140, number 11.) [N. XI., 79.]

Wᴀʟᴛᴇʀ Wʀᴏᴛᴛᴇsʟᴇʏ to Sɪʀ Sᴀᴍᴘsᴏɴ Eᴠᴇʀs.

1642, April 20. Wrottesley.—Enclosing a particular of the conduct of Mr. Thomas Leveson, and desiring him to move the House for a *Nc Exeat Regnum*, "that the House may be acquainted with his carriages before he goes." *Enclosed :*

The said Particular.

1642, April 9.—"The said day Mr. Thomas Leveson sent . . . to John Tanner, . . an armourer in Wolverhampton to demand his horseman's arms, who gave them answer he was not to deliver them without command from the Deputy-Lieutenants. . . . Mr. Leveson" then "came himself in person . . . to the said John Tanner's shop, and spoke these words, 'Sirrah! why did you not send me my armes.'? John Tanner submissively replied with his hat in his hand . . . that he was not to deliver them without order from the Deputy-Lieutenants, and therefore wished him not to take it ill. Whereupon Mr. Leveson asked, 'who were Deputy-Lieutenants?' to which John Tanner told him, Mr. Crompton and Mr. Wrottesley and others ; and thereupon Mr. Leveson in a violent passion said that Mr. Wrottesley was a fool and a knave, and he, meaning the said John Tanner, was a stinking rogue, and he would whip him and have him set by the heels ; and with those words with a cane which he had in his hand stroke him two or three blows, one whereof hit him on the head and made a great knob in the skin thereof." (See *Commons' Journals*, ii. 554.) [N. XI., 87.]

Sɪʀ Hᴜɢʜ Cʜᴏʟᴍʟᴇʏ, Sɪʀ Pʜɪʟɪᴘ Sᴛᴀᴘɪʟᴛᴏɴ, and Sɪʀ Hᴇɴʀʏ
Cʜᴏʟᴍʟᴇʏ, to Wɪʟʟɪᴀᴺ Lᴇɴᴛʜᴀʟʟ.

1642, June 13. York.—(Identical *mutatis mutandis* with the letter to the Speaker of the House of Peers, printed in *Lords' Journals*, v. 138.) [N. XI., 94.]

Sɪʀ Nɪᴄʜᴏʟᴀs Lᴏғᴛᴜs to Rᴏʙᴇʀᴛ Rᴇʏɴᴏʟᴅs.

1642, September 16. Dublin.—I find all things here in a miserable condition. All the soldiers are wasted away with sickness, death, and slaughter; all the provisions of powder, match, and ammunition, are spent. If the enemy were to know our weakness, we should hardly be able to hold out for six weeks. Unless some governor be sent having the countenance of the state in England, all things will fall into lamentable confusion. The army is so weak that it cannot do any service or go abroad ten miles from the city. What is done in the provinces of Munster, Ulster, and Connaught, we cannot learn. The rebels here rejoice in the distractions of England. They have divers agents in England, from whom they expect great comfort. If the 28,000*l.* designed to be sent hither do not come, we shall have this small army in a confusion of mutiny. I wish I were out of the kingdom before they hear of the stay of it. I wish that the Parliament had sent a committee to Dublin, as I desired. [N. XI., 131.]

Isaac Pennington, Lord Mayor of London, to William Lenthall.

1643, March 27.—Concerning the commitment of Sir Kenelm Digby. (See *Commons' Journals*, iii. 22.) [N. XI., 200.]

Sir John Hotham to William Lenthall.

1643, April 1. Hull.—(The substance appears from *Commons' Journals*, iii. 27.) [N. XI., 208.]

Captain John Hotham to the Earl of Newcastle.

1643, April 1. Beverley.—"I am very sorry you should ever harbour such an opinion of me, as to think that any motive whatsoever could ever move me to betray the public trust I have undertaken, unless they had unquestionably fallen from principles of honour and honesty, I could never have satisfied myself but I should have been the scorn and byeword of every boy in the street. . . . My particular affection to your person was a motive to me to be glad to serve you if a way might be found out to do it as befitted a gentleman, otherwise I will not serve the greatest Emperor, although reward and punishment were proposed in the highest measure, and therefore for an end of the treaty as you please. I shall speak no more of it at all ; but now to give you a taste that all is not as you think at Court I shall freely tell you this, that within this four days some very near her Majesty spoke such words of contempt and disgrace of you as truly for my part I could not hear them repeated with patience, and you will plainly see if they dare venture it, you will have a successor. This . . is not fiction, and further such offers of grace and favour and honour have been made within this few days to your servants here with a very great under-valuing of you as may be you will not believe ; but it shall not be said that an answer shall be returned to any of them. . . I speak not this for myself, I can shift in any fortune, but for the great esteem I have of your worth, that you be not abused and ungratefully used by the malice of your enemies that envy your virtues. . . . *Postscript.*—For the Lincolnshire business you know my near relations there, and I confess, at the instance of such friends as I could not deny, and with great importunity, made me seem content they should use my name, which they persuaded themselves would do their business good, stand-ing but then in a reasonable condition." [N. XI., 209.]

The Same to the Same.

1643, April 3. Beverley.—" I received your two letters, and for my promise that you write of I believe that I might write some such thing, and I am in the same mind still that I should be glad of an opportunity to serve his Majesty, but it must be such a one as not to bring upon me the odious name of knavery ; but now for the particular you write of, upon your engagement, which I confess I trust above all, that it shall be made use of as to your private, I shall give you all the particulars. The words were these, 'that you were a sweet General, lay in bed until eleven o'clock and combed till 12, then came to the Queen, and so the work was done, and that General King did all the business.' They were spoken by my Lady Cornwallis in the hearing of Mr. Portington, a fellow cunning enough ; and this to my father and another gentleman with many other words of undervaluing, which he said were spoken by others ; for the great offers that were made, they came from my Lord Goring, the instrument Mr. George Butler, and it was offered that he should meet my father in any place upon his word, and strange things to be really performed. The great esteem that I have of your private friendship leads me to do this, and not anything of the public; and if you think the friendship of a gentleman worth your acceptance you shall have it with as much affection and integrity to your particular as you can expect, and I shall be faithful to you, whatsoever become of the public, and for their Court tricks I value them not, as never intending to be within the reach of them, God saying Amen; for I have taken such course as if the times be bad to me my wife and children have to put meat in their mouths, and if I live I shall shark for meat and drink, and if I be knockt in the head the care is taken, I need not a winter jerkin. For attending you I doubt I cannot, Sir Hugh Cholmeley's business hath drawn such a jealousy upon me and our people talk at large. . . You can expect nothing at Court, truly the women rule all, and what certainty can be hoped from them he that knows them may easily guess ; strengthen yourself with such friends as will not forsake you upon every   of the Court   . Although I am not worthy to advise you, this course all wise men have taken. You have now done great service, that will be forgotten when they think they can shift without you." *Blanks in transcript.* [N. XI., 210.]

The KENTISH COMMITTEE to WILLIAM LENTHALL.

1643, April 4, 5, 5. Rochester.—Concerning the apprehension of Sir H. Compton; the tumult at the election of overseers at Dartford raised by one Summers, a brewer; and the bad attendance of Deputy-Lieutenants who were members of the House. (For all three see *Commons' Journals,* iii. 31, 33, 31.)   [N. XI., 211, 212, 213.]

The BAILIFFS OF YARMOUTH to MILES CORBETT.

1643, April 6.—Enclosing the information of a Scotchman from Ostend concerning great forces prepared at Dunkirk to invade England, supposed to be intended for either Yarmouth or Burlington. [N. XI., 214.]

The KENTISH COMMITTEE to WILLIAM LENTHALL.

1643, April 6. Rochester.—Again desiring that Sir Edward Hales and other gentlemen be commanded to attend their future meetings. [N. XI., 215.]

PETER SEALE, Mayor, and others, to WILLIAM LENTHALL.

1643, April 10. Southampton.—(The effect appears from *Commons' Journals,* iii. 42.)   [N. XI., 217.]

Captain JOHN HOTHAM to the EARL OF NEWCASTLE.

1643, April 14. Lincoln.—" It is a part of my unhappiness that I am necessitated by my employment to be so far distant from you, and not to hear of your well-being by a line or two ; I have not been idle since you writt last to do his Majesty and your Lordship the best service I could, although to bring that about I was glad to go seemingly the contrary. I have since I came into this town dealt with some of my friends that they would not be so violent against his Majesty's service, and was bold to promise them a pardon if they would retire and give way that this country might be wholly at his devotion, the gentlemen are so considerable that of my knowledge, if they desist, there shall not be a man here to hold up his hand against his Majesty ; I was so

earnest with them that I am confident it will be done, if your Lordship
will be pleased to return me an assurance that they shall have his
Majesty's favour and pardon. The gentlemen are Sir Christopher
Wray and Sir Edward Ayscough, men as considerable as any in the
North, and for myself, your interest in me must wholly guide me. I
shall submit to such a course as you shall think fit for him that you
were pleased to name your friend; and . . when this is done I hope
it will appear, that none hath done that great considerable service as
you have done, and I doubt not but his Majesty's grace and favour will
be on you accordingly. . ." [N. XI., 220.]

The EARL of STAᴺFORD to the SPEAKER OF THE HOUSE OF PEERS,
pro tempore.

1643, April 15. Exeter.—"The last week during our cessation I
went to Bristol, where I was in hopes to have found Sir William
Waller, but he was then employed upon very good service, and could
not have leisure to give me a meeting; so in my return back to this
place I visited Bridgewater and Taunton . . . where I have placed
some few men to garrison there; and I have given order to make some
works in both places, that in short time I trust in God I shall secure
those places from all danger. From thence I went to Barnstaple,
Bideford, and Appledore, and those places likewise I have taken care
of, and doubt not but by God's blessing to prevent by those works and
the good affection of the inhabitants . . . all invasions whatsoever
 . . . either by sea or land. I intended to have come thence as upon
Monday last, but meeting with some intelligence from Wales I stayed
one day more, I hope to very good purpose, if it shall please God to
send favourable winds, for I dispatched out two small barques with 50
musketeers in each, and made ready for the next day three good ships
all well manned, and so gave them my commission to ply to and again
upon the Severn Sea, for I was informed from very honest men that
came from Wales, that the Earl of Worcester with his whole family
were come down in very great haste to . . Swansey, there intending
to take shipping, for one of the revolted ships of Bristol did then ride
in that harbour, so I gave command that those two small barques,
having in them above 14 oars to row if the wind served not, ...
should make an attempt to take that ship; if they failed, the other
three ships, being good able ships, might in time and by God's blessing
do the work. I have likewise placed both horse and foot upon all the
seacoast, that in case any of the Malignants that are fled into Wales
should attempt to return home . . they might be apprehended. The
later design hath wrought so good effect that some hath been already
taken. I shall give your Lordships a further account concerning our
new levies. Our men come in plentifully, especially the seamen, and
grow very conformable to our land commanders, being all of them
ambitious to be taught the land discipline, which is a thing very rare
amongst seamen. I believe that I shall have near 2,000 seamen in my
army, so that our foot I esteem shall be about 3,500 men besides our
towns well garrisoned, and about some eight troops of horse, of
dragoons none at all, for I have found that they serve their own turns
by plundering and robbing, but do little service or duty at all. It
pleased·God to favour us with the blessing of such a prosperous wind
that we received from Holland about 1,500 good muskets, of which we
stood in great need, so that now we shall be fitted to march into the
field within a few days, all other materials being in a good readiness, as
tents and ammunition. . . The gentlemen of the counties of Devon

and Somerset take infinite pains and deserve a favourable acceptance from both Houses and the whole Kingdom. I shall not fail on my part to use . . my best endeavours to deserve the title of a faithful and painful labourer in this vineyard. *Postscript.*—Our Commissioners at Plymouth now upon the treaty are in expectation of 10 days more cessation, which in all our judgements may advantage us exceedingly, by reason our men understand no discipline as yet." [N. XI., 221.]

Arthur Dakins to the Deputy-Lieutenants of Essex.

1643, April 17. Watford.—Desiring them to take into their serious consideration what upon the general and earnest entreaty both of officers and soldiers I am to present by the bearer. On our march out of Essex by the directions of Lord Grey of Warke we, as far as we could, obeyed all his orders, and we are now quartered at Watford on the edge of Hertfordshire, out of which neither officer or soldier is willing to move, being out of the Association, without some special and authentic order, and such accommodation as may relieve them in their marches, and secure them from the enemy. They expect, and I doubt not, resolve with alacrity and courage suddenly to fall upon the enemy, but the want of the necessaries I shall propound is a main stop and hindrance to their better resolutions. First, the want of close waggons to transport and keep dry our ammunition, next a surgeon, to look to the hurt, maimed, or sick, as we have divers already, and have left some behind not able to travel for want of these conveniences, next an able and religious teacher to apply and administer comfort and courage to our soldiers. We want likewise a sutler, a quarter-master, a provost-marshal, and an armourer, but for these three last we shall not trouble you, because we have partly provided them already. A larger supply of ammunition is also required. [N. XI., 222.]

Captain John Hotham to the Earl of Newcastle.

1643, April 18. Lincoln.—" I received your letter and your safe conduct by my trumpet, but with them a message, that I must either come this day to you or not at all, and indeed the safe conduct is only until Wednesday night. I was very sorry to see myself put upon an impossibility, for it was 12 o'clock before the boy came, and then I had to acquaint those gentlemen with it, and ride 26 miles after, which could not be done in that time. . . If your occasions do at this time call you northward that I cannot for the present attend you, yet I doubt not but to make it appear when I have the honour to wait upon you that his Majesty's service here hath all that time by your means made a very large progress ; for I hope to gain my Lord Willoughby and all those that have here either power or reputation. One thing yesterday disadvantaged me much, a letter that I received from some gentlemen at Newark about the exchanging of prisoners, so full of pride and folly, and what is not in a gentleman, that those men of quality here said nothing in the whole business troubled them so much as joining with men of so great folly and little worth ; the letter I have sent you ; they had an answer sharp enough, and they will never be treated with again by any that understands himself." [N. XI., 223.]

The Kentish Committee to William Lenthall.

1643, April 19. Rochester.—" We find the weekly tax would go cheerfully on, were it not for some obstacles that must be removed. And although there be many branches, yet we find they all spring from one head, that is the Malignant Clergy, who both privately whisper and publickly speak against the unlawfulness of it, and so stagger the minds of their parishioners, for we find not much opposition, but where such are who are as malicious to this as the subscriptions. We shall humbly offer these two cures for this disease ; first when any such minister hath two livings, that one be sequestered and put in the hands of some man better affected, when but one, if he persist in instilling such principles into his ignorant parishioners he be also sequestered until these distrac-tions shall have an end. Then that where any shall refuse that some two or three in a parish so refusing be retuined up to the House to receive such punishment as will be a warning to others, for it will be a toil to any Collector to distrain for so many petty sums, and infinitely retard the payment which had need to be quickened." [N. XI., 224.]

WILLIAM LENTHALL to LORD GREY OF GROBY.

1643, April 20.—(The effect appears from *Commons' Journals*, iv. 52.) [N. XI., 225.]

SIR JOHN GELL and others to the HOUSE OF LORDS.

1643, April 20. Derby.—(The effect appears from *Lords' Journals*, vi. 16 ; and *Commons' Journals*, iii. 58.) [N. XI , 226.]

The COMMITTEE OF SUFFOLK to WILLIAM LENTHALL.

1643, April 20. Bottesdale.—Desiring that all former Committee-men for subsidies and taxes in the county might be added to the Com-mittee for sequestering the rents of Malignants and Recusants, and that the knights of the shire and other members for the county might be sent down. (See *Commons' Journals*, iii. 59.) [N. XI., 227.]

The EARL OF PEMBROKE, JOHN PYM, and others, to the EARL OF ESSEX.

1643, April 21.—Concerning the seizure of four horses by Cornet Corbett from Thomas Southol's stable, two being his own, and two belonging to Mr. De Valls, page of the backstairs to the Queen, both Frenchmen, on whose behalf the French Agent had interfered, and sug-gesting it would be fit to restore them, as the Parliament was likely to send some person into France, for which this act would be but an ill preparation. (See *Commons' Journals*, iii. 55, 75.) [N. XI., 228.]

WILLIAM PALMER, Mayor, and two Aldermen, to WILLIAM LENTHALL.

1643, April 21. Barnstaple.—Desiring authority to proceed with their fortifications and indemnity for any damage to private property they might thereby cause. (See *Commons' Journals*, iii. 63, 67 ; and *Lords' Journals*, vi. 27.) [N. XI., 229.]

SIR JOHN SELBY to WILLIAM LENTHALL.

1643, April 24. St. Cleers in East Kent.—Accusing Mr. Dixon, whom he is sending up. (The effect appears from *Commons' Journals*, iii. 58.) [N. XI., 234.]

EDMUND PRIDEAUX to WILLIAM LENTHALL.

1643, April 26, past 12 at night. Exeter.— . . . "Our intelli-gence came just as did from Keinton field, the rogues that ran away brought certain advice that all our army was routed, which put all the city of Exon into a great distraction ; some time after, others came that gave better hopes ; at last we received the certain intelligence. . . . The Major got as much honour by his honourable retreat from Lanceston, as by his victory at Okehampton. In his return he lost not one man, nor in the skirmish lost not any musket or any considerable thing, though he slew divers of the enemy in his retreat, and it is confest 100 were slain in the whole whereof Captain Basset of the isle of Scilly was one . . . and he that succeeded him in that command was also taken prisoner, and some others of quality were slain also. One of Chudleigh's field pieces being in danger in the retreat to be lost, and he being resolved to adventure his life rather than leave anyone behind him, and having given command to a prime officer to fetch him off, being danger in it he refused, then the Major himself did it, and had 500 shot at him, yet brought him away clear, drove the oxen himself that carried it and had no hurt. For the business at Okehampton, it was so full of discreet valour and resolution, as if the particulars were related it would be admired how it could be managed by so young a man. The enemy had 500 horse and dragoons and 5,000 foot having 57 colours as the prisoners confess, the work was done by 108 horse without any other help. The thing is almost incredible . . that 108 horse should . . . defeat 500 horse and dragoons and 5,000 foot, and yet it is most certain true it was done the last night in the night, and he had some advantage of ground. He hath taken some prisoners, three colours, Captain Digbie's standard, twelve drums, some hundreds of muskets and pikes and seven barrels of powder and many other things ; had his foot seconded him, or those horse not gone a plundering he had taken his ordnance and wholly defeated that army. . . . . . Chudleigh lost not one man . . had only two hurt. We have taken bags of letters, books of accounts, and other things, which will discover much of their wicked purposes. You will perceive in part what was intended . . by what was written from the King. . . . The truth for so much as is written is not to be doubted, for I have it from Major Chudleigh and the captains who are all come to . . . Exon this evening, and the enemy with his forces left, not run away nor slain, are returned into Cornwall. . . . r. The mariners and seamen, to say no worse, were a little too willing homewards, though Captain Chudleigh used them with all civil and winning respects. He hath much won the hearts of the soldiers, in fetching them off so bravely and safely in the retreat from Lanceston." [N. XI., 235.]

HENRY MARTEN to Mr. BAKER.

1643, May 2.—(Printed in *Commons' Journals*, iii. 68.) [N. XI., 241.]

SIR EDWARD AYSCOGHE and SIR CHRISTOPHER WRAY to WILLIAM LENTHALL.

1643, May 2. Lincoln.—" Necessity inforceth us still to let you know how much those forces with Colonel Cromwell are retarded, which long since were promised to our assistance. . . . 'Tis not fear makes us doubt the defence of this place, for by the great industry and care of Lieutenant-General Hotham it is now made considerable to any force but my Lord Newcastle's whole army." (For the effect of the rest see *Commons' Journals*, iii. 75.) [N. XI., 243.]

WILLIAM LENTHALL to Major-General CHUDLEIGH.

1643, May 2.—Thanking him and his officers for their services at Okehampton. [N. XI., 245.]

Robert Knollys to Henry Jermyn.

1643, May 3. The Hague.—" I have twice sent unto you, first by my man, whom I have now heard was unfortunately cast away at Hartlepool, the other . . . by way of Scotland. . . . Mr. Strickland is as busy as ever, he hath and continues his going to all the particular States as he did to those of Arnehem in order to their association to assist the Parliament. His information of the Prince of Orange's giving license for 22 Dunkirk ships hath been a great occasion of his being not so well entertained as formerly." [N. XI., 247.]

Captain John Hotham to the Earl of Newcastle.

1643, May 4. Lincoln.—" I am somewhat ashamed that I should make you believe more certainly than I doubt you will find in some gentlemen here. The truth is, they are divided ; some, upon the business of the South going high, are off again, others still the same men. I should desire your opinion what to do in it, for my Lord Willoughby hangs most off. I think you are mistaken in my father, for the reason of his standing a little aloof is, that he so infinitely wishes the peace of the kingdom, which he thinks the King's last answer tends not to, that I know it hath staggered him much, and my not having opportunity to speak with him since, and some other that do very ill offices in that place; but I hope to remedy all. There have been those ladies treating that you write of, and they were as well fitted with an answer of nothing, but there is another manner of treater there than they, and it was said from a good hand, that the Queen thought much you did not enough communicate with her and take her directions, but you were not yet to be displeased. . . . For myself I am as much your servant as ever, and twenty such businesses as Reading shall make no alteration, but these tickle people put me to my wits' end, yet there is hope to overcome the difficulty with a little patience, if his Majesty's affairs suffer not too much by it, it may do well yet. Our lieing still and not hasting Cromwell to join is, I am sure, some advantage ; for he is still kept to eat up the fat clergy at Peterborough, although my Lord of Essex hath writt often to the contrary to him. For what Sir Hugh Cholmeley says it is no matter, it is not the first time he hath scandall'd his friends, and then denied it. I confess I am in a very great strait in these businesses, your Lordship's wisdom can best give directions in it." [N. XI., 248.]

Captain John Hotham, Sir Edward Ayscoghe, and Sir Christopher Wray to William Lenthall.

1643, May 5. Lincoln.—" We cannot but hear that some to colour their own fears, others, that the blame should rather light upon others than themselves, have reported that we have not been so diligent to promote the public service in these parts as we ought to have been ; to vindicate ourselves . . . we have thought fit to give you a narrative of some particulars ; there hath not at any time this three weeks passed one day that we have not writt both to Colonel Cromwell, the Norfolk Gentlemen, and my Lord Grey to appoint a place of meeting, and we would march to them wheresoever it were ; their answer always was they would meet, but something of importance was first to be done in those countries they then were in, which hitherto hath been the cause that little is done, only the particular countries where we quarter put to a very great charge without benefit to the public. We have sent you here inclosed the last letter that came from Colonel Cromwell, that you may see we are in no fault. The Committee here is grown to two, all else at London or Hull, and so they may with great ease sit safe and talk of what they please of those actions and particulars they take up at second hand. We shall desire this justice, that those of this county may be sent down, and . . . some soldiers of knowledge with them, and they shall have all here surrendered into their hands to manage, and it shall be delivered to them in as good or better condition than it was yet in Lincolnshire." (See *Commons' Journals*, iii. 75.) [N. XI, 253.] *Enclosed:*

OLIVER CROMWELL to the LORDS AND GENTLEMEN, COMMITTEES AT LINCOLN.

1643, May 3.—(Printed in Carlyle, Letter IX., from the original in the Tanner MSS. A copy is N. XI., 246.)

SIR ANTHONY WELDON and others to WILLIAM LENTHALL.

1643, May 5. Dartford.—Desiring that those persons who hindered the subscriptions should be sent for and made examples of.

And

SIR ANTHONY WELDON to SIR HENRY HAYMOND and others.

[1643, May 7.] Sunday night.—Concerning Mr. Mathias Allen of Stone parish. (For both these, see *Commons' Journals*, iii. 74.) [N. XI., 252, 251.]

The EARL OF ESSEX to WILLIAM LENTHALL.

1643, May 8. Reading.—Concerning the seizure of horses in Hertfordshire by Captain Andrews by virtue of a warrant from himself, and the subsequent taking away of some of them from him by Sir Thomas Dacres and Mr. Barbor. (See *Commons' Journals*, iii. 101.) [N. XI., 249.]

WILLIAM LENTHALL to the COMMITTEE AT LINCOLN.

1643, May 9.—In reply to their letters of the 2nd and 5th stating that orders had already been given for sending down their Committee men about London, and sending powder to Lord Grey. " Colonel Cromwell is already advanced and by this time in your county with a considerable force, as it is informed. My Lord General hath sent to Sir John Gell and the Nottingham forces to draw all into a body with you." (See *Commons' Journals*, iii. 75.) [N.XI., 254.]

Colonel WALTER LONG to the COMMITTEE AT HABERDASHERS' HALL.

1643, May 9. Chelmsford.—Concerning a discovery of plate, &c. concealed in a secret vault at Sir Thomas Wiseman's, by some of his troop. (See *Commons' Journals*, iii. 79.) [N. XI., 255.]

EDWARD MARTIN to WILLIAM LENTHALL.

1643, May 9. Canterbury.—Desiring that the Receiver of Church Rates should pay directly to the Collectors of the weekly Assessment the sums assessed upon the Prebendaries. (See *Commons' Journals*, iii. 142.) [N. XI., 256.]

Five thousand SHIP-CARPENTERS to WILLIAM LENTHALL.

1643, May 9.—Petition, praying that their former petition might be considered and promising to pay his fees. (See *Commons' Journals*, iii. 79.) [N. XI., 257.]

RICHARD ALDWORTH, Mayor, and the ALDERMEN and COMMON COUNCIL MEN to the EARL OF ESSEX.

1643, May 12. Bristol.—Interceding for the persons sentenced to death for the late plot to surrender the city. [N. XI., 258.]

JOHN CLARKE to the EARL OF WARWICK.

1643, May [21-]31. Dunkirk.—Concerning frigates sailing with Irish Commissions. (The effect appears from *Commons' Journals*, iii. 99.) [N. XI., 266.]

The EARL OF ESSEX to WILLIAM LENTHALL.

1643, May 22. Reading.—Concerning Mr. Starkey's complaints. (The effect appears from *Commons' Journals*, iii. 104.) [N. XI., 264.]

Colonel HERBERT MORLEY to WILLIAM LENTHALL.

1643, May 23. Lewes.—Concerning the loan of 1,000*l.* by Mr. John Fagge, and a riot at West Hedly fair, when Ancient Streater was beating for volunteers, in which the Ancient was dangerously hurt, and the head of his drum beaten in, and enclosing a petition from divers well affected, who desired that a certain minister to be appointed in the place of the present one, and also sending some additional names for Committees. [N. XI., 263.]

The EARL OF MULGRAVE to the EARL OF MANCHESTER.

1643, May 29.—Kensington.—(The effect appears from *Lords' Journals*, iii. 70.) [N. XI., 265.]

THOMAS GURLYN, Mayor, and others to MILES CORBETT.

[1643, May.] King's Lynn.—As many gentlemen had lately crowded into the town, desiring power for the Mayor to examine any strangers now in the town or that might come thereafter, and also to deal with delinquents, should any come thither. (See *Commons' Journals*, iii. 76.) [N. XI., 250.]

WILLIAM LENTHALL to the EARL OF ESSEX.

1643, June [2.]—"Yours of the 1st of June touching the various reports of your stay at Causam (Caversham) being read in the House of Commons they have commanded me, in answer thereto, to let you know, that the great care and good affection, with which your Excellency hath constantly proceeded in the management of this weighty and public affair, doth so far supersede all vain reports and vulgar censures, that with them they can make no impression to impute the least unto your Excellency, and your letter rather gives them fresh cause of comfort and acknowledgement that your truly noble and most Christian resolution can freely pass such rumours as these without variation or discouragement which, as it is your Excellency's honour, so it cannot but produce God's glory and the Kingdom's peace." (See *Commons' Journals*, iii. 113.) [N. XI., 267.]

SIR ROBERT COOKE to WILLIAM LENTHALL.

1 6 43, June 2. Gloucester.—"The success of Sir William Waller's late design upon Worcester was not so prosperous as to hasten an account

especially the opportunity of sending it being wanting, yet not so ill as perhaps report may render it. Sir William, finding a necessity of drawing his forces from these parts, was desirous to have in as good condition as he might this county afflicted on the one side with the Worcester garrison, and the rather because it was impossible for him to march away with a convenient strength, unless he withdrew the garrison from Teuxbury, consisting with officers of near 1,000 horse and foot. In this regard he held it both necessary for this country and of great consequence to the main to attempt the taking in of Worcester; that so the works being slighted it might not remain a strength for the Parliament's enemies and give assurance to their chief body of retreat upon occasion of disaster. Upon Monday morning he presented his forces before it, all that day assaulted it, and especially at two gates, Sudbury and St. John's; the cannon played on both sides all day, the defence was obstinate, yet within less than four hours we had beaten the enemy out of all their outworks and gained the suburb, and lodged our musketeers at the very port, and were in as fair a way in so short a time of gaining the town as could be. But Sir William Brereton's forces not coming in according as was expected, and Sir William Waller being called away by no less than five packets that evening out of the West, exclaiming that all would be lost there, if he did not immediately advance that way; it was held necessary to rise to attend that service, as of greater importance. What their loss was we cannot certify, but are credibly informed, a sergeant-major and a cannoneer, besides others, were slain. We lost the day before Captain Lower, killed by scouts, that day Captain Balls, an ensign, and in all about sixteen. Sir William Waller's trumpeter, after he had delivered his summons, was unsoldierly shot in the thigh by one Sterner at the animation of the Governor Colonel Beaumont. On Tuesday morning Sir William Waller drew from thence to Teuxbury and so to Gloucester, leaving order with me to throw down as much of the works as the conveniency of my time would afford, which I believe is so done that they are made unuseful, though not fully slighted, and to withdraw the forces from Teuxbury to Gloucester from whence he had sooner departed, had not the impossibility of either marching without money or getting it without the employment of his troops to collect it, a little hindered his speed. The country is much troubled at his departure, and unless my Lord General's motion shall divert the other forces they fear the worst." [N. XI., 269.]

Sir Walter Erle to William Lenthall.

1643, June 3. Dorchester.—"Had not the enemy's sudden and near approach . . cut off all intercourse betwixt this and London, necessity as well as duty would have obliged me to have given you an account ere this of the . . . condition of this county. . . The enemy is now removed though to a place no further distant from us than that where they formerly were yet the way is more open, and so the opportunity of conveying letters better than it was. . . . Presently on their approach to Salisbury, seeing this county to be in a weak condition, and the forces we had in readiness being but a troop of horse and a company of dragoons and a foot company or two more, no way considerable for the opposing of such a force as was coming toward it, I resorted to Sir William Waller, being then but a day's journey from me. To him I represented the condition that we were in, making it plainly to appear that unless he came speedily with succours, ... not only this place but the whole county would in all likelihood be lost, urging therewithal the consequences of it in regard of the port towns and the magazines, which I have often mentioned in the House to be of great importance. Him I found very ready and willing to answer my desires and to give order for the drawing of his forces together that he might presently march; so I returned full of hopes, that, he once advancing towards the enemy then at Salisbury, the course would be diverted. But I know not how, some other direction . . . intervening, he went a quite contrary way and sat down before Worcester, the enemies in the mean space increasing in strength, and after awhile advancing towards us and coming to Blandford 12 miles distant from us, there to take up their quarter. This, together with the being in a manner out of hope of receiving any aid . . in time, was enough to startle us, the rather for that this place being our chief quarter could not by men of judgment be thought tenable, besides that those slender works which we had, wanted men wherewith to man them. Yet . . . we resolved to cast ourselves upon God Almighty's providence and protection, and, in case the enemy should come on, to defend ourselves the best that we could; and thereupon having some spare armes gotten in from the county, we got in more men, and put ourselves in a reasonable good posture; our soldiers upon all occasions being ready to answer the alarms, and manifesting much courage and resolution; all the magistrates, commanders, and officers obliging themselves by solemn protestation to live and die together in the defence of the place; which as it is supposed, coming to the enemy's knowledge made him to balk us, and to march away towards Sherborne, where he now is. Whilst our eyes were thus fixed upon Prince Maurice and the Marquess of Hertford, upon a sudden tidings came unto us, that the Cornish were advancing towards us on the other side, and were come within little more than a day's march of us. You may imagine what apprehensions this might cause; in plain truth, we thought the case so altered by our being beset with two armies that might upon a day's warning join . . and sit down before this place, as that we were fain to betake ourselves to new counsels, the strength that we were to encounter being treble to what we had prepared for. Whilst we were with much anxiety deliberating what course to take, it pleased God to resolve our doubts by some intelligence . . . of the advancing of Colonel Popham with a good strength both of horse and foot towards us, and immediately thereupon also of Sir William Waller's being come away from Worcester and making all the haste he could to be with us. These tidings were and are a good comfort . . . to us, but . . . the enemy's forces on both sides by the help of the *Posse Comitatus* increase so fast, as that, unless some other force come in the rear, it will be a hard pull to clear these parts, as it is intended and desired. They get in all the arms, horses, &c., they make men compound for their arms that were by us taken from them, they plunder the best affected, and commit all manner of outrages. God of His mercy deliver this poor country from such guests as these. . . . Be pleased to acquaint the House with our miserable condition which is likely to be much worse and more miserable, if some speedy course be not taken. We were in a good way of raising money and of settling the peace of the county, but you see how we are interrupted. . . . . . I humbly desire that I may not be cast upon impossibilities, as I shall be if help be not afforded, when extreme necessity calls for it. I have a great burthen lying upon me, my fellow Deputy-Lieutenants being for their better safety retired into Poole and leaving me alone to manage the whole business.

Postscript:—Since the sealing up of my letter I have certain intelligence that the Cornish with all or most part of their army are advanced as far as Axminster within 22 miles of this place, and, as some of them give out and by the providing of carriages yesterday at Sherborne it seems probable, that both armies are to meet this day about Crookhorne ; this being so, you may judge in what a condition we are." [N. XI., 270.]

Sir ROBERT COOKE, Colonel BURGHILL, and others the COMMITTEE AT GLOUCESTER to WILLIAM LENTHALL.

Same date. Gloucester.—"It is true that God's blessing upon Sir William Waller's weak forces hath often raised our admiration and engaged our thankfulness. . . . But at this time Sir Ralph Hopton is marching very strong from Cornwall, Prince Maurice with the Lord Marquess strong and increasing in power are advancing towards him ; if they meet the conjunction will in time prove dangerous to you, presently to us. Our desires are to interfere and with hazard to endeavour a prevention, but our men are not only too few to encounter theirs, but, which is worse, too many to be paid by us, and the want of money hath bred such mutinous dispositions in the soldiers that no arguments will make them stir. If by your advice his Excellency would be pleased to supply us with forces proportionable to that party that is advanced from Oxford, whence we little expected spare forces for remote attempts, and that you would be pleased to supply us speedily with a good sum of money, we should hope, by God's assistance, to afford you such an account as may justify your thrift for the Commonwealth in redeeming a heavy rent with a reasonable fine. You may perhaps hear a noise of new regiments raising, and so over-value the strength of these parts, but the truth is, for want of money neither can the new be completed, nor the old encouraged. If we can obtain no supply we must wait upon God, and petition him to list our preservation amongst his wonders ; or if we sink under the burden, it must suffice that we have done our duty to our country in troubling you with these necessary though unpleasant lines." (For these three letters see *Commons' Journals*, iii. 116.) [N. XI., 272.]

SIR EDWARD AYSCOGH and JOHN BROXOLME to WILLIAM LENTHALL.

1643, June 3. Lincoln.—"The cloud which hath long hung over this county, it hath pleased God . . . in some measure to disperse. For the malignant party at Gainsborough, being assured that the strength of our horse was joined to the great body about Nottingham, were puffed up with such boldness as . . . . to range over the county to assess towns, to take prisoners and to drive men's horses, and this course being long held by them, the 1° June with some troops and horse and dragoons they passed to Market Rasen and from thence to many other places in this county, still doing their pleasure to the pre-judice of the people. 2° June they marched to and lodged at Louth. Their leaders were Sir John Brook, Sir Charles Dallyson, and Captain Whitchcoat. We being advertised of the way they took, and assisted with 300 horse brought out of several parts to this town the day before, sent our men to waylay them in their return homewards, but such was the valour and vigilancy of the commanders and soldiers, as without rest to themselves or ease to their horses they arrived at Louth very early this morning, which they entered and subdued, and have this day by noon brought hither near 100 prisoners and as many horses with some arms and other considerable booty. The chief commanders of the enemy saved themselves by flight." . . . . [N. XI., 271.]

The KENTISH COMMITTEE to WILLIAM LENTHALL.

1643, June 3. Maidstone.—Again complaining of the neglect of the Kentish members of the House, except Sir E. Patherich, to assist them in the weekly tax, sequestrations, and assessment. [N. XI., 273.]

WILLIAM LENTHALL to the COMMITTEE AT DERBY.

1643, June 3.—Replying to their letter of May 27th, and stating the arms, &c. to be delivered to their agents. (See *Commons' Journals*, iii. 111, 113.) [N. XI., 268.]

WILLIAM LENTHALL to SIR WILLIAM WALLER.

1643, June 9.—On behalf of the House, thanking him and his officers and assuring him " that although for the present they cannot send you relief proportionable to their desires and your merit, yet they have resolved to send you a further supply with as much speed as the condition of their affairs can admit, and have given an express command to two worthy members . . . to take a more particular care of you in the absence of Sir Arthur Hasilrigg." [N. XI., 274.]

SIR WILLIAM BREREION and WILLIAM MOWBRAY to WILLIAM LENTHALL.

1643, June 15. Namptwich.—" By the letters . . . from Sir Nicholas Byron, Governor of Chester, to the Lord Capel, taken amongst many others at Whitchurch, . . . dated April 5° and . . . 28 . . it appears that they then hoped shortly to receive good supplies out of Ireland, which are not to be taken notice of until they come, such is the expression of the letter dated Apr. 5° 1643. In the other letter . . . Sir Nicholas Byron expresseth, that next the business of Reading, if it should miscarry, our retreat must be into these parts with those forces the King can make, and not stay in the midst of an enemy to be surrounded on all sides, but where we may countenance such succours as may easily come out of Ireland. . . In pursuance hereof some rebels are already landed and entertained, many more are daily expected, and this morning I was advertised from Liverpool that there were two barques of Irish rebels come into Chester Water, which our ships could not prevent, the wind having been constantly averse since their coming to Liverpool. The fortifications are as strong as the judgement and art of those men that command there can contrive them: their preparation of ordnance is suitable thereto, there being no less than 40 cannons as we have heard and the Castle victualled for three years . . . Some of them in their letters which I have seen have affirmed this city impregnable . . . We will only add the conclusion of Sir Nicholas Byron's letter. However things happen, Shrewsbury and Chester must be our last refuge, and so to provide for them in time, as no thought of quitting them must be entertained." (See *Commons' Journals*, iii. 143.) [N. XI., 275.]

PHILIP FRANCIS, Mayor, and others, to SIR JOHN YOUNG.

1643, June 15. Plymouth.—" We are here in a deplorable condition, our whole county being harrowed by Sir Ralph Hopton lately in their going forth, and the forces left behind them, joining with those of the Sheriff raised by his power, plunder as well in our parts in the

South as those in the East about Exon, stopping all intelligence between us and them. It is no small addition to our unhappiness that our garrison soldiers being necessitated for want of pay . . . are many of them stolen out of town, and now that our Committees are come hither upon our earnest and often solicitations to levy money upon the 20th part of men's estates, we . . . perceive their purpose is to carry it all from us, unless they receive orders from the House to dispose of such money here as may be . . . necessary for our occasions." We there. fore desire orders to them to leave as much money as they raise in this south division for the use of this garrison, the loss whereof is the loss of the whole county. [N. XI., 276.]

The EARL OF ESSEX to WILLIAM LENTHALL.

1643, June 16. Thame.—Concerning Mr. Fagg. (The purport appears from *Commons' Journals*, iii. 134.) [N. XI., 277.]

WILLIAM LENTHALL to the CITIZENS OF CANTERBURY.

1643, June 17.—(The purport appears from *Commons' Journals*, iii. 133.) [N. XI., 278.]

The COMMITTEE OF SEQUESTRATIONS FOR KENT to ¡ WILLIAM LENTHALL.

1643, June 17.—Concerning Mr. Roper's estate. (The purport sufficiently appears from the resolution thereon in *Commons' Journals*, iii. 135.) [N. XI., 279.]

The KENTISH COMMITTEE to WILLIAM LENTHALL.

1643, June 23. Gravesend.—Concerning Sir Norton Knatchbull. (The purport appears from *Commons' Journals*, iii. 144.) [N. XI., 284.]

The SAME to the SAME.

1643, June 24. Gravesend.—Concerning Sir Thomas Peyton and Sir Francis Barnham, whom they conceive to be liable to sequestration. [N. XI., 285.]

SIR WILLIAM WALLER to WILLIAM LENTHALL.

1643, June 25. Bath.—Returning thanks to the House for the provision for "these poor troops, which came very seasonably to keep life in us, even then when we were in a gasping condition." [N. XI., 286.]

SIR PHILIP STAPILTON and others to WILLIAM LENTHALL.

1643, June 26. Thame.—"Being commanded by my Lord General to acquaint you with the condition of the army we thought fit to inform you that the last money being paid out to the soldiers will provide them victuals until Monday next and no longer, if so long; for we find our living in the field so near the enemy altereth much the condition of our men, who whilst they lay in garrison, and had necessaries and victuals, they were in some measure contented, but now they are not, nor will be without constant pay, their provisions not being to be got without present money, which when the country find to grow short, they will forbear to bring in at all, without which the army cannot subsist. . . . We likewise offer to you other considerations, which are the continual decay of our horses occasioned by the daily hard service they are now put upon, since we took the field; the present supply whereof is of absolute necessity, yet orders for recruiting of our horse being only put into the hands of the Deputy-Lieutenants hath already weakened our strength in horse, the Deputy-Lieutenants to whom his Excellency writt not furnishing him with horses according to his letters, for remedy whereof we desire you would take some speedy and effectual course for the future, and that there being a great want of pistols and saddles you would please to take order for the provision of and sending down to the army such convenient provision of both as can be for the present procured. We further present unto you our want of men for recruits which we desire may be to the number of 2,000 to be sent up with all speed, as also of muskets, pikes, swords, bandaleers for those and other recruits of foot without which all those recruits will be altogether unserviceable." [N. XI., 287.]

The EARL OF ESSEX to WILLIAM LENTHALL.

1643, June 28. T[h]ame.—" The displeasure that the officers of this army are fallen into in general and I in particular came unexpected to me ; however I received it with all obedience ; for the plundering of the Cavaliers at Wickham, Newport, and other parts, thus much I can say, that I have often writt up, that it is impossible, if this army was three times as strong, to preserve the enemies from plundering ; we had neither foot nor horse at any of those places, but one troop of the Association which was without order ; and the enemy did not stay, as those that speaks with the most, above three quarters of an hour at Wickham. Sir Philip Stapilton and Colonel Middleton with most of the horse were sent presently out, but they were all retreated and in some confusion. I am sorry it should be conceived that through our neglect the countrys should be discouraged from sending any more men or money for the relief of the army. Sir, hitherto it is but the cries of poor people that suffer which have grieved me ; but the last, that our neglect should bring dishonour to the Parliament in making men believe the subjects are much safer in the protection of the King's army than of the Parliament's, wounds us so deeply that I must be forced to say, that never army served with more fidelity than this ; for my own particular, I thank God, my heart cannot accuse me either of want of care or hazard that I could conceive might be for the service of the State. It is well known to divers that sits in your House, how little ambitious I was of the great honour the Parliament was pleased to put upon me, not out of any want of respect to venture my life for the service of the State, I knowing my own disabilities to undertake so great a charge.

I shall take all the care I can that the army may secure these parts from the ranging of the King's horse and secure the counties between London and the army. My only suit is, that my imperfections may not be a means the army should disband for want of supply; but rather that the army may be paid, and there may be somebody placed in the head of it, in whom they may put confidence in." (For both these letters, see *Commons' Journals*, iii. 148.) [N. XI., 288.]

[Captain MOYER] to Mr. RIPPLEY.

[1643, June 28.]—Warning him of the danger of Hull. (The substance is in Rushworth, iii. 2, 276.) [N. XI., 289.]

The EARL OF ESSEX to the EARL OF MANCHESTER.

1643, June 30. Thame.—(Printed in *Lords' Journals*, vi. 110) [N. XI., 291.]

TORRELL JOCELYN to SIR HENRY MILDMAY.

1643, June 30. The fort at the Hermitage.—"I was counselled by you to repair to the House and there to declare the state of the Isle of Ely. But that very evening a messenger was sent unto me to let me know that those forces that were left under my command at Ely for the security of the Isle were in my absence thrust forth, and fearing that the like should be done at this fort, which is a very considerable passage, I made haste to secure it, and here I have been ever since and though daily threatened, yet I shall be able to make it good for one week." [N. XI., 292.]

The COMMITTEE FOR CAMBRIDGESHIRE to WILLIAM LENTHALL.

1643, June 30. Cambridge.—Recommending Mr. George Green for the incumbency of Sutton, in the Isle of Ely. [N. XI., 293.]

SIR WALTER ERLE to WILLIAM LENTHALL.

1643, June 30. Wareham.— . . . "Since the departure of Prince Maurice, and the Marquess of Hertford with their forces out of these parts, and their joining with the Cornish men upon the taking of . . . Taunton and Bridgewater, and the besieging of . . . Exeter, the consequence whereof hath been the overrunning and in effect the conquest of two of the greatest and richest counties of this kingdom, men's hearts fail them exceedingly, so as we find them not anything so forward to engage their persons or estates as formerly; and as for the levying of moneys, whereupon depends the maintaining of those forces which we have gotten together ; it is by reason thereof, and of the nearness of that great army, and those other forces, grown to be quite at a stand, every man being afraid, lest the bringing in of his money may be a means to expose him and his estate to rapine and plunder, if any strong party should break in upon us, as is likely enough there may, so as our troops are fallen much in arrear. And now when . . . we had escaped the danger of being swallowed up by that army that passed through our country, and by the way stayed well nigh a fortnight amongst us, we are come to be in a worse condition than ever ; and for my part, I am sure, may truly say it, for such commands are laid upon us, as if they be obeyed will in all likelihood utterly ruin us, and if they be not obeyed, what censure we shall incur we know not. For instance now at this present time a command comes from Sir William Waller for me to march towards him with all the strength that I can make ; at the very same instant, comes another to require me to provide 300 musketeers to be laid aboard my Lord of Warwick's fleet, which is bound for the west, neither of which can any way consist with the safety of this county and those places of impor- tance in it which hitherto have been kept for your service. . . . The demands are such, as if either of them be yielded unto, I shall . . . be brought into a far worse condition than ever I was in before, for whereas in the lowest estate that ever I was in for this twelvemonth, I was able to draw out two or three foot companies to assist me upon occasion, besides my troop of horse ; now when as within 30 or 40 miles of me, there are upon the matter three several bodies of the enemy that may, whenever they will, send out parties to molest us, I shall not be able to look abroad with so small a number, and that one troop of mine will be the only troop remaining within 40 miles compass, those of the enemy excepted which are many ; and this at such a time as we are upon the point of besieging, or at least blocking up of Corfe Castle, that begins exceedingly to annoy us; and when the Isle of Portland lately reduced begins to incline to a second revolt, which will with much more ease take effect, when Weymouth shall be left without a garrison, as it will be if both those commands be obeyed. . . . I rather was in hope . . . that we should have been reinforced with two or three troops of horse, with which I hope we not only should have cleared the western parts of this county, where a party or two, newly raised, begins to spoil and plunder, but all that part of Devonshire, which is betwixt us and Exeter. Thus you see what straits I am brought into. My humble request . . . is that the House may be made acquainted herewith, that so there may be some better course taken for the safety of this county . . . or at least, if businesses through want thereof should miscarry, it may not reflect upon me. . . . In the meantime in obedience to those commands . . . . I have in the first place given order for two troops of horse, such as they are, to join with those of Hampshire, and to march towards Sir William Waller, though with no small hazard, and am now giving order for 200 musketeers to be put aboard the fleet, which I suppose will this day come in Portland Road." *Postscript.*—Desiring the presence of Mr. Brown, which will be very useful in raising money and other business. [N. XI., 294.]

THOMAS STOCKDALE to WILLIAM LENTHALL.

1643, July 1. Halifax.—"I writt to you . . . on Thursday last, since which time the state of our affairs are much altered, being changed from ill into worse. . . . Yesterday morning we drew our forces together consisting of 1,200 commanded men of the garrison of Leeds, seven companies of Bradford, 500 men of Halifax, Pomfret, Paddleworth, Almonberry, and the country thereabouts, twelve companies of foot brought out of Lancashire, and of horse we had ten troops of our own and three from Lancashire, but the troops for the most part weak ; we had four pieces of brass ordnance with us and a great part of our powder and match, and many club-men followed us, who are fit to do execution upon a flying enemy, but unfit for other service, for I am sure they did us none ; and with this strength, being not full 4,000 men horse and foot armed, we marched from Bradford against the enemy who lay about three miles of us in a village called Aldwalton or Atherton and the places thereabouts. They hearing of our preparation had left their quarters about Howley and chosen that place of advantage being both a great hill and an open moor or common, where our foot could not be able to stand their horse. Their army consisted of 8,000 of their old foot, and about 7,000 new men raised by the Commission of Array, and, as most men say, 4,000 horse, which I could not conceive by view, though the truth is they had 80 cornets, and so might have had more, if their companies had been full and well armed, but indeed there are many both of their horse and foot very slenderly armed. Upon Atherton moor they planted their ordnance and ordered their battalia, but they manned divers houses standing in the enclosed grounds betwixt Bradford and Atherton moor with musketeers, and sent out great parties of horse and foot by the lanes and enclosed grounds to give us fight. Our forlorn hope consisting of horse and foot and dragoons was led by Captain Mildmay, to whom was joined Captain Askwith, Captain Morgan, Captain Farrar, Captain Salmon, and Captain Mudd. The van, wherein were placed the 1,200 commanded men from Leeds was led by Major-General Gifford, and the main battle wherein [were] the forces of Lancashire and 500 from the parts about Halifax and the moors had the Lord General himself,

Colonel Ashton, and Colonel Holland in it, and the rear with the garrison forces of Bradford were led by Lieutenant-Colonel Forbes. The horse were commanded by Sir Thomas Fairfax, who should have led the main battle, if the Lord General could have been persuaded to absent himself. Our forlorn hope beat back the enemies out of the lanes and enclosed grounds, killing many and taking some prisoners, and then the van coming up fell upon the enemies on the left hand and the main battle upon those on the right hand, and after some dispute beat the enemy both out of the houses they had manned and from the skirts of the moor to the height, killing very many and amongst them two Colonels, one of them, as by description I conclude was Colonel Herne, and our horse very bravely recovered part of the moor from the enemy, and maintained it and the rear fell on in the middle and did good service. Thus far we had a fair day, but the success of our men at the first drew them unawares to engage themselves too far upon the enemies, who having the advantage of the ground, and infinitely exceeded us in numbers, at least five for one, they sent some regiments of horse and foot by a lane on the left hand to encompass our army, and fall on their rear, which forced us to retreat, and our men, being unacquainted with field service, would not be drawn off in any order, but instead of marching fell into running; the commanders did their best to stay them, but in vain, for away they went in disorder, yet they brought off two pieces of the ordnance, and lost the other two and many prisoners, but the estimate of the number I cannot give you. Sir Thomas Fairfax with five or six troops of horse brought off the most part of the main battle, wherein the Lancashire men were, and made his retreat to Halifax very well, for the enemy was gotten so far before him towards Bradford, as he could not reach that place, and with much importunity I persuaded the Lord General to retire, who stayed so long upon the field, until the enemies were got betwixt him and Bradford, yet he took byways and recovered the town. Our loss was not great in commanders, for I do not yet hear of any save Major Talbot killed and Lieutenant-Colonel Forbes taken prisoner. Our loss of prisoners taken by the enemy was great, but the number is not equal to the fear and distraction it hath begotten in the country, which is increased by the Lancashire forces, who are retired home, the commanders not being able to persuade them to stay, as they allege, only we have got some 20 horse and 200 foot of them to stay with us at Halifax, upon promise to pay them ready money for their entertainment, which otherwise absolutely refused. . . . The country is wasted and exhausted and tired out with the weight of the troubles continually falling upon this part of Yorkshire, the soldiers want pay, and, which is worse, arms and powder and other ammunition, and are over-charged with the most potent strength that opposeth the Parliament; insomuch as the soldiers disband and desert the service, and the country overawed cannot longer assist the army; and if speedy supply be not sent with some considerable succour of men, the Lord General will be constrained to accept of some dishonourable conditions from the enemy. . . . I am now at Halifax, to which place I came last night . . . and take opportunity to send this bearer with Sir Thomas Fairfax's warrant to get you speedy notice, lest we be so shut up in Bradford and Leeds as we cannot send. Sir Thomas Fairfax is gone himself to Bradford with some horse and foot that he brought hither yesterday. Hasten some relief to preserve the most constant part of the kingdom. *Postscript.*—As I was closing this letter, I received a letter and after that a messenger from the Lord General to tell me that the enemy have made eight great shot at the town this day, and have even now recovered certain houses without the works, which if he cannot get fired, will much endanger the loss of the town. Sir Thomas is gone with some succours from hence, and what can be had more, I will get up, but the people stir with fear seeing no succours appear." [N. XI., 295.]

Sir Thomas Pelham, Sir Thomas Parker, and others, to
William Lenthall.

164[8(?)], June 29. Lewes.—"The magazine at Horsham long since seized upon by the disaffected party, is now employed to arm themselves and adherents, and some numbers are already drawn into a body, which we fear will soon increase, unless timely course be taken . . . for they continue together, and by beating of drum invite men unto them; what influence this disaster may have upon other parts of this county we know not, but have just cause to suspect the worst." (Dated 1643, but this is almost certainly a mistake for 1648. See letter of June 22, on p. 465.) [N. XI., 290.]

At the end of the Index Volume are " Collections out of a manuscript intituled ' Memoirs written by the late Earl of Manchester, son to the Lord Privy Seal, made by his own hand.' " The first extract is identical with the latter part of the MS. in the British Museum numbered MSS. Additional 15,567 from page 30 to the end, parts of which are printed in Nalson, and in Gardiner, and then follows a fragment beginning with the passage printed in Nalson, ii. 272, and concluding thus:

" All things proving thus contrary to the endeavours of the king and cross to the hopes and expectations of the Earl of Strafford, his friends proposed to attempt the integrity of Sir William Balfore, then Lieutenant of the Tower, in order to his escape, and the Earl himself, not long before his death, did endeavour to persuade him to give way to his escape, assuring him that if he would connive thereunto he would give him 20,000l. and provide a good marriage for his son. But Sir William Balfour replied, he would not falsify the trust reposed in him by the Parliament, and that he was so far from concurring with his Lordship's desires, as that he would not hearken to any motion tending to his escape."

Fragment 2.

" In order to the trial of this great man, who was now fallen under so public an odium, as that by the clamour of the people and their tumultuary pressing for justice, it might have been thought that the three kingdoms had owned their hopes of present and future security to have depended on Strafford's trial and sentence, whatsoever was desired of the Lords was granted and nothing omitted by either House that might [lead] to the discovery of truth. Therefore the House of Commons within few days after they had brought up their general accusation against the Earl of Strafford sent unto the Lords to let them know that they had divers witnesses which they were to produce, some were members of their own House, whom they had ordered to be ready to be examined, when their Lordships should require. Others were members or assistants of the House of Lords, and for those they desired that the Lords would order that they might be examined upon oath, if need required. And because some of the witnesses to be produced were of his Majesty's Privy Council, it was desired that the Lords would take such course as should seem best to their judgement that they also might be examined upon oath if need required. It was further urged by the Commons that Treason was such a crime as in the first preparation and design for the most part it walked in the dark, or, if it came abroad, it was with such disguise as it was hardly to be discovered and therefore it was with great instance recommended to the care and wisdom of their Lordships so to provide, that when any witnesses were produced they might be speedily examined, and both the name of the party and the matter of the interrogatory and answer might be kept secret, till there was occasion to make use of them; by this way subtle practices and combinations might be prevented and the truth secured from corruption and concealment. And it was desired by the Commons that some of their members might be present at those examinations to offer to the Lords such new interrogatories as should be thought necessary."

Fragment 3.

Begins with the first paragraph of the passage printed in Nalson, ii. 206, "When the king" down to "a false and unworthy servant." Then follows (out of order) Sir Henry Vane's paper printed on pages 208, 209, and then follows the rest of page 207 from "yet he thought" to the bottom of the page. It continues thus:

"In order to these preparatory examinations a Committee of the Lords was appointed, to whom an injunction was given that they should not reveal anything concerning the examination of witnesses touching the Earl of Strafford.

The Attorney-General and Mr. Sergeant Glanvil [were] appointed by the Lords to attend the Committee to set down in writing the examinations of witnesses and had an oath of secrecy administered unto them.

The Earl of Strafford being thus removed from power, sequestered from Parliament, and secured in the Tower, and all things in order to the discovery of his Treason being in a way of examination, the House of Commons fell upon the consideration of other persons, who were esteemed criminal, and in so long corruption of government by the intermission and dissolution of Parliaments they found many offenders in ecclesiastical and civil concerns."

Fragment 4.

"By this time the preparatory examinations in the case of the Earl of Strafford were finished; therefore the House of Commons sent to the House of Lords to desire that those examinations might be delivered to a Committee of their House that they might make use of them by way of addition, not of new matter but by reducing the generals into particulars, to the end that what shall appear in the examinations might be applied to the fortifying of the general articles.

They further signified to the Lords that they had entered a protestation in their House and desired it might likewise be entered in their Lordships' Books of Record, that they were not bound up to any course of proceeding, nor that this should be any precedent hereafter to bind them, but that they might proceed in generals, and that they would do so if they saw cause.

Upon this desire the Lords ordered that the examinations should be delivered to the House of Commons.

And now divers particulars coming into debate concerning the trial of the Earl of Strafford, it was referred to the Committee of Privileges to consider of the form and manner of proceeding against him, and likewise what time should be given him to put in his answer, and it was resolved to allow him fourteen days' time to put in his answer in writing to the further impeachment of the House of Commons. They likewise ordered that the Earl of Strafford should make use of counsel no further than the necessity for his defence did require, and wherein counsel might, with the justice of the House of Peers, be afforded to him, and that no delay should be in the proceedings, but all convenient expedition used, according to the desires of the House of Commons.

When the day came wherein the Earl was appointed to put in his answer, the King came to the House of Peers without any notice given, therefore the Lords were without their robes, which was unparliamentary, the King being present. The King being set, made this speech: 'My Lords, before the Earl of Strafford comes to the bar, I give you this reason of my coming, hearing that your Lordships have appointed this day for the Earl of Strafford to bring in his answer to the charge of High Treason. I am come to hear it read, the better to inform myself truly of the business whereby to govern myself the better. I desire you not to think that I do this in any kind to alter justice, nor to put you out of your ordinary way of debate, but I do it to know all that may be said on both sides.'

Then the Lord Keeper, kneeling to his Majesty, according to that reverend custom of that House, and returning to his own place, signified to the Lords that his Majesty's pleasure was that the prisoner should be brought to the bar and his answer read.

According to this direction, the Gentleman Usher of the Black Rod, who is the attendant of that House, brought the Earl of Strafford to the bar, and the first general Articles were read by the Clerk of the Parliament, and then his Lordship's answer was read by one of his Counsel.

After this the particular Articles were read one by one by the Clerk of the Parliament, and the answers by one of the Earl's Counsel.

This being done, the Earl was appointed to withdraw and his Majesty departed from the House.

The Lords, taking into consideration the danger of such a precedent, as that the King should come to the House of Peers and take notice of what business was there to be consulted of: Resolved that they would proceed in the intended business of the day as if nothing had been done when the King was present, ordering that the Earl of Strafford should be commanded to put in his answer, according to former Order. And the Earl was again called to the bar, and demanded to put in his answer, but his Counsel was appointed to read it, and the Earl allowed a stool to sit on, because he was not well and had stood long before, during the King's sitting in the House.

When the Earl came in the Bishops withdrew.

The answer being read the Earl made these desires—

1. To have time to examine his own witnesses.
2. To have the names of those that were examined against him.
3. To cross-examine those witnesses or liberty to except against them.
4. To have liberty to examine his witnesses in writing.
5. To have warrants to bring in his witnesses.

But the Lords would give no answer to these particulars till they had communicated them to the House of Commons. But after a few days the Earl presented a petition to the Lords for an answer to his desires formerly made unto them, and it was ordered that the Earl of Strafford should have varrant from the Lords to produce such vitnesses as vould not come vithout varrant (Affidavit being made thereof), and this not to be any occasion of delay in his trial. It vas further ordered that the Earl of Strafford should have liberty to examine such vitnesses (vithout oath) at his trial as vere necessary for his defence, and also that he might cross-examine vitnesses at the Bar, *viva voce* (but not upon oath), if it were needful for his defence.

The Lords having considered the Earl of Strafford's answer, sent a copy of it to the House of Commons, whereupon they sent a message to the Lords.

(This message with one or two verbal differences is that printed in Rushvorth, *Trial of Strafford*, p. 33.)

At the Conference the House of Commons declared that they thought it fit to have all their members present at the trial, that thereby they might be better satisfied in their consciences vhen they came to vote in demanding judgement. They likewise desired their Lordships to give directions for conveniency of room for so great a number, and that intimation was given that the space in the Lords' House vithout the Bar vould be too strait to contain such as would be necessary to be present at the trial.

The Lords taking these propositions into consideration thought fit to put it upon the House of Commons to show precedents, vhen and where the place had been changed, for locally the judicature had been in their House. The House having received this answer from the Lords, they insisted on their desire of having a larger room than the Lords' House, and concerning precedents they instanced in the case of Gonime in 1° R. II., the Parliament sat in the Black Chamber, and they further urged that the Parliament being summoned to appear at the King's Palace at Westminster, if one room were not convenient another might be appointed which was more proper.

The Lords being convinced that their House was not so fit as a larger place they acquainted the King with the desires of the Commons, and propounded to his Majesty Westminster Hall to be the place for the trial to vhich the King consented, and order vas given to the Lord High Chamberlain to have all things prepared in order to the trial. And the Earl of Arundel, then Lord Steward for the time of Parliament, was appointed Speaker of the House of Peers during the trial.

Some things vere offered for the resolutions of the Peers as relating to their ovn members.

First, vhether those Lords who had proxies of absent Lords should make use of them, and it vas resolved that at that time and in that case proxies should not be made use of yet with this salvo, saving to those absent Lords the right of Peers.

It vas likevise questioned whether the Bishops should be alloved their votes in this cause of the Earl of Strafford, it being a charge of High Treason, and punishable by death, vhereupon one of the Lords alleged that to his best remembrance the Bishop of Lincoln had at the Committee two or three days before deserted his claim therein both in his ovn name and in the name of the rest of the Bishops. But the Bishop of Lincoln replied that he did not desert his claim, nor durst he do so, knoving vhat his vrit of summons to Parliament enjoined him to, but he said by his Majesty's gracious favour, and the favour of their Lordships, he vould forbear to vote or to speak anything to the merits of the cause, vhich vas now prosecuted against the Earl of Strafford, and he conceived his brethren the Bishops vere also inclined so to do.

This was taken by the Lords as a modest expression, in confirmation whereof, when any question was put concerning the trial of the Earl of Strafford, the Bishops did forbear to vote.

They did further declare that at that time and in that case they would not make any procurator, saving to themselves their ancient rights.

All things being now so resolved in order to the trial, that the House of Commons should be present in Westminster Hall as a Committee, and that some of their members should manage the evidence against the Earl, the Lords thought fit to order, that the Earl of Strafford in matter of mere fact should not make use of his Counsel, but in matter of Law he might make use of Counsel; and if any doubt did arise concerning what was matter of fact and what was matter of Law the Lords would refer unto themselves the judgement thereof.

The House of Commons having these resolutions communicated unto them made this declaration. (Printed in Rushworth, *Trial of Strafford*, p. 38.)"

The fragment here ends.